American Government

The Essentials

American Government

The Essentials

EIGHTH EDITION

James Q. Wilson
University of California, Los Angeles

John J. DiIulio, Jr.
University of Pennsylvania

Houghton Mifflin Company   Boston   New York

Sponsoring editor: Mary Dougherty
Development editor: Katherine Meisenheimer
Senior project editor: Carol Newman
Manufacturing manager: Florence Cadran
Marketing manager: Jay Hu

Cover design: Harold Burch, Harold Burch Design, Inc.
Cover image: © Omel Curtis/Photonica.

Photo credits appear on page C1.

Printed in the U.S.A.

Library of Congress Catalog Card Number: 00-104954

ISBN: 0-618-04360-8

1 2 3 4 5 6 7 8 9—VH—2004 2003 2002 2001 2000

Contents

Preface   xiii
About the Authors   xv

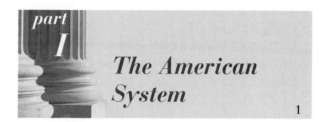

part
1

The American System   1

1 The Study of American Government   2

What Is Political Power?   4
What Is Democracy?   5
Direct Versus Representative Democracy: Which Is Best?   6
How Is Power Distributed in a Democracy?   8
  Four Theories of Who Governs   8
Political Change   11
Finding Out Who Governs   12

2 The Constitution   16

The Problem of Liberty   17
  The Colonial Mind   18
  The Real Revolution   20
  Weaknesses of the Confederation   21
The Constitutional Convention   22
  The Lessons of Experience   22
  The Framers   23

The Challenge   25
  The Virginia Plan   25
  The New Jersey Plan   26
  The Compromise   27
The Constitution and Democracy   28
  Key Principles   28
  Government and Human Nature   29
The Constitution and Liberty   30
  The Antifederalist View   31
  Need for a Bill of Rights   35
  The Constitution and Slavery   36
The Motives of the Framers   38
  Economic Interests at the Convention   38
  Economic Interests and Ratification   39
  The Constitution and Equality   39
Constitutional Reform—Modern Views   41
  Reducing the Separation of Powers   41
  Making the System Less Democratic   43
  Who Is Right?   44

3 Federalism   48

Governmental Structure   50
  Federalism: Good or Bad?   51
  Increased Political Activity   52
The Founding   52
  A Bold, New Plan   53
  Elastic Language   54
The Debate on the Meaning of Federalism   55
  The Supreme Court Speaks   56
  Nullification   57
  Dual Federalism   57
  State Sovereignty   58
Federal-State Relations   59
  Grants-in-Aid   60
  Meeting National Needs   61

The Intergovernmental Lobby   62
Categorical Grants Versus Revenue
  Sharing   62

The Slowdown in "Free" Money   64
Rivalry Among the States   65

Federal Aid and Federal Control   66
Mandates   66
Conditions of Aid   68

A Devolution Revolution?   70
Block Grants for Entitlements   70
What's Driving Devolution?   71

Congress and Federalism   72

4 American Political Culture 78

Political Culture   80
The Political System   80
The Economic System   83

**Comparing America with Other
  Nations**   84
Political System   84
Economic System   85
The Role of Religion   86

The Sources of Political Culture   88
The Culture War   90

Mistrust of Government   92

Political Efficacy   93

Political Tolerance   94

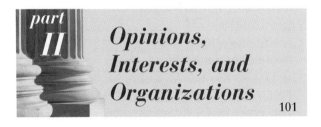

part II Opinions, Interests, and Organizations 101

5 Public Opinion 102

What Is Public Opinion?   104

The Origins of Political Attitudes   106
The Role of the Family   106
Religion   107
The Gender Gap   109
Schooling and Information   110

Cleavages in Public Opinion   112
Social Class   112
Race and Ethnicity   114
Region   117

Political Ideology   118
Consistent Attitudes   120
What Do *Liberalism* and *Conservatism*
  Mean?   120
Various Categories   121
Analyzing Consistency   122
Political Elites   123
Is There a "New Class"?   124

**Political Elites, Public Opinion, and Public
  Policy**   125

6 Political Participation 128

A Closer Look at Nonvoting   129

The Rise of the American Electorate   132
From State to Federal Control   132
Voter Turnout   135

Who Participates in Politics?   137
Forms of Participation   137
The Causes of Participation   138
The Meaning of Participation Rates   141

7 Political Parties 148

Parties—Here and Abroad   150
Political Culture   152

**The Rise and Decline of the Political
  Party**   152
The Founding   152
The Jacksonians   153
The Civil War and Sectionalism   154
The Era of Reform   156

The National Party Structure Today   157
National Conventions   159

State and Local Parties 161
The Machine 161
Ideological Parties 163
Solidary Groups 164
Sponsored Parties 164
Personal Following 165
The Two-Party System 165
Minor Parties 169
Nominating a President 172
Are the Delegates Representative of the
Voters? 172
Who Votes in Primaries? 173
Who Are the New Delegates? 174
Parties Versus Voters 174

8 Elections and Campaigns 178

**Presidential Versus Congressional
Campaigns** 180
Running for President 181
Primary Versus General Campaigns 183
Two Kinds of Campaign Issues 185
Television, Debates, and Direct Mail 187
Money 191
The Sources of Campaign Money 191
Campaign Finance Rules 192
The Effects of the 1974 Reforms 194
Proposals for More Reform 195
Money and Winning 196
What Decides the Election? 199
Party 199
Issues, Especially the Economy 201
The Campaign 203
Finding a Winning Coalition 204
Election Outcomes 207
Party Realignments 208
Party Decline 211
The Effects of Elections on Policy 212

9 Interest Groups 216

Explaining Proliferation 217

The Birth of Interest Groups 219
Kinds of Organizations 221
Institutional Interests 221
Membership Interests 222
Incentives to Join 223
The Influence of the Staff 225
**Interest Groups and Social
Movements** 225
The Environmental Movement 226
The Feminist Movement 226
The Union Movement 227
Funds for Interest Groups 229
Foundation Grants 229
Federal Grants and Contracts 229
Direct Mail 229
The Problem of Bias 230
The Activities of Interest Groups 232
Information 232
Public Support: The Rise of the New
Politics 233
Money and PACs 236
The "Revolving Door" 238
Trouble 239
Regulating Interest Groups 240

10 The Media 244

**Journalism in American Political
History** 246
The Party Press 246
The Popular Press 247
Magazines of Opinion 249
Electronic Journalism 249
The Internet 251
The Structure of the Media 251
Degree of Competition 252
The National Media 253
Rules Governing the Media 255
Confidentiality of Sources 256
Regulating Broadcasting 256
Campaigning 258
The Effects of the Media on Politics 259
Government and the News 261
Prominence of the President 261

Coverage of Congress   262

Interpreting Political News   263
Are News Stories Slanted?   264
Why Do We Have So Many News
  Leaks?   266
Sensationalism in the Media   269
Government Constraints on Journalists   271

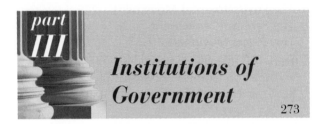

part
III

*Institutions of
Government*

273

11 **Congress**   274

The Evolution of Congress   279
Phase One: The Powerful House   279
Phase Two: A Divided House   280
Phase Three: The Rise of a Powerful
  Speaker   280
Phase Four: The Revolt Against the
  Speaker   281
Phase Five: The Empowerment of Individual
  Members   282
Phase Six: The Return of Leadership   282
The Future?   282
The Evolution of the Senate   283

Who Is in Congress?   284
Sex and Race   284
Incumbency   284
Party   287

Getting Elected to Congress   289
Determining Fair Representation   290
Majority-Minority Districts   291
Winning the Primary   292

**Do Members Represent Their
  Voters?**   295
Representational View   295
Organizational View   296
Attitudinal View   296

Ideology and Civility in Congress   298

**The Organization of Congress: Parties and
  Caucuses**   298
Party Organization of the Senate   298
Party Structure in the House   300
The Strength of Party Structures   301
Party Unity   302
Caucuses   304

**The Organization of Congress:
  Committees**   306

**The Organization of Congress: Staffs and
  Specialized Offices**   309
Tasks of Staff Members   310
Staff Agencies   311

How a Bill Becomes Law   311
Introducing a Bill   312
Study by Committees   313
Floor Debate—The House   316
Floor Debate—The Senate   317
Methods of Voting   318

Reforming Congress   319
Representative or Direct Democracy?   319
Proper Guardians of the Public Weal?   320
A Decisive Congress or a Deliberative
  One?   320
Imposing Term Limits   320
Reducing Powers and Perks   322

Ethics and Congress   324

12 **The Presidency**   332

Presidents and Prime Ministers   334
Divided Government   335
Does Gridlock Matter?   336
Is Policy Gridlock Bad?   336
The Evolution of the Presidency   337
Concerns of the Founders   337
The Electoral College   338
The President's Term of Office   338
The First Presidents   339
The Jacksonians   342
The Reemergence of Congress   342
The Powers of the President   344
The Office of the President   345
The White House Office   346

The Executive Office of the President 348
The Cabinet 349
Independent Agencies, Commissions, and
Judgeships 350

Who Gets Appointed 350

Presidential Character 353

The Power to Persuade 354
The Three Audiences 355
Popularity and Influence 356
The Decline in Popularity 357

The Power to Say No 358
Veto 358
Executive Privilege 360
Impoundment of Funds 362

The President's Program 362
Putting Together a Program 362
Attempts to Reorganize 364

Presidential Transition 365
The Vice President 366
Problems of Succession 367
Impeachment 369

How Powerful Is the President? 371

13 The Bureaucracy 374

**Distinctiveness of the American
Bureaucracy** 376

The Growth of the Bureaucracy 376
The Appointment of Officials 377
A Service Role 378
A Change in Role 379

The Federal Bureaucracy Today 380
Recruitment and Retention 381
Personal Attributes 386
Do Bureaucrats Sabotage Their Political
Bosses? 387
Culture and Careers 389
Constraints 389
Agency Allies 392

Congressional Oversight 393
The Appropriations Committee and
Legislative Committees 394
The Legislative Veto 394
Congressional Investigations 395

Bureaucratic "Pathologies" 395
Reforming the Bureaucracy 397

14 The Judiciary 402

**The Development of the Federal
Courts** 405
National Supremacy and Slavery 405
Government and the Economy 407
Government and Political Liberty 409
The Revival of State Sovereignty 411

The Structure of the Federal Courts 411
Selecting Judges 411

**The Jurisdiction of the Federal
Courts** 414

Getting to Court 417
Fee Shifting 418
Standing 418
Class-Action Suits 419

The Supreme Court in Action 420

The Power of the Federal Courts 422
The Power to Make Policy 423
Views of Judicial Activism 424
Legislation and the Courts 426

Checks on Judicial Power 426
Congress and the Courts 427
Public Opinion and the Courts 429

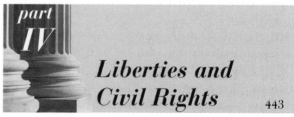

part
IV

*Liberties and
Civil Rights* 443

15 Civil Liberties 434

Politics, Culture, and Civil Liberties 436
Rights in Conflict 437

Policy Entrepreneurs 437
Cultural Conflicts 439

Interpreting and Applying the First Amendment 440
Speech and National Security 441

What Is Speech? 443
Libel 443
Obscenity 444
Symbolic Speech 446

Who Is a Person? 447

Church and State 448
The Free-Exercise Clause 448
The Establishment Clause 449

Crime and Due Process 451
The Exclusionary Rule 452
Search and Seizure 452
Confessions and Self-Incrimination 456
Relaxing the Exclusionary Rule 457

16 Civil Rights 460

The Black Predicament 462

The Campaign in the Courts 464
"Separate but Equal" 465
Can Separate Schools Be Equal? 467
Brown v. Board of Education 467

The Campaign in Congress 472

Women and Equal Rights 477
Sexual Harassment 479
Abortion 480

Affirmative Action 481
Equality of Results 481
Equality of Opportunity 482

Gays and the Supreme Court 488

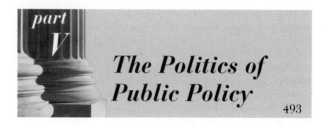

part
V

The Politics of Public Policy 493

17 Politics and Public Policy 494

How the American System Affects Policy-Making 496

How the American System Has Changed 499

Restraints on Growth 500

Relaxing the Restraints 501
The Old System 502
The New System 502

Should the System Be Changed? 506
Reducing the Barriers to Action 506
Increasing the Barriers to Action 508
Term Limits 510
Who Is Right? 510

Appendix A1
The Declaration of Independence A1
The Constitution of the United States A4
The *Federalist* No. 10 A21
The *Federalist* No. 51 A26
Presidents and Congresses, 1789–2000 A30

Glossary G1

Notes N1

Index I1

Photo Credits C1

Preface

Books, like children, tend to grow. In preparing this edition, we have taken a look at how the book has grown in recent years and have tried to cut its length judiciously, without sacrificing any important content. We have also been alert to some major issues that have come to influence politics, analyzing some extensively and minimizing a few that, in retrospect, seem less important. In 1999, the press was devoted to the impeachment of President Clinton, and although we have described that event briefly, we have focused much more on things that will have more lasting importance. These include

- The effort of the Supreme Court to reestablish the idea that the states have certain rights that cannot be trumped even with the use of the commerce clause of the Constitution.
- The devolution of the old Aid to Families with Dependent Children back to the states, a move that stimulated a remarkable variety of state approaches to welfare.
- The end, at least for the time being, of annual budget deficits so that politicians can now talk freely of what to do with the surplus.
- The renewed but difficult effort to find new ways of regulating campaign finance.
- The continued but confused expansion by the Supreme Court of rules governing sexual harassment.
- The preoccupation of the mass media with any hint of sexual scandal to an extent not seen before.
- The continued polarization of opinion in Congress, especially in the House of Representatives.

While attending to all of this, we also brought the text up to date through the 2000 elections.

These changes have not altered the essential structure or themes of the text. It remains an effort to show not only who governs but what difference—in policies adopted or rejected—it makes who governs. As always, we stress the historical evolution of our practices and institutions, focusing on the importance of the Constitution and American political culture in shaping governmental activities.

Features that have proved popular and useful have also been retained in this edition, such as "Politically Speaking" and "Trivia." Students seem to share our interest in knowing these interesting, often humorous aspects of political life. Other helpful features have been renamed as "The 'Rules' of Politics" and "How Things Work" in order to clarify their purpose. Finally, one feature has become so essential to instructors that we added more. There is now a "What Would You Do?" box in almost every chapter. These ask students to put themselves in the shoes of policymakers so that they can appreciate some of the tough decisions that have to be made.

Two new features are, we think, likely to prove very helpful to readers. First, to help students identify and remember the most important issues, each chapter now begins with a list of Enduring Questions. Second, almost every chapter now contains a list of related World Wide Web addresses that will enable students and professors to access political information online.

To help make the text shorter, we have combined into a single, briefer chapter the old chapters on foreign and military policy, and we have omitted the chapter on state and local government. However, for those instructors who wish it, that chapter, completely updated, is available as a free pamphlet that can be ordered with the text.

For the Instructor

The outstanding ancillary program that has always supported *American Government* has been improved and enlarged for the Eighth Edition.

The **Instructor's Resource Manual** helps instructors plan their course, lectures, and discussion sections. Professor MaryAnne Borelli (Connecticut College) has thoroughly integrated the IRM with the textbook so instructors can capitalize upon the richness of *American Government*. Elements new to this edition are summarized, and the resources and references sections have been thoroughly updated.

The **Test Item File,** revised by J. Edwin Benton (University of South Florida) contains over 4,000 questions. Each chapter has multiple choice, true/false, and essay questions. These test items are also available in electronic format for both Windows and Macintosh platforms. The **HM Testing** software provides a complete testing solution, with test generation, classroom administration, and online testing features.

The **Transparency Package** contains fifty full-color transparencies from the illustration program of *American Government,* Eighth Edition.

New! The illustrations in the transparency package are also available as **PowerPoint Slides,** downloadable from the *American Government,* Eighth Edition web site **Instructor's Resource Page** (go to http://www.college.hmco.com). Adopters of the text may obtain the password for this page from their Houghton Mifflin sales representative.

New! For instructors who wish to include a unit on state and local politics in their course, a chapter-length **State and Local Government Supplement** may be packaged with the text at no extra cost.

New! The *American Government,* Eighth Edition **WebCT Webcourselet** and **Blackboard Course Cartridge** provide text-specific student study aids in customizable, Internet-based education platforms. Both platforms provide a full array of course management features for instructors who wish to incorporate educational technology in their traditional classrooms or for those who are creating distance learning courses.

For the Student

New! Each new copy of the Eighth Edition comes packaged with a free **Real Deal UpGrade CD-ROM.** Designed to enhance students' understanding of their textbook, this CD contains chapter outlines, learning objectives, study skills tips, self-tests, primary source documents, web links, video clips, and footage of nine key campaign advertisements with activities that help students analyze the ads.

The **Student Handbook** has been thoroughly updated by J. Edwin Benton (University of South Florida) to help students using *American Government* master the facts and principles introduced in the text and prepare for examinations. For each chapter, the handbook includes focus points, a study outline, key terms, notes about possible misconceptions, a data

check, practice exam questions, and special application projects, as well as answers to all chapter exercises (excluding the essay questions).

The ***American Government,* Eighth Edition Web Site,** accessible via the Houghton Mifflin College Division web site at http://www.college.hmco.com, contains other student study aids, including chapter outlines, ACE self-quizzes, *What Would You Do? Interactive* simulations, additional "Trivia" features, and chapter-specific web links. The Eighth Edition web site also links to **Political SourceNet,** Houghton Mifflin's American Government resource, containing primary source documents, Internet exercises, and **Crosstabs 4.0.** Crosstabs allows students to cross-tabulate survey data on the 1996 Presidential election and the 105th Congress voting records in order to analyze voter attitudes and behavior.

Acknowledgments

A number of scholars reviewed the Seventh Edition and made many useful suggestions for the Eighth. They include John R. Baker, Wittenberg University; Evelyn Ballard, Houston Community College; Donald Brand, College of the Holy Cross; Gary Bryner, Brigham Young University; Mark Byrnes, Middle Tennessee State University; Mike Caldwell, University of Illinois; Anita Chadha, University of Tennessee at Chattanooga; David E. Dupree, Victor Valley College; John Gerring, Boston University; Eugene R. Goss, Long Beach City College; W. Gary Howard, University of West Florida; E. Terrence Jones, University of Missouri-St. Louis; John R. Kayser, University of New Hampshire; Gary Malecha, University of Portland; Bonnie G. Mani, East Carolina University; Don Melton, Arapahoe Community College; Keith Nicholls, University of South Alabama; Steven Puro, St. Louis University; James A. Rhodes, Luther College; James M. Scott, University of Nebraska at Kearney; Sanford R. Silverburg, Catawba College; Robert L. Silvey, John Jay College; Morton Sipress, University of Wisconsin-Eau Claire; and Bedford Umez, Lee College.

In producing this edition, we are especially grateful to our research assistants: Erin Architzel, Christopher Blunt, Russell Burgos, and Sean Trende.

J.Q.W. and J.J.D.

About the Authors

James Q. Wilson
is an emeritus professor of management and public policy at the University of California, Los Angeles. From 1961 to 1987, he was a professor of government at Harvard University. Raised in California, he received a B.A. degree from the University of Redlands and a Ph.D. from the University of Chicago. Wilson is the author or coauthor of fourteen books, including *Moral Judgment* (1997), *The Moral Sense* (1993), *Bureaucracy* (1989), *Crime and Human Nature* (1985, with Richard J. Herrnstein), *Thinking about Crime* (1983), and *Political Organizations* (1974).

Wilson has served in a number of advisory posts in the federal government. He was chairman of the White House Task Force on Crime in 1967, chairman of the National Advisory Council on Drug Abuse Prevention in 1972–1973, a member of the Attorney General's Task Force on Violent Crime in 1981, and a member of the President's Foreign Intelligence Advisory Board in 1986–1990.

In 1977 the American Political Science Association conferred on him the Charles E. Merriam Award for advancing the art of government through the application of social science knowledge and in 1990 the James Madison Award for distinguished scholarship. In 1991–1992 he was President of the Association.

He is a Fellow of the American Academy of Arts and Sciences and a member of the American Philosophical Society. When not writing, teaching, or advising, he goes scuba diving. He says that it clears the brain.

John J. DiIulio, Jr.
is Frederic Fox Leadership Professor of Politics, Religion, and Civil Society at the University of Pennsylvania. From 1986 to 1999, he was a professor of politics and public affairs at Princeton University's Woodrow Wilson School of Public and International Affairs. He is also a senior fellow at the Brookings Institution and the Manhattan Institute, and a senior counsel to Public/Private Ventures. He received a B.A. from The University of Pennsylvania and a Ph.D. from Harvard University. He is the author, coauthor, or editor of a dozen books, including *What's God Got to Do with the American Experiment?* (2000, with E. J. Dionne); *Medicaid and Devolution* (1998, with Frank Thompson); *Deregulating the Public Service* (1994); *Courts, Corrections, and the Constitution* (1990); and *Governing Prisons* (1987).

DiIulio has served on the National Commission on the State and Local Public Service and advised officials at the National Performance Review, the Office of Management and Budget, the General Accounting Office, the Office of National Drug Control Policy, the U.S. Justice Department, and other federal agencies.

In 1995 the Association of Public Policy Analysis and Management conferred on him the David N. Kershaw Award for outstanding research achievements by a scholar under age 40, and in 1987 he received the American Political Science Association's Leonard D. White Award in public administration. In 1991–1994 he chaired the latter association's standing committee on professional ethics. He spends all his free time with family and old friends from Philadelphia.

part I The American System

In framing a government which is to be administered by men over men, the great difficulty lies in this: You must first enable the government to control the governed; and in the next place oblige it to control itself.

FEDERALIST No. 51

Madison

p. 25

1

The Study of American Government

Enduring Questions

1. If average citizens are fit to select their leaders (representative democracy), how can they be unfit to govern themselves directly (direct democracy)?
2. What is political power, and how is it actually distributed in America?
3. Why does government expand and contract, and what accounts for major political change?

What Is Political Power?

What Is Democracy?

Direct Versus Representative Democracy: Which Is Best?

How Is Power Distributed in a Democracy?
    Four Theories of Who Governs

Political Change

Finding Out Who Governs

There are two questions about politics: Who governs? To what ends?

We want to know the answer to the first question because we believe that those who rule—their personalities and beliefs, their virtues and vices—will affect what they do to and for us. Many people think they already know the answer to the question, and they are prepared to talk and vote on that basis. That is their right, and the opinions they express may be correct. But they may also be wrong. Indeed, many of these opinions *must* be wrong because they are in conflict. When asked, "Who governs?" some people will say "the unions" and some will say "big business"; others will say "the politicians," "the people," or "the special interests." Still others will say "Wall Street," "the military," "crackpot liberals," "the media," "the bureaucrats," or "white males." Not all these answers can be correct—at least not all of the time.

The answer to the second question is important because it tells us how government affects our lives. We want to know not only who governs, but what difference it makes who governs. In our day-to-day lives we may not think government makes much

3

difference at all. In one sense that is right, because our most pressing personal concerns—work, play, love, family, health—are essentially private matters on which government touches but slightly. But in a larger and longer perspective government makes a substantial difference. Consider: in 1935, 96 percent of all American families paid no federal income tax, and for the 4 percent or so who did pay, the average rate was only about 4 percent of their incomes. Today almost all families pay federal income taxes, and the average rate is 20 percent of their incomes. Through laws that have been enacted since the 1930s, the federal government has taken charge of an enormous amount of the nation's income, with results that are still being debated. Or consider: in 1960, in many parts of the country, African Americans could ride only in the backs of buses, had to use washrooms and drinking fountains that were labeled "colored," and could not be served in most public restaurants. Such restrictions have been almost eliminated, in large part because of decisions by the federal government.

It is important to bear in mind that we wish to answer two different questions, and not two versions of the same question. You cannot always predict what goals government will establish knowing only who governs, nor can you always tell who governs by knowing what activities government undertakes. Most people holding national political office are middle-class, middle-aged, white Protestant males, but we cannot then conclude that the government will adopt only policies that are to the narrow advantage of the middle class, the middle-aged, whites, Protestants, or men. If we thought that, we would be at a loss to explain why the rich are taxed more heavily than the poor, why the War on Poverty was declared, why constitutional amendments giving rights to African Americans and women passed Congress by large majorities, or why Catholics and Jews have been appointed to so many important governmental posts.

This book is chiefly devoted to answering the question, Who governs? It is written in the belief that this question cannot be answered without looking at how government makes—or fails to make—decisions about a large variety of concrete issues. Thus in this book we shall inspect government policies to see what individuals, groups, and institutions seem to exert the greatest power in the continuous struggle to define the purposes of gov-

ernment. We shall see that power and purpose are inextricably intertwined.

What Is Political Power?

By **power** we mean the ability of one person to get another person to act in accordance with the first person's intentions. Sometimes an exercise of power is obvious, as when the president tells the air force that it can or cannot build the B-1 bomber. More often power is exercised in subtle ways that may not be evident even to the participants, as when the president's economic advisers persuade him to impose or lift wage and price controls. The advisers may not think they are using power—after all, they are the president's subordinates—but if the president acts in accord with their intentions as a result of their arguments, they have used power.

Power is found in all human relationships, but we shall be concerned here only with power as it is used to affect who will hold government office and how government will behave. This fails to take into account many important things. If a corporation closes a factory in a small town where it was the major employer, it is using power in ways that affect deeply the lives of people. When a university refuses to admit a student or a medical society refuses to license a would-be physician, it is also using power. But to explain how all these things happen would be tantamount to explaining how society as a whole, and in all its particulars, operates. We limit our view here to government, and chiefly to the American federal government. However, we shall repeatedly pay special attention to how things once thought to be "private" matters become "public"— that is, how they manage to become objects of governmental action. Indeed, one of the most striking transformations of American politics has been the extent to which, in recent decades, almost every aspect of human life has found its way onto the governmental agenda. In the 1950s the federal government would have displayed no interest in a factory closing its doors, a university refusing an applicant, or a profession not accrediting a member. Now government actions can and do affect all these things.

People who exercise political power may or may not have the authority to do so. By **authority** we mean the right to use power. The exercise of rightful power—that is, of authority—is ordinarily easier than the exercise of power that is not supported by any persuasive claim of right. We accept decisions, often without question, if they are made by people who we believe have the right to make them; we may bow to naked power because we cannot resist it, but by our recalcitrance or our resentment we put the users of naked power to greater trouble than the wielders of authority. In this book we will on occasion speak of "formal authority." By this we mean that the right to exercise power is vested in a governmental office. A president, a senator, and a federal judge have formal authority to take certain actions.

What makes power rightful varies from time to time and from country to country. In the United States we usually say that a person has political authority if his or her right to act in a certain way is conferred by a law or by a state or national constitution. But what makes a law or constitution a source of right? That is the question of **legitimacy.** In the United States the Constitution today is widely, if not unanimously, accepted as a source of legitimate authority, but that was not always the case.

Much of American political history has been a struggle over what constitutes legitimate authority. The Constitutional Convention in 1787 was an effort to see whether a new, more powerful federal government could be made legitimate; the succeeding administrations of George Washington, John Adams, and Thomas Jefferson were in large measure preoccupied with disputes over the kinds of decisions that were legitimate for the federal government to make. The Civil War was a bloody struggle over the legitimacy of the federal union; the New Deal of Franklin Roosevelt was hotly debated by those who disagreed over whether it was legitimate for the federal government to intervene deeply in the economy.

In the United States today no government at any level would be considered legitimate if it were not in some sense democratic. That was not always the prevailing view, however; at one time people disagreed over whether democracy itself was a good idea. In 1787 Alexander Hamilton worried that the new government he helped create might be too democratic, while George Mason, who refused to sign the Constitution, worried that it was not democratic enough. Today virtually everyone believes that "democratic government" is the only proper kind. Most people probably believe that our existing gov-

Dramatic changes have occurred in what people believe it is legitimate for the government to do. Some students are now searched for weapons after shootings occurred in schools.

ernment is democratic; and a few believe that other institutions of public life—schools, universities, corporations, trade unions, churches—should be run on democratic principles if they are to be legitimate. We shall not discuss the question of whether democracy is the best way of governing all institutions. Rather we shall consider the different meanings that have been attached to the word *democratic* and which, if any, best describes the government of the United States.

What Is Democracy?

Democracy is a word used to describe at least three different political systems. In one system the government is said to be democratic if its decisions will serve the "true interests" of the people, whether or not those people directly affect the making of those decisions. It is by using this definition of democracy that various authoritarian regimes—China, Cuba, and certain European, Asian, and Latin American dictatorships—have been able to claim that they were "democratic." Presidents of the now defunct Soviet Union, for example, used to claim that they operated on the principle of **democratic centralism,** whereby the true interests of the masses were discovered through discussion within the Communist party and then decisions were made under central leadership to serve those interests. The collapse of the Soviet Union occurred in part because many

China has tried to create a country with both a market economy and an authoritarian political system. Will that work?

average Russians doubted that the Communist party knew or would act in support of the people's true interests.

Second, the term *democracy* is used to describe those regimes that come as close as possible to Aristotle's definition—the "rule of the many."[1] A government is democratic if all, or most, of its citizens participate directly in either holding office or making policy. This is often called **direct or participatory democracy.** In Aristotle's time—Greece in the fourth century B.C.—such a government was possible. The Greek city-state, or *polis*, was quite small, and within it citizenship was extended to all free adult male property holders. (Slaves, women, minors, and those without property were excluded from participation in government.) In more recent times the New England town meeting approximates the Aristotelian ideal. In such a meeting the adult citizens of a community gather once or twice a year to vote directly on all major issues and expenditures of the town. As towns have become larger and issues more complicated, many town governments have abandoned the pure town meeting in favor of either the representative town meeting (in which a large number of elected representatives, perhaps two or three hundred, meet to vote on town affairs) or representative government (in which a small number of elected city councillors make decisions).

The third definition of democracy is the principle of governance of most nations that are called democratic. It was most concisely stated by the economist Joseph Schumpeter: "The democratic method is that institutional arrangement for arriving at political decisions in which individuals [that is, leaders] acquire the power to decide by means of a competitive struggle for the people's vote."[2] Sometimes this method is called, approvingly, **representative democracy;** at other times it is referred to, disapprovingly, as the elitist theory of democracy. It is justified by one or both of two arguments: First, it is impractical, owing to limits of time, information, energy, interest, and expertise, for the people to decide on public policy, but it is not impractical to expect them to make reasonable choices among competing leadership groups. Second, some people (including, as we shall see in the next chapter, many of the Framers of the Constitution) believe that direct democracy is likely to lead to bad decisions, because people often decide large issues on the basis of fleeting passions and in response to popular demagogues. This fear of direct democracy persists today, as can be seen from the statements of those who do not like what the voters have decided. For example, politicians who favored Proposition 13, the referendum measure that in 1978 sharply cut property taxes in California, spoke approvingly of the "will of the people." Politicians who disliked Proposition 13 spoke disdainfully of "mass hysteria."

Direct Versus Representative Democracy: Which Is Best?

Whenever the word *democracy* is used alone in this book, it will have the meaning Schumpeter gave it. As we shall see in the next chapter, the men who wrote the Constitution did not use the word *democracy* in that document. They wrote instead of a "republican form of government," but by that they meant what we call "representative democracy." Whenever we refer to that form of democracy involving the direct participation of all or most citizens, we shall use the term *direct* or *participatory democracy.*

For representative government to work, there must, of course, be an opportunity for genuine leadership competition. This requires in turn that

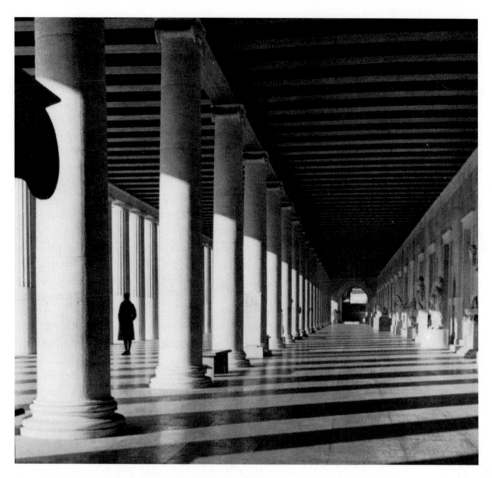

In ancient Athens citizens participated directly in politics by meeting in the Agora.

individuals and parties be able to run for office, that communication (through speeches or the press, and in meetings) be free, and that the voters perceive that a meaningful choice exists. Many questions still remain to be answered. For instance: How many offices should be elective and how many appointive? How many candidates or parties can exist before the choices become hopelessly confused? Where will the money come from to finance electoral campaigns? There is more than one answer to such questions. In some European democracies, for example, very few offices—often just those in the national or local legis-lature—are elective, and much of the money for cam-paigning for these offices comes from the government. In the United States many offices—executive and judi-cial as well as legislative—are elective, and most of the money the candidates use for campaigning comes from industry, labor unions, and private individuals.

Some people have argued that the virtues of direct or participatory democracy can and should be reclaimed even in a modern, complex society. This can be done either by allowing individual neighborhoods in big cities to govern themselves (community control) or by requiring those affected by some government program to participate in its formulation (citizen participation). In many states a measure of direct democracy exists when voters can decide on referendum issues—that is, policy choices that appear on the ballot. The proponents of direct democracy defend it as the only way to ensure that the "will of the people" prevails.

The Framers of the Constitution did not think that the "will of the people" was synonymous with the "common interest" or the "public good." They strongly favored representative democracy over direct democracy. They believed that government should mediate, not mirror, popular views, and that elected officials should represent, not register, majority sentiments. They supposed that most citizens did not have the time, information, interest, and expertise to make reasonable choices among competing policy positions. They suspected that even highly educated people could be manipulated by demagogic leaders who played on their fears and prejudices. They granted that representative democracy often proceeds slowly and prevents sweeping changes in policy, but they cautioned that a government capable of doing great good quickly also can do great harm quickly. They agreed that majority opinion should figure in the enactment of many or most government policies, but they insisted that the protection of civil rights and civil liberties—the right to a fair trial; the freedom of speech, press, and religion; or the right to vote itself—ought never to hinge on a popular vote. Above all, they embraced representative democracy because they saw it as a way of minimizing the chances that power would be abused either by a tyrannical popular majority or by self-serving officeholders.

How Is Power Distributed in a Democracy?

Representative democracy is any system of government in which leaders are authorized to make decisions by winning a competitive struggle for the popular vote. It is obvious then that very different sets of hands can control political power, depending on what kinds of people can become leaders, how the struggle for votes is carried on, how much freedom to act is given to those who win the struggle, and what other sorts of influence (besides the desire for popular approval) affect the leaders' actions.

In some cases the leaders will be so sharply constrained by what most people want that the actions of officeholders will follow the preferences of citizens very closely. We shall call such cases examples of *majoritarian politics*. In this case elected officials are the delegates of the people, acting as the people (or a majority of them) would act were the matter put to a popular vote. The issues handled in a majoritarian fashion can be only those that are suf-

ficiently important to command the attention of most citizens, sufficiently clear to elicit an informed opinion from citizens, and sufficiently feasible to address so that what citizens want done can in fact be done.

When circumstances do not permit majoritarian decision-making, then some group of officials will have to act without knowing (and perhaps without caring) exactly what people want. Indeed, even on issues that do evoke a clear opinion from a majority of citizens, the shaping of the details of a policy will reflect the views of those people who are sufficiently motivated to go to the trouble of becoming active participants in policy-making. These active participants usually will be a small, and probably an unrepresentative, minority. Thus the actual distribution of political power, even in a democracy, will depend importantly on the composition of the political elites who are actually involved in the struggles over policy. By **elite** we mean an identifiable group of persons who possess a disproportionate share of some valued resource—in this case, political power.

Four Theories of Who Governs

At least four theories purport to describe and explain the actions of political elites. One theory is associated with the writings of Karl Marx. To **Marxists**—or at least to some of them, since not all Marxists agree—government, whatever its outward form, is merely a reflection of underlying economic forces, primarily the pattern of ownership of the means of production. All societies, they claim, are divided into classes on the basis of the relationships of people to the economy—capitalists (the bourgeoisie), workers, farmers, intellectuals. In modern society two major classes contend for power—capitalists and workers. Whichever class dominates the economy also controls the government, which is nothing more than a piece of machinery designed to express and give legal effect to underlying class interests. In the United States the government "is but a committee for managing the common affairs of the whole bourgeoisie."[3] To a traditional Marxist it would be pointless to study the government since, as it is controlled by the dominant social class, it would have no independent power. There are many variations, some quite subtle, on this fundamental argument, and some newer Marxists find it more interesting to

Karl Marx (left, 1818–1883), a German philosopher and radical political leader, was the founder of modern socialist thought. A brilliant, complex, and vituperative writer, Marx was best known for his Communist Manifesto. *His major work was* Das Kapital, *a four-volume analysis of nineteenth-century capitalism. Max Weber (right, 1864–1920), a German scholar, was a founder of sociology. Trained in law and history, he produced a major analysis of the evolution of modern society, which stressed the role of bureaucracy.*

study how the government actually operates than did Marx himself, for whom government was a mere "epiphenomenon." But even neo-Marxists believe that the answers to the questions of who really governs and to what ends are to be found in the pattern of economic interests, especially those represented by the large corporation.

A second theory, closely related to the first, argues that a nongovernmental elite makes most of the major decisions but that this elite is not composed exclusively, or even primarily, of corporate leaders. C. Wright Mills, an American sociologist, expresses this view in his book *The Power Elite.*[4] To him the most important policies are set by a loose coalition of three groups—corporate leaders, top military officers, and a handful of key political leaders. Different people have different versions of the "power elite" theory. Some would add to the triumvirate listed by Mills the leaders of the major

communications media; others would add major labor leaders or the heads of various special-interest groups. The essential argument is the same, however: government is dominated by a few top leaders, most of whom are outside the government and enjoy great advantages in wealth, status, or organizational position. They act in concert, and the policies they make serve the interests of the elite. Some people have such leaders in mind when they use the term *the Establishment*, though when that expression was first coined, it referred to the influence exercised by Wall Street lawyers who alternated between governmental and private employment.[5]

A third theory directs attention to the appointed officials—the **bureaucrats**—who operate government agencies from day to day. Max Weber, a German historian and sociologist who wrote in the early years of this century, criticized the Marxist position because it assigned exclusive significance to economic power. Weber thought Marx had neglected the dominant social and political fact of modern times—that all institutions, governmental and nongovernmental, have fallen under the control of large bureaucracies whose expertise and specialized competence are essential to the management of contemporary affairs. Capitalists or workers may come to power, but the government agencies they create will be dominated by those who operate them on a daily basis. This dominance would have advantages, Weber thought, because decisions would be made more rationally; but it would also have disadvantages, because the political power of the bureaucrats would become "overtowering."[6]

A fourth answer has no single intellectual parent but can be described loosely as the **pluralist** view. Political resources, such as money, prestige, expertise, organizational position, and access to the mass media, are so widely scattered in our society and in the hands of such a variety of persons that no single elite has anything like a monopoly on them. Furthermore there are so many governmental institutions in which power may be exercised—city, state, and federal governments and, within these, the offices of mayors, managers, legislators, governors, presidents, judges, bureaucrats—that no single group, even if it had many political resources, could dominate most, or even much, of the political process. Policies are the outcome of a complex pattern of political haggling, innumerable compromises, and shifting alliances.[7] Pluralists do not argue that political resources are distributed equally—that would be tantamount to saying that all decisions are made on a majoritarian basis. They believe that political resources are sufficiently divided among such different kinds of elites (businesspeople, politicians, union leaders, journalists, bureaucrats, professors, environmentalists, lawyers, and whomever else) that all, or almost all, relevant interests have a chance to affect the outcome of decisions. Not only are the elites divided, they are responsive to their followers' interests, and thus they provide representation to almost all citizens affected by a policy.

Contemplating these contending theories may lead some people to the cynical conclusion that, whichever theory is correct, politics is a self-seeking enterprise in which everybody is out for personal gain. Though there is surely plenty of self-interest among political elites (at least as much as there is

among college students!), it does not necessarily follow that the resulting policies will be wholly self-serving. For one thing, a policy may be good or bad independent of the motives of the person who decided it, just as a product sold on the market may be useful or useless regardless of the profit-seeking or wage-seeking motives of those who produced it. For another thing, the self-interest of individuals is often an incomplete guide to their actions. People must frequently choose between two courses of action, neither of which has an obvious "payoff" to them. We caution against the cynical explanation of politics that Americans seem especially prone to adopt. Alexis de Tocqueville, the French author of a perceptive account of American life and politics in the early nineteenth century, noticed this trait among us.

> Americans . . . are fond of explaining almost all the actions of their lives by the principle of self-interest rightly understood. . . . In this respect I think they frequently fail to do themselves justice; for in the United States as well as elsewhere people are sometimes seen to give way to those disinterested and spontaneous impulses that are natural to man; but the Americans seldom admit that they yield to emotions of this kind; they are more anxious to do honor to their philosophy than to themselves.[8]

The belief that people will usually act on the basis of their self-interest, narrowly defined, is a theory to be tested, not an assumption to be made. Two examples of how such an assumption can prove misleading will suffice for now. In the 1960s leaders of the AFL-CIO in Washington were among the most influential forces lobbying Congress for the passage of certain civil rights bills. Yet at the time they did this, the leaders did not stand to benefit either personally (they were almost all white) or organizationally (rank-and-file labor union members were not enthusiastic about such measures).[9] Another example: In the late 1970s many employees of the Civil Aeronautics Board worked hard to have their agency abolished, even though this meant that they would lose their jobs. To understand why they took these positions, it is not enough to know their incomes or their jobs; one must also know something about their attitudes, their allies, and the temper of the times. In short political preferences cannot

Soup kitchens, such as this one created by the Great Depression, helped redefine the responsibilities of government.

invariably be predicted simply by knowing economic or organizational position.

Political Change

The question of who governs will be answered differently at different times. Circumstances change, as does our knowledge about politics. As we shall see in Part III, the presidency and Congress in the second half of the nineteenth century were organized rather differently from how they are today. Throughout this book we shall make frequent reference to the historical evolution of institutions and policies. We shall do this partly because what government does today is powerfully influenced by what it did yesterday, and partly because the evolution of our institutions and policies has not stopped but is continuing. If we get some sense of how the past has shaped the government, we may better understand what we see today and are likely to see tomorrow.

When we view American government from the perspective of the past, we will find it hard to accept as generally true any simple, mechanistic theory of politics. Economic interests, powerful elites, entrenched bureaucrats, and competing pressure groups have all played a part in shaping our policies, but the great shifts in the direction of that policy respond to changing *beliefs* about what government is supposed to do.

In the 1920s it was widely assumed that the federal government would play a small role in our lives. From the 1930s through the 1970s it was generally believed that the federal government would try to solve whatever social or economic problem existed. From 1981 through 1988 the administration of Ronald Reagan sought to reverse that assumption and to cut back on the taxes Washington levied, the money it spent, and the regulations it imposed. It is clear that no simple theory of politics is likely to explain both the growth of federal power after 1932 and the effort to cut back on that power starting in 1981. Every student of politics sooner or later learns that the hardest things to explain are usually the most important ones.

Take the case of foreign affairs. During certain periods in our history we have taken an active interest in the outside world—at the time the nation was founded, when France and England seemed to have it in their power to determine whether or not America would survive as a nation; in the 1840s, when we sought to expand the nation into areas where Mexico and Canada had claims; in the late 1890s, when many leaders believed we had an obligation to acquire an overseas empire in the Caribbean and the Pacific; and in the period from the 1940s to the 1960s, when we openly accepted the role of the world's police officer. At other times America has looked inward, spurning opportunities for expansion and virtually ignoring events that in other periods would have been a cause for war, or at least mobilization.

Deep-seated beliefs, major economic developments, and widely shared (or competing) opinions about what constitutes the dominant political problem of the time shape the nature of day-to-day political conflict. What this means is that, in any broad historical or comparative perspective, politics is not just about "who gets what," though that is part of the story. It is about how people, or elites claiming to speak for people, define the public interest. Lest one think that such definitions are mere window dressing, signifying nothing of importance, bear in mind that on occasion men and women have been prepared to fight and die for one definition or another. Suppose you had been alive in 1861. Do you think you would have viewed slavery as a matter of gains and losses, costs and benefits, winners and losers? Some people did. Or do you think you would have been willing to fight to abolish or preserve it? Many others did just that. The differences in these ways of thinking about such an issue are at least as important as how institutions are organized or elections conducted.

Finding Out Who Governs

Ideally political scientists ought to be able to give clear answers, amply supported by evidence, to the questions, How is political power distributed? And to what purposes will it be used under various circumstances? In reality they can (at best) give partial, contingent, and controversial answers. The reason is to be found in the nature of our subject. Unlike economists, who assume that people have more or less stable preferences and can compare ways of satisfying those preferences by looking at the relative prices

of various goods and services, political scientists are interested in how preferences are formed, especially for those kinds of services, such as national defense or pollution control, that cannot be evaluated chiefly in terms of monetary costs.

Understanding preferences is vital to understanding power. Who did what in government is not hard to find out, but who wielded power—that is, who made a difference in the outcome and for what reason—is much harder to discover. *Power* is a word that conjures up images of deals, bribes, power plays, and arm-twisting. In fact most power exists because of shared understanding, common friendships, communal or organizational loyalties, and different degrees of prestige. These are hard to identify and almost impossible to quantify.

Nor can the distribution of political power be inferred simply by knowing what laws are on the books or what administrative actions have been taken. The enactment of a consumer protection law does not mean that consumers are powerful, any more than the absence of such a law means that corporations are powerful. The passage of such a law could reflect an aroused public opinion, the lobbying of a small group claiming to speak for consumers, the ambitions of a senator, or the intrigues of one business firm seeking to gain a competitive advantage over another. A close analysis of what the law entails and how it was passed and administered is necessary before much of anything can be said.

This book will avoid sweeping claims that we have an "imperial" presidency (or an impotent one), an "obstructionist" Congress (or an innovative one), or "captured" regulatory agencies. Such labels do an injustice to the different roles that presidents, members of Congress, and administrators play in different kinds of issues and in different historical periods.

The view taken in this book is that judgments about institutions and interests can be made only after one has seen how they behave on a variety of important issues or potential issues, such as economic policy, the regulation of business, social welfare, civil rights and liberties, and foreign and military affairs. The policies adopted or blocked, the groups heeded or ignored, the values embraced or rejected—these constitute the raw material out of which one can fashion an answer to the central questions we have asked: Who rules? and To what ends?

MEMORANDUM
To: Governor Steve Finore
From: Edward Heron, chief policy adviser
Subject: Initiative Repeal

You have supported several successful initiatives (life imprisonment for thrice-convicted violent felons, property tax limits), but you have never publicly stated a view on the initiative itself, and the repeal proposal will probably surface during tomorrow's press briefing.

Arguments for a ban:

1. Ours is a representative, not a direct, democracy in which voters elect leaders and elected leaders make policy decisions subject to review by the courts.

2. Voters are often neither rational nor respectful of constitutional rights. For example, many people demand both lower taxes and more government services, and polls find that most voters would prohibit people with certain views from speaking and deprive all persons accused of a violent crime from getting out on bail while awaiting trial.

3. Over the past 100 years nearly 800 statewide ballot initiatives have been passed in 24 states, including 35 in 1998 alone. Rather than giving power to the people, special-interest groups have spent billions of dollars manipulating voters to pass initiatives that enrich or benefit them, not the public at large.

Arguments against a ban:

1. When elected officials fail to respond to persistent public majorities favoring tougher crime measures, lower property taxes, and other popular concerns, direct democracy via the initiative is legitimate, and the courts can still review the law.

2. More Americans than ever have college degrees and easy access to information about public affairs. Studies find that most average citizens are able to figure out which candidates, parties, or advocacy groups come closest to supporting their own economic interests and personal values.

3. All told, the 24 states that passed 35 laws by initiative in 1998 also passed more than 14,000 laws by the regular legislative process (out of more than 70,000 bills they considered). Studies find that special-interest groups are severely limited in their ability to pass new laws by initiative, while citizens' groups with broad-based public support are behind most initiatives that pass.

Your decision:

Favor ban _____ Oppose ban _____

Legal and Policy Experts Call for a Ban on Ballot Initiatives

December 11
SACRAMENTO, CA

A report released yesterday and signed by more than 100 law and public policy professors statewide urges that the state's constitution be amended to ban legislation by initiative. The initiative allows state voters to place legislative measures directly on the ballot by getting enough signatures. The initiative "has led to disastrous policy decisions on taxes, crime, and other issues," the report declared . . .

The way in which our institutions of government handle social welfare, for example, differs from the way other democratic nations handle it, and it differs as well from the way our own institutions once treated it. The description of our institutions in Part III will therefore include not only an account of how they work today but also a brief historical background on their workings and a comparison with similar institutions in other countries. There is a tendency to assume that how we do things today is the only way they could possibly be done. In fact there are other ways to operate a government based on some measure of popular rule. History, tradition, and belief weigh heavily on all that we do.

In any event the place to begin a search for how power is distributed in national politics and what purposes that power serves is with the founding of the federal government in 1787: the Constitutional Convention and the events leading up to it. Though the decisions of that time were not made by philosophers or professors, the practical men who made them had a philosophic and professorial cast of mind, and thus they left behind a fairly explicit account of what values they sought to protect and what arrangements they thought ought to be made for the allocation of political power.

Summary

There are two major questions about politics: Who governs? To what ends? This book focuses mainly on answering the first.

Four answers have traditionally been given to the question of who governs.

- The *Marxist*—those who control the economic system will control the political one.
- The *elitist*—a few top leaders, not all of them drawn from business, make the key decisions without reference to popular desires.
- The *bureaucratic*—appointed civil servants run things.
- The *pluralist*—competition among affected interests shapes public policy.

To choose among these theories or to devise new ones requires more than describing governmental institutions and processes. In addition one must examine the kinds of issues that do (or do not) get taken up by the political system and how that system resolves them.

The distinction between different types of democracies is important. The Framers of the Constitution intended that America be a representative democracy in which the power to make decisions is determined by means of a free and competitive struggle for the citizens' votes.

Key Terms

power *p. 4*	democratic centralism *p. 5*	representative democracy *p. 6*	bureaucrats *p. 9*
authority *p. 4*			pluralist *p. 10*
legitimacy *p. 5*	direct or participatory democracy *p. 6*	elite *p. 8*	
democracy *p. 5*		Marxists *p. 8*	

Suggested Readings

Banfield, Edward C. *Political Influence*. New York: Free Press, 1961. A method of analyzing politics—in this case, in the city of Chicago—comparable to the approach adopted in this book.

Crick, Bernard, *The American Science of Politics*, London: Routledge & Kegan Paul, 1959. A critical review of the methods of studying government and politics.

Marx, Karl, and Friedrich Engels. "The Manifesto of the Communist Party." In *The Marx-Engels Reader*. 2nd ed., edited by Robert C. Tucker. New York: Norton, 1978, 469–500. The classic statement of the Marxist view of history and politics. Should be read in conjunction with Engels, "Socialism: Utopian and Scientific," in the same collection, 683–717.

Mills, C. Wright. *The Power Elite*. New York: Oxford University Press, 1956. An argument that self-serving elites dominate American politics.

Schumpeter, Joseph A. *Capitalism, Socialism, and Democracy*. 3rd ed. New York: Harper Torchbooks, 1950, chs. 20–23. A lucid statement of the theory of representative democracy and how it differs from participatory democracy.

Truman, David B. *The Governmental Process*. 2nd ed. New York: Knopf, 1971. A pluralist interpretation of American politics.

Weber, Max. *From Max Weber: Essays in Sociology*. Translated and edited by H. H. Gerth and C. Wright Mills. London: Routledge & Kegan Paul, 1948, ch. 8. A theory of bureaucracy and its power.

The Constitution

2

Enduring Questions

1. What view of human nature is embodied in the Constitution?
2. Is representative democracy possible without political compromise?
3. How can any government be strong enough to govern without threatening freedom?
4. Has the system of separate institutions sharing powers protected liberty and promoted equality as the Framers envisioned it would?

The Problem of Liberty
The Colonial Mind • The Real Revolution • Weaknesses of the Confederation

The Constitutional Convention
The Lessons of Experience • The Framers

The Challenge
The Virginia Plan • The New Jersey Plan • The Compromise

The Constitution and Democracy
Key Principles • Government and Human Nature

The Constitution and Liberty
The Antifederalist View • Need for a Bill of Rights • The Constitution and Slavery

The Motives of the Framers
Economic Interests at the Convention • Economic Interests and Ratification • The Constitution and Equality

Constitutional Reform—Modern Views
Reducing the Separation of Powers • Making the System Less Democratic • Who Is Right?

The goal of the American Revolution was liberty. It was not the first revolution with that object; it may not have been the last; but it was perhaps the clearest case of a people altering the political order violently, simply in order to protect their liberties. Subsequent revolutions had more complicated, or utterly different, objectives. The French Revolution in 1789 sought not only liberty, but "equality and fraternity." The Russian Revolution (1917) and the Chinese Revolution (culminating in 1949) chiefly sought equality and were little concerned with liberty as we understand it.

The Problem of Liberty

What the American colonists sought to protect when they signed the Declaration of Independence in 1776 were the traditional liberties to which they thought they were entitled as British subjects. These liberties included the right to bring their legal cases before truly independent judges rather than ones subordinate to the king; to be free of the burden of having

*Even before the Revolutionary War, many felt that some form of union would be necessary if
the rebellious colonies were to survive. In 1774, the* Massachusetts Spy *portrayed the colonies
as segments of a snake that must "Join or Die."*

British troops quartered in their homes; to engage in trade without burdensome restrictions; and, of course, to pay no taxes voted by a British Parliament in which they had no direct representation. During the ten years or more of agitation and argument leading up to the War of Independence, most colonists believed that their liberties could be protected while they remained a part of the British Empire.

Slowly but surely opinion shifted. By the time war broke out in 1775, a large number of colonists (though perhaps not a majority) had reached the conclusion that the colonies would have to become independent of Great Britain if their liberties were to be assured. The colonists had many reasons for regarding independence as the only solution, but one is especially important: they no longer had confidence in the English constitution. This constitution was not a single written document but rather a collection of laws, charters, and traditional understandings that proclaimed the liberties of British subjects. Yet these liberties, in the eyes of the colonists, were regularly violated despite their constitutional protection. Clearly, then, the English constitution was an inadequate check on the abuses of political power. The revolutionary leaders sought an explanation of the insufficiency of the constitution and found it in human nature.

The Colonial Mind

"A lust for domination is more or less natural to all parties," one colonist wrote.[1] Men will seek power,

many colonists believed, because they are ambitious, greedy, and easily corrupted. John Adams denounced the "luxury, effeminacy, and venality" of English politics; Patrick Henry spoke scathingly of the "corrupt House of Commons"; and Alexander Hamilton described England as "an old, wrinkled, withered, worn-out hag."[2] This was in part flamboyant rhetoric designed to whip up enthusiasm for the conflict, but it was also deeply revealing of the colonial mind. Their belief that English politicians—and by implication, most politicians—tended to be corrupt was the colonists' explanation of why the English constitution was not an adequate guarantee of the liberty of the citizens. This opinion was to persist and, as we shall see, profoundly affect the way the Americans went about designing their own governments.

The liberties the colonists fought to protect were, they thought, widely understood. They were based not on the generosity of the king or the language of statutes but on a "higher law" embodying "natural rights" that were ordained by God, discoverable in nature and history, and essential to human progress. These rights, John Dickinson wrote, "are born with us; exist with us; and cannot be taken away from us by any human power."[3] There was general agreement that the essential rights included life, liberty, and property long before Thomas Jefferson wrote them into the Declaration of Independence. (Jefferson changed "property" to "the pursuit of happiness," but almost everybody else went on talking about property.)

The American colonists' desire to assert their liberties led in time to a deep hostility to British government, as when these New Yorkers toppled a statue of King George III, melted it down, and used the metal to make bullets.

This emphasis on property did not mean that the American Revolution was thought up by the rich and wellborn to protect their interests or that there was a struggle between property owners and the propertyless. In late-eighteenth-century America most people (except the black slaves) had property of some kind. The overwhelming majority of citizens were self-employed—as farmers or artisans—and rather few people benefited financially by gaining independence from England. Taxes were higher during and after the war than before, trade was disrupted by the conflict, and debts mounted perilously as various expedients were invented to pay for the struggle. There were, of course, war profiteers and those who tried to manipulate the currency to their own advantage, but most Americans at the time of the war saw the conflict clearly in terms of political rather than economic issues. It was a war of ideology.

Everyone recognizes the glowing language with which Jefferson set out the case for independence in the second paragraph of the Declaration:

> We hold these truths to be self-evident, that all men are created equal, that they are endowed by their Creator with certain unalienable Rights, that among these are Life, Liberty, and the pursuit of Happiness.—That to secure these rights, Governments are instituted among Men, deriving their just powers from the consent of the governed—that whenever any Form of Government becomes destructive of these ends, it is the Right of the People to alter or to abolish it, and to institute new Government, having its foundation on such principles, and organizing its powers in such form, as to them shall seem most likely to effect their Safety and Happiness.

What almost no one recalls, but what are an essential part of the Declaration, are the next twenty-seven paragraphs, in which Jefferson listed, item by item, the specific complaints the colonists had against George III and his ministers. None of these items spoke of social or economic conditions in the colonies; all spoke instead of specific violations of political liberties. The Declaration was in essence a lawyer's brief prefaced by a stirring philosophical claim that the rights being violated were **unalienable**—that is, based on nature and Providence, and not on the whims or preferences of people. Jefferson, in his original draft, added a

North America in 1787

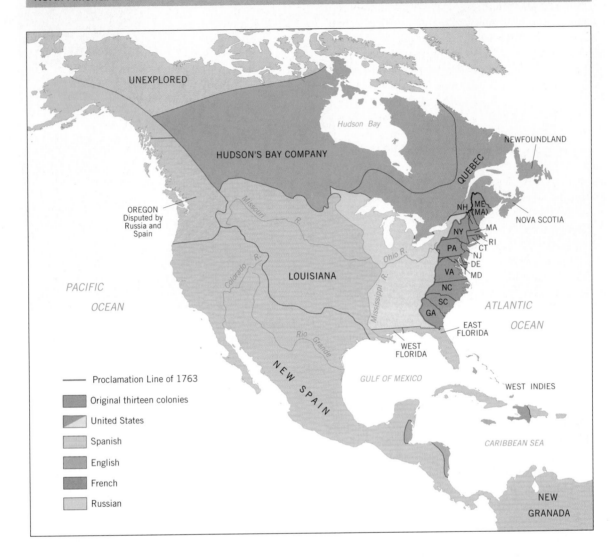

twenty-eighth complaint—that the king had allowed the slave trade to continue *and* was inciting slaves to revolt against their masters. Congress, faced with so contradictory a charge, decided to include a muted reference to slave insurrections and omit all reference to the slave trade.

The Real Revolution

The Revolution was more than the War of Independence. It began before the war, continued after it, and involved more than driving out the British army by force of arms. The *real* Revolution, as John Adams afterward explained in a letter to a friend, was the "radical change in the principles, opinions, and sentiments, and affections of the people."[4] This radical change had to do with a new vision of what could make political authority legitimate and personal liberties secure. Government by royal prerogative was rejected; instead legitimate government would require the consent of the governed. Political power could not be exercised on the basis of tradition but only as a result of a direct grant of power contained in a written constitution. Human liberty existed before government was organized, and government must respect that liberty. The legislative branch of government, in which the people were directly represented, should be superior to the executive branch.

These were indeed revolutionary ideas. No government at the time had been organized on the basis of these principles. And to the colonists such notions were not empty words but rules to be put into immediate practice. In 1776 eight states adopted written constitutions. Within a few years every former colony had adopted one except Connecticut and Rhode Island, two states that continued to rely on their colonial charters. Most state constitutions had detailed bills of rights defining personal liberties, and most placed the highest political power in the hands of elected representatives.

Written constitutions, representatives, and bills of rights are so familiar to us now that we forget how bold and unprecedented those innovations were in 1776. Indeed, many Americans did not think they would succeed: such arrangements would be either so strong that they would threaten liberty or so weak that they would permit chaos.

The eleven years that elapsed between the Declaration of Independence and the signing of the Constitution in 1787 were years of turmoil, uncertainty, and fear. George Washington had to wage a bitter, protracted war without anything resembling a strong national government to support him. The supply and financing of his army were based on a series of hasty improvisations, most badly administered and few adequately supported by the fiercely independent states. When peace came, many parts of the nation were a shambles. At least a quarter of New York City was in ruins, and many other communities were nearly devastated. Though the British lost the war, they still were powerful on the North American continent, with an army available in Canada (where many Americans loyal to Britain had fled) and a large navy at sea. Spain claimed the Mississippi River valley and occupied what are now Florida and California. Men who had left their farms to fight came back to discover themselves in debt with no money and heavy taxes. The paper money printed to finance the war was now virtually worthless.

Weaknesses of the Confederation

The thirteen states had formed only a faint semblance of a national government with which to

The Articles of Confederation had made it plain that the United States was not to have a true national government but was to be governed by a compact among sovereign and independent states.

bring order to the nation. The **Articles of Confederation,** which went into effect in 1781, created little more than a "league of friendship" that could not levy taxes or regulate commerce. Each state retained its sovereignty and independence, each state (regardless of size) had one vote in Congress, nine (of thirteen) votes were required to pass any measure, and the delegates who cast these votes were picked and paid for by the state legislatures. Congress did have the power to make peace, and thus it was able to ratify the treaty with England in 1783. It could coin money, but there was precious little to coin; it could appoint the key army officers, but the army was small and dependent for support on independent state militias; it was allowed to run the post office, then, as now, a thankless task that nobody else wanted. John Hancock, who in 1785 was elected to the meaningless office of "president" under the Articles, never showed up to take the job.

John Hancock was proud to have signed the Declaration of Independence but thought so little of the presidency under the Articles of Confederation that he never bothered to accept the job.

The Constitutional Convention

The delegates assembled at Philadelphia for what was advertised (and authorized by Congress) as a meeting to revise the Articles; they adjourned four months later having written a wholly new constitution. When they met, they were keenly aware of the problems of the confederacy but far from agreeing as to what should be done about those problems. The protection of life, liberty, and property was their objective in 1787 as it had been in 1776, but they had no accepted political theory that would tell them what kind of national government, if any, would serve that goal.

The Lessons of Experience

They had read ancient and modern political history, only to learn that nothing seemed to work. James Madison spent a good part of 1786 studying books sent to him by Thomas Jefferson, then in Paris, in hopes of finding some model for a workable American republic. He took careful notes on various confederacies in ancient Greece and on the more modern confederacy of the United Netherlands. He reviewed the history of Switzerland and Poland and the ups and downs of the Roman republic. He concluded that there was no model; as he later put it in one of the *Federalist* papers, history consists only of beacon lights "which give warning of the course to be shunned, without pointing out that which ought to be pursued."[5] The problem seemed to be that confederacies were too weak to govern and tended to collapse from internal dissension, while all stronger forms of government were so powerful as to trample the liberties of the citizens.

Several states claimed the unsettled lands in the West, and they occasionally pressed those claims with guns. Pennsylvania and Virginia went to war near Pittsburgh, and Vermont threatened to become part of Canada. There was no national judicial system to settle these or other claims among the states. To amend the Articles of Confederation, all thirteen states had to agree.

Many of the leaders of the Revolution, such as George Washington and Alexander Hamilton, believed that a stronger national government was essential. They lamented the disruption of commerce and travel caused by the quarrelsome states and deeply feared the possibility of foreign military intervention, with England or France playing one state off against another. A small group of men, conferring at Washington's home at Mount Vernon in 1785, decided to call a meeting to discuss trade regulation. That meeting, held at Annapolis, Maryland, in September 1786, was not well attended (no delegates arrived from New England), and so another meeting, this one in Philadelphia, was called for the following spring—in May 1787—to consider ways of remedying the defects of the Confederation.

State Constitutions   Madison and the others did not need to consult history, or even the defects of the Articles of Confederation, for illustrations of the problem. These could be found in the government of the American states at the time. Pennsylvania and Massachusetts exemplified two aspects of the problem. The Pennsylvania constitution, adopted in 1776, created the most radically democratic of the new state regimes. All power was given to a one-house (unicameral) legislature, the Assembly, the members of which were elected annually for one year terms. No legislator could serve more than four years. There was no governor or president, only an

Quakers

Executive Council that had few powers. Thomas Paine, whose pamphlets had helped precipitate the break with England, thought the Pennsylvania constitution was the best in America, and in France philosophers hailed it as the very embodiment of the principle of rule by the people. Though popular in France, it was a good deal less popular in Philadelphia. The Assembly disfranchised the Quakers, persecuted conscientious objectors to the war, ignored the requirement of trial by juries, and manipulated the judiciary.[6] To Madison and his friends the Pennsylvania constitution demonstrated how a government, though democratic, could be tyrannical as a result of concentrating all powers into one set of hands.

The Massachusetts constitution, adopted in 1780, was a good deal less democratic. There was a clear separation of powers among the various branches of government, the directly elected governor could veto acts of the legislature, and judges served for life. Both voters and elected officials had to be property owners; the governor, in fact, had to own at least £1,000 worth of property. The principal officeholders had to swear that they were Christians.

Shays's Rebellion   But if the government of Pennsylvania was thought to be too strong, that of Massachusetts seemed too weak, despite its "conservative" features. In January 1787 a group of ex-Revolutionary War soldiers and officers, plagued by debts and high taxes and fearful of losing their property to creditors and tax collectors, forcibly prevented the courts in western Massachusetts from sitting. This became known as **Shays's Rebellion**, after one of the officers, Daniel Shays. The governor of Massachusetts asked the Continental Congress to send troops to suppress the rebellion, but it could not raise the money or the manpower. Then he turned to his own state militia, but discovered he did not have one. In desperation private funds were collected to hire a volunteer army, which marched on Springfield and, with the firing of a few shots, dispersed the rebels, who fled into neighboring states.

Shays's Rebellion, occurring between the aborted Annapolis and the coming Philadelphia conventions, had a powerful effect on opinion. Delegates who might have been reluctant to attend the Philadelphia meeting, especially those from New England, were galvanized by the fear that state gov-

The presiding officer at the Constitutional Convention was George Washington (1732–1799). He participated just once in the debates, but the effect of his presence was great. He was a national military hero, and it was generally expected that he would be the nation's first president.

ernments were about to collapse from internal dissension. George Washington wrote a friend despairingly: "For God's sake, if they [the rebels] have *real* grievances, redress them; if they have not, employ the force of government against them at once."[7] Thomas Jefferson, living in Paris, took a more detached view: "A little rebellion now and then is a good thing," he wrote. "The tree of liberty must be refreshed from time to time with the blood of patriots and tyrants."[8] Though Jefferson's detachment might be explained by the fact that he was in Paris and not in Springfield, there were others, like Governor George Clinton of New York, who shared the view that no strong central government was required. (Whether Clinton would have agreed about the virtues of spilled blood, especially his, is another matter.)

The Framers

The Philadelphia convention attracted fifty-five delegates, only about thirty of whom participated regularly in the proceedings. One state, Rhode Island, refused to send anyone. The convention met during a miserably hot Philadelphia summer, with the delegates pledged to keep their deliberations secret. The

Shays's Rebellion in western Massachusetts in 1786–1787 stirred deep fears of anarchy in America. The ruckus was put down by a hastily assembled militia, and the rebels were eventually pardoned.

Commonwealth of MASSACHUSETTS,

By BENJAMIN LINCOLN, ESQUIRE,

Commanding General of the Troops now in the Field, by Order of
GOVERNMENT.

WHEREAS there are some of the Citizens of this Commonwealth, who have acted in Arms as Non-Commissioned Officers and Privates against the Government of this State, who have caused it to be represented, that they would willingly return to their Allegiance and Duty, could they hope for a Pardon.

To all such I declare, That if they will come in, surrender their Arms, and take and subscribe the Oath of Allegiance to this Commonwealth, that they will be recommended to a Pardon.

B. *LINCOLN.*

Dated at Head-Quarters, Pittsfield, *February* 19, 1787.

talkative and party-loving Benjamin Franklin was often accompanied by other delegates to make sure that neither wine nor his delight in telling stories would lead him to divulge delicate secrets.

Those who attended were for the most part young (Hamilton was thirty; Madison thirty-six) but experienced. Eight delegates had signed the Declaration of Independence, seven had been governors, thirty-four were lawyers and reasonably well-to-do, a few were wealthy. They were not "intellectuals," but men of practical affairs. Thirty-nine had served in the ineffectual Congress of the Confederation; a third were veterans of the Continental army.

Some names made famous by the Revolution were conspicuously absent. Thomas Jefferson and John Adams were serving as ministers abroad; Samuel Adams was ill; Patrick Henry was chosen to attend but refused, commenting that he "smelled a rat in Philadelphia, tending toward monarchy."

The convention produced not a revision of the Articles of Confederation, as it had been authorized to do, but instead a wholly new written constitution creating a true national government unlike any that had existed before. That document is today the world's oldest written national constitution. Those who wrote it were neither saints nor schemers, and the deliberations were not always lofty or philosophical—much hard bargaining, not a little confusion, and the accidents of personality and time helped shape the final product. The delegates were split on many issues—what powers should be given to a central government, how the states should be represented, what was to be done about slavery, the role of the people—each of which was resolved by a compromise. The speeches of the delegates (known to us from the detailed notes kept by Madison) did not explicitly draw on political philosophy or quote from the writings of philosophers. Everybody present was quite familiar with the traditional arguments and, on the whole, well-read in history. But though the leading political philosophers were only rarely mentioned, the debate was profoundly influenced by philosophical beliefs, some formed by the revolutionary experience and others by the eleven-year attempt at self-government.

From the debates leading up to the Revolution, the delegates had drawn a commitment to liberty, which, despite the abuses sometimes committed in its name, they continued to share. Their defense of liberty as a natural right was derived from the writings of the English philosopher John Locke and based on his view that such rights are discoverable by reason. In a "state of nature," Locke argued, all men cherish and seek to protect their life, liberty, and property. But in a state of nature—that is, a society without a government—the strong can use their liberty to deprive the weak of theirs. The instinct for self-preservation leads people to want a government that will prevent this exploitation. But if the government is not itself to deprive its subjects of their liberty, it must be limited. The chief limitation on it, he said, should derive from the fact that it is created, and governs, by the consent of the governed. People will not agree to be ruled by a government that threatens their liberty; therefore the government to which they freely choose to submit themselves will be a limited government designed to protect liberty.

The Pennsylvania experience as well as the history of British government led the Framers to doubt whether popular consent alone would be a sufficient guarantor of liberty. A popular government may prove too weak (as in Massachusetts) to prevent one faction from abusing another, or a popular majority can be tyrannical (as in Pennsylvania). In fact the tyranny of the majority can be an even graver threat than rule by the few. In the former case there may be no defenses for the individual—one lone person cannot count on the succor of public opinion or the possibility of popular revolt.

The problem, then, was a delicate one: how to devise a government strong enough to preserve order but not so strong that it would threaten liberty. The answer, the delegates believed, was not "democracy" as it was then understood. To many conservatives in the late eighteenth century, democracy meant mob rule—it meant, in short, Shays's Rebellion (or, if they had been candid about it, the Boston Tea Party). On the other hand, *aristocracy*—the rule of the few—was no solution, since the few were likely to be self-seeking. Madison, writing later in the *Federalist* papers, put the problem this way:

If men were angels, no government would be necessary. If angels were to govern men, neither external nor internal controls on government would be necessary. In framing a govern-

ment which is to be administered by men over men, the great difficulty lies in this: you must first enable the government to control the governed; and in the next place oblige it to control itself.[9]

Striking this balance could not be done, Madison believed, simply by writing a constitution that set limits on what government could do. The example of British rule over the colonies proved that laws and customs were inadequate checks on political power. As he expressed it, "A mere demarcation on parchment of the constitutional limits [of government] is not a sufficient guard against those encroachments which lead to a tyrannical concentration of all the powers of government in the same hands."[10]

The Challenge

The resolution of political issues, great and small, often depends crucially on how the central question is phrased. The delegates came to Philadelphia in general agreement that there were defects in the Articles of Confederation that ought to be remedied. Had they, after convening, decided to make their business that of listing these defects and debating alternative remedies for them, the document that emerged would in all likelihood have been very different from what in fact was adopted. But immediately after the convention had organized itself and chosen Washington to be its presiding officer, the Virginia delegation, led by Governor Edmund Randolph but relying heavily on the draftsmanship of James Madison, presented to the convention a comprehensive plan for a wholly new national government. The plan quickly became the major item of business of the meeting; it, and little else, was debated for the next two weeks.

The Virginia Plan

When the convention decided to make the Virginia Plan its agenda, it had fundamentally altered the nature of its task. The business at hand was not to be the Articles and their defects, but rather how one should go about designing a true national government. The Virginia Plan called for a strong national union organized into three governmental branches—the legislative, executive, and judicial. The legislature was to be composed of two houses, the first elected directly by the people and the second chosen by the first house from among the people nominated by state legislatures. The executive was to be chosen by the national legislature, as were members of a national judiciary. The executive and some members of the judiciary were to constitute a "council of revision" that could veto acts of the legislature; that veto, in turn, could be overridden by the legislature. There were other interesting details, but the key features of the Virginia Plan were two: (1) a national legislature would have supreme powers on all matters on which the separate states were not competent to act, as well as the power to veto any and all state laws, and (2) at least one house of the legislature would be elected directly by the people.

The New Jersey Plan

As the debate went on, the representatives of New Jersey and other small states became increasingly worried that the convention was going to write a constitution in which the states would be represented in both houses of Congress on the basis of population. If this happened, the smaller states feared they would always be outvoted by the larger ones, and so, with William Paterson of New Jersey as their spokesman, they introduced a new plan. The New Jersey Plan proposed to amend, not replace, the old Articles of Confederation. It enhanced the power of the national government (though not as much as the Virginia Plan), but it did so in a way that left the states' representation in Congress unchanged from the Articles—each state would have one vote. Thus not only would the interests of the small states be protected, but Congress itself would remain to a substantial degree the creature of state governments.

If the New Jersey resolutions had been presented first and taken up as the major item of business, it is quite possible that they would have become the framework for the document that finally emerged. But they were not. Offered after the convention had been discussing the Virginia Plan for two weeks, the resolutions encountered a reception very different from what they would have received if introduced earlier. The debate had the delegates already thinking in terms of a national government that was more independent of the states, and thus it had accustomed them to proposals that, under other cir-

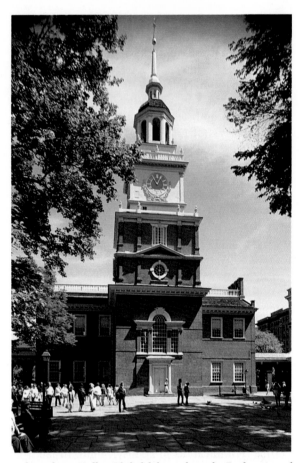

Independence Hall in Philadelphia, where the Declaration of Independence and the Constitution were signed.

cumstances, might have seemed quite radical. On June 19 the first decisive vote of the convention was taken: seven states preferred the Virginia Plan, three states the New Jersey Plan, and one state was split.

With the tide running in favor of a strong national government, the supporters of the small states had to shift their strategy. They now began to focus their efforts on ensuring that the small states could not be outvoted by the larger ones in Congress. One way was to have the members of the lower house elected by the state legislatures rather than the people, with each state getting the same number of seats rather than seats proportional to its population.

The debate was long and feelings ran high, so much so that Benjamin Franklin, at eighty-one the oldest delegate present, suggested that each day's meeting begin with a prayer. It turned out that the convention could not even agree on this: Hamilton is supposed to have objected that the convention did not need "foreign aid," and others pointed out that the group had no funds with which to hire a minister. And so the argument continued.

The Compromise

Finally, a committee was appointed to meet during the Fourth of July holidays to work out a compromise, and the convention adjourned to await its report. Little is known of what went on in that committee's session, though some were later to say that Franklin played a key role in hammering out the plan that finally emerged. That compromise, the most important reached at the convention, and later called the **Great Compromise** (or sometimes the Connecticut Compromise), was submitted to the full convention on July 5 and debated for another week and a half. The debate might have gone on even longer, but suddenly the hot weather moderated, and Monday, July 16, dawned cool and fresh after a month of misery. On that day the plan was adopted: five states were in favor, four were opposed, and two did not vote.* Thus, by the narrowest of margins, the structure of the national legislature was set as follows:

- A House of Representatives consisting initially of sixty-five members apportioned among the states roughly on the basis of population and elected by the people
- A Senate consisting of two senators from each state to be chosen by the state legislatures

The Great Compromise reconciled the interests of small and large states by allowing the former to predominate in the Senate and the latter in the House. This reconciliation was necessary to ensure that there would be support for a strong national government from small as well as large states. It represented major concessions on the part of several groups. Madison, for one, was deeply opposed

to the idea of having the states equally represented in the Senate. He saw in that a way for the states to hamstring the national government and much preferred some measure of proportional representation in both houses. Delegates from other states worried that representation on the basis of population in the House of Representatives would enable the large states to dominate legislative affairs. Although the margin by which the compromise was accepted was razor-thin, it held firm. In time most of the delegates from the dissenting states accepted it.

After the Great Compromise many more issues had to be resolved, but by now a spirit of accommodation had developed. When one delegate proposed having Congress choose the president, another, James Wilson, proposed that he be elected directly by the people. When neither side of that argument prevailed, a committee invented a plan for an "electroal college" that would choose the president. When some delegates wanted the president chosen for a life term, others proposed a seven-year term, and still others wanted the term limited to three years without eligibility for reelection. The convention settled on a four-year term with no bar to reelection. Some states wanted the Supreme Court picked by the Senate; others wanted it chosen by the president. They finally agreed to let the justices be nominated by the president and then confirmed by the Senate.

Finally, on July 26, the proposals that were already accepted, together with a bundle of unresolved issues, were handed over to the Committee of Detail, consisting of five delegates. This committee included Madison and Gouverneur Morris, who was to be the chief draftsman of the document that finally emerged. The committee hardly contented itself with mere "details," however. It inserted some new proposals and made changes in old ones, drawing for inspiration on existing state constitutions and the members' beliefs as to what the other delegates might accept. On August 6 the report—the first complete draft of the Constitution—was submitted to the convention. There it was debated, item by item, revised, amended, and finally, on September 17, approved by all twelve states in attendance. (Not all *delegates* approved, however; three, including Edmund Randolph, who first submitted the Virginia Plan, refused to sign.)

---

*The states in favor were Connecticut, Delaware, Maryland, New Jersey, and North Carolina. Those opposed were Georgia, Pennsylvania, South Carolina, and Virginia. Massachusetts was split down the middle; the New York delegates had left the convention. New Hampshire and Rhode Island were absent.

The Constitution and Democracy

A debate continues to rage over whether the Constitution created, or was even intended to create, a democratic government. The answer is complex. The Framers did not intend to create a "pure democracy"—one in which the people rule directly. For one thing the size of the country and the distances between settlements would have made that physically impossible. But more important the Framers worried that a government in which all citizens directly participate, as in the New England town meeting, would be a government excessively subject to temporary popular passions and one in which minority rights would be insecure. They intended instead to create a **republic,** by which they meant a government in which a system of representation operates. In designing that system the Framers chose, not without argument, to have the members of the House of Representatives elected directly by the people. Some delegates did not want to go even that far. Elbridge Gerry of Massachusetts, who refused to sign the Constitution, argued that though "the people do not want [that is, lack] virtue," they are often the "dupes of pretended patriots." Roger Sherman of Connecticut agreed. But George Mason of Virginia and James Wilson of Pennsylvania carried the day when they argued that "no government could long subsist without the confidence of the people," and this required "drawing the most numerous branch of the legislature directly from the people." Popular elections for the House were approved: six states were in favor, two opposed.

But though popular rule was to be one element of the new government, it was not to be the only one. State legislatures, not the people, would choose the senators; electors, not the people directly, would choose the president. As we have seen, without these arrangements, there would have been no Constitution at all, for the small states adamantly opposed any proposal that would have given undue power to the large ones. And direct popular election of the president would clearly have made the populous states the dominant ones. In short the Framers wished to observe the principle of majority rule, but they felt that, on the most important questions, two kinds of majorities were essential—a majority of the voters and a majority of the states.

The power of the Supreme Court to declare an act of Congress unconstitutional—**judicial review**—is also a way of limiting the power of popular majorities. It is not clear whether the Framers intended that there be judicial review, but there is little doubt that in the Framers' minds the fundamental law, the Constitution, had to be safeguarded against popular passions. They made the process for amending the Constitution easier than it had been under the Articles but still relatively difficult.

An amendment can be proposed either by a two-thirds vote of both houses of Congress *or* by a national convention called by Congress at the request of two-thirds of the states.* Once proposed, an amendment must be ratified by three-fourths of the states, either through their legislatures or through special ratifying conventions in each state. Twenty-seven amendments have survived this process, all of them proposed by Congress and all but one (the Twenty-first Amendment) ratified by state legislatures rather than state conventions.

In short the answer to the question of whether the Constitution brought into being a democratic government is yes, if by *democracy* one means a system of representative government based on popular consent. The degree of that consent has changed since 1787, and the institutions embodying that consent can take different forms. One form, rejected in 1787, gives all political authority to one set of representatives, directly elected by the people. (That is the case, for example, in most parliamentary regimes, such as Great Britain, and in some city governments in the United States.) The other form of democracy is one in which different sets of officials, chosen directly or indirectly by different groups of people, share politcal power. (That is the case with the United States and a few other nations where the separation of powers is intended to operate.)

Key Principles

The American version of representative democracy was based on two major principles, the separation of powers and federalism. In America political power was to be shared by three separate branches of gov-

---

*There have been many attempts to get a new constitutional convention. In the 1960s thirty-three states, one short of the required number, requested a convention to consider the reapportionment of state legislatures. In the 1980s efforts were made to call a convention to consider amendments to ban abortions and to require a balanced federal budget.

Checks and Balances

The Constitution creates a system of *separate* institutions that *share* powers. Because the three branches of government share powers, each can (partially) check the powers of the others. This is the system of **checks and balances**. The major checks possessed by each branch are listed below.

Congress

1. Can check the president in these ways:
   a. By refusing to pass a bill the president wants
   b. By passing a law over the president's veto
   c. By using the impeachment powers to remove the president from office
   d. By refusing to approve a presidential appointment (Senate only)
   e. By refusing to ratify a treaty the president has signed (Senate only)
2. Can check the federal courts in these ways:
   a. By changing the number and jurisdiction of the lower courts
   b. By using the impeachment powers to remove a judge from office
   c. By refusing to approve a person nominated to be a judge (Senate only)

The President

1. Can check Congress by vetoing a bill it has passed
2. Can check the federal courts by nominating judges

The Courts

1. Can check Congress by declaring a law unconstitutional
2. Can check the president by declaring actions by him or his subordinates to be unconstitutional or not authorized by law

In addition to these checks specifically provided for in the Constitution, each branch has informal ways of checking the others. For example, the president can try to withhold information from Congress (on the grounds of "executive privilege"), and Congress can try to get information by mounting an investigation.

The exact meaning of the various checks is explained in Chapter 11 on Congress, Chapter 12 on the presidency, and Chapter 14 on the courts.

---

ernment; in parliamentary democracies that power was concentrated in a single, supreme legislature. In America political authority was divided between a national government and several state governments—**federalism**—whereas in most European systems authority was centralized in the national government. Neither of these principles was especially controversial at Philadelphia. The delegates began their work in broad agreement that separated powers and some measure of federalism were necessary, and both the Virginia and New Jersey plans contained a version of each. How much federalism should be written into the Constitution was quite controversial, however.

Government and Human Nature

The desirability of separating powers and leaving the states equipped with a broad array of rights and responsibilities was not controversial at the Philadelphia convention because the Framers' experiences with British rule and state government under the Articles had shaped their view of human nature.

These experiences had taught most of the Framers that people would seek their own advantage in and out of politics; this pursuit of self-interest, unchecked, would lead some people to exploit others. Human nature was good enough to make it possible to have a decent government that was based on popular consent, but it was not good enough to make it inevitable. One solution to this problem would be to improve human nature. Ancient political philosophers such as Aristotle believed that the first task of any government was to cultivate virtue among the governed.

Many Americans were of the same mind. To them Americans would first have to become good people before they could have a good government. Samuel Adams, a leader of the Boston Tea Party, said that the new nation must become a "Christian Sparta." Others spoke of the need to cultivate frugality, industry, temperance, and simplicity.

But to James Madison and the other architects of the Constitution, the deliberate cultivation of virtue would require a government too strong and thus too dangerous to liberty, at least at the national level. Self-interest, freely pursued within reasonable limits, was a more practical and durable solution to the problem of government than any effort to improve the virtue of the citizenry. He wanted, he said, to make republican government possible "even in the absence of political virtue."

Madison argued that the very self-interest that leads people toward factionalism and tyranny might, if properly harnessed by appropriate constitutional arrangements, provide a source of unity and a guarantee of liberty. This harnessing was to be accomplished by dividing the offices of the new government among many people and giving to the holder of each office the "necessary means and personal motives to resist encroachments of the others." In this way "ambition must be made to counteract ambition" so that "the private interest of every individual may be a sentinel over the public rights."[11] If men were angels, all this would be unnecessary. But Madison and the other delegates pragmatically insisted on taking human nature pretty much as it was, and therefore they adopted "this policy of supplying, by opposite and rival interests, the defect of better motives."[12] The **separation of powers** would work, not in spite of the imperfections of human nature, but because of them.

So also with federalism. By dividing power between the states and the national government, one level of government can serve as a check on the other. This should provide a "double security" to the rights of the people: "The different governments will control each other, at the same time that each will be controlled by itself."[13] This was especially likely to happen in America, Madison thought, because it was a large country filled with diverse interests—rich and poor, Protestant and Catholic, northerner and southerner, farmer and merchant, creditor and debtor. Each of these interests would constitute a **faction** that would seek its own advantage. One faction might come to dominate government, or a part of government, in one place, and a different and

rival faction might dominate it in another. The pulling and hauling among these factions would prevent any single government—say, that of New York—from dominating all of government. The division of powers among several governments would give to virtually every faction an opportunity to gain some—but not full—power.

The Constitution and Liberty

A more difficult question is whether the Constitution created a system of government that would respect personal liberties. And that in fact is the question that was debated in the states when the document was presented for ratification. The proponents of the Constitution called themselves the **Federalists** (though they might more accurately have been called "nationalists"). The opponents came to be known as the **Antifederalists** (though they might more accurately have been called "states' righters").* To be put into effect, the Constitution had to be approved at ratifying conventions in at least nine states. This was perhaps the most democratic feature of the Constitution: it had to be accepted, not by the existing Congress (still limping along under the Articles of Confederation), nor by the state legislatures, but by special conventions elected by the people.

Though democratic, the process established by the Framers for ratifying the Constitution was technically illegal. The Articles of Confederation, which still governed, could be amended only with the approval of all thirteen state legislatures. The Framers wanted to bypass these legislatures because they feared that, for reasons of ideology or out of a desire to retain their powers, the legislators would oppose the Constitution. The Framers wanted ratification with less than the consent of all thirteen states because they knew that such unanimity could not be attained.

---

*To the delegates a truly "federal" system was one, like the New Jersey Plan, that allowed for very strong states and a weak national government. When the New Jersey Plan lost, the delegates who defeated it began using the word *federal* to describe their plan even though it called for a stronger national government. Thus men who began as "Federalists" at the convention ultimately became known as "Antifederalists" during the struggle over ratification.

And indeed the conventions in North Carolina and Rhode Island did initially reject the Constitution.

The Antifederalist View

The great issue before the state conventions was liberty, not democracy. The opponents of the new Constitution, the Antifederalists, had a variety of objections but were in general united by the belief that liberty could be secure only in a small republic in which the rulers were physically close to—and closely checked by—the ruled. Their central objection was stated by a group of Antifederalists at the ratifying convention in an essay published just after they had lost: "a very extensive territory cannot be governed on the principles of freedom, otherwise than by a confederation of republics."[14]

These dissenters argued that a strong national government would be distant from the people and would use its powers to annihilate or absorb the functions that properly belonged to the states. Congress would tax heavily, the Supreme Court would overrule state courts, and the president would come to head a large standing army. (Since all these things have occurred, we cannot dismiss the Antifederalists as cranky obstructionists who opposed without justification the plans of the Framers.) These critics argued that the nation needed, at best, a loose confederation of states, with most of the powers of government kept firmly in the hands of state legislatures and state courts.

But if a stronger national government was to be created, the Antifederalists argued, it should be hedged about with many more restrictions than those in the constitution then under consideration. They proposed several such limitations, including narrowing the jurisdiction of the Supreme Court, checking the president's power by creating a council that would review his actions, leaving military affairs in the hands of the state militias, increasing the size of the House of Representatives so that it would reflect a greater variety of popular interests, and reducing or eliminating the power of Congress to levy taxes. And some of them insisted that a *bill of rights* be added to the Constitution.

James Madison gave his answer to these criticisms in *Federalist* No. 10 and No. 51 (reprinted in the Appendix). It was a bold answer, for it flew squarely in the face of widespread popular sentiment and much philosophical writing. Following the great

Ratification of the Federal Constitution by State Conventions, 1787–1790

Strongly in favor, ratified early

Initially opposed, later ratified

Ratified initially after close struggle

French political philosopher Montesquieu, many Americans believed that liberty was safe only in small societies governed either by direct democracy or by large legislatures with small districts and frequent turnover among members.

Madison argued quite the opposite—that liberty is safest in *large* (or as he put it, "extended") republics. In a small community, he said, there will be relatively few differences in opinion or interest; people will tend to see the world in much the same way. If anyone dissents or pursues an individual interest, he or she will be confronted by a massive majority and will have few, if any, allies. But in a large republic there will be many opinions and interests; as a result it will be hard for a tyrannical majority to form or organize,

The Federalist Papers

In 1787, to help win ratification of the new Constitution in the New York state convention, Alexander Hamilton decided to publish a series of articles defending and explaining the document in the New York City newspapers. He recruited John Jay and James Madison to help him, and the three of them, under the pen name "Publius," wrote eighty-five articles that appeared from late 1787 through 1788. The identity of the authors was kept secret at the time, but we now know that Hamilton wrote fifty-one of them, Madison twenty-six, and Jay five, and that Hamilton and Madison jointly authored three.

The ***Federalist* papers** probably played only a small role in securing ratification. Like most legislative battles, this one was not decisively influenced by philosophical writings. But these essays have had a lasting value as an authoritative and profound explanation of the Constitution. Though written for political purposes, the *Federalist* has become the single most important piece of American political philosophy ever produced. Ironically Hamilton and Madison were later to become political enemies; even at the Philadelphia convention they had different views of the kind of government that should be created. But in 1787–1788 they were united in the belief that the new constitution was the best that could have been obtained under the circumstances.

Although Hamilton wrote most of the *Federalist* papers, Madison wrote the two most famous articles—Numbers 10 and 51, reprinted here in the Appendix. After you have finished this chapter, turn to the Appendix and try to read them. On your first reading of the papers you may find Madison's language difficult to understand and his ideas overly complex. The following pointers will help you decipher his meaning.

In *Federalist* No. 10 Madison begins by stating that "a well constructed Union" can "break and control the violence of faction." He goes on to define a "faction" as any group of citizens who attempt to advance their ideas or economic interests at the expense of other citizens, or in ways that

James Madison

John Jay

Alexander Hamilton

conflict with "the permanent and aggregate interests of the community" or "public good." Thus what Madison terms "factions" are what we today call "special interests."

One way to defeat factions, according to Madison, is to remove whatever causes them to arise in the first place. This can be attempted in two ways. First, government can deprive people of the liberty they need to organize: "Liberty is to faction what air is to fire." But that is surely a cure "worse than the disease." Second, measures can be taken to make all citizens share the same ideas, feelings, and economic interests. However, as Madison observes, some people are smarter or more hard working than others, and this "diversity in the faculties" of citizens is bound to result

For the Independent Journal.

The FŒDERALIST. No. X.

To the People of the State of New-York.

AMONG the numerous advantages promised by a well constructed Union, none deserves to be more accurately developped than its tendency to break and control the violence of faction. The friend of popular governments, never finds himself so much alarmed for their character and fate, as when he contemplates their propensity to this dangerous vice. He will not fail therefore to set a due value on any plan which, without violating the principles to which he is attached, provides a proper cure for it. The instability, injustice and confusion introduced into the public councils, have in truth been the mortal diseases under which popular governments have every where perished; as they continue to be the favorite and fruitful topics from which the adversaries to liberty derive their most specious declamations. The valuable improvements made by the American Constitutions on the popular models, both ancient and modern, cannot certainly be too much admired; but it would be an unwarrantable partiality, to contend that they have as effectually obviated the danger on this side as was wished and expected. Complaints are every where heard from our most considerate and virtuous citizens, equally the friends of public and private faith, and of public and personal liberty; that our governments are too unstable; that the public good is disregarded in the conflicts of rival parties; and that measures are too often decided, not according to the rules of justice, and the rights of the minor party; but by the superior force of an interested and over-bearing majority. However anxiously we may

in different economic interests as some people acquire more property than others. Consequently, protecting property rights, not equalizing property ownership, "is the first object of government." Even if everyone shared the same basic economic interests, they would still find reasons "to vex and oppress each other" rather than cooperate "for their common good." Religious differences, loyalties to different leaders, even "frivolous and fanciful distinctions" (not liking how other people dress or their taste in music) can be fertile soil for factions. In Madison's view people are factious by nature; the "causes of faction" are "sown" into their very being.

Madison thus proposes a second and, he thinks, more practical and desirable way of defeating faction. The way to cure "the mischiefs of faction" is not by removing its causes but by "controlling its effects." Factions will always exist, so the trick is to establish a form of government that is likely to serve the public good through the even-handed "regulation of these various and interfering interests." Wise and public-spirited leaders can "adjust these clashing interests and render them all subservient to the public good," but, he cautions, "enlightened statesmen will not always be at the helm." (Madison implies that "enlightened statesmen"—such as himself, Washington, and Jefferson—were at the "helm" of government in 1787.)

Madison's proposed cure for the evils of factions is in fact nothing other than a republican form of government. Use the following questions to guide your own analysis of Madison's ideas. Why does Madison think the problem of a "minority" faction is easy to handle? Conversely, why is he so troubled by the potential of a majority faction? How does he distinguish direct democracy from republican government? What is he getting at when he terms elected representatives "proper guardians of the public weal," and why does he think that "extensive republics" are more likely to produce such representatives than small ones?

When you are finished with *Federalist* No. 10, try your hand at *Federalist* No. 51. You will find that the ideas in the former paper anticipate many of those in the latter. And you will find many points on which you may or may not agree with Madison. For example, do you agree with his assumption that people—even your best friends or college roommates—are factious by nature? Likewise, do you agree with his view that government is "the greatest of all reflections on human nature"?

By attempting to meet the mind of James Madison, you can sharpen your own mind and deepen your understanding of American government.

and anyone with an unpopular view will find it easier to acquire allies. If Madison's argument seems strange or abstract, ask yourself the following question: if I have an unpopular opinion, an exotic lifestyle, or an unconventional interest, will I find greater security living in a small town or a big city?

By favoring a large republic Madison was not trying to stifle democracy. Rather he was attempting to show how democratic government really works, and what can make it work better. To rule, different interests must come together and form a **coalition**—that is, an alliance. In *Federalist* No. 51 he argued that the coalitions that formed in a large republic would be more moderate than those that formed in a small one because the bigger the republic, the greater the variety of interests, and thus the more a coalition of the majority would have to accommodate a diversity of interests and opinions if it hoped to succeed. He concluded that in a nation the size of the United States, with its enormous variety of interests, "a coalition of a majority of the whole society could seldom take place on any other principles than those of justice and the general good." Whether he was right in that prediction is a matter to which we shall return repeatedly.

The implication of Madison's arguments was daring, for he was suggesting that the national government should be at some distance from the people and insulated from their momentary passions, because the people did not always want to do the right thing. Liberty was threatened as much (or even more) by public passions and popularly based factions as by strong governments. Now the Antifederalists themselves had no very lofty view of human nature, as is evidenced by the deep suspicion with which they viewed "power-seeking" officeholders. What Madison did was take this view to its logical conclusion, arguing that if people could be corrupted by office, they could also be corrupted by factional self-interest. Thus the government had to be designed to prevent both the politicians and the people from using it for ill-considered or unjust purposes.

To argue in 1787 against the virtues of small democracies was like arguing against motherhood, but the argument prevailed, probably because many citizens were convinced that a reasonably strong national government was essential if the nation were to stand united against foreign enemies, facilitate commerce among the states, guard against domestic insurrections, and keep one faction from oppressing another. The political realities of the moment and the recent bitter experiences with the Articles probably counted for more in ratifying the Constitution than did Madison's arguments. His cause was helped by the fact that, for all their legitimate concerns and their uncanny instinct for what the future might bring, the Antifederalists could offer no agreed-upon alternative to the new Constitution. In politics, then as now, you cannot beat something with nothing.

But this does not explain why the Framers failed to add a bill of rights to the Constitution. If they were so preoccupied with liberty, why didn't they take this most obvious step toward protecting liberty, especially since the Antifederalists were demanding it? Some historians have suggested that this omission was evidence that liberty was not as important to the Framers as they claimed. In fact when one delegate suggested that a bill of rights be drawn up, the state delegations at the convention unanimously voted the idea down. There were several reasons for this.

First, the Constitution, as written, *did* contain a number of specific guarantees of individual liberty, including the right of trial by jury in criminal cases and the privilege of the writ of habeas corpus. The liberties guaranteed in the Constitution (before the Bill of Rights was added) are listed below.

- **Writ of habeas corpus*** may not be suspended (except during invasion or rebellion).
- No **bill of attainder** may be passed by Congress or the states.
- No **ex post facto law** may be passed by Congress or the states.
- Right of trial by jury in criminal cases is guaranteed.
- The citizens of each state are entitled to the privileges and immunities of the citizens of every other state.
- No religious test or qualification for holding federal office is imposed.
- No law impairing the obligation of contracts may be passed by the states.

Second, most states in 1787 had bills of rights. When Elbridge Gerry proposed to the convention

---

*For a definition of this and the following terms used in connection with certain rights, see the Glossary.

The Bill of Rights

The First Ten Amendments to the Constitution Grouped by Topic and Purpose

Protections Afforded Citizens to Participate in the Political Process

Amendment 1: Freedom of religion, speech, press, and assembly; the right to petition the government.

Protections Against Arbitrary Police and Court Action

Amendment 4: No unreasonable searches or seizures.

Amendment 5: Grand jury indictment required to prosecute a person for a serious crime.

No "double jeopardy" (being tried twice for the same offense).

Forcing a person to testify against himself or herself prohibited.

No loss of life, liberty, or property without due process.

Amendment 6: Right to speedy, public, impartial trial with defense counsel and right to cross-examine witnesses.

Amendment 7: Jury trials in civil suits where value exceeds $20.

Amendment 8: No excessive bail or fines, no cruel and unusual punishments.

Protections of States' Rights and Unnamed Rights of People

Amendment 9: Unlisted rights are not necessarily denied.

Amendment 10: Powers not delegated to the United States or denied to states are reserved to the states.

Other Amendments

Amendment 2: Right to bear arms.

Amendment 3: Troops may not be quartered in homes in peacetime.

---

that a federal bill of rights be drafted, Roger Sherman rose to observe that it was unnecessary because the state bills of rights were sufficient.[15]

But third, and perhaps most important, the Framers thought they were creating a government with specific, limited powers. It could do, they thought, only what the Constitution gave it the power to do, and nowhere in that document was there permission to infringe on freedom of speech or of the press or to impose cruel and unusual punishments. Some delegates probably feared that if any serious effort were made to list the rights that were guaranteed, later officials might assume that they had the power to do anything not explicitly forbidden.

Need for a Bill of Rights

Whatever their reasons, the Framers made at least a tactical and perhaps a fundamental mistake. It quickly became clear that without at least the promise of a **bill of rights,** the Constitution would not be ratified. Though the small states, pleased by their equal representation in the Senate, quickly ratified (in Delaware, New Jersey, and Georgia, the vote in the conventions was unanimous), the battle in the large states was intense and the outcome uncertain. In Pennsylvania Federalist supporters dragged boycotting Antifederalists to the legislature in order to ensure that a quorum was present so that a convention could be called. There were rumors of other rough tactics.

In Massachusetts the Constitution was approved by a narrow majority, but only after key leaders promised to obtain a bill of rights. In Virginia James Madison fought against the fiery Patrick Henry, whose climactic speech against ratification was dramatically punctuated by a noisy thunderstorm outside. The Federalists won by ten votes. In New York Alexander Hamilton argued the case for six weeks against the determined opposition of most of the state's key political leaders; he carried the day, but only by three votes, and then only after New York City threatened to secede from the state if it did not ratify. By June 21, 1788, the ninth state—New Hampshire—had ratified, and the Constitution was law.

Despite the bitterness of the ratification struggle, the new government that took office in 1789–1790, headed by President Washington, was greeted enthusiastically. By the spring of 1790 all thirteen states had ratified. There remained, however, the task of fulfilling the promise of a bill of rights. To that end James Madison introduced into the first session of the First Congress a set of proposals, many based on the existing Virginia bill of rights. Twelve were approved by Congress; ten of these were ratified by the states and went into effect in 1791. These amendments did not limit the power of state governments over citizens, only the power of the federal government. Later the Fourteenth Amendment, as interpreted by the Supreme Court, extended many of the guarantees of the Bill of Rights to cover state governmental action.

The Constitution and Slavery

Though black slaves amounted to one-third of the population of the five southern states, nowhere in the Constitution can one find the word *slave* or *slav-ery*. There are three provisions bearing on the matter, all designed to placate the slave owning states. The apportionment of seats in the House of Representatives was to be made by counting all free persons and three-fifths of all "other persons." This meant giving a few extra seats in the House to those states that had a lot of "other persons"—that is, slaves. Congress was forbidden to prohibit the "importation" of "persons" (that is, slaves) before the year 1808. And if any "person held to service or labour" (that is, any slave) were to escape from a slave owning state and get to a free state, that person would not become free but would have to be returned to his or her master.

To some the failure of the Constitution to address the question of slavery was a great betrayal of the promise of the Declaration of Independence that "all men are created equal."[16] For the Constitution to be silent on the subject of slavery, and thereby to allow that odious practice to continue, was to convert, by implication, the wording of the Declaration to "all white men are created equal."

The Constitution was silent on slavery, and so buying and selling slaves continued for many years.

It is easy to accuse the signers of the Declaration and the Constitution of hypocrisy. They knew of slavery, many of them owned slaves, and yet they were silent. Indeed, British opponents of the independence movement took special delight in taunting the colonists about their complaints of being "enslaved" to the British Empire while ignoring the slavery in their very midst. Increasingly, revolutionary leaders during this period spoke to this issue. Thomas Jefferson had tried to get a clause opposing the slave trade put into the Declaration of Independence. James Otis of Boston had attacked slavery and argued that black as well as white men should be free. As revolutionary fervor mounted, so did northern criticism of slavery. The Massachusetts legislature and then the Continental Congress voted to end the slave trade; Delaware prohibited the importation of slaves; Pennsylvania voted to tax it out of existence; and Connecticut and Rhode Island decided that all slaves brought into those states would automatically become free.

Slavery continued unabated in the South, defended by some whites because they thought it right, by others because they found it useful. But even in the South there were opponents, though rarely conspicuous ones. George Mason, a large Virginia slaveholder and a delegate to the convention, warned prophetically that "by an inevitable chain of causes and effects, providence punishes national sins [slavery] by national calamities."[17]

The blunt fact, however, was that any effort to use the Constitution to end slavery would have meant the end of the Constitution. The southern states would never have signed a document that seriously interfered with slavery. Without the southern states there would have been a continuation of the Articles of Confederation, which would have left each state entirely sovereign and thus entirely free of any prospective challenge to slavery.

Thus the Framers compromised with slavery; political scientist Theodore Lowi calls this their Greatest Compromise.[18] Slavery is dealt with in three places in the Constitution, though never by name. In determining the representation each state was to have in the House, "three-fifths of all other persons" (that is, of slaves) are to be added to "the whole number of free persons."[19] The South originally wanted slaves to count fully even though, of course, none would be elected to the House; they settled for counting 60 percent of them. The convention also agreed not to allow the new government by law or even constitutional amendment to prohibit the importation of slaves until the year 1808.[20] The South thus had twenty years in which it could acquire more slaves from abroad; after that Congress was free (but not required) to end the importation. Finally, the Constitution guaranteed that if a slave were to escape his or her master and flee to a nonslave state, the slave would be returned by that state to "the party to whom . . . service or labour may be due."[21]

The unresolved issue of slavery was to prove the most explosive question of all. Allowing slavery to continue was a fateful decision, one that led to the worst social and political catastrophe in the nation's history—the Civil War. The Framers chose to sidestep the issue in order to create a union that, they hoped, would eventually be strong enough to deal with the problem when it could no longer be postponed. The legacy of that choice continues to this day.

The Motives of the Framers

The Framers were not saints or demigods. They were men with political opinions who also had economic interests and human failings. It would be a mistake to conclude that everything they did in 1787 was motivated by a disinterested commitment to the public good. But it would be an equally great mistake to think that what they did was nothing but an effort to line their pockets by producing a government that would serve their own narrow interests. As in almost all human endeavors, the Framers acted out of a mixture of motives. What is truly astonishing is that economic interests played only a modest role in their deliberations.

Economic Interests at the Convention

Some of the Framers were wealthy; some were not. Some owned slaves; some had none. Some were creditors (having loaned money to the Continental Congress or to private parties); some were deeply in debt. For nearly a century scholars have argued over just how important these personal interests were in shaping the provisions of the Constitution.

In 1913 Charles Beard, a historian, published a book—*An Economic Interpretation of the Constitution*—arguing that the better-off urban and commercial classes, especially those members who held the IOUs issued by the government to pay for the Revolutionary War, favored the new Constitution because they stood to benefit from it.[22] But in the 1950s that view was challenged by historians who, after looking carefully at what the Framers owned or owed, concluded that one could not explain the Constitution exclusively or even largely in terms of the economic interests of those who wrote it.[23] Some of

Elbridge Gerry (left, 1744–1814) was a wealthy Massachusetts merchant and politician who participated in the convention but refused to sign the Constitution. James Wilson (right, 1742–1798) of Pennsylvania, a brilliant lawyer and terrible businessman, was the principal champion of the popular election of the House. Near the end of his life he was jailed repeatedly for debts incurred as a result of his business speculations.

the richest delegates, such as Elbridge Gerry of Massachusetts and George Mason of Virginia, refused to sign the document, while many of its key backers—James Madison and James Wilson, for example—were men of modest means or heavy debts.

In the 1980s a new group of scholars, primarily economists applying more advanced statistical techniques, found evidence that some economic considerations influenced how the Framers voted on some issues during the Philadelphia convention. Interestingly, however, the economic position of the *states* from which they came had a greater effect on their votes than did their *own* monetary condition.[24]

We have already seen how delegates from small states fought to reduce the power of large states and how those from slaveowning states made certain that the Constitution would contain no provision that would threaten slavery.

But contrary to what Beard asserted, the individual interests of the Framers themselves did not dominate the convention except in a few cases where a constitutional provision would have affected them directly. As you might expect, all slaveowning delegates, even those who did not live in states where slavery was commonplace (and several northern delegates owned slaves), tended to vote for provisions that would have kept the national government's power over slavery as weak as possible. However, the effects of other personal business interests were surprisingly weak. Some delegates owned a lot of public debt that they had purchased for low prices. A strong national government of the sort envisaged by the Constitution was more likely than the weak Continental Congress to pay off this debt at face value, thus making the delegates who owned it much richer. Despite this, the ownership of public debt had no significant effect on how the Framers voted in Philadelphia. For example, five men who among them owned one-third of all the public securities held by all the delegates voted against the Constitution. Nor did the big land speculators vote their interests. Some, such as George Washington and Robert Morris, favored the Constitution, while others, such as George Mason and William Blount, opposed it.[25]

In sum the Framers tended to represent their states' interests on important matters. Since they were picked by the states to do so, this is exactly what

one would expect. If they had not met in secret, perhaps they would have voted even more often as their constituents wanted. But except with respect to slavery, they usually did not vote their own economic interests. They were reasonably but not wholly disinterested delegates who were probably influenced as much by personal beliefs as by economics.

Economic Interests and Ratification

At the popularly elected state ratifying conventions, economic factors played a larger role. Delegates who were merchants, who lived in cities, who owned large amounts of western land, who held government IOUs, and who did not own slaves were more likely to vote to ratify the new Constitution than were delegates who were farmers, who did not own public debt, and who did own slaves.[26] There were plenty of exceptions, however. Small farmers dominated the conventions in some states where the vote to ratify was unanimous.

Though interests made a difference, they were not simply elite interests. In most states the great majority of adult white males could vote for delegates to the ratifying conventions. This means that women and blacks were excluded from the debates, but by the standards of the time—standards that did not change for over a century—the ratification process was remarkably democratic.

The Constitution and Equality

Ideas counted for as much as interests. At stake were two views of the public good. One, espoused by the Federalists, was that a reasonable balance of liberty, order, and progress required a strong national government. The other, defended by the Antifederalists, was that liberty would not be secure in the hands of a powerful, distant government; freedom required decentralization.

Today that debate has a new focus. The defect of the Constitution, to some contemporary critics, is not that the government it created is too strong but that it is too weak. In particular the national government is too weak to resist the pressures of special interests that reflect and perpetuate social inequality.

This criticism reveals how our understanding of the relationship between liberty and equality has changed since the Founding. To Jefferson and Madison citizens naturally differed in their talents and qualities. What had to be guarded against was

Were Women Left Out of the Constitution?

In one sense, yes: Women were nowhere mentioned in the Constitution when it was written in 1787. Moreover, Article I, which set forth the provisions for electing members of the House of Representatives, granted the vote to those people who were allowed to vote for members of the lower house of the legislature in the states in which they resided. In no state at the time could women participate in those elections. In no state could they vote in any elections or hold any offices. Furthermore, wherever the Constitution uses a pronoun, it uses the masculine form—*he* or *him*.

In another sense, no: Wherever the Constitution or the Bill of Rights defines a right that people are to have, it either grants that right to "persons" or "citizens," not to "men," or it makes no mention at all of people or gender. For example:

- "The *citizens* of each State shall be entitled to all privileges and immunities of citizens of the several States."   [Art. I, sec. 9]

- "No *person* shall be convicted of treason unless on the testimony of two witnesses to the same overt act, or on confession in open court."   [Art. III, sec. 3]

- "No bill of attainder or ex post facto law shall be passed."   [Art. I, sec. 9]

- "The right of the *people* to be secure in their persons, houses, papers, and effects, against unreasonable searches and seizures, shall not be violated."   [Amend. IV]

- "No *person* shall be held to answer for a capital, or otherwise infamous crime, unless on presentment or indictment of a grand jury . . . nor shall any *person* be subject for the same offense to be twice put in jeopardy of life or limb; . . . nor be deprived of life, liberty, or property, without due process of law."   [Amend. V]

- "In all criminal prosecutions the *accused* shall enjoy the right to a speedy and public trial, by an impartial jury."   [Amend. VI]

Moreover, when the qualifications for elective office are stated, the word *person*, not *man*, is used.

- "No *person* shall be a Representative who shall not have attained to the age of twenty-five years."   [Art. I, sec. 2]

- "No *person* shall be a Senator who shall not have attained to the age of thirty years."   [Art. I, sec. 3]

- "No *person* except a natural born citizen . . . shall be eligible to the office of President; neither shall any *person* be eligible to that office who shall not have attained to the age of thirty-five years."   [Art. II, sec. 1]

In places the Constitution and the Bill of Rights used the pronoun *he*, but always in the context of referring back to a *person* or *citizen*. At the time, and until quite recently, the male pronoun was often used in legal documents to refer generically to both men and women.

Thus, though the Constitution did not give women the right to vote until the Nineteenth Amendment was ratified in 1920, it did use language that extended fundamental rights, and access to office, to women and men equally.

Of course what the Constitution permitted did not necessarily occur. State and local laws denied to women rights that in principle they ought to have enjoyed. Except for a brief period in New Jersey, no women voted in statewide elections until, in 1869, they were given the right to cast ballots in territorial elections in Wyoming.

When women were first elected to Congress, there was no need to change the Constitution; nothing in it restricted office holding to men.

When women were given the right to vote by constitutional amendment, it was not necessary to amend any existing language in the Constitution, because nothing in the Constitution itself denied women the right to vote; the amendment simply added a new right:

- "The right of citizens of the United States to vote shall not be denied or abridged by the United States or any state on account of sex."   [Amend. XIX]

Source: Adapted from Robert Goldwin, "Why Blacks, Women and Jews Are Not Mentioned in the Constitution," *Commentary* (May 1987): 28–33.

Ways of Amending the Constitution

Under Article V there are two ways to *propose* **amendments** to the Constitution and two ways to *ratify* them.

To Propose an Amendment

1. Two-thirds of both houses of Congress vote to propose an amendment, *or*
2. Two-thirds of the state legislatures ask Congress to call a national convention to propose amendments.

To Ratify an Amendment

1. Three-fourths of the state legislatures approve it, *or*
2. Ratifying conventions in three-fourths of the states approve it.

Some Key Facts

- Only the first method of proposing an amendment has been used.
- The second method of ratification has been used only once, to ratify the Twenty-first Amendment (repealing Prohibition).
- Congress may limit the time within which a proposed amendment must be ratified. The usual limitation has been seven years.
- Thousands of proposals have been made, but only thirty-three have obtained the necessary two-thirds vote in Congress.
- Twenty-seven amendments have been ratified.
- The first ten amendments, ratified on December 15, 1791, are known as the Bill of Rights.

---

the use of governmental power to create *un*natural and undesirable inequalities. This might happen, for example, if political power was concentrated in the hands of a few people (who could use that power to give themselves special privileges) or if it was used in ways that allowed some private parties to acquire exclusive charters and monopolies. To prevent the inequality that might result from having too strong a government, its powers must be kept strictly limited.

Today some people think of inequality quite differently. To them it is the natural social order—the marketplace and the acquisitive talents of people operating in that marketplace—that leads to undesirable inequalities, especially in economic power. The government should be powerful enough to restrain these natural tendencies and produce, by law, a greater degree of equality than society allows when left alone.

To the Framers liberty and (political) equality were not in conflict; to some people today these two principles are deeply in conflict. To the Framers the task was to keep government so limited as to prevent it from creating the worst inequality—political privilege. To some modern observers the task is to make government strong enough to reduce what they believe is the worst inequality—differences in wealth.

Constitutional Reform—Modern Views

Almost from the day it was ratified, the Constitution has been the object of debate over ways in which it might be improved. These debates have rarely involved the average citizen, who tends to revere the document even if he or she cannot recall all its details. Because of this deep and broad popular support, scholars and politicians have been wary of attacking the Constitution or suggesting many wholesale changes. But such attacks have occurred. During the 1980s—the decade in which we celebrated the bicentennial of its adoption—we heard a variety of suggestions for improving the Constitution, ranging from particular amendments to wholesale revisions. In general there are today, as in the eighteenth century, two kinds of critics: those who think the federal government is too weak and those who think it is too strong.

Reducing the Separation of Powers

To the first kind of critic the chief difficulty with the Constitution is the separation of powers. By making every decision the uncertain outcome of the pulling and hauling between the president and

Congress, the Constitution precludes the emergence—except perhaps in times of crisis—of the kind of effective national leadership the country needs. In this view our nation today faces a number of challenges that require prompt, decisive, and comprehensive action. Our problem is gridlock. Our position of international leadership, the dangerous and unprecedented proliferation of nuclear weapons among the nations of the globe, and the need to find ways of stimulating economic growth while reducing our deficit and conserving our environment—all these situations require that the president be able to formulate and carry out policies free of some of the pressures and delays from interest groups and members of Congress tied to local interests.

Not only would this increase in presidential authority make for better policies, these critics argue, it would also help the voters hold the president and his party accountable for their actions. As matters now stand, nobody in government can be held responsible for policies: everybody takes the credit for successes and nobody takes the blame for failures. Typically the president, who tends to be the major source of new programs, cannot get his policies adopted by Congress without long delays and much bargaining, the result of which often is some watered-down compromise that neither the president nor Congress really likes but that each must settle for if anything is to be done at all.

Finally, critics of the separation of powers complain that the government agencies responsible for implementing a program are exposed to undue interference from legislators and special interests. In this view the president is supposed to be in charge of the bureaucracy but in fact must share this authority with countless members of Congress and congressional committees.

Not all critics of the separation of powers agree with all these points, nor do they all agree on what should be done about the problems. But they all have in common a fear that the separation of powers makes the president too weak and insufficiently accountable. Their proposals for reducing the separation of powers include the following:

- Allow the president to appoint members of Congress to serve in the cabinet (the Constitution forbids members of Congress from holding any federal appointive office while in Congress).

- Allow the president to dissolve Congress and call for a special election (elections now can be held only on the schedule determined by the calendar).
- Allow Congress to require a president who has lost its confidence to face the country in a special election before his term would normally end.
- Require the presidential and congressional candidates to run as a team in each congressional district; thus a presidential candidate who carries a given district could be sure that the congressional candidate of his party would also win in that district.
- Have the president serve a single six-year term instead of being eligible for up to two four-year terms; this would presumably free the president to lead without having to worry about reelection.
- Lengthen the terms of members of the House of Representatives from two to four years so that the entire House would stand for reelection at the same time as the president.[27]

Some of these proposals are offered by critics out of a desire to make the American system of government work more like the British parliamentary system, in which, as we shall see in Chapters 11 and 12, the prime minister is the undisputed leader of the majority in the British Parliament. The parliamentary system is the major alternative in the world today to the American separation-of-powers system.

Both the diagnosis and the remedies proposed by these critics of the separation of powers have been challenged. Many defenders of our present constitutional system believe that nations, such as Great Britain, with a different, more unified political system have done no better than the United States in dealing with the problems of economic growth, national security, and environmental protection. Moreover, they argue, close congressional scrutiny of presidential proposals has improved these policies more often than it has weakened them. Finally, congressional "interference" in the work of government agencies is a good way of ensuring that the average citizen can fight back against the bureaucracy; without that so-called interference, citizens and interest groups might be helpless before big and powerful agencies.

Each of the specific proposals, defenders of the present constitutional system argue, would either make matters worse or have, at best, uncertain effects. Adding a few members of Congress to the president's cabinet would not provide much help in getting his program through Congress; there are 535 senators and representatives, and probably only about half a dozen would be in the cabinet. Giving either the president or Congress the power to call a special election in between the regular elections (every two or four years) would cause needless confusion and great expense; the country would live under the threat of being in a perpetual political campaign with even weaker political parties. Linking the fate of the president and congressional candidates by having them run as a team in each district would reduce the stabilizing and moderating effect of having them elected separately. A Republican presidential candidate who wins in the new system would have a Republican majority in the House; a Democratic candidate winner would have a Democratic majority. We might as a result expect dramatic changes in policy as the political pendulum swung back and forth. Giving presidents a single six-year term would indeed free them from the need to worry about reelection, but it is precisely that worry that keeps presidents reasonably concerned about what the American people want.

Making the System Less Democratic

The second kind of critic of the Constitution thinks the government does too much, not too little. Though the separation of powers at one time may have slowed the growth of government and moderated the policies it adopted, in the last few decades government has grown helter-skelter. The problem, these critics argue, is not that democracy is a bad idea but that democracy can produce bad, or at least unintended, results if the government caters to the special-interest claims of the citizens rather than to their long-term values.

To see how these unintended results might occur, imagine a situation in which every citizen thinks the government grows too big, taxes too heavily, and spends too much. Each citizen wants the government made smaller by reducing the benefits other people get—but not by reducing the benefits he or she gets. In fact such citizens may even be willing to see their own benefits cut, provided everybody else's are cut as well, and by a like amount.

But the political system attends to individual wants, not general preferences. It gives aid to farmers, contracts to industry, grants to professors, pensions to the elderly, and loans to students. As someone once said, the government is like an adding machine: during elections candidates campaign by promising to do more for whatever group is dissatisfied with what the incumbents are doing for it. As a result most elections bring to office men and women who are committed to doing more for somebody. The grand total of all these additions is more for everybody. Few politicians have an incentive to do less for anybody.

To remedy this state of affairs, these critics suggest various mechanisms, but principally a constitutional amendment that would either set a limit on the amount of money the government could collect in taxes each year or require that each year the government have a balanced budget (that is, not spend more than it takes in in taxes), or both. In some versions of these plans an extraordinary majority (say, 60 percent) of Congress could override these limits, and the limits would not apply in wartime.

The effect of such amendments, the proponents claim, would be to force Congress and the president to look at the big picture—the grand total of what they are spending—rather than just to operate the adding machine by pushing the "add" button over and over again. If they could spend only so much during a given year, they would have to allocate what they spend among all rival claimants. For example, if more money were to be spent on the poor, less could then be spent on the military, or vice versa.

Some critics of an overly powerful federal government think these amendments will not be passed or may prove unworkable; instead they favor enhancing the president's power to block spending by giving him a **line-item veto.** Most state governors can veto a particular part of a bill and approve the rest using a line-item veto. The theory is that such a veto would better equip the president to stop unwarranted spending without vetoing the other provisions of a bill. In 1996 President Clinton signed the Line Item Veto Act, passed by the 104th Congress. But despite its name, the new law did not give the president full line-item veto power (only a change in the Constitution could confer that power). Instead the law gave the president authority to selectively eliminate individual items in large appropriations bills, expansions in certain income-transfer programs, and tax breaks (giving the president what budget experts call *enhanced rescission authority*). But it also left Congress free to craft bills in ways that would give the president few opportunities to veto (or *rescind*) favored items. For example, Congress could still force the president to accept or reject an entire appropriations bill simply by tagging on this sentence: "Appropriations provided under this act (or title or section) shall not be subject to the provisions of the Line Item Veto Act." In *Clinton et al. v. New York et al.* (1998), the Supreme Court struck down the 1996 law, holding 6 to 3 that the Constitution does not allow the president to cancel specific items in tax and spending legislation.

Finally, some of these critics of a powerful government feel that the real problem arises not from an excess of "adding-machine" democracy but from the growth in the power of the federal courts, as described in Chapter 14. What these critics would like to do is devise a set of laws or constitutional amendments that would narrow the authority of federal courts.

The opponents of these suggestions argue that constitutional amendments to restrict the level of taxes or to require a balanced budget are unworkable, even assuming—which they do not—that a smaller government is desirable. There is no precise, agreed-upon way to measure how much the government spends or to predict in advance how much it will receive in taxes during the year; thus defining and enforcing a "balanced budget" is no easy matter. Since the government can always borrow money, it might easily evade any spending limits. It has also shown great ingenuity in spending money in ways that never appear as part of the regular budget.

The line-item veto may or may not be a good idea. Unless the Constitution is amended to permit it, future presidents will have to do without it. The states, where some governors have long had the veto, are quite different from the federal government in power and responsibilities. Whether a line-item veto would work as well in Washington, D.C.,

as it does in many state capitals is something that we may simply never know.

Finally, proposals to curtail judicial power are thinly veiled attacks, the opponents argue, on the ability of the courts to protect essential citizen rights. If Congress and the people do not like the way the Supreme Court has interpreted the Constitution, they can always amend the Constitution to change a specific ruling; there is no need to adopt some across-the-board limitation on court powers.

Who Is Right?

Some of the arguments of these two sets of critics of the Constitution may strike you as plausible or even entirely convincing. Whatever you may ultimately decide, decide nothing for now. One cannot make or remake a constitution based entirely on abstract reasoning or unproven factual arguments. Even when the Constitution was first written in 1787, it was not an exercise in abstract philosophy but rather an effort to solve pressing, practical problems in the light of a theory of human nature, the lessons of past experience, and a close consideration of how governments in other countries and at other times had worked.

Just because the Constitution is over two hundred years old does not mean that it is out-of-date. The crucial questions are these: How well has it worked over the long sweep of American history? How well has it worked compared to the constitutions of other democratic nations?

The only way to answer those questions is to study American government closely—with special attention to its historical evolution and to the practices of other nations. That is what this book is about. Of course, even after close study, people will still disagree about whether our system should be changed. People want different things and evaluate human experience according to different beliefs. But if we first understand how, in fact, the government works and why it has produced the policies it has, we can then argue more intelligently about how best to achieve our wants and give expression to our beliefs.

MEMORANDUM

To: Senator Marty Lieb
From: Joseph Miceli, general counsel
Subject: Line-Item Veto Amendment

In 1996 you voted in favor of the Line Item Veto Act, which authorized the president to selectively eliminate items in certain appropriations bills subject to such exemptions as Congress might make. Despite its narrow application, the Supreme Court has declared the law unconstitutional. The amendment being debated next week would confer full line-item veto power on the president.

Arguments for:
1. Forty-three state constitutions, most of them explicitly modeled on the U.S. Constitution, confer line-item veto power on governors.
2. The line-item veto has equipped many governors to stop unwarranted spending without stopping the sensible provisions of a bill.
3. Most people favor giving the president this authority and holding him accountable.

Arguments against:
1. The national government is different. The Founding Fathers considered many veto alternatives and limited the president's "qualified negative" power to rejecting a bill in its entirety, subject to an override by a two-thirds vote of Congress.
2. There is no clear evidence that the line-item veto restrains state spending or that the aforementioned 1996 law restrained federal spending.
3. Popular support for the line-item veto dwindles when people are reminded about our system's separation of powers and checks and balances.

Your decision:
Favor amendment _____
Oppose amendment _____

House Backs Amendment to Give President New Veto Power

June 27
WASHINGTON
    Yesterday the House of Representatives, by a 315-to-120 vote, proposed an amendment to the U.S. Constitution that would give future presidents the power to veto a particular part of a bill and approve the rest. The Senate will debate the bill next week . . .

Summary

The Framers of the Constitution sought to create a government capable of protecting both liberty and order. The solution they chose—one without precedent at that time—was a government that was based on a written constitution that combined the principles of popular consent, the separation of powers, and federalism.

Popular consent was embodied in the procedure for choosing the House of Representatives but limited by the indirect election of senators and the electoral college system for selecting the president. Political authority was to be shared by three branches of government in a manner deliberately intended to produce conflict among these branches. This conflict, motivated by the self-interest of the people occupying each branch, would, it was hoped, prevent tyranny, even by a popular majority.

Federalism came to mean a system in which both the national and state governments had independent authority. Allocating powers between the two levels of government and devising means to ensure that neither large nor small states would dominate the national government required the most delicate compromises at the Philadelphia convention. The decision to do nothing about slavery was another such compromise.

In the drafting of the Constitution and the struggle over its ratification in the states, the positions people took were chiefly determined not by their economic interests but by a variety of factors. Among these were profound differences of opinion over whether the state governments or the national government would be the best protector of personal liberty.

World Wide Web Resources

To find historical and legal documents:
- FedLaw's constitutional and early government documents: www.legal.gsa.gov/legal9.htm
- Emory University Law School: www.law.emory.edu/FEDERAL/conpict.html
- National Constitution Center: www.constitutioncenter.org
- Congress: www.thomas.loc.gov/ (choose Historical Documents)

To look at court cases about the Constitution:
- Yale University Law School: www.yale.edu/lawweb/avalon/avalon.htm
- Washington, D.C., newspapers:
  Washington Post: www.washingtonpost.com
  Washington Times: www. washtimes.com

Key Terms

unalienable *p. 19*
Articles of Confederation *p. 21*
Constitutional Convention *p. 22*
Shays's Rebellion *p. 23*
Great Compromise *p. 27*

republic *p. 28*
judicial review *p. 28*
federalism *p. 29*
checks and balances *p. 29*
separation of powers *p. 30*

faction *p. 30*
Federalists *p. 30*
Antifederalists *p. 30*
Federalist papers *p. 32*
coalition *p. 34*
writ of habeas corpus *p. 34*

bill of attainder *p. 34*
ex post facto law *p. 34*
bill of rights *p. 35*
amendments *p. 41*
line-item veto *p. 43*

Suggested Readings

Bailyn, Bernard. *The Ideological Origins of the American Revolution.* Cambridge: Harvard University Press, 1967. A brilliant account of how the American colonists formed and justified the idea of independence.

Becker, Carl L. *The Declaration of Independence.* New York: Vintage, 1942. The classic account of the meaning of the Declaration.

Farrand, Max. *The Framing of the Constitution of the United States.* New Haven, Conn.: Yale University Press, 1913. A good, brief account of the Philadelphia convention by the editor of Madison's notes on the convention.

Federalist papers. By Alexander Hamilton, James Madison, and John Jay. The definitive edition, edited by Jacob E. Cooke, was published in Middletown, Conn., in 1961, by the Wesleyan University Press.

Goldwin, Robert A., and William A. Schambra, eds. *How Capitalistic Is the Constitution?* Washington, D.C.: American Enterprise Institute, 1982. Essays from different viewpoints discussing the relationship between the Constitution and the economic order.

———. *How Democratic Is the Constitution?* Washington, D.C.: American Enterprise Institute, 1980. Collection of essays offering differ-ent interpretations of the political meaning of the Constitution.

McDonald, Forrest. *Novus Ordo Seclorum.* Lawrence: University of Kansas Press, 1985. A careful study of the intellectual origins of the Constitution. The Latin title means "New World Order," which is what the Framers hoped they were creating.

Robinson, Donald L., ed. *Reforming American Government.* Boulder, Colo.: Westview Press, 1985. Collection of essays advocating con-stitutional reform.

Storing, Herbert J. *What the Anti-Federalists Were For.* Chicago: University of Chicago Press, 1981. Close analysis of the political views of those opposed to the ratification of the Constitution.

Wood, Gordon S. *The Creation of the American Republic.* Chapel Hill: University of North Carolina Press, 1969. A detailed study of American political thought before the Philadelphia convention.

———. *The Radicalism of the American Revolution.* New York: Knopf, 1992. Magisterial study of the nature and effects of the American Revolution and the relationship between the socially radical Revolution and the Constitution.

Federalism

3

Enduring Questions

1. Where is sovereignty located in the American political system?
2. How is power divided between the national government and the states under the Constitution?
3. How has America's federal system changed since the first days of the Republic?
4. Is dual federalism the friend or foe of liberty, equality, political participation, and policy innovation?

Governmental Structure
  Federalism: Good or Bad? • Increased Political Activity

The Founding
  A Bold, New Plan • Elastic Language

The Debate on the Meaning of Federalism
  The Supreme Court Speaks • Nullification • Dual Federalism • State Sovereignty

Federal-State Relations
  Grants-in-Aid • Meeting National Needs • The Intergovernmental Lobby • Categorical Grants Versus Revenue Sharing

The Slowdown in "Free" Money
  Rivalry Among the States

Federal Aid and Federal Control
  Mandates • Conditions of Aid

A Devolution Revolution?
  Block Grants for Entitlements • What's Driving Devolution?

Congress and Federalism

Since the adoption of the Constitution in 1787, the single most persistent source of political conflict has been the relations between the national and state governments. The political conflict over slavery, for example, was intensified because some state governments condoned or supported slavery, while others took action to discourage it. The proponents and opponents of slavery were thus given territorial power centers from which to carry on the dispute. Other issues, such as the regulation of business and the provision of social welfare programs, were in large part fought out, for well over a century, in terms of "national interests" versus "states' rights." While other nations, such as Great Britain, were debating the question of whether the national government *ought* to provide old-age pensions or regulate the railroads, the United States debated a different question—whether the national government *had the right* to do these things. Even after these debates had ended—almost invariably with a decision favorable to the national government—the administration and financing of the programs that resulted have usually involved a large role for the states.

Today an effort is under way to scale back the size and activities of the national government and to shift responsibility for a wide range of domestic programs from Washington to the states. In recent years the effort to devolve onto the states the national government's functions in areas such as welfare, health care, and job training has become known as **devolution.** In the 104th Congress (1994–1996) Republican majorities in the House and Senate made proposals, several of them enacted into law, to accelerate the devolution of national power. Many of these proposals involved giving the states **block grants**—money from the national government for programs in certain general areas that the states can use at their discretion within broad guidelines set by Congress.

In 1908 Woodrow Wilson observed that how we structure the relationship between the national government and the states "is the cardinal question of our constitutional system," a question that cannot be settled by "one generation, because it is a question of growth, and every successive stage of our political and economic development gives it a new aspect, makes it a new question."[1]

As the nation enters the twenty-first century, is the American political system in the early stages of a "devolution revolution" that will make the states, not the national government, the dominant force in domestic affairs? Do most Americans support devolution? Have recent court decisions returned power to the states? What, if any, differences will devolution reforms make in who governs and to what ends? Before one can begin to address these questions, it is important to master the basic concepts and understand the political history of federalism.

Governmental Structure

Federalism refers to a political system in which there are local (territorial, regional, provincial, state, or municipal) units of government, as well as a national government, that can make final decisions with respect to at least some governmental activities and whose existence is specially protected.[2] Almost every nation in the world has local units of government of some kind, if for no other reason than to decentralize the administrative burdens of governing. But these governments are not federal unless the local units exist independent of the preferences of the national government and can make decisions on at least some matters without regard to those preferences.

The United States, Canada, Australia, India, Germany, and Switzerland are federal systems, as are a few other nations. France, Great Britain, Italy, and Sweden are not: they are unitary systems, because such local governments as they possess can be altered or even abolished by the national government and cannot plausibly claim to have final authority over any significant governmental activities.

The special protection that subnational governments enjoy in a federal system derives in part from the constitution of the country but also from the habits, preferences, and dispositions of the citizens and the actual distribution of political power in society. The constitution of the former Soviet Union in theory created a federal system, as claimed by that country's full name—the Union of Soviet Socialist Republics—but for most of their history, none of these "socialist republics" were in the slightest degree independent of the central government. Were the American Constitution the only guarantee of the independence of the American states, they would long since have become mere administrative subunits of the government in Washington. Their independence results in large measure from the commitment of Americans to the idea of local self-government and from the fact that Congress consists of people who are selected by and responsive to local constituencies.

"The basic political fact of federalism," writes David B. Truman, "is that it creates separate, self-sustaining centers of power, prestige, and profit."[3] Political power is locally acquired by people whose careers depend for the most part on satisfying local interests. As a result, though the national government has come to have vast powers, it exercises many of those powers through state governments. What many of us forget when we think about "the government in Washington" is that it spends much of its money and enforces most of its rules not on citizens directly but on other, local units of government. A large part of the welfare system, all of the interstate highway system, virtually every aspect of programs to improve cities, the largest part of the effort to supply jobs to the unemployed, the entire program to clean up our water, and even much of our military manpower (in the form of the National

Guard) are enterprises in which the national government does not govern so much as it seeks, by regulation, grant, plan, argument, and cajolery, to get the states to govern in accordance with nationally defined (though often vaguely defined) goals.

In France welfare, highways, education, the police, and the use of land are all matters that are directed nationally. In the United States highways and some welfare programs are largely state functions (though they make use of federal money), while education, policing, and land-use controls are primarily local (city, county, or special-district) functions.

Federalism: Good or Bad?

A measure of the importance of federalism is the controversy that surrounds it. To some federalism means allowing states to block action, prevent progress, upset national plans, protect powerful local interests, and cater to the self-interest of hack politicians. Harold Laski, a British observer, described American states as "parasitic and poisonous,"[4] and William H. Riker, an American political scientist, argued that "the main effect of federalism since the Civil War has been to perpetuate racism."[5] By contrast, another political scientist, Daniel J. Elazar, believes that the "virtue of the federal system lies in its ability to develop and maintain mechanisms vital to the perpetuation of the unique combination of governmental strength, political flexibility, and individual liberty, which has been the central concern of American politics."[6]

So diametrically opposed are the Riker and Elazar views that one wonders whether they are talking about the same subject. They are, of course, but they are stressing different aspects of the same phenomenon. Whenever the opportunity to exercise political power is widely available (as among the fifty states, three thousand counties, and many thousands of municipalities in the United States), it is obvious that in different places different people will make use of that power for different purposes. There is no question that allowing states and cities to make autonomous, binding political decisions will allow some people in some places to make those decisions in ways that maintain racial segregation, protect vested interests, and facilitate corruption. It is equally true, however, that this arrangement also enables other people in other places to pass laws that attack segregation, regulate harmful economic practices,

---

★ **POLITICALLY**
SPEAKING ★

Sovereignty, Federalism, and the Constitution

Sovereignty means supreme or ultimate political authority: a sovereign government is one that is legally and politically independent of any other government.

A **unitary system** is one in which sovereignty is wholly in the hands of the national government, so that the states and localities are dependent on its will.

A **confederation or confederal system** is one in which the states are sovereign and the national government is allowed to do only that which the states permit.

A **federal system** is one in which sovereignty is shared, so that in some matters the national government is supreme and in other matters the states are supreme.

The Founding Fathers often took *confederal* and *federal* to mean much the same thing. Rather than establishing a government in which there was a clear division of sovereign authority between the national and state governments, they saw themselves as creating a government that combined some characteristics of a unitary regime with some of a confederal one. Or, as James Madison expressed the idea in *Federalist* No. 39, the Constitution "is, in strictness, neither a national nor a federal Constitution, but a composition of both." Where sovereignty is located in this system is a matter that the Founders did not clearly answer.

In this text, a **federal regime** is defined in the simplest possible terms—as one in which local units of government have a specially protected existence and can make some final decisions over some governmental activities.

---

and purify politics, often long before these ideas gain national support or become national policy.

For example, in a unitary political system, such as that of France, a small but intensely motivated group could not have blocked civil rights legislation for as long as some southern senators blocked it in

Federalism has permitted experimentation. Women were able to vote in the Wyoming Territory in 1888, long before they could do so in most states.

this country. But by the same token it would have been equally difficult for another small but intensely motivated group to block plans to operate a nuclear power plant in their neighborhood, as citizens have done in this country but not in France.

The existence of independent state and local governments means that different political groups pursuing different political purposes will come to power in different places. The smaller the political unit, the more likely it is to be dominated by a single political faction. James Madison understood this fact perfectly and used it to argue (in *Federalist* No. 10) that it would be in a large (or "extended") republic, such as the United States as a whole, that one would find the greatest opportunity for all relevant interests to be heard. When William Riker condemns federalism, he is thinking of the fact that in some places the ruling factions in cities and states have opposed granting equal rights to African Americans. When Daniel

Elazar praises federalism, he is recalling that, in other states and cities, the ruling factions have taken the lead (long in advance of the federal government) in developing measures to protect the environment, extend civil rights, and improve social conditions. If you live in California, whether you like federalism depends in part on whether you like the fact that California has, independent of the federal government, cut property taxes, strictly controlled coastal land use, heavily regulated electric utilities, and increased (at one time) and decreased (at another time) its welfare rolls.

Increased Political Activity

Federalism has many effects, but its most obvious effect has been to facilitate the mobilization of political activity. Unlike Don Quixote, the average citizen does not tilt at windmills. He or she is more likely to become involved in organized political activity if he or she feels there is a reasonable chance of having a practical effect. The chances of having such an effect are greater where there are many elected officials and independent governmental bodies, each with a relatively small constituency, than where there are few elected officials, most of whom have the nation as a whole for a constituency. In short a federal system, by virtue of the decentralization of authority, lowers the cost of organized political activity; a unitary system, because of the centralization of authority, raises the cost. We may disagree about the purposes of organized political activity, but the fact of widespread organized activity can scarcely be doubted—or if it can be doubted, it is only because you have not yet read Chapters 6 and 9.

It is impossible to say whether the Founders, when they wrote the Constitution, planned to produce such widespread opportunities for political participation. Unfortunately they were not very clear (at least in writing) about how the federal system was supposed to work, and thus most of the interesting questions about the jurisdiction and powers of our national and state governments had to be settled by a century and a half of protracted, often bitter, conflict.

The Founding

The goal of the Founders seems clear: federalism was one device whereby personal liberty was to be protected. (The separation of powers was another.) They feared that placing final political authority in any one set of hands, even in the hands of persons popularly elected, would so concentrate power as to risk tyranny. But they had seen what happened when independent states tried to form a compact, as under the Articles of Confederation; what the states put together, they could also take apart. The alliance among the states that existed from 1776 to 1787 was a confederation: that is, a system of government in which the people create state governments, which, in turn, create and operate a national government (see Figure 3.1). Since the national government in a confederation derives its powers from the states, it is dependent on their continued cooperation for its survival. By 1786 that cooperation was barely forthcoming.

A Bold, New Plan

A federation—or a "federal republic," as the Founders called it—derives its powers directly from the people, as do the state governments. As the Founders envisioned it, both levels of government, the national and the state, would have certain powers, but neither would have supreme authority over the other. Madison, writing in *Federalist* No. 46, said that both the state and federal governments "are in fact but different agents and trustees of the people, constituted with different powers." In *Federalist* No. 28 Hamilton explained how he thought the system would work: the people could shift their support between state and federal levels of government as needed to keep the two in balance. "If their rights are invaded by either, they can make use of the other as the instrument of redress."

It was an entirely new plan, for which no historical precedent existed. Nobody came to the Philadelphia convention with a clear idea of what a federal (as opposed to a unitary or a confederal) system would look like, and there was not much discussion at Philadelphia of how the system would work in practice. Few delegates then used the word *federalism* in the sense in which we now employ it (it was originally used as a synonym for *confederation* and only later came to stand for something different).[7] The Constitution does not spell out the powers that the states are to have, and until the Tenth Amendment was added at the insistence of various states, there was not even a clause in it saying (as did the amend-

Figure 3.1   Lines of Power in Three Systems of Government

UNITARY SYSTEM

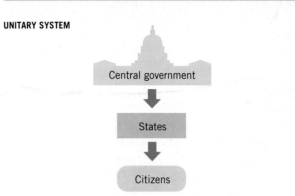

Power centralized.
State or regional governments derive authority from central government.
Examples: United Kingdom, France.

FEDERAL SYSTEM

Power divided between central and state or local governments.
Both the government and constituent governments act directly
    upon the citizens.
Both must agree to constitutional change.
Examples: Canada, United States since adoption of Constitution.

**CONFEDERAL SYSTEM
(or CONFEDERATION)**

Power held by independent states.
Central government is a creature of the constituent governments.
Example: United States under the Articles of Confederation.

ment) that "the powers not delegated to the United States by the Constitution, nor prohibited by it to the states, are reserved to the states respectively, or to

The States and the Constitution

The Framers made some attempt to define the relations between the states and the federal government and how the states were to relate to one another. The following points were made in the original Constitution—before the Bill of Rights was added.

Restrictions on Powers of the States

States may not make treaties with foreign nations, coin money, issue paper currency, grant titles of nobility, pass a bill of attainder or an ex post facto law,* or, without the consent of Congress, levy any taxes on imports or exports, keep troops and ships in time of peace, or enter into an agreement with another state or with a foreign power.

[Art. I, sec. 10]

Guarantees by the Federal Government to the States

The national government guarantees to every state a "republican form of government" and protection against foreign invasion and (provided the states request it) protection against domestic insurrection.

[Art. IV, sec. 4]

An existing state will not be broken up into two or more states or merged with all or part of another state without that state's consent.

[Art. IV, sec. 3]

*For definitions of *bill of attainder* and *ex post facto law,* see the Glossary.

Congress may admit new states into the Union.

[Art. IV, sec. 3]

Taxes levied by Congress must be uniform throughout the United States: they may not be levied on some states but not others.

[Art. I, sec. 8]

The Constitution may not be amended to give states unequal representation in the Senate.

[Art. V]

Rules Governing How States Deal with Each Other

"Full faith and credit" shall be given by each state to the laws, records, and court decisions of other states. (For example, a civil case settled in the courts of one state cannot be retried in the courts of another.)

[Art. IV, sec. 1]

The citizens of each state shall have the "privileges and immunities" of the citizens of every other state. (No one is quite sure what this is supposed to mean.)

[Art. IV, sec. 2]

If a person charged with a crime by one state flees to another, he or she is subjected to extradition—that is, the governor of the state that finds the fugitive is supposed to return the person to the governor of the state that wants him or her.

[Art. IV, sec. 2]

---

the people." The Founders assumed from the outset that the federal government would have only those powers given to it by the Constitution; the Tenth Amendment was an afterthought, added to make that assumption explicit and allay fears that something else was intended.[8]

The Tenth Amendment has rarely had much practical significance, however. From time to time the Supreme Court has tried to interpret that amendment as putting certain state activities beyond the reach of the federal government, but invariably the Court has later changed its mind and allowed Washington to regulate such matters as the hours that employees of a city-owned mass-transit system may work. The Court did not find that running such a transportation system was one of the powers "reserved to the states."[9] But, as we explain later in this chapter, the Court has begun to give new life to the Tenth Amendment and the doctrine of state sovereignty.

Elastic Language

The need to reconcile the competing interests of large and small states and of northern and southern states, especially as they affected the organization of Congress, was sufficiently difficult without trying to spell out exactly what relationship ought to exist between the national and state systems. For example, Congress was given the power to regulate commerce "among the several states." The Philadelphia convention would have gone on for four years rather than four months if the Founders had decided that it was necessary to describe, in clear language, how one was to tell where commerce *among* the states ended and commerce wholly *within* a single state began. The Supreme Court, as we shall see, devoted over a century to that task before giving up.

Though some clauses bearing on federal-state relations were reasonably clear (see the box on page 54), other clauses were quite vague. The Founders knew, correctly, that they could not make an exact and exhaustive list of everything the federal government was empowered to do—circumstances would change, new exigencies would arise. Thus they added the following elastic language to Article I: Congress shall have the power to "make all laws which shall be necessary and proper for carrying into execution the foregoing powers."

The Founders themselves carried away from Philadelphia different views of what federalism meant. One view was championed by Hamilton. Since the people had created the national government, since the laws and treaties made pursuant to the Constitution were "the supreme law of the land" (Article VI), and since the most pressing needs were the development of a national economy and the conduct of foreign affairs, Hamilton thought that the national government was the superior and leading force in political affairs and that its powers ought to be broadly defined and liberally construed.

The other view, championed by Jefferson, was that the federal government, though important, was the product of an agreement among the states; and though "the people" were the ultimate sovereigns, the principal threat to their liberties was likely to come from the national government. (Madison, a strong supporter of national supremacy at the convention, later became a champion of states' rights.) Thus the powers of the federal government should be narrowly construed and strictly limited. As Madison put it in *Federalist* No. 45, in language that probably made Hamilton wince, "The powers delegated by the proposed Constitution to the federal government are few and defined. Those which are to

Thomas Jefferson (1743–1826) was not at the Constitutional Convention. His doubts about the new national government led him to oppose the Federalist administration of John Adams and to become an ardent champion of states' rights.

remain in the State governments are numerous and indefinite."

Hamilton argued for national supremacy, Jefferson for states' rights. Though their differences were greater in theory than in practice (as we shall see in Chapter 12, Jefferson while president sometimes acted in a positively Hamiltonian manner), the differing interpretations they offered of the Constitution were to shape political debate in this country until well into the 1960s.

The Debate on the Meaning of Federalism

The Civil War was fought, in part, over the issue of national supremacy versus states' rights, but it settled only one part of that argument—namely, that the national government was supreme, its sovereignty derived directly from the people, and thus the states could not lawfully secede from the Union. Virtually every other aspect of the national-supremacy issue continued to animate political and legal debate for another century.

The Supreme Court Speaks

As arbiter of what the Constitution means, the Supreme Court became the focal point of that debate. In Chapter 14 we shall see in some detail how the Court made its decisions. For now it is enough to know that during the formative years of the new Republic, the Supreme Court was led by a staunch and brilliant advocate of Hamilton's position, Chief Justice John Marshall. In a series of decisions he and the Court powerfully defended the national-supremacy view of the newly formed federal government.

The most important decision was in a case, seemingly trivial in its origins, that arose when James McCulloch, the cashier of the Baltimore branch of the Bank of the United States, which had been created by Congress, refused to pay a tax levied on that bank by the state of Maryland. He was hauled into state court and convicted of failing to pay a tax. In 1819 McCulloch appealed all the way to the Supreme Court in a case known as *McCulloch v. Maryland*. The Court, in a unanimous opinion, answered two questions in ways that expanded the powers of Congress and confirmed the supremacy of the federal government in the exercise of those powers.

The first question was whether Congress had the right to set up a bank, or any other corporation, since such a right is nowhere explicitly mentioned in the Constitution. Marshall said that, though the federal government possessed only those powers enumerated in the Constitution, the "extent"—that is, the meaning—of those powers required interpretation. Though the word *bank* is not in that document, one finds there the power to manage money: to lay and collect taxes, issue a currency, and borrow funds. To carry out these powers Congress may reasonably decide that chartering a national bank is "necessary and proper." Marshall's words were carefully chosen to endow the "**necessary and proper**" **clause** with the widest possible sweep:

> Let the end be legitimate, let it be within the scope of the Constitution, and all means which are appropriate, which are plainly adapted to that end, which are not prohibited, but consistent with the letter and spirit of the Constitution, are constitutional.[10]

The second question was whether a federal bank could lawfully be taxed by a state. To answer it, Marshall went back to first principles. The government of the United States was not established by the states, but by the people, and thus the federal government was supreme in the exercise of those powers conferred upon it. Having already concluded that chartering a bank was within the powers of Congress, Marshall then argued that the only way for such powers to be supreme was for their use to be immune from state challenge and for the products of their use to be protected against state destruction. Since "the power to tax involves the power to destroy," and since the power to destroy a federal agency would confer upon the states using it supremacy over the federal government, the states may not tax any federal instrument. Hence the Maryland law was unconstitutional.

McCulloch won, and so did the federal government. Half a century later the Court decided that what was sauce for the goose was sauce for the gander. It held that just as state governments could not tax federal bonds, the federal government could not tax the interest people earn on state and municipal bonds. In 1988 the Supreme Court changed its mind and decided that Congress was now free, if it wished, to tax the interest on such state and local bonds. Municipal bonds, which for nearly a century were a tax-exempt investment protected, so their holders

At one time the states could issue their own paper money, such as this New York currency worth twenty-five cents in 1776. Under the Constitution this power was reserved to Congress.

thought, by the Constitution, were now protected only by politics. So far Congress hasn't wanted to tax them.[11]

Nullification

The Supreme Court can decide a case without settling the issue. The struggle over states' rights versus national supremacy continued to rage in Congress, during presidential elections, and ultimately on the battlefield. The issue came to center on the doctrine of **nullification.** When Congress passed laws (in 1798) to punish newspaper editors who published stories critical of the federal government, James Madison and Thomas Jefferson opposed the laws, suggesting (in statements known as the Virginia and Kentucky Resolutions) that the states had the right to "nullify" (that is, declare null and void) a federal law that, in the states' opinion, violated the Constitution. The laws expired before the claim of nullification could be settled in the courts.

Later the doctrine of nullification was revived by John C. Calhoun of South Carolina, first in opposition to a tariff enacted by the federal government and later in opposition to federal efforts to restrict slavery. Calhoun argued that if Washington attempted to ban slavery, the states had the right to declare such acts unconstitutional and thus null and void. This time the issue was settled—by war. The northern victory in the Civil War determined once and for all that the federal union is indissoluble and that states cannot declare acts of Congress unconstitutional, a view later confirmed by the Supreme Court.[12]

Dual Federalism

After the Civil War the debate about the meaning of federalism focused on the interpretation of the commerce clause of the Constitution. Out of this debate there emerged the doctrine of **dual federalism,** which held that though the national government was supreme in its sphere, the states were equally supreme in theirs, and that these two spheres of action should and could be kept separate. Applied to commerce the concept of dual federalism implied that there were such things as *inter*state commerce, which Congress could regulate, and *intra*state commerce, which only the states could regulate, and that the Court could tell which was which.

For a long period the Court tried to decide what was interstate commerce based on the kind of business that was being conducted. Transporting things between states was obviously interstate commerce, and so subject to federal regulation. Thus federal laws affecting the interstate shipment of lottery tickets,[13] prostitutes,[14] liquor,[15] and harmful foods and drugs[16] were upheld. On the other hand manufacturing,[17] insurance,[18] and farming,[19] were in the past considered *intra*state commerce, and so only the state governments were allowed to regulate them.

Such product-based distinctions turned out to be hard to sustain. For example, if you ship a case of whiskey from Kentucky to Kansas, how long is it in interstate commerce (and thus subject to federal law), and when does it enter intrastate commerce and become subject only to state law? For a while the Court's answer was that the whiskey was in interstate commerce so long as it was in its "original package,"[20] but that only precipitated long quarrels as to what was the original package and how one is to treat things, like gas and grain, that may not be shipped in packages at all. And how could one distinguish between manufacturing and transportation when one company did both or when a single manufacturing corporation owned factories in different states? And if an insurance company sold policies to customers both inside and outside a given state, were there to be different laws regulating identical policies that happened to be purchased from the same company by persons in different states?

In time the effort to find some clear principles that distinguished interstate from intrastate commerce was pretty much abandoned. Commerce was like a stream flowing through the country, drawing to itself contributions from thousands of scattered enterprises and depositing its products in millions of individual homes. The Court began to permit the federal government to regulate almost anything that affected this stream, so that by the 1940s not only had farming and manufacturing been redefined as part of interstate commerce,[21] but even the janitors and window washers in buildings that housed companies engaged in interstate commerce were now said to be part of that stream.[22]

The current Court interpretation of various laws pertaining to commerce is immensely complex, difficult to summarize, and impossible to explain. For example, lawyers are said to engage in interstate commerce, but professional baseball players are not, so federal antitrust laws affect the former but not the latter.[23]

State Sovereignty

It would be a mistake to think that the doctrine of dual federalism is entirely dead. Until recently Congress, provided that it had a good reason, could pass a law regulating almost any kind of economic activity anywhere in the country, and the Supreme Court would call it constitutional. But in *United States v. Lopez* (1995) the Court held that Congress had exceeded its commerce clause power by prohibiting guns in schools.

The Court reaffirmed the view that the commerce clause does not justify any federal action when, in May 2000, it overturned the Violence Against Women Act of 1994. This law allowed women who were the victims of a crime of violence motivated by gender to sue the guilty party in federal court. In *United States v. Morrison* the Court, in a five-to-four decision, said that attacks against women are not, and do not substantially affect, interstate commerce, and hence Congress cannot constitutionally pass such a law. Chief Justice William Rehnquist said that "the Constitution requires a distinction between what is truly national and what is truly local." The states, of course, can pass such laws, and many have.

The Court has moved to strengthen states' rights on other grounds as well. In *Printz v. United States* (1997) the Court invalidated a federal law that required local police to conduct background checks on all gun purchasers. The Court ruled that the law violated the Tenth Amendment by commandeering state governments to carry out a federal regulatory program. Writing for the five-to-four majority, Justice Antonin Scalia declared, "The Federal government may neither issue directives requiring the states to address particular problems, nor command the states' officers, or those of their political subdivisions, to administer or enforce a Federal regulatory program. . . . Such commands are fundamentally incompatible with our constitutional system of dual sovereignty."

The Court has also given new life to the Eleventh Amendment, which protects states from lawsuits by citizens of other states or foreign nations. In 1999 the Court shielded states from suits by copyright owners who claimed infringement from state agencies and immunized states from lawsuits by people who argued that state regulations create unfair eco-

The Terms of Local Governance

Legally a **city** is a **municipal corporation** or **municipality** that has been chartered by a state to exercise certain defined powers and provide certain specific services. There are two kinds of charters: special-act charters and general-act charters.

A **special-act charter** applies to a certain city (for example, New York City) and lists what that city can and cannot do. A **general-act charter** applies to a number of cities that fall within a certain classification, usually based on city population. Thus in some states all cities over 100,000 population will be governed on the basis of one charter, while all cities between 50,000 and 99,999 population will be governed on the basis of a different one.

Under **Dillon's rule** the terms of these charters are to be interpreted very narrowly. This rule (named after a lawyer who wrote a book on the subject in 1911) authorizes a municipality to exercise only those powers expressly given, implied by, or essential to the accomplishment of its enumerated powers. This means, for example, that a city cannot so much as operate a peanut stand at the city zoo unless the state has specifically given the city that power by law or charter.

A **home-rule charter,** now in effect in many cities, reverses Dillon's rule and allows a city government to do anything that is not prohibited by the charter or state law. Even under a home-rule charter, however, city laws (called **ordinances**) cannot be in conflict with state laws, and the states can pass laws that preempt or interfere with what home-rule cities want to do.

There are in this country more than 86,000 local governments, less than one-fourth (19,000) of which are cities or municipalities. **Counties** (3,000) are the largest territorial units between a state and a city or town. Every state but Connecticut and Rhode Island has county governments. (In Louisiana counties are called parishes, in Alaska boroughs.)

There are more than 33,000 **special-district governments or authorities,** which have responsibility for some single governmental function—handling sewage treatment, managing airports, or getting rid of mosquitoes, for example. **School districts** (more than 14,000) are the most familiar special-district governments. Often the voters elect school board members, who then choose a school superintendent.

nomic competition. In *Alden v. Maine* (1999) the Court held that state employees could not sue to force state compliance with federal fair-labor laws. In the Court's five-to-four majority opinion, Justice Anthony M. Kennedy stated, "Although the Constitution grants broad powers to Congress, our federalism requires that Congress treat the states in a manner consistent with their status as residuary sovereigns and joint participants in the governance of the nation."

Not all recent Court decisions, however, support greater state sovereignty. In 1999, for example, the Court ruled seven to two that state welfare programs may not restrict new residents to the welfare benefits they would have received in the states from which they moved. In addition, each of the Court's major pro–state sovereignty decisions has been decided by a tenuous five-to-four margin. More generally, to empower states is not to disempower Congress, which, as it has done since the late 1930s, can still make federal laws on almost anything as long as it does not go too far in "commandeering" state resources or gutting states' rights.

New debates over state sovereignty call forth old truths about the constitutional basis of state and local government. In general a state can do anything that is not prohibited by the Constitution or preempted by federal policy and that is consistent with its own constitution. One generally recognized state power is the **police power,** which refers to those laws and regulations, not otherwise unconstitutional, that promote health, safety, and morals. Thus the states can enact and enforce criminal codes, require children to attend school and citizens to be vaccinated, and restrict (subject to many limitations) the availability of pornographic materials or the activities of prostitutes and drug dealers. As a practical matter the most important activities of state and local governments involve public education, law enforcement and criminal justice, health and hospitals, roads and highways, public welfare, and control over the use of public land and water supplies.

As we saw in Chapter 2, the federal Constitution is based on a republican, not a democratic, principle: laws are to be made by the representatives of citizens, not by the citizens directly. But many state constitutions open one or more of three doors to direct democracy. About half of the states provide for some form of legislation by initiative. The **initiative** allows voters to place legislative measures (and

sometimes constitutional amendments) directly on the ballot by getting enough signatures (usually between 5 and 15 percent of those who voted in the last election) on a petition. About half of the states permit the **referendum,** a procedure that enables voters to reject a measure adopted by the legislature. Sometimes the state constitution specifies that certain kinds of legislation (for example, tax increases) must be subject to a referendum whether the legislature wishes it or not. The **recall** is a procedure, in effect in about one-third of the states, whereby voters can remove an elected official from office. If enough signatures are gathered on a petition, the official must go before voters, who can vote to leave the person in office, remove the person from office, or remove the person and replace him or her with someone else.

The existence of the states is guaranteed by the federal Constitution: no state can be divided without its consent, each state must have two representatives in the Senate (the only provision of the Constitution that may not be amended), every state is assured of a republican form of government, and the powers not granted to Congress are reserved for the states. By contrast, cities, towns, and counties enjoy no such protection; they exist at the pleasure of the states. Indeed, states have frequently abolished certain kinds of local governments, such as independent school districts. Without exception the legal terms of local governance (see the box on the opposite page) are determined by the states.

This explains why there is no debate about city sovereignty comparable to the debate about state sovereignty. The constitutional division of power between them is settled: the state is supreme. But federal-state relations can be complicated, because the Constitution invites elected leaders to struggle over sovereignty. Which level of government has the ultimate power to decide where nuclear waste gets stored, how much welfare beneficiaries are paid, what rights prisoners enjoy, or whether supersonic jets can land at local airports? American federalism answers such questions, but on a case-by-case basis through intergovernmental politics and court decisions.

Federal-State Relations

Though constitutionally the federal government may be supreme, politically it must take into account the fact that the laws it passes have to be approved by members of Congress selected from, and responsive to, state and local constituencies. Thus what Washington lawfully may do is not the same thing as what it politically may wish to do. For example, in 1947 the Supreme Court decided that the federal government and not the states had supreme authority over oil beneath the ocean off the nation's coasts.[24] Six years later, after an intense debate, Congress passed and the president signed a law transferring title to these tideland oil reserves back to the states.

Grants-in-Aid

The best illustration of how political realities modify legal authority can be found in federal **grants-in-aid.** The first of these programs began even before the Constitution was adopted, in the form of land

Some of the nation's greatest universities, such as the University of California at Berkeley, began as land-grant colleges.

grants made by the national government to the states in order to finance education. (State universities all over the country were built with the proceeds from the sale of these land grants; hence the name *land-grant colleges.*) Land grants were also made to support the building of wagon roads, canals, railroads, and flood-control projects. These measures were hotly debated in Congress (President Madison thought some were unconstitutional), even though the use to which the grants were put was left almost entirely to the states.

Cash grants-in-aid began almost as early. In 1808 Congress gave $200,000 to the states to pay for their militias, with the states in charge of the size, deployment, and command of these troops. However, grant-in-aid programs remained few in number and small in price until the twentieth century, when scores of new ones came into being. In 1915 less than $6 million was spent per year in grants-in-aid; by 1925 over $114 million was spent; by 1937 the figure was nearly $300 million.[25] The greatest growth began in the 1960s: between 1960 and 1966 federal grants to the states doubled; from 1966 to 1970 they doubled again; between 1970 and 1975 they doubled yet again. By 1985 they amounted to over $100 billion a year and were spent through more than four hundred separate programs. The five largest programs accounted for over half the money spent and reflected the new priorities that federal policy had come to serve: housing assistance for low-income families, Medicaid, highway construction, services to the unemployed, and welfare programs for mothers with dependent children and for the disabled.

The grant-in-aid system, once under way, grew rapidly because it helped state and local officials resolve a dilemma. On the one hand they wanted access to the superior taxing power of the federal government. On the other hand prevailing constitutional interpretation, at least until the late 1930s, held that the federal government could not spend money for purposes not authorized by the Constitution. The solution was obviously to have federal money put into state hands: Washington would pay the bills; the states would run the programs.

There were four reasons why federal money seemed, to state officials, so attractive. First, the money was there. During most of the nineteenth century and the early decades of the twentieth, the federal government was taking in more money than it was spending. The high-tariff policies of the Republicans produced a large budget surplus; in the 1880s Washington literally had more money than it knew what to do with. Some went to pay off a big part of the national debt, some was given to Civil War veterans as pensions, and some went to the states or was otherwise used for internal improvements.[26]

By the mid-twentieth century, when budget surpluses had pretty much become a thing of the past, a second reason for turning to Washington became evident: the federal income tax. Inaugurated in the 1920s it proved to be a marvelously flexible tool of public finance, for it automatically brought in more money as economic activity (and thus personal income) grew.

Third, the federal government, unlike the states, managed the currency and thus could print more money whenever it needed it. (Technically it borrowed this money, and of course it paid interest on what it had borrowed, but it was under no obligation to pay it all back, because, as a practical matter, it had borrowed, from itself.) The size of the federal public debt stayed more or less constant, or even declined, in the second half of the nineteenth century. By the mid-twentieth century people no longer worried about the national debt so much, or at least they worried about it for reasons other than the fear of being in debt. Thus the federal government came to accept, as a matter of policy, the proposition that when it needed money, it would print it. States could not do this: if they borrowed (and many could not), they had to pay it all back, in full.

These three economic reasons for the attractiveness of federal grants were probably not as important as a fourth reason: politics. Federal money seemed to a state official to be "free" money. If Alabama could get Washington to put up the money for improving navigation on the Tombigbee River, the citizens of the entire nation, not just those of Alabama, would pay for it. Of course if Alabama gets money for that purpose, every state will want it (and will get it). Even so it was still an attractive political proposition: the governor of Alabama did not have to propose, collect, or take responsibility for federal taxes. Indeed, the governor could denounce the federal government for being profligate in its use of the people's money. Mean-

while he would cut the ribbon opening the new dam on the Tombigbee.

That every state had an incentive to ask for federal money to pay for local programs meant, of course, that it would be very difficult for one state to get money for a given program without every state's getting it. The senator from Alabama who votes for the project to improve navigation on the Tombigbee will have to vote in favor of projects improving navigation on every other river in the country if the senator expects his or her Senate colleagues to support such a request. Federalism as practiced in the United States means that when Washington wants to send money to one state or congressional district, it must send money to many states and districts.

In 1966, for example, President Lyndon Johnson proposed a "Model Cities" plan, under which federal funds would be spent on experimental programs in a small number of large cities that had especially acute problems. When the bill went to Congress, it quickly became clear that no such plan could be passed unless the number of cities to benefit was increased. Senator Edmund Muskie of Maine, whose support was crucial, would not vote for a bill that did not make Augusta, Bangor, and Portland eligible for aid originally intended to help New York, Chicago, and Philadelphia.[27]

Meeting National Needs

Until the 1960s most federal grants-in-aid were conceived by or in cooperation with the states and were designed to serve essentially state purposes. Large blocs of voters and a variety of organized interests would press for grants to help farmers, build highways, or support vocational education. During the 1960s, however, an important change occurred: the federal government began devising grant programs based less on what states were demanding and more on what federal officials perceived to be important *national* needs (see Figure 3.2). Federal officials, not state and local ones, were the principal proponents of grant programs to aid the urban poor, combat crime, reduce pollution, and deal with drug abuse. Some of these programs even attempted to bypass the states, providing money directly to cities or event to local citizen groups. These were worrisome developments for governors, who were accustomed to being the conduit for money on its way from Washington to local communities.

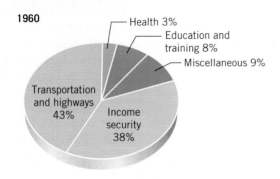

Figure 3.2   The Changing Purpose of Federal Grants to State and Local Governments

1960
- Health 3%
- Education and training 8%
- Miscellaneous 9%
- Transportation and highways 43%
- Income security 38%

1997
- Transportation and highways 11%
- Income security 23%
- Health 42%
- Miscellaneous 9%
- Education and training 15%

Note: Totals may not add up to 100 percent because of rounding.
Source: Budget of the U.S. Government, Fiscal Year 1999, Table 12.2, 205–210.

The rise in federal activism in setting goals and the efforts, on occasion, to bypass state officials occurred at a time when the total amount of federal aid to states and localities had become so vast that many jurisdictions were completely dependent on it for the support of vital services. Whereas federal aid amounted to less than 2 percent of state and local spending in 1927, by 1980 it amounted to 26 percent, and total aid to state and local governments was 15.4 percent of the federal budget (see Figure 3.3). Some older, larger cities had become what one writer called "federal-aid junkies," so dependent were they on these grants. In 1978 in Detroit 77 percent of the revenue the city raised came from Washington.[28]

The Intergovernmental Lobby

State and local officials, both elected and appointed, began to form an important new lobby—the "intergovernmental lobby," made up of mayors, governors, superintendents of schools, state directors of public health, country highway commissioners, local police chiefs, and others who had come to count on federal funds.[29] The four largest of these lobbies employed, in 1998, nearly four hundred people and spent about $62 million (see Table 3.1), about 10 percent of which came from the federal government. Even this has proved insufficient. After all, national organizations of governors or mayors can press for more federal money but not for increased funding for any particular state or city. Thus over thirty-one individual states, more than two dozen counties, and over one hundred cities have opened their own offices in Washington. Some are small, some share staff with other communities, but a few are quite large. Texas alone employs two dozen people in Washington to look after its interests.

The purpose of this intergovernmental lobby was the same as that of any private lobby—to obtain more federal money with fewer strings attached. For a while the cities and states did in fact get more money, but by 1980 federal grants had stopped growing.

Categorical Grants Versus Revenue Sharing

The effort to loosen the strings took the form of shifting, as much as possible, the federal aid from **categorical grants** to block grants or to **revenue sharing.** A categorical grant is one for a specific purpose defined by federal law: to build an airport or a college dormitory, for example, or to make welfare payments to low-income mothers. Such grants usually require that the state or locality put up money to "match" some part of the federal grant, though the amount of matching funds can be quite small. (In the federal highway program Washington pays about 90 percent of the construction costs and the states only about 10 percent.) Governors and mayors complained about these categorical grants because their purposes were often so narrow that it was impossible for a state to adapt federal grants to local needs. A mayor seeking federal money to build parks might have discovered that the city could get money only if it launched an urban-renewal program that entailed

Figure 3.3   Federal Aid to State and Local Governments, 1980–2000

Total federal aid to state and local governments, in billions of constant 1992 dollars, and the aid as a percentage of total federal spending, for each fiscal year.

■ Total aid (scale at left)
□ Percentage of federal spending

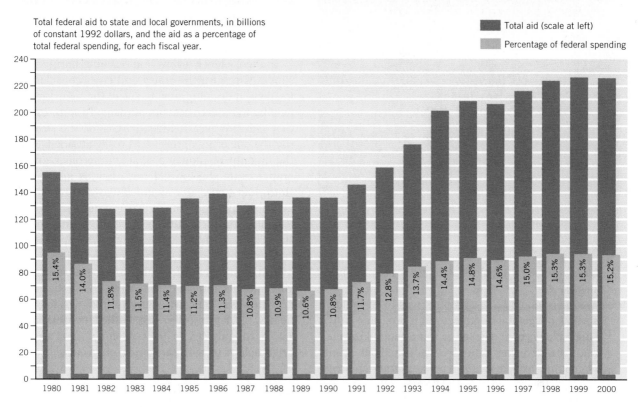

Note: Data for the years 1997–2000 are estimated.
Source: Budget of the U.S. Government, Fiscal Year 1998, Historical Tables, Table 6.1, 99.

Table 3.1   Some State and Local Government Lobbies in Washington

Organization	Number of Employees 1998	Approximate Budget 1998	Percentage of Budget from Federal Government 1980	Percentage of Budget from Federal Government 1998
National Governors' Association (55 state and territorial governors)	93	$14 million	42%	30%
National Conference of State Legislatures (7,424 state legislators)	125	$20 million	36	22
National League of Cities (18,000 cities)	75	$12 million	43	1
National Association of Counties (1,954 counties)	79	$16 million	30	13

Source: Compiled by Russell Burgos.

The federal government requires city transportation services to be accessible to the handicapped.

bulldozing several blocks of housing or small businesses.

One response to this problem was to consolidate several categorical or project grant programs into a single block grant devoted to some general purpose and with fewer restrictions on its use. Block grants (sometimes called *special revenue sharing* or *broad-based aid*) began in the mid-1960s, when such a grant was created in the health field. Though many block grants were proposed between 1966 and 1980, only five were enacted. Of the three largest, one consolidated various categorical grant programs aimed at cities (Community Development Block Grants), another created a program to aid local law enforcement (Law Enforcement Assistance Act), and a third authorized new kinds of locally managed programs for the unemployed (CETA, or the Comprehensive Employment and Training Act). Between 1980 and 1995 the number of block grants in effect rose from five to sixteen.

Revenue sharing (sometimes called *general revenue sharing,* or GRS) was even more permissive. Adopted in 1972 with the passage of the State and Local Fiscal Assistance Act, GRS provided for the distribution of about $6 billion a year in federal funds to states and localities, with no requirement as to matching funds and freedom to spend the money on almost any governmental purpose. Distribution of the money was determined by a statistical formula that took into account population, local tax effort, and the wealth of the state in a way intended to send more money to poorer, heavily taxed states and less to richer, lightly taxed ones. In 1986 the program was ended after having distributed about $85 billion over a fourteen-year period.

In theory block grants and revenue sharing were supposed to give the states and cities considerable freedom in deciding how to spend the money while helping to relieve their tax burdens. To some extent they did. However, neither the goal of "no strings" nor the one of fiscal relief was really attained. First, the amount of money available from block grants and revenue sharing did not grow as fast as the states had hoped nor as quickly as did the money available through categorical grants. Second, the federal government steadily increased the number of strings attached to the spending of this supposedly "unrestricted" money. Thus between 1993 and 1995 the number of federal grants to state and local governments increased from 599 to 633. The entire growth was in categorical grants (from 578 to 618); no new block grants were established. In 1995, as in 1975, roughly 85 to 90 percent of total federal grant dollars were in categorical programs.

The Slowdown in "Free" Money

Block grants grew more slowly than categorical grants because of the different kinds of political coalitions supporting each. Congress and the federal bureaucracy liked categorical grants for the same reason the states disliked them—the specificity of these programs enhanced federal control over how the money was to be used. Federal officials, joined by liberal interest groups and organized labor, tended to distrust state governments. Whenever Congress wanted to address some national problem, its natural inclination was to create a categorical grant program so that it, and not the states, would decide how the money would be spent.

Moreover, even though governors and mayors like block grants and revenue sharing, these programs cover such a broad range of activities that no single interest group has a vital stake in pressing for their enlargement. Revenue sharing, for example, provided a little money to many city agencies but rarely provided all or even most of the money for any single agency. Thus no single agency acted as if the expansion of revenue sharing were a life-and-death matter. Categorical grants, on the other hand, are often a matter of life and death for many agencies—state departments of welfare, of highways, and of health, for example, are utterly dependent on federal aid. Accordingly the administrators in charge of these programs will press strenuously for their expansion. Moreover, categorical programs are supervised by special committees of Congress, and as we shall see in Chapter 11, many of these committees have an interest in seeing their programs grow.

As a result of the political differences between categorical grants and block grants or revenue sharing, the amount spent on the former tends to increase faster than the amount spent on the latter. Between 1975 and 1978 the amount spent on revenue sharing increased by 11 percent, but that spent on categorical grants increased by 56 percent.[30] One observer explained: "You dilute the constituency when you make aid more general. Say you had a program to control a disease. You'd get everyone in the country interested in that disease to focus on that one subject, and a congressman to become the champion of it. . . . There just is not that much sympathy to increase revenue sharing."[31] So little support did general revenue sharing have that, in their debate over the 1986 budget, almost the only thing Democrats and Republicans could agree on was abolishing revenue sharing, which they did.

Not only did general revenue sharing lack a constituency, but it was a wasteful way of trying to help poor communities. The waste resulted from the fact that *every* community—some thirty-nine thousand in all-got revenue-sharing money, whether it was rich or poor. Paw Paw, West Virginia, a town devastated by a loss of jobs, received only $11,874 from revenue sharing, but that amounted to more than one-third of all the tax money it collected and was enough to pay the salary of its lone police officer. Beverly Hills, California, a city so affluent and exclusive that, as the joke goes, the police department has an unlisted phone number, also got revenue-sharing money.

Rivalry Among the States

The more important that federal money becomes to the states, the more likely they are to compete among themselves for the largest share of it. For a century or better the growth of the United States—in population, business, and income—was concentrated in the industrial Northeast. In recent decades, however, that growth—at least in population and employment, if not in income—has shifted to the South, Southwest, and Far West. This change has precipitated an intense debate over whether the federal government, by the way it distributes its funds and awards its contracts, is unfairly helping some regions and states at the expense of others. Journalists and politicians have dubbed the struggle as one between Snowbelt (or Frostbelt) and Sunbelt states.

Whether in fact there is anything worth arguing about is far from clear: the federal government has had great difficulty in figuring out where it ultimately spends what funds for what purposes. For example, a $1 billion defense contract may go to a company with headquarters in California, but much of the money may actually be spent in Connecticut or New York, as the prime contractor in California buys from subcontractors in the other states. It is even less clear whether federal funds actually affect the growth rate of the regions. The uncertainty about the facts has not prevented a debate about the issue, however. That debate focuses on the formulas written into federal laws by which block grants are allocated. These formulas take into account such factors as a county's or city's population, personal income in the area, and housing quality. A slight change in a formula can shift millions of dollars in grants in ways that favor either the older, declining cities of the Northeast or the newer, still-growing cities of the Southwest.

With the advent of grants based on distributional formulas (as opposed to grants for a particular project), the results of the census, taken every ten years, assume monumental importance. A city or state shown to be losing population may, as a result, forfeit millions of dollars in federal aid. There are over one hundred programs (out of some five hundred federal grant programs in all) that distribute money on the basis of population. When the director of the census in 1960 announced figures showing that many big cities had lost population, he was generally ignored. When he made the same announcement in 1980, after the explosion in federal grants, he was roundly denounced by the mayors of those cities.

Senators and representatives now have access to computers that can tell them instantly the effect on their states and districts of even minor changes in a formula by which federal aid is distributed. These formulas rely on objective measures, but the exact measure is selected with an eye to its political consequences. There is nothing wrong with this in principle, since any political system must provide some benefits for everybody if it is to stay together. Given the competition among states in a federal system, however, the struggle over allocation formulas becomes especially acute. The results are sometimes plausible, as when Congress decides to distribute money intended to help disadvantaged local school systems in large part on the basis of the proportion of poor children in each school district. But some-

times the results are a bit strange, as when the formula by which federal aid for mass transit is determined gives New York, a city utterly dependent on mass transit, a federal subsidy of two cents per transit passenger but gives Grand Rapids, a city that relies chiefly on the automobile, a subsidy of forty-five cents per passenger.[32]

Federal Aid and Federal Control

So important has federal aid become for state and local governments that mayors and governors, along with others, began to fear that Washington was well on its way to controlling other levels of government. "He who pays the piper calls the tune," they muttered. In this view the constitutional protection of state government to be found in the Tenth Amendment was in jeopardy as a result of the strings being attached to the grants-in-aid on which the states were increasingly dependent.

Block grants and revenue sharing were efforts to reverse this trend by allowing the states and localities freedom (considerable in the case of block grants; almost unlimited in the case of revenue sharing) to spend money as they wished. But as we have seen, these new devices did not in fact reverse the trend. Until 1978 block grants and revenue sharing increased until they amounted to 27 percent of all federal grants to states and localities but then began to decline, so that by 1986 they accounted for only 18 percent of such aid. Categorical grants—those with strings attached—continued to grow even faster.

There are two kinds of federal controls on state governmental activities. The traditional control tells the state government what it must do if it wants to get some grant money. These strings are often called **conditions of aid.** The newer form of control tells the state government what it must do, period. These rules are called **mandates.** Sometimes the mandates must be observed only if the state takes any federal grants, but sometimes the mandates have nothing to do with federal aid—they apply to all state governments whether or not they accept grants.

Mandates

Most mandates concern civil rights and environmental protection. States may not discriminate in

The federal government helps shape the character of cities by giving money to build parts of the federal highway system.

the operation of their programs, no matter who pays for them. Initially the antidiscrimination rules applied chiefly to distinctions based on race, sex, age, and ethnicity, but of late they have been broadened to include physical and mental disabilities as well. Various pollution control laws require the states to comply with federal standards for clean air, pure drinking water, and sewage treatment.[33]

Stated in general terms, these mandates seem reasonable enough. It is hard to imagine anyone arguing that state governments should be free to discriminate against people because of their race or national origin. In practice, however, some mandates create administrative and financial problems, especially when the mandates are written in vague language, thereby giving federal administrative agencies the power to decide for themselves what state and local governments are supposed to do.

In 1980 there were thirty-six mandates affecting state and local governments, twenty-two of them enacted in the 1970s. Both the Reagan administration and the Bush administration opposed the growth of mandates. Nevertheless, between 1981 and 1986 some 140 regulations, representing nearly six thousand new requirements on state and local government, were added to eighteen existing mandates. And between 1982 and 1991 Congress passed twenty-seven additional mandates (see Table 3.2).

All mandates are not created equal. Some mandates take the form of regulatory statutes and amendments that expand on previous legislation; the 1982 Voting Rights Act Amendments were based on federal civil rights laws dating back to the 1960s. Other mandates represent new areas of federal involvement. For example, the 1986 Handicapped Children's Protection Act introduced federal regulations intended to improve the life prospects of disabled youngsters. Some mandates are easy to understand, simple to administer, and relatively inexpensive—for example, the 1988 Ocean Dumping Ban Act, which prohibits any additional dumping of municipal sewage sludge in ocean waters. However, many mandates are hard to interpret, difficult to administer, and have high or uncertain costs. The 1990 Americans with Disabilities Act (ADA), which required businesses and state and local governments to provide the disabled with equal access to services, employment, buildings, and

Table 3.2	Major Mandate Enactments Regulating State and Local Governments, 1982–1991
1982	Surface Transportation Assistance Act
	Voting Rights Act Amendments
1983	Social Security Amendments
1984	Child Abuse Amendments
	Hazardous and Solid Waste Amendments
	Highway Safety Amendments
	Voting Accessibility for the Elderly and Handicapped Act
1985	Consolidated Omnibus Budget Reconciliation Act
1986	Age Discrimination in Employment Act Amendments
	Asbestos Hazard Emergency Response Act
	Commercial Motor Vehicle Safety Act
	Education of the Handicapped Act Amendments
	Emergency Planning and Community Right-to-Know Act
	Handicapped Children's Protection Act
	Safe Drinking Water Act Amendments
1987	Civil Rights Restoration Act
	Water Quality Act
1988	Drug-Free Workplace Act
	Fair Housing Act Amendments
	Lead Contamination Control Act
	Ocean Dumping Ban Act
1990	Americans with Disabilities Act
	Cash Management Improvement Act
	Clean Air Act Amendments
	Education of the Handicapped Act Amendments
	Older Workers Benefit Protection Act
1991	Social Security Fiscal Budget Reconciliation Act

Source: Adapted from Timothy J. Conlan and David R. Beam, "Federal Mandates: The Record of Reform and Future Prospects," *Intergovernmental Perspective* (Fall 1992): 8.

transportation systems, was one of twenty mandates signed into law by President Bush in 1990. Unfortunately the ADA was enacted with no clear-cut definition of "equal access," no unambiguous blueprint of how it was to be administered, and no reliable estimates of how much it would cost to implement.

Republican leaders in the 104th Congress promised to roll back mandates. They took special aim at requirements from Washington that dictate actions by state and local governments without providing the money to carry them out. For example, in 1993 the U.S. Conference of Mayors claimed that it cost 314 cities $6.5 billion to comply with just ten federal laws that contained such "unfunded mandates."[34] In

1995 Congress passed and President Clinton signed a law that directed the Congressional Budget Office to identify any bill, amendment, or conference report that would impose a new mandate of more than $50 million on state and local governments. But the law neither repealed existing unfunded mandates nor prohibited new ones, and it exempted all antidiscrimination legislation.

Mandates are not the only way in which the federal government imposes costs on state and local governments. According to a 1994 study by the U.S. Advisory Commission on Intergovernmental Relations, certain federal tax and regulatory policies make it difficult or expensive for state and local governments to raise revenues, borrow funds, or privatize public functions. Other federal laws expose state and local governments to financial liability, and numerous federal court decisions and administrative regulations require state and local governments to do or not do various things, either by statute or through an implied constitutional obligation.[35]

It is clear that the federal courts have helped fuel the growth of mandates. As interpreted in this century by the U.S. Supreme Court, the Tenth Amendment provides state and local officials no protection against the march of mandates. Indeed, many of the more controversial mandates result not from congressional action but from court decisions. For example, many state prison systems have been, at one time or another, under the control of federal judges who required major changes in prison construction and management in order to meet standards the judges derived from their reading of the Constitution.

School-desegregation plans are of course the best-known example of federal mandates. Those involving busing—an unpopular policy—have typically been the result of court orders rather than of federal law or regulation.

Judges—usually, but not always, in federal courts—have ordered Massachusetts to change the way it hires fire fighters, required Philadelphia to institute new procedures to handle complaints of police brutality, and altered the location in which Chicago was planning to build housing projects. Note that in most of these cases nobody in Washington was placing a mandate on a local government; rather a local citizen was using the federal courts to change a local practice.

The Supreme Court has made it much easier of late for citizens to control the behavior of local officials. A federal law, passed in the 1870s to protect newly freed slaves, makes it possible for a citizen to sue any state or local official who deprives that citizen of any "rights, privileges, or immunities secured by the Constitution and laws" of the United States.[36] In 1980 the Court decided that this law permitted a citizen to sue a local official if the official deprived the citizen of *anything* to which the citizen was entitled under federal law (and not just those federal laws protecting civil rights).[37] For example, a citizen can now use the federal courts to obtain from a state welfare office a payment to which he or she may be entitled under federal law. No one yet knows how this development will affect the way local government operates.

Conditions of Aid

By far the most important federal restrictions on state action are the conditions attached to the grants the states receive. In theory accepting these conditions is voluntary—if you don't want the strings, don't take the money. But when the typical state depends for a quarter or more of its budget on federal grants, many of which it has received for years and on which many of its citizens depend for their livelihoods, it is not clear exactly how "voluntary" such acceptance is. During the 1960s some strings were added, the most important of which had to do with civil rights. But beginning in the 1970s the number of conditions proliferated. One study of federal grant programs in five large states found that between 1951 and 1978 over a thousand conditions had been added to these programs; nearly 90 percent had been added after 1971.[38]

Some conditions are specific to particular programs. For example, if a state does not establish a highway beautification program, it will lose 10 percent of its federal highway aid money.[39] Others are general, covering most or all grants. For instance, if a state builds something with federal money, it must first conduct an environmental impact study, it must pay construction workers the "prevailing wage" in the area, it often must provide an opportunity for citizen participation in some aspects of the design or location of the project, and it must ensure that the contractors who build the project have nondiscriminatory hiring policies.

The states and the federal government, not surprisingly, disagree about the costs and benefits of such rules. Members of Congress and federal officials feel they have an obligation to develop uniform national policies with respect to important matters and to prevent states and cities from misspending federal tax dollars. State officials, on the other hand, feel these national rules fail to take into account diverse local conditions, require the states to do things that the states must then pay for, and create serious inefficiencies.

What state and local officials discovered, in short, was that "free" federal money was not quite free after all. In the 1960s federal aid seemed to be entirely beneficial; what mayor or governor would not want such money? But just as local officials found it attractive to do things that another level of government then paid for, in time federal officials learned the same thing. Passing laws to meet the concerns of national constituencies—leaving the cities and states to pay the bills and manage the problems—began to seem attractive to Congress.

One's perspective depends on what office one holds, as is revealed by this statement by former New York City mayor Edward I. Koch, who once had been a congressman:

> As a member of Congress I voted for many of the laws imposing grant conditions, and did so with every confidence that we were enacting sensible permanent solutions to critical problems. It took a plunge into the mayor's job to drive home how misguided my congressional outlook had been. The bills I voted for came to the floor in a form that compelled approval. After all, who can vote against clean air and water or better access and education for the handicapped? But as I look back it is hard to believe I could have been taken in by the simplicity of what the Congress was doing and by the flimsy empirical support . . . offered to persuade the members that the proposed solution would work throughout the country.[40]

As is evident from the mayor's remarks, the tensions in the federal system do not arise from one level of government or another being callous or incompetent, but from the kinds of political demands with which each must cope. Because of these competing demands, federal and local officials find themselves in a bargaining situation in which each side is trying to get some benefit (solving a problem, satisfying a pressure group) while passing on to the other side most of the costs (taxes, administrative problems).

The bargains struck in this process used to favor the local officials, because members of Congress were essentially servants of local interests: they were elected by local political parties, they were part of local political organizations, and they supported local autonomy. Beginning in the 1960s, however, changes in American politics that will be described in later chapters—especially the weakening of political parties, the growth of public-interest lobbies in Washington, and the increased activism of the courts—shifted the orientation of many in Congress toward favoring Washington's needs over local needs.

Various presidents have tried to reverse this trend, but with little success. President Nixon proclaimed the "new federalism" and helped create revenue sharing and block grants, but as we shall see, federal mandates and conditions of aid grew rather than declined during his administration.

In 1981 President Reagan asked Congress to consolidate eighty-three categorical grants into six large block grants, none of which would seriously restrict how the states could spend the money. Congress went along in name only—it consolidated fifty-seven

Federal aid now supplies training for the unemployed, as with these Job Corps members.

programs into nine small block grants, each of which had many restrictions attached.

In general the states did not respond to Reagan-era block grants and budget cuts simply by slashing programs. A state-by-state study led by Richard P. Nathan found that "state and local government responses to the 1981 federal aid cuts—through replacement funding, through a wide variety of financial coping and delaying measures, and through administrative reforms"—actually produced "higher service levels than otherwise would have been the case."[41] Likewise, another study concluded that on balance the Reagan block grants had promoted greater state flexibility in program design, reduced administrative costs, and necessitated little reduction in services despite the fact that states had to operate with about 13 percent fewer federal dollars.[42]

In fact it appears that the Reagan-era cutbacks in the amount of federal money, and the threat of more to come, led many governors and mayors to find new ways of delivering old services. Many cities turned over trash collection and other tasks to private firms, often realizing financial savings. Many states experimented with ways of inducing welfare recipients to take jobs, thereby saving on welfare payments. During the prosperous 1980s the cutback in federal aid was made easier to bear because the economy brought in more tax money to the states without their having to raise new taxes. In tough times, such as the early 1990s, the states struggled to make ends meet. By the mid-1990s, however, the economy was back on track, and the effort begun by the Reagan administration to devolve federal power to the states got a powerful new push by the 104th Congress.

A Devolution Revolution?

With the election of Republican majorities in the House and Senate in 1994, a renewed effort was led by Congress to shift important functions back to the states. The key first issue was welfare—that is, Aid to Families with Dependent Children (AFDC). Since 1935 there had been a federal guarantee of cash assistance to states that offered support to low-income, unmarried mothers and their children. AFDC had become bitterly controversial as the num-

ber of women using it and the proportion of births out of wedlock rose dramatically. President Clinton vetoed the first two bills to cut it back but signed the third. It ended any federal guarantee of support and, subject to certain rules, turned the management of the program entirely over to the states, aided by federal block grants. The rules said that every aided woman should begin working within two years and no woman could receive benefits for more than five years.

These and other Republican initiatives were part of a new effort called devolution, which aimed to pass on to the states many federal functions. It is an old idea but one that acquired new vitality because Congress, rather than the president, was leading the effort. Traditionally members of Congress liked voting for federal programs and categorical grants; that way members could take credit for what they were doing for particular constituencies. Under its new conservative leadership Congress, and especially the House, was looking for ways to scale back the size and activities of the national government. Even Clinton seemed to agree when, in his 1996 State of the Union address, he said that the era of big national government was over. But whatever politicians say, no one really knows how best to divide the responsibility between Washington and the states.

Block Grants for Entitlements

Consider what happened with block grants. Basically, there are three types of block grants: *operational grants,* for purposes such as running state child-care programs; *capital grants,* for purposes such as building local wastewater treatment plants; and *entitlement grants,* for transferring income to families and individuals. From 1966 to 1994 a total of twenty-three block grants were enacted, and fifteen were still in place when the 104th Congress came to power. But all of these block grants, including all nine of the Reagan-era block grants, were for operating and capital purposes; none were for major entitlement programs. Thus in 1995, of the $38.4 billion in federal block grant money, 29 percent was for operating programs, 67 percent was for capital programs, and only 4 percent was for entitlement programs. Block grant programs represented about 15 percent of the $238.5 billion in federal grants to states, localities, and nonprofit organizations.

The federal government's two biggest grant-in-aid programs—AFDC, often referred to simply as "welfare," which provides cash assistance to the poor, and Medicaid, which finances the majority of medical and long-term care services for low-income and disabled adults and children—were not created as block grant programs. Together AFDC and Medicaid accounted for half of all federal grant-in-aid spending. Both AFDC and Medicaid were operated as entitlement programs. Each state was entitled to federal dollars for AFDC and Medicaid based on the amount of money it paid to poor families and individuals. In turn each state determined the level and range of benefits eligible individuals received, within a framework defined by federal laws and regulations.

The Reagan administration once considered making AFDC a block grant program in exchange for centralizing Medicaid, but this "swap and turn back plan" was never even introduced in Congress. By contrast, Republicans in the 104th Congress made a flurry of proposals for making *both* AFDC and Medicaid into block grant programs, as well as federal job training, vocational education, employment, childcare, foster care, school nutrition, and food programs. All told these proposals, had they been enacted, would have increased federal block grants to about $183 billion and catapulted the amount of block grant funds in income-transfer programs from only 4 percent to nearly 79 percent.

In the end the devolution revolutionaries of the 104th Congress did not succeed in turning Medicaid into a block grant program. But they did succeed with AFDC and a number of related programs. And they did put the devolution of Medicaid and other important federal programs squarely on the national political agenda, possibly to stay.

There is also some early evidence that the devolution of federal welfare programs has triggered **second-order devolution,** a flow of power and responsibility from the states to local governments, and **third-order devolution,** the increased role of nonprofit organizations and private groups in policy implementation. For example, until the 1996 federal welfare reform law took effect, few states administered their welfare systems in close working partnerships with city or county governments. By 2000, however, fifteen states, including two of the biggest (California and New York), were using so-called county-administered systems. Subject to state direction, scores of local governments are now designing and administering welfare programs (job placement, job training, childcare, and others) through for-profit firms and a wide variety of nonprofit organizations, including local religious congregations.

The total number of people on welfare in America fell from 14.1 million in January 1993 to 8.9 million in March 1998, a 37 percent decline. Between 1994 and 1998 the welfare rolls in thirty of the largest cities declined by 35 percent. Observers disagree about how much the devolution of welfare policy (independent of good economic times and other factors) had to do with these drops. But one thing is clear: with fewer people on welfare rolls receiving cash assistance, states have amassed billions of dollars in unspent federal welfare funds. It appears, however, that many states are spending at least part of their so-called welfare surpluses on other social service programs. So far, for example, devolution has been associated with increased, not decreased, spending by all levels of government on such intergovernmental programs as child welfare services (see Figure 3.4). In fact in some states the spending increases have been so large that total welfare spending is up despite steep declines in spending on cash-assistance programs.

What's Driving Devolution?

The drive for devolution has complex roots, but three forces stand out: the beliefs of devolution's proponents, the realities of deficit politics, and the views of most citizens. According to R. Kent Weaver, the House Republicans who spearheaded the devolution effort harbored a "deep-seated ideological mistrust of the federal government reinforced by the belief that governments closer to the people were more responsive to popular sentiment, and more likely to constrain the growth of programs that were wasteful and redistributive."[43] At the same time, by 1994 many governors of both parties were convinced that the time had come to let state capitals take the lead in figuring out how best to address social problems and administer public health and welfare programs.

But deficit politics also played a role. Congressional Republicans sought not only to fund entitlement programs with block grants instead of categorical grants but also to make major cuts in entitlement spending. For example, one of their bills

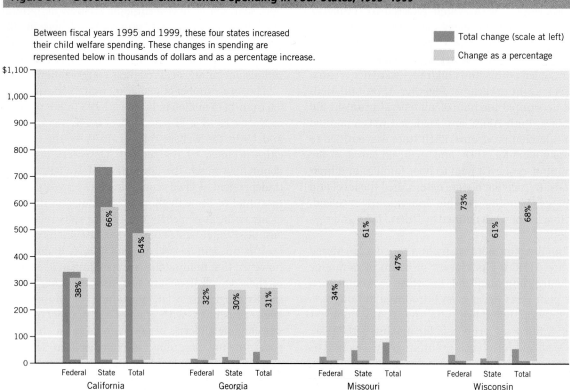

Figure 3.4   Devolution and Child Welfare Spending in Four States, 1995–1999

Between fiscal years 1995 and 1999, these four states increased their child welfare spending. These changes in spending are represented below in thousands of dollars and as a percentage increase.

■ Total change (scale at left)
■ Change as a percentage

Source: Deborah A. Ellwood and Donald J. Boyd, *Changes in State Spending on Social Services Since the Implementation of Welfare Reform* (Albany, N.Y.: Nelson A. Rockefeller Institute of Government, February 2000), 13.

would have reduced Medicaid spending by $163 billion and various welfare entitlements by $175 billion over seven years. In the words of Richard P. Nathan, there is probably no way any big "federal deficit-reduction targets can be met without striking a deal whereby governors get more power in exchange for going along with growth caps on grants-in-aid. Once you put a growth cap on these programs, you have to give the states added flexibility to meet them. Whether you call this a block grant or not does not matter. The result is programs that look and function like block grants."[44]

As Figure 3.5 suggests, most Americans favor devolution, at least in principle. But it remains unclear how deep public sentiment in favor of devolution runs when "shifting responsibility to the states" also means cutting specific program benefits. For example, when asked in 1995 which federal programs "should be cut back in order to reduce the federal budget deficit," most Americans opposed cuts in Medicaid (73 percent), environmental spending (67 percent), unemployment insurance (64 percent), and many other programs. The one main exception was AFDC (only 35 percent opposed cutting it).[45]

Congress and Federalism

Just as it remains to be seen whether the Supreme Court will continue to revive the doctrine of state sovereignty, so it is not yet clear whether the devolution movement will gain momentum, stall, or be reversed. But whatever the movement's fate, the United States will not become a wholly centralized nation. There remains more political and pol-

Figure 3.5   Devolution in the Polls: The States over Washington

QUESTION

Which do you favor—concentration of power in the federal government or in the state government?

QUESTION*

Would you still favor shifting responsibility for programs from the federal government to state governments if it meant your state taxes would increase to offset a decrease in your federal taxes?

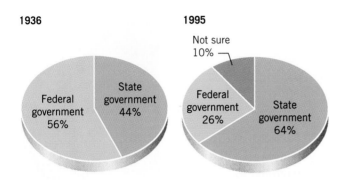

1936

Federal government 56%

State government 44%

1995

Not sure 10%

Federal government 26%

State government 64%

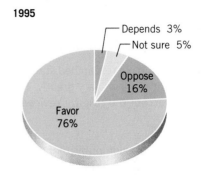

1995

Depends 3%

Not sure 5%

Oppose 16%

Favor 76%

QUESTION

What if some of the tax dollars that go to the federal government now went to your state government instead? Generally speaking, do you think that would result in better government services, or in worse government services, or wouldn't it have much impact on the quality of government services?

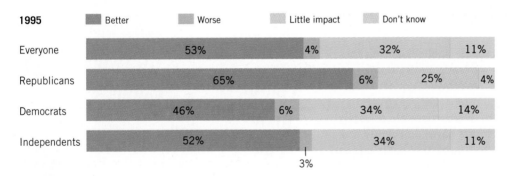

1995   ■ Better   ■ Worse   ■ Little impact   ■ Don't know

	Better	Worse	Little impact	Don't know
Everyone	53%	4%	32%	11%
Republicans	65%	6%	25%	4%
Democrats	46%	6%	34%	14%
Independents	52%	3%	34%	11%

*Asked of those who favored giving states more responsibility (75%). Survey by the Hart and Teeter Research Companies for the Council for Excellence in Government, March 16–18, 1995.

Source: Polling results on devolution as compiled by Richard P. Nathan, Director, Rockefeller Institute at SUNY-Albany, with the assistance of the Roper Center for Public Opinion Research at the University of Connecticut. Data for bottom graph: Survey by the *Los Angeles Times,* January 19–22, 1995, as published in *The Public Perspective* (Storrs: Roper Center for Public Opinion Research, University of Connecticut), April/May 1995): 28. © The Public Perspective. Reprinted by permission.

icy diversity in America than one is likely to find in any other large industrialized nation. The reason is not only that state and local governments have retained certain constitutional protections but also that members of Congress continue to think of themselves as the representatives of localities *to* Washington and not as the representatives *of* Washington to the localities. As we shall see in Chapter 11, American politics, even at the national level, remains local in its orientation.

But if this is true, why do these same members of Congress pass laws that create so many problems for,

MEMORANDUM

To: Judge Grace Viola
From: Robert George, law clerk
Subject: State abortion-funding policies

As requested, I have researched state abortion-funding policies. The main finding is that the laws vary greatly. The first question before you is whether to accept the case for review.

Arguments for:

1. Three states provide public financing for abortion only in cases of life endangerment. Sixteen states provide it in all or most circumstances.
2. About two hundred thousand women nationwide receive government-funded abortions each year.
3. Advocates argue that just as the federal courts have narrowed state discretion in domains such as state prisoners' appeal rights, the courts should set and enforce national standards for women's abortion rights. Who gets what should not depend on who lives where.

Arguments against:

1. Twenty-six states provide public financing for abortions only in cases of rape, incest, or life endangerment. Only five provide it under those and other health circumstances.
2. About 85 percent of all abortions are privately funded, and federal courts have consistently upheld the right of states to restrict abortions and withhold public funding.
3. Opponents argue that just as the Supreme Court has begun to restore state sovereignty and revive the Eleventh Amendment, it would be a mistake, especially on such a morally controversial issue as abortion, to prevent the citizens of each state from setting and enforcing policies that are in accord with their preferences. Who gets what should sometimes depend on who lives where.

Your decision:
Accept case _____
Reject case _____

Out-of-Towner with Twins to Sue State for Failing to Fund Abortion

January 4
PIERRE, SD

An abortion rights group has filed a multimillion-dollar federal lawsuit against the South Dakota Department of Human Services. The suit is brought on behalf of a welfare-dependent Minnesota woman who was denied public funding for an abortion. Across the state line in Minnesota, public funding for abortions is available to adult welfare recipients in all or most circumstances, but in South Dakota it is available only in cases of life endangerment. The woman claimed that while her life was not endangered, the abortion that she sought was "medically necessary" because she had previously been diagnosed as suffering from chronic fatigue syndrome. Agency doctors disagreed and denied her the procedure. While in the state seeking work, she was temporarily housed in a public shelter. On her return trip home, she went into premature labor and gave birth to twins . . .

and stimulate so many complaints from, mayors and governors? One reason is that members of Congress represent different constituencies from the same localities. For example, one member of Congress from Los Angeles may think of the city as a collection of businesspeople, homeowners, and taxpayers, while another may think of it as a group of African Americans, Hispanics, and nature lovers. If Washington wants to simply send money to Los Angeles, these two representatives could be expected to vote together. But if Washington wants to impose mandates or restrictions on the city, they might very well vote on opposite sides, each voting as his or her constituents would most likely prefer.

Another reason is that the organizations that once linked members of Congress to local groups have eroded. As we shall see in Chapter 7, the political parties, which once allowed many localities to speak with a single voice in Washington, have decayed to the point where most members of Congress now operate as free agents, judging local needs and national moods independently. In the 1960s these needs and moods seemed to require creating new grant programs; in the 1970s they seemed to require voting for new mandates; in the 1980s they seemed to require letting the cities and states alone to experiment with new ways of meeting their needs.

There are exceptions. In some states the parties continue to be strong, to dominate decision-making in the state legislatures, and to significantly affect the way their congressional delegations behave. Democratic members of Congress from Chicago, for example, typically have a common background in party politics and share at least some allegiance to important party leaders.

But these exceptions are becoming fewer and fewer. As a result, when somebody tries to speak "for" a city or state in Washington, that person has little claim to any real authority. The mayor of Philadelphia may favor one program, the governor of Pennsylvania may favor another, and individual local and state officials—school superintendents, the insurance commissioner, public health administrators—may favor still others. In bidding for federal aid, those parts of the state or city that are best-organized often do the best, and increasingly the best-organized groups are not the political parties but rather specialized occupational groups such as doctors or schoolteachers. If one is to ask, therefore, why a member of Congress does not listen to his or her state anymore, the answer is, "What do you mean by *the state?* Which official, which occupational group, which party leader speaks for the state?"

Finally, Americans differ in the extent to which we like federal as opposed to local decisions. When people are asked which level of government gives them the most for their money, relatively poor citizens are likely to mention the federal government first, whereas relatively well-to-do citizens are more likely to mention local government. If we add to income other measures of social diversity—race, religion, and region—there emerge even sharper differences of opinion about which level of government works best. It is this social diversity, and the fact that it is represented not only by state and local leaders but also by members of Congress, that keeps federalism alive and makes it so important. Americans simply do not agree on enough things, or even on which level of government ought to decide on those things, to make possible a unitary system.

Summary

States participate actively both in determining national policy and in administering national programs. Moreover, they reserve to themselves or the localities within them important powers over public services, such as schooling and law enforcement, and public decisions, such as land-use control, that in unitary systems are dominated by the national government.

How one evaluates federalism depends in large part on the value one attaches to the competing criteria of equality and participation. Federalism means that citizens living in different parts of the country will be treated differently, not only in spending programs, such as welfare, but in legal systems that assign in different places different penalties to similar offenses or that differentially enforce civil rights laws. But federalism also means that there are more opportunities for participation in making decisions—in influencing what is taught in the schools and in deciding where highways and government projects are to be built. Indeed, differences in public policy—that is, unequal treatment—are in large part the result of participation in decision-making. It is difficult, perhaps impossible, to have more of one of these values without having less of the other.

From the 1930s to the present American politics and public policy have become decidedly more nationalized, with the federal government, and especially the federal courts, imposing increasingly uniform standards on the states in the form of both mandates and conditions of aid. Efforts begun in the 1960s and 1970s to reverse this trend by shifting to revenue sharing and block grants have been only partially successful. In the mid-1990s the Supreme Court began to revive the doctrine of state sovereignty, and a political movement to devolve power from Washington to the states gained momentum. But whether these developments will effect large and lasting changes in American federalism remains to be seen.

World Wide Web Resources

- Information on state governments:
  www.stateline.org
  www.csg.org

- National Governors' Association: www.nga.org
- Supreme Court decisions:
  www.findlaw.com/casecode/supreme.html

Key Terms

devolution *p. 50*
block grants *p. 50*
federalism *p. 50*
sovereignty *p. 51*
unitary system *p. 51*
confederation or confederal system *p. 51*
federal system *p. 51*
federal regime *p. 51*
"necessary and proper" clause *p. 56*

nullification *p. 57*
dual federalism *p. 57*
city *p. 58*
municipal corporation or municipality *p. 58*
special-act charter *p. 58*
general-act charter *p. 58*
Dillon's rule *p. 58*
home-rule charter *p. 58*
ordinances *p. 58*
counties *p. 58*

special-district governments or authorities *p. 58*
school districts *p. 58*
police power *p. 59*
initiative *p. 59*
referendum *p. 59*
recall *p. 59*
grants-in-aid *p. 60*
categorical grants *p. 62*
revenue sharing *p. 62*

conditions of aid *p. 66*
mandates *p. 66*
second-order devolution *p. 71*
third-order devolution *p. 71*

Suggested Readings

Beer, Samuel H. *To Make a Nation: The Rediscovery of American Federalism.* Cambridge: Harvard University Press, 1993. The definitive study of the philosophical bases of American federalism.

Conlan, Timothy. *From New Federalism to Devolution.* Washington, D.C.: Brookings Institution, 1998. A masterful overview of the politics of federalism from Richard Nixon to Bill Clinton.

Diamond, Martin. "The Federalist's View of Federalism." In *Essays in Federalism,* edited by George C.S. Benson. Claremont, Calif.: Institute for Studies in Federalism of Claremont Men's College, 1961,

21–64. A profound analysis of what the Founders meant by federalism.

Grodzins, Morton. *The American System.* Chicago: Rand McNally, 1966. Argues that American federalism has always involved extensive sharing of functions between national and state governments.

Melnick, R. Shep. *Between the Lines: Interpreting Welfare Rights.* Washington, D.C.: Brookings Institution, 1994. An examination of how trends in statutory interpretation have affected broader policy developments, including the expansion of the agenda of national government, the persistence of divided government, and the resurgence and decentralization of Congress.

Peterson, Paul E., Barry G. Rabe, and Kenneth K. Wong. *When Federalism Works*. Washington, D.C.: Brookings Institution, 1986. A careful analysis of how various federal grant-in-aid programs actually work.

Riker, William H. *Federalism: Origin, Operation, Significance*. Boston: Little, Brown, 1964. An explanation and critical analysis of federalism here and abroad.

Thompson, Frank, and John J. DiIulio, Jr., eds. *Medicaid and Devolution: A View from the States*. Washington, D.C.: Brookings Institution, 1998. Essays on the devolution of the largest federal-state social welfare program for the poor.

Wright, Deil S. *Understanding Intergovernmental Relations*. 2nd ed. Monterey, Calif.: Brooks/Cole, 1982. Useful survey of how state and local officials try to influence federal policies.

American Political Culture

4

Enduring Questions

1. What distinctive set of beliefs is fundamental to how most Americans, past and present, think about politics and government?
2. How has American political culture changed over the past hundred years, and how does it differ from the political cultures of other democratic nations?
3. How much do Americans really believe in civil liberty and political toleration?
4. To what extent have Americans come to mistrust government, and what difference does it make?

Political Culture
   The Political System • The Economic System

Comparing America with Other Nations
   Political System • Economic System • The Role of
   Religion

The Sources of Political Culture
   The Culture War

Mistrust of Government

Political Efficacy

Political Tolerance

If the Republic, created in 1787, had depended for its survival entirely on the constitutional machinery designed by the Founders, it probably would not have endured. That machinery has been copied by many other nations, notably those of Latin America, but in virtually no other country have devices such as federalism, an elected president, a bicameral legislature, and the separation of powers produced a political system capable of both effective government and the protection of liberty. In many nations (such as Argentina, Brazil, and the Philippines) that adopted the American model, there have been, at best, brief periods of democratic rule interrupted by military takeovers, the rise to power of demagogues, or the spread of wholesale corruption. The Constitution of the United States, like an old wine, has rarely survived an ocean crossing.

Alexis de Tocqueville, the perceptive French observer of American politics, noticed this as early as the 1830s. One reason a democratic republic took root in the United States but not in other countries that copied its constitution was that this country offered more abundant and fertile soil in which the roots could grow.[1] The vast territory of the United

Alexis de Tocqueville (1805–1859) was a young French aristocrat who came to the United States to study the American prison system. He wrote the brilliant Democracy in America *(2 vols., 1835–1840), a profound analysis of our political culture.*

States created innumerable opportunities for people to acquire land and make a living. No feudal aristocracy monopolized the land, the government imposed only minimal taxes, and few legal restraints existed. As one place after another filled up, people kept pushing west to find new opportunities. A nation of small, independent farmers, unlike the traditional European one of landless peasants and indentured servants, could make democracy work.

But other nations that were similarly favored did not achieve the same result. As Tocqueville noted, much of South America contains fertile land and rich resources, but democracy has not flourished there.[2] Had he returned to the United States fifty years later, when the frontier was no longer expanding and Americans were crowding into big cities, he would have found that democratic government was still more or less intact.

The Constitution and the physical advantages of the land cannot by themselves explain the persist-

ence of the nation's democratic institutions. In addition we must consider the customs of the people—what Tocqueville called their "moral and intellectual characteristics"[3] and what modern social scientists call our political culture.

Political Culture

If you travel abroad, you will quickly become aware that other people often behave differently from Americans. Spaniards may eat dinner at 10:00 P.M., whereas Americans eat at 6:00 or 7:00 P.M. Italians may close their shops for three hours in the middle of the day, while American shops are open continuously from 9:00 to 5:00. Germans address people more formally than Americans, using last names when we would use first names. Japanese business executives attach a lot of importance to working together as a group, while their American counterparts often are more individualistic. In these and countless other ways we can observe cultural differences among people.

Such differences are not limited to eating, shopkeeping, or manners. They include differences in political culture as well. A **political culture** is a distinctive and patterned way of thinking about how political and economic life ought to be carried out (see the box on page 81). Beliefs about economic life are part of the political culture because politics affects economics.

Americans do not judge their political and economic systems in the same way. As we shall see, this difference makes them somewhat unique, for in many other nations people apply the same standards to both systems. For example, Americans think it very important that everybody should be equal politically, but they do not think it important that everybody should be equal economically. By contrast, people in some other nations believe that the principle of equality should be applied to both economic and political life.

The Political System

There are at least five important elements in the American view of the political system:

- *Liberty:* Americans are preoccupied with their rights. They believe they should be free to do pretty much as they please, with some exceptions, so long as they don't hurt other people.

- *Equality:* Americans believe everybody should have an equal vote and an equal chance to participate and succeed.
- *Democracy:* Americans think government officials should be accountable to the people.
- *Civic duty:* Americans generally feel people ought to take community affairs seriously and help out when they can.[4]
- *Individual responsibility:* A characteristically American view is that, barring some disability, individuals are responsible for their own actions and well-being.

By vast majorities Americans believe that every citizen should have an equal chance to influence government policy and to hold public office, and they oppose the idea of letting people have titles such as "Lord" or "Duke," as in England. By somewhat smaller majorities they believe that people should be allowed to vote even if they can't read or write or vote intelligently.[5] Though Americans recognize that people differ in their abilities, they overwhelmingly agree with the statement that "teaching children that all people are really equal recognizes that all people are equally worthy and deserve equal treatment."[6]

At least three questions can be raised about this political culture. First, how do we know that the American people share these beliefs? For most of our history there were no public opinion polls, and even after they became commonplace, they were rather crude tools for measuring the existence and meaning of complex, abstract ideas. There is in fact no way to prove that values such as those listed above are important to Americans. But neither is there good reason for dismissing the list out of hand. One can infer, as have many scholars, the existence of certain values by a close study of the kinds of books Americans read, the speeches they hear, the slogans to which they respond, and the political choices they make, as well as by noting the observations of insightful foreign visitors. Personality tests as well as opinion polls, particularly those asking similar questions in different countries, also supply useful evidence, some of which will be reviewed in the following paragraphs.

Second, if these values are important to Americans, how can we explain the existence in our society of behavior that is obviously inconsistent with them? For example, if white Americans believe in equality of opportunity, why did so many of them for so long deny that equality to African Americans? That people act contrary to their professed beliefs is an everyday

---

★ POLITICALLY SPEAKING ★

Political Culture/Political Ideology

A political culture is a patterned set of ways of thinking about how politics and government ought to be carried out. It consists of a people's fundamental assumptions about how the political process should operate. For instance, Americans assume that a person who loses an election should not try to prevent the winner from taking office, and we eschew political violence: "ballots, not bullets," should decide who holds office. Likewise, Americans believe that nobody should have a greater claim to political authority simply because he or she comes from a rich or aristocratic family. In many societies these are not widely shared assumptions, and in some societies the opposite is believed. Most nations, however, are made up of distinctive regions, religions, and ethnic groups. Each of these may have a distinctive **political subculture.** For example, the American South has a political subculture that differs in important ways from that of the Northeast.

A political ideology is not the same as a political culture. **Political ideology** refers to more or less consistent sets of views concerning the policies government ought to pursue. A doctrinaire liberal or conservative has an ideology. Up to a point people can disagree on ideology (a viewpoint on what government should do) but still share a common political culture (basic beliefs about how government ought to operate). Some ideologies, however, are so critical of existing government policies and practices that they require a fundamental change in the way politics is carried on and thus embody a different political culture as well. The concept of political ideology is explained in Chapter 5.

---

fact of life: people believe in honesty, yet they steal from their employers and sometimes underreport their taxable income. Besides values, self-interest and social circumstances also shape behavior. Gunnar Myrdal, a Swedish observer of American society, described race relations in this country as "an American dilemma" resulting from the conflict between the "American creed" (a belief in equality of opportunity) and American behavior (denying African

At the height of immigration to this country there was a striking emphasis on creating a shared political culture. Schoolchildren, whatever their national origin, were taught to salute this country's flag.

Americans full citizenship).[7] But the creed remains important because it is a source of change: as more and more people become aware of the inconsistency between their values and their behavior, that behavior slowly changes.[8] Race relations in this country would take a very different course if instead of an abstract but widespread belief in equality there were an equally widespread belief that one race is inherently inferior to another. (No doubt some Americans believe that, but most do not.)

Third, if there is agreement among Americans on certain political values, why has there been so much political conflict in our history? How could a people who agree on such fundamentals fight a bloody civil war, engage in violent labor-management disputes, take to the streets in riots and demonstrations, and sue each other in countless court battles? Conflict, even violent struggles, can occur over specific policies even among those who share, at some level of abstraction, common beliefs. Many political values may be irrelevant to specific controversies: there is no abstract value, for example, that would settle the question of whether steelworkers ought to organize unions. More important, much of our conflict has occurred precisely because we have strong beliefs that happen, as each of us interprets them, to be in conflict. Equality of opportunity seems an attractive idea, but sometimes it can be pursued only by curtailing

personal liberty, another attractive idea. The states went to war in 1861 over one aspect of that conflict—the rights of slaves versus the rights of slaveowners.

Indeed, the Civil War illustrates the way certain fundamental beliefs about how a democratic regime ought to be organized have persisted despite bitter conflict over the policies adopted by particular governments. When the southern states seceded from the Union, they formed not a wholly different government but one modeled, despite some important differences, on the U.S. Constitution. Even some of the language of the Constitution was duplicated, suggesting that the southern states believed not that a new form of government or a different political culture ought to be created but that the South was the true repository of the existing constitutional and cultural order.[9]

Perhaps the most frequently encountered evidence that Americans believe themselves bound by common values and common hopes has been the persistence of the word *Americanism* in our political vocabulary. Throughout the nineteenth and most of the twentieth centuries *Americanism* and *American way of life* were familiar terms not only in Fourth of July speeches but also in everyday discourse. For many years the House of Representatives had a committee called the House Un-American Activities Committee. There is hardly any example to be found abroad of such a way of thinking: there is no "Britishism" or "Frenchism," and when Britons and French people become worried about subversion, they call it a problem of internal security, not a manifestation of "un-British" or "un-French" activities.

The Economic System

Americans judge the economic system using many of the same standards by which they judge the political system, albeit with some very important differences. As it is in American politics, liberty is important in the U.S. economy. Thus Americans support the idea of a free-enterprise economic system, calling the nation's economy "generally fair and efficient" and denying that it "survives by keeping the poor down."[10] However, there are limits to how much freedom they think should exist in the marketplace. People support government regulation of business in order to keep some firms from becoming too powerful and to correct specific abuses.[11]

Americans are more willing to tolerate economic inequality than political inequality. They believe in maintaining "equality of opportunity" in the economy but not "equality of results." If everyone has an equal opportunity to get ahead, then it is all right for people with more ability to earn higher salaries and for wages to be set based on how hard people work rather than on their economic needs.[12] Although Americans are quite willing to support education and training programs to help disadvantaged people get ahead, they are strongly opposed to anything that looks like preferential treatment (for example, hiring quotas) in the workplace.[13]

The leaders of very liberal political groups, such as civil rights and feminist organizations, are more willing than the average American to support preferential treatment in the hiring and promoting of minorities and women. They do so because, unlike most citizens, they believe that whatever disadvantages minorities and women face are the result of failures of the economic system rather than the fault of individuals.[14] Even so, these leaders strongly support the idea that earnings should be based on ability and oppose the idea of having any top limit on what people can earn.[15]

This popular commitment to economic individualism and personal responsibility may help explain how Americans think about particular public policies, such as welfare and civil rights. Polls show that Americans are willing to help people "truly in need" (this includes the elderly and the disabled) but not

In the 1950s a committee of the House of Representatives investigating alleged subversion was called the House Un-American Activities Committee. The term un-American activities *seemed strange to nations that did not understand the great appeal of the concept of "Americanism."*

those deemed "able to take care of themselves" (this includes, in the public's mind, people "on welfare"). Also, Americans dislike preferential hiring programs and the use of quotas to deal with racial inequality.

At the core of these policy attitudes is a widely (but not universally) shared commitment to economic individualism and personal responsibility. Some scholars, among them Donald Kinder and David Sears, interpret these individualistic values as "symbolic racism"—a kind of plausible camouflage for antiblack attitudes.[16] But other scholars, such as Paul M. Sniderman and Michael Gray Hagen, argue that these views are not a smoke screen for bigotry or insensitivity but a genuine commitment to the ethic of self-reliance.[17] Since there are many Americans on both sides of this issue, debates about welfare and civil rights tend to be especially intense. What is striking about the American political culture is that in this country the individualist view of social policy is by far the most popular.[18]

Views about specific economic policies change. Americans now are much more inclined than they once were to believe that the government should help the needy and regulate business. But the commitment to certain underlying principles has been remarkably enduring. In 1924 most of the high school students in Muncie, Indiana, said that "it is

Table 4.1 **Responsibility for Success or Failure**		
	Percentage of High School Students Agreeing	
Statement	**1924**	**1977**
It is entirely the fault of the man himself if he cannot succeed.	47%	47%
The fact that some men [in 1977: people] have so much more money than others shows there is an unjust condition in this country that ought to be changed.	30	34

Source: Theodore Caplow and Howard M. Bahr, "Half a Century of Change in Adolescent Attitudes: A Replication of a Middletown Survey by the Lynds," *Public Opinion Quarterly* 43 (Spring 1979): 1–17, table 1. Copyright © 1979, reprinted by permission of University of Chicago Press.

entirely the fault of the man himself if he cannot succeed" and disagreed with the view that differences in wealth showed that the system was unjust. In 1977, over half a century later, the students in this same high school were asked the same questions again, with the same results (see Table 4.1).[19]

Comparing America with Other Nations

The best way to learn what is distinctive about the American political culture is to compare it with that of other nations. This comparison shows that Americans have somewhat different beliefs about the political system, the economic system, and religion.

Political System

Sweden has a well-developed democratic government, with a constitution, free speech, an elected legislature, competing political parties, and a reasonably honest and nonpartisan bureaucracy. But the Swedish political culture is significantly different from ours; it is more deferential than participatory. Though almost all adult Swedes vote in national elections, few participate in politics in any other way. They defer to the decisions of experts and specialists who work for the government, rarely challenge governmental decisions in court, believe leaders and legislators ought to decide issues on the basis of

"what is best" more than on "what the people want," and value equality as much as (or more than) liberty.[20] Whereas Americans are contentious, Swedes value harmony; while Americans tend to assert their rights, Swedes tend to observe their obligations.

The contrast in political cultures is even greater when one looks at a nation, such as Japan, with a wholly different history and set of traditions. One study compared the values expressed by a small number of upper-status Japanese with those of some similarly situated Americans. Whereas the Americans emphasized the virtues of individualism, competition, and equality in their political, economic, and social relations, the Japanese attached greater value to maintaining good relations with colleagues, having decisions made by groups, preserving social harmony, and displaying respect for hierarchy. The Americans were more concerned than the Japanese with rules and with treating others fairly but impersonally, with due regard for their rights. The Japanese, on the other hand, stressed the importance of being sensitive to the personal needs of others, avoiding conflict, and reaching decisions through discussion rather than the application of rules.[21] These cultural differences affect in profound but hard-to-measure ways the workings of the political and economic systems of the two countries, making them function quite differently despite the fact that both are industrialized, capitalist nations.

It is easy to become carried away by the more obvious differences among national cultures and to overgeneralize from them. Thinking in stereotypes about the typical American, the typical Swede, or the typical Japanese is as risky as thinking of the typical white or the typical black American. This can be especially misleading in nations, such as the United States and Canada, that have been settled by a variety of ethnic and religious groups (English-speaking versus French-speaking Canadians, for example, or Jewish, Protestant, and Catholic Americans). But it is equally misleading to suppose that the operation of a political system can be understood entirely from the nation's objective features—its laws, economy, or physical terrain.

In 1959–1960 Gabriel Almond and Sidney Verba published a study of political culture in five nations. In general they found that Americans, and to a lesser degree citizens of Great Britain, had a stronger sense of **civic duty** (a belief that one has an obligation to participate in civic and political affairs) and a stronger sense of **civic competence** (a belief that one can affect government policies) than did the citizens of Germany, Italy, or Mexico. Over half of all Americans and a third of all Britons believed that the average citizen ought to "be active in one's community," compared to only a tenth in Italy and a fifth in Germany. Moreover, many more Americans and Britons than Germans, Italians, or Mexicans believed that they could "do something" about an unjust national law or local regulation.[22] Since 1960 nobody has asked people in these five countries the same questions, and hence we do not know whether these views have changed in recent years. But in a 1995 study of citizen participation in politics, Verba and others reported that while America lagged behind Austria, the Netherlands, West Germany, and the United Kingdom in voter participation, when it came to campaigning, attending political meetings, becoming active in the local community, and contacting government officials, Americans were as active—or substantially more active—than citizens elsewhere.[23]

Nevertheless, today the American people have less trust in government than they once did. But even so, popular confidence in political institutions remains higher here than in many places abroad. In 1987 a survey in the United States and four European nations showed that Americans and Britons were much more likely than people in West Germany, France, or Spain to say that they had a "great deal of" or "some" confidence in their country's armed forces, police, and business. With respect to the nation's judicial system and labor unions, Amer-

Though Japan is a democracy, one group, the Liberal Democratic party, has ruled the country since the end of the Second World War.

icans displayed less confidence but still more than did Europeans (see Table 4.2).[24]

By the same token Americans were more likely to say that they were "very patriotic" and that, if a war came, they would be "willing to fight" for their country (see Table 4.3).[25] Of course Americans know that their country has a lot of faults. But even the most disaffected voters believe the United States needs to change only certain policies, not its system of government.[26]

Economic System

The political culture of Sweden is not only more deferential than ours but also more inclined to favor

---

Table 4.2 Popular Confidence in Institutions in Europe and America, 1987

Institution					
	Percentage Saying They Have a "Great Deal of" or "Some" Confidence				
	U.S.	**Great Britain**	**West Germany**	**France**	**Spain**
Armed forces	86%	79%	69%	59%	36%
Police	88	80	80	72	44
Congress (Parliament)	83	52	64	55	30
Schools	82	53	82	82	59
Church	85	56	66	53	38
Business	84	55	44	30	26
Press/media/TV	69	38	41	48	46
Labor unions	52	29	43	36	26
Judicial system	77	56	72	62	35

Source: Laurence Parisot, "Attitudes About the Media: A Five-Country Comparison," *Public Opinion* (January-February 1988): 18. Reprinted with the permission of the American Enterprise Institute for Public Policy Research, Washington, D.C.

Table 4.3   Patriotism in America and Europe

	Percentage Agreeing				
Statement	U.S.	Germany	Great Britain	Italy	France
I am very patriotic.	88%	77%	72%	69%	64%
We should all be willing to fight for our country whether it is right or wrong.	55	28	56	39	37

Source: Adapted from *The Public Perspective* (November/December 1991): 6. Reprinted by permission of *The Public Perspective,* a publication of the Roper Center for Public Opinion Research, University of Connecticut.

equality of results over equality of opportunity. In 1985 Sidney Verba and Gary Orren compared the views of Swedish and American trade union and political party leaders on a variety of economic issues. In both countries the leaders were chosen from either blue-collar unions or the major liberal political party (the Democrats in the United States, the Social Democrats in Sweden).

The results (see Table 4.4) are quite striking. By margins of four or five to one the Swedish leaders were more likely to believe in giving workers equal pay than were their American counterparts. Moreover, by margins of at least three to one, the Swedes were more likely than the Americans to favor putting a top limit on incomes.[27]

Just what these differences in beliefs mean in dollars-and-cents terms was revealed by the answers to another question. Each group was asked what should be the ratio between the income of an executive and that of a menial worker (a dishwasher in Sweden, an elevator operator in the United States). The Swedish leaders said the ratio should be a little

over two to one. That is, if the dishwasher earned $200 a week, the executive should earn no more than $440 to $480 a week. But the American leaders were ready to let the executive earn between $2,260 and $3,040 per week when the elevator operator was earning $200.

Americans, compared to people in many other countries, are more likely to think that freedom is more important than equality and less likely to think that hard work goes unrewarded or that the government should guarantee citizens a basic standard of living (see Table 4.5). These cultural differences make a difference in politics. In fact there is less income inequality in Sweden than in the United States—the government sees to that.

The Role of Religion

In the 1830s Tocqueville was amazed at how religious Americans were in comparison to his fellow Europeans. As political sociologist Seymour Martin Lipset has observed, "from the early nineteenth century down to the present, the United States has been

Table 4.4   Commitment to Income Equity in Sweden and the United States

	Political Party Leaders		Blue-Collar Union Leaders	
	Sweden (Social Democrats)	U.S. (Democrats)	Sweden	U.S.
Favor equality of results (%)	21%	9%	14%	4%
Favor equal pay (%)	58	12	68	11
Favor top limit on income (%)	44	17	51	13
Fair income ratio of executive to menial worker*	2:1	15:1	2:1	11:1

*In Sweden menial worker was a dishwasher; in U.S. menial worker was an elevator operator.

Source: Reprinted by permission of the publisher from *Equality in America: The View from the Top* by Sidney Verba and Gary R. Orren, Cambridge: Harvard University Press, Copyright © 1985 by the Presidents and Fellows of Harvard College.

Table 4.5   Attitudes Toward Economic Equality in America and Europe, 1991

Statement	Percentage Agreeing				
	U.S.	Great Britain	Germany	Italy	France
It is government's responsibility to take care of the very poor who can't take care of themselves.	23%	62%	50%	66%	62%
Hard work guarantees success.	63	46	38	51	46
Government should *not* guarantee every citizen food and basic shelter.	34	9	13	14	10

Source: Adapted from *The Public Perspective* (November/December 1991): 5, 7. Reprinted by permission of *The Public Perspective,* a publication of the Roper Center for Public Opinion Research, University of Connecticut.

Table 4.6   Religious Belief in America and Europe, 1991

Statement	Percentage Agreeing				
	U.S.	Great Britain	Germany	Italy	France
I never doubt the existence of God.	60%	31%	20%	56%	29%
Prayer is an important part of my daily life.	77	37	44	69	32
There are clear guidelines about what is good and evil.	79	65	54	56	64

Source: Adapted from *The Public Perspective* (November/December 1991): 5, 8. Reprinted by permission of *The Public Perspective,* a publication of the Roper Center for Public Opinion Research, University of Connecticut.

among the most religious countries in the world."[28] The average American is more likely than the average European to believe in God, to pray on a daily basis, and to acknowledge clear standards of right and wrong (see Table 4.6). Surveys in forty-five countries conducted from 1990 to 1993 revealed that America was the only industrial nation in which over 80 percent of citizens identified themselves as religious. Only 1 percent of Americans claimed they were atheists (see Table 4.7).

Religious beliefs have always played a significant role in American politics. The religious revivalist movement of the late 1730s and early 1740s (known as the First Great Awakening) transformed the political life of the American colonies. Religious ideas fueled the break with England, which, in the words of the Declaration of Independence, had violated "the laws of nature and nature's God." Religious leaders were central to the struggle over slavery in the nineteenth century and the temperance movement of the early twentieth century.

Both liberals and conservatives have used the pulpit to promote political change. The civil rights move-

ment of the 1950s and 1960s was led mainly by black religious leaders, most prominently Martin Luther King, Jr. In the 1980s a conservative religious

Religion plays a larger role in the lives of Americans than it does for citizens in most other Western democracies.

Table 4.7   Religion in Industrial Nations, 1990–1993

Statement	Percentage Answering Yes							
	U.S.	Sweden	France	W. Germany	Britain	Spain	Canada	Mexico
Would you say you are...								
A religious person?	82%	29%	48%	54%	55%	64%	69%	72%
Not a religious person?	15	56	36	27	37	27	26	22
A convinced atheist?	1	7	11	2	4	4	3	2
Not sure	2	9	5	17	4	5	2	4

Source: Adapted from *The Public Perspective,* reporting data from surveys conducted from 1990 to 1993 by the Inter-University Consortium for Political and Social Research. *The Public Perspective* (Storrs: Roper Center for Public Opinion Research, University of Connecticut, April/May 1995): 2. © The Public Perspective. Reprinted by permission.

group known as the Moral Majority advocated constitutional amendments that would allow prayer in public schools and ban abortion. In the 1990s another conservative religious group, the Christian Coalition, attracted an enormous amount of media attention and became a prominent force in many national, state, and local elections. If history is any guide, religious beliefs will continue to shape American political culture for many generations to come.

The Sources of Political Culture

That Americans bring a distinctive way of thinking to their political life is easier to demonstrate than to explain. But even a brief, and necessarily superficial, effort to understand the sources of our political culture can help make its significance clearer.

The American Revolution, as we discussed in Chapter 2, was essentially a war fought over liberty: an assertion by the colonists of what they took to be their rights. Though the Constitution, produced eleven years after the Revolution, had to deal with other issues as well, its animating spirit reflected the effort to reconcile personal liberty with the needs of social control. These founding experiences, and the political disputes that followed, have given to American political thought and culture a preoccupation with the assertion and maintenance of rights. This tradition has imbued the daily conduct of U.S. politics with a kind of adversarial spirit quite foreign to the political life of countries that did not undergo a libertarian revolution or that were formed out of an interest in other goals, such as social equality, national independence, or ethnic supremacy.

The adversarial spirit of the American political culture reflects not only our preoccupation with rights but also our long-standing distrust of authority and of people wielding power. The colonies' experiences with British rule was one source of that distrust. But another, older source was the religious belief of many Americans, which saw human nature as fundamentally depraved. To the colonists all of mankind suffered from original sin, symbolized by Adam and Eve eating the forbidden fruit in the Garden of Eden. Since no one was born innocent, no one could be trusted with power. Thus the Constitution had to be designed in such a way as to curb the darker side of human nature. Otherwise everyone's rights would be in jeopardy.

The contentiousness of a people animated by a suspicion of government and devoted to individualism could easily have made democratic politics so tumultuous as to be impossible. After all one must be willing to trust others with power if there is to be any kind of democratic government, and sometimes those others will be people not of one's own choosing. The first great test case took place around 1800 in a battle between the Federalists, led by John Adams and Alexander Hamilton, and the Democratic-Republicans, led by Thomas Jefferson and James Madison. The two factions deeply distrusted each other: the Federalists had passed laws designed to suppress Jeffersonian journalists; Jefferson suspected the Federalists were out to subvert the Constitution; and the Federalists believed Jefferson intended to sell out the country to France. But as we shall see in Chapter 7, the threat of civil war never materialized, and the Jeffersonians came to power peacefully. Within a few years the role of an opposition party

Three kinds of modern families: A traditional mother-father family, a single-mother one, and one with adopted children.

became legitimate, and people abandoned the idea of making serious efforts to suppress their opponents. By happy circumstance people came to accept that liberty and orderly political change could coexist.

The Constitution, by creating a federal system and dividing political authority among competing institutions, provided ample opportunity for widespread—though hardly universal—participation in politics. The election of Jefferson in 1800 produced no political catastrophe, and those who had predicted one were, to a degree, discredited. But other, more fundamental features of American life contributed to the same end. One of the most important of these was religious diversity.

The absence of an established or official religion for the nation as a whole, reinforced by a constitutional prohibition of such an establishment and by the migration to this country of people with different religious backgrounds, meant that religious diversity was inevitable. Since there could be no orthodox or official religion, it became difficult for a corresponding political orthodoxy to emerge. Moreover, the conflict between the Puritan tradition, with its emphasis on faith and good works, and the Catholic Church, with its devotion to the sacraments and priestly authority, provided a recurrent source of cleavage in American public life. The differences in values between these two groups showed up not only in their religious practices but also in areas involving the regulation of manners and morals, and even in people's choice of political party. For more than a century candidates for state and national office were deeply divided over whether the sale of liquor should be prohibited, a question that arose ultimately out of competing religious doctrines.

Even though there was no established church, there was certainly a dominant religious tradition—Protestantism, and especially Puritanism. The Protestant churches provided people with both a set of beliefs and an organizational experience that had profound effects on American political culture.

Those beliefs encouraged, or even required, a life of personal achievement as well as religious conviction: a believer had an obligation to work, save money, obey the secular law, and do good works. Max Weber explained the rise of capitalism in part by what he called the Protestant ethic—what we now sometimes call the **work ethic.**[29] Such values had political consequences, as people holding them were motivated to engage in civic and communal action.

Churches offered ready opportunities for developing and practicing civic and political skills. Since most Protestant churches were organized along congregational lines—that is, the church was controlled by its members, who put up the building, hired the preacher, and supervised the finances—they were, in effect, miniature political systems, with leaders and committees, conflict and consensus. Developing a participatory political culture was undoubtedly made easier by the existence of a participatory religious culture. Even some Catholic churches in early America were under a degree of lay control. Parishioners owned the church property, negotiated with priests, and conducted church business.

All aspects of culture, including the political, are preserved and transmitted to new generations primarily by the family. Though some believe that the weakening of the family unit has eroded the extent to which it transmits anything, particularly culture, and has enlarged the power of other sources of values— the mass media and the world of friends and fashion, leisure and entertainment—there is still little doubt that the ways in which we think about the world are largely acquired within the family. In Chapter 5 we shall see that the family is the primary source of one kind of political attitude—identification with one or another political party. Even more important, the family shapes in subtle ways how we think and act on political matters. Erik Erikson, the psychologist, noted certain traits that are more characteristic of American than of European families—the greater freedom enjoyed by children, for example, and the larger measure of equality among family members. These familial characteristics promote a belief, carried through life, that every person has rights deserving protection and that a variety of interests have a legitimate claim to consideration when decisions are made.[30]

The combined effect of religious and ethnic diversity, an individualistic philosophy, fragmented political authority, and the relatively egalitarian American family can be seen in the absence of a high degree of **class consciousness** among Americans. Class consciousness means thinking of oneself as a worker whose interests are in opposition to those of management, or vice versa. In this country most people, whatever their jobs, think of themselves as "middle class."

If any group of Americans were likely to think and act in terms of their economic class, one would suppose it would be the unemployed. Nonetheless, a careful study in 1976 showed that, though unemployed people feel deprived, the great majority do not identify with other unemployed people or think that their interests as a class are in opposition to those of management. The political views of the unemployed do not seem to differ much from those of the employed, and even when the former think in class terms, their political views do not seem to be affected. Moreover, we know that even in the late 1930s, when the country was in the grip of a massive depression, only a small minority of the unemployed expressed a strong sense of class consciousness.[31]

Though the writings of Horatio Alger are no longer popular, Americans still seem to believe in the message of those stories—that the opportunity for success is available to people who work hard. This may help explain why the United States is the only large industrial democracy without a significant socialist party and why the nation has been slow to adopt certain welfare programs.

The Culture War

Almost all Americans share some elements of a common political culture. Why, then, is there so much cultural conflict in American politics? For many years, the most explosive political issues have included abortion, gay rights, drug use, school prayer, and pornography. Viewed from a Marxist perspective, politics in the United States is utterly baffling: instead of two economic classes engaged in a bitter struggle over wealth, we have two cultural classes locked in a war over values.

To say that there are two cultural classes is, of course, an oversimplification, but to say that there is a culture war is not an exaggeration.[32] Groups supporting and opposing the right to abortion have had many angry confrontations in recent years. The latter have been arrested while attempting to block access to abortion clinics; some clinics have been firebombed; and at least one physician has been killed. A controversy over what schoolchildren should be taught about homosexuals was responsible, in part, for the firing of the head of the New York City school system; in other states there have been fierce arguments in state legislatures and before the courts over whether gay and lesbian couples should be allowed to adopt children. Although most Americans want to keep heroin, cocaine, and other drugs illegal, a significant number of people want to legalize (or at least decriminalize) their use. The Supreme Court has ruled that children cannot pray in public schools, but this has not stopped many parents and school authorities from trying to reinstate school prayer, or at least prayerlike moments of silence. The discovery that a federal agency, the National Endowment for the Arts, had given money to support exhibitions and performances that many people thought were obscene led to a furious congressional struggle over the future of the agency. The 1992 presidential election centered, in part, on a passionate argument over which candidate best exemplified "family values."

The culture war differs from other political disputes (over such matters as taxes, business regulations, and foreign policy) in several ways: money is not at stake, compromises are almost impossible to arrange, and the conflict is more profound. It is animated by deep differences in people's beliefs about private and public morality—that is, about the standards that ought to govern individual behavior and social arrangements. It is about what kind of country we ought to live in, not just about what kinds of policies our government ought to adopt.

To simplify, there are two opposed camps, the **orthodox** and the **progressive.** On the orthodox side are people who believe that morality is as important as, or more important than, self-expression and that moral rules derive from the commands of God or the laws of nature—commands and laws that are relatively clear, unchanging, and independent of individual preferences. On the progressive side are people who think that personal freedom is as important as, or more important than, certain traditional moral rules and that those rules must be evaluated in light of the circumstances of modern life—circumstances that are quite complex, changeable, and dependent on individual preferences.

Most conspicuous among the orthodox are fundamentalist Protestants and born-again Christians, and so critics who dislike orthodox views often dismiss them as the fanatical expressions of "the Religious Right." But many people who hold orthodox views are not fanatical or deeply religious or right-

wing on most issues; they simply have strong views about drugs, pornography, and sexual morality. Similarly, the progressive side often includes members of liberal Protestant denominations (for example, Episcopalians and Unitarians) and people with no strong religious beliefs, and so their critics often denounce them as immoral, anti-Christian radicals who have embraced the ideology of secular humanism, the belief that moral standards do not require religious justification. But in all likelihood few progressives are immoral or anti-Christian, and most do not regard secular humanism as their defining ideology.

Moreover, the culture war is occurring not just between different religious denominations but also within them. Catholic, Protestant, and Jewish leaders with an orthodox perspective tend to assign great importance to two-parent families, condemn pornography, denounce homosexuality, and think the United States is in general a force for good in the world. Leaders of the same faiths who have a progressive outlook are more likely to say that many legitimate alternatives to the traditional two-parent family exist, that pornography and homosexuality are private matters protected by individual rights, and that the United States has been at best a neutral and at worst a bad force in world affairs.[33] This conflict between the orthodox and progressive view of American culture is similar to, and has many of the same causes, as the cleavage (described in Chapter 5) between the traditional middle class and the new middle class.

American history has always had conflicts of this sort, but they have acquired special importance today as a result of two major changes in American society. The first is the great increase in the proportion of people who consider themselves progressive. Once almost everyone was religiously orthodox, even if politically liberal; today fewer are. The second factor is the rise of media (such as television, direct-mail advertising, and the Internet) that make it easy to wage a cultural war on a large scale. In the past preachers, writers, and lecturers could reach at most a few hundred people at a time; today television evangelists, radio talk-show hosts, and the authors of direct-mail messages or websites can wage a furious war of words reaching tens of millions of people and recruiting hundreds of thousands of followers. A cultural war that once enlisted only a few activists can now mobilize mass armies.

The tensions generated by the culture war affect our views as to how well our government works, how much influence ordinary people can have over it, and how large a measure of freedom we ought to grant to our opponents. Trust in government, a sense of political efficacy, and tolerance for views we dislike are fragile under the best of circumstances. Have the cultural tensions of recent decades made matters worse? In the rest of this chapter we shall try to answer these questions.

Mistrust of Government

In 1979 President Jimmy Carter, taking note of numerous public opinion polls that showed a dramatic decline in the proportion of Americans who said they had a great deal of confidence in our system, made a nationwide television address on the subject of "the American malaise," which he defined as a crisis of confidence evident in Americans' "growing disrespect" for government, schools, churches, and other institutions.

Though it probably wasn't a politically astute speech—Americans don't like to be told they suffer from a malaise, and the following year they voted against Carter and for a man, Ronald Reagan, who offered a much more upbeat assessment of the American condition—it was based on some solid factual evidence. As Figure 4.1 shows, in 1972, 53 percent of Americans trusted the federal government to "do what is right" all or most of the time. By

1974 that number had fallen to 36 percent and has remained below 50 percent ever since.

In part this decline in trust was the result of some dramatic events. The largest single increase in mistrust occurred between 1972 and 1974—the time of the Watergate scandal, when close aides to President Nixon authorized a burglary of Democratic party headquarters and the president himself participated in the cover-up of the bungled break-in. But the decline began long before Watergate (or the war in Vietnam) and continued after both events were history.

This rising mistrust is worrisome, but it should be viewed in context. There is evidence that the mistrust is chiefly aimed not at our *system* of government but at specific leaders and policies.[34] We have already seen that Americans have more confidence in their governmental institutions than do citizens of many other countries. Even in 1972–1974, when distrust of government was especially high, 86 percent of those interviewed in a national survey agreed with the following statement: "I am proud of many things about our form of government."[35] It is also important to note that from the early 1970s through the mid-1990s, high public trust in the presidency and Congress was cut in half, but public confidence in the Supreme Court remained virtually unchanged, and the percentage of Americans expressing a "great deal" of confidence in state and local government increased.[36]

Moreover, there are reasons for thinking that the current level of trust in government is close to the

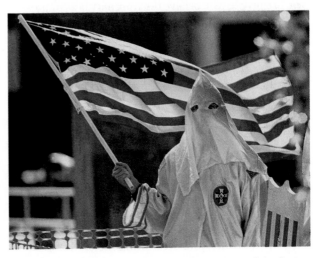

When people think things have gone wrong, they often demonstrate, as did these marchers during the Great Depression and this member of the Ku Klux Klan.

Figure 4.1   Trust in the Federal Government, 1958–1998

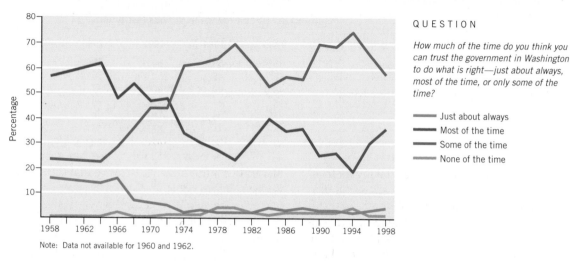

QUESTION

How much of the time do you think you can trust the government in Washington to do what is right—just about always, most of the time, or only some of the time?

— Just about always
— Most of the time
— Some of the time
— None of the time

Note: Data not available for 1960 and 1962.

Source: University of Michigan, *The National Election Studies* (September 1999), table 5A.1.

historical norm and that the much higher levels of trust of the late 1950s and early 1960s were unusual. Though polling was then in its infancy, there is evidence that Americans in the 1930s were not much more trustful of their government than they are now.[37] Between the 1930s and the 1960s this nation overcame an economic depression and won World War II, events that gave citizens an unusually high degree of confidence in the capacity of their government. The 1960s and 1970s, when that confidence weakened, were years of great turmoil—the civil rights movement, the war in Vietnam, a sharp rise in crime rates, the assassination of various leaders, urban riots and campus demonstrations, and economic inflation. Small wonder that people thought that things were getting out of hand and that political leaders ought to take some of the blame.

There was a brief and small improvement in trust during the early Reagan years,[38] but that gain was washed out, and then some, by a big drop in the early 1990s. Owing to the combined effects of an economic recession, political scandals (such as the revelation that members of the House of Representatives were writing checks without having money in the House bank to cover them), and the continued growth in problems such as crime, drug abuse, and the federal debt, Americans in record numbers expressed disgust at politics and politicians.

The decline in popular confidence in national government that began in the 1960s is real, but it ought not to be overstated or overgeneralized. As Table 4.8 suggests, whereas Americans have lost confidence in some institutions, they have retained or gained confidence in others. In addition certain group differences in confidence have diminished. African Americans, for example, have more confidence in organized religion and less confidence in the criminal justice system than do white Americans.[39] But both blacks and whites have far more confidence in churches than they do in criminal courts, three-quarters of both say that they are "proud to live under our political system," and 95 percent of both say that there are no "countries better than the United States."[40] In sum, without regard to race or other factors, most Americans no longer give to political leaders and their policies the kind of support they gave in the 1950s, but they have never lost confidence in either the political system or each other.

Political Efficacy

Perhaps the most worrisome aspect of recent changes in the American political culture is the decline in the extent to which citizens feel that the political system will respond to their needs and beliefs. These changes

Table 4.8   Public Confidence in Institutions, 1973–1999

Institution	Percentage Saying They Have a "Great Deal" or "Quite a Lot" of Confidence in Various Institutions						
	1973	1979	1985	1991	1997	1998	1999
Church/organized religion	66%	65%	66%	59%	56%	59%	58%
U.S. Supreme Court	44	45	56	48	50	50	49
Public schools	58	53	48	44	40	37	36
Newspapers	39	51	35	32	35	33	33
Big business	26	32	31	26	28	30	30
Small business	—	—	—	—	63	56	—
Congress	42	34	39	30	22	28	26
State government	63[a]	—	—	—	68	—	—
Local government	63[a]	—	—	—	69	—	—
Criminal justice system	—	—	—	—	19	24	23

[a]Data for 1972.

Sources: The Gallup Organization, *Poll Releases: Confidence in Institutions* (2000), 3–5; *Poll Releases: Confidence in Federal Government* (June 19, 1997), 3–5.

are in what scholars call a citizen's sense of **political efficacy,** by which they mean a citizen's capacity to understand and influence political events.

This sense of efficacy has two parts—**internal efficacy** (the ability to understand and take part in political affairs) and **external efficacy** (the ability to make the system respond to the citizenry). Since the mid-1960s there has been a fairly sharp drop in the sense of external efficacy (or system responsiveness) but not much change in the sense of internal efficacy (personal competence).

As we can see in Figure 4.2, people today are not much different from people in 1952 with respect to whether they can understand what is going on in government (most find it too complicated to fathom) and whether they have much say in what the government does. But there has been a big change in how responsive people think the government is to their interests. In 1980 people were twice as likely as they were in the late 1950s to say that public officials don't "care much what people like me think." And in 1980 they were much more likely than they had been (even as recently as 1968) to say "those we elect to Congress in Washington lose touch with the people pretty quickly" and "parties are only interested in people's votes, not their opinions."[41]

Unlike the increase in the mistrust of government, the increase in the feeling that government was unresponsive was not shaped by any particular events; the sense of external efficacy dropped more or less steadily throughout the 1960s and 1970s. What seems to

have happened is that Americans gradually have come to the view that government has become too big and pervasive for it to be sensitive to citizen preferences. In 1964 less than a third of Americans thought the federal government was too powerful; in 1976 half did.[42]

Though Americans may feel less effective as citizens than they once did, their sense of efficacy remains much higher than it is among Europeans. In 1974 a poll taken in five nations found that the average American scored significantly higher on the efficacy scale than the average person in Austria, Germany, Great Britain, or the Netherlands. Moreover, Americans were much more likely than Europeans to say that they regularly discussed politics, signed petitions, and worked to solve community problems.[43] Though Americans are less likely to vote than Europeans, they are more likely to do the harder chores that make up democratic politics.

Because Americans are less likely than they once were to hold their leaders in high esteem, to have confidence in government policies, and to believe the system will be responsive to popular wishes, some observers like to say that Americans today are more "alienated" from politics. It probably would be better to say that they are simply more realistic.

Political Tolerance

Democratic politics depends crucially on citizens' being reasonably tolerant of the opinions and

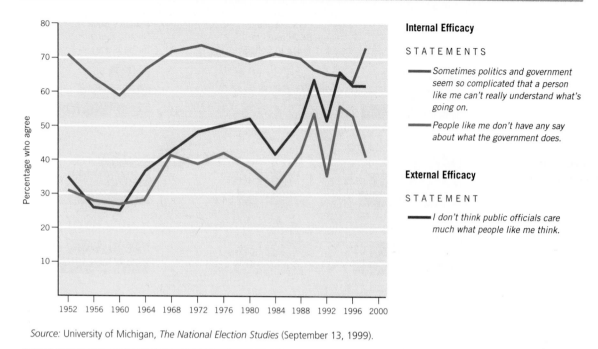

Figure 4.2   Changes in the Sense of Political Efficacy, 1952–1998

Internal Efficacy

STATEMENTS

— *Sometimes politics and government seem so complicated that a person like me can't really understand what's going on.*

— *People like me don't have any say about what the government does.*

External Efficacy

STATEMENT

— *I don't think public officials care much what people like me think.*

Source: University of Michigan, *The National Election Studies* (September 13, 1999).

actions of others. If unpopular speakers were always shouted down, if government efforts to censor newspapers were usually met with popular support or even public indifference, if peaceful demonstrations were regularly broken up by hostile mobs, if the losing candidates in an election refused to allow their victorious opponents to take office, then the essential elements of a democratic political culture would be missing, and democracy would fail. Democracy does not require perfect tolerance; if it did, the passions of human nature would make democracy forever impossible. But at a minimum citizens must have a political culture that allows the discussion of ideas and the selection of rulers in an atmosphere reasonably free of oppression.

Public opinion surveys show that the overwhelming majority of Americans agree with concepts such as freedom of speech, majority rule, and the right to circulate petitions—at least in the abstract.[44] But when we get down to concrete cases, a good many Americans are not very tolerant of groups they dislike. Suppose you must decide which groups will be permitted to espouse their causes at meetings held in your community's civic auditorium. Which of these groups would *you* allow to run such a meeting?

1. Protestants holding a revival meeting
2. Right-to-life groups opposing abortion
3. People protesting a nuclear power plant
4. Feminists organizing a march for the Equal Rights Amendment
5. Gays organizing for homosexual rights
6. Atheists preaching against God
7. Students organizing a sit-in to shut down city hall

In a national opinion poll conducted by Herbert McClosky and Alida Brill in 1978–1979, a majority of Americans would have allowed the first four groups to hold their meetings but would have refused to allow the last three. (Similar findings from another opinion survey are shown in Figure 4.3.) Leaders in the communities where this survey was performed would have allowed the first five groups to meet. Lawyers and judges in these communities would have allowed all seven to meet.[45]

Clearly community leaders, and especially lawyers and judges, are more tolerant of specific political activities than are most citizens. But three things need to be said on behalf of the average citizen.

First, one person's civic intolerance can be another person's heartfelt display of civic concern. As is suggested by Figure 4.4, most Americans

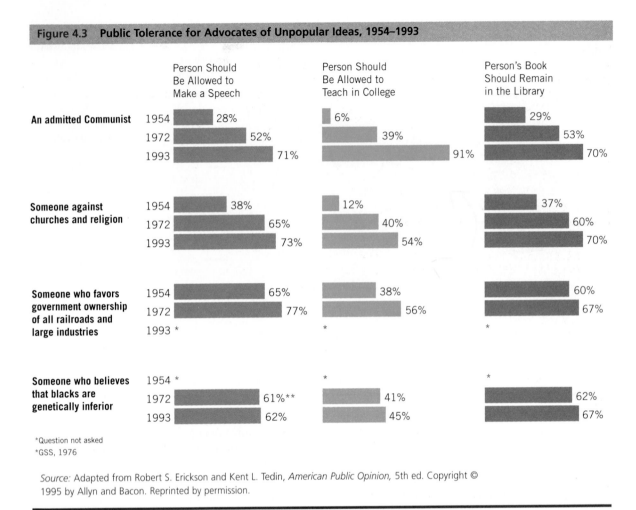

Figure 4.3   Public Tolerance for Advocates of Unpopular Ideas, 1954–1993

*Question not asked
*GSS, 1976

Source: Adapted from Robert S. Erickson and Kent L. Tedin, *American Public Opinion,* 5th ed. Copyright © 1995 by Allyn and Bacon. Reprinted by permission.

believe that serious civic problems are rooted in a breakdown of moral values. Correctly or not, most citizens worry that the nation is becoming too tolerant of behaviors that harm society, and they favor defending common moral standards over protecting individual rights.

Second, Americans are willing to allow many people with whom they disagree to do a great deal politically. In the McClosky-Brill study, for example, the general public supported the right of the movie industry to make movies on any subjects it chooses, upheld the right of reporters to keep confidential their sources of information, defended the right of newspapers and television stations to hire "radical reporters," said that college officials should allow nonviolent protest demonstrations by students, and supported freedom of worship even for extremist religious groups.[46]

Third, Americans have become more tolerant over the last few decades. For instance, in the 1970s people were much more willing to allow communists, socialists, and atheists to meet and disseminate their views than they were in the early 1950s, even though Americans in the 1970s were probably no more sympathetic to these causes than they were in the 1950s.[47] Similarly, there has been a general increase in the willingness of citizens to say that they would vote for a Catholic, Jew, black, or woman for president (see Figure 4.5 on page 99).

Nonetheless, this majority tolerance for many causes should not blind us to the fact that for most of us there is some group or cause from which we are willing to withhold political liberties—even though we endorse those liberties in the abstract.

If most people dislike one or another group strongly enough to deny it certain political rights

---

Figure 4.4   Views of Toleration and Morality

QUESTION

Which worries you more, that the country will become too tolerant of behaviors that are bad for sociey, or that the country will become too intolerant of behaviors that don't do any real harm to society?

1998

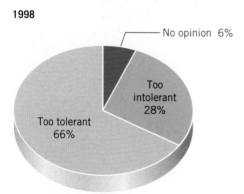

QUESTION

Is it more important to defend standards of right and wrong, to protect the rights of individuals, or are both equally important?

1998

Source: The American Enterprise (January/February 1999): 37, reporting data from Roper, *Washington Post,* Harvard, and Kaiser Family Foundation polls.

---

that we usually take for granted, how is it that such groups (and such rights) survive? The answer, in part, is that most of us don't act on our beliefs. We rarely take the trouble—or have the chance—to block another person from making a speech or teaching school. And among people who are in a position to deny other people rights—officeholders and political activists, for example—the level of political tolerance is somewhat greater than among the public at large.[48]

But another reason may be just as important. Most of us are ready to deny *some* group its rights, but we

MEMORANDUM

To: Representative Heidi Unruh
From: Ron Sider, chief of staff
Subject: Charitable Choice Expansion Act

Section 104 of the 1996 federal welfare reform law encouraged states to utilize "faith-based organizations" as providers of federal welfare services. Known as Charitable Choice, the law prohibits participating organizations from discriminating against beneficiaries on the basis of religion but permits them to control "the definition, development, practice, and expression" of their religious convictions. The proposed act would expand Charitable Choice to crime prevention and other areas.

Arguments for:

1. Over 90 percent of Americans believe in God, and 80 percent favor government funding for faith-based social programs.
2. Local religious groups are the main nongovernmental providers of social services in poor urban neighborhoods. The primary beneficiaries of faith-based programs are needy neighborhood children who are not affiliated with any congregation.
3. So long as the religious organizations serve civic purposes and do not proselytize, the law is constitutional.

Arguments against:

1. Americans are a richly religious people precisely because we have never mixed church and state in this way.
2. Community-serving religious groups succeed because over 97 percent of their funding is private and they can flexibly respond to people's needs without government or other interference.
3. Constitutional or not, the law threatens to undermine both church and state: children will have religion slid (if not jammed) down their throats, and religious leaders will be tempted to compromise their convictions.

Your decision:
Favor expansion _____
Oppose expansion _____

Religious Leaders Rally to Expand Federal Funding for "Charitable Choice"

August 28
WASHINGTON
Yesterday an interfaith coalition of religious leaders conducted an all-day prayer vigil on Capitol Hill and called for increased federal funding for antipoverty programs run by local religious congregations . . .

Figure 4.5   Changes in Levels of Political Tolerance, 1930–1999

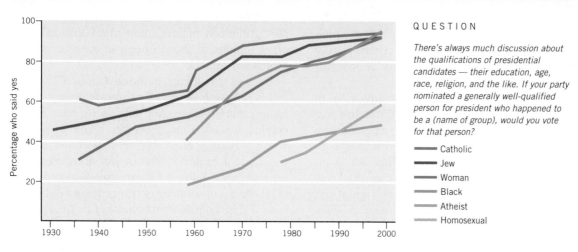

QUESTION

There's always much discussion about the qualifications of presidential candidates — their education, age, race, religion, and the like. If your party nominated a generally well-qualified person for president who happened to be a (name of group), would you vote for that person?

— Catholic
— Jew
— Woman
— Black
— Atheist
— Homosexual

Sources: Gallup poll data, various years, as compiled by Professor John Zaller, Department of Political Science, UCLA; The Gallup Organization, *Poll Releases* (March 29, 1999), 2–6.

usually can't agree on which group that should be. Sometimes we can agree, and then the disliked group may be in for real trouble. There have been times (1919–1920, and again in the early 1950s) when socialists or communists were disliked by most people in the United States. The government on each occasion took strong actions against them. Today fewer people agree that these left-wing groups are a major domestic threat, and so their rights are now more secure.

Finally, the courts are sufficiently insulated from public opinion that they can act against majority sentiments and enforce constitutional protections (see Chapter 14). Most of us are not willing to give all rights to all groups, but most of us are not judges.

These facts should be a sober reminder that political liberty cannot be taken for granted. Men and women are not, it would seem, born with an inclination to live and let live, at least politically, and many—possibly most—never acquire that inclination. Liberty must be learned and protected. Happily the United States during much of its recent history has not been consumed by a revulsion for any one group that has been strong enough to place the group's rights in jeopardy.

Nor should any part of society pretend that it is always more tolerant than another. In the 1950s, for example, ultraconservatives outside the universities were attacking the rights of professors to say and teach certain things. In the 1960s and 1970s ultraliberal students and professors inside the universities were attacking the rights of other students and professors to say certain things.

Summary

The American system of government is supported by a political culture that fosters a sense of civic duty, takes pride in the nation's constitutional arrangements, and provides support for the exercise of essential civil liberties (albeit out of indifference or diversity more than principle at times). In recent decades mistrust of government officials (though not of the system itself) has increased, and confidence in their responsiveness to popular feelings has declined.

Although Americans value liberty in both the political system and the economy, they believe equality is important only in the political realm. In economic affairs they wish to see equality of opportunity but accept inequality of results.

Not only is our culture generally supportive of democratic rule, it also has certain distinctive features that make our way of governing different from what one finds in other democracies. Americans are preoccupied with their rights, and this fact, combined with a political system that (as we shall see) encourages the vigorous exercise of rights and claims, gives to our political life an *adversarial* style.

Unlike Swedes or Japanese, we do not generally reach political decisions by consensus, and we often do not defer to the authority of administrative agencies. American politics, more than that of many other nations, is shot through at every stage with protracted conflict.

But as we shall learn in the next chapter, that conflict is not easily described as always pitting liberals against conservatives. Not only do we have a lot of conflict, it is often messy conflict, a kind of political Tower of Babel. Foreign observers sometimes ask how we stand the confusion. The answer, of course, is that we have been doing it for over two hundred years. Maybe our Constitution is two centuries old not in spite of this confusion but because of it. We shall see.

World Wide Web Resources

- Polling organizations that frequently measure aspects of political culture:
    www.roper.com
    www.gallup.com

- U.S. Census Bureau: www.census.gov

Key Terms

political culture *p. 80*	civic duty *p. 84*	class consciousness *p. 90*	political efficacy *p. 94*
political subculture *p. 81*	civic competence *p. 85*	orthodox *p. 91*	internal efficacy *p. 94*
political ideology *p. 81*	work ethic *p. 90*	progressive *p. 91*	external efficacy *p. 94*

Suggested Readings

Almond, Gabriel, and Sidney Verba. *The Civic Culture*. Princeton, N.J.: Princeton University Press, 1963. A survey of the political cultures of five nations—the United States, Germany, Great Britain, Italy, and Mexico—as they were in 1959.

Gallup, George, Jr., and D. Michael Lindsay. *Surveying the the Religious Landscape: Trends in U.S. Beliefs*. Harrisburg, Pa.: Morehouse Publishing, 1999. Masterful summary of polling data on religion and American life in the second half of the twentieth century.

Hartz, Louis. *The Liberal Tradition in America*. New York: Harcourt Brace Jovanovich, 1955. A stimulating interpretation of American political thought since the Founding, emphasizing the notion of a liberal consensus.

Lipset, Seymour Martin. *The First New Nation*. Rev. ed. New York: Norton, 1979. How the origins of American society gave rise to the partially competing values of equality and achievement and the ways in which these values shape political institutions.

McClosky, Herbert, and Alida Brill. *Dimensions of Tolerance: What Americans Believe About Civil Liberties*. New York: Russell Sage Foundation, 1983. How—and whether—different kinds of Americans learn political tolerance.

McClosky, Herbert, and John Zaller. *The American Ethos: Public Attitudes Toward Capitalism and Democracy*. Cambridge: Harvard University Press, 1984. Study of the ways in which Americans evaluate political and economic arrangements.

Nye, Joseph S., Philip D. Zelikow, and David C. King. *Why People Don't Trust Government*. Cambridge: Harvard University Press, 1997. An effort explain distrust.

Putnam, Robert D. *Bowling Alone: The Collapse and Revival of American Community*. New York: Simon & Schuster, 2000. An important argument that American political culture has been harmed by the decline in membership in organizations that bring people together for communal activities.

Tocqueville, Alexis de. *Democracy in America*. Edited by Phillips Bradley. 2 vols. New York: Knopf, 1951. First published in 1835–1840, this was and remains the greatest single interpretation of American political culture.

Verba, Sidney, and Gary R. Orren. *Equality in America: The View from the Top*. Cambridge: Harvard University Press, 1985. Elite views on political and economic equality.

part II

Opinions, Interests, and Organizations

*The latent causes of faction
are thus sown in the nature
of man; and we see them
everywhere brought into
different degrees of activity,
according to the different
circumstances of civil society.*

FEDERALIST No. 10

101

Public Opinion

Enduring Questions

1. According to the Framers of the Constitution, what, if any, part should public opinion play in America's representative democracy?

2. How, if at all, does public opinion in America today vary by race, religion, region, and other differences?

3. What is political ideology, and to what extent are ideological differences reflected in political behavior?

4. How responsive is contemporary American government to the opinion of persistent popular majorities, and to what extent do political elites shape how average citizens debate and decide policy issues?

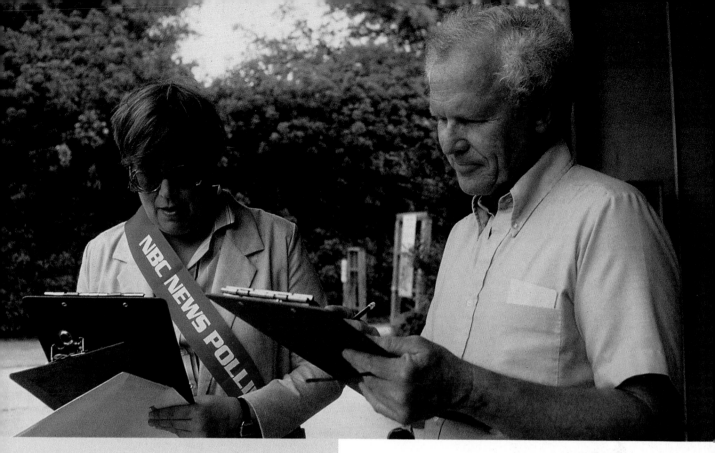

What Is Public Opinion?

The Origins of Political Attitudes
The Role of the Family • Religion • The Gender Gap • Schooling and Information

Cleavages in Public Opinion
Social Class • Race and Ethnicity • Region

Political Ideology
Consistent Attitudes • What Do *Liberalism* and *Conservatism* Mean? • Various Categories • Analyzing Consistency • Political Elites • Is There a "New Class"?

Political Elites, Public Opinion, and Public Policy

I n the Gettysburg Address Abraham Lincoln said that the United States has a government "of the people, by the people, and for the people." That suggests that the government should do what the people want. If that is the case, it is puzzling that:

- The federal government has often had a large budget deficit, but the people want a balanced budget.
- Courts have ordered that children be bused in order to balance the schools racially, but the people opposed busing.
- The Equal Rights Amendment to the Constitution was not ratified, but polls showed that most people supported it.
- The House of Representatives voted to impeach President Bill Clinton even though most Americans opposed this.
- Most people believe that there should be a limit on the number of terms to which U.S. senators and members of the U.S. House of Representatives can be elected, but Congress has not approved term limits.

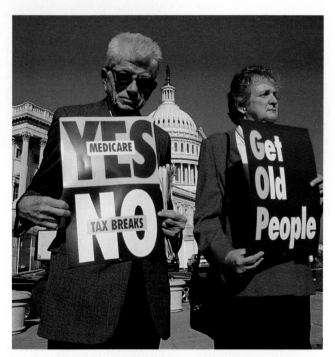

Elderly Americans express—vocally—their opinions about Medicare benefits.

Some people, reflecting on the many gaps between what the government does and what the people want, may become cynical and think our system is democratic in name only. That would be a mistake. There are several very good reasons why government policy will often appear to be at odds with public opinion.

First, the Framers of the Constitution did not try to create a government that would do from day to day "what the people want." They created a government for the purpose of achieving certain substantive goals. The preamble to the Constitution lists six of these: "to form a more perfect Union, establish Justice, ensure domestic Tranquility, provide for the common defence, promote the general Welfare, and secure the Blessings of Liberty."

One means of achieving these goals was popular rule, as provided for by the right of the people to vote for members of the House of Representatives (and later for senators and presidential electors). But other means were provided as well: representative government, federalism, the separation of powers, a Bill of Rights, and an independent judiciary. These were all intended to be checks on public opinion. In addition the Framers knew that in a nation as large and diverse as the United States there would rarely be any such thing as "public opinion"; rather there would be many "publics" (that is, factions) holding many opinions. The Framers hoped that the struggle among these many publics would protect liberty (no one "public" would dominate) while at the same time permitting the adoption of reasonable policies that commanded the support of many factions.

Second, it is not as easy as one may suppose to know what the public thinks. We are so inundated these days with public opinion polls that we may imagine that they tell us what the public believes. That may be true on a few rather simple, clear-cut, and widely discussed issues, but it is not true with respect to most matters on which the government must act. The best pollsters know the limits of their methods, and the citizen should know them as well.

Third, the more people are active in and knowledgeable about politics, the more weight their opinions carry in governmental circles. For most of us, politics ranks way down on the list of things to think about, well below our families, jobs, health, sweethearts, entertainment, and sports. Some people, however, are political activists, and so come to know as much about politics as the rest of us know about batting averages, soap operas, and car repair. Not only do these activists, or political elites, *know more* about politics than the rest of us, they *think differently* about it—they have different views and beliefs. The government attends more to the elite views than to popular views, at least on many matters.

In this chapter we take a close look at what "public opinion" is, how it is formed, the major cleavages in public opinion, and, especially, how political elites differ from ordinary citizens. In later chapters we examine the workings of political parties, interest groups, and government institutions and consider what impact they have on whether public opinion affects government policy.

What Is Public Opinion?

A few years ago some researchers at the University of Cincinnati asked twelve hundred local residents whether they favored passage of the Monetary Control Bill of 1983. About 21 percent said that they favored the bill, 25 percent said that they opposed it, and the rest said that they hadn't thought much about the matter or didn't know.

The members of Congress from Cincinnati would have been surprised to learn of this expression of public opinion from their constituents, for there was no such thing as the Monetary Control Bill. The researchers had made it up. Nor is there anything unusual about people in Cincinnati. A few years earlier about 26 percent of the people questioned in a national survey also expressed opinions on the same nonexistent piece of legislation.[1] Given this information, how much confidence should we place in polls that presumably tell us "what the American people think" about legislation and other issues?

Even if people have heard of a given person or issue, how a pollster words a question can dramatically affect the answer he or she gets. Suppose we want to know whether the public believes that the federal government should provide housing for people. One poll asked that question in three different ways. In the first example people were asked whether they agreed or disagreed with a one-sided statement ("The federal government should see to it that all people have adequate housing"). A majority agreed. In the second example people were given a choice between two statements, one favoring a federal housing policy (mentioned first) and the other favoring individual responsibility ("each person should provide for his own housing"). Given this choice, a small majority opposed federal housing programs. In the third example the question was repeated, but this time with the individual responsibility option mentioned first. Now over 70 percent of the respondents opposed federal housing programs. Simply altering the order in which people were presented with options affected which option they chose and changed "public opinion" on housing programs.

Moreover, opinions on public issues may not be stable—that is, they may not be firmly held. In a study conducted in 1980, the same people were asked the same questions in January and again in June of the same year. The first had to do with how tough we should be in dealing with the Soviet Union, the second with whether spending should be cut on things like health and education programs. Many people gave one opinion in January and then a different one in June. Of those who said in January that we should cooperate more with the Soviets, only one-quarter said in June that we should get together with them. Of those who said in January that the government should cut the services it provides, more than one-quarter said in June that they wanted to

keep those services at the same level or expressed a middle-of-the-road position.

In sum public opinion on many matters suffers from ignorance, instability, and sensitivity to the way questions are worded in polls. This does not mean that the American people are ignorant, unstable, or gullible, only that most Americans do not find it worth their while to spend the amount of time thinking about politics that they spend on their jobs, families, and friends. Moreover, just because people do not

---

★ POLITICALLY SPEAKING ★

John Q. Public, Middle America, and the Silent Majority

John Q. Public is the average man or woman on the street, often portrayed by cartoonists as bespectacled and befuddled. The "little guy," the "common man" (or woman), John Doe or Jane Doe. John Q. Public is sometimes confused with James Q. Wilson, to whom he is only distantly related.

Middle America is a phrase coined by the late Joseph Kraft in 1968 to refer to Americans who have moved out of poverty but are not yet affluent and who cherish the traditional middle-class values.

The **silent majority** consists of those people, whatever their economic status, who uphold traditional values, especially against the counterculture of the 1960s.

Source: Adapted from *Safire's Political Dictionary* by William Safire. Copyright © 1968, 1972, 1978 by William Safire. Reprinted by permission of Random House, Inc. and the author.

think much about politics does not mean that democracy is impossible, only that it can work best when people are given relatively simple, clear-cut choices—like the choice between Democrats and Republicans or between one presidential candidate and another.

Furthermore, our specific attitudes about particular matters may be much less important for the health of society than our underlying political culture—our commitment, discussed in Chapter 4, to liberty, equality, individualism, and civic duty. As we shall see, different people give different weight to the various parts of this culture, producing what can be described as a political ideology.

The Origins of Political Attitudes

Because our attitudes are often unstable or uninformed, some critics of American society have argued that we are brainwashed—duped by television or demagogic leaders into thinking one way or another. Often we are told that presidential candidates are "sold," as if they were boxes of soap flakes. Naturally these critics never say that *they* are brainwashed, only the rest of us.

However shallow their analysis, the argument is a serious one. If the government (or the media) were able to manipulate our political attitudes, then democracy would be a joke. It is akin to what would happen in the marketplace if automobile dealers were able to "brainwash" us into buying Chevrolets, Fords, Chryslers, or Toyotas. The car manufacturers would no longer have to strive to achieve greater effi-ciency and produce better products; they would only have to "persuade" us what to like. We would be happy not because we owned a good car but because Madison Avenue *told* us we owned a good car.

Of course advertising does affect our choice of candidates and policies, just as it affects our choice of automobiles. Otherwise why would companies and politicians spend so much money on advertising? But there are real and important limits to the impact of that advertising. Those limits exist because we have learned, independent of government and the market, some things that help us make our own choices.

The Role of the Family

The best-studied (though not necessarily the most important) case of opinion formation is that of party identification. The majority of young people identify with their parents' political party. A study of high school seniors showed that, of these young men and women, almost all (91 percent) knew accurately the presidential preference of their parents, the great majority (71 percent) knew accurately their parents' party identification, and most shared that identification (only 9 percent identified with the party opposite to that of their parents).[2] (See Table 5.1.) This process begins fairly early in life: by the time they are in the fifth grade (age eleven), over half of all schoolchildren identify with one party or the other, and another fifth claim to be independents.[3]

Naturally, as people grow older, they become more independent of their parents in many ways, including politically, but there nonetheless remains a great deal of continuity between youthful partisanship, learned from one's parents, and adult partisanship. One study of adults found that around 60 percent still had the party identification—Democrat, Republican, or independent—of their parents. Of those who differed with their parents, the overwhelming majority did so not by identifying with the opposite party but by describing themselves as "independents."[4]

The ability of the family to inculcate a strong sense of party identification has declined in recent years. The proportion of citizens who say they consider themselves to be Democrats or Republicans has become steadily smaller since the early 1950s. This drop has been greatest among those who *strongly* identify with one party or another. In 1952 fully 22 percent of voters said they were strong Democrats

Table 5.1	Parent and Child Agreement in Party Identification		
	Parents		
Child	**Democrat**	**Independent**	**Republican**
Democrat	66%	29%	13%
Independent	27	53	36
Republican	7	17	51
Number	914	442	495

Source: M. Kent Jennings and Richard G. Niemi, *The Political Character of Adolescence: The Influence of Families and Schools* (Princeton, N.J.: Princeton University Press, 1974), 41. Copyright © by Princeton University Press. Reprinted by permission.

and 13 percent said they were strong Republicans; by 1976 only 15 percent claimed to be strong Democrats and 9 percent to be strong Republicans. Accompanying this decline in partisanship has been a sharp rise in the proportion of citizens describing themselves as independents.

Part of this change results from the fact that young voters have always had a weaker sense of partisanship than older ones, and today there are proportionally a larger number of young voters than there were thirty years ago. But the youthfulness of the population cannot explain all the changes, for the decline in partisanship has occurred at all age levels. Moreover, those who reached voting age in the 1960s were less apt than those who matured in the 1950s to keep the party identification of their parents.[5]

Though we still tend to acquire some measure of partisanship from our parents, the meaning of that identification is far from clear. There are, after all, liberal and conservative Democrats, as well as liberal and conservative Republicans. So far the evidence suggests that children are more independent of their parents in policy preferences than in party identification. The correlation of children's attitudes with parental attitudes on issues involving civil liberties and racial questions is much lower than the correlation in their party identification. This may be because issues change from one generation to the next, because children are more idealistic than their parents, or because most parents do not communicate to their children clear, consistent positions on a range of political issues. The family dinner table is not a seminar in political philosophy but a place where people discuss jobs, school, dates, and chores.

In some families, however, the dinner table is a political classroom. Fairly clear political ideologies (a term we shall define in a later section) seem to be communicated to that small proportion of children raised in families where politics is a dominant topic of conversation and political views are strongly held. Studies of the participants in various student radical movements in the 1960s suggested that college radicals were often the sons and daughters of people who had themselves been young radicals; some commentators dubbed them the "red-diaper babies." Presumably, deeply conservative people come disproportionately from families that were also deeply conservative. This transfer of political beliefs from

"Yes, son, we're Republicans."

Drawing by Richter; © *The* New Yorker *Magazine, Inc.*

one generation to the next does not appear in large national studies, because such a small proportion of the population is at either the far left or the far right of the political spectrum.

Religion

One way in which the family forms and transmits political beliefs is by its religious tradition. In general Catholic families are somewhat more liberal on economic issues than white Protestant ones, while Jewish families are much more liberal on both economic and social issues than families of either Catholics or Protestants.[6]

There are two theories as to why this should be so. The first has to do with the **social status** of religious groups in America. When they immigrated to this country, Catholics and Jews were often poor and the object of discrimination. As a result they often affiliated themselves with whichever party and social doctrine seemed most sympathetic to their plight. In many places the Democratic party and a liberal social doctrine seemed to offer the most support. Today Catholics and Jews enjoy greater economic prosperity and face much less discrimination, and so their support for Democrats and liberal candidates has weakened.

The status explanation cannot be the whole story, for if it were simply a matter of low status and discrimination, born-again Christians, many of whom are poor, would be liberal Democrats. The second theory emphasizes the content of the **religious tradition** more than the social status of its adherents. In

The Christian Coalition has emerged as a significant political force. Here it is addressed by Rev. Pat Robertson, a founder.

this view the Jewish religion has always emphasized social justice as much as personal rectitude. By contrast, evangelical Protestant denominations emphasize personal salvation (becoming "born again") more than questions of social policy. This difference in teachings has led Jews to be disproportionately liberal and fundamentalist Protestants to be disproportionately conservative on many social issues.

Whatever the reason, religious differences make for political differences. In Table 5.2 we can see how the religious beliefs of white voters affected their policy preferences in 1992. Fundamentalists believe that the Bible is God's word and literally true. They are more likely than those who doubt that the Bible is inspired by God to oppose cuts in defense spending, to want cuts in domestic spending, to oppose abortions, and to favor prayer in schools. (These differences remain essentially the same even after you divide the respondents between those who have a lot of political information and those who have rather little.)

Interestingly there are no significant differences in how people holding differing views of the Bible feel about economic issues, as opposed to social or foreign policy issues. Fundamentalists and nonfundamentalists have about the same opinion on government job guarantees and spending on government services. This suggests that both social status and religious tradition help explain the effect of religion on politics: the poor status of many fundamentalists inclines them to back liberal government economic policies, but the religious tradition of this group leads them to take a conservative position on social and foreign policy matters.

In the early 1990s a broad-based political movement arose to represent the views of conservative evangelical Christians. The movement was spearheaded by the Christian Coalition, an activist organi-

	Religious Orientation		
Political Opinion	**Secular**	**In Between**	**Fundamentalist**
Increase domestic spending	48%	41%	32%
Institute national health insurance	63	56	38
Guarantee good standard of living	38	23	21
Permit all abortions	70	50	14
Prohibit mandatory school prayers	67	60	51
Allow gays in the military	68	59	32
Encourage equal role for women	99	93	71
Fund more AIDS research	63	52	46
Cut defense spending	77	70	42
Oppose Gulf War	17	11	10
Increase aid to Russia	35	33	24
Percent Democratic (of party identifiers)	41	40	30
Percent liberal (of ideological identifiers)	48	38	7
Percent for Clinton (1992)	57	49	23

Table 5.2   Religious Orientation

Source: From Robert S. Erikson and Kent L. Tedin, *American Public Opinion,* 5th ed. Copyright © 1995 by Allyn and Bacon. Reprinted by permission.

zation founded by Pat Robertson and led by Ralph Reed. Unlike the older Moral Majority, the Christian Coalition took seriously the task of entering politics at the grassroots and recognized the need to build working alliances with mainstream politicians. Within a short time people allied with the Christian Coalition have won power in many local Republican party organizations, and its national conferences have become important places for Republican presidential candidates to appear. Although the Christian Coalition is strongest in the South, Midwest, and West, it is unmistakably a national force in American politics. During the 1994 elections, for example, it distributed some 30 million voter guides nationwide, and affiliated local organizations may have distributed several million more. Recent opinion surveys show that since 1960 evangelical Christians have become more attached to Republican presidential candidates (except in 1976, when Jimmy Carter ran), while Jews and those without a religious orientation have been consistently supportive of the Democratic party.

The Gender Gap

Journalists often point out that women have "deserted" Republican candidates to favor Democratic ones. In some cases that is true. But it would be more correct to say that men have "deserted" Democratic candidates for Republican ones. The **gender gap** is the difference in political views between men and women. That gap has existed for a long time, and it is a problem for both political parties.

A recent study found that men have become increasingly Republican since the mid-1960s, while the voting behavior of women has remained unchanged. As Figure 5.1 shows, in 1952 men and women identified with the Democratic party at about the same level, around 58 or 59 percent. In 1996 women still identified with the Democrats at about the same level, while men had abandoned the Democratic party and identified more with the Republicans.[7]

The biggest reason for this shift seems to involve attitudes about the size of government, gun control, spending programs aimed at the poor, and gay rights. Men have always been more conservative than women in their views on these social issues, but by the late 1960s and early 1970s men had changed their party loyalty to match their policy preferences. As Table 5.3 shows, in 1996 men and women were similar in their views on abortion but quite different

Figure 5.1   Party Identification of Men and Women, 1952–1996

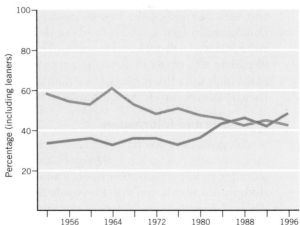

Source: Karen M. Kaufman and John R. Petrocik, "The Changing Politics of American Men: Understanding the Sources of the Gender Gap," *American Journal of Political Sciences* 43 (1999): 864–887.

Table 5.3	The Gender Gap: Differences in Political Views of Men and Women		
Issue		**Men**	**Women**
Federal spending for welfare programs should be increased.		8%	14%
Abortion should be permitted by law.		57	60
Sexual harassment is a very serious problem in the workplace.		24	38
This country would be better off if we just stayed home and did not concern ourselves with problems in other parts of the world.		24	29
I voted for Clinton in 1996.		45	59
Generally speaking, I think of myself as a Democrat.		32	44
The United States should increase defense spending.		37	26
The United States should increase spending on solving the problems of the homeless.		51	63
Ban all handguns except for the police.		33	58

Source: ICPSR American National Election Survey, 1996. Pre- and Post-Election Surveys.

in their opinions about welfare, spending money to help the homeless or to increase military defense, and sexual harassment in the workplace. In the 1996 election women were much more likely than men to vote for Clinton even though he had been involved in extramarital affairs. In 1998 women were much more inclined than men to vote for female Senate candidates. Part of that difference was because most of the women candidates were Democrats; in fact, in one race where the woman candidate was a Republican, the male (Democratic) candidate got a bigger share of the female vote than of the male vote. This gender gap is not unique to the United States; it can be found throughout the world.

Schooling and Information

Studies going back over half a century seem to show that attending college has a big impact on political attitudes, usually making them more liberal. College students are more liberal than the population generally, and students at the most prestigious or selective colleges are the most liberal of all.[8] For example, the undergraduates at Harvard College in 1984 preferred Mondale to Reagan 61 percent to 28 percent, while the country at large favored Reagan over Mon-

dale 59 percent to 41 percent.[9] Moreover, the longer students stay in college, the more liberal they are, with seniors more liberal than freshmen and graduate students more liberal than undergraduates.[10] Harvard seniors were more supportive of Mondale than were Harvard freshmen. Students studying the social sciences tend to be more liberal than those studying engineering or the physical sciences.[11] As we shall see in the next chapter, having gone to college increases the rate at which people participate in politics.

Why schooling should have this effect on attitudes is not clear. One possibility is that it has nothing to do with schooling but rather with the individual traits typically possessed by people who go to college and beyond. Some combination of temperament, intelligence, and family background may lead to greater liberalism, with the contents of a college education playing no role at all.

A second possibility is that college and postgraduate schooling expose people to more information about politics from all sources. College graduates, compared to high school graduates, read more newspapers and periodicals, join more organizations and social movements, and participate in more election campaigns and lobbying efforts. Their political beliefs may be shaped by these experiences as much as, or more than, by what they learn in the college classroom. In addition evidence collected by John Zaller shows that the level of political information one has is the best single predictor of being liberal on some kinds of issues, such as civil liberties and civil rights.[12] Information on these matters, he suggests, is today produced by a predominantly liberal cultural elite (see Chapter 10). The longer you stay in school, the more you are exposed to the views of that elite.

The third possibility is that college somehow teaches liberalism. We know that professors are more liberal than members of other occupations, that professors at the most prestigious schools are more liberal than those at the less-celebrated ones, that professors in the social sciences are more liberal than those in engineering or business, and that younger faculty members are more liberal than older ones.[13]

The political disposition of professors is in part the result of the kinds of people who become college teachers, but it is also the result of the nature of intellectual work. Intellectuals require freedom to

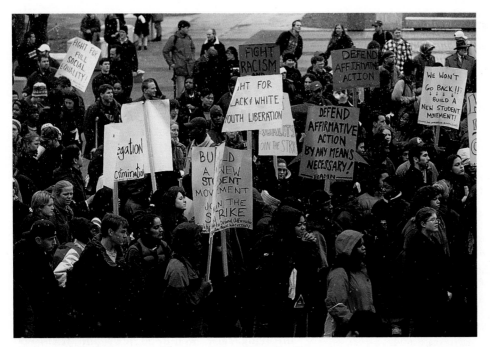

Students tend to become more liberal as they go through college.

explore new or unpopular ideas and thus tend to be strong supporters of civil liberties. Intellectuals work with words and numbers to develop general or abstract ideas; frequently they do not take personal responsibility for practical matters. Thus they are often critical of people who do take such responsibility and who, in the management of complex human affairs, inevitably make compromises. Intellectuals are by training and profession skeptical of common opinions, and thus they are often critical of accepted values and existing institutions. They are interested in ideas and the ideal and thus are sometimes disdainful of the interests and institutions of society.

At one time the liberalizing effect of college had only a small impact on national politics, because so few persons were college graduates. In 1900 only 6 percent of Americans seventeen years of age had even graduated from high school, and less than 1 percent of twenty-three-year-olds were college graduates. By 1982 fully 71 percent of all Americans age twenty-five and over were high school graduates, and 18 percent of those age twenty-five and over were college graduates.[14] College, or the exposure to ideas and movements that one encounters there, has become, along with the family, an important source of political opinion for the American electorate.

Some people believe that college students today are more conservative than students were ten or twenty years ago. That is partly true and partly false. As indicated in Table 5.4 college freshmen in 1993 were less likely than freshmen in the 1970s to favor legalizing marijuana or abortion and less willing to support increased military spending. Their opinions about government-sponsored consumer protection changed slightly.

How long the liberalizing effect of college persists depends on a number of factors. One study found that former college students still described themselves as more liberal than their parents seven years after graduation.[15] Another study found that students who changed in college from being conservative to being liberal tended to maintain that liberalism for at least twenty years if they acquired, after graduation, liberal friends and spouses.[16] College graduates who go on to get a postgraduate degree—say, a law degree or a Ph.D.—tend to become decidedly more liberal than those who stop with just a B.A. degree.[17] A scholar who tracked students graduating from college in 1969 found that those who had taken part in protests remained very liberal well into the 1980s, while nonprotesters became somewhat more conservative over the years.[18]

Table 5.4   The Changing College Student

Since the 1970s college freshmen have become more conservative on some issues and more liberal on others.

Issue	Percentage Agreeing	
	1970s[a]	1993
Abolish death penalty	33%	22%
Legalize abortion	83	62
Legalize marijuana	47	28
Increase military spending	39	23
Criminals have too many rights	52	68
Government not doing enough to:		
Control pollution	91	84
Protect consumers	77	72

Note: We have no comparable figures for college seniors. Freshmen may change their opinions on these matters while in school.

[a]Exact year the question was asked in 1970s varies between 1970 and 1976, depending on the question.

Sources: Richard C. Braungart and Margaret M. Braungart, "Black Colleges: Freshmen Attitudes," *Public Opinion* (May–June 1989): 14. Reprinted with the permission of the American Enterprise Institute for Public Policy Research, Washington, D.C. Updated to 1993 from Alexander W. Astin, William S. Korn, and Ellyne R. Riggs, *The American Freshman* (Los Angeles: UCLA Graduate School of Education, 1993), 25.

Cleavages in Public Opinion

The way in which political opinions are formed helps explain the cleavages that exist among these opinions and why these cleavages do not follow any single political principle but instead overlap and crosscut in bewildering complexity. If, for example, the United States lacked regional differences and was composed almost entirely of white Protestants who had never attended college, there would still be plenty of political conflict—the rich would have different views from the poor; workers would have different views from farmers—but that conflict would be much simpler to describe and explain. It might even lead to political parties that were more clearly aligned with competing political philosophies than those we now have. In fact some democratic nations in the world today do have a population very much like the one we have asked you to imagine, and the United States itself, during the first half of the nineteenth century, was overwhelmingly white, Protestant, and without much formal schooling.

Today, however, there are crosscutting cleavages based on race, ethnicity, religion, region, and educa-

tion, in addition to those created by income and occupation. To the extent that politics is sensitive to public opinion, it is sensitive to a variety of different and even competing publics. Not all these publics have influence proportionate to their numbers or even to their numbers adjusted for the intensity of their feelings. As will be described later, a filtering process occurs that makes the opinions of some publics more influential than those of others.

Whatever this state of affairs may mean for democracy, it creates a messy situation for political scientists. It would be so much easier if everyone's opinion on political affairs reflected some single feature of his or her life, such as income, occupation, age, race, or sex. Of course some writers have argued that political opinion is a reflection of one such feature, social class, usually defined in terms of income or occupation, but that view, though containing some truth, is beset with inconsistencies: poor blacks and poor whites disagree sharply on many issues involving race; well-to-do Jews and well-to-do Protestants often have opposing opinions on social welfare policy; and low-income elderly people are much more worried about crime than are low-income graduate students. Plumbers and professors may have similar incomes, but they rarely have similar views, and businesspeople in New York City often take a very different view of government than businesspeople in Houston or Birmingham.

In some other democracies a single factor such as class may explain more of the differences in political attitudes than it does in the more socially heterogeneous United States. Most blue-collar workers in America think of themselves as being "middle-class," whereas most such workers in Britain and France describe themselves as "working-class." In England the working class prefers the Labour party by a margin of three to one, while in the United States workers prefer the Democratic party by less than two to one, and in 1980 and 1984 they gave most of their votes to the Republican Ronald Reagan.[19]

Social Class

Americans speak of "social class" with embarrassment. The norm of equality tugs at our consciences, urging us to judge people as individuals, not as parts of some social group (such as "the lower class"). Social scientists speak of "class" with confusion. They know it exists but quarrel constantly about how to define it: By income? Occupation? Wealth? Schooling? Prestige? Personality?

Let's face up to the embarrassment and skip over the confusion. Truck drivers and investment bankers look different, talk differently, and vote differently. There is nothing wrong with saying that the first group consists of "working-class" (or "blue-collar") people and the latter of "upper-class" (or "management") people. Moreover, though different definitions of class produce slightly different groupings of people, most definitions overlap to such an extent that it does not matter too much which we use.

However defined, public opinion and voting have been less determined by class in the United States than in Europe, and the extent of class cleavage has declined in the last few decades in both the United States and Europe. In the 1950s V. O. Key, Jr., found that differences in political opinion were closely associated with occupation. He noted that people holding managerial or professional jobs had distinctly more conservative views on social welfare policy and more internationalist views on foreign policy than did manual workers.[20]

During the next decade this pattern changed greatly. Opinion surveys done in the late 1960s showed that business and professional people had views quite similar to those of manual workers on matters such as the poverty program, health insurance, American policy in Vietnam, and government efforts to create jobs.[21]

The voting patterns of different social classes have also become somewhat more similar. Class voting has declined sharply since the late 1940s in the United States, France, Great Britain, and West Germany and declined moderately in Sweden.

Class differences remain, of course. Unskilled workers are more likely than affluent white-collar workers to be Democrats and to have liberal views on economic policy. And when economic issues pinch—for example, when farmers are hurting or steelworkers are being laid off—the importance of economic interests in differentiating the opinions of various groups rises sharply. Moreover, there is some evidence that during the Reagan administration, income once again began to make a large difference in the party affiliation of voters.

Why should social class, defined along income lines, have become less important over the long term? One reason has to do largely with schooling. At one time the income of people did not depend so

The traditional labor unions have lost members, but they still try to be a force in elections.

heavily as it now does on having educational credentials. Most people had only a high school education, whatever their job might be, and only a small minority had a college or postgraduate degree. Today access to higher-paying jobs (outside of sports and entertainment) is increasingly restricted to people with extensive schooling. Since, as we have seen, college and (especially) postgraduate education tends to make people more liberal than they would otherwise be, the arrival of millions of college graduates, lawyers, and Ph.D.'s into the ranks of the financially affluent has brought into the upper classes a more liberal political outlook than once was the case. This development probably favors Democrats. For example, an analysis of voting in a hundred of America's richest communities found that the Democratic share of the vote increased steadily, from 25 percent in 1980 to 41 percent in 1996, a gain of 16 points.[22]

Still many of the issues that now lead us to choose which party to support and that determine whether we think of ourselves as liberals or conservatives are noneconomic issues. In recent years our political posture has been shaped by the positions we take on race relations, abortion, school prayer, arms control, and environmentalism, issues that do not clearly affect the rich differently from the poor (or at least do not affect them as differently as do the union movement, the minimum wage, and unemployment). Moral, symbolic, and foreign policy matters do not divide rich and poor in the same way as economic ones. Thus we have many well-off people who think of themselves as liberals because they take liberal

The Art of Public Opinion Polling

A survey of public opinion—popularly called a **poll**—can provide us with a reasonably accurate measure of how people think, provided certain conditions are met. There are five key criteria that must be met in designing and interpreting surveys.

1. **The persons interviewed must be a random sample of the entire population.** In a **random sample** poll any given person, or any given voter or adult, has an equal chance of being interviewed. Most national surveys draw a sample of between a thousand and fifteen hundred persons by a process called stratified or multistage area sampling. The pollster makes a list of all the geographical units in the country (say, all the counties) and groups (or "stratifies") them by the size of their population. The pollster then selects at random units from each group or stratum in proportion to its total population. For example, if one stratum's total population is 10 percent of the national population, then 10 percent of the counties in the sample will be drawn from this stratum. Within each selected county smaller and smaller geographical units (cities, towns, census tracts, blocks) are chosen, and then, within the smallest unit, individuals are selected at random (by, for example, choosing the occupant of every fifth house). The key is to stick to the sample and not let people volunteer to be interviewed—volunteers often have views different from those who do not volunteer.

2. **The questions must be comprehensible.** The questions must ask people about things they have

some knowledge of and some basis for forming an opinion about. Most people know, at least at election time, whom they would prefer as president; most people also have views about what they think the most important national problems are. But relatively few voters will have any opinion about our policy toward El Salvador (if indeed they have even heard of it) or about the investment tax credit. If everybody refused to answer questions about which they are poorly informed, no problem would arise, but unfortunately many of us like to pretend that we know things that in fact we don't or to be "helpful" to interviewers by inventing opinions on the spur of the moment.

3. **The questions must be asked fairly.** They should be worded in clear language, without the use of "loaded" or "emotional" words. They must give no indication of what the "right" answer is but offer a reasonable explanation, where necessary, of the consequences of each possible answer. For example, in 1971 a Gallup poll asked people whether they favored a proposal "to bring home all U.S. troops [from Vietnam] before the end of the year." Two-thirds of the public agreed with that. Then the question was asked in a different way: Do you agree or disagree with a proposal to withdraw all U.S. troops by the end of the year "regardless of what happens there [in Vietnam] after U.S. troops leave"? In this form substantially less than half the public agreed.

4. **The answer categories offered to a person must be carefully considered.** This is no problem when

positions on these noneconomic matters, and many not-so-well-off people who think of themselves as conservatives because that is the position they take on these issues.

Race and Ethnicity

Social class clearly has become a less clear-cut source of political cleavage, but it is harder to know what to make of race and ethnicity. In some ways racial differences are of central importance. African Ameri-

cans are overwhelming Democrats while whites are much more likely to be Republicans. African Americans thought that O. J. Simpson was innocent of killing his wife, but white Americans thought that he was guilty. Blacks believe that the criminal justice system is biased against them; whites disagree. Blacks favor a stronger affirmative action program; whites are opposed to it (see Table 5.5).

But in other respects the opinions of whites and blacks are similar. Majorities of both groups oppose there are only two candidates for office—say, Al Gore and George W. Bush—and you want only to know which one the voters prefer. But it can be a big problem when you want more complex information. For example, if you ask people (as does George Gallup) whether they "approve" or "disapprove" of how the president is handling his job, you will get one kind of answer—let us say that 55 percent approve and 45 percent disapprove. On the other hand, if you ask them (as does Louis Harris) how they rate the job the president is doing, "excellent, pretty good, only fair, or poor," you will get very different results. It is quite possible that only 46 percent will pick such positive answers as "excellent" or "pretty good," and the rest will pick the more negative answers, "only fair" and "poor." If you are president, you can choose to believe Mr. Gallup (and feel pleased) or Mr. Harris (and be worried). The differences in the two polls do not arise from the competence of the two pollsters but entirely from the choice of answers that they include with their questions.

5. **Not every difference in answers is a significant difference.** A survey is based on a sample of people. Select another sample, by equally randomized methods, and you might get slightly different results. This difference is called a **sampling error,** and its likely size can be computed mathematically. In general the bigger the sample and the bigger the differences between the percentage of people giving one answer and the percentage giving another, the smaller the sampling

error. If a poll of fifteen hundred voters reveals that 47 percent favor Bill Clinton, we can be 95 percent certain that the actual proportion of all voters favoring Clinton is within three percentage points of this figure—that is, it lies somewhere between 44 and 50 percent. In a close race an error of this size could be quite important. It could be reduced by using a bigger sample, but the cost of interviewing a sample big enough to make the error much smaller is huge.

As a result of sampling error and for other reasons, it is very hard for pollsters to predict the winner in a close election. Since 1952 every major national poll has in fact picked the winner of the presidential election, but there may have been some luck involved in such close races as the 1960 Kennedy-Nixon and the 1976 Carter-Ford contests. In 1980 the polls greatly underestimated the Reagan vote, partly because many voters made up their minds at the last minute and partly because a bigger percentage of Carter supporters decided not to vote at all. By contrast, pollsters did remarkably well in forecasting the results of the 1992 presidential election, a volatile three-way race between Bill Clinton, George Bush, and Ross Perot. Although they tended to overestimate Clinton's margin and to underestimate Perot's, twenty of the most frequently cited national polls came close to predicting the actual results. In 1996, however, most pollsters overestimated Clinton's margin of victory over Bob Dole. Polling is not an exact science, but done right, it is a highly skilled art.

---

the use of racial quotas, want the courts to get tougher on criminals, oppose making abortion legal in all cases, and nearly identical percentages wish that the Census Bureau would stop collecting data on race and ethnicity. Huge majorities in both groups think that too much is made of racial differences and would be willing to vote for an African American presidential candidate.

There is some evidence that the differences between white and black Americans may be narrow-

ing. About 26 percent of African Americans ages twenty-six to thirty-five (as opposed to only 3 percent of those ages fifty-one to sixty-four) identify themselves as Republicans.[23] Likewise, African American teenagers are only half as likely as African American adults to think that the social and economic differences between whites and blacks are mainly due to racial discrimination.[24] Some hints of these differences can be seen in Table 5.6, which shows that between 1974 and 1996 African Americans became

Table 5.5   African American and White Opinion

	African American	White
Favor expanding affirmative action programs[a]	53%	22%
Believe the justice system is racially biased against blacks[a]	72	44
Favor harsher treatment of criminals by the courts[b]	78	76
Favor more spending on national defense[c]	13	18
Favor national health insurance by government[c]	39	23
Believe the U.S. Census Bureau should stop collecting information on race and ethnicity[d]	48	47
Believe abortion should be legal in all cases[e]	24	28
Approve of black/white marriages[a]	77	61
Willing to vote for a black person for president[a]	93	91
Believe that too much is made of the differences between blacks and whites and not enough of what they have in common[f]	89	92

Sources: (a) *Black/White Perspectives in the United States* (Princeton, N.J.: The Gallup Organization, June 1997), 14, 16, 23, 24; (b) Gallup Polls, 1993 and 1994; (c) American National Election Survey, 1996; (d) "The Newsweek Poll," *Newsweek* (February 13, 1995): 65; (e) *The Public Perspective* (May 1995): 19; (f) *The American Enterprise* (November/December 1998): 92, reporting results of a March–April 1998 Public Agenda survey of white and black parents or guardians of children in kindergarten through twelfth grade.

less convinced that the government should help them and more convinced that they should help themselves. It remains to be seen whether this generation gap between younger and older African Americans will persist or have any important political effects.

In the meantime, however, it is clear that there is a big opinion gap between the leaders of African American organizations and African Americans in general. A 1985 survey of more than a hundred African American leaders and six hundred African American citizens found that the leaders were much more likely than the rank and file to favor abortions, school busing, and affirmative action. Most African American leaders deny that blacks are making progress, while most African American citizens think that they are.[25] This cleavage should not surprise us; as we shall see, there is a similar cleavage between white leaders and white citizens.

Though there are an estimated 30 million Hispanics and 10 million Asian Americans in this country, they tend to be concentrated in a few locations (half of all Latinos, for example, live in California and Texas), and so not enough appear in the usual national opinion polls to permit us to say much about their views.

However, a 1984 survey of ethnic groups in California, a state where fully one-third of all recent immigrants to this country live, gives us some knowledge of how Latinos and Asian Americans feel about political parties and issues. As you can see in Table 5.7, Latinos identify themselves as Democrats, but much less so than do blacks, and Asian Americans are even more identified with the Republican

Table 5.6   Changes in Racial Opinion

	Whites		African Americans	
	1974	1996	1974	1996
Government should help blacks	25%	16%	63%	40%
Blacks should help themselves	50	61	12	40

Source: Robert S. Erikson and Kent L. Tedin, *American Public Opinion,* 5th ed. Copyright © 1995 by Allyn and Bacon. Reprinted by permission. Updated for 1996 with National Election Survey figures.

Table 5.7   Party Identification and Political Attitudes of Ethnic Groups in California

	Anglo White	Black	Latino	Asian American
Party Identification				
Democrat	37%	78%	54%	35%
Republican	35	3	20	38
In between, other	28	18	26	27
Political Attitude				
Favor increased military spending	32	18	28	38
Favor increased welfare spending	59	84	73	66
Favor prayer in public schools	50	62	53	46
Favor death penalty for murder	75	47	57	73
Favor abortion on demand	60	47	40	53
Favor bilingual education programs	41	63	69	51
Number	409	335	593	305

Source: Bruce Cain and Roderick Kiewiet, "California's Coming Minority Majority," *Public Opinion* (February–March 1986): 50–52. Reprinted with permission of American Enterprise Institute for Public Policy Research.

party than Anglo whites. On issues such as spending on the military and welfare programs, prayer in public schools, and the imposition of the death penalty for murder, Asian American views are much more like those of Anglo whites than those of either blacks or Hispanics. Latinos are somewhat more liberal than Anglos or Asian Americans, but much less liberal than blacks, except with respect to bilingual education programs.[26]

These figures conceal important differences within these ethnic groups. For example, Japanese Americans are among the more conservative Asian Americans, whereas Korean Americans (perhaps because they are among the most recent immigrants) are more liberal. Similarly, Latinos, the fastest-growing ethnic group in the United States, are a diverse mix of Cuban Americans, Mexican Americans, Central Americans, and Puerto Ricans, each with distinct political views. A study of Latino voting in the 1988 presidential election found that Mexican Americans were the most Democratic, Cuban Americans were the most Republican, and Puerto Ricans were in between the other two groups.[27] But no group of Latino voters has become predictably partisan. In 1998, 78 percent of California's Latino (predominantly Mexican American) vote went to Democrat Gray Davis in the governor's race, but in Texas half of the Latino (also predominantly Mexican American) vote went to reelect Republican governor George W. Bush.[28]

Region

It is widely believed that geographic region affects political attitudes and in particular that southerners and northerners disagree significantly on many policy questions. As we will see, southern members of Congress tend to vote differently—and more conservatively—than northern ones, and it should stand to reason that this is because their constituents, southern voters, expect them to vote differently. At one time white southerners were conspicuously less liberal than easterners, midwesterners, or westerners on questions such as aid to minorities, legalizing marijuana, school busing, and enlarging the rights of those accused of crimes. Although more conservative on these issues, they held views on economic issues similar to those of whites in other regions of the country. This helps to explain why the South was for so long a part of the Democratic party coalition: on national economic and social welfare policies, southerners expressed views not very different from those of northerners. That coalition was always threatened, however, by the divisiveness produced by issues of race and liberty.

Today the political views of white southerners are less distinct from those of whites living in other parts of the country. As Table 5.8 illustrates, the proportion of white Protestants in the South who gave liberal answers to questions regarding both civil liberties/civil rights issues and economic/welfare issues in 1992 was only somewhat different from that of

Table 5.8   Does the South Differ?

Percentage giving "liberal" response among white Protestants living in different regions, 1992.

Issue	Northeast[a]	North Central[b]	South[c]	West[d]
Economic and Welfare Issues				
More government services	26.4%	27.4%	28.8%	26.5%
More government job guarantees	23.0	19.2	20.7	21.2
Increase social security	55.1	39.7	43.8	42.0
Cut defense spending	47.3	36.4	37.0	44.4
Civil Rights and Civil Liberties Issues				
Government aid to black citizens	10.4	13.8	12.0	21.7
Laws to protect homosexuals against job discrimination	61.1	45.8	50.3	56.8
Women's equality	72.5	66.8	72.1	75.8
Right to abortion	50.0	40.6	34.7	53.8
Average Percentage Liberal, All Issues	43.2	36.2	37.4	42.8

[a]Northeast: Connecticut, Massachusetts, New Hampshire, New Jersey, New York, Pennsylvania

[b]North Central: Illinois, Indiana, Iowa, Kansas, Michigan, Minnesota, Missouri, Nebraska, Ohio, Wisconsin

[c]South: Alabama, Arkansas, Delaware, District of Columbia, Florida, Georgia, Louisiana, Maryland, North Carolina, Tennessee, Texas, Virginia, West Virginia

[d]West: Arizona, California, Colorado, Oregon, Washington, Wyoming

Source: Compiled by Meenekshi Bose, using data from the ICPSR *1992 American National Election Survey,* University of Michigan.

white Protestants in other regions. (The table is limited to white Protestants to eliminate the effect of the very different proportions of Catholics, Jews, African Americans, and other ethnic groups living in various regions.)

The southern lifestyle is in fact different from that of other regions of the country. The South has, on the whole, been more accommodating to business enterprise and less so to organized labor than, for example, the Northeast; it gave greater support to the third-party candidacy of George Wallace in 1968, which was a protest against big government and the growth of national political power as well as against civil rights; and it was in the South that the greatest opposition arose to income-redistribution plans such as the Family Assistance Plan of 1969. Moreover, there is some evidence that white southerners became by the 1970s more conservative than they had been in the 1950s, at least when compared to white northerners.[29] Finally, white southerners have become less attached to the Democratic party: whereas over three-fourths described themselves as Democrats in 1952, only a third did by 1996 (see Figure 5.2).

These changes in the South can have great significance, as we shall see in the next three chapters

when we consider how elections are fought. It is enough for now to remember that, without the votes of the southern states, no Democrat except Lyndon Johnson in 1964 would have been elected president from 1940 through 1976. (Without the South Roosevelt would have lost in 1944, Truman in 1948, Kennedy in 1960, and Carter in 1976. And even though Carter carried the South, he did not win a majority of white southern votes.) Clinton won in 1992 and 1996 without carrying the South, but those were three-man races.

Political Ideology

Up to now the words **liberal** and **conservative** have been used here as if everyone agreed on what they meant and as if they accurately described general sets of political beliefs held by large segments of the population. Neither of these assumptions is correct. Like many useful words—*love, justice, happiness*—they are as vague as they are indispensable.

When we refer to people as liberals, conservatives, socialists, or radicals, we are implying that they have a patterned set of beliefs about how government and other important institutions in fact operate and how

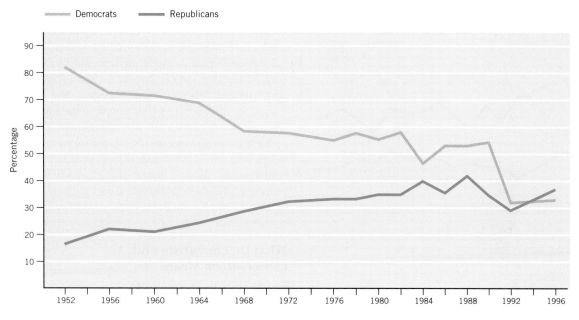

Figure 5.2   Whites in the South Leaving the Democrats

Percentage of southern white registered voters who identified with each party.

Source: ICPSR National Election Studies, Cumulative Data File, 1952–1996.

they ought to operate, and in particular about what kinds of policies government ought to pursue. They are said to display to some degree a **political ideology**—that is, a coherent and consistent set of beliefs about who ought to rule, what principles rulers ought to obey, and what policies rulers ought to pursue. Political scientists measure the extent to which people have a political ideology in two ways: first, by seeing how frequently people use broad political categories (such as "liberal," "conservative," "radical") to describe their own views or to justify their preferences for various candidates and policies, and second, by seeing to what extent the policy preferences of a citizen are consistent over time or are based at any one time on consistent principles.

This second method involves a simple mathematical procedure: measuring how accurately one can predict a person's view on a subject at one time based on his or her view on that subject at an earlier time, or measuring how accurately one can predict a person's view on one issue based on his or her view on a different issue. The higher the accuracy of such predictions (or correlations), the more we say a person's political opinions display "constraint," or ideol-

ogy. Despite annual fluctuations, ideological self-identification surveys typically find that moderates are the largest group among American voters, conservatives the second largest, and liberals the smallest (see Figure 5.3). This pattern held throughout the 1990s. In 1998 one-fifth of voters described themselves as liberal, one-third described themselves as conservative, and a plurality called themselves moderate.[30]

Except when asked by pollsters, most Americans do not actually employ the words *liberal* or *conservative* in explaining or justifying their preferences for candidates or policies, and not many more than half can give plausible definitions of these terms. Furthermore, there are relatively low correlations among the answers to similar questions asked by pollsters at different times and to comparable questions asked at the same time. From this, many scholars have concluded that the great majority of Americans do not think about politics in an ideological or even in a very coherent manner and that they make little use of such concepts, so dear to political commentators and professors alike, as "liberal" and "conservative."[31]

Figure 5.3   Ideological Self-Identification, 1976–1993

QUESTION

How would you describe your views on most political matters? Generally, do you think of yourself as a liberal, moderate, or conservative?

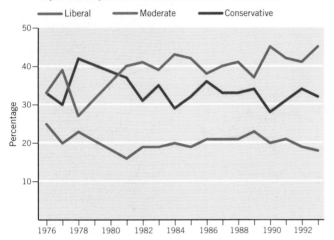

Source: The American Enterprise (March/April 1993): 84, citing surveys by CBS/*New York Times.* Reprinted from *The American Enterprise,* a Washington-based magazine of politics, business and culture.

Consistent Attitudes

This does not settle the question entirely, however. Critics of the view that Americans are nonideological have argued that people can have general, and strongly felt, political predispositions even though they are not able to use terms such as *liberal* correctly. Moreover, public opinion polls must of necessity ask rather simple questions, and the apparent "inconsistency" in the answers people give at different times may mean only that the nature of the problem and the wording of the question have changed in ways not obvious to the people analyzing the surveys.[32]

People can have an ideology without using the words *liberal* or *conservative* and without having beliefs that line up neatly along the conventional liberal-versus-conservative dimension. We saw in Chapter 4 that most Americans share a distinctive political culture—a belief in freedom, equality (of political condition and economic opportunity), and civic duty. They also attach a great deal of importance to "Americanism." Though these words may be vague, they are not trivial—at some level they are an ideology.

Scholars regularly discover that people have what some would consider "inconsistent" opinions. For example, a voter may want the government to spend more on education and the environment and at the same time favor a bigger military budget and a tough posture toward unfriendly nations. These views are "inconsistent" only in the sense that they violate a political rule of thumb, common in the media and in national policy debates, that expects people who favor a bigger welfare state to favor a smaller military establishment as well. That is the conventional "liberal" view. Similarly, the rule of thumb in the media is that people who support a strong military posture are also going to favor prayer in the schools and oppose abortion on demand. That is the conventional "conservative" position. But of course many citizens violate these rules of thumb, picking and choosing their positions without regard to the conventional definitions of liberalism and conservatism.

What Do *Liberalism* and *Conservatism* Mean?

Just because most people are not consistent liberals or consistent conservatives does not prove that these terms are meaningless. As we shall see, they are very meaningful for political elites. And they even have meaning for ordinary citizens, but this meaning is a complicated one that requires careful analysis.

The definition of these words has changed since they first came into use in the early nineteenth century. At that time a liberal was a person who favored personal and economic liberty—that is, freedom from the controls and powers of the state. An economic liberal, for example, supported the free market and opposed government regulation of trade. A conservative was originally a person who opposed the excesses of the French Revolution and its emphasis on personal freedom and favored instead a restoration of the power of the state, the church, and the aristocracy.

Beginning around the time of Franklin Roosevelt and the New Deal, the meaning of these terms began to change. Roosevelt used the term *liberal* to refer to his political program—one that called for an active national government that would intervene in the economy, create social welfare programs, and help certain groups (such as organized labor) acquire greater bargaining power. In time the opponents of an activist national government began using the term *conservative* to describe themselves. (Barry Goldwater, in 1964, was the first major U.S. politician to proclaim himself a conservative.) In general a conservative favored a free market rather than a regulated one, states' rights over national supremacy, and greater reliance on individual choice in economic affairs.

Though the meaning of these terms changed, it did not in the process become more precise. Two persons may describe themselves as liberals even though the first favors both the welfare state and a strong national defense and the second favors the welfare state but wants a sharp reduction in military spending. Similarly, one conservative may favor enforcement of laws against drug abuse, and another may believe that the government should let people decide for themselves what drugs to take. Once, liberals favored laws guaranteeing equality of opportunity among the races; now some liberals favor "affirmative action" plans involving racial quotas or goals. Once, conservatives opposed American intervention abroad; today many conservatives believe the United States should play an active role in foreign affairs.

In view of this confusion one is tempted to throw up one's hands in disgust and consign words like *liberal* and *conservative* to the garbage can. While understandable, such a reaction would be a mistake, because in spite of their ambiguities, these words remain in general use, convey some significant meaning, and point to real differences between, for example, the liberal and conservative wings of the Democratic and Republican parties. Our task is to clarify these differences by showing the particular meanings these words have. One way to do this is by considering how self-described liberals and conservatives differ in their opinions on prominent issues, such as those listed in Table 5.9.

Various Categories

We can imagine certain broad categories of opinion to which different people subscribe. These categories are found by analyzing the answers people give to dozens of questions about political issues. Different analysts come up with slightly different categories, but on the whole there is a substantial amount of agreement. Three categories in particular have proved useful.

The first category involves questions about government policy with regard to the *economy*. We will describe as liberal those persons who favor government efforts to ensure that everyone has a job, to

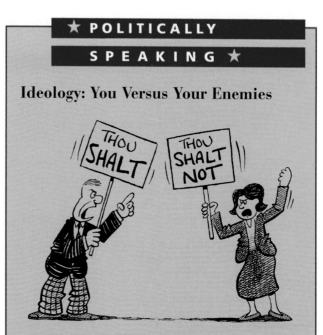

Ideology: You Versus Your Enemies

A political ideology is a coherent set of political rules for explaining how the world works and prescribing how it ought to work.

Liberals describe

- *themselves* as "caring," "committed," "an activist," or "progressive";
- *their enemies* as "reactionary," "right-wing," and "extremist."

Conservatives describe

- *themselves* as "moderate," "responsible," "prudent," or "mainstream";
- *their enemies* as "crackpot," "knee-jerk," "left-wing," or "bleeding-heart."

An easy way to tell whether a politician, newspaper, or magazine is liberal or conservative is to see whether, in describing liberals or conservatives, it uses terms from the "nice" (themselves) list or the "hostile" (their enemies) list.

spend more money on medical and educational programs, and to increase rates of taxation for well-to-do persons.

The second involves questions about *civil rights* and race relations. We will describe as liberal those who favor strong federal action to desegregate schools, to increase hiring opportunities for minorities, to

Table 5.9 How Liberals and Conservatives Differ		
Belief	Support Among Self-Declared Liberals	Support Among Self-Declared Conservatives
The government should provide "more services even if it means an increase in spending."	73%	32%
The government should guarantee "that every person has a job and a good standard of living."	55	21
Favor "government insurance plan which would cover all medical and hospital expenses for everyone."	82	27
The government "should make every effort to improve the social and economic position of blacks."	55	18
The U.S. "should spend less on defense."	85	65
"Aid to [Russia] should be increased."	36	32
"Women should have an equal role in running business, industry, and government."	96	81
The United States should always permit abortion "as a matter of personal choice."	72	36
"Homosexuals should be allowed to serve in U.S. Armed Forces."	70	45
"Oppose death penalty for persons convicted of murder."	35	15

Source: Robert S. Erikson and Kent L. Tedin, *American Public Opinion,* 5th ed. (Boston: Allyn and Bacon, 1995), 69. © 1995 by Addison-Wesley Educational Publishers, Inc. Reprinted by permission.

provide compensatory programs for minorities, and to enforce civil rights laws strictly.

The third involves questions about public and political *conduct.* We will describe as liberal those who are tolerant of protest demonstrations, who favor legalizing marijuana and in other ways wish to "decriminalize" so-called victimless crimes, who emphasize protecting the rights of the accused over punishing criminals, and who see the solution to crime in eliminating its causes rather than in getting tough with offenders.

Analyzing Consistency

Now it is obvious that people can take a liberal position on one of these issues and a conservative position on another without feeling in the slightest degree "inconsistent." Several studies, such as those by Seymour Martin Lipset and Earl Raab and by Herbert McClosky and John Zaller, show that this is exactly what most people do.[33]

This fact does not mean that people are unideological but that we need more than two labels to describe their ideology. If we considered all possible combinations of the three sets of views described above, we would have nine categories of opinion; if people always stuck with whichever category they were in, we would need nine different ideological labels to describe those people.

To invent those labels and describe the people who have those views would take countless pages and bore readers to tears. To avoid all that pain and suffering, let's use just two sets of views—those on economic policy and those on personal conduct—and describe the kinds of people who have each of the four combinations (liberal or conservative on each set). The data are from a study by William S. Maddox and Stuart A. Lilie.

1. *Pure liberals*[34]   These people are liberal on both economic policy and personal conduct. They want the government to reduce economic inequality, regulate business, tax the rich heavily, cure the (presumably) economic causes of crime, allow abortions, protect the rights of the accused, and guarantee the broadest possible freedoms of speech and press.
Number: In 1994 about 17 percent of the population were pure liberals.
Traits: Pure liberals are more likely than the average citizen to be young, college-educated, and either Jewish or nonreligious. They voted heavily against Ronald Reagan.

2. *Pure conservatives*   These people are conservative on both economic and conduct issues. They want the government to cut back on the welfare state, allow the market to allocate goods and services,

keep taxes low, lock up criminals, and curb forms of conduct they regard as antisocial.

Number: In 1994 about 28 percent of the population were pure conservatives.

Traits: Pure conservatives are more likely than the average citizen to be older, to have higher incomes, to be white, and to live in the Midwest. They voted overwhelmingly for Ronald Reagan.

3. *Libertarians* These people are conservative on economic matters and liberal on social ones. The common theme is that they want a small, weak government—one that has little control over either the economy or the personal lives of citizens.

Number: In 1994 about 21 percent of the population were libertarians.

Traits: **Libertarians** are more likely than the average citizen to be young, college-educated, and white, to have higher incomes and no religion, and to live in the West. They voted for Ronald Reagan, but many also supported the third-party ticket of John Anderson.

4. *Populists* These people are liberal on economic matters and conservative on social ones. They want a government that will reduce economic inequality and control business, but they also want it to regulate personal conduct, lock up criminals, and permit school prayer.

Number: In 1994 about 24 percent of the population were populists.

Traits: **Populists** are more likely than the average citizen to be older, poorly educated, low-income, religious, and female and to live in the South or Midwest. In 1980 they voted for Jimmy Carter, but in 1984 they voted for Reagan.

Obviously this classification is an oversimplification. There are many exceptions, and the number of people in each category changes from time to time. Moreover, this categorization leaves out about one-seventh of the population—their views do not fit any of these categories. Nonetheless, it is a useful way to explain how complex are the political ideologies in this country and why terms such as *liberal* and *conservative,* in their "pure" form, describe the views of relatively few people.

Political Elites

There is one group that can be classified as liberals or conservatives in a pure sense, and it is made up of people who are in the **political elite.** By "elite" we

Activists tend to take political ideology more seriously than do most voters.

do not mean people who are "better" than others. *Elite* is a technical term used by social scientists to refer to people who have a disproportionate amount of some valued resource—money, schooling, prestige, athletic ability, political power, or whatever. Every society, capitalist or communist, has an elite, because in every society government officials will have more power than ordinary folk, some persons will make more money than others, and some people will be more popular than others. (In the former Soviet Union they even had an official name for the political elite—the *nomenklatura.*)

In this country we often refer to the political elite as "activists"—people who hold office, run for office, work in campaigns or on newspapers, lead interest groups and social movements, and speak out on public issues. Being an activist is not an all-or-nothing proposition; people display differing degrees of activism, from full-time politicians to persons who occasionally get involved in a campaign (see Chapter 6). But the more a person is an activist, the more likely it is that he or she will display ideological consistency on the conventional liberal-conservative spectrum.

The reasons for this greater consistency seem to be information and peers. First, information: in general the better informed people are about politics and the more interest they take in politics, the more likely they are to have consistently liberal or conservative views.[35] This higher level of information and interest may lead them to find relationships among issues that others don't see and to learn from the media and elsewhere what are the "right" things to believe. This does not mean that there are no differences within liberal elites (or within conservative ones), only that the differences occur within a liberal (or conservative) consensus that is more well defined, more consistent, and more important to those who share it than would be the case among ordinary citizens.

Second, peers: politics does not make strange bedfellows. On the contrary politics is a process of likes attracting likes. The more active you are in politics, the more you will associate with people who agree with you on some issues; and the more time you spend with those people, the more your other views will shift to match theirs.

The greater ideological consistency of political elites can be seen in Congress. As we shall note in Chapter 11, Democratic members of Congress tend to be consistently liberal, and Republican members of Congress tend to be consistently conservative— *far more* consistently than Democratic voters and Republican voters. By the same token we shall see in Chapter 7 that the delegates to presidential nominating conventions are far more ideological (liberal in the Democratic convention, conservative in the Republican one) than is true of voters who identify with the Democratic or Republican party.

Is There a "New Class"?

Some writers have speculated that political elites now represent a "new class" in American politics. The old classes were those who owned the means of production (the capitalists) and those who were employed by those owners (the workers). The "new class" consists of people who possess certain advantages conferred not by the power, resources, and growth of business but by the power, resources, and growth of government.[36]

Politicians, bureaucrats, members of the media, interest group leaders—these people and others like them have, it is claimed, a stake in the growth of government. Because of that, they often have liberal (that is, progovernment) views even though they also have high incomes. The emergence of the new class helps explain, in this theory, why affluent people are not as consistently conservative as they were in the 1940s and 1950s.

It is true, as we have already seen, that many well-off people are liberals. That these people benefit from big government may be one explanation for this fact. But there is another explanation: the spread of higher education.

High levels of schooling, especially at the postgraduate level, tend to make people more liberal. This was not always the case. For example, in the 1940s and 1950s a clear majority of Harvard students, and probably of most college students, preferred Republican candidates for president.[37] For whatever reason things are different now. Some people with law degrees and Ph. D.'s may favor government because they get grants and jobs from it, but most people probably favor it because they have acquired an ideology that is consistent with a more activist government.

In any event, it is striking how strongly postgraduate education affects political preferences. John McAdams has analyzed the voting results for several presidential, gubernatorial, and senatorial elections and for various state referenda elections on issues such as the death penalty, school busing, nuclear energy, gun control, environmental protection, and the Equal Rights Amendment. In each and every case he discovered that those with a postgraduate education were much more likely to take a liberal position, even after holding constant age, race, and income.[38]

On the basis of his findings, McAdams suggests that the middle class in the United States has been split in two—one part he calls the "traditional middle class," and the other he calls the "new class" (though it might more appropriately be called the "liberal middle class").[39] The traditional middle class consists of people who often have gone to college but not graduate school and who live in the suburbs, go to church, are well disposed toward business, have conservative views on social issues, and usually vote Republican. The liberal middle class is more likely to consist of people who have a postgraduate education, live in or near big cities, are critical of business, have liberal views on social issues, and usually vote Democratic. The cleavage between the traditional and the liberal middle class has many of the same causes as the growing rift between orthodox and progressive ideologies discussed in Chapter 4.

As we shall see in Chapter 7, the strain within the middle class has been particularly felt by the Democratic party. That strain has made it harder to hold together the coalition (often called the New Deal coalition) that once made that party so strong, a coalition among blue-collar workers, southerners, African Americans, and intellectuals. Increasingly the workers and white southerners have displayed conservatism on social issues, while members of the liberal middle class have displayed liberalism on these issues. Each side has a label for the other: the workers in the Democratic party call the members of the liberal middle class the "cheese and white wine set," while the people in the liberal middle class call the workers "Joe Six-Pack."

Political Elites, Public Opinion, and Public Policy

Though the elites and the public see politics in very different ways, and though there are often intense antagonisms between the two groups, the elites influence public opinion in at least two important ways.

First, elites, especially those in or having access to the media (see Chapter 10), raise and frame political issues. At one time environmentalism was not on the political agenda; at a later time not only was it on the agenda, it was up near the top of government concerns. At some times the government had little interest in what it should do in South Africa or Central America; at other times the government was preoccupied with these matters. Though world events help shape the political agenda, so also do political elites. A path-breaking study by John Zaller shows in fact that elite views shape mass views by influencing both what issues capture the public's attention and how those issues are debated and decided.[40] Contrary to the myth of the pandering politician, recent evidence suggests that what scholars of the subject call opinion-policy congruence (essentially the rate at which governments adopt crime, health, trade, and other policies supported by majorities in polls) has been declining, not rising, since 1980, a trend that may reflect greater elite influence over how policy options are presented to the public.[41]

Second, elites state the norms by which issues should be settled. (A **norm** is a standard of right or proper conduct.) By doing this they help determine the range of acceptable and unacceptable policy options. For example, elites have for a long time emphasized that racism is wrong. Of late they have emphasized that sexism is wrong. Over a long period the steady repetition of views condemning racism and sexism will at least intimidate, and perhaps convince, those of us who are racist and sexist.

A recent example of this process has been the public discussion of AIDS and its relationship to

The media help shape public opinion about some issues, as when these television photographers focus on an environmental issue.

homosexuality. The initial public reaction to AIDS was one of fear and loathing. But efforts to quarantine people infected with AIDS were met with firm resistance from the medical community and from other policy elites. The elites even managed to persuade some legislatures to bar insurance companies from testing insurance applicants for the disease.

There are limits to how much influence elites can have on the public. For instance, elites do not define economic problems—people can see for themselves that there is or is not unemployment, that there is or is not raging inflation, that there are or are not high interest rates. Elite opinion may shape the policies, but it does not define the problem. Similarly, elite opinion has little influence on whether we think there is a crime or drug problem; it is, after all, *our* purses being snatched, cars being stolen, and children being drugged. On the other hand, elite opinion does define the problem as well as the policy options with respect to most aspects of foreign affairs; the public has little firsthand experience with which to judge what is going on in Panama or Iraq.

Because elites affect how we see some issues and determine how other issues get resolved, it is important to study the differences between elite and public opinion. But it is wrong to suppose that there is one elite, unified in its interests and opinions. Just as there are many publics, and hence many public opinions, there are many elites, and hence many different elite opinions. Whether there is enough variety of opinion and influence among elites to justify calling our politics "pluralist" is one of the central issues confronting any student of government.

MEMORANDUM

To: Senator P. J. Jacobs
From: Tanya Jones, legislative intern
Subject: Reducing legal immigration

Your constituents are evenly divided over restrictions. Having declared yourself "neutral pending further study and debate," you are nonetheless being urged by valued colleagues on both sides of the issue and by the press to take a position on cutting legal immigration.

Arguments for:

1. Since Congress liberalized U.S. immigration laws in 1965, nearly 25 million legal immigrants have settled in America, and the percentage of foreign-born U.S. residents has risen to 10 percent. At this rate, by 2050 the total U.S. population will rise by about 125 million, to nearly 400 million. Two-thirds of the increase will be due to legal immigration.
2. For every ten legal immigrants, about three undocumented aliens enter the country. Together they take jobs away from native-born Americans.
3. Most immigrants settle in one of four states (California, Florida, New York, and Texas), placing an undue burden on those states to pay for services such as health care and welfare for immigrants.

Arguments against:

1. From 1860 to 1930 over 10 percent of U.S. residents were foreign born. Without immigration the U.S. population will reach 310 million by 2035 and then decline. Immigrants not only consume public services but also pay taxes and provide a younger, more vital labor pool.
2. All told only about 5 million noncitizens are living unlawfully in the United States. Legal immigrants include people with advanced degrees and highly marketable skills. Low-skilled immigrants often take menial jobs that nobody else wants.
3. Immigrants have always tended to settle in a few areas. In the first half of the twentieth century, most settled in a half dozen big cities. Today the federal government provides funds to the states to pay for at least some of the costs of social services for residents, including immigrants.

Your decision:
Favor curbs _____
Oppose curbs _____

U.S. Senate to Debate New Curbs on Legal Immigration

May 22
WASHINGTON
Legal immigration to the United States has reached record highs. From 1991 to 2000 more than 9 million people, or about 300,000 more than entered the country during the first decade of the twentieth century, came to America. Next week the Senate begins debate on several bills that would slow or stop the flow of legal immigrants . . .

Summary

"Public opinion" is a slippery notion, partly because there are many publics, with many different opinions, and partly because opinion on all but relatively simple matters tends to be uninformed, unstable, and sensitive to different ways of asking poll questions.

The chief sources of political opinion are the family, religion, information, and schooling. Once, occupation (or income) was a central determinant of opinion, but with the spread of higher education, the connection between occupational status (or income) and opinion is no longer quite as close.

The chief source of cleavages in opinion are race and ethnicity, class (in which schooling is an important component), and region.

Americans are divided by their political ideologies but not along a single liberal-conservative dimension. There are several kinds of issues on which people may take "liberal" or "conservative" positions, and they often do not take the same position on all issues. Just using two kinds of issues—economic and social—it is possible to define four kinds of ideologies: pure liberal, pure conservative, libertarian, and populist.

Political elites are much more likely to display a consistently liberal or consistently conservative ideology. Elites are important because they have a disproportionate influence on public policy and even an influence on mass opinion (through the dissemination of information and the evocation of political norms).

World Wide Web Resources

- CBS News poll: cbsnews.cbs.com
- Gallup opinion poll: www.gallup.com
- *Los Angeles Times* poll: www.latimes.com/ HOME/NEWS/POLITICS/POLLS

Key Terms

John Q. Public *p. 105*
Middle America *p. 105*
silent majority *p. 105*
social status *p. 107*

religious tradition *p. 107*
gender gap *p. 109*
poll *p. 114*
random sample *p. 114*

sampling error *p. 115*
liberal *p. 118*
conservative *p. 118*
political ideology *p. 119*

libertarians *p. 123*
populists *p. 123*
political elite *p. 123*
norm *p. 125*

Suggested Readings

Converse, Philip E. "The Nature of Belief Systems in Mass Publics." In *Ideology and Discontent*, edited by David Apter. Glencoe, Ill.: Free Press, 1964. The classic discussion of inconsistencies in public opinion.

Dionne, E. J. *Why Americans Hate Politics*. New York: Simon and Schuster, 1991. Misnamed, this book actually describes the emergence of various elite ideologies since the 1960s and why, in the author's view, none is relevant to actually solving problems.

Erikson, Robert S., and Kent L. Tedin. *American Public Opinion*. 5th ed. Boston: Allyn and Bacon, 1995. An excellent summary of how opinion is measured, what it shows, and how it affects politics.

Jennings, M. Kent, and Richard G. Niemi. *The Political Character of Adolescence: The Influence of Families and Schools*. Princeton, N.J.: Princeton University Press, 1974. A study of political attitudes among high school students.

———. *Generations and Politics*. Princeton, N.J.: Princeton University Press, 1981. A study of persistence and change in the political views of young adults and their parents.

Key, V. O., Jr. *The Responsible Electorate*. Cambridge: Harvard University Press, 1966. An argument, with evidence, that American voters are not fools.

Lipset, Seymour Martin. *Political Man: The Social Bases of Politics*. Garden City, N.Y.: Doubleday, 1959. An exploration of the relationship between society, opinion, and democracy in America and abroad.

Nie, Norman H., Sidney Verba, and John R. Petrocik. *The Changing American Voter*. Cambridge: Harvard University Press, 1976. Traces shifts in American voter attitudes since 1960.

Zaller, John. *The Nature and Origins of Mass Opinion*. Cambridge: Cambridge University Press, 1992. A path-breaking study of how the public forms an opinion, illustrating the ways in which elite views help shape mass views.

Political Participation

6

Enduring Questions

1. *What role did the Framers of the Constitution believe average citizens should play in America's representative democracy?*
2. *Who votes, who doesn't, and why?*
3. *Why do some people participate in politics at higher rates than others?*
4. *How, if at all, do differences in political participation affect what government actually does?*

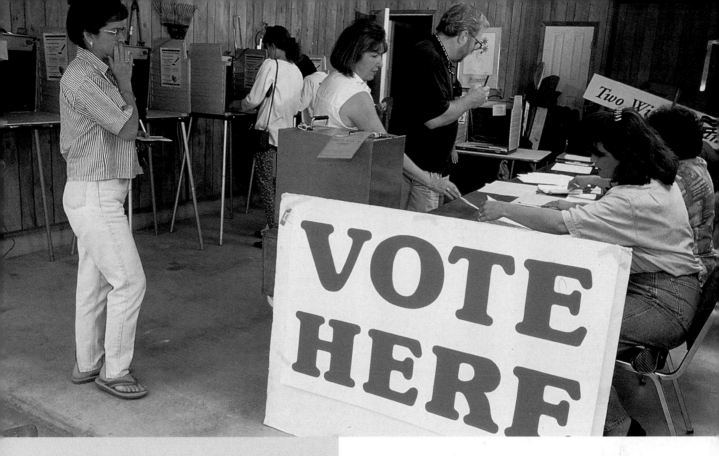

A Closer Look at Nonvoting

The Rise of the American Electorate
From State to Federal Control • Voter Turnout

Who Participates in Politics?
Forms of Participation • The Causes of
Participation • The Meaning of Participation Rates

A
mericans are often embarrassed by their low rate of participation in national elections. Data such as those shown in Table 6.1 are frequently used to make the point: whereas well over 80 percent of the people vote in many European elections, only about half of the people vote in American presidential elections (and a much smaller percentage vote in congressional contests). Many observers blame this low turnout on voter apathy and urge the government and private groups to mount campaigns to get out the vote.

There are only three things wrong with this view. First, it is a misleading description of the problem; second, it is an incorrect explanation of the problem; and third, it proposes a remedy that won't work.

A Closer Look at Nonvoting

First, let's look at how best to describe the problem. The conventional data on voter turnout here and abroad are misleading, because they compute participation rates by two different measures. In this country only two-thirds of the voting-age population is

129

Table 6.1	Two Ways of Calculating Voter Turnout		
A Turnout as Percentage of Voting-Age Population		**B** Turnout as Percentage of Registered Voters	
Austria	89.3%	Belgium	94.6%
Belgium	88.7	Australia	94.5
Sweden	86.8	Austria	91.6
Netherlands	84.7	Sweden	90.7
Australia	83.1	New Zealand	89.0
Denmark	82.1	West Germany	88.6
Norway	81.8	Netherlands	87.0
West Germany	81.1	UNITED STATES	86.8
New Zealand	78.5	France	85.9
France	78.0	Denmark	83.2
United Kingdom	76.0	Norway	82.0
Japan	74.4	United Kingdom	76.3
Canada	67.4	Japan	74.5
Finland	63.0	Canada	69.3
UNITED STATES	52.6	Finland	64.3
Switzerland	39.4	Switzerland	48.3

Source: Adapted from tables in David Glass, Peverill Squire, and Raymond Wolfinger, "Voter Turnout: An International Comparison," *Public Opinion* (December–January 1984): 50, 52. Reprinted with permission of American Enterprise Institute for Public Policy Research.

registered to vote. To understand what this means, look at Table 6.1. In column A are several countries ranked in terms of the percentage of the **voting-age population** that voted in the 1984 national election. As you can see, the United States, where 52.6 percent voted, ranked near the bottom; only Switzerland was lower. Now look at column B, where the same countries are ranked in terms of the percentage of **registered voters** who participated in the last national election. The United States, where almost 87 percent of registered voters turned out at the polls, is now up in the middle of the pack.[1]

Second, let's consider a better explanation for the problem. Apathy on election day is clearly not the source of the problem. Of those who are registered, the overwhelming majority vote. The real source of the participation problem in the United States is that a relatively low percentage of the adult population is registered to vote.

Third, let's look at how to cure the problem. Mounting a get-out-the-vote drive wouldn't make much difference. What might make a difference is a plan that would get more people to register to vote. But doing that does not necessarily involve overcoming the "apathy" of unregistered voters. Some people

may not register because they don't care about politics or their duty as citizens. But there are other explanations for being unregistered. In this country the entire burden of registering to vote falls on the individual voters. They must learn how and when and where to register; they must take the time and trouble to go someplace and fill out a registration form; and they must reregister in a new county or state if they happen to move. In most European nations registration is done for you, automatically, by the government. Since it is costly to register in this country and costless to register in other countries, it should not be surprising that fewer people are registered here than abroad.

In 1993 Congress passed a law designed to make it easier to register to vote. Known as the **motor-voter law,** the law requires states to allow people to register to vote when applying for driver's licenses and to provide registration through the mail and at some state offices that serve the disabled or provide public assistance (such as welfare checks). The motor-voter law took effect in 1995. In just two months, 630,000 new voters signed up in twenty-seven states. Even so, the results of the law so far have been mixed.

Only 49 percent of eligible voters went to the polls in 1996, and in North Dakota, where voters are not required to register, turnout was still only 56 percent.[2] In 1998 only 17.6 percent of the eligible electorate voted in primary elections, and a record-low 36.1 percent of the voting-age population cast ballots in the midterm congressional elections.[3] On the other hand, registration among the voting-age population rose to 70.1 percent in 1998, the highest in a nonpresidential year since 1970, and turnout was less depressed in states that had fully implemented the motor-voter law or instituted universal election-day registration programs.[4] Contrary to the fears of congressional Republicans (90 percent of whom opposed the motor-voter law) and the hopes of congressional Democrats (95 percent of whom supported it), the adoption of motor-voter programs has not changed the two-party balance of registrants, but it has increased independent registrations.[5] The motor-voter law has allowed a lot of people to register that way (see Figure 6.1), but it has not had much of an impact on election results.

A final point: voting is only one way of participating in politics. It is important (we could hardly be considered a democracy if nobody voted), but it is not all-important. Joining civic associations, supporting

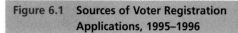

Figure 6.1   Sources of Voter Registration Applications, 1995–1996

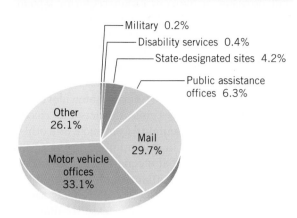

Source: Federal Election Commission, *Executive Summary—Report to the Congress,* June 1997.

ures, Americans participate in politics *more* than most Europeans—or anybody else, for that matter. Moreover, it is possible that low rates of registration indicate that people are reasonably well satisfied with how the country is governed. If 100 percent of all adult Americans registered and voted (especially under a system that makes registering relatively difficult), it could mean that people were deeply upset about how things were run. In short it is not at all clear whether low voter turnout is a symptom of political disease or a sign of political good health.

The important question about participation is not how much participation there is but how different kinds of participation affect the kind of government we get. This question cannot be answered just by looking at voter turnout, the subject of this chapter; it also requires us to look at the composition and activities of political parties, interest groups, and the media (the subjects of later chapters).

Nonetheless, voting is important. To understand why participation in American elections takes the form that it does, we must first understand how laws have determined who shall vote and under what circumstances.

social movements, writing to legislators, fighting city hall—all these and other activities are ways of participating in politics. It is possible that, by these meas-

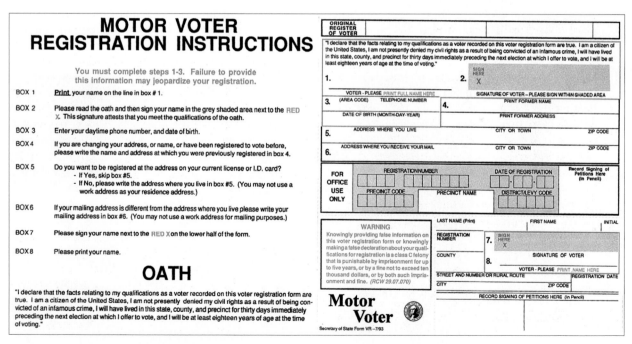

When you apply for a driver's license in the state of Washington, you are given this form so that you can register to vote at the same time. This "motor-voter" idea became the basis of a federal law passed in 1993.

The Rise of the American Electorate

It is ironic that relatively few citizens vote in American elections, since it was in this country that the mass of people first became eligible to vote. At the time the Constitution was ratified, the vote was limited to property owners or taxpayers, but by the administration of Andrew Jackson (1829–1837) it had been broadened to include virtually all white male adults. Only in a few states did property restrictions persist: they were not abolished in New Jersey until 1844 or in North Carolina until 1856. And, of course, African American males could not vote in many states, in the North as well as the South, even if they were not slaves. Women could not vote in most states until the twentieth century; Chinese Americans were widely denied the vote; and being in prison is grounds for losing the franchise even today. Aliens, on the other hand, were often allowed to vote if they had at least begun the process of becoming citizens. By 1880 only an estimated 14 percent of all adult males in the United States could not vote; in England in the same period about 40 percent of adult males were disfranchised.[6]

From State to Federal Control

Initially it was left entirely to the states to decide who could vote and for what offices. The Constitution gave Congress the right to pick the day on which presidential electors would gather and to alter state regulations regarding congressional elections. The only provision of the Constitution requiring a popular election was the clause in Article I stating that members of the House of Representatives be chosen by the "people of the several states."

Because of this permissiveness, early federal elections varied greatly. Several states picked their members of the House at large (that is, statewide) rather than by district; others used districts but elected more than one representative from each. Still others had their elections in odd-numbered years, and some even required that a congressional candidate win a majority, rather than simply a plurality, of votes to be elected (when that requirement was in effect, runoff elections—in one case as many as twelve—were necessary). Furthermore, presidential electors were at first picked by state legislatures rather than by the voters directly.

Congress, by law and constitutional amendment, has steadily reduced state prerogatives in these matters. In 1842 a federal law required that all members of the House be elected by districts; other laws over the years required that all federal elections be held in even-numbered years on the Tuesday following the first Monday in November.

The most important changes in elections have been those that extended the suffrage to women,

In the first years of the republic, voting was frequently restricted to male property owners.

WHITE SUPREMACY!

Attention, White Men!

Grand Torch-Light Procession

At JACKSON,

On the Night of the

Fourth of January, 1890.

**The Final Settlement of Democratic Rule
and White Supremacy in Mississippi.**

GRAND PYROTECHNIC DISPLAY!
Transparencies and Torches Free for all.

**All in Sympathy with the Grand Cause
are Cordially and Earnestly Invited to be
on hand, to aid in the Final Overthrow of
Radical Rule in our State.**

Come on foot or on horse-back; come any way, but
be sure to get there.
Brass Bands, Cannon, Flambeau Torches, Transparencies, Sky-rockets, Etc.

A GRAND DISPLAY FOR A GRAND CAUSE.

After Reconstruction ended in 1876, black voting shrank under the attack of white supremacists.

After the Civil War, while Union forces were still in control, African Americans began to vote in the South, as shown here in Richmond, Virginia, in 1871.

African Americans, and eighteen-year-olds and made mandatory the direct popular election of U.S. senators. The Fifteenth Amendment, adopted in 1870, said that the "right of citizens of the United States to vote shall not be denied or abridged by the United States or by any state on account of race, color, or previous condition of servitude." Reading those words today, one would assume that they gave African Americans the right to vote. That is not what the Supreme Court during the 1870s thought they meant. By a series of decisions, it held that the Fifteenth Amendment did not necessarily confer the right to vote on anybody; it merely asserted that if someone was denied that right, the denial could not be explicitly on the grounds of race. And the burden of proving that it was race that led to the denial fell on the black who was turned away at the polls.[7]

This interpretation opened the door to all manner of state stratagems to keep blacks from voting. One

was a **literacy test** (a large proportion of former slaves were illiterate); another was a requirement that a **poll tax** be paid (most former slaves were poor); a third was the practice of keeping blacks from voting in primary elections (in the one-party South the only meaningful election was the Democratic primary). To allow whites who were illiterate or poor to vote, a **grandfather clause** was added to the law, saying that a person could vote, even if he did not meet the legal requirements, if he or his ancestors voted before 1867 (blacks, of course, could not vote before 1867). When all else failed, blacks were intimidated, threatened, or harassed if they showed up at the polls.

There began a long, slow legal process of challenging in court each of these restrictions in turn. One by one the Supreme Court set most of them aside. The grandfather clause was declared unconstitutional in 1915,[8] and the **white primary** finally fell in 1944.[9] Some of the more blatantly discriminatory literacy tests were also overturned.[10] The practical result of these rulings was slight: only a small proportion of voting-age blacks were able to register and vote in the South, and they were found mostly in the larger cities. A dramatic change did not begin until 1965, with the passage of the Voting Rights Act. This act suspended the use of literacy tests and authorized the appointment of federal examiners who could order the registration of blacks in states and counties (mostly in the South) where fewer than 50 percent of the voting-age population were registered or had voted in the last presidential election. It also provided criminal penalties for interfering with the right to vote.

Though implementation in some places was slow, the number of African Americans voting rose sharply throughout the South. For example, in Mississippi the proportion of voting-age blacks who registered rose from 5 percent to over 70 percent in just ten years (see Table 6.2). These changes had a profound effect on the behavior of many white southern politicians: Governor George Wallace stopped making prosegregation speeches and began courting the black vote.

Women were kept from the polls by law more than by intimidation, and when the laws changed, women almost immediately began to vote in large numbers. By 1915 several states, mostly in the West, had begun to permit women to vote. But it was not until the Nineteenth Amendment to the Constitution was ratified in 1920, after a struggle lasting many decades, that women generally were allowed to vote. At one stroke the size of the eligible voting population almost doubled. Contrary to the hopes of some and the fears of others, no dramatic changes occurred in the conduct of elections, the identity of the winners, or the substance of public policy. Initially, at least, women voted more or less in the same manner as men, though not quite as frequently.

The political impact of the youth vote was also less than expected. The Voting Rights Act of 1970 gave eighteen-year-olds the right to vote in federal elections beginning January 1, 1971. It also contained a provision lowering the voting age to eighteen in state elections, but the Supreme Court declared this unconstitutional. As a result a constitutional amendment, the Twenty-sixth, was proposed by Congress and ratified by the states in 1971. The 1972 elections became the first in which all people between the ages of eighteen and twenty-one could cast ballots (before then, four states had allowed those under twenty-one to vote). About 25 million people suddenly became eligible to participate in elections, but their turnout (42 percent) was lower than for the population as a whole, and they did not flock to any particular party or candidate. George McGovern, the Democratic candidate for president in 1972, counted heavily on attracting the youth vote but did not succeed. Most young voters supported Richard Nixon (though college students favored McGovern).[11]

In the midterm congressional elections of 1994, only one-fifth of those between the ages of eighteen and twenty-four cast ballots, and in 1996 only 30 percent of young adults went to the polls.[12] At the same time, however, young Americans' rates of participation in civic activities such as community service rose to nearly 70 percent.[13] Senator Paul Wellstone of Minnesota, a liberal Democrat who taught political science and was a campus political protester during the 1970s and 1980s, believes that among young people today, "community service is viewed as good, and political service is viewed as disrep-

Table 6.2   Voter Registration in the South

		Ala.	Ark.	Fla.	Ga.	La.	Miss.	N.C.	S.C.	Tenn.	Tex.	Va.	Total
		Percentage of Voting-Age Population That Is Registered											
1960	White	63.6%	60.9%	69.3%	56.8%	76.9%	63.9%	92.1%	57.1%	73.0%	42.5%	46.1%	61.1%
	Black*	13.7	38.0	39.4	29.3	31.1	5.2	39.1	13.7	59.1	35.5	23.1	29.1
1970	White	85.0	74.1	65.5	71.7	77.0	82.1	68.1	62.3	78.5	62.0	64.5	62.9
	Black	66.0	82.3	55.3	57.2	57.4	71.0	51.3	56.1	71.6	72.6	57.0	62.0
1986	White	77.5	67.2	66.9	62.3	67.8	91.6	67.4	53.4	70.0	79.0	60.3	69.9
	Black	68.9	57.9	58.2	52.8	60.6	70.8	58.4	52.5	65.3	68.0	56.2	60.8

*Includes other minority races.

Source: Voter Education Project, Inc., of Atlanta, Georgia, as reported in *Statistical Abstract of the United States, 1990,* 264.

utable."[14] Systematic studies of the subject are few, but the senator is probably right.

National standards now govern almost every aspect of voter eligibility. All persons eighteen years of age and older may vote; there may be no literacy test or poll tax; states may not require residency of more than thirty days in that state before a person may vote; areas with significant numbers of citizens not speaking English must give those people ballots written in their own language; and federal voter registrars and poll watchers may be sent into areas where less than 50 percent of the voting-age population participates in a presidential election. Before 1961 residents of the District of Columbia could not vote in presidential elections; the Twenty-third Amendment to the Constitution gave them this right.

Voter Turnout

Given all these legal safeguards, one might expect that participation in elections would have risen sharply. In fact the proportion of the voting-age population that has gone to the polls in presidential elections has remained about the same—between 50 and 60 percent of those eligible—at least since 1928 and appears today to be much smaller than it was in the

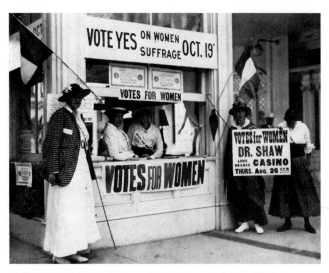

The campaign to win the vote for women nationwide succeeded with the adoption of the Nineteenth Amendment in 1920.

latter part of the nineteenth century (see Figure 6.2). In every presidential election between 1860 and 1900, at least 70 percent of the eligible population apparently went to the polls, and in some years (1860 and 1876) almost 80 percent seem to have voted. Since 1900 not a single presidential election turnout

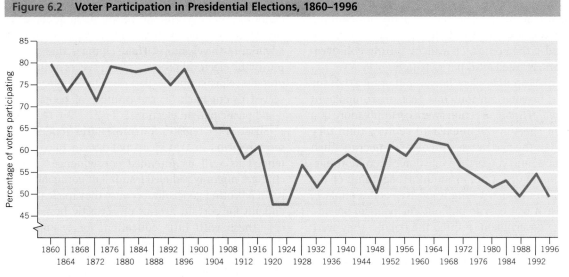

Figure 6.2   Voter Participation in Presidential Elections, 1860–1996

Note: Several southern states did not participate in the 1864 and 1868 elections.
Sources: For 1860–1928: Bureau of the Census, *Historical Statistics of the United States, Colonial Times to 1970*, part 2, 1071; 1932–1992: *Statistical Abstract of the United States, 1992*, 517.

has reached 70 percent, and on two occasions (1920 and 1924) it did not even reach 50 percent.[15] Even outside the South, where efforts to disfranchise African Americans make data on voter turnout especially hard to interpret, turnout seems to have declined: over 84 percent of the voting-age population participated in presidential elections in non-southern states between 1884 and 1900, but only 68 percent participated between 1936 and 1960, and even fewer have done so since 1960.[16]

Scholars have vigorously debated the meaning of these figures. One view is that this decline in turnout, even allowing for the shaky data on which the estimates are based, has been real and is the result of a decline of popular interest in elections and a weakening of the competitiveness of the two major parties. During the nineteenth century, according to this theory, the parties fought hard, worked strenuously to get as many voters as possible to the polls, afforded the mass of voters a chance to participate in party politics through caucuses and conventions, kept the legal barriers to participation (such as complex registration procedures) low, and looked forward to close, exciting elections. After 1896, by which time the South had become a one-party Democratic region and the North heavily Republican, both parties became more conservative, national elections usually resulted in lopsided victories for the Republicans, and citizens began to lose interest in politics because it no longer seemed relevant to their needs. The parties ceased functioning as organizations to mobilize the mass of voters and fell under the control of leaders, mostly conservative, who resisted mass participation.[17]

There is another view, however. It argues that the decline in voter turnout has been more apparent than real. Though elections were certainly more of a popular sport in the nineteenth century than they are today, the parties were no more democratic then than now, and voters then may have been more easily manipulated. Until around the beginning of the twentieth century, voting fraud was commonplace, because it was easy to pull off. The political parties, not the government, printed the ballots; they were often cast in public, not private, voting booths; there were few serious efforts to decide who was eligible to vote, and the rules that did operate were easily evaded.

Under these circumstances it was easy for a person to vote more than once, and the party machines made heavy use of these "floaters," or repeaters. "Vote early and often" was not a joke but a fact. The parties often controlled the counting of votes, padding the totals whenever they feared losing. As a result of these machinations, the number of votes counted was often larger than the number cast, and the number cast was in turn often larger than the number of individuals eligible to vote.

Around 1890 the states began adopting the **Australian ballot.** This was a government-printed ballot of uniform size and shape that was cast in secret, created to replace the old party-printed ballots cast in public. By 1910 only three states were without the Australian ballot. Its use cut back on (but certainly did not eliminate) vote buying and fraudulent vote counts.

In short, if votes had been legally cast and honestly counted in the nineteenth century, the statistics on election turnout might well be much lower than the inflated figures we now have.[18] To the extent that this is true, we may not have had a decline in voter participation as great as some have suggested. Nevertheless, most scholars believe that turnout probably did actually decline somewhat after the 1890s. One reason was that voter-registration regulations became more burdensome: there were longer residency requirements; aliens who had begun but not completed the process of becoming citizens could no longer vote in most states; it became harder for African Americans to vote; educational qualifications for voting were adopted by several states; and voters had to register long in advance of the elections. These changes, designed to purify the electoral process, were aspects of the progressive reform impulse (described in Chapter 7) and served to cut back on the number of people who could participate in elections.

Strict voter-registration procedures tended, like most reforms in American politics, to have unintended as well as intended consequences. These changes not only reduced fraudulent voting but also reduced voting generally, because they made it more difficult for certain groups of perfectly honest voters—those with little education, for example, or those who had recently moved—to register and vote. This was not the first time, and it will not be the last, that a reform designed to cure one problem created another.

Even after all the legal changes are taken into account, there has still been a decline in citizen participation in elections. Between 1960 and 1980 the proportion of voting-age people casting a ballot in presidential elections fell by about 10 percentage points, a drop that cannot be explained by how ballots were printed or how registration rules were rewritten. Nor can these factors explain why 1996 witnessed not only the lowest level of turnout (49 percent) in a presidential election since 1924 but also the single steepest four-year decline (from 55 percent in 1992) since 1920.

Actual trends in turnout aside, what if they gave an election and everyone came? Would universal turnout change national election outcomes and the content of public policy? It has long been argued that because the poor, less educated, and minorities are overrepresented among nonvoters, universal turnout would strongly benefit Democratic candidates and liberal causes. But a careful study of this question found that the "party of nonvoters" largely mirrors the demographically diverse and ideologically divided population that goes to the polls.[19] In 1992 and 1996, for example, the two most common demographic features of nonvoters were residential mobility and youth: "fully 43 percent of nonvoters had moved within two years of the election and one third were under the age of thirty."[20] If everyone who was eligible had voted in those elections, Bill Clinton's winning margin over George Bush and Bob Dole, respectively, would have been a bit wider, but there would have been "no Mother Lode of votes for Democratic candidates or pressure for liberal causes."[21]

Who Participates in Politics?

To understand better why voter turnout declined and what, if anything, that decline may mean, we must first look at who participates in politics.

Forms of Participation

Voting is by far the most common form of political participation, while giving money to a candidate and being a member of a political organization are the least common. Many Americans exaggerate how frequently they vote or how active they are in politics. In a study by Sidney Verba and Norman Nie, 72 percent of those interviewed said that they voted "regularly" in presidential elections. Yet we know that since 1960, on average only 56 percent of the

---

HOW THINGS WORK

Voter Turnout: Some Myths and Realities

Myth

Turnout is declining because the poor are dropping out of politics.

Today's voters see no differences between Democrats and Republicans.

Nonvoters don't vote because the policies they prefer haven't been debated or adopted.

Many elections are decided by levels of voter turnout.

Registration reform (for example, the "motor-voter" law, Figure 6.1) would definitely help the Democrats and hurt the Republicans.

Reality

Turnout is declining because *all* groups—the poor, the middle class, and the rich—have become less likely to vote.

More voters see more important differences between the parties today than they did in the 1960s.

Voters and nonvoters differ very little in their policy preferences.

Levels of turnout do not, as a rule, make much of a difference in election outcomes.

Nobody really knows, but surveys suggest that the political leanings of voters and nonvoters do not differ enough for the addition of even millions of nonvoters to make much of a partisan impact.

Source: Adapted from Ruy A. Teixeria, "Voter Turnout in America," *The Brookings Review* (Fall 1992): 28–31. Reprinted with permission of the Brookings Institution.

---

voting-age population has actually cast presidential ballots. Careful studies of this discrepancy suggest that 8 to 10 percent of Americans interviewed misreport their voting habits: they claim to have voted when in fact they have not. Young, low-income, less-educated, and nonwhite people are more likely to misreport than others.[22] If people misreport their voting behavior, it is likely that they also misreport—that is, exaggerate—the extent to which they participate in other ways.

Indeed, most research shows that "politics is not at the heart of the day-to-day life of the American people."[23] Work, family, church, and other voluntary activities come first, both in terms of how Americans spend their time and in terms of the money they donate. For example, a study by Verba and others found that a higher proportion of citizens take part in nonpolitical than political activities: "More citizens reported giving time to church-related or charitable activities than indicated contacting a government official or working informally on a community problem, two of the most frequent forms of political participation beyond the vote"[24] (see Figure 6.3).

In an earlier study Verba and Nie analyzed the ways in which people participate in politics and came up with six forms of participation that are characteristic of six different kinds of U.S. citizens. About one-fifth (22 percent) of the population is completely inactive: they rarely vote, they do not get involved in organizations, and they probably do not even talk about politics very much. These inactives typically have little education and low incomes and are relatively young. Many of them are African American. At the opposite extreme are the complete **activists,** constituting about one-ninth of the population (11 percent). These people are highly educated, have high incomes, and tend to be middle-aged rather than young or old. They tend to participate in all forms of politics.

Between these extremes are four categories of limited forms of participation. The *voting specialists* are people who vote but do little else; they tend not to have much schooling or income and to be substantially older than the average person. *Campaigners* not only vote but also like to get involved in campaign activities. They are better educated than the average voter, but what seems to distinguish them most is their interest in the conflicts, passions, and struggle of politics; their clear identification with a political party; and their willingness to take strong positions. *Communalists* are much like campaigners in social background but have a very different temperament: they do not like the conflict and tension of partisan campaigns. They tend to reserve their energy for community activities of a more nonpartisan nature—forming and joining organizations to deal with local problems and contacting local officials about these problems. Finally, there are some *parochial participants*, who do not vote and stay out of

Figure 6.3   Nonpolitical Voluntary Activity Among Citizens

- Affiliated with nonpolitical organization — 68%
- Attend meeting of nonpolitical organization — 37%
- Attend church services once a month or more — 57%
- Attend church services weekly — 32%
- Give time to church work — 25%
- Church contribution — 62%
- Give time to charitable work — 36%
- Charitable contribution — 66%

Percent active

Source: Sidney Verba et al., *Voice and Equality: Civic Voluntarism in American Politics* (Cambridge: Harvard University Press, 1995), 77–79.

election campaigns and civic associations but are willing to contact local officials about specific, often personal, problems.[25]

The Causes of Participation

Whether participation takes the form of voting or being a complete activist, it is higher among people who have gone to college than among those who have not and higher among people who are over forty-four years of age than among those who are under thirty-five. (The differences in voting rates for these groups are shown in Figure 6.4.) Even after controlling for differences in income and occupation, the more schooling one has, the more likely one is to vote. Of course it may not be schooling itself that causes participation but something that is strongly correlated with schooling, such as high levels of political information.[26]

In fact the differences in participation that are associated with schooling (or its correlates) are probably even greater than reported in this figure, since we have already seen that less-educated people exaggerate how frequently they vote. An excellent

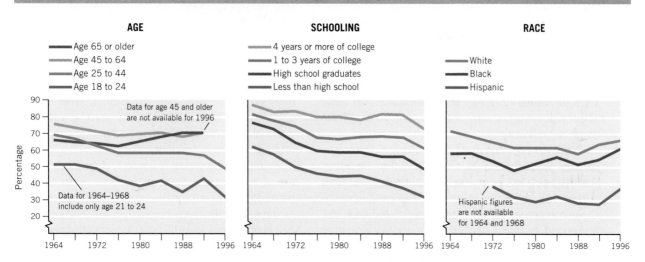

Figure 6.4   Voter Turnout in Presidential Elections, by Age, Schooling, and Race, 1964–1996

Sources: Updated from Gary R. Orren, "The Linkage of Policy to Participation," in *Presidential Selection,* ed. Alexander Heard and Michael Nelson (Durham, N.C.: Duke University Press, 1987). Data for 1996 are from *Statistical Abstract of the United States 1998,* 296, as supplied by Christopher Blunt.

study of turnout concludes that people are more likely to vote when they have those personal qualities that "make learning about politics easier and more gratifying."[27]

Religious involvement also increases political participation. If you are a regular churchgoer who takes your faith seriously, the chances are that you will be more likely to vote and otherwise take part in politics than if you are a person of the same age, sex, income, and educational level who does not go to church. Church involvement leads to social connectedness, teaches organizational skills, increases one's awareness of larger issues, and puts one in contact with like-minded people.[28]

Men and women vote at about the same rate, but blacks and whites do not. Although at one time that difference was largely the result of discrimination, today it can be explained mostly by differences in social class—blacks are poorer and have less schooling, on average, than whites. However, among people of the same socioeconomic status—that is, having roughly the same level of income and schooling—blacks tend to participate *more* than whites.[29]

Because the population has become younger (due to the baby boom of the 1960s and 1970s) and because blacks have increased in numbers faster

than whites, one might suppose that these demographic changes would explain why the turnout in presidential elections has gone down a bit since the early 1960s. And they do—up to a point. But there is another factor that ought to make turnout go *up*—schooling. Since college graduates are much more likely to vote than those with less educational experience, and since the college-graduate proportion of the population has gone up sharply, turnout should have risen. But it has not. What is going on here?

Perhaps turnout has declined despite the higher levels of schooling due to the rising level of distrust of government. We saw in Chapter 4 that, well into the 1990s, more and more people were telling pollsters that they lacked confidence in political leaders. Rising distrust seems a plausible explanation for declining turnout, until one looks at the facts. The data show that there is *no correlation* between expressing distrust of political leaders and not voting.[30] People who are cynical about our leaders are just as likely to vote as people who are not.

As we have seen, turnout is powerfully affected by the number of people who have registered to vote; perhaps in recent years it has become harder to register. But in fact exactly the opposite is true. Since 1970 federal law has prohibited residency requirements longer than thirty days for presidential elections, and a Supreme Court decision in 1972 held that requirements much in excess of this were invalid for state and local elections.[31] By 1982 twenty-one states and the District of Columbia, containing about half the nation's population, had adopted laws permitting voters to register by mail. In four states—Maine, Minnesota, Oregon, and Wisconsin—voters can register and vote on the same day, all at once.

What is left? Several small things. First, the greater youthfulness of the population, together with the presence of growing numbers of African Americans and other minorities, has pushed down the percentage of voters who are registered and vote.

Second, political parties today are no longer as effective as they once were in mobilizing voters, ensuring that they are registered, and getting them to the polls. As we shall see in Chapter 7, the parties once were grassroots organizations with which many people strongly identified. Today the parties are somewhat distant, national bureaucracies with which most of us do not identify very strongly.

Third, the remaining impediments to registration exert some influence. One study estimated that if every state had registration requirements as easy as the most permissive states, turnout in a presidential election would be about 9 percent higher.[32] The

Latino voters tend to participate less in elections than do other groups. This billboard is an effort to change that: "Your vote is your voice."

experience of the four states where you can register and vote on the same day is consistent with this: in 1976, when same-day registration first went into effect, three of the four states that had it saw their turnout go up by 3 or 4 percent, while those states that did not have it saw their turnout go down.[33] If an even bolder plan were adopted, such as the Canadian system of universal enrollment, whereby the government automatically puts on the voter list every eligible citizen, there would probably be some additional gain in turnout.[34]

Fourth, if *not* voting is costless, then there will be more nonvoting. Several nations with higher turnouts than ours make voting compulsory. For example, in Italy a person who does not vote has his or her government identification papers stamped "*DID NOT VOTE.*"[35] In Australia and other countries fines can be levied on nonvoters. As a practical matter such fines are rarely imposed, but just the threat of them probably induces more people to register and vote.

Finally, voting (and before that, registering) will go down if people do not feel that elections matter much. There has been a decline in the proportion of people who feel that elections matter a lot, corresponding to the decrease in those who do participate in elections.

In short there are a number of reasons why we register and vote less frequently in the United States than do citizens of other countries. Two careful studies of all these factors found that almost all of the differences in turnout among twenty-four democratic nations, including the United States, could be explained by party strength, automatic registration, and compulsory voting laws.[36]

The presence of these reasons does not necessarily mean that somebody ought to do something about them. We could make registration automatic—but that might open the way to voter fraud, since people move around and change names often enough to enable some of them, if they wanted to, to vote more than once. We could make voting compulsory, but Americans have an aversion to government compulsion in any form and probably would object strenuously to any plan for making citizens carry identification papers that the government would stamp.

Democrats and Republicans fight over various measures designed to increase registration and voting because one party (usually the Democrats) thinks that higher turnout will help them and the other (usually the Republicans) fears that higher

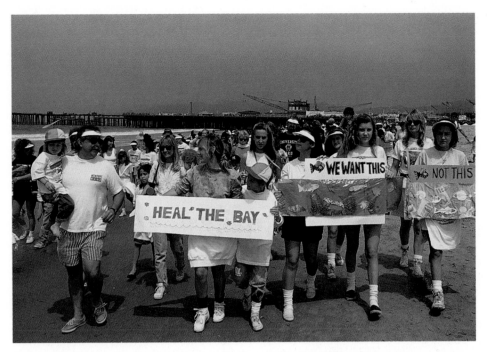

Demonstrations are almost as important as elections in shaping public policy.

turnout will hurt them. In fact no one really knows whether either party would be helped or hurt by higher voter turnout.

Nonvoters are more likely than voters to be poor, black or Hispanic, or uneducated. However, the proportion of nonvoters with some college education rose from 7 percent in 1960 to 18 percent in 1980. In addition the percentage of nonvoters who held white-collar jobs rose from 33 percent to 50 percent in the same period. Many of these better-off nonvoters might well have voted Republican had they gone to the polls. And even if the turnout rates only of blacks and Hispanics had increased, there would not have been enough votes added to the Democratic column to affect the outcome of the 1984 or 1988 presidential elections.[37]

Both political parties try to get a larger turnout among voters likely to be sympathetic to them, but it is hard to be sure that these efforts will produce real gains. If one party works hard to get its nonvoters to the polls, the other party will work just as hard to get its people there. For example, when Jesse Jackson ran for the presidency in 1984, registration of southern blacks increased, but registration of southern whites increased even more.

The Meaning of Participation Rates

Americans may be voting less, but there is evidence that they are participating more. As Table 6.3 shows, between 1967 and 1987 the percentage of Americans who voted regularly in presidential and local elections dropped, but the percentage who participated in ten out of twelve other political activities increased, steeply in some cases. Thus, although Americans are going to the polls less, they are campaigning, contacting government officials, and working on community issues more. And while the proportion of the population that votes is lower in the United States than in many other democracies, the percentage of Americans who engage in one or more political activities beyond voting is higher (see Table 6.4).

Public demonstrations such as sit-ins and protest marches have become much more common in recent decades than they once were. By one count there were only 6 demonstrations per year between 1950 and 1959 but over 140 per year between 1960 and 1967. Though the demonstrations of the 1960s began with civil rights and antiwar activists, public protests were later employed by farmers demanding government aid, truckers denouncing

Table 6.3   How Citizens Participate

Specific Activity	Percentage Engaging in Fourteen Acts of Participation, 1967 and 1987		
	1967	1987	Absolute Change
Voting			
Regularly vote in presidential elections	66%	58%	−8%
Always vote in local elections	47	35	−12
Campaigning			
Persuade others how to vote	28	32	+4
Actively work for party or candidate	26	27	+1
Attend political meetings or rallies	19	19	0
Contribute money to a party or candidate	13	23	+10
Participate in a political club	8	4	−4
Contacting Government			
Contact local officials: issue-based	14	24	+10
Contact state or national officials: issue-based	11	22	+11
Contact local officials: particularized	7	10	+3
Contact state or national officials: particularized	6	7	+1
Taking Action in the Community			
Work with others on a local problem	30	34	+4
Actively participate in community problem-solving organization	31	34	+3
Form group to help solve local problem	14	17	+3

Source: Reprinted by permission of the publisher from *Voice and Equality: Civic Voluntarism in American Politics* by Sidney Verba, Kay Lehman Scholzman, and Henry A. Brady, Cambridge, Mass.: Harvard University Press, Copyright © 1995 by the Presidents and Fellows of Harvard College. Data from p. 72.

Table 6.4   Participation Beyond Voting in Fourteen Democracies

Percentage of adult population who engaged in some form of political participation beyond voting in 1990.

Britain	77%	Italy	56
Sweden	74	Iceland	55
Norway	68	Netherlands	54
UNITED STATES	66	Belgium	51
Denmark	59	Ireland	46
France	57	Finland	38
West Germany	57	Spain	32

Sources: U.S. percentage calculated from Sidney Verba et al., *Voice and Equality: Civic Voluntarism in American Politics* (Cambridge: Harvard University Press, 1995), 83; other percentages calculated from Max Kaase and Kenneth Newton, *Beliefs in Government,* vol. 5 (New York: Oxford University Press, 1995), 51.

the national speed limit, people with disabilities seeking to dramatize their needs, parents objecting to busing to achieve racial balance in the schools, conservationists hoping to block nuclear power plants, and construction workers urging that nuclear power *not* be blocked.[38]

Although we vote at lower rates here than people do abroad, the meaning of our voting is different. For one thing we elect far more public officials than do the citizens of any other nation. One scholar has estimated that there are 521,000 elective offices in the United States and that almost every week of the year there is an election going on somewhere in this country.[39]

A citizen of Massachusetts, for example, votes not only for the U.S. president but also for two senators, the state governor, the member of the House of Representatives for his or her district, a state representative, a state senator, the state attorney general, the state auditor, the state treasurer, the secretary of state, a county commissioner, a sheriff, and clerks of various courts, as well as (in the cities) for the mayor, the city councillor, and school committee members and (in towns) for selectmen, town-meeting members, a town moderator, library trustees, health board members, assessors, water commissioners, the town clerk, housing authority members, the tree warden, and the commissioner of the public burial ground. (There are probably others that we have forgotten.)

In many European nations, by contrast, the voters get to make just one choice once every four or five years: they can vote for or against a member of parliament. When there is only one election for one office every several years, that election is bound to assume more importance to voters than many elections for scores of offices. But one election for one office probably has less effect on how the nation is governed than many elections for thousands of offices. Americans may not vote at high rates, but voting affects a far greater part of the political system here than abroad.

The kinds of people who vote here are also different from those who vote abroad. Since almost everybody votes in many other democracies, the votes cast there mirror almost exactly the social composition of those nations. Since only slightly over half of the voting-age population turns out even for presidential elections here, the votes cast in the United States may not truly reflect the country.

That is in fact the case. Figure 6.5 shows the proportion of each major occupational group that

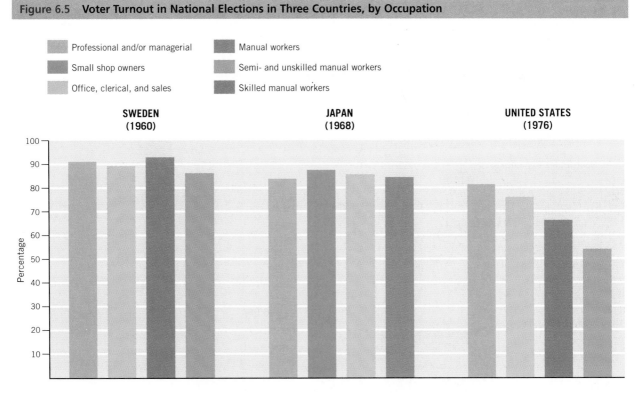

Figure 6.5   Voter Turnout in National Elections in Three Countries, by Occupation

Sources: For Japan: The Society for Promotion of Clean Elections, Survey of 34th General Election, 1976. Reprinted from an unpublished paper by Gary Orren, "Political Participation and Public Policy: The Case for Institutional Reform," Cambridge, Mass., November 1985, 16A. For U.S. and Sweden: Samuel P. Huntington and Joan M. Nelson, *No Easy Choice* (Cambridge: Harvard University Press, 1976), 88.

usually votes in Japan, Sweden, and the United States. Each occupational group—or, if you prefer, social class—votes at about the same rate in Japan and Sweden. But in the United States the turnout is heavily skewed toward higher-status persons: those in professional, managerial, and other white-collar occupations are overrepresented among the voters.

Although nonwhites and Latinos are the fastest-growing segment of the U.S. population, they tend to be the most underrepresented groups among American voters. Little is known about the relationship between political participation and variables such as command of the language and

involvement in nonpolitical institutions that provide information or impart skills relevant to politics (such as workplaces and voluntary associations). However, such factors could be quite important in explaining differences in political participation rates among poor and minority citizens. As we can see in Figure 6.6, blacks, though less involved than whites, participate in voting and political activities at higher rates than do Latinos. One excellent study suggests that these differences are due in part to the fact that blacks are more likely than Latinos to be members of churches that stimulate political interest, activity, and mobilization.[40] Language barriers

Figure 6.6   Electoral and Nonelectoral Political Participation Among Anglo Whites, African Americans, and Latinos

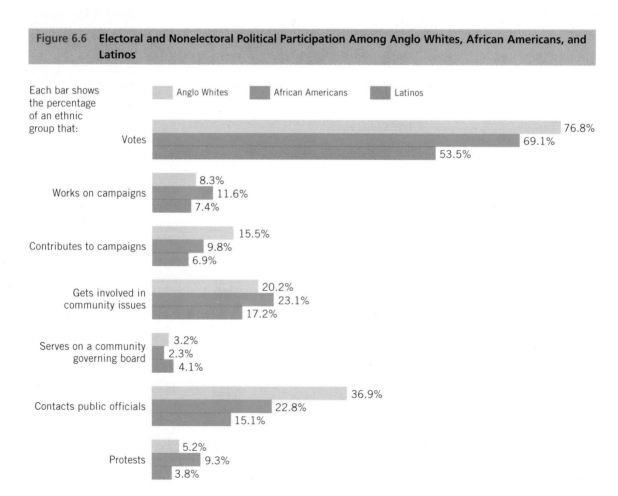

Source: Adapted from Sidney Verba, Kay Lehman Scholzman, Henry Brady, and Norman H. Nie, "Race, Ethnicity, and the Resources for Participation: The Role of Religion," paper delivered at the 1992 Annual Meeting of the American Political Science Association, September 3–6, 1992. Reprinted by permission.

MEMORANDUM

To: Angela Richards, state senator
From: Ted Mitchell, legislative analyst
Subject: Caucus proposal to fine nonvoters

In the 1990s barely half of the electorate voted for president, and only a third or so cast ballots for the U.S. House of Representatives. In a few recent presidential primaries and statewide special elections, turnout has run 10 percent or below. In the mid-1960s, 47 percent of people who did not finish high school and one-third of people in their early twenties voted in the most recent election, but by the mid-1990s only one-quarter of the former group and one-fifth of the latter group did so. Does fining nonvoters make good sense, and would it work?

Arguments for:

1. Australia instituted compulsory voting after its turnout rate fell below 60 percent in 1922. Italy did the same after World War II. Since the early 1920s Australia's turnout has never fallen below 90 percent, and since the early 1950s Italy's has averaged between 85 and 90 percent.
2. The usual fine for nonvoting in these countries is under fifty dollars. Judges or other officials excuse people who are too sick to vote or have other valid excuses.
3. The law sends a moral message that voting is a civic duty in a democracy. More citizens will feel morally obliged to vote if all citizens are legally obliged to vote.

Arguments against:

1. Americans vote in more elections and participate in more political activities beyond voting than other democratic peoples do. Other reforms—streamlining voter registration requirements, holding elections on weekends, making election day a national holiday, increasing get-out-the-vote public service ads—are worth trying instead.
2. Most Americans would probably assert that they have a right not to vote, and many would simply refuse to pay even a small fine for not voting. What then, jail them?
3. Compelling people with limited or no political knowledge to vote leads to what Australians aptly call the "donkey vote." It is both unwise and undemocratic to legally oblige people to vote.

Your decision:
Favor proposal _____
Oppose proposal _____

Caucus Declares "Saving Democracy" Means Fining Nonvoters

May 30
SACRAMENTO, CA
Voting has never been America's favorite pastime, but a report issued by the state senate's Democracy Caucus declares that "nonvoting is now a civic epidemic" that "can best be cured by fining nonvoters as they do in some other democracies" . . .

also make it harder for many Latinos to get in touch with a public official, serve on local governing boards, and engage in other forms of political participation in which command of English is an asset. The lower participation rates of minority citizens are likely compounded by their being disproportionately of low socioeconomic status compared to white Americans.

Exactly what these differences in participation mean in terms of how the government is run is not entirely clear. But since we know from evidence presented in the last chapter that upper-status persons are more likely to have an ideological view of politics, it may suggest that governance here is a bit more sensitive not only to the interests of upper-status white people but also to their (conflicting) ideologies.

Summary

The popular view that Americans don't vote as a result of apathy is not quite right. The correct view is that we don't register to vote (but once registered, we do vote) and that there are many factors having nothing to do with apathy that shape our participation rates—age, race, party organization, the barriers to registration, and popular views about the significance of elections.

The most powerful determinants of participation are schooling and information; the next most power-

ful is age. Race makes a difference, but black participation rates approximate white rates once you control for socioeconomic status.

Compared to other nations, Americans vote at lower rates but more frequently and for many more offices, so elections make a bigger difference in the conduct of public affairs here than abroad. We also engage somewhat more frequently than do people abroad in various nonelectoral forms of participation.

World Wide Web Resources

- Information for voters
  Democracy Network: http://www.dnet.org/
  League of Women Voters: http://www.lwv.org/
  Voter Information Services: http://www.vis.org/
  Women's Voting Guide:
  http://www.womenvote.org/
- National Mail Voter Registration Form:
  http://www.fec.gov/votregis/vr.htm

- The Vanishing Voter:
  http://www.vanishingvoter.org/
- Voter turnout statistics:
  http://clerkweb.house.gov/histrecs/history/
  elections/elections.htm
  http://www.fec.gov/elections.html

Key Terms

voting-age population *p. 130*	motor-voter law *p. 130*	grandfather clause *p. 133*	activists *p. 138*
registered voters *p. 130*	literacy test *p. 133*	white primary *p. 133*	
	poll tax *p. 133*	Australian ballot *p. 136*	

Suggested Readings

Burnham, Walter Dean. *Critical Elections and the Mainsprings of American Politics.* New York: Norton, 1970. An argument about the decline of voter participation, linking is to changes in the economic system.

Conway, M. Margaret. *Political Participation in the United States.* 2nd ed. Washington, D.C.: Congressional Quarterly Press, 1991. Good brief summary of what we need to know about who participates in politics and why.

Orren, Gary R. "The Linkage of Policy to Participation." In *Presidential Selection,* edited by Alexander Heard and Michael Nelson. Durham, N.C.: Duke University Press, 1987. Carefully evaluates various proposals for increasing electoral turnout in the United States.

Teixera, Ruy. *Why Americans Don't Vote.* Westport, Conn.: Greenwood Press, 1987. Good summary of what we know about nonvoting.

Verba, Sidney, et al. *Voice and Equality: Civic Voluntarism in American Politics.* Cambridge.: Harvard University Press, 1995.

Verba, Sidney, Norman H. Nie, and Jae-on Kim. *Participation and Political Equality.* Cambridge: Cambridge University Press, 1978. Comparative study of political participation in seven nations.

Wolfinger, Raymond E., and Steven R. Rosenstone. *Who Votes?* New Haven, Conn.: Yale University Press, 1980. Excellent analysis of what factors determine turnout.

Political Parties

Enduring Questions

1. What did the Founding Fathers believe about political parties?
2. How has America's two-party system changed over the past century and a half? How does it differ today from the party systems of other representative democracies?
3. To what extent has the decline of mass attachment to the two major parties affected how Americans vote?
4. Is the future of the two-party system increasingly shaky or virtually ensured?

Parties—Here and Abroad
Political Culture

The Rise and Decline of the Political Party
The Founding • The Jacksonians • The Civil War
and Sectionalism • The Era of Reform

The National Party Structure Today
National Conventions

State and Local Parties
The Machine • Ideological Parties • Solidary
Groups • Sponsored Parties • Personal Following

The Two-Party System

Minor Parties

Nominating a President
Are the Delegates Representative of the Voters? •
Who Votes in Primaries? • Who Are the New
Delegates?

Parties Versus Voters

One of the reasons why voter turnout is higher abroad than in this country is that political parties in other democratic nations are more effective at mobilizing voters than those here. The sense of being a party member and the inclination to vote the party ticket are greater in France, Italy, and Sweden than in the United States. From this fact you might suppose that political parties here are recent inventions with little experience at organizing and no history of attracting voter identification.

Quite the contrary. American political parties are the oldest in the world, and at one time being a Democrat or a Republican was a serious commitment that people did not make lightly or abandon easily. In those days it would have been hard to find anything in Europe that could match the vote-getting power of such party organizations as those in Chicago, New York, and Philadelphia.

Parties in the United States are relatively weak today, not because they are old but because the laws and rules under which they operate have taken away much of their power at the same time that many voters have lost their sense of commitment to party identification. This weakening has proceeded

149

Figure 7.1   Decline in Party Identification, 1952–1998

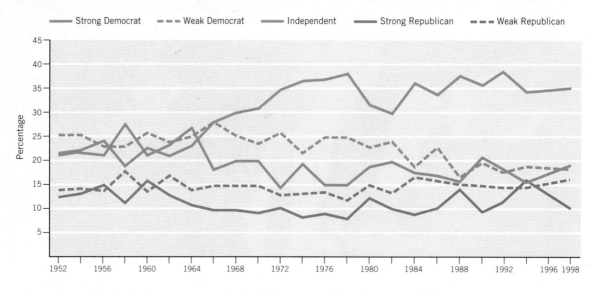

Source: National Election Studies data as reported in Harold W. Stanley and Richard G. Niemi, *Vital Statistics on American Politics, 1999–2000* (Washington, D.C.: Congressional Quarterly Press, 2000), 112.

unevenly, however, because our constitutional system has produced a decentralized party system just as it has produced a decentralized governmental system, with the result that parties in some places are strong and in other places almost nonexistent.

Parties—Here and Abroad

A **political party** is a group that seeks to elect candidates to public office by supplying them with a label—a "party identification"—by which they are known to the electorate.[1] This definition is purposefully broad so that it will include both familiar parties (Democratic, Republican) and unfamiliar ones (Whig, Libertarian, Socialist Workers) and will cover periods in which a party is very strong (having an elaborate and well-disciplined organization that provides money and workers to its candidates) as well as periods in which it is quite weak (supplying nothing but the label to candidates). The label by which a candidate is known may or may not actually be printed on the ballot opposite the candidate's name: in the United States it does appear on the ballot in all national elections but in only a minority of municipal ones; in Australia and Israel (and in Great Britain before 1969) it never appears on the ballot at all.

This definition suggests the three political arenas within which parties may be found. A party exists as a *label* in the minds of the voters, as an *organization* that recruits and campaigns for candidates, and as a *set of leaders* who try to organize and control the legislative and executive branches of government. A powerful party is one whose label has a strong appeal for the voters, whose organization can decide who will be candidates and how their campaigns will be managed, and whose leaders can dominate one or all branches of government.

American parties have become weaker in all three arenas. As a *label* with which voters identify, the parties are probably much weaker than they were in the nineteenth century but only somewhat weaker than they were forty years ago (see Figure 7.1). In 1952 a total of 22 percent of the voters described themselves as "strong" Democrats; by 1998 only 19 percent did. In 1952 a total of 13 percent said that they were "strong" Republicans; in 1998 only 10 percent did. There has been an increase in the proportion of people saying that they either are "independent" or have no preference between the two major parties. (Many of the "independents," of course, lean more toward one party than the other, and many of the "no preference" voters simply don't care about politics, period.) After

1980 the number of Republicans increased, owing, apparently, to the popularity of President Reagan; however, scholars are not sure that this increase will last. But the best evidence of weakening party identification is what voters *do*. As we shall see in the next chapter, they have been increasingly voting split tickets—that is, supporting a president from one party and members of Congress from the other.

As a *set of leaders* who organize government, especially Congress, political parties remain somewhat strong in ways that will be described in Chapter 11. As *organizations* that nominate and elect candidates, parties have become dramatically weaker since the 1960s. In most states parties have very little control over who gets nominated to office. The causes and consequences of that change are the subject of this chapter.

In Europe things are very different. Almost the only way a person can become a candidate for elective office is to be nominated by party leaders. Campaigns are run by the party, using party funds and workers, not by the candidate. Once in office the elected officials are expected to vote and act together with other members of their party. The principal criterion by which voters choose among candidates is their party identification or label. This has been changing somewhat of late: European parties, like American ones, have not been able to count as heavily as in the past on party loyalty among the voters.

Several factors explain the striking differences between American and European political parties. First, the federal system of government in the United States decentralizes political authority and thus decentralizes political party organizations. For nearly two centuries most of the important governmental decisions were made at the state and local levels—decisions regarding education, land use, business regulation, and public welfare—and thus it was at the state and local levels that the important struggles over power and policy occurred. Moreover, most people with political jobs—either elective or appointive—worked for state and local government, and thus a party's interest in obtaining these jobs for its followers meant that it had to focus attention on who controlled city hall, the county courthouse, and the state capitol. Federalism, in short, meant that political parties would acquire jobs and money from local sources and fight local contests. This, in turn, meant that the national political parties would be coalitions of local parties, and though these coalitions would have a keen interest in capturing the presidency (with it,

Political parties mean more in parliamentary regimes than in the United States, as is evident in this rally of leftist voters in India.

after all, went control of large numbers of federal jobs), the national party leaders rarely had as much power as the local ones. The Republican leader of Cuyahoga County, Ohio, for example, could often ignore the decisions of the Republican national chairman and even of the Ohio state chairman.

Political authority in the United States has of late come to be far more centralized: the federal government now makes decisions affecting almost all aspects of our lives, including those—such as schooling and welfare—once left entirely in local hands. Yet the political parties have not become more centralized as a result. If anything, they have become even weaker and more decentralized. One reason for this apparent paradox is that in the United States, unlike in most other democratic nations, political parties are closely regulated by state and federal laws, and these regulations have had the effect of weakening the power of parties substantially. Perhaps the most important of these regulations are those that prescribe how a party's candidates are to be selected.

In the great majority of American states, the party leaders do not select people to run for office; by law those people are chosen by the voters in primary elections. Though sometimes the party can influence who will win a primary contest, in general people running for state or national office in this country owe little to party leaders. In Europe, by contrast, there is no such thing as a primary election—the only way to become a candidate for office is to persuade party leaders to put your name on the ballot. In a later section of this chapter, the impact of the direct primary will be discussed in more detail; for now, it is enough to note that its use removes from the hands of the party leadership its most important source of power over officeholders.

Furthermore, if an American political party wins control of Congress, it does not—as in most European nations with a parliamentary system of government—also win the right to select the chief executive of the government. The American president, as we have seen, is independently elected, and this means that he will choose his principal subordinates not from among members of Congress but from among persons out of Congress. Should be pick a representative or senator for his cabinet, the Constitution requires that person to resign from Congress in order to accept the job. Thus an opportunity to be a cabinet secretary is not an important reward for members of Congress, and so the president cannot use the prospect of that reward as a way of controlling congressional action. All this weakens the significance and power of parties in terms of organizing the government and conducting its business.

Political Culture

The attitudes and traditions of American voters reinforce the institutional and legal factors that make American parties relatively weak. Political parties in this country have rarely played an important part in the life of the average citizen; indeed, one does not usually "join" a party here except by voting for its candidates. In many European nations, on the other hand, large numbers of citizens will join a party, pay dues, and attend regular meetings. Furthermore, in countries such as France, Austria, and Italy, the political parties sponsor a wide range of activities and dominate a variety of associations to which a person may belong—labor unions, youth groups, educational programs, even chess clubs.

In the United States we tend to keep parties separate from other aspects of our lives. As Democrats or Republicans, we may become excited by a presidential campaign, and a few of us may even participate in helping elect a member of Congress or state senator. Our social, business, working, and cultural lives, however, are almost entirely nonpartisan. Indeed, most Americans, unlike many Europeans, would resent partisanship's becoming a conspicuous feature of other organizations to which they belong. All this is a way of saying that American parties play a segmen-

tal, rather than a comprehensive, role in our lives and that even this role is diminishing as more and more of us proclaim ourselves to be "independents."

The Rise and Decline of the Political Party

Our nation began without parties, and today's parties, though far from extinct, are about as weak as at any time in our history. In between the Founding and the present, however, parties arose and became powerful. We can see this process in four broad periods of party history: when political parties were created (roughly from the Founding to the 1820s); when the more or less stable two-party system emerged (roughly from the time of President Jackson to the Civil War); when parties developed a comprehensive organizational form and appeal (roughly from the Civil War to the 1930s); and finally when party "reform" began to alter the party system (beginning in the early 1900s but taking effect chiefly since the New Deal).

The Founding

The Founders disliked parties, thinking of them as "factions" motivated by ambition and self-interest. George Washington, dismayed by the quarreling between Hamilton and Jefferson in his cabinet, devoted much of his Farewell Address to condemning parties. This hostility toward parties was understandable: the legitimacy and success of the newly created federal government were still very much in doubt. When Jefferson organized his followers to oppose Hamilton's policies, it seemed to Hamilton and *his* followers that Jefferson was opposing not just a policy or a leader but also the very concept of a national government. Jefferson, for his part, thought that Hamilton was not simply pursuing bad policies but was subverting the Constitution itself. Before political parties could become legitimate, it was necessary for people to be able to separate in their minds quarrels over policies and elections from disputes over the legitimacy of the new government itself. The ability to make that distinction was slow in coming, and thus parties were objects of profound suspicion, defended, at first, only as temporary expedients.

The first organized political party in American history was made up of the followers of Jefferson, who, beginning in the 1790s, called themselves *Republicans* (hoping to suggest thereby that their

"The man who has filled the measure of his Country's Glory."
JEFFERSON.

Jackson,

DEMOCRACY,   And our Country.

"*The Union must be Preserved.*"
1. Samuel M'Kean.

When Andrew Jackson ran for president in 1828, over a million votes were cast for the first time in American history. This poster, from the 1832 election, was part of the emergence of truly mass political participation.

opponents were secret monarchists).* The followers of Hamilton kept the label *Federalist,* which once had been used to refer to all supporters of the new Constitution (hoping to imply that their opponents were "Antifederalists," or enemies of the Constitution).

These parties were loose caucuses of political notables in various localities, with New England being strongly Federalist and much of the South passionately Republican. Jefferson and his ally James Madison thought that their Republican party was a temporary arrangement designed to defeat John Adams, a Federalist, in his bid to succeed Washington in 1796. (Adams narrowly defeated Jefferson, who, under the system then in effect, became vice president because he had the second most electoral votes.) In 1800 Adams's bid to succeed himself intensified party activity even more, but this time Jefferson won and the Republicans assumed office.

---

*The Jeffersonian Republicans were not the party that today we call Republican. In fact present-day Democrats consider Jefferson to be the founder of their party.

The Federalists feared that Jefferson would dismantle the Constitution, but Jefferson adopted a conciliatory posture, saying in his inaugural address that "we are all Republicans, we are all Federalists."[2] It was not true, of course: the Federalists detested Jefferson, and some were planning to have New England secede from the Union. But it was good politics, expressive of the need that every president has to persuade the public that, despite partisan politics, the presidency exists to serve all the people.

So successful were the Republicans that the Federalists virtually ceased to exist as a party. Jefferson was reelected in 1804 with almost no opposition; Madison easily won two terms; James Monroe carried sixteen out of nineteen states in 1816 and was reelected without opposition in 1820. Political parties had seemingly disappeared, just as Jefferson had hoped. The weakness of this so-called first party system can be explained by the fact that it was the first: nobody had been born a Federalist or a Republican; there was no ancestral party loyalty to defend; the earliest political leaders did not think of themselves as professional politicians; and the Federalist party had such a limited sectional and class base that it could not compete effectively in national elections. The parties that existed in these early years were essentially small groups of local notables. Political participation was limited, and nominations for most local offices were arranged rather casually.

Even in this early period, the parties, though they had very different views on economic policy and somewhat different class bases, did not represent clear, homogeneous economic interests. Farmers in Virginia were Republicans, but farmers in Delaware were Federalists; the commercial interests of Boston were firmly Federalist, but commercial leaders in urban Connecticut were most likely to be Republican.

From the beginning to the present elections have created heterogeneous coalitions, as Madison anticipated.

The Jacksonians

What is often called the second party system emerged around 1824 with Andrew Jackson's first run for the presidency and lasted until the Civil War became inevitable. Its distinctive feature was that political participation became a mass phenomenon. For one thing, the number of voters to be reached had become quite large. Only about 365,000 popular votes were cast in 1824. But as a result of laws that enlarged the number of people eligible to vote and of

★ POLITICALLY SPEAKING ★

The Donkey and the Elephant

Since 1874, when Thomas Nast published political cartoons using these figures, the elephant has been the symbol of the Republican party and the donkey (originally the jackass) the symbol of the Democratic party.

The association of the Democrats with donkeys may have begun with a remark by Ignatius Donnelly, a Republican in the Minnesota legislature, who said that the "Democratic party is like a mule—without pride of ancestry or hope of posterity." An equally uncharitable explanation for the link between Republicans and elephants was offered by Democratic presidential candidate Adlai Stevenson, who

in the 1950s made the observation that "the elephant has a thick skin, a head full of ivory, and as everyone who has seen a circus parade knows, proceeds best by grasping the tail of its predecessor."

Source: Adapted from *Safire's Political Dictionary* by William Safire. Copyright © 1968, 1972, 1978 by William Safire. Reprinted by permission of Random House, Inc. and the author.

an increase in the population, by 1828 well over a million votes were tallied. By 1840 the figure was well over 2 million. (In England at this time there were only 650,000 eligible voters.) In addition, by 1832 presidential electors were selected by popular vote in virtually every state. (As late as 1816 electors were chosen by the state legislatures, rather than by the people, in about half the states.) Presidential politics had become a truly national, genuinely popular activity; indeed, in many communities election campaigns had become the principal public spectacle.

The party system of the Jacksonian era was built from the bottom up rather than—as during the period of the Founding—from the top down. No change better illustrates this transformation than the abandonment of the system of having caucuses composed of members of Congress nominate presidential candidates. The caucus system was an effort to unite the legislative and executive branches by giving the former some degree of control over who would have a chance to capture the latter. The caucus system became unpopular when the caucus candidate for president in 1824 ran third in a field of four in the general election, and it was completely discredited that same year when Congress denied the presidency to Jackson, the candidate with the greatest share of the popular vote.

To replace the caucus, the party convention was invented. The first convention in American history was that of the Anti-Masonic party in 1831; the first convention of a major political party was that of the anti-Jackson Republicans later that year (it nominated Henry Clay for president). The Democrats held a convention in 1832 that ratified Jackson's nomination for reelection and picked Martin Van Buren as his running mate. The first convention to select a man who would be elected president and who was not already the incumbent president was held by the Democrats in 1836; it chose Van Buren.

Considering the many efforts made in recent years to curtail or even abolish the national nominating convention, it is worth remembering that the convention system was first developed in part as a reform—a way of allowing for some measure of local control over the nominating process. Virtually no other nation adopted this method, just as no other nation was later to adopt the direct primary after the convention system became the object of criticism. It is interesting, but perhaps futile, to speculate on how American government would have evolved if the legislative caucus had remained the method for nominating presidents.

The Civil War and Sectionalism

Though the party system created in the Jacksonian period was the first truly national system, with

Democrats (followers of Jackson) and Whigs (opponents of Jackson) fairly evenly balanced in most regions, it could not withstand the deep split in opinion created by the agitation over slavery. Both parties tried, naturally, to straddle the issue, since neither wanted to divide its followers and thus lose the election to its rival. But slavery and sectionalism were issues that could not be straddled. The old parties divided and new ones emerged. The modern Republican party (not the old Democratic-Republican party of Thomas Jefferson) began as a third party. As a result of the Civil War it came to be a major party (the only third party ever to gain major-party status) and to dominate national politics, with only occasional interruptions, for three-quarters of a century.

Republican control of the White House, and to a lesser extent of Congress, was in large measure the result of two events that gave to Republicans a marked advantage in the competition for the loyalties of voters. The first of these was the Civil War. This bitter, searing crisis deeply polarized popular attitudes. Those who supported the Union side became, for generations, Republicans; those who supported the Confederacy, or who had opposed the war, became Democrats.

As it turned out, this partisan division was, for a while, nearly even: though the Republicans usually won the presidency and the Senate, they often lost control of the House. There were many northern Democrats. In 1896, however, another event—the presidential candidacy of William Jennings Bryan—further strengthened the Republican party. Bryan, a Democrat, alienated many voters in the populous northeastern states while attracting voters in the South and Midwest. The result was to confirm and deepen the split in the country, especially North versus South, begun by the Civil War. From 1896 to the 1930s, with rare exceptions northern states were solidly Republican, southern ones solidly Democratic.

This split had a profound effect on the organization of political parties, for it meant that most states were now one-party states. As a result, competition for office at the state level had to go on *within* a single dominant party (the Republican party in Massachusetts, New York, Pennsylvania, Wisconsin, and elsewhere; the Democratic party in Georgia, Mississippi, South Carolina, and elsewhere). Consequently there emerged two major factions within each party, but especially within the Republican party. One was composed of the party regulars—the professional politicians, the "stalwarts," the Old Guard. They were preoccupied with building up the party machinery,

developing party loyalty, and acquiring and dispensing patronage—jobs and other favors—for themselves and their faithful followers. Their great skills were in organization, negotiation, bargaining, and compromise; their great interest was in winning.

The other faction, variously called **mugwumps** or **progressives** (or "reformers"), was opposed to the heavy emphasis on patronage; disliked the party machinery, because it permitted only bland candidates to rise to the top; was fearful of the heavy influx of immigrants into American cities and of the ability of the party regulars to organize them into "machines"; and wanted to see the party take unpopular positions on certain issues (such as free trade). Their great skills lay in the areas of advocacy and articulation; their great interest was in principle.

At first the mugwumps tried to play a balance-of-power role, sometimes siding with the Republican

This was Tammany Hall in its heyday as Democratic party headquarters in Manhattan.

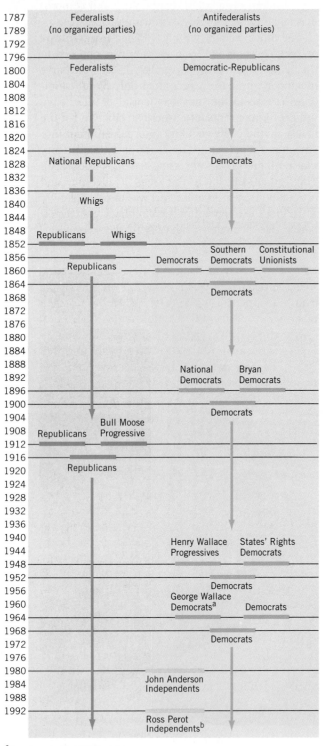

Figure 7.2 Cleavages and Continuity in the Two-Party System

^aAmerican Independent party.

^bUnited We Stand America or Reform Party.

party of which they were members, at other times defecting to the Democrats (as when they bolted the Republican party to support Grover Cleveland, the Democratic nominee, in 1884). But later, as the Republican strength in the nation grew, progressives within that party became less and less able to play a balance-of-power role, especially at the state level. Wisconsin, Michigan, Ohio, and Iowa were solidly Republican; Georgia, the Carolinas, and the rest of the Old South had by 1880 become so heavily Democratic that the Republican party in many areas had virtually ceased to exist. If the progressives were to have any power, it would require, they came to believe, an attack on the very concept of partisanship itself.

The Era of Reform

Progressives began to espouse measures to curtail or even abolish political parties. They favored primary elections to replace nominating conventions, because the latter were viewed as being manipulated by party bosses; they favored nonpartisan elections at the city level and in some cases at the state level as well; they argued against corrupt alliances between parties and businesses. They wanted strict voter-registration requirements that would reduce voting fraud (but would also, as it turned out, keep ordinary citizens who found the requirements cumbersome from voting); they pressed for civil service reform to eliminate patronage; and they made heavy use of the mass media as a way of attacking the abuses of partisanship and of promoting their own ideas and candidacies.

The progressives were more successful in some places than in others. In California, for example, progressives led by Governor Hiram Johnson in 1910–1911 were able to institute the direct primary and to adopt procedures—called the *initiative* and the *referendum*—so that citizens could vote directly on proposed legislation, thereby bypassing the state legislature. Governor Robert La Follette brought about similar changes in Wisconsin.

The effect of these changes was to reduce substantially the worst forms of political corruption and ultimately to make boss rule in politics difficult if not impossible. But they also had the effect of making political parties, whether led by bosses or by statesmen, weaker, less able to hold officeholders accountable, and less able to assemble the power necessary for governing the fragmented political institutions created by the Constitution. In Congress party lines began to grow fainter, as did the power of congressional leadership. Above all, the progressives did not have an answer to the problem first faced by Jefferson: if there is not a strong political party, by what other means will candidates for office be found, recruited, and supported? Political candidacies, like people, are not the products of a virgin birth. Some group or organization must arrange a candidacy, and if that group is not a party, then it can only be another kind of interest group, the mass media, or the personal supporters and family of the candidate. These alternatives are best seen by looking at the forms of party structure now operating.

The National Party Structure Today

Despite many changes and challenges (see Figure 7.2), America's two-party system remains strong. Since political parties exist at the national, state, and local levels, you might suppose that they are arranged like a big corporation, with a national board of directors giving orders to state managers, who in turn direct the activities of rank-and-file workers at the county and city level.

Nothing could be further from the truth. At each level a separate and almost entirely independent organization exists that does pretty much what it wants, and in many counties and cities there is virtually no organization at all.

On paper the national Democratic and Republican parties look quite similar. In both parties ultimate authority is in the hands of the **national convention** that meets every four years to nominate a presidential candidate. Between these conventions party affairs are managed by a **national committee,** made up of delegates from each state and territory. In Congress each party has a **congressional campaign committee** that helps members of Congress who are running for reelection or would-be members running for an open seat or challenging a candidate from the opposition party. The day-to-day work of the party is managed by a full-time, paid **national chairman,** who is elected by the committee.

For a long time the two national parties were alike in behavior as well as description. The national chairman, if his party held the White House, would help decide who among the party faithful would get federal jobs. Otherwise the parties did very little.

But beginning in the late 1960s and early 1970s the Republicans began to convert their national party into a well-financed, highly staffed organization devoted to finding and electing Republican can-

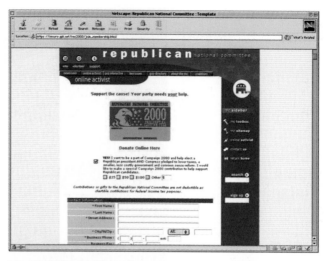

The World Wide Web has become an important way to raise money for candidates and political parties.

didates, especially to Congress. At about the same time, the Democrats began changing the rules governing how presidential candidates are nominated in ways that profoundly altered the distribution of power within the party. As a consequence the Republicans became a bureaucratized party and the Democrats became a factionalized one. After the Republicans won four out of five presidential elections from 1968 to 1984 and briefly took control of the Senate, the Democrats began to suspect that maybe an efficient bureaucracy was better than a collection of warring factions, and so they made an effort to emulate the Republicans.

What the Republicans had done was to take advantage of a new bit of technology—computerized mailings. They built up a huge file of names of people who had given or might give money to the party, usually in small amounts, and used that list to raise a big budget for the national party. In 1983 the Republican National Committee (RNC) raised $35 million from over 1.7 million individual donors; by the time of the 1994 election, the Republican Party committees—the National Committee, the Senatorial Committee, and the Congressional Committee—had raised $246 million from 2.8 million donors.

The RNC used this money to run, in effect, a national political consulting firm. Money went to recruit and train Republican candidates, give them legal and financial advice, study issues and analyze voting trends, and conduct national advertising campaigns on behalf of the party as a whole. No one can be sure how much political success this money

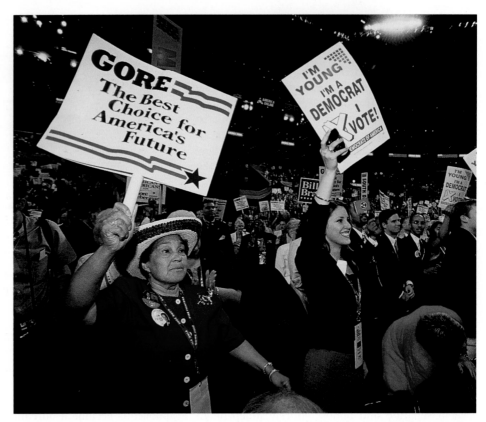

No longer functioning as deliberate bodies, party conventions have become arenas for made-for-television hoopla.

bought (after all, the Republicans lost control of the Senate in 1986), but many observers believed that Republican losses in Congress in 1982 and 1986 would have been even greater if the RNC had not worked so vigorously on behalf of its candidates.

When the Democratic National Committee (DNC) decided to play catch-up, it followed the RNC strategy. Using the same computerized direct-mail techniques, the Democratic party committees—the National Committee, Senatorial Committee, and Congressional Committee—raised $131 million from 2.2 million contributors, about half of what the Republican equivalents had raised. This was a great improvement over what it had managed to do just ten years earlier. The Democrats, like the Republicans, ship a lot of their national party money to state organizations to finance television ads supporting their parties. By doing this the national parties sidestep a restriction on how their money can be used. By law the national parties can spend only $12 million each directly on their presidential candidates. But by sending money to state parties to spend, they can get around this limitation.

A lot of RNC money goes to commission public opinion polls, not only to find out which candidate is likely to win an election but also, more importantly, to find out what issues are troubling the voters, how different segments of the population respond to different kinds of issues and news stories, and how people react to the campaign efforts of specific candidates. During the Reagan administration the RNC's principal pollster, Richard Wirthlin, was taking polls at least monthly and sometimes daily.[3] For reasons explained in Chapter 5, these polls can take you just so far; they are helpful, but they are not a sure-fire guide to public opinion or how to change it.

In 1996 both Democrats and Republicans redoubled their efforts to raise what is called *soft money*—that is, funds to aid parties (and their ads and polls). Both totals were two or three times larger than the soft money raised in 1992. Afterward a Senate investigating committee found evidence that illegal foreign contributions were funneled through intermediaries into both parties, that President Clinton and Vice President Gore made many White House phone calls to raise funds, and that big donors were invited to spend the night in the White House's Lincoln Bedroom.

National Conventions

The national committee selects the time and place of the next national convention and issues a "call" for the convention that sets forth the number of delegates each state and territory is to have and also the rules under which delegates must be chosen. The number of delegates and their manner of selection can significantly influence the chances of various presidential candidates, and considerable attention is thus devoted to these matters. In the Democratic party, for example, a long struggle took place between those who wished to see southern states receive a large share of delegates to the convention, in recognition of their firm support of Democratic candidates in presidential elections, and those who preferred to see a larger share of delegates allotted to northern and western states, which, though less solidly Democratic, were larger or more liberal. A similar conflict within the Republican party has pitted conservative Republican leaders in the Midwest against liberal ones in the East.

A compromise formula is usually chosen; nevertheless, over the years these formulas have gradually changed, shifting voting strength in the Democratic convention away from the South and toward the North and West and in the Republican convention away from the East and toward the South and Southwest. These delegate allocation formulas are but one sign (others will be mentioned later in this chapter) of the tendency of the two parties' conventions to move in opposite ideological directions—Democrats more to the left, Republicans more to the right.

The exact formula for apportioning delegates is extremely complex. For the Democrats it takes into account the vote each state cast for Democratic candidates in past elections and the number of electoral votes of each state; for the Republicans it takes into account the number of representatives in Congress and whether the state in past elections cast its electoral votes for the Republican presidential candidate and elected Republicans to the Senate, the House, and the governorship. Thus the Democrats give extra delegates to large states while the Republicans give extra ones to loyal states.

The way in which delegates are chosen can be even more important than their allocation. The Democrats, beginning in 1972, have developed an elaborate set of rules designed to weaken the control over delegates by

T·R·I·V·I·A

Political Parties

First national political convention	Anti-Masonic party, 1831, in Baltimore
First time incumbent governors were nominated for president	Rutherford B. Hayes of Ohio, by Republicans in 1876 Samuel J. Tilden of New York, by Democrats in 1876
First African American to receive a vote at a national party convention	Frederick Douglass, at Republican convention in 1888
First year in which women attended conventions as delegates	1900 (one woman at both Democratic and Republican conventions)
Most ballots needed to choose a presidential nominee	103, by Democrats in 1924 to select John W. Davis
Closest vote in convention history	$543\frac{1}{20}$ to $542\frac{7}{20}$, defeating a motion to condemn the Ku Klux Klan at 1924 Democratic convention
First Catholic nominated for president by a major party	Al Smith, by Democrats in 1928
Only person nominated for president four times by a major political party	Franklin D. Roosevelt, by Democrats in 1932, 1936, 1940, and 1944
First presidential nominee to make an acceptance speech at the party convention	Franklin D. Roosevelt

local party leaders and to increase the proportion of women, young people, African Americans, and Native Americans attending the convention. These rules were first drafted by a party commission chaired by Senator George McGovern (who was later to make skillful use of these new procedures in his successful bid for the Democratic presidential nomination). They were revised in 1974 by another commission chaired by Barbara Mikulski, whose decisions were ratified by the 1974 midterm convention. After the 1976 election yet a third commission, chaired by Morley Winograd, produced still another revision of the rules, which took effect in 1980. Then a fourth commission, chaired by North Carolina governor James B. Hunt, recommended in 1981 yet another set of rules, which became effective with the 1984 convention.

The general thrust of the work of the first three rules commissions was to broaden the antiparty changes started by the progressives at the beginning of this century. Whereas the earlier reformers had tried to minimize the role of parties in the election process, those of the 1970s sought to weaken the influence of leaders within the party. In short the newer reforms were aimed at creating *intra*party democracy as well as *inter*party democracy. This was done by rules that, for the 1980 convention, required:

- Equal division of delegates between men and women
- Establishment of "goals" for the representation of African Americans, Hispanics, and other groups in proportion to their presence in a state's Democratic electorate
- Open delegate selection procedures, with advance publicity and written rules
- Selection of 75 percent of the delegates at the level of the congressional district or lower
- No "unit rule" that would require all delegates to vote with the majority of their state delegation
- Restrictions on the number of party leaders and elected officials who could vote at the convention
- A requirement that all delegates pledged to a candidate vote for that candidate

In 1981 the Hunt Commission changed some of these rules—in particular, the last two—in order to increase the influence of elected officials and to make the convention a somewhat more deliberative body. The commission reserved about 14 percent of the delegate seats for party leaders and elected officials, who would not have to commit themselves in advance to a presidential candidate, and it repealed the rule requiring that delegates pledged to a candidate vote for that candidate.

Rules have consequences. Whereas in 1980 only one-seventh of the Democratic senators and representatives got to be delegates to the national convention, in 1984 more than half were delegates. In the 1984 presidential primaries, Walter Mondale was the chief beneficiary of the delegate selection rules. He won the support of the overwhelming majority of elected officials—the so-called **superdelegates**—and he did especially well in those states that held winner-take-all primaries. Had different rules been in effect (if, for

Table 7.1	Who Are the Party Delegates?	

Characteristics of delegates to Democratic and Republican national conventions in 2000.

	Democrats	Republicans
Sex and Race		
Women	48%	35%
Blacks	19	4
Religion		
Protestant	47	63
Catholic	31	27
Jewish	8	2
Education		
College degree and beyond	74	77
Post graduate	49	46
Family Income		
Under $50,000	18	10
$100,000 and over	36	41
Belong to union	31	4
Born-again Christian	12	27
Gun owner in household	35	57

Source: New York Times (August 14, 2000): A17.

example, the delegates had been allocated strictly in proportion to the primary votes that the candidates won), Mondale probably would not have entered the Democratic convention with an assured majority.

But the "reform" of the parties, especially the Democratic party, has had far more profound consequences than merely helping one candidate or another. Before 1968 the Republican party represented, essentially, white-collar voters and the Democratic party represented blue-collar ones. After a decade of "reform" the Republican and the Democratic parties each represented two ideologically different sets of upper-middle-class voters (see Table 7.1). In the terminology of Chapter 5, the Republicans came to represent the more conservative wing of the traditional middle class and the Democrats the more leftist wing of the liberal middle class (or the "new class").

This was more troubling to the Democrats than to the Republicans, because the traditional middle class is somewhat closer to the opinions of most citizens than is the liberal middle class (and thus the Republican national convention more closely reflected public opinion than did the Democratic national convention). And for whatever reason, the Republicans won five out of six presidential races between 1968 and 1988.

Before the 1988 convention the Democrats took a long, hard look at their party procedures. Under the leadership of DNC chairman Paul Kirk, they decided against making any major changes, especially ones that would increase the power of grassroots activists at the expense of elected officials and party leaders. The number of such officials (or superdelegates) to be given delegate seats was increased. For example, 80 percent of the Democratic members of Congress and all Democratic governors were automatically made convention delegates in 1988. The official status of some special-interest caucuses (such as those organized to represent African Americans, homosexuals, and various ethnic groups) was reduced in order to lessen the perception that the Democrats were simply a party of factions.

The surface harmony was a bit misleading, however, as some activists, notably supporters of Jesse Jackson, protested that the rules made it harder for candidates like Jackson to win delegates in proportion to their share of the primary vote. (In 1984 Jackson got 18 percent of the primary vote but only 12 percent of the delegates.) The DNC responded by changing the rules for the 1992 campaign. Former DNC chairman Ronald H. Brown (later President Clinton's secretary of commerce) won approval for three important requirements:

- The winner-reward systems of delegate distribution, which gave the winner of a primary or caucus extra delegates, were banned. (In 1988 fifteen states used winner-reward systems, including such vote-rich states as Florida, Illinois, New Jersey, and Pennsylvania.)
- The proportional representation system was put into use. This system divides a state's publicly elected delegates among candidates who receive at least 15 percent of the vote.
- States that violate the rules are now penalized with the loss of 25 percent of their national convention delegates.

Even though the Democrats have retreated a bit from the reforms of the 1960s and 1970s, the conventions of both parties have changed fundamentally, and probably permanently. Delegates once selected by party leaders are now chosen by primary elections and grassroots caucuses. As a result the national party conventions are no longer places where party leaders meet to bargain over the selection of their presidential candidates; they are instead places where delegates come together to ratify choices already made by party activists and primary voters.

Most Americans dislike bosses, deals, and manipulation and prefer democracy, reform, and openness.

These are commendable instincts. But such instincts, unless carefully tested against practice, may mislead us into supposing that anything carried out in the name of reform is a good idea. Rules must be judged by their practical results as well as by their conformity to some principle of fairness. Rules affect the distribution of power: they help some people win and others lose. Later in this chapter we shall try to assess delegate selection rules by looking more closely at how they affect who attends conventions and which presidential candidates are selected there.

State and Local Parties

While the national party structures have changed, the grassroots organizations have withered. In between, state party systems have struggled to redefine their roles.

In every state there is a Democratic and a Republican state party organized under state law. Typically each consists of a state central committee, below which are found county committees and sometimes city, town, or even precinct committees. The members of these committees are chosen in a variety of ways—sometimes in primary elections, sometimes by conventions, sometimes by a building-block process whereby people elected to serve on precinct or town committees choose the members of county committees, who in turn choose state committee members.

Knowing these formal arrangements is much less helpful than knowing the actual distribution of power in each state party. In a few places strong party bosses handpick the members of these committees; in other places powerful elected officials—key state legislators, county sheriffs, or judges—control the committees. And in many places no one is in charge, so that either the party structure is largely meaningless or it is made up of the representatives of various local factions.

To understand how power is distributed in a party, we must first know what *incentives* motivate people in a particular state or locality to become active in a party organization. Different incentives lead to different ways of organizing parties.

The Machine

A **political machine** is a party organization that recruits its members by the use of tangible incentives—money, political jobs, an opportunity to get favors from government—and that is characterized by a high degree of leadership control over member

Ex-senator George Washington Plunkitt of Tammany Hall explains machine politics from atop the bootblack stand in front of the New York County Courthouse around 1905.

activity. At one time many local party organizations were machines, and the struggle over political jobs—patronage—was the chief concern of their members. Though Tammany Hall in New York City began as a caucus of well-to-do notables in the local Democratic party, by the late nineteenth century it had become a machine organized on the basis of political clubs in each assembly district. These clubs were composed of party workers whose job it was to get out the straight party vote in their election districts and who hoped for a tangible reward if they were successful.

And there were abundant rewards to hope for. During the 1870s it was estimated that one out of every eight voters in New York City had a federal, state, or city job.[4] The federal bureaucracy was one important source of those jobs. The New York Customhouse alone employed thousands of people, virtually all of whom were replaced if their party lost the presidential election. The postal system was another source, and it was frankly recognized as such. When James N. Tyner became postmaster general in 1876, he was "appointed not to see that the mails were carried, but to see that Indiana was carried."[5] Elections and conventions were so frequent and the intensity of party competition so great that being a party worker was for many a full-time paid occupation.

Well before the arrival of vast numbers of poor immigrants from Ireland, Italy, and elsewhere, old-stock Americans had perfected the machine, run up the cost of government, and systematized voting fraud. Kickbacks on contracts, payments extracted from officeholders, and funds raised from businesspeople made some politicians rich but also paid the huge bills of the elaborate party organization. When the immigrants began flooding the eastern cities, the party machines were there to provide them with all manner of services in exchange for their support at the polls: the machines were a vast welfare organization operating before the creation of the welfare state.

The abuses of the machine were well known and gradually curtailed. Stricter voter registration laws reduced fraud, civil service reforms cut down the number of patronage jobs, and competitive-bidding laws made it harder to award overpriced contracts to favored businesses. The Hatch Act (passed by Congress in 1939) made it illegal for federal civil service employees to take an active part in political management or political campaigns by serving as party officers, soliciting campaign funds, running for partisan office, working in a partisan campaign, endorsing partisan candidates, taking voters to the polls, counting ballots, circulating nominating petitions, or being delegates to a party convention. (They may still vote and make campaign contributions.)

These restrictions gradually took federal employees out of machine politics, but they did not end the machines. In many cities—Chicago, Philadelphia, and Albany—ways were found to maintain the machines even though city employees were technically under the civil service. Far more important than the various progressive reforms that weakened the machines were changes among voters. As voters grew in education, income, and sophistication, they depended less and less on the advice and leadership of local party officials. And as the federal government created a bureaucratic welfare system, the parties' welfare systems declined in value.

It is easy either to scorn the political party machine as a venal and self-serving organization or to romanticize it as an informal welfare system. In truth it was a little of both. Above all it was a frank recognition of the fact that politics requires organization; the machine was the supreme expression of the value of organization. Even allowing for voting fraud, in elections where party machines were active, voter turnout was huge: more people participated in politics when mobilized by a party machine than when appealed to by television or good-government associations.[6] Moreover, because the party machines were interested in winning, they would subordinate any other consideration to that end. This has meant that the machines were usually willing to support the presidential candidate with the best chance of winning, regardless of his policy views (provided, of course, that he was not determined to wreck the machines once in office). Republican machines helped elect Abraham Lincoln as well as Warren G. Harding; Democratic machines were of crucial importance in electing Franklin D. Roosevelt and John F. Kennedy.

The old-style machine is almost extinct, though important examples still can be found in the Democratic organization in Cook County (Chicago) and the Republican organization in Nassau County (New York). But a new-style machine has emerged in a few places. It is a machine in the sense that it uses money to knit together many politicians, but it is new in that the money comes not from patronage and contracts but from campaign contributions supplied by wealthy individuals and the proceeds of direct-mail campaigns.

The political organization headed by Democratic congressmen Henry A. Waxman and Howard L.

The Christian Coalition, founded by evangelist Pat Robertson (center), is a powerful conservative group.

Berman on the west side of Los Angeles is one such new-style machine. By the astute use of campaign funds, the "Waxman-Berman organization" builds loyalties to it among a variety of elected officials at all levels of government. Moreover, this new-style machine, unlike the old ones, has a strong interest in issues, especially at the national level. In this sense it is not a machine at all, but a cross between a machine and an ideological party.

Ideological Parties

At the opposite extreme from the machine is the **ideological party.** Where the machine values winning above all else, the ideological party values principle above all else. Where the former depends on money incentives, the latter spurns them. Where the former is hierarchical and disciplined, the latter is usually contentious and factionalized.

The most firmly ideological parties have been independent "third parties," such as the Socialist, Socialist Workers, Libertarian, and Right-to-Life parties. But there have been ideological factions within the Democratic and Republican parties as well, and in some places these ideological groups have taken over the regular parties.

In the 1950s and 1960s these ideological groups were "reform clubs" within local Democratic and Republican parties. In Los Angeles, New York, and many parts of Wisconsin and Minnesota issue-oriented activists fought to take over the party from election-oriented regulars. Democratic reform clubs managed to defeat the head of Tammany Hall in Manhattan; similar activist groups became the dominant force in California state politics.[7] Democratic club leaders were more liberal than rank-and-file Democrats, and Republican club leaders were often more conservative than rank-and-file Republicans.

The 1960s and 1970s saw these "reform" movements replaced by more focused social movements. The "reform" movement was based on a generalized sense of liberalism (among Democrats) or conservatism (among Republicans). With the advent of social movements concerned with civil rights, peace, feminism, environmentalism, libertarianism, and abortion, the generalized ideology of the clubs was replaced by the specific ideological demands of single-issue activists.

Today, for example, the Christian Coalition is an active group within the Republican party. Strongly pro-life and conservative on social issues, these religiously oriented Republican party activists were influential in the early 1990s in everything from local school board races to congressional races.

The result is that in many places the party has become a collection of people drawn from various social movements. For a candidate to win the party's support, he or she often has to satisfy the "litmus test" demands of the ideological activists in the party. Democratic senator Barbara Mikulski put it this way: "The social movements are now our farm clubs."

With social movements as their farm clubs, the big-league teams—the Democrats and Republicans at the state level—behave very differently than they did when political machines were the farm clubs. Internal factionalism is more intense, and the freedom of action of the party leader (say, the chairperson of the state committee) has been greatly reduced. A leader who demands too little or gives up too much, or who says the wrong thing on a key issue, is quickly accused of having "sold out." Under these circumstances many "leaders" are that in name only.

Solidary Groups

Many people who participate in state and local politics do so not in order to earn money or vindicate some cause, but simply because they find it fun. They enjoy the game, they meet interesting people, and they like the sense of being "in the know" and rubbing shoulders with the powerful. When people get together out of gregarious or game-loving instincts, we say that they are responding to **solidary incentives;** if they form an organization, it is a solidary association.

Some of these associations were once machines. When a machine loses its patronage, some of its members—especially the older ones—may continue to serve in the organization out of a desire for camaraderie. In other cases precinct, ward, and district committees are built up on the basis of friendship networks. One study of political activists in Detroit found that most of them mentioned friendships and a liking for politics, rather than an interest in issues, as their reasons for joining the party organization.[8] Members of ward and town organizations in St. Louis County gave the same answers when asked why they joined.[9] Since patronage has declined in value and since the appeals of ideology are limited to a minority of citizens, the motivations for participating in politics have become very much like those for joining a bowling league or a bridge club.

The advantage of such groups is that they are neither corrupt nor inflexible; the disadvantage is that they often do not work very hard. Knocking on doors on a rainy November evening to try to talk people into voting for your candidate is a chore under the best of circumstances; it is especially unappealing if you joined the party primarily because you like to attend meetings or drink coffee with your friends.[10]

Sponsored Parties

Sometimes a relatively strong party organization can be created among volunteers without heavy reliance on money or ideology and without depending entirely on people's finding the work fun. This type of **sponsored party** occurs when another organization exists in the community that can create, or at least sponsor, a local party structure. The clearest example of this is the Democratic party in and around Detroit, which has been developed, led, and to a degree financed by the political-action arm of the United Auto Workers union. The UAW has had a long tradition of rank-and-file activism, stemming from its formative struggles in the 1930s, and since the city is virtually a one-industry town, it was not hard to transfer some of this activism from union organizing to voter organizing.

By the mid-1950s union members and leaders made up over three-fourths of all the Democratic

The personal following of former President George Bush was passed on to his sons, George W. (left) and Jeb (right), both of whom were successful in major elections.

party district leaders within the city.[11] On election day union funds were available for paying workers to canvass voters; between elections political work on an unpaid basis was expected of union leaders. Though the UAW-Democratic party alliance in Detroit has not always been successful in city elections (the city is nonpartisan), it has been quite successful in carrying the city for the Democratic party in state and national elections.

Not many areas have organizations as effective or as dominant as the UAW that can bolster, sponsor, or even take over the weak formal party structure. Thus sponsored local parties are not common in the United States.

Personal Following

Because most candidates can no longer count on the backing of a machine, because sponsored parties are limited to a few unionized areas, and because solidary groups are not always productive, a person wanting to get elected will often try to form a **personal following** that will work for him or her during a campaign and then disband until the next election rolls around. Sometimes a candidate tries to meld a personal following with an ideological group, especially during the primary election campaign, when candidates need the kind of financial backing and hard work that only highly motivated activists are likely to supply.

To form a personal following, the candidate must have an appealing personality, a lot of friends, or a big bank account. The Kennedy family has all three, and the electoral success of the personal followings of John F. Kennedy, Edward M. Kennedy, Robert Kennedy, and Joseph P. Kennedy II are legendary. President George Bush also established such a following. After he left office, one son (Jeb) became governor of Florida and another one (George W.) became governor of Texas and Republican presidential nominee.

Southern politicians who have to operate in one-party states with few, if any, machines have become grand masters at building personal followings, such as those of the Talmadge family in Georgia, the Long family in Louisiana, and the Byrd family in Virginia. But the strategy is increasingly followed wherever party organization is weak. The key asset is to have a known political name. That has helped the electoral victories of the son of Hubert Humphrey in Minnesota, the son and daughter of Pat Brown in California, the son of Birch Bayh in Indiana, the son of George Wallace in Alabama, and the son and grandson of Robert La Follette in Wisconsin.

The traditional party organization—one that is hierarchical, lasting, based on material incentives, and capable of influencing who gets nominated for office—exists today, according to political scientist David Mayhew, in only about eight states, mostly the older states of the Northeast. Another five states, he feels, have faction-ridden versions of the traditional party organization.[12] The states in the rest of the country display the weak party system of solidary clubs, personal followings, ideological groups, and sponsored parties. What that means can be seen in the composition of recent Democratic national conventions. More than half of the delegates have been drawn from the ranks of the AFL-CIO, the National Education Association, and the National Organization for Women.[13]

The Two-Party System

With so many different varieties of local party organizations (or nonorganizations), and with such a great range of opinion found within each party, it is remarkable that we have had only two major political parties for most of our history. In the world at large a **two-party system** is a rarity; by one estimate only fifteen nations have one.[14] Most European democracies are multiparty systems. We have only two parties with any chance of winning nationally, and these parties have been, over time, rather evenly balanced—between 1888

Table 7.2 The Rise of Republican Politics in the South, 1956–2000

Year	Number of Representatives		Number of Senators		Number of Governors		Number of States Voting for Presidential Nominee	
	Dem.	Rep.	Dem.	Rep.	Dem.	Rep.	Dem.	Rep.
1956	99	7	22	0	11	0	6	5
1958	99	7	22	0	11	0	—	—
1960	99	7	22	0	11	0	8[a]	2
1962	95	11	21	1	11	0	—	—
1964	89	17	21	1	11	0	6	5
1966	83	23	19	3	9	2	—	—
1968	80	26	18	4	9	2	1	5[b]
1970	79	27	16 (1)[c]	5	9	2	—	—
1972	74	34	14 (1)[c]	7	8	3	0	11
1974	81	27	15 (1)[c]	6	8	3	—	—
1976	82	26	16 (1)[c]	5	9	2	10	1
1978	77	31	15 (1)[c]	6	8	3	—	—
1980	55	53	11 (1)[c]	10	6	5	1	10
1982	80	33	11	11	11	0	—	—
1984	72	41	11	11	10	1	0	11
1986	77	39	16	6	6	5	—	—
1988	80	36	15	7	6	5	0	11
1990	77	39	15	7	8	3	—	—
1992	82	43	14	8	8	3	4	7
1994	61	64	9	13	5	6	—	—
1996	54	71	9	13	4	7	4	7
1998	54	71	8	14	4	7	—	—
2000	54	71	7	15	6	5	0	11

[a]Eight Mississippi electors voted for Harry Byrd.

[b]George Wallace won five states on the American Independent ticket.

[c]Harry Byrd, Jr., was elected in Virginia in 1970 and 1976 as an independent.

and 1996, the Republicans won fifteen presidential elections and the Democrats thirteen. Furthermore, whenever one party has achieved a temporary ascendancy and its rival has been pronounced dead (as were the Democrats in the first third of this century and the Republicans during the 1930s and the 1960s), the "dead" party has displayed remarkable powers of recuperation, coming back to win important victories.

At the state and congressional district levels, however, the parties are not evenly balanced. For a long time the South was so heavily Democratic at all levels of government as to be a one-party area, while upper New England and the Dakotas were strongly Republican. All regions are more competitive today than once was the case, but even now one party tends to enjoy a substantial advantage in at least half the states and in perhaps two-thirds of the congres-

sional districts. Nevertheless, though the parties are not as competitive in state elections as they are in presidential ones, states have rarely had, at least for any extended period, politcal parties other than the Democratic and Republican (see Table 7.2).

Scholars do not entirely agree on why the two-party system should be so permanent a feature of American political life, but two explanations are of major importance. The first has to do with the system of elections, the second with the distribution of public opinion.

Elections at every level of government are based on the plurality, winner-take-all method. The **plurality system** means that in all elections for representative, senator, governor, or president, and in almost all elections for state legislator, mayor, or city councillor, the winner is that person who gets the *most* votes, even if he or she does not get a *majority*

Table 7.3 Party Voting in Presidential Elections

Party Affiliation of Voter	1984		1988		1992			1996		
	Dem.	Rep.	Dem.	Rep.	Dem.	Rep.	Ind.	Dem.	Rep.	Ind.
Democrat	79%	21%	85%	15%	82%	8%	10%	84%	10%	5%
Republican	4	96	7	93	7	77	16	13	80	6
Independent	33	67	43	57	39	30	31	43	35	17

Source: Gallup poll, as reported in Harold W. Stanley and Richard G. Niemi, *Vital Statistics on American Politics,* 6th ed. (Washington, D.C.: Congressional Quarterly Press, 1998), 128.

of all votes cast. We are so familiar with this system that we sometimes forget that there are other ways of running an election. For example, one could require that the winner get a majority of the votes, thus producing runoff elections if nobody got a majority on the first try. France does this in choosing its national legislature. In the first election candidates for parliament who win an absolute majority of the votes cast are declared elected. A week later remaining candidates who received at least one-eighth but less than one-half of the vote go into a runoff election; those who then win an absolute majority are also declared elected.

The French method encourages many political parties to form, each hoping to win at least one-eighth of the vote in the first election and then to enter into an alliance with its ideologically nearest rival in order to win the runoff. In the United States the plurality system means that a party must make all the alliances it can before the first election—there is no second chance. Hence every party must be as broadly based as possible; a narrow, minor party has no hope of winning.

The winner-take-all feature of American elections has the same effect. Only one member of Congress is elected from each district. In many European countries the elections are based on proportional representation. Each party submits a list of candidates for parliament, ranked in order of preference by the party leaders. The nation votes. A party winning 37 percent of the vote gets 37 percent of the seats in parliament; a party winning 2 percent of the vote gets 2 percent of the seats. Since even the smallest parties have a chance of winning something, minor parties have an incentive to organize.

The most dramatic example of the winner-take-all principle is the electoral college (see pages 338–341). In every state but Maine and Nebraska,

the candidate who wins the most popular votes in a state wins *all* of that state's electoral votes. In 1992, for example, Bill Clinton won only 45 percent of the popular vote in Missouri, but he got all of Missouri's eleven electoral votes because his two rivals (George Bush and Ross Perot) each got fewer popular votes. Minor parties cannot compete under this system. Voters are often reluctant to "waste" their votes on a minor-party candidate who cannot win.

The United States has experimented with other electoral systems. Proportional representation was used for municipal elections in New York City at one time and is still in use for that purpose in Cambridge, Massachusetts. Many states have elected more than one state legislator from each district. In Illinois, for example, three legislators have been elected from each district, with each voter allowed to cast two votes, thus virtually guaranteeing that the minority party will be able to win one of the three seats. But none of these experiments has altered the national two-party system, probably because of the existence of a directly elected president chosen by a winner-take-all electoral college.

The presidency is the great prize of American politics; to win it you must form a party with as broad appeal as possible. As a practical matter that means there will be, in most cases, only two serious parties—one made up of those who support the party already in power, and the other made up of everybody else. Only one third party ever won the presidency—the Republicans in 1860—and it had by then pretty much supplanted the Whig party. No third party is likely to win, or even come close to winning, the presidency anytime soon. Despite the decline in mass party attachment, among Americans who actually vote in presidential elections, party voting is almost as strong today as it was in the early 1950s. As Table 7.3 shows, in the

Table 7.4 The Public Rates the Two Parties		
Question *Do you think the Republican party or the Democratic party would do a better job of dealing with each of the following issues and problems?*		
	Democrats	**Republicans**
Advantage Republicans		
National defense*	37%	53%
Foreign trade	35	48
Crime	36	43
Campaign finance reform	31	37
Split Between the Parties		
Economic prosperity	44	42
Taxes	43	42
Advantage Democrats		
Poverty*	61	27
Environment	54	31
Health care	51	34
Social Security	46	35

*Question on this item asked as "Which party, the Democrats or the Republicans, do you trust to do a better job on . . . ?"

Source: The Public Perspective (April/May 1998): 13, reporting the results of a survey by the Gallup Organization for CNN/*USA Today,* October 27–28, 1997, and a survey by ABC News/*Washington Post,* January 15–19, 1998.

presidential elections of 1984 through 1996 the vast majority of Democrats voted for the Democrat, and the vast majority of Republicans voted for the Republican. Meanwhile, most independents voted for the winning Republican in 1984 and 1988, and pluralities of independents voted for the winning Democrat in 1992 and 1996.

The second explanation for the persistence of the two-party system is to be found in the opinions of the voters. There remains a kind of rough parity between the two parties regarding which of them most citizens think is likely to govern best on given issues. For example, in public opinion surveys conducted in 1997 and 1998, respondents favored the Republicans over the Democrats on national defense and crime, favored the Democrats over the Republicans on poverty and the environment, and were split evenly between the two parties on taxes and economic prosperity (see Table 7.4).

Though there have been periods of bitter dissent, most of the time most citizens have agreed enough to permit them to come together into two broad coalitions. There has not been a massive and persistent body of opinion that has rejected the prevailing economic system (and thus we have not had a Marxist party with mass appeal); there has not been in our history an aristocracy or monarchy (and thus there has been no party that has sought to restore aristocrats or monarchs to power). Churches and religion have almost always been regarded as matters of private choice that lie outside politics (and thus there has not been a party seeking to create or abolish special government privileges for one church or another). In some European nations the organization of the economy, the prerogatives of the monarchy, and the role of the church have been major issues with long and bloody histories. So divisive have these issues been that they have helped prevent the formation of broad coalition parties.

But Americans have had other deep divisions—between white and black, for example, and between North and South—and yet the two-party system has endured. This suggests that our electoral procedures are of great importance—the winner-take-all, plurality election rules have made it useless for anyone to attempt to create an all-white or an all-black national party except as an act of momentary defiance or in the hope of taking enough votes away from the two major parties to force the presidential election into the House of Representatives. (That may have been George Wallace's strategy in 1968.)

For many years there was an additional reason for the two-party system: the laws of many states made it difficult, if not impossible, for third parties to get on the ballot. In 1968, for example, the American Independent party of George Wallace found that it would have to collect 433,000 signatures (15 percent of the votes cast in the last statewide election) in order to get on the presidential ballot in Ohio. Wallace took the issue to the Supreme Court, which ruled, six to three, that such a restriction was an unconstitutional violation of the equal-protection clause of the Fourteenth Amendment.[15] Wallace got on the ballot. In 1980 John Anderson, running as an independent, was able to get on the ballot in all fifty states; in 1992 Ross Perot did the same. But for the reasons already indicated, the two-party system will probably persist even without the aid of legal restrictions.

Minor Parties

The electoral system may prevent minor parties from winning, but it does not prevent them from forming. Minor parties—usually called, erroneously, "third parties"—have been a permanent feature of American political life. Four major kinds of minor parties, with examples of each, are described in the box on page 170.

The minor parties that have endured have been the ideological ones. Their members feel themselves to be outside the mainstream of American political life and sometimes, as in the case of various Marxist parties, look forward to a time when a revolution or some other dramatic change in the political system will vindicate them. They are usually not interested in immediate electoral success and thus persist despite their poor showing at the polls. One such party, however, the Socialist party of Eugene Debs, won nearly 6 percent of the popular vote in the 1912 presidential election and during its heyday elected some twelve hundred candidates to local offices, including seventy-nine mayors. Part of the Socialist appeal arose from its opposition to municipal corruption, part from its opposition to American entry into World War I, and part from its critique of American society. No ideological party has ever carried a state in a presidential election.

Apart from the Republicans, who quickly became a major party, the only minor parties to carry states and thus win electoral votes were one party of economic protest (the Populists, who carried five states in 1892) and several factional parties (most recently, the States' Rights Democrats in 1948 and the American Independent party of George Wallace in 1968). Though factional parties may hope to cause the defeat of the party from which they split, they have not always been able to achieve this. Harry Truman was elected in 1948 despite the defections of both the leftist progressives, led by Henry Wallace, and the right-wing Dixiecrats, led by J. Strom Thurmond. In 1968 it seems likely that Hubert Humphrey would have lost even if George Wallace had not been in the race (Wallace voters would probably have switched to Nixon rather than to Humphrey, though of course one cannot be certain). It is quite possible, on the other hand, that a Republican might have beaten Woodrow Wilson in 1912 if the Republican party had not split in two (the regulars supporting William Howard Taft, the progressives supporting Theodore Roosevelt).

When Jesse Ventura became governor of Minnesota, the Reform party finally elected someone to an important office.

What is striking is not that we have had so many minor parties but that we have not had more. There have been several major political movements that did not produce a significant third party: the civil rights movement of the 1960s, the antiwar movement of the same decade, and, most important, the labor movement of the twentieth century. African Americans were part of the Republican party after the Civil War and part of the Democratic party after the New Deal (even though the southern wing of that party for a long time kept them from voting). The antiwar movement found candidates with whom it could identify within the Democratic party (Eugene McCarthy, Robert F. Kennedy, George McGovern), even though it was a Democratic president, Lyndon B. Johnson, who was chiefly responsible for the U.S. commitment in Vietnam. After Johnson only narrowly won the 1968

Types of Minor Parties

Ideological parties: Parties professing a comprehensive view of American society and government that is radically different from that of the established parties. Most have been Marxist in outlook, but some are quite the opposite, such as the Libertarian party.

Examples:
Socialist party (1901 to 1960s)
Socialist Labor party (1888 to present)
Socialist Workers party (1938 to present)
Communist party (1920s to present)
Libertarian party (1972 to present)

One-issue parties: Parties seeking a single policy, usually revealed by their names, and avoiding other issues.

Examples:
Free-Soil party—to prevent the spread of slavery (1848–1852)
American or "Know-Nothing" party—to oppose immigration and Catholics (1856)
Prohibition party—to ban the sale of liquor (1869 to present)
Woman's party—to obtain the right to vote for women (1913–1920)

Economic-protest parties: Parties, usually based in a particular region, especially involving farmers, that protest against depressed economic conditions. These tend to disappear as conditions improve.

Examples:
Greenback party (1876–1884)
Populist party (1892–1908)

Factional parties: Parties that are created by a split in a major party, usually over the identity and philosophy of the major party's presidential candidate.

Examples:
Split off from the Republican party:
  "Bull Moose" Progressive party (1912)
  La Follette Progressive party (1924)
Split off from the Democratic party:
  States' Rights ("Dixiecrat") party (1948)
  Henry Wallace Progressive party (1948)
  American Independent (George Wallace) party (1968)
Split off from both Democrats and Republicans:
  Reform party (Ross Perot)

New Hampshire primary, he withdrew from the race. Unions have not tried to create a labor party—indeed, they were for a long time opposed to almost any kind of national political activity. Since labor became a major political force in the 1930s, the largest industrial unions have been content to operate as a part (a very large part) of the Democratic party.

One reason why some potential sources of minor parties never formed such parties, in addition to the dim chance of success, is that the direct primary and the national convention have made it possible for dissident elements of a major party, unless they become completely disaffected, to remain in the party and influence the choice of candidates and policies. The antiwar movement had a profound effect on the Democratic conventions of 1968 and 1972; African Americans have played a growing role in the Democratic party, especially with the candidacy of Jesse Jackson in 1984 and 1988; only in 1972 did the unions feel that the Democrats nominated a presidential candidate (McGovern) unacceptable to them.

The impact of minor parties on American politics is hard to judge. One bit of conventional wisdom holds that minor parties develop ideas that the major parties later come to adopt. The Socialist party, for example, is supposed to have called for major social and economic policies that the Democrats under Roosevelt later embraced and termed the New Deal. It is possible that the Democrats did steal the thunder of the Socialists, but it hardly seems likely that they did it because the Socialists had proposed these

The Socialist party and the Progressive party were both minor parties, but their origins were different. The Socialist party was an ideological party; the "Bull Moose" Progressive party split off from the Republicans to support Theodore Roosevelt.

things or proved them popular. (In 1932 the Socialists got only 2 percent of the vote and in 1936 less than one-half of 1 percent.) Roosevelt probably adopted the policies he did in part because he thought them correct and in part because dissident elements within his *own* party—leaders such as Huey Long of Louisiana—were threatening to bolt the Democratic party if it did not move to the left. Even Prohibition was adopted more as a result of the efforts of interest groups such as the Anti-Saloon League than as the consequence of its endorsement by the Prohibition party.

The minor parties that have probably had the greatest influence on public policy have been the factional parties. Mugwumps and liberal Republicans, by bolting the regular party, may have made that party more sensitive to the issue of civil service reform; the Bull Moose and La Follette Progressive parties probably helped encourage the major parties

to pay more attention to issues of business regulation and party reform; the Dixiecrat and Wallace movements probably strengthened the hands of those who wished to go slow on desegregation. The threat of a factional split is a risk that both major parties must face, and it is in the efforts that each makes to avoid such splits that one finds the greatest impact, at least in this century, of minor parties.

In 1992 and again in 1996, Ross Perot led the most successful recent third-party movement. Begun as United We Stand America and later renamed the Reform party, Perot's appeal seemed to reflect a growing American dissatisfaction with the existing political parties and a heightened demand for bringing in a leader who would "run the government without politics." Of course it is no more possible to take politics out of governing than it is to take churches out of religion. Though unrealistic, people seem to want policies without bargaining.

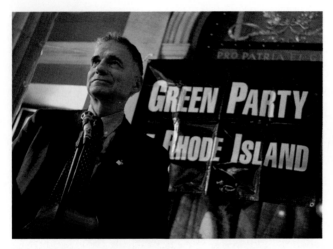

Ralph Nader campaigned in 2000 as a candidate of the Green party.

Nominating a President

The major parties face, as we have seen, two contrary forces: one, generated by the desire to win the presidency, pushes them in the direction of nominating a candidate who can appeal to the majority of voters and who will thus have essentially middle-of-the-road views. The other, produced by the need to keep dissident elements in the party from bolting and forming a third party, leads them to compromise with dissidents or extremists in ways that may damage the party's standing with the voters.

The Democrats and Republicans have always faced these conflicting pressures, but of late they have become especially acute. When the presidential nomination was made by a party convention that was heavily influenced, if not controlled, by party leaders and elected officials, it was relatively easy to ignore dissident factions and pick candidates on the basis of who could win. The *electoral* objectives of the party were predominant. The result was that often a faction left the party and ran a separate ticket—as in 1912, 1924, 1948, 1968, and 1980. Today the power of party leaders and elected officials within the parties is greatly diminished, with most delegates now selected by primary elections. A larger proportion of the delegates is likely to be more interested in issues and to be less amenable to compromise over those issues than formerly. In these circumstances the *policy* interests of the party activists are likely to be important.

Are the Delegates Representative of the Voters?

There would be no conflict between the electoral and policy interests of a political party if the delegates to its nominating convention had the same policy views as most voters, or at least as most party supporters. In fact this is not the case: in parties, as in many organizations, the activists and leaders tend to have views different from those of the rank and file.[16] In American political parties in recent years this difference has become very great.

In 1964 the Republican party nominated the highly conservative Barry Goldwater for president. We have no opinion data for delegates to that convention as detailed and comprehensive as those available for subsequent conventions, but it seems clear that the Republican delegates selected as their nominee a person who was not the most popular candidate among voters at large and thus not the candidate most likely to win.

At every Democratic national convention since 1972 the delegates have had views on a variety of important issues that were vastly different from those of rank-and-file Democrats. On welfare, military policy, school desegregation, crime, and abortion, Democratic delegates expressed opinions almost diametrically opposed to those of most Democrats. The delegates to the 1980, 1984, and (to a lesser extent) 1988, 1992, and 1996 conventions were ideologically very different from the voters at large. The Democratic delegates were more liberal than the Democratic voters, and the Republican delegates were more conservative than the Republican voters (see Table 7.5).[17]

What accounts for the sharp disparity between delegate opinion (and often delegate candidate preference) and voter attitudes? Some blame the discrepancy on the rules, described earlier in this chapter, under which Democratic delegates are chosen, especially those that require increased representation for women, minorities, and the young. Close examination suggests that this is not a complete explanation. For one thing, it does not explain why the Republicans nominated Goldwater in 1964 (and almost nominated Ronald Reagan instead of Gerald Ford in 1976). For another, women, minorities, and youth have among them all shades of opinions: there are many middle-of-the-road women and young people, as well as very liberal or very conservative ones. (There are not many very conservative African

Americans, at least on race issues, but there are certainly plenty who are moderate on race and conservative on other issues.) The question is why only *certain* elements of these groups are heavily represented at the conventions.

Who Votes in Primaries?

Maybe delegates are unrepresentative of the party rank and file because they are chosen in caucuses and primary elections whose participants are unrepresentative. Before 1972 most delegates were picked by party leaders; primaries were relatively unimportant, and voter caucuses were almost unheard-of. Adlai Stevenson in 1952 and Hubert Humphrey in 1968 won the Democratic presidential nominations without even entering a primary. Harry Truman once described primaries as "eyewash."[18]

After 1972 they were no longer eyewash. The vast majority of delegates were selected in primaries and caucuses. In 1992 forty states and territories held primaries, and twenty held caucuses (some places had both primaries and caucuses).

Only about half as many people vote in primaries as in general elections. If these primary voters have more extreme political views than do the rank-and-file party followers, then they might support presidential delegates who also have extreme views. However, there is not much evidence that such is the case. Studies comparing the ideological orientations of primary voters with those of rank-and-file party voters show few strong differences.[19]

When it comes to presidential primaries, a good fight draws a crowd. For example, in twelve of the first eighteen Republican presidential primaries in 2000, voter turnout hit record highs as Governor George W. Bush battled state by state to stay ahead of Senator John McCain. But the "crowd" represented only 13.6 percent of the voting-age population, up 4.3 percent from the 1996 turnout, and the highest since Senator Barry Goldwater's campaign for the nomination divided Republicans in 1964.[20] In the states that voted after Bush had the nomination all but won, turnout was considerably lower. Likewise, the contest between Vice President Al Gore and Senator Bill Bradley resulted in the second-lowest Democratic presidential primary turnout since 1960.

Primaries differ from caucuses. A **caucus** is a meeting of party followers, often lasting for hours and held in the dead of winter in a schoolhouse

Table 7.5	How Party Delegates and Party Voters Differ in Liberal Ideology			
Liberal Ideology	1984	1988	1992	1996
Democrats				
Delegates	66%	39%	47%	43%
Voters	31	25	28	27
Republicans				
Delegates	2	1	1	0
Voters	15	12	12	7

Sources: For 1984: *Los Angeles Times* (August 19, 1984); for 1988: *New York Times*/CBS News poll, in *New York Times* (August 14, 1988); for 1992: *New York Times* (July 13 and August 17, 1992) and unpublished CBS News poll, "The 1992 Republican Convention Delegates"; for 1996: *New York Times* (August 12 and 26, 1996).

miles from home, in which party delegates are picked. Only the most dedicated partisans attend. For the Democrats these have been liberals; for the Republicans conservatives. In 1988 the most liberal Democratic candidate, Jesse Jackson, got more delegates in the Alaska, Delaware, Michigan, and Vermont caucuses than did Michael Dukakis, the eventual nominee. Republican evangelist Pat Robertson did not win any primary, but he won the caucuses in Alaska, Hawaii, and Washington.

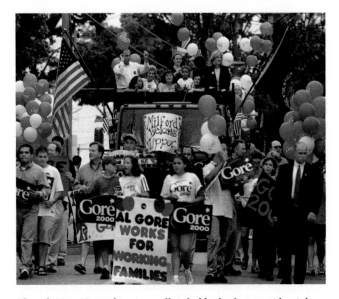

Though New Hampshire is small, it holds the first presidential primary, and so it produces a lot of election hoopla.

Who Are the New Delegates?

However delegates are chosen, they are a different breed today than they once were. Whether picked by caucuses or primaries, and whatever their sex and race, a far larger proportion of convention delegates, both Republican and Democratic, are issue-oriented activists—people with an "amateur" or "purist" view of politics. Far fewer delegates are in it for the money (there is no longer much patronage to pass around) or to help their own reelection prospects. For example, in 1980 only 14 percent of the Democratic senators and 15 percent of the Democratic members of the House were delegates to the national convention. In 1956, by contrast, 90 percent of the senators and 33 percent of the representatives were delegates.[21]

Party activists, especially those who work without pay and who are in politics out of an interest in issues, are not likely to resemble the average citizen, for whom politics is merely an object of observation, discussion, and occasional voting. In 1972 such activists at the Democratic convention were most likely to support one of the two candidates with the strongest ideological appeal—McGovern or Wallace—and least likely to support those candidates that represented party regularity (Edmund Muskie and Hubert Humphrey).[22] It seems likely that the same thing was true at the Republican conventions of 1964, 1976, and 1980; the activists favored the more ideological candidates.

The changing incentives for participation in party work, in addition to the effects of the primary system, have contributed to the development of a national presidential nominating system different from that which once existed. The advantage of the new system is that it increases the opportunity for those with strong policy preferences to play a role in the party and thus reduces the chance that they will bolt the party and form a factional minor party. The disadvantage of the system is that it increases the chances that one or both parties may nominate presidential candidates who are not appealing to the average voter or even to a party's rank and file.

In sum presidential nominating conventions are now heavily influenced by ideologically motivated activists. Democratic conventions have heavy representation from organized feminists, unionized schoolteachers, and abortion rights activists; Republican conventions have large numbers of antiabortion activists, Christian conservatives, and small-government libertarians. As a result the presidential nominating system is now fundamentally different from what it was as late as the mid-1960s.

Parties Versus Voters

Since 1968 the Democratic party has had no trouble winning congressional elections but great difficulty winning presidential contests. Except for 1980–1986 and since 1994, the Democrats have controlled both houses of Congress; except for 1976, 1992, and 1996, they have lost every presidential election. The Republican party has had the opposite problem: though it won five out of seven presidential elections between 1968 and 1992, it did not control Congress for the forty years preceding its big win in 1994.

There are many reasons for this odd state of affairs, most of which will be discussed later. But one requires attention here. The difficulty the Democrats have had in competing for the presidency is in part because their candidates for the presidency have had, on certain issues—chiefly social and taxation issues—views very different from those of the average voter. That disparity to a large degree mirrors (and may be caused by) the gulf that separates the opinions of delegates to Democratic nominating conventions from the opinions of most citizens.

The Republicans have not been immune to this problem. In 1964 they nominated a candidate, Barry Goldwater, whose beliefs placed him well to the right of most voters. Not surprisingly, he lost. And the delegates to recent Republican conventions have held opinions on some matters that continue to be very different from most people's. Still, the problem has been more acute for the Democrats.

The problem can be seen in Table 7.6. A lot of information is shown there; to understand it, study the table step by step. First, look at the middle column, which summarizes the views of voters in 1996. (Because there are about the same number of Democratic and Republican voters, the opinion of the average voter is about halfway between those of the followers of the two parties.) Now look at the columns on the far left and the far right. These show the views of delegates to the 1996 Democratic and Republican conventions. On almost every issue the delegates are in sharp disagreement. There were hardly any conservatives at the Democratic convention or liberals at the Republican convention. On every social issue and

MEMORANDUM

To: Harry Bower, president of Republicans for Life
From: Patricia Nucanon, political consultant
Subject: Forming a third party

Without regard to your organization's particular cause or issue, I have been employed to brief you on the general pros and cons of backing independent candidates and forming a third party.

Arguments for:
1. Independent and third-party candidates can garner votes and even win. In 1992 independent candidate Ross Perot won nearly a fifth of the vote for president. In 1998 the Reform party candidate Jesse Ventura became governor of Minnesota.
2. Even losing independent candidates (Eugene Debs, Robert La Follette, and George Wallace, to name just three) have made real marks on American politics. "Unsuccessful" third parties were the first to advocate policy positions later championed by the two main parties: abolishing slavery (Free-Soil party), giving women the vote (Woman's Party), the direct election of senators (Progressive party), and many others.
3. Splitting off from a major party courts public attention and eventually gets policy results.

Arguments against:
1. The two-party system is supported by more than 150 years of political tradition featuring winner-take-all, single-member election districts. Since the 1850s more than 100 third parties and thousands of independent candidates have come, gone, and been forgotten by all except historians.
2. Usually the two main parties adapt and co-opt, not adopt, third-party ideas and positions. In the 1930s the Democrats watered down the Socialist party's plan and gave birth to the Social Security system. In the 1980s the Republican position on tax relief was but a faint echo of the Libertarian party's.
3. Splitting off from a major party courts political oblivion and reduces the chances that the issue or cause will be raised or represented even halfheartedly by either main party.

Your decision:
Favor a third party _____
Oppose third party _____

Pro-Life Group Threatens to Bolt GOP

February 1
HARRISBURG, PA
At a televised press conference last week several top Republican officials called for "moderating" their party's pro-life platform. Yesterday a leading antiabortion political action committee responded by running full-page newspaper ads calling for "independent candidates and a third party to represent the views" of pro-life Republicans and Democrats alike" . . .

Table 7.6   Political Opinions of Delegates and Voters, 1996

	Democratic Delegates	Voters	Republican Delegates
Who They Are			
Male	47%	46%	64%
Female	53	54	36
White	71	84	91
Black	17	11	3
Income over $75,000	46	11	47
What They Think			
Abortion should be permitted in all cases.	61	27	11
Government should do more to solve national problems.	76	36	4
Trade restrictions are necessary to protect domestic industries.	54	60	31
Government should protect traditional values.	27	42	56
Laws are necessary to protect racial minorities.	88	51	30
There should be a nationwide ban on assault weapons.	91	72	34
Most affirmative action programs should be continued.	81	45	9
Children of illegal immigrants should be allowed to attend public schools.	79	54	26

Source: New York Times/CBS News polls, as reported in New York Times (August 12 and 26, 1996).

every tax orspending issue, the delegates were at opposite ends of the spectrum.

Still, either party can win if its delegates nominate a candidate whose views put him or her closer to the average citizen than to the average delegate or if the campaign is fought out over issues on which the delegates and the voters agree. For example, if the election turned on what to do about an economic recession, the delegates, the voters, and the candidate would probably all agree: do whatever is necessary to end the recession. Exactly that happened in 1992, and the Democrats won.

Of course, even without a scandal, recession, or some other unifying issue, the need to win an election will lead all candidates to move toward the middle of the road. That is where the votes are. But this creates a dilemma for a candidate of either party. The stance one takes to win support from party activists in the caucuses and primaries will often be quite different from the stance one should take to win votes from the general public. In the next chapter we shall look more closely at how politicians try to cope with that dilemma.

Summary

A political party exists in three arenas: among the voters who psychologically identify with it, as a grassroots organization staffed and led by activists, and as a group of elected officials who follow its lead in lawmaking. In this chapter we have looked at the party primarily as an organization and seen the various forms it takes at the local level—the machine, the ideological party, the solidary group, the sponsored party, and the personal following.

Nationally the parties are weak, decentralized coalitions of these local forms. As organizations that influence the political systems, parties are getting weaker. Voters no longer strongly identify with one of the major parties as they once did. The spread of the direct primary has made it harder for parties to control who is nominated for elective office, thus making it harder for the parties to influence the behavior of these people once elected. Delegate selection rules, especially in the Democratic party, have helped shift the center of power in the national nominating convention. Because of the changes in rules, power has moved away from officeholders and party regulars and toward the more ideological wings of the parties.

Minor parties have arisen from time to time, but the only ones that have affected the outcome of presidential elections have been those that represented a splinter group within one of the major parties (such as the Bull Moose Progressives). The two-party system is maintained, and minor parties are discouraged, by an election system (winner-take-all, plurality elections) that makes voters reluctant to waste a vote on a minor party and by the ability of potential minor parties to wield influence within a major party by means of the primary system.

In the next chapter we shall look at the role of parties in shaping voter attitudes, and in Chapter 11 we shall look at the role of parties in Congress. In each of these areas we will find more evidence of party decay.

World Wide Web Resources

- Democratic National Committee: www.democrats.org
- Republican National Committee: www.rnc.org
- Green party: www.greens.org
- Libertarian party: www.lp.org
- Reform party: www.reformparty.org

Key Terms

political party *p. 150*

mugwumps or
  progressives *p. 155*

national convention
  p. 157

national committee
  p. 157

congressional campaign
  committee *p. 157*

national chairman *p. 157*

superdelegates *p. 160*

political machine *p. 161*

ideological party *p. 163*

solidary incentives *p. 164*

sponsored party *p. 164*

personal following *p. 165*

two-party system *p. 165*

plurality system *p. 166*

caucus *p. 173*

Suggested Readings

Chambers, William Nisbet, and Walter Dean Burnham, eds. *The American Party Systems: Stages of Political Development.* 2nd ed. New York: Oxford University Press, 1975. Essays tracing the rise of the party system since the Founding.

Goldwin, Robert A., ed. *Political Parties in the Eighties.* Washington, D.C.: American Enterprise Institute, 1980. Essays evaluating parties and efforts at reform.

Kayden, Xandra, and Eddie Mahe, Jr. *The Party Goes On.* New York: Basic Books, 1985. How the two major parties have adjusted to new political conditions.

Key, V. O., Jr. *Southern Politics.* New York: Knopf, 1949. A classic account of the one-party South.

Mayhew, David R. *Placing Parties in American Politics.* Princeton, N.J.: Princeton University Press, 1986. A state-by-state description of state party organizations.

Polsby, Nelson W. *Consequences of Party Reform.* New York: Oxford University Press, 1983. Fine analysis of how changed party rules have affected the parties and the government.

Ranney, Austin. *Curing the Mischiefs of Faction: Party Reform in America.* Berkeley: University of California Press, 1975. History and analysis of party "reforms," with special attention to the 1972 changes in the Democratic party rules.

Riordan, William L. *Plunkitt of Tammany Hall.* New York: Knopf, 1948. (First published in 1905.) Insightful account of how an old-style party boss operated.

Schattschneider, E. E. *Party Government.* New York: Holt, Rinehart and Winston, 1942. An argument for a more disciplined and centralized two-party system.

Shafer, Byron E. *Quiet Revolution: The Struggle for the Democratic Party and the Shaping of Post-Reform Politics.* New York: Russell Sage Foundation, 1983. Detailed, insightful history of how the Democratic party came to be reformed.

Sundquist, James L. *Dynamics of the Party System.* Rev. ed. Washington, D.C.: Brookings Institution, 1983. History of the party system, emphasizing the impact of issues on voting.

Wilson, James Q. *The Amateur Democrat.* Chicago: University of Chicago Press, 1962. Analysis of the issue-oriented political clubs that rose in the 1950s and 1960s.

Elections and Campaigns

Enduring Questions

1. How have primaries and general election campaigns changed over the past century and a half?
2. What matters most in deciding who wins presidential and congressional elections?
3. What are valence issues, and why do average citizens tend to vote retrospectively?
4. Do elections really make a difference in what laws get passed?

Presidential Versus Congressional Campaigns
Running for President

Primary Versus General Campaigns
Two Kinds of Campaign Issues • Television, Debates, and Direct Mail

Money
The Sources of Campaign Money • Campaign Finance Rules • The Effects of the 1974 Reforms • Proposals for More Reform • Money and Winning

What Decides the Election?
Party • Issues, Especially the Economy • The Campaign • Finding a Winning Coalition

Election Outcomes
Party Realignments • Party Decline

The Effects of Elections on Policy

I f you want to be elected to Congress or to the presidency, you must develop a game plan that is in tune with the unique legal, political, and financial realities of American politics. A plan that will work here would be useless in almost any other democratic nation; one that would work abroad would be useless here.

Elections have two crucial phases—getting nominated and getting elected. Getting nominated means getting your name on the ballot. In the great majority of states winning your party's nomination for either the presidency or Congress requires an *individual* effort—*you* decide to run, *you* raise money, *you* and your friends collect signatures to get your name on the ballot, and *you* appeal to voters in primary elections on the basis of your personality and your definition of the issues. In most European nations winning your party's nomination for parliament involves an *organizational* decision—*the party* looks you over, *the party* decides whether to allow you to run, and *the party* puts your name on its list of candidates.

American political parties do play a role in determining the outcome of the final election, but even that role involves parties more as labels in the voters'

179

minds than as organizations that get out the vote. By contrast, many other democratic nations conduct campaigns that are almost entirely a contest between parties as organizations. In Israel and the Netherlands the names of the candidates for the legislature do not even appear on the ballot; only the party names are listed there. And even where candidate names are listed, as in Great Britain, the voters tend to vote "Conservative" or "Labour" more than they vote for Smith or Jones. European nations (except France) do not have a directly elected president; instead the head of the government—the prime minister—is selected by the party that has won the most seats in parliament.

At one time parties played a much larger role in elections in the United States than they do now. Until well into this century they determined, or powerfully influenced, who got nominated. In the early nineteenth century the members of Congress from a given party would meet in a caucus to pick their presidential candidate. After these caucus were replaced by national nominating conventions, the real power over presidential nominations was wielded by local party leaders, who came together (sometimes in the legendary "smoke-filled rooms") to choose the candidate, whom the rest of the delegates would then endorse.

Congressional candidates were often handpicked by powerful local party bosses. In the past people were much more likely to vote a straight party ticket than they are today.

Chapter 7 described the factors that weakened the parties' ability to control nominations. There is little chance that they will ever regain that control. Thus candidates are now pretty much on their own. So if you want to be a candidate, what do you do?

Presidential Versus Congressional Campaigns

Presidential and congressional races differ in important ways. The most obvious, of course, is size: more voters participate in the former than the latter contests, and so presidential candidates must work harder and spend more. But there are some less obvious differences that are equally important.

First, presidential races are more competitive than those for the House of Representatives. In the thirty-three elections from 1932 to 1996 the Republicans won control of the House only four times (12.5 percent of the time); in the seventeen presidential elections during the same period the Republicans won the White House on seven occasions (41 percent of the time). In the typical presidential race the winner gets less than 55 percent of the two-party vote; in the typical House race, the **incumbent** wins with over 60 percent of the vote. A president cannot serve more than two terms, so at least once every eight years you have a chance of running against a nonincumbent; members of Congress can serve for an unlimited number of terms, and so the chances are you will run against an incumbent. If you do, the odds are very much against you. Most years over 90 percent of all House incumbents who stand for reelection are reelected; in 1988 and 1998 *over 98 percent* retained their seats.

Second, a much smaller proportion of people vote in congressional races during off years (that is, when there is no presidential contest) than vote for president. This lower turnout (around 36 percent of the voting-age population) means that candidates in congressional races must be appealing to the more motivated and partisan voter.

Third, members of Congress can do things for their constituents that a president cannot. They take credit—sometimes deserved, sometimes not—for every grant, contract, bridge, canal, and highway that the federal government provides the district or state. They send letters (at the government's expense) to large fractions of their constituents and visit their districts every weekend. Presidents get little credit for district improvements and must rely on the mass media to communicate with voters.

Fourth, a candidate for Congress can deny that he or she is responsible for "the mess in Washington," even when the candidate is an incumbent. As we shall see in Chapter 11, incumbents tend to run as individuals, even to the point of denouncing the very Congress of which they are a part. An incumbent president can't get away with this; rightly or wrongly, he is often held responsible for whatever has gone wrong, not only in the government but in the nation as a whole.

These last three factors—low voter turnout, services to constituents, and the ability to duck responsibility—probably help explain why so high a percentage of congressional incumbents get reelected.

But they do not enjoy a completely free ride. Members of Congress who belong to the same party as the president often feel voters' anger about national affairs, particularly economic conditions. When the economy turns sour and a Republican is in the White House, Republican congressional candidates lose votes; if a Democrat is in the White House, Democratic congressional candidates lose votes.

At one time the **coattails** of a popular presidential candidate could help congressional candidates in his own party. But there has been a sharp decline in the value of presidential coattails; indeed, some scholars doubt that they still exist.

The net effect of all these factors is that, to a substantial degree, congressional elections have become independent of presidential ones. Though economic factors may still link the fate of a president and some members of his party, by and large the incumbent members of Congress enjoy enough of a cushion to protect them against whatever political storms engulf an unpopular president. This fact further reduces the meaning of party—members of Congress can get reelected even though their party's "leader" in the White House has lost popular support, and nonincumbent candidates for Congress may lose despite the fact that a very popular president from their party is in the White House.

Running for President

The first task facing anyone who wishes to be president is to get "mentioned" as someone who is of "presidential caliber." No one is quite sure why some people are mentioned and others are not. The journalist David Broder has suggested that somewhere there is "The Great Mentioner," who announces from time to time who is of presidential caliber (and only The Great Mentioner knows how big that caliber is).

But if The Great Mentioner turns out to be as unreal as the Easter Bunny, you have to figure out for yourself how to get mentioned. One way is to let it be known to reporters, "off the record," that you are thinking about running for president. Another is to travel around the country making speeches (Ronald Reagan, while working for General Electric, made a dozen or more speeches *a day* to audiences all over the country). Another way is to already have a famous name (John Glenn, the former astronaut, was in the public eye long before he declared for the presidency in 1984). Another way to get mentioned is to be identified with a major piece of legislation.

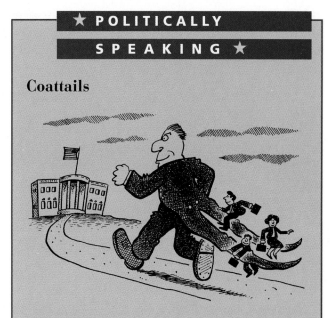

★ POLITICALLY SPEAKING ★

Coattails

Today the word is used in the sense of riding into office on the coattails of a better-known or more popular candidate. The political carrying power of coattails depends on the voters' casting a straight-ticket ballot so that their support for a popular presidential candidate is translated into support for lesser candidates on the same party ticket. Scholars are skeptical that such an effect exists today.

The word first came into popular usage in 1848, when Abraham Lincoln defended the Whig party's effort to take shelter under the military coattails of that party's presidential candidate, General Zachary Taylor. Lincoln argued that in the past the Democrats had run under the coattails of General Andrew Jackson.

Later the military connotation of *coattails* fell by the wayside, and the term came to mean any effort to obtain straight-ticket voting.

Source: Adapted from *Safire's Political Dictionary* by William Safire. Copyright © 1968, 1972, 1978 by William Safire. Reprinted by permission of Random House, Inc. and the author.

Senator Bill Bradley of New Jersey was known as an architect of the Tax Reform Act of 1986; Representative Richard Gephardt of Missouri was known as an author of a bill designed to reduce foreign imports. Still another way is to be the governor of a big state. New York governors, such as Mario Cuomo, are often viewed as presidential prospects,

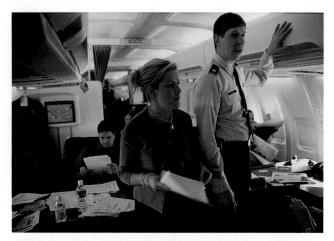

Political campaigns are hard work, even when you get to fly on the vice president's airplane.

partly because New York City is the headquarters of the television and publishing industries.

Once you are mentioned, it is wise to set aside a lot of time to run, especially if you are only "mentioned" as opposed to being really well known. Ronald Reagan devoted the better part of six years to running; Walter Mondale spent four years campaigning; Howard Baker resigned from the Senate in 1984 to prepare to run in 1988 (he finally dropped out of the race). However, most post-1988 candidates—senators Bob Dole, Tom Harkin, Bob Kerrey, and Paul Simon; governors Michael Dukakis, Bill Clinton, and George W. Bush; vice presidents George Bush and Al Gore; and House members Richard Gephardt and Jack Kemp—made the run while holding elective office.

Money   One reason why running takes so much time is that it takes so long to raise the necessary money and build up an organization of personal followers. As we shall see later in this chapter, federal law restricts the amount that any single individual can give a candidate to $1,000 in each election. (A **political action committee,** or PAC, which is a committee set up by and representing a corporation, labor union, or other special-interest group, can give up to $5,000.) Moreover, to be eligible for federal matching grants to pay for your primary campaign, you must first raise at least $5,000, in individual contributions of $250 or less, in each of twenty states.

Organization   Raising and accounting for this money requires a staff of fund-raisers, lawyers, and accountants. You also need a press secretary, a travel scheduler, an advertising specialist, a direct-mail company, and a pollster, all of whom must be paid, plus a large number of volunteers in at least those states that hold early primary elections or party caucuses. These volunteers will brief you on the facts of each state, try to line up endorsements from local politicians and celebrities, and put together a group of people who will knock on doors, make telephone calls, organize receptions and meetings, and try to keep you from mispronouncing the name of the town in which you are speaking. Finally, you have to assemble advisers on the issues. These advisers will write "position papers" for you on all sorts of things that you are supposed to know about (but probably don't). Because a campaign is usually waged around a few broad themes, these position papers rarely get used or even read. The papers exist so that you can show important interest groups that you have taken "sound" positions, so that you can be prepared to answer tough questions, and so that journalists can look up your views on matters that may become topical.

Strategy and Themes   Every candidate picks a strategy for the campaign. In choosing one, much depends on whether you are the incumbent. Incumbents must defend their records, like it or not. (An incumbent ran for president in 1964, 1972, 1976, 1980, 1984, 1992, and 1996.) The challenger attacks the incumbent. When there is no incumbent (as in 1960, 1968, 1988, and 2000), both candidates can announce their own programs; however, the candidate from the party that holds the White House must take, whether he thinks he deserves it or not, some of the blame for whatever has gone wrong in the preceding four years. Within these limits a strategy consists of the answers to questions about tone, theme, timing, and targets:

- What *tone* should the campaign have? Should it be a positive (build-me-up) or negative (attack-the-opponent) campaign? In 1988 George Bush began with a negative campaign; Michael Dukakis followed suit.
- What *theme* can I develop? A theme is a simple, appealing idea that can be repeated over and over again. For Jimmy Carter in 1976 it was "trust";

The Road to the Nomination

A campaign for the presidential nomination must begin early. Among the key steps are these.

Create an organization: A campaign manager, fund-raiser, pollster, and several lawyers and accountants must be hired early—two or even three years before the election. Money cannot legally be raised until an organization exists to receive and account for it.

Start raising money: To be eligible for federal matching dollars for your primary-election campaign, you must raise $250 from each of at least twenty donors in each of twenty states. You cannot receive more than $1,000 from any individual or $5,000 from any PAC. There are national and state-by-state limits on what you can spend.

Prepare for the early primaries and caucuses: To show that you are a serious contender and have "momentum," you should enter the early primaries and caucuses. In 1996 some key early ones were:

- February 12: Iowa caucus
- February 20: New Hampshire primary
- March 12: "Super Tuesday" (primaries in six states, mostly in the South)

- March 19: "Big 10 Tuesday" (primaries in the Midwest)

To win a primary you must campaign hard and often; to win a caucus you must have an organization that can get your supporters to attend and vote at the local caucus.

Pick a strategy: If you are relatively unknown, you must campaign heavily in the early primaries (this is called a "front-loaded" campaign). But then you risk running out of money before the later primaries in the big states. If you are the front-runner, you are in better shape, but then you must worry about losing even one primary (as did Dole to Buchanan in New Hampshire in 1996), thereby tarnishing your "unbeatable" image.

Control the convention: If you win the most delegates in the primaries and caucuses, you will be nominated. (From 1956 through 1996 the winning candidate was nominated on the first ballot at the Democratic and Republican conventions.) Then your problem is to control everything else that goes on at the convention—the platform, the speeches, the vice-presidential nomination—so nothing happens that will embarrass you.

---

for Ronald Reagan in 1980 it was "competence" and in 1984 it was "it's morning again in America"; for Bush in 1988 it was "stay the course"; for Clinton in 1992 it was "we need to change."
- What should be the *timing* of the campaign? If you are relatively unknown, you will have to put everything into the early primaries and caucuses, try to emerge a front-runner, and then hope for the best. If you are already the front-runner, you may either go for broke early (and try to drive out all your opponents) or hold back some reserves for a long fight.
- Whom should you *target?* Only a small percentage of voters change their vote from one election to the next. Who is likely to change this time—unemployed steelworkers? Unhappy farmers? People upset by inflation?

Primary Versus General Campaigns

These four strategic decisions are not easily made, however, because you are (you hope) entering two elections, not just one. The first consists of primary elections and caucuses, which select the nominees; the second is the general election, which decides who wins the office. Each election attracts a different mix of voters, workers, and media attention. What works in the primary election may not work in the general one, and vice versa.

To win the nomination you must mobilize political activists who will give money, do volunteer work, and attend local caucuses. As we saw in Chapters 5 and 6, activists are more ideologically stringent than the voters at large. To motivate these activists you must be more liberal (if you are a Democrat) in your

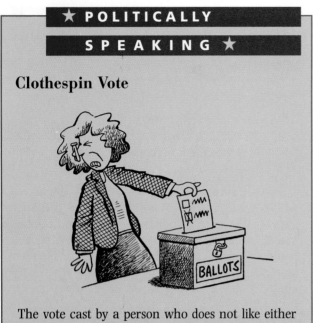

★ **POLITICALLY**

SPEAKING ★

Clothespin Vote

The vote cast by a person who does not like either candidate and so votes for the less objectionable of the two, putting a clothespin over his or her nose to keep out the unpleasant stench.

tone and theme than are rank-and-file Democrats, or more conservative (if you are a Republican) than are rank-and-file Republicans.

Consider the caucuses held in Iowa in early February of a presidential election year. This is the first real test of the candidates vying for the nomination. Anyone who does poorly here is at a disadvantage, in terms of media attention and contributor interest, for the rest of the campaign.

The several thousand Iowans who participate in their parties' caucuses are not representative of the followers of their party in the state, much less nationally. In 1988 Senator Robert Dole came in first and evangelist Pat Robertson came in second in the Iowa Republican caucus, with Vice President George Bush finishing third. As it turned out, there was little support for Dole or Robertson in the rest of the country.

Democrats who participate in the Iowa caucus tend to be more liberal than Democrats generally.[1] Moreover, the way the caucuses are run is a far cry from how most elections are held. To vote in the Republican caucus, you need not prove you are a Republican or even a voter. The Democratic caucus is not an election at all; instead a person supporting

The Iowa caucuses are the first in the nation, and so this small state draws almost all of the contenders. Here, left to right, are the Republicans in 2000: Alan Keyes, Orrin Hatch, Gary Bauer, Steve Forbes, George W. Bush, and John McCain.

a certain candidate stands in one corner of the room with people who also support him, while those supporting other candidates stand in other corners with other groups. There is a lot of calling back and forth, intended to persuade people to leave one group and join another. No group with fewer than 15 percent of the people in attendance gets to choose any delegates, so people in these small groups then go to other, larger ones. It is a cross between musical chairs and fraternity pledge week.

Suppose you are a Democrat running for president and you do well in the Iowa caucus. Suppose you go on to win your party's nomination. Now you have to go back to Iowa to campaign for votes in the general election. Since 1940 Iowa has voted Republican in every presidential election but five (1948, 1964, 1988, 1996, and 2000). Your Republican opponent is not going to let you forget all of the liberal slogans you uttered nine months before. The Republican candidate faces the mirror image of this problem—sounding very conservative to get support from Republican activists in states such as Massachusetts and New York and then having to defend those speeches when running against his Democratic opponent in those states.

The problem is not limited to Iowa but exists in every state where activists are more ideologically polarized than the average voter. To get activist support for the nomination, candidates move to the ideological extremes; to win the general election, they try to move back to the ideological center. The typical voter looks at the results and often decides that neither candidate appeals to him or her very much, and so casts a "clothespin vote" (see the box on page 184).

Occasionally even the voters in the primary elections will be more extreme ideologically than are the general-election voters. This certainly happened in 1972. George McGovern won the Democratic nomination with the support of voters who were well to the left of the public at large (and even of rank-and-file Democratic voters) on issues such as U.S. policy in Vietnam, amnesty for draft resisters, decriminalizing marijuana, and helping minorities.[2] His general-election opponent, Richard Nixon, was able to take advantage of this by portraying McGovern as a leftist. But even when primary voters are not too different from general-election voters, the activists who contribute the time, money, and effort to mount a campaign are very different from the voters—in both parties.

T·R·I·V·I·A

Elections

Only two men to have been elected president by the House of Representatives after failing to win a majority in the electoral college	Thomas Jefferson (1800) and John Quincy Adams (1824)
Only Democratic senator to be the running mate of a Republican presidential candidate	Andrew Johnson (1864)
A candidate for president who received more popular votes than his opponent but was not elected	Grover Cleveland got more popular votes but fewer electoral votes than Benjamin Harrison in 1888
President who won the largest percentage of the popular vote	Lyndon B. Johnson, 61.7 percent (1964)
Only person to serve as vice president and president without having been elected to either post	Gerald Ford (1973–1976)
President who won the most electoral votes	Ronald Reagan (525 in 1984)
First woman to run for national office on a major-party ticket	Geraldine Ferraro (Democratic candidate for vice president, 1984)

Two Kinds of Campaign Issues

In election campaigns there are two different kinds of issues.[3] A **position issue** is one in which the rival candidates have opposing views on a question that also divides the voters. For example, in the 2000 election George W. Bush wanted to let people put some of their Social Security money into private savings accounts; Al Gore opposed this.

Since 1860 many of the great party realignments have been based on differing position issues. After the Civil War the question was whether African Americans should be slaves or free. In the 1890s it was whether tariffs should be high or low and whether the dollar should be made cheaper. In the 1960s it was whether broad new civil rights legislation was needed.

Kinds of Elections

There are two kinds of elections in the United States: general and primary. A **general election** is used to fill an elective office. A **primary election** is used to select a party's candidates for an elective office, though in fact those who vote in a primary election may not consider themselves party members. Some primaries are closed. In a **closed primary** you must declare in advance (sometimes several weeks in advance) that you are a registered member of the political party in whose primary you wish to vote. About forty states have closed primaries.

Other primaries are open. In an **open primary** you can decide when you enter the voting booth which party's primary you wish to participate in. You are given every party's ballot; you may vote on one. Idaho, Michigan, Minnesota, Montana, North Dakota, Utah, Vermont, and Wisconsin have open primaries. A variant on the open primary is the **blanket** (or "free love") **primary**—in the voting booth you mark a ballot that lists the candidates of all the parties, and thus you can help select the Democratic candidate for one office and the Republican candidate for another. Alaska and Washington have blanket primaries.

The differences among these kinds of primaries should not be exaggerated, for even the closed primary does not create any great barrier for a voter who wishes to vote in the Democratic primary in one election and the Republican in another. Some states also have a **runoff primary**: if no candidate gets a majority of the votes, there is a runoff between the two with the most votes. Runoff primaries are common in the South.

A special kind of primary, a **presidential primary**, is that used to pick delegates to the presidential nominating conventions of the major parties. Presidential primaries come in a bewildering variety. A simplified list looks like this:

- **Delegate selection only**   Only the names of prospective delegates to the convention appear on the ballot. They may or may not indicate their presidential preferences.
- **Delegate selection with advisory presidential preference**   Voters pick delegates and indicate their preferences among presidential candidates. The delegates are not legally bound to observe these preferences.
- **Binding presidential preference**   Voters indicate their preferred presidential candidates. Delegates must observe these preferences, at least for a certain number of convention ballots. The delegates may be chosen in the primary or by a party convention.

In 1981 the Supreme Court ruled that political parties, not state legislatures, have the right to decide how delegates to national conventions are selected. Thus Wisconsin could not retain an open primary if the national Democratic party objected (*Democratic Party v. La Follette*, 101 Sup. Ct. 1010, 1981). Now the parties can insist that only voters who declare themselves Democrats or Republicans can vote in presidential primaries. The Supreme Court's ruling may have relatively little practical effect, however, since the "declaration" might occur only an hour or a day before the election.

But sometimes voters are not divided on important issues. Instead the question is whether a candidate fully supports the public's view on a matter about which nearly everyone agrees. These are called **valence issues.** For example, everybody wants a strong economy and low crime rates, and so no candidate favors high unemployment or more crime. What voters look for on valence issues is which candidate seems most closely linked to a universally shared view.

Valence issues are quite common. In 1968 Richard Nixon seemed to be more supportive of anticrime measures than his rival; in 1976 Jimmy Carter seemed more likely to favor honesty in government than his opponent; in 1984 Ronald Reagan seemed more closely identified with a strong economy than his opponent; in 1988 George Bush seemed more closely linked to patriotism than his opponent. Notice that we have said "seemed." This is how voters perceived the winners; it does not mean that the opponents favored crime, corruption, unemployment, or anti-Americanism.

In 1992 Bill Clinton was beset with charges that he was guilty of dodging the draft, marital infidelity, and smoking pot. But his strategists decided to focus the campaign on the valence issue of the economy, and they went about rescuing Clinton from the other criticisms. One observer later reported, "Retooling the image of a couple who had already been in the public eye for five battering months required a campaign of behavior modification and media manipulation so elaborate that its outline ran to fourteen single-spaced pages."[4] Bill Clinton and his wife, Hillary, made joint appearances on television during which they demonstrated their affection for each other. The plan even called for staging an event where Bill Clinton and his daughter would surprise Hillary Clinton on Mother's Day.[5]

The 1996 campaign was run almost entirely in valence terms. Clinton took credit for improving the economy and putting more police on the street. He took swipes at Bob Dole's advanced age and criticized him as an "extremist" who would abolish Medicare. Clinton won easily.

Likewise, the 2000 campaign relied on valence issues, but some position issues also became important. George W. Bush and Al Gore disagreed about the need for across-the-board cuts in the federal income tax, on the value of a national missile defense system, and on whether parents could use public money to send their children to whichever schools they chose.

Campaigns have usually combined both position and valence questions, but the latter have increased in importance in recent years. This has happened in part because presidential campaigns are now conducted largely on television, where it is important to project popular symbols and manipulate widely admired images. Candidates try to show that they are likable, and they rely on televised portraits of their similarity to ordinary people.

Television, Debates, and Direct Mail

Once campaigns mostly involved parades, big rallies, "whistle-stop" train tours, and shaking hands outside factory gates and near shopping centers. All of this still goes on, but increasingly presidential and senatorial candidates (and those House candidates with television stations in their districts) use broadcasting.

There are two ways to use television—by running paid advertisements and by getting on the nightly

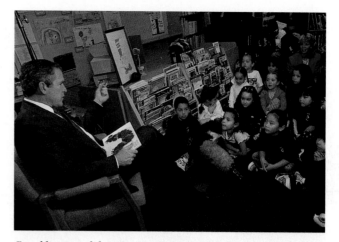

Republican candidate George W. Bush emphasized "compassionate conservatism" in his campaign and illustrated it by talking to schoolchildren.

news broadcasts. In the language of campaigners, short television ads are called *spots,* and a campaign activity that appears on a news broadcast is called a *visual.* Much has been written about the preparation of spots, usually under titles such as "the selling of the president" or "packaging the candidate" (and mostly by advertising executives, who are not especially known for underestimating their own influence). No doubt spots can have an important effect in some cases. A little-known candidate can increase his or her visibility by frequent use of spots (this is what Jimmy Carter did in the 1976 presidential primaries). Sometimes a complete unknown can win a primary by clever use of television, as allegedly happened when Mike Gravel became the Democratic nominee for senator from Alaska in 1968 and Milton Shapp became the Democratic nominee for governor of Pennsylvania in 1966.

The effect of television advertising on general elections is probably a good deal less than its effect on primaries; indeed, as we shall see in Chapter 10, most scientific studies of television's influence on voting decisions have shown that either it has no effect or the effect is subtle and hard to detect. Nor is it surprising that this should be the case. In a general election, especially one for a high-visibility office (such as president or governor), the average voter has many sources of information—his or her own party or ideological preference, various kinds of advertising, the opinions of friends and family, and newspaper and magazine stories. Furthermore, both sides will use TV spots; if well done, they are likely to

In the 1888 presidential campaign, supporters of Benjamin Harrison rolled a huge ball covered with campaign slogans across the country. The gimmick, first used in 1840, gave rise to the phrase "keep the ball rolling."

cancel each other out. In short it is not yet clear that a gullible public is being sold a bill of goods by slick Madison Avenue advertisers, whether the goods are automobiles or politicians.

Visuals are a vital part of any major campaign effort because, unlike spots, they cost the campaign little and, as "news," they may have greater credibility with the viewer. A visual is a brief filmed episode showing the candidate doing something that a reporter thinks is newsworthy. Simply making a speech, unless the speech contains important new facts or charges, is often thought by TV editors to be uninteresting: television viewers are not attracted by pictures of "talking heads," and in the highly competitive world of TV, audience reactions are all-important determinants of what gets on the air. Knowing this, campaign managers will strive to have their candidates do something visually interesting every day, no later than 3:00 P.M. (if the visual is to be on the 6:00 P.M. news)—talk to elderly folks in a nursing home, shake hands with people waiting in an unemployment line, or sniff the waters of a polluted lake. Obviously all these efforts are for naught if a TV camera crew is not around; great

Candidates first made phonographic recordings of their speeches in 1908. Warren G. Harding is shown here recording a speech during the 1920 campaign.

pains are therefore taken to schedule these visuals at times and in places that make it easy for the photographers to be present.

Ironically, visuals—and television newscasts generally—may give the viewer less information than commercial spots. This, of course, is the exact opposite of what many people believe. It is commonplace to deplore political advertising, especially the short spot, on the grounds that it is either devoid of information or manipulative, and to praise television news programs, especially longer debates and interviews, because they are informative and balanced. In fact the best research we have so far suggests that the reverse is true: news programs covering elections tend to convey very little information (they often show scenes of crowds cheering or candidates shouting slogans) and make little or no impression on viewers, if indeed they are watched at all. Paid commercials, on the other hand, especially the shorter spots, often contain a good deal of information that is seen, remembered, and evaluated by a public that is quite capable of distinguishing between fact and humbug.[6]

A special kind of television campaigning is the campaign debate. Incumbents or well-known candidates have little incentive to debate their opponents; by so doing, they only give more publicity to lesser-known rivals. Despite the general rule among politicians never to help an opponent, Vice President Nixon debated the less-well-known John Kennedy in 1960, and President Gerald Ford debated the less-well-known Jimmy Carter in 1976. Nixon and Ford lost. Lyndon Johnson would not debate Barry Goldwater in 1964, nor would Nixon debate Humphrey in 1968 or McGovern in 1972. Johnson and Nixon won. Carter debated the equally well-known Reagan in 1980 (but refused to join in a three-way debate with Reagan and John Anderson). Carter lost. It is hard to know what effect TV debates have on election outcomes, but poll data suggest that in 1980 voters who watched the debates were reassured by Reagan's performance; after the second debate with Carter, he took a lead in the polls that he never relinquished.[7] In 1984 most people thought that Mondale did better than Reagan in the first debate, but there is little evidence that the debate affected the outcome of the election. In 1992 and 1996 Clinton was probably the better debater, but he most likely would have won even if he had stumbled.

Urbanization and the movement of people to big cities made railroad tours of small towns an increasingly inefficient way to meet voters. Thus the motorcade through city streets began to take its place, such as this one in 1968 where the public greets Robert F. Kennedy.

In 1988 the televised debate became a major activity during—and even before—the primary elections. The half dozen or so contenders for both the Democratic and the Republican presidential nominations participated in so many debates that one journalist was led to compare the campaign to a political version of the television program "The Dating Game," with the candidates, like bachelors trying to impress a woman, describing over and over again all their good qualities. Other than providing free television exposure (and probably boring the candidates to tears), it is hard to see what this accomplished.

Though TV visuals and debates are free, they are also risky. The risk is the slip of the tongue. You may have spent thirty years of your life in unblemished public service, you may have thought through your position on the issues with great care, you may have rehearsed your speeches until your dog starts to howl, but just make one verbal blunder and suddenly the whole campaign focuses on your misstep. In 1976 President Ford erroneously implied that Poland was not part of the Soviet bloc. For days the press

The first televised presidential campaign debate took place in 1960 between John F. Kennedy and Richard M. Nixon.

dwelt on this slip. His opponent, Jimmy Carter, admitted in a *Playboy* interview that he had sometimes had lust in his heart. It is hard to imagine anyone who has not, but apparently presidents are supposed to be above that sort of thing. In 1980 Ronald Reagan said that trees cause pollution—oops, here we go again.

Because of the fear of a slip, because the voters do not want to hear long, fact-filled speeches about complex issues, and because general-election campaigns

Presidential debates offer voters an opportunity to see and hear candidates in a forum where differences between their visions for the country often come into sharp focus, such as they did during the first presidential debate between Al Gore and George W. Bush held in Boston on October 3, 2000.

are fights to attract the centrist voter, the candidates will rely on a stock speech that sets out the campaign theme as well as on their ability to string together several proven applause-getting lines. For reporters covering the candidate every day, it can be a mind-numbing experience. Nelson Rockefeller spoke so often of the "brotherhood of man and the fatherhood of God" that the reporters started referring to it as his BOMFOG speech. Occasionally this pattern is interrupted by a "major" address—that is, a carefully composed talk on some critical issue, usually delivered before a live audience and designed to provide issue-related stories for the reporters to write.

If you dislike campaign oratory, put yourself in the candidate's shoes for a moment. Every word you say will be scrutinized, especially for slips of the tongue. Interest group leaders and party activists will react sharply to any phrase that departs from their preferred policies. Your opponent stands ready to pounce on any error of fact or judgment. You must give countless speeches every day. The rational reaction to this state of affairs is to avoid controversy, stick to prepared texts and tested phrases, and shun anything that sounds original (and hence untested). You therefore wind up trying to sell yourself as much as or more than your ideas. Voters may *say* that they admire a blunt, outspoken person, but in a tough political campaign they would probably find such bluntness a little unnerving.

Television is the most visible example of modern technology's effect on campaigns. Since 1960 presidential elections have been contested largely through television. Without television the campaign waged in 1992 by independent candidate Ross Perot might not have happened at all. Perot launched his candidacy with successive appearances on Cable News Network's call-in program "Larry King Live," and he bought several half-hour chunks of television time to air his views on the federal budget deficit. In early October, before the first of three televised debates featuring Perot, Republican incumbent George Bush, and Democratic challenger Bill Clinton, most national polls showed Perot with only 10 percent of the vote. But after the debates Perot's support in the polls doubled, and he ended up with about 19 percent of the votes cast on election day.

In 1996 the big television networks agreed to make some free television time available to the major presidential candidates. The Federal Communications Commission approved the plan to limit the free

TV to "major" candidates, thus denying it to minor third-party nominees.

Less visible than television but perhaps just as important is the computer. The computer makes possible sophisticated direct-mail campaigning, and this in turn makes it possible for a candidate to address specific appeals to particular voters easily and rapidly solicit campaign contributions. In the 2000 presidential campaign, Republican John McCain and Democrat Bill Bradley raised substantial money via the Internet. Both lost their primary challenge, but fundraising via the Internet is surely here to stay.

Whereas television is heard by everybody—and thus leads the candidate using it to speak in generalities to avoid offending anyone—direct mail is aimed at particular groups (college students, Native Americans, bankers, autoworkers), to whom specific views can be expressed with much less risk of offending someone. So important are the lists of names of potential contributors to whom a computer may send appeals that a prized resource of any candidate, guarded as if it were a military secret, is "The List." Novices in politics must slowly develop their own lists or beg sympathetic incumbents for a peek at theirs.

The chief consequence of the new style of campaigning is not, as some think, that it is more manipulative than old-style campaigning (picnics with free beer and $5 bills handed to voters can be just as manipulative as TV ads); rather it is that running campaigns has become divorced from the process of governing. Previously the party leaders who ran the campaigns would take part in the government once it was elected, and since they were *party* leaders, they had to worry about getting their candidate *re*elected. Modern political consultants take no responsibility for governing, and by the time the next election rolls around, they may be working for someone else.

Money

All these consultants, TV ads, and computerized mailings cost money—lots of it. A powerful California politician once observed that "money is the mother's milk of politics," and many people think that our democracy is drowning in it. In 1998 winning House and Senate candidates spent a combined total of $448 million (see Figure 8.1). When that kind of money is spent, many people will cynically

conclude that elections are being bought and sold. Clever television producers are being paid huge sums, so the theory goes, to put on TV ads that sell candidates as if they were boxes of soap.

But matters are a good deal more complicated and less sinister than the popular theory supposes. Money is important in politics as in everything else, but it is not obvious that the candidates with the most money always win or that the donors of the money buy big favors in exchange for their big bucks. In Chapter 9 we will consider what, if anything, interest groups get for the money they give to politicians, and in Chapter 10 we shall summarize what we know about the effects of television advertising on elections. Here let us try to answer four questions: Where does campaign money come from? What rules govern how it is raised and spent? What has been the effect of campaign finance reform? What new reform proposals are being debated? What does campaign spending buy?

The Sources of Campaign Money

Presidential candidates get part of their money from private donors and part from the federal government; congressional candidates get all of their

Figure 8.1   The Cost of Winning

Source: Federal Election Commission Report, April 28, 1999.

money from private sources. In the presidential primaries candidates raise money from private citizens and interest groups. The federal government will provide matching funds, dollar for dollar, for all monies raised from individual donors who contribute no more than $250. Since every candidate wants as much of this "free" federal money as possible, each has an incentive to raise money from small, individual givers. (To prove they are serious candidates, they must first raise $5,000 in each of twenty states from such small contributors.) The government also gives a lump-sum grant to each political party to help pay the costs of its nominating convention. In the general election the government pays all the costs of each candidate, up to a limit set by law (in 1996 that limit was $61.8 million for each major candidate and $29 million for Perot).

Congressional candidates get no government funds; all their money must come out of their own pockets or be raised from individuals, interest groups (PACs), or the political parties. Contrary to what many people think, most of that money comes—and has always come—from individual donors (see Table 8.1). Because the rules sharply limit how much any individual can give, these donors tend not to be fat cats but people of modest means who contribute $100 or $200 per person.

Since the typical individual contribution is very small (and in no case larger than $1,000), some candidates have turned to rock bands and movie stars to put on benefit performances. If five thousand people will each pay $25 for a performance by Slipped Disc, a lot of money can be raised in a hurry.

The most a PAC can give a candidate in any election is $5,000, but the typical PAC does not donate anything approaching the maximum amount; usually it gives a few hundred dollars to each candidate it supports.

These figures conceal some important differences among kinds of candidates, however. As Table 8.1 shows, incumbent members of Congress running for reelection get over a third of their money from PACs and spend next to nothing out of their own pockets. Their challengers, by contrast, spend only half as much and are able to get only one-tenth of that from PACs. Challengers have to put up much more of their own money. As we shall see in the next section, these money problems weaken the ability of challengers to mount effective campaigns.

Campaign Finance Rules

During the 1972 presidential election men hired by President Nixon's campaign staff broke into the headquarters of the Democratic National Committee in the Watergate office building. They were caught by an alert security guard. The subsequent investigation disclosed that the Nixon people had engaged in dubious or illegal money-raising schemes, including taking large sums from wealthy contributors in exchange for appointing them to ambassadorships. Many individuals and corporations were indicted for making illegal donations

Table 8.1 Sources of Campaign Funds: All House and Senate Candidates in 1997–1998, by Incumbents, Challengers, and Open

	Incumbents		Challengers		Open	
	Sum (millions)	Percent	Sum	Percent	Sum	Percent
Individuals	$292.4	57.5%	$109.1	51.9%	$71.2	50.7%
PACs	158.3	37.6	21.4	10.2	26.9	19.2
Candidates	0.07	0.02	4.1	2.0	2.5	1.8
Loans	5.6	1.3	62.6	29.8	33.7	24.0
Parties	14.9	3.5	12.9	6.1	6.1	4.3
Total	$421.3		$210.1		$140.4	

Note: The data on candidates, loans, and parties are especially messy. "Candidates" includes only direct personal contributions by the office seekers. "Loans" includes money lent to the campaigns by the candidates as well as other loans. Loans from incumbents are almost always repaid by campaign committees. "Parties" includes both direct party contributions and a variety of "party-coordinated expenditures."

Source: Federal Election Commission Report, April 28, 1999.

Major Federal Campaign Finance Rules

General

- All federal election contributions and expenditures are reported to the six-person Federal Election Commission, which has the power to investigate and prosecute violators.
- All contributions over $100 must be disclosed, with name, address, and occupation of contributor.
- No cash contributions over $100, no foreign contributions.
- No ceiling on amount a candidate or campaign may spend (unless a presidential candidate accepts federal funding).

Individual Contributions

- May not exceed $1,000 to any candidate in any election per year.
- May not exceed $20,000 per year to a national party committee or $5,000 to a political action committee.
- No limit on expenditures for "independent advertising."

Political Action Committees (PACs)

- A corporation, union, or other association may each establish one PAC.
- A PAC must register six months in advance, have at least fifty contributors, and give to at least five candidates.
- PAC contributions to a candidate may not exceed $5,000 per election, or to a national party $15,000 per year.

Presidential Primaries

- Federal matching funds, dollar for dollar, are available for all money raised by candidates from individual donors giving $250 or less.
- To be eligible a candidate must raise $5,000 in each of twenty states, in contributions of $250 or less.

Presidential Election

- Federal government will pay all campaign costs of major-party candidates and part of the costs of minor-party candidates (those winning between 5 and 25 percent of the vote).

(since 1925 it had been against the law for corporations or labor unions to contribute money to candidates, but the law had been unenforceable). Some of the accused had given money to Democratic candidates as well as to Nixon.

To prevent these abuses, in 1974 Congress passed a new federal campaign finance reform law. It created a six-person Federal Election Commission (FEC) charged with enforcing a new, tougher set of restrictions on political spending as well as a system of public financing of presidential campaigns. The key provisions of this law are summarized in the box above.

If you want to run for Congress today, you must report to the FEC every contribution of $100 or more, and you cannot accept more than $1,000 from any individual during any election. (If you run in both the primary and the general election, you can take up to $1,000 in each campaign from the same person.) The law against taking money from corpora-

tions or labor unions was reaffirmed, but such organizations were allowed to form PACs that could raise money in voluntary contributions from their employees or members. (Trade associations, professional societies, and other groups were also allowed to form PACs.) No PAC can give more than $5,000 to any candidate in any election, with the primary and the general contest counted as separate elections.

Initially the law also set limits on how much an individual candidate could spend on his or her own campaign, but the Supreme Court ruled that this was an unconstitutional infringement of the First Amendment's guarantee of free speech.[8] The right to run for office and to express your views includes the right to spend your own money on the effort. However, the Court let stand a limit of $50,000 on how much a presidential candidate could spend out of his pocket on his own campaign if he accepted federal financing. They reasoned that anybody taking the taxpayers' money was getting plenty of help in exercising his First Amendment rights, and so it was not unreasonable to restrict his own spending on that cause.

The law sets no limits on how much individuals or organizations can spend for "independent" political advertising on behalf of a candidate. To be considered independent, an expenditure cannot be made at the request of or in cooperation or consultation with the candidate or the candidate's campaign organization. These independent expenditures are typically made by ideologically oriented PACs and sometimes take the form of "negative ads"—that is, advertisements attacking an opposing candidate for his or her position on the environment, abortion, or whatever.

No law regulating a powerful human desire, such as ambition for office, can ever be entirely successful, and campaign finance rules are no exception. Though the law has ended many of the worst abuses, it leaves a number of loopholes that candidates can exploit. Among them are these:

- The political parties can solicit unlimited funds from individuals, corporations, and unions, provided that they spend the money on local party activities such as voter registration campaigns and get-out-the-vote drives and not on behalf of specific candidates. But of course a successful campaign by a party to get voters to the polls will tend to help the candidate of that party. The funds are called **soft money,** as opposed to the hard money that must be reported to the FEC. In 1996 political parties raised huge amounts of soft money, leading to new demand for another law to change campaign finance.
- Many small contributions from different individuals or PACs can be bundled together and delivered at one time in order to increase the impact of the contributions on the campaign and, presumably, better promote the interests of the contributors before those of the candidate.

The Effects of the 1974 Reforms

The intent of the reforms was to get political fundraising out in the open and subject to clearly understood rules that would minimize the chances of some fat cat's buying a pet politician. By and large the law has succeeded at that.

But the reforms have also had some unintended effects. First, by authorizing PACs to raise money, the law made possible a vast increase in the amount of money spent on elections by special interests. Figure 8.2 shows how PACs have grown from several hundred in 1977 to over three thousand in 1998. During that same period their contributions to federal candidates rose from about $25 million to more than $200 million.

Second, the reforms have shifted the control of campaign money away from the political parties and toward individual candidates, thus further weakening the power of the parties. Some people might think this is a good thing, but there is another side to the story. To the extent that people vote for parties rather than for individuals (and many people still do), the party ought to have some way of influencing the selection and behavior of its candidates. It is harder for this to occur when parties play so small a role in financing campaigns.

Third, the reforms provide an advantage to wealthy challengers. If you want to take on a well-entrenched incumbent and have no money of your own, you will find that the rules make raising the necessary funds a slow and painful process involving endless appeals to countless individuals to obtain small donations. It can easily take half a million dollars to mount a credible congressional campaign; that adds up to a lot of phone calls and coffee parties. But if you can write a check for half a million dollars, you can spare yourself all the trouble.

Fourth, the reforms give an advantage to candidates with strong ideological appeal. Unless you are rich, the easiest way to get money from lots of small donors is to use direct-mail pieces that evoke powerful emotions such as feelings for or against abortion, gun control, school prayer, or the death penalty. Never mind whether these are the most important issues—they generate cash.

Fifth, the reforms penalize people who start late in a campaign. Fund-raising takes a lot of time; if you decide at the last minute to run, you may discover you have no chance of raising the money you need before it is too late. Incumbents know this, so many of them spend their time in office raising huge war chests well in advance of the election in order to scare off would-be challengers.

Finally, the reforms help incumbents and hurt challengers. Incumbents find it easier to raise money from PACs, regardless of the incumbent's party and of the type of PAC. As we shall see in Chapter 9, cor-

Figure 8.2   Growth of PACs

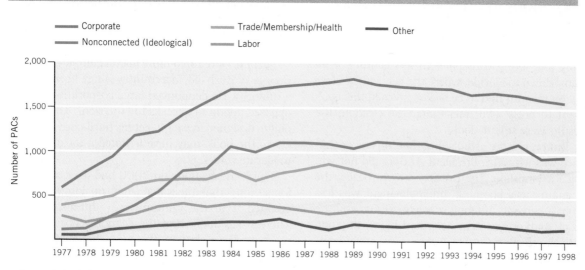

Source: Federal Election Commission.

porate PACs are more likely to support incumbents of either party than they are to support challengers.

Proposals for More Reform

Not only do the present campaign finance rules create some problems, but voters in general also seem to think that political money buys politicians. As a result candidates who emphasize reforming the rules, as John McCain did in the 2000 Republican primaries, get a lot of attention.

But it is very hard to think of a way to make the rules both better and constitutional. Even worse, it is hard to find evidence—as opposed to opinion—that many votes in Congress are bought with campaign money. Money does buy access. If you help raise money, your member of Congress will listen to you. But a lot of people help raise money, so the member must listen to all kinds of opinions, including ones with which you disagree.

Here are some popular ideas for reforming campaign finance laws, together with the problems they would create.

- *Idea:* Keep or even sharpen limits on how much each person can contribute to a candidate. *Problem:* This would make it harder for challengers to run against incumbents, who find it easier to raise money.

- *Idea:* Provide free television ads to candidates. *Problem:* This would impose heavy financial burdens on radio and television stations and would do nothing for the many House candidates who do not use television.

- *Idea:* Ban the soft money that people give to political parties or spend in independent advertisements. *Problem:* You cannot ban money without banning the speech it pays for, and that is unconstitutional.

- *Idea:* Use government money to pay for campaigns, as four states now do. *Problem:* This would do nothing to limit how much interest groups and individuals could spend on their own advertising for and against candidates. Also, should the government pay the primary campaign expenses of anybody who wants to get the nomination?

- *Idea:* Prevent PACs from spending money on candidates. *Problem:* Committees, like individuals, have a First Amendment right to make their views known. In addition, if PAC money were banned, where would the candidates get the money to pay their bills?

Reforming campaign finance practices always sounds like a good idea, but figuring out how to reform them is a big challenge.

The 2000 Election

The presidential race in 2000 was a cliffhanger, producing the narrowest margin between the winning and losing candidates in this century. It all came down to Florida, where the vote was so close that a recount had to be ordered. When this book went to press, two weeks after the election, the results were still in doubt.

But even more astonishing than this razor-thin race was why Vice President Al Gore did not win with a landslide. The country was at peace, the economy was booming, unemployment was less than 4 percent, inflation scarcely existed, and the stock market was near its record high, yet going into the election Gore trailed in most public-opinion polls, and in the election his popular vote was only slightly ahead of that of Governor Bush.

This is not supposed to have happened. In general, a good economy helps the party that controls the White House. Take a look at Figure 8.3 on page 203. It shows that the better the economy, the better the candidate of that party does in the presidential race. Never in this century has the economy been stronger than it was in 2000, yet Gore rarely led in the polls (he should have been ahead by eight points) and was in a squeaker of an election. What went wrong for him?

No one is quite sure, but here are some guesses. First, Gore had to run in the face of President Clinton's sexual and fund-raising scandals in the White House. Though Americans liked the job Clinton did as president, Gore believed they didn't think he was a good man. Gore, as the vice president, believed he had to confront a lot of anti-Clinton hostility. Gore did what he could to deal with this problem by choosing as his vice presidential nominee Senator Joe Lieberman, one of the first Democrats to speak out against Clinton, and by not letting Clinton campaign for him except in a few carefully chosen places. Maybe this was not enough.

Second, Gore ran a more liberal campaign than George W. Bush did, in a country where liberals are a minority. He denounced large corporations and opposed giving tax breaks to "the rich." His campaign, designed in part to get his hard-core followers to the polls, may have irritated a lot of more moderate voters.

Third, the economy in 2000 had been so good for so long that the voters may no longer have credited it to the Clinton-Gore administration. There is no doubt that the economy does affect most elections, but in the past that effect has occurred when a good economy has suddenly gone sour or a bleak one has suddenly gotten better. When Franklin Roosevelt beat Herbert Hoover in 1932 and when Ronald Reagan beat Jimmy Carter in 1980, the victors both took advantage of a sudden economic downturn. When George Bush (George W. Bush's father) beat Michael Dukakis in 1988, the elder Bush took advantage of an upturn in economic news. In 2000 there was no recent change on which to capitalize.

Long before the election, several political scientists predicted its outcome, using economic models to estimate that Gore would win between 53 and 60 percent of the vote. All were wrong.

The Vice President

Gore, in picking Lieberman, chose to emphasize a moderate Democrat who was an Orthodox Jew and had been critical of Clinton. Bush, in picking former Secretary of Defense Dick Cheney, chose to emphasize long Washington experience and a deep familiarity with military and foreign-policy issues. The Lieberman choice was especially interesting, not

Money and Winning

In the general election for president money does not make much difference, because both major-party candidates have the same amount, contributed by the federal government. Of course the candidates may have more or less soft money that has been contributed to their political parties and more or fewer independent advertisements paid for by friends and supporters. But these other sources of support probably do not make a big difference. Rather, during peacetime presidential elections are usually decided by three things: political party affilonly because he was the first Jew to be on a major-party ticket for national office, but because he did not hesitate to discuss the importance of religion in public affairs, a subject that many politicians avoid because they fear that people will criticize them for relaxing a barrier that is supposed to exist, in the eyes of some people, between church and state.

The Campaign

The campaign was concentrated in a few key states that held the balance of power. Everyone knew that Bush would do well in the South and much of the Midwest; everyone knew that Gore would do well in New York, most of New England, and California. That meant that the battleground would be in states like Michigan, Missouri, Ohio, Pennsylvania, and Wisconsin. Both Bush and Gore campaigned repeatedly in those states, but not exclusively, because some odd things happened in unexpected states.

One such state was Florida, which Bush assumed he would easily win. (His brother, Jeb Bush, was governor of Florida.) But Gore did well in Florida, turning it, as we have seen, into the place where ultimately the identity of the next president was determined. Two other states were Arkansas and Tennessee, the first the home of Clinton (he was governor there), the second that of Gore (he was a senator from there). Bush managed to capture both states, one of the few times when the incumbent party did not carry the states of its key national figures. And a third was California, a state Gore was expected to win and did win. Despite that, Bush campaigned intensively there.

The Role of Third Parties

Ross Perot led the Reform Party to a major showing in 1992, when he got 19 percent of the vote, and in 1996, when he won 9 percent. But in 2000, Pat Buchanan, a conservative Republican, left his own party and won the Reform nomination. This enabled him to get access to the federal election money available to parties that have won at least 5 percent of the vote (in this case, around $12 million), but Buchanan wound up with nothing to show for it, getting less than 1 percent of the vote. The Reform Party will have no federal money in 2004, and so it may not be long for this world.

The major third-party effort was led by Ralph Nader, who became the nominee of the Green Party, an ultra-liberal group. Nader campaigned hard on a slim budget, hoping to win at least 5 percent of the vote and thus become eligible for federal funds. But he won only 2 percent, meaning he will have no federal money in 2004. But he did frighten the Gore campaign: the polls showed that the great majority of Green Party backers would have voted for Gore if Nader had not been in the race.

Congress

The Republicans managed to control both houses of Congress, though with reduced majorities. Traditionally, the party that wins the White House picks up more seats in Congress, though that did not happen with Bush in 1988, with Clinton (in the House) in 1992, or with Clinton (in the Senate) in 1996. The Democrats had counted on at least winning the House, but they did not. The Republicans won a majority of about nine seats in the House and about one in the Sentate; though the final numbers may differ after all the counts are finished.

iation, the state of the economy, and the character of the candidates.

For all the talk about voting for "the person, not the party," history teaches that at least 80 percent of the presidential vote will go to the candidates of the two main parties. This means that a presidential election will normally be decided by the 20 percent of voters who cannot be counted on to vote either Democratic or Republican.

In good economic times the party holding the White House normally does well; in poor times it does badly. This is sometimes called the "pocketbook vote."

HOW THINGS WORK

What Other Countries Do

	Public Financing	Limits on Fund-Raising or Spending	Television
Britain	No	Yes	Free time, allocated according to party's strength in previous election
Denmark	Allowance to parties, based on strength in previous election	No	Parties given equal and free time on public stations
France	Reimbursement to candidates, according to votes received	Yes	Free and equal time to candidates
Italy	Reimbursement to candidates, according to votes received	No	Free and equal time to candidates on state-run stations, but parties control major private stations
Israel	No	Yes	Parties given equal and free time on public stations
Japan	No	Yes	Candidates given some free time for speeches: no negative advertising
Germany	Reimbursement to parties, according to votes received	No	Free time to candidates on public stations

Source: New York Times (March 21, 1990): A12. Copyright © 1990 by the New York Times Company. Reprinted by permission.

But it is not clear whose pocketbook determines how a person will vote. Many people who are doing well financially will vote against the party in power if the country as a whole is not doing well. A person who is doing well may have friends or family members who are doing poorly. Or the well-off voter may think that if the country is doing poorly, he or she will soon feel the pinch by losing a job or losing customers.

Voters also care about character, and so some money from presidential campaign coffers goes to fund "character ads." *Character* here means several things: Is the candidate honest and reliable? Does the candidate think as the voter thinks about social issues such as crime, abortion, and school prayer? Does the candidate act presidential? Acting presidential seems to mean being an effective speaker, displaying dignity and compassion, sounding like someone who can take charge and get things done, and coming across consistently as a reasonable, likable person. Rash, disagreeable extremists need not apply.

Since both major candidates get the same amount of federal money for the general-election campaign, money does not make much of a difference in determining the winner. Other factors that

also do not make much of a difference include the following:

- *Vice-presidential nominee:* There has rarely been an election in which his or her identity has made a difference.
- *Political reporting:* It may make a difference in some elections, but not in presidential ones.
- *Religion:* Being a Catholic was once a barrier, but since John F. Kennedy was elected president in 1960, this is no longer true.
- *Abortion:* This probably affects who gets a party's nomination, but in the general election ardent supporters and ardent opponents are about evenly balanced.
- *New voting groups:* Political scientists have shown that, whatever reporters may say, "angry white males" did not elect the Republican Congress in 1994 and "soccer moms" did not elect Bill Clinton in 1996.[9]

In congressional races, however, in general it seems that money does make a decisive difference. Scholars are not entirely agreed on the facts, but there is strong evidence that how much the challenger spends is most important, because the chal-

Table 8.2	**The Incumbency Advantage in Congressional Campaign Spending (constant 1992 dollars)**				
Year	Average Incumbent Spending	Average Challenger Spending	Number of Races	Incumbent-to-Challenger Spending Ratio	Median Ratio
1978	$284,577	$202,863	235*	1.40	1.93
1980	$298,510	$174,031	338	1.72	3.82
1982	$400,630	$202,689	315	1.98	3.24
1984	$417,815	$192,433	338	2.17	4.47
1986	$488,447	$175,418	319	2.78	5.39
1988	$496,894	$148,723	328	3.34	7.08
1990	$479,969	$124,899	321	3.84	10.02
1992	$609,060	$172,802	307	3.52	5.35
1994	$573,374	$223,664	328	2.56	4.68
1996	$630,852	$254,964	357	2.47	5.11
Total	$473,421	$187,587	3,186	2.52	4.66

*Number of cases is small due to nonfilers.

Source: Stephen Ansolabehere and James Snyder, "The Sources of the Incumbency Advantage in Congressional Campaign Finance," Department of Political Science, Massachusetts Institute of Technology, June 1997, 29.

lenger usually must become known to the public. Buying name recognition is expensive. Gary Jacobson has shown that, other things being equal, in every congressional election from 1972 to the mid-1980s, challengers who spent more money did better than those who spent less.[10] Jacobson also suggested that how much the incumbents spent was not very important, presumably because they already had all the name recognition they needed (as well as the other benefits of holding office, such as free mail and travel). Other scholars, applying different statistical methods to the same facts, have come to different conclusions. It now seems that, other things being equal, high-spending incumbents do better than low-spending ones.[11] It also now seems that ever higher spending by incumbents, both in absolute dollars and relative to what challengers spend, has become the congressional campaign norm. As Table 8.2 shows, in 1978 average incumbent spending in congressional races was $284,577, average challenger spending was $202,863, and the incumbent-to-challenger spending ratio was 1.40. By 1996 the average for incumbents had soared to $630,852, the average for challengers had grown to $254,964, and the incumbency spending advantage was 2.47.

That money makes a difference does not mean it makes the only difference. In 1986 and 1988 Republican challengers for Senate seats spent more money than the Democratic incumbents to whom they lost. Political party, incumbency, and issues also affect the outcomes of congressional elections.

Incumbents find it easier to raise money than do challengers; incumbents provide services to their districts that challengers cannot; incumbents regularly send free ("franked") mail to their constituents, while challengers must pay for their mailings; incumbents can get free publicity by sponsoring legislation or conducting an investigation. Thus it is hardly surprising that incumbents who run for reelection win in the overwhelming majority of races.

What Decides the Election?

To the voter it all seems quite simple—he or she votes for "the best person" or maybe "the least-bad person." To scholars it is all a bit mysterious. How do voters decide who the best person is? What does "best" mean, anyway?

Party

One answer to these questions is party identification. People may say that they are voting for the "best person," but for many people the best person is always a Democrat or a Republican. Moreover, we have seen in Chapter 5 that many people know rather little about the details of political issues. They may not even know what position their favored candidate has taken on issues that the voters care about. Given these facts many scholars have argued that party identification is the principal determinant of how people vote.[12]

If it were only a matter of party identification, though, the Democrats would always win the presidency, since more people identify with the Democratic than the Republican party (that gap narrowed, however, in the early 1980s). But we know that the Democrats lost five of the seven presidential elections between 1968 and 1992. There are at least three reasons for this.

First, those people who consider themselves Democrats are less firmly wedded to their party than are Republicans. Table 8.3 shows how people identifying themselves as Democrats, Republicans, or Independents voted in presidential elections from 1960 to 2000. In every election except 1992, at least 80 percent of Republican voters supported the Republican candidate in each election. By contrast, there have been more defections among Democratic voters—in 1972 a third of Democrats supported Nixon, and in 1984 some 26 percent supported Reagan.

The second reason, also clear from Table 8.3, is that the Republicans do much better than the Democrats among the self-described "independent" voters. In every election since 1960 (except 1964, 1992, and 1996), the Republican candidate has won a larger percentage of the independent vote than the Democratic nominee; in fact the Republicans usually got a majority of the independents, who tend to be younger whites.

Finally, a higher percentage of Republicans than Democrats vote in elections. In every presidential

Table 8.3	**Percentage of Popular Vote by Groups in Presidential Elections, 1960–2000**				
		National	**Republicans**	**Democrats**	**Independents**
1960	Kennedy	50%	5%	84%	43%
	Nixon	50	95	16	57
1964	Johnson	61	20	87	56
	Goldwater	39	80	13	44
1968	Humphrey	43	9	74	31
	Nixon	43	86	12	44
	Wallace	14	5	14	25
1972	McGovern	38	5	67	31
	Nixon	62	95	33	69
1976	Carter	51	11	80	48
	Ford	49	89	20	52
1980[a]	Carter	41	11	66	30
	Reagan	51	84	26	54
	Anderson	7	4	6	12
1984	Mondale	41	7	73	35
	Reagan	59	92	26	63
1988	Dukakis	46	8	82	43
	Bush	54	91	17	55
1992	Clinton	43	10	77	38
	Bush	38	73	10	32
	Perot	19	17	13	30
1996	Clinton	49	13	84	43
	Dole	41	80	10	35
	Perot	8	6	5	17
2000	Gore	50	8	86	45
	Bush	50	91	11	47

[a]The figures for 1980, 1984, 1988, and 1996 fail to add up to 100 percent because of missing data.

Sources: Gallup poll data, compiled by Robert D. Cantor, *Voting Behavior and Presidential Elections* (Itasca, Ill.: F. E. Peacock, 1975), 35; Gerald M. Pomper, *The Election of 1976* (New York: David McKay, 1977), 61; Gerald M. Pomper et al., *The Election of 1980* (Chatham, N.J.: Chatham House, 1981), 71; *New York Times*/CBS Poll, November 5, 1992.

The Congressional Election of 1998

In 1994 the Republicans won control of both the House and the Senate and retained that control in 1996 even though Clinton, a Democrat, was reelected president. Then came 1998, an off-year election in which the president's party almost always loses seats in Congress. But the Democrats did not lose seats—they gained five in the House and held even in the Senate.

What happened? There has not been another off-year election during a twentieth-century president's second term when his party gained seats in the House. No one can be certain, but here is what probably occurred.

The Economy   Times were good in 1998, with low inflation, little unemployment, falling crime rates, and a booming stock market. Good times help a president. People who felt that their standard of living had gotten worse voted for the Republicans, but there were not many of them.

The Speaker   Speaker Newt Gingrich was an unpopular figure in the press and among the public. There had even been an effort among House Republicans to dump him as Speaker. Although it failed, it showed that he was vulnerable. In addition Congress enjoyed little popular approval. A lot of voters supported Democrats as a way of voting against the Republican leadership.

The President   Bill Clinton was being threatened by impeachment over his alleged perjury and obstruction of justice in the Monica Lewinsky affair. It probably would have destroyed anyone else, but Clinton, an extraordinary campaigner, is not anyone else. A lot of voters decided that what he had done did not merit impeachment, and when the Republicans insisted on it, they voted for Clinton's party.

A Confession   We do not know of a single professor of political science who predicted a Democratic victory. Now you know what it is that we don't know.

---

contest in the past thirty years, those describing themselves as "strongly Republican" have been much more likely to vote than those describing themselves as "strongly Democratic."

Issues, Especially the Economy

Even though voters may not know a lot about the issues, that does not mean that issues play no role in elections or that voters respond irrationally to them. For example, V. O. Key, Jr., looked at those voters who switched from one party to another between elections and found that most of them switched in a direction consistent with their own interests. As Key put it, the voters are not fools.[13]

Moreover, voters may know a lot more than we suppose about issues that really matter to them. They may have hazy, even erroneous, views about monetary policy, Central America, and the trade deficit, but they are likely to have a very good idea about whether unemployment is up or down, prices at the supermarket are stable or rising, or crime is a problem in their neighborhoods. And on some issues—such as abortion, school prayer, and race relations—they are likely to have some strong principles that they want to see politicians obey.

Contrary to what we learn in our civics classes, representative government does not require voters to be well informed on the issues. If it were our duty as citizens to have accurate facts and sensible ideas about how best to negotiate with foreign adversaries, stabilize the value of the dollar, revitalize failing industries, and keep farmers prosperous, we might as well forget about citizenship and head for the beach. It would be a full-time job, and then some, to be a citizen. Politics would take on far more importance in our lives than most of us would want, given our need to earn a living and our belief in the virtues of limited government.

To see why our system can function without well-informed citizens, we must understand the differences between two ways in which issues can affect elections.

Prospective Voting   *Prospective* means "forward-looking"; we vote prospectively when we examine the views that the rival candidates have on the issues of the day and then cast our ballots for the person we think has the best ideas for handling these matters. **Prospective voting** requires a lot of information about issues and candidates. Some of us do vote

When the economy is strong, the incumbent party usually (but not always) wins.

prospectively. Those who do tend to be political junkies. They are either willing to spend a lot of time learning about issues or are so concerned about some big issue (abortion, school busing, nuclear energy) that all they care about is how a candidate stands on that question.

Prospective voting is more common among people who are political activists, have a political ideology that governs their voting decision, or are involved in interest groups with a big stake in the election. They are a minority of all voters, but (as we saw in Chapters 5 and 6) they are more influential than their numbers would suggest. Some prospective voters (by no means all) are organized into single-issue groups, to be discussed in the next section.

Retrospective Voting   *Retrospective* means "backward-looking"; **retrospective voting** involves looking at how things have gone in the recent past and then voting for the party that controls the White House if we like what has happened and voting against that party if we don't like what has happened. Retrospective voting does not require us to have a lot of information—all we need to know is whether things have, in our view, gotten better or worse.

Elections are decided by retrospective voters.[14] In 1980 they decided to vote against Jimmy Carter because inflation was rampant, interest rates were high, and we seemed to be getting the worst of things overseas. The evidence suggests rather clearly that they did not vote *for* Ronald Reagan; they voted for *an alternative to* Jimmy Carter. (Some people did

vote for Reagan and his philosophy; they were voting prospectively, but they were in the minority.) In 1984 people voted for Ronald Reagan because unemployment, inflation, and interest rates were down and because we no longer seemed to be getting pushed around overseas. In 1980 retrospective voters wanted change; in 1984 they wanted continuity. In 1988 there was no incumbent running, but George Bush portrayed himself as the candidate who would continue the policies that had led to prosperity and depicted Michael Dukakis as a "closet liberal" who would change those policies. In 1992 the economy had once again turned sour, and so voters turned away from Bush and toward his rivals, Bill Clinton and Ross Perot.

Though most incumbent members of Congress get reelected, those who lose do so, it appears, largely because they are the victims of retrospective voting. After Reagan was first elected, the economy went into a recession in 1981–1982. As a result Republican members of Congress were penalized by the voters, and Democratic challengers were helped. But it is not just the economy that can hurt congressional candidates. Since 1860 every midterm election but one (1934) has witnessed a loss of congressional seats by the party holding the White House. Just why this should be is not entirely clear, but it probably has something to do with the tendency of some voters to change their opinions of the presidential party once that party has had a chance to govern—which is to say, a chance to make some mistakes, disappoint some supporters, and irritate some interests.

Some scholars believe that retrospective voting is based largely on economic conditions. Figure 8.3 certainly provides support for this view. Each dot represents a presidential election (fourteen of them, from 1948 to 2000). The horizontal axis is the percentage increase or decrease in per capita disposable income (adjusted for inflation) during the election year. The vertical axis is the percentage of the two-party vote won by the party already occupying the White House. You can see that, as per capita income goes up (as you move to the right on the horizontal axis), the incumbent political party tends to win a bigger share of the vote.

Other scholars feel that matters are more complicated than this. As a result a small industry has grown up consisting of people who use different techniques to forecast the outcome of elections. If you know how the president stands in the opinion polls several months before the election and how well the economy is performing, you can make a pretty good guess as to who is going to win the presidency. For congressional races predicting is a lot tougher, because so many local factors affect these contests. Election forecasting remains an inexact science. As one study of the performance of presidential election forecasting models and the 1992 election concluded, "Models may be no improvement over pundits."[15]

The Campaign

If party loyalty and national economic conditions play so large a role in elections, is the campaign just sound and fury, signifying nothing?

No. Campaigns can make a difference in three ways. First, they reawaken the partisan loyalties of voters. Right after a party's nominating convention selects a presidential candidate, that person's standing with voters of both parties goes way up in the polls. The reason is that the just-nominated candidate has received a lot of media attention during the summer months, when not much else is happening. When the campaign gets under way, however, both candidates get publicity, and voters return to their normal Democratic or Republican affiliations.[16]

Second, campaigns give voters a chance to watch how the candidates handle pressure, and they give candidates a chance to apply that pressure. The two rivals, after promising to conduct a campaign "on the issues" without mudslinging, immediately start searching each other's personal histories and records to find acts, statements, or congressional votes that can be shown in the worst possible light in newspaper or television ads. In 1988 George Bush asserted that as governor, Michael Dukakis had vetoed a bill to make the Pledge of Allegiance mandatory in the Massachusetts schools; Dukakis retaliated by saying that Bush had to accept responsibility for some of the scandals of the Reagan administration, because "a fish rots from the head." Many voters don't like these "negative ads"—but they work. As a result every politician constantly worries about how an opponent might portray his or her record, a fact that helps explain why so many politicians never do or say anything that can't be explained in a thirty-second television spot.

Third, campaigns allow voters an opportunity to judge the character and core values of the candi-

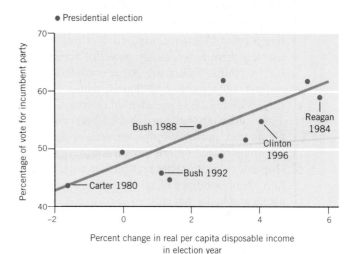

Figure 8.3 Economic Performance and Vote for the Incumbent President's Party

Note: Each dot represents a presidential election, showing the popular vote received by the incumbent president's party; 1992 data do not include votes for independent candidate H. Ross Perot.
Source: Robert S. Erikson and Kent L. Tedin, *American Public Opinion,* 5th ed. (Boston: Allyn and Bacon, 1995), 271.

dates. Most voters don't study in detail a candidate's positions on issues; even if they had the time, they know that you can't predict how politicians will behave just from knowing what a campaign manager has written in a position paper. The voters want some guidance as to how a candidate will behave once elected. They get that guidance by listening not to the details of what a candidate says but to the themes and tone of those statements. Is the candidate tough on crime and drugs? Are his or her statements about the environment sincere or perfunctory? Does the candidate favor having a strong military? Does the candidate care more about not raising taxes or more about helping the homeless?

The desire of voters to discern character, combined with the mechanics of modern campaigning—short radio and television ads and computer-targeted direct mail—lend themselves to an emphasis on themes at the expense of details. This tendency is reinforced by the expectations of ideological party activists and single-issue groups.

Thematic campaigning, negative ads, and the demands of single-issue groups are not new; they

The Hispanic Vote

Some people call the Hispanic vote the "sleeping giant." In 1998 there were an estimated 30 million people of Hispanic origin in the United States, making them a potentially powerful voting bloc. But two things reduce this power considerably.

First, only about 2 million Hispanics voted in the 1980 and 1984 presidential elections. And in 1998, although they were about 10 percent of the population, they cast only 5 percent of the votes. The main reason for this low turnout is that many Hispanic citizens are not registered to vote. In addition about one-third of all Hispanics are resident aliens and hence not entitled to register.

Second, the Hispanic vote is not homogeneous. Cuban Americans, many of them concentrated in the Miami area, tend to be strongly Republican, while Mexican Americans are strongly Democratic. But Mexican Americans outnumber Cuban Americans, and the Hispanic vote nationally has favored Democrats in every election since 1980, albeit more strongly in recent presidential-election years (by seven to three in 1992 and 1996) than in midterm congressional elections (by six to four in 1994 and 1998).

Because the Hispanic vote is chiefly located in a few key states—California, Texas, and New York—any presidential candidate who can succeed in get-

The Hispanic vote has picked up as more and more of these voters have worked for Latino candidates.

ting Hispanic voters to the polls could enjoy a big advantage. These three states have almost half of the total number of electoral votes needed to win the presidency. In nearly two dozen congressional districts in these states the Hispanic vote has already become crucial to winning election to Congress; it remains to be seen how or when the Hispanic vote will take on the same importance on the national level.

Source: New York Times (November 9, 1998): A20.

are as old as the republic. In the nineteenth century the theme was slavery and the single-issue groups were abolitionists and their opponents; their negative ads make the ones we have today sound like Sunday school sermons. At the turn of the century the themes were temperance and the vote for women; both issues led to no-holds-barred, rough-and-tumble campaigning. In the 1970s and 1980s new themes were advanced by fundamentalist Christians and by pro- and antiabortion groups.

What has changed is not the tone of campaigning but the advent of primary elections. Once, political parties picked candidates out of a desire to win elections. Today activists and single-issue groups influence the selection of candidates, sometimes out of a belief that it is better to lose with the "right" candidate than to win with the wrong one. In a five-

candidate primary, only 21 percent of the voters can pick the winner. Single-issue groups can make a big difference under these conditions, even though they may not have much influence in the general election.

Finding a Winning Coalition

Putting together a winning electoral coalition means holding on to your base among committed partisans and attracting the swing voters who cast their ballots in response to issues (retrospectively or prospectively) and personalities.

There are two ways to examine the nature of the parties' voting coalitions. One is to ask what percentage of various identifiable groups in the population supported the Democratic or Republican candidate for president. The other is to ask what proportion of a party's total vote came from each of these groups. The answer to the first question tells us how *loyal* African Americans, farmers, union members, and others are to the Democratic or Republican party or candidate; the answer to the second question tells us how *important* each group is to a candidate or party.

For the Democratic coalition African Americans are the most loyal voters. In every election but one since 1952, two-thirds or more of all African Americans voted Democratic; since 1964 four-fifths have gone Democratic. At one time Jewish voters were almost as solidly Democratic, but in 1980 only a minority supported Jimmy Carter (the rest split their votes between Reagan and John Anderson). Most Hispanics have been Democrats, though the label "Hispanic" conceals differences among Cuban Americans (who often vote Republican) and Mexican Americans and Puerto Ricans (who are strongly Democratic). The turnout among most Hispanic groups has been quite low (many are not yet citizens), so their political power is not equivalent to their numbers (see the box on page 204).

The Democrats have lost their once strong hold on Catholics, southerners, and union members. In 1960 Catholics supported John F. Kennedy (a Democrat and fellow Catholic), but they also voted for Eisenhower, Nixon, and Reagan, all Republicans. Union members deserted the Democrats in 1968 and 1972, came back in 1980 and 1988, and divided about evenly between the two parties in 1952, 1956, and 1980. White southerners have voted Republican in national elections but Democratic in many local ones (see Table 8.4).

The Republican party is often described as the party of business and professional people. The loyalty of these groups to Republicans is in fact strong: only in 1964 did they desert the Republican candidate to support Lyndon Johnson. Farmers have usually been Republican, but they are a volatile group, highly sensitive to the level of farm prices—and thus quick to change parties. They abandoned the Republicans in 1948 and 1964. Contrary to popular wisdom, the Republican party usually wins a majority of the votes of poor people (defined as those earning less than roughly $5,000 a year). Only in 1964 did most poor people support the Democratic candidate. This can be explained by the fact that the poor include quite different elements—low-income blacks (who are Demo-

Union members were once heavily Democratic, but since Ronald Reagan began winning white union votes in 1980, these votes have been up for grabs.

crats) and many elderly, retired persons (who usually vote Republican).

In sum the loyalty of most identifiable groups of voters to either party is not overwhelming. Only African Americans, businesspeople, and Jews usually give two-thirds or more of their votes to one party or the other; other groups display tendencies, but none that cannot be overcome.

The contribution that each of these groups makes to the party coalitions is a different matter. Though African Americans are overwhelmingly and persistently Democratic, they make up so small a portion of the total electorate that they have never accounted for more than a quarter of the total Democratic vote (see Table 8.5). The groups that make up the largest part of the Democratic vote—Catholics, union members, southerners—are also the least dependable parts of that coalition.[17]

When representatives of various segments of society make demands on party leaders and presidential candidates, they usually stress their numbers or their loyalty, but rarely both. African American leaders, for example, sometimes describe the black vote as being of decisive importance to Democrats and thus deserving of special consideration from a Democratic

Table 8.4   Who Likes the Democrats?

Percentage of various groups saying that they voted for the Democratic presidential candidate, 1964–2000.

	1964	1968[a]	1972	1976	1980[c]	1984	1988	1992[d]	1996	2000
Sex										
Men	60%	41%	37%	53%	37%	37%	41%	41%	43%	42%
Women	62	45	38	48	45	42	49	46	54	54
Race										
White	59	38	32	46	36	34	40	39	43	42
Nonwhite	94	85	87	85	82	90	86	82	84	90
Education										
College	52	37	37	42	35	40	43	44	47	45
Grad school	66	52	49	58	43	49	56	55	52	52
Occupation										
Professional and business	54	34	31	42	33	37	40	NA	NA	NA
Blue-collar	71	50	43	58	46	46	50	NA	NA	NA
Age										
Under 30	64	47	48	53	43	41	47	44	53	48
50 and over	59	41	36	52	41[e]	39	49	50	48[g]	48
Religion										
Protestant	55	35	30	46	NA	NA	33[f]	33	36	42
Catholic	76	59	48	57	40	44	47	44	53	50
Jewish[b]	89	85	66	68	45	66	64	78	78	79
Southerners	52	31	29	54	47	36	41	42	46	NA

[a]1968 election had three major candidates (Humphrey, Nixon, and Wallace). [b]Jewish vote estimated from various sources; since the number of Jewish persons interviewed is often less than 100, the error in this figure, as well as that for nonwhites, may be large. [c]1980 election had three major candidates (Carter, Reagan, and Anderson). [d]1992 election had three major candidates (Clinton, Bush, and Perot). [e]For 1980–1992, refers to age 60 and over. [f]For 1988, white Protestants only. [g]For 1996, refers to age 45 and over.

Sources: For 1964–1976: Gallup poll data, as tabulated in Jeane J. Kirkpatrick, "Changing Patterns of Electoral Competition," in *The New American Political System*, ed. Anthony King (Washington, D.C.: American Enterprise Institute, 1978), 264–256. For 1980–1992: Data from *New York Times*/CBS News exit polls. For 1996: *Congressional Quarterly Weekly Report*, 1997, p. 188; For 2000: Exit polls supplied by ABC news.

Table 8.5   The Contribution Made to Democratic Vote Totals by Various Groups, 1956–1996[a]

	1956	1960	1964	1968	1972	1976	1980	1984	1988	1992	1996
Poor (income under $3,000 before 1980, $5,000 in 1990)	19%	16%	15%	12%	10%	7%	5%	8%	5%	5%	5%
Black (and nonwhite)	5	7	12	19	22	16	22	24	15	23	25
Union member (or union member in family)	36	31	32	28	32	33	32	32	27	21	23
Catholic (and other non-Protestant)	38	47	36	40	34	35	32	47	43	46	44
South (including border states)	23	27	21	24	25	36	39	29	24	33	31
Central cities (12 largest metropolitan areas)	19	19	15	14	14	11	12	12	14	NA	6

[a]The figures shown represent the percentage of the party's vote in any specific election attributable to the group in question.

Source: Extracted from figures presented by Robert Axelrod, "Communications," *American Political Science Review* (June 1981). Updated by Daron Shaw; ICPSR American National Election Study, 1992, Pre- and Post-Election Surveys. 1996 estimates based on analyses of NES data by Daron R. Shaw.

president. But African Americans are so loyal that a Democratic candidate can almost take their votes for granted, and in any event they are not as numerous as other groups. Union leaders emphasize how many union voters there are, but a president will know that union leaders cannot "deliver" the union vote and that this vote may go to the president's opponent, whatever the leaders say. For any presidential candidate a winning coalition must be put together anew for each election. Only a few voters can be taken for granted or written off as a lost cause.

Election Outcomes

To the candidates, and perhaps to the voters, the only interesting outcome of an election is who won. To a political scientist the interesting outcomes are the broad trends in winning and losing and what they imply about the attitudes of voters, the operation of the electoral system, the fate of political parties, and the direction of public policy.

Figure 8.4 shows the trend in the popular vote for president since before the Civil War. From 1876 to 1896 the Democrats and Republicans were hotly competitive. The Republicans won three times, the Democrats twice in close contests. Beginning in 1896 the Republicans became the dominant party, and except for 1912 and 1916, when Woodrow Wilson, a Democrat, was able to win owing to a split in the Republican party, the Republicans carried every presidential election until 1932. Then Franklin Roosevelt put together what has since become known as the "New Deal coalition," and the Democrats became the dominant party. They won every election until 1952, when Eisenhower, a Republican and a popular military hero, was elected for the first of his two terms.

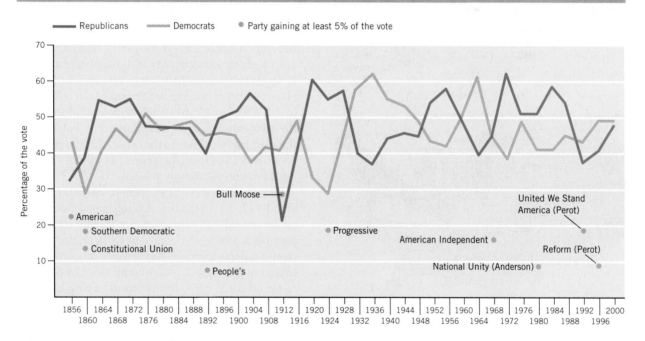

Figure 8.4   Partisan Division of the Presidential Vote in the Nation, 1856–1996

Sources: For 1856–1988: Historical Data Archive, Inter-University Consortium for Political Research, as reported in William H. Flanigan and Nancy H. Zingale, *Political Behavior of the American Electorate*, 3rd ed., 32. Copyright © 1975 by Allyn and Bacon, Inc., Boston. Reprinted with permission of William C. Brown Publishers, Dubuque, Iowa. For 1992: Reprinted with permission from *The World Almanac and Book of Facts 1994*, 73. Copyright © 1993 K-III Reference Corporation. All rights reserved.

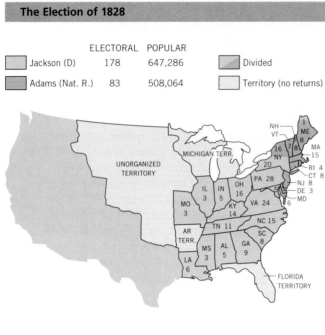

The Election of 1828

	ELECTORAL	POPULAR
Jackson (D)	178	647,286
Adams (Nat. R.)	83	508,064

Divided

Territory (no returns)

The Election of 1860

	ELECTORAL	POPULAR
Lincoln (R)	180	1,866,452
Douglas (No. D)	12	1,375,157
Breckenridge (So. D)	76	847,953
Bell (Const. Union)	39	590,631

Divided

Territory (no returns)

Party Realignments

There have clearly been important turning points in the strength of the major parties, especially in the twentieth century, when for long periods we have not so much had close competition between two parties

as we have had an alternation of dominance by one party and then the other. To help explain these major shifts in the tides of politics, scholars have developed the theory of **critical or realigning periods.** During such periods a sharp, lasting shift occurs in the popular coalition supporting one or both parties. The issues that separate the two parties change, and so the kinds of voters supporting each party change. This shift may occur at the time of the election or just after, as the new administration draws in new supporters.[18] There seem to have been five realignments so far, during or just after these elections: 1800 (when the Jeffersonian Republicans defeated the Federalists), 1828 (when the Jacksonian Democrats came to power), 1860 (when the Whig party collapsed and the Republicans under Lincoln came to power), 1896 (when the Republicans defeated William Jennings Bryan), and 1932 (when the Democrats under Roosevelt came into office). Some observers, noting that these realignments have occurred with marked regularity every twenty-eight to thirty-six years, have speculated on whether they are the result of inevitable cycles in American political life.

Such speculations need not concern us, for what is more important is to understand why a realignment occurs at all. That is not entirely clear. For one thing there are at least two kinds of realignments— one in which a major party is so badly defeated that it disappears and a new party emerges to take its place (this happened to the Federalists in 1800 and to the Whigs in 1856–1860), and another in which the two existing parties continue but voters shift their support from one to the other (this happened in 1896 and 1932). Furthermore, not all critical elections have been carefully studied.

The three clearest cases seem to be 1860, 1896, and 1932. By 1860 the existing parties could no longer straddle the fence on the slavery issue. The Republican party was formed in 1856 on the basis of clear-cut opposition to slavery; the Democratic party split in half in 1860, with one part (led by Stephen A. Douglas and based in the North) trying to waffle on the issue and the other (led by John C. Breckinridge and drawing its support from the South) categorically denying that any government had any right to outlaw slavery. The remnants of the Whig party, renamed the Constitutional Union party, tried to unite the nation by writing no platform at all, thus remaining silent on slavery. Lincoln and the antislavery Republicans won in 1860; Breckinridge and the proslavery Southern Democrats came in second. From that moment on, the two major political parties had acquired different sources of support and stood (at least for a decade) for different principles. The parties that had tried to straddle the fence were eliminated. The Civil War fixed these new party loyalties deep in the popular mind, and the structure of party competition was set for nearly forty years.

In 1896 a different kind of realignment occurred. Economics rather than slavery was at issue. A series of depressions during the 1880s and 1890s fell especially hard on farmers in the Midwest and parts of the South. The prices paid to farmers for their commodities had been falling more or less steadily since the Civil War, making it increasingly difficult for them to pay their bills. A bitter reaction against the two major parties, which were straddling this issue as they had straddled slavery, spread like a prairie fire, leading to the formation of parties of economic protest—the Greenbackers and the Populists. Reinforcing the economic cleavages were cultural ones: populists tended to be fundamentalist Protestants; urban voters were increasingly Catholic. Matters came to a head in 1896 when William Jennings Bryan captured the Democratic nomination for president and saw to it that the party adopted a populist platform. The existing Populist party endorsed the Bryan candidacy. In the election anti-Bryan Democrats deserted the party in droves to support the Republican candidate, William McKinley. Once again a real issue divided the two parties: the Republicans stood for industry, business, hard money, protective tariffs, and urban interests; the Democrats for farmers, small towns, low tariffs, and rural interests. The Republicans won, carrying the cities, workers and businesspeople alike; the Democrats lost, carrying most of the southern and midwestern farm states. The old split between North and South that resulted from the Civil War was now replaced in part by an East versus West, city versus farm split.[19] It was not, however, only an economic cleavage—the Republicans had been able to appeal to Catholics and Lutherans, who disliked fundamentalism and its hostility toward liquor and immigrants.

This alignment persisted until 1932. Again change was triggered by an economic depression; again more than economic issues were involved. The New Deal coalition that emerged was based on bringing together into the Democratic party urban workers, northern blacks, southern whites, and Jewish

The Election of 1896

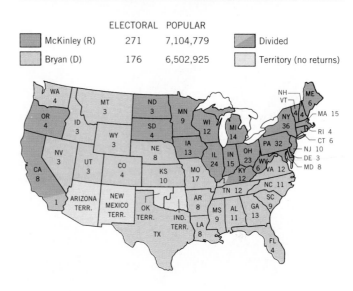

	ELECTORAL	POPULAR	
McKinley (R)	271	7,104,779	Divided
Bryan (D)	176	6,502,925	Territory (no returns)

The Election of 1932

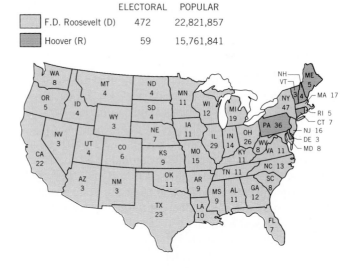

	ELECTORAL	POPULAR
F.D. Roosevelt (D)	472	22,821,857
Hoover (R)	59	15,761,841

voters. Unlike 1860 and 1896, it was not preceded by any third-party movement; it occurred suddenly (though some groups had begun to shift their allegiance in 1928) and gathered momentum throughout the 1930s. The Democrats, isolated since 1896 as a southern and midwestern sectional party, had now become the majority party by finding a candidate and a cause that could lure urban workers,

The 1896 election was a watershed in American politics—a "realigning election" that brought together new party coalitions. It pitted William McKinley, the Republican defender of the gold standard (left), against William Jennings Bryan, a fiery midwestern champion of strict religion and easy money (right).

blacks, and Jews away from the Republican party, where they had been for decades. It was obviously a delicate coalition—blacks and southern whites disagreed on practically everything except their liking for Roosevelt; Jews and the Irish bosses of the big-city machines also had little in common. But the federal government under Roosevelt was able to supply enough benefits to each of these disparate groups to keep them loyal members of the coalition and to provide a new basis for party identification.

These critical elections may have involved not converting existing voters to new party loyalties but recruiting into the dominant party new voters— young people just coming of voting age, immigrants just receiving their citizenship papers, and blacks just receiving, in some places, the right to vote. But there were also genuine conversions—northern blacks, for example, had been heavily Republican before Roosevelt but became heavily Democratic after his election.

In short an electoral realignment occurs when a new issue of utmost importance to the voters (slav-

ery, the economy) cuts across existing party divisions and replaces old issues that were formerly the basis of party identification. Some observers have speculated that we are due for a new party realignment as the tensions within the New Deal coalition become more evident. As the memory of Roosevelt and the Great Depression fades and as new voters come of age, the ability of the Democrats to hold on to both people who are liberal and those who are conservative on social issues may decline.

Some people wondered whether the election of 1980, since it brought into power the most conservative administration in half a century, signaled a new realignment. Many of President Reagan's supporters began talking of their having a "mandate" to adopt major new policies in keeping with the views of the "new majority." But Reagan won in 1980 less because of what he stood for than because he was not Jimmy Carter, and he was reelected in 1984 primarily because people were satisfied with how the country was doing, especially economically.[20]

Just because we have had periods of one-party dominance in the past does not mean that we will have them in the future. Reagan's election could not have been a traditional realignment, because it left Congress in the hands of the Democratic party. Moreover, some scholars are beginning to question the theory of critical elections, or at least the theory that they occur with some regularity.

Nevertheless, one major change has occurred of late—the shift in the presidential voting patterns of the South. From 1972 through 1996 the South was more Republican than the nation as a whole. The proportion of white southerners describing themselves to pollsters as "strongly Democratic" fell from more than one-third in 1952 to about one-seventh in 1984. There has been a corresponding increase in "independents." As it turns out, southern white independents have voted overwhelmingly Republican in recent presidential elections.[21] If you lump independents together with the parties for which they actually vote, the party alignment among white southerners has gone from six-to-one Democratic in 1952 to about fifty-fifty Democrats and Republicans. If this continues, it will constitute a major realignment in a region of the country that is growing rapidly in population and political clout.

In general, however, the kind of dramatic realignment that occurred in the 1860s or after 1932 may not occur again, because party labels have lost their meaning for a growing number of voters. For these people politics may *de*align rather than *re*align.

Party Decline

The evidence that the parties are decaying, not realigning, is of several sorts. We have already noted (see Chapter 7) that the proportion of people identifying with one or the other party declined between 1960 and 1980. Simultaneously, the proportion of those voting a **split ticket** (as opposed to a **straight ticket**) increased. Figure 8.5, for example, shows the steep increase in the percentage of congressional districts carried by one party for the presidency and by the other for Congress. Whereas in the 1940s one party would carry a given district for both its presidential and congressional candidates, today about a quarter of the districts split their votes between one party's presidential candidate and the other's congressional candidate.

In 1988 more than *half* of all House Democrats were elected in districts that voted for Republican

Franklin Roosevelt greets George Washington Carver at Tuskegee Institute in Alabama. Blacks had long voted Republican; during the New Deal they shifted to the Democratic party. This change was part of the political realignment that occurred in the elections of 1932 and 1936.

George Bush as president. This ticket splitting was greatest in the South, but it was common everywhere. If every district that voted for Bush had also elected a Republican to Congress, the Republican party would have held a two-to-one majority in the

Figure 8.5   Trends in Split-Ticket Voting for President and Congress, 1920–1996

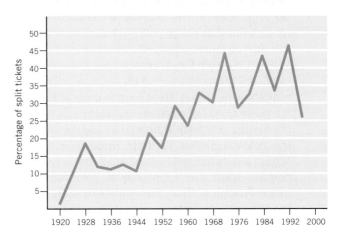

Note: The figure is the percentage of congressional districts carried by presidential and congressional candidates of different parties in each election year.

House of Representatives. Ticket splitting creates divided government—the White House and Congress are controlled by different parties (see Chapter 12). Ticket splitting helped the Democrats keep control of the House of Representatives from 1954 to 1994.

Ticket splitting was almost unheard-of in the nineteenth century, and for a very good reason. In those days the voter was either given a ballot by the party of his choice and he dropped it, intact, into the ballot box (thereby voting for everybody listed on the ballot), or he was given a government-printed ballot that listed in columns all the candidates of each party. All the voter had to do was mark the top of one column in order to vote for every candidate in that column. (When voting machines came along, they provided a single lever that, when pulled, cast votes for all the candidates of a particular party.) Progressives around the turn of the century began to persuade states to adopt the **office-bloc** (or "Massachusetts") **ballot** in place of the **party-column** (or "Indiana") **ballot.** The office-bloc ballot lists all candidates by office; there is no way to vote a straight party ticket by making one mark. Not surprisingly, states using the office-bloc ballot show much more ticket splitting than those without it.[22]

The Effects of Elections on Policy

Cynics complain that elections are meaningless: no matter who wins, crooks, incompetents, or self-serving politicians still hold office. The more charitable argue that elected officials are usually decent enough but that public policy remains more or less the same no matter which official or party is in office.

There is no brief and simple response to this latter view. Much depends on which office or policy you examine. One reason it is so hard to generalize about the policy effects of elections is that the offices to be filled by the voters are so numerous and the ability of the political parties to unite these officeholders behind a common policy is so weak that any policy proposal must run a gauntlet of potential opponents. Though we have but two major parties, and though only one party can win the presidency, each party is a weak coalition of diverse elements that reflect the many divisions in public opinion. The proponents of a new law must put together a majority coalition almost from scratch, and a winning coalition on one issue tends to be somewhat different—

quite often dramatically different—from a winning coalition on another issue.

In a parliamentary system with strong parties, such as that in Great Britain, an election can often have a major effect on public policy. When the Labour party won office in 1945, it put several major industries under public ownership and launched a comprehensive set of social services, including a nationalized health care plan. Its ambitious and controversial campaign platform was converted, almost item by item, into law. When the Conservative party returned to power in 1951, it accepted some of these changes but rejected others (for example, it denationalized the steel industry).

American elections, unless accompanied by a national crisis such as a war or a depression, rarely produce changes of the magnitude of those that occurred in Britain in 1945. The constitutional system within which our elections take place was designed to moderate the pace of change—to make it neither easy nor impossible to adopt radical proposals. But the fact that the system is intended to moderate the rate of change does not mean that it will always work that way.

The election of 1860 brought to national power a party committed to opposing the extension of slavery and southern secession; it took a bloody war to vindicate that policy. The election of 1896 led to the dominance of a party committed to high tariffs, a strong currency, urban growth, and business prosperity—a commitment that was not significantly altered until 1932. The election of that year led to the New Deal, which produced the greatest single enlargement of federal authority since 1860. The election of 1964 gave the Democrats such a large majority in Congress (as well as control of the presidency) that there began to issue forth an extraordinary number of new policies of sweeping significance—Medicare and Medicaid, federal aid to education and to local law enforcement, two dozen environmental and consumer protection laws, the Voting Rights Act of 1965, a revision of the immigration laws, and a new cabinet-level Department of Housing and Urban Development.

The election of 1980 brought into office an administration determined to reverse the direction of policy over the preceding half century. Reagan's administration succeeded in obtaining large tax cuts, significant reductions in spending (or in the rate of increase of spending) on some domestic pro-

MEMORANDUM

To: Senator Bob Edison
From: Jill Long, campaign manager
Subject: Responding to negative ads

Never in your political career have you been attacked so viciously. The fact is that your lead is now in the single digits, and we think it is because of the negative ads. With only a few weeks left until election day, you need to decide whether you want us to fight fire with fire.

Arguments for:

1. Negative ads work. In particular some studies, and lots of political lore, suggest that "going negative" helps lesser-known, less-well-financed challengers against better-known, better-financed incumbents who fail to respond in kind and in time.
2. In the age of the political sound bite, it is much easier to dish dirt on an opponent's personal history and official record than it is to explain the complexities behind one's own past votes or to put one's past public statements back into context.
3. If you don't sling the mud back, it will stick to you, and people will question not only your integrity but also your toughness.

Arguments against:

1. Negative ads can backfire. People don't like them, esecially when the charges are harshly personal or otherwise over the top.
2. A tit-for-tat sound bite volley can be positive: "I am a person of integrity. I vote my conscience. I live to serve."
3. If you stay positive and "wrap yourself in the flag," the mud will melt away and people will question your opponent's decency and character.

Your decision:
Go negative _____
Stay positive _____

U.S. Senate Challenger Launches Blistering Media Attack

TV and Radio Ads Call Incumbent "Callous" Puppet of Big Money

October 20
PHOENIX, AZ
Until last week every statewide poll showed U.S. senator Bob Edison coasting to a comfortable reelection victory. Today, however, the Edison campaign is reeling. Polls show the race tightening fast, thanks to thirty-second negative ads depicting the senator's votes against certain gun control bills and prescription drug price control plans as evidence of his "heartless approach to public safety and callous disregard for the lives of the medically needy." The ads call Edison's votes "political payoffs to the gun makers and big drug companies who have owned him" for years . . .

grams, and changes in the policies of some regulatory agencies. The election of 1982, in which the Democrats made gains in the House of Representatives, stiffened congressional resistance to further spending cuts and stimulated renewed interest in tax increases as a way of reducing the deficit. Following the election of 1984 a major tax reform plan was passed. After the 1996 election Clinton and Republican congressional leaders agreed on a plan to balance the budget.

In view of all these developments it is hard to argue that the pace of change in our government is always slow or that elections never make a difference. Studies by scholars confirm that elections are often significant, despite the difficulty of getting laws passed. One analysis of about fourteen hundred promises made between 1944 and 1964 in the platforms of the two major parties revealed that 72 percent were put into effect.[23]

Another study examined the party platforms of the Democrats and Republicans from 1844 to 1968 and all the laws passed by Congress between 1789 and 1968. By a complex statistical method, the author of the study was able to show that during certain periods the differences between the platforms of the two parties were especially large (1856, 1880, 1896, 1932) and that there was at about the same time a high rate of change in the kinds of laws being passed.[24] This study supports the general impression conveyed by history that elections can often be central to important policy changes.

Why then do we so often think that elections make little difference? It is because public opinion and the political parties enter a phase of consolidation and continuity between periods of rapid change. During this phase the changes are, so to speak, digested, and party leaders adjust to the new popular consensus, which may (or may not) evolve around the merits of these changes. During the 1870s and 1880s Democratic politicians had to come to terms with the failure of the southern secessionist movement and the abolition of slavery; during the 1900s the Democrats had to adjust again, this time to the fact that national economic policy was going to support industrialization and urbanization, not farming; during the 1940s and 1950s the Republicans had to learn to accept the popularity of the New Deal.

Elections in ordinary times are not "critical"— they do not produce any major party realignment, they are not fought out over a dominant issue, and they provide the winners with no clear mandate. In most cases an election is little more than a retrospective judgment on the record of the incumbent president and the existing congressional majority. If times are good, incumbents win easily; if times are bad, incumbents may lose even though their opponents may have no clear plans for change. But even a "normal" election can produce dramatic results if the winner is a person such as Ronald Reagan, who helped give his party a distinctive political philosophy.

Summary

Political campaigns have increasingly become personalized, with little or no connection to formal party organizations, as a result of the decay of parties, the rise of the direct primary and the electronic media, and campaign finance laws. Candidates face the problem of creating a temporary organization that can raise money from large numbers of small donors, mobilize enthusiastic supporters, and win a nomination in a way that will not harm their ability to appeal to a broader, more diverse constituency in the general election. Campaigning has an uncertain effect on election outcomes, but election outcomes can have important effects on public policy, especially at those times—during critical or "realigning" elections— when new voters are coming into the electorate in large numbers, old party loyalties are weakening, or a major issue is splitting the majority party. Most people vote retrospectively rather than prospectively.

World Wide Web Resources

- Federal Election Commission: www.fec.gov
- Project Vote Smart: www.vote-smart.org
- Election history: clerkweb.house.gov
- Electoral college: www.avagara.com/e_c
- Campaign finance: www.opensecrets.org

Key Terms

incumbent *p. 180*

coattails *p. 181*

political action committee *p. 182*

position issue *p. 185*

general election *p. 186*

primary election *p. 186*

closed primary *p. 186*

open primary *p. 186*

blanket primary *p. 186*

runoff primary *p. 186*

presidential primary *p. 186*

valence issue *p. 186*

soft money *p. 194*

prospective voting *p. 201*

retrospective voting *p. 202*

critical or realigning periods *p. 208*

split ticket *p. 211*

straight ticket *p. 211*

office-bloc ballot *p. 212*

party-column ballot *p. 212*

Suggested Readings

Asher, Herbert. *Presidential Elections and American Politics*. 5th ed. Pacific Grove, Calif.: Brooks/Cole, 1992. A useful, brief analysis of how Americans have voted.

Burnham, Walter Dean. *Critical Elections and the Mainsprings of American Politics*. New York: Norton, 1970. An argument about the decline in voting participation and the significance of the realigning election of 1896.

Jacobson, Gary C. *The Politics of Congressional Elections*. 2nd ed. Boston: Little, Brown, 1987. Careful analysis of how people get elected to Congress.

Kayden, Xandra. *Campaign Organization*. Lexington, Mass.: D. C. Heath, 1978. A close look at how political campaigns are organized, staffed, and led at the state level.

Malbin, Michael J., ed. *Money and Politics in the United States: Financing Elections in the 1980s*. Chatham, N.J.: Chatham House, 1984. Articles on the sources and uses of campaign money, with special attention to political parties and political action committees.

Page, Benjamin I. *Choices and Echoes in Presidential Elections*. Chicago: University of Chicago Press, 1978. Analyzes the interaction between the behavior of candidates and of voters in American elections.

Sorauf, Frank. *Money in American Elections*. Glenview, Ill.: Scott Foresman, 1988. The best summary of what we know about the sources and effects of campaign spending.

Sundquist, James L. *Dynamics of the Party System: Alignment and Realignment of Political Parties in the United States*. Rev. ed. Washington, D.C.: Brookings Institution, 1983. Historical analysis of realigning elections from 1860 to the nonrealignment of 1980.

Interest Groups

Enduring Questions

1. Why do people join interest groups?
2. Why do interest groups differ in their tactics?
3. With so many interest groups active, has America succeeded in "curing the mischiefs of faction"?
4. Are there any ways, both feasible and desirable, of regulating interest groups?

Explaining Proliferation

The Birth of Interest Groups

Kinds of Organizations
Institutional Interests • Membership Interests • Incentives to Join • The Influence of the Staff

Interest Groups and Social Movements
The Environmental Movement • The Feminist Movement • The Union Movement

Funds for Interest Groups
Foundation Grants • Federal Grants and Contracts • Direct Mail

The Problem of Bias

The Activities of Interest Groups
Information • Public Support: The Rise of the New Politics • Money and PACs • The "Revolving Door" • Trouble

Regulating Interest Groups

lmost every tourist arriving in Washington visits the White House and the Capitol. Many look at the Supreme Court building. But hardly any walk down K Street, where much of the political life of the country occurs.

K Street? From the sidewalk it is just a row of office buildings, no different from what one might find in downtown Seattle or Kansas City. What's to see? But in these buildings, and in similar ones lining nearby streets, are the offices of the nearly seven thousand organizations that are represented in Washington.

It is doubtful whether there is any other nation in which so many organizations are represented in its capital. They are there to participate in politics. They are interest groups, or, if you prefer, lobbies.

Explaining Proliferation

There are at least three reasons why interest groups are so common in this country. First, the more cleavages there are in a society, the greater the variety of interests that will exist. In addition to divisions along

217

★ POLITICALLY

SPEAKING ★

Lobby

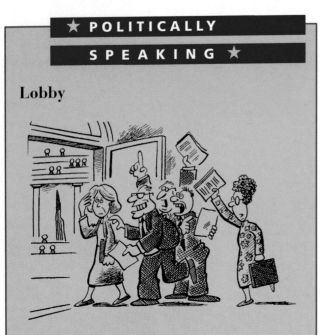

To **lobby** means to attempt to influence governmental decisions, especially legislation. A lobby is a group organized for this purpose, and a **lobbyist** is an individual who engages in lobbying.

The term came into vogue in the mid-seventeenth century to refer to a large anteroom near the English House of Commons, wherein members of Parliament could be approached by people pleading their cases.

In the United States lobbyists were people who met members of Congress just outside the chambers of the House or Senate to argue their cause. In the nineteenth century *lobbyist* became synonymous with *vote buyer*, because of the widespread belief that lobbyists were using money to corrupt legislators.

Today lobbying is no longer regarded as an inevitably corrupt activity, and lobbyists in Washington are no longer embarrassed to refer to themselves by this term.

Source: Adapted from *Safire's Political Dictionary* by William Safire. Copyright © 1968, 1972, 1978 by William Safire. Reprinted by permission of Random House, Inc. and the author.

cans are scattered over a vast land made up of many regions with distinctive traditions and cultures. These social facts make for a great variety of interests and opinions. As James Madison said in *Federalist* No. 10, "The latent causes of faction are thus sown in the nature of man."

Second, the American constitutional system contributes to the number of interest groups by multiplying the points at which such groups can gain access to the government. In a nation such as Great Britain, where most political authority is lodged in a single official such as the prime minister, there are only a few places where important decisions are made—and thus only a few opportunities for affecting those decisions. But when political authority is shared by the president, the courts, and Congress (and within Congress among two houses and countless committees and subcommittees), there are plenty of places where one can argue one's case. And the more chances there are to influence policy, the more organizations there will be that seek to exercise that influence.

This fact helps explain why in Great Britain there is often only one organization representing a given interest, whereas in the United States there are several. In London only one major association represents farmers, one represents industry, one represents veterans, and one represents doctors. In the United States, by contrast, at least three organizations represent farmers (the American Farm Bureau Federation, the National Farmers' Union, and the Grange), and each of these is made up of state and county branches, many of which act quite independently of national headquarters. Though there is one major American labor organization, the AFL-CIO, it is in fact a loose coalition of independent unions (plumbers, steelworkers, coal miners), and some large unions, such as the Teamsters, were for many years not part of the AFL-CIO at all.

Third, the weakness of political parties in this country may help explain the number and strength of our interest groups. Where parties are strong, interests work through the parties; where parties are weak, interests operate directly on the government. That at least is the theory. Though scholars are not certain of its validity, it is a plausible theory and can be illustrated by differences among American cities. In cities such as Chicago where a party (in this case, the Democrats) has historically been very strong, labor unions, business associations, and citizens

lines of income and occupation found in any society, America is a nation of countless immigrants and many races. There are at least eighty-five religions that claim fifty thousand members or more. Amerigroups have had to work with the party and on its terms. But in cities such as Boston and Los Angeles where the parties are very weak, interest groups proliferate and play a large role in making policy.[1]

In Austria, France, and Italy many if not most interest groups are closely linked to one or another political party. In Italy, for example, each party—Socialist, Communist, and Christian Democrat—has a cluster of labor unions, professional associations, and social clubs allied with it.[2] Though American interest groups often support one party (the AFL-CIO, for example, almost always backs Democratic candidates for office), the relationship between party and interest group here is not as close as it is in Europe.

The Birth of Interest Groups

The number of interest groups has grown rapidly since 1960. A study of Washington-based political associations revealed that roughly 70 percent of them established their Washington offices after 1960, and nearly half opened their doors after 1970.[3]

The 1960s and 1970s were boom years for interest groups, but there have been other periods in our history when political associations were created in especially large numbers. During the 1770s many groups arose to agitate for American independence; during the 1830s and 1840s the number of religious associations increased sharply, and the anti-slavery movement began. In the 1860s trade unions based on crafts emerged in significant numbers, farmers formed the Grange, and various fraternal organizations were born. In the 1880s and 1890s business associations proliferated. The great era of organization building, however, was in the first two decades of the twentieth century. Within this twenty-year period many of the best-known and largest associations with an interest in national politics were formed: the Chamber of Commerce, the National Association of Manufacturers, the American Medical Association, the National Association for the Advancement of Colored People (NAACP), the Urban League, the American Farm Bureau, the Farmers' Union, the National Catholic Welfare Conference, the American Jewish Committee, and Anti-Defamation League. The wave of interest group formation that occurred in the 1960s led to the emergence of environmental, consumer, and political reform organizations such as those sponsored by consumer activist Ralph Nader.

The fact that associations in general, and political interest groups in particular, are created more rapidly in some periods than in others suggests that

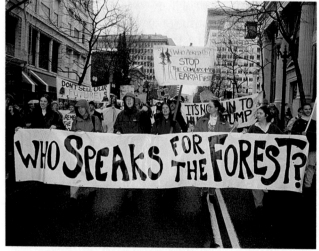

The greater the activity of government—for example, in regulating the timber industry—the greater the number of interest groups.

Almost any group today is prepared to stage a demonstration. Here is the "Million Mom March" organized to press for tougher gun laws.

these groups do not arise inevitably out of natural social processes. There have always been farmers in this country, but there were no national farm organizations until the latter part of the nineteenth century. Blacks had been victimized by various white-supremacy policies from the end of the Civil War on, but the NAACP did not emerge until 1910. Men and women worked in factories for decades before industrial unions were formed.

At least four factors help explain the rise of interest groups. The first consists of broad economic developments that create new interests and redefine old ones. Farmers had little reason to become organized for political activity so long as most of them consumed what they produced. The importance of regular political activity became evident only after most farmers began to produce cash crops for sale in markets that were unstable or affected by forces (the weather, the railroads, foreign competition) that farmers could not control. Similarly, for many decades most workers were craftspeople working alone or in small groups. Such unions as existed were little more than craft guilds interested in protecting members' jobs and in training apprentices. The reason for large, mass-membership unions did not exist until there arose mass-production industry operated by large corporations.

Second, government policy itself helped create interest groups. Wars create veterans, who in turn demand pensions and other benefits. The first large veterans organization, the Grand Army of the Republic, was made up of Union veterans of the Civil

War. By the 1920s these men were receiving about a quarter of a billion dollars a year from the government, and naturally they created organizations to watch over the distribution of this money. The federal government encouraged the formation of the American Farm Bureau Federation (AFBF) by paying for county agents who would serve the needs of farmers under the supervision of local farm organizations; these county bureaus eventually came together as the AFBF. The Chamber of Commerce was launched at a conference attended by President William Howard Taft.

Professional societies, such as those made up of lawyers and doctors, became important in part because state governments gave to such groups the authority to decide who was qualified to become a lawyer or a doctor. Workers had a difficult time organizing so long as the government, by the use of injunctions enforced by the police and the army, prevented strikes. Unions, especially those in mass-production industries, began to flourish after Congress passed laws in the 1930s that prohibited the use of injunctions in private labor disputes, that required employers to bargain with unions, and that allowed a union representing a majority of the workers in a plant to require all workers to join it.[4]

Third, political organizations do not emerge automatically, even when government policy permits them and social circumstances seem to require them. Somebody must exercise leadership, often at substantial personal cost. These organizational entrepreneurs are found in greater numbers at certain times than at others. They are often young, caught up in a social movement, drawn to the need for change, and inspired by some political or religious doctrine. Antislavery organizations were created in the 1830s and 1840s by enthusiastic young people influenced by a religious revival then sweeping the country. The period from 1890 to 1920, when so many national organizations were created, was a time when the college-educated middle class was growing rapidly. (The number of men and women who received college degrees each year tripled between 1890 and 1920.)[5] During this era natural science and fundamentalist Christianity were locked in a bitter contest, with the Gospels and Darwinism offering competing ideas about personal salvation and social progress. The 1960s, when many new organizations were born, was a decade in which young people were powerfully influenced by the civil rights and antiwar movements and when college enrollments more than doubled.

Finally, the more activities government undertakes, the more organized groups there will be that are interested in those activities. As can be seen from Table 9.1, most Washington offices representing corporations, labor unions, and trade and professional associations were established before 1960—in some cases many decades before—because it was during the 1930s or even earlier that the government began making policies important to business and labor. The great majority of "public-interest" lobbies (those concerned with the environment or consumer protection), social welfare associations, and organizations concerned with civil rights, the elderly, and the handicapped established offices in Washington after 1960. Policies of interest to these groups, such as the major civil rights and environmental laws, were adopted after that date. In fact over half the public-interest lobbies opened their doors after 1970.

Kinds of Organizations

An **interest group** is any organization that seeks to influence public policy. When we think of an organization, we usually think of something like the Boy Scouts or the League of Women Voters—a group consisting of individual members. In Washington, however, many organizations do not have individual members at all but are offices—corporations, law firms, public relations firms, or "letterhead" organizations that get most of their money from foundations or from the government—out of which a staff operates. It is important to understand the differences between the two kinds of interest groups—institutional and membership interests.[6]

Institutional Interests

Institutional interests are individuals or organizations representing other organizations. General Motors, for example, has a Washington representative. Over five hundred firms have such representatives in the capital, most of whom have opened their offices since 1970.[7] Firms that do not want to place their own full-time representative in Washington can hire a Washington lawyer or public relations expert on a part-time basis. Between 1970 and 1980 the number of lawyers in Washington more

Table 9.1	Dates of Founding of Organizations Having Washington Offices	
	Percentage Founded	
Organization	**After 1960**	**After 1970**
Corporations	14%	6%
Unions	21	14
Professional	30	14
Trade	38	23
Civil rights	56	46
Women/elderly/disabled	56	46
"Public interest"	76	57
Social welfare	79	51

Source: Kay Lehman Schlozman and John T. Tierney, *Organized Interests and American Democracy* (New York: Harper & Row, 1986), 76. Copyright © 1986 by Kay Lehman Schlozman and John T. Tierney. Reprinted by permission of Addison-Wesley Educational Publishers, Inc.

than tripled; Washington now has more lawyers (over 38,000) than Los Angeles, a city three times its size.[8] Another kind of institutional interest is the trade or governmental association, such as the National Independent Retail Jewelers or the National Association of Counties.

Individuals or organizations that represent other organizations tend to be interested in bread-and-butter issues of vital concern to their clients. Some of the people who specialize in this work can earn very large fees. Top public relations experts and Washington lawyers can charge $400 an hour or more for their time. Since they earn a lot, they are expected to deliver a lot.

Just what they are expected to deliver, however, varies with the diversity of the groups making up the organization. The American Cotton Manufacturers Institute represents southern textile mills. Those mills are few enough in number and similar enough in outlook to allow the institute to carry out clear policies squarely based on the business interests of its clients. For example, the institute works hard to get the federal government to adopt laws and rules that will keep foreign-made textiles from competing too easily with American-made goods. Sometimes the institute is successful, sometimes not, but it is never hard to explain what it is doing.

By contrast, the U.S. Chamber of Commerce represents thousands of different businesses in hundreds of different communities. Its membership is so large and diverse that the Chamber in Washington can speak out clearly and forcefully on only those relatively few matters in which all, or most, businesses take the same position. Since all businesses would like lower taxes, the Chamber favors that. On the other hand, since some businesses (those that import goods) want low tariffs and other businesses (those that face competition from imported goods) want higher tariffs, the Chamber says little or nothing about tariffs.

Institutional interests do not just represent business firms; they also represent governments, foundations, and universities. For example, the American Council on Education claims to speak for most institutions of higher education, the American Public Transit Association represents local mass-transit systems, and the National Association of Counties argues on behalf of county governments.

Membership Interests

It is often said that Americans are a nation of joiners, and so we take for granted the many organizations around us supported by the activities and contributions of individual citizens. But we should not take this multiplicity of organizations for granted; in fact their existence is something of a puzzle.

Americans join only certain kinds of organizations more frequently than do citizens of other democratic countries. We are no more likely than the British, for example, to join social, business, professional, veterans, or charitable organizations, and we are *less* likely to join labor unions. Our reputation as

W.E.B. Du Bois (center) was one of the founders of the NAACP in 1910 and the editor of its magazine, The Crisis.

a nation of joiners arises chiefly out of our unusually high tendency to join religious and civic or political associations. About three times as many Americans as Britons say that they are members of a civic or political organization.[9]

This proclivity of Americans to get together with other citizens to engage in civic or political action reflects, apparently, a greater sense of political efficacy and a stronger sense of civic duty in this country. When Gabriel Almond and Sidney Verba asked citizens of five nations what they would do to protest an unjust local regulation, 56 percent of the Americans—but only 34 percent of the British and 13 percent of the Germans—said that they would try to organize their neighbors to write letters, sign petitions, or otherwise act in concert.[10] Americans are also more likely than Europeans to think that organized activity is an effective way to influence the national government, remote as that institution may seem. And this willingness to form civic or political groups is not a product of higher levels of education in this country; Americans of every level of schooling are political joiners.[11]

But explaining the American willingness to join politically active groups by saying that Americans feel a "sense of political efficacy" is not much of an explanation; we might as well say that people vote because they think that their vote makes a difference. But one vote clearly makes no difference at all in almost any election; similarly, one member, more or less, in the Sierra Club, the Christian Coalition, or the NAACP clearly will make no difference in the success of those organizations.

And in fact most people who are sympathetic to the aims of a mass-membership interest group do not join it. The NAACP, for example, enrolls as members only a tiny fraction of all African Americans. This is not because people are selfish or apathetic but because they are rational and numerous. A single African American, for example, knows that he or she can make no difference in the success of the NAACP, just as a single nature enthusiast knows that he or she cannot enhance the power of the Sierra Club. Moreover, if the NAACP or the Sierra Club succeeds, African Americans and nature lovers will benefit even if they are not members. Therefore rational people who value their time and money would no more join such organizations than they would attempt to empty a lake with a cup—unless they got something out of joining.

Incentives to Join

To get people to join mass-membership organizations, they must be offered an **incentive**—something of value they cannot get without joining. There are three kinds of incentives.

Solidary incentives are the sense of pleasure, status, or companionship that arises out of meeting together in small groups. Such rewards are extremely important, but because they tend to be available only from face-to-face contact, national interest groups offering them often have to organize themselves as coalitions of small local units. For example, the League of Women Voters, the Parent Teacher Association (PTA), the NAACP, the Rotary Club, and the American Legion all consist of small local chapters that support a national staff. It is the task of the local chapters to lure members and obtain funds from them; the state or national staff can then pursue political objectives by using these funds. Forming organizations made up of small local chapters is probably easier in the United States than in Europe because of the great importance of local government in our federal system. There is plenty for a PTA, an NAACP, or a League of Women Voters to do in its own community, and so its members can be kept busy with local affairs while the national staff pursues larger goals.

A second kind of incentive consists of **material incentives**—that is, money, or things and services readily valued in monetary terms. Farm organizations have recruited many members by offering a wide range of services. The Illinois Farm Bureau, for example, offers to its members—and *only* to its members—a chance to buy farm supplies at discount prices, to market their products through cooperatives, and to purchase low-cost insurance. These material incentives help explain why the Illinois Farm Bureau has been able to enroll nearly every farmer in the state as well as many nonfarmers who also value these rewards.[12]

Similarly, the American Association of Retired Persons (AARP) has recruited over 30 million members by supplying them with everything from low-cost life insurance and mail-order discount drugs to tax advice and group travel plans. About 45 percent of the nation's population that is fifty and older—one out of every four registered voters—belongs to the AARP. With an annual operating budget of over $200 million and a cash flow estimated at a whopping $10 billion, the AARP seeks to influence public policy in many areas, from health and housing to taxes and transportation.

The third—and most difficult—kind of incentive is the *purpose* of the organization. Many associations rely chiefly on this **purposive incentive**—the appeal of their stated goals—to recruit members. If the attainment of those goals will also benefit people who do not join, individuals who do join will have to be those who feel passionately about the goal, who have a strong sense of duty (or who cannot say no to a friend who asks them to join), or for whom the cost of joining is so small that they are indifferent to joining or not. Organizations that attract members by appealing to their interest in a coherent set of (usually) controversial principles are sometimes called **ideological interest groups.**

When the purpose of the organization, if attained, will principally benefit nonmembers, it is customary to call the group a **public-interest lobby.** (Whether the public at large will really benefit, of course, is a matter of opinion, but at least the group members think that they are working selflessly for the common good.)

Though some public-interest lobbies may pursue relatively noncontroversial goals (for example, persuading people to vote or raising money to house orphans), the most visible of these organizations are highly controversial. It is precisely the controversy that attracts the members, or at least those members who support one side of the issue. Many of these

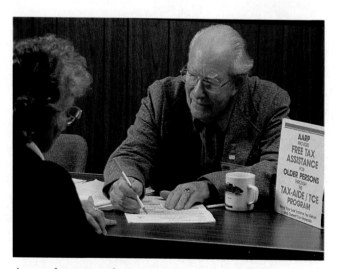

Among the services the American Association of Retired Persons provides the elderly is free assistance in preparing tax returns.

Ralph Nader

Funded by Public Citizen: Ralph Nader, President

Funded by Center for Study of Responsive Law: Ralph Nader, Managing Trustee

Litigation Group

Congress Watch

Funded by Nader Personal Income

Consumer Complaint Research Center

Health Research Group

Corporate Accountability Research Group

Clean Water Action Project

Tax Reform Research Group

Public Interest Research Group

Freedom of Information Clearinghouse

Critical Mass

Public Citizens Visitor Center

State Public Interest Research Group and Citizen Action Group

Independent Groups With Close Ties to Nader

Aviation Consumer Action Project

Center for Auto Safety
Center for Concerned Engineering
Consumers Union Washington Office
Professional Drivers Council for Safety and Health
Disability Rights Group
Pension Rights Center

Retired Professional Action Group

The Nader Network

Since the mid-1960s consumer activist Ralph Nader has spawned more than a dozen interest groups. In 2000 Nader ran for president as a Green party candidate.

groups can be described as markedly liberal or decidedly conservative in outlook.

Perhaps the best known of the liberal public-interest groups are those founded by or associated with Ralph Nader. Nader became a popular figure in the mid-1960s after General Motors made a clumsy attempt to investigate and discredit his background at a time when he was testifying in favor of an auto-safety bill. Nader won a large out-of-court settlement against General Motors, his books began to earn royalties, and he was able to command substantial lecture fees. Most of this money was turned over to various organizations he created that dealt with matters of interest to consumers. In addition he founded a group called Public Citizen that raised money by direct-mail solicitation from thousands of small contributors and sought foundation grants. Finally, he helped create Public Interest Research Groups (PIRGs) in a number of states, supported by donations from college students (voluntary at some colleges, a compulsory assessment levied on all students at others) and concerned with organizing student activists to work on local projects.

Recently cracks have begun to appear in the Nader movement. When Hawaii and California considered plans to develop no-fault automobile insurance, some former allies of Nader led the effort to reduce auto insurance prices by adopting a no-fault system. Nader denounced this effort and urged Hawaii's governor to veto the no-fault bill. Each side criticized the other.

Conservatives, though slow to get started, have also adopted the public-interest organizational strategy. As with such associations run by liberals, they are of two kinds: those that engage in research and lobbying and those that bring lawsuits designed to advance their cause. The boxes on pages 225 and 226 list some examples of public-interest organizations that support liberal or conservative causes.

Membership organizations that rely on purposive incentives, especially appeals to deeply controversial purposes, tend to be shaped by the mood of the times. When an issue is hot—in the media or with the public—such organizations can grow rapidly. When the spotlight fades, the organization may lose support. Thus such organizations have a powerful motive to stay in the public eye. To remain visible public-interest lobbies devote a lot of attention to generating publicity by developing good contacts with the media and issuing dramatic press releases about crises and scandals.

Because of their need to take advantage of a crisis atmosphere, public-interest lobbies often do best when the government is in the hands of an administration that is *hostile*, not sympathetic, to their views. Environmentalist organizations could mobilize more resources when James Watt, an opponent of much of the environmental movement, was secretary of the interior than they could when Cecil D. Andrus, his proenvironment predecessor, was in office. By the same token many conservative interest groups were able to raise more money with the relatively liberal Jimmy Carter or Bill Clinton in the White House than with the conservative Ronald Reagan.

The Influence of the Staff

We often make the mistake of assuming that what an interest group does politically is simply to exert influence on behalf of its members. That is indeed the case when all the members have a clear and similar stake in an issue. But many issues affect different members differently. In fact, if the members joined to obtain solidary or material benefits, they may not care at all about many of the issues with which the organization gets involved. In such cases what the interest group does may reflect more what the staff wants than what the members believe.

For example, a survey of the white members of a large labor union showed that one-third of them believed that the desegregation of schools, housing, and job opportunities had gone too fast; only one-fifth thought that it had gone too slowly. But among the staff members of the union, *none* thought that desegregation had gone too fast, and over two-thirds thought that it had gone too slowly.[13] As a result the union staff aggressively lobbied Congress for the passage of tougher civil rights laws, even though most of the union's members did not feel that they were needed. The members stayed in the union for reasons unrelated to civil rights, giving the staff the freedom to pursue its own goals.

The National Council of the Churches of Christ (NCC), an organization of various Protestant denominations claiming several million members, has spoken out frequently on political questions, generally by taking a strongly liberal position. But opinion surveys show that most white Protestants are relatively conservative, especially those in the South. Thus it is quite likely that the staff of the NCC does not, on many political questions, actually represent the majority of the churchgoers for whom it claims to speak.[14] It can ignore them because people

Public-Interest Law Firms

A special kind of public-interest lobby is an organization that advances its cause by bringing lawsuits to challenge existing practices or proposed regulations. A public-interest law firm will act in one of two ways: First, it will find someone who has been harmed by some public or private policy and bring suit on his or her behalf. Second, it will file a brief with a court supporting somebody else's lawsuit (this is called an amicus curiae brief; it is explained in Chapter 14).

Here are some examples of liberal and conservative public-interest law firms:

Liberal	*Conservative*
American Civil Liberties Union	Atlantic Legal Foundation
Asian American Legal Defense Fund	The Center for Individual Rights
Lawyers' Committee for Civil Rights	Criminal Justice Legal Foundation
Mexican American Legal Defense Fund	Landmark Legal Foundation
NAACP Legal Defense and Education Fund	Mountain States Legal Foundation
Natural Resources Defense Council	Pacific Legal Foundation
Women's Legal Defense Fund	Washington Legal Foundation

join churches, by and large, for reasons other than how staff members in New York or Washington think.

Interest Groups and Social Movements

Because it is difficult to attract people with purposive incentives, interest groups employing them tend to arise out of social movements. A **social movement** is a widely shared demand for change in some aspect of the social or political order. The civil rights movement of the 1960s was such an event, as was the environmentalist movement of the 1970s. A social movement need not have liberal goals. In the nineteenth

Think Tanks in Washington

Think tanks are public-interest organizations that do research on policy questions and disseminate their findings in books, articles, conferences, op-ed essays for newspapers, and (occasionally) testimony before Congress. Some are nonpartisan and ideologically more or less neutral, but others—and many of the most important ones—are aligned with liberal or conservative causes. Here are some examples of each:

Liberal	*Conservative*
Center on Budget and Policy Priorities	American Enterprise Institute
Center for Defense Information	Cato Institute
Children's Defense Fund	Center for Strategic and International Studies
Economic Policy Institute	Competitive Enterprise Institute
Institute for Policy Studies	Ethics and Public Policy Center
Joint Center for Political and Economic Studies	Free Congress Foundation
Progressive Policy Institute	Heritage Foundation

Note that the labels "liberal" and "conservative," while generally accurate, conceal important differences among the think tanks in each list.

century, for example, there were various nativist movements that sought to reduce immigration to this country or to keep Catholics or Masons out of public office. Broad-based religious revivals are social movements.

No one is quite certain why social movements arise. At one moment people are largely indifferent to some issue; at another moment many of these same people care passionately about religion, civil rights, immigration, or conservation. A social movement may be triggered by a scandal (an oil spill on the Santa Barbara beaches helped launch the environmental movement), the dramatic and widely publicized activities of a few leaders (lunch counter sit-ins helped stimulate the civil rights movement),

or the coming of age of a new generation that takes up a cause advocated by eloquent writers, teachers, or evangelists.

The Environmental Movement

Whatever its origin, the effect of a social movement is to increase the value some people attach to purposive incentives. As a consequence new interest groups are formed that rely on these incentives. In the 1890s, as a result of the emergence of conservation as a major issue, the Sierra Club was organized. In the 1930s conservation once again became popular, and the Wilderness Society and the National Wildlife Federation took form. In the 1960s and 1970s environmental issues again came to the fore, and we saw the emergence of the Environmental Defense Fund and Environmental Action.

The smallest of these organizations (Environmental Action and the Environmental Defense Fund) tend to have the most liberal members.[15] This is often the case with social movements. A movement will spawn many organizations. The most passionately aroused people will be the fewest in number, and they will gravitate toward the organizations that take the most extreme positions; as a result these organizations are small but vociferous. The more numerous and less passionate people will gravitate toward more moderate, less vociferous organizations, which will tend to be larger.

The Feminist Movement

There have been several feminist social movements in this country's history—in the 1830s, in the 1890s, in the 1920s, and in the 1960s. Each period has brought into being new organizations, some of which have endured to the present. For example, the League of Women Voters was founded in 1920 to educate and organize women for the purpose of using effectively their newly won right to vote.

Though a strong sense of purpose may lead to the creation of organizations, each will strive to find some incentive that will sustain it over the long haul. These permanent incentives will affect how the organization participates in politics.

There are at least three kinds of feminist organizations. First, there are those that rely chiefly on solidary incentives, enroll middle-class women with relatively high levels of schooling, and tend to support those causes that command the widest support among women generally. The League of Women

Voters and the Federation of Business and Professional Women are examples. Both supported the campaign to ratify the Equal Rights Amendment (ERA), but as Jane Mansbridge has observed in her history of the ERA, they were uneasy with the kind of intense, partisan fighting displayed by some other women's organizations and with the tendency of more militant groups to link the ERA to other issues, such as abortion. The reason for their uneasiness is clear: to the extent they relied on solidary incentives, they had a stake in avoiding issues and tactics that would divide their membership or reduce the extent to which membership provided camaraderie and professional contacts.[16]

Second, there are women's organizations that attract members with purposive incentives. The National Organization for Women (NOW) and the National Abortion Rights Action League (NARAL) are two of the largest such groups, though there are many smaller ones. Because they rely on purposes, these organizations must take strong positions, tackle divisive issues, and employ militant tactics. Anything less would turn off the committed feminists who make up the rank and file and contribute the funds. But because these groups take controversial stands, they are constantly embroiled in internal quarrels between those who think that they have gone too far and those who think that they have not gone far enough, between women who want NOW or NARAL to join with lesbian and socialist organizations and those who want them to steer clear. Moreover, as Mansbridge showed, purposive organizations often cannot make their decisions stick on the local level (local chapters will do pretty much as they please).[17]

The third kind of women's organization is the caucus that takes on specific issues that have some material benefit to women. The Women's Equity Action League (WEAL) is one such group. Rather than relying on membership dues for financial support, it obtains grants from foundations and government agencies. Freed of the necessity of satisfying a large rank-and-file membership, WEAL has concentrated its efforts on bringing lawsuits aimed at enforcing or enlarging the legal rights of women in higher education and other institutions. In electoral politics the National Women's Political Caucus (officially nonpartisan, but generally liberal and Democratic) and the National Federation of Republican Women (openly supportive of the Republican party)

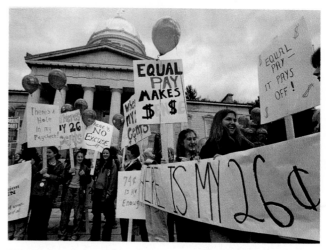

Women have become more visible as an interest group. Here in Vermont they claim that women are not paid equally with men.

work to get more women active in politics and more women elected or appointed to office.

The feminist movement has, of course, spawned an antifeminist movement, and thus feminist organizations have their antifeminist counterparts. The campaign by NOW for the ERA was attacked by a women's group called STOP ERA; the proabortion position of NARAL has been challenged by the various organizations associated with the right-to-life movement. These opposition groups have their own tactical problems, which arise in large part from their reliance on different kinds of incentives. In the chapter on civil rights we shall see how the conflict between these opposing groups shaped the debate over the ERA.

The Union Movement

When social movements run out of steam, they leave behind organizations that continue the fight. But with the movement dead or dormant, the organizations often must struggle to stay alive. This has happened to labor unions.

The major union movement in this country occurred in the 1930s, when the Great Depression, popular support, and a sympathetic administration in Washington led to a rapid growth in union membership. In 1945 union membership peaked; at that time nearly 36 percent of all nonfarm workers were union members.

Since then union membership has fallen more or less steadily, so that by 1998 only 14 percent of all

Figure 9.1   The Decline in Union Membership

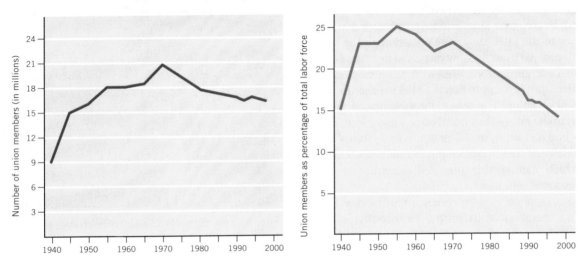

Sources: *Historical Statistics of the United States*, vol. 1, 178; *Statistical Abstract of the United States*, 1998, 444.

workers were unionized (see Figure 9.1). This decline has been caused by several factors. There has been a shift in the nation's economic life away from industrial production (where unions have traditionally been concentrated) and toward service delivery (where unions have usually been weak). But accompanying this decline, and perhaps contributing to it, has been a decline in popular approval of unions. Approval has moved down side by side with a decline

in membership and declines in union victories in elections held to see whether workers in a plant want to join a union. The social movement that supported unionism has faded.

But unions will persist, because most can rely on incentives other than purposive ones to keep them going. In many industries they can require workers to join if they wish to keep their jobs, and in other industries workers believe that they get sufficient

Table 9.2   The Rise in Four Government Employee Unions

| | Number of Members | | | |
Union	1979	1983	1993	2000
National Association of Letter Carriers	151,000	201,000	210,000	220,000
Postal Workers	245,000	213,999	249,000	366,000
American Federation of Teachers	423,000	544,000	574,000	1 million*
American Federation of State and County Municipal Employees	889,000	1 million	1.16 million	1.3 million

Four-Union Total 1979: 1.71 million
Four-Union Total 2000: 2.89 million
Percent Change, 1979–2000: +69%

*Data for 1999.

Sources: *Statistical Abstract of the United States, 1994*, table 696, 443; post-1998 press releases and fact sheets by each organization.

benefits from the union to make even voluntary membership worthwhile. And in a few industries, such as teaching and government, there has been a growth in membership, as some white-collar workers have turned to unions to advance their interests.

Unions composed of government workers are becoming the most important part of the union movement. They are almost the only part that is growing in size. For example, from 1983 to 1994 the number of private sector union members fell from 11.9 million to 9.6 million, a 19 percent drop. Over the same period, however, the number of public sector union members rose from 5.7 million to 7 million, a 22 percent increase. Especially significant has been the membership growth in certain government employee unions affiliated with the AFL-CIO (see Table 9.2). These unions have gained new members and political clout at a time when almost every industrial union was losing both.

Funds for Interest Groups

All interest groups have some trouble raising money, but membership organizations have more trouble than most, especially membership organizations relying on appeals to purpose—to accomplishing stated goals. As a result the Washington office of a public-interest lobbying group is likely to be small, stark, and crowded, whereas that of an institutional lobby, such as the AFL-CIO or the American Council on Education, will be rather lavish.

To raise more money than members supply in dues, lobbying organizations have turned to three sources that have become important in recent years: foundation grants, government grants, and direct-mail solicitation.

Foundation Grants

One study of eighty-three (primarily liberal) public-interest lobbying groups found that one-third of them received half or more of all their funds from foundation grants; one-tenth received over 90 percent from such sources.[18] Between 1970 and 1980 the Ford Foundation alone contributed about $21 million to liberal public-interest groups. Many of these organizations were law firms that, other than the staff lawyers, really had no members at all. The Environmental Defense Fund is supported almost entirely by grants from foundations such as the

Rockefeller Family Fund. The more conservative Scaife foundations gave $1.8 million to a conservative public-interest group, the National Legal Center for the Public Interest.[19]

Federal Grants and Contracts

The expansion of federal grants during the 1960s and 1970s benefited interest groups as well as cities and states; the cutbacks in those grants during the early 1980s hurt interest groups even more than they hurt local governments. Of course the federal government usually does not give the money to support lobbying itself; it is given instead to support some project that the organization has undertaken. For example, the National Alliance of Business received $20 million in 1980 from Washington, much of it for summer youth job programs and the like. But money for a project helps support the organization as a whole and thus enables the organization to press Congress for policies it favors (including, of course, policies that will supply it with more grants and contracts).

Before running for president in 1984, the Reverend Jesse Jackson had been heavily supported for several years by federal grants to his community-development organization, PUSH. Between 1978 and 1982 PUSH received in excess of $5 million from various federal agencies.

Since most public-interest groups pursue liberal policies, the Reagan administration became interested in saving money by reducing grants to interest groups and was particularly interested in cutting back on money being spent to lobby for liberal causes. Some writers called this an effort to "de-fund the left."

Direct Mail

If there is any one technique that is unique to the modern interest group, it is the sophistication with which mailings are used both to raise money and to mobilize supporters. By using computers, membership interest groups can mail directly to specialized audiences identified from lists developed by the staff or purchased from other organizations. Letters can be tailor-made, for example, to appeal to upper-income residents of Oregon who belong to the Sierra Club, live near the Columbia River, own four-wheel-drive vehicles, and thus might be interested in maintaining a local wilderness area.

A classic example of an interest group that was created and maintained by direct-mail solicitation is

Common Cause, a liberal organization founded in 1970. Its creator, John Gardner, sent letters to tens of thousands of people selected from mailing lists it had acquired, urging them to join the organization and to send in money. Over two hundred thousand members were obtained in this way, each of whom mailed in dues (initially $15 a year) in return for nothing more than the satisfaction of belonging.

But raising money by mail costs money—lots of money. To bring in more money than it spends, the interest group must write a letter that will galvanize enough readers to send in a check. "Enough" usually amounts to at least 2 percent of the names on the list. Techniques include the following:

- Put a "teaser" on the outside of the envelope so that it won't be thrown out as "junk mail." If the letter is going to African Americans, put a picture of Reverend Martin Luther King, Jr. on the envelope.
- Arouse emotions, preferably by portraying the threat posed by some "devil." To environmentalists, a typical devil would be former secretary of the interior James Watt; to civil libertarians, former Moral Majority leader Jerry Falwell; to conservatives, Senator Ted Kennedy.
- Have the endorsement of a famous name. For liberals it is often Senator Kennedy; for conservatives it may be Senator Jesse Helms.
- Personalize the letter by instructing the computer to insert the recipient's name into the text of the letter to create the impression that it was written personally to him or her.

The Problem of Bias

Many observers believe that the interest groups active in Washington reflect an upper-class bias. There are two reasons for this belief: first, well-off people are more likely than poor people to join and be active in interest groups, and second, interest groups representing business and the professions are much more numerous and better financed than organizations representing minorities, consumers, or the disadvantaged.

Doubtless both these facts are true. As we can see from Table 9.3, a survey of citizens done in 1976 showed that those with higher incomes, those whose schooling went through college or beyond, and those in professional or technical jobs were

Table 9.3   Organizational Membership and Social Class

	Percentage Who Are Members of an Organization, Union, or Both
Total	53%
Education	
Grade school	35
Some high school	43
High school graduate	44
Some college	49
College graduate	60
Graduate school	80
Occupation	
Sales	39
Service	40
Clerical	41
Operative	48
Manager/administrator	51
Laborer	56
Crafts	64
Professional/technical	70
Income	
Under $6,000	29
$6,000–10,999	42
$11,000–15,999	52
$16,000 and over	65

Source: 1976 Metropolitan Work Force Survey, as reported in Kay Lehman Schlozman and John T. Tierney, *Organized Interests and American Democracy* (New York: Harper & Row, 1986), 60. Copyright © 1986 by Kay Lehman Schlozman and John T. Tierney. Reprinted by permission of Addison-Wesley Educational Publishers Inc.

much more likely to belong to a voluntary association than people with the opposite characteristics. Just as we would expect, higher-income people can afford more organizational memberships than lower-income ones; people in business and the professions find it both easier to attend meetings (they have more control over their own work schedules) and more necessary to do so than people in blue-collar jobs; and people with college degrees often have a wider range of interests than those without.

Of the nearly seven thousand groups that were represented in Washington in 1976, over half were corporations, and another third were professional and trade associations. Only 4 percent were public-interest groups; fewer than 2 percent were civil

How Political Mail Piles Up

One day Daniel Aaron Schlozman of Massachusetts joined eight interest groups, four liberal and four conservative.

Over the next eighteen months, he received 248 pieces of mail, weighing a total of *eighteen pounds.* Included were 135 separate appeals for money.

Of the total, 63 pieces of mail were from organizations that he had not joined but that, apparently, had bought or borrowed mailing lists from organizations that he had joined. The conservative organizations allowed their mailing lists to be used by other conservatives; the liberal organizations by other liberals.

For example, by joining the National Conservative Caucus, he found himself on the mailing lists of Young Americans for Freedom, the Committee for the Survival of a Free Congress, the National Tax Limitation Committee, and the Senator Orrin Hatch Election Committee.

By joining Common Cause, he found himself on the mailing lists of the NAACP, the League of Women Voters, the National Organization for Women, the Campaign to Save the Massachusetts Bottle Bill, and the Union of Concerned Scientists.

But it didn't do any of these organizations much good. Daniel Schlozman was only four months old. His mother, Professor Kay Schlozman, a political scientist at Boston College, had enrolled him just to find out who shares mailing lists.

Source: Adapted from Kay Lehman Schlozman and John T. Tierney, *Organized Interests and American Democracy* (New York: Harper & Row, 1986), 94–95.

---

rights or minority groups.[20] About 170 organizations represented in Washington were concerned just with the oil industry.

But the question of an upper-class bias cannot be settled by these two facts taken alone. In the first place, they describe only certain *inputs* into the political system; they say nothing about the *outputs*—that is, who wins and who loses on particular issues. Even if 170 interest groups are trying to protect the oil industry, this is important only if the oil industry in fact gets protected. Sometimes it does; sometimes it does not. At one time, when oil prices were low, oil companies were able to get Congress to pass a law that sharply restricted the importation of foreign oil. A few years later, after oil prices had risen and people were worried about energy issues, these restrictions were ended.

In the second place, business-oriented interest groups are often divided among themselves. Take one kind of business: farming. Once, farm organizations seemed so powerful in Washington that scholars spoke of an irresistible "farm bloc" in Congress that could get its way on almost anything. Today dozens of agricultural organizations operate in the capital, with some (such as the Farm Bureau) attempting to speak for all farmers and others (such as the Tobacco Institute and Mid-America Dairymen) representing particular commodities and regions.

Farmers still have a great deal of influence, especially when it comes to blocking a bill that they oppose. But it is proving difficult for them to get Congress to approve a bill that they want passed. In part this political weakness reflects the decline in the number of farmers and thus in the number of legislators who must take their interests into account. (Only 2.5 percent of all Americans live on farms—just one-sixth of the number who lived there thirty years ago.) In part their political weakness reflects splits among the farmers themselves, with southern cotton growers often seeing things differently from midwestern wheat growers or New England dairy farmers. And to some extent it reflects the context within which interest group politics must operate. In the 1950s few people thought that providing subsidies for farmers was too expensive—if indeed they knew of such programs at all. But by the 1980s consumers were acutely aware of food prices, and their legislators were keenly aware of the cost of farm-support programs.[21]

Whenever American politics is described as having an upper-class bias, it is important to ask exactly what this bias is. Most of the major conflicts in American politics—over foreign policy, economic affairs, environmental protection, or equal rights for women—are conflicts *within* the upper middle class; they are conflicts, that is, among politically active elites. As we saw in

Farmers once had great influence in Congress and could get their way with a few telephone calls. Today they often must use mass protest methods.

Chapter 5, there are profound cleavages of opinion among these elites. Interest group activity reflects these cleavages.

Nonetheless, it would be a mistake to ignore the overrepresentation of business in Washington. A student of politics should always take differences in the availability of political resources as an important clue to possible differences in the outcomes of political conflicts. But they are only clues, not conclusions.

The Activities of Interest Groups

Size and wealth are no longer entirely accurate measures of an interest group's influence—if indeed they ever were. Depending on the issue, the key to political influence may be the ability to generate a dramatic newspaper headline, mobilize a big letter-writing campaign, stage a protest demonstration, file a suit in federal court to block (or compel) some government action, or quietly supply information to key legislators. All of these things require organization, but only some of them require big or expensive organizations.

Information

Of all these tactics, the single most important one—in the eyes of virtually every lobbyist and every academic student of lobbying—is supplying credible information. The reason why information is so valuable is that, to busy legislators and bureaucrats, information is in short supply. Legislators in particular must take positions on a staggering number of issues about which they cannot possibly become experts.

Though there are nonpolitical sources of information, such as encyclopedias, they often do not provide the kind of detailed, specific, up-to-date information that politicians need. This kind of information will ordinarily be gathered only by a group that has a strong interest in some issue. Lobbyists, for the most part, are not flamboyant, party-giving arm-twisters; they are specialists who gather information (favorable to their clients, naturally) and present it in as organized, persuasive, and factual a manner as possible. All lobbyists no doubt exaggerate, but few can afford to misrepresent the facts or mislead a legislator, and for a very simple reason: almost every lobbyist must develop and maintain the confidence of a legislator over the long term, with an eye on tomorrow's issues as well as today's. Misrepresentation or bad advice can embarrass a legislator who accepts it or repel one who detects it, leading to distrust of the lobbyist. Maintaining contacts and channels of communication is vital; to that end, maintaining trust is essential.

The value of the information provided by a lobbyist is often greatest when the issue is fairly narrow, involving only a few interest groups or a complex economic or technical problem. The value of information, and thus the power of the lobbyist, is likely to be least when the issue is one of broad and highly visible national policy.

Sometimes the nature of an issue or the governmental process by which an issue is resolved gives a great advantage to the suppliers of certain information and imposes a great burden on would-be suppliers of contrary information. This is an example of what is called "client politics." For example, the Civil Aeronautics Board (CAB) once set airline fares and decided what airlines would fly to what cities. Historically the only organizations with any incentive to appear before the CAB and supply the necessary information were, naturally, the airlines. Until the CAB began to deregulate civil aviation, CAB decisions often tended to favor the established airlines.

For a long time only radio and television broadcasters had any incentive (or could afford) to appear before the Federal Communications Commission (FCC), which decides which broadcasters shall be licensed and on what terms. Owing to changes in the industry (such as the rise of cable and satellite television) and to the growth of consumer groups, FCC hearings are now often hotly contested. When the Federal Energy Administration (FEA) was trying to allocate scarce oil and gasoline supplies among competing users, it discovered that the information it needed was possessed only by the oil companies. (It later took steps to develop its own sources of data.)

Public officials not only want technical information; they also want political cues. A **political cue** is a signal telling the official what values are at stake in an issue—who is for, who against a proposal—and how that issue fits into his or her own set of political beliefs. Some legislators feel comfortable when they are on the liberal side of an issue, and others feel comfortable when they are on the conservative side, especially when they are not familiar with the details of the issue. A liberal legislator will look to see whether the AFL-CIO, the NAACP, the Americans for Democratic Action, the Farmers' Union, and various consumer organizations favor a proposal; if so, that is often all he or she has to know. If these liberal groups are split, then the legislator will worry about the matter and try to look into it more closely. Similarly, a conservative legislator will feel comfortable taking a stand on an issue if the Chamber of Commerce, the Christian Coalition, the American Medical Association, various business associations, and Americans for Constitutional Action are in agreement about it; he or she will feel less comfortable if such conservative groups are divided. As a result of this process lobbyists often work together in informal coalitions based on general political ideology.

One important way in which these cues are made known is by **ratings** that interest groups make of legislators. These are regularly compiled by the AFL-CIO (on who is prolabor), by the Americans for Democratic Action (on who is liberal), by the Americans for Constitutional Action (on who is conservative), by the Consumer Federation of America (on who is proconsumer), and by the League of Conservation Voters (on who is pro-environment). These ratings are designed to generate public support for (or opposition to) various legislators. They can be helpful sources of information, but they are sometimes biased by the arbitrary determination of what constitutes a liberal, proconsumer, or conservative vote.

Both political information and political cues now arrive in the offices of politicians at a faster rate than ever before, thanks to fax machines and the Internet. Many interest groups and political activists have banks of computer-operated fax machines that can get a short, snappy document into the hands of every legislator within minutes. William Kristol, a Republican activist, used this technique to good effect in 1993 when he bombarded Republican members of Congress with arguments concerning why they should oppose President Clinton's health care plan. Many credit him with having played a major role in the defeat of that plan.

Public Support: The Rise of the New Politics

Once upon a time, when the government was small, Congress was less individualistic, and television was nonexistent, lobbyists mainly used an *insider strategy:* they worked closely with a few key members of Congress, meeting them privately to exchange information and (sometimes) favors. Matters of mutual interest could be discussed at a leisurely pace, over dinner or while playing golf. Public opinion was important on some highly visible issues, but there were not many of these.

Following an insider strategy is still valuable, but increasingly interest groups have turned to an *outsider strategy*. The newly individualistic nature of Congress has made this tactic useful, and modern technology has made it possible. Radio, fax machines, and the Internet can now get news out almost immediately. Satellite television can be used to link interested citizens in various locations across the country. Toll-free phone numbers can be publicized, enabling voters to call the offices of their members of Congress without charge. Public opinion polls can be done by telephone, virtually overnight, to measure (and help generate) support for or opposition to proposed legislation. Mail can be directed by computers to people already known to have an interest in a particular matter.

This kind of *grassroots lobbying* is central to the outsider strategy. It is designed to generate public pressure directly on government officials. The "public" that exerts this pressure is not every voter or even most voters; it is that part of the public (sometimes called an *issue public*) that is directly affected by or deeply concerned with a government policy. What modern technology has made possible is the overnight mobilization of specific issue publics.

Not every issue lends itself to an outsider strat-

Members of Congress must depend on lobbyists, such as these from the farming industry, to get information about how government policies affect people.

egy: it is hard to get many people excited about, for example, complex tax legislation affecting only a few firms. But as the government does more and more, its policies affect more and more people, and so more and more will join in grassroots lobbying efforts over matters such as abortion, Medicare, Social Security, environmental protection, and affirmative action.

Undoubtedly the new politics creates new conflicts. Since conflict is the essence of politics, it may seem strange that politicians dislike controversy. But they do, and for perfectly human reasons: no one enjoys dealing with people who are upset or who find one's viewpoint objectionable or unworthy. Consequently, most legislators tend to hear what they want to hear and to deal with interest groups that agree with them.[22] Two senators from the same state may choose to listen to very different constituencies in that state and to take very different policy positions. Neither senator may feel "pressured" or "lobbied," because each has heard mostly from groups or persons who share his or her views. (Politicians define "pressure" as arguments and inducements supplied by somebody with whom they disagree.)

Members of an interest group will also tend to work primarily with legislators with whom they agree; lobbyists do not like to argue with people who are suspicious of them or who are unlikely to change their minds no matter what is said. For the lobbyist the key target is the undecided or wavering legislator or bureaucrat. Sometimes lobbyists will make a major effort to persuade an undecided legislator that public opinion is strongly inclined in one direction. A lobbyist will do this by commissioning public opinion polls, stimulating local citizens to write letters or send telegrams, arranging for constituents to pay personal visits to the legislator, or getting newspapers to run editorials supporting the lobbyist's position.

Though most lobbying organizations cultivate the goodwill of government officials, there are important exceptions. Some groups, especially those that use an ideological appeal to attract supporters or that depend for their maintenance and influence on media publicity, will deliberately attack actual or potential allies in government in order to embarrass them. Ralph Nader is as likely to denounce as to praise those officials who tend to agree with him, if their agreement is not sufficiently close or public. He did this with Senator Edmund Muskie, the author of the Clean Air Act, and with William Haddon, Jr., an early administrator of the National Highway Traffic Safety Administration. The head of the Fund for Animals is not reluctant to attack those officials in the Forest Service and the Interior Department on whose cooperation the fund must rely if it is to achieve its goals.[23] Sometimes, as we shall see later in this chapter, the use of threats instead of rewards extends to physical confrontations.

It is not clear how often public pressure works. Members of Congress are skilled at recognizing and discounting organized mail campaigns and feel that they can occasionally afford to go against even legitimate expressions of hostile public opinion. Only a few issues of great symbolic significance and high visibility are so important that a member of Congress would think that to ignore public opinion would mean losing the next election. In 1978 the proposed Panama Canal treaties were one such case; since the 1980s abortion has been another. Issues such as these can make or break a member of Congress.

Of late, interest groups have placed great emphasis on developing grassroots support. Sometimes it is impossible to develop such support, as when a complicated tax regulation of interest to only a few firms is being changed. But sometimes a proposed bill touches a public nerve such that even businesses can help generate an outpouring of mail: when the Food and Drug Administration announced it was going to ban saccharin on the grounds that it caused cancer in laboratory animals, the Calorie Control Council (closely tied to the Coca-Cola Company, a big user of saccharin in soft drinks such as Tab) ran newspaper ads denouncing the policy. The public, worried about losing access to an artificial sweetener important to dieters, responded with an avalanche of mail to Congress, which promptly passed a law reversing the ban.

Usually, however, the public at large doesn't care that much about an issue, and so interest groups will try by direct-mail campaigns to arouse a small but passionate group to write letters or vote (or not vote) for specified candidates. Beginning in 1970 Environmental Action designated certain members of the House of Representatives as the "Dirty Dozen" because of their votes against bills that the lobbying group claimed were necessary to protect the environment. Of the thirty-one members of Congress so listed in various elections, only seven survived in office. Many members of Congress believe that the

"Dirty Dozen" label hurts them with pro-environment voters in their districts, and though they are angry over what they feel is the unfair use of that label, they strive to avoid it if at all possible.

The press sometimes depicts certain large, well-funded interest groups as all-powerful, but few are. Take, for example, the National Rifle Association (NRA). Founded in 1871 as a group dedicated to shooting instruction, the NRA in the 1960s and 1970s became a lobby opposing policies that would restrict citizens' rights to own and use firearms for sporting and other legal purposes. By the 1980s the NRA's dues-paying membership had increased from one million to nearly three million. Its members receive magazines, decals, and other direct benefits. From 1983 to 1992 the NRA spent $8 million on congressional races both in direct contributions to their favored candidates and in independent expenditures supporting or opposing various candidates. Still, in the mid-1990s the NRA lost a major battle to repeal New Jersey's ban on certain types of semiautomatic weapons and lost similar battles in Connecticut, Virginia, and other states. In 1993, over fierce opposition from the NRA, Congress passed the Brady bill, a major piece of gun control legislation named after Jim Brady, the press secretary who was shot and permanently disabled during an attempt to assassinate President Reagan. By the late 1990s the NRA had a negative image even among most gun owners, and the organization found itself constantly in the political cross hairs of small but media-savvy

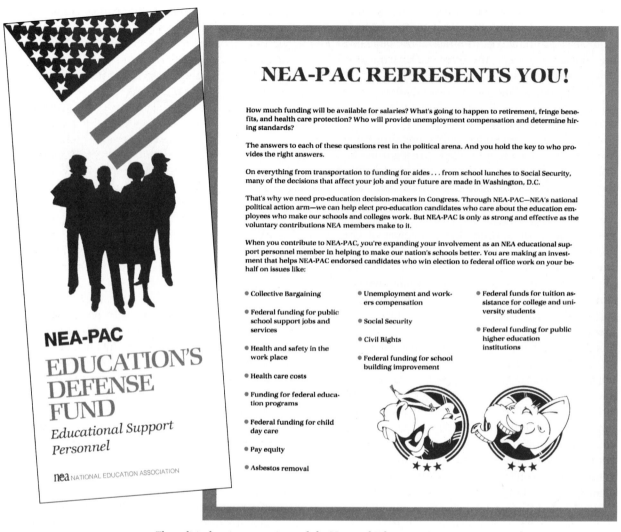

NEA-PAC REPRESENTS YOU!

How much funding will be available for salaries? What's going to happen to retirement, fringe benefits, and health care protection? Who will provide unemployment compensation and determine hiring standards?

The answers to each of these questions rest in the political arena. And you hold the key to who provides the right answers.

On everything from transportation to funding for aides . . . from school lunches to Social Security, many of the decisions that affect your job and your future are made in Washington, D.C.

That's why we need pro-education decision-makers in Congress. Through NEA-PAC—NEA's national political action arm—we can help elect pro-education candidates who care about the education employees who make our schools and colleges work. But NEA-PAC is only as strong and effective as the voluntary contributions NEA members make to it.

When you contribute to NEA-PAC, you're expanding your involvement as an NEA educational support personnel member in helping to make our nation's schools better. You are making an investment that helps NEA-PAC endorsed candidates who win election to federal office work on your behalf on issues like:

- Collective Bargaining
- Federal funding for public school support jobs and services
- Health and safety in the work place
- Health care costs
- Funding for federal education programs
- Federal funding for child day care
- Pay equity
- Asbestos removal
- Unemployment and workers compensation
- Social Security
- Civil Rights
- Federal funding for school building improvement
- Federal funds for tuition assistance for college and university students
- Federal funding for public higher education institutions

NEA-PAC
EDUCATION'S DEFENSE FUND
Educational Support Personnel

nea NATIONAL EDUCATION ASSOCIATION

The political action committee of the National Education Association—a teachers union—is one of the biggest in the nation.

pro–gun control lobbies such as Handgun Control, Inc. As the NRA's recent history teaches, in American politics no interest group, no matter how big its budget or mammoth its membership, is a lobby that cannot be beat.

Money and PACs

Contrary to popular suspicions, money is probably one of the less effective ways by which interest groups advance their causes. That was not always the case. Only a few decades ago powerful interests used their bulging wallets to buy influence in Congress. The passage of the campaign finance reform law in 1973 changed that. The law had two effects.

First, it sharply restricted the amount that any interest could give to a candidate for federal office (see Chapter 8). Second, it made it legal for corporations and labor unions to form political action committees (PACs) that could make political contributions.

The effect of the second change was to encourage the rapid growth of PACs. By 1993 some 4,200 PACs existed, over six times the number that existed in 1975. In 1997–1998 they gave nearly $200 million to congressional candidates. Some people worry that the existence of all this political money has resulted in our having, as Senator Edward Kennedy put it, "the finest Congress that money can buy." More likely the increase in the number of PACs has had just the opposite effect. The reason is simple: with PACs so numerous and so easy to form, it is now probable that there will be money available on every side of almost every conceivable issue. As a result members of Congress can take money and still decide for themselves how to vote. As we shall see, there is not much scholarly evidence that money buys votes in Congress.

Indeed, some members of Congress tell PACs what to do rather than take orders from them. Members will frequently inform PACs that they "expect" money from them; grumbling PAC officials feel that they have no choice but to contribute for fear of alienating the members. Moreover, some members have created their *own* PACs—organizations set up to raise money from individual donors that is then given to favored political allies in and out of Congress or used to advance the members' own political ambitions. When Charles Rangel, congressman from New York, was hoping to be elected whip of the Democratic party in the House, he set up a PAC that made campaign contributions to fellow representatives in hopes that they might vote for him as whip. There are many other examples from both sides of the aisle. An ironic consequence of this is that a conservative Republican may give money to a PAC set up by a moderate Democrat, who then gives the money to a liberal Democrat (or vice versa), with the result that the original donor winds up having his or her money go to somebody that he or she profoundly dislikes.

Almost any kind of organization—corporation, labor union, trade association, public-interest lobby, citizens group—can form a PAC. Over half of all PACs are sponsored by corporations, about a tenth by labor unions, and the rest by various groups, including ideological ones.

The rise of ideological PACs has been the most remarkable development in interest group activity in recent years. They have increased in number at a faster rate than business or labor PACs, and in the 1980 and 1982 elections they raised more money than either business or labor. In the 1992 election there were more than one thousand ideological PACs; about one-third were liberal, about two-thirds conservative.[24]

Though the ideological PACs raised more money than business or labor ones, they spent less on campaigns and gave less to candidates. The reason for this anomaly is that an ideological PAC usually has to raise its money by means of massive direct-mail solicitations, expensive efforts that can consume all the money raised, and more. By contrast, a typical business or labor PAC solicits money from within a single corporation or union. Even a well-run ideological PAC must spend fifty cents to raise a dollar; some spend much more than that.[25]

As Table 9.4 shows, of the ten PACs that gave the most money to candidates in the 1998 election, most were labor unions, business organizations, and groups that represented doctors, lawyers, realtors, and government employees. Except for Democratic Republican Voter Education, none was an ideological PAC.

Table 9.5 shows that, as we learned in Chapter 8, incumbents received more PAC money than challengers and that, whereas labor PACs gave almost exclusively to Democrats, business PACs favored Republicans.

Both parties have become dependent on PAC money. Still, the popular image of rich PACs stuffing huge sums into political campaigns and thereby buying the attention and possibly the favors of the grateful candidates is a bit overdrawn. For one thing, the typical PAC contribution is rather small. The average PAC donation to a House candidate is only a few hundred dollars and accounts for less than 1 percent of the candidate's total receipts. Most PACs spread small sums of money over many

Table 9.4 Spending by Political Action Committees (PACs), 1998

Ten largest PAC contributors to federal candidates during the 1998 election.

Committee	Contribution
Realtors Association	$2,474,133
Association of Trial Lawyers	2,428,300
State, County, and Municipal Employees	2,374,950
American Medical Association	2,336,281
Democratic Republican Voter Education	2,183,250
National Automobile Dealers Association	2,107,800
United Auto Workers	1,915,460
International Brotherhood of Electrical Workers	1,884,470
National Education Association	1,853,390
National Association of Home Builders	1,807,240

Source: Federal Election Commission.

Table 9.5	How PACs Spent Their Money in 1998									

During the 1998 campaign nearly four thousand PACs divided up their contributions as follows (in millions of dollars).

	House					Senate				
PAC Sponsor	Dem.	Rep.	Incumbent	Challenger	Open	Dem.	Rep.	Incumbent	Challenger	Open
Corporate	$16.1	$34.1	$43.9	$2.0	$4.2	$6.9	$13.9	$15.2	$2.6	$2.9
Trade/professional	17.6	28.7	38.1	2.9	4.2	4.6	7.8	8.9	1.5	1.9
Labor	34.0	3.1	26.1	5.3	5.4	5.4	0.6	3.9	0.9	1.0
Nonconnected	7.6	12.2	11.6	4.1	4.2	3.0	4.0	4.7	1.2	1.0

Source: Federal Election Commission.

candidates, and despite their great growth in numbers and expenditures, PACs still provide only about one-third of all the money spent by candidates for the House.[26]

Moreover, scholars have yet to find systematic evidence that PAC contributions generally affect how members of Congress vote. On most issues how legislators vote can be explained primarily by their general ideological outlooks and the characteristics of their constituents; how much PAC money they have received turns out to be a small factor. On the other hand, when an issue arises in which most of their constituents have no interest and ideology provides little guidance, there is a slight statistical correlation between PAC contributions and votes. But even here the correlation may be misleading. The same groups that give money also wage intensive lobbying campaigns, flooding representatives with information, press releases, and letters from interested constituents. What these studies may be measuring is the effect of persuasive arguments, not dollars; no one can be certain.[27]

It is possible that money affects legislative behavior in ways that will never appear in studies of roll-call votes in Congress. Members of Congress may be more willing to set aside time in their busy schedules for a group that has given money than for a group that has not. What the money has bought is access: it has helped open the door. Or contributions might influence how legislators behave on the committees on which they serve, subtly shaping the way in which they respond to arguments and the facts on which they rely. No one knows, because the research has not been done.

In any event, if interest group money makes a difference at all, it probably makes it on certain kinds of issues more than others. In the chapter on policy-making we define the kind of issues—we call them "client politics"—on which a given interest group is likely to be especially influential, whether by means of arguments, money, or both. After reading that chapter and considering the examples given there, it will be easier to put the present discussion of PAC money into context.

The "Revolving Door"

Every year, hundreds of people leave important jobs in the federal government to take more lucrative positions in private industry. Some go to work as lobbyists, others as consultants to business, still others as key executives in corporations, foundations, and universities. Many people worry that this "revolving door" may give private interests a way of improperly influencing government decisions. If a federal official uses his or her government position to do something for a corporation in exchange for a cushy job after leaving government, or if a person who has left government uses his or her personal contacts in Washington to get favors for private parties, then the public interest may suffer.

From time to time there are incidents that seem to confirm these fears. Michael K. Deaver, once the deputy chief of staff in the Reagan White House, was convicted of perjury in connection with a grand jury investigation of his having used his former government contacts to help the clients of his public relations firm. Lyn Nofziger, a former Reagan White House aide, was convicted of violating the Ethics in Government Act (see the box above) by lobbying the White House, soon after he left it, on behalf of various businesses and labor unions.

In 1988 federal investigators revealed evidence of corrupt dealings between some Defense Department officials and industry executives. Contractors and

Conflict of Interest

In 1978 a new federal law, the Ethics in Government Act, codified and broadened the rules governing possible conflicts of interest among senior members of the executive branch. The key provisions were as follows.

The president, vice president, and top-ranking (GS-16 and above) executive branch employees must each year file a public financial disclosure report that lists:

- The source and amount of all earned income as well as income from stocks, bonds, and property; the worth of any investments or large debts; and the source of a spouse's income, if any
- Any position held in business, labor, or certain nonprofit organizations

Employment after government service is restricted. Former executive branch employees may *not*:

- Represent anyone before their former agencies in connection with any matter that the former employees had been involved in before leaving the government

- Appear before an agency, for two years after leaving government service, on matters that came within the former employees' official sphere of responsibility, even if they were not personally involved in the matter
- Represent anyone on any matter before their former agencies, for one year after leaving them, even if the former employees had no connection with the matter while in the government

In addition, another law prohibits bribery. It is illegal to ask for, solicit, or receive anything of value in return for being influenced in the performance of one's duties.

Finally, an executive order forbids outside employment. An official may not hold a job or take a fee, even for lecturing or writing, if such employment or income might create a conflict of interest or an apparent conflict of interest.

Sources: National Journal (November 19, 1977): 1796–1803; *Congressional Quarterly Weekly Report* (October 28, 1978): 3121–3127.

---

their consultants, many of whom were former Pentagon personnel, obtained favors from procurement officials, gaining an edge on their competitors.

How systematic is this pattern of abuse? We don't know. Studies of the revolving door in federal regulatory agencies have found no clear pattern of officials' tilting their decisions in hopes of landing a lucrative business job.[28]

Agencies differ in their vulnerability to outside influences. If the Food and Drug Administration is not vigilant, people in that agency who help decide whether a new drug should be placed on the market may have their judgment affected somewhat by the possibility that, if they approve the drug, the pharmaceutical company that makes it will later offer them a lucrative position.

On the other hand, lawyers in the Federal Trade Commission who prosecute businesses that violate the antitrust laws may decide that their chances for getting a good job with a private law firm later on will increase if they are particularly vigorous and effective prosecutors. The firm, after all, wants to

hire competent people, and winning a case is a good test of competence.[29]

Trouble

Public displays and disruptive tactics—protest marches, sit-ins, picketing, and violence—have always been a part of American politics. Indeed, they were among the favorite tactics of the American colonists seeking independence in 1776.

Both ends of the political spectrum have used display, disruption, and violence. On the left feminists, antislavery agitators, coal miners, autoworkers, welfare mothers, African Americans, anti–nuclear power groups, public housing tenants, the American Indian Movement, the Students for a Democratic Society, and the Weather Underground have created "trouble" ranging from peaceful sit-ins at segregated lunch counters to bombings and shootings. On the right the Ku Klux Klan has used terror, intimidation, and murder; parents opposed to forced busing of schoolchildren have demonstrated; business firms have used strong-arm squads against

Disruptive tactics have been a part of American politics since the Boston Tea Party. These gay rights activists are blocking a road.

workers; right-to-life groups have blockaded abortion clinics; and an endless array of "anti-" groups (anti-Catholics, anti-Masons, anti-Jews, anti-immigrants, antisaloons, antiblacks, antiprotesters, and probably even anti-antis) have taken their disruptive turns on stage. These various activities are not morally the same—a sit-in demonstration is quite different from a lynching—but politically they constitute a similar problem for a government official.

An explanation of why and under what circumstances disruption occurs is beyond the scope of this book. To understand interest group politics, however, it is important to remember that making trouble has, since the 1960s, become a quite conventional political resource and is no longer simply the last resort of extremist groups. Making trouble is now an accepted political tactic of ordinary middle-class citizens as well as the disadvantaged or disreputable.

There is of course a long history of the use of disruptive methods by "proper" people. In a movement that began in England at the turn of the century and then spread here, feminists would chain themselves to lampposts or engage in what we now call "sit-ins" as part of a campaign to win the vote for women. The object then was much the same as the object of similar tactics today: to disrupt the working of some institution so that it is forced to negotiate with you, or, failing that, to enlist the sympathies of third parties (the media, other interest groups) who will come to your aid and press your target to negotiate with you, or, failing that, to goad the police into making attacks and arrests so that martyrs are created.

The civil rights and antiwar movements of the 1960s gave experience in these methods to thousands of young people and persuaded others of the effectiveness of such methods under certain conditions. Though these movements have abated or disappeared, their veterans and emulators have put such tactics to new uses—trying to block the construction of a nuclear power plant, for example, or occupying the office of a cabinet secretary to obtain concessions for a particular group.

Government officials dread this kind of trouble. They usually find themselves in a no-win situation. If they ignore the disruption, they are accused of being "insensitive," "unresponsive," or "arrogant." If they give in to the demonstrators, they encourage more demonstrations by proving that this is a useful tactic. If they call the police, they run the risk of violence and injuries, followed not only by bad publicity but by lawsuits.

Regulating Interest Groups

Interest group activity is a form of political speech protected by the First Amendment to the Constitution: it cannot lawfully be abolished or even much curtailed. In 1946 Congress passed the Federal Regulation of Lobbying Act, which requires groups and individuals seeking to influence legislation to register with the secretary of the Senate and the clerk of the House and to file quarterly financial reports. The Supreme Court upheld the law but restricted its application to lobbying efforts involving direct contacts with members of Congress.[30] More general "grassroots" interest group activity may not be restricted by the government. The 1946 law had little practical effect. Not all lobbyists took the trouble to register, and there was no guarantee that the financial statements were accurate. There was no staff in charge of enforcing the law.

After years of growing popular dissatisfaction with Congress, prompted in large measure by the (exaggerated) view that legislators were the pawns of powerful special interests, Congress in late 1995 unanimously passed a bill that tightened up the registration and disclosure requirements. Signed by the president, the law restates the obligation of lobbyists to register with the House and Senate, but it broadens the definition of a lobbyist to include the following:

- People who spend at least 20 percent of their time lobbying

- People who are paid at least $5,000 in any six-month period to lobby
- Corporations and other groups that spend more than $20,000 in any six-month period on their own lobbying staffs

The law covers people and groups who lobby the executive branch and congressional staffers as well as elected members of Congress, and it includes law firms that represent clients before the government. Twice a year, all registered lobbyists must report the following:

- The names of their clients
- Their income and expenditures
- The issues on which they worked

The registration and reporting requirements do not, however, extend to so-called grassroots organizations—that is, campaigns (sometimes led by volunteers, sometimes by hired professionals) to mobilize citizens to write or call the government about some issue. Nor was any new enforcement organization created, although congressional officials may refer violations to the Justice Department for investigation. Fines for breaking the law could amount to $50,000. In addition, the law bars tax-exempt, nonprofit advocacy groups that lobby from getting federal grants, a provision aimed at organizations such as the American Association of Retired Persons (AARP).

The most significant legal constraints on interest groups come not from the current federal lobbying law (though that may change) but from the tax code and the campaign finance laws. A nonprofit organization—which includes not only charitable groups but almost all voluntary associations that have an interest in politics—need not pay income taxes, and financial contributions to it can be deducted on the donor's income tax return, provided that the organization does not devote a "substantial part" of its activities to "attempting to influence legislation."[31] Many tax-exempt organizations do take public positions on political questions and testify before congressional committees. If the organization does any serious lobbying, however, it will lose its tax-exempt status (and thus find it harder to solicit donations and more expensive to operate). Exactly this happened to the Sierra Club in 1968 when the Internal Revenue Service revoked its tax-exempt status because of its extensive lobbying activities. Some voluntary associations try to deal with this problem by setting up separate organizations to collect tax-exempt money—for example, the NAACP, which lobbies, must pay taxes, but the NAACP Legal Defense and Education Fund, which does not lobby, is tax-exempt.

Finally, the campaign finance laws, described in detail in Chapter 8, limit to $5,000 the amount any political action committee can spend on a given candidate in a given election. These laws have sharply curtailed the extent to which any *single* group can give money, though they have increased the *total* amount that different groups are providing.

Many now believe that regulating interest groups requires regulating campaign expenditures. The basic pros and cons of key reform proposals can be summarized as follows:

- Putting a limit on campaign contributions would make it hard to buy a candidate—and harder to fund a challenger.
- Providing free television to candidates would cut the costs for campaigns but impose costs on television companies and fail to cut costs in the many House races that do not use television.
- Restricting issue advocacy would reduce the need for money but violate the Constitution.
- Banning soft money would bring all campaign dollars under federal regulation but restrict individuals' freedom to spend on political causes.
- Requiring all campaign money to be reported immediately on the Internet would keep the public informed but be hard to implement and monitor for compliance.
- Using government money to finance campaigns with no private donations would end political fundraising but not prevent people other than candidates from spending as they like on campaigns.

Beyond making bribery or other manifestly corrupt forms of behavior illegal and restricting the sums that campaign contributors can donate, there is probably no system for controlling interest groups that would both make a useful difference and leave important constitutional and political rights unimpaired. Ultimately the only remedy for imbalances or inadequacies in interest group representation is to devise and sustain a political system that gives all affected parties a reasonable chance to be heard on matters of public policy. That, of course, is exactly what the Founders thought they were doing. Whether they succeeded or not is a question to which we shall return at the end of this book.

MEMORANDUM

To: Senator Rita McCord
From: Jack Smith, chief of staff
Subject: Federal finance of campaigns

Every presidential election since 1976 has been financed in part by federal funds, but the proposal in question would start by limiting major presidential candidates to federal financing.

Arguments for:

1. The legal precedents are promising. Federal matching funds already go to presidential-primary candidates who have raised at least a total of $5,000, in contributions of $250 or less, in each of twenty states, and each major party nominee is already eligible for federal grants if he or she agrees to spend no more than the grant amount (about $62 million in 1996).
2. The sums required would be trivial. The hard money spent on the 1996 presidential campaigns (about $400 million) plus the soft money spent on them (about $260 million) totaled less than $700 million—hardly a fiscal drain were it paid out of a nearly $2 trillion annual federal budget.
3. The effects would be pervasive. Candidates and party leaders would stop covertly courting soft-money suppliers, stop compromising themselves with big-money donors (phone calls, luncheons, personal visits), and start focusing on the needs of average citizens.

Arguments against:

1. The constitutional precedents are prohibitive. The Supreme Court's *Buckley v. Valeo* (1976) decision upheld legal limits on campaign contributions but defined spending money for political purposes as a form of political expression protected by the First Amendment.
2. The sums spent would soon spiral. The federal government would be unable to restrict spending by individuals or organizations working independently, and federal funds would supplement, not supplant, new private money.
3. The effects would be perverse. Candidates would rely less on party leaders, which would further weaken the political parties. Many average citizens (most of whom have not opted to help pay for campaigns through voluntary federal income tax checkoffs) and nonvoters would feel as if they were being bullied into bankrolling a process that serves the politicians, not the people.

Your decision:
Favor proposal _____
Oppose proposal _____

U.S. Senator Wants Feds to Foot the Bill for Political Campaigns

September 4
WASHINGTON

Calling the country's campaign finance system "corrupt and complicated beyond comprehension," an ex-presidential contender and sitting senator is corralling congressional cosponsors for a new law that would have the federal government pay the entire cost of presidential races and lead to full federal funding for congressional campaigns as well . . .

Summary

Interest groups in the United States are more numerous and more fragmented than those in nations such as Great Britain, where the political system is more centralized. The goals and tactics of interest groups reflect not only the interests of their members but also the size of the groups, the incentives with which they attract supporters, and the role of their professional staffs. Because of the difficulty of organizing large numbers of people, a group purporting to speak for mass constituencies will often have to provide material benefits to members or acquire an affluent sponsor (such as a foundation). The chief source of interest group influence is information; public support, money, and the ability to create "trouble" are also important. The right to lobby is protected by the Constitution, but the tax and campaign finance laws impose significant restrictions on how money may be used.

World Wide Web Resources

- Index of interest groups: www.policy.com/community/advoc.html
- Conservative interest groups
  American Conservative Union: www.conservative.org
  Christian Coalition: www.cc.org
- Liberal interest groups
  American Civil Liberties Union: www.aclu.org
  Americans for Democratic Action: www.adaction.org
- Environmental groups
  Environmental Defense Fund: www.edf.org
  National Resources Defense Council: www.nrdc.org
- Civil rights groups
  NAACP: www.naacp.org
  Center for Equal Opportunity: www.ceousa.org
- Feminist group
  National Organization for Women: www.now.org

Key Terms

lobby *p. 218*
lobbyist *p. 218*
interest group *p. 221*
incentive *p. 223*

solidary incentives *p. 223*
material incentives *p. 223*
purposive incentive *p. 223*

ideological interest groups *p. 223*
public-interest lobby *p. 223*

social movement *p. 225*
political cue *p. 233*
ratings *p. 233*

Suggested Readings

Bauer, Raymond A., Ithiel de Sola Pool, and Lewis A. Dexter. *American Business and Public Policy*. New York: Atherton, 1963. A classic study of how business groups tried to shape foreign-trade legislation, set in a broad analysis of pressure groups and Congress.

Berry, Jeffrey M. *Lobbying for the People*. Princeton, N.J.: Princeton University Press, 1977. Analyzes more than eighty "public-interest" lobbies, with a detailed discussion of two.

Cigler, Allan J., and Burdett A. Loomis, eds. *Interest Group Politics*. 3rd ed. Washington, D.C.: Congressional Quarterly Press, 1991. Essays on several interest groups active in Washington.

Lowi, Theodore J. *The End of Liberalism*. New York: Norton, 1969. A critique of the role of interest groups in American government.

Malbin, Michael J., ed. *Money and Politics in the United States*. Chatham, N.J.: Chatham House, 1984. Excellent studies of PACs and of the influence of money in elections.

Mansbridge, Jane J. *Why We Lost the ERA*. Chicago: University of Chicago Press, 1986. Insightful analysis of the relationship between organizational incentives and tactics in the ERA campaign.

Olson, Mancur. *The Logic of Collective Action*. Cambridge: Harvard University Press, 1965. An economic analysis of interest groups, especially the "free-rider" problem.

Sabato, Larry. *PAC Power*. New York: Norton, 1985. A full discussion of the nature and activities of political action committees.

Schlozman, Kay Lehman, and John T. Tierney. *Organized Interests and American Democracy*. New York: Harper & Row, 1985. Comprehensive treatise on interest groups based on original research.

Truman, David B. *The Governmental Process*. 2nd ed. New York: Knopf, 1971. First published in 1951, this was the classic analysis—and defense—of interest group pluralism.

Wilson, James Q. *Political Organizations*. Rev. ed. Princeton, N.J.: Princeton University Press, 1995. A theory of interest groups emphasizing the incentives they use to attract members.

The Media

Enduring Questions

1. *Why do politicians worry so much about the media?*
2. *Why do the media focus on scandal?*
3. *Can we trust the media to be fair?*
4. *Should people care more about getting political information?*
5. *Why do people rely more on television than newspapers?*

Journalism in American Political History
The Party Press • The Popular Press • Magazines of Opinion • Electronic Journalism • The Internet

The Structure of the Media
Degree of Competition • The National Media

Rules Governing the Media
Confidentiality of Sources • Regulating Broadcasting • Campaigning

The Effects of the Media on Politics

Government and the News
Prominence of the President • Coverage of Congress

Interpreting Political News
Are News Stories Slanted? • Why Do We Have So Many News Leaks? • Sensationalism in the Media • Government Constraints on Journalists

All public officials have a love-hate relationship with newspapers, television, and the other media of mass communication. They depend on the media for the advancement of their careers and policies but fear the media's power to criticize, expose, and destroy. As political parties have declined—especially, strong local party organizations—politicians have become increasingly dependent on the media. Their efforts to woo the press have become ever greater, and their expressions of rage and dismay when that courtship is spurned, ever stronger. At the same time, the media have been changing, especially in regard to the kinds of people who have been attracted to leading positions in journalism and the attitudes they have brought with them. There has always been an adversarial relationship between those who govern and those who write, but events of recent decades have, as we shall see, made that conflict especially keen.

The relationships between government and the media in this country are shaped by laws and understandings that accord the media a degree of freedom greater than that found in almost any other nation.

245

Though many public officials secretly might like to control the media, and though no medium of communication in the United States or elsewhere is totally free of government influence, the press in this country is among the freest in the world. A study of ninety-four countries found only sixteen in which the press enjoyed a high degree of freedom; the United States was one of these.[1] Some democratic nations, such as France and Great Britain, place more restrictions on the communications media than are found here. The laws governing libel in England are so strict that public figures frequently sue newspapers for printing statements that tend to defame or ridicule them—and they collect. In the United States, as will be explained, the law of libel is loose enough to permit intense and even inaccurate criticism of anybody in the public eye. England also has an Official Secrets Act that can be used to punish any present or past public official who divulges to the press private government business.[2] In this country, by contrast, the Freedom of Information Act, together with a long tradition of leaking inside stories and writing memoirs of one's public service, virtually guarantees that very little can be kept secret for very long.

Almost all American radio and television stations are privately owned, though they require government licenses (issued for seven- and five-year terms, respectively) to operate. In France broadcasting is operated by a government agency (Radio-diffusion-Télévision Française) under the control of the minister of information, who is not averse to using that control to protect the government's image. Until recently the French government had the power to ban the showing of any motion picture that was thought likely to "disturb the public order" or for other "reasons of state."[3] A French newspaper editor was heavily fined by a court for having written an article critical of the president of France.[4] While the federal government does impose rules on American broadcasters, it does not have the power to censor or dictate the contents of particular stories. As we shall see, though, its power to license broadcasters has been used, on occasion, to harass station owners who were out of favor with the White House.

The freedom from government control that comes with the private ownership of the media of mass communication has a price, of course: newspapers, magazines, and broadcast stations are businesses that must earn a profit. Some critics believe that the need for profit leads publishers and station owners to distort the news coverage of politics to satisfy the desires of advertisers, the pecuniary interests of stockholders, or the private ideology of the managers. This is much too simple a view, however. Every owner of a communications medium must satisfy the often competing interests of a number of distinct constituencies—advertisers, readers or viewers, editors and reporters, and organized external pressure groups. How each newspaper or broadcaster balances the preferences of these groups varies from case to case. Moreover, the relative strength of these groups has changed over time. In general the history of American journalism, at least among newspapers, has been the history of the growing power and autonomy of editors and reporters.

Journalism in American Political History

Important changes in the nature of American politics have gone hand in hand with major changes in the organization and technology of the press. It is the nature of politics, being essentially a form of communication, to respond to changes in how communications are carried on. This can be seen by considering four important periods in journalistic history.

The Party Press

In the early years of the Republic, politicians of various factions and parties created, sponsored, and controlled newspapers to further their interests. This was possible because circulation was of necessity small (newspapers could not easily be distributed to large audiences, owing to poor transportation) and newspapers were expensive (the type was set by hand and the presses printed copies slowly). Furthermore, there were few large advertisers to pay the bills. These newspapers circulated chiefly among the political and commercial elites, who could afford the high subscription prices. Even with high prices, the newspapers, to exist, often required subsidies. That money frequently came from the government or from a political party.

The National Gazette, *edited by Philip Freneau, supported the Thomas Jefferson faction in national politics. Jefferson, as secretary of state, helped Freneau by giving him a job in the State Department. The* Gazette of the United States, *published by John Fenno, supported Jefferson's rival, Alexander Hamilton.*

During the Washington administration the Federalists, led by Alexander Hamilton, created the *Gazette of the United States.* The Republicans, led by Thomas Jefferson, retaliated by creating the *National Gazette* and made its editor, Philip Freneau, "clerk for foreign languages" in the State Department at $250 a year to help support him. After Jefferson became president, he induced another publisher, Samuel Harrison Smith, to start the *National Intelligencer,* subsidizing him by giving him a contract to print government documents. Andrew Jackson, when he became president, aided in the creation of the *Washington Globe.* By some estimates there were over fifty journalists on the government payroll during this era.[5] Naturally these newspapers were relentlessly partisan in their views. Citizens could choose among different party papers, but only rarely could they find a paper that presented both sides of an issue.

The Popular Press

Changes in society and technology made possible the rise of a self-supporting, mass-readership daily newspaper. The development of the high-speed rotary press enabled publishers to print thousands of copies of a newspaper cheaply and quickly. The invention of the telegraph in the 1840s meant that news from Washington could be flashed almost immediately to New York, Boston, Philadelphia, and Charleston, thus providing local papers with access to information that once only the Washington

POLITICALLY SPEAKING ★

Muckraker

A **muckraker** is a journalist who searches through the activities of public officials and organizations, especially business firms, seeking to expose conduct contrary to the public interest.

Anyone who has been around stables knows that *muck* means "manure"; by extension it can refer to anything that is filthy or disgusting.

The word was first used in a political sense by President Theodore Roosevelt, who warned in a 1906 speech that antibusiness journalism could go too far. He said that "the men with the muckrakes are often indispensable to the well-being of society; but only if they know when to stop raking the muck, and to look upward to the celestial crown above them, to the crown of worthy endeavor."

Roosevelt was referring to a character named the Man with the Muck Rake in John Bunyan's book *Pilgrim's Progress*; this fellow was so preoccupied with raking the muck on the stable floor that he could never look any way but down.

Source: Adapted from *Safire's Political Dictionary* by William Safire. Copyright © 1968, 1972, 1978 by William Safire. Reprinted by permission of Random House, Inc. and the author.

brief and that went to newspapers of every political hue, it could not afford to be partisan or biased; to attract as many subscribers as possible, it had to present the facts objectively. Meanwhile the nation was becoming more urbanized, with large numbers of people brought together in densely settled areas. These people could support a daily newspaper by paying only a penny per copy and by patronizing merchants who advertised in its pages. Newspapers no longer needed political patronage to prosper, and soon such subsidies began to dry up. In 1860 the Government Printing Office was established, thereby putting an end to most of the printing contracts that Washington newspapers had once enjoyed.

The mass-readership newspaper was scarcely nonpartisan, but the partisanship it displayed arose from the convictions of its publishers and editors rather than from the influence of its party sponsors. And these convictions blended political beliefs with economic interest. The way to attract a large readership was with sensationalism: violence, romance, and patriotism, coupled with exposés of government, politics, business, and society. As practiced by Joseph Pulitzer and William Randolph Hearst, founders of large newspaper empires, this editorial policy had great appeal for the average citizen and especially for the immigrants flooding into the large cities.

Strong-willed publishers could often become powerful political forces. Hearst used his papers to agitate for war with Spain when the Cubans rebelled against Spanish rule. Conservative Republican political leaders were opposed to the war, but a steady diet of newspaper stories about real and imagined Spanish brutalities whipped up public opinion in favor of intervention. At one point Hearst sent the noted artist Frederic Remington to Cuba to supply paintings of the conflict. Remington cabled back: "Everything is quiet.... There will be no war." Hearst supposedly replied: "Please remain. You furnish the pictures and I'll furnish the war."[6] When the battleship USS *Maine* blew up in Havana harbor, President William McKinley felt helpless to resist popular pressure, and war was declared in 1898.

For all their excesses, the mass-readership newspapers began to create a common national culture, to establish the feasibility of a press free of government control or subsidy, and to demonstrate how

papers enjoyed. The creation in 1848 of the Associated Press allowed telegraphic dissemination of information to newspaper editors on a systematic basis. Since the AP provided stories that had to be exciting (and profitable) could be the criticism of public policy and the revelation of public scandal.

Magazines of Opinion

The growing middle class was often repelled by what it called "yellow journalism" and was developing, around the turn of the century, a taste for political reform and a belief in the doctrines of the progressive movement. To satisfy this market, a variety of national magazines appeared that, unlike those devoted to manners and literature, discussed issues of public policy. Among the first of these were the *Nation*, the *Atlantic Monthly*, and *Harper's*, founded in the 1850s and 1860s; later there came the more broadly based mass-circulation magazines such as *McClure's*, *Scribner's*, and *Cosmopolitan*. They provided the means for developing a national constituency for certain issues, such as regulating business (or in the language of the times, "trustbusting"), purifying municipal politics, and reforming the civil service system. Lincoln Steffens and other so-called muckrakers were frequent contributors to the magazines, setting a pattern for what we now call "investigative reporting."

The national magazines of opinion provided an opportunity for individual writers to gain a nationwide following. The popular press, though initially under the heavy influence of founder-publishers, made the names of certain reporters and columnists household words. In time the great circulation wars between the big-city daily newspapers started to wane, as the more successful papers bought up or otherwise eliminated their competition. This reduced the need for the more extreme forms of sensationalism, a change that was reinforced by the growing sophistication and education of America's readers. And the founding publishers were gradually replaced by less flamboyant managers. All of these changes—in circulation needs, in audience interests, in managerial style, in the emergence of nationally known writers—helped increase the power of editors and reporters and make them a force to be reckoned with.

Although politics dominated the pages of most national magazines in the late nineteenth century, today national magazines that focus mainly on politics and government affairs account for only a small and declining portion of the national magazine market. Among all magazines in circulation today, only a fraction focus on politics—the majority of today's magazines focus on popular entertainment and leisure activities.

Electronic Journalism

Radio came on the national scene in the 1920s, television in the late 1940s. They represented a major change in the way news was gathered and disseminated, though few politicians at first understood the importance of this change. A broadcast permits public officials to speak directly to audiences without their remarks being filtered through editors and reporters. This was obviously an advantage to politicians, provided they were skilled enough to use it: they could in theory reach the voters directly on a national scale without the services of political parties, interest groups, or friendly editors.

But there was an offsetting disadvantage—people could easily ignore a speech broadcast on a radio or television station, either by not listening at all or by tuning to a different station. By contrast, the views of at least some public figures would receive prominent and often unavoidable display in newspapers, and in a growing number of cities there was only one daily paper. Moreover, space in a newspaper is cheap compared to time on a television broadcast. Adding one more story, or one more name to an existing story, costs the newspaper little. By contrast, less news can be carried on radio or television, and each news segment must be quite brief to avoid boring the audience. As a result, the number of political personalities that can be covered by radio and television news is much smaller than is the case with newspapers, and the cost (to the station) of making a news item or broadcast longer is often prohibitively large.

Thus, to obtain the advantages of electronic media coverage, public officials must do something sufficiently bold or colorful to gain free access to radio and television news—or they must find the money to purchase radio and television time. The president of the United States, of course, is routinely covered by radio and television and can ordinarily get free time to speak to the nation on matters of importance. All other officials must struggle for access to the electronic media by making controversial statements, acquiring a national reputation, or purchasing expensive time.

As we discussed in Chapter 8, the rise of the talk show as a political forum has increased politicians' access to the electronic media, as has the televised

In 1933 White House press conferences were informal affairs, as when reporters gathered around Franklin Roosevelt's desk in the Oval Office. Today they are huge gatherings held either in a special conference room or (as here) outside in the Rose Garden.

"town meeting." But such developments need to be understood as part of a larger story.

Until the 1990s, the "big three" television networks (ABC, CBS, and NBC) together claimed 80 percent or more of all viewers (see Table 10.1). Their evening newscasts dominated electronic media coverage of politics and government affairs. When it came to presidential campaigns, for example, the three networks were the only television games in town—they reported on the primaries, broadcast the party conventions, and covered the general election campaigns, including any presidential debates. But over the last few decades, the networks' evening newscasts have changed in ways that have made it harder for candidates to use them to get their messages across. For instance, the average **sound bite**—a video clip of a presidential contender speaking—dropped from about forty-two seconds in 1968 to less than ten seconds in 1988.[7]

Today politicians have sources other than the network news for sustained and personalized television exposure. Cable television, early-morning news and entertainment programs, and prime-time "newsmagazine" shows have greatly increased and diversified politicians' access to the electronic media. One of the most memorable moments of the 1992 presidential campaign—Ross Perot's declaring his willingness to run for president on CNN's "Larry King Live"—occurred on cable television. And while the networks' evening news programs feature only small sound bites, their early-morning programs and newsmagazine shows feature lengthy interviews with candidates.

Naturally many politicians favor the call-in format, town-meeting setups, lengthy human interest interviews, and casual appearances on entertainment shows to televised confrontations on policy

Table 10.1	Decline in Viewership of the Television Networks

"Big Three" Networks: Average Shares of Prime-Time Viewing Audience	
Year	Share
1961	94%
1971	91
1981	83
1991	41
1997	33

Source: Updated from *The Public Perspective* (September/October 1992): 6, reporting data provided by Nielsen Media Research and NBC. Used by permission of *The Public Perspective,* a publication of the Roper Center for Public Opinion Research, University of Connecticut.

issues with seasoned network journalists who push, probe, and criticize. And naturally they favor being a part of visually interesting programs rather than traditional "talking heads" news shows. But what is preferable to candidates is not necessarily helpful to the selection process that voters must go through in choosing a candidate. No one has yet systematically analyzed what, if any, positive or negative consequences these recent changes in politicians' access to the electronic media hold for campaigns, elections, or governance. Nor, for that matter, is there yet any significant research on the broader societal consequences of so-called narrowcasting—the proliferation of television and radio stations that target highly segmented listening and viewing audiences, and the relative decline of electronic and print media that reach large and heterogeneous populations.

One thing is clear: most politicians crave the media spotlight, both on the campaign trail and in office. The efforts made by political candidates to get "visuals"—filmed stories—on television continue after they are elected. Since the president is always news, a politician wishing to make news is well advised to attack the president. Even better, attack him with the aid of a photogenic prop: when the late Senator John Heinz III of Pennsylvania wanted to criticize a president's bridge-repair program, Heinz had himself filmed making the attack not in his office but standing on a bridge.

The Internet

The newest electronic source of news is the Internet and the World Wide Web. In a 1998 survey more than forty million people, especially young people, said that they had used the Internet within the past thirty days. The political news that is found there ranges from summaries of news stories from newspapers and magazines to political rumors and hot (but often unverified) news tips. Users can get gossip before it is printed or broadcast, learn about (or even join) political organizations, and participate in chat rooms with people who have similar political views. The Internet is the ultimate free market in political news: no one can ban, control, or regulate it, and no one can keep either facts or nonsense off of it.

During the discussion of the sexual liaison between former White House intern Monica Lewin-

News moves in a fast and focused way on the Internet, where not only can you stay up to date, you can be in contact with like-minded people.

sky and President Bill Clinton, the Internet was a source of facts, gossip, and news leads. In the 2000 presidential campaign every major candidate had a web site both to promote his or her views and to raise money. When Senator John McCain won the Republican primary in New Hampshire, the number of people going to his web site, and the money he raised through it, shot up.

The rise of the Internet has completed a remarkable transformation in American journalism. In the days of the party press only a few people read newspapers. When mass-circulation newspapers arose, there also arose mass politics. When magazines of opinion developed, there also developed interest groups. When radio and television became dominant, politicians could build their own bridges to voters without party or interest group influence. And now, with the Internet, voters and political activists can talk to each other.

The Structure of the Media

The relationship between journalism and politics is a two-way street: though politicians take advantage as best they can of the communications media available

Figure 10.1   Young People Have Become Less Interested in Political News

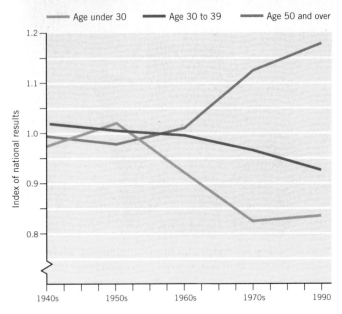

The three lines show how attentive people of different ages were to news stories during the 1940s, 1950s, 1960s, and 1990. The dashed line represents those under age 30, the blue line those 30–49, and the black line those 50 and older.

Source: Los Angeles Times, Times Mirror Center for the People and the Press (June 28, 1990).

to them, these media in turn attempt to use politics and politicians as a way of both entertaining and informing their audiences. The mass media, whatever their disclaimers, are not simply a mirror held up to reality or a messenger that carries the news. There is inevitably a process of selection, of editing, and of emphasis, and this process reflects, to some degree, the way in which the media are organized, the kinds of audiences they seek to serve, and the preferences and opinions of the members of the media.

Degree of Competition

There has been a significant decline in the number of daily newspapers in this country, as well as in the number of cities in which there are competing daily papers. There were competing newspapers in 60 percent of American cities in 1900 but in only 4 percent by 1972. The largest cities—New York,

Chicago, Detroit, Philadelphia, Los Angeles, Washington, Atlanta, Boston—have at least two central-city newspapers, but most other cities have just one. This is partially offset by the fact that in many metropolitan areas, two or more neighboring cities will each have a newspaper whose readership overlaps. Residents of Manchester, New Hampshire, for example, can easily obtain the *Manchester Union Leader,* the *Boston Globe,* and the *Boston Herald.* But newspaper circulation overall has fallen since 1967. People now get most of their news from television. Young people especially have turned away from political news (see Figure 10.1).

Radio and television, by contrast, are intensely competitive and becoming more so. Almost every American home has a radio and a television set. Though there are only five major television networks, there are over one thousand television stations, each of which has its own news programs. Local stations affiliated with a network are free to accept or reject network programs. There are more than eleven thousand cable TV systems, serving over fifty million people (and a typical cable can carry dozens of channels). In addition there are nearly ten thousand radio stations; some broadcast nothing but news, and others develop a specialized following among blacks, Hispanics, or other minorities. Magazines exist for every conceivable interest. The number of news sources available to an American is vast—more than even dedicated readers and viewers can keep up with.

To a degree that would astonish most foreigners, the American press—radio, television, and newspapers—is made up of locally owned and managed enterprises. In Britain, France, Germany, Japan, Sweden, and elsewhere, the media are owned and operated with a national audience in mind. The *Times* of London may be published in that city, but it is read throughout Great Britain, as are the *Guardian,* the *Daily Telegraph,* and the *Daily Mirror.* Radio and television broadcasts are centrally planned and nationally aired.

The American newspaper, however, is primarily oriented to its local market and local audience, and there is typically more local than national news in it. Radio and television stations accept network programming, but the early- and late-evening news programs provide a heavy diet of local political, social, and sports news. Government regulations developed by the Federal Communications Commission (FCC) are in part responsible for this. Until the mid-1990s, no one could own and operate more than one newspaper, one AM radio station, one FM radio station, or one television station in a given market. The networks still today may not compel a local affiliate to accept any particular broadcast. (In fact almost all network news programs are carried by the affiliates.) The result has been the development of a decentralized broadcast industry.

The National Media

The local orientation of much of the American communications media is partially offset, however, by the emergence of certain publications and broadcast services that constitute a kind of national press. The wire services—the Associated Press and United Press International—supply most of the national news that local papers publish. Certain newsmagazines—*Time, Newsweek, U.S. News & World Report*—have a national readership. The network evening news broadcasts produced by ABC, CBS, and NBC are carried by most television stations with a network affiliation. CNN—the Cable News Network—broadcasts national news around the clock. There are only three truly national newspapers, the *Wall Street Journal,* the *Christian Science Monitor,* and *USA Today,* but the *New York Times* and the *Washington Post* have acquired national influence because they are read daily by virtually every important official in Washington (and thus have become an important channel by which these officials keep track of one another) and because the television networks and many local newspapers use the stories that the *Times* and the *Post* print. In fact one study found that the front page of the morning *Times* significantly shapes the contents of each network's evening news broadcasts.[8]

The existence of a national press is important for two reasons: First, government officials in Washington pay great attention to what these media say about them and their programs. They pay much less attention to what local papers and broadcasters say (if, indeed, they even know about their comments). Politicians read and worry about newspaper editorials, something the average citizen rarely does. Second, reporters and editors for the national press tend to differ from those who work for the local press. They are usually better paid than most other journalists, they have often graduated from the most

To help reach the voters directly without going through reporters, presidential candidates increasingly use talk show hosts. Here, Elizabeth Dole and Larry King in 1999.

prestigious colleges and universities, and in general they have more liberal political views.[9] Above all they seek—and frequently obtain—the opportunity to write stories that are not accounts of a particular news event but "background," investigative, or interpretive stories about issues and policies.[10]

The national press plays the role of gatekeeper, scorekeeper, and watchdog for the federal government.

Gatekeeper   As gatekeeper it can influence what subjects become national political issues and for how long. Automobile safety, water pollution, and the quality of prescription drugs were not major political issues before the national press began giving substantial attention to these matters and thus helped place them on the political agenda. When crime rates rose in the early 1960s, the subject was given little political attention in Washington, in part because the media did not cover it extensively. Media attention to crime increased in the late 1960s and early 1970s, slackened in the late 1970s, and rose again in the 1980s and early 1990s. Throughout most of these years crime went up. In short *reality* did not change during this time; only the focus of media and political attention shifted. Elite opinion about the war in Vietnam also changed significantly as the attitude toward the war expressed by the national media changed.

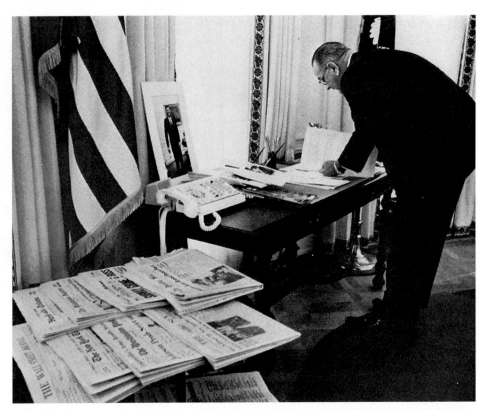

The national press wields great influence because it is read by presidents and virtually every other top government official. President Lyndon Johnson surveys his daily collection of newspapers in the Oval Office.

Scorekeeper As scorekeepers the national media keep track of and help make political reputations, note who is being "mentioned" as a presidential candidate, and help decide who is winning and losing in Washington politics. When Jimmy Carter, a virtually unknown former governor of Georgia, was planning his campaign to get the Democratic nomination for president, he understood clearly the importance of being "mentioned." So successful was he in cultivating members of the national press that between November 1975 and February 1976, before the first primary election was held, he was the subject of more stories in the *New York Times*, the *Washington Post*, and the *Columbus Dispatch* than any other potential Democratic presidential candidate, even though the others (Henry Jackson, Hubert Humphrey, and George Wallace) were much better known. He did almost as well in getting mentioned on the three television networks.

The scorekeeper role of the media often leads the press to cover presidential elections as if they were horse races rather than choices among policies. Consider the enormous attention the media give to the Iowa caucus and the New Hampshire primary election, despite the fact that these states produce only a tiny fraction of the delegates to either party's nominating convention and that neither state is representative of the nation as a whole. The results of the Iowa caucus, the first in the nation, are given great importance by the press. Consequently the coverage received by a candidate who does well in Iowa constitutes a tremendous amount of free publicity that can help him or her in the New Hampshire primary election. Doing well in that primary results in even more media attention, thus boosting the candidate for the next primaries, and so on.

For example, in 2000 John McCain won the Republican primary in New Hampshire. Even though New Hampshire is a small state and lots of candidates who win its primary fail to win the presidency, McCain became a major political figure, just as Gary Hart did in 1984. The media were already fascinated by McCain, but their coverage of him increased greatly, and he became the key rival to George W. Bush. The horse race—once involving six candidates—was then a two-horse contest.

This is not the only time that the press has decided that New Hampshire is important. In 1972 George McGovern became part of the horse race after he lost the primary to Edmund Muskie, and in 1968 Eugene McCarthy won what the press called a "moral victory" after he lost to Lyndon Johnson.

Watchdog   Once the scorekeepers decide that you are the person to watch, they adopt their watchdog role. Before his New Hampshire victory in 1984, Hart's background went largely unexamined; after he had been declared a "front-runner," stories began appearing about how he had changed his name and altered his birth date by a year. In 1987, when Hart was already the front-runner for the 1988 Democratic presidential nomination, the press played its watchdog role right from the start. When rumors circulated that he was unfaithful to his wife, the *Miami Herald* staked out his apartment in Washington, D.C., and discovered that he had spent several evening hours there with an attractive young woman, Donna Rice. Soon there appeared other stories about his having taken Ms. Rice on a boat trip to Bimini. Not long thereafter Hart dropped out of the presidential race, accusing the press of unfair treatment. Then, in late 1987, Hart reentered the race only to drop out again after getting little popular support.

This close scrutiny is natural. The media have an instinctive—and profitable—desire to investigate personalities and expose scandals. To some degree all reporters probably share H. L. Mencken's belief that the role of the press is to "comfort the afflicted and afflict the comfortable." They tend to be tolerant of underdogs, tough on front-runners. Though some reporters develop close relations with powerful personages, many—especially younger ones—find the discovery of wrongdoing both more absorbing and more lucrative. Bob Woodward and Carl Bernstein, who wrote most of the Watergate stories for the *Washington Post*, simultaneously performed an important public service, received the accolades of their colleagues, and earned a lot of money.

Newspapers and television stations play these three roles in somewhat different ways. A newspaper can cover more stories in greater depth than a TV station and faces less competition from other papers than TV stations face from other broadcasters. A TV station faces brutal competition, must select its programs in part for their visual impact, and must keep its stories short and punchy. As a result newspaper reporters have more freedom to develop their own stories, but they earn less money than television news broadcasters. The latter have little freedom (the fear of losing their audience is keen), but they can make a lot of money (if they are attractive personalities who photograph well).

Rules Governing the Media

Ironically, the least competitive media outlets—the big-city newspapers—are almost entirely free from government regulation, while the most competitive ones—radio and television stations—must have a government license to operate and must adhere to a variety of government regulations.

Newspapers and magazines need no license to publish, their freedom to publish may not be restrained in advance, and they are liable for punishment for what they do publish only under certain highly restricted circumstances. The First Amendment to the Constitution has been interpreted as meaning that no government, federal or state, can place "prior restraints" (that is, censorship) on the press except under very narrowly defined circumstances.[11] When the federal government sought to prevent the *New York Times* from publishing the Pentagon Papers, a set of secret government documents stolen by an antiwar activist, the Court held that the paper was free to publish them.[12]

Once something is published, a newspaper or magazine may be sued or prosecuted if the material is libelous or obscene or if it incites someone to commit an illegal act. But these are usually not very serious restrictions, because the courts have defined *libelous*, *obscene*, and *incitement* so narrowly as to make it more difficult here than in any other nation to find the press guilty of such conduct. For example, for a paper to be found guilty of libeling a public official or other prominent person, the person must not only show that what was printed was wrong and damaging but must also show, with "clear and convincing evidence," that it was printed maliciously—that is, with "reckless disregard" for its truth or falsity.[13] When in 1984 Israeli General Ariel Sharon sued *Time* magazine for libel, the jury decided that the story that *Time* had printed was false and defamatory but that *Time* had not published it as the result of malice, and so Sharon did not collect any damages.

There are also laws intended to protect the privacy of citizens, but they do not really inhibit newspapers. In general, your name and picture can be printed without your consent if they are part of a news story of some conceivable public interest. And if a paper attacks you in print, the paper has no legal obligation to give you space for a reply.[14]

It is illegal to use printed words to advocate the violent overthrow of the government if by your advocacy you incite others to action, but this rule has been applied to newspapers only rarely, and in recent years, never.[15]

Confidentiality of Sources

Reporters believe that they should have the right to keep confidential the sources of their stories. Some states agree and have passed laws to that effect. Most states and the federal government do not agree, so the courts must decide in each case whether the need of a journalist to protect confidential sources does or does not outweigh the interest of the government in gathering evidence in a criminal investigation. In general the Supreme Court has upheld the right of the government to compel reporters to divulge information as part of a properly conducted criminal investigation, if it bears on the commission of a crime.[16]

This conflict arises not only between reporters and law enforcement agencies but also between reporters and persons accused of committing a crime. Myron Farber, a reporter for the *New York Times*, wrote a series of stories that led to the indictment and trial of a physician on charges that he had murdered five patients. The judge ordered Farber to show him his notes to determine whether they should be given to the defense lawyers. Farber refused, arguing that revealing his notes would infringe upon the confidentiality that he had promised to his sources. Farber was sent to jail for contempt of court. On appeal the New Jersey Supreme Court and the U.S. Supreme Court decided against Farber, holding that the accused person's right to a fair trial includes the right to compel the production of evidence, even from reporters.

In another case the Supreme Court upheld the right of the police to search newspaper offices, so long as they have a warrant. But Congress then passed a law forbidding such searches (except in special cases), requiring instead that the police subpoena the desired documents.[17]

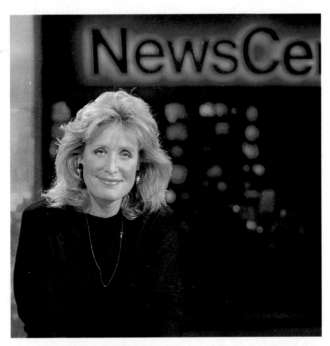

Reporter Susan Wornick in Boston was arrested when she refused to divulge the name of a person who told her that police officers had broken into a drugstore. Eventually the source revealed himself, and the charges against her were dropped.

Regulating Broadcasting

Although newspapers and magazines by and large are not regulated, broadcasting is regulated by the government. No one may operate a radio or television station without a license from the Federal Communications Commission, renewable every seven

How to Read a Newspaper

Newspapers don't simply report the news; they report somebody's idea of what is news, written in language intended to *persuade* as well as inform. To read a newspaper intelligently, look for three things: what is covered, who are the sources, and how language is used.

Coverage Every newspaper will cover a big story, such as a flood, fire, or presidential trip, but newspapers can pick and choose among lesser stories. One paper will select stories about the environment, business fraud, and civil rights; another will prefer stories about crime, drug dealers, and "welfare cheats." What do these choices tell you about the beliefs of the editors and reporters working for these two papers? What do these people want you to believe are the important issues?

Sources For some stories, the source is obvious: "The Supreme Court decided . . . ," "Congress voted . . . ," or "The president said. . . ." For others, the source is not so obvious. There are two kinds of sources you should beware of. The first is an anonymous source. When you read phrases such as "a high official said today . . . " or "White House sources revealed that . . . " always ask yourself this question: why does the source want me to know this? The answer usually will be this: because if I believe what he or she said, it will advance his or her interests. This can happen in one of three ways. First, the source may support a policy or appointment and want to test public reaction to it. This is called floating a **trial balloon.** Second, the source may oppose a policy or appointment and hope that by leaking word of it, the idea will be killed. Third, the source may want to take credit for something good that happened or shift blame onto somebody else for something bad that happened. When you read a story that is based on anonymous sources, ask yourself these questions: Judging from the tone of the story, is this leak designed to support or kill an idea? Is it designed to take credit or shift blame? In whose interest is it to accomplish these things? By asking these questions, you often can make a pretty good guess as to the identity of the anonymous source.

Some stories depend on the reader's believing a key fact, previously unknown. For example: "The world's climate is getting hotter because of man-made pollution," "drug abuse is soaring," "the death penalty will prevent murder," "husbands are more likely to beat up on their wives on Super Bowl Sunday." Each of these "facts" is either wrong, grossly exaggerated, or stated with excessive confidence. But each comes from an advocate organization that wants you to believe it, because if you do, you will take that organization's solution more seriously. Be skeptical of key facts if they come from an advocacy source. Don't be misled by the tendency of many advocacy organizations to take neutral or scholarly names like "Center for the Public Interest" or "Institute for Policy Research." Some of these really are neutral or scholarly, but many aren't.

Language Everybody uses words to persuade people of something without actually making a clear argument for it. This is called using **loaded language.** For example: if you like a politician, call him "Senator Smith"; if you don't like him, refer to him as "right-wing (or left-wing) senators such as Smith." If you like an idea proposed by a professor, call her "respected"; if you don't like the idea, call her "controversial." If you favor abortion, call somebody who agrees with you "pro-choice" ("choice" is valued by most people); if you oppose abortion, call those who agree with you "pro-life" ("life," like "choice," is a good thing). Recognizing loaded language in a newspaper article can give you important clues to the writer's own point of view.

---

years for radio and every five for television stations. An application for renewal is rarely refused, but until recently the FCC required the broadcaster to submit detailed information about its programming and how it planned to serve "community needs" in order to get a renewal. Based on this information or on the complaints of some group, the FCC could use its powers of renewal to influence what the station put on the air. For example, it could induce stations to reduce the amount of violence shown, increase the proportion of "public service" programs on the air, or alter the way it portrayed various ethnic groups.

Of late a movement has arisen to deregulate broadcasting, on the grounds that so many stations are now on the air that competition should be allowed to determine how each station defines and serves community needs. In this view citizens can choose what they want to hear or see without the government's shaping the content of each station's programming. For example, since the early 1980s a station can simply submit a postcard requesting that its license be renewed, a request automatically granted unless some group formally opposes the renewal. In that case the FCC holds a hearing. As a result some of the old rules—for instance, that each hour on TV could contain only sixteen minutes of commercials—are no longer rigidly enforced.

Radio broadcasting has been deregulated the most. Before 1992 one company could own one AM and one FM station in each market. In 1992 this number was doubled. And in 1996 the Telecommunications Act allowed one company to own as many as eight stations in large markets (five in smaller ones) and as many as it wished nationally. This trend has had two results. First, a few large compa-

nies now own most of the big-market radio stations. Second, the looser editorial restrictions that accompanied deregulation mean that a greater variety of opinions and shows can be found on radio. There are many more radio talk shows than would have been heard when content was more tightly controlled.

The content of radio and television is still regulated in ways that newspapers and magazines are not. These include the following:

- **Equal time rule:** If a station sells time to one candidate for office, it must be willing to sell equal time to opposing candidates.
- **Right-of-reply rule:** If a person is attacked on a broadcast (other than in a regular news program), that person has the right to reply over that same station.
- **Political editorializing rule:** If a broadcaster endorses a candidate, the opposing candidate has a right to reply.

For many years there was also in place the **fairness doctrine,** which required broadcasters to give time to opposing views if they broadcast a program giving one side of a controversial issue. In 1987 the FCC, believing that the doctrine inhibited the free discussion of issues, abolished it; Congress has tried to pass a law to reinstate it (so far without success). Most broadcasters still follow the rule voluntarily.

Campaigning

When candidates wish to campaign on radio or television, the equal time rule applies. A broadcaster must provide equal access to candidates for office and charge them rates no higher than the cheapest rate applicable to commercial advertisers for comparable time.

At one time this rule meant that a station or network could not broadcast a debate between the Democratic and Republican candidates for an office without inviting all other candidates as well—Libertarian, Prohibitionist, or whatever. Thus a presidential debate in 1980 could be limited to the major candidates, Reagan and Carter (or Reagan and Anderson), only by having the League of Women Voters sponsor it and then allowing radio and TV to cover it as a "news event." Now stations and networks can themselves sponsor debates limited to major candidates.

To be successful in an election, candidates have to win the support of a diverse group of people. This advertisement in Spanish is directed toward the Hispanic community. It says, "Al Gore and the Democrats: We Can Trust Them."

Though laws guarantee that candidates can buy time at favorable rates on television, not all candidates take advantage of this. The reason is that television is not always an efficient way to reach voters. A television message is literally "broad cast"—spread out to a mass audience without regard to the boundaries of the district in which a candidate is running. Presidential candidates, of course, always use television, because their constituency is the whole nation. Candidates for senator or representative, however, may or may not use television, depending on whether the boundaries of their state or district conform well to the boundaries of a television market.

A **market** is an area easily reached by a television signal; there are about two hundred such markets in the country. Congressman Tim Roemer comes from a district in Indiana centered on the city of South Bend, which is also the hub of a distinct TV market. Roemer can use television effectively and relatively cheaply (in terms of dollars per viewer reached). By contrast, when Adam K. Levin ran for a congressional seat in New Jersey in 1982, he spent large sums on television ads on the only stations—those in New York City—that reach his district. But just 4 percent of the viewers of those stations lived in Levin's district, and so most of the money was wasted. As a more experienced politician commented, he "might as well give the money away at a bus station." Because of these factors, a far higher proportion of Senate than of House candidates buy television ads.[18]

The Effects of the Media on Politics

Everyone believes that the media have a profound effect, for better or for worse, on politics. A small but growing body of research indicates that what appears in print or on the air probably does have an effect on how citizens think and what they think about—what they cite as "important problems," how they attribute responsibility for problems, what policy preferences they hold—and what policymakers do.[19] But there is as of yet relatively little scholarly evidence that enables us to know precisely how large that effect is or under what conditions it exists. The reason for this gap between what everyone knows and what no one can prove is probably that

until recently scholars have chiefly tried to measure the effect of the media on election outcomes. But as we have seen (Chapter 8), elections—especially those for important, highly visible offices—are occasions when the voter is bombarded with all manner of cues from friends, family, interest groups, candidates, memories, and loyalties, as well as radio, television, and newspapers. It would be surprising if the effect of the media were very strong, or at least very apparent, under these circumstances.

Efforts to determine whether voters who watch a lot of television or who see candidates on television frequently vote differently from those who do not watch television at all (or who watch only nonpolitical messages) have generally proved unavailing.[20] This is quite consistent with studies of political propaganda generally. At least in the short run, television and radio suffer from processes called **selective attention** (the citizen sees and hears only what he or she wants) and mental tune-out (the citizen simply ignores or gets irritated by messages that are not in accord with existing beliefs). Radio and television may tend to reinforce existing beliefs, but it is not clear that they change them.[21]

But if this is true, why do companies spend millions of dollars advertising deodorants and frozen pizza? And if advertising can sell these products, why can't it sell candidates? The answer is quite simple: citizens are not idiots. They can tell the difference between a deodorant and a Democrat, between a pizza and a Republican. If an ad persuades them to try a deodorant or a pizza, they will do so, knowing that not much is at stake, the costs are small, and if they do not like it, they can change brands in an instant. But they know that government is a more serious business, that one is stuck with the winning candidate for two, four, or even six years, and that as citizens they have accumulated a lot of information about the past behavior of the two major parties and their principal figures.

Local newspapers have generally endorsed Republican candidates for president throughout this century. Indeed, only in 1964 did more newspapers endorse the Democrat (Johnson) than the Republican (Goldwater). Since the Democrats won eight of the fourteen presidential elections between 1932 and 1984, you might think that newspaper endorsements are worthless. They may have some value,

The "Rules" of Politics

The Maxims of Media Relations

The importance of the national media to politicians has given rise to some shared understandings among officeholders about how one deals with the media. Some of these are caught in the following maxims:

- All secrets become public knowledge. The more important the secret, the sooner it becomes known.

- All stories written about me are inaccurate; all stories written about you are entirely accurate.

- The rosier the news, the higher ranking the official who announces it.

- Always release bad news on Saturday night. Fewer people notice it.

- Never argue with a person who buys ink by the barrel.

however. A careful study of the effect of such endorsements on the 1964 presidential election found that, at least in the North, a newspaper endorsement may have added about five percentage points to what the Democratic candidate would otherwise have obtained.[22]

There are some elections, however, in which voters have few sources of information beyond what the media provide. Primary elections involving political unknowns and general elections for low-visibility offices (for example, tax assessor or superior court judge) may make voters dependent on newspaper and broadcast ads for information. Skillful ads may have a big effect on the results of these contests.

The major effects of the media, however, probably have much less to do with how people vote in an election and much more to do with how politics is conducted, how candidates are perceived, and how policies are formulated. National nominating conventions have been changed to fit the needs of television broadcasters. Some candidates have found it

possible to win their party's nomination for senator or governor with expensive advertising campaigns that bypass the parties and ultimately weaken them. Unknown politicians can acquire a national reputation overnight by being shrewd enough—or lucky enough—to be at the center of an event heavily covered by the press.

In 1950 Estes Kefauver was a little-known senator from Tennessee. Then he chaired a special Senate investigating committee that brought before it various figures in organized crime. When these dramatic hearings were televised to audiences numbering in the millions, Kefauver became a household word, and in 1952 he became a leading contender for the Democratic nomination for president. He was a strong vote getter in the primaries and actually led on the first ballot at the Chicago convention, only to lose to Adlai Stevenson.

The lesson was not lost on other politicians. From that time on, developing through the media a recognized name and a national constituency became important to many senators. It also became a strategy whereby a variety of issues could be placed on the national agenda and pressed on Congress. Environmental and consumer issues benefited especially from the attention given them by the national press.

A survey of public opinion in North Carolina found that the issues that citizens believed to be important politically were very similar to the issues that newspapers and television newscasts had featured. Experiments conducted in New Haven, Connecticut, also showed that watching television news programs affected the importance people attached to various issues. TV influenced the political agenda.[23] On the other hand, people are much less likely to take their cues from the media on matters that affect them personally. Everybody who is unemployed, the victim of crime, or worried about high food prices will identify these matters as issues whether or not the media emphasize them.[24] In short the media help set the political agenda on matters with which citizens have little personal experience, but they have much less influence over how people react to things that touch their lives directly.

The media also affect how we perceive certain issues and candidates. A study of the differences between voters who get their news primarily from

Senator Estes Kefauver pioneered the televised Senate investigation with hearings into organized crime and (pictured here) teenage drug addiction.

television and those who get it chiefly from newspapers found that the two groups did not view political matters the same way. On a variety of issues, newspaper readers thought that Gerald Ford was more conservative and Jimmy Carter more liberal than did television viewers. This difference persisted even after taking into account the fact that newspaper readers tend to have more schooling than do television viewers. Put another way, newspaper readers saw bigger differences between the 1976 presidential candidates than did television viewers.[25]

Another study found that television news stories affect the popularity of presidents and that television "commentary"—that is, the expression by newscasters of their personal opinions—tends to have a large effect, at least in the short run.[26] This will not come as a surprise to White House officials, who spend almost every waking minute trying to get the television networks to say something nice about the president. The data support much anecdotal evidence on this score, such as Lyndon Johnson's belief that his war policy in Vietnam was doomed when Walter Cronkite, in his heavily watched CBS News programs, turned against the war.

Government and the News

Every government agency, every public official, spends a great deal of time trying to shape public opinion. From time to time somebody publishes an exposé of the efforts of the Pentagon, the White House, or some bureau to "sell" itself to the people, but in a government of separated powers, weak parties, and a decentralized legislature, any government agency that fails to cultivate public opinion will sooner or later find itself weak, without allies, and in trouble.

Prominence of the President

Theodore Roosevelt was the first president to raise the systematic cultivation of the press to an art form. From the day he took office, he made it clear that he would give inside stories to friendly reporters and withhold them from hostile ones. He made sure that scarcely a day passed without his doing something newsworthy. In 1902 he built the West Wing of the White House and included in it, for the first time, a special room for reporters near his office, and he invited the press to become fascinated by the antics of his children. In return the reporters adored

When President Theodore Roosevelt cultivated the media, reporters were usually unknown and poorly paid.

him. Teddy's nephew Franklin Roosevelt institutionalized this system by making his press secretary (a job created by Herbert Hoover) a major instrument for cultivating and managing, as well as informing, the press.[27]

Today the press secretary heads a large staff that meets with reporters, briefs the president on questions he is likely to be asked, attempts to control the flow of news from cabinet departments to the press, and arranges briefings for out-of-town editors (to bypass what many presidents think are the biases of the White House press corps).

The press makes news, as when it covered Elian Gonzalez who had escaped from Cuba with his mother, who drowned.

All this effort is directed primarily at the White House press corps, a group of men and women who have a lounge in the White House itself where they wait for a story to break, attend the daily press briefing, or take advantage of a "photo op"—an opportunity to photograph the president with some newsworthy person.

No other nation in the world has brought the press into such close physical proximity to the head of its government. The result is that the actions of our government are personalized to a degree not found in most other democracies. Whether the president rides a horse, comes down with a cold, greets a Boy Scout, or takes a trip in his airplane, the press is there. The prime minister of Great Britain does not share his home with the press or expect to have his every sneeze recorded for posterity.

Coverage of Congress

Congress has watched all this with irritation and envy. It resents the attention given the president, but it is not certain how it can compete. The 435 members of the House are so numerous and play such specialized roles that they do not get much individualized press attention. In the past the House was quite restrictive about television or radio coverage of its proceedings. Until 1978 it prohibited television cameras on the floor except on purely ceremonial occasions (such as the annual State of the Union message delivered by the president). From 1952 to 1970 the House would not even allow electronic coverage of its committee hearings (except for a few occasions during those periods when the Republicans were in the majority). Significant live coverage of committee hearings began in 1974 when the House Judiciary Committee was discussing the possible impeachment of President Nixon.[28] Since 1979 cable TV (C-SPAN) has provided gavel-to-gavel coverage of speeches on the House floor.

The Senate has used television much more fully, heightening the already substantial advantage that senators have over representatives in getting the public eye. Although radio and television coverage of the Senate floor was not allowed until 1978 (when the debates on the Panama Canal treaties were broadcast live), Senate committee hearings have frequently been televised for either news films or live broadcasts ever since Estes Kefauver demonstrated the power of this medium in 1950. Since

1986 the Senate has allowed live C-SPAN coverage of its sessions.

Senatorial use of televised committee hearings has helped turn the Senate into the incubator for presidential candidates. At least in most states, if you are a governor, you are located far from network television news cameras; the best you can hope for is that some disaster—a flood or a blizzard—will bring the cameras to you and focus them on your leadership. But senators all work in Washington, a city filled with cameras. No disaster is necessary to get on the air; only an investigation, a scandal, a major political conflict, or an articulate and telegenic personality is needed.

Interpreting Political News

News stories, especially those about events of which we have no firsthand knowledge, are apt to be accepted without question. This may be particularly true of television news stories, since they enable us to judge not only what is said but how it is said.

Americans tell pollsters that they get most of their news from television, not newspapers, and that they regard TV as more reliable than the printed press. Though in general the public has a favorable view of the media, between 1985 and 1989 there was a sharp increase in the proportion of Americans who thought the media tended to favor one side of a story—from 53 percent in 1985 to 68 percent in 1989. Between 1985 and 1998, there was also a sharp increase in the percentage who thought stories were inaccurate (see Figure 10.2). This is in sharp contrast to how the press sees itself. Two-thirds of all journalists think that the press deals fairly with all sides of political and social questions. Among the biggest losers in public confidence were Dan Rather and Ted Koppel; the biggest gainer was CNN (Cable News Network).

Bias is difficult to define and harder to measure, but in general the popular worry is that editors and reporters allow their personal political beliefs to influence the stories that they choose to run and to color the way in which they report them.

Once people worried that the press was slanted because newspaper editorial pages usually endorsed Republicans. In 1948, 85 percent of all newspapers endorsed a presidential candidate, and of those 77 percent endorsed the Republican. (He lost.) In 1996

only 30 percent of the papers made an endorsement, and of those 63 percent endorsed the Republican. (He lost.)

In a presidential election it is unlikely that editorial endorsements make any difference (which is one reason papers have stopped issuing them). The question today is whether the liberal views of reporters bias the news. According to polls, journalists are much more liberal than the public at large, and those in the national media are the most liberal of all. In Table 10.2 we can see how the beliefs of some 2,700 journalists from around the country compared with those of about three thousand ordinary citizens in the 1980s. On most issues the journalists were more liberal. In Table 10.3 we see the views of the members of the "elite" or "national" media, also in the 1980s. Unfortunately this survey did not ask the same questions of the public as it did of the journalists. Nonetheless, on such questions as abortion and affirmative action there is little doubt that the media elite were significantly to the left of the public. This has been confirmed by a comparison of their voting patterns. In 1972, for example, when 61 percent of the American people voted for Richard Nixon, only 19 percent of persons in the national media voted for him.[29] Likewise, in 1992 over 80

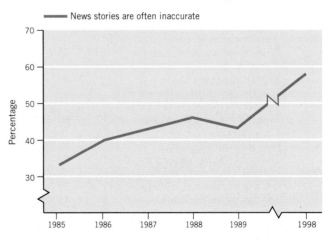

Figure 10.2 Public Perception of Accuracy in the Media

Source: Pew Research Center, "The People and the Press" (February 1999), 13.

Table 10.2 Journalist Opinion Versus Public Opinion		
	Journalists	**The Public**
Self-described ideology:		
Liberal	55%	23%
Conservative	17	29
Favor government regulation of business	49	22
U.S. should withdraw investments from South Africa	62	31
Allow women to have abortions	82	49
Allow prayer in public schools	25	74
Favor "affirmative action"	81	56
Favor death penalty for murder	47	75
Want stricter controls on handguns	78	50
Increase defense budget	15	38
Favor hiring homosexuals	89	55

Sources: Los Angeles Times poll of about 3,000 citizens and 2,700 journalists nationwide, as reported in William Schneider and I. A. Lewis, "Views on the News," *Public Opinion* (August–September 1985): 7. Reprinted with permission of American Enterprise Institute for Public Policy Research.

Table 10.3 The Political Attitudes of the Media Elite	
	Percentage Agree
People with ability should earn more.	86%
Less regulation of business is good for the United States.	63
Government should reduce the income gap.	68
There should be a strong affirmative-action program for blacks.	80
A woman has a right to decide on an abortion.	90
Homosexuality is wrong.	25
The United States exploits the Third World and causes poverty.	56
U.S. use of resources is immoral.	57
The CIA should sometimes undermine hostile governments.	45

Sources: Survey of 240 journalists and broadcasters employed by the national media, reported in S. Robert Lichter and Stanley Rothman, "Media and Business Elites," *Public Opinion* (October–November 1981): 44.

Table 10.4 Self-Identified Ideology Among American Elites			
	Percentages		
	Liberal	**Conservative**	**Moderate**
Television	75	14	12
Labor	73	6	20
Bureaucrats	56	27	17
Media	55	17	28
Judges	54	23	22
Lawyers	47	32	22
Business	14	63	17
Military	14	75	12

Source: Table adapted from Robert Lerner et al., *American Elites* (New Haven, Conn.: Yale University Press, 1996), 50, table 3.2. Reprinted by permission of Yale University Press.

percent of media leaders in Washington, D.C., versus 43 percent of the public, voted for Bill Clinton.[30] And as can be seen in Table 10.4, in the 1990s members of the media, especially those who worked in television, were more likely than members of many other professions to identify themselves as politically liberal.

Are News Stories Slanted?

The fact that reporters tend to have liberal views does not mean that their stories will inevitably have a liberal slant. Other factors influence how stories are written, including the need to meet an urgent deadline, the desire to attract an audience, a professional obligation to be fair and to tell the truth, and the need to develop sources among people holding different views. For example, whatever their views, the national media gave, according to a careful study, quite evenhanded treatment to both the Republican and Democratic presidential candidates during the 1980 campaign, although they gave quite decidedly anti-Reagan coverage during the 1984 campaign and appeared to have been consistently tougher on George Bush than on his 1992 campaign rivals, especially in the primaries.[31]

Still, it would be astonishing if strongly held beliefs had *no* effect on what is written or broadcast. To understand the circumstances under which a reporter's or editor's opinion is more or less likely to affect a story—and thus to be able to interpret intelligently what we read and hear—we must distinguish among these three *kinds* of stories:

1. **Routine stories:** These are public events regularly covered by reporters, involving relatively simple, easily described acts or statements. For example, the president takes a trip, a bill passes Congress, the Supreme Court rules on an important case.
2. **Feature stories:** These are public events knowable to any reporter who cares to inquire but involving acts and statements not routinely covered by a group of reporters. Thus a reporter must take the initiative and select a particular event as newsworthy, decide to write about it, and persuade an editor to run it. Examples: an obscure agency issues a controversial ruling, an unknown member of Congress conducts an investigation, an interest group works for the passage of a bill.
3. **Insider stories:** Information not usually made public becomes public because someone with inside knowledge tells a reporter. The reporter may have worked hard to learn these facts, in which case we say it is "investigative reporting," or some official may have wanted a story to get out, in which case we call it a "leak."

Routine stories are covered in almost exactly the same way by almost all the media, differing only in their length, the kinds of headlines written, and the position the story occupies on the pages or the evening news. The wire services—AP and UPI—supply routine stories immediately to practically every daily newspaper in America. (The headlines and placement, however, can make a big difference in how the same story is perceived.) The political opinions of journalists have the least effect on these stories, especially if several competing journalists are covering the same story over a protracted period of time.

Even a routine news story can be incorrectly reported, however, if something dramatic or unique occurs. For example, toward the end of the Vietnam War the North Vietnamese army launched a massive, all-out attack on cities held by the South Vietnamese and their American allies. The attack failed—it was repulsed, and there were heavy North Vietnamese casualties. But the news stories reported exactly the opposite: the North Vietnamese could move and fight at will, and the Americans were helpless to defend the cities or even their own fortified positions. Peter Braestrup, who later ana-

lyzed the Tet Offensive and its journalistic coverage, painstakingly described the errors and omissions that led to the misleading versions published. He did not conclude that the political views of reporters explained the mistakes, and surely it would be difficult for any reporters, however fair, to grasp quickly and accurately an event as complex, dramatic, and violent as a major military struggle. But it is also probably the case that the antiwar attitudes of most reporters reinforced the interpretation of Tet that they wrote.[32]

Feature and insider stories must be selected, and thus someone must do the selecting. The grounds on which the selections are made include not only the intrinsic interest of a story but also the reporter's or editor's beliefs about what *ought* to be interesting. Among these beliefs are the political ideologies of the journalists. A liberal paper may well select for coverage stories about white-collar crime, consumerism, the problems of minorities, and environmentalism; a conservative paper might instead select stories about street crime, the decline of a city's central business district, and the need for family values.

Nor are selected stories rare. In order to compete with television, newspapers increasingly print feature stories, thereby becoming more like a magazine, with something for everybody. As a result, a large part of a newspaper consists of precisely the kinds of stories that are most likely to be influenced by the ideological attitudes of reporters.

In one of the few studies of the effect of journalistic opinions on news stories, the authors found that in two examples of selected stories—articles concerning nuclear power and stories on the use of busing to integrate schools—the coverage provided by the national press reflected more the views of the press than those of experts or the public. But different segments of the media differed in how much slant they gave to their stories.

On nuclear power plants the vast majority of the stories in the *New York Times* gave a balanced view of the issue; the national newsmagazines (especially *Time* and *Newsweek*) and network television news programs, however, gave a predominately antinuclear slant to their stories. Moreover, though the great majority of scientists and engineers working in the field favor the rapid development of nuclear power plants, very few of the experts quoted on this subject by the national press favored nuclear power.[33] On school busing the majority of the stories run by the *New York Times*, the *Washington Post, Time,* and CBS News had a probusing slant.

If a nonroutine story is a major, complex, somewhat unusual event, such as the congressional investigation of Irangate in 1987, all the media will cover it, but each will choose what themes to emphasize and what questions to raise. Almost inevitably the media will put some "spin" on the story. (For example, was the star witness, Lieutenant Colonel Oliver North, a "hero," a "loose cannon," or a "Rambo"? It depended on whom you read or listened to.) If it is an offbeat story, it will be covered by one newspaper or TV station but not others; the very act of selection usually involves some political perspective. In evaluating feature and insider stories, every reader or viewer should keep these questions in mind:

- What beliefs or opinions led the editors to run this story?
- How representative of expert and popular opinion are the views of the people quoted in the story?
- What adjectives are being used to color the story?

Insider stories raise the most difficult questions of all—those of motive. When somebody inside government with private or confidential information gives a story to a reporter, that somebody must have a reason for doing so. But the motives of those who leak information are almost never reported. Sometimes the reporter does not know the motives. More often, one suspects, the reporter is dependent on his or her "highly placed source" and is reluctant to compromise it.

The reliance on the insider leak is as old as the Republic. At one time reporters were grateful for "background briefings" at which top government officials tried to put themselves in the best possible light while explaining the inner meaning of American policy. In the aftermath of Vietnam and Watergate, which weakened the credibility of "the Establishment," many reporters became even more interested in the leaks from insiders critical of top officials. In neither case were the motives of the sources discussed, leaving the reader or viewer to accept at face value whatever remarks are attributed to unnamed "highly placed sources" or "well-informed observers."

Why Do We Have So Many News Leaks?

American government is the leakiest in the world. The bureaucracy, members of Congress, and the White House staff regularly leak stories favorable to their interests. Of late the leaks have become geysers, gushing forth torrents of insider stories. Many people in and out of government find it depressing that our government seems unable to keep anything secret for long. Others think that the public has a right to know even more and that there are still too many secrets.

However you view leaks, you should understand why we have so many. The answer is found in the Constitution. Because we have separate institutions that must share power, each branch of government competes with the others to get power. One way to compete is to try to use the press to advance your pet projects and to make the other side look bad. There are far fewer leaks in other democratic nations in part because power is centralized in the hands of a prime minister, who does not need to leak in order to get the upper hand over the legislature, and because the legislature has too little information to be a good source of leaks. In addition we have no Official Secrets Act of the kind that exists in England; except for a few matters, it is not against the law for the press to receive and print government secrets.

Even if the press and the politicians loved each other, the competition between the various branches of government would guarantee plenty of news leaks. But since the Vietnam War, the Watergate scandal, and the Iran-contra affair, the press and the politicians have come to distrust one another. As a result, journalists today are far less willing to accept at face value the statements of elected officials and are far more likely to try to find somebody who will leak "the real story." We have come, in short, to have an **adversarial press**—that is, one that (at least at the national level) is suspicious of officialdom and eager to break an embarrassing story that will win for its author honor, prestige, and (in some cases) a lot of money.

This cynicism and distrust of government and elected officials have led to an era of attack journalism—seizing upon any bit of information or rumor that might call into question the qualifications or character of a public official. Media coverage of gaffes—misspoken words, misstated ideas, clumsy moves—has become a staple of political journalism. At one time, such "events" as President Ford slipping down some stairs, Governor Dukakis dropping the ball while playing catch with a Boston Red Sox player, or Vice President Quayle misspelling the word *potato* would have been ignored, but now they are hot news items. Attacking public figures has become a professional norm, where once it was a professional taboo.

During the 1992 election, most of the national press clearly supported Bill Clinton. The love affair between Clinton and reporters lasted for several months after his inauguration. But when stories began to appear about Whitewater (an Arkansas real estate deal in which the Clintons were once involved), Clinton's alleged sexual escapades while governor, and Hillary Rodham Clinton's profits in commodities trading, the press went into a feeding frenzy. The Clintons learned the hard way the truth of an old adage: if you want a friend in Washington, buy a dog.

Many people do not like this type of journalism, and the media's rising cynicism about the government is mirrored by the public's increasing cynicism about the media. As Figure 10.3 shows, most Americans had less confidence in the news media in 1993 than they did when they first began paying attention to the news. Most people surveyed also believed that the press slanted its coverage, had too much influence over events, and abused its constitutional protections.

Furthermore, the public's confidence in big business has eroded along with its confidence in government, and the media are increasingly big business. As noted earlier in this chapter, network television has become a highly competitive industry. Under these circumstances, every contribution to "market share" is vitally important, and the newsroom is no exception. In a highly competitive environment that is rich in information, those who aspire to reach a mass market must find a mass theme into which they can tap with visually dramatic, quick-tempo messages. In politics the theme is obvious: politics is a corrupt, self-serving enterprise. Many people include the profit-driven press in their antipolitical sentiments.

Given their experiences with Watergate and Irangate, given the highly competitive nature of national newsgathering, and given their political ideology

★ POLITICALLY SPEAKING ★

On Background

When politicians talk to the press, they set certain ground rules that the press usually observes. These rules specify who, if anyone, is quoted as the source of the story.

On the record. The official is quoted by name. For example: "I say that water runs downhill, and you can quote me on that."

Off the record. What the official says cannot be printed. For example: "Off the record, the head of my party is a complete wacko."

On background. What the official says can be printed, but it may not be attributed to him or her by name. For example: "A well-placed source said today that the sun will continue to rise in the east."

On deep background. What the official says can be printed, but it cannot be attributed to anybody. The reporter must say it on his or her own authority. For example: "In my opinion this administration secretly believes that two plus two equals five."

(which tends to put them to the left of the administration in power), American editors and reporters, at least at the national level, are likely to have an adver-

---

Figure 10.3   Decline in Public Trust of the Media

QUESTION

Do you have more or less or about the same amount of confidence in the news media today as you did when you first began paying attention to news and current events?

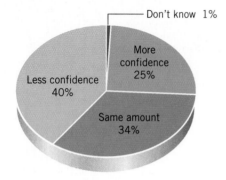

- Don't know 1%
- More confidence 25%
- Less confidence 40%
- Same amount 34%

QUESTION

Do you agree or disagree with this statement: "The news media give more coverage to stories that support their own point of view than to those that don't"?

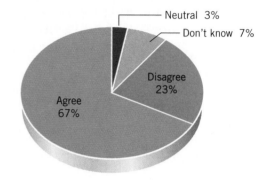

- Neutral 3%
- Don't know 7%
- Disagree 23%
- Agree 67%

QUESTION

Generally speaking, do you feel that the news media have too much or too little or the right amount of influence over what happens today?

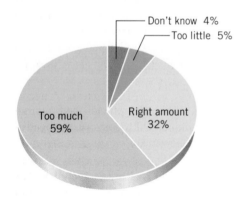

- Don't know 4%
- Too little 5%
- Too much 59%
- Right amount 32%

QUESTION

The Bill of Rights of the U.S. Constitution guarantees freedom of the press so that the news media can be a watchdog over the government and other powerful institutions. And the courts have ruled that the news media should be protected even in some cases when they have been unfair or inaccurate. Do you think the news media are careful to use this power responsibly?

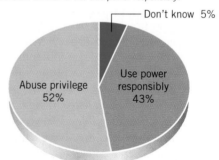

- Don't know 5%
- Abuse privilege 52%
- Use power responsibly 43%

Source: David Shaw, "Trust in Media Is on Decline," *Los Angeles Times* (March 31, 1993): A16, reporting data a Times poll conducted March 6–9,1993. Copyright © 1993, Los Angeles Times. Reprinted by permission.

---

sarial relationship with government for a long time to come. Given our constitutional system, there will always be plenty of people in government eager to help them with leaks hostile to one faction or another.

One side effect of the increasingly adversarial nature of the press is the increased prevalence of negative campaign advertising—that is, of ads that lambaste opponents and attack them on a personal level. Adversarial media coverage has helped make these types of ads more socially acceptable. The reason candidates use attack ads is simple: they work. A good negative ad will change the preferences of some voters. But this change is purchased at a price. Research shows that a negative ad not only changes voter preferences, it reduces voter turnout. Negative advertising may help a candidate win, but only by turning other people against elections.

Sensationalism in the Media

Back in the 1930s newspaper reporters knew that President Franklin Roosevelt had a romantic affair with a woman other than his wife. They did not report it. In the early 1960s many reporters knew that President John Kennedy had many sexual affairs outside his marriage. They did not report this. In 1964 the director of the Federal Bureau of Investigation played for reporters secret tape recordings of the Reverend Martin Luther King, Jr., having sex with women other than his wife. They did not report it.

By the 1980s sex and politics were extensively covered. When presidential candidate Gary Hart was caught in adultery and when President Bill Clinton was accused of adultery by Gennifer Flowers, of asking for sexual favors by Paula Jones, and of having sex with Monica Lewinsky in the Oval Office, these were headline news stories.

What had changed? Not politics: all of the people whom the press protected or reported on were Democrats. The big change was in the economics of journalism and the ideas of reporters.

Until the 1970s Americans gathered their political news from one of three networks—ABC, CBS, or NBC. For a long time these networks had only one half-hour news show a day. By the 1990s, however, viewers had the same three networks plus three cable news networks, two sports networks, countless radio talk shows, and the Internet. Many of the cable networks, such as CNN, carried news 24 hours a day. The result of this intense competition was that each radio or television network had a small share of the audience. Today less than half the public watches the evening network news shows—a big decline even since 1993. Dozens of news programs are trying to reach a shrinking audience, with the result that the audience share of each program is small. To attract any audience at all, each program has a big incentive to rely on sensational news stories—sex, violence, and intrigue. Reinforcing this desire to go with sensationalism is the fact that covering such stories is cheaper than investigating foreign policy or analyzing the tax code. During its first month, the Lewinsky story consumed more than one-third of the on-air time of the news networks—more than the U.S. showdown with Iran, the Winter Olympics, the pope's visit to Cuba, and the El Niño weather pattern combined.[34]

"Those are the headlines, and we'll be back in a moment to blow them out of proportion."

Since the days of Vietnam and Watergate, journalists have become adversaries of the government. They instinctively distrust people in government. But to that attitude change can be added an economic one: in their desperate effort to reclaim market share, journalists are much more likely to rely on unnamed sources than once was the case. When the *Washington Post* broke the Watergate story in the 1970s, it required the reporters to have at least two sources for their stories. Now many reporters break stories that have only one unnamed source, and often not a source at all but a rumor posted on the Internet.

As a result, reporters are more easily manipulated by sources than once was the case. Spokesmen for President Clinton tried to "spin" the news about his affairs, usually by attacking his critics. Gennifer Flowers, Paula Jones, and Monica Lewinsky were portrayed as bimbos, liars, or stalkers. Much of the press used the spin. To see how successful spin can be, compare independent counsel Lawrence Walsh's investigation of aides to President Ronald Reagan over the sale of arms to Iran with independent counsel Kenneth Starr's investigation of the Clinton administration. Walsh's inquiry got full press support, while Starr was regularly attacked by the press.

Government Constraints on Journalists

An important factor works against the influence of ideology and antiofficial attitudes on reporters—the need every reporter has for access to key officials. A reporter is only as good as his or her sources, and it is difficult to cultivate good sources if you regularly

MEMORANDUM

To: Editor in chief, Washington Post
From: Foreign news editor
Subject: Ruritania

One of our best reporters has information that the United States plans to invade Ruritania three days from now. His source is a top military official who has been reliable in the past. As of now we do not think that any other newspaper has this story. As you know, opinion in the government is deeply divided over the wisdom of any action against Ruritania. So far all official sources in the White House and the State Department have denied that anything is afoot. But we all know that the president is deeply upset by the continuation of Ruritanian-sponsored terrorism against U.S. personnel overseas. Your options are:

1. Print the story in tomorrow's edition.

Advantages: (a) This is important news, and we have an obligation to publish news. (b) We get a major scoop that no other newspaper can match. (c) In our editorials we have said that we think an invasion of Ruritania would be a mistake. This story, if printed now, may lead to a cancellation of the military action.

Disadvantages: (a) There is a small chance that we could be wrong and no invasion is planned. (b) We will be criticized for leaking military secrets. (c) If the invasion takes place despite our story, the United States may lose the element of surprise, and this may affect the outcome and cause additional casualties.

2. Do not print the story.

Advantages: (a) We avoid charges that we are leaking military secrets. (b) If an invasion occurs, we will not have alerted the enemy.

Disadvantages: (a) There is the possibility that another newspaper may learn of this story in the next two days; if we don't publish now, they may publish later and we will look foolish. (b) We will be failing in our duty to inform the people about the activities of their government. (c) The Ruritanians may already know of the planned invasion, and so our story will not have alerted them.

Your decision:
Option 1 _____
Option 2 _____

Tensions Mount Between U.S. and Ruritania

U.S. 6th Fleet Maneuvering near African Nation

February 23
WASHINGTON
The State Department today denied Ruritanian claims that the United States is planning military action against Ruritania in the wake of Ruritanian-sponsored terrorist actions . . .

antagonize them. Thus Washington reporters must constantly strike a balance between expressing their own views (and risk losing a valuable source) and keeping a source (and risk becoming its mouthpiece).

The great increase in the number of congressional staff members has made striking this balance easier than it once was. Since it is almost impossible to keep anything secret from Congress, the existence of fifteen thousand to twenty thousand congressional staffers means that there is a potential source for every conceivable issue and cause. Congress has become a gold mine for reporters. If a story annoys one congressional source, another source can easily be found.

The government is not without means to fight back. The number of press officers on the payroll of the White House, Congress, and the executive agencies has grown sharply in recent decades. Obviously these people have a stake in putting out news stories that reflect favorably on their elected superiors. They can try to do this with press releases, but adversarial journalists are suspicious of "canned news" (although they use it nonetheless). Or the press officers can try to win journalistic friends by offering leaks and supplying background stories to favored reporters. (A **background story** is one that purportedly explains current policy and is given on condition that the source not be identified by name.) Finally, the press officers can try to bypass the national press and directly reach the local press—the hometown newspapers and radio stations. Members of the local press are less likely to feel an adversarial attitude toward official Washington and perhaps are more likely to have a political ideology akin to that of the national administration.

The ultimate weapon in the government's effort to shape the press to its liking is the president's

Though President Clinton denied he had sex with Monica Lewinsky, this photo suggested he certainly knew her.

rewarding of reporters and editors who treat him well and his punishing of those who treat him badly. President Kennedy regularly called in offending reporters for brutal tongue-lashings and favored friendly reporters with tips and inside stories. Johnson did the same, with special attention to television reporters. Nixon made the mistake of attacking the press publicly, thereby allowing it to defend itself with appeals to the First Amendment. (Kennedy's and Johnson's manipulative skills were used privately.) Probably every president tries to use the press with whatever means are at his disposal, but in the long run it is the press, not the president, who wins. Johnson decided not to run again in 1968 in part because of press hostility to him; Nixon was exposed by the press; Carter came to be disliked by national reporters. The press and the president need but do not trust one another; it is inevitably a stormy relationship.

Summary

Changes in the nature of American politics have been accompanied by—and influenced by—changes in the nature of the mass media. The rise of strong national political party organizations was facilitated by the emergence of mass-circulation daily newspapers. Political reform movements depended in part on the development of national magazines catering to middle-class opinion. The weakening of political parties was accelerated by the ability of candidates to speak directly to constituents by radio and television.

The role of journalists in a democratic society poses an inevitable dilemma: if they are to serve well their functions as information gatherer, gatekeeper, scorekeeper, and watchdog, they must be free of government controls. But to the extent that they are free of such controls, they are also free to act in their own interests, whether political or economic. In the United States a competitive press largely free of government controls (except in the area of broadcast licenses) has produced both a substantial diversity of opinion and a general (though not unanimous) commitment to the goal of fairness in news reporting. The national media are in general more liberal than the local media, but the extent to which a reporter's beliefs affect reporting varies greatly with the kind of story—routine, feature, or insider.

World Wide Web Resources

- To search many newspapers: www.ipl.org
- CNN/*Time* news: www.allpolitics.com
- *New York Times*: www.nytimes.com

- Washington, D.C., newspapers:
  Washington Post: www.washingtonpost.com
  Washington Times: www. washtimes.com

Key Terms

muckraker *p. 248*
sound bite *p. 250*
trial balloon *p. 257*
loaded language *p. 257*
equal time rule *p. 258*

right-of-reply rule *p. 258*
political editorializing rule
    p. 258
fairness doctrine *p. 258*
market (television) *p. 259*

selective attention *p. 259*
routine stories *p. 265*
feature stories *p. 265*
insider stories *p. 265*
adversarial press *p. 266*

background story (news)
    p. 271

Suggested Readings

Braestrup, Peter. *Big Story: How the American Press and Television Reported and Interpreted the Crises of Tet 1968 in Vietnam and Washington.* 2 vols. Boulder, Colo.: Westview Press, 1977. A massive, detailed account of how the press reported one critical event; the factual accuracy or inaccuracy of each story is carefully checked.

Crouse, Timothy. *The Boys on the Bus.* New York: Random House, 1973. A lively, irreverent account by a participant of how reporters cover a presidential campaign.

Epstein, Edward J. *Between Fact and Fiction: The Problem of Journalism.* New York: Random House, 1975. Essays by a perceptive student of the press on media coverage of Watergate, the Pentagon Papers, the deaths of Black Panthers, and other major stories.

————. *News from Nowhere.* New York: Random House, 1973. Analysis of how television network news programs are produced and shaped.

Garment, Suzanne. *Scandal.* New York: Random House, 1991. A careful look at the role of the media (and others) in fostering the "culture of mistrust."

Graber, Doris A. *Mass Media and American Politics.* 3rd ed. Washington, D.C.: Congressional Quarterly Press, 1989. A good summary of what we know about the press and politics.

Iyengar, Shanto, and Donald R. Kinder. *News That Matters.* Chicago: University of Chicago Press, 1987. The report of experiments testing the effect of television news on public perceptions of politics.

Kurtz, Howard. *Spin Cycle: Inside the Clinton Propaganda Machine.* New York: Free Press, 1998. A journalistic account of how one president's staff tried to influence the media.

Lichter, S. Robert, Stanley Rothman, and Linda S. Lichter. *The Media Elite.* Bethesda, Md.: Adler & Adler, 1986. A study of the political beliefs of "elite" journalists and how those beliefs influence what we read and hear.

Patterson, Thomas W. *The Mass Media Election.* New York: Praeger, 1980. Analyzes what effect, if any, the media had on the 1976 election.

Robinson, Michael J., and Margaret A. Sheehan. *Over the Wire and on TV.* New York: Russell Sage Foundation, 1983. Analyzes how CBS News and United Press International covered the 1980 election.

Sabato, Larry J. *Feeding Frenzy.* New York: Free Press, 1991. Explains the press focus on political misconduct.

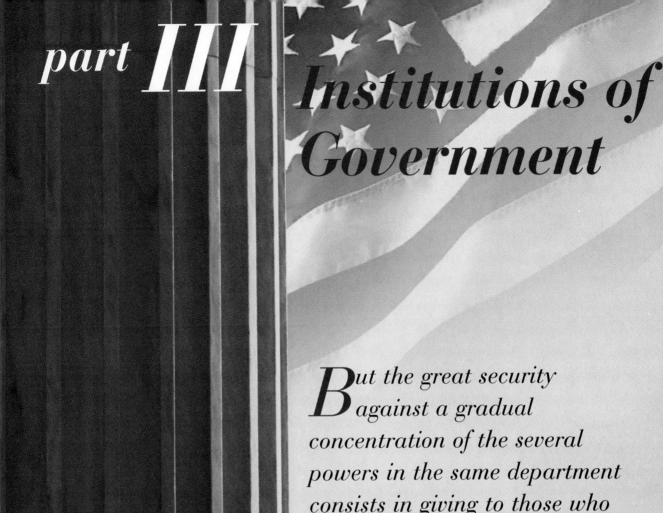

part *III* *Institutions of Government*

*B*ut the great security against a gradual concentration of the several powers in the same department consists in giving to those who administer each department the necessary constitutional means and personal motives to resist encroachments of the others.

FEDERALIST No. 51

Congress

Enduring Questions

1. Are the members of Congress representative of the American people?
2. Should Congress run under strong leadership, or should it allow its members a lot of freedom?
3. Why do the seats one party gets in Congress not match the vote it gets in the election?
4. Why does it take so long for Congress to act?
5. Why is Congress an unpopular institution?

The Evolution of Congress

Who Is in Congress?

Getting Elected to Congress

Do Members Represent Their Voters?

Ideology and Civility in Congress

The Organization of Congress: Parties and Caucuses

The Organization of Congress: Committees

The Organization of Congress: Staffs and Specialized Offices

How a Bill Becomes Law

Reforming Congress

Ethics and Congress

Senator Daniel Patrick Moynihan of New York once remarked that the United States is the only democratic government that has a legislative branch. Of course lots of democracies have parliaments that pass laws. What he meant is that among the large democracies of the world, only the U.S. Congress has great powers that it can exercise independently of the executive branch. To see why this is the case, we must understand the difference between a congress and a parliament.

The United States (along with most Latin American nations) has a congress; Great Britain (along with most Western European nations) has a parliament. A hint as to the difference between the two kinds of legislatures can be found in the original meanings of the words: *Congress* derives from a Latin term that means "a coming together," a meeting, as of representatives from various places. *Parliament* comes from a French word, *parler*, that means "to talk."

There is of course plenty of talking—some critics say that there is nothing *but* talking—in the U.S. Congress, and certainly members of a parliament

275

represent to a degree their local districts. But the differences implied by the names of the lawmaking groups are real ones, with profound significance for how laws are made and how the government is run. These differences affect two important aspects of lawmaking bodies: how one becomes a member and what one does as a member.

Ordinarily a person becomes a member of a parliament (such as the British House of Commons) by persuading a political party to put his or her name on the ballot. Though usually a local party committee selects a person to be its candidate, that committee often takes suggestions from national party headquarters. In any case the local group selects as its candidate someone willing to support the national party program and leadership. In the election voters in the district choose not between two or three personalities running for office, but between two or three national parties.

By contrast, a person becomes a candidate for representative or senator in the U.S. Congress by running in a primary election. Except in a very few places, political parties exercise little control over the choice of who is nominated to run for congressional

The work of Congress takes place in committees with members of both parties—here Senators Orrin Hatch (R-Utah) and Patrick Leahy (D-Vt.).

office. (This is the case even though the person who wins the primary will describe himself or herself in the general election as a Democrat or a Republican.) Voters select candidates in the primaries because of their personalities, positions on issues, or overall reputation. Even in the general election, where the party label affects who votes for whom, many citizens vote "for the man" (or for the woman), not for the party. As a result of these different systems a parliament tends to be made up of people loyal to the national party leadership who meet to debate and vote on party issues. A congress, on the other hand, tends to be made up of people who think of themselves as independent representatives of their districts or states and who, while willing to support their party on many matters, expect to vote as their (or their constituents') beliefs and interests require.

Once they are in the legislature, members of a parliament discover that they can make only one important decision—whether or not to support the government. The government in a parliamentary system such as Britain's consists of a prime minister and various cabinet officers selected from the party that has the most seats in parliament. As long as the members of that party vote together, that government will remain in power (until the next election). Should members of a party in power in parliament decide to vote against their leaders, the leaders lose office, and a new government must be formed. With so much at stake, the leaders of a party in parliament have a powerful incentive to keep their followers in line. They insist that all members of the party vote together on almost all issues. If someone refuses, the penalty is often drastic: the party does not renominate the offending member in the next election.

Members of the U.S. Congress do not select the head of the executive branch of government—that is done by the voters when they choose a president. Far from making members of Congress less powerful, this makes them more powerful. Representatives and senators can vote on proposed laws without worrying that their votes will cause the government to collapse and without fearing that a failure to support their party will lead to their removal from the ballot in the next election. Congress has independent powers, defined by the Constitution, that it can exercise without regard to presidential preferences. Political parties do not control nominations for office, and thus they cannot discipline members of Congress who fail to support the party leadership. Because Congress is constitutionally independent of the president, and because its members are not tightly disciplined by a party leadership, individual members of Congress are free to express their views and vote as they wish. They are also free to become involved in the most minute details of lawmaking, budget making, and supervision of the administration of laws. They do this through an elaborate set of committees and subcommittees.

During the first months of the 104th Congress (1994–1996) it appeared that parliamentary governance of a sort had at last come to Capitol Hill. For the first time in four decades Republicans controlled both houses of Congress. On January 4, 1995, their very first day in power, the members of the House adopted procedural changes that enhanced the powers of the Speaker to control the legislative agenda. Mindful of these changes, a reporter declared that the "mini-universe known as Capitol Hill turned upside down January 4."[1] For a while at least, those words seemed prophetic. For example, the new Republican leadership proved so cohesive that it was able to pass a budget resolution promising tax cuts, deep spending cuts, and a balanced budget. Only one House Republican broke ranks on the resolution, and none did so in the Senate. It was not long, however, before congressional Republicans fought among themselves and with their leadership on funding for the B-2 bomber, Medicare, the National Endowment for the Arts, abortion policy, and environmental issues. In late September disaffected House Republicans joined Democrats to defeat the Republican leadership on certain defense and appropriations bills. Meanwhile President Clinton and congressional Democrats blocked or stalled many of the Republican leadership's major proposals. By the end of the first session of the 104th Congress, only 67 bills had been enacted (the previous post-1950 low was 145, in 1981), and any notion that parliamentary governance had come to Washington was laid to rest.

A real parliament, such as that in Britain, is an assembly of party representatives who choose a government and discuss major national issues. The principal daily work of a parliament is debate. A congress, such as that in the United States, is a meeting place of the representatives of local constituencies—districts and states. Members of the U.S. Congress can initiate, modify, approve, or reject laws, and they share with the president supervision of the administrative agencies of the government. The principal work of a congress is representation and action, most of which takes place in committees.

What this means in practical terms to the typical legislator is easy to see. Since members of the British House of Commons have little independent power, they get rather little in return. They are poorly paid, may have no offices of their own and virtually no staff, are allowed only small sums to buy stationery, and can make a few free local telephone calls. Each is given a desk, a filing cabinet, and a telephone, but not always in the same place.

By contrast, a member of the U.S. House of Representatives, even a junior one, has power and is rewarded accordingly. For example, in 2000 each member earned a substantial salary ($141,300) and was entitled to a large office (or "clerk-hire") allowance, to pay for as many as twenty-two staffers. Each member also received individual allowances for travel, computer services, and the like. In addition each member could mail newsletters and certain other documents to constituents for free using the

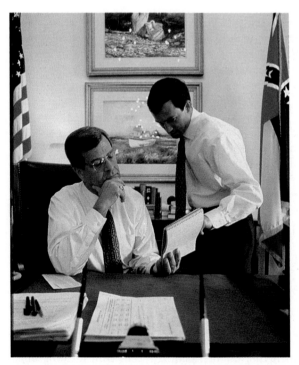

Every member of Congress, including Senator Trent Lott, has a large staff.

The Powers of Congress

The powers of Congress are found in Article I, section 8, of the Constitution.

- To lay and collect taxes, duties, imposts, and excises
- To borrow money
- To regulate commerce with foreign nations and among the states
- To establish rules for naturalization (that is, becoming a citizen) and bankruptcy
- To coin money, set its value, and punish counterfeiting
- To fix the standard of weights and measures
- To establish a post office and post roads
- To issue patents and copyrights by inventors and authors
- To create courts inferior to (that is, below) the Supreme Court
- To define and punish piracies, felonies on the high seas, and crimes against the law of nations
- To declare war
- To raise and support an army and navy and make rules for their governance
- To provide for a militia (reserving to the states the right to appoint militia officers and to train the militia under congressional rules)
- To exercise exclusive legislative powers over the seat of government (that is, the District of Columbia) and other places purchased to be federal facilities (forts, arsenals, dockyards, and "other needful buildings")
- To "make all laws which shall be necessary and proper for carrying into execution the foregoing powers, and all other powers vested by this Constitution in the government of the United States" (*Note*: This "necessary and proper," or "elastic," clause has been generously interpreted by the Supreme Court, as explained in Chapter 14.)

"franking privilege." Senators, and representatives with seniority, received even larger benefits. Each senator was entitled to a generous office budget and legislative assistance allowance and was free to hire as many staff members as he or she wished with the money. These examples are not given to suggest that members of Congress are overrewarded, but only that their importance, as individuals, in our political system can be inferred from the resources that they command.

Because the United States has a congress made up of people chosen to represent their states and districts, rather than a parliament made up to represent competing political parties, no one should be surprised to learn that members of the U.S. Congress are more concerned with their own constituencies and careers than with the interests of any organized party or program of action. And since Congress does not choose the president, members of Congress know that worrying about the voters they represent is much more important than worrying about whether the president succeeds with his programs. These two factors taken together mean that Congress tends to be a decentralized institution, with

each member more interested in his or her own views and those of his or her voters than with the programs proposed by the president.

Indeed, Congress was designed by the Founders in ways that almost inevitably make it unpopular with voters. Americans want government to take action, follow a clear course of action, and respond to strong leaders. Americans dislike political arguments, the activities of special-interest groups, and the endless pulling and hauling that often precede any congressional decision. But the people who feel this way are deeply divided about what government should do: Be liberal? Be conservative? Spend money? Cut taxes? Support abortions? Stop abortions? Since they are divided, and since members of Congress must worry about how voters feel, it is inevitable that on controversial issues Congress will engage in endless arguments, worry about what interest groups (who represent different groups of voters) think, and work out compromise decisions. When it does those things, however, many people feel let down and say that they have a low opinion of Congress.

Of course a member of Congress might explain all these constitutional facts to the people, but not many members are eager to tell their voters that they do not really understand how Congress was created and organized. Instead they run for reelection by promising voters that they will go back to Washington and "clean up that mess."

The Evolution of Congress

The Framers chose to place legislative powers in the hands of a congress rather than a parliament for philosophical and practical reasons. They did not want to have all powers concentrated in a single governmental institution, even one that was popularly elected, because they feared that such a concentration could lead to rule by an oppressive or impassioned majority. At the same time, they knew that the states were jealous of their independence and would never consent to a national constitution if it did not protect their interests and strike a reasonable balance between large and small states. Hence they created a **bicameral** (two-chamber) **legislature**—with a House of Representatives, to be elected directly by the people, and a Senate, consisting of two members from each state, to be chosen by the legislatures of each state. Though "all legislative powers" were to be vested in Congress, those powers would be shared with the president (who could veto acts of Congress), limited to powers explicitly conferred on the federal government, and, as it turned out, subject to the power of the Supreme Court to declare acts of Congress unconstitutional.

Although they designed these checks and balances to prevent legislative tyranny, the Framers nonetheless expected that Congress would be the dominant institution in the national government. And for at least a century and a half it was, except for a few brief periods when activist presidents (such as Andrew Jackson, Abraham Lincoln, Theodore Roosevelt, and Woodrow Wilson) were able to challenge congressional supremacy. Until the twentieth century, and during some periods since, the major struggles for national political power have been *within* Congress, over the rules and leadership of that body, rather than between Congress and the president.

The struggles within Congress were generally over issues of great national significance—slavery, the admission of new states, the development of internal improvements, tariffs against foreign goods,

and the regulation of business—but cutting across most of these substantive issues was a conflict over the distribution of power within Congress itself. Two competing values were at stake: centralization versus decentralization. If Congress were to act quickly and decisively as a body, then there must be strong central leadership, restrictions on debate, few opportunities for stalling tactics, and minimal committee interference. If, on the other hand, the interests of individual members—and the constituencies that they represent—were to be protected or enhanced, then there must be weak leadership, rules allowing for delay and discussion, and many opportunities for committee activity.

Though there have been periods of strong central leadership in Congress, the general trend, especially in this century, has been toward decentralizing decision-making and enhancing the power of the individual member at the expense of the congressional leadership. This decentralization may not have been inevitable. Most American states have constitutional systems quite similar to the federal one, yet in many state legislatures, such as those in New York, Massachusetts, and Indiana, the leadership is quite powerful. In part the position of these strong state legislative leaders may be the result of the greater strength of political parties in some states than in the nation as a whole. In large measure, however, it is a consequence of permitting state legislative leaders to decide who shall chair what committee and who shall receive what favors.

The House of Representatives, though always powerful, has often changed the way in which it is organized and led. In some periods it has given its leader, the Speaker, a lot of power; in other periods it has given much of that power to the chairmen of the House committees; and in still other periods it has allowed individual members to acquire great influence. In the 1990s it seemed for a while that the Speaker would permanently reclaim powers previously given away to individual members, but it is too early to tell whether that change will endure. To simplify a complicated story, here are six snapshots of how the House operated at six different periods in our history.

Phase One: The Powerful House

During the first three administrations—of George Washington, John Adams, and Thomas Jefferson—leadership in Congress was often supplied by the

One of the most powerful Speakers of the House, Henry Clay, is shown here addressing the U.S. Senate around 1850.

president or his cabinet officers. Alexander Hamilton, as secretary of the treasury, acted as Washington's leader in Congress, even though he was not a member of that body. Albert Gallatin, Jefferson's secretary of the treasury, performed essentially the same function, working through intermediaries.

Rather quickly, however, Congress began to assert its independence and to develop its own leadership. The House of Representatives was the preeminent institution, overshadowing the tiny Senate. It originated most legislation. Henry Clay, as Speaker of the House, was a powerful leader who appointed the members and chairmen of the committees and kept his party, the Democratic-Republicans, under reasonable control. The party caucus, dominated by Clay, was often influential in shaping policy questions before they were debated on the floor of the House. Indeed, during these early years, the caucus selected its party's candidate for president. For example, the Democratic-Republican caucus nominated Jefferson in 1804, James Madison in 1808 and again in 1812, and James Monroe in 1816. The caucus system of nomination enhanced the power of the House, for it meant that the president of the United States, though not elected by Congress, was nominated for that office by impor-

tant members of Congress. This political fact of life helped make the presidents quite sensitive to congressional desires.

Phase Two: A Divided House

In the late 1820s the preeminence of the House began to wane. Andrew Jackson asserted the power of the presidency by vetoing legislation that he did not like. The caucus system of nominations had fallen into disrepute and was replaced (as we saw in Chapter 7) with a system of national nominating conventions. Most important the party unity necessary for a Speaker, or any other leader, to control the House was shattered by the issue of slavery. So divided were the parties over this question that the choice of a Speaker became a protracted struggle; one contest in 1856 took 133 ballots before the outcome was decided. A Speaker chosen under these circumstances could hardly wield much power.

The Civil War led to the end of slavery, and hence to the end of the argument in the House over that issue. Of course representatives from the South did not attend during the war, and their seats remained vacant for several years after it ended. This meant that a group called the Radical Republicans, led by men such as Thaddeus Stevens of Pennsylvania, could produce strong majorities for measures aimed at punishing the defeated South. The House even voted to impeach President Andrew Johnson for being too soft on the South. (The Senate, by a margin of one vote, failed to convict Johnson on the impeachment.) But such measures were driven more by shared beliefs among the representatives than by people in powerful leadership positions. As time passed, the hot passions the war had generated began to cool, and it became clear that the leadership of the House remained weak.

Phase Three: The Rise of a Powerful Speaker

Toward the end of the nineteenth century the Speaker of the House gained power. When Thomas B. Reed of Maine became Speaker in 1889, he obtained by vote of the Republican majority more authority than any of his predecessors. He had the right to select the chairmen and members of all committees, and he used this power to reward friends and punish enemies. He chaired the Rules Committee and had the authority to decide what business would come up for a vote and what the limitations on debate would be. He decided who would be allowed to speak and who would not, which allowed him to thwart the delaying tactics of other members. While he was in power, Reed produced a great deal of party unity in the House.

Not long after Reed resigned in 1899, another powerful man, Joseph G. Cannon of Illinois, became Speaker. He sought to maintain the Reed tradition, but by now circumstances had changed. Whereas Reed had political views quite similar to those of most Republicans, Cannon was distinctly more conservative than many Republicans around the turn of the century. Moreover, the desire of individual members to act independently was becoming more pronounced. Within a few years the revolt came.

Phase Four: The Revolt Against the Speaker

In 1910–1911 the House revolted against Cannon, voting to strip the Speaker of his right to appoint committee members and chairmen and to remove him from membership on the powerful Rules Committee. What power Cannon lost did not flow imme-diately into the hands of individual members, however. Instead three other sources of power emerged.

One was the party caucus. For a time the members of each political party in the House, meeting in their caucuses, would take positions on issues coming before the House and induce each member to support them. On occasion the leader of a caucus was an especially influential or respected figure, and the caucus was strong. But the caucuses lacked any real authority, and soon their influence waned. Individual members increasingly discovered that they could defy them without penalty. Individual members increasingly discovered that they could defy them without penalty.

A second was the Rules Committee. Though the Speaker was no longer a member, the committee still decided what bills would come up for a vote and in what order, and it still set restrictions on the length of debate and on members' ability to offer amendments.

Third, the power of the chairmen of the standing committees rose as the power of the Speaker fell. Until the 1970s these chairmen had substantial

Three powerful Speakers of the House: Thomas B. Reed (1889–1891, 1895–1899) (left), Joseph G. Cannon (1903–1911) (center), and Sam Rayburn (1941–1947, 1949–1953, 1955–1961) (right). Reed put an end to the filibuster in the House by refusing to allow dilatory motions and by counting as "present"—for purposes of a quorum—members in the House even though they were not voting. Cannon further enlarged the Speaker's power by refusing to recognize members who wished to speak without Cannon's approval and increased the power of the Rules Committee, over which he presided. Cannon was stripped of much of his power in 1910. Rayburn's influence rested more on his ability to persuade than on his formal powers.

ability to decide what business the committees they chaired would take up, what bills would be sent out of the committees to the full House, and even what some of these bills would contain. In the days when these chairmen were chosen by the Speaker, they often used their power to follow his leadership or that of the party as a whole. But once the Speaker no longer appointed them, they acquired office strictly on the basis of seniority.

Phase Five: The Empowerment of Individual Members

In the 1960s and 1970s the House struck out against almost all forms of leadership. The defining issue was civil rights. Newly elected Democrats could not get the House to vote on a meaningful civil rights bill until 1965 because powerful committee chairmen, most of them from the South, kept such legislation bottled up. To make certain that never happened again, Democrats changed the rules so that chairmen lost much of their authority. Beginning in the 1970s committee chairmen would no longer be selected simply on the basis of seniority; they had to be elected by the members of the majority party. Committees without subcommittees had to create them and allow their members to choose subcommittee chairmen. Chairmen could no longer refuse to call committee meetings, and most meetings had to be public. Individual members' staffs were greatly enlarged.

Individual members of the House became more powerful. Each member could introduce bills, and half of all majority party members were chairmen of at least one committee or subcommittee. There was no way old-style committee chairmen could block legislation any longer.

Phase Six: The Return of Leadership

The new individualistic system had its costs of course. Since every member had power, it was harder for the House to get anything done. By slow steps, culminating in some sweeping changes made in 1995, there were efforts to restore some of the power the Speaker had once had. In the late 1970s and early 1980s the Speaker acquired the power to choose a majority of the members of the Rules Committee (which still schedules legislation for a vote) and of the committee that chooses which members will serve on which committees. He also acquired the authority to assign a bill to several different committees for consideration.

When the Republicans took control of the House after the 1994 election, they retained many of the changes the Democrats had made during the 1970s and added several of their own, many designed to ensure more open debate. Some of the changes they introduced, such as a decision that no one could chair a committee for more than six years, seemed to weaken leadership. But other changes strengthened it. The number of committees and subcommittees was reduced, thus reducing the chance for a member to become a chairman. They continued the policy of ignoring seniority in the selection of some committee chairmen. Speaker Newt Gingrich dominated the choice of committee chairmen, often passing over more senior members for more agreeable junior ones. The Speaker set the agenda for the House—and got it to vote on every item in the "Contract with America" within the first few months of 1995. In many of these votes virtually every Republican voted with the party leadership, while most Democrats opposed it.

The forceful leadership of Gingrich had its costs. He ran roughshod over some of his own party members, his decision not to pass some appropriations bills forced many government offices to close down for a short period, he had to pay a fine for using tax-exempt funds for political purposes, and then the Republicans lost a number of seats in the 1998 election. Gingrich resigned as Speaker and as a member of the House, replaced by a more moderate Speaker (Dennis Hastert of Illinois) with a penchant for accommodating his colleagues.

The Future?

All of these changes suggest that the House has trouble deciding once and for all how to run itself. Sometimes it has a strong Speaker, sometimes a weak one; sometimes committee chairmen are selected by seniority, sometimes by the Speaker, and sometimes by party vote.

These fluctuations reveal the fundamental problem the House faces: it wants to be both big (it has 435 members) and powerful, and its members want to be powerful both as individuals and as a group. But being big makes it hard for the House to be powerful unless some small group is given the authority to run it. If a group runs the place, however, the individual members lack much power. Individuals can gain power, but only at the price of making the House harder to run and thus reducing its collective power in government. There is no lasting solution to these dilemmas, and so the House will always be undergoing changes.

The Evolution of the Senate

The Senate does not face any of these problems. It is small enough (100 members) that it can be run without giving much authority to any small group of leaders. In addition it has escaped some of the problems the House once faced. During the period leading up to the Civil War it was carefully balanced so that the number of senators from slaveowning states exactly equaled the number from free states. Hence fights over slavery rarely arose in the Senate.

From the first the Senate was small enough that no time limits had to be placed on how long a senator could speak. This meant that there never was anything like a Rules Committee that controlled the amount of debate.

Finally, senators were not elected by the voters until this century. Prior to that they were picked instead by state legislatures. Thus senators were often the leaders of local party organizations, with an interest in funneling jobs and contracts back to their states.

The big changes in the Senate came not from any fight about how to run it (nobody ever really ran it) but from a dispute over how its members should be chosen. For more than a century after the Founding members of the Senate were chosen by state legislatures. Though often these legislatures picked popular local figures to be senators, just as often there was intense political maneuvering among the leaders of various factions, each struggling to win (and sometimes buy) the votes necessary to become senator. By the end of the nineteenth century the Senate was known as the Millionaires' Club because of the number of wealthy party leaders and businessmen in it. There arose a demand for the direct, popular election of senators.

Naturally the Senate resisted, and without its approval the necessary constitutional amendment could not pass Congress. When some states threatened to demand a new constitutional convention, the Senate feared that such a convention would change more than just the way in which senators were chosen. A protracted struggle ensued, during which many state legislatures devised ways to ensure that the senators they picked would already have won a popular election. The Senate finally

agreed to a constitutional amendment that required the popular election of its members, and in 1913 the Seventeenth Amendment was approved by the necessary three-fourths of the states. Ironically, given the intensity of the struggle over this question, no great change in the composition of the Senate resulted; most of those members who had first been chosen by state legislatures managed to win reelection by popular vote.

The other major issue in the development of the Senate was the filibuster. A **filibuster** is a prolonged speech, or series of speeches, made to delay action in a legislative assembly. It had become a common—and unpopular—feature of Senate life by the end of the nineteenth century. It was used by liberals and conservatives alike and for lofty as well as self-serving purposes. The first serious effort to restrict the filibuster came in 1917, after an important foreign policy measure submitted by President Wilson had been talked to death by, as Wilson put it, "eleven willful men." Rule 22 was adopted by a Senate fearful of tying a president's hands during a

THE WAY WE BECOME SENATOR NOWADAYS.

A cartoon from Puck *in 1890 expressed popular resentment over the "Millionaires' Club," as the Senate had become known.*

★ POLITICALLY SPEAKING ★

Filibuster

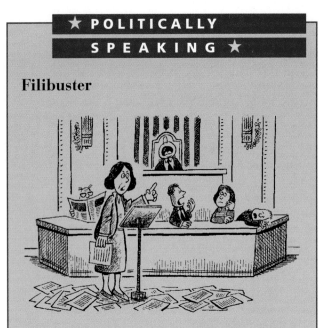

A filibuster is a technique by which a small number of senators attempt to defeat a measure by talking it to death—that is, by speaking continuously and at such length as to induce the supporters of the measure to drop it in order to get on with the Senate's business.

The right to filibuster is governed by the Senate's Rule 22, which allows for unlimited debate unless at least sixty senators agree to a motion to cut it off.

Originally *filibusterers* were sixteenth-century English and French pirates and buccaneers who raided Spanish treasure ships. The term came from a Dutch word, *vrijbuiter,* meaning "freebooter," which was converted into the English word *filibuster.*

The word came into use in America as a term for "continuous talking" in the mid-nineteenth century. One of its first appearances was in 1854, when a group of senators tried to talk to death the Kansas-Nebraska Act.

Source: From *Safire's Political Dictionary* by William Safire. Copyright © 1968, 1972, 1978 by William Safire. Reprinted by permission of Random House, Inc. and the author.

wartime crisis. The rule provided that debate could be cut off if two-thirds of the senators present and voting agreed to a "cloture" motion (it has since been revised to allow sixty senators to cut off debate). Two years later it was first invoked successfully when the Senate voted cloture to end, after fifty-five days, the debate over the Treaty of Versailles. Despite the existence of Rule 22, the tradition of unlimited debate remains strong in the Senate.

Who Is in Congress?

With power so decentralized in Congress, the kind of person elected to it is especially important. Since each member exercises some influence, the beliefs and interests of each individual affect policy. Viewed simplistically, most members of Congress seem the same: the typical representative or senator is a middle-aged white Protestant male lawyer. If all such persons usually thought and voted alike, that would be an interesting fact, but they do not, and so it is necessary to explore the great diversity of views among seemingly similar people.

Sex and Race

Congress has gradually become less male and less white. Between 1950 and 1999 the number of women in the House increased from nine to fifty-eight and the number of African Americans from two to thirty-nine. There are also nineteen Hispanic members.

Until recently the Senate changed much more slowly (see Table 11.1). Before the 1992 election there were no African Americans and only two women in the Senate. But in 1992 four more women, including one black woman, Carol Mosely Braun of Illinois, were elected. Two more were elected in 1994, when a Native American, Ben Nighthorse Campbell of Colorado, also became a senator. Braun lost her seat in 1998, leaving no African Americans and nine women in the Senate.

The relatively small number of African Americans and Hispanics in the House understates their influence, at least when the Democrats are in the majority. In 1994 four House committees were chaired by blacks and three by Hispanics. In the same year, however, no woman chaired a committee. The reason for this difference in power is that the former tend to come from safe districts (see page 286) and thus to have more seniority than the latter. Republican control of the House in 1995 reduced minority influence.

Incumbency

The most important change that has occurred in the composition of Congress has been so gradual that

| Table 11.1 | Blacks, Hispanics, and Women in Congress, 1971–2000 |

	Senate			House		
Congress	Blacks	Hispanics	Women	Blacks	Hispanics	Women
106th (1999–2000)	0	0	9	39	19	58
105th	1	1	9	37	18	51
104th	1	0	8	38	18	48
103rd	1	0	6	38	17	47
102nd	0	0	2	26	10	29
101st	0	0	2	24	11	25
100th	0	0	2	23	11	23
99th	0	0	2	20	11	22
98th	0	0	2	21	10	22
97th	0	0	2	17	6	19
96th	0	0	1	16	6	16
95th	1	0	2	16	5	18
94th	1	1	0	15	5	19
93rd	1	1	0	15	5	14
92nd (1971–1972)	1	1	2	12	5	13

Source: Congressional Quarterly Almanac, various years.

most people have not noticed it. In the nineteenth century a large fraction—often a majority—of congressmen served only one term. In 1869, for example, more than half the members of the House were serving their first term in Congress. Being a congressman in those days was not regarded as a career. This was in part because the federal government was not very important (most of the interesting political decisions were made by the states); in part because travel to Washington, D.C., was difficult and the city was not a pleasant place in which to live; and in part because being a congressman did not pay well. Furthermore, many congressional districts were highly competitive, with the two political parties fairly evenly balanced in each.

By the 1950s, however, serving in Congress had become a career. Between 1863 and 1969 the proportion of first-termers in the House fell from 58 percent to 8 percent (see Figure 11.1).[2] As the public took note of this shift, people began to complain about "professional politicians" being "out of touch with the people." A movement to impose term limits was started. In 1995 the House approved a constitutional amendment to do just that, but it died in the Senate. Then the Supreme Court struck down an effort by a state to impose term limits on its own members of Congress.

As it turned out, natural political forces were already doing what the term limits amendment was

supposed to do. The 1992 and 1994 elections brought scores of new members to the House, with the result that by 1995 the proportion of members who were serving their first or second terms had risen sharply. Three things were responsible for this change. First, when congressional district lines were redrawn after the 1990 census, a lot of incumbents found themselves running in new districts that they couldn't carry. Second, voter disgust at a variety of Washington political scandals made them receptive to appeals from candidates who could describe themselves as "outsiders." And third, the Republican victory in 1994—made possible in part by the conversion of the South from a Democratic bastion to a Republican stronghold—brought a lot of new faces to the Capitol.

This influx of freshman members should not obscure the fact that incumbents still enjoy enormous advantages in congressional elections.[3] Even in 1994, when thirty-five incumbent Democrats lost to Republicans, over 90 percent of all House members who ran for reelection were reelected. In the Senate 92 percent of incumbents who ran again were reelected. In 1996 over 90 percent of House incumbents were reelected, and only one in twenty Senate incumbents who stood for reelection was defeated.

The arrival of scores of new faces in the 1990s should not obscure the fact that most House members

Figure 11.1   Changing Percentage of First-Term Members in Congress

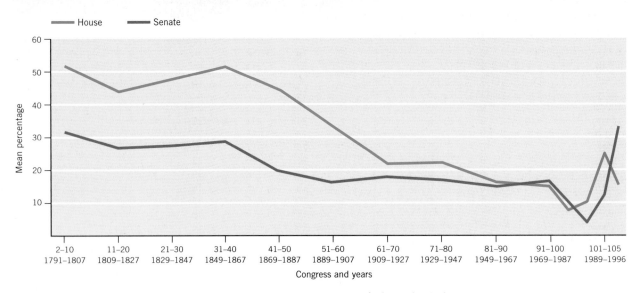

Notes: The 1989 freshman class in the House was the smallest in history. The 1993 freshman class in the House was the largest since 1949.

Sources: Data for 90th through 103rd congresses are from *Congressional Quarterly Weekly Reports.* Data for 69th through 89th congresses are adapted from Nelson W. Polsby, "The Institutionalization of the U.S. House of Representatives," *American Political Science Review* (March 1968): 146. Data for 1st through 68th congresses are from Stuart A. Rice, *Quantitative Methods in Politics* (New York: Knopf, 1928), 296–297, as reported in Polsby, 146. Data for Senate are from N. J. Ornstein, T. J. Mann, and M. J. Malbin, *Vital Statistics on Congress, 1989–1990* (Washington, D.C.: Congressional Quarterly Press, 1990), 56–57, 59–60.

still win big in their districts. Political scientists call districts that have close elections (when the winner gets less than 55 percent of the vote) **marginal districts** and districts where incumbents win by wide margins (55 percent or more) **safe districts.** The proportion of House incumbents who have won reelection with at least 60 percent of the vote increased from about three-fifths in the 1950s and early 1960s to three-quarters in the 1970s and almost nine-tenths in the late 1980s (see Figure 11.2). Even as this trend began to change in 1990, most House districts remained safe. Senators remained less secure: the rule, to which the period 1980–1990 and the year 1998 are the exceptions, is that fewer than half of Senate incumbents win with as much as 60 percent of the vote (see Table 11.2).

Why congressional seats have become less marginal—that is, safer—is a matter on which scholars do not agree. Some feel that it is the result of television and other media. But challengers can go on television, too, so why should this benefit incumbents?

Another possibility is that voters are becoming less and less likely to automatically support whatever candidate wins the nomination of their own party. They are more likely, in short, to vote for the person rather than the party. And they are more likely to have heard of a person who is an incumbent: incumbents can deluge the voter with free mailings, they can travel frequently (and at public expense) to meet constituents, and they can get their names in the newspaper by sponsoring bills or conducting investigations. Simply having a familiar name is important in getting elected, and incumbents find it easier than challengers to make their names known.

Finally, some scholars argue that incumbents can use their power to get programs passed or funds spent to benefit their districts—and thereby to benefit themselves. They can help keep an army base open, support the building of a new highway (or block the building of an unpopular one), take credit for federal grants to local schools and hospitals, make certain that a particular industry or labor union is protected by tariffs against foreign competition, and so on.[4]

Probably all of these factors make some difference. Whatever the explanation, the tendency of voters to return incumbents to office means that in ordinary times no one should expect any dramatic changes in the composition of Congress.

Party

From 1933 to 1998 thirty-three Congress convened (a new Congress convenes every two years). The Democrats controlled both houses in twenty-five of these Congresses and at least one house in twenty-eight of them. Scholars differ in their explanations of why the Democrats have so thoroughly dominated Congress. Most of the research on the subject has focused on the reasons for Democratic control of the House.

As Table 11.3 shows, in every election from 1968 to 1998 the percentage of the popular vote for Republican candidates to the House was higher than the percentage of House seats that actually went to Republicans. For example, in 1976 the Republicans won 42.1 percent of the vote but received only 32.9 percent of the seats. Some have argued that this gap between votes and seats has occurred because Democratic-controlled state legislatures have redrawn congressional district maps in ways that make it hard for Republicans to win House seats. There is some striking anecdotal evidence to support this conclusion. For example, following the 1990 census, the Democratic-controlled Texas legislature crafted a new congressional district map clearly designed to benefit Democrats. In 1992 Republicans won 48 percent of the House vote in Texas but received only 30 percent of the seats. Similarly, in 1984 Democrats in California won nine more congressional seats than did Republicans, even though the latter received about one hundred thousand more votes statewide. After 1990 California's congressional map was redrawn by a state court, and in 1992 Republican House candidates won 41 percent of the statewide vote and 42 percent of the seats.[5] Only in 1994, with the historic election of the first Republican majorities in Congress in four decades, did the gap close.

Partisan tinkering with district maps and other structural features of House elections is not a sufficient explanation of why Democrats dominated the House until 1994. As one study concluded, "Virtu-

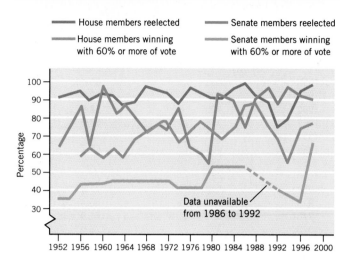

Figure 11.2   Percentage of Incumbents Reelected to Congress

- House members reelected
- Senate members reelected
- House members winning with 60% or more of vote
- Senate members winning with 60% or more of vote

Data unavailable from 1986 to 1992

Source: Harold W. Stanley and Richard G. Niemi, *Vital Statistics on American Politics, 1999–2000* (Washington, D.C.: Congressional Quarterly Press, 2000), table 1-18.

ally all the political science evidence to date indicates that the electoral system has little or no partisan bias, and that the net gains nationally from redistricting for one party over another are very small."[6] To control the redistricting process, one party must control both houses of the legislature, the governor's office, and, where necessary, the state courts. These conditions simply do not exist in most states. And even if district lines were consistently drawn with scrupulous fairness, the Democrats would still win control of the House, because they win more votes. The Republican vote-seat gap is accounted for in part by the fact that the Democrats tend to do exceptionally well in low-turnout districts such as minority-dominated inner cities, while the Republicans tend to do well in high-turnout districts such as affluent white suburbs (see Figure 11.3).

In 1994, however, the year the gap closed, Republican candidates for the House ran especially strong in the roughly half of all districts that have predominantly suburban constituencies. Thus even though only 19 percent of eligible voters cast a vote for a Republican, it was enough to best the Democrats, who won the votes of only 16.6 percent of all eligible voters.

Table 11.2 Incumbents in Congress Reelected by 60 Percent or More

House, 1956–1998

Year	Number of Incumbents Running in General Election	Percentage of Incumbents Reelected with at Least 60 Percent of the Vote
1956	403	59.1%
1958	390	63.1
1960	400	58.9
1962	376	63.6
1964	388	58.5
1966	401	67.7
1968	397	72.2
1970	389	77.3
1972	373	77.8
1974	383	66.4
1976	381	71.9
1978	377	78.0
1980	392	72.9
1982	383	68.9
1984	406	74.6
1986	391	86.4
1988	407	88.5
1990	406	76.4
1992	349	65.6
1994	383	64.5
1996	383	73.6
1998	400	77.2

Senate, 1944–1998

Election Period	Number of Incumbents Running in General Election	Percentage of Incumbents Reelected with at Least 60 Percent of the Vote
1944–1948	61	39.3%
1950–1954	76	35.5
1956–1960	84	42.9
1962–1966	86	44.2
1968–1972	74	44.6
1974–1978	70	41.4
1980–1984	84	54.1
1986–1990	87	57.5
1992–1994	53	43.4
1996–1998	49	57.1

Source: Harold W. Stanley and Richard G. Niemi, *Vital Statistics on American Politics, 1999–2000* (Washington, D.C.: Congressional Quarterly Press, 2000), table 1-18.

Table 11.3 Republican Vote-Seat Gap, 1968–1998

Year	Percentage of Popular Vote for Republican House Candidates	Percentage of House Seats Held by Republicans
1968	48.2%	44.1%
1970	44.5	41.4
1972	46.4	44.2
1974	40.5	33.1
1976	42.1	32.9
1978	44.7	36.3
1980	48.0	44.1
1982	43.3	38.2
1984	47.0	41.8
1986	44.6	40.7
1988	45.5	40.2
1990	45.0	38.4
1992	45.6	40.5
1994	52.4	52.9
1996	48.9	52.2
1998	48.7	51.3

Source: Harold W. Stanley and Richard G. Niemi, *Vital Statistics on American Politics, 1999–2000* (Washington, D.C.: Congressional Quarterly Press, 2000), table 1–12.

that the incumbency advantage was worth about two percentage points prior to the 1960s but has grown to six to eight points today.

But as political scientist Gary C. Jacobson has observed, the historical Democratic dominance of the House cannot be explained simply by reference to incumbency advantages. Instead Jacobson argues that "Democrats' continued dominance of the House (as well as of other lower offices) despite a string of Republican presidential victories is a consequence of electoral politics."[7] In comparison with the Republicans, the Democrats, he finds, generally have fielded better, more experienced congressional candidates, have more closely reflected district-level voters' policy preferences, and have been able to fashion winning, district-level coalitions from among national Democratic constituencies such as organized labor, civil rights activists, feminists, and environmentalists. This implies that more than mere changes in the structural features of House elections (incumbency advantages, partisan redistricting) would be necessary to keep the GOP's vote-seat gap closed.

It is important to remember that from time to time major electoral convulsions do alter the mem-

Congressional incumbents have come to enjoy certain built-in electoral advantages over challengers, and the Democrats were in the majority as the advantages of incumbency grew. Studies suggest bership patterns in Congress. For example, in the election of 1938 the Democrats lost seventy seats in the House; in 1942 they lost fifty; in 1950 they lost twenty-nine; and in 1966 they lost forty-eight. Despite these big losses, the Democrats retained a majority in the House in each of these years. Not so, however, in 1994, when the Democrats lost fifty-two House seats (the largest loss by either party since the Republicans lost seventy-five seats in 1948), and Republicans gained majorities in both the House and the Senate.

Just as it is not easy to explain why Democrats dominated Congress for half a century, so it is not easy to explain why that domination ended when and as it did. Several reasons, however, stand out. By the 1990s the advantages of incumbency had turned into disadvantages: voters increasingly came to dislike "professional politicians," whom they held responsible for "the mess in Washington." Just what "the mess" was varied according to which voter you asked, but it included chronic budget deficits, the congressional habit of exempting itself from laws that affected everybody else, constant bickering between Congress and the White House, and various congressional scandals. During the 1980s about forty members of Congress were charged with misconduct ranging from having sex with minors to accepting illegal gifts. When it was disclosed that the House had its own bank that would cash checks even for members who (temporarily) had no funds in their accounts, public indignation exploded, even though almost no taxpayer money was lost. Public respect for Congress, as measured by the polls, plummeted.

The Democrats had the misfortune of being the majority party in Congress when all of this happened. The anti-incumbent mood, coupled with the effects of redistricting after the 1990 census and the shift of the South to the Republican party, brought the Republicans into power in the House and Senate in the 1994 elections.

In the past the Democratic party was more deeply divided than the Republicans, because of the presence in Congress of conservative Democrats from the South. Often these southern Democrats would vote with the Republicans in the House or Senate, thereby forming what came to be called the **conservative coalition.** During the 1960s and 1970s that coalition came together in about one-fifth of all

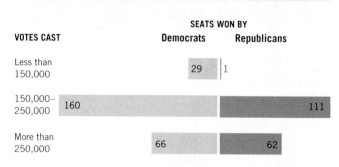

Figure 11.3   Results of 1992 House Election by Turnout

	SEATS WON BY	
VOTES CAST	**Democrats**	**Republicans**
Less than 150,000	29	1
150,000–250,000	160	111
More than 250,000	66	62

Source: "House Republicans Scored a Quiet Victory in '92," *Congressional Quarterly* (April 17, 1993): 967.

roll-call votes. When it did, it usually won, defeating northern Democrats. But since the 1980s, and especially since the watershed election of 1994, the conservative coalition has become much less important. The reason is simple: many southern Democrats in Congress have been replaced by southern Republicans, and the southern Democrats who remain (many of them African Americans) are as liberal as northern Democrats. The effect of this change is to make Congress, and especially the House, more ideologically partisan—Democrats are liberals, Republicans are conservatives—and this in turn helps explain why there is more party unity in voting.

Getting Elected to Congress

Who serves in Congress, and what interests are represented there, is affected by the mechanisms by which its members are elected. Each state is entitled to two senators, who serve six-year terms, and at least one representative, who serves a two-year term. How many more representatives a state has depends on its population; what local groups these representatives speak for depends in part on how the district lines are drawn.

The Constitution says very little about how representatives will be selected except to require that they be inhabitants of the states from which they are chosen. It says nothing about districts and originally left it up to the states to decide who would be eligible to

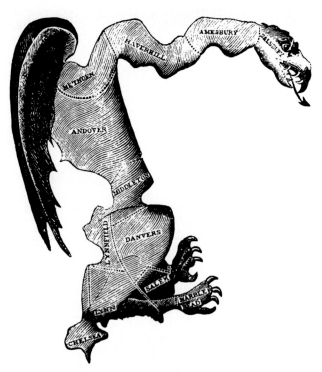

The original Gerrymander: Elbridge Gerry had this Massachusetts district drawn to ensure the election of a Republican. Cartoonist Elkanah Tinsdale in 1812 compared the district to a salamander and termed it a "Gerry-Mander."

vote for representatives. The size of the first House was set by the Constitution at sixty-five members, and the apportionment of the seats among the states was spelled out in Article I, section 2. From that point on it has been up to Congress to decide how many representatives each state would have (provided that each had at least one).

Determining Fair Representation

Initially some states did not create congressional districts; all their representatives were elected at large. In other states representatives were elected from multimember as well as single-member districts. In time all states with more than one representative elected each from a single-member district. How those district boundaries were drawn, however, could profoundly affect the outcomes of elections. There were two problems. One was **malapportionment,** which results from having districts of very unequal size. If one district is twice as populous as another, twice as many votes are needed in the larger district to elect a representative. Thus a citizen's vote in the smaller district is worth twice as much as a vote in the larger.

The other problem was **gerrymandering,** which means drawing a district boundary in some bizarre or unusual shape to make it easy for the candidate of one party to win election in that district. In a state entitled to ten representatives, where half the voters are Democrats and half are Republicans, district lines could be drawn so that eight districts would have a slight majority of citizens from one party and two districts would have lopsided majorities from the other. Thus it can be made easy for one party to win eight of the ten seats.

Malapportionment and gerrymandering have been conspicuous features of American congressional politics. In 1962, for example, one district in Texas had nearly a million residents, while another had less than a quarter million. In California Democrats in control of the state legislature drew district lines in the early 1960s so that two pockets of Republican strength in Los Angeles separated by many miles were connected by a thin strip of coastline. In this way most Republican voters were thrown into one district, while Democratic voters were spread more evenly over several.

Hence there are four problems to solve in deciding who gets represented in the House:

1. Establishing the total size of the House
2. Allocating seats in the House among the states
3. Determining the size of congressional districts within states
4. Determining the shape of those districts

By and large Congress has decided the first two questions, and the states have decided the last two—but under some rather strict Supreme Court rules.

In 1911 Congress decided that the House had become large enough and voted to fix its size at 435 members. There it has remained ever since (except for a brief period when it had 437 members owing to the admission of Alaska and Hawaii to the Union in 1959). Once the size was decided upon, it was necessary to find a formula for performing the painful task of apportioning seats among the states as they gained and lost population. The Constitution requires such reapportionment every ten years. A more or less automatic method was selected in 1929 based on a complex statistical system that has withstood decades of political and scientific testing. Under this system many states—such as New York,

Ohio, Pennsylvania, and Illinois—have lost representation in the House as other states have grown more rapidly in population. The largest gainers have been California, Florida, and Texas (see Table 11.4). The average congressional district in 1990 had about 575,000 residents.

The states did little about malapportionment and gerrymandering until ordered to do so by the Supreme Court. In 1964 the Court ruled that the Constitution requires that districts be drawn so that, as nearly as possible, one person's vote would be worth as much as another's.[8] The Court rule, "one person, one vote," seems clear but in fact leaves a host of questions unanswered. How much deviation from equal size is allowable? Should other factors be considered besides population? (For example, a state legislature might want to draw district lines to make it easier for African Americans, Italian Americans, farmers, or some other group with a distinct interest to elect a representative; the requirement of exactly equal districts might make this impossible.) And the gerrymandering problem remains: districts of the same size can be drawn to favor one party or another. The courts have struggled to find answers to these questions, but they remain far from settled.

Majority-Minority Districts

Perhaps the most vexing legal questions concern **majority-minority districts**—congressional districts designed to make it easier for minority citizens to elect minority representatives. For many years geographically concentrated communities of African Americans in the South and in many big cities throughout the country were carved up in ways that kept black politicians out of power. Even as recently as 1991 African Americans constituted about 25 percent of the southern population but held barely 4 percent of the congressional seats in the South. In response some southern states created majority-minority districts. For example, in 1991 the North Carolina General Assembly created two majority-black districts (shown on the map on page 292). One of these districts, the twelfth, was a 160-mile path no wider at some points than the interstate highway it traced.[9] The redistricting paid off. In 1992 Democratic representatives Melvin Watt and Eva Clayton became the first African Americans to represent North Carolina in Congress since 1901.[10] Similarly, New York City's X-shaped twelfth district

	Number of Seats			
States	**Before Census**	**After Census**	**Change**	**Party Control of State, 1991**
Gained Seats				
Arizona	5	6	+1	Split
California	45	52	+7	Split
Florida	19	23	+4	Democrats
Georgia	10	11	+1	Democrats
North Carolina	11	12	+1	Democrats
Texas	27	30	+3	Democrats
Virginia	10	11	+1	Democrats
Washington	8	9	+1	Split
Lost Seats				
Illinois	22	20	−2	Split
Iowa	6	5	−1	Split
Kansas	5	4	−1	Split
Kentucky	7	6	−1	Democrats
Louisiana	8	7	−1	Democrats
Massachusetts	11	10	−1	Split
Michigan	18	16	−2	Split
Montana	2	1	−1	Split
New Jersey	14	13	−1	Democrats
New York	34	31	−3	Split
Ohio	21	19	−2	Split
Pennsylvania	23	21	−2	Split
West Virginia	4	3	−1	Democrats

Table 11.4 Changes in State Representation in the House of Representatives After the 1990 Census

Note: "Split" means that the same party does not control the governorship, House, and Senate in that state.

Source: U.S. Bureau of the Census.

snakes through a dozen different school districts and police precincts and is only a block wide at one point. It was designed to pool Hispanic voters in Manhattan, Queens, and Brooklyn.[11] In the 1992 Democratic primary in this district, a Hispanic challenger, Nydia M. Velasquez, defeated a Jewish incumbent, Stephen Solarz, and went on to win a House seat.

The constitutionality of majority-minority redistricting efforts has been called into question. In a five-to-four decision issued on June 28, 1993, in the case of *Shaw v. Reno*, the U.S. Supreme Court reinstated a suit by five white North Carolinians who maintained that the state's congressional map violated their Fourteenth Amendment right to "equal protection under the law."[12] The *Shaw* decision sent

Districts 1 and 12 in North Carolina

■ 1st District

■ 12th District

Source: *Congressional Quarterly* (May 22, 1993): 1323.

the case back to the lower courts for review, telling them that race could be a factor in drawing congressional district lines only if there was a "compelling governmental interest" in doing so. The states took a fresh look, but when the issue came back to the Supreme Court, the justices were not persuaded that such a compelling interest had been established. In two 5–4 decisions the Court said that race had been used so heavily and with so little justification in drawing the lines of districts like North Carolina's twelfth that they were unlawful "racial gerrymanders."[13] Since the Court did not spell out the meaning of a "compelling governmental interest" that might justify using race as the main factor in drawing districts, we can expect that it will have to hear a lot more cases like these.

In 1993 there were twenty Hispanic-majority districts and thirty-two black-majority districts nationwide. Not all are drawn as oddly as the ones the Court rejected (in North Carolina and Texas), and so they will likely survive. In any case African Americans were elected even from districts that were redrawn to conform to Supreme Court opinions. But it seems clear that the current Court majority will want to take a hard look at any new districts that use race in a way that makes for bizarre-appearing districts.

It is important to recognize that two conceptions of representation are at odds in the debate over majority-minority districts. The political theorist Hannah F. Pitkin has distinguished between **descriptive representation,** the statistical correspondence of the demographic characteristics of representatives with those of their constituents, and **substantive representation,** the correspondence

between representatives' opinions and those of their constituents.[14]

To those who favor descriptive (also sometimes referred to as categorical) representation, majority-minority districts are desirable for their own sake, and creating them is a legitimate way of ensuring that citizens of a given racial or ethnic background are represented by persons of the same background. To those who favor substantive representation, however, the key question is whether representatives work to support the interests and opinions of the voters in their districts.

One challenging question is whether the substantive interests of minority voters are adequately represented by nonminority representatives in Congress. In a sophisticated analysis political scientist Carol M. Swain has explored this question by studying the constituency relations and roll-call votes of black members of Congress from a variety of districts (historically black, newly black, heterogeneous, and primarily white) and of white members from districts with either a black majority or a significant black minority. Among other things she found that liberal white members of Congress represented black interests as strongly as did black representatives (their voting records on key economic and other issues of import to the black community were virtually the same) and that "creating newly black districts will not significantly increase black substantive representation."[15]

Winning the Primary

Once the district lines are set, the other major procedural arrangement that affects the election of a candidate has to do with the system for getting one's name on the ballot. At one time the political parties nominated candidates and even printed ballots with the party slates listed on them. All the voter had to do was take the ballot of the preferred party and put it in the ballot box. Today, with rare exceptions, a candidate wins a party's nomination by gathering enough voter signatures to get on the ballot in a primary election, the outcome of which is often beyond the ability of political parties to influence. Candidates tend to form organizations of personal followings and win "their party's" nomination simply by getting more primary votes than the next candidate. It is quite unusual for an incumbent to lose a primary: from 1946 to 1988 only 6 percent of incumbent senators and fewer than 2 percent of incumbent representatives seeking reelection failed to win renomination in primaries. These statistics suggest how little opportunity parties have to control or punish their congressional members.

Nor are the voters much inclined to punish their members of Congress. We have already seen that typically over 90 percent of incumbent House members are reelected. Most newly elected members become strong in their districts very quickly; this is called the **sophomore surge.** It is the difference between the votes candidates get the first time they are elected (and thus become freshman members) and the votes they get when they run for reelection (in hopes of becoming sophomore members). Before the 1960s House candidates did not do much better the second time they ran than the first. Beginning then, however, the sophomore surge kicked in, so that today freshman candidates running for reelection will get 8 to 10 percent more votes than when they were first elected. Senate candidates also benefit now from a sophomore surge, though to a lesser degree.

The reason for this surge is that members of Congress have figured out how to use their offices to run *personal* rather than party campaigns. They make use of free ("franked") mail, frequent trips home, radio and television broadcasts, and the distribution of services to their districts to develop among their constituents a good opinion of themselves, not their party. They also cater to their constituents' distrust of the federal government by promising to "clean things up" if reelected. They run *for* Congress by running *against* it.[16]

To the extent that they succeed, they enjoy great freedom in voting on particular issues and have less need to explain away votes that their constituents might not like. If, however, any single-issue groups are actively working in their districts for or against abortion, gun control, nuclear energy, or tax cuts, muting the candidates' voting record may not be possible.

The way people get elected to Congress has two important effects. First, it produces legislators who are closely tied to local concerns (their districts, their states), and second, it ensures that party leaders will have relatively weak influence over them (because those leaders cannot determine who gets nominated for office).

The local orientation of legislators has some important effects on how policy is made. For example:

- Every member of Congress organizes his or her office to do as much as possible for people back home.
- If your representative serves on the House Transportation and Infrastructure Committee, your state has a much better chance of getting a new bridge or canal than if you do not have a representative on this committee.[17]

Qualifications for Entering Congress and Privileges of Being in Congress

QUALIFICATIONS

Representative

- Must be twenty-five years of age (when seated, not when elected)
- Must have been a citizen of the United States for seven years
- Must be an inhabitant of the state from which elected (*Note:* Custom, but *not* the Constitution, requires that a representative live in the district that he or she represents.)

Senator

- Must be thirty years of age (when seated, not when elected)
- Must have been a citizen of the United States for nine years
- Must be an inhabitant of the state from which elected

JUDGING QUALIFICATIONS

Each house is the judge of the "elections, returns, and qualifications" of its members. Thus Congress alone can decide disputed congressional elections. On occasion it has excluded a person from taking a seat on the grounds that the election was improper.

Either house can punish a member—by reprimand, for example—or, by a two-thirds vote, expel a member.

PRIVILEGES

Members of Congress have certain privileges, the most important of which, conferred by the Constitution, is that "for any speech or debate in either house they shall not be questioned in any other place." This doctrine of "privileged speech" has been interpreted by the Supreme Court to mean that members of Congress cannot be sued or prosecuted for anything that they say or write in connection with their legislative duties.

When Senator Mike Gravel read the Pentagon Papers—some then-secret government documents about the Vietnam War—into the *Congressional Record* in defiance of a court order restraining their publication, the Court held that this was "privileged speech" and beyond challenge [*Gravel v. United States*, 408 U.S. 606 (1972)]. But when Senator William Proxmire issued a press release critical of a scientist doing research on monkeys, the Court decided that the scientist could sue him for libel because a press release was not part of the legislative process [*Hutchinson v. Proxmire*, 443, U.S. 111 (1979)].

- If your representative serves on the House Appropriations Committee, your district is more likely to get approval for a federal grant to improve your water and sewage-treatment programs than if your representative does not serve on that committee.[18]

Former House Speaker Thomas P. "Tip" O'Neill had this in mind when he said, "All politics is local." Some people think that this localism is wrong; in their view members of Congress should do what is best for "the nation as a whole." This argument is about the role of legislators: are they supposed to be

delegates who do what their district wants or *trustees* who use their best judgment on issues without regard to the preferences of their district?

Naturally most members are some combination of delegate and trustee, with the exact mix depending on the nature of the issue. But some, as we shall see, definitely lean one way or the other. All members want to be reelected, but "delegates" tend to value this over every other consideration and so seek out committee assignments and projects that will produce benefits for their districts. On the other hand, "trustees" will seek out committee assignments that give them a chance to address large questions, such as foreign affairs, that may have no implications at all for their districts.

Do Members Represent Their Voters?

In a decentralized, individualistic institution such as Congress, it is not obvious how its members will behave. They could be devoted to doing whatever their constituents want or, since most voters are not aware of what their representatives do, act in accordance with their own beliefs, the demands of pressure groups, or the expectations of congressional leaders. You may think it would be easy to figure out whether members are devoted to their constituents by analyzing how they vote, but that it not quite right. Members can influence legislation in many ways other than by voting: they can conduct hearings, help mark up bills in committee meetings, and offer amendments to the bills proposed by others. A member's final vote on a bill may conceal as much as it reveals: some members may vote for a bill that contains many things they dislike because it also contains a few things they value.

There are at least three theories about how members of Congress behave: representational, organizational, and attitudinal.

The *representational* explanation is based on the reasonable assumption that members want to get reelected, and therefore they vote to please their constituents. The *organizational* explanation is based on the equally reasonable assumption that since most constituents do not know how their legislator has voted, it is not essential to please them. But it is important to please fellow members of Congress, whose goodwill is valuable in getting things done and in acquiring status and power in Congress. The *attitudinal* explanation is based on the assumption that there are so many conflicting pressures on members of Congress that they cancel one another out, leaving them virtually free to vote on the basis of their own beliefs.

Political scientists have studied, tested, and argued about these (and other) explanations for decades, and nothing like a consensus has emerged. Some facts have been established, however.

Representational View

The representational view has some merit under certain circumstances—namely, when constituents

Elections may raise national issues, but campaigning is an intensely local affair, as when Rep. Patrick Kennedy cultivated voters in a Rhode Island company.

have a clear view on some issue and a legislator's vote on that issue is likely to attract their attention. Such is often the case for civil rights laws: representatives with significant numbers of black voters in their districts are not likely to oppose civil rights bills; representatives with few African Americans in their districts are comparatively free to oppose such bills. (Until the late 1960s many southern representatives were able to oppose civil rights measures because the African Americans in their districts were prevented from voting. On the other hand, many representatives without black constituents have supported civil rights bills, partly out of personal belief and partly, perhaps, because certain white groups in their districts—organized liberals, for example—have insisted on such support.)

One study of congressional roll-call votes and constituency opinion showed that the correlation between the two was quite strong on civil rights bills. There was also a positive (though not as strong) correlation between roll-call votes and constituency opinion on social welfare measures. Scarcely any correlation, however, was found between congressional votes and hometown opinion on foreign policy measures.[19] Foreign policy is generally remote from the daily interests of most Americans, and public opinion about such matters can change rapidly. It is not surprising, therefore, that congressional votes and constituent opinion should be different on such questions.

From time to time an issue arouses deep passions among the voters, and legislators cannot escape the need either to vote as their constituents want, whatever their personal views, or to anguish at length about which side of a divided constituency to support. Gun control has been one such question, the use of federal money to pay for abortions has been another, and the effort to impeach President Clinton was a third. Some fortunate members of Congress get unambiguous cues from their constituents on these matters, and no hard decision is necessary. Others get conflicting views, and they know that whichever way they vote, it may cost them dearly in the next election. Occasionally members of Congress in this fix will try to be out of town when the matter comes up for a vote. One careful study found that constituency influences were an important factor in Senate votes,[20] but no comparable study has been done for the House.

You might think that members of Congress who won a close race in the last election—who come from a "marginal" district—would be especially eager to vote the way that their constituents want. Research so far has shown that is not generally the case. There seem to be about as many independent-minded members of Congress from marginal as from safe districts. Perhaps it is because opinion is so divided in a marginal seat that one cannot please everybody; as a result the representative votes on other grounds.

In general the problem with the representational explanation is that public opinion is not strong and clear on most measures on which Congress must vote. Many representatives and senators face constituencies that are divided on key issues. Some constituents go to special pains to make their views known (these interest groups were discussed in Chapter 9). But as we indicated, the power of interest groups to affect congressional votes depends, among other things, on whether a legislator sees them as united and powerful or as disorganized and marginal.

This does not mean that constituents rarely have a direct influence on voting. The influence that they have probably comes from the fact that legislators risk defeat should they steadfastly vote in ways that can be held against them by a rival in the next election. Though most congressional votes are not known to most citizens, blunders (real or alleged) quickly become known when an electoral opponent exploits them.

Still, any member of Congress can choose the positions that he or she takes on most roll-call votes (and on all voice or standing votes, where names are not recorded). And even a series of recorded votes that are against constituency opinion need not be fatal: a member of Congress can win votes in other ways—for example, by doing services for constituents or by appealing to the party loyalty of the voters.

Organizational View

When voting on matters where constituency interests or opinions are not vitally at stake, members of Congress respond primarily to cues provided by their colleagues. This is the organizational explanation of their votes. The principal cue is party; as already noted, what party a member of Congress belongs to explains more about his or her voting record than any other single factor. Additional organizational cues come from the opinions of colleagues with whom the member of Congress feels a close ideological affinity: for liberals in the House it is the Democratic Study Group; for conservatives it has often been the Republican Study Committee or the Wednesday Club. But party and other organizations do not have clear positions on all matters. For the scores of votes that do not involve the "big questions," a representative or senator is especially likely to be influenced by the members of his or her party on the sponsoring committee.

It is easy to understand why. Suppose you are a Democratic representative from Michigan who is summoned to the floor of the House to vote on a bill to authorize a new weapons system. You haven't the faintest idea what issues might be at stake. There is no obvious liberal or conservative position on this matter. How do you vote? Simple. You take your cue from several Democrats on the House Armed Services Committee that handled the bill. Some are liberal; others are conservative. If both liberals and conservatives support the bill, you vote for it unhesitatingly. If they disagree, you vote with whichever Democrat is generally closest to your own political ideology. If the matter is one that affects your state, you can take your cue from members of your state's delegation to Congress.

Attitudinal View

Finally, there is evidence that the ideology of a member of Congress affects how he or she votes. We have seen that Democratic and Republican legislators differ sharply on a liberal-versus-conservative scale. On both domestic and foreign policy issues many tend to be consistently liberal or conservative.[21]

This consistency isn't surprising. As we saw in Chapter 5, political elites think more ideologically than the public generally.

On many issues the average member of the House has opinions close to those of the average voter, as seen in Figure 11.4. Senators, by contrast, are often less in tune with public opinion. In the 1970s they were much more liberal than voters; in the early 1980s more conservative. Two senators from the same state often mobilize quite different bases of support. The result is that many states, such as California, Delaware, and New York, have been represented by senators with almost diametrically opposed views.

Of late the Senate has gone through three phases. In the first, during the 1950s and early 1960s, it was a cautious, conservative institution dominated by southern senators and displaying many of the features of a "club" that welcomed members into its inner circle only after they had displayed loyalty to its gentlemanly (and, in effect, conservative) customs. This was the era when the Senate was the graveyard of civil rights bills.

The second period began in the mid-1960s as liberal senators rose steadily in number, seniority, and influence, helped along by the Johnson reforms, which made it easier for junior senators to gain chairmanships. The decentralization of the Senate gave more power to individual senators, including liberals. In 1972 there were about twenty-four liberal senators, but among them they held forty subcommittee chairmanships.[22]

The third period began in the late 1970s and became most visible after the 1980 elections, when many liberals lost their seats to conservative Republicans. The conservatism of the present Senate is based more on ideology than on the rules of the southern "club" that characterized it in the 1950s.

The Democratic party is more deeply divided than the Republican. There are only a few liberal Republicans, but there have been many more conservative Democrats from the South and West. Southern Democrats often teamed up with Republicans to form a conservative coalition. In a typical year a majority of Republicans and southern Democrats would vote together against a majority of northern Democrats about 20 to 25 percent of the time. When the conservative coalition did form, it usually

Figure 11.4 Comparison of Public and Congressional Opinion on Policy Issues, 1978

■ Public   ■ House members

Defense: Favor more money for national defense

23%

26%

Arms control: Favor Strategic Arms Limitation Talks (SALT)

67%

74%

Health insurance: Favor national health insurance fully paid for by the government

47%

45%

Tax cut: Oppose a "large" federal income-tax cut

53%

51%

Abortion: Favor government paying for abortions for the poor

41%

35%

Source: CBS—*New York Times* poll, as reported in Robert S. Erikson, Norman R. Luttbeg, and Kent L. Tedin, *American Public Opinion,* 2nd ed. (New York: Wiley, 1980), 240.

won: between 1970 and 1982 it won about two-thirds of the votes on which it held together. After the Reagan victory and the Republican gain of thirty seats in the House in 1981, the conservative coalition became even more effective, dominating key votes on the Reagan budget and tax plans.

But the conservative coalition was important only when there were a lot of conservative southern Democrats. Many of these have now been replaced with southern Republicans. As a result almost all of the conservatives are now in the Republican party, so there is not much of a coalition left to form. In 1998 this coalition—that is, a majority of Republicans and southern Democrats voting against a majority of northern Democrats—existed in only 6 percent of all congressional votes. In the 1970s, by contrast, it appeared in about one-quarter of all votes.

Ideology and Civility in Congress

Congress has become an increasingly ideological organization. By that we mean its members are more sharply divided by political ideology than it once was and certainly more divided than are American voters. In short the attitudinal explanation of how members vote has increased in importance, while the organizational explanation has declined. All of Congress's most liberal members are Democrats, and all of its most conservative ones are Republicans. That is not what you would find among ordinary voters. A lot of us split our tickets, voting for one party's presidential nominee and a different party's congressional candidate.

This higher level of congressional ideology does not mean that its existing members have changed how they think. Rather it means that new kinds of members have been elected, bringing to Congress a more ideological perspective.[23] In 1974 (the election right after Watergate) a large number of more ideological Democrats entered Congress. In 1994 there was a large influx of more ideological Republicans.

Congress has become more polarized than voters in terms of political beliefs. Among voters the average Democrat and the average Republican, though they surely disagree, nonetheless have views that put them close to the center of the political spectrum. But among members of Congress the average Democrat is very liberal and the average Republican very conservative, a fact that keeps them far from the political center. There are, of course, some conservative Democrats and some liberal Republicans, but their numbers have been getting smaller and smaller.

One result of this polarization is that members of Congress, especially those in the House, do not get along as well as they once did with members who disagree with them, and they are more likely to challenge, investigate, and denounce one another. Two speakers of the House, Jim Wright and Newt Gingrich, were investigated and resigned. Many presidential nominees have been subjected to withering investigations, some based on ideological differences and some on charges of ethical violations, many of which were dubious. President Clinton was impeached on a nearly party-line vote. Members regularly accuse one another of misconduct. When they run for reelection, they often use negative ads of the sort discussed in Chapter 5. The mass media feed on and aggravate this tendency because of their interest in scandal.

The result is that the public—already puzzled by the constitutional need members have to discuss policy matters for long periods, listen to interest groups, and reach compromise settlements—are now put off even more by the political disposition members have to attack one another. At one time the constitutional need to negotiate was facilitated by reasonably good relationships between Democrats and Republicans, most of whom treated one another with politeness and socialized together after hours. This congenial social relationship no longer exists in most cases, and the public has noticed.

The Organization of Congress: Parties and Caucuses

Congress is not a single organization; it is a vast and complex collection of organizations by which the business of the legislative branch is carried on and through which its members form alliances. If we were to look inside the British House of Commons, we would find only one kind of organization of any importance—the political party. Though party organization is important in the U.S. Congress, it is only one of many important elements. In fact other organizations have grown in number as the influence of the parties has declined.

The Democrats and Republicans in the House and the Senate are organized by party leaders. The key leaders in turn are elected by the full party membership within the House and Senate. The description that follows is confined to the essential positions.

Party Organization of the Senate

The majority party (in 2000, the Republicans) chooses one of its members—usually the person with the greatest seniority—to be president pro tempore of the Senate. It is largely an honorific position, required by the Constitution so that the Senate will have a presiding officer in the absence of the vice president of the

United States (who is also, according to the Constitution, the president of the Senate). In fact presiding over the Senate is a tedious chore that neither the vice president nor the president pro tem relishes, and so the actual task of presiding is usually assigned to some junior senator.

The real leadership is in the hands of the **majority leader** (chosen by the senators of the majority party) and the **minority leader** (chosen by the senators of the other party). In addition the senators of each party elect a whip. The principal task of the majority leader is to schedule the business of the Senate, usually in consultation with the minority leader. The majority leader has the right to be recognized first in any floor debate. A majority leader with a strong personality who is skilled at political bargaining may do much more. Lyndon Johnson, who was Senate majority leader for the Democrats during much of the 1950s, used his prodigious ability to serve the needs of fellow senators. He helped them with everything from obtaining extra office space to getting choice committee assignments, and in this way he acquired substantial influence over the substance as well as the schedule of Senate business. Johnson's successor, Mike Mansfield, was a less assertive majority leader and had less influence.

The **whip** is a senator who helps the party leader stay informed about what party members are thinking, rounds up members when important votes are to be taken, and attempts to keep a nose count on how the voting on a controversial issue is likely to go. The whip has several senators who assist him or her in this task.

Each party in the Senate also chooses a Policy Committee composed of a dozen or so senators who help the party leader schedule Senate business, choosing what bills are to be given major attention and in what order.

From the point of view of individual senators, however, the key party organization is the group that assigns senators to the standing committees of the Senate. The Democrats have a Steering Committee that does this; the Republicans have a Committee on Committees. These assignments are especially important for newly elected senators: their political careers, their opportunities for favorable publicity, and their chances for helping their states and their supporters depend in great part on the committees to which they are assigned. For example, when

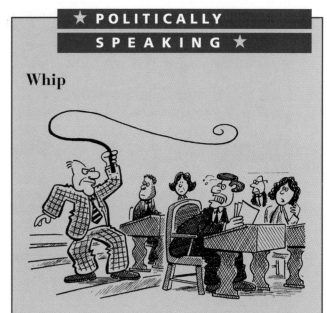

★ POLITICALLY SPEAKING ★

Whip

A whip is a party leader who makes certain that party members are present for a vote and vote the way the party wishes. In the British House of Commons the whips produce strong party votes; in the U.S. Congress whips are a lot less successful.

The word comes from *whipper-in*, a term from fox hunting denoting the person whose job it is to keep the hounds from straying off the trail. It became a political term in England in the eighteenth century, and from there came to the United States.

Source: From *Safire's Political Dictionary* by William Safire. Copyright © 1968, 1972, 1978 by William Safire. Reprinted by permission of Random House, Inc. and the author.

Daniel Patrick Moynihan was elected to the Senate from New York in 1976, he waged an intensive and successful effort to get appointed to the Finance Committee. That body handles bills providing aid to cities and welfare recipients—two concerns of great importance to the big urban areas in Moynihan's state. When Lloyd Bentsen of Texas left the Senate to become the Clinton administration's secretary of the treasury, Moynihan succeeded him as chairman of the Finance Committee. During the 1960s many new senators fought to get on the Foreign Relations Committee because of the controversy surrounding the war in Vietnam and the highly visible role of members of that committee in criticizing or defending American policy.

Minority leader Richard Gephardt (left) and House Speaker Dennis Hastert (right).

The key—and delicate—aspect of selecting party leaders, of making up the important party committees, and of assigning freshman senators to Senate committees is achieving ideological and regional balance. Liberals and conservatives in each party will fight over the choice of majority and minority leader, but factors in addition to ideology play a part in the choice. These include personal popularity, the ability of the leader to make an effective television appearance, and who owes whom what favors.

Party Structure in the House

Though the titles of various posts are different, the party structure is essentially the same in the House as in the Senate. Leadership carries more power in the House than in the Senate because of the House rules. Being so large (435 members), the House must restrict debate and schedule its business with

great care; thus leaders who do the scheduling and who determine how the rules shall be applied usually have substantial influence.

The Speaker is the most important person in the House. He is elected by whichever party has a majority, and he presides over all House meetings. Unlike the president pro tem of the Senate, however, his position is anything but honorific. He is the principal leader of the majority party as well as the presiding officer of the entire House. Though Speakers-as-presiders are expected to be fair, Speakers-as-party-leaders are expected to use their powers to help pass legislation favored by their party.

In helping his party, the Speaker has some important formal powers at his disposal: he decides who shall be recognized to speak on the floor of the House; he rules whether a motion is relevant and germane to the business at hand; and he decides (subject to certain rules) the committees to which new bills shall be assigned. He influences what bills are brought up for a vote and appoints the members of special and select committees (to be explained on pages 306–307). Since 1975 the Speaker has been able to nominate the majority-party members of the Rules Committee. He also has some informal powers: he controls some patronage jobs in the Capitol building and the assignment of extra office space. Even though he is far less powerful than in the days of Clay, Reed, and Cannon, the Speaker is still an important person to have on one's side. Sam Rayburn of Texas exercised great influence as Speaker, and Tip O'Neill, Jim Wright, Tom Foley, and Newt Gingrich tried to do the same.

In the House, as in the Senate, the majority party elects a floor leader, called the majority leader. The other party also chooses a leader—the minority leader. Traditionally the majority leader becomes Speaker when the person in that position dies or retires—provided, of course, that the departing Speaker's party is still in the majority. Each party also has a whip, with several assistant whips in charge of rounding up votes from various state delegations. Committee assignments are made and the scheduling of legislation is discussed, by the Democrats, in a Steering and Policy Committee, chaired by the Speaker. The Republicans have divided committee assignments and policy discussions, with the former task assigned to a Committee on Committees and the latter to a Policy Committee. Each party also has a congressional campaign committee to provide

Party Leadership Structure

SENATE

President Pro Tempore Selected by majority party

Democrats

Majority Leader Leads the party

Majority Whip Assists the leader, rounds up votes, heads group of deputy whips

Chairman of the Conference Presides over meetings of all Senate Democrats

Policy Committee Schedules legislation

Steering Committee Assigns Democratic senators to committees

Democratic Senatorial Campaign Committee Provides funds, assistance to Democratic candidates for the Senate

Republicans

Minority Leader Leads the party

Assistant Minority Leader Assists the leader, rounds up votes

Chairman of the Conference Presides over meetings of all Senate Republicans

Policy Committee Makes recommendations on party policy

Committee on Committees Assigns Republican senators to committees

Republican Senatorial Committee Provides funds, advice to Republican candidates for the Senate

HOUSE

Speaker of the House Selected by majority party

Democrats

Majority Leader Leads the party

Majority Whip Assists the leader, rounds up votes, heads group of deputy and assistant whips

Chairman of the Caucus Presides over meetings of all House Democrats

Steering and Policy Committee Schedules legislation, assigns Democratic representatives to committees

Democratic Congressional Campaign Committee Provides funds, advice to Democratic candidates for the House

Republicans

Minority Leader Leads the party

Minority Whip Assists the leader, rounds up votes, heads large group of deputy and assistant whips

Chairman of the Conference Presides over meetings of all House Republicans

Committee on Committees Assigns Republican representatives to committees

Policy Committee Advises on party policy

National Republican Congressional Committee Provides funds, advice to Republican candidates for the House

Research Committee On request, provides information about issues

---

funds and other assistance to party members running for election or reelection to the House.

The Strength of Party Structures

One important measure of the strength of the parties in Congress is the ability of party leaders to get their members to vote together on the rules and structure of Congress. When Newt Gingrich became Speaker of the Republican-controlled House in 1995, he proposed sweeping changes in House rules, many not popular with some Republican members. For example, he wanted no one to serve as a committee chairman for more than six years, for three committees to be abolished, and for other committees to lose either functions or members. He also wanted to pass over some senior members in picking committee chairmen. Though these moves adversely affected some Republican representatives, they all voted in favor of the new rules.[24] Of course Gingrich would not have made these proposals unless he was certain he could get them adopted. But it was a measure of his influence and support among newly elected Republicans that even major changes in congressional procedures would get unanimous party

The U.S. Congress

HOUSE OF REPRESENTATIVES
1. House Minority Whip
2. Lobby
3. House chamber
4. Cloakrooms
5. Speaker of the House
6. Ways and Means Committee
7. House Minority Leader

SENATE
8. Senate Minority Leader
9. Office of the Secretary
10. Senate chamber
11. Cloakrooms
12. Senate Majority Leader
13. Vice President

The House and Senate meet at opposite ends of the Capitol building. When there is a joint session of Congress—for example, to hear the president's State of the Union address—the senators sit with the representatives in the House chamber. Though the most important work of Congress goes on in committee meetings, which are held in office buildings behind the Capitol, some important political negotiations occur in the offices surrounding the chambers—especially in the cloakrooms (actually, lounges) and the offices of the majority and minority leaders, the Speaker and the vice president, and the secretary of the Senate.

support.[25] Getting support on proposed legislation is a harder task.

The Senate is another matter. As Barbara Sinclair has argued, in the last few decades the Senate has been transformed by changes in norms (informal understandings governing how members ought to behave toward their colleagues), without any far-reaching changes in the written Senate rules.[26] Compared to the Senate of the 1950s and 1960s, today's Senate is less party-centered, less leader-oriented, more hospitable to freshmen (who no longer have to "pay their dues" before assuming major roles as legislators), more heavily staffed, and more subcommittee-oriented.

Party Unity

The strength of Congress's elaborate party machinery can also be measured by the extent to which members of a party vote together in the House and Senate. **Party polarization** is defined as a vote in which a majority of voting Democrats oppose a majority of voting Republicans. In seven of the thirteen years from 1953 to 1965, at least half of all House votes pitted a majority of voting Democrats against a majority of voting Republicans (see Table 11.5). But in 1966 the number dropped to 41 percent, and it was not until 1983 that voting in the House once again took on a distinctively partisan cast. By the 1990s party unity voting was the norm

Table 11.5   Party Polarization in Congressional Voting, 1953–1998 (percentage of all votes)

Year	House	Senate	Year	House	Senate
1953	52%	N.A.	1976	36%	37%
1954	38	47%	1977	42	42
1955	41	30	1978	33	45
1956	44	53	1979	47	47
1957	59	36	1980	38	46
1958	40	44	1981	37	48
1959	55	48	1982	36	43
1960	53	37	1983	56	44
1961	50	62	1984	47	40
1962	46	41	1985	61	50
1963	49	47	1986	57	52
1964	55	36	1987	64	41
1965	52	42	1988	47	42
1966	41	50	1989	55	35
1967	36	35	1990	49	54
1968	35	32	1991	55	49
1969	31	36	1992	64	53
1970	27	35	1993	65	67
1971	38	42	1994	62	52
1972	27	36	1995	73	69
1973	42	40	1996	56	62
1974	29	44	1997	50	50
1975	48	48	1998	56	56

Source: Harold W. Stanley and Richard G. Niemi, *Vital Statistics on American Politics, 1999–2000* (Washington, D.C.: Congressional Quarterly Press, 2000), 211.

in both the House and the Senate. A kindred measure of party strength is the cohesion of the parties on votes that elicit a party split. By this measure, between 1991 and 1994 over 80 percent of all House and Senate Democrats voted with a majority of their party on party unity votes, as did over 80 percent of House and Senate Republicans.

As these recent trends make plain, party unity in Congress is hardly a thing of the past. Specific issues can trigger an extraordinary degree of party cohesion. For example, in 1993 every single Republican in both the House and Senate voted against the Clinton budget plan, the first budget offered by a Democratic president since Jimmy Carter left office in 1980. This may be an extreme example, but it reflects the increasingly adversarial relationship between Democrats and Republicans, especially in the House.

Still, it is worth remembering that even today's Congress is less divided along party lines than many of its predecessors were. During the years 1890–1910,

for example, two-thirds of all votes evoked a party split, and in several sessions more than half the roll calls found 90 percent of each party's members opposing the other party.[27] Whereas the party splits of the past often reflected the routine operations of highly disciplined parties interested mainly in winning elections, dispensing patronage, and keeping power, today's party splits often reflect sharp ideological differences between the parties (or at least between their respective leaders).

The party polarization of today's Congress poses something of a puzzle. Given that the parties do not tightly control legislators' ability to get elected and that members of both parties are far more interested in getting reelected than in scoring ideological points debating their colleagues across the aisle, why do the members of one party vote en masse against the other party? There are several reasons. First, members of Congress do not randomly decide to be Democrats or Republicans; these choices reflect some broad ideological orientation, at least for most members. Democrats vote alike in part because they are ideologically alike.

Several interest groups tabulate the votes of legislators on important issues to see who is most and least sympathetic to their positions. By combining the scores given by many such organizations—including Americans for Democratic Action (liberal), Americans for Constitutional Action (conservative), the AFL-CIO, and the Chamber of Commerce—it is possible to rank each member of Congress from most to least liberal in three policy areas: economic affairs (taxes, job programs, and so forth), social questions (abortion, civil rights, school prayer), and foreign affairs (defense spending, support for military intervention). Democrats in the House and Senate have been much more liberal than Republicans in most recent years. So pronounced are the ideological differences between the parties that, even allowing for the existence of conservative southern Democrats, the average southern Democrat in the House is more liberal than the average northern Republican.

In addition to their personal views, members of Congress have other reasons for supporting their party's position at least some of the time. On many matters that come to a vote, members have little information and no opinion. They have no chance of becoming personally familiar with more than a small fraction of the hundreds of items with which Congress deals each session. They must get advice on how to vote, and it is only natural that Democrats look to Democratic leaders and fellow partisans for that advice, and Republicans look to Republicans.

Furthermore, supporting the party position can work to the long-term advantage of a member interested in rising in status and influence in Congress. As a number of recent studies have shown, though party leaders are weaker today than in the past, they are hardly powerless.[28] If you are a member of Congress who wants to get a committee assignment, obtain a favorable hearing for a bill, become chairman of an important subcommittee, or be taken seriously by other members in the party caucus, it pays not to insult, ignore, or challenge party leaders. Sam Rayburn, who served as Speaker for seventeen years (in the 1940s and 1950s), reputedly told freshman members of Congress that "if you want to get along, go along." That is less true today, but it's still good advice.

In short party *does* make a difference in Congress—not as much as it once did, and not nearly as much as it does in a parliamentary system, but party affiliation is still the most important thing to know about a member of Congress. Knowing whether a member is a Democrat or a Republican will not tell you everything about the member, but it will tell you more than any other single fact.

Caucuses

Congressional caucuses are a growing rival to the parties as a source of policy leadership. A **caucus** is an association of members of Congress created to advocate a political ideology or a regional or economic interest. In 1959 there were only four caucuses; by the late 1980s there were over one hundred.

As Congress expert Susan Webb Hammond has observed, "The pace of caucus formation accelerated rapidly during the 1970s as members, operating with increased and more equitably distributed resources within a decentralized institution, sought to respond to increased external demands. . . .

The Congressional Black Caucus.

Members derive benefits—gaining information, being identified as a 'leader,' symbolically showing that they care about an issue of importance to constituents—from caucus activities."[29] In January 1995, at the beginning of the Republican-led 104th Congress, it was widely reported that the House of Representatives would "abolish" congressional caucuses. Yet as of January 1996 there were 129 congressional caucuses—111 from the 103rd Congress and 18 new ones established by the 104th. What the Republicans did do was to adopt a rule making the operation of caucuses more difficult. All aides working on caucus matters must be housed in members' offices. Therefore aides are often scattered among several offices, and coordination becomes more difficult. Some caucuses responded by spinning off informational functions to new outside groups. Clearly the death of the caucuses was greatly exaggerated.

The caucuses are alive, well, and changing. Hammond has identified six types, four of which are constituency-based (see Table 11.6). Intraparty caucuses are formed by groups whose members share a similar ideology; for example, the Democratic Study Group was established by liberal Democrats. Personal-interest caucuses form around a common interest in an issue—for example, the environment, the arts, or human rights. Constituency caucuses are established to represent certain groups (African Americans, women, Vietnam veterans), regions (New England, the western states), or both (in states or congressional districts with diffuse constituents, such as different ethnic populations or family and corporate farms).

One long-established national constituency caucus is the Congressional Black Caucus (CBC). Founded in 1970, its membership increased from nine members that year to forty in the 104th Congress. Most CBC members have been liberal House Democrats. J. C. Watts, a black Republican from Oklahoma, was elected in 1994 but refused to join the CBC. In the Democratic-controlled 103rd Congress, CBC members chaired three standing committees and eighteen subcommittees.

But in the Republican-controlled 104th Congress, CBC committee leaders became ranking minority members, and some caucus Democrats lost their seats on major House committees—Appropriations, Ways and Means, and Rules. Moreover, the CBC grew less unified as liberal Democratic members

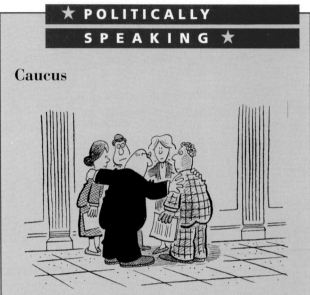

★ POLITICALLY SPEAKING ★

Caucus

A *caucus* is a closed meeting of the members of a political party either to select a candidate for office or to agree on a legislative position.

The term is from an American Indian word meaning "elder" or "counsellor." It quickly entered political usage in the United States, there being a Caucus Club in Boston as early as 1763.

The first national political caucuses were in Congress, where legislators would gather to select their party's candidate for president. Persons who did not get a caucus endorsement soon began denouncing the entire procedure, referring contemptuously to the "decrees of King Caucus." Popular resentment led in the 1830s to the creation of the nominating convention as a way of choosing presidential candidates.

Today congressional caucuses are organizations of legislators from a single party (Democrats or Republicans), with a common background (for example, women, African Americans, Hispanics), sharing a particular ideology (liberals or conservatives), or having an interest in a single issue (such as mushrooms, steel mills, or the environment).

Source: From *Safire's Political Dictionary* by William Safire. Copyright © 1968, 1972, 1978 by William Safire. Reprinted by permission of Random House, Inc. and the author.

from northern districts were forced to share power with more centrist members representing southern rural and suburban districts.

Table 11.6   Congressional Caucuses

Type	Typical Examples
Intraparty	Class Clubs The Coalition Conservative Opportunity Society Democratic Study Group Tuesday Lunch Bunch Wednesday Groups
Personal interest	Arts Caucuses Constitutional Caucus Constitutional Forum Congressional Family Caucus Human Rights Caucuses Military Reform Caucus Population and Development Coalition Senate Children's Caucus
Constituency concerns, national	Congressional Black Caucus Congressional Caucus for Women's Issues Congressional Hispanic Caucus Vietnam Veterans Caucus
Constituency concerns, regional	Congressional Border Caucus Congressional Sunbelt Council Northeast-Midwest Congressional Coalition Tennessee Valley Authority Caucus Western Caucus Western States Senate Coalition

Constituency concerns, state/district	Congressional Caucus on
	  American Issues
	Export Caucus
	Irish Caucuses
	Rural Caucus
	Suburban Caucus
	Task Force on Industrial
	  Innovation and Productivity

Constituency concerns, industry	Automotive Caucus Boating Caucus Depot Caucus Steel Caucuses Textile Caucus Travel and Tourism Caucus

Source: Lawrence C. Dodd and Bruce I. Oppenheimer, eds., *Congress Reconsidered,* 6th ed. Washington, D.C.: Congressional Quarterly Press, 1997), table 12-1 by Susan Hammond.

By contrast, other caucuses (and not only Republican ones), have fared better in recent years. For example, an intraparty caucus of "Blue Dog Democrats" known as the Coalition was born in February 1995. The Coalition's two dozen moderate-to-conservative members favor "middle-of-the-road" policies, especially on welfare and budget issues. For example, in 1995 the Coalition introduced its own welfare and budget bills, and although neither proposal was enacted, certain provisions of each strongly influenced final House deliberations. As Hammond has concluded, although the political fortunes of the CBC, the Coalition, and other caucuses may change from year to year, caucuses will continue and thrive as congressional institutions "because they help members to achieve personal goals of policy, representation, or power."[30]

The Organization of Congress: Committees

The most important organizational feature of Congress is the set of legislative committees of the House and Senate. It is there that the real work of Congress is done, and it is in the chairmanships of these committees and their subcommittees that most of the power in Congress is found. The number and jurisdiction of these committees are of the greatest interest to members of Congress, since decisions on these subjects determine what group of members, with what political views, will pass on legislative proposals, oversee the workings of agencies in the executive branch, and conduct investigations.

There are three kinds of committees: **Standing committees** (more or less permanent bodies with specified legislative responsibilities), **select committees** (groups appointed for a limited purpose and usually lasting for only a few congresses), and **joint committees** (those on which both representatives and senators serve). An especially important kind of joint committee is the **conference committee,** made up of representatives and senators appointed to resolve differences in the Senate and House versions of the same piece of legislation before final passage.

In the 104th Congress (1995–1996) the new Republican majority reduced the number of committees as part of its larger plan to reform House operations. Similar efforts were made in the Senate. When the dust settled on Capitol Hill, the total number of House and Senate committees had fallen from 252 in the previous Congress to 198, a smaller total even than the 242 committees of the 84th Congress

(1955–1956). The House went from 22 to 19 standing committees and from 115 to 84 subcommittees of standing committees. The Senate maintained 17 committees but reduced the number of subcommittees of standing committees from 86 to 68.

Though members of the majority party could, in theory, occupy all the seats on all the committees, in practice they take the majority of the seats on each committee, name the chairman, and allow the minority party to have the remainder of the seats. The number of seats varies with the committee, from about six to over fifty. Usually the ratio of Democrats to Republicans on a committee roughly corresponds to their ratio in that house of Congress. In 1981 the Democrats held 56 percent of the House seats but tried to keep a two-to-one majority on key committees. After the Republicans complained, a compromise still left the Democrats overrepresented (with 66 percent of the seats on Ways and Means, 60 percent on Appropriations and Budget). In 1999 Democrats complained that they were underrepresented on key committees.

Standing committees are the important ones, because, with a few exceptions, they are the only ones that can propose legislation by reporting a bill out to the full House or Senate. Each member of the House usually serves on two standing committees, unless he or she is on an "exclusive" committee—Appropriations, Rules, or Ways and Means. In such a case the representative is limited to one. Each senator may serve on two "major" committees and one "minor" committee.

When party leaders were strong, as under Speakers Reed and Cannon, committee chairmen were picked on the basis of loyalty to the leader. Now that this leadership has been weakened, seniority on the committee governs the selection of chairmen. Of late, however, even seniority has been under attack. In 1971 House Democrats decided in their caucus to elect committee chairmen by secret ballot. From then through 1991 they used that procedure to remove six committee chairmen. In 1975 three were deposed, in 1985 another, and in 1992 two more. When the Republicans took control of the House in 1995, they could have returned to the strict seniority rule, but they did not. House Speaker Gingrich passed over three senior representatives in favor of more junior ones as committee chairmen. Though most chairmen still get and hold their posts through seniority, these changes have made all

HOW THINGS WORK

Standing Committees of the Senate

Major Committees
No senator is supposed to serve on more than two (but some do).

Agriculture, Nutrition, and Forestry
Appropriations
Armed Services
Banking, Housing, and Urban Affairs
Budget
Commerce, Science, and Transportation
Energy and Natural Resources
Environment and Public Works
Finance
Foreign Relations
Governmental Affairs
Health, Education, Labor, and Pensions
Judiciary

Minor Committees
No senator is supposed to serve on more than one (but some do).

Indian Affairs
Rules and Administration
Small Business
Veterans' Affairs

Select Committees

Aging
Ethics
Intelligence

chairmen worry about pleasing their rank-and-file members and the party leaders.

Traditionally the committees of Congress were dominated by the chairmen. They often did their most important work behind closed doors (though their hearings and reports were almost always published in full). In the early 1970s Congress further decentralized and democratized its operations by a series of changes that some members regarded as a "bill of rights" for representatives and senators, especially those with relatively little seniority. These

Standing Committees of the House

Exclusive Committees
Members may not serve on any other committee except Budget.

Appropriations
Rules
Ways and Means

Major Committees
Members may serve on only one major committee.

Agriculture
Armed Services
Banking and Financial Services
Commerce
Education and the Workforce
International Relations
Judiciary
Transportation and Infrastructure

Nonmajor Committees
Members may serve on one major and one nonmajor committee, or on two nonmajor committees.

Administration
Budget
Government Reform
Resources
Science
Small Business
Standards of Official Conduct
Veterans' Affairs

Select Committee

Intelligence

Note: In 1995 the House Republican majority abolished three committees—District of Columbia, Post Office and Civil Service, and Merchant Marine and Fisheries—and gave their duties to other standing committees.

House

- Committee chairmen to be elected by secret ballot in party caucus
- No member to chair more than one committee
- All committees with more than twenty members to have at least four subcommittees (at the time, Ways and Means had no subcommittees)
- Committee and personal staffs to be increased in size
- Committee meetings to be public unless members vote to close them

Senate

- Committee meetings to be public unless members vote to close them
- Committee chairmen to be selected by secret ballot at the request of one-fifth of the party caucus
- Committees to have larger staffs
- No senator to chair more than one committee

The effect of these changes, especially in the House, was to give greater power to individual members and to lessen the power of party leaders and committee chairmen. The decentralization of the House meant that it was much harder for chairmen to block legislation they did not like or to discourage junior members from playing a large role. House members were quick to take advantage of these enlarged opportunities. In the 1980s they proposed three times as many amendments to bills as they had in the 1950s.[31]

There was a cost to be paid, however, for this empowerment of the membership. The 435 members of the House could not get much done if everyone talked as much as they liked and introduced as many amendments as they wished. And with the big increase in the number of subcommittees, many subcommittee meetings were attended by (and thus controlled by) only one person, the chairman. To deal with this, the Democratic leaders began reclaiming some of their lost power. They made greater use of restrictive rules that sharply limited debate and the introduction of amendments. Committee chairmen began casting proxy votes. (A proxy is a written authorization to cast another person's vote.) In this way a chairman could control the results of committee deliberations by casting the proxies of absent members.

Republican House members were angered by all of this. They suspected that restrictive rules and proxy

changes were by and large made by the Democratic Caucus, but since the Democrats were in the majority, the changes, in effect, became the rules of Congress. The more important ones were as follows.

voting were designed to keep them from having any voice in House affairs. When they took control of the House in 1995, they announced some changes:

- They banned proxy voting.
- They limited committee and subcommittee chairmen's tenures to three terms (six years) and the Speaker's to four terms (eight years).
- They allowed more frequent floor debate under open rules.
- They reduced the number of committees and subcommittees.
- They authorized committee chairmen to hire subcommittee staffs.

The endless arguments about rules illustrate a fundamental problem that the House faces. Closed rules, proxy voting, powerful committee chairmen, and strong Speakers make it easier for business to get done; they put the House in a good bargaining position with the president and the Senate; and they make it easier to reduce the number of special-interest groups with legislative power. But this system also keeps individual members weak. The opposite arrangements—open rules, weak chairmen, many subcommittees, meetings open to the public—help individual members be heard and increase the amount of daylight shining on congressional processes. But if everyone is heard, no one is heard, because the noise is deafening and the speeches endless. And though open meetings and easy amending processes may be intended to open up the system to "the people," the real beneficiaries are the lobbyists.

The House Republican rules of 1995 gave back some power to the chairmen (for example, by letting them pick all staff members) but further reduced it in other ways (for example, by imposing term limits and banning proxy voting). The commitment to public meetings remained.

In the Senate there have been fewer changes, in part because individual members of the Senate have always had more power than their counterparts in the House. Two important changes made by the Republicans in 1995:

- A six-year term limit on all committee chairmen (no limit on the majority leader's term)
- A requirement that committee members select their chairmen by secret ballot

Despite these new rules, the committees remain the place where the real work of Congress is done.

Committee hearings are an important means of defining issues, as when Bill Gates spoke to a committee about the claim that Microsoft was a monopoly.

The different types of committees tend to attract different kinds of members. Some, such as the committees that draft tax legislation (the Senate Finance Committee and the House Ways and Means Committee) or that oversee foreign affairs (the Senate Foreign Relations Committee and the House International Relations Committee) are attractive to members who want to shape public policy, become experts on important issues, or have influence with their colleagues. Others, such as the House and Senate committees dealing with public lands, small business, and veterans' affairs, are attractive to members who want to serve particular constituents.[32]

The Organization of Congress: Staffs and Specialized Offices

In 1900 representatives had no personal staffs, and senators averaged fewer than one staff member each. As recently as 1935 the typical representative had but two aides. In 1998 the average representative had seventeen assistants and the average senator over forty. To the more than ten thousand individuals who served on the personal staffs of members of the 103rd Congress must be added three thousand more who worked for congressional committees and yet another three thousand employed by various congressional research agencies. Until the 1990s Congress had the most rapidly growing bureaucracy in Washington—the personal staffs of legislators

Figure 11.5   The Growth in Staffs of Members and Committees in Congress, 1891–1993

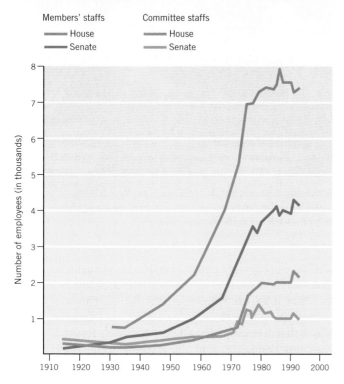

Sources: Ornstein et al., *Vital Statistics on Congress* (Washington, D.C.: American Enterprise Institute, 1984 and 1996), from David C. Kozak and John D. Macartney, eds., *Congress and Public Policy,* 2nd ed. (Chicago: Dorsey Press, 1987), 95; *Statistical Abstract of the United States,* 1992, 264.

increased more than fivefold from 1947 to 1991, then leveled off and declined slightly (see Figure 11.5). Though some staffers perform routine chores, many help draft legislation, handle constituents, and otherwise shape policy and politics.

Tasks of Staff Members

Staff members assigned to a senator or representative spend most of their time servicing requests from constituents—answering mail, handling problems, sending out newsletters, and meeting with voters. In short a major function of a member of Congress's staff is to help constituents solve problems and thereby help that member get reelected. Indeed, over the last two decades a larger and larger portion of congressional staffs—now about one-third—work in the local (district or state) office of the member of Congress rather

than in Washington. Almost all members of Congress have such offices on a full-time basis; about half maintain two or more offices in their constituencies. Some scholars believe that this growth in constituency-serving staffs helps explain why it is so hard to defeat an incumbent representative or senator.

The legislative function of congressional staff members is also important. With each senator serving on an average of more than two committees and seven subcommittees and each representative serving on an average of six committees and subcommittees, it is virtually impossible for members of Congress to become familiar in detail with all the proposals that come before them or to write all the bills that they feel ought to be introduced. As the workload of Congress has grown (over six thousand bills are introduced, about six hundred public laws are passed, and uncounted hearings and meetings are held during a typical Congress), the role of staff members in devising proposals, negotiating agreements, organizing hearings, writing questions for members of Congress to ask of witnesses, drafting reports, and meeting with lobbyists and administrators has grown correspondingly.

Those who work for individual members of Congress, as opposed to committees, see themselves entirely as advocates for their bosses. As the mass media have supplanted political parties as ways of communicating with voters, the advocacy role of staff members had led them to find and promote legislation for which a representative or senator can take credit. This is the entrepreneurial function of the staff. While it is sometimes performed under the close supervision of the member of Congress, just as often a staff member takes the initiative, finds a policy, and then "sells" it to his or her employer. Lobbyists and reporters understand this completely and therefore spend a lot of time cultivating congressional staffers, both as sources of information and as consumers of ideas.

One reason for the rapid growth in the size and importance of congressional staffs is that a large staff creates conditions that seem to require an even larger staff. As the staff grows in size, it generates more legislative work. Subcommittees proliferate to handle all the issues with which legislators are concerned. But as the workload increases, legislators complain that they cannot keep up and need more help.

The increased reliance on staff has changed Congress, not because staffers do things against the wishes of their elected masters but because the staff has altered the environment within which Congress does its work. In addition to their role as entrepreneurs promoting new policies, staffers act as negotiators. As a result members of Congress today are more likely to deal with one another through staff intermediaries than personally. Congress has thereby become less collegial, more individualistic, and less of a deliberative body.[33]

Staff Agencies

In addition to increasing the number of staff members, Congress has also created a set of staff agencies that work for Congress as a whole. These staff agencies have come into being in large part to give Congress specialized knowledge equivalent to what the president has by virtue of his position as chief of the executive branch.

Congressional Research Service (CRS)   Formerly the Legislative Reference Service, the CRS is part of the Library of Congress. Since 1914 it has responded to congressional requests for information and now employs nearly nine hundred people, many with advanced academic training, to respond to more than a quarter of a million questions each year. As a politically neutral body, it does not recommend policy, but it will look up facts and indicate the arguments for and against a proposed policy. CRS also keeps track of the status of every major bill before Congress and produces a summary of each bill introduced. This information is instantly available to legislators via computer terminals located in almost all Senate and most House offices.

General Accounting Office (GAO)   Created in 1921, this agency once performed primarily routine financial audits of the money spent by executive-branch departments. Today it also investigates agencies and policies and makes recommendations on almost every aspect of government—defense contracting, drug enforcement policies, the domestic security investigations of the FBI, Medicare and Medicaid programs, water pollution programs, and so forth. Though the head of the GAO—the comptroller general—is appointed by the president (with the consent of the Senate), he or she serves for a fifteen-year term and is very much the servant of Congress rather than of the president. The GAO employs about five thousand people, many of whom are permanently assigned to work with various congressional committees.

Office of Technology Assessment (OTA)   Established in 1972 to study and evaluate policies and programs with a significant use of or impact on technology, the OTA had a staff of more than one hundred. Staff members looked into matters such as a plan to build a pipeline to transport coal slurry. The agency had little impact and was abolished in 1995.

Congressional Budget Office (CBO)   Created in 1974, the CBO advises Congress on the likely economic effects of different spending programs and provides information on the costs of proposed policies. This latter task has been more useful to Congress than the more difficult job of estimating future economic trends. The CBO prepares analyses of the president's budget and economic projections that often come to conclusions different from those of the administration, thus giving members of Congress arguments to use in the budget debates.

How a Bill Becomes Law

Some bills zip through Congress; others make their way slowly and painfully. Congress, an English observer once remarked, is like a crowd, moving either sluggishly or with great speed.

Bills that have sped through on the fast track include ones to reduce drug abuse, reform Defense Department procurement procedures, end the mandatory retirement age, and help the disabled. Those that have plodded through on the slow track include ones dealing with health care, tax laws, energy conservation, and foreign trade, as well as several appropriations bills.

Why the difference? Studying the list above gives some clues. Bills to spend a lot of money move slowly, especially during times (such as the 1980s and early 1990s) when the government is running up big deficits. Bills to tax or regulate businesses move slowly because so many different interests have to be heard and accommodated. On the other hand, bills that seem to embody a clear, appealing idea ("stop drugs," "help old folks," "end scandal") gather momentum quickly, especially if the government doesn't have to spend a lot of its money (as opposed to requiring other people to spend their money) on the idea.

In the following account of how a bill becomes law, keep in mind the central fact that the complexity of these procedures ordinarily gives a powerful advantage to the opposition. There are many points at which action can be blocked. This does not mean that nothing gets done but that, to get something

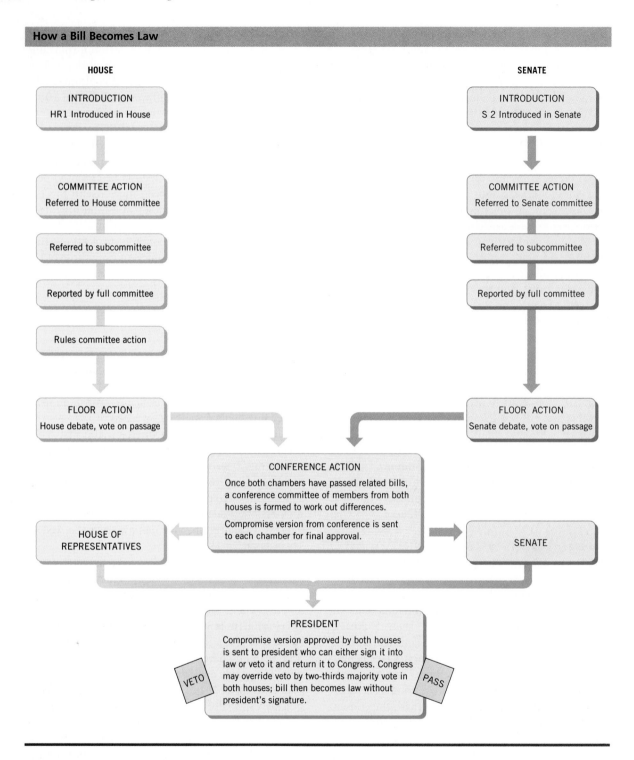

How a Bill Becomes Law

HOUSE

INTRODUCTION
HR1 Introduced in House

COMMITTEE ACTION
Referred to House committee

Referred to subcommittee

Reported by full committee

Rules committee action

FLOOR ACTION
House debate, vote on passage

SENATE

INTRODUCTION
S 2 Introduced in Senate

COMMITTEE ACTION
Referred to Senate committee

Referred to subcommittee

Reported by full committee

FLOOR ACTION
Senate debate, vote on passage

CONFERENCE ACTION
Once both chambers have passed related bills, a conference committee of members from both houses is formed to work out differences.

Compromise version from conference is sent to each chamber for final approval.

HOUSE OF REPRESENTATIVES

SENATE

PRESIDENT
Compromise version approved by both houses is sent to president who can either sign it into law or veto it and return it to Congress. Congress may override veto by two-thirds majority vote in both houses; bill then becomes law without president's signature.

VETO

PASS

done, a member of Congress must *either* assemble a majority coalition slowly and painstakingly *or* take advantage of temporary enthusiasm for some new cause that sweeps away the normal obstacles.

Introducing a Bill

Any member of Congress may introduce a bill—in the House simply by handing it to a clerk or dropping it in a box (the "hopper"), in the Senate by being rec-

---

H.R.1661

Children's Health Insurance Accountability Act of 1999 (Introduced in the House)

HR 1661 IH

106th CONGRESS

1st Session

H. R. 1661

To amend title XXVII of the Public Health Service Act and part 7 of subtitle B of title I of the Employee Retirement Income Security Act of 1974 to establish standards for the health quality improvement of children in managed care plans and other health plans.

IN THE HOUSE OF REPRESENTATIVES

May 4, 1999

Mrs. MORELLA (for herself, Mr. BALDACCI, Mr. SAWYER, and Mr. HILLIARD) introduced the following bill; which was referred to the Committee on Commerce, and in addition to the Committee on Education and the Workforce, for a period to be subsequently determined by the Speaker, in each case for consideration of such provisions as fall within the jurisdiction of the committee concerned

---

A BILL

To amend title XXVII of the Public Health Service Act and part 7 of subtitle B of title I of the Employee Retirement Income Security Act of 1974 to establish standards for the health quality improvement of children in managed care plans and other health plans.

Be it enacted by the Senate and House of Representatives of the United States of America in Congress assembled,

---

A bill (H.R. 1661) as it looks when introduced in the House.

ognized by the presiding officer and announcing the bill's introduction. Bills are numbered and sent to the printer: a House bill bears the prefix *H.R.,* a Senate bill the prefix S. A bill can be either a **public bill** (pertaining to public affairs generally) or a **private bill** (pertaining to a particular individual, such as a person pressing a financial claim against the government or seeking special permission to become a naturalized citizen). Private bills were once very numerous; today many such matters have been delegated to administrative agencies or the courts. If a bill is not passed by both houses and signed by the president within the life of one Congress, it is dead and must be reintroduced during the next Congress. Pending legislation does not carry over from one Congress to the next. (A new Congress is organized every two years.)

We often hear that legislation is initiated by the president and enacted by Congress—the former proposes, the latter disposes. The reality is more complicated. Congress frequently initiates legislation; in fact most of the consumer and environmental protection legislation passed since 1966 began in Congress, not in the executive branch. And even laws formally proposed by the president often represent presidential versions of proposals that have incubated in Congress. This was the case, for example, with some civil rights laws and with the proposal that eventually became Medicare. Even when the president is the principal author of a bill, he usually submits it (if he is prudent) only after careful consultation with key congressional leaders. In

any case the president cannot himself introduce legislation; he must get a member of Congress to do it for him.

One study showed that of ninety major laws passed between 1880 and 1945, seventy-seven were introduced without presidential sponsorship. In shaping the final contents, congressional influence dominated in thirty-five cases, presidential influence dominated in nineteen, and influence was mixed in the remaining thirty-six. Another study, covering the period 1940 to 1967, found that Congress was the major contributor to the contents of about half of all laws passed.[34]

In addition to bills, Congress can pass resolutions. A **simple resolution** (passed by either the House or the Senate) is used for matters such as establishing the rules under which each body will operate. A **concurrent resolution** settles housekeeping and procedural matters that affect both houses. Simple and concurrent resolutions are not signed by the president and do not have the force of law. A **joint resolution** requires the approval of both houses and the signature of the president; it is essentially the same as a law. A joint resolution is also used to propose a constitutional amendment; in this case it must be approved by a two-thirds vote of both houses, but it does not require the signature of the president.

Study by Committees

A bill is referred to a committee for consideration by either the Speaker of the House or the presiding

The House is a collection of powerful committees.

officer of the Senate. Rules govern which committee will get which bill, but sometimes a choice is possible. In the House the right of the Speaker to make such choices is an important component of his powers. (His decisions can be appealed to the full House.) In 1963 a civil rights bill was referred by the presiding officer of the Senate to the Commerce Committee in order to keep it out of the hands of the chairman of the Judiciary Committee, who was hostile to the bill. In the House the same piece of legislation was referred by the Speaker to the Judiciary Committee in order to keep it out of the grasp of the hostile chairman of the Interstate and Foreign Commerce Committee.

The Constitution requires that "all bills for raising revenue shall originate in the House of Representatives." The Senate can and does amend such bills, but only after the House has acted first. Bills that are not for raising revenue—that is, bills that do not change the tax laws—can originate in either house. In practice the House also originates appropriations bills—that is, bills directing how money shall be spent. Because of the House's special position in relation to revenue legislation, the committee that handles those bills—the Ways and Means Committee—is particularly powerful.

Most bills die in committee. They are often introduced only to get publicity for the member of Con-

gress or to enable the member to say to constituents or pressure groups that he or she "did something" on a matter concerning them. Bills of general interest— many of which are drafted in the executive branch but introduced by a member of Congress—are assigned to a subcommittee for a hearing, where witnesses appear, evidence is taken, and questions are asked. These hearings are used to inform members of Congress, to permit interest groups to speak out (whether or not they have anything helpful to say), and to build public support for a measure favored by the majority of the committee.

Though committee hearings are necessary and valuable, they also fragment the process of considering bills dealing with complex matters. Both power and information are dispersed in Congress, and thus it is difficult to take a comprehensive view of matters cutting across committee boundaries.

To deal with this problem Congress has established a process whereby a bill may now be referred to several committees that simultaneously consider it in whole or in part. This process, called **multiple referral,** was used in 1977 to send President Carter's energy proposals to six different committees in both the House and Senate. An even bigger multiple referral was used for the 1988 trade bill, which was considered by fourteen committees in the House and nine in the Senate. The advantage of this procedure is that all views have a chance to be heard; the disadvantage is that it takes a lot of time and gives opponents a greater chance to kill or modify the bill. And if the different committees disagree about the bill, their members have to come together in a gargantuan joint meeting to iron out their differences. In these cases the advantages of the committee system—providing expert knowledge and careful deliberation—are often lost. Before the practice was abolished in 1995, about a quarter of all House bills and resolutions went through multiple referrals. Under the new rules, the Speaker is allowed to send a bill to a second committee after the first is finished acting, or he may refer parts of a bill to separate committees. This process, called **sequential referral,** did not noticeably slow down the pace of legislative activity in the 104th Congress.

After the hearings the committee or subcommittee will "mark up" the bill—that is, make revisions and additions, some of which are extensive. These changes do not become part of the bill unless they are approved by the house of which the committee is a part. If a majority of the committee votes to report a bill out to the House or Senate, it goes forward. It is accompanied by a report that explains why the committee favors the bill and why it wishes to see its amendments, if any, adopted. Committee members who oppose the bill have an opportunity to include their dissenting opinions in the report.

If the committee does not report the bill out favorably, that ordinarily kills it. There is a procedure whereby the full House or Senate can get a bill that is stalled in committee out and onto the floor, but it is rarely used. In the House a **discharge petition** must be signed by 218 members; if the petition is approved by a vote of the House, the bill comes before it directly. In the Senate a member can move to discharge a committee of any bill, and if the motion passes, the bill comes before the Senate. During this century there have been over eight hundred efforts in the House to use discharge petitions; only two dozen have succeeded. Discharge is rarely tried in the Senate, in part because Senate rules permit almost any proposal to get to the floor as an amendment to another bill.

For a bill to come before either house, it must first be placed on a calendar. There are five such calendars in the House and two in the Senate (see the box above).

Though the bill goes onto a calendar, it is not necessarily considered in chronological order or even

> ## HOW THINGS WORK
>
> # Congressional Calendars
>
> **House**
>
> *Union Calendar*   Bills to raise revenue or spend money
>   Example: an appropriations bill
> *House Calendar*   Nonmoney bills of major importance
>   Example: a civil rights bill
> *Private Calendar*   Private bills
>   Example: a bill to waive the immigration laws so that a Philadelphia woman could be joined by her Italian husband
> *Consent Calendar*   Noncontroversial bills
>   Example: a resolution creating National Stenographers Week
> *Discharge Calendar*   Discharge petitions
>
> **Senate**
>
> *Executive Calendar*   Presidential nominations, proposed treaties
> *Calendar of Business*   All legislation

considered at all. In the House the Rules Committee reviews most bills and adopts a rule that governs the procedures under which they will be considered by the House. A **closed rule** sets a strict time limit on debate and forbids the introduction of any amendments from the floor, or forbids amendments except those offered by the sponsoring committee. Obviously such a rule can make it very difficult for opponents to do anything but vote yes or no on the measure. An **open rule** permits amendments from the floor. A **restrictive rule** permits some amendments but not others.

In the early 1970s most bills were debated under open rules. In the 1980s the Rules Committee—which is controlled by the Speaker—increasingly introduced bills for consideration under closed or restrictive rules in an effort to reduce the number of amendments from the floor (and, the Republicans claimed, to reduce Republican influence). By the end of the 1980s roughly half of all bills, and nearly three-fourths of all important ones, were debated under restrictive or closed rules. In 1992 only one-third of all bills were considered under an open

★ POLITICALLY SPEAKING ★

Riders and Christmas Trees

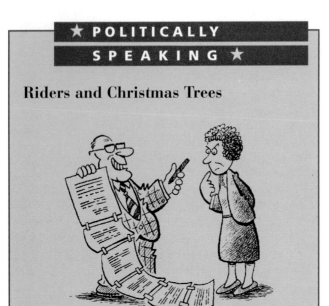

A **rider** is a provision added to a piece of legislation that is not germane to the bill's purpose. The goal is usually to achieve one of two outcomes: either to get the president (or governor) to sign an otherwise objectionable bill by attaching to it, as an amendment, a provision that the chief executive desperately wants to see enacted, or to get the president to veto a bill that he would otherwise sign by attaching to it, as an amendment, a provision that the chief executive strongly dislikes.

A rider is a convenient way for a legislator to get a pet project approved that might not be approved if it had to be voted on by itself. The term can be traced back to seventeenth-century England.

When a bill has lots of riders, it becomes a **Christmas tree bill.** In 1966, for example, the Foreign Investors Act, a bill designed to solve the balance-of-payments problem, had added to it riders giving assistance to hearse owners, the mineral ore business, importers of scotch whiskey, and presidential candidates.

Source: From *Safire's Political Dictionary* by William Safire. Copyright © 1968, 1972, 1978 by William Safire. Reprinted by permission of Random House, Inc. and the author.

the rules be suspended, which requires a two-thirds vote; (2) a discharge petition, as explained above, can be filed; or (3) the House can use the "Calendar Wednesday" procedure.* These methods are not used very often, but they are available if the Rules Committee departs too far from the sentiments of the House.

In theory few such barriers to floor consideration exist in the Senate. There bills may be considered in any order at any time whenever a majority of the Senate chooses. The majority leader, in consultation with the minority leader, schedules bills for consideration. In practice, however, getting proposals to the Senate floor is far more complicated. Whereas the House normally plows through its legislative schedule, ignoring individual members' complaints in favor of getting its work done, the Senate majority leader must accommodate the interests of individual senators before proceeding with the Senate's business.

Floor Debate—The House

Once on the floor, the bills are debated. In the House all revenue and most other bills are discussed by the "Committee of the Whole," which is nothing more than whoever happens to be on the floor at the time. The **quorum,** or minimum number of members who must be present for business to be conducted, is only 100 members for the Committee of the Whole. Obviously this number is easier to assemble than a quorum for the House itself, which the Constitution specifies as a majority, or 218 members. The Speaker does not preside but chooses another person to wield the gavel. The Committee of the Whole debates, amends, and generally decides the final shape of the bill, but technically cannot pass it. To do that the Committee of the Whole reports the bill back to the House (that is, to itself), which takes final action. During the debate in the Committee of the Whole, the committee sponsoring the bill guides the discussion, divides the time equally between proponents and opponents, and decides how long each member will be permitted

rule.[35] In 1995 the Republicans allowed more debate under open rules.

The House has at least three ways of bypassing the Rules Committee: (1) a member can move that

*On Wednesdays the list of committees of the House is called more or less in alphabetical order, and any committee can bring up for action a bill of its own already on a calendar. Action on a bill brought to the floor on Calendar Wednesday must be completed that day, or the bill goes back to committee. Since major bills rarely can be voted on in one day, this procedure is not often used.

to speak. If amendments are allowed under the rule, they must be germane to the purpose of the bill—extraneous matters (riders) are not allowed—and no one may speak for more than five minutes on an amendment. During this process people wishing to take time out to huddle about strategy or to delay action can demand a **quorum call**—a calling of the roll to find out whether the necessary minimum number of members are present. If a quorum is not present, the House must either adjourn or dispatch the sergeant at arms to round up missing members. The sponsoring committee almost always wins; its bill, as amended by it, usually is the version that the House passes.

Floor Debate—The Senate

Things are a good deal more casual in the Senate. Short of cloture (discussed below), there is no rule limiting debate, and members can speak for as long as they can stay on their feet. A senator's remarks need not be relevant to the matter under consideration (some senators have read aloud from the Washington telephone directory), and anyone can offer an amendment at any time. There is no Committee of the Whole. Amendments need not be germane to the purpose of the bill, and thus the Senate often attaches riders to bills.

In fact the opportunity to offer nongermane amendments gives a senator a chance to get a bill onto the floor without regard to the calendar or the schedule of the majority leader: he or she need only offer a pet bill as an "amendment" to a bill already under discussion. (This cannot be done to an appropriations bill.) Indeed, the entire committee hearing process can be bypassed in the Senate if the House has already passed the bill. In that case a senator can get the House-passed measure put directly onto the Senate calendar without committee action. In 1957 and again in 1964 this was done with House-passed civil rights bills to make certain that they would not be bottled up in the conservative Senate Judiciary Committee.

A Senate filibuster is difficult to break. The current **cloture rule** requires that sixteen senators sign a petition to move cloture. The motion is voted on two days after the petition is introduced; to pass, three-fifths of the entire Senate membership (sixty senators if there are no vacancies) must vote for it. If it passes, each senator is thereafter limited to one hour of debate on the bill under consideration. The total debate, including roll calls and the introduction of amendments, cannot exceed one hundred hours.

In recent years both filibusters and cloture votes have become more common. The filibuster occurs more frequently because it is now easier to stage one. Often it consists not of a senator's making a long speech but of endless requests for the clerk to call the roll. More filibusters means more cloture votes, which are now easier to win since the 1975 change lowering the required number of supporters from two-thirds to three-fifths of all senators. During the 100th Congress (1987–1988) there were almost as many cloture votes—forty-three—as there had been in the half century after the procedure was invented. Since 1975 about 40 percent of all cloture votes have succeeded in cutting off debate.

Conservatives have used the filibuster to try to block civil rights laws; liberals have used it to try to block decontrol of gas prices. Since both factions have found the filibuster useful, it seems most unlikely that it will ever be abolished, though it has been somewhat curtailed. One way to keep the Senate going during a filibuster is **double-tracking,** whereby the disputed bill is shelved temporarily so that the Senate can get on with other business. Because double-tracking permits the Senate to discuss and vote on matters other than the bill that is being filibustered, it is less costly to individual senators to stage a filibuster. In the past, before double-tracking, a senator and his allies had to keep talking around the clock to keep their filibuster alive. If they stopped talking, the Senate was free to take up other business. Opponents of the filibuster would bring cots and blankets to the Senate so that they could sleep and eat there, ready to take the floor the moment the filibuster faltered. But with double-tracking other business can go on while the stalled bill is temporarily set aside. As a result the number of filibusters has skyrocketed. In the words of two expert Senate watchers, the "Senate has become increasingly unmanageable as filibusters have become virtually commonplace on both major and minor pieces of legislation, raising the standard for passage of even routine bills from fifty to sixty votes and resulting in frequent delays in scheduling, stop-and-go patterns of floor debate," and the use of other procedures "that make the institution hostage to the whims of individual senators."[36]

What the threat of a filibuster means in practice is this: neither political party can control the Senate

The electronic voting system in the House of Representatives allows each member to vote by inserting a plastic card into a box fastened to the backs of many chairs and choosing "yea," "nay," or "present."

unless it has at least sixty votes. Neither party has had that many Senate seats since 1979, and so for the Senate to act there must be a bipartisan majority.

Methods of Voting

Some observers of Congress make the mistake of deciding who was for and who was against a bill by the final vote. This can be misleading—often a member of Congress will vote for final passage of a bill after having supported amendments that, if they had passed, would have made the bill totally different. To keep track of various members' voting records, therefore, it is often more important to know how they voted on key amendments than to know how they voted on the bill itself.

Finding that out is not always easy, though it has become more so in recent years. There are four procedures for voting in the House. A **voice vote** consists of the members' shouting "yea" or "nay"; a **division** (or standing) **vote** involves the members' standing and being counted. In neither a voice nor a standing vote are the names of members recorded as having voted one way or the other.

To learn how an individual votes there must be either a recorded teller vote or a roll call. In a **teller vote** the members pass between two tellers, the yeas first and then the nays. Since 1971 a teller vote can be "recorded," which means that, at the request of twenty members, clerks write down the names of those favoring or opposing a bill as they pass the tellers. Since teller votes but not roll calls may be taken in the Committee of the Whole, the use of a

recorded teller vote enables observers to find out how members voted in those important deliberations.

A **roll-call vote,** of course, consists of people answering "yea" or "nay" to their names. It can be done at the request of one-fifth of the representatives present in the House. When roll calls were handled orally, it was a time-consuming process, since the clerk had to drone though 435 names. Since 1973 an electronic voting system has been in operation that permits each member, by inserting a plastic card into a slot, to record his or her own vote and to learn the total automatically. Owing to the use of recorded teller votes and the advent of electronic roll-call votes, the number of recorded votes has gone up sharply in the House. There were only seventy-three House roll calls in 1955; twenty years later there were over eight times that many. Voting in the Senate is much the same, only simpler: there is no such thing as a teller vote, and no electronic counters are used.

If a bill passes the House and Senate in different forms, the differences must be reconciled if the bill is to become law. If they are minor, the last house to act may simply refer the bill back to the other house, which then accepts the alterations. If the differences are major, it is often necessary to appoint a conference committee to iron them out. Only a minority of bills require a conference. Each house must vote to form such a committee. The members are picked by the chairmen of the House and Senate standing committees that have been handling the legislation, with representation given to the minority as well as the majority party. There are usually between three and fifteen members from each house. No decision can be made unless approved by a majority of both delegations.

Bargaining is long and hard; in the past it was also secret. Now some conference sessions are open to the public. Often—as with President Carter's energy bill—the legislation is substantially rewritten in conference. Complex bills can lead to enormous conference committees. The 1988 trade bill went before a conference committee of two hundred members. Theoretically the conferees are not supposed to change anything already agreed to by both the House and Senate, but in the inevitable give-and-take even matters already approved may be changed.

In most cases the conference reports tend to favor, slightly, the Senate version of the bill. Several studies have suggested that the Senate wins in 57 to 65 per-

> **HOW THINGS WORK**
>
> # House-Senate Differences: A Summary
>
> | House | Senate |
> |---|---|
> | 435 members serve two-year terms. | 100 members serve rotating six-year terms. |
> | House members have only one major committee assignment, thus tend to be policy specialists. | Senators have two or more major committee assignments, thus tend to be policy generalists. |
> | Speaker's referral of bills to committee is hard to challenge. | Referral decisions are easy to challenge. |
> | Committees almost always consider legislation first. | Committee consideration is easily bypassed. |
> | Scheduling and rules are controlled by the majority party. | Scheduling and rules are generally agreed to by majority and minority leaders. |
> | Rules Committee is powerful; controls time of debate, admissibility of amendments. | Rules Committee is weak; few limits on debate or amendments. |
> | Debate is usually limited to one hour. | Debate is unlimited unless shortened by unanimous consent or by invoking cloture. |
> | Nongermane amendments may not be introduced from the floor. | Nongermane amendments may be introduced. |

cent of cases.[37] Whoever wins (and both sides always claim that they got everything out of the bargaining that they possibly could have), conferees report their agreement back to their respective houses, which usually consider the report immediately. The report can be accepted or rejected; it cannot be amended. In the great majority of cases it is accepted: the alternative is to have no bill at all, at least for that Congress. The bill, now in final form, goes to the president for signature or veto. If a veto is cast, the bill returns to the house of origin. There an effort can be made to override the veto. This requires that two-thirds of those present (provided that there is a quorum) must vote to override; this vote must be a roll call. If both houses override in this manner, the bill becomes law without the president's approval.

Reforming Congress

Most citizens are less interested in why members of Congress vote the way they do than they are in whether Congress as an institution serves the public interest and fulfills its mission as a democratic body. In recent years a number of proposals have been made to reform Congress—term limitations, new ethics and campaign finance laws, and organizational changes intended to reduce the power and perks of members while making it easier for Congress to pass needed legislation in a timely fashion.

It is important to recognize that the kind of reform proposed depends not only on what is feasible but also on an underlying idea of what Congress ought to be. For example, which of the two conceptions of democracy discussed in Chapter 1—direct or representative—should Congress embody? What definition of "the public interest" should Congress favor? And by what criteria should one decide whether a given piece of legislation is so badly needed that a failure to pass it promptly constitutes a failure of Congress?

Representative or Direct Democracy?

The Framers of the Constitution believed that representatives should refine, not reflect, public wishes. Today, however, many believe that elected officials should mirror, not mediate, the majority's views. Some would go so far as to bypass Congress entirely. A survey conducted in 1993 found that two-thirds of Americans favored having binding national referenda on policy questions and about half favored selecting members of Congress randomly from lists of eligible voters. (One in six even supported the idea of auctioning seats in Congress to the highest bidders as a way of retiring the national debt.)[38] A more moderate vision of direct democracy in Congress would have citizen legislators serving short terms as the people's delegates (voting as a majority of their constituents want them to vote), with small staffs and no perks. By contrast, representative democracy in Congress would mean professional legislators serving as the people's trustees (consulting their constituents' views but voting their consciences), with expert staffs, no term limits, and such work-related perks (travel allowances, mailing privileges) as they required to fulfill their duties.

Proper Guardians of the Public Weal?

Everyone agrees that Congress should serve the public interest, but what is the public interest? In *Federalist* No. 10 James Madison offered one answer. To him the public interest—"the permanent and aggregate interests of the community"—was to be expressed concretely in national laws that transcended "local prejudices" and frustrated the "sinister designs" of factions.

In Madison's view the public interest was not the simple sum of whatever societal interests demanded from government. Instead members of Congress were to be "proper guardians of the public weal," representatives who served "the great and aggregate interests" of the country. To Madison the art of the public-spirited legislator was to know the true ends of the body politic and to effect reasonable compromises among competing societal interests via the legislative process. He held that "the regulation of these various and interfering interests" was the "principal task" of representatives, and he argued that a congress fashioned institutionally as a representative body, rather than one that carried out direct democracy, would be best able to balance contending societal interests without succumbing to the demands of factions.

Madison's conception of the public interest lives on in contemporary calls for reforming Congress to make the body less captive of so-called special interests, our modern term for factions. Some people believe that by outlawing political action committees, fine-tuning congressional ethics regulations, or taking related measures Congress would become less accessible to special interests and more solicitous of the public interest.

The difficulty, however, is that one person's special-interest group is often another's professional association, trade group, or public-interest lobby. If you were a member of Congress, would you listen to the views of the National Abortion Federation, the U.S. Catholic Conference, both, or neither?

A Decisive Congress or a Deliberative One?

Madison and the other Framers recognized that Congress, as a representative body designed to protect the public interest while balancing the competing views and interests of the citizenry, would normally proceed slowly. Congress was designed for deliberative, not decisive, action. It was intended to check and balance strong leaders in the executive branch, not automatically cede its authority to them. Its institutional mission was more to block or delay popular legislative action than it was to speed it along.

But many contemporary critics of Congress do not share the Framers' vision of what Congress ought to be. Many wish to reform Congress in ways that might end "policy gridlock" by making Congress capable of speedily adopting sweeping changes in national policies. The problem, however, is that a Congress capable of doing much good quickly would also be capable of doing much bad quickly. A Congress that could move decisively to adopt wise budget, health, or trade policies could also move decisively to adopt unwise ones, and a Congress that could suddenly endorse and enact popular laws could do the same for unpopular ones.

Imposing Term Limits

As explained in Chapter 2, the Antifederalists (those who opposed the new Constitution in the late 1780s) believed that a strong national government would grow corrupt, distant from the people, and contemptuous of states' rights. Among other measures to check the national government's power and ensure its responsiveness to the popular will, many Antifederalists believed that members of Congress should stand for election annually and that no citizen should serve more than a few terms in Congress.

Today many Americans have come to the view that the Antifederalists were right about the need for some type of term limits in Congress. When around 95 percent of House incumbents are reelected, people worry that popular control of Congress has weakened, while state and local officials complain that there is no room for them to move up the political

MEMORANDUM

To: Representative Peter Skerry
From: Martha Bayles, legislative aide
Subject: The Size of the House of Representatives

The House can decide how big it wishes to be. When it was created, there was one representative for every 30,000 people. Now there is one for every 600,000. In most other democracies each member of parliament represents far fewer than 600,000 people. Doubling the size of the House may be a way of avoiding term limits.

Arguments for:

1. Doubling the size of the House would reduce the huge demand for constituent services each member now faces.
2. A bigger House would represent more shades of opinion more fairly.
3. Each member could raise less campaign money because his or her campaign would be smaller.

Arguments against:

1. A bigger House would be twice as hard to manage, and it would take even longer to pass legislation.
2. Campaigns in districts of 300,000 people would cost as much as ones in districts with 600,000 people.
3. Interest groups do a better job of representing public opinion than would a House with more members.

Your decision:
Increase size of House _____
Do not increase size of House _____

Should We Have a Bigger Congress?

November 15
WASHINGTON

A powerful citizens organization has demanded that the House of Representatives be made larger so that voters can feel closer to their members. Each representative now speaks for about 600,000 people—far too many, the group argues, to make it possible for all points of view to be heard. In its petition . . .

ladder. A 1992 survey showed that about 80 percent of Americans felt there should be a limit on the number of terms to which a senator or member of the House can be elected.[39]

The contemporary term-limit movement began in the fall of 1990, when term-limit measures passed in three statewide initiatives (California, Colorado, and Oklahoma). By 1994 twenty-two states had voted, in most places by large majorities, to impose limits on the number of years their representatives could serve in Congress, but the Supreme Court has ruled that such state-imposed limits on members of Congress are unconstitutional.

Proposals that would place a lifetime limit on legislative service would result in an amateur legislature. Let us assume, as many supporters of these measures do, that amateurs in Congress would act out of personal conviction rather than from the desire to be reelected. Reelection-minded professional politicians must be concerned about what their constituents think and want; principled amateur legislators need not be. Would a Congress composed of such legislators be good or bad, better or worse? The answer, of course, depends largely on whether you favor representative or direct democracy.

But whichever you favor, do not suppose that amateur legislators would eliminate policy gridlock: people who act out of conviction are more prone to disagree and less apt to compromise than people whose profession it is to practice the ABC's of democratic politics—making *a*lliances, striking *b*argains, and forging *c*ompromises.[40] In a diverse, pluralistic, and multicultural society, a politics of unbending

principle can be a recipe for political stalemate—or worse.

By the same token do not suppose that all the amateur legislators would be true political novices. As should be obvious, the typical American is simply not well positioned to quit work in order to spend a year or two in Washington, D.C. But there are people for whom such a brief tour of duty in Congress would be both feasible and desirable. With lifetime term limits many of tomorrow's citizen legislators on Capitol Hill could well be yesterday's lawyer lobbyists from K Street.

On the other hand, were term limits to take the form of limiting continuous service in one legislative branch without restricting eligibility for other elected offices, the probable result would be a Congress of office-hopping political professionals who must constantly prepare to run for the other chamber or some other office. In a Congress dominated by members who played electoral "musical chairs," it is probable that seniority would fade as the basis for distributing committee assignments, party leadership would change hands every few years, and individual members would probably keep one eye fixed on their next constituencies (local, regional, statewide, or national) and would have every incentive to act in ways that brought them public attention rather than work behind the scenes to get things done.

Reducing Powers and Perks

To many term-limitation enthusiasts and other would-be reformers, Congress is grossly overstaffed and self-indulgent. It is quick to impose new laws on states, cities, businesses, and average citizens but slow to apply those same laws to itself and its members. It is quick to pass **pork-barrel legislation**—bills that give tangible benefits (highways, dams, post offices) to constituents in the hope of winning their votes in return—but slow to tackle complex and controversial questions of national policy. The reformers' image of Congress is unflattering, but is it wholly unwarranted?

Fencing in the Frank   No perk is more treasured by members of Congress than the frank. Members of Congress are allowed by law to send material through the mail free of charge by substituting their facsimile signature (*frank*) for postage. But rather than using this **franking privilege** to keep their constituents informed about the government, most members use franked newsletters and questionnaires as campaign literature. That is why use of the frank soars in the months before an election. For example, more than 30 million newsletters were sent out in March 1992, the last month in which members facing June primaries could send franked mailings.[41]

Thus the frank amounts to a taxpayer subsidy of members' campaigns, a perk that bolsters the electoral fortunes of incumbents. Some reformers do not believe that it is possible to fence in congressional use of the frank for public education or other legitimate purposes, and so they propose abolishing it outright. Other reformers argue that the frank can be fenced in by prohibiting mailings just before primaries and general elections (to dilute any electoral impact) and by placing a prominent notice, "Paid For at Taxpayer Expense," on the front of every franked piece of mail.[42] Such measures could well discourage members from abusing their franking privilege. Reformers cheered in 1995 when the House resolved to limit the use of the frank and to prevent members from using the frank as a campaign tool. The House Oversight Committee voted to cut franking authorization by one-third of the 1994 level.

Placing Congress Under the Law   For years Congress routinely exempted itself from many of the laws it passed. In defense of this practice members said that if members of Congress were subject to, for example, the minimum wage laws, the executive branch, charged with enforcing these laws, would acquire excessive power over Congress. This would violate the separation of powers. But as public criticism of Congress grew and confidence in government declined, more and more people demanded that Congress subject itself to the laws that applied to everybody else. In 1995 the 104th Congress did this by passing a bill that obliges Congress to obey eleven important laws governing things such as civil rights, occupational safety, fair labor standards, and family leave.

The bipartisan Congressional Accountability Act of 1995 had to solve a key problem: under the constitutional doctrine of separated powers, it would have been unwise and perhaps unconstitutional for the executive branch to enforce congressional compliance with executive-branch regulations. So Congress created the independent Office of Compliance and an employee grievance procedure to deal with implementation. Now Congress, too, must obey laws such as the Civil Rights Act, the Equal Pay Act, the Age Discrimination Act, and the Family and Medical Care Leave Act.

★ POLITICALLY SPEAKING ★

Pork Barrel

Before the Civil War it was the custom to take salt pork from barrels and distribute it to the slaves. Often the eagerness of the slaves to get the food would result in a rush on the barrels, with each slave trying to get as much as possible.

By the 1870s members of Congress were using the term *pork* to refer to benefits for their districts and *pork barrel* to mean the piece of legislation containing those benefits.

Today the classic example of pork-barrel legislation is the rivers and harbors bill, which provides appropriations for countless dams, bridges, and canals to be built in congressional districts all over the country.

Source: From *Safire's Political Dictionary* by William Safire. Copyright © 1968, 1972, 1978 by William Safire. Reprinted by permission of Random House, Inc. and the author.

Trimming the Pork   Bills containing money for local dams, bridges, roads, and monuments are referred to disparagingly as pork-barrel legislation. Reformers complain that when members act to "bring home the bacon," Congress misallocates tax dollars by supporting projects with trivial social benefits in order to bolster their reelection prospects.

No one can doubt the value of trimming unnecessary spending, but pork is not necessarily the villain it is made out to be. For example, the main cause of the budget deficit was the increase in spending on entitlement programs (like health care and interest on the national debt) without a corresponding increase in taxes. Spending on pork is a small fraction of spending on entitlements, and most categories of pork spending have decreased in the last ten or fifteen years. Furthermore, one person's pork is another person's necessity. No doubt some congressional districts get an unnecessary bridge or highway, but others get bridges and highways that are long overdue. The notion that every bridge or road a member of Congress gets for his or her district is wasteful pork is tantamount to saying that no member attaches any importance to merit.

Even if all pork were bad, it would still be necessary. Congress is an independent branch of government, and each member is, by constitutional design, the advocate of his or her district or state. No member's vote can be won by coercion, and few can be had by mere appeals to party loyalty or presidential needs. Pork is a way of obtaining consent. The only alternative is bribery, but bribery, besides being wrong, would benefit only the member, whereas pork usually benefits voters in the member's district. If you want to eliminate pork, you must eliminate Congress, by converting it into a parliament under the control of a powerful party leader or prime minister. In a tightly controlled parliament no votes need be bought; they can be commanded. But members of such a parliament can do little to help their constituents cope with government or to defend them against bureaucratic abuses, nor can they investigate the conduct of the executive branch. The price of a citizen-oriented Congress is a pork-oriented Congress.

Ethics and Congress

Most contemporary proposals to reform Congress are motivated at least in part by a belief that "congressional ethics" has become an oxymoron.* The Framers of the Constitution hoped that members of Congress would be virtuous citizens, but they feared that some would not. They had, as stated earlier, a rather sober view of human nature and designed the system of checks and balances in part to minimize the chance that anybody, by gaining undue influence over one part of the government, would be able to tyrannize over the other parts.

It could be argued that this very separation of power made corruption more, rather than less, likely. If power were concentrated in one set of hands—say, those of a prime minister—nobody would have any incentive to bribe or even influence any other political figure; there is little that subordinate officials could do for that person. And though a favor seeker might try to influence the prime minister, few could pay the price of bribing someone with so much power. When bits and pieces of power are placed in many different hands, as in the United States, there are many opportunities to exercise influence: lots of officials have something that they could sell, and at a price that many favor seekers could afford.

For example, the appointive power is shared by the president and the Senate. Since the Senate will not confirm anybody for appointment to federal office who is personally obnoxious to either senator from the candidate's state (the rule of "senatorial courtesy"), the opportunity exists for an office seeker to try to influence a senator to get the desired appointment. The stage is also set for a senator, who may want the president to nominate a certain person, to delay some piece of presidential legislation until the nomination is made, or for the president to try to get a piece of legislation passed by offering to appoint the senator's campaign manager, brother-in-law, or law partner to a lucrative federal post.

Some of these attempts at influence may involve money; some may not. The point is that divided power means divided responsibility, and divided responsibility creates the possibility for evaded responsibility. It also creates the need to use influence to assemble enough power to get anything done. What the Constitution has separated, individuals must pull together; sometimes the pulling together involves mere persuasion, sometimes an exchange of favors, occasionally the payment of money.

Though the moral climate of American politics has improved in the last century, scandals continue. From 1941 to 1989 nearly fifty members of Congress faced criminal charges; most were convicted. From 1978 to 1992 Congress considered charges involving sixty-three members; thirty-one were sanctioned or convicted, and sixteen resigned or announced their intention to retire.[43] Charges of congressional misconduct included misuse of funds, having sex with minors, failing to disclose income, and accepting illegal gifts.

---

*An oxymoron is a phrase that combines contradictory terms ("deafening silence").

The two most dramatic events were the 1980–1981 Abscam investigation and the 1989 Jim Wright hearings. In the former six House members and one senator were convicted of having accepted money from an FBI agent posing as a wealthy Arab seeking political favors. In the latter House Speaker Wright was found by the House Ethics Committee to have broken rules against taking certain gifts and exceeding limits on outside income. The Speaker resigned.

In 1995 Senator Robert Packwood (R-Oreg.) was forced to resign from Congress after the Ethics Committee recommended that he be expelled for having sexually harassed various women and for refusing to be completely cooperative with the ethics investigation. In 1997 Speaker Gingrich was fined $300,000 for having improperly raised money.

These scandals, together with the large amount of PAC money given to legislators, have led many people to conclude that "we have the best Congress money can buy." No doubt there are moral failings, as there would be among any group of 535 powerful men and women, but it is not clear that Congress is inherently corrupt. Ethics codes and related reforms enacted in 1978, 1989, and 1995 have placed members of Congress under tight rules governing financial disclosure, accepting gifts, and other practices that were already regulated, while also prohibiting numerous practices (such as the use of office accounts for campaign purposes) that had been unregulated. There "are more rules than there used to be and more rules than in any other political system. A comparative study of twenty-five countries with the most developed ethics rules for national legislators found that regulations in the United States are clearly the most restrictive."[44]

Each successive wave of ethics laws has been predicated on the assumption that improper influence is associated with financial transactions, yet obviously that is not always the case. Many members of Congress who in the past earned substantial incomes from speaking and writing did not have their votes corrupted by such activities; other members of Congress who rarely take such fees may be heavily influenced, perhaps unduly so, by personal friendships and political alliances that have no direct monetary value at all. And no ethics code can address the bargaining among members of Congress, or between members of Congress and the president, involving the exchange of favors and votes.

HOW THINGS WORK

Rules on Congressional Ethics

Senate

Gifts: No gifts (in money, meals, or things) totaling $100 or more from anyone except a spouse or personal friend.

Lobbyists may not pay for gifts, official travel, legal defense funds, or charitable contributions to groups controlled by senators.

Fees: No fees for lectures or writing ("honoraria"), except that fees of up to $2,000 may go to a senator-designated charity.

Outside earned income may not exceed 15 percent of a senator's salary.

Ex-senators may not try to influence members of Congress for one year after leaving the Senate.

Mass mailings: No senator may receive more than $50,000 from the Senate to send out a mailing to constituents.

House

Gifts: No gifts (in money, meals, or things) totaling $100 or more from anyone except a spouse or personal friend.

Lobbyists may not offer gifts or pay for travel, even if lobbyist is a spouse or personal friend.

Travel: House members may travel at the expense of others if travel is for officially connected meetings.

Fees: No honoraria for House members.

Ex–House members may not lobby Congress for one year after leaving office.

Moreover, the ethics rules seem to favor people with inherited wealth or those who earned large sums before entering Congress. When the Senate voted in 1990 to limit the outside income its members could earn (mostly by writing and speaking) to 15 percent of their Senate salary, Senator Daniel Patrick Moynihan, who can earn a lot from writing and speaking, proposed an amendment to limit what senators could receive from their "unearned income" (that is, their investments and inherited

How Congress Raises Its Pay

For over two hundred years Congress has tried to find a politically painless way to raise its own pay. It has managed to vote itself a pay increase twenty-three times in those two centuries, but usually at the price of a hostile public reaction. Twice during the nineteenth century a pay raise led to a massacre of incumbents in the next election.

Knowing this, Congress has invented various ways to get a raise without actually appearing to vote for it. These have included the following:

- Voting for a tax deduction for expenses incurred as a result of living in Washington
- Creating a citizens commission that could recommend a pay increase that would take effect automatically provided Congress did not vote *against* it
- Linking increases in pay to decreases in honoraria (that is, speaking fees)

In 1989 a commission recommended a congressional pay raise of over 50 percent (from $89,500 to $135,000) and a ban on honoraria. The House planned to let it take effect automatically. But the public wouldn't have it, demanding that Congress vote on the raise—and vote it down. It did.

Embarrassed by its maneuvering, Congress retreated. At the end of 1989 it voted itself (as well as most top executive and judicial branch members) a small pay increase (7.9 percent for representatives, 9.9 percent for senators) that also provided for automatic cost-of-living adjustments (up to 5 percent a year) in the future. But the automatic adjustments in congressional pay have been rejected every year in recorded roll-call votes. Apparently nobody in Congress wants to be accused of "getting rich" at the taxpayers' expense.

wealth) to 15 percent of their Senate salaries. It passed. Had the bill become law (which it did not, lacking presidential approval), it would have meant that the many Senate millionaires would have had either to leave their money to charity or leave the Senate. Moynihan reasoned that calling senators unethical if they made too much money by working, while calling them ethical if they did no work more arduous than collecting dividends, made no sense.

It might not have made sense to the Framers either. Their object was not to create a simon-pure Congress but to create one that was powerful, one that would be composed of representatives who (at least in the lower house) could be closely checked by the voters, and one that would offer manifold opportunities for competing interests and opinions to check one another. Their goal was liberty more than morality, though they knew that in the long run the latter was essential to the former.

Summary

Over the last half century or so Congress, especially the House, has evolved through three stages. The modern Congress is an uneasy combination of stages two and three.

During the first stage, lasting from the end of World War I until the early 1960s, the House was dominated by powerful committee chairmen who controlled the agenda, decided which members would get what services for their constituents, and tended to follow the leadership of the Speaker. Newer members were expected to be seen but not heard; power and prominence came only after a long apprenticeship. Congressional staffs were small, and so members dealt with each other face to face. In

How to Look Up Facts About Congress

To find out how Congress is organized, staffed, and run:

Congressional Quarterly, *Guide to Congress*. 3rd ed. Washington, D.C.: Congressional Quarterly, 1982. One volume that covers almost everything.

Congressional Directory (published annually by Congress). Lists members of Congress, committee assignments, telephone numbers, maps of districts.

Congressional Staff Directory. Lists all staffers and gives biographical sketches.

To find out about the political inclinations and constituency characteristics of members of Congress:

Michael Barone et al. *The Almanac of American Politics*. Revised every two years, this is a candid description of districts, states, members of Congress, and how they vote.

Congressional District Data Book. Published by the Census Bureau, it compiles all relevant census data by congressional district.

To find out what is going on in Congress currently:

Congressional Quarterly Weekly Report. A weekly summary of issues, votes, and politics. Commercially published.

Congressional Record. The official, verbatim account of what is said (after being revised by members of Congress who do the saying). Published daily by the Government Printing Office while Congress is in session.

To find out what Congress did in the past:

Congressional Quarterly Almanac. Published each year as a summary of issues, votes, and politics.

Congressional Quarterly: Congress and the Nation. 8 vols., 1945–1992. Convenient compilation of past Almanacs.

To find out the exact wording of bills and laws:

United States Statutes at Large. Published by the Government Printing Office; the laws and volumes are chronologically arranged.

Digest of Public Bills. Published by the Congressional Research Service.

---

dealing with other members it helped to have a southern accent: half of all committee chairmen in both the House and the Senate were from the South. Not many laws were passed over their objections.

The second stage emerged in the early 1970s, in part as the result of trends already under way (for example, the steady growth in the number of staffers assigned to each member) and in part as a result of changes in procedures and organization brought about by younger, especially northern, members. Dissatisfied with southern resistance to civil rights bills and emboldened by a sharp increase in the number of liberals who had been elected in the Johnson landslide of 1964, the House Democratic caucus adopted rules that allowed the caucus to select committee chairmen without regard to seniority, dramatically increased the number and staffs of subcommittees (for the first time, the Ways and Means Committee was required to have subcommittees), authorized individual committee members (instead of the chairman) to choose the chairmen of these subcommittees, ended the ability of chairmen to refuse to call meetings, and made it much harder for those meetings to be closed to the public. The installation of electronic voting made it easier to require recorded votes, and so the number of times each member had to go on record rose sharply. The Rules Committee was instructed to issue more rules that would allow floor amendments.

At the same time, the number of southern Democrats in leadership positions began to decline, and the conservatism of the remaining ones began to lessen. (In 1990 southerners held only a quarter of committee chairmanships in the House and none of the major party leadership posts.) Moreover, northern and southern Democrats began to vote together a bit more frequently (though the conservative Boll Weevils remained a significant—and often swing—group).

These changes created a House ideally suited to serve the reelection needs of its members. Each representative could be an individual political entrepreneur, seeking publicity, claiming credit, introducing bills, holding subcommittee hearings, and assigning staffers to work on constituents' problems. There was

MEMORANDUM

To: Representative Sally Brook
From: Joe Tell, chief of staff
Subject: Proposal for Appointment by Party Leaders

You are on record as opposing the seniority system, but you have hitherto expressed no views in public about other methods by which committee chairs can be selected. One is election by party caucus. Letting party members elect committee chairs has some advantages: autocratic chairs can be ousted and committee chairs are likely to reflect the views of most party members. But it also has several disadvantages: it invites bruising fights for chairships that can divide party members and produce committee chairs who are not loyal to party leaders. Another method, now being debated around town and about which you might be asked at tomorrow's press briefing, is appointment by party leaders.

Arguments for:

1. Having the speaker, majority leader, or minority leader choose chairs would increase party discipline and accountability.
2. Appointment by party leaders would make it easier for party programs to be enacted.

Arguments against:

1. Concentrating so much power in the hands of party leaders could corrupt even the best or most public-spirited of them.
2. Chairships could be denied to qualified and worthy members just because they are out of favor with party leaders.

Your decision:
Favor proposal _____
Oppose proposal _____

Nonpartisan Panel Proposes Letting Party Chiefs Pick Committee Chairs

February 14
WASHINGTON

Traditionally, there has been only one way to become a congressional committee chair: outlast everyone else. The so-called seniority system let the person with the longest tenure on a committee chair it. This eliminated fights over selection, and made it easier for legislators with unpopular views and for African Americans with tenure to become chairs. But, critics claim, it also sometimes landed incompetent people atop important committees, and made it harder for party leaders to move major legislation. Yesterday, a nonpartisan group of experts called for giving the seniority system "a decent but deep burial" and letting party leaders appoint committee chairs . . .

no need to defer to powerful party leaders or committee chairmen. But because representatives in each party were becoming more alike ideologically, there was a rise in party voting. Congress became a career attractive to men and women skilled in these techniques, and these people entered Congress in large numbers. Their skill was manifest in the growth of the sophomore surge—the increase in their winning percentage during their first reelection campaign.

Even junior members could now make their mark on legislation. In the House more floor amendments were offered and passed; in the Senate filibusters became more commonplace. Owing to multiple referrals and overlapping subcommittee jurisdictions, more members could participate in writing bills and overseeing government agencies.

But lurking within the changes that defined the second stage were others, less noticed at the time, that created the beginnings of a new phase. The third stage was an effort in the House to strengthen and centralize party leadership. The Speaker acquired the power to appoint a majority of the members of the Rules Committee. That body, worried by the flood of floor amendments, began issuing more restrictive rules. By the mid-1980s this had reached the point where Republicans were complaining that they were being gagged. The Speaker also got control of the Democratic Steering and Policy Committee (it assigns new members to committees) and was given the power to refer bills to several committees simultaneously.

These opportunities for becoming a powerful Speaker were not noticed while the affable Tip O'Neill of Massachusetts held that post, but when Jim Wright of Texas replaced O'Neill, he began making full use of those powers. Perhaps if he had not stumbled over his ethical problems, Wright might have succeeded in becoming the policy leader of the House, setting the agenda and getting much of it adopted. The replacement of Wright by Tom Foley of Washington signaled a return to a more accommodative leadership style. Foley's replacement, Republican Newt Gingrich, was a more assertive policy leader. The evolution of the House remains an incomplete story; it is not yet clear whether it will remain in stage two or find some way of moving decisively into stage three. For now it has elements of both.

Congress is a collection of individual representatives from states and districts who play no role in choosing the president and hence are free to serve the interests of their constituents, their personal political views, and (to a limited extent) the demands of congressional leaders. In serving those interests members of necessity must rely on investigating, negotiating, and compromising, all of which may annoy voters who want Congress to be "decisive." The unpopularity of Congress is made worse by the recent tendency of its members to become ideologically more polarized.

Women and African Americans have increased their membership in Congress. The more important change, however, has been the increased ability of incumbents to get reelected. This reflects not how congressional districts are defined but instead the growth of constituent service and name familiarity, and the weakening of party loyalties, among voters.

Meanwhile the Senate remains as individualistic and decentralized as ever—a place where it has always been difficult to exercise strong leadership.

Though its members may complain that Congress is collectively weak, to any visitor from abroad it seems extraordinarily powerful, probably the most powerful legislative body in the world. Congress has always been jealous of its constitutional independence and authority. Three compelling events led to Congress's reasserting its authority: the increasingly unpopular war in Vietnam; the Watergate scandals, which revealed a White House meddling illegally in the electoral process; and the advent of divided governments—with one party in control of the presidency and the other in control of Congress.

In 1973 Congress passed, over a presidential veto, the War Powers Act, giving it a greater voice in the use of American forces abroad. The following year it passed the Congressional Budget and Impoundment Control Act, which denied the president the right to refuse to spend money appropriated by Congress and allowed Congress to play a greater role in the budget process. It passed more laws to provide a legislative veto over proposed presidential actions, especially with respect to the sale of arms abroad. Not all these steps have withstood the tests of time or Supreme Court review, but taken together they symbolize the resurgence of congressional authority and helped set the stage for sharper conflicts between Congress and the presidency.

Claims that Congress became weak as the president grew stronger are a bit overdrawn. As we shall see in the next chapter, the view from the White House is quite different. Recent presidents have complained bitterly of their inability to get Congress even to act on, much less approve, many of their key proposals and have resented what they regard as congressional interference in the management of executive-branch agencies and the conduct of foreign affairs.

World Wide Web Resources

- House of Representatives: www.house.gov
- Senate: www.senate.gov
- Library of Congress
  thomas.loc.gov
  lcweb.loc.gov/global/legislative/congress

- For news about Congress
  Roll Call magazine: www.rollcall.com
  C-SPAN: www.c-span.org

Key Terms

bicameral legislature
  p. 279
filibuster *p. 283*
marginal districts *p. 286*
safe districts *p. 286*
conservative coalition
  p. 289
malapportionment
  p. 290
gerrymandering *p. 290*
majority-minority
  districts *p. 291*
descriptive representation
  p. 292

substantive representa-
  tion *p. 292*
sophomore surge *p. 293*
majority leader *p. 299*
minority leader *p. 299*
whip *p. 299*
party polarization
  p. 302
caucus (congressional)
  p. 304
standing committees
  p. 306
select committees *p. 306*
joint committees *p. 306*

conference committee
  p. 306
public bill *p. 313*
private bill *p. 313*
simple resolution *p. 313*
concurrent resolution
  p. 313
joint resolution *p. 313*
multiple referral *p. 314*
sequential referral *p. 315*
discharge petition *p. 315*
closed rule *p. 315*
open rule *p. 315*
restrictive rule *p. 315*

rider *p. 316*
Christmas tree bill *p. 316*
quorum *p. 316*
quorum call *p. 317*
cloture rule *p. 317*
double-tracking *p. 317*
voice vote *p. 318*
division vote *p. 318*
teller vote *p. 318*
roll-call vote *p. 318*
pork-barrel legislation
  p. 322
franking privilege *p. 322*

Suggested Readings

Davidson, Roger H., and Walter J. Oleszek. *Congress and Its Members.* 7th ed. Washington, D.C.: Congressional Quarterly Press, 2000. Complete and authoritative account of who is in Congress and how it operates.

Dodd, Lawrence C., and Bruce I. Oppenheimer, eds. *Congress Reconsidered.* 6th ed. Washington, D.C.: Congressional Quarterly Press, 1997. Recent studies of congressional politics.

Fenno, Richard F., Jr. *Congressmen in Committees.* Boston: Little, Brown, 1973. Study of the styles of twelve standing committees.

Fiorina, Morris P. *Congress: Keystone of the Washington Establishment.* 2nd ed. New Haven, Conn.: Yale University Press, 1989. Argues that congressional behavior is aimed at guaranteeing their chances for reelection.

Jacobson, Gary. *The Politics of Congressional Elections.* 4th ed. New York: Longman, 1997. Authoritative study of how members of Congress are elected.

Maass, Arthur. *Congress and the Common Good.* New York: Basic Books, 1983. Insightful account of congressional operations, especially those involving legislative-executive relations. Disputes Fiorina's argument that reelection needs explain congressional behavior.

Malbin, Michael J. *Unelected Representatives.* New York: Basic Books, 1980. Study of the influence of congressional staff members.

Mann, Thomas E., and Norman J. Ornstein. *Renewing Congress.* 2 vols. Washington, D.C.: Brookings Institution and American Enterprise Institute, 1993. Superb, up-to-date overview of what's really wrong with Congress and how to fix it.

Smith, Steven S., and Christopher J. Deering. *Committees in Congress.* Washington, D.C.: Congressional Quarterly, 1984. Analysis of how different kinds of congressional committees operate.

Sundquist, James L. *The Decline and Resurgence of Congress.* Washington, D.C.: Brookings Institution, 1981. A history of the fall and, after 1973, the rise of congressional power vis-à-vis the president.

The Presidency

12

Enduring Questions

1. Should we want our president to be stronger or weaker than Congress?
2. How can we get the best people to run for president?
3. Does the personal character of a president make a difference in how he does his job?
4. Should we abolish the Electoral College?

Presidents and Prime Ministers

Divided Government
Does Gridlock Matter? • Is Policy Gridlock Bad?

The Evolution of the Presidency
Concerns of the Founders • The Electoral College •
The President's Term of Office • The First Presidents •
The Jacksonians • The Reemergence of Congress

The Powers of the President

The Office of the President
The White House Office • The Executive Office of
the President • The Cabinet • Independent
Agencies, Commissions, and Judgeships

Who Gets Appointed

Presidential Character

The Power to Persuade
The Three Audiences • Popularity and Influence •
The Decline in Popularity •

The Power to Say No
Veto • Executive Privilege • Impoundment of Funds

The President's Program
Putting Together a Program • Attempts to
Reorganize

Presidential Transition
The Vice President • Problems of Succession •
Impeachment

How Powerful Is the President?

rofessor Jones speaks to his political science class: "The president of the United States occupies one of the most powerful offices in the world. Presidents Kennedy and Johnson sent American troops to Vietnam, President Bush sent them to Saudi Arabia, and President Clinton sent them to Kosovo, all without war being declared by Congress. President Nixon imposed wage and price controls on the country. Between them, Presidents Carter and Reagan selected most of the federal judges now on the bench; thus the political philosophies of these two men were stamped on the courts. No wonder people talk about our having an 'imperial presidency.'"

A few doors down the hall, Professor Smith speaks to her class: "The president, compared to the prime ministers of other democratic nations, is one of the weakest chief executives anywhere. President Carter signed an arms-limitation treaty with the Soviets, but the Senate wouldn't ratify it. President Reagan was not allowed even to test antisatellite weapons, and in 1986 Congress rejected his budget before the ink was dry. President Clinton's health care plan was ignored, and the House voted to

The first cabinet: left to right, Secretary of War Henry Knox, Secretary of State Thomas Jefferson, Attorney General Edmund Randolph, Secretary of the Treasury Alexander Hamilton, and President George Washington.

impeach him. Regularly, subordinates who are supposed to be loyal to the president leak his views to the press and undercut his programs before Congress. No wonder people call the U.S. president a 'pitiful, helpless giant.' "

Can Professors Jones and Smith be talking about the same office? Who is right? In fact they are both right. The American presidency is a unique office, with elements of great strength *and* profound weakness built into it by its constitutional origins.

Presidents and Prime Ministers

The popularly elected president is an American invention. Of the roughly five dozen countries in which there is some degree of party competition and thus, presumably, some measure of free choice for the voters, only sixteen have a directly elected president, and thirteen of these are nations of North and

South America. The democratic alternative is for the chief executive to be a prime minister, chosen by and responsible to the parliament. This system prevails in most Western European countries as well as in Israel and Japan. There is no nation with a purely presidential political system in Europe; France combines a directly elected president with a prime minister and parliament.[1]

In a parliamentary system the prime minister is the chief executive. The prime minister is chosen not by the voters but by the legislature, and he or she in turn selects the other ministers from the members of parliament. If the parliament has only two major parties, the ministers will usually be chosen from the majority party; if there are many parties (as in Italy), several parties may participate in a coalition cabinet. The prime minister remains in power as long as his or her party has a majority of the seats in the legislature or as long as the coalition he or she has assembled holds together. The voters choose who is to be a member of parliament—usually by voting for one or another party—but cannot choose who is to be the chief executive officer.

Whether a nation has a presidential or a parliamentary system makes a big difference in the identity and powers of the chief executive.

Presidents Are Often Outsiders People become president by winning elections, and sometimes winning is easier if you can show the voters that you are not part of "the mess in Washington." Prime ministers are selected from among people already in parliament, and so they are always insiders.

Jimmy Carter, Ronald Reagan, and Bill Clinton did not hold national office before becoming president. Franklin Roosevelt had been assistant secretary of the navy, but his real political experience was as governor of New York. Dwight Eisenhower was a general, not a politician. John F. Kennedy, Lyndon Johnson, and Richard Nixon had been in Congress, but only Nixon had had top-level experience in the executive branch (he had been vice president). George Bush had had a great deal of executive experience in Washington—as vice president, director of the CIA, and representative to China, whereas Bill Clinton's executive experience was as governor of Arkansas.

Presidents Choose Cabinet Members from Outside Congress Under the Constitution, no sitting member of Congress can hold office in the executive branch. The persons chosen by a prime minister to be in the cabinet are almost always members of parliament.

Of the fourteen heads of the cabinet-level government departments in the first Clinton administration, only three had been members of Congress. The rest, as is customary with most presidents, were close personal friends or campaign aides, representatives of important constituencies (for example, farmers, blacks, or women), experts on various policy issues, or some combination of all three.

The prime minister of Great Britain, by contrast, picks all of his or her cabinet ministers from among members of Parliament. This is one way by which the prime minister exercises control over the legislature. If you were an ambitious member of Parliament, eager to become prime minister yourself someday, and if you knew that your main chance of realizing that ambition was to be appointed to a series of ever-more-important cabinet posts, then you would not be likely to antagonize the person doing the appointing.

Presidents Have No Guaranteed Majority in the Legislature A prime minister's party (or coalition) always has a majority in parliament; if it did not, somebody else would be prime minister. A president's party often does not have a congressional majority; instead, Congress is often controlled by the opposite party, creating a divided government. Divided government means that cooperation between the two branches, hard to achieve under the best of circumstances, is often further reduced by partisan bickering.

Even when one party controls both the White House and Congress, the two branches often work at cross-purposes. The U.S. Constitution created a system of separate branches sharing powers. The authors of the document expected that there would be conflict between the branches, and they have not been disappointed.

When Kennedy was president, his party, the Democrats, held a big majority in the House and the Senate. Yet Kennedy was frustrated by his inability to get Congress to approve proposals to enlarge civil rights, supply federal aid for school construction, create a Department of Urban Affairs and Housing, or establish a program of subsidized medical care for the elderly. During his last year in office, Congress passed only about one-fourth of his proposals.

Carter did not fare much better; even though the Democrats controlled Congress, many of his most important proposals were defeated or greatly modified. Only Franklin Roosevelt (1933–1945) and Lyndon Johnson (1963–1969) had even brief success in leading Congress, and for Roosevelt most of that success was confined to his first term or to wartime.

Divided Government

In the forty-six years between 1952 and 1998, there were twenty-three congressional or presidential elections. Sixteen of the twenty-three produced **divided government**—that is, a government in which one party controls the White House and a different party controls one or both houses of Congress. When Bill Clinton became president in 1992, it was the first time since 1981 (and only the second time since 1969) that the same party was in charge of both the presidency and Congress, creating a **unified government.** And it only lasted two years.

Americans say they don't like divided government. They, or at least the pundits who claim to speak for them, think divided government produces partisan bickering, political paralysis, and policy

British prime minister Tony Blair, unlike the president of the United States, knows that almost any bill he submits to his legislature will be approved.

gridlock. During the 1990 battle between President Bush and a Democratic Congress, one magazine compared it to a movie featuring the Keystone Kops, characters from the silent movies who wildly chased each other around while accomplishing nothing.[2] In the 1992 campaign, Bush, Clinton, and Ross Perot bemoaned the "stalemate" that had developed in Washington. When Clinton was sworn in as president, many commentators spoke approvingly of the "end of gridlock."

There are two things wrong with these complaints. First, it is not clear that divided government produces a gridlock that is any worse than that which exists with unified government. Second, it is not clear that, even if gridlock does exist, it is always, or even usually, a bad thing for the country.

Does Gridlock Matter?

Despite the well-publicized stories about presidential budget proposals being ignored by Congress (Democrats used to describe Reagan's and Bush's budgets as being "dead on arrival"), it is not easy to tell whether divided governments produce fewer or worse policies than unified ones. The scholars who have looked closely at the matter have, in general, concluded that divided governments do about as well as unified ones in passing important laws, conducting important investigations, and ratifying significant treaties.[3] Political scientist David Mayhew studied 267 important laws that were enacted between 1946 and 1990. These laws were as likely to be passed when different parties controlled the White House and Congress as when the same party controlled both branches.[4] For example, divided governments produced the 1946 Marshall Plan to rebuild war-torn Europe and the 1986 Tax Reform Act.

Why do divided governments produce about as much important legislation as unified ones? The main reason is that "unified government" is something of a myth. Just because the Democrats control both the presidency and Congress does not mean that the Democratic president and the Democratic senators and representatives will see things the same way. For one thing, Democrats are themselves divided between conservatives (mainly from the South) and liberals (mainly from the Northeast and the West). They disagree about policy almost as much as Republicans and Democrats disagree. For another thing, the Constitution ensures that the

president and Congress will be rivals for power and thus rivals in policy-making. That's what the separation of powers and checks and balances are all about.

As a result, periods of unified government often turn out not to be so unified. Democratic president Lyndon Johnson could not get many Democratic members of Congress to support his war policy in Vietnam. Democratic president Jimmy Carter could not get the Democratic-controlled Senate to ratify his strategic arms limitation treaty. Democratic president Bill Clinton could not get the Democratic Congress to go along with his policy on gays in the military or his health proposals; and when the heavily revised Clinton budget did pass in 1993, it was by just one vote.

The only time there really is a unified government is when not just the same party but the same *ideological wing* of that party is in effective control of both branches of government. This was true in 1933 when Franklin Roosevelt was president and change-oriented Democrats controlled Congress, and it was true again in 1965 when Lyndon Johnson and liberal Democrats dominated Congress. Both were periods when many major policy initiatives became law: Social Security, business regulations, Medicare, and civil rights legislation. But these periods of ideologically unified government are very rare.

Is Policy Gridlock Bad?

An American president has less ability to decide what laws get passed than does a British prime minister. If you think that the job of a president is to "lead the country," that weakness will worry you. The only cure for that weakness is either to change the Constitution so that our government resembles the parliamentary system in effect in Great Britain or always to vote into office members of Congress who not only are of the same party as the president but also agree with him on policy issues.

We suspect that even Americans who hate gridlock and want more leadership aren't ready to make sweeping constitutional changes or to stop voting for presidents and members of Congress from different parties. This unwillingness suggests that they like the idea of somebody being able to block a policy they don't like. Since all of us don't like something, we all have an interest in some degree of gridlock.

And we seem to protect that interest. In a typical presidential election, about one-fourth of all voters will vote for one party's candidate for president and the other party's candidate for Congress. As a result, about one-third of all congressional districts will be represented in the House by a person who does not belong to the party of the president who carried that district. Some scholars believe that voters split tickets deliberately in order to create divided government and thus magnify the effects of the checks and balances built into our system, but the evidence supporting this belief is not conclusive.

Gridlock, to the extent that it exists, is a necessary consequence of a system of **representative democracy.** Such a system causes delays, intensifies deliberations, forces compromises, and requires the creation of broad-based coalitions to support most new policies. This system is the opposite of **direct democracy.** If you believe in direct democracy, you believe that what the people want on some issue should become law with as little fuss and bother as possible. Political gridlocks are like traffic gridlocks—people get overheated, things boil over, nothing moves, and nobody wins except journalists who write about the mess and lobbyists who charge big fees to steer their clients around the tie-up. In a direct democracy, the president would be a traffic cop with broad powers to decide in what direction the traffic should move and to make sure that it moves that way.

But if unified governments are not really unified—if in fact they are split by ideological differences within each party and by the institutional rivalries between the president and Congress—then this change is less important than it may seem. What *is* important is the relative power of the president and Congress. That has changed greatly.

The Evolution of the Presidency

In 1787 few issues inspired as much debate or concern among the Framers as the problem of defining the chief executive. The delegates feared anarchy and monarchy in about equal measure. When the Constitutional Convention met, the existing state constitutions gave most, if not all, power to the legislatures. In eight states the governor was actually chosen by the legislature, and in ten states the governor could not serve more than one year. Only in New York, Massachusetts, and Connecticut did governors have much power or serve for any length of time.

Some of the Framers proposed a plural national executive (that is, several people would each hold the executive power in different areas, or they would exercise the power as a committee). Others wanted the executive power checked, as it was in Massachusetts, by a council that would have to approve many of the chief executive's actions. Alexander Hamilton strongly urged the exact opposite: in a five-hour speech he called for something very much like an elective monarchy, patterned in some respects after the British kind. No one paid much attention to this plan or even, at first, to the more modest (and ultimately successful) suggestion of James Wilson for a single, elected president.

In time those who won out believed that the governing of a large nation, especially one threatened by foreign enemies, required a single president with significant powers. Their cause was aided, no doubt, by the fact that everybody assumed that George Washington would be the first president, and confidence in him—and in his sense of self-restraint—was widely shared. Even so, several delegates feared that the presidency would become, in the words of Edmund Randolph of Virginia, "the foetus of monarchy."

Concerns of the Founders

The delegates in Philadelphia, and later the critics of the new Constitution during the debate over its ratification, worried about aspects of the presidency that were quite different from those that concern us today. In 1787–1789 some Americans suspected that the president, by being able to command the state militia, would use the militia to overpower state governments. Others were worried that if the president were allowed to share treaty-making power with the Senate, he would be "directed by minions and favorites" and become a "tool of the Senate."

But the most frequent concern was over the possibility of presidential reelection: Americans in the late eighteenth century were sufficiently suspicious of human nature and sufficiently experienced in the arts of mischievous government to believe that a president, once elected, would arrange to stay in office in perpetuity by resorting to bribery, intrigue, and force. This might happen, for example, every time the presidential election was thrown into the House of Representatives because no candidate had received a majority of the votes in the electoral college, a situation that most people expected to happen frequently.

In retrospect these concerns seem misplaced, even foolish. The power over the militia has had little significance; the election has gone to the House only twice (1800 and 1824); and though the Senate dominated the presidency off and on during the second half of the nineteenth century, it has not done so recently. The real sources of the expansion of presidential power—the president's role in foreign affairs, his ability to shape public opinion, his position as head of the executive branch, and his claims to have certain "inherent" powers by virtue of his office—were hardly predictable in 1787. And not surprisingly. There was nowhere in the world at that time, nor had there been at any time in history, an example of an American-style presidency. It was a unique and unprecedented institution, and the Framers and their critics can easily be forgiven for not predicting accurately how it would evolve. At a more general level, however, they understood the issue quite clearly. Gouverneur Morris of Pennsylvania put the problem of the presidency this way: "Make him too weak: the Legislature will usurp his powers. Make him too strong: he will usurp on the Legislature."

The Framers knew very well that the relations between the president and Congress and the manner in which the president is elected were of profound importance, and they debated both at great length. The first plan was for Congress to elect the president—in short, for the system to be quasi-parliamentary. But if that were done, some delegates pointed out, Congress could dominate an honest or lazy president, while a corrupt or scheming president might dominate Congress.

After much discussion it was decided that the president should be chosen directly by voters. But by which voters? The emerging nation was large and diverse. It seemed unlikely that every citizen would be familiar enough with the candidates to cast an informed vote for a president directly. Worse, a direct popular election would give inordinate weight to the large, populous states, and no plan with that outcome had any chance of adoption by the smaller states.

The Electoral College

Thus the electoral college was invented, whereby each of the states would select electors in whatever manner it wished. The electors would then meet in each state capital and vote for president and vice president. Many Framers expected that this procedure would lead to each state's electors' voting for a favorite son, and thus no candidate would win a majority of the popular vote. In this event, it was decided, the House of Representatives should make the choice, with each state delegation casting one vote.

The plan seemed to meet every test: large states would have their say, but small states would be protected by having a minimum of three electoral votes no matter how tiny their population. The small states together could wield considerable influence in the House, where, it was widely expected, most presidential elections would ultimately be decided. Of course it did not work out quite this way: the Framers did not foresee the role that political parties would play in producing nationwide support for a slate of national candidates.

Once the manner of electing the president was settled, the question of his powers was much easier to decide. After all, if you believe that the procedures are fair and balanced, then you are more confident in assigning larger powers to the president within this system. Accordingly, the right to make treaties and the right to appoint lesser officials, originally reserved for the Senate, were given to the president "with the advice and consent of the Senate."

The President's Term of Office

Another issue was put to rest soon thereafter. George Washington, the unanimous choice of the electoral college to be the first president, firmly limited himself to two terms in office (1789–1797), and no president until Franklin D. Roosevelt (1933–1945) dared to run for more (though Ulysses S. Grant tried). In 1951 the Twenty-second Amendment to the Constitution was ratified, formally limiting all subsequent presidents to two terms. The remaining issues concerning the nature of the presidency, and especially the relations between the president and Congress, have been the subject of continuing dispute. The pattern of relationships that we see today is the result of an evolutionary process that has extended over more than two centuries.

The first problem was to establish the legitimacy of the presidency itself: that is, to ensure, if possible, public acceptance of the office, its incumbent, and its powers and to establish an orderly transfer of power from one incumbent to the next.

Today we take this for granted. When Bill Clinton was inaugurated in January 1993 as our forty-second president, George Bush, the forty-first president, quietly left the White House and went home. In the world today such an uneventful succession is unusual. In many nations a new chief executive comes to power with the aid of military force or as a result of political intrigue; his predecessor often leaves office disgraced, exiled, or dead. At the time that the Constitution was written, the Founders could only hope that an orderly transfer of power from one president to the next would occur. France had just undergone a bloody revolution; England in the not-too-distant past had beheaded a king; and in Poland the ruler was elected by a process so manifestly corrupt and so open to intrigue that Thomas Jefferson, in what may be the first example of ethnic humor in American politics, was led to refer to the proposed American presidency as a "bad edition of a Polish king."

Yet by the time Abraham Lincoln found himself at the helm of a nation plunged into a bitter, bloody civil war, fifteen presidents had been elected, served their time, and left office without a hint of force being used to facilitate the process and with the people accepting the process—if not admiring all the presidents. This orderly transfer of authority occurred despite passionate opposition and deeply divisive elections (such as that which brought Jefferson to power). And it did not happen by accident.

The First Presidents

Those who first served as president were among the most prominent men in the new nation, all active either in the movement for independence or in the Founding or in both. Of the first five presidents, four (all but John Adams) served two full terms. Washington and Monroe were not even opposed. The first administration had at the highest levels the leading spokesmen for all of the major viewpoints: Alexander Hamilton was Washington's secretary of the treasury (and was sympathetic to the urban commercial interests), and Thomas Jefferson was secretary of state (and more inclined toward rural, small-town, and farming views). Washington spoke out strongly against political parties, and though parties soon emerged, there was a stigma attached to them: many people believed that it was wrong to take advantage of divisions in the country, to organize deliberately to acquire political office, or to

America has witnessed peaceful transfers of power not only between leaders of different parties (such as Woodrow Wilson and William Howard Taft in 1913) but also after a popular leader has been assassinated (Lyndon Johnson is sworn in after Kennedy's death).

The Electoral College

Each state is allotted by the Constitution as many electoral votes as it has senators and representatives in Congress. Thus no state has fewer than three electoral votes. (The District of Columbia also gets three, even though it has no members of Congress.)

In each state each party runs a slate of electors pledged to that party's presidential and vice-presidential candidates. The names of these electors usually do not appear on the ballots. The slate whose candidate wins more popular votes than any other is authorized to cast all the votes of that state in the electoral college.

This results in a "winner-take-all" effect. Since it is up to the state legislatures to decide how electors are chosen, they could devise systems that would produce a split in the state's electoral votes. Maine and Nebraska are the only states that have done this. In these two states, one electoral vote goes to the winner of the popular vote in each district, and two electoral votes go to the top vote getter statewide.

The winning slates of electors assemble in their state capitals about six weeks after the election to cast their ballots. Ordinarily this is a pure formality. Occasionally, however, an elector will vote for a presidential candidate other than the one who carried the state. Such "faithless electors" have appeared in nine elections since 1796. The most recent case was in 1988, when a West Virginia elector pledged to Michael Dukakis voted instead for Lloyd Bentsen.

The state electoral ballots are opened and counted before a joint session of Congress during the first week of January. The candidate with a majority of votes is declared elected.

If no candidate wins a majority, the House of Representatives chooses the president from among the three leading candidates, with each state casting one vote. By House rule, each state's vote is allotted to the candidate preferred by a majority of the state's House delegation. If there is a tie within a delegation, that state's vote is not counted.

The House has had to decide two presidential contests. In 1800 Thomas Jefferson and Aaron Burr tied in the electoral college because of a defect in the language of the Constitution—each state cast two electoral votes, without indicating which was for president and which for vice president. (Burr was supposed to be vice president, and after much maneuvering he was.) This problem was corrected by the Twelfth Amendment, ratified in 1804. The only House decision under the modern system was in 1824, when it chose John Quincy Adams over Andrew Jackson and William H. Crawford, even though Jackson had more electoral votes (and probably more popular votes) than his rivals.

The chief political effects of the electoral college are these: The winner-take-all system probably discourages the emergence of serious third parties. The system encourages candidates to focus their campaigns on states, especially states whose vote may be in doubt. It especially encourages candidates to emphasize large, doubtful states. A candidate who carries the ten largest states wins 254 electoral votes, only 16 short of a majority. These states tend to be the most urbanized, industrialized, and politically competitive ones. A president seeking reelection has reason to be attentive to the needs of such states.

---

make legislation depend upon party advantage. As it turned out, this hostility to party (or "faction," as it was more commonly called) was unrealistic: parties are as natural to democracy as churches are to religion.

Establishing the legitimacy of the presidency in the early years was made easier by the fact that the national government had relatively little to do. It

had, of course, to establish a sound currency and to settle the debt accrued during the Revolutionary War. The Treasury Department inevitably became the principal federal office, especially under the strong leadership of Hamilton. Relations with England and France were important—and difficult—but otherwise government took little time and few resources.

Electoral Votes per State for 2000 Election

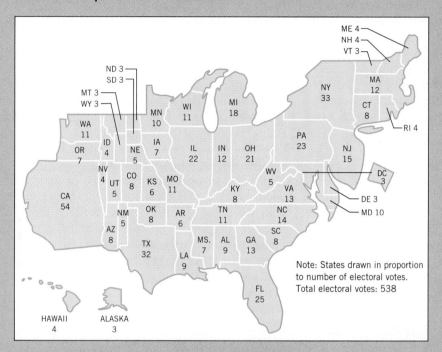

Note: States drawn in proportion to number of electoral votes.
Total electoral votes: 538

Proposals to alter or abolish the electoral college have been made, but none has come close to adoption. Among these are plans to elect the president by direct, national, popular vote; to divide each state's electoral votes in proportion to the popular vote received by each candidate in that state; to have electors chosen by congressional district rather than at large; and to retain the electoral system but abolish the office of elector and thus the chance of a faithless elector.

The issues and arguments are complex. Those who want to preserve the electoral college believe that it is important for the states to have a role in choosing the president and for the president to have an electoral reason to attend to state interests. Moreover, the electoral college helps maintain the two-party system. Those favoring direct popular election argue that the states are irrelevant in presidential elections and that each person's vote should count the same as every other person's, regardless of where he or she lives.

In appointing people to federal office, a general rule of "fitness" emerged: those appointed should have some standing in their communities and be well thought of by their neighbors. Appointments based on partisanship soon arose, but community stature could not be neglected.

The presidency was kept modest. Washington clearly had not sought the office and did not relish the exercise of its then modest powers. He traveled widely so that as many people as possible could see their new president. His efforts to establish a semiregal court etiquette were quickly rebuffed; the presidency was to be kept simple. Congress decided that not until after a president was dead might his likeness appear on a coin or on currency; no president until Eisenhower was given a pension on his retirement.

The president's relations with Congress were correct but not close. Washington appeared before the Senate to ask its advice on a proposed treaty with some Indian tribes. He got none and instead was politely told that the Senate would like to consider the matter in private. He declared that he would be "damned if he ever went there again," and he never did. Thus ended the responsibility of the Senate to "advise" the president. Vetoes were sometimes cast by the president, but sparingly, and only when the president believed that the law was not simply unwise but unconstitutional. Washington cast only two vetoes; Jefferson and Adams cast none.

The Jacksonians

At a time roughly corresponding to the presidency of Andrew Jackson (1829–1837), broad changes began to occur in American politics. These changes, together with the personality of Jackson himself, altered the relations between president and Congress and the nature of presidential leadership. As so often happens, few people at the time Jackson took office had much sense of what his presidency would be like. Though he had been a member of the House of Representatives and of the Senate, he was elected as a military hero—and an apparently doddering one at that. Sixty-one years old and seemingly frail,

President Andrew Jackson thought of himself as the "Tribune of the People," and he symbolized this by throwing a White House party that anyone could attend. Hundreds of people showed up and ate or carried away most of a 1,400-pound block of cheese.

he nonetheless used the powers of his office as no one before him had.

Jackson vetoed twelve acts of Congress, more than all his predecessors combined and more than any subsequent president until Andrew Johnson thirty years later. His vetoes were not simply on constitutional grounds but on policy ones: as the only official elected by the entire voting citizenry, he saw himself as the "Tribune of the People." None of his vetoes were overridden. He did not initiate many new policies, but he struck out against the ones that he did not like. He did so at a time when the size of the electorate was increasing rapidly, and new states, especially in the West, had entered the Union. (There were then twenty-four states in the Union, nearly twice the original number.)

Jackson demonstrated what could be done by a popular president. He did not shrink from conflict with Congress, and the tension between the two branches of government that was intended by the Framers became intensified by the personalities of those in government: Jackson in the White House, and Henry Clay, Daniel Webster, and John Calhoun in Congress. These powerful figures walked the political stage at a time when bitter sectional conflicts—over slavery and commercial policies—were beginning to split the country. Jackson, though he was opposed to a large and powerful federal government and wished to return somehow to the agrarian simplicities of Jefferson's time, was nonetheless a believer in a strong and independent presidency. This view, though obscured by nearly a century of subsequent congressional dominance of national politics, was ultimately to triumph—for better or for worse.

The Reemergence of Congress

With the end of Jackson's second term, Congress quickly reestablished its power, and except for the wartime presidency of Lincoln and brief flashes of presidential power under James Polk (1845–1849) and Grover Cleveland (1885–1889, 1893–1897), the presidency for a hundred years was the subordinate branch of the national government. Of the eight presidents who succeeded Jackson, two (William H. Harrison and Zachary Taylor) died in office, and none of the others served more than one term. Schoolchildren, trying to memorize the list of American presidents, always stumble in this era of the "no-name" presidents. This is hardly a coincidence: Congress was the leading institution, struggling, unsuccessfully, with slavery and sectionalism.

It was also an intensely partisan era, a legacy of Jackson that lasted well into the twentieth century. Public opinion was closely divided. In nine of the seventeen presidential elections between the end of Jackson's term in 1837 and Theodore Roosevelt's election in 1904, the winning candidate received less than half the popular vote. Only two candidates (Lincoln in 1864 and Ulysses S. Grant in 1872) received more than 55 percent of the popular vote.

During this long period of congressional—and usually senatorial—dominance of national government, only Lincoln broke new ground for presidential power. Lincoln's expansive use of that power, like Jackson's, was totally unexpected. He was first elected in 1860 as a minority president, receiving less than 40 percent of the popular vote in a field of four candidates. Though a member of the new Republican party, he had been a member of the Whig party, a group that had stood for limiting presidential power. He had opposed America's entry into the Mexican War and had been critical of Jackson's use of executive authority. But as president during the Civil War, he made unprecedented use of the vague gift of powers in Article II of the Constitution, especially those that he felt were "implied" or "inherent" in the phrase "take care that the laws be faithfully executed" and in the express authorization for him to act as commander in chief. Lincoln raised an army, spent money, blockaded southern ports, temporarily suspended the writ of habeas corpus, and issued the Emancipation Proclamation to free the slaves—all without prior congressional approval. He justified this, as most Americans probably would have, by the emergency conditions created by civil war. In this he acted little differently from Thomas Jefferson, who while president waged undeclared war against various North African pirates.

After Lincoln, Congress reasserted its power and became, during Reconstruction and for many decades thereafter, the principal federal institution. But it had become abundantly clear that a national emergency could equip the president with great powers and that a popular and strong-willed president could expand his powers even without an emergency.

Except for the administrations of Theodore Roosevelt (1901–1909) and Woodrow Wilson (1913–1921), the president was, until the New Deal, at best a negative force—a source of opposition to Congress, not a source of initiative and leadership for it. Grover Cleveland was a strong personality, but for all his efforts he was able to do little more than veto bills that he did not like. He cast 414 vetoes—more than any other president until Franklin Roosevelt. A frequent target of his vetoes were bills to confer special pensions on Civil War veterans.

Today we are accustomed to thinking that the president formulates a legislative program to which Congress then responds, but until the 1930s the opposite was more the case. Congress ignored the initiatives of such presidents as Grover Cleveland, Rutherford Hayes, Chester Arthur, and Calvin Coolidge. Woodrow Wilson in 1913 was the first president since John Adams to deliver personally the State of the Union address, and he was one of the first to develop and argue for a presidential legislative program.

Our popular conception of the president as the central figure of national government, devising a legislative program and commanding a large staff of advisers, is very much a product of the modern era and of the enlarged role of government. In the past the presidency became powerful only during a national crisis (the Civil War, World War I) or because of an extraordinary personality (Andrew Jackson, Theodore Roosevelt, Woodrow Wilson). Since the 1930s, however, the presidency has been powerful no matter who occupied the office and whether or not there was a crisis. Because government now plays such an active role in our national life, the president is the natural focus of attention and the titular head of a huge federal administrative system (whether he is the real boss is another matter).

But the popular conception of the president as the central figure of national government belies the realities of present-day legislative-executive relations. In a thorough analysis of national policy-making from the Eisenhower years through the Reagan administration, Mark A. Peterson demonstrated that Congress, not the president, often took the lead in setting the legislative agenda.[5] For example, the 1990 Clean Air Act, like the 1970 Clean Air Act before it, was born and bred mainly by congressional, not presidential, action. Indeed, administration officials played almost no role in the legislative process that culminated in these laws.[6] When President Bush signed the 1990 Clean Air Act or President Clinton signed the 1996 Welfare Reform Act, each took credit for it, but in fact both bills were designed by members of Congress, not by the president.[7] Likewise, although presidents dominated budget policy-making from the 1920s into the early 1970s, they no longer do. Instead, the "imperatives of the budgetary process have pushed congressional leaders to center stage."[8] Thus, as often as not, Congress proposes, the president disposes, and legislative-executive relations involve hard bargaining and struggle between these two branches of government.

The Powers of the President

Though the president, unlike a prime minister, cannot command an automatic majority in the legislature, he does have some formidable, albeit vaguely defined, powers. These are mostly set forth in Article II of the Constitution and are of two sorts: those he can exercise in his own right without formal legislative approval, and those that require the consent of the Senate or of Congress as a whole.

Powers of the President Alone

- Serve as commander in chief of the armed forces
- Commission officers of the armed forces
- Grant reprieves and pardons for federal offenses (except impeachment)
- Convene Congress in special sessions
- Receive ambassadors
- Take care that the laws be faithfully executed
- Wield the "executive power"
- Appoint officials to lesser offices

Powers of the President That Are Shared with the Senate

- Make treaties
- Appoint ambassadors, judges, and high officials

Powers of the President That Are Shared with Congress as a Whole

- Approve legislation

Taken alone and interpreted narrowly, this list of powers is not very impressive. Obviously the president's authority as commander in chief is important, but literally construed, most of the other constitutional grants seem to provide for little more than a president who is chief clerk of the country. A

hundred years after the Founding, that is about how matters appeared to even the most astute observers. In 1884 Woodrow Wilson wrote a book about American politics titled *Congressional Government*, in which he described the business of the president as "usually not much above routine," mostly "*mere* administration." The president might as well be an officer of the civil service. To succeed, he need only obey Congress and stay alive.[9]

But even as Wilson wrote, he was overlooking some examples of enormously powerful presidents, such as Lincoln, and was not sufficiently attentive to the potential for presidential power to be found in the more ambiguous clauses of the Constitution as well as in the political realities of American life. The president's authority as commander in chief has grown—especially, but not only, in wartime—to

A military officer carrying "the football," the briefcase containing the secret codes the president can use to launch a nuclear attack.

encompass not simply the direction of the military forces but also the management of the economy and the direction of foreign affairs as well. A quietly dramatic reminder of the awesome implications of the president's military powers occurs at the precise instant that a new president assumes office. An army officer carrying a locked briefcase moves from the side of the outgoing president to the side of the new one. In the briefcase are the secret codes and orders that permit the president to authorize the launching of American nuclear weapons.

The president's duty to "take care that the laws be faithfully executed" has become one of the most elastic phrases in the Constitution. By interpreting this broadly, Grover Cleveland was able to use federal troops to break a labor strike in the 1890s, and Dwight Eisenhower was able to send troops to help integrate a public school in Little Rock, Arkansas, in 1957.

The greatest source of presidential power, however, is not found in the Constitution at all but in politics and public opinion. Increasingly since the 1930s, Congress has passed laws that confer on the executive branch broad grants of authority to achieve some general goals, leaving it up to the president and his deputies to define the regulations and programs that will actually be put into effect. In Chapter 13 we shall see how this delegation of legislative power to the president has contributed to the growth of the bureaucracy. Moreover, the American people—always in times of crisis, but increasingly as an everyday matter—look to the president for leadership and hold him responsible for a large and growing portion of our national affairs. The public thinks, wrongly, that the presidency is the "first branch" of government.

The Office of the President

It was not until 1857 that the president was allowed to have a private secretary paid for with public funds, and it was not until after the assassination of President McKinley in 1901 that the president was given a Secret Service bodyguard. He was not able to submit a single presidential budget until after 1921, when the Budget and Accounting Act was passed and the Bureau of the Budget (now called the Office of Management and Budget) was created. Grover Cleveland personally answered the White House

---

HOW THINGS WORK

The President: Qualifications and Benefits

Qualifications

- A natural-born citizen (can be born abroad of parents who are American citizens)
- Thirty-five years of age
- A resident of the United States for at least fourteen years (but not necessarily the fourteen years just preceding the election)

Benefits

- A nice house
- A salary of $400,000 per year (taxable)
- An expense account of $50,000 per year (taxable)
- Travel expenses of $100,000 per year (tax-free)
- A pension, on retirement, equal to the pay of a cabinet member (taxable)
- Staff support and Secret Service protection on leaving the presidency
- A White House staff of 400 to 500 persons
- A place in the country—Camp David
- A personal airplane—Air Force One
- A fine chef

---

telephone, and Abraham Lincoln often answered his own mail.

Today, of course, the president has hundreds of people assisting him, and the trappings of power—helicopters, guards, limousines—are plainly visible. The White House staff has grown enormously. (Just how big the staff is, no one knows. Presidents like to pretend that the White House is not the large bureaucracy that it in fact has become.) Add to this the opportunities for presidential appointments to the cabinet, the courts, and various agencies, and the resources at the disposal of the president would appear to be awesome. That conclusion is partly true and partly false, or at least misleading, and for a simple reason. If the president was once helpless for lack of assistance, he now confronts an army of assistants so large that it constitutes a bureaucracy that he has difficulty controlling (see Figure 12.1). Note that Figure 12.1 ends in 1985. Recent presidents have made

Figure 12.1   Growth of the White House Office, 1935–1985

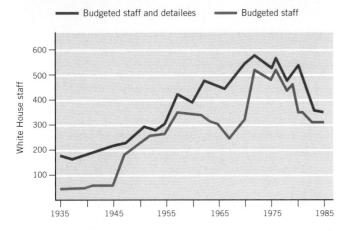

— Budgeted staff and detailees   — Budgeted staff

White House staff

600
500
400
300
200
100

1935   1945   1955   1965   1975   1985

Note: Detailees are people who are employed by and paid by another federal agency but are assigned to work in the White House. Number of detailees for 1981 unavailable.

Sources: For 1935–1977: *Congressional Record* (April 13, 1978), 10111; for 1979–1985: annual reports filed by the White House with the House of Representatives Committee on Post Office and Civil Service, titled "Aggregate Report on Personnel; Pursuant to Title 3, United States Code, Section 113"; and *Budget of the United States Government.* From Samuel Kernell and Samuel Popkin, eds., *Chief of Staff* (Berkeley: University of California Press, 1986), 201.

it very hard to find out how many people work for them and, as a result, we cannot tell you how many employees Presidents Reagan, Bush, and Clinton have had.

The ability of a presidential assistant to affect the president is governed by the rule of propinquity: in general power is wielded by people who are in the room when a decision is made. Presidential appointments can thus be classified in terms of their proximity, physical and political, to the president. There are three degrees of propinquity: the White House Office, the Executive Office, and the cabinet.

The White House Office

The president's closest assistants have offices in the White House, usually in the West Wing of that building. Their titles often do not reveal the functions that they actually perform: "counsel," "counselor," "assistant to the president," "special assistant," "special consultant," and so forth. The actual titles vary from one administration to another, but

in general the men and women who hold them oversee the political and policy interests of the president. As part of the president's personal staff, these aides do not have to be confirmed by the Senate; the president can hire and fire them at will. In 1993 the Clinton White House had five hundred staff members and a budget of $35.4 million.

There are essentially three ways in which a president can organize his personal staff—the "pyramid," "circular," and "ad hoc" methods. In a **pyramid structure,** used by Eisenhower, Nixon, Reagan, Bush, and (after a while) Clinton, most assistants report through a hierarchy to a chief of staff, who then deals directly with the president. In a **circular structure,** used by Carter, cabinet secretaries and assistants report directly to the president. In an **ad hoc structure,** used for a while by President Clinton, task forces, committees, and informal groups of friends and advisers deal directly with the president. For example, the Clinton administration's health care policy planning was spearheaded not by Health and Human Services secretary Donna E. Shalala but by First Lady Hillary Rodham Clinton and a White House adviser, Ira Magaziner. Likewise, its initiative to reform the federal bureaucracy (the National Performance Review) was led not by Office of Management and Budget director Leon E. Panetta but by an adviser to Vice President Gore, Elaine Kamarck.[10]

It is common for presidents to mix methods; for example, Franklin Roosevelt alternated between the circular and ad hoc methods in the conduct of his domestic policy and sometimes employed a pyramid structure when dealing with foreign affairs and military policy. Taken individually, each method of organization has advantages and disadvantages. A pyramid structure provides for an orderly flow of information and decisions but does so at the risk of isolating or misinforming the president. The circular method has the virtue of giving the president a great deal of information, but at the price of confusion and conflict among cabinet secretaries and assistants. An ad hoc structure allows great flexibility, minimizes bureaucratic inertia, and generates ideas and information from disparate channels, but it risks cutting the president off from the government officials who are ultimately responsible for translating presidential decisions into policy proposals and administrative action.

The Myth and Reality of the White House Office

The Myth

The White House Office was created in the 1930s following recommendations made by the President's Commission on Administrative Management. The principles underlying those recommendations have been endorsed by almost every presidential chief of staff since then. The key ones are:

1. *Small is beautiful.* The presidential staff should be small. At first there were only six assistants.
2. *A passion for anonymity.* The president's personal assistants should stay out of the limelight.
3. *Honest brokers.* The presidential staff should not make decisions for the president; it should only coordinate the flow of information to the president.

The Reality

Increasingly the operations of the White House Office seem to reflect almost the exact opposite of these principles.

1. *Big is better.* The White House staff has grown enormously in size. Hundreds now work there.
2. *Get out front.* Key White House staffers have become household words—Henry Kissinger (under Nixon and Ford), H. R. Haldeman (under Nixon), Hamilton Jordan (under Carter), Donald Regan and Howard Baker (under Reagan), George Stephanopoulos (under Clinton).
3. *Be in charge.* Cabinet officers regularly complain that White House staffers are shutting them out and making all the important decisions. Congressional investigations have revealed the power of such White House aides as Haldeman, John Poindexter, and Lieutenant Colonel Oliver North.

Why the Gap Between Myth and Reality?

The answer is—the people and the government. The people expect much more from presidents today; no president can afford to say, "We're too busy here to worry about that." The government is much more complex, and so leadership requires more resources. Even conservatives such as Ronald Reagan have been activist presidents.

Source: Adapted from Samuel Kernell and Samuel L. Popkin, eds., *Chief of Staff* (Berkeley: University of California Press, 1986), 193–232.

All presidents claim that they are open to many sources of advice, and some presidents try to guarantee that openness by using the circular method of staff organization. President Carter liked to describe his office as a wheel with himself as the hub and his several assistants as spokes. But most presidents discover, as did Carter, that the difficulty of managing the large White House bureaucracy and of conserving their own limited supply of time and energy makes it necessary for them to rely heavily on one or two key subordinates. Carter, in July 1979, dramatically altered the White House staff organization by elevating Hamilton Jordan to the post of chief of staff, with the job of coordinating the work of the other staff assistants.

At first President Reagan adopted a compromise between the circle and the pyramid, putting the White House under the direction of three key aides. At the beginning of his second term in 1985, however, the president shifted to a pyramid, placing all his assistants under a single chief of staff. Clinton began with an ad hoc system and then changed to one more like a pyramid. Each assistant has, of course, others working for him or her, sometimes a large number. There are, at a slightly lower level of status, "special assistants to the president" for various purposes. (Being "special" means, paradoxically, being less important.)

Typically senior White House staff members are drawn from the ranks of the president's campaign staff—longtime associates in whom he has confidence. A few members, however, will be experts brought in after the campaign: such was the case, for example, with Henry Kissinger, a former Harvard professor who became President Nixon's assistant for national security affairs. The offices

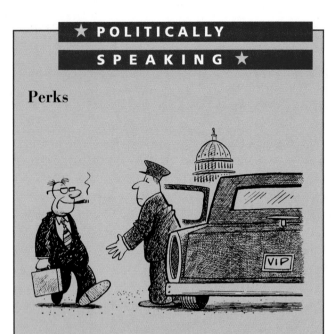

Perks

Perks is the short form of *perquisites*, meaning "the fringe benefits of office." Among the perks of political office for high-ranking officials are limousines, expense accounts, free air travel, fancy offices, and staff assistants.

The word comes to us from Great Britain, probably in the 1960s, and was first applied to the fringe benefits given to top executives in business firms.

Among the kinds of perks are:

- Freebies (small gifts)
- Annie Oaklies (free tickets or passes to theatrical or sporting events)
- Junkets (free trips abroad)

Source: From *Safire's Political Dictionary* by William Safire. Copyright © 1968, 1972, 1978 by William Safire. Reprinted by permission of Random House, Inc. and the author.

that these men and women occupy are often small and crowded (Kissinger's was not much bigger than the one that he had while a professor at Harvard), but their occupants willingly put up with any discomfort in exchange for the privilege (and the power) of being *in* the White House. The arrangement of offices—their size, and especially their proximity to the president's Oval Office—is a good measure of the relative influence of the people in them.

To an outsider, the amount of jockeying among the top staff for access to the president may seem comical or even perverse. The staff attaches enormous significance to whose office is closest to the president's, who can see him on a daily as opposed to a weekly basis, who can get an appointment with the president and who cannot, and who has a right to see documents and memoranda just before they go to the Oval Office. To be sure, there is ample grist here for Washington political novels. But there is also something important at stake: it is not simply a question of power plays and ego trips. Who can see the president and who sees and "signs off" on memoranda going to the president affect in important ways who influences policy and thus whose goals and beliefs become embedded in policy.

For example, if a memo from a secretary of the treasury who believes in free trade can go directly to the president, the president may be more likely to support free trade (low tariffs). On the other hand, if that memo must be routed through the office of the assistant to the president for political affairs, who is worried about the adverse effects of foreign competition on jobs in the American steel industry because the votes of steelworkers are important to the president's reelection campaign, then the president may be led to support higher tariffs.

The Executive Office of the President

Agencies in the Executive Office report directly to the president and perform staff services for him but are not located in the White House itself. Their members may or may not enjoy intimate contact with him; some agencies are rather large bureaucracies. The top positions in these organizations are filled by presidential appointment, but unlike the White House staff positions, these appointments must be confirmed by the Senate.

The principal agencies in the Executive Office are:

- Office of Management and Budget (OMB)
- Central Intelligence Agency (CIA)
- Council of Economic Advisers (CEA)
- Office of Personnel Management (OPM)
- Office of the U.S. Trade Representative

Of all the agencies in the Executive Office of the President, perhaps the most important in terms of the president's need for assistance in administering the federal government is the Office of Management and Budget. First called the Bureau of the Budget when it was created in 1921, it became OMB in 1970 to reflect its broader responsibilities. Today it does considerably more than assemble and analyze the figures that go each year into the national budget that the president submits to Congress. It also studies the organization and operations of the executive branch, devises plans for reorganizing various departments and agencies, develops ways of getting better information about government programs, and reviews proposals that cabinet departments want included in the president's legislative program.

OMB has a staff of over five hundred people, almost all career civil servants, many of high professional skill and substantial experience. Traditionally OMB has been a nonpartisan agency—experts serving all presidents, without regard to party or ideology. In recent administrations, however, OMB has played a major role in advocating policies rather than merely analyzing them. David Stockman, President Reagan's OMB director, was the primary architect of the 1981 and 1985 budget cuts that were proposed by the president and enacted by Congress. Stockman's proposals were often adopted over the objections of the affected department heads.

The Cabinet

The **cabinet** is a product of tradition and hope. At one time the heads of the federal departments met regularly with the president to discuss matters, and some people, especially those critical of strong presidents, would like to see this kind of collegial decision-making reestablished. But in fact this role of the cabinet is largely a fiction. Indeed, the Constitution does not even mention the cabinet (though the Twenty-fifth Amendment implicitly defines it as consisting of "the principal offices of the executive departments"). When Washington tried to get his cabinet members to work together, its two strongest members—Alexander Hamilton and Thomas Jefferson—spent most of their time feuding. The cabinet, as a presidential committee, did not work any better for John Adams or Abraham Lincoln, for Franklin Roosevelt or John Kennedy. Dwight Eisenhower is almost the only modern president who came close to making the cabinet a truly deliberative body: he gave it a large staff, held regular meetings, and listened to opinions expressed there. But even under Eisen-

Table 12.1   The Cabinet Departments

Department	Created	Approximate Employment (1997)
State	1789	24,100
Treasury	1789	140,400
Defense[a]	1947	749,500
Justice	1789	117,200
Interior	1849	67,900
Agriculture[b]	1889	106,500
Commerce	1913	34,800
Labor	1913	15,800
Health and Human Services[c]	1953	59,500
Housing and Urban Development	1965	10,900
Transportation	1966	64,200
Energy	1977	17,100
Education	1979	4,600
Veterans Affairs	1989	243,300

[a]Formerly the War Department, created in 1789. Figures are for civilians only.

[b]Agriculture Department created in 1862; made part of cabinet in 1889.

[c]Originally Health, Education and Welfare; reorganized in 1979.

Source: *Statistical Abstract of the United States, 1998,* 353.

hower, the cabinet did not have much influence over presidential decisions, nor did it help him gain more power over the government.

By custom, cabinet officers are the heads of the fourteen major executive departments. These departments, together with the dates of their creation and the approximate number of their employees, are given in Table 12.1. The order of their creation is unimportant except in terms of protocol: where one sits at cabinet meetings is determined by the age of the department that one heads. Thus the secretary of state sits next to the president on one side and the secretary of the treasury next to him on the other. Down at the foot of the table are found the heads of the newer departments.

The president appoints or directly controls vastly more members of his cabinet departments than does the British prime minister (see Table 12.2). The reason is simple: the president must struggle with Congress for control of these agencies, while the prime minister has no rival branch of government that seeks this power. Presidents get more appointments

Table 12.2	Number of Political Appointments in Cabinet Departments	
Department	**Political Appointees***	**Percentage of All Appointees**
Education	139	2.9%
State	176	1.3
Housing and Urban Development	113	0.8
Labor	114	0.7
Energy	126	0.6
Commerce	196	0.5
Justice	349	0.3
Agriculture	271	0.2
Health and Human Services	127	0.2
Transportation	75	0.1
Interior	76	0.1
Treasury	110	0.08
Defense (civilians)	280	0.04
Veterans Affairs	30	0.01

*Personnel appointed by the president with or without Senate confirmation, Senior Executive Service positions filled by non-career personnel, and confidential or policy-making personnel exempt from the civil service by Schedule C.

Source: Committee on Government Reform and Oversight, *Policy and Supporting Positions*, November 13, 1996.

than do prime ministers to make up for what the separation of powers denies them.

This abundance of political appointments, however, does not give the president ample power over the departments. Each of these organizations seeks to defend, explain, and enlarge itself. The secretary of Housing and Urban Development (HUD) spends most of his or her time on departmental business and vastly less on talking to the president. It is hardly surprising that the secretary is largely a representative of HUD to the president than his representative to HUD. And no one should be surprised that the secretary of HUD rarely finds much to talk about with the secretary of defense at cabinet meetings.

Having the power to make these appointments does give the president one great advantage: he has a lot of opportunities to reward friends and political supporters. In the Education Department, for example, President Clinton found jobs for onetime mayors, senators, state legislators, and campaign aides.

Independent Agencies, Commissions, and Judgeships

The president also appoints people to four dozen or so agencies and commissions that are not considered part of the cabinet and that by law often have a quasi-independent status. The difference between an "executive" and an "independent" agency is not precise. In general it means that the heads of executive agencies serve at the pleasure of the president and can be removed at his discretion. On the other hand, the heads of many independent agencies serve for fixed terms of office and can be removed only "for cause."

The president can also appoint federal judges, subject to the consent of the Senate. Judges serve for life unless they are removed by impeachment and conviction. The reason for the special barriers to the removal of judges is that they represent an independent branch of government as defined by the Constitution, and limits on presidential removal powers are necessary to preserve that independence.

One new feature of appointing top government officials is the increasing use of "acting" appointments. An acting appointee holds office until the Senate acts on his or her nomination. In 1998 acting officials held one-fifth of all of the Clinton administration's cabinet-level (or subcabinet-level)* jobs. Some were in office for many months. Many senators feel that this violates their right to consent to appointments and in particular violates the Vacancies Act passed in 1868. That law limits acting appointees to 120 days in office. If the Senate takes no action during those 120 days, the acting official may stay in office until he or she, or someone else, is confirmed for the post. Administration officials defend the practice as necessary given the slow pace of confirmations; senators attack it as an opportunity for a president to fill up his administration with unconfirmed officials.

Who Gets Appointed

As we have seen, a president can make lot of appointments but he rarely knows more than a few of the people whom he does appoint.

---

*Subcabinet refers to under secretary, deputy secretary, and assistant secretaries in each cabinet department.

Federal Agencies

The following agencies are classified by whether the president has unlimited or limited right of removal.

"Executive" Agencies
Head can be removed at any time.

Action
Arms Control and Disarmament Agency
Commission on Civil Rights
Energy Research and Development Agency
Environmental Protection Agency
Federal Mediation and Conciliation Service
General Services Administration
National Aeronautics and Space Administration
Postal Service
Small Business Administration
All cabinet departments
Executive Office of the President

"Independent" or "Quasi-Independent" Agencies
Members serve for a fixed term.

Federal Reserve Board (14 years)
Consumer Product Safety Commission (6 years)
Equal Employment Opportunity Commission (5 years)
Federal Communications Commission (7 years)
Federal Deposit Insurance Corporation (6 years)
Federal Energy Regulatory Commission (5 years)
Federal Maritime Commission (5 years)
Federal Trade Commission (7 years)
National Labor Relations Board (5 years)
National Science Foundation (6 years)
Securities and Exchange Commission (5 years)
Tennessee Valley Authority (9 years)

Unlike cabinet members in a parliamentary system, the president's cabinet officers and their principal deputies usually have not served with the chief executive in the legislature. Instead they come from private business, universities, "think tanks," foundations, law firms, labor unions, and the ranks of former and present members of Congress as well as past state and local government officials. A president is fortunate if most cabinet members turn out to agree with him on major policy questions. President Reagan made a special effort to ensure that his cabinet members were ideologically in tune with him, but even so Secretary of State Alexander Haig soon got into a series of quarrels with senior members of the White House staff and had to resign.

The men and women appointed to the cabinet and to the "subcabinet" (a loose term for those holding posts as deputy secretary or assistant secretary in the cabinet departments) will usually have had some prior federal experience. One study of over a thousand such appointments made by five presidents (Franklin Roosevelt through Lyndon Johnson) found that about 85 percent of the cabinet, subcabinet, and independent-agency appointees had some prior federal experience. In fact most were in government service (at the federal, state, or local levels) just before they received their cabinet or subcabinet appointment.[11] Clearly the executive branch is not, in general, run by novices.

Many of these appointees are what Richard Neustadt has called "in-and-outers": people who alternate between jobs in the federal government and ones in the private sector, especially in law firms and in universities. Cyrus Vance, before becoming secretary of state to President Carter, had been general counsel in the Defense Department, secretary of the army, and deputy secretary of defense under President Johnson. Before and after these federal jobs he was a member of a large Wall Street law firm. This pattern is quite different from that of parliamentary systems, where all the cabinet officers come from the legislature and are typically full-time career politicians.

At one time the cabinet had in it many people with strong political followings of their own—former senators and governors and powerful local party leaders. Under Franklin Roosevelt, Truman, and Kennedy, the postmaster general was the president's campaign manager. George Washington, Abraham Lincoln, and other presidents had to contend with

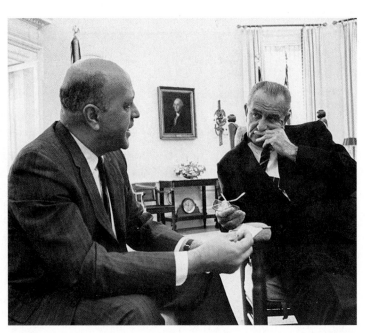

Secretary of Labor Frances Perkins (left), appointed by President Franklin Roosevelt, was the first woman cabinet member. When Robert Weaver (right) was made Secretary of Housing and Urban Development by President Johnson, he became the first African American to hold a cabinet post.

cabinet members who were powerful figures in their own right: Alexander Hamilton and Thomas Jefferson worked with Washington; Simon Cameron (a Pennsylvania political boss) and Salmon P. Chase (formerly governor of Ohio) worked for—and against—Lincoln. Before 1824 the post of secretary of state was regarded as a steppingstone to the presidency; and after that at least ten persons ran for president who had been either secretary of state or ambassador to a foreign country.[12]

Of late, however, a tendency has developed for presidents to place in their cabinets people known for their expertise or administrative experience rather than for their political following. This is in part because political parties are now so weak that party leaders can no longer demand a place in the cabinet and in part because presidents want (or think they want) "experts." A remarkable illustration of this is the number of people with Ph.D.'s who have entered the cabinet. President Nixon, who supposedly did not like Harvard professors, appointed two—Henry Kissinger and Daniel Patrick Moynihan—to important posts; Gerald Ford added a third, John Dunlop.

A president's desire to appoint experts who do not have independent political power is modified—but

not supplanted—by his need to recognize various politically important groups, regions, and organizations. Since Robert Weaver became the first African American to serve in the cabinet (as secretary of HUD under President Johnson), it is clear that it would be quite costly for a president *not* to have one or more blacks in his cabinet. The secretary of labor must be acceptable to the AFL-CIO, the secretary of agriculture to at least some organized farmers. Women have been in several cabinets since Franklin Roosevelt's; with the growing importance of the feminist movement, it is now essential that they be in every cabinet. Traditionally the interior secretary comes from the resource- and land-conscious West. And so on and on.

Because political considerations must be taken into account in making cabinet and agency appointments and because any head of a large organization will tend to adopt the perspective of that organization, there is an inevitable tension—even a rivalry—between the White House staff and the department heads. Staff members see themselves as extensions of the president's personality and policies; department heads see themselves as repositories of expert knowledge (often knowledge of why something will not work as the president hopes). White House staffers, many of them young men and women in their twenties or early thirties with little executive experience, will call department heads, often persons in their fifties with substantial executive experience, and tell them that "the president wants" this or that or that "the president asked me to tell you" one thing or another. Department heads try to conceal their irritation and then maneuver for some delay so that they can develop their own counterproposals. On the other hand, when department heads call a White House staff person and ask to see the president, unless they are one of the privileged few in whom the president has special confidence, they are often told that "the president can't be bothered with that" or "the president doesn't have time to see you."

Presidential Character

Every president brings to the White House a distinctive personality; the way the White House is organized and run will reflect that personality. Moreover, the public will judge the president not only in terms of what he accomplished but also in terms of its perception of his character. Thus personality plays a more important role in explaining the presidency than it does in explaining Congress.

DWIGHT EISENHOWER brought an orderly, military style to the White House. He was accustomed to delegating authority and to having careful and complete staff work done for him by trained specialists. Though critics often accused him of having a bumbling, incoherent manner of speaking, in fact much of that was a public disguise—a strategy for avoiding being pinned down in public on matters where he wished to retain freedom of action. His private papers reveal a very different Eisenhower—sharp, precise, deliberate.

JOHN KENNEDY brought a very different style to the presidency. He projected the image of a bold, articulate, and amusing leader who liked to surround himself with talented amateurs. Instead of clear, hierarchical lines of authority, there was a pattern of personal rule and an atmosphere of improvisation. Kennedy did not hesitate to call very junior subordinates directly and tell them what to do, bypassing the chain of command.

LYNDON JOHNSON was a master legislative strategist who had risen to be majority leader of the Senate on

T·R·I·V·I·A

Presidents

Only divorced president	Ronald Reagan
Only bachelor president	James Buchanan
Three presidents who died on the Fourth of July	Thomas Jefferson (1826) John Adams (1826) James Monroe (1831)
The shortest presidential term	William Henry Harrison (1 month)
The longest presidential term	Franklin D. Roosevelt (12 years and 1 month)
The youngest president when inaugurated	Theodore Roosevelt (42)
The oldest president when inaugurated	Ronald Reagan (69)
First president born in a hospital	Jimmy Carter
First presidential automobile	Owned by William Howard Taft
Only former presidents elected to Congress	John Quincy Adams (to House) and Andrew Johnson (to Senate)
Only president who never attended school	Andrew Johnson

the strength of his ability to persuade other politicians in face-to-face encounters. He was a consummate deal maker who, having been in Washington for thirty years before becoming president, knew everybody and everything. As a result he tried to make every decision himself. But the style that served him well in political negotiations did not serve him well in speaking to the country at large, especially when trying to retain public support for the war in Vietnam.

RICHARD NIXON was a highly intelligent man with a deep knowledge of and interest in foreign policy, coupled with a deep suspicion of the media, his political rivals, and the federal bureaucracy. In contrast to Johnson, he disliked personal confrontations and tended to shield himself behind an elaborate staff system. Distrustful of the cabinet agencies, he tried first

Three presidents—George Bush, Bill Clinton, and Jimmy Carter—at a summit to encourage volunteer activity.

to centralize power in the White House and then to put into key cabinet posts former White House aides loyal to him. Like Johnson, his personality made it difficult for him to mobilize popular support. Eventually he was forced to resign under the threat of impeachment arising out of his role in the Watergate scandal.

GERALD FORD, before being appointed vice president, had spent his political life in Congress and was at home with the give-and-take, discussion-oriented procedures of that body. He was also a genial man who liked talking to people. Thus he preferred the circular to the pyramid system of White House organization. But this meant that many decisions were made in a disorganized fashion in which key people—and sometimes key problems—were not taken into account.

JIMMY CARTER was an outsider to Washington and boasted of it. A former Georgia governor, he was determined not to be "captured" by Washington insiders. He also was a voracious reader with a wide range of interests and an appetite for detail. These

dispositions led him to try to do many things and to do them personally. Like Ford, he began with a circular structure; unlike Ford, he based his decisions on reading countless memos and asking detailed questions. His advisers finally decided that he was trying to do too much in too great detail, and toward the end of his term he shifted to a pyramid structure.

RONALD REAGAN was also an outsider, a former governor of California. But unlike Carter, he wanted to set the broad directions of his administration and leave the details to others. He gave wide latitude to subordinates and to cabinet officers, within the framework of an emphasis on lower taxes, less domestic spending, a military buildup, and a tough line with the Soviet Union. He was a superb leader of public opinion, earning the nickname "The Great Communicator."

GEORGE BUSH lacked Reagan's speaking skills and was much more of a hands-on manager. Drawing on his extensive experience in the federal government (he had been vice president, director of the CIA, ambassador to the United Nations, representative to China, and a member of the House), Bush made decisions on the basis of personal contacts with key foreign leaders and Washington officials.

BILL CLINTON, like Carter, paid a lot of attention to public policy and preferred informal, ad hoc arrangements for running his office. Unlike Carter, he was an effective speaker who could make almost any idea sound plausible. He was elected as a centrist Democrat but immediately pursued liberal policies such as comprehensive health insurance. When those failed and the Republicans won control of Congress in 1994, Clinton became a centrist again. His sexual affairs became the object of major investigations, and he was impeached by the House but acquitted by the Senate.

Professor James David Barber has attempted to study presidential personality systematically and use the results to predict presidential performance in office. Scholars are divided over whether this approach works, but none disputes the fact that personality affects how the White House is run.[13]

The Power to Persuade

The sketchy constitutional powers given the president, combined with the lack of an assured legislative majority, mean that he must rely heavily on

Lyndon Johnson's great political skill was not his ability to make speeches but his knack for deal-ing effectively with people singly or in small groups. Left, he relaxes while talking informally with reporters in the White House; right, his face shows the strain of making a public address.

persuasion if he is to accomplish much. Here the Constitution gives him some advantages: he and the vice president are the only officials elected by the whole nation, and he is the ceremonial head of state as well as the chief executive of the government. The president can use his national constituency and ceremonial duties to enlarge his power, but he must do so quickly: the second half of his first term in office will be devoted to running for reelection, especially if he faces opposition for his own party's nomination (as was the case with Carter and Ford).

The Three Audiences

The president's persuasive powers are aimed at three audiences. The first, and often the most important, is his Washington, D.C., audience of fellow politicians and leaders. As Richard Neustadt points out in his book *Presidential Power*, a president's reputation among his Washington colleagues is of great importance in affecting how much deference his views receive and thus how much power he can wield.[14] If a president is thought to be "smart," "sure of himself," "cool," "on top of things," or "shrewd," and thus "effective," he *will* be effective. Franklin Roosevelt had that reputation, and so did Lyndon John-

son, at least for his first few years in office. Truman, Ford, and Carter often did not have that reputation, and they lost ground accordingly. Power, like beauty, exists largely in the eye of the beholder.

A second audience is composed of party activists and officeholders outside Washington—the partisan grassroots. These persons want the president to exemplify their principles, trumpet their slogans, appeal to their fears and hopes, and help them get reelected. Since, as we explained in Chapter 7, partisan activists increasingly have an ideological orientation toward national politics, these people will expect "their" president to make fire-and-brimstone speeches that confirm in them a shared sense of purpose and, incidentally, help them raise money from contributors to state and local campaigns.

The third audience is "the public." But of course that audience is really many publics, each with a different view or set of interests. A president on the campaign trail speaks boldly of what he will accomplish; a president in office speaks quietly of the problems that must be overcome. Citizens are often irritated at the apparent tendency of officeholders, including the president, to sound mealy-mouthed and equivocal. But it is easy to criticize the cooking when you haven't been the cook. A president learns quickly that his every utterance will be scrutinized closely by the media and by organized groups here and abroad, and his errors of fact, judgment, timing, or even inflection will be immediately and forcefully pointed out. Given the risks of saying too much, it is a wonder that presidents say anything at all.

Presidents have made fewer and fewer impromptu remarks in the years since Franklin Roosevelt held office and have instead relied more and more on prepared speeches from which political errors can be removed in advance. Hoover and Roosevelt held six or seven press conferences each month, but every president from Nixon through Clinton has held barely one a month. Instead modern presidents make formal speeches. These speeches help them wage media politics by saying things, using phrases, and displaying attitudes that opinion polls tell them are politically useful.

Popularity and Influence

The object of all this talk is to convert personal popularity into congressional support for the president's legislative programs (and improved chances for reelection). It is not obvious, of course, why Congress should care about a president's popularity. After all, as we saw in Chapter 11, most members of Congress are secure in their seats, and few need fear any "party bosses" who might deny them renomination. Moreover, the president cannot ordinarily provide credible electoral rewards or penalties to members of Congress. By working for their defeat in the 1938 congressional election, President Roosevelt attempted to "purge" members of Congress who opposed his program, but he failed. Nor does presidential support help a particular member of Congress: most representatives win reelection anyway, and the few who are in trouble are rarely saved by presidential intervention. When President Reagan campaigned hard for Republican senatorial candidates in 1986, he, too, failed to have much impact.

For a while scholars thought that congressional candidates might benefit from the president's coattails: they might ride into office on the strength of the popularity of a president of their own party. It is true, as can be seen from Table 12.3, that a winning president will find that his party's strength in Congress increases.

Table 12.3	Partisan Gains or Losses in Congress in Presidential Election Years			
			Gains or Losses of President's Party In:	
Year	President	Party	House	Senate
1932	Roosevelt	Dem.	+90	+9
1936	Roosevelt	Dem.	+12	+7
1940	Roosevelt	Dem.	+7	−3
1944	Roosevelt	Dem.	+24	−2
1948	Truman	Dem.	+75	+9
1952	Eisenhower	Rep.	+22	+1
1956	Eisenhower	Rep.	−3	−1
1960	Kennedy	Dem.	−20	+1
1964	Johnson	Dem.	+37	+1
1968	Nixon	Rep.	+5	+7
1972	Nixon	Rep.	+12	−2
1976	Carter	Dem.	+1	+1
1980	Reagan	Rep.	+33	+12
1984	Reagan	Rep.	+16	−2
1988	Bush	Rep.	−3	−1
1992	Clinton	Dem.	−9	+1
1996	Clinton	Dem.	+9	−2

Sources: Updated from Congressional Quarterly, *Guide to U.S. Elections,* 928; and *Congress and the Nation,* vol. 4 (1973–1976), 28.

But there are good reasons to doubt whether the pattern observed in Table 12.3 is the result of presidential coattails. For one thing, there are some exceptions. Eisenhower won 57.4 percent of the vote in 1956, but the Republicans lost seats in the House and Senate. Kennedy won in 1960, but the Democrats lost seats in the House and gained but one in the Senate. When Nixon was reelected in 1972 with one of the largest majorities in history, the Republicans lost seats in the Senate.

Careful studies of voter attitudes and of how presidential and congressional candidates fare in the same districts suggest that, whatever may once have been the influence of coattails, their effect has declined in recent years and is quite small today. The weakening of party loyalty and of party organizations, combined with the enhanced ability of members of Congress to build secure relations with their constituents, have tended to insulate congressional elections from presidential ones. When voters choose as members of Congress people of the same party as an incoming president, they probably do so out of a desire for a general change and as an adverse judgment about the outgoing party's performance as a whole, not because they want to supply the new president with members of Congress favorable to him.[15] The big increase in Republican senators and representatives that accompanied the election of Ronald Reagan in 1980 was probably as much a result of the unpopularity of the outgoing president and the circumstances of various local races as it was of Reagan's coattails.

Nonetheless, a president's personal popularity may have a significant effect on how much of his program Congress passes, even if it does not affect the reelection chances of those members of Congress. Though they do not fear a president who threatens to campaign against them (or cherish one who promises to support them), members of Congress do have a sense that it is risky to oppose too adamantly the policies of a popular president. Politicians share a sense of a common fate: they tend to rise or fall together. Statistically a president's popularity, as measured by the Gallup poll (see Figure 12.2), is associated with the proportion of his legislative proposals that are approved by Congress (see Figure 12.3). Other things being equal, the more popular the president, the higher the proportion of his bills that Congress will pass.

But use these figures with caution. How successful a president is with Congress depends not just on the numbers reported here but on a lot of other factors as well. First, he can be "successful" on a big bill or on a trivial one. If he is successful on a lot of small matters and never on a big one, the measure of presidential victories does not tell us much. Second, a president can keep his victory score high by not taking a position on any controversial measure. (President Carter made his views known on only 22 percent of the House votes, while President Eisenhower made his views known on 56 percent of those votes.) Third, a president can appear successful if a few bills he likes are passed but most of his legislative program is bottled up in Congress and never comes to a vote. Given these problems, "presidential victories" are hard to measure accurately.

The Decline in Popularity

Though presidential popularity is an asset, its value tends inexorably to decline. As can be seen from Figure 12.2, every president except Eisenhower, Reagan, and Clinton lost popular support between his inauguration and the time that he left office, except when his reelection gave him a brief burst of renewed popularity. Truman was hurt by improprieties among his subordinates and by the protracted Korean War; Johnson was crippled by the increasing unpopularity of the Vietnam War; Nixon was severely damaged by the Watergate scandal; Ford was hurt by having pardoned Nixon for his part in Watergate; Carter was weakened by continuing inflation, staff irregularities, and the Iranian kidnapping of American hostages; Bush was harmed by a protracted economic recession. Remarkably, Clinton's approval rating was not greatly harmed by his affair with Monica Lewinsky and his impeachment.

Because a president's popularity tends to be highest right after an election, political commentators like to speak of a "honeymoon," during which, presumably, the president's love affair with the people and with Congress can be consummated. Certainly Roosevelt enjoyed such a honeymoon. In the legendary "first hundred days" of his presidency, from March to June 1933, FDR obtained from a willing Congress a vast array of new laws creating new agencies and authorizing new powers. But those were extraordinary times: the most serious economic depression of this century had put millions out of work, closed banks, impoverished farmers, and ruined the stock market. It would have been political suicide for Congress to have blocked, or even delayed, action on measures that appeared designed to help the nation out of the crisis.

Other presidents, serving in more normal times, have not enjoyed such a honeymoon. Truman had little success with what he proposed; Eisenhower proposed little. Kennedy, Nixon, Ford, and Carter had some victories in their first year in office, but nothing that could be called a honeymoon. Only Lyndon Johnson enjoyed a highly productive relationship with Congress; until the Vietnam War sapped his strength, he rarely lost. Reagan began his administration with important victories in his effort to cut expenditures and taxes, but in his second year in office he ran into trouble.

The decay in the reputation of the president and his party in midterm is evident in Table 12.4 (see page 360). Since 1934, in every off-year election but

Figure 12.2   Presidential Popularity

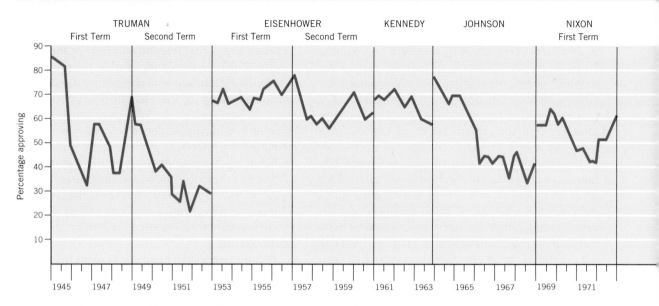

Note: Popularity was measured by asking every few months, "Do you approve of the way _____ is handling his job as president?"

Source: Thomas E. Cronin, *The State of the Presidency* (Boston: Little, Brown, 1975), 110–111. Copyright © 1975 by Little, Brown and Company, Inc. Reprinted by permission. Updated with Gallup poll data, 1976–1993. Reprinted by permission of the Gallup Poll News Service.

one, the president's party has lost seats in one or both houses of Congress. In 1998 the Democrats won five seats in the House and lost none in the Senate. The ability of the president to persuade is important but limited. However, he also has a powerful bargaining chip to play: the ability to say no.

The Power to Say No

The Constitution gives the president the power to veto legislation. In addition most presidents have asserted the right of "executive privilege," or the right to withhold information that Congress may want to obtain from the president or his subordinates, and some presidents have tried to impound funds appropriated by Congress. These efforts by the president to say no are not only a way of blocking action but also a way of forcing Congress to bargain with him over the substance of policies.

Veto

If a president disapproves of a bill passed by both houses of Congress, he may veto it in one of two ways. One is by a **veto message.** This is a statement that the president sends to Congress accompanying the bill, within ten days (not counting Sundays) after the bill has been passed. In it he sets forth his reasons for not signing the bill. The other is the **pocket veto.** If the president does not sign the bill within ten days *and* Congress has adjourned within that time, then the bill will not become law. Obviously a pocket veto can be used only during a certain time of the year—just before Congress adjourns at the end of its second session. At times, however, presidents have pocket-vetoed a bill just before Congress recessed for a summer vacation or to permit its members to campaign during an off-year election. In 1972 Senator Edward M. Kennedy of Massachusetts protested that this was unconstitutional, since a recess is not the same thing as an adjournment. In

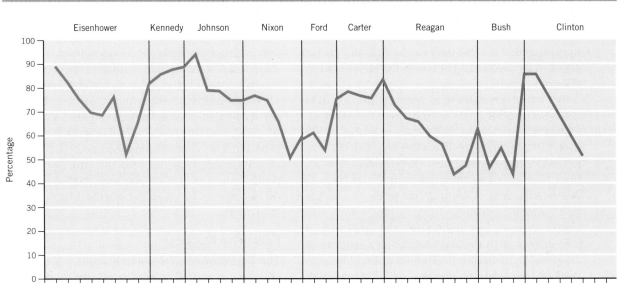

Figure 12.3   Presidential Victories on Votes in Congress, 1953–1999

Note: Percentages indicate number of congressional votes supporting the president divided by the total number of votes on which the president has taken a position.

Source: Updated from Norman J. Ornstein, Thomas E. Mann, and Michael J. Malbin, *Vital Statistics on Congress*, 1995–1996, Congressional Quarterly Inc., 1996: 205. Reprinted with permission.

Table 12.4	Partisan Gains or Losses in Congress in Off-Year Elections			
			Gains or Losses of President's Party In:	
Year	President	Party	House	Senate
1934	Roosevelt	Dem.	+9	+9
1938	Roosevelt	Dem.	−70	−7
1942	Roosevelt	Dem.	−50	−8
1946	Truman	Dem.	−54	−11
1950	Truman	Dem.	−29	−5
1954	Eisenhower	Rep.	−18	−1
1958	Eisenhower	Rep.	−47	−13
1962	Kennedy	Dem.	−5	+2
1966	Johnson	Dem.	−48	−4
1970	Nixon	Rep.	−12	+1
1974	Ford	Rep.	−48	−5
1978	Carter	Dem.	−12	−3
1982	Reagan	Rep.	−26	0
1986	Reagan	Rep.	−5	−8
1990	Bush	Rep.	−9	−1
1994	Clinton	Dem.	−52	−9
1998	Clinton	Dem.	+5	0

Source: Harold W. Stanley and Richard G. Niemi, *Vital Statistics on American Politics, 1997–1998* (Washington, D.C.: Congressional Quarterly, 1998), 46.

a case brought to federal court, Kennedy was upheld, and it is now understood that the pocket veto can be used only just before the life of a given Congress expires.

A bill that is not signed or vetoed within ten days while Congress is still in session becomes law automatically, without the president's approval. A bill that has been returned to Congress with a veto message can be passed over the president's objections if at least two-thirds of each house votes to override the veto. A bill that has received a pocket veto cannot be brought back to life by Congress (since Congress has adjourned), nor does such a bill carry over to the next session of Congress. If Congress wants to press the matter, it will have to start all over again by passing the bill anew in its next session, and then hope that the president will sign it or, if he does not, that they can override his veto.

Until 1996 the president had to either accept or reject the entire bill. Presidents did not have the power, possessed by most governors, to exercise a

line-item veto, with which the chief executive can approve some provisions of a bill and disapprove others. Congress could take advantage of this by putting items the president did not like into a bill he otherwise favored, forcing him to approve those provisions along with the rest of the bill or reject the whole thing. But in 1996 Congress passed a bill, which the president signed into law, that gives the president the power of "enhanced rescission." This means the president could cancel parts of a spending bill passed by Congress without vetoing the entire bill. The president had five days after signing a bill to send a message to Congress rescinding some parts of what he had signed. These rescissions would take effect unless Congress, by a two-thirds vote, overturned them. Congress could choose which parts of the president's cancellations it wanted to overturn. But the Supreme Court has decided that this law is unconstitutional. The Constitution gives the president no such power to carve up a bill: he must either sign the whole bill, veto the whole bill, or allow it to become law without his signature.[16]

Nevertheless, the veto power is a substantial one, because Congress rarely has the votes to override it. From George Washington to Bill Clinton, over 2,500 presidential vetoes were cast; about 4 percent were overridden (see Table 12.5). Cleveland, Franklin Roosevelt, Truman, and Eisenhower made the most extensive use of vetoes, accounting for 65 percent of all vetoes ever cast. Often the vetoed legislation is revised by Congress and passed in a form suitable to the president. There is no tally of how often this happens, but it is frequent enough so that both branches of government recognize that the veto, or even the threat of it, is part of an elaborate process of political negotiation in which the president has substantial powers.

Executive Privilege

The Constitution says nothing about whether the president is obliged to divulge private communications between himself and his principal advisers, but presidents have acted as if they do have that privilege of confidentiality. The presidential claim is based on two grounds. First, the doctrine of the separation of powers means that one branch of government does not have the right to inquire into the

Table 12.5   **Presidential Vetoes, 1789–1997**

	Regular Vetoes	Pocket Vetoes	Total Vetoes	Vetoes Overridden
Washington	2	—	2	—
Madison	5	2	7	—
Monroe	1	—	1	—
Jackson	5	7	12	—
Tyler	6	3	9	1
Polk	2	1	3	—
Pierce	9	—	9	5
Buchanan	4	3	7	—
Lincoln	2	4	6	—
A. Johnson	21	8	29	15
Grant	45	49	94	4
Hayes	12	1	13	1
Arthur	4	8	12	1
Cleveland	304	109	413	2
Harrison	19	25	44	1
Cleveland	43	127	170	5
McKinley	6	36	42	—
T. Roosevelt	42	40	82	1
Taft	30	9	39	1
Wilson	33	11	44	6
Harding	5	1	6	—
Coolidge	20	30	50	4
Hoover	21	16	37	3
F. Roosevelt	372	263	635	9
Truman	180	70	250	12
Eisenhower	73	108	181	2
Kennedy	12	9	21	—
L. Johnson	16	14	30	—
Nixon	26	17	43	7
Ford	48	18	66	12
Carter	13	18	31	2
Reagan	39	39	78	9
Bush	29	15	44	1
Clinton	31	0	31	2

Source: Harold W. Stanley and Richard G. Niemi, *Vital Statistics on American Politics, 1997–1998* (Washington, D.C.: Congressional Quarterly, 1998), 252.

internal workings of another branch headed by constitutionally named officers. Second, the principles of statecraft and of prudent administration require that the president have the right to obtain confidential and candid advice from subordinates; such advice could not be obtained if it would quickly be exposed to public scrutiny.

For almost two hundred years there was no serious challenge to the claim of presidential confiden-

tiality. The Supreme Court did not require the disclosure of confidential communications to or from the president.[17] Congress was never happy with this claim but until 1973 did not seriously dispute it. Indeed, in 1962 a Senate committee explicitly accepted a claim by President Kennedy that his secretary of defense, Robert S. McNamara, was not obliged to divulge the identity of Defense Department officials who had censored certain speeches by generals and admirals.

In 1973 the Supreme Court for the first time met the issue directly. A federal special prosecutor sought tape recordings of White House conversations between President Nixon and his advisers as part of his investigation of the Watergate scandal. In the case of *United States v. Nixon*, the Supreme Court, by a vote of eight to zero, held that while there may be a sound basis for the claim of executive privilege, especially where sensitive military or diplomatic matters are involved, there is no "absolute unqualified Presidential privilege of immunity from judicial process under all circumstances."[18] To admit otherwise would be to block the constitutionally defined function of the federal courts to decide criminal cases.

Thus Nixon was ordered to hand over the disputed tapes and papers to a federal judge so that the judge could decide which were relevant to the case at hand and allow those to be introduced into evidence. In the future another president may well persuade the Court that a different set of records or papers is so sensitive as to require protection, especially if there is no allegation of criminal misconduct requiring the production of evidence in court. As a practical matter it seems likely that presidential advisers will be able, except in unusual cases such as Watergate, to continue to give private advice to the president.

In 1997 and 1998 President Clinton was sued while in office by a private person, Paula Jones, who claimed that he had solicited sex from her in ways that hurt her reputation. In defending himself against that and other matters, his lawyers attempted to claim executive privilege for Secret Service officers and government-paid lawyers who worked with him, but federal courts held that not only could a president be sued, but these other officials could not claim executive privilege.[19] One unhappy consequence of this episode is that the courts have greatly weakened the number of officials with whom the president can speak in confidence. It is not easy to run an organization when the courts can later compel your associates to testify about everything you said.

Impoundment of Funds

From time to time presidents have refused to spend money appropriated by Congress. Truman did not spend all that Congress wanted spent on the armed forces, and Johnson did not spend all that Congress made available for highway construction. Kennedy refused to spend money appropriated for new weapons systems that he did not like. Indeed, the precedent for impounding funds goes back at least to the administration of Thomas Jefferson.

But what has precedent is not thereby constitutional. The Constitution is silent on whether the president *must* spend the money that Congress appropriates; all it says is that the president cannot spend money that Congress has *not* appropriated. The major test of presidential power in this respect occurred during the Nixon administration. Nixon wished to reduce federal spending. He proposed in 1972 that Congress give him the power to reduce federal spending so that it would not exceed $250 billion for the coming year. Congress, under Democratic control, refused. Nixon responded by pocket-vetoing twelve spending bills and then impounding funds appropriated under other laws that he had not vetoed.

Congress in turn responded by passing the Budget Reform Act of 1974, which, among other things, requires the president to spend all appropriated funds unless he first tells Congress what funds he wishes not to spend and Congress, within forty-five days, agrees to delete the items. If he wishes simply to delay spending the money, he need only inform Congress, but Congress then can refuse the delay by passing a resolution requiring the immediate release of the money. Federal courts have upheld the rule that the president must spend, without delay for policy reasons, money that Congress has appropriated.

The President's Program

Imagine that you have just spent three or four years running for president, during which time you have given essentially the same speech over and over again. You have had no time to study the issues in any depth. To reach a large television audience, you have couched your ideas largely in rather simple— if not simple-minded—slogans. Your principal advisers are political aides, not legislative specialists.

You win. You are inaugurated. Now you must *be* a president instead of just talking about it. You must fill hundreds of appointive posts, but you know personally only a handful of the candidates. You must deliver a State of the Union message to Congress only two or three weeks after you are sworn in. It is quite possible that you have never read, much less written, such a message before. You must submit a new budget; the old one is hundreds of pages long, much of it comprehensible only to experts. Foreign governments, as well as the stock market, hang on your every word, interpreting many of your remarks in ways that totally surprise you. What will you do?

The Constitution is not much help. It directs you to report on the state of the union and to recommend "such measures" as you shall judge "necessary and expedient." Beyond that you are charged to "take care that the laws be faithfully executed."

At one time, of course, the demands placed on a newly elected president were not very great, because the president was not expected to do very much. The president, on assuming office, might speak of the tariff, or relations with England, or the value of veterans' pensions, or the need for civil service reform, but he was not expected to have something to say (and offer) to everybody. Today he is.

Putting Together a Program

To develop policies on short notice, a president will draw on several sources, each with particular strengths and weaknesses:

- **Interest groups**
  Strength: Will have specific plans and ideas.
  Weakness: Will have narrow view of the public interest.

- **Aides and campaign advisers**
  Strength: Will test new ideas for their political soundness.
  Weakness: Will not have many ideas to test, being inexperienced in government.

- **Federal bureaus and agencies**
  Strength: Will know what is feasible in terms of governmental realities.
  Weakness: Will propose plans that promote own agencies and will not have good information on whether plans will work.

- **Outside, academic, and other specialists and experts**
  Strength: Will have many general ideas and criticisms of existing programs.
  Weakness: Will not know the details of policy or have good judgment as to what is feasible.

There are essentially two ways for a president to develop a program. One, exemplified by Presidents Carter and Clinton, is to have a policy on almost everything. To do this they worked endless hours and studied countless documents, trying to learn something about, and then state their positions on, a large number of issues. The other method, illustrated by President Reagan, is to concentrate on three or four major initiatives or themes and leave everything else to subordinates.

But even when a president has a governing philosophy, as did Reagan, he cannot risk plunging ahead on his own. He must judge public and congressional reaction to this program before he commits himself fully to it. Therefore he will often allow parts of his program to be "leaked" to the press, or to be "floated" as a trial balloon. Reagan's commitment to a 30 percent tax cut and larger military expenditures was so well known that it required no leaking, but he did have to float his ideas on Social Security and certain budget cuts to test popular reaction. His opponents in the bureaucracy did exactly the same thing, hoping for the opposite effect. They leaked controversial parts of the program in an effort to discredit the whole policy. This process of testing the winds by a president and his critics helps explain why so many news stories coming from Washington mention no person by name but only an anonymous "highly placed source."

In addition to the risks of adverse reaction, the president faces three other constraints on his ability to plan a program. One is the sheer limit of his time and attention span. Every president works harder than he has ever worked before. A ninety-hour week is typical. Even so, he has great difficulty keeping up with all the things that he is supposed to know and make decisions about. For example, Congress during an average year passes between four hundred and six hundred bills, each of which the president must sign, veto, or allow to take effect without his signature. Scores of people wish to see him. Hundreds of phone calls must be made to members of Congress and others in order to ask for help, to smooth ruffled feathers, or to get information. He must receive all newly appointed ambassadors and visiting heads of state and in addition have his picture taken with countless people, from a Nobel Prize winner to a child whose likeness will appear on the Easter Seal.

The second constraint is the unexpected crisis. Franklin Roosevelt obviously had to respond to a depression and to the mounting risks of world war. But most presidents get their crises when they least expect them. Consider these crises:

Kennedy

- Failure of Bay of Pigs invasion of Cuba
- Soviets put missiles in Cuba
- China invades India
- Federal troops sent to the South to protect blacks

Johnson

- Vietnam War
- Black riots in major cities
- War between India and Pakistan
- Civil war in Dominican Republic
- Arab-Israeli war
- Civil rights workers murdered in South

Nixon

- Watergate scandal
- Arab-Israeli war
- Value of dollar falls in foreign trade
- Arabs raise the price of oil

Carter

- OMB director Bert Lance accused of improprieties
- Lengthy coal strike
- Seizure of American hostages in Iran
- Soviet invasion of Afghanistan

Reagan

- Poland suppresses Solidarity movement
- U.S. troops sent to Lebanon
- U.S. hostages held in Lebanon

- Civil war in Nicaragua
- Iran-contra crisis

Bush

- Soviet Union dissolves
- Iraq invades Kuwait
- China suppresses student rebellion in Tiananmen Square, Beijing

Clinton

- Civil war continues in Bosnia and other parts of the former Yugoslavia
- North Korea resists inspections designed to detect possible manufacture of nuclear weapons
- Investigation of possible wrongdoing of President and Mrs. Clinton in Whitewater real estate development
- Charges of sexual harassment made against Clinton
- Clinton impeached

The third constraint is the fact that the federal government and most federal programs, as well as the federal budget, can only be changed marginally, except in special circumstances. The vast bulk of federal expenditures are beyond control in any given year: the money must be spent whether the president likes it or not. Many federal programs have such strong congressional or public support that they must be left intact or modified only slightly. And this means that most federal employees can count on being secure in their jobs, whatever a president's views on reducing the bureaucracy.

The result of these constraints is that the president, at least in ordinary times, has to be selective about what he wants. He can be thought of as having a stock of influence and prestige the way that he might have a supply of money. If he wants to get the most "return" on his resources, he must "invest" that influence and prestige carefully in enterprises that promise substantial gains—in public benefits and political support—at reasonable costs. Each president tends to speak in terms of changing everything at once, calling his approach a "New Deal," a "New Frontier," a "Great Society," or the "New Federalism." But beneath the rhetoric he must identify a few specific proposals on which he wishes to bet his resources, mindful of the need to leave a substantial stock of resources in reserve to handle the inevitable crises and emergencies. In recent decades events have required

every president to devote much of his time and resources to two key issues: the state of the economy and foreign affairs. What he manages to do beyond this will depend on his personal views and his sense of what the nation, as well as his reelection, requires.

And it will depend on one other thing: opinion polls. The last president who never used polls was Herbert Hoover. Franklin Roosevelt began making heavy use of them, and every president since has relied on them. Bill Clinton had voters polled about almost everything—where he should go on vacation (the West) and how to deal with Bosnia (no ground troops).

Once, when polls did not exist, politicians often believed that they should do what they thought the public interest required. Now that polls are commonplace, some politicians act on the basis of what their constituents want. Scholars call the first view the **trustee approach:** do what the public good requires, even if the voters are skeptical. The second view is the **delegate model:** do what your constituents want you to do.

But there is another way of looking at polls. They may be a device not for picking a policy but for deciding what language to use in explaining that policy. Choose a policy that helps you get reelected or that satisfies an interest group, but then explain it with poll-tested words. President Clinton wanted to keep affirmative action (described in the chapter titled "Civil Rights") but knew that most voters disliked it. So he used a poll-tested phrase—"mend it but don't end it"—and then did nothing to mend it.

Attempts to Reorganize

One item on the presidential agenda has been the same for almost every president since Herbert Hoover: reorganizing the executive branch of government. With few exceptions every president since 1928 has tried to change the structure of the staff, departments, and agencies that are theoretically subordinate to him. Every president has been appalled by the number of agencies that report to him and by the apparently helter-skelter manner in which they have grown up. But this is only one—and often not the most important—reason for wanting to reorganize. If a president wants to get something done, put new people in charge of a program, or recapture political support for a policy, it is often easier to do so by creating a new agency or reorganizing an old one than by abolishing a program, firing a subordinate, or passing a new law. Reorganization serves many objectives and thus is a recurring theme.

Legally the president can reorganize his personal White House staff anytime that he wishes. To reorganize in any important way the larger Executive Office of the President or any of the executive departments or agencies, however, Congress must first be consulted. For over forty years this consultation usually took the form of submitting to Congress a reorganization plan that would take effect provided that neither the House nor the Senate passed, within sixty days, a concurrent resolution disapproving the plan (such a resolution was called a **legislative veto**). This procedure, first authorized by the Reorganization Act of 1939, could be used to change, but not create or abolish, an executive agency. In 1981 authority under that act expired, and Congress did not renew it. Two years later the Supreme Court declared that all legislative vetoes were unconstitutional (see Chapter 13), and so today any presidential reorganization plan would have to take the form of a regular law, passed by Congress and signed by the president.

What has been said so far may well give the reader the impression that the president is virtually helpless. That is not the case. The *actual* power of the president can only be measured in terms of what he can accomplish. What this chapter has described so far is the office as the president finds it—the burdens, restraints, demands, complexities, and resources that he encounters on entering the Oval Office for the first time. Every president since Truman has commented feelingly on how limited the powers of the president seem from the inside compared to what they appear to be from the outside. Franklin Roosevelt compared his struggles with the bureaucracy to punching a feather bed; Truman wrote that the power of the president was chiefly the power to persuade people to do what they ought to do anyway. After being in office a year or so, Kennedy spoke to interviewers about how much more complex the world appeared than he had first supposed. Johnson and Nixon were broken by the office and the events that happened there.

"15% LIKE YOU AS A CONSERVATIVE, 15% LIKE YOU LIBERAL, AND 70% DON'T CARE ... SO MY ADVICE IS TO REINVENT YOURSELF AS THE 'I DON'T CARE' CANDIDATE."

Polling dominates not only politics, but government, as some presidents rely on them to decide how to discuss issues.

Yet Franklin Roosevelt helped create the modern presidency, with its vast organizational reach, and directed a massive war effort. Truman ordered two atomic bombs dropped on Japanese cities. Eisenhower sent American troops to Lebanon; Kennedy supported an effort to invade Cuba. Johnson sent troops to the Dominican Republic and to Vietnam; Nixon ordered an invasion of Cambodia; Reagan launched an invasion of Grenada and sponsored an antigovernment insurgent group in Nicaragua; Bush invaded Panama and sent troops to the Persian Gulf to fight Iraq; Clinton sent troops to Haiti and Bosnia. Obviously Europeans, Russians, Vietnamese, Cambodians, Dominicans, Panamanians, and Iraqis do not think of the American president as "helpless."

Presidential Transition

No president but Franklin Roosevelt has ever served more than two terms, and since the ratification of the Twenty-second Amendment in 1951, no president will ever again have the chance. But more than tradition or the Constitution escorts presidents from office. Only about one-third of the forty-two presidents since George Washington have been elected to a second term. Of the twenty-seven not reelected, four died in office during their first term. But the

President Reagan, moments before he was shot on March 30, 1981, by a would-be assassin.

remainder either did not seek or (more usually) could not obtain reelection.

Of the eight presidents who died in office, four were assassinated: Lincoln, Garfield, McKinley, and Kennedy. At least six other presidents were the objects of unsuccessful assassination attempts: Jackson, Theodore Roosevelt, Franklin Roosevelt, Truman, Ford, and Reagan. (There may have been attempts on other presidents that never came to public notice; the attempts mentioned here involved public efforts to fire weapons at presidents.)

The presidents who served two or more terms fall into certain periods, such as the Founding (Washington, Jefferson, Madison, Monroe) or wartime (Lincoln, Wilson, Roosevelt), or they happened to be in office during especially tranquil times (Monroe, McKinley, Eisenhower, Clinton), or some combination of the above. When the country was deeply divided, as during the years just before the Civil War and during the period of Reconstruction after it, it was the rare president who was reelected.

The Vice President

Eight times a vice president has become president because of the death of his predecessor. It first happened to John Tyler, who became president in 1841 when William Henry Harrison died peacefully after only one month in office. The question for Tyler and for the country was substantial: was

Tyler simply to be the acting president and a kind of caretaker until a new president was elected, or was he to be *president* in every sense of the word? Despite criticism and despite what might have been the contrary intention of the Framers of the Constitution, Tyler decided on the latter course and was confirmed in that opinion by a decision of Congress. Ever since, the vice president has automatically become president, in title and in powers, when the occupant of the White House has died or resigned.

But if vice presidents frequently acquire office because of death, they rarely acquire it by election. Since the earliest period of the Founding, when John Adams and Thomas Jefferson were each elected president after having first served as vice president under their predecessors, there have only been three occasions when a vice president was later able to win the presidency without his president's having died in office. One was in 1836, when Martin Van Buren was elected president after having served as Andrew Jackson's vice president; the second was in 1968, when Richard Nixon became president after having served as Dwight Eisenhower's vice president eight years earlier; the third was in 1988, when George Bush succeeded Ronald Reagan. Many vice presidents who entered the Oval Office because their predecessors died were subsequently elected to terms in their own right—Theodore Roosevelt, Calvin Coolidge, Harry Truman, and Lyndon Johnson. But no one who wishes to become president should assume that to become vice president first is the best way to get there.

The vice-presidency is just what so many vice presidents have complained about its being: a rather empty job. John Adams described it as "the most insignificant office that ever the invention of man contrived or his imagination conceived," and most of his successors would have agreed. Thomas Jefferson, almost alone, had a good word to say for it: "The second office of the government is honorable and easy, the first is but a splendid misery."[20] Daniel Webster rejected a vice-presidential nomination in 1848 with the phrase, "I do not choose to be buried until I am really dead."[21] (Had he taken the job, he would have become president after Zachary Taylor died in office, thereby achieving a remarkable secular resurrection.) For all the good and bad jokes about the vice-presidency, however, candidates still struggle mightily for it. John Nance Garner gave up the speakership of the House to become Franklin Roosevelt's vice president (a job he valued as "not worth a pitcher of warm spit"*), and Lyndon Johnson gave up the majority leadership of the Senate to become Kennedy's. Truman, Nixon, Humphrey, Mondale, and Gore all left reasonably secure Senate seats for the vice-presidency.

The only official task of the vice president is to preside over the Senate and to vote in case of a tie. Even this is scarcely time-consuming, as the Senate chooses from among its members a president pro tempore, as required by the Constitution, who (along with others) presides in the absence of the vice president. The vice president's leadership powers in the Senate are weak, especially when the vice president is of a different party from the majority of the senators. Presidents have from time to time found tasks for their vice presidents—attending the funerals of world figures, being the chairman of governmental commissions, and the like—but all in all the vice president can do little more than endorse whatever the president does and wait. And if a vice president should run for president after his former boss retires (as Al Gore did in 2000), he has to walk the fine line between appearing loyal to the president and having opinions of his own. It isn't easy.

Problems of Succession

If the president should die in office, the right of the vice president to assume that office has been clear since the time of John Tyler. But two questions remain: What if the president falls seriously ill but does not die? And if the vice president steps up, who then becomes the new vice president?

The first problem has arisen on a number of occasions. After President James A. Garfield was shot in 1881, he lingered through the summer before he died. President Woodrow Wilson collapsed from a stroke and was a virtual recluse for seven months in 1919 and an invalid for the rest of his term. Eisenhower had three serious illnesses while in office; Reagan was shot during his first term and hospitalized during his second.

The second problem has arisen on eight occasions when the vice president became president

When President Woodrow Wilson suffered a stroke in 1919, his wife, Edith Galt Wilson, became the power behind the scenes. The Twenty-fifth Amendment solves the problem of presidential disability by providing for an orderly transfer of power to the vice president.

owing to the death of the incumbent. In these cases no elected person was available to succeed the new president should he die in office. For many decades the problem was handled by law. The Succession Act of 1886, for example, designated the secretary of state as next in line for the presidency should the vice president die, followed by the other cabinet officers in order of seniority. But this meant that a vice president who became president could pick his own successor by choosing his own secretary of state. In 1947 the law was changed to make the Speaker of the House and then the president pro tempore of the Senate next in line for the presidency. But that created still other problems: a Speaker or a president pro tempore is likely to be chosen because of seniority,

---

*The word he actually used was a good deal stronger than spit, but historians are decorous.

MEMORANDUM

To: Delegate James Nagle
From: Robert Gilbert, legal staff
Subject: Six-year presidential term

The proposal to give the president a single six-year term is perhaps the most popular amendment now before the convention. Polls suggest that it is supported by a sizable percentage of the American people.

Arguments for:

1. Today a president no sooner learns the ropes after being elected for the first time than he or she has to start preparing for the next election. A six-year term will give the president a chance to govern for several years after learning how to be president. This will lessen the extent to which political pressures dictate what the president does.
2. Limited to a single term, the president need not cater to special-interest groups or the media in deciding on policy. He or she can concentrate on what is good for the country.
3. Many states have limited their governors to a single term.

Arguments against:

1. It is the need to win reelection that keeps the president (like any politician) attentive to what the people want. A president unable to succeed himself or herself will be tempted to ignore public opinion.
2. Limiting a president to a single term will not free him or her from the need to play to the media or special-interest groups, since the formal powers of the presidency are too weak to permit the incumbent to govern without the aid of Congress and the press.
3. There is no evidence that presidents (such as Dwight Eisenhower) who served a second term knowing that they could not run for reelection did a better or less "political" job in the second term than in the first.

Your decision:
Favor amendment _____
Oppose amendment _____

Six-Year Term for President

Delegates Divided on Big Issue

October 15
EUDORA, KS
    Here at the convention called to propose amendments to the United States Constitution, the major issue facing the delegates is the proposal to limit the president to a single six-year term. Proponents of the measure claim . . .

not executive skill, and in any event might well be of the party opposite to that occupying the White House.

Both problems were addressed in 1967 by the Twenty-fifth Amendment to the Constitution. It deals with the disability problem by allowing the vice president to serve as "acting president" whenever the president declares that he is unable to discharge the powers and duties of his office or whenever the vice president and a majority of the cabinet declare that the president is incapacitated. If the president disagrees with the opinion of his vice president and a majority of the cabinet, then Congress decides the issue. A two-thirds majority is necessary to confirm that the president is unable to serve.

The amendment deals with the succession problem by requiring a vice president who assumes the presidency (after a vacancy is created by death or resignation) to nominate a new vice president. This person takes office if the nomination is confirmed by a majority vote of both houses of Congress. When there is no vice president, then the 1947 law governs: next in line are the Speaker, the Senate president, and the fourteen cabinet officers, beginning with the secretary of state.

The disability problem has not arisen since the adoption of the amendment, but the succession problem has. In 1973 Vice President Spiro Agnew resigned, having pleaded no contest to criminal charges. President Nixon nominated Gerald Ford as vice president, and after extensive hearings he was confirmed by both houses of Congress and sworn in. Then on August 9, 1974, Nixon resigned the presidency—the first man to do so—and Ford became president. He nominated as his vice president Nelson Rockefeller, who was confirmed by both houses of Congress—again, after extensive hearings—and was sworn in on December 19, 1974. For the first time in history, the nation had as its two principal executive officers men who had not been elected to either the presidency or the vice-presidency. It is a measure of the legitimacy of the Constitution that this arrangement caused no crisis in public opinion.

Impeachment

There is one other way—besides death, disability, or resignation—by which a president can leave office before his term expires, and that is by impeachment.

President Clinton was impeached for lying to the grand jury and others about his sexual relations with Monica Lewinsky, but the Senate did not convict him.

Not only the president and vice president but also all "civil officers of the United States" can be removed by being impeached and convicted. As a practical matter civil officers—cabinet secretaries, bureau chiefs, and the like—are not subject to impeachment, because the president can remove them at any time and usually will if their behavior makes them a serious political liability. Federal judges, who serve during "good behavior"* and who are constitutionally independent of the president and Congress, have been the most frequent objects of impeachment.

An **impeachment** is like an indictment in a criminal trial: a set of charges against somebody, voted by (in this case) the House of Representatives. To be removed from office, the impeached officer must be convicted by a two-thirds vote of the Senate, which sits as a court, hears the evidence, and makes its decision under whatever rules it wishes to adopt. Sixteen persons have been impeached by the House, and seven have been convicted by the Senate. The last conviction was in 1989, when two federal judges were removed from office.

Only two presidents have ever been impeached—Andrew Johnson in 1868 and Bill Clinton in 1998. Richard Nixon would surely have been impeached in 1974 had he not resigned after the House Judiciary Committee voted to recommend impeachment.

The Senate did not convict either Johnson or Clinton by the necessary two-thirds vote. The case

★ **POLITICALLY**

SPEAKING ★

Lame Duck

A **lame duck** is a politician whose power has diminished because he or she is about to leave office as a result of electoral defeat or statutory limitation (for example, the president can serve no more than two terms).

The expression was first used in eighteenth-century England, where it meant a "bankrupt businessman." Soon it was used to refer to "bankrupt" politicians. Perhaps they were called "lame ducks" because they had been shot on the wing and, though still alive, could no longer fly.

A lame duck is not to be confused with a "sitting duck" (somebody who is an easy target).

Source: From *Safire's Political Dictionary* by William Safire. Copyright © 1968, 1972, 1978 by William Safire. Reprinted by permission of Random House, Inc. and the author.

ciary Committee). The vote to impeach was passed by the House along party lines. A majority, but not two-thirds, of the Senate voted to convict.

Why did Clinton survive? There were many factors. The public disliked his private behavior but did not think it amounted to an impeachable offense. (In fact right after Lewinsky revealed her sexual affair with him, his standing in opinion polls went up.) The economy was strong, and the nation was at peace. Clinton was a centrist Democrat who did not offend most voters.

The one casualty of the entire episode was the death of the law creating the office of the Independent Counsel. Passed in 1978 by a Congress that was upset by the Watergate crisis, the law directed the attorney general to ask a three-judge panel to appoint an independent counsel whenever a high official is charged with serious misconduct. (In 1993, when the 1978 law expired, President Clinton asked that it be passed again. It was.) Eighteen people were investigated by various independent counsels from 1978 to 1999. In about half the cases, no charges were brought to court.

For a long time Republicans disliked the law because the counsels were investigating them. After Clinton came to office, the counsels started investigating him and his associates, and so the Democrats began to oppose it. In 1999, when the law expired, it was not renewed.

A problem remains, however. How will any high official, including the president, be investigated when the attorney general, who does most investigations, is part of the president's team? One answer is to let Congress do it, but Congress may be controlled by the president's party. No one has yet solved this puzzle.

Some Founders may have thought that impeachment would be used frequently against presidents, but as a practical matter it is so complex and serious an undertaking that we can probably expect it to be reserved in the future only for the gravest forms of presidential misconduct. No one quite knows what a high crime or misdemeanor is, but most scholars agree that the charge must involve something illegal or unconstitutional, not just unpopular. Unless a president or vice president is first impeached and

against Johnson was entirely political—Radical Republicans, who wished to punish the South after the Civil War, were angry at Johnson, a southerner, who had a soft policy toward the South. The argument against him was flimsy.

The case against Clinton was more serious. The House Judiciary Committee, relying on the report of independent counsel Kenneth Starr, charged Clinton with perjury (lying under oath about his sexual affair with Monica Lewinsky), obstruction of justice (trying to block the Starr investigation), and abuse of power (making false written statements to the Judi-

---

*"Good behavior" means a judge can stay in office until he retires or dies, unless he or she is impeached and convicted.

convicted, many experts believe that he is not liable to prosecution as would be an ordinary citizen. (No one is certain, because the question has never arisen.) President Ford's pardon of Richard Nixon meant that he could not be prosecuted under federal law for things that he may have done while in office.

Students may find the occasions of misconduct or disability remote and the details of succession or impeachment tedious. But the problem is not remote—succession has occurred nine times and disability at least twice—and what may appear tedious goes, in fact, to the heart of the presidency. The first and fundamental problem is to make the office legitimate. That was the great task George Washington set himself, and that was the substantial accomplishment of his successors. Despite bitter and sometimes violent partisan and sectional strife, beginning almost immediately after Washington stepped down, presidential succession has always occurred peacefully, without a military coup or a political plot. For centuries, in the bygone times of kings as well as in the present times of dictators and juntas, peaceful succession has been a rare event among the nations of the world. Many of the critics of the Constitution believed in 1787 that peaceful succession would not happen in the United States either: somehow the president would connive to hold office for life or to handpick his successor. Their predictions were wrong, though their fears are understandable.

How Powerful Is the President?

Just as members of Congress bemoan their loss of power, so presidents bemoan theirs. Can both be right?

In fact they can. If Congress is less able to control events than it once was, it does not mean that the president is thereby more able to exercise control. The federal government *as a whole* has become more constrained, so it is less able to act decisively. The chief source of this constraint is the greater complexity of the issues with which Washington must deal.

It was one thing to pass the Social Security Act in 1935; it is quite another thing to keep the Social Security system adequately funded. It was one thing for the nation to defend itself when attacked in 1941; it is quite another to maintain a constant military preparedness while simultaneously exploring possibilities for arms control. It was not hard to give pensions to veterans; it seems almost impossible today to find the cure for drug abuse or juvenile crime.

In the face of modern problems, all branches of government, including the presidency, seem both big and ineffectual. Add to this the much closer and more critical scrutiny of the media and the proliferation of interest groups, and it is small wonder that both presidents and members of Congress feel that they have lost power.

Presidents have come to acquire certain rules of thumb for dealing with their political problems. Among them are these:

- *Move it or lose it.* A president who wants to get something done should do it early in his term, before his political influence erodes.
- *Avoid details.* President Carter's lieutenants regret having tried to do too much. Better to have three or four top priorities and forget the rest.
- *Cabinets don't get much accomplished; people do.* Find capable White House subordinates and give them well-defined responsibility; then watch them closely.[22]

Summary

A U.S. president, chosen by the people and with powers derived from a written constitution, has less power than does a British prime minister, even though the latter depends entirely on the support of his or her party in Parliament. The separation of powers between the executive and legislative branches, the distinguishing feature of the American system, means that the president must deal with a competitor—Congress—in setting policy and even in managing executive agencies.

Presidential power, though still sharply limited, has grown from its constitutional origins as a result of congressional delegation, the increased importance of foreign affairs, and public expectations. But if the president today has more power, more is also demanded of him. As a result how effective he is depends not on any general grant of authority but on the nature of the issue that he confronts and the extent to which he can mobilize informal sources of power (public opinion, congressional support).

Though the president seemingly controls a vast executive-branch apparatus, in fact he appoints but a small portion of the officials, and the behavior of even these is often beyond his easy control. Moreover, public support, high at the beginning of any new presidency, usually declines as the term proceeds. Consequently each president must conserve his power (and his energy and time), concentrating these scarce resources to deal with a few matters of major importance. Virtually every president since Franklin Roosevelt has tried to enlarge his ability to manage the executive branch—by reorganization, by appointing White House aides, by creating specialized staff agencies—but no president has been satisfied with the results.

The president, in dealing with Congress, can rely to some degree on party loyalty; thus presidents whose party controls Congress tend to have more of their proposals approved. But such loyalty is insufficient; every president must in addition cajole, award favors, and threaten vetoes to influence legislation. Few presidents can count on a honeymoon; most discover that their own plans are at the mercy of unexpected crises.

The extent to which a president will be weak or powerful will vary with the kind of issue and the circumstances of the moment. It is a mistake to speak of an "imperial presidency" or of an ineffectual one. A president's power is better assessed by considering how he behaves in regard to specific issues.

World Wide Web Resources

- www.whitehouse.gov
- www.ipl.org/ref/POTUS/

- lcweb.loc.gov/global/executive/fed.html
- www.interlink-cafe.com/uspresidents

Key Terms

divided government p. 335
unified government p. 335
representative democracy p. 337

direct democracy p. 337
pyramid structure p. 346
circular structure p. 346
ad hoc structure p. 346
perks p. 348

cabinet p. 349
veto message p. 358
pocket veto p. 358
line-item veto p. 360
trustee approach p. 364

delegate model p. 364
legislative veto p. 365
impeachment p. 369
lame duck p. 370

Suggested Readings

General

Barber, James David. *The Presidential Character*. 3rd ed. Englewood Cliffs, N.J.: Prentice-Hall, 1985. How a president's personality evolves and shapes his conduct in office.

Corwin, Edward S. *The President: Office and Powers*. 5th ed. New York: New York University Press, 1985. Historical, constitutional, and legal development of the office.

Jones, Charles O. *Passage to the Presidency* (Washington, D.C.: Brookings Institution, 1998). Insightful account of how four presidents—Nixon, Carter, Reagan, and Clinton—moved from the campaign to the presidency.

Neustadt, Richard E. *Presidential Power: The Politics of Leadership*. Rev. ed. New York: Wiley, 1976. How presidents try to acquire and hold political power in the competitive world of official Washington, by a man who has been both a scholar and an insider.

Peterson, Mark A. *Legislating Together: The White House and Congress from Eisenhower to Reagan*. Cambridge: Harvard University Press, 1990. Challenges the conventional view that "the president proposes, Congress disposes." Contains many excellent examples of bargaining and cooperation between Congress and the executive branch.

On Franklin D. Roosevelt

Leuchtenberg, William E. *Franklin D. Roosevelt and the New Deal, 1932–1940*. New York: Harper & Row, 1963.

Maney, Richard J. *The Roosevelt Presence*. New York: Twayne, 1992.

On Harry S Truman

Hamby, A. L. *Beyond the New Deal: Harry S Truman and American Liberalism*. New York: Columbia University Press, 1973.

McCullough, David. *Truman*. New York: Simon & Schuster, 1984.

On Dwight D. Eisenhower

Ambrose, Stephen E. *Eisenhower*. New York: Simon & Schuster, 1984.

Greenstein, Fred I. *The Hidden-Hand Presidency: Eisenhower as Leader*. New York: Basic Books, 1982.

On John F. Kennedy

Paper, Lewis J. *The Promise and the Performance: The Leadership of John F. Kennedy*. New York: Crown, 1975.

Parmet, Herbert C. *Jack*. New York: Dial Press, 1980.

On Lyndon B. Johnson

Dallek, Robert. *Lone Star Rising* and *Flawed Giant*. New York: Oxford University Press, 1991 and 1996.

Kearns, Doris. *Lyndon Johnson and the American Dream*. New York: Harper & Row, 1976.

On Richard M. Nixon

Ambrose, Stephen E. ———. *Nixon*. 3 vols. New York: Simon & Schuster, 1987, 1989, 1991.

On Jimmy Carter

Bourne, Peter G. *Jimmy Carter*. New York: Scribner, 1997.

On Ronald Reagan

Cannon, Lou. *President Reagan*. New York: Simon & Schuster, 1991.

On George Bush

Parmet, Herbert C. *George Bush*. New York: Scribner, 1997.

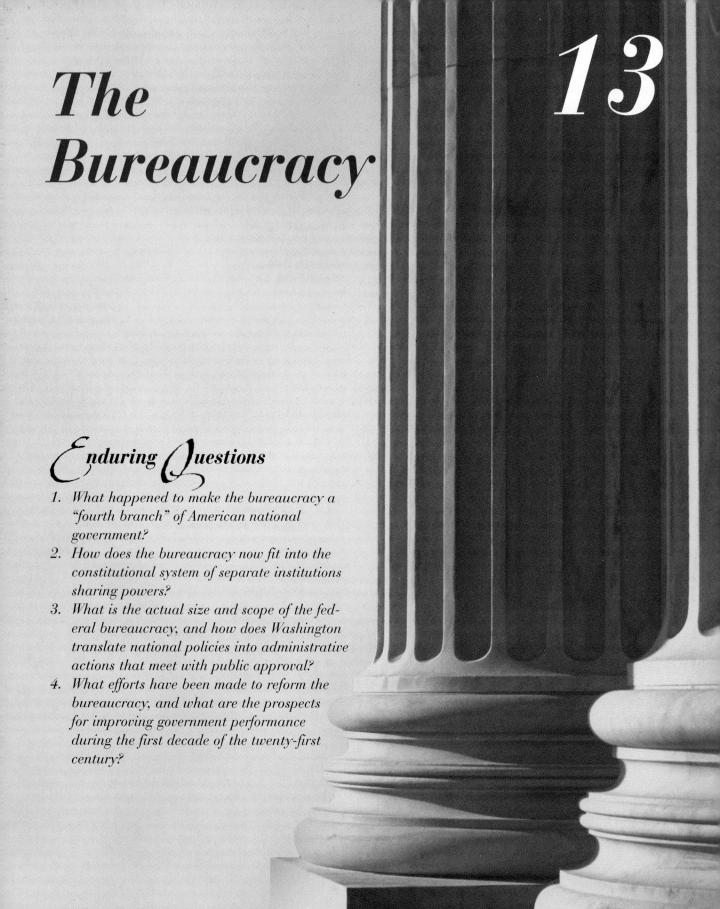

The Bureaucracy

13

Enduring Questions

1. *What happened to make the bureaucracy a "fourth branch" of American national government?*

2. *How does the bureaucracy now fit into the constitutional system of separate institutions sharing powers?*

3. *What is the actual size and scope of the federal bureaucracy, and how does Washington translate national policies into administrative actions that meet with public approval?*

4. *What efforts have been made to reform the bureaucracy, and what are the prospects for improving government performance during the first decade of the twenty-first century?*

Distinctiveness of the American Bureaucracy

The Growth of the Bureaucracy
The Appointment of Officials • A Service Role •
A Change in Role

The Federal Bureaucracy Today
Recruitment and Retention • Personal Attributes •
Do Bureaucrats Sabotage Their Political Bosses? •
Culture and Careers • Constraints • Agency Allies

Congressional Oversight
The Appropriations Committee and Legislative
Committees • The Legislative Veto • Congressional
Investigations

Bureaucratic "Pathologies"

Reforming the Bureaucracy

There is probably not a man or woman in the United States who has not, at some time or other, complained about "the bureaucracy." Your letter was slow in getting to Aunt Minnie? The Internal Revenue Service took months to send you your tax refund? The Defense Department paid $400 for a hammer? The Occupational Safety and Health Administration told you that you installed the wrong kind of portable toilet for your farm workers? The "bureaucracy" is to blame.

For most people and politicians *bureaucracy* is a pejorative word implying waste, confusion, red tape, and rigidity. But for scholars—and for bureaucrats themselves—*bureaucracy* is a word with a neutral, technical meaning. A **bureaucracy** is a large, complex organization composed of appointed officials. By *complex* we mean that authority is divided among several managers; no one person is able to make all the decisions. A large corporation is a bureaucracy; so also are a big university and a government agency. With its sizable staff, even Congress has become, to some degree, a bureaucracy.

What is it about complex organizations in general, and government agencies in particular, that leads so many people to complain about them? In part the answer is to be found in their very size and complexity. But in large measure the answer is to be found in the political context within which such agencies must operate. If we examine that context carefully, we will discover that many of the problems that we blame on "the bureaucracy" are in fact the result of what Congress, the courts, and the president do.

Distinctiveness of the American Bureaucracy

Bureaucratic government has become an obvious feature of all modern societies, democratic and nondemocratic. In the United States, however, three aspects of our constitutional system and political traditions give to the bureaucracy a distinctive character. First, political authority over the bureaucracy is not in one set of hands but is shared among several institutions. In a parliamentary regime, such as in Great Britain, the appointed officials of the national government work for the cabinet ministers, who are in turn dominated by the prime minister. In theory, and to a considerable extent in practice, British bureaucrats report to and take orders from the ministers in charge of their departments, do not deal directly with Parliament, and rarely give interviews to the press. In the United States the Constitution permits both the president and Congress to exercise authority over the bureaucracy. Every senior appointed official has at least two masters: one in the executive branch and the other in the legislative. Often there are many more than two: Congress, after all, is not a single organization but a collection of committees, subcommittees, and individuals. This divided authority encourages bureaucrats to play one branch of government off against the other and to make heavy use of the media.

Second, most of the agencies of the federal government share their functions with related agencies in state and local government. Though some federal agencies deal directly with American citizens—the Internal Revenue Service collects taxes from them, the Federal Bureau of Investigation looks into crimes for them, the Postal Service delivers mail to them—many agencies work with other organizations at other levels of government. For example, the Department of Education gives money to local school systems; the Health Care Financing Administration in the Department of Health and Human Services reimburses states for money spent on health care for the poor; the

Department of Housing and Urban Development gives grants to cities for community development; and the Employment and Training Administration in the Department of Labor supplies funds to local governments so that they can run job-training programs. In France, by contrast, government programs dealing with education, health, housing, and employment are centrally run, with little or no control exercised by local governments.

Third, the institutions and traditions of American life have contributed to the growth of what some writers have described as an "adversary culture," in which the definition and expansion of personal rights, and the defense of rights and claims through lawsuits as well as political action, are given central importance. A government agency in this country operates under closer public scrutiny and with a greater prospect of court challenges to its authority than in almost any other nation. Virtually every important decision of the Occupational Safety and Health Administration or of the Environmental Protection Agency is likely to be challenged in the courts or attacked by an affected party; in Sweden the decisions of similar agencies go largely uncontested.

The scope as well as the style of bureaucratic government differs. In most Western European nations the government owns and operates large parts of the economy: the French government operates the railroads and owns companies that make automobiles and cigarettes, and the Italian government owns many similar enterprises and also the nation's oil refineries. In just about every large nation except the United States, the telephone system is owned by the government. Publicly operated enterprises account for about 12 percent of all employment in France but less than 3 percent in the United States.[1] The U.S. government regulates privately owned enterprises to a degree not found in many other countries, however. Why we should have preferred regulation to ownership as the proper government role is an interesting question to which we shall return.

The Growth of the Bureaucracy

The Constitution made scarcely any provision for an administrative system other than to allow the president to appoint, with the advice and consent of the Senate, "ambassadors, other public ministers and consuls, judges of the Supreme Court, and all other officers of the United States whose appointments are not herein otherwise provided for, and which shall be established by law."[2] Departments and bureaus were not mentioned.

In the first Congress, in 1789, James Madison introduced a bill to create a Department of State to assist the new secretary of state, Thomas Jefferson, in carrying out his duties. People appointed to this department were to be nominated by the president and approved by the Senate, but they were "to be removable by the president" alone. These six words, which would confer the right to fire government officials, occasioned six days of debate in the House. At stake was the locus of power over what was to become the bureaucracy. Madison's opponents argued that the Senate should consent to the removal of officials as well as their appointment. Madison responded that, without the unfettered right of removal, the president would not be able to control his subordinates, and without this control he would not be able to discharge his constitutional obligation to "take care that the laws be faithfully executed."[3] Madison won, twenty-nine votes to twenty-two. When the issue went to the Senate, another debate resulted in a tie vote, broken in favor of the president by Vice President John Adams. The Department of State, and all cabinet departments subsequently created, would be run by people removable only by the president.

That decision did not resolve the question of who would really control the bureaucracy, however. Congress retained the right to appropriate money, to investigate the administration, and to shape the laws that would be executed by that administration—more than ample power to challenge any president who claimed to have sole authority over his subordinates. And many members of Congress expected that the cabinet departments, even though headed by people removable by the president, would report to Congress.

The government in Washington was at first minuscule. The State Department started with only nine employees; the War Department did not have eighty civilian employees until 1801. Only the Treasury Department, concerned with collecting taxes and finding ways to pay the public debt, had much power, and only the Post Office Department provided any significant service.

The Appointment of Officials

Small as the bureaucracy was, people struggled, often bitterly, over who would be appointed to it. From George Washington's day to modern times, presidents have found appointment to be one of

their most important and difficult tasks. The officials that they select affect how the laws are interpreted (thus the political ideology of the job holders is important), what tone the administration will display (thus personal character is important), how effectively the public business is discharged (thus competence is important), and how strong the political party or faction in power will be (thus party affiliation is important). Presidents trying to balance the competing needs of ideology, character, fitness, and partisanship have rarely pleased most people. As John Adams remarked, every appointment creates one ingrate and ten enemies.

Because Congress, during most of the nineteenth and twentieth centuries, was the dominant branch of government, congressional preferences often controlled the appointment of officials. And since Congress was, in turn, a collection of people who represented local interests, appointments were made with an eye to rewarding the local supporters of members of Congress or building up local party organizations. These appointments made on the basis of political considerations—patronage—were later to become a major issue. They galvanized various reform efforts that sought to purify politics and to raise the level of competence of the public service. Many of the abuses that the reformers complained about were real enough, but patronage served some useful purposes as well. It gave the president a way to ensure that his subordinates were reasonably supportive of his policies; it provided a reward that the president could use to induce recalcitrant members of Congress to vote for his programs; and it enabled party organizations to be built up to perform the necessary functions of nominating candidates and getting out the vote.

Though at first there were not many jobs to fight over, by the middle of the nineteenth century there were a lot. From 1816 to 1861 the number of federal employees increased eightfold. This expansion was not, however, the result of the government's taking on new functions but simply a result of the increased demands on its traditional functions. The Post Office alone accounted for 86 percent of this growth.[4]

The Civil War was a great watershed in bureaucratic development. Fighting the war led, naturally, to hiring many new officials and creating many new offices. Just as important, the Civil War revealed the administrative weakness of the federal government and led to demands by the civil service reform movement for an improvement in the quality and organization of federal employees. And finally, the war was

★ **POLITICALLY**
SPEAKING ★

Spoils System

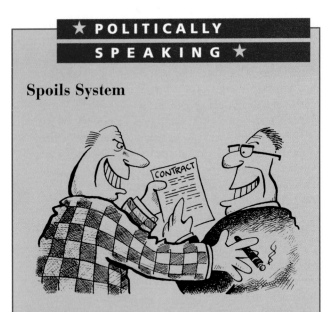

The **spoils system** is another phrase for *political patronage*—that is, the practice of giving the fruits of a party's victory, such as jobs and contracts, to the loyal members of that party.

Spoils became a famous word when it was used in 1832 by Senator William Marcy of New York in a speech that he made defending the decision of President Andrew Jackson to appoint one of his supporters, Martin Van Buren, as ambassador to Great Britain. New York politicians, he said, "boldly preach what they practice. . . . If they are successful, they claim, as a matter of right, the advantages of success. They see nothing wrong in the rule, that to the victor belong the spoils of the enemy."

In fact both the word and the practice are much older than Marcy and Jackson. Thomas Jefferson had appointed his partisans to office when he won the presidency from John Adams. Though Jackson is remembered as a heavy user of spoils, in fact he only replaced about 20 percent of all the officeholders that he inherited from his predecessor.

By the late nineteenth century the spoils system was both more extensively used and sharply criticized. Ending the system and replacing it with appointments based on merit was a major goal of the progressive movement around the turn of the century.

Today most federal appointments are based on merit, but in many state governments there continues to be a heavy reliance on patronage.

Source: From *Safire's Political Dictionary* by William Safire. Copyright © 1968, 1972, 1978 by William Safire. Reprinted by permission of Random House, Inc. and the author.

followed by a period of rapid industrialization and the emergence of a national economy. The effects of these developments could no longer be managed by state governments acting alone. With the creation of a nationwide network of railroads, commerce among the states became increasingly important. The constitutional powers of the federal government to regulate interstate commerce, long dormant for want of much commerce to regulate, now became an important source of controversy.

A Service Role

From 1861 to 1901 new agencies were created, many to deal with particular sectors of society and the economy. Over two hundred thousand new federal employees were added, with only about half of this increase in the Post Office. The rapidly growing Pension Office began paying benefits to Civil War veterans; the Department of Agriculture was created in 1862 to help farmers; the Department of Labor was founded in 1882 to serve workers; and the Department of Commerce was organized in 1903 to assist businesspeople. Many more specialized agencies, such as the National Bureau of Standards, also came into being.

These agencies had one thing in common: their role was primarily to serve, not to regulate. Most did research, gathered statistics, dispensed federal lands, or passed out benefits. Not until the Interstate Commerce Commission (ICC) was created in 1887 did the federal government begin to regulate the economy (other than by managing the currency) in any large way. Even the ICC had, at first, relatively few powers.

There were several reasons why federal officials primarily performed a service role. The values that had shaped the Constitution were still strong: these included a belief in limited government, the importance of states' rights, and the fear of concentrated discretionary power. The proper role of government in the economy was to promote, not to regulate, and a commitment to **laissez-faire**—a freely competitive economy—was strongly held. But just as important, the Constitution said nothing about giving any regulatory powers to bureaucrats. It gave to *Congress* the power to regulate commerce among the states. Now obviously Congress could not make the necessary day-to-day decisions to regulate, for example, the rates that interstate railroads charged to farmers and other shippers. Some agency or commission composed of appointed officials and experts would have to be created to do that. For a long time, however, the prevail-

The Hollerith machine (left) was invented by Herman Hollerith (1860–1929) to help the government take the census. It analyzed statistical data by sorting and counting punched paper cards. Today high-speed computers (right) read data optically and analyze them electronically.

ing interpretation of the Constitution was that no such agency could exercise such regulatory powers unless Congress first set down clear standards that would govern the agency's decisions. As late as 1935 the Supreme Court held that a regulatory agency could not make rules on its own; it could only apply the standards enacted by Congress.[5] The Court's view was that the legislature may not delegate its powers to the president or to an administrative agency.[6]

These restrictions on what administrators could do were set aside in wartime. During World War I, for example, President Woodrow Wilson was authorized by Congress to fix prices, operate the railroads, manage the communications system, and even control the distribution of food.[7] This kind of extraordinary grant of power usually ended with the war.

Some changes in the bureaucracy did not end with the war. During the Civil War, World War I, World War II, the Korean War, and the war in Vietnam, the number of civilian (as well as military) employees of the government rose sharply. These increases were not simply in the number of civilians needed to help serve the war effort; many of the additional people were hired by agencies, such as the Treasury Department, not obviously connected with the war. Furthermore, the number of federal officials did not return to prewar levels after each war. Though there was some reduction, each war left the number of federal employees larger than before.[8]

It is not hard to understand how this happens. During wartime almost every government agency argues that its activities have *some* relation to the war effort, and few legislators want to be caught voting against something that may help that effort. Hence in 1944 the Reindeer Service in Alaska, an agency of the Interior Department, asked for more employees because reindeer are "a valued asset in military planning."

A Change in Role

Today's bureaucracy is largely a product of two events: the depression of the 1930s (and the concomitant New Deal program of President Roosevelt) and World War II. Though many agencies have been added since then, the basic features of the bureaucracy were set mainly as a result of changes in public attitudes and in constitutional interpretation that occurred during these periods. The government was now expected to play an active role in dealing with economic and social problems. In the late 1930s the Supreme Court reversed its earlier decisions (see Chapter 14) on the question of delegating legislative powers to administrative agencies and upheld laws by which Congress merely instructs agencies to make decisions that serve "the public interest" in some area.[9] As a result it was possible for President Nixon to set up in 1971 a system of price and wage controls based on a statute that simply authorized the president "to issue such orders and regulations as he may deem appropriate to stabilize prices, rents, wages, and salaries."[10] The Cost of Living Council and other agencies that Nixon established to carry out this order were run by appointed officials who had the legal authority to make sweeping decisions based on general statutory language.

World War II was the first occasion during which the government made heavy use of federal income taxes—on individuals and corporations—to finance its activities. Between 1940 and 1945 total federal tax collections increased from about $5 billion to nearly $44 billion. The end of the war brought no substantial tax reduction: the country believed that a high level of military preparedness continued to be necessary and that various social programs begun before the war should enjoy the heavy funding made possible by wartime taxes. Tax receipts continued, by and large, to grow. Before 1913, when the Sixteenth Amendment to the Constitution was passed, the federal government could not collect income taxes at all (it financed itself largely from customs duties and excise taxes). From 1913 to 1940 income taxes were small (in 1940 the average American paid only $7 in federal income taxes). World War II created the first great financial boom for the government, permitting the sustained expansion of a wide variety of programs and thus entrenching a large number of administrators in Washington.[11]

The Federal Bureaucracy Today

No president wants to admit that he has increased the size of the bureaucracy. He can avoid saying this by pointing out that the number of civilians working for the federal government, excluding postal workers, has not increased significantly in recent years and is about the same today (2 million persons) as it was in 1960, and less than it was during World War II. This explanation is true but misleading, for it neglects the roughly 13 million people who work *indirectly* for Washington as employees of private firms and state or local agencies that are largely, if not entirely, supported by federal funds. As Figure 13.1 shows, there are nearly three persons earning their living indirectly from the federal government for every one earning it directly. While federal employment has remained quite stable, employment among federal contractors and consultants and in state and local governments has mushroomed. Indeed, most federal bureaucrats, like most other people who work for the federal government, live outside Washington, D.C. (see Figure 13.3 later in this chapter).

The power of the federal bureaucracy cannot be measured by the number of employees, however. A bureaucracy of five million persons would have little power if each employees did nothing but type letters or file documents, whereas a bureaucracy of only one hundred persons would have awesome power if each member were able to make arbitrary life-and-death decisions affecting the rest of us. The power of the bureaucracy depends on the extent to which appointed officials have **discretionary authority**— that is, the ability to choose courses of action and to make policies that are not spelled out in advance by laws. In Figure 13.2 we see how the volume of regulations issued and the amount of money spent have risen much faster than the number of federal employees who write the regulations and spend the money.

By this test the power of the federal bureaucracy has grown enormously. Congress has delegated substantial authority to administrative agencies in three areas: (1) paying subsidies to particular groups and organizations in society (farmers, veterans, scientists, schools, universities, hospitals); (2) transferring money from the federal government to state and local governments (the grant-in-aid programs described in Chapter 3); and (3) devising and enforcing regulations for various sectors of society and the economy. Some of these administrative functions, such as grants-in-aid to states, are closely monitored by Congress; others, such as the regulatory programs, usually operate with a greater degree of independence. These delegations of power, especially in the areas of paying subsidies and regulating the economy, did not become commonplace until the 1930s, and then only after the

---

Figure 13.1   The Real "Washington" Bureaucracy

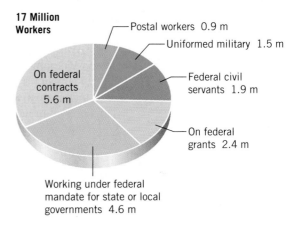

17 Million Workers

- Postal workers 0.9 m
- Uniformed military 1.5 m
- Federal civil servants 1.9 m
- On federal grants 2.4 m
- Working under federal mandate for state or local governments 4.6 m
- On federal contracts 5.6 m

Source: Paul C. Light, *The True Size of Government* (Washington, D.C.: Brookings Institution, 1999). Data for 1996.

Supreme Court decided that such delegations were constitutional. Today, by contrast, appointed officials can decide, within rather broad limits, who shall own a television station, what safety features automobiles shall have, what kinds of scientific research shall be specially encouraged, what drugs shall appear on the market, which dissident groups shall be investigated, what fumes an industrial smokestack may emit, which corporate mergers shall be allowed, what use shall be made of national forests, and what prices crop and dairy farmers shall receive for their products.

If appointed officials have this kind of power, then how they use it is of paramount importance in understanding modern government. There are, broadly, four factors that may explain the behavior of these officials:

1. The manner in which they are recruited and rewarded
2. Their personal attributes, such as their socioeconomic backgrounds and their political attitudes
3. The nature of their jobs
4. The constraints that outside forces—political superiors, legislators, interest groups, journalists—impose on their agencies

Recruitment and Retention

The federal civil service system was designed to recruit qualified people on the basis of merit, not political patronage, and to retain and promote employees on the basis of performance, not political favoritism. Many appointed federal officials belong to the **competitive service.** This means that they are appointed only after they have passed a written examination administered by the Office of Personnel Management (OPM) or met certain selection criteria (such as training, educational attainments, or prior experience) devised by the hiring agency and approved by the OPM. Where competition for a job exists and candidates can be ranked by their scores or records, the agency must usually appoint one of the three top-ranking candidates.

In recent years the competitive service system has become decentralized, so that each agency now hires its own people without an OPM referral, and examinations have become less common. In 1952 more than 86 percent of all federal employees were civil servants hired by the competitive service; by 1996 that figure had fallen to less than 54 percent. This decentralization and the greater use of ways other than exams to hire employees was caused by three

Figure 13.2 Federal Government: Money, People, and Regulations, 1940–1996

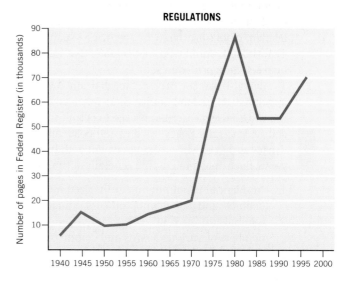

Sources: Expenditures: *Statistical Abstract of the United States, 1996,* table 517; *Historical Statistics of the United States,* Series F-32 and Y-340. Civilian employment and regulations: Harold W. Stanley and Richard G. Niemi, *Vital Statistics on American Politics* (Washington, D.C.: Congressional Quarterly Press, 1998), tables 6-12, 6-14.

things. First, the old OPM system was cumbersome and often not relevant to the complex needs of departments. Second, these agencies had a need for more professionally trained employees—lawyers, biologists, engineers, and computer specialists—who could not be ranked on the basis of some standard exam. And third, civil rights groups pressed Washington to make the racial composition of the federal bureaucracy look more like the racial composition of the nation.

Thus it is wrong to suppose that a standardized, centralized system governs the federal service. As one recent study concluded, today much of the "real responsibility for recruiting, testing, and hiring has shifted to the agencies from OPM and its central system."[12]

Moreover, the kinds of workers being recruited into the federal civil service have changed. For example, blue-collar employment fell from 26 percent of the federal work force in 1973 to 16 percent in 1993. Meanwhile, the federal government's white-collar work force has become more diverse occupationally. As one writer on civil service reform has noted, the "need to recruit and retain physicists, biologists, oceanographers, nurses, statisticians, botanists, and epidemiologists, as well as large numbers of engineers, lawyers, and accountants, now preoccupies federal personnel managers."[13]

Employees hired outside the competitive service are part of the excepted service. They now make up almost half of all workers. Though not hired by the OPM, they still are typically hired in a nonpartisan fashion. Some are hired by agencies—such as the CIA, the FBI, and the Postal Service—that have their own selection procedures.

About 3 percent of the excepted employees are appointed on grounds other than or in addition to merit. These legal exceptions exist to permit the president to select, for policy-making and politically sensitive posts, people who are in agreement with his policy views. Such appointments are generally of three kinds:

1. Presidential appointments authorized by statute (cabinet and subcabinet officers, judges, U.S. marshals and U.S. attorneys, ambassadors, and members of various boards and commissions).
2. "Schedule C" appointments to jobs that are described as having a "confidential or policy-determining character" below the level of cabinet or subcabinet posts (including executive assistants, special aides, and confidential secretaries).
3. Noncareer executive assignments (NEAs) given to high-ranking members of the regular competitive civil service or to persons brought into the civil service at these high levels. These people are deeply involved in the advocacy of presidential programs or participate in policy-making.

Federal employees aren't just paper shufflers; many, such as this biologist, perform skilled professional tasks.

These three groups of excepted appointments constitute the patronage available to a president and his administration. When President Kennedy took office in 1961, he had 451 political jobs to fill. When President Clinton took office in 1993, he had more than four times that number, including nearly four times the number of top cabinet posts (see Table 13.1 on page 384). Scholars disagree over whether this proliferation of political appointees has improved or worsened Washington's performance, but one thing is clear: widespread presidential patronage is hardly unprecedented. In the nineteenth century practically every federal job was a patronage job. For example, when Grover Cleveland, a Democrat, became president in 1885, he replaced

HOW THINGS WORK

A Day in the Life of a Bureaucrat

Here is how the commissioner of the Social Security Administration (SSA), a high-level bureaucrat, spent a typical day:

5:45 A.M.	Arise.
6:50 A.M.	Leave for the office.
7:30 A.M.	Read newspapers.
8:00 A.M.	Meet with deputy commissioner.
8:30 A.M.	Brief cabinet secretary on Social Security data.*
9:45 A.M.	Decide how to respond to press criticisms.
10:05 A.M.	Leave for meeting in another building.
11:30 A.M.	Meet with top staff.
1:00 P.M.	Meet with bureau chiefs on half a dozen issues.
2:45 P.M.	Meet with a deputy to discuss next year's budget.
3:30 P.M.	Meet with business executive about use of computers in SSA.
4:30 P.M.	Meet with deputy in charge of Medicare to discuss plan for national health insurance.
5:10 P.M.	Catch up on phone calls; meet with committee concerned with drug abuse.
6:10 P.M.	Leave for home. Get out of attending a dinner meeting in Washington.

As is obvious, high-level bureaucrats spend most of their time discussing things in meetings. It is in such meetings that government policy is made.

*SSA was part of the Department of Health and Human Services but no longer is.

Source: Adapted from "A Day in the Life of a Government Executive," in *Inside the System*, ed. Charles Peters and Nicholas Leamann, 4th ed. (New York: Holt, Rinehart and Winston, 1979), 205–213.

some forty thousand Republican postal employees with Democrats.

Ironically, two years earlier, in 1883, the passage of the Pendleton Act had begun a slow but steady transfer of federal jobs from the patronage to the merit system. It may seem strange that a political party in power (the Republicans) would be willing to relinquish its patronage in favor of a merit-based appointment system. Two factors made it possible for the Republicans to pass the Pendleton Act: (1) public outrage over the abuses of the spoils system, highlighted by the assassination of President James Garfield by a man always described in the history books as a "disappointed office seeker" (*lunatic* would be a more accurate term); and (2) the fear that if the Democrats came to power on a wave of antispoils sentiment, existing Republican officeholders would be fired. (The Democrats won anyway.)

The merit system spread to encompass most of the federal bureaucracy, generally with presidential support. Though presidents may have liked in theory the idea of hiring and firing subordinates at will, most felt that the demands for patronage were impossible either to satisfy or to ignore. Furthermore, by increasing the coverage of the merit system a president could "blanket in" patronage appointees already holding office, thus making it difficult or impossible for the next administration to fire them.

The Buddy System   The actual recruitment of civil servants, especially in middle- and upper-level jobs, is somewhat more complicated, and slightly more political, than the laws and rules might suggest. Though many people enter the federal bureaucracy by learning of a job, filling out an application, perhaps taking a test, and being hired, many also enter on a "name-request" basis. A **name-request job** is one that is filled by a person whom an agency has already identified. In this respect the federal government is not so different from private business. A person learns of a job from somebody who already has one, or the head of a bureau decides in advance whom he or she wishes to hire. The agency must still send a form describing the job to the OPM, but it also names the person whom the agency wants to appoint. Sometimes the job is even described in such a way that the person named is the only one who can qualify for it. Occasionally this tailor-made, name-request job is offered to a person at the insistence of a member of Congress who wants a political supporter taken care of; more often it is made available because the bureaucracy itself knows whom it wishes to hire and wants to circumvent an elaborate search. This is the "buddy system."

The buddy system does not necessarily produce poor employees. Indeed, it is frequently a way of hiring people known to the agency as being capable of handling the position. It also opens up the possibility

Table 13.1 The Rise in Top Political Jobs		
	Administration	
	Kennedy	**Clinton**
Top cabinet posts		
Secretary	10	14
Deputy secretary	6	21
Undersecretary	14	32
Assistant secretary	81	212
Deputy assistant secretary	77	507
Deputy administrator	52	190
Total top cabinet posts	240	976
Total top political jobs	451	2,393

Source: Paul C. Light, *Thickening Government* (Washington, D.C.: Brookings Institution, 1995).

of hiring people whose policy views are congenial to those already in office. Such networking is based on shared policy views, not (as once was the case) on narrow partisan affiliations. For example, bureaucrats in consumer protection agencies recruit new staff from private groups with an interest in consumer protection, such as the various organizations associated with Ralph Nader, or from academics who have a proconsumer inclination.

There has always been an informal "old boys' network" among those who move in and out of high-level government posts; with the increasing appointment of women to these jobs, there has begun to emerge an old girls' network as well.[14] In a later section we will consider whether, or in what ways, these recruitment patterns make a difference.

Firing a Bureaucrat   The great majority of bureaucrats who are part of the civil service and who do not hold presidential appointments have jobs that are, for all practical purposes, beyond reach. An executive must go through elaborate steps to fire, demote, or suspend a civil servant. Realistically this means that no one is fired or demoted unless his or her superior is

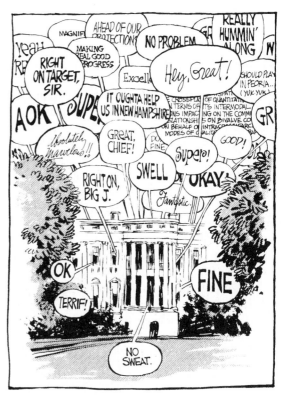

One barrier to improving presidential control of the federal bureaucracy is that even the White House has become a large bureaucracy.

Firing a Bureaucrat

To fire or demote a member of the competitive civil service, these procedures must be followed:

1. The employee must be given written notice at least thirty days in advance that he or she is to be fired or demoted for incompetence or misconduct.
2. The written notice must contain a statement of reasons, including specific examples of unacceptable performance.
3. The employee has the right to an attorney and to reply, orally or in writing, to the charges.

4. The employee has the right to appeal any adverse action to the Merit Systems Protection Board (MSPB), a three-person, bipartisan body appointed by the president with the consent of the Senate.
5. The MSPB must grant the employee a hearing, at which the employee has the right to have an attorney present.
6. The employee has the right to appeal the MSPB decision to a U.S. court of appeals, which can hold new hearings.

prepared to invest a great deal of time and effort in the attempt. In 1987 about 2,600 employees who had completed their probationary period were fired for misconduct or poor performance. That is about one-tenth of 1 percent of all federal employees. It is hard to believe that a large private company would fire only one-tenth of 1 percent of its workers in a given year. It's also impossible to believe that, as is often the case in Washington, it would take a year to fire anyone. To cope with this problem, federal executives have devised a number of stratagems for bypassing or forcing out civil servants with whom they cannot work—denying them promotions, transferring them to undesirable locations, or assigning them to meaningless work.

With the passage of the Civil Service Reform Act of 1978 Congress recognized that many high-level positions in the civil service have important policy-making responsibilities and that the president and his cabinet officers ought to have more flexibility in recruiting, assigning, and paying such people. Accordingly, the act created the Senior Executive Service (SES), about eight thousand top federal managers who can (in theory) be hired, fired, and transferred more easily than ordinary civil servants. Moreover, the act stipulated that members of the SES would be eligible for substantial cash bonuses if they performed their duties well. (To protect the rights of SES members, anyone who is removed from the SES is guaranteed a job elsewhere in the government.)

Things did not work out quite as the sponsors of the SES had hoped. Though most eligible civil servants joined it, there was only a modest increase in the proportion of higher-ranking positions in agencies that were filled by transfer from another agency; the cash bonuses did not prove to be an important incentive (perhaps because the base salaries of top bureaucrats did not keep up with inflation); and hardly any member of the SES was actually fired. Two years after the SES was created, less than one-half of 1 percent of its members had received an unsatisfactory rating, and none had been fired. Nor does the SES give the president a large opportunity to make political appointments: only 10 percent of the SES can be selected from outside the existing civil service. And no SES member can be transferred involuntarily.

The Agency's Point of View When one realizes that most agencies are staffed by people who were recruited by those agencies, sometimes on a name-request basis, and who are virtually immune from dismissal, it becomes clear that the recruitment and retention policies of the civil service work to ensure that most bureaucrats will have an "agency" point of view. Even with the encouragement for transfers created by the SES, most government agencies are dominated by people who have not served in any other agency and who have been in government service most of their lives. This fact has some advantages: it means that most top-tier bureaucrats are experts in the procedures and policies of their agencies and that there will be a substantial degree of continuity in agency behavior no matter which political party happens to be in power.

But the agency point of view has its costs as well. A political executive entering an agency with responsibility for shaping its direction will discover that he or she must carefully win the support of career subordinates. A subordinate has an infinite capacity for discreet sabotage and can make life miserable for a political superior by delaying action, withholding information, following the rule book with literal exactness, or making an "end run" around a superior to mobilize members of Congress who are sympathetic to the bureaucrat's point of view. For instance, when one political executive wanted to downgrade a bureau in his department, he found, naturally, that the bureau chief was opposed. The bureau chief spoke to some friendly lobbyists and a key member of Congress. When the political executive asked the congressman whether he had any problem with the contemplated reorganization, the congressman replied, "No, you have the problem, because if you touch that bureau, I'll cut your job out of the budget."[15]

Personal Attributes

A second factor that might shape the way bureaucrats use their power is their personal attributes. These include their social class, education, and personal political beliefs. The federal civil service as a whole looks very much like a cross section of American society in the education, sex, race, and social origins of its members (see Figure 13.3). But as with many other employers, African Americans and other minorities are most likely to be heavily represented in the lowest grade levels and tend to be underrepresented at the executive level (see Table 13.2). At the higher-ranking levels, where the most power is found—say, in the supergrade ranks of GS 16 through GS 18—the typical civil servant is a middle-aged white male with a college degree whose father was somewhat more advantaged than the average citizen. In the great majority of cases this individual is in fact very different from the typical American in both background and personal beliefs.

Because political appointees and career bureaucrats are unrepresentative of the average American, and because of their supposed occupational self-interest, some critics have speculated that the people holding these jobs think about politics and government in ways very different from the public at large.

The results of a 1998 survey would seem to prove them right: 57 percent of average citizens, versus 76 percent of career bureaucrats and 88 percent of Clinton administration appointees, described themselves as pro-government; 60 percent of all Americans, compared to just 4 percent of all career bureaucrats and Clinton appointees, agreed that most popular criticisms of the federal government were justified; about a third of the public, but under a fifth of the career and appointed public servants, described themselves as conservative; and only 13 or 14 percent of those in government agreed that the public knew enough about the issues to form wise opinions on policy.[16]

It is important, however, not to overgeneralize from such differences. For example, whereas Clinton appointees (virtually all of them strong Democrats) were more liberal than average citizens, Reagan appointees (virtually all of them loyal Republicans) were undoubtedly more conservative than average citizens. Likewise, career civil servants are more pro-government than the public at large, but on most specific policy questions, federal bureaucrats do not have extreme positions. They don't, for example, think that the government should take over the big corporations, they support some amount of business deregulation, and a majority (by a slim margin) don't think that the goal of U.S. foreign policy has been to protect business.[17]

We can also see, however, that the kind of agency for which a bureaucrat works makes a difference. Those employed in "activist" agencies, such as the Federal Trade Commission, Environmental Protection Agency, and Food and Drug Administration, have much more liberal views than those who work for the more "traditional" agencies, such as the departments of Agriculture, Commerce, and the Treasury.

This association between attitudes and kind of agency has been confirmed by other studies. Even when the bureaucrats come from roughly the same social backgrounds, their policy views seem to reflect the type of government work that they do. For example, people holding foreign service jobs in the State Department tended to be more liberal than those coming from similar family backgrounds and performing similar tasks (such as working on foreign affairs) in the Defense Department.[18] It is not clear whether these differences in attitudes were produced by the jobs that they held or whether certain jobs attract people with certain beliefs. Probably both forces were at work.

Whatever the mechanism involved, there seems little doubt that different agencies display different polit-

Figure 13.3   Characteristics of Federal Civilian Employees, 1960 and 1994

Total number of employees   1960   2.2 million
                             1994   2.1 million

Sex

1960   Male 75%   Female 25%

1994   Male 57%   Female 43%

Race

1960   White/Minority data for 1960 unavailable

1994   White 71.8%   Minority* 28.2%

Employing Agency

1960   Defense Department 44%   Postal Service 23%   All other 33%

1994   Defense Department 30.2%   Postal Service 38.3%   All other 31.5%

Location

1960   11%   Elsewhere 89%

1994   11%   Elsewhere 89%

└─> In Washington area

*Blacks, Native Americans, Hispanics, Asians, and Pacific Islanders

Sources: Statistical Abstract of the United States, 1961, 392–394; Statistical Abstract of the United States, 1992, 330–331.

ical ideologies. A study done in 1976 revealed that Democrats and people with liberal views tended to be overrepresented in social service agencies, whereas Republicans and people with conservative views tend to be overrepresented in defense agencies.[19]

Do Bureaucrats Sabotage Their Political Bosses?

Because it is so hard to fire career bureaucrats, it is often said that these people will sabotage any actions by their political superiors with which they disagree. And since civil servants tend to have liberal views, it has been conservative presidents and cabinet secretaries who have usually expressed this worry.

There is no doubt that some bureaucrats will drag their heels if they don't like their bosses, and a few will block actions they oppose. However, most bureaucrats try to carry out the policies of their superiors even when they personally disagree with them. When David Stockman was director of the

OMB, he set out to make sharp cuts in government spending programs in accordance with the wishes of his boss, President Reagan. He later published a book complaining about all the people in the White House and Congress who worked against him.[20] But nowhere in the book is there any major criticism of the civil servants at the OMB. It appears that whatever these people thought about Stockman and Reagan, they loyally tried to carry out Stockman's policies.

Bureaucrats tend to be loyal to political superiors who deal with them cooperatively and constructively. An agency head who tries to ignore or discredit them can be in for a tough time, however. The powers of obstruction available to aggrieved bureaucrats are formidable. Such people can leak embarrassing stories to Congress or to the media, help interest groups mobilize against the agency head, and discover a thousand procedural reasons why a new course of action won't work.

Table 13.2	Minority Employment in the Federal Bureaucracy by Rank, 1995					
					Percentage of Total	
Grade	Black	Hispanic	All Races	Black	Hispanic
GS 1–4	41,381	11,081	131,657	31.4%	8.4%
GS 5–8	112,962	31,152	432,869	26.1	7.2
GS 9–12	79,795	34,056	579,759	13.8	5.9
GS 13–15	24,448	10,473	302,171	8.1	3.5
SES	942	382	14,631	6.4	2.6
Total	259,528	87,144	1,461,087	17.8	6.0

Note: GS stands for "General Service." The higher the number, the higher the rank of people with that number.

Source: Statistical Abstract of the United States, 1998, 354.

The exercise of some of those bureaucratic powers is protected by the Whistle Blower Protection Act. Passed in 1989, the law created the Office of Special Counsel, charged with investigating complaints from bureaucrats that they were punished after reporting to Congress about waste, fraud, or abuse in their agencies.

It may seem odd that bureaucrats, who have great job security, would not always act in accordance with their personal beliefs instead of in accordance with the wishes of their bosses. Bureaucratic sabotage, in this view, ought to be very common. But bureaucratic cooperation with superiors is not odd, once you take into account the nature of a bureaucrat's job.

If you are a voter at the polls, your beliefs will clearly affect how you vote (see Chapter 5). But if you are the second baseman for the Boston Red Sox, your political beliefs, social background, and education will have nothing to do with how you field ground balls. Sociologists like to call the different things that people do in their lives "roles" and to distinguish between roles that are loosely structured (such as the role of voter) and those that are highly structured (such as that of second baseman). Personal attitudes greatly affect loosely structured roles and only slightly affect highly structured ones. Applied to the federal bureaucracy, this suggests that civil servants performing tasks that are routinized (such as filling out forms), tasks that are closely defined by laws and rules (such as issuing welfare checks), or tasks that are closely monitored by others (supervisors, special-interest groups, the media) will probably perform them in ways that can only partially be explained, if at all, by their personal attitudes. Civil servants performing complex, loosely defined tasks that are not closely monitored may carry out their work in ways powerfully influenced by their attitudes.

Among the loosely defined tasks are those performed by professionals, and so the values of these people may influence how they behave. An increasing number of lawyers, economists, engineers, and physicians are hired to work in federal agencies. These men and women have received extensive training that produces not only a set of skills but also a set of attitudes as to what is important and valuable. For example, the Federal Trade Commission (FTC), charged with preventing unfair methods of competition among businesses, employs two kinds of professionals—lawyers, organized into a Bureau of Competition, and economists, organized into a Bureau of Economics. Lawyers are trained to draw up briefs and argue cases in court and are taught the legal standards by which they will know whether they have a chance of winning a case or not. Economists are trained to analyze how a competitive economy works and what costs consumers must bear if the goods and services are produced by a monopoly (one firm controlling the market) or an oligopoly (a small number of firms dominating the market).

Because of their training and attitudes, lawyers in the FTC prefer to bring cases against a business firm that has done something clearly illegal, such as attending secret meetings with competitors to rig the prices that will be charged to a purchaser. These cases appeal to lawyers because there is usually a victim (the purchaser or a rival company) who complains to the government, the illegal behavior can be proved in a court of law, and the case can be completed rather quickly.

Economists, on the other hand, are trained to measure the value of a case not by how quickly it can be proved in court but by whether the illegal practice imposes large or small costs on the consumer. FTC economists often dislike the cases that appeal to lawyers. The economists feel that the amount of money that such cases save the consumer is often small and that the cases are a distraction from the major issues—such as whether IBM unfairly dominates the computer business or whether General Motors is too large to be efficient. Lawyers, in turn, are leery of big cases, because the facts are hard to prove and they may take forever to decide (one blockbuster case can drag through the courts for ten years). In many federal agencies divergent professional values such as these help explain how power is used.

Culture and Careers

Unlike the lawyers and economists working in the FTC, the government bureaucrats in a typical agency don't have a lot of freedom to choose a course of action. Their jobs are spelled out not only by the laws, rules, and routines of their agency but also by the informal understandings among fellow employees as to how they are supposed to act. These understandings are the *culture* of the agency.[21]

If you belong to the air force, you can do a lot of things, but only one thing really counts: flying airplanes, especially advanced jet fighters and bombers. The culture of the air force is a pilots' culture. If you belong to the navy, you have more choices: fly jet aircraft or operate nuclear submarines. Both jobs provide status and a chance for promotion to the highest ranks. By contrast, sailing minesweepers or transport ships (or worse, having a desk job and not sailing anything at all) is not a very rewarding job. The culture of the CIA emphasizes working overseas as a clandestine agent; staying in Washington as a report writer is not as good for your career. The culture of the State Department rewards skill in political negotiations; being an expert on international economics or embassy security is much less rewarding.

You can usually tell what kind of culture an agency has by asking an employee, "If you want to get ahead here, what sort of jobs should you take?" The jobs that are career enhancing are part of the culture; the jobs that are not career enhancing (NCE in bureaucratic lingo) are not part of it.

Being part of a strong culture is good—up to a point. It motivates employees to work hard in order to win the respect of their coworkers as well as the approval of their bosses. But a strong culture also makes it hard to change an agency. FBI agents for many years resisted getting involved in civil rights or organized crime cases, and diplomats in the State Department didn't pay much attention to embassy security. These important jobs were not a career-enhancing part of the culture.

Constraints

The biggest difference between a government agency and a private organization is the vastly greater number of constraints on the agency. Unlike a business firm, the typical government bureau can-

T·R·I·V·I·A

Famous Bureaucrats

The federal government has employed as bureaucrats people who were later to become famous in other careers.

Clara Barton, founder of the American Red Cross	Clerk in the U.S. Patent Office, 1854–1861
Alexander Graham Bell, inventor of the telephone	Special agent of the U.S. Census Bureau, 1890
Nathaniel Hawthorne, author	Weigher in the Boston Custom House, 1839–1841, and surveyor of the Port of Salem, Massachusetts, 1845–1849
Washington Irving, author	U.S. foreign service
Abraham Lincoln, president	Postmaster of New Salem, Illinois, 1833–1836
Knute Rockne, football coach	Clerk in Chicago Post Office, 1907–1910
James Thurber, humorist	Code clerk in State Department
James Whistler, painter	Draftsman, U.S. Coast Survey, 1854–1855
Walt Whitman, poet	Clerk, U.S. Department of the Interior, 1865

not hire, fire, build, or sell without going through procedures set down in laws. How much money it pays its members is determined by statute, not by the market. Not only the goals of an agency but often its exact procedures are spelled out by Congress.

At one time the Soil Conservation Service was required by law to employ at least 14,177 full-time workers. The State Department is forbidden by law from opening a diplomatic post in Antigua or Barbuda but forbidden from closing a post anywhere else. The Agency for International Development (which administers our foreign-aid program) has been given by Congress 33 objectives and 75 priorities and must send to Congress 288 reports each year. When it buys military supplies, the Defense Department must give a "fair proportion" of its contracts to small businesses, especially those

The "Rules" of Politics

How to Get Rid of a Career Civil Servant Without Going Through the System

The frontal assault   Tell him that he is no longer wanted and that if he quits, he will get a nice letter of recommendation and a farewell luncheon. If he won't quit but later wants to leave for a better job, he will get a nasty letter of recommendation.

The transfer technique   Find out where in the country the civil servant does *not* want to live and threaten to transfer her there. Send Bostonians to Texas and Texans to Maine.

The special-assignment technique   Useful for a family person who does not like to travel. Tell him that to keep his job he must inspect all the agency's offices in cities with a population under twenty thousand and stay in bad motels. Even if he doesn't quit, at least you will have him out of the office.

The layering technique   Put loyal subordinates in charge of disloyal ones, or put the objectionable civil servant into an out-of-the-way post where you can ignore her.

Source: Adapted from "Federal Political Personnel Manual," printed in "Presidential Campaign Activities of 1972," Hearings Before the Select Committee on Presidential Campaign Activities, Ninety-third Congress, 2nd Session, vol. 19 (1974). This manual was produced by members of the Nixon administration, but in some version its principles have been applied by all administrations.

operated by "socially and economically disadvantaged individuals," and must buy from American firms even if, in some cases, buying abroad would be cheaper. Some of the more general constraints include the following:

- Administrative Procedure Act (1946). Before adopting a new rule or policy, an agency must give notice, solicit comments, and (often) hold hearings.
- Freedom of Information Act (1966). Citizens have the right to inspect all government records except those containing military, intelligence, or trade secrets or revealing private personnel actions.
- National Environmental Policy Act (1969). Before undertaking any major action affecting the environment, an agency must issue an environmental impact statement.
- Privacy Act (1974). Government files about individuals, such as Social Security and tax records, must be kept confidential.
- Open Meeting Law (1976). Every part of every agency meeting must be open to the public unless certain matters (for example, military or trade secrets) are being discussed.

One of the biggest constraints on bureaucratic action is that Congress rarely gives any job to a single agency. Stopping drug trafficking is the task of the Customs Service, the FBI, the Drug Enforcement Administration, the Border Patrol, and the Defense Department (among others). Disposing of the assets of failed savings-and-loan associations is the job of the Resolution Funding Corporation, Resolution Trust Corporation, Federal Housing Finance Board, Office of Thrift Supervision in the Treasury Department, Federal Deposit Insurance Corporation, Federal Reserve Board, and Justice Department (among others).

The effects of these constraints on agency behavior are not surprising.

- The government will often act slowly. (The more constraints that must be satisfied, the longer it will take to get anything done.)
- The government will sometimes act inconsistently. (What is done to meet one constraint—for example, freedom of information—may endanger another constraint—for example, privacy.)
- It will be easier to block action than to take action. (The constraints ensure that lots of voices will be heard; the more voices that are heard, the more they may cancel each other out.)
- Lower-ranking employees will be reluctant to make decisions on their own. (Having many constraints means having many ways to get into trouble; to avoid trouble, let your boss make the decision.)
- Citizens will complain of red tape. (The more constraints to serve, the more forms to fill out.)

These constraints do not mean that government bureaucracy is powerless, only that, however great its power, it tends to be clumsy. That clumsiness arises not from the fact that the people who work for agencies are

Learning Bureaucratese

A few simple rules, if remembered, will enable you to speak and write in the style of a government official.

- **Use nouns as if they were verbs.** Don't say, "We must set priorities"; say instead, "We must prioritize."

- **Use adjectives as if they were verbs.** Don't say, "We put the report in final form"; say instead, "We finalized the report."

- **Use several words where one word would do.** Don't say, "now"; say instead, "at this point in time."

- **Never use ordinary words where unusual ones can be found.** Don't say that you "made a choice"; say that you "selected an option."

- **No matter what subject you are discussing, employ the language of sports and war.** Never say, "progress"; say, "breakthrough." Never speak of a "compromise"; instead consider "adopting a fallback position."

- **Avoid active verbs.** Never say, "Study the problem"; say instead, "It is felt that the problem should be subjected to further study."

dull or incompetent but from the complicated political environment in which that work must be done.

The moral of the story: the next time you get mad at a bureaucrat, ask yourself, Why would a rational, intelligent person behave that way? Chances are you will discover that there are good reasons for that action. You would probably behave the same way if you were working for the same organization.

Why So Many Constraints? Government agencies behave as they do in large part because of the many different goals they must pursue and the complex rules they must follow. Where does all this red tape come from?

From us. From us, the people.

Every goal, every constraint, every bit of red tape, was put in place by Congress, the courts, the White House, or the agency itself responding to the demands of some influential faction. Civil rights groups want every agency to hire and buy from women and minorities. Environmental groups want every agency to file environmental impact statements. Industries being regulated want every new agency policy to be formulated only after a lengthy public hearing with lots of lawyers present. Labor unions also want those hearings so that they can argue against industry lawyers. Everybody who sells something to the government wants a "fair chance" to make the sale, and so everybody insists that government contracts be awarded only after complex procedures are followed. A lot of people don't trust the government, and so they insist that everything it does be done in the sunshine—no secrets, no closed meetings, no hidden files.

If we want agencies to pursue their main goal with more vigor and less encumbering red tape, we would have to ask Congress, the courts, or the

The "Rules" of Politics

"Laws" of Bureaucratic Procedure

Acheson's Rule A memorandum is written not to inform the reader but to protect the writer.

Boren's Laws
When in doubt, mumble.
When in trouble, delegate.
When in charge, ponder.

Chapman's Rules of Committees
Never arrive on time, or you will be stamped a beginner.
Don't say anything until the meeting is half over; this stamps you as being wise.
Be as vague as possible; this prevents irritating others.
When in doubt, suggest that a subcommittee be appointed.

Meskimen's Law There's never time to do it right but always time to do it over.

Murphy's Law If anything can go wrong, it will.

O'Toole's Corollary to Murphy's Law Murphy was an optimist.

Parkinson's First Law Work expands to fill the time available for its completion.

Parkinson's Second Law Expenditure rises to meet income.

Peter Principle In every hierarchy, each employee tends to rise to his level of incompetence; thus, every post tends to be filled by an incompetent employee.

Robertson's Rule The more directives you issue to solve a problem, the worse it gets.

Smith's Principle Never do anything for the first time.

White House to repeal some of these constraints. In other words, we would have to be willing to give up something we want in order to get something else we want even more But politics does not encourage people to make these trade-offs; instead it encourages us to expect to get everything—efficiency, fairness, help for minorities—all at once.

Agency Allies

Despite these constraints, government bureaucracies are not powerless. In fact some of them actively seek certain constraints. They do so because it is a way of cementing a useful relationship with a congressional committee or an interest group.

At one time scholars described the relationship among an agency, a committee, and an interest group as an **iron triangle.** For example, the Department of Veterans Affairs, the House and Senate committees on veterans affairs, and veterans' organizations (such as the American Legion) would form a tight, mutually advantageous alliance. The department would do what the committees wanted and in return get political support and budget appropriations; the committee members would do what the veterans' groups wanted and in return get votes and campaign contributions. Iron triangles are examples of what are called *client politics.*

Many agencies still have important allies in Congress and the private sector, especially those bureaus that serve the needs of specific sectors of the economy or regions of the country. The Department of Agriculture works closely with farm organizations, the Department of the Interior with groups interested in obtaining low-cost irrigation or grazing rights, and the Department of Housing and Urban Development with mayors and real-estate developers.

Sometimes these allies are so strong that they can defeat a popular president. For years President Reagan tried to abolish the Small Business Administration (SBA), arguing that its program of loans to small firms was wasteful and ridden with favoritism. But Congress, reacting to pressures from small-business groups, rallied to the SBA's defense. As a result Reagan had to oversee an agency that he didn't want.

But iron triangles are much less common today than once was the case. Politics of late has become far more complicated. For one thing, the number and variety of interest groups has increased so much in recent years that there is scarcely any agency that is not subject to pressures from several competing interests instead of only from one powerful interest. For another, the growth of subcommittees in Congress has meant that most agencies are subject to control by many different legislative groups, often with very different concerns. Finally, the courts have made it much easier for all kinds of individuals and interests to intervene in agency affairs.

As a result, nowadays government agencies face a bewildering variety of competing groups and legislative subcommittees that constitute not a loyal group of allies but a fiercely contentious collection of critics. The Environmental Protection Agency is caught between the demands of environmentalists and those of industry organizations, the Occupational Safety and Health Administration between the pressures of labor and those of business, and the Federal Communications Commission between the desires of broadcasters and those of cable television companies. Even the Department of Agriculture faces not a unified group of farmers but many different farmers split into rival groups, depending on the crops they raise, the regions in which they live, and the attitudes they have toward the relative merits of farm subsidies or free markets.

Political scientist Hugh Heclo has described the typical government agency today as being embedded not in an iron triangle but in an **issue network**.[22] These issue networks consist of people in Washington-based interest groups, on congressional staffs, in universities and think tanks, and in the mass media, who regularly debate government policy on a certain subject—say, health care or auto safety. The networks are contentious, split along political, ideological, and economic lines. When a president takes office, he often recruits key agency officials from those members of the issue network who are most sympathetic to his views.

When Jimmy Carter, a Democrat, became president, he appointed to key posts in consumer agencies people who were from that part of the consumer issue network associated with Ralph Nader. Ronald Reagan, a conservative Republican, filled these same jobs with people who were from that part of the issue network holding free market or antiregulation views. When George Bush, a more centrist Republican, took office, he filled these posts with more centrist members of the issue network. Bill Clinton brought back the consumer activists.

Congressional Oversight

The main reason why some interest groups are important to agencies is that they are important to Congress. Not every interest group in the country has substantial access to Congress, but those that do and that are taken seriously by the relevant committees or subcommittees must also be taken seriously by the agency. Furthermore, even apart from interest groups, members of Congress have constitutional powers over agencies and policy interests in how agencies function.

The real federal bureaucracy is bigger than just who works for the national government. Because defense contractors depend on government contracts, the bureaucracy includes people who work in these private firms.

Congressional supervision of the bureaucracy takes several forms. First, no agency may exist (except for a few presidential offices and commissions) without congressional approval. Congress influences—and sometimes determines precisely—agency behavior by the statutes it enacts.

Second, no money may be spent unless it has first been authorized by Congress. **Authorization legislation** originates in a legislative committee (such as Agriculture, Education and Labor, or Public Works) and states the maximum amount of money that an agency may spend on a given program. This authorization may be permanent, it may be for a fixed number of years, or it may be annual (that is, it must be renewed each year, or the program or agency goes out of business).

Third, even funds that have been authorized by Congress cannot be spent unless (in most cases) they are also appropriated. Appropriations are usually made annually, and they originate not with the legislative committees but with the House Appropriations Committee and its various (and influential) subcommittees. An **appropriation** (money formally set aside for a specific use) may be, and often is, for less than the amount authorized. The Appropriations Committee's action thus tends to have a budget-cutting effect. There are some funds that can be spent without an appropriation, but in virtually every part of the bureaucracy each agency is keenly sensitive to congressional concerns at the time that the annual appropriations process is going on.

The Appropriations Committee and Legislative Committees

The fact that an agency budget must be both authorized and appropriated means that each agency serves not one congressional master but several, and that these masters may be in conflict. The real power over an agency's budget is exercised by the Appropriations Committee; the legislative committees are especially important when a substantive law is first passed or an agency is first created, or when an agency is subject to annual authorization.

In the past the power of the Appropriations Committee was rarely challenged: from 1947 through 1962, fully 90 percent of the House Appropriations Committee's recommendations on expenditures were approved by the full House without change.[23] Furthermore, the Appropriations Committee tends to recommend less money than an agency requests (though some specially favored agencies, such as the FBI, the Soil Conservation Service, and the Forest Service, have tended to get almost everything that they have asked for). Finally, the process of "marking up" (revising, amending, and approving) an agency's budget request gives to the Appropriations Committee, or one of its subcommittees, substantial influence over the policies that the agency follows.

Of late the appropriations committees have lost some of their great power over government agencies. This has happened in three ways:

First, Congress has created trust funds to pay for the benefits many people receive. The Social Security trust fund is the largest of these. In 1990 it took in about $260 billion in Social Security taxes and paid out about $220 billion in old-age benefits. There are several other trust funds as well. **Trust funds** operate outside the regular government budget, and the appropriations committees have no control over these expenditures. They are automatic.

Second, Congress has changed the authorization of many programs from permanent or multiyear to **annual authorizations.** This means that every year the legislative committees, as part of the reauthorization process, get to set limits on what these agencies can spend. This limits the ability of the appropriations committees to determine the spending limits. Before 1959 most authorizations were permanent or multiyear. Now a long list of agencies must be reauthorized every year—the State Department, NASA, military procurement programs of the Defense Department,

the Justice Department, the Energy Department, and parts or all of many other agencies.

Third, the existence of huge budget deficits during the 1980s and early 1990s has meant that much of Congress's time has been taken up with trying (usually not very successfully) to keep spending down. As a result there has rarely been much time to discuss the merits of various programs or how much ought to be spent on them; instead attention has been focused on meeting a target spending limit. In 1981 the budget resolution passed by Congress mandated cuts in several programs before the appropriations committees had even completed their work.[24]

In addition to the power of the purse, there are informal ways by which Congress can control the bureaucracy. An individual member of Congress can call an agency head on behalf of a constituent. Most such calls merely seek information, but some result in, or attempt to second, special privileges for particular people. Congressional committees may also obtain the right to pass on certain agency decisions. This is called **committee clearance,** and though it is usually not legally binding on the agency, few agency heads will ignore the expressed wish of a committee chair that he or she be consulted before certain actions (such as transferring funds) are taken.

The Legislative Veto

For many decades Congress made frequent use of the legislative veto to control bureaucratic or presidential actions. A **legislative veto** is a requirement that an executive decision must lie before Congress for a specified period (usually thirty or ninety days) before it takes effect. Congress could then veto the decision if a resolution of disapproval were passed by either house (a "one-house veto") or both houses (a "two-house veto"). Unlike laws, such resolutions were not signed by the president. Between 1932 and 1980 about two hundred laws were passed providing for a legislative veto, many of them involving presidential proposals to sell arms abroad.

But in June 1983 the Supreme Court declared the legislative veto to be unconstitutional. In the *Chadha* case the Court held that the Constitution clearly requires in Article I that "every order, resolution, or vote to which the concurrence of the Senate and House of Representatives may be necessary" (with certain minor exceptions) "shall be presented to the President of the United States," who must either approve it or return it with his veto attached. In short

Congress cannot take any action that has the force of law unless the president concurs in that action.[25] At a stroke of the pen parts of some two hundred laws suddenly became invalid.

At least that happened in theory. In fact since the *Chadha* decision Congress has passed a number of laws that contain legislative vetoes, despite the Supreme Court's having ruled against them! (Someone will have to go to court to test the constitutionality of these new provisions.)

Opponents of the legislative veto hope that future Congresses will have to pass laws that state much more clearly than before what an agency may or may not do. But it is just as likely that Congress will continue to pass laws stated in general terms and require that agencies implementing those laws report their plans to Congress so that it will have a chance to enact and send to the president a regular bill disapproving the proposed action. Or Congress may rely on informal (but scarcely weak) means of persuasion, including threats to reduce the appropriations of an agency that does not abide by congressional preferences.

Congressional Investigations

Perhaps the most visible and dramatic form of congressional supervision of an agency is the investigation. Since 1792, when Congress investigated an army defeat by a Native American tribe, congressional investigations of the bureaucracy have been a regular feature—sometimes constructive, sometimes destructive—of legislative-executive relations. The investigative power is not mentioned in the Constitution but has been inferred from the power to legislate. The Supreme Court has consistently upheld this interpretation, though it has also said that such investigations should not be solely for the purpose of exposing the purely personal affairs of private individuals and must not operate to deprive citizens of their basic rights.[26] Congress may compel a person to attend an investigation by issuing a subpoena; anyone who ignores the subpoena may be punished for contempt. Congress can vote to send the person to jail or can refer the matter to a court for further action. As explained in Chapter 12, the president and his principal subordinates have refused to answer certain congressional inquiries on grounds of "executive privilege."

Although many areas of congressional oversight—budgetary review, personnel controls, investigations—are designed to control the exercise of bureaucratic discretion, other areas are intended to ensure the freedom of certain agencies from effective control, especially by the president. In dozens of cases Congress has authorized department heads and bureau chiefs to operate independent of presidential preferences. Congress has resisted, for example, presidential efforts to ensure that policies to regulate pollution do not impose excessive costs on the economy, and interest groups have brought suit to prevent presidential coordination of various regulatory agencies. If the bureaucracy sometimes works at cross-purposes, it is usually because Congress—or competing committees in Congress—wants it that way.

Bureaucratic "Pathologies"

Everyone complains about bureaucracy in general (though rarely about bureaucratic agencies that everyone believes are desirable). This chapter should persuade you that it is difficult to say anything about bureaucracy "in general"; there are too many different kinds of agencies, kinds of bureaucrats, and kinds of programs to label the entire enterprise with some single adjective. Nevertheless, many people who recognize the enormous variety among government agencies still believe that they all have some general features in common and suffer from certain shared problems or pathologies.

This is true enough, but the reasons for it—and the solutions, if any—are not often understood. There are five major (or at least frequently mentioned) problems with bureaucracies: red tape, conflict, duplication, imperialism, and waste. **Red tape** refers to the complex rules and procedures that must be followed to get something done. *Conflict* exists because some agencies seem to be working at cross-purposes with other agencies. (For example, the Agricultural Research Service tells farmers how to grow crops more efficiently, while the Agricultural Stabilization and Conservation Service pays farmers to grow fewer crops or to produce less.) *Duplication* (usually called "wasteful duplication") occurs when two government agencies seem to be doing the same thing, as when the Customs Service and the Drug Enforcement Administration both attempt to intercept illegal drugs being smuggled into the country. *Imperialism* refers to the tendency of agencies to grow without regard to the benefits that their programs confer or the costs that they entail. *Waste* means spending more than is necessary to buy some product or service.

These long lines of cars at the border between the United States and Mexico may be a symbol of "bureaucratic red tape" to some travelers, but they are a sign of "effective law enforcement" to people who want to cut off the flow of drugs and illegal immigrants.

These problems all exist, but they do not necessarily exist because bureaucrats are incompetent or power-hungry. Most exist because of the very nature of government itself. Take red tape: partly we encounter cumbersome rules and procedures because any large organization, governmental or not, must have some way of ensuring that one part of the organization does not operate out of step with another. Business corporations have red tape also; it is to a certain extent a consequence of bigness. But a great amount of governmental red tape is also the result of the need to satisfy legal and political requirements. Government agencies must hire on the basis of "merit," must observe strict accounting rules, must supply Congress with detailed information on their programs, and must allow for citizen access in countless ways. Meeting each need requires rules; enforcing the rules requires forms.

Or take conflict and duplication: they do not occur because bureaucrats enjoy conflict or duplication. (Quite the contrary!) They exist because Congress, in setting up agencies and programs, often wants to achieve a number of different, partially inconsistent goals or finds that it cannot decide which goal it values the most. Congress has 535 members and little strong leadership; it should not be surprising that 535 people will want different things and will sometimes succeed in getting them.

Imperialism results in large measure from government agencies' seeking goals that are so vague and so difficult to measure that it is hard to tell when they have been attained. When Congress is unclear as to exactly what an agency is supposed to do, the agency will often convert that legislative vagueness into bureaucratic imperialism by taking the largest possible view of its powers. It may do this on its own; more often it does so because interest groups and judges rush in to fill the vacuum left by Congress. As we saw in Chapter 3, the 1973 Rehabilitation Act was passed with a provision barring discrimination against people with disabilities in any program receiving federal aid. Under pressure from people with disabilities, that lofty but vague goal was converted by the Department of Transportation into a requirement that virtually every big-city bus have a device installed to lift people in wheelchairs on board.

Waste is probably the biggest criticism that people have of the bureaucracy. Everybody has heard stories of the Pentagon's paying $91 for screws that cost 3 cents in the hardware store. President Reagan's "Private Sector Survey on Cost Control," generally known as the Grace Commission (after its chairman, J. Peter Grace), publicized these and other tales in a 1984 report.

No doubt there is waste in government. After all, unlike a business firm worried about maximizing profits, in a government agency there are only weak incentives to keep costs down. If a business employee cuts costs, he or she often receives a bonus or raise, and the firm gets to add the savings to its profits. If a government official cuts costs, he or she receives no reward, and the agency cannot keep the savings—they go back to the Treasury.

But many of the horror stories are either exaggerations or unusual occurrences.[27] Most of the screws, hammers, and light bulbs purchased by the government are obtained at low cost by means of competitive bidding among several suppliers. When the government does pay outlandish amounts, the reason typically is that it is purchasing a new or one-of-a-kind item not available at your neighborhood hardware store—for example, a new bomber or missile.

Even when the government is not overcharged, it still may spend more money than a private firm in buying what it needs. The reason is red tape—the rules and procedures designed to ensure that when the government buys something, it will do so in a way that serves the interests of many groups. For example, it must often buy from American rather than foreign suppliers, even if the latter charge a lower price; it must make use of contractors that employ minorities; it must hire only union laborers and pay them the "prevailing" (that is, the highest) wage; it must allow public inspection of its records; it frequently is required to choose contractors favored by influential members of Congress; and so on. Private firms do not have to comply with all these rules and thus can buy for less.

From this discussion it should be easy to see why these five basic bureaucratic problems are so hard to correct. To end conflicts and duplication Congress would have to make some policy choices and set some clear priorities, but with all the competing demands that it faces, Congress finds it difficult to do that. You make more friends by helping people than by hurting them, and so Congress is more inclined to add new programs than to cut old ones, whether or not the new programs are in conflict with existing ones. To check imperialism some way would have to be found to measure the benefits of government, but that is often impossible; government exists in part to achieve precisely those goals—such as national defense—that are least measurable. Furthermore, what might be done to remedy some problems would make other problems worse: if you simplify rules and procedures to cut red tape, you are likely also to reduce the coordination among agencies and thus to increase the extent to which there is duplication or conflict. If you want to reduce waste, you will have to have more rules and inspectors—in short more red tape. The problem of bureaucracy is inseparable from the problem of government generally.

Just as people are likely to say that they dislike Congress but like their own member of Congress, they are inclined to express hostility toward "the bureaucracy" but goodwill for that part of the bureaucracy with which they have dealt personally. In 1973 a survey of Americans found that over half had had some contact with one or more kinds of government agencies, most of which were either run directly or funded indirectly by the federal government. The great majority of people were satisfied with these contacts and felt that they had been treated fairly and given useful assistance. When these people were asked their feelings about government officials in general, however, they expressed much less favorable attitudes. Whereas about 80 percent liked the officials with whom they had dealt, only 42 percent liked officials in general.[28] This finding helps explain why government

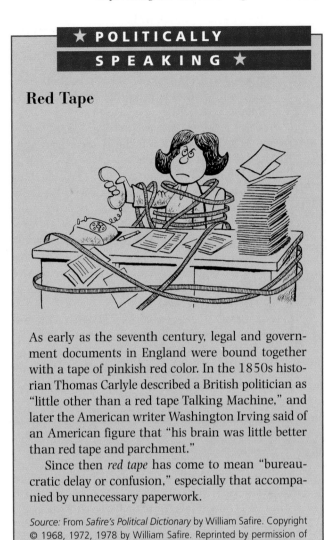

★ POLITICALLY SPEAKING ★

Red Tape

As early as the seventh century, legal and government documents in England were bound together with a tape of pinkish red color. In the 1850s historian Thomas Carlyle described a British politician as "little other than a red tape Talking Machine," and later the American writer Washington Irving said of an American figure that "his brain was little better than red tape and parchment."

Since then *red tape* has come to mean "bureaucratic delay or confusion," especially that accompanied by unnecessary paperwork.

Source: From *Safire's Political Dictionary* by William Safire. Copyright © 1968, 1972, 1978 by William Safire. Reprinted by permission of Random House, Inc. and the author.

agencies are rarely reduced in size or budget: whatever the popular feelings about the bureaucracy, any given agency tends to have many friends.

Reforming the Bureaucracy

The history of American bureaucracy has been punctuated with countless efforts to make it work better and cost less. There have been eleven major attempts in this century alone (see the box on page 398). The latest was the National Performance Review (NPR)—popularly called the plan to "reinvent government"—led by Vice President Al Gore. The results of the review were published in 1993.

Reforming the Federal Bureaucracy

Keep Commission (1905–1909) Personnel management, government contracting, information management.

President's Commission on Economy and Efficiency (1910–1913) Recommended creating a national executive budget.

Joint Committee on Reorganization (1921–1924) Proposed ways of distributing executive functions among the departments.

President's Committee on Administrative Management (1936–1937) Known as the Brownlow Commission, after its chairman, Louis Brownlow. Recommended creation of the Executive Office of the President. Famous conclusion: "The president needs help."

First Hoover Commission (1947–1949) Comprehensive review of the executive branch.

Second Hoover Commission (1953–1955) Follow-up to the First Hoover Commission; focused mainly on policy problems rather than organizational structure.

Study commission on executive reorganization (1953–1968) Series of low-key reforms that produced small but significant changes.

Ash Council (1969–1971) Proposed creation of new "super departments" to encompass existing departments.

Carter reorganization effort (1977–1979) Attempted to reorganize agencies from the bottom up; new cabinet departments created independently of effort.

Grace Commission (1982–1984) Large-scale, politically contentious effort to determine how government could be operated for less money.

National Performance Review (1993–present) Attempt to "reinvent" government to improve its performance.

Source: Adapted from Ronald C. Moe, *Reorganizing the Executive Branch in the Twentieth Century* (Congressional Research Service, March 1992).

The NPR differed from many of the preceding reform efforts in one important way. Most of the earlier ones suggested ways of increasing central (that is, presidential) control of government agencies: the Brownlow Commission (1936–1937) recommended giving the president more assistants, the First Hoover Commission (1947–1949) suggested ways of improving top-level management, and the Ash Council (1969–1971) called for consolidating existing agencies into a few big "super departments." The intent was to make it easier for the president and his cabinet secretaries to run the bureaucracy. The key ideas were efficiency, accountability, and consistent policies.

The NPR, by contrast, emphasized customer satisfaction (the "customers" in this case being the citizens who come into contact with federal agencies). To the authors of the NPR report, the main problem with the bureaucracy was that it had become too centralized, too rule-bound, too little concerned with making programs work, and too much concerned with avoiding scandal. The NPR report contained many horror stories about useless red tape, excessive regulations, and cumbersome procurement systems that make it next to impossible for agencies to do what they were created to do. (For example, before it could buy an ashtray, the General Services Administration issued a nine-page document that described an ashtray and specified how many pieces it must break into should it be hit with a hammer.)[29] To solve these problems the NPR called for less centralized management and more employee initiative, fewer detailed rules and more emphasis on customer satisfaction. It sought to create a new kind of organizational culture in government agencies, one more like that found in the more innovative, quality-conscious American corporations. The NPR was reinforced legislatively by the Government Performance and Results Act (GPRA) of 1993, which required agencies "to set goals, measure performance, and report on the results."

But making these changes is easier said than done. Most of the rules and red tape that make it hard for agency heads to do a good job are the result either of the struggle between the White House and Congress for control over the agencies or of the agencies' desire to avoid irritating influential voters. Silly as the rules for ashtrays may sound, they were written so that the government could say it had an "objective" standard

MEMORANDUM

To: Dr. Robert Smith, president of Cybersystems Engineering
From: James Logan, secretary of defense
Subject: Becoming an assistant secretary of defense

As both secretary and a dear old college buddy of yours, I write again to express my hope that you will accept the president's call to service. We all desperately want you aboard. Yes, conflict-of-interest laws will require you to sell your stock in your present company and drop out of its generous pension plan. No, the government won't even pay moving costs. And once you leave office, you will be barred for life from lobbying the executive branch on matters in which you were directly involved while in office, and you will be barred for two years from lobbying on matters that were under your general official authority. Your other concerns have teeth, too, but let me help you weigh your options.

Arguments for:
1. I hate to preach, but it is one's duty to serve one's country when called. Your sacrifice would honor your family and benefit your fellow Americans for years to come.
2. As an accomplished professional and the head of a company that has done business with the government, you could help the president succeed in reforming the department so that it works better and costs less.
3. Despite the restrictions, you could resume your career once your public service was complete.

Arguments against:
1. Since you will have to be confirmed by the Senate, your life will be put under a microscope, and everything (even some of our old college mischief together) will be fair game for congressional staffers and reporters.
2. You will face hundreds of rules telling you what you can't do and scores of congressmen telling you what you should do. Old friends will get mad at you for not doing them favors. The president will demand loyalty. The press will pounce on your every mistake, real or imagined.
3. Given the federal limits on whom in the government you can deal with after you leave office, your job at Cybersystems may well suffer.

Your decision:
Accept position _____ Reject position _____

New Administration Struggling to Fill Top Posts

Cabinet Secretaries Say "The President Needs Help!"

May 20
WASHINGTON

Four months into the new administration, hundreds of assistant secretary and deputy assistant secretary positions remain unfilled. In 1960 the total number of presidential political appointees was just 450. Today the total is over 2,400, but sheer growth is not the whole story. Rather, say experts on federal bureaucracy, plumb public service posts go unfilled because the jobs have become so unrewarding, even punishing . . .

Most bureaucrats are people we like, such as the letter carriers in the Postal Service.

for buying ashtrays. If it simply went out and bought ashtrays at a department store the way ordinary people do, it would risk being accused by the Acme Ashtray Company of buying trays from its competitor, the A-1 Ashtray Company, because of political favoritism.

The rivalry between the president and Congress for control of the bureaucracy makes bureaucrats nervous about irritating either branch, and so they issue rules designed to avoid getting into trouble, even if these rules makes it hard to do their job. Matters become even worse during periods of divided government when different parties control the White House

and Congress. As we saw in Chapter 12, divided government may not have much effect on *making* policy, but it can have a big effect on *implementing* it. Presidents of one party have tried to increase political control over the bureaucracy ("executive micromanagement"), and Congresses of another party have responded by increasing the number of investigations and detailed rule-making ("legislative micromanagement"). Divided government intensifies the cross-fire between the executive and legislative branches, making bureaucrats dig into even deeper layers of red tape to avoid getting hurt.

This does not mean that reform is impossible, only that it is very difficult. For example, despite a lack of clear-cut successes in other areas, the NPR's procurement reforms stuck: government agencies can now buy things costing as much as $100,000 without following any complex regulations.

It might be easier to make desirable changes if the bureaucracy were accountable to but one master—say, the president—instead of to several. But that situation, which exists in many parliamentary democracies, creates its own problems. When the bureaucracy has but one master, it often ends up having none: it becomes so powerful that it controls the prime minister and no longer listens to citizen complaints. A weak, divided bureaucracy, such as exists in the United States, may strike us as inefficient, but that very inefficiency may help protect our liberties.

Summary

Bureaucracy is characteristic of almost all aspects of modern life, not simply the government. Government bureaucracies, however, pose special problems because they are subject to competing sources of political authority, must function in a constitutional system of divided powers and federalism, have vague goals, and lack incentive systems that will encourage efficiency. The power of a bureaucracy should be measured by its discretionary authority, not by the number of its employees or the size of its budget.

War and depression have been the principal sources of bureaucratic growth, aided by important changes in constitutional interpretation in the 1930s that permitted Congress to delegate broad grants of authority to administrative agencies. With only partial success Congress seeks to check or recover those grants by controlling budgets, personnel, and policy decisions and by the exercise of legislative vetoes. The uses to which bureaucrats put their authority can be explained in part by their recruitment and security (they have an agency orientation), their personal political views, and the nature of the tasks that their agencies are performing.

Many of the popular solutions for the problems of bureaucratic rule—red tape, duplication, conflict, agency imperialism, and waste—fail to take into account that these problems are to a degree inherent in any government that serves competing goals and is supervised by rival elected officials. Nevertheless, some reform efforts have succeeded in making government work better and cost less to operate.

World Wide Web Resources

- For addresses and reports of various cabinet departments
  Web addresses:
  www.whitehouse.gov/WH/Cabinet/
     html/cabinet_links.html
  Documents and bulletin boards:
  www.fedworld.gov
  National Performance Review: www.npr.gov

- A few specific Web sites of federal agencies
  Department of Defense: www.defenselink.mil
  Department of Education: www.ed.gov
  Department of Health and Human Services:
  www.dhhs.gov
  Department of State: www.state.gov
  Federal Bureau of Investigation: www.fbi.gov

Key Terms

bureaucracy *p. 375*
spoils system *p. 378*
laissez-faire *p. 378*
discretionary authority
   p. 380
competitive service *p. 381*

name-request job *p. 383*
iron triangle *p. 392*
issue network *p. 393*
authorization legislation
   p. 393

appropriation *p. 393*
trust funds *p. 394*
annual authorizations
   p. 394

committee clearance
   p. 394
legislative veto *p. 394*
red tape *p. 395*

Suggested Readings

Burke, John P. *Bureaucratic Responsibility*. Baltimore: Johns Hopkins University Press, 1986. Examines the problem of individual responsibility—for example, when to be a whistle blower—in government agencies.

DiIulio, John J., Gerald Garvey, and Donald F. Kettl. *Improving Government Performance: An Owner's Manual*. Washington, D.C.: Brookings Institution, 1993. A concise overview of the history of federal bureaucracy and ideas about how to reform it.

Downs, Anthony. *Inside Bureaucracy*. Boston: Little, Brown, 1967. An economist's explanation of why bureaucrats and bureaus behave as they do.

Halperin, Morton H. *Bureaucratic Politics and Foreign Policy*. Washington, D.C.: Brookings Institution, 1974. Insightful account of the strategies by which diplomatic and military bureaucracies defend their interests.

Heclo, Hugh. *A Government of Strangers*. Washington, D.C.: Brookings Institution, 1977. Analyzes how political appointees attempt to gain control of the Washington bureaucracy and how bureaucrats resist those efforts.

Johnson, Ronald L., and Gary Libecap. *The Federal Civil Service System and the Problem of Bureaucracy*. Chicago: University of Chicago Press, 1994. Two economists analyze how federal bureaucrats acquire positions and salaries.

Light, Paul C. *The True Size of Government*. Washington, D.C.: Brookings Institution, 1999. A revealing explanation of why the federal government is a lot bigger than is suggested by simply counting employees.

Moore, Mark H. *Creating Public Value: Strategic Management in Government*. Cambridge: Harvard University Press, 1995. A thoughtful account of how wise bureaucrats can make government work better.

Parkinson, C. Northcote. *Parkinson's Law*. Boston: Houghton Mifflin, 1957. Half-serious, half-joking explanation of why government agencies tend to grow.

Wilson, James Q. *Bureaucracy: What Government Agencies Do and Why They Do It*. New York: Basic Books, 1989. A comprehensive review of what we know about bureaucratic behavior in the United States.

The Judiciary

Enduring Questions

1. Should judges be limited to interpreting what the law says?
2. Should Congress care what a judge thinks about controversial issues before it votes on his appointment?
3. Why should federal courts have the right to declare an act of Congress unconstitutional?

The Development of the Federal Courts
National Supremacy and Slavery • Government and the Economy • Government and Political Liberty • The Revival of State Sovereignty

The Structure of the Federal Courts
Selecting Judges

The Jurisdiction of the Federal Courts

Getting to Court
Fee Shifting • Standing • Class-Action Suits

The Supreme Court in Action

The Power of the Federal Courts
The Power to Make Policy • Views of Judicial Activism • Legislation and the Courts

Checks on Judicial Power
Congress and the Courts • Public Opinion and the Courts

resident Bush nominated Clarence Thomas to the Supreme Court on July 1, 1991. He was confirmed by a Senate vote of 52 to 48 on October 15. Thomas's margin of confirmation was the closest in more than one hundred years, and the second closest in U.S. history. His hearings were dominated by allegations of sexual harassment lodged against him by Anita F. Hill, a former subordinate during his tenure at the Equal Employment Opportunity Commission and later a University of Oklahoma law professor. Apart from the sexual harassment allegations, which both sides estimated cost him about ten votes, opponents of his confirmation claimed that his judicial philosophy was outside the mainstream, while supporters claimed that he would be sensitive to the rights of the disadvantaged, having himself risen from childhood poverty.

Only in the United States would the selection of a judge produce so dramatic and bitter a conflict. The reason is simple: only in the United States do judges play so large a role in making public policy.

One aspect of this power is **judicial review**—the right of the federal courts to declare laws of Congress

403

and acts of the executive branch void and unenforceable if they are judged to be in conflict with the Constitution. Since 1789 the Supreme Court has declared over one hundred federal laws to be unconstitutional. In Britain, by contrast, Parliament is supreme, and no court may strike down a law that it passes. As the second earl of Pembroke is supposed to have said, "A parliament can do anything but make a man a woman and a woman a man." All that prevents Parliament from acting contrary to the (unwritten) constitution of Britain are the consciences of its members and the opinions of the citizens. About sixty nations do have something resembling judicial review, but in only a few cases does this power mean much in practice. Where it means something—in Australia, Canada, Germany, India, and some other nations—one finds a stable, federal system of government with a strong tradition of an independent judiciary.[1] (Some other nations—France, for example—have special councils, rather than courts, that can under certain circumstances decide that a law is not authorized by the constitution.)

Judicial review is the federal courts' chief weapon in the system of checks and balances on which the American government is based. Today few people would deny to the courts the right to decide that a legislative or executive act is unconstitutional, though once that right was controversial. What

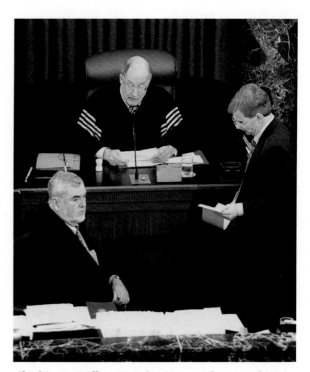

Chief Justice William H. Rehnquist presiding over the Clinton impeachment trial

remains controversial is the method by which such review is conducted.

There are two competing views, each ardently pressed during the fight to confirm Clarence Thomas. The first holds that judges should only judge—that is, they should confine themselves to applying those rules that are stated in or clearly implied by the language of the Constitution. This is often called the **strict-constructionist approach.** The other argues that judges should discover the general principles underlying the Constitution and its often vague language, amplify those principles on the basis of some moral or economic philosophy, and apply them to cases. This is sometimes called the **activist approach.**

Note that the difference between activist and strict-constructionist judges is not necessarily the same as the difference between liberals and conservatives. Judges can be political liberals and still believe that they are bound by the language of the Constitution. A liberal justice, Hugo Black, once voted to uphold a state law banning birth control because nothing in the Constitution prohibited such a law. Or judges can be conservative and still think

Table 14.1	Chief Justices of the United States	
Chief Justice	**Appointed By**	**Years of Service**
John Jay	Washington	1789–1795
Oliver Ellsworth	Washington	1796–1800
John Marshall	Adams	1801–1835
Roger B. Taney	Jackson	1836–1864
Salmon P. Chase	Lincoln	1864–1873
Morrison R. Waite	Grant	1874–1888
Melville W. Fuller	Cleveland	1888–1910
Edward D. White	Taft	1910–1921
William Howard Taft	Harding	1921–1930
Charles Evans Hughes	Hoover	1930–1941
Harlan Fiske Stone	F. Roosevelt	1941–1946
Fred M. Vinson	Truman	1946–1953
Earl Warren	Eisenhower	1953–1969
Warren E. Burger	Nixon	1969–1986
William H. Rehnquist	Reagan	1986–present

Note: Omitted is John Rutledge, who served for only a few months in 1795 and who was not confirmed by the Senate.

that they have a duty to use their best judgment in deciding what is good public policy. Rufus Peckham, one such conservative, voted to overturn a state law setting maximum hours of work because he believed that the Fourteenth Amendment guaranteed something called "freedom of contract," even though those words are not in the amendment.

Fifty years ago judicial activists tended to be conservatives and strict-constructionist judges tended to be liberals; today the opposite is usually the case.

The Development of the Federal Courts

Most of the Founders probably expected the Supreme Court to have the power of judicial review (though they did not say that in so many words in the Constitution), but they did not expect federal courts to play so large a role in making public policy. The traditional view of civil courts was that they judged disputes between people who had direct dealings with each other—they had entered into a contract, for example, or one had dropped a load of bricks on the other's toe—and decided which of the two parties was right. The court then supplied relief to the wronged party, usually by requiring the other person to pay him or her money ("damages").

This traditional understanding was based on the belief that judges would find and apply existing law. The purpose of a court case was not to learn what the judge believes but what the law requires. The later rise of judicial activism occurred when judges questioned this traditional view and argued instead that judges do not merely find the law, they make the law.

The view that judges interpret the law and do not make policy made it easy for the Founders to justify the power of judicial review and led them to predict that the courts would play a relatively neutral, even passive, role in public affairs. Alexander Hamilton, writing in *Federalist* No. 78, described the judiciary as the branch "least dangerous" to political rights. The president is commander in chief and thus holds the "sword of the community"; Congress appropriates money and thus "commands the purse" as well as decides what laws shall govern. But the judiciary "has no influence over either the sword or the purse" and "can take no active resolution whatever." It has "neither force nor will but merely judgment," and thus is "beyond comparison the weakest of the three

departments of power." As a result "liberty can have nothing to fear from the judiciary alone." Hamilton went on to state clearly that the Constitution intended to give to the courts the right to decide whether a law is contrary to the Constitution. But this authority, he explained, was designed not to enlarge the power of the courts but to confine that of the legislature.

Obviously things have changed since Hamilton's time. The evolution of the federal courts, especially the Supreme Court, toward the present level of activism and influence has been shaped by the political, economic, and ideological forces of three historical eras. From 1787 to 1865 nation building, the legitimacy of the federal government, and slavery were the great issues; from 1865 to 1937 the dominant issue was the relationship between the government and the economy; from 1938 to the present the major issues confronting the Court have involved personal liberty and social equality and the potential conflict between the two. In the first period the Court asserted the supremacy of the federal government; in the second it placed important restrictions on the powers of that government; and in the third it enlarged the scope of personal freedom and narrowed that of economic freedom.

National Supremacy and Slavery

"From 1789 until the Civil War, the dominant interest of the Supreme Court was in that greatest of all the questions left unresolved by the Founders—the nation-state relationship."[2] The answer that the Court gave, under the leadership of Chief Justice John Marshall, was that national law was in all instances the dominant law, with state law having to give way, and that the Supreme Court had the power to decide what the Constitution meant. In two cases of enormous importance—*Marbury v. Madison* in 1803 and *McCulloch v. Maryland* in 1819—the Court, in decisions written by Marshall, held that the Supreme Court could declare an act of Congress unconstitutional; that the power granted by the Constitution to the federal government flows from the people and thus should be generously construed (and thus any federal laws that are "necessary and proper" to the attainment of constitutional ends are permissible); and that federal law is supreme over state law, even to the point that a state may not tax an enterprise (such as a bank) created by the federal government.[3]

Marbury v. Madison

The story of *Marbury v. Madison* is often told, but it deserves another telling because it illustrates so many features of the role of the Supreme Court—how apparently small cases can have large results, how the power of the Court depends not simply on its constitutional authority but also on its acting in ways that avoid a clear confrontation with other branches of government, and how the climate of opinion affects how the Court goes about its task.

When President John Adams lost his bid for reelection to Thomas Jefferson in 1800, he—and all members of his party, the Federalists—feared that Jefferson and the Republicans would weaken the federal government and turn its powers to what the Federalists believed were wrong ends (states' rights, an alliance with the French, hostility to business). Feverishly, as his hours in office came to an end, Adams worked to pack the judiciary with fifty-nine loyal Federalists by giving them so-called midnight appointments before Jefferson took office.

John Marshall, as Adams's secretary of state, had the task of certifying and delivering these new judicial commissions. In the press of business he delivered all but seventeen; these he left on his desk for the incoming secretary of state, James Madi-

son, to send out. Jefferson and Madison, however, were furious at Adams's behavior and refused to deliver the seventeen. William Marbury and three other Federalists who had been promised these commissions hired a lawyer and brought suit against Madison to force him to produce the documents. The suit requested the Supreme Court to issue a writ of mandamus (from the Latin, "we command") ordering Madison to do his duty. The right to issue such writs had been given to the Court by the Judiciary Act of 1789.

Marshall, the man who had failed to deliver the commissions to Marbury and his friends in the first place, had become the chief justice and was now in a position to decide the case. These days a justice who had been involved in an issue before it came to the Court would probably disqualify himself or herself, but Marshall had no intention of letting others decide this question. He faced, however, not simply a partisan dispute over jobs but what was nearly a constitutional crisis. If he ordered the commission delivered, Madison might still refuse, and the Court had no way—if Madison was determined to resist—to compel him. The Court had no police force, whereas Madison had the support of the president of

The supremacy of the federal government was reaffirmed by other decisions as well. In 1816 the Supreme Court rejected the claim of the Virginia courts that the Supreme Court could not review the decisions of state courts. The Virginia courts were ready to acknowledge the supremacy of the U.S. Constitution but believed that they had as much right as the U.S. Supreme Court to decide what the Constitution meant. The Supreme Court felt otherwise, and in this case and another like it the Court asserted its own broad powers to review any state court decision if that decision seemed to violate federal law or the federal Constitution.[4]

The power of the federal government to regulate commerce among the states was also established. When New York gave to Robert Fulton, the inventor of the steamboat, the monopoly right to operate his steamboats on the rivers of that state, the Marshall Court overturned the license because the rivers connected New York and New Jersey and thus trade on

those rivers would involve *inter*state commerce, and federal law in that area was supreme. Since there was a conflicting federal law on the books, the state law was void.[5]

All of this may sound rather obvious to us today, when the supremacy of the federal government is largely unquestioned. In the early nineteenth century, however, these were almost revolutionary decisions. The Jeffersonian Republicans were in power and had become increasingly devoted to states' rights; they were aghast at the Marshall decisions. President Andrew Jackson attacked the Court bitterly for defending the right of the federal government to create a national bank and for siding with the Cherokee Indians in a dispute with Georgia. In speaking of the latter case, Jackson is supposed to have remarked, "John Marshall has made his decision; now let him enforce it!"[6]

Though Marshall seemed to have secured the supremacy of the federal government over the state the United States. And if the order were given, whether or not Madison complied, the Jeffersonian Republicans in Congress would probably try to impeach Marshall. On the other hand, if Marshall allowed Madison to do as he wished, the power of the Supreme Court would be seriously reduced.

Marshall's solution was ingenious. Speaking for a unanimous Court, he announced that Madison was wrong to withhold the commissions, that courts could issue writs to compel public offcials to do their prescribed duty—*but* that the Supreme Court had no power to issue such writs in this case because the law (the Judiciary Act of 1789) giving it that power was unconstitutional. The law said that the Supreme Court could issue such writs as part of its "original jurisdiction"—that is, persons seeking such writs could go *directly* to the Supreme Court with their request (rather than go first to a lower federal court and then, if dissatisfied, appeal to the Supreme Court). Article III of the Constitution, Marshall pointed out, spelled out precisely the Supreme Court's original jurisdiction; it did not mention issuing writs of this sort and plainly indicated that on all matters not mentioned in the Constitution, the Court would have only appellate

James Madison   *John Adams*

jurisdiction. Congress may not change what the Constitution says; hence the part of the Judiciary Act attempting to do this was null and void.

The result was that a showdown with the Jeffersonians was avoided—Madison was not ordered to deliver the commissions—but the power of the Supreme Court was unmistakably clarified and enlarged. As Marshall wrote, "It is emphatically the province and duty of the judicial department to say what the law is." Furthermore, "a law repugnant to the Constitution is void."

governments, another even more divisive issue had arisen; that, of course, was slavery. Roger B. Taney succeeded Marshall as chief justice in 1836. He was deliberately chosen by President Jackson because he was an advocate of states' rights, and he began to chip away at federal supremacy, upholding state claims that Marshall would have set aside. But the decision for which he is famous—or infamous—came in 1857, when in the *Dred Scott* case he wrote perhaps the most disastrous judicial opinion ever issued. A slave, Dred Scott, had been taken by his owner to a territory (near what is now St. Paul, Minnesota) where slavery was illegal under federal law. Scott claimed that since he had resided in a free territory, he was now a free man. Taney held that Negroes were not citizens of the United States and could not become so, and that the federal law—the Missouri Compromise—prohibiting slavery in northern territories was unconstitutional.[7] The public outcry against this view was enormous, and the Court and

Taney were discredited in the North, at least. The Civil War was ultimately fought over what the Court mistakenly had assumed was a purely legal question.

Government and the Economy

The supremacy of the federal government may have been established by John Marshall and the Civil War, but the scope of the powers of that government or even of the state governments was still to be defined. During the period from the end of the Civil War to the early years of the New Deal, the dominant issue the Supreme Court faced was deciding when the economy would be regulated by the states and when by the nation.

The Court revealed a strong though not inflexible attachment to private property. In fact that attachment had always been there: the Founders thought that political and property rights were inextricably linked, and Marshall certainly supported the sanctity of contracts. But now, with the muting of the federal

Roger B. Taney, chief justice from 1836 to 1864, wrote the Dred Scott *decision, which asserted that blacks were not citizens of the United States. Dred Scott claimed that when his master brought him north to a free state, he ceased to be a slave. The public outcry against the decision was intense, at least in the North, as is evident from this poster announcing a mass meeting "to consider the atrocious decision."*

supremacy issue and the rise of a national economy with important unanticipated effects, the property question became the dominant one. In general the Court developed the view that the Fourteenth Amendment, adopted in 1868 primarily to protect African American claims to citizenship from hostile state action, also protected private property and the corporation from unreasonable state action. The crucial phrase was this: no state shall "deprive any person of life, liberty, or property, without due process of law." Once it became clear that a "person" could be a firm or a corporation as well as an individual, business and industry began to flood the courts with cases challenging various government regulations.

The Court quickly found itself in a thicket: it began ruling on the constitutionality of virtually every effort by any government to regulate any aspect of business or labor, and its workload rose sharply. Judicial activism was born in the 1880s and 1890s as the Court set itself up as the arbiter of what kind of regulation was permissible. In the first seventy-five years of this country's history, only 2 federal laws were held to be unconstitutional; in the next seventy-five years, 71 were.[8] Of the roughly 900 state laws held to be in conflict with the federal Constitution since 1789, about 800 were overturned after 1870. In one

decade alone—the 1880s—5 federal and 48 state laws were declared unconstitutional.

Many of these decisions provided clear evidence of the Court's desire to protect private property: it upheld the use of injunctions to prevent labor strikes,[9] struck down the federal income tax,[10] sharply limited the reach of the antitrust law,[11] restricted the powers of the Interstate Commerce Commission to set railroad rates,[12] prohibited the federal government from eliminating child labor,[13] and prevented the states from setting maximum hours of work.[14] In 184 cases between 1899 and 1937, the Supreme Court struck down state laws for violating the Fourteenth Amendment, usually by economic regulation.[15]

But the Court also rendered decisions that authorized various kinds of regulation. It allowed states to regulate businesses "affected with a public interest,"[16] changed its mind about the Interstate Commerce Commission and allowed it to regulate railroad rates,[17] upheld rules requiring railroads to improve their safety,[18] approved state antiliquor laws,[19] approved state mine safety laws,[20] supported state workers' compensation laws,[21] allowed states to regulate fire-insurance rates,[22] and in time upheld a number of state laws regulating wages and hours.

Indeed, between 1887 and 1910, in 558 cases involving the Fourteenth Amendment, the Supreme Court upheld state regulations over 80 percent of the time.[23]

To characterize the Court as probusiness or anti-regulation is both simplistic and inexact. More accurate, perhaps, is to characterize it as supportive of the rights of private property but unsure how to draw the lines that distinguish "reasonable" from "unreasonable" regulation. Nothing in the Constitution clearly differentiates reasonable from unreasonable regulation, and the Court has been able to invent no consistent principle of its own to make this determination. For example, what kinds of businesses are "affected with a public interest"? Grain elevators and railroads are, but are bakeries? Sugar refiners? Saloons? And how much of commerce is "interstate"—anything that moves? Or only something that actually crosses a state line? The Court found itself trying to make detailed judgments that it was not always competent to make and to invent legal rules where no clear legal rules were possible.

In one area, however, the Supreme Court's judgments were clear: the Fourteenth and Fifteenth Amendments were construed so narrowly as to give African Americans only the most limited benefits of their provisions. In a long series of decisions the Court upheld segregation in schools and on railroad cars and permitted blacks to be excluded from voting in many states.

Government and Political Liberty

After 1936 the Supreme Court stopped imposing any serious restrictions on state or federal power to regulate the economy, leaving such matters in the hands of the legislatures. From 1937 to 1974 the Supreme Court did not overturn a single federal law designed to regulate business but did overturn thirty-six congressional enactments that violated personal political liberties. It voided as unconstitutional laws that restricted freedom of speech,[24] denied passports to communists,[25] permitted the government to revoke a person's citizenship,[26] withheld a person's mail,[27] or restricted the availability of government benefits.[28]

This new direction began when one justice changed his mind, and it continued as the composition of the Court changed. At the outset of the New Deal the Court was, by a narrow margin, dominated by justices who opposed the welfare state and federal regulation based on broad grants of discretionary authority to administrative agencies. President Franklin Roosevelt, who was determined to get just such legislation implemented, found himself powerless to alter the composition of the Court during his first term (1933–1937): because no justice died or retired, he had no vacancies to fill. After his

The "nine old men": The Supreme Court in 1937, not long after President Franklin D. Roosevelt tried, unsuccessfully, to "pack" it by appointing six additional justices who would have supported his New Deal legislation. Justice Owen J. Roberts (standing, second from the left) changed his vote on these matters, and the Court ceased to be a barrier to the delegation of power to the bureaucracy.

U.S. District and Appellate Courts

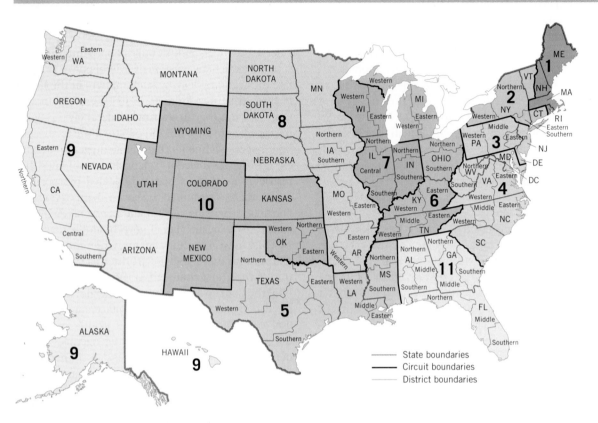

Note: Washington, D.C., is in a separate court. Puerto Rico is in the first circuit; the Virgin Islands are in the third; Guam and the Northern Mariana Islands are in the ninth.
Source: Administrative Office of the United States Courts (January 1983).

overwhelming reelection in 1936, he moved to remedy this problem by "packing" the Court.

Roosevelt proposed a bill that would have allowed him to appoint one new justice for each one over the age of seventy who refused to retire, up to a total membership of fifteen. Since there were six men in this category then on the Supreme Court, he would have been able to appoint six new justices, enough to ensure a comfortable majority supportive of his economic policies. A bitter controversy ensued, but before the bill could be voted on, the Supreme Court, perhaps reacting to Roosevelt's big win in the 1936 election, changed its mind. Whereas it had been striking down several New Deal measures by votes of five to four, now it started approving them by the same vote. One justice, Owen Roberts, had switched his position. This was called the "switch in time that

saved nine," but in fact Roberts had changed his mind *before* the FDR plan was announced.

The "Court-packing" bill was not passed, but it was no longer necessary. Justice Roberts had yielded before public opinion in a way that Chief Justice Taney a century earlier had not, thus forestalling an assault on the Court by the other branches of government. Shortly thereafter several justices stepped down, and Roosevelt was able to make his own appointments (he filled seven seats during his four terms in office). From then on the Court turned its attention to new issues—political liberties and, in time, civil rights.

With the arrival in office of Chief Justice Earl Warren in 1953, the Court began its most active period yet. Activism now arose to redefine the relationship of citizens to the government and especially to protect the rights and liberties of citizens from governmental trespass. Although the Court has always seen itself as protecting citizens from arbitrary government, before 1937 that protection was of a sort that conservatives preferred; after 1937 it was of a kind that liberals preferred.

The Revival of State Sovereignty

For many decades the Supreme Court allowed Congress to pass almost any law authorized by the Constitution, no matter how it affected the states. As we saw in Chapter 3, the Court had long held that Congress could regulate almost any activity if it affected interstate commerce, and in the Court's opinion virtually every activity did affect it. The states were left with few rights to challenge federal power. But since around 1992 the Court has backed away from this view. By narrow majorities it has begun to restore the view that states have the right to resist some forms of federal action.

When Congress passed a bill that forbade anyone from carrying a gun near a school, the Court held that carrying guns did not affect interstate commerce, and so the law was invalid.[29] One year later it struck down a law that allowed Indian tribes to sue the states in federal courts, arguing that Congress lacks the power to ignore the "sovereign immunity" of states—that is, the right, protected by the Eleventh Amendment, not to be sued in federal court. (It has since upheld that view in two more cases.) And the next year it held that the Brady gun control law could not be used to require local law enforcement officers to do background checks on people trying to buy weapons.[30] These cases are all hints that there are some real limits to the supremacy of the federal government created by the existence and powers of the several states.

The Structure of the Federal Courts

The only federal court that the Constitution requires is the Supreme Court, as specified in Article III. All other federal courts and their jurisdictions are creations of Congress. Nor does the Constitution indicate how many justices shall be on the Supreme Court (there were originally six, now there are nine) or what its appellate jurisdiction shall be.

Congress has created two kinds of lower federal courts to handle cases that need not be decided by the Supreme Court: constitutional and legislative courts. A **constitutional court** is one exercising the judicial powers found in Article III of the Constitution, and therefore its judges are given constitutional protection: they may not be fired (they serve during "good behavior"), nor may their salaries be reduced while they are in office. The most important of the constitutional courts are the **district courts** (a total of ninety-four, with at least one in each state, the District of Columbia, and the commonwealth of Puerto Rico) and the **courts of appeals** (one in each of eleven regions, or circuits, plus one in the District of Columbia). There are also certain specialized courts having constitutional status, such as the Court of International Trade, but we shall not be concerned with them.

A **legislative court** is one set up by Congress for some specialized purpose and staffed with people who have fixed terms of office and can be removed or have their salaries reduced. Legislative courts include the Court of Military Appeals and the territorial courts.

Selecting Judges

Since the judges on the constitutional courts serve for life and have the power of judicial review, how they are selected and what attitudes they bring to the bench are obviously important. All are nominated by the president and confirmed by the Senate. Almost invariably the president nominates a member of his own political party.

Party background does have some effect on how judges behave. A study by Robert A. Carp and C. K. Rowland of over twenty-seven thousand district court cases decided between 1933 and 1977 revealed that Democratic judges took somewhat more liberal positions than Republican ones (see Table 14.2). The biggest differences were in cases alleging discrimination based on race or sex and in those involving the rights of the accused in criminal prosecutions. In these matters Democratic judges reached a "liberal" decision 13 to 18 percent more frequently than Republican ones. Comparable findings have come from studies of appeals court and Supreme Court justices.[31] This is consistent with what we have already learned about public opinion: within political elites partisanship is associated with ideology, and this affects behavior.

But ideology does not determine behavior. So many other things shape court decisions—the facts of

Table 14.2   How Partisanship Affects Judicial Attitudes

In 1984 over one hundred federal judges were interviewed to learn about their background and attitudes. There were about equal numbers of Democrats and Republicans, and they were quite similar in social background. The overwhelming majority were white males; their average age was sixty. Most had attended a prestigious college. Despite these similarities, they expressed quite different political views and applied quite different judicial philosophies.

	Judges Appointed By:	
Attitudes	**Democrats**	**Republicans**
Political Ideology		
Liberal	75%	28%
Conservative	11	37
Policy Positions		
Favor less government regulation of business	54	85
Government should reduce income gap between rich and poor	78	44
Special preference should be given to blacks in hiring	62	41
Special preference should be given to women in hiring	47	22
A woman has right to decide on abortion	81	80
Judicial Philosophy		
Courts show too much concern for criminals	16	44
Judges should just apply the law, leave the rest to legislators	51	69
Judges need to supervise public bureaucracies	81	64

Source: Althea K. Nagai, Stanley Rothman, and S. Robert Lichter, "The Verdict of Federal Judges," *Public Opinion* (November–December 1987): 52–56. Reprinted with the permission of the American Enterprise Institute for Public Policy Research, Washington, D.C.

the case, prior rulings by other courts, the arguments presented by lawyers—that there is no reliable way of predicting how judges will behave in all matters. Presidents often make the mistake of thinking that they know how their appointees will behave, only to be surprised by the facts. Theodore Roosevelt appointed Oliver Wendell Holmes to the Supreme Court, only to remark later, after Holmes had voted in a way that Roosevelt did not like, that "I could carve out of a banana a judge with more backbone than that!" Holmes, who had plenty of backbone, said that he did not "give a damn" what Roosevelt thought. Richard Nixon, an ardent foe of court-ordered school busing, appointed Warren Burger to be chief justice. Burger promptly sat down and wrote the opinion upholding busing. Another Nixon appointee, Harry Blackmun, wrote the opinion declaring the right to an abortion to be constitutionally protected.

Senatorial Courtesy   In theory the president nominates a "qualified" person to be a judge, and the

Senate approves or rejects the nomination based on those "qualifications." In fact the tradition of *senatorial courtesy* gives heavy weight to the preferences of the senators from the state where a federal district judge is to serve. Ordinarily the Senate will not confirm a district court judge if the senior senator from the state where the district is located objects (if he is of the president's party). The senator can exercise this veto power by means of the "blue slip"—a blue piece of paper on which the senator is asked to record his or her views on the nominee. A negative opinion, or even failure to return the blue slip, usually kills the nomination. This means that as a practical matter the president nominates only persons recommended to him by that key senator. Someone once suggested that, at least with respect to district judges, the Constitution has been turned on its head. To reflect reality, he said, Article II, section 2, ought to read: "The senators shall nominate, and by and with the consent of the President, shall appoint" federal judges.

The "Litmus Test" Of late, presidents have tried to exercise more influence on the selection of federal district and appellate court judges by getting the Justice Department to find candidates that not only are supported by their party's senators but also reflect the political and judicial philosophy of the president. Presidents Carter and Clinton sought out liberal, activist judges; President Reagan sought out conservative, strict-constructionist ones. The party membership of federal judges makes a difference in how they vote. A review of eighty-four studies shows that Democratic judges are more liberal than Republican ones.[32]

Because different courts of appeals have different combinations of judges, some will be more liberal than others. For example, there are more liberal judges in the court of appeals for the ninth circuit (which includes most of the far western states) and more conservative ones in the fifth circuit (Texas, Louisiana, and Mississippi). The ninth circuit takes liberal positions, the fifth more conservative ones. Since the Supreme Court does not have time to settle every disagreement among appeals courts, different interpretations of the law may exist in different circuits. In the fifth circuit, for instance, it is unconstitutional for state universities to have affirmative action programs.

These differences make some people worry about the use of a political **litmus test**—a test of ideological purity—in selecting judges. When conservatives are out of power, they complain about how liberal presidents use such a test; when liberals are out power, they complain about how conservative presidents use it. Many people would like to see judges picked on the basis of professional qualifications, without reference to ideology, but the courts are now so deeply involved in political issues that it is hard to imagine what an ideologically neutral set of professional qualifications might be.

The litmus test has grown in importance. During the Clinton administration it was hard for the president to get his candidates for judgeships approved by the Senate. This was not just a result of his being a Democrat and the Senate being under Republican control. That has happened before, but without producing a logjam. The real problem is the litmus test: Democrats want judges that support abortion, look favorably on affirmative action, and oppose giving public money to students who attend private schools. Republicans tend to have the opposite views. These differences in opinion would not be so

important if the courts did not play an active role in making decisions on these matters. At one time they did not. But now the courts are settling these issues, and so politicians increasingly want them to be decided the "right way." With divided government, the litmus test has become much more important.

Figure 14.1 Female and Minority Judicial Appointments, 1963–1998

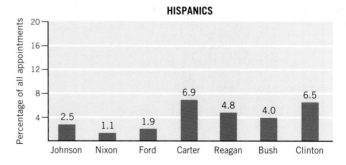

Source: Harold W. Stanley and Richard G. Niemi, *Vital Statistics on American Politics, 1997–1998* (Washington, D.C.: Congressional Quarterly, 1998), 272–273.

Litmus Test

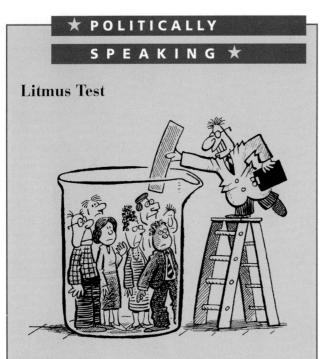

In chemistry a litmus test is a way of finding out whether a liquid is acid or alkaline. It involves exposing the fluid to an organic dye that turns red in acids, blue in alkalines.

The term is used in politics to mean a test of ideological purity, a way of finding out whether a person is a dyed-in-the-wool liberal or a conservative. For liberals a litmus test issue might be support for abortion or opposition to school prayer; for conservatives it might be holding the opposite of these views, or perhaps favoring tax cuts.

Source: From *Safire's Political Dictionary* by William Safire. Copyright © 1968, 1972, 1978 by William Safire. Reprinted by permission of Random House, Inc. and the author.

The litmus test issue is of greatest importance in selecting Supreme Court justices. Here there is no tradition of senatorial courtesy. The president takes a keen personal interest in the choices and, of late, has sought to find nominees who share his philosophy. In the Reagan administration there were bruising fights in the Senate over the nomination of William Rehnquist to be chief justice (he won) and Robert Bork to be an associate justice (he lost), with liberals pitted against conservatives. When President Bush nominated David Souter, there were lengthy hearings as liberal senators tried to pin down Souter's views on issues such as abortion. Souter refused to discuss matters on which he might later have to judge, however. Clarence Thomas, another Bush nominee, also tried to avoid the litmus test by saying that he had not formed an opinion on prominent abortion cases. In his case, however, the litmus test issue was overshadowed by sensational allegations from a former employee, Anita Hill, that Thomas had sexually harassed her.

Of the 145 Supreme Court nominees presented to it, the Senate has rejected 29. Only 5 of these were in the twentieth century. The reasons for rejecting a Supreme Court nominee are complex—each senator may have a different reason—but have involved such matters as the nominee's alleged hostility to civil rights, questionable personal financial dealings, a poor record as a lower-court judge, and Senate opposition to the nominee's political or legal philosophy. Nominations of district court judges are rarely defeated, because typically no nomination is made unless the key senators approve in advance.

The Jurisdiction of the Federal Courts

We have a dual court system—one state, one federal—and this complicates enormously the task of describing what kinds of cases federal courts may hear and how cases beginning in the state courts may end up before the Supreme Court. The Constitution lists the kinds of cases over which federal courts have jurisdiction (in Article III and the Eleventh Amendment); by implication all other matters are left to state courts. Federal courts (see Figure 14.2) can hear all cases "arising under the Constitution, the laws of the United States, and treaties" (these are **federal-question cases**), and cases involving citizens of different states (called **diversity cases**).

Some kinds of cases can be heard in either federal or state courts. For example, if citizens of different states wish to sue one another and the matter involves more than $75,000, they can do so in either a federal or a state court. Similarly, if someone robs a federally insured bank, he or she has broken both state and federal law and thus can be prosecuted in state or federal courts, or both. Lawyers have become quite sophisticated in deciding

Figure 14.2 The Jurisdiction of the Federal Courts

Original jurisdiction
Cases begin in the Supreme Court over controversies involving:

1. Two or more states
2. The United States and a state
3. Foreign ambassadors and other diplomats
4. A state and a citizen of a different state (if begun by the state)

Supreme Court of the United States
(1 court with 9 justices)
Appellate jurisdiction
Cases begin in another, lower court. Hears appeals, at its discretion, from:

State Supreme Courts
(if federal questions are raised)

United States Courts of Appeals
(1 in each of 11 "circuits" or regions plus 1 in the District of Columbia and 1 Federal Circuit Court)
Hear appeals only from:

Court of Military Appeals

U.S. regulatory commissions

United States District Courts
(1 in each of 94 districts)
Have only original jurisdiction, over cases involving:

1. Federal crimes
2. Civil suits under federal law
3. Civil suits between citizens of different states where the amount exceeds $50,000
4. Admiralty and maritime disputes
5. Bankruptcy
6. Review of actions of certain federal administrative agencies
7. Other matters assigned to them by Congress

Claims Court
Tax Court
Court of International Trade

whether, in a given civil case, their clients will get better treatment in a state or federal court. Prosecutors often send a person who has broken both federal and state law to whichever court system is likelier to give the toughest penalty.

Sometimes defendants may be tried in both state and federal courts for the same offense. In 1992 four Los Angeles police officers accused of beating Rodney King were tried in a California state court and acquitted of assault charges. They were then prosecuted in federal court for violating King's civil rights. This time two of the four were convicted. Under the dual sovereignty doctrine, state and federal authorities can prosecute the same person for the same conduct. The Supreme Court has upheld this doctrine on two grounds: First, each level of government has the right to enact laws serving its own purposes.[33] As a result federal civil rights charges could have been brought against the officers even if they had already been convicted of assault in state court (though as a

---

★ POLITICALLY
SPEAKING ★

Kinds of Law

The differences between *civil* and *criminal* law are not precise. Generally speaking:

- **Civil law** is the body of rules defining relationships among private citizens. It consists of both statutes and the accumulated customary law embodied in judicial decisions (the "common law").
- **Criminal law** is the body of rules defining offenses that, though they harm an individual (such as murder, rape, and robbery), are considered to be offenses against society as a whole and thus warrant punishment by and in the name of society.

You can go to prison if convicted of a crime but not if you lose a civil suit.

---

practical matter this would have been unlikely). Second, neither level of government wants the other to be able to block prosecution of an accused person who has the sympathy of the authorities at one level. For example, when certain southern state courts were in sympathy with whites who had lynched blacks, the absence of the dual sovereignty doctrine would have meant that a trumped-up acquittal in state court would have barred federal prosecution.

Furthermore, a matter that is exclusively within the province of a state court—for example, a criminal case in which the defendant is charged with violating only a state law—can be appealed to the U.S. Supreme Court under certain circumstances (described below). Thus federal judges can overturn state court rulings even when they had no jurisdiction over the original matter. Under what circumstances this should occur has been the subject of long-standing controversy between the state and federal courts.

Some matters, however, are exclusively under the jurisdiction of federal courts. When a federal criminal law is broken—but not a state one—the case is heard in federal district court. If you wish to appeal the decision of a federal regulatory agency, such as the Federal Communications Commission, you can

do so only before a federal court of appeals. And if you wish to declare bankruptcy, you do so in federal court. If there is a controversy between two state governments—say, California and Arizona sue each other over which state is to use how much water from the Colorado River—the case can be heard only by the Supreme Court.

The vast majority of all cases heard by federal courts begin in the district courts. The volume of business there is huge. In 1996 the 600 or so district court judges received over 300,000 cases (about 500 per judge). Most of the cases heard in federal courts involve rather straightforward applications of law; few lead to the making of new public policy. Cases that do affect how the law or the Constitution is interpreted can begin with seemingly minor events. For example, a major broadening of the Bill of Rights—requiring for the first time that all accused persons in *state* as well as federal criminal trials be supplied with a lawyer, free if necessary—began when impoverished Clarence Earl Gideon, imprisoned in Florida, wrote an appeal in pencil on prison stationery and sent it to the Supreme Court.[34]

The Supreme Court does not have to hear any appeal it does not want to hear. At one time it was required to listen to certain appeals, but Congress has changed the law so that now the Court can pick the cases it wants to consider.

It does this by issuing a **writ of certiorari.** *Certiorari* is a Latin word meaning, roughly, "made more certain"; lawyers and judges have abbreviated it to *cert*. It works this way: The Court considers all the petitions it receives to review lower-court decisions. If four justices agree to hear a case, cert is issued and the case is scheduled for a hearing.

In deciding whether to grant certiorari, the Court tries to reserve its time for cases decided by lower federal courts or by the highest state courts in which a significant federal or constitutional question has been raised. For example, the Court will often grant certiorari when one or both of the following is true:

- Two or more federal circuit courts of appeals have decided the same issue in different ways.
- The highest court in a state has held a federal or state law to be in violation of the Constitution or has upheld a state law against the claim that it is in violation of the Constitution.

In a typical year the Court may consider over seven thousand petitions asking it to review deci-

Clarence Earl Gideon studied law books while in prison so that he could write an appeal to the Supreme Court. His handwritten appeal asked that his conviction be set aside because he had not been provided with an attorney. His appeal was granted.

sions of lower or state courts. It rarely accepts more than about one hundred of them for full review.

In exercising its discretion in granting certiorari, the Supreme Court is on the horns of a dilemma. If it grants it frequently, it will be inundated with cases. As it is, the Court's workload has quintupled in the last fifty years. If, on the other hand, the Court grants certiorari only rarely, then the federal courts of appeals have the last word on the interpretation of the Constitution and federal laws, and since there are twelve of these, staffed by about 168 judges, they may well be in disagreement. In fact this has already happened: because the Supreme Court reviews only about 1 or 2 percent of appeals court cases, applicable federal law may be different in different parts of the country.[35] One proposal to deal with this dilemma is to devote the Supreme Court's time entirely to major questions of constitutional interpretation and to create a national court of appeals that would ensure that the twelve circuit courts of appeals are producing uniform decisions.[36]

Because the Supreme Court has a heavy workload, the influence wielded by law clerks has grown. These clerks—recent graduates of law schools hired by the justices—play a big role in deciding which cases should be heard under a writ of certiorari. Indeed, some of the opinions written by the justices are drafted by the clerks. Since the reasons for a decision may be as important as the decision itself, and since these reasons are sometimes cre-

ated by the clerks, the power of the clerks can be significant.

Getting to Court

In theory the courts are the great equalizer in the federal government. To use the courts to settle a question, or even to alter fundamentally the accepted interpretation of the Constitution, one need not be elected to any office, have access to the mass media, be a member of an interest group, or be otherwise powerful or rich. Once the contending parties are before the courts, they are legally equal.

It is too easy to believe this theory uncritically or to dismiss it cynically. In fact it is hard to get before the Supreme Court: it rejects over 96 percent of the applications for certiorari that it receives. And the costs involved in getting to the Court can be high. To apply for certiorari costs only $300 (plus forty copies of the petition), but if certiorari is granted and the case is heard, the costs—for lawyers and for copies of the lower-court records in the case—can be very high. And by then one has already paid for the cost of the first hearing in the district court and probably one appeal to the circuit court of appeals. Furthermore, the time it takes to settle a matter in federal court can be quite long.

But there are ways to make these costs lower. If you are indigent—without funds—you can file and be heard as a pauper for nothing; about half the petitions arriving before the Supreme Court are **in forma pauperis** (such as the one from Gideon, described earlier). If your case began as a criminal trial in the district courts and you are poor, the government will supply you with a lawyer at no charge. If the matter is not a criminal case and you cannot afford to hire a lawyer, interest groups representing a wide spectrum of opinion sometimes are willing to take up the cause if the issue in the case seems sufficiently important. The American Civil Liberties Union (ACLU), a liberal group, represents some people who believe that their freedom of speech has been abridged or that their constitutional rights in criminal proceedings have been violated. The Center for Individual Rights, a conservative group, represents some people who feel that they have been victimized by racial quotas.

But interest groups do much more than just help people pay their bills. Many of the most important cases decided by the Court got there because an interest group organized the case, found the plaintiffs, chose the legal strategy, and mobilized legal allies. The NAACP has brought many key civil rights cases on behalf of individuals. Although in the past most such cases were brought by liberal interest groups, of late conservative interest groups have entered the courtroom on behalf of individuals. One helped sue CBS for televising a program that allegedly libeled General William Westmoreland, once the American commander in Vietnam. (Westmoreland lost the case.) And many important issues are raised by attorneys representing state and local governments. Several price-fixing cases have been won by state attorneys general on behalf of consumers in their states.

Fee Shifting

Unlike what happens in most of Europe, each party to a lawsuit in this country must pay its own way. (In England, by contrast, if you sue someone and lose, you pay the winner's costs as well as your own.) But various laws have made it easier to get someone else to pay. **Fee shifting** enables the **plaintiff** (the party that initiates the suit) to collect its costs from the defendant if the defendant loses, at least in certain kinds of cases. For example, if a corporation is found to have violated the antitrust laws, it must pay the legal fees of the winner. If an environmentalist group sues the Environmental Protection Agency, it can get the EPA to pay the group's legal costs. Even more important to individuals, Section 1983 of Chapter 42 of the *United States Code* allows a citizen to sue a state or local government official—say, a police officer or a school superintendent—who has deprived the citizen of some constitutional right or withheld some benefit to which the citizen is entitled. If the citizen wins, he or she can collect money damages and lawyers' fees from the government. Citizens, more aware of their legal rights, have become more litigious, and a flood of such "Section 1983" suits has burdened the courts. The Supreme Court has restricted fee shifting to cases authorized by statute,[37] but it is clear that the drift of policy has made it cheaper to go to court—at least for some cases.

Standing

There is, in addition, a nonfinancial restriction on getting into federal court. To sue, one must have **standing,** a legal concept that refers to who is entitled to bring a case. It is especially important in determining who can challenge the laws or actions of the government itself. A complex and changing set of rules governs standings; some of the more important ones are these:

- There must be an actual controversy between real adversaries. (You cannot bring a "friendly" suit against someone, hoping to lose in order to prove your friend right. You cannot ask a federal court for an opinion on a hypothetical or imaginary case or ask it to render an advisory opinion.)
- You must show that you have been harmed by the law or practice about which you are complaining. (It is not enough to dislike what the government or a corporation or a labor union does; you must show that you were actually harmed by that action.)
- Merely being a taxpayer does not ordinarily entitle you to challenge the constitutionality of a federal governmental action. (You may not want your tax money to be spent in certain ways, but your remedy is to vote against the politicians doing the spending; the federal courts will generally require that you show some other personal harm before you can sue.)

Congress and the courts have recently made it easier to acquire standing. It has always been the rule that a citizen could ask the courts to order federal officials to carry out some act that they were under a legal obligation to perform or to refrain from some action that was contrary to law. A citizen can also sue a government official personally in order to collect damages if the official acted contrary to law. For example, it was for long the case that if an FBI agent broke into your office without a search warrant, you could sue the agent and, if you won, collect money. However, you cannot sue the government itself without its consent. This is the doctrine of **sovereign immunity.** For instance, if the army accidentally kills your cow while testing a new cannon, you cannot sue the government to recover the cost of the cow unless the government agrees to be sued. (Since testing cannons is legal, you cannot sue the army officer who fired the cannon.) By statute Congress has given its consent for the government to be sued in many cases involving a dispute over a contract or damage done as a result of negligence (for example, the dead cow). Over the years these statutes have made it easier to take the government into court as a defendant.

Even some of the oldest rules defining standing have been liberalized. The rule that merely being a taxpayer does not entitle you to challenge in court a government decision has been relaxed where the citizen claims that a right guaranteed under the First Amendment is being violated. The Supreme Court allowed a taxpayer to challenge a federal law that would have given financial aid to parochial (or church-related) schools on the grounds that this aid violated the constitutional requirement of separation between church and state. On the other hand, another taxpayer suit to force the CIA to make public its budget failed because the Court decided that the taxpayer did not have standing in matters of this sort.[38]

Class-Action Suits

Under certain circumstances a citizen can benefit directly from a court decision, even though the citizen himself or herself has not gone into court. This can happen by means of a **class-action suit:** a case brought into court by a person on behalf not only of himself or herself but of all other persons in similar circumstances. Among the most famous of these was the 1954 case in which the Supreme Court found that Linda Brown, a black girl attending the fifth grade in the Topeka, Kansas, public schools, was denied the equal protection of the laws (guaranteed under the Fourteenth Amendment) because the schools in Topeka were segregated. The Court did not limit its decision to Linda Brown's right to attend an unsegregated school but extended it—as Brown's lawyers from the NAACP had asked—to cover all "others similarly situated."[39] It was not easy to design a court order that would eliminate segregation in the schools, but the principle was clearly established in this class action.

Since the *Brown* case, many other groups have been quick to take advantage of the opportunity created by class-action suits. By this means the courts could be used to give relief not simply to a particular person but to all those represented in the suit. A landmark class-action case was that which challenged the malapportionment of state legislative districts (see Chapter 11).[40] There are thousands of class-action suits in the federal courts involving civil rights, the rights of prisoners, antitrust suits against corporations, and other matters. These suits

became more common partly because people were beginning to have new concerns that were not being met by Congress and partly because some class-action suits became quite profitable. The NAACP got no money from Linda Brown or from the Topeka Board of Education in compensation for its long and expensive labors, but beginning in the 1960s court rules were changed to make it financially attractive for lawyers to bring certain kinds of class-action suits.

Suppose, for example, that you think your telephone company overcharged you by $75. You could try to hire a lawyer to get a refund, but not many lawyers would take the case, because there would be no money in it. Even if you were to win, the lawyer would stand to earn no more than perhaps one-third of the settlement, or $25. Now suppose that you bring a class action against the company on behalf of everybody who was overcharged. Millions of

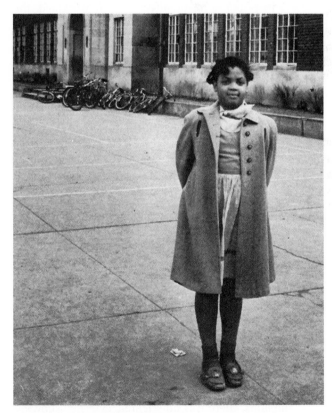

Linda Brown was refused admission to a white elementary school in Topeka, Kansas. On her behalf the NAACP brought a class-action suit that resulted in the 1954 landmark Supreme Court decision Brown v. Board of Education.

Table 14.3 Supreme Court Justices in Order of Seniority, 1999			
Name (Birth Date)	**Home State**	**Prior Experience**	**Appointed By (Year)**
William H. Rehnquist, Chief Justice (1924)	Arizona	Justice; assistant attorney general	Reagan (1986) as chief; Nixon (1971) as justice
John Paul Stevens (1916)	Illinois	Federal judge	Ford (1975)
Sandra Day O'Connor (1930)	Arizona	State judge	Reagan (1981)
Antonin Scalia (1936)	New York	Federal judge	Reagan (1986)
Anthony Kennedy (1936)	California	Federal judge	Reagan (1988)
David Souter (1939)	New Hampshire	State judge	Bush (1990)
Clarence Thomas (1948)	Georgia	Federal judge	Bush (1991)
Ruth Bader Ginsburg (1933)	New York	Federal judge	Clinton (1993)
Stephen Breyer (1938)	Massachusetts	Federal judge	Clinton (1994)

dollars might be at stake; lawyers would line up eagerly to take the case, because their share of the settlement, if they won, would be huge. The opportunity to win profitable class-action suits, combined with the possibility of having the loser pay the attorneys' fees, led to a proliferation of such cases.

In response to the increase in its workload, the Supreme Court decided in 1974 to tighten drastically the rules governing these suits. It held that it would no longer hear (except in certain cases defined by Congress, such as civil rights matters) class-action suits seeking monetary damages unless each and every ascertainable member of the class was individually notified of the case. To do this is often prohibitively expensive (imagine trying to find and send a letter to every customer that may have been overcharged by the telephone company!), and so the number of such cases declined and the number of lawyers seeking them out dropped.[41]

But it remains easy to bring a class-action suit in most state courts. State Farm automobile insurance company was told by a state judge in a small Illinois town that it must pay over $1 billion in damages on behalf of a "national" class, even though no one in this class had been notified. Big class-action suits powerfully affect how courts make public policy. Such suits have forced into bankruptcy companies making asbestos and silicone breast implants and have threatened to put out of business tobacco companies and gun manufacturers. (Ironically, in some of these cases, such as the one involving breast implants, there was no scientific evidence showing that the product was harmful.) Some class-action suits, such as the one ending school segregation, are good, but others are frivolous efforts to get companies to pay large fees to the lawyers who file the suits.

In sum, getting into court depends on having standing and having resources. The rules governing standing are complex and changing, but generally they have been broadened to make it easier to enter the federal courts, especially for the purpose of challenging the actions of the government. Obtaining the resources is not easy but has become easier because laws in some cases now provide for fee shifting, private interest groups are willing to finance cases, and it is sometimes possible to bring a class-action suit that lawyers find lucrative.

The Supreme Court in Action

If your case should find its way to the Supreme Court—and of course the odds are that it will not—you will be able to participate in one of the more impressive, sometimes dramatic ceremonies of American public life. The Court is in session in its white marble building for thirty-six weeks out of each year, from early October until the end of June. The nine justices read briefs in their individual offices, hear oral arguments in the stately courtroom, and discuss their decisions with one another in a conference room where no outsider is ever allowed.

Most cases, as we have seen, come to the Court on a writ of certiorari. The lawyers for each side may then submit their briefs. A **brief** is a document that sets forth the facts of the case, summarizes the lower-court decision, gives the arguments for the side represented by the lawyer who wrote the brief, and discusses the other cases that the Court has decided bear on the issue. Then the lawyers are allowed to present their oral arguments in open court. They usually summarize their briefs or

This photo of the Supreme Court in session on February 8, 1932, may be the only one ever taken while the justices were actually hearing a case.

emphasize particular points in them, and they are strictly limited in time—usually to no more than a half hour. (The lawyer speaks from a lectern that has two lights on it. When the white light goes on, the attorney has five minutes remaining; when the red flashes, he or she must stop—instantly.) The oral arguments give the justices a chance to question the lawyers, sometimes searchingly.

Since the federal government is a party—as either plaintiff or defendant—to about half the cases that the Supreme Court hears, the government's top trial lawyer, the solicitor general of the United States, appears frequently before the Court. The solicitor general is the third-ranking officer of the Department of Justice, right after the attorney general and deputy attorney general. The solicitor general decides what cases the government will appeal from lower courts and personally approves every case the government presents to the Supreme Court. In recent years the solicitor general has often been selected from the ranks of distinguished law school professors.

In addition to the arguments made by lawyers for the two sides in a case, written briefs and even oral arguments may also be offered by "a friend of the court," or **amicus curiae.** An amicus brief is from an interested party not directly involved in the suit. For example, when Allan Bakke complained that he had been the victim of "reverse discrimination"

when he was denied admission to a University of California medical school, fifty-eight amicus briefs were filed supporting or opposing his position. Before such briefs can be filed, both parties must agree or the Court must grant permission. Though these briefs sometimes offer new arguments, they are really a kind of polite lobbying of the Court that declare which interest groups are on which side. The ACLU, the NAACP, the AFL-CIO, and the U.S. government itself have been among the leading sources of such briefs.

These briefs are not the only source of influence on the justices' views. Legal periodicals such as the *Harvard Law Review* and the *Yale Law Journal* are frequently consulted, and citations to them often appear in the Court's decisions. Thus the outside world of lawyers and law professors can help shape, or at least supply arguments for, the conclusions of the justices.

The justices retire every Friday to their conference room, where in complete secrecy they debate the cases they have heard. The chief justice speaks first, followed by the other justices in order of seniority. After the arguments they vote, traditionally in reverse order of seniority: the newest justice votes first, the chief justice last. By this process an able chief justice can exercise considerable influence—in guiding or limiting debate, in setting forth the issues,

The members of the U.S. Supreme Court: from left to right, Antonin Scalia, Ruth Bader Ginsburg, John Paul Stevens, David Souter, William Rehnquist, Clarence Thomas, Sandra Day O'Connor, Stephen Breyer, Anthony Kennedy.

and in handling sometimes temperamental personalities. In deciding a case, a majority of the justices must be in agreement: if there is a tie, the lower-court decision is left standing. (There can be a tie among nine justices if one is ill or disqualifies himself or herself because of prior involvement in the case.)

Though the vote is what counts, by tradition the Court usually issues a written opinion explaining its decision. Sometimes the opinion is brief and unsigned (called a **per curiam opinion**); sometimes it is quite long and signed by the justices agreeing with it. If the chief justice is in the majority, he will either write the opinion or assign the task to a justice who agrees with him. If he is in the minority, the senior justice on the winning side will decide who writes the Court's opinion. There are three kinds of opinions—an **opinion of the Court** (reflecting the majority's view), a **concurring opinion** (an opinion by one or more justices who agree with the majority's conclusion but for different reasons that they wish to express), and a **dissenting opinion** (the opinion of the justices on the losing side). Each justice has three or four law clerks to help him or her review the many petitions the Court receives, study cases, and write opinions.

People like to think of the courts as expressing "liberal" or "conservative" opinions, and in many cases they seem to do just that. But that is far from the whole story. In many cases, perhaps one-third of those decided by the Supreme Court, the decisions are unanimous. Even two justices as different as Antonin Scalia and Ruth Bader Ginsburg vote the same way much of the time. The most important thing to remember is not the decision but the reasons behind the decision. Many times judges will vote for a position that they don't personally like but feel obliged to support because that is how the law reads.

The Power of the Federal Courts

The great majority of the cases heard in the federal courts have little or nothing to do with changes in public policy: people accused of bank robbery are tried, disputes over contracts are settled, personal-injury cases are heard, and the patent law is applied. In most instances the courts are simply applying a relatively settled body of law to a specific controversy.

The Power to Make Policy

The courts make policy whenever they reinterpret the law or the Constitution in significant ways, extend the reach of existing laws to cover matters not previously thought to be covered by them, or design remedies for problems that involve the judges' acting in administrative or legislative ways. By any of these tests the courts have become exceptionally powerful.

One measure of that power is the fact that more than 130 federal laws have been declared unconstitutional, although since 1937 relatively few of these have had broad national significance. And as we shall see, on matters where Congress feels strongly, it can often get its way by passing slightly revised versions of a voided law.

Another measure, and perhaps a more revealing one, is the frequency with which the Supreme Court changes its mind. An informal rule of judicial decision-making has been **stare decisis,** meaning "let the decision stand." It is the principle of precedent: a court case today should be settled in accordance with prior decisions on similar cases. (What constitutes a similar case is not always clear; lawyers are especially gifted at finding ways of showing that two cases are different in some relevant way.) There are two reasons why precedent is important. The practical reason should be obvious: if the meaning of the law continually changes, if the decisions of judges become wholly unpredictable, then human affairs affected by those laws and decisions become chaotic. A contract signed today might be invalid tomorrow. The other reason is at least as important: if the principle of equal justice means anything, it means that similar cases should be decided in a similar manner. On the other hand, times change, and the Court can make mistakes. As Justice Felix Frankfurter once said, "Wisdom too often never comes, and so one ought not to reject it merely because it comes late."[42]

However compelling the arguments for flexibility, the pace of change can become dizzying. By one count the Court has overruled its own previous decisions in over 260 cases since 1810.[43] In fact it may have done it more often, because sometimes the Court does not say that it is abandoning a precedent, claiming instead that it is merely distinguishing the present case from a previous one.

A third measure of judicial power is the degree to which courts are willing to handle matters once left to the legislature. For example, the Court refused for a long time to hear a case about the size of congressional districts, no matter how unequal their populations.[44] The determination of congressional district boundaries was regarded as a **political question**—that is, as a matter that the Constitution left entirely to another branch of government (in this case, Congress) to decide for itself. Then in 1962 the Court decided that it was competent after all to handle this matter, and the notion of a "political question" became a much less important (but by no means absent) barrier to judicial power.[45]

By all odds the most powerful indicator of judicial power can be found in the kinds of remedies that the courts will impose. A **remedy** is a judicial order setting forth what must be done to correct a situation that a judge believes to be wrong. In ordinary cases, such as when one person sues another, the remedy is straightforward: the loser must pay the winner for some injury that he or she has caused, the loser must agree to abide by the terms of a contract he or she has broken, or the loser must promise not to do some unpleasant thing (such as dumping garbage on a neighbor's lawn). Today, however, judges design remedies that go far beyond what is required to do justice to the individual parties who actually appear in court. The remedies now imposed often apply to large groups and affect the circumstances under which thousands or even millions of people work, study, or live. For example, when a federal district judge in Alabama heard a case brought by a prison inmate in that state, he issued an order not simply to improve the lot of that prisoner but to revamp the administration of the entire prison system. The result was an improvement in the living conditions of many prisoners, at a cost to the state of an estimated $40 million a year. Similarly, a person who feels entitled to welfare payments that have been denied him or her may sue in court to get the money, and the court order will in all likelihood affect all welfare recipients. In one case certain court orders made an additional one hundred thousand people eligible for welfare.[46]

The basis for sweeping court orders can sometimes be found in the Constitution; the Alabama prison decision, for example, was based on the judge's interpretation of the Eighth Amendment, which prohibits "cruel and unusual punishments."[47] Others are based on court interpretations of federal laws. The Civil Rights Act of 1964 forbids discrimination on grounds of "race, color, or national origin" in any program receiving federal financial assistance. The Supreme Court interpreted that as meaning that the San Francisco school system was obliged to teach English to Chinese students unable to speak it.[48] Since a Supreme Court decision is the law of the land, the impact of that ruling was not limited to San Francisco. Local courts and legislatures elsewhere decided that that decision meant that classes must be taught in Spanish for Hispanic children. What Congress meant by the Civil Rights Act is not clear; it may or may not have believed that teaching Hispanic children in English rather than Spanish was a form of discrimination. What is important is that it was the Court, not Congress, that decided what Congress meant.

Views of Judicial Activism

Judicial activism has, of course, been controversial. Those who support it argue that the federal courts must correct injustices when the other branches of the federal government, or the states, refuse to do so. The courts are the institution of last resort for those without the votes or the influence to obtain new laws, and especially for the poor and powerless. After all, Congress and the state legislatures tolerated segregated public schools for decades. If the Supreme Court had not declared segregation unconstitutional in 1954, it might still be law today.

Those who criticize judicial activism rejoin that judges usually have no special expertise in matters of school administration, prison management, environmental protection, and so on; they are lawyers, expert in defining rights and duties but not in designing and managing complex institutions. Furthermore, however desirable court-declared rights and principles may be, implementing those principles means balancing the conflicting needs of various interest groups, raising and spending tax monies, and assessing the costs and benefits of complicated alternatives. Finally, federal judges are not elected; they are appointed and are thus immune to popular control. As a result, if they depart from their traditional role of making careful and cautious interpretations of what a law or the Constitution means and instead begin formulating wholly new policies, they become unelected legislators.

Some people think that we have activist courts because we have so many lawyers. The more we take matters to courts for resolution, the more likely it is that the courts will become powerful. It is true that we have more lawyers in proportion to our population than most other nations. There is one lawyer for every 325 Americans but only one for every 970 Britons, every 1,220 Germans, and every 8,333 Japanese.[49] But that may well be a symptom, not a cause, of court activity. As we suggested in Chapter 4, we have an adversary culture based on an emphasis on individual rights and an implicit antagonism between the people and the government. Generally speaking, lawyers do not create cases; contending interests do, thereby generating a demand for lawyers.[50] Furthermore, we had more lawyers in relation to our population in 1900 than in 1970, yet the courts at the turn

The activism of federal courts is exemplified by the sweeping orders they have issued to correct such problems as overcrowded prisons.

MEMORANDUM

To: Justice Robert Gilbert
From: David Wilson, law clerk

Before I draft your opinion, I want to know how you feel about declaring the death penalty unconstitutional.

Arguments for:

1. As enforced, the death penalty tends to be discriminatory. Black convicts are, in some cases, more likely to be executed than white ones.
2. The death penalty is irrevocable. If an innocent man is executed, he cannot be brought back to life when his innocence becomes known.
3. The death penalty is "cruel and unusual punishment" that is banned by the Constitution.

Arguments against:

1. The Constitution does not ban the death penalty.
2. The death penalty existed when the Constitution and Bill of Rights were written. Their authors meant by "cruel and unusual punishment" the use of torture.
3. When a legislature decides to punish murder by death, its views are entitled to deference.
4. There is no strong evidence that the death penalty is imposed in a discriminatory manner.

Your decision:
Ban death penalty _____
Do not ban death penalty _____

Supreme Court to Decide Constitutionality of Capital Punishment

March 20
WASHINGTON
The Supreme Court has been asked to decide whether the death penalty is constitutional. A decision in this important case is expected by June . . .

of the twentieth century were far less active in public affairs. In fact, in 1932 there were more court cases per 100,00 people than there were in 1972.

A more plausible reason for activist courts has been the developments discussed earlier in this chapter that have made it easier for people to get standing in the courts, to pay for the costs of litigation, and to bring class-action suits. The courts and Congress have gone a long way toward allowing private citizens to become "private attorneys general." Making it easier to get into court increases the number of cases being heard. For example, in 1961 civil rights cases, prisoners' rights cases, and cases under the Social Security laws were relatively uncommon in federal court. Between 1961 and 1990 the increase in the number of such matters was phenomenal: civil rights cases rose over sixtyfold and prisoners' petitions over fortyfold. Such matters are the fastest-growing portion of the courts' civil workload.

Legislation and the Courts

An increase in cases will not by itself lead to sweeping remedies. For that to occur, the law must be sufficiently vague to permit judges wide latitude in interpreting it, and the judges must want to exercise that opportunity fully. The Constitution is filled with words of seemingly ambiguous meaning—"due process of law," the "equal protection of the laws," the "privileges or immunities of citizens." Such phrases may have been clear to the Framers, but to the Supreme Court they have become equivocal or elastic. How the Court has chosen to interpret such phrases has changed greatly over the last two centuries in ways that can be explained in part by the personal political beliefs of the justices.

Increasingly Congress has passed laws that also contain vague language, thereby adding immeasurably to the courts' opportunities for designing remedies. Various civil rights acts outlaw discrimination but do not say how one is to know whether discrimination has occurred or what should be done to correct it if it does occur. That is left to the courts and the bureaucracy. Various regulatory laws empower administrative agencies to do what the "public interest" requires but say little about how the public interest is to be defined. Laws intended to alleviate poverty or rebuild neighborhoods speak of "citizen participation" or "maximum feasible participation" but do not explain who the citizens are that should participate, or how much power they should have.

In addition to laws that require interpretation, other laws induce litigation. Almost every agency that regulates business will make decisions that cause the agency to be challenged in court—by business firms if the regulations go too far, by consumer or labor organizations if they do not go far enough. One study showed that the federal courts of appeals heard over three thousand cases in which they had to review the decision of a regulatory agency. In two-thirds of them the agency's position was supported; in the other third the agency was overruled.[51] Perhaps one-fifth of these cases arose out of agencies or programs that did not even exist in 1960. The federal government today is much more likely to be on the defensive in court than it was twenty or thirty years ago.

Finally, the attitudes of the judges powerfully affect what they will do, especially when the law gives them wide latitude. There have been very few studies of the attitudes of federal judges, but their decisions and opinions have been extensively analyzed—well enough, at least, to know that different judges often decide the same case in different ways. Conservative southern federal judges in the 1950s, for example, often resisted plans to desegregate public schools while judges with a different background authorized bold plans.[52] Some of the greatest disparities in judicial behavior can be found in the area of sentencing criminals.[53]

Checks on Judicial Power

No institution of government, including the courts, operates without restraint. The fact that judges are not elected does not make them immune to public opinion or to the views of the other branches of government. How important these restraints are varies from case to case, but in the broad course of history they have been significant.

One restraint exists because of the very nature of courts. A judge has no police force or army; decisions that he or she makes can sometimes be resisted or ignored, *if* the person or organization resisting is not highly visible and is willing to run the risk of being caught and charged with contempt of court. For example, long after the Supreme Court had decided that praying and Bible reading could not take place in public schools,[54] schools all over the country were still allowing prayers and Bible reading.[55] Years after the Court declared segregated schools to be unconstitutional, scores of school systems remained segregated. On the other hand, when a failure to comply is easily detected and punished, the courts' power is usually unchallenged. When the Supreme Court declared the income tax to be unconstitutional in 1895, income tax collections promptly ceased. When the Court in 1952 declared illegal President Truman's effort to seize the steel mills in order to stop a strike, the management of the mills was immediately returned to their owners.

Congress and the Courts

Congress has a number of ways of checking the judiciary. It can gradually alter the composition of the judiciary by the kinds of appointments that the Senate is willing to confirm, or it can impeach judges that it does not like. Fifteen federal judges have been the object of impeachment proceedings in our history, and nine others have resigned when such proceedings seemed likely. Of the fifteen who were impeached, seven were acquitted, four were convicted, and one resigned. The most recent convictions were those of Alcee Hastings of Florida and Walter Nixon of Mississippi, both in 1989.[56] In practice, however, confirmation and impeachment proceedings do not make much of an impact on the federal courts because simple policy disagreements are not generally regarded as adequate grounds for voting against a judicial nominee or for starting an impeachment effort.

Congress can alter the number of judges, though, and by increasing the number sharply, it can give a president a chance to appoint judges to his liking. As described above, a "Court-packing" plan was proposed (unsuccessfully) by Franklin Roosevelt in 1937 specifically to change the political persuasion of the Supreme Court. In 1978 Congress passed a bill creating 152 new federal district and appellate judges to help ease the workload of the federal judiciary. This bill gave President Carter a chance to appoint over 40 percent of the federal bench. In 1984 an additional eighty-four judgeships were created; by 1988 President Reagan had appointed about half of all federal judges. In 1990 an additional seventy-two judges were authorized.

During and after the Civil War, Congress may have been trying to influence Supreme Court decisions when it changed the size of the Court three times in six years (raising it from nine to ten in 1863, lowering it again from ten to seven in 1866, and raising it again from seven to nine in 1869).

Congress and the states can also undo a Supreme Court decision interpreting the Constitution by amending that document. This happens, but rarely: the Eleventh Amendment was ratified to prevent a citizen from suing a state in federal court; the Thirteenth, Fourteenth, and Fifteenth were ratified to undo the *Dred Scott* decision regarding slavery; the Sixteenth was added to make it constitutional for Congress to pass an income tax; and the Twenty-sixth was added to give the vote to eighteen-year-olds in state elections.

On over thirty occasions Congress has merely repassed a law that the Court has declared unconsti-

---

T·R·I·V·I·A

The Supreme Court

Supreme Court justice who served the longest	William O. Douglas: 36 years (1939–1975)
Only Supreme Court justice to run for president	Charles Evans Hughes (resigned from Court in 1916 to seek presidency; lost to Woodrow Wilson)
Only president to become Supreme Court justice	William Howard Taft (president, 1909–1913; chief justice, 1921–1930)
First Catholic Supreme Court justice	Roger B. Taney (1836–1864)
First Jewish Supreme Court justice	Louis Brandeis (1916–1939)
First black Supreme Court justice	Thurgood Marshall (1967–1991)
First woman Supreme Court justice	Sandra Day O'Connor (1981 to present)
Only Supreme Court justice to be impeached	Samuel Chase (impeached by House in 1804; acquitted by Senate)
Only Supreme Court justice whose grandson also served on the Court	John Harlan (1877–1911), whose grandson John Harlan served from 1954 to 1971

Judicial Review in Canada and Europe

Courts outside the United States can declare laws to be unconstitutional, but most can do so in ways that are very different from that in the United States.

Canada: The highest court can declare a law unconstitutional, but not if the legislature has passed it with a special provision that says the law will survive judicial scrutiny notwithstanding the country's Charter of Rights. Such laws must be renewed every five years.

Europe: The European Court of Human Rights in Strasbourg can decide human rights cases that begin in any of fifteen nations that make up the European Community.

France: Its Constitutional Council can declare a law unconstitutional, but only if asked to do so by government officials and only before (not after) the law goes into effect.

Germany: The Federal Constitutional Court can declare in an advisory opinion, before a case has emerged, that a law is unconstitutional, and it can judge the constitutionality of laws when asked to do so by a lower court (which itself cannot rule a law unconstitutional). The Federal Constitutional Court may hold an administrative or judicial action to be unjustified when a citizen, having exhausted all other remedies, files a petition.

---

tutional. In one case a bill to aid farmers, voided in 1936, was accepted by the Court in slightly revised form three years later.[57] (In the meantime, of course, the Court had changed its collective mind about the New Deal.)

One of the most powerful potential sources of control over the federal courts, however, is the authority of Congress, given by the Constitution, to decide what the entire jurisdiction of the lower courts and the appellate jurisdiction of the Supreme Court shall be. In theory Congress could prevent matters on which it did not want federal courts to act from ever coming before the courts. This happened in 1868. A Mississippi newspaper editor named McCardle was jailed by federal military authorities who occupied the defeated South. McCardle asked the federal district court for a writ of habeas corpus to get him out of custody; when the district court rejected his plea, he appealed to the Supreme Court. Congress at that time was fearful that the Court might find the laws on which its Reconstruction policy was based (and under which McCardle was in jail) unconstitutional. To prevent that from happening, it passed a bill withdrawing from the Supreme Court appellate jurisdiction in cases of this sort. The Court conceded that Congress could do this and thus dismissed the case because it no longer had jurisdiction.[58]

Congress has threatened to withdraw jurisdiction on other occasions, and the mere existence of the threat may have influenced the nature of Court deci-

sions. In the 1950s, for example, congressional opinion was hostile to Court decisions in the field of civil liberties and civil rights, and legislation was proposed that would have curtailed the Court's jurisdiction in these areas. It did not pass, but the Court may have allowed the threat to temper its decisions.[59] On the other hand, as congressional resistance to the Roosevelt Court-packing plan shows, the Supreme Court enjoys a good deal of prestige in the nation, even among people who disagree with some of its decisions, and so passing laws that would frontally attack it would not be easy except perhaps in times of national crisis.

Furthermore, laws narrowing jurisdiction or restricting the kinds of remedies that a court can impose are often blunt instruments that might not achieve the purposes of their proponents. Suppose that you, as a member of Congress, would like to prevent the federal courts from ordering schoolchildren to be bused for the purpose of achieving racial balance in the schools. If you denied the Supreme Court appellate jurisdiction in this matter, you would leave the lower federal courts and all state courts free to do as they wished, and many of them would go on ordering busing. If you wanted to attack that problem, you could propose a law that would deny to all federal courts the right to order busing as a remedy for racial imbalance. But the courts would still be free to order busing (and of course a lot of busing goes on even without court orders), provided that they did not say that it was for the purpose of achieving racial balance. (It could be for the purpose of "facilitating desegregation" or making possible "redistricting.") Naturally you could always make it illegal for children to enter a school bus for any reason, but then many children would not be able to get to school at all. Finally, the Supreme Court might well decide that if busing were essential to achieve a constitutional right, then any congressional law prohibiting such busing would itself be unconstitutional. Trying to think through how *that* dilemma would be resolved is like trying to visualize two kangaroos simultaneously jumping into each other's pouches.

Public Opinion and the Courts

Though they are not elected, judges read the same newspapers as members of Congress, and thus they, too, are aware of public opinion, especially elite opinion. Though it may be going too far to say that the Supreme Court follows the election returns, it is nonetheless true that the Court is sensitive to certain bodies of opinion, especially of those elites—liberal or conservative—to which its members happen to be attuned. The justices will keep in mind historical cases in which their predecessors, by blatantly disregarding public opinion, very nearly destroyed the legitimacy of the Court itself. This was the case with the *Dred Scott* decision, which infuriated the North and was widely disobeyed. No such crisis exists today, but it is altogether possible that changing political moods affect the kinds of remedies that judges will think appropriate.

Opinion not only restrains the courts; it may also energize them. The most activist periods in Supreme Court history have coincided with times when the political system was undergoing profound and lasting changes. The assertion by the Supreme Court, under John Marshall's leadership, of the principles of national supremacy and judicial review occurred at the time when the Jeffersonian Republicans were coming to power and their opponents, the Federalists, were collapsing as an organized party. The proslavery decisions of the Taney Court came when the nation was so divided along sectional and ideological lines as to make almost any Court decision on this matter unpopular. Supreme Court review of economic regulation in the 1890s and 1900s came at a time when the political parties were realigning and the Republicans were acquiring dominance that would last for several decades. The Court decisions of the 1930s corresponded to another period of partisan realignment. (The meaning of a realigning election was discussed in Chapter 8.)

Pollsters have been measuring how much confidence the public has in the Supreme Court. The results are shown in Figure 14.3. The percentage of people saying that they had a "great deal of confidence" in the Court rose sharply from 1971 to 1974, fell again until 1976, seesawed up and down until 1989, took a sharp dip and then recovered from 1989 to 1991, and again seesawed before declining in 1996. These movements seem to reflect the public's reaction not only to what the Court does but also to what the government as a whole is doing. The upturn in the early 1970s was probably caused by the Watergate scandal, an episode that simultaneously discredited the presidency and boosted the stock of those institutions (such as the courts) that seemed to be checking the abuses of the White House. The gradual upturn in the 1980s may have reflected a general restoration of public confidence in government during that decade.[60]

Though popular support is now relatively low for the Supreme Court, this decline has so far not resulted in any legal checks being placed on it. In the 1970s and 1980s several bills were introduced in Congress that would have restricted the jurisdiction of federal courts over busing for purposes of racial integration or altered the Supreme Court's decisions regarding school prayer and abortion. None passed.

The changes that have occurred in the Court have been caused by changes in its personnel. Presidents Nixon and Reagan attempted to produce a less activist Court by appointing justices who were more inclined to be strict constructionists and conservatives. To some extent they succeeded: Justices Kennedy, O'Connor, Rehnquist, and Scalia were certainly less inclined than Justice Thurgood Marshall to find new rights in the Constitution or to overturn the decisions of state legislatures. But as of yet there has been no wholesale retreat from the positions staked out by the Warren Court. As noted above, a Nixon appointee, Justice Blackmun, wrote the decision making antiabortion laws unconstitutional; and another Nixon appointee, Chief Justice Burger, wrote the opinion upholding court-ordered school busing to achieve racial integration. A Reagan appointee, Justice O'Connor, voted to uphold a right to an abortion. The Supreme Court has become somewhat less

Figure 14.3	Patterns of Public Confidence in the Court, 1974–1998

Source: The Gallup Poll: Public Opinion 1991 (Wilmington, Del.: Scholarly Resources, Inc., 1992), 213.

willing to impose restraints on police practices, and it has not blocked the use of the death penalty. But in general the major features of Court activism and liberalism during the Warren years—school integration, sharper limits on police practice, greater freedom of expression—have remained intact.

The reasons for the growth in court activism are clear. One is the sheer growth in the size and scope of the government as a whole. The courts have come to play a larger role in our lives because Congress, the bureaucracy, and the president have come to play larger ones. In 1890 hardly anybody would

have thought of asking Congress—much less the courts—to make rules governing the participation of women in college sports or the district boundaries of state legislatures. Today such rules are commonplace, and the courts are inevitably drawn into interpreting them.

The other reason for increased activism is the acceptance by a large number of judges, conservative as well as liberal, of the activist view of the function of the courts. If courts once existed solely to "settle disputes," today they also exist in the eyes of their members to "solve problems."

Summary

An independent judiciary with the power of judicial review—the right to decide the constitutionality of acts of Congress, the executive branch, and state governments—can be a potent political force in American life. That influence has been realized from the earliest days of the nation, when Marshall and Taney put the Supreme Court at the center of the most important issues of the time. From 1787 to 1865 the Supreme Court was preoccupied with the establishment of national supremacy. From 1865 to 1937 it struggled with defining the scope of political power over the economy. In the present era it has sought to expand personal liberties.

The scope of the courts' political influence has increasingly widened as various groups and interests have acquired access to the courts, as the judges serving on them have developed a more activist stance, and as Congress has passed more laws containing vague or equivocal language. Whereas in other political arenas (the electorate, Congress, the bureaucracy) the influence of contending groups is largely dependent on their size, intensity, prestige, and political resources, the influence of contending groups before the courts depends chiefly on their arguments and the attitudes of the judges.

Though the Supreme Court is the pinnacle of the federal judiciary, most decisions, including many important ones, are made by the twelve courts of appeals and the ninety-four district courts. The Supreme Court can control its own workload by deciding when to grant certiorari. It has become easier for citizens and groups to gain access to the federal courts (through class-action suits, by amicus curiae briefs, by laws that require government agencies to pay legal fees, and because of the activities of private groups such as the NAACP and the ACLU).

At the same time, the courts have widened the reach of their decisions by issuing orders that cover whole classes of citizens or affect the management of major public and private institutions. However, the courts can overstep the bounds of their authority and bring upon themselves a counterattack from both the public and Congress. Congress has the right to control much of the courts' jurisdiction, but it rarely does so. As a result the ability of judges to make law is only infrequently challenged directly.

World Wide Web Resources

- Federal Judicial Center: www.fjc.gov
- Federal courts: www.uscourts.gov
- Supreme Court decisions: www.law.cornell.edu
- Finding laws and reports: www.findlaw.com

Key Terms

judicial review *p. 403*
strict-constructionist approach *p. 404*
activist approach *p. 404*
constitutional court *p. 411*
district courts *p. 411*
courts of appeals *p. 411*
legislative court *p. 411*

litmus test *p. 413*
federal-question cases *p. 414*
diversity cases *p. 414*
civil law *p. 416*
criminal law *p. 416*
writ of certiorari *p. 416*
in forma pauperis *p. 417*

fee shifting *p. 418*
plaintiff *p. 418*
standing *p. 418*
sovereign immunity *p. 418*
class-action suit *p. 419*
brief *p. 420*
amicus curiae *p. 421*
per curiam opinion *p. 422*

opinion of the Court *p. 422*
concurring opinion *p. 422*
dissenting opinion *p. 422*
stare decisis *p. 423*
political question *p. 423*
remedy *p. 423*

Suggested Readings

Abraham, Henry J. *The Judicial Process.* 6th ed. New York: Oxford University Press, 1993. An excellent, comprehensive survey of how the federal courts are organized and function.

Cardozo, Benjamin N. *The Nature of the Judicial Process.* New Haven, Conn.: Yale University Press, 1921. Important statement of how judges make decisions, by a former Supreme Court justice.

Carp, Robert A., and Ronald Stidham. *The Federal Courts.* Washington, D.C.: Congressional Quarterly Press, 1985. Excellent summary of the workings of the lower federal courts.

Ely, John Hart. *Democracy and Distrust.* Cambridge: Harvard University Press, 1980. Effort to create a theory of judicial review that is neither strict-constructionist nor activist.

Hall, Kermit L., ed. *The Oxford Companion to the Supreme Court of the United States.* New York: Oxford University Press, 1992. Everything you ever wanted to know about the Supreme Court, its justices, and its major decisions, arranged in more than one thousand alphabetical entries.

Lasser, William. *The Limits of Judicial Power.* Chapel Hill: University of North Carolina Press, 1988. Shows how the Court through history has withstood the political storms created by its more controversial decisions.

Lazarus, Edward. *Closed Chamber*. (New York: Times Books, 1998). An eyewitness account of how the Supreme Court operates. Written by a former law clerk, it is filled with both interesting facts and personal opinions.

McCloskey, Robert G. *The American Supreme Court*. 2nd ed. Edited by Sanford Levinson. Chicago: University of Chicago Press, 1994. Superb brief history of the Supreme Court, updated by one of McCloskey's former students who now teaches law at the University of Texas.

Rabkin, Jeremy. *Judicial Compulsions*. New York: Basic Books, 1989. Explains (and argues against) the extensive Court intervention in the work of administrative agencies.

Wolfe, Christopher. *The Rise of Modern Judicial Review*. New York: Basic Books, 1986. An excellent history of judicial review from 1787 to the present.

part IV

Liberties and Rights

*I*n the extended republic of
the United States, and among
the great variety of interests,
parties and sects which it
embraces, a coalition of a
majority of the whole society
could seldom take place on any
other principles than those of
justice and the general good.

FEDERALIST No. 51

Civil
Liberties

Enduring Questions

1. Should it be all right for religious symbols to be displayed on government property?
2. If a person confesses that he committed a crime, is there any reason why the confession should not be used in court?
3. Should the government have the right to test you to see if you are using drugs?
4. What does the Supreme Court mean by "pornography"?

Politics, Culture, and Civil Liberties
  Rights in Conflict • Policy Entrepreneurs • Cultural
  Conflicts

Interpreting and Applying the First Amendment
  Speech and National Security

What Is Speech?
  Libel • Obscenity • Symbolic Speech

Who Is a Person?

Church and State
  The Free-Exercise Clause • The Establishment
  Clause

Crime and Due Process
  The Exclusionary Rule • Search and Seizure •
  Confessions and Self-Incrimination • Relaxing the
  Exclusionary Rule

D ogs trained to sniff out drugs go down your high school corridors and detect marijuana in some lockers. The school authorities open and search your locker without permission or a court order. You are expelled from school without any hearing. Have your liberties been violated?

Angry at what you consider unfair treatment, you decide to wear a cloth American flag sewn to the seat of your pants, and your fellow students decide to wear black armbands to class to protest how you were treated. The police arrest you for wearing a flag on your seat, and the school punishes your classmates for wearing armbands contrary to school regulations. Have your liberties, or theirs, been violated?

You go into federal court to find out. We cannot be certain how the court would decide the issues in this particular case, but in similar cases in the past the courts have held that school authorities can use dogs to detect drugs in schools and that these officials can conduct a "reasonable" search of you and your effects if they have a "reasonable suspicion" that you are violating a school rule. But they cannot

435

punish your classmates for wearing black armbands, they cannot expel you without a hearing,
and the state cannot make it illegal to treat the flag
"contemptuously" (by sewing it to the seat of your
pants, for example).[1]

Your claim that these actions violated your constitutional rights would have astonished the
Framers of the Constitution. They thought that they
had written a document that stated what the federal
government *could* do, not one that specified what
state governments (such as school systems) *could not*
do. And they thought that they had created a
national government of such limited powers that it
was not even necessary to add a list—a bill of
rights—stating what that government was forbidden from doing. It would be enough, for example,
that the Constitution did not authorize the federal
government to censor newspapers; an amendment
prohibiting censorship would be superfluous.

The people who gathered in the state ratifying
conventions weren't so optimistic. They suspected—
rightly, as it turned out—that the federal government
might well try to do things that it was not authorized
to do, and so they insisted that the Bill of Rights be
added to the Constitution. But even they never imagined that the Bill of Rights would affect what *state*
governments could do. Each state would decide that
for itself, in its own constitution. And if by chance the
Bill of Rights did apply to the states, surely its guarantees of free speech and freedom from unreasonable
searches and seizures would apply to big issues—the
freedom to attack the government in a newspaper
editorial, for example, or to keep the police from
breaking down the door of your home without a warrant. The courts would not be deciding who could
wear what kinds of armbands or under what circumstances a school could expel a student.

To understand the nature of civil liberties today, it
is necessary to understand why the liberties mentioned in the Bill of Rights were thought to be important, how they came to apply to the states, and why
they have grown in scope and meaning.

Politics, Culture, and Civil Liberties

The Bill of Rights is an important limitation on popular rule. It says that there are things that a government cannot do even if a majority wants them done.
But why would the government, to say nothing of a

popular majority, ever want to do these things? In
our review of the politics of policy-making, we have
repeatedly observed the ability of small but intensely
motivated minorities to block actions that would
impose heavy costs on them. Milk producers for a
long time resisted efforts that would reduce government subsidies for their products, and ship owners
and merchant seamen have been able to block
efforts to introduce more competition (and presumably lower prices) into their industry. The political
system has facilitated this kind of client politics.

If a largely indifferent public permits various economic, occupational, or professional minorities to
safeguard their own interests, why should other
kinds of minorities—religious or ideological ones—
require special constitutional protection? Just as the
average citizen bears only slight costs created by the
advantages enjoyed by milk producers or truck drivers, presumably the average citizen bears only slight
(if any) costs from the publication of a Communist
party newspaper or from the refusal of a member of
the Jehovah's Witnesses to recite the pledge of allegiance to the flag. If costs are small and widely distributed, then one would expect that political activity to reduce those costs would be infrequent and
often ineffective. Moreover, some of these "costs"—
such as the consequences of reading a Communist
party newspaper—will occur in the distant future, if
at all. Ordinarily people are not politically sensitive
to such distant or hypothetical burdens.

So why do the liberties claimed by some people
ever become a major issue? There are three reasons.
In two of the three the politics surrounding civil liberties are similar to those around any other issue.
First, there may be rights in conflict (in which case
we have interest group politics). Second, passions
may be inflamed by a skilled policy entrepreneur (in
which case we have entrepreneurial politics). But
the third reason makes the politics of civil liberties
different from that of most issues: the political culture of the United States, described in Chapter 4,
contains principles that are in conflict with one
another. Most Americans accept that culture and
thus accept the contradictions built into it. From
time to time we tend to favor one part of that culture
(say, a belief in "Americanism") over another part
(say, a belief in personal freedom). When that happens, we find ourselves fighting over matters such as
flag burning with an intensity that seems out of proportion to what is actually at stake.

Rights in Conflict

We often think of "civil liberties" as a set of principles that protect the freedoms of all of us all of the time. That is true—up to a point. But in fact the Constitution and the Bill of Rights contain a list of *competing* rights and duties. That competition becomes obvious when one person asserts one constitutional right or duty and another person asserts a different one. For example:

- Dr. Samuel H. Sheppard of Cleveland, Ohio, asserted his right to have a fair trial on the charge of having murdered his wife. Bob Considine and Walter Winchell, two radio commentators, as well as other reporters, asserted their right to broadcast whatever facts and rumors they heard about Dr. Sheppard and his love life. Two rights in conflict.

- The U.S. government has an obligation to "provide for the common defense" and, in pursuit of that duty, has claimed the right to keep secret certain military and diplomatic information. The *New York Times* claimed the right to publish such secrets as the "Pentagon Papers" without censorship, citing the Constitution's guarantee of freedom of the press. A duty and a right in conflict.

- Carl Jacob Kunz delivered inflammatory anti-Jewish speeches on the street corners of a Jewish neighborhood in New York City, suggesting, among other things, that Jews be "burnt in incinerators." The Jewish people living in that area were outraged. The New York police commissioner revoked Kunz's license to hold public meetings on the streets. When he continued to air his views on the public streets, Kunz was arrested for speaking without a permit. Freedom of speech versus the preservation of public order.

Even a disruptive high school student's right not to be a victim of arbitrary or unjustifiable expulsion is in partial conflict with the school's obligation to maintain an orderly environment in which learning can take place.

Political struggles over civil liberties follow much the same pattern as interest group politics involving economic issues, even though the claims in question are made by individuals. Indeed, there are formal, organized interest groups concerned with civil liberties. The Fraternal Order of the Police complains about restrictions on police powers, whereas the American Civil Liberties Union defends and seeks to enlarge those restrictions. Catholics have pressed for public support of parochial schools; Protestants and Jews have argued against it. Sometimes the opposed groups are entirely private; sometimes one or both are government agencies. Often their clashes end up in the courts. (When the Supreme Court decided the cases given earlier, Sheppard, the *New York Times*, and Kunz all won.[2])

Policy Entrepreneurs

Just as a skilled policy entrepreneur can sometimes arouse legislators to act against the normally undisputed claims of an interest group, so also can such an entrepreneur sometimes arouse people to take action against the rights and liberties claimed by political or religious dissidents. The success of entrepreneurial politics, whether involving money interests or civil liberties, often depends on the existence of a crisis.

War has usually been the crisis that has facilitated entrepreneurial politics aimed at restricting the liberty of some minority. For example:

- The Sedition Act was passed in 1798, making it a crime to write, utter, or publish "any false, scandalous, and malicious writing" with the intention of defaming the president, Congress, or the

A 1919 cartoon expresses popular fears of "Reds" (that is, leftist radicals) threatening American institutions.

★ **POLITICALLY**
SPEAKING ★

McCarthyism

In 1950 Senator Joseph R. McCarthy of Wisconsin began making a long series of charges, usually unsubstantiated, that people working for various government agencies were communists. Since then anyone making a charge that unfairly impugns the motives, attacks the patriotism, or violates the rights of individuals is often criticized for engaging in **McCarthyism.** The word has become a synonym for "character assassination." Senator McCarthy was a conservative, and so liberals today are often quick to denounce conservative attacks on them as "McCarthyism." But increasingly conservatives have used the term against liberals, usually by modifying it to read "McCarthyism of the left."

Source: From *Safire's Political Dictionary* by William Safire. Copyright © 1968, 1972, 1978 by William Safire. Reprinted by permission of Random House, Inc. and the author.

- The Espionage and Sedition Acts were passed in 1917–1918, making it a crime to utter false statements that would interfere with the American military, to send through the mails material "advocating or urging treason, insurrection, or forcible resistance to any law of the United States," or to utter or write any disloyal, profane, scurrilous, or abusive language intended to incite resistance to the United States or to curtail war production. The occasion was World War I; the impetus was the fear that Germans in this country were spies and that radicals were seeking to overthrow the government. Under these laws more than two thousand persons were prosecuted (about half were convicted), and thousands of aliens were rounded up and deported. The policy entrepreneur leading this massive crackdown (the so-called Red Scare) was Attorney General A. Mitchell Palmer.

- The Smith Act was passed in 1940, the Internal Security Act in 1950, and the Communist Control Act in 1954. These laws made it illegal to advocate the overthrow of the U.S. government by force or violence (Smith Act), required members of the Communist party to register with the government (Internal Security Act), and declared the Communist party to be part of a conspiracy to overthrow the government (Communist Control Act). The occasion was World War II and the Korean War, which, like earlier wars, inspired fears that foreign agents (Nazi and Soviet) were trying to subvert the government. For the latter two laws the policy entrepreneur was Senator Joseph McCarthy, who attracted a great deal of attention with his repeated (and sometimes inaccurate) claims that Soviet agents were working inside the U.S. government.

These laws had in common an effort to protect the nation from threats, real and imagined, posed by people who claimed to be exercising their freedom to speak, publish, organize, and assemble. In each case a real threat (a war) led the government to narrow the limits of permissible speech and activity. Almost every time such restrictions were imposed, the Supreme Court was called upon to decide whether Congress (or sometimes state legislatures) had drawn those limits properly. In most instances the Court tended to uphold the legislatures. But as time passed and the war or crisis ended, popular passions abated and many of the laws proved to be unimportant.

government or of exciting against the government "the hatred of the people." The occasion was a kind of half-war between the United States and France, stimulated by fear in this country of the violence following the French Revolution of 1789. The policy entrepreneurs were Federalist politicians who believed that Thomas Jefferson and his followers were supporters of the French Revolution and would, if they came to power, encourage here the kind of anarchy that seemed to be occurring in France.

Though it is uncommon, some use is still made of the sedition laws. In the 1980s various white supremacists and Puerto Rican nationalists were charged with sedition. In each case the government alleged that the accused had not only spoken in favor of overthrowing the government, they had actually engaged in violent actions such as bombings. Later in this chapter we shall see how the Court has increasingly restricted the power of Congress and state legislatures to outlaw political speech; to be found guilty of sedition now it is usually necessary to do something more serious than just talk about it.

Cultural Conflicts

In the main the United States was originally the creation of white European Protestants. Blacks were, in most cases, slaves, and American Indians were not citizens. Catholics and Jews in the colonies com-posed a small minority, and often a persecuted one. The early schools tended to be religious—that is, Protestant—ones, many of them receiving state aid. It is not surprising that under these circumstances a view of America arose that equated "Americanism" with the values and habits of white Anglo-Saxon Protestants.

But immigration to this country brought a flood of new settlers, many of them coming from very different backgrounds (see Figure 15.1). In the mid-nineteenth century the potato famine led millions of Irish Catholics to migrate here. At the turn of the century religious persecution and economic disadvantage brought more millions of people, many Catholic or Jewish, from southern and eastern Europe.

In recent decades political conflict and economic want have led Hispanics (mostly from Mexico but increasingly from all parts of Latin America),

Figure 15.1 Annual Immigration, 1840–1996

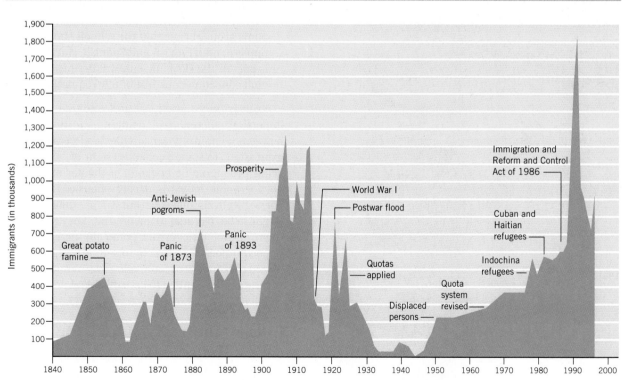

Note: Figures for 1989 and 1990 include persons who were granted permanent residence under the legalization program of the Immigration and Reform and Control Act of 1986.
Source: Statistical Abstract of the United States, 1998, 10.

Figure 15.2   Changing Composition of U.S. Immigration, 1901–1996

1901–1920

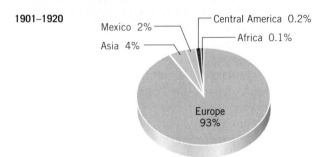

Mexico 2%
Asia 4%
Central America 0.2%
Africa 0.1%
Europe 93%

1921–1940

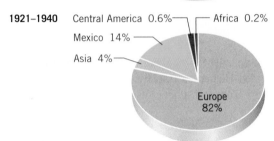

Central America 0.6%
Mexico 14%
Asia 4%
Africa 0.2%
Europe 82%

1941–1960

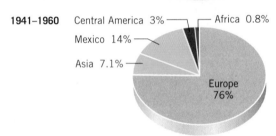

Central America 3%
Mexico 14%
Asia 7.1%
Africa 0.8%
Europe 76%

1961–1980

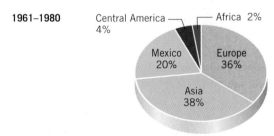

Central America 4%
Africa 2%
Mexico 20%
Europe 36%
Asia 38%

1981–1996

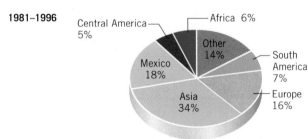

Central America 5%
Africa 6%
Other 14%
Mexico 18%
South America 7%
Asia 34%
Europe 16%

Sources: For 1901–1980: Associated Press, adapted from a *Boston Globe* graphic by Steven Nelson. Reprinted courtesy of the *Boston Globe*. For 1981–1996: *Statistical Abstract of the United States, 1998,* 11.

Caribbeans, Africans, Middle Easterners, Southeast Asians, and Asians to cross our borders—some legally, some illegally (see Figure 15.2). Among them have been Buddhists, Catholics, Muslims, and members of many other religious and cultural groups.

Ethnic, religious, and cultural differences have given rise to different views as to the meaning and scope of certain constitutionally protected freedoms. For example:

- Many Jewish groups find it offensive for a crèche (that is, a scene depicting the birth of Christ in a manger) to be displayed in front of a government building such as city hall at Christmastime, while many Catholics and Protestants regard such displays as an important part of our cultural heritage. Does a religious display on public property violate the First Amendment requirement that the government pass on law "respecting an establishment of religion"?

- Many English-speaking people believe that the public schools ought to teach all students to speak and write English, because the language is part of our nation's cultural heritage. Some Hispanic groups argue that the schools should teach pupils in both English and Spanish, since Spanish is part of the Hispanic cultural heritage. Is bilingual education constitutionally required?

Even within a given cultural tradition there are important differences of opinion as to the balance between community sensitivities and personal self-expression. To some people the sight of a store carrying pornographic books or a theater showing a pornographic movie is deeply offensive; to others pornography is offensive but such establishments ought to be tolerated to ensure that laws restricting them do not also restrict politically or artistically important forms of speech; to still others pornography itself is not especially offensive. What forms of expression are entitled to constitutional protection?

Interpreting and Applying the First Amendment

The First Amendment contains the language that has been at issue in most of the cases to which we have thus far referred. It has roughly two parts: one protecting **freedom of expression** ("Congress shall make no law . . . abridging the freedom of speech, or of the press, or of the right of people peaceably to assemble, and to petition the government for a redress of grievances") and the other protecting **freedom of religion** ("Congress shall make no law respecting an establishment of religion; or abridging the free exercise thereof"). In this section we shall discuss freedom of expression, and in the next freedom of religion.

Speech and National Security

The traditional view of free speech and a free press was expressed by William Blackstone, the great English jurist, in his *Commentaries*, published in 1765. A free press is essential to a free state, he wrote, but the freedom that the press should enjoy is the freedom from **prior restraint**—that is, freedom from censorship, or rules telling a newspaper in advance what it can publish. Once a newspaper has published an article or a person has delivered a speech, that paper or speaker has to take the consequences if what was written or said proves to be "improper, mischievous, or illegal."[3]

The U.S. Sedition Act of 1798 was in keeping with traditional English law. Like it, the act imposed no prior restraint on publishers; it did, however, make them liable to punishment after the fact. The act was an improvement over the English law, however, because unlike the British model, it entrusted the decision to a jury, not a judge, and allowed the defendant to be acquitted if he or she could prove the truth of what had been published. Although several newspaper publishers were convicted under the act, none of these cases reached the Supreme Court. When Jefferson became president in 1801, he pardoned everyone who had been convicted under the Sedition Act. Though Jeffersonians objected vehemently to the law, their principal objection was not to the idea of holding newspapers accountable for what they published but to letting the *federal* government do this. Jefferson was perfectly prepared to have the *states* punish what he called the "overwhelming torrent of slander" by means of "a few prosecutions of the most prominent offenders."[4]

It would be another century before the federal government would attempt to define the limits of free speech and writing. Perhaps recalling the widespread opposition to the sweep of the 1798 act, Congress in 1917–1918 placed restrictions not on publications that were critical of the government but only on those that advocated "treason, insurrection, or forcible resistance" to federal laws or attempted to foment disloyalty or mutiny in the armed services.

Women picketed in front of the White House, urging President Warren Harding to release political radicals arrested during his administration.

In 1919 this new law was examined by the Supreme Court when it heard the case of Charles T. Schenck, who had been convicted of violating the Espionage Act because he had mailed circulars to men eligible for the draft, urging them to resist. At issue was the constitutionality of the Espionage Act and, more broadly, the scope of Congress's power to control speech. One view held that the First Amendment prevented Congress from passing *any* law restricting speech; the other held that Congress could punish dangerous speech. For a unanimous Supreme Court, Justice Oliver Wendell Holmes announced a rule by which to settle the matter. It soon became known as the **clear-and-present-danger test:**

> The question in every case is whether the words used are used in such circumstances and are of such a nature as to create a clear and present danger that they will bring about the substantive evils that Congress has a right to prevent.[5]

The Court held that Schenck's leaflets did create such a danger, and so his conviction was upheld. In explaining why, Holmes said that not even the Constitution protects a person who has been "falsely shouting fire in a theatre and causing a panic." In this case things that might safely be said in peacetime may be punished in wartime.

The clear-and-present-danger test may have clarified the law, but it kept no one out of jail. Schenck went, and so did the defendants in five other cases in the period 1919–1927, even though during this time Holmes, the author of the test, shifted his position and began writing dissenting opinions in which he urged that the test had not been met and so the defendant should go free.

During the same period the Court for the first time came to grips with the power of state governments to punish speech. As we saw in Chapter 2, the Bill of Rights was originally intended only to limit the powers of the *federal* government. The adoption in 1868 of the Fourteenth Amendment, however, brought into the Constitution language that for the first time created the possibility that some or all of the Bill of Rights might now restrict the states' actions. The key phrase was the **due-process clause:**

> No state shall . . . deprive any person of life, liberty or property, without due process of law.

For over half a century after 1868, the Supreme Court steadfastly denied that the due-process clause made the Bill of Rights applicable to the states. Therefore, state legislatures could pass sedition laws or antiobscenity laws without fear of having them overturned by the Supreme Court.

Then in 1925 Benjamin Gitlow was convicted of violating New York's sedition law—a law similar to the federal Sedition Act of 1918—by passing out some leaflets. The Supreme Court upheld his conviction but added a statement that changed constitutional history: freedom of speech and of the press were now among the "fundamental personal rights" protected by the due-process clause of the Fourteenth Amendment from infringements by *state* action.[6] Thereafter state laws involving speech, the press, and peaceful assembly were struck down by the Supreme Court for being in violation of the freedom-of-expression guarantees of the First Amendment, made applicable to the states by the Fourteenth Amendment.[7]

The clear-and-present-danger test was a way of balancing the competing demands of free expression and national security. As the memory of World War I and the ensuing Red Scare evaporated, the Court began to develop other tests, ones that shifted the balance more toward free expression. Some of these tests are listed in the box on page 445.

But when a crisis reappears, as it did in World War II and the Korean conflict, the Court has tended to defer, up to a point, to legislative judgments about the need to protect national security. For example, it upheld the conviction of eleven leaders of the Communist party for having advocated the violent overthrow of the U.S. government, a violation of the Smith Act of 1940.

This conviction once again raised the hard question of the circumstances under which words can be punished. Hardly anybody would deny that actually *trying* to overthrow the government is a crime; the question is whether *advocating* its overthrow is a crime. In the case of the eleven Communist leaders, the Court said that the government did not have to wait to protect itself until "the *putsch* [rebellion] is about to be executed, the plans have been laid and the signal is awaited." Even if the Communists were not likely to be successful in their effort, the Court held that specifically advocating violent overthrow could be punished. "In each case," the opinion read, the courts "must ask whether the gravity of the 'evil,' discounted by its improbability, justifies such invasion of free speech as is necessary to avoid the danger."[8]

But as the popular worries about communists began to subside and the membership of the Supreme Court changed, the Court began to tip the balance even farther toward free expression. By 1957 the Court made it clear that for advocacy to be punished, the government would have to show not just that a person believed in the overthrow of the government but also that he or she was using words "calculated to incite" that overthrow.[9]

By 1969 the pendulum had swung to the point where the speech would have to be judged likely to incite "imminent" unlawful action. In this case Clarence Brandenburg, a leader of the Ku Klux Klan in Ohio, staged a cross-burning rally during which he reviled blacks and Jews. The police told him to clear the street; as he left, he said, "We'll take the [expletive] street later." He was convicted of attempting to incite lawless mob action. The Supreme Court overturned the conviction, holding that any speech that does not call for illegal action is protected, and even speech that *does* call for illegal action is protected if the action is not "imminent" or there is reason to believe that the listeners will not take action.[10]

This means that no matter how offensive or provocative some forms of expression may be, this expression has powerful constitutional protections. In 1977 a group of American Nazis wanted to parade through the streets of Skokie, Illinois, a community with a large Jewish population. The residents, outraged, sought to ban the march. Many feared violence if it occurred. But the lower courts, under prodding from the Supreme Court, held that, noxious and provocative as the anti-Semitic slogans of the Nazis may be, the Nazi party had a constitutional right to speak and parade peacefully.[11]

Similar reasoning led the Supreme Court in 1992 to overturn a Minnesota statute that made it a crime to display symbols or objects, such as a Nazi swastika or a burning cross, that are likely to cause alarm or resentment among an ethnic or racial group, such as Jews or African Americans.[12] On the other hand, if you are convicted of actually hurting someone, you may be given a tougher sentence if it can be shown that you were motivated to assault them by racial or ethnic hatred.[13] To be punished for such a hate crime, your bigotry must result in some direct and physical harm and not just the display of an odious symbol.

What Is Speech?

If most political speaking or writing is permissible, save that which actually incites someone to take illegal actions, what *kinds* of speaking and writing qualify for this broad protection? Though the Constitution says that the legislature may make "no law" abridging freedom of speech or the press, and although some justices have argued that this means literally *no* law, the Court has held that there are at least four forms of speaking and writing that are not automatically granted full constitutional protection: libel, obscenity, symbolic speech, and false advertising.

Libel

A **libel** is a written statement that defames the character of another person. (If the statement is oral, it is called a slander.) In some countries, such as England, it is easy to sue another person for libel and to collect. In this country it is much harder. For one thing, you must show that the libelous statement

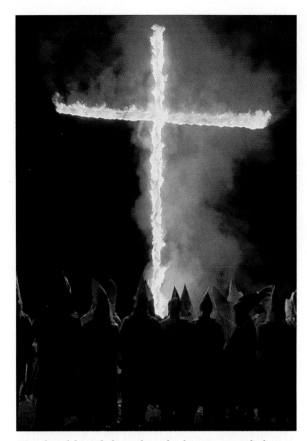

Even hateful symbols, such as this burning cross lit by members of the Ku Klux Klan, enjoy constitutional protection.

was false. If it was true, you cannot collect no matter how badly it harmed you.

A beauty contest winner was awarded $14 million (later reduced on appeal) when she proved that *Penthouse* magazine had libeled her. The actress Carol Burnett collected a large sum from a libel suit brought against a gossip newspaper. But when Theodore Roosevelt sued a newspaper for falsely claiming that he was a drunk, the jury awarded him damages of only six cents.[14]

If you are a public figure, it is much harder to win a libel suit. A public figure such as an elected official, an army general, or a well-known-celebrity must prove not only that the publication was false and damaging but also that the words were published with "actual malice"—that is, with reckless disregard for their truth or falsity or with knowledge that they were false.[15] As we saw in Chapter 10, that is not easily done. General Ariel Sharon was able to

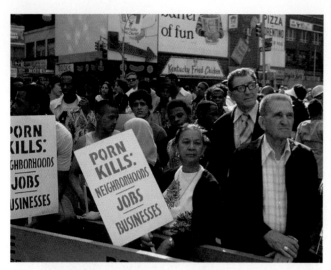

Pornography: People protest to keep it away from desirable neighborhoods, as here in Times Square, New York City.

prove that the statements made about him by *Time* magazine were false and damaging but not that they were the result of "actual malice."

Obscenity

Obscenity is not protected by the First Amendment. The Court has always held that obscene materials, because they have no redeeming social value and are calculated chiefly to appeal to one's sexual rather than political or literary interests, can be regulated by the state. The problem, of course, arises with the meaning of *obscene*. In the eleven-year period from 1957 to 1968 the Court decided thirteen major cases involving the definition of obscenity, which resulted in fifty-five separate opinions.[16] Some justices, such as Hugo Black, believed that the First Amendment protected all publications, even wholly obscene ones. Others believed that obscenity deserved no protection and struggled heroically to define the term. Still others shared the view of former Justice Potter Stewart, who objected to "hard-core pornography" but admitted that the best definition he could offer was "I know it when I see it."[17]

It is unnecessary to review in detail the many attempts by the Court at defining obscenity. The justices have made it clear that nudity and sex are not, by definition, obscene and that they will provide First Amendment protection to anything that has

political, literary, or artistic merit, allowing the government to punish only the distribution of "hard-core pornography." Their most recent (1973) definition of this is as follows: to be obscene, the work, taken as a whole, must be judged by "the average person applying contemporary community standards" to appeal to the "prurient interest" or to depict "in a patently offensive way, sexual conduct specifically defined by applicable state law" and to lack "serious literary, artistic, political, or scientific value."[18]

After Albany, Georgia, decided that the movie *Carnal Knowledge* was obscene by contemporary local standards, the Supreme Court overturned the distributor's conviction on the grounds that the authorities in Albany failed to show that the film depicted "patently offensive hard-core sexual conduct."[19]

It is easy to make sport of the problems the Court has faced in trying to decide obscenity cases (one conjures up images of black-robed justices leafing through the pages of *Hustler* magazine, taking notes), but these problems reveal, as do other civil liberties cases, the continuing problem of balancing competing claims. One part of the community wants to read or see whatever it wishes; another part wants to protect private acts from public degradation. The first part cherishes liberty above all; the second values decency above liberty. The former fears that *any* restriction on literature will lead to *pervasive* restrictions; the latter believes that reasonable people can distinguish (or reasonable laws can require them to distinguish) between patently offensive and artistically serious work.

Anyone strolling today through an "adult" bookstore must suppose that no restrictions at all exist on the distribution of pornographic works. This condition does not arise simply from the doctrines of the Court. Other factors operate as well, including the priorities of local law enforcement officials, the political climate of the community, the procedures that must be followed to bring a viable court case, the clarity and workability of state and local laws on the subject, and the difficulty of changing the behavior of many people by prosecuting one person. The current view of the Court is that localities can decide for themselves whether to tolerate hard-core pornography; but if they choose not to, they must meet some fairly strict constitutional tests.

Testing Restrictions on Expression

The Supreme Court has employed various standards and tests to decide whether a restriction on freedom of expression is constitutionally permissible.

1. **Preferred position** The right of free expression, though not absolute, occupies a higher, or more preferred, position than many other constitutional rights, such as property rights. This is still a controversial rule; nonetheless, the Court always approaches a restriction on expression skeptically.

2. **Prior restraint** With scarcely any exceptions, the Court will not tolerate a prior restraint on expression, such as censorship, even when it will allow subsequent punishment of improper expressions (such as libel).

3. **Imminent danger** Punishment for uttering inflammatory sentiments will be allowed only if there is an imminent danger that the utterances will incite an unlawful act.

4. **Neutrality** Any restriction on speech, such as a requirement that parades or demonstrations not disrupt other people in the exercise of their rights, must be neutral—that is, it must not favor one group more than another.

5. **Clarity** If you must obtain a permit to hold a parade, the law must set forth clear (as well as neutral) standards to guide administrators in issuing that permit. Similarly, a law punishing obscenity must contain a clear definition of obscenity.

6. **Least-restrictive means** If it is necessary to restrict the exercise of one right to protect the exercise of another, the restriction should employ the least-restrictive means to achieve its end. For example, if press coverage threatens a person's right to a fair trial, the judge may only do what is minimally necessary to that end, such as transferring the case to another town rather than issuing a "gag order."

Cases cited, by item: (1) *United States v. Carolene Products,* 304 U.S. 144 (1938). (2) *Near v. Minnesota,* 283 U.S. 697 (1931). (3) *Brandenburg v. Ohio,* 395 U.S. 444 (1969). (4) *Kunz v. New York,* 340 U.S. 290 (1951). (5) *Hynes v. Mayor and Council of Oradell,* 425 U.S. 610 (1976). (6) *Nebraska Press Association v. Stuart,* 427 U.S. 539 (1976).

The protections given by the Court to expressions of sexual or erotic interest have not been limited to books, magazines, or films. Almost any form of visual or auditory communication can be considered "speech" and thus protected by the First Amendment. In one case even nude dancing was given protection as a form of "speech,"[20] although in 1991 the Court held that nude dancing was only "marginally" within the purview of First Amendment protections, and so it upheld an Indiana statute that banned *totally* nude dancing.[21]

Of late some feminist organizations have attacked pornography on the grounds that it exploits and degrades women. They persuaded Indianapolis to pass an ordinance that defined pornography as portrayals of the "graphic, sexually explicit subordination of women" and allowed people to sue the producers of such material. Sexually explicit portrayals of women in positions of equality were not defined as pornography. The Court disagreed. In 1986 it affirmed a lower-court ruling that such an ordinance was a violation of the First Amendment because it represented a legislative preference for one form of expression (women in positions of equality) over another (women in positions of subordination).[22]

One constitutionally permissible way to limit the spread of pornographic materials has been to establish rules governing where in a city they can be sold. When one city adopted a zoning ordinance prohibiting an "adult" movie theater from locating within one thousand feet of any church, school, park, or residential area, the Court upheld the ordinance, nothing that the purpose of the law was not to regulate speech but to regulate the use of land. And in any case the adult theaters still had much of the city's land area in which to find a location.[23]

With the advent of the Internet it has become more difficult for the government to regulate

WHO GOVERNS? TO WHAT ENDS?

Flag Burning

Texas passed a law that made burning the American flag a crime. In 1989 the U.S. Supreme Court declared, by a five-to-four vote, that the law was unconstitutional because it violated a citizen's right to free speech.* The public was outraged, thinking that flag burning was inexcusable. Within a few days the House passed by a vote of 380 to 38 a bill that would make flag burning a federal crime. Not long after, the Senate agreed by a vote of 91 to 9. Under the law a person could be sent to prison for up to one year if he or she "knowingly mutilates, defaces, physically defiles, burns, maintains on the floor or ground, or tramples upon" any U.S. flag.

The Supreme Court was not satisfied. In 1990 by a similar five-to-four vote, it struck down the new federal law as unconstitutional, repeating its view that flag burning was a form of constitutionally protected speech.† The public was still upset, but now it was clear that only a constitutional amendment could make flag burning a crime.

But the constitutional amendment, which would have required a two-thirds majority vote in both the House and the Senate, never passed. Why? A year earlier both houses of Congress had approved a sim-

ilar law by margins well in excess of a two-thirds vote, and the public still wanted such a law. In fact many veterans' organizations argued vigorously in favor of an amendment.

Who governed? The answer, it seems, is those members of Congress who were reluctant to amend the Constitution even for a popular cause. The amendment that would have made flag burning illegal passed both houses, but without enough votes to meet the two-thirds requirement. The missing votes were cast by members who said that although flag burning was wrong, it was a mistake to limit the Bill of Rights to deal with this rare and unhappy form of "speech."

The congressional action cannot be explained by public opinion, interest groups, or electoral politics. More Republicans than Democrats favored the amendment, but there were members from both parties on both sides of the issue. In this case members of Congress voted to a large degree on the basis of their personal convictions.

†*Texas v. Johnson*, 491 U.S. 397 (1989).
United States v. Eichman, 496 U.S. 310 (1990).

obscenity. The Internet spans the globe. It offers an amazing variety of materials—some educational, some entertaining, some sexually explicit. But it is difficult to apply the Supreme Court's standard for judging whether sexual material is obscene—the "average person" applying "contemporary community standards"—to the Internet, because there is no easy way to tell what "the community" is. Is it the place where the recipient lives or the place where the material originates? And since no one is in charge of the Internet, who can be held responsible for controlling offensive material? Since anybody can send anything to anybody else without knowing the age or location of the recipient, how can the Internet protect children? When Congress tried to ban obscene, indecent, or "patently offensive" materials from the Internet, the Supreme Court struck down the law as unconstitutional.[24]

Symbolic Speech

You cannot ordinarily claim that an illegal act should be protected because that action is meant to convey a political message. For example, if you burn your draft card in protest against the foreign policy of the United States, you can be punished for the illegal act (burning the card), even if your intent was to communicate your beliefs. The Court reasoned that giving such **symbolic speech** the same protection as real speech would open the door to permitting all manner of illegal actions—murder, arson, rape—if the perpetrator meant thereby to send a message.[25]

On the other hand, a statute that makes it illegal to burn the American flag is an unconstitutional infringement of free speech.[26] Why is there a difference between a draft card and the flag? The Court argues that the government has a right to run a military draft and so can protect draft cards, even if this incidentally restricts speech. But the only motive that the government has in banning flag burning is to restrict this form of speech, and that would make such a restriction improper. In 1989–1990 Congress refused to endorse a proposed constitutional amendment that, if ratified, would have reversed this Court ruling. It did pass a bill making flag burning a crime, but the Supreme Court, consistent with its decision in an earlier Texas case, held that this law was an unconstitutional infringement of free speech.[27]

Who Is a Person?

If people have a right to speak and publish, do corporations, interest groups, and children have the same right? By and large the answer is yes, though there are some exceptions.

When the attorney general of Massachusetts tried to prevent the First National Bank of Boston from spending money to influence votes in a local election, the Court stepped in and blocked him. The Court held that a corporation, like a person, has certain First Amendment rights. Similarly, when the federal government tried to limit the spending of a group called Massachusetts Citizens for Life (an antiabortion organization), the Court held that such organizations have First Amendment rights.[28] The Court has also told states that they cannot forbid liquor stores to advertise their prices and informed federal authorities that they cannot prohibit casinos from plugging gambling.[29]

When the California Public Utility Commission tried to compel one of the utilities that it regulates, the Pacific Gas and Electric Company, to enclose in its monthly bills to customers statements written by groups attacking the utility, the Supreme Court blocked the agency, saying that forcing it to disseminate political statements violated the firm's free speech rights. "The identity of the speaker is not decisive in determining whether speech is protected," the Court said. "Corporations and other associations, like individuals, contribute to the 'discussion, debate, and the dissemination of information and ideas' that the First Amendment seeks to foster." In this case the right to speak includes the choice of what *not* to say.[30]

Even though corporations have some First Amendment rights, the government can place more

"Symbolic speech": When young men burned their draft cards during the 1960s to protest the Vietnam War, the Supreme Court ruled that it was an illegal act for which they could be punished.

limits on commercial than on noncommercial speech. The legislature can place restrictions on advertisements for cigarettes, liquor, and gambling; it can even regulate advertising for some less harmful products provided that the regulations are narrowly tailored and serve a substantial public interest.[31] If the regulations are too broad or do not serve a clear interest, then ads are entitled to some constitutional protection. For example, the states cannot bar lawyers from advertising or accountants from personally soliciting clients.[32]

Under certain circumstances, young people may have less freedom of expression than adults. In 1988 the Supreme Court held that the principal of Hazelwood High School could censor articles appearing in the student-edited newspaper. The newspaper was published using school funds and was part of a journalism class. The principal ordered the deletion of stories dealing with student pregnancies and the impact of parental divorce on students. The student editors sued, claiming their First Amendment rights had been violated. The Court agreed that students do not "shed their constitutional rights to freedom of speech or expression at the schoolhouse gate" and that they cannot be punished for expressing on campus their personal views. But students do not have exactly the same rights as adults if the exercise of those rights impedes the educational mission of the school. Students may lawfully say things on campus, as individuals, that they cannot say if they are part of school-sponsored activities, such as plays or school-run newspapers, that are part of the curriculum.

School-sponsored activities can be controlled so long as the controls are "reasonably related to legitimate pedagogical concerns."[33]

Church and State

Everybody knows, correctly, the language of the First Amendment that protects freedom of speech and the press, though most people are not aware of how complex the legal interpretations of these provisions have become. But many people also believe, wrongly, that the language of the First Amendment clearly requires the "separation of church and state." It does not.

What that amendment actually says is quite different and maddeningly unclear. It has two parts. The first, often referred to as the **free-exercise clause,** states that Congress shall make no law prohibiting the "free exercise" of religion. The second, which is called the **establishment clause,** states that Congress shall make no law "respecting an establishment of religion."

The Free-Exercise Clause

The free-exercise clause is the clearer of the two, though by no means is it lacking in ambiguity. It obviously means that Congress cannot pass a law prohibiting Catholics from celebrating Mass, requiring Baptists to become Episcopalians, or preventing Jews from holding a bar mitzvah. Since the First Amendment has been applied to the states via the due-process clause of the Fourteenth Amendment, it means that state governments cannot pass such laws either. In general the courts have treated religion like speech: you can pretty much do or say what you want so long as it does not cause some serious harm to others.

Even some laws that do not appear on their face to apply to churches may be unconstitutional if their enforcement imposes particular burdens on churches or greater burdens on some churches than others. For example, a state cannot apply a license fee on door-to-door solicitors when the solicitor is a Jehovah's Witness selling religious tracts.[34] By the same token, the courts ruled that the city of Hialeah, Florida, cannot ban animal sacrifices by members of an Afro-Caribbean religion called Santeria. Since killing animals is generally not illegal (if it were, there could be no hamburgers or chicken sand-wiches served in Hialeah's restaurants, and rat traps would be unlawful), the ban in this case was clearly directed against a specific religion and hence was unconstitutional.[35]

Having the right to exercise your religion freely does not mean, however, that you are exempt from laws binding other citizens, even when the law goes against your religious beliefs. A man cannot have more than one wife, even if (as once was the case with Mormons) polygamy is thought desirable on religious grounds.[36] For religious reasons you may oppose being vaccinated or having blood transfusions, but if the state passes a compulsory vaccination law or orders that a blood transfusion be given to a sick child, the courts will not block them on grounds of religious liberty.[37] Similarly, if you belong to an Indian tribe that uses a drug, peyote, in religious ceremonies, you cannot claim that your freedom was abridged if the state decides to ban the use of peyote, provided the law applies equally to all.[38] Since airports have a legitimate need for tight security measures, begging can be outlawed in them even if some of the people doing the begging are part of a religious group (in this case, the Hare Krishnas).[39]

Unfortunately some conflicts between religious belief and public policy are even more difficult to settle. What if you believe on religious grounds that war is immoral? The draft laws have always exempted a conscientious objector from military duty, and the Court has upheld such exemptions. But the Court has gone further: it has said that people cannot be drafted even if they do not believe in a Supreme Being or belong to any religious tradition, so long as their "consciences, spurred by deeply held moral, ethical, or religious beliefs, would give them no rest or peace if they allowed themselves to become part of an instrument of war."[40] Do exemptions on such grounds create an opportunity for some people to evade the draft because of their political preferences? In trying to answer such questions, the courts often have had to try to define a religion—no easy task.

And even when there is no question about your membership in a bona fide religion, the circumstances under which you may claim exemption from laws that apply to everybody else are not really clear. What if you, a member of the Seventh-Day Adventists, are fired by your employer for refusing on religious grounds to work on Saturday, and then it turns out that you cannot collect unemployment insurance because you refuse to take an available job—one that also requires you to work on Saturday? Or what if you are a member of the Amish sect, which refuses, contrary to state law, to send its children to public schools past the eighth grade? The Court has ruled that the state must pay you unemployment compensation and cannot require you to send your children to public schools beyond the eighth grade.[41]

These last two decisions, and others like them, show that even the "simple" principle of freedom of religion gets complicated in practice and can lead to the courts' giving, in effect, preference to members of one church over members of another.

The Establishment Clause

What in the world did the members of the First Congress mean when they wrote into the First Amendment language prohibiting Congress from making a law "respecting" an "establishment" of religion? The Supreme Court has more or less consistently interpreted this vague phrase to mean that the Constitution erects a "wall of separation" between church and state.

That phrase, so often quoted, is not in the Bill of Rights nor in the debates in the First Congress that drafted the Bill of Rights; it comes from the pen of Thomas Jefferson, who was opposed to having the Church of England as the established church of his native Virginia. (At the time of the Revolutionary War there were established churches—that is, official, state-supported churches—in at least eight of the thirteen former colonies.) But it is not clear that Jefferson's view was the majority view.

During much of the debate in Congress the wording of this part of the First Amendment was quite different and much plainer than what finally emerged. Up to the last minute the clause was intended to read "no religion shall be established by law" or "no national religion shall be established." The meaning of those words seems quite clear: whatever the states may do, the federal government cannot create an official, national religion or give support to one religion in preference to another.[42]

But Congress instead adopted an ambiguous phrase, and so the Supreme Court had to decide what it meant. It has declared that these words do not simply mean "no national religion" but mean as well no government involvement with religion at all,

even on a nonpreferential basis. They mean, in short, erecting a "wall of separation" between church and state.[43] Though the interpretation of the establishment clause remains a topic of great controversy among judges and scholars, the Supreme Court has more or less consistently adopted this **wall-of-separation principle.**

Its first statement of this interpretation was in 1947. The case involved a New Jersey town that reimbursed parents for the costs of transporting their children to school, including parochial (in this case Catholic) schools. The Court decided that this reimbursement was constitutional, but it made it clear that the establishment clause of the First Amendment applied (via the Fourteenth Amendment) to the states and that it meant, among other things, that the government cannot require a person to profess a belief or disbelief in any religion; it cannot aid one religion, some religions, or all religions; and it cannot spend any tax money, however small the amount might be, in support of any religious activities or institutions.[44] The reader may wonder, in view of the Court's reasoning, why it allowed the town to pay for busing children to Catholic schools. The answer that it gave is that busing is a religiously neutral activity, akin to providing fire and police protection to Catholic schools. Busing, available to public- and private-school children alike, does not breach the wall of separation.

Since 1947 the Court has applied the wall-of-separation theory to strike down as unconstitutional

Students pray in front of a high school in Virginia. The Supreme Court will not let this happen inside a public school.

every effort to have any form of prayer in public schools, even if it is nonsectarian,[45] voluntary,[46] or limited to reading a passage of the Bible.[47] Since 1992 it has even been unconstitutional for a public school to ask a rabbi or minister to offer a prayer—an invocation or a benediction—at the school's graduation ceremony.[48] Moreover, the Court has held that laws prohibiting teaching the theory of evolution or requiring giving equal time to "creationism" (the biblical doctrine that God created mankind) are religiously inspired and thus unconstitutional.[49] A public school may not allow its pupils to take time out from their regular classes for religious instruction if this occurs within the schools, though "released-time" instruction is all right if it is done outside the public school building.[50] The school prayer decisions in particular have provoked a storm of controversy, but efforts to get Congress to propose to the states a constitutional amendment authorizing such prayers have failed.

Almost as controversial have been Court-imposed restrictions on public aid to parochial schools, though here the wall-of-separation principle has not been used to forbid any and all forms of aid. For example, it is permissible for the federal government to provide aid for constructing buildings on denominational (as well as nondenominational) college campuses[51] and for state governments to loan free textbooks to parochial-school pupils,[52] grant tax-exempt status to parochial schools,[53] allow parents of parochial-school children to deduct their tuition payments on a state's income tax returns,[54] and pay for computers and a deaf child's sign language interpreter at private and religious schools.[55] But the government cannot pay a salary supplement to teachers who teach secular subjects in parochial schools,[56] reimburse parents for the cost of parochial-school tuition,[57] supply parochial schools with services such as counseling,[58] give money with which to purchase instructional materials, require that "creationism" be taught in public schools, or create a special school district for Hasidic Jews.[59]

The Court sometimes changes its mind on these matters. In 1985 it said that the states could not send teachers into parochial schools to teach remedial courses for needy children, but twelve years later it decided that they could. "We no longer presume," the Court wrote, "that public employees will inculcate religion simply because they happen to be in a sectarian environment."[60]

If you find it confusing to follow the twists and turns of Court policy in this area, you are not alone. The wall-of-separation principle has not been easy to apply, and with its membership undergoing change, the Court has begun to alter its position on church-state matters. (O'Connor, Rehnquist, Scalia, Kennedy, and Thomas have generally supported lowering—or perhaps perforating—the wall a bit.) The Court has tried to sort out the confusion by developing a three-part test to decide under what circumstances government involvement in religious activities is improper.[61] That involvement is constitutional if it meets these tests:

1. It has a secular purpose.
2. Its primary effect neither advances nor inhibits religion.
3. It does not foster an excessive government entanglement with religion.

No sooner had the test been developed than the Court decided that it was all right for the government of Pawtucket, Rhode Island, to erect a Nativity scene as part of a Christmas display in a local park. But five years later it said that Pittsburgh could not put a Nativity scene in front of the courthouse but could display a menorah (a Jewish symbol of Chanukah) next to a Christmas tree and a sign extolling liberty. The Court claimed that the crèche had to go (because, being too close to the courthouse, a government endorsement was implied) but the menorah could stay (because, being next to a Christmas tree, it would not lead people to think that Pittsburgh was endorsing Judaism).[62]

Confused? It gets worse. Though the Court has struck down prayer in public schools, it has upheld prayer in Congress (since 1789, the House and Senate open each session with a prayer).[63] A public school cannot have a chaplain, but the armed services can. The Court has said that the government cannot "advance" religion, but it has not objected to the printing of the phrase "In God We Trust" on the back of every dollar bill.

It is obvious that despite its efforts to set forth clear rules governing church-state relations, the Court's actual decisions are hard to summarize. It is deeply divided—some would say deeply confused—on these matters, and so the efforts to define the "wall of sep-

How Would You Decide?

Suppose that you are on the Supreme Court. In each of the actual cases summarized below, you are asked to decide whether the First Amendment to the Constitution permits or prohibits a particular action. What would be your decision? (How the Supreme Court actually decided is given on page 514.)

Case 1: Jacksonville, Florida, passed a city ordinance prohibiting drive-in movies from showing films containing nudity if the screen was visible to passersby on the street. A movie theater manager protested, claiming that he had a First Amendment right to show such films, even if they could be seen from the street. Who is correct?

Case 2: Dr. Benjamin Spock wanted to enter Fort Dix Military Reservation in New Jersey to pass out campaign literature and discuss issues with service personnel. The military denied him access on grounds that regulations prohibit partisan campaigning on military bases. Who is correct?

Case 3: A town passed an ordinance forbidding the placing of "For Sale" or "Sold" signs in front of homes in racially changing neighborhoods. The purpose was to reduce "white flight" and panic selling. A realty firm protested, claiming that its

freedom of speech was being abridged. Who is correct?

Case 4: A girl in Georgia was raped and died. A local television station broadcast the name of the girl, having obtained it from court records. Her father sued, claiming that his family's right to privacy had been violated, and pointed to a Georgia law that made it a crime to broadcast the name of a rape victim. The television station claimed that it had a right under the First Amendment to broadcast the name. Who is correct?

Case 5: Florida passed a law giving a political candidate the right to equal space in a newspaper that had published attacks on him. A newspaper claimed that this violated the freedom of the press to publish what it wants. Who is correct?

Case 6: Zacchini is a "human cannonball" whose entire fifteen-second act was filmed and broadcast by an Ohio television station. Zacchini sued the station, claiming that his earning power had been reduced by the film because the station showed for free what he charges people to see at county fairs. The station replied that it had a First Amendment right to broadcast such events. Who is correct?

aration" will continue to prove to be as difficult as the Court's earlier efforts to decide what is interstate and what is local commerce (see Chapter 3).

Crime and Due Process

Whereas the central problem in interpreting the religion clauses of the First Amendment has been to decide what they mean, the central problems in interpreting those parts of the Bill of Rights that affect people accused of a crime have been to decide not only what they mean but also how to put them into effect. It is not obvious what constitutes an "unreasonable search," but even if we settle that question, we still must decide how best to protect people against such searches in ways that do not unduly hinder criminal investigations.

There are at least two ways to provide that protection. One is to let the police introduce in court evidence relevant to the guilt or innocence of a person, no matter how it was obtained and then, after the case is settled, punish the police officer (or his or her superiors) if the evidence was gathered improperly (for example, by an unreasonable search). The other way is to exclude improperly gathered evidence from the trial in the first place, even if it is relevant to determining the guilt or innocence of the accused.

Most democratic nations, including England, use the first method; the United States uses the second. Because of this, many of the landmark cases decided by the Supreme Court have been bitterly controversial. Opponents of these decisions have argued that a guilty person should not go free just because the police officer blundered, especially if the mistake was

A man is arrested in Texas.

minor. Supporters rejoin that there is no way to punish errant police officers effectively other than by excluding tainted evidence; moreover, nobody should be convicted of a crime except by evidence that is above reproach.[64]

The Exclusionary Rule

The American method relies on what is called the **exclusionary rule.** That rule holds that evidence gathered in violation of the Constitution cannot be used in a trial. The rule has been used to implement two provisions of the Bill of Rights—the right to be free from unreasonable searches and seizures (Fourth Amendment) and the right not to be compelled to give evidence against oneself (Fifth Amendment).*

Not until 1949 did the Supreme Court consider whether to apply the exclusionary rule to the states. In a case decided that year the Court made it clear that the Fourth Amendment prohibited the police from carrying out unreasonable searches and obtaining improper confessions but held that it was not necessary to use the exclusionary rule to enforce those prohibitions. It noted that other nations did

---

*We shall consider here only two constitutional limits—those bearing on searches and confessions. Thus we will omit many other important constitutional provisions affecting criminal cases, such as rules governing wiretapping, prisoner rights, the right to bail and to a jury trial, the bar on ex post facto laws, the right to be represented by a lawyer in court, the ban on "cruel and unusual" punishment, and the rule against double jeopardy.

not require that evidence improperly gathered had to be excluded from a criminal trial. The Court said that the local police should not improperly gather and use evidence, but if they did, the remedy was to sue the police department or punish the officer.[65]

But in 1961 the Supreme Court changed its mind about the use of the exclusionary rule. It all began when the Cleveland police broke into the home of Dollree Mapp in search of drugs and, finding none, arrested her for possessing some obscene pictures that they found there. The Court held that this was an unreasonable search and seizure because the police had not obtained a search warrant, though they had had ample time to do so. Furthermore, such illegally gathered evidence could not be used in the trial of Mapp.[66] Beginning with this case—*Mapp v. Ohio*—the Supreme Court required the use of the exclusionary rule as a way of enforcing a variety of constitutional guarantees.

Search and Seizure

After the Court decided to exclude improperly gathered evidence, the next problem was to decide what evidence was improper. What happened to Dollree Mapp was an easy case: hardly anybody argued that it was reasonable for the police to break into someone's home without a warrant, ransack their belongings, and take whatever they could find that might be incriminating. But that left a lot of hard choices still to be made.

When can the police search you without its being unreasonable? Under two circumstances—when they have a search warrant and when they have lawfully arrested you. A **search warrant** is an order from a judge authorizing the search of a place; the order must describe what is to be searched and seized, and the judge can issue it only if he or she is persuaded by the police that good reason **(probable cause)** exists to believe that a crime has been committed and that the evidence bearing on that crime will be found at a certain location. (The police can also search a building if the occupant gives them permission.)

In addition, you can be searched if the search occurs when you are being lawfully arrested. When can you be arrested? You can be arrested if a judge has issued an arrest warrant for you, if you commit a crime in the presence of a police officer, or if the officer has probable cause to believe that you have committed a serious crime (usually a felony). If you are arrested and no search warrant has been issued,

What would you do?

MEMORANDUM

To: Senator Edward Cortez
From: Mary Briscoe, legislative assistant

Federal courts have been required to exclude improperly gathered evidence since 1886 and state courts since 1961. The rule is an effort to prevent unconstitutional searches and seizures. The constitutional amendment would ban the rule and create instead a procedure for punishing police officers who violate the Constitution.

Arguments for:

1. The rule makes it easy for defense attorneys to attack police evidence by having the judge declare it inadmissible. As a result a guilty person may go free because a police officer made a mistake.
2. The rule does not punish a police officer who violates the Constitution. Instead it benefits only accused persons.
3. No other democratic country uses the exclusionary rule.

Arguments against:

1. The rule protects the privacy of every individual by discouraging illegal searches.
2. There is no easy way to punish police officers who gather illegal evidence except by preventing them from using it in court.
3. There is no strong evidence that guilty people go free because of the rule.

Your decision:
Favor amendment _____
Oppose amendment _____

Congress Debates the Exclusionary Rule

October 15
WASHINGTON
Congress takes up tomorrow a proposed constitutional amendment that would ban the exclusionary rule from trials. The Supreme Court has required courts to exclude improperly gathered evidence from criminal cases . . .

How the Court Decided

The United States Supreme Court answered the questions on page 511 in the following ways:

Case 1:   The drive-in movie won. The Supreme Court, 6–3, decided that the First Amendment protects the right to show nudity; it is up to the unwilling viewer on the public streets to avert his or her eyes.   *Erznoznik v. Jacksonville,*
420 U.S. 205 (1975)

Case 2:   The military won. The Supreme Court, 6–2, decided that military reservations are not like public streets or parks, and thus civilians can be excluded from them, especially if such exclusion prevents the military from appear-ing to be the handmaiden of various political causes.
Greer v. Spock,
424 U.S. 828 (1976)

Case 3:   The realty firm won. The Supreme Court, 8–0, decided that the First Amendment prohibits the banning of signs, even of a commercial nature, without a strong, legitimate state interest. Banning the signs would not obviously reduce "white flight," and the government has no right to withhold information from citizens for fear that they will act unwisely.
Linmark Associates, Inc. v. Willingboro,
431 U.S. 85 (1977)

Case 4:   The television station won. The Court, 8–1, decided that the First Amendment protects the right to broadcast the names of rape victims obtained from public (that is, court) records.
Cox Broadcasting Corp. v. Cohn,
420 U.S. 469 (1975)

Case 5:   The newspaper won. The Supreme Court decided unanimously that the First Amendment prohibits the state from intruding into the function of editors.
Miami Herald Publishing Co. v. Tornillo,
418 U.S. 241 (1974)

Case 6:   Zacchini, the human cannonball, won. The Supreme Court, 5–4, decided that broadcasting the entire act without the performer's consent jeopardized his means of livelihood, even though the First Amendment would guarantee the right of the station to broadcast newsworthy facts about the act.
Zacchini v. Scripps-Howard Broadcasting Co.,
433 U.S. 562 (1977)

---

the police, and not a judge, decide what they can search. What rules should they follow?

In trying to answer that question, the courts have elaborated a set of rules that are complex, subject to frequent change, and quite controversial. In general the police, after arresting you, can search:

• You
• Things in plain view
• Things or places under your immediate control

As a practical matter, things "in plain view" or "under your immediate control" mean the room in which you are arrested but not other rooms of the house.[67] If the police want to search the rest of your house or a car parked in your driveway, they will first have to go to a judge to obtain a search warrant. But if the police arrest a college student on campus for drinking under age and then accompany that student back to his or her dormitory room so that the

student can get proof that he or she was old enough to drink, the police can seize drugs that are in plain view in that room.[68] And if marijuana is growing in plain view in an open field, the police can enter and search that field even though it is fenced off with a locked gate and a "No Trespassing" sign.[69]

But what if you are arrested while driving your car—how much of it can the police search? The answer to that question has changed almost yearly. In 1979 the Court ruled that the police could not search a suitcase taken from a car of an arrested person, and in 1981 it extended this protection to any "closed, opaque container" found in the car.[70] But the following year the Court decided that all parts of a car, closed or open, could be searched if the officers had probable cause to believe that the contained contraband (that is, goods illegally possessed). And recently the rules governing car searches have been relaxed even further. Officers who have probable cause to search a car can also search the things passengers are carrying in the car. And if the car is stopped to give the driver a traffic ticket, the car can be searched if the officer develops a "reasonable, articulable suspicion" that the car is involved in other illegal activity.[71]

In this confusing area of the law the Court is attempting to protect those places in which a person has a "reasonable expectation of privacy." Your body is one such place, and so the Court has held that the police cannot compel you to undergo surgery to remove a bullet that might be evidence of your guilt or innocence in a crime.[72] But the police can require you to take a Breathalyzer test to see whether you have been drinking while driving.[73] Your home is another place where you have an expectation of privacy, but a barn next to your home is not, nor is your backyard viewed from an airplane, nor is your home if it is a motor home that can be driven away, and so the police need not have a warrant to look into these places.[74]

If you work for the government, you have an expectation that your desk and files will be private; nonetheless, your supervisor may search the desk and files without a warrant, provided that he or she is looking for something related to your work.[75] But bear in mind that the Constitution protects you only against *the government*; a private employer has a great deal of freedom to search your desk and files.

Some people had hoped that the Court would develop a general right of privacy so that nothing done in your home among consenting adults would be subject to government regulation. Support for this hope was given by the Court's decisions forbidding states from prohibiting the sale of contraceptives. But when the Court was asked to pass on the constitutionality of a Georgia statute that made it illegal to engage in homosexual activities, it held, by a narrow five-to-four vote, that the right to privacy does not extend to such activities, and so the Georgia statute may stand.[76]

Testing for Drugs and AIDS   If the government can under some circumstances search your desk and files without a warrant, can it require you to undergo a test for AIDS or for drug use?

In the mid-1980s the deadly AIDS virus became a major public health issue. Because it disproportionately affected homosexuals, testing people to see whether they had the disease raised fears among

Since the U.S. Constitution controls only government actions, it does not affect drug testing by private businesses.

some that the tests would be used to discriminate against homosexuals in employment and the issuance of life insurance. But others worried that failing to test for the virus would cause people to be needlessly exposed to the risk of death. In 1987 President Reagan called for AIDS tests for new immigrants, federal prisoners, and certain other categories of people.

In the wake of growing public concern about the spread of drug abuse, President Reagan in 1986 signed an executive order requiring many federal-government employees to be tested. Numerous private firms and major-league sports organizations had already required such testing of job applicants and athletes. There is no obvious constitutional reason why a *private* organization should not be able to test its members. But the Constitution restricts what the *government* may do; so is drug testing by a government agency a proper or an improper "search" of a person?

At first some federal district courts took the view that the mandatory drug testing of, say, fire fighters was an unreasonable search unless the fire fighter who was tested had been suspected of some wrongdoing. But in 1989 the Supreme Court held that certain kinds of employees could be subjected to drug tests without a search warrant or even any individualized suspicion. These were employees involved in law enforcement (in particular, Customs Service agents) and railroad employees involved in accidents. In short, a concern for public safety or national security can justify government-ordered

HOW THINGS WORK

The Miranda Rule

The Supreme Court has interpreted the due-process clause to require that local police departments issue warnings of the sort shown below to people whom they are arresting.

PHILADELPHIA POLICE DEPARTMENT

STANDARD POLICE INTERROGATION CARD

WARNINGS TO BE GIVEN ACCUSED

We are questioning you concerning the crime of (state specific crime).

We have a duty to explain to you and to warn you that you have the following legal rights:

A. You have a right to remain silent and do not have to say anything at all.

B. Anything you say can and will be used against you in Court.

C. You have a right to talk to a lawyer of your own choice before we ask you any questions, and also to have a lawyer here with you while we ask questions.

D. If you cannot afford to hire a lawyer, and you want one, we will see that you have one provided to you free of charge before we ask you any questions.

E. If you are willing to give us a statement, you have a right to stop any time you wish.

75-Misc.-3   (Over)

(6-24-70)

Ernesto A. Miranda was convicted in Arizona of rape and kidnapping. When the Supreme Court overturned the conviction, it issued a set of rules—the "Miranda rules"—governing how police must conduct an arrest and interrogation.

drug tests. Using the same reasoning, the Court has upheld state laws that authorize the police to set up roadblocks and randomly check drivers to see if they are sober and the random drug testing of high school athletes.[77]

But when there is no threat to safety, the Court has been skeptical of drug testing. Georgia passed a law saying that all political candidates there must take a drug test, but the Court decided that this was unconstitutional. There was no evidence that drugs were a problem in the state legislature, and even if some local politicians were taking drugs, they were not likely to hurt (at least physically) anyone else.[78]

Confessions and Self-Incrimination

The constitutional ban on being forced to give evidence against oneself was originally intended to prevent the use of torture or "third-degree" police tactics to extract confessions. But it has since been extended to cover many kinds of statements uttered not out of fear of torture but from lack of awareness of one's rights, especially the right to remain silent, whether in the courtroom or in the police station.

For many decades the Supreme Court had held that involuntary confessions could not be used in federal criminal trials but had not ruled that they were barred from state trials. But in the early 1960s it changed its mind in two landmark cases—*Escobedo* and *Miranda*.[79] The story of the latter and of the controversy that it provoked is worth telling.

Ernesto A. Miranda was convicted in Arizona of the rape and kidnapping of a young woman. The conviction was based on a written confession that Miranda signed after two hours of police questioning. (The victim also identified him.) Two years earlier the Court had decided that the rule against self-incrimination applied to state courts.[80] Now the question arose of what constitutes an "involuntary" confession. The Court decided that a confession should be presumed involuntary unless the person in custody had been fully and clearly informed of his or her right to be silent, to have an attorney present during any questioning, and to have an attorney provided free of charge if he or she could not afford one. The accused may waive these rights and offer to talk, but the waiver must be truly voluntary. Since Miranda did not have a lawyer present when he was questioned and had not knowingly waived his right to a lawyer, the confession was excluded from evidence in the trial and his conviction was overturned.[81]

Miranda was tried and convicted again, this time on the basis of evidence supplied by his girlfriend, who testified that he had admitted to her that he was guilty. Nine years later he was released from prison; four years after that he was killed in a barroom fight.

When the Phoenix police arrested the prime suspect in Ernesto Miranda's murder, they read him his rights from a "Miranda card."

Everyone who watches cops-and-robbers shows on television probably knows the "Miranda warning" by heart (see the box on page 456). The police now read it routinely to people whom they arrest. It is not clear whether it has much impact on who does or does not confess or what effect, if any, it may have on the crime rate.

In time the Miranda rule was extended to mean that you have a right to a lawyer when you appear in a police lineup[82] and when you are questioned by a psychiatrist to determine whether you are competent to stand trial.[83] The Court threw out the conviction of a man who had killed a child, because the accused, without being given the right to have a lawyer present, had led the police to the victim's body.[84] You do not have a right to a Miranda warning, however, if while in jail you confess a crime to another inmate who turns out to be an undercover police officer.[85]

A recent case may change the meaning of the Miranda rule. The U.S. Court of Appeals for the Fourth Circuit (a court that covers Atlantic coast states between Maryland and South Carolina) ruled that the Miranda warning is only one of several ways by which the right not to incriminate oneself might be protected. Congress, the court said, had passed a law that did not require a Miranda warning if the confession was made voluntarily.[86] But the Supreme Court disagreed, deciding that the Miranda rule was required by the Constitution and Congress could not alter it.[87]

Relaxing the Exclusionary Rule

Cases such as *Miranda* were highly controversial and led to efforts in Congress to modify or overrule the decisions by statute—without much coming of the attempts. But as the rules governing police conduct became increasingly more complex, pressure mounted to find an alternative. Some thought that any evidence should be admissible, with the question of police conduct left to lawsuits or other ways of punishing official misbehavior. Others felt that the exclusionary rule served a useful purpose but had simply become too technical to be an effective deterrent to police misconduct (the police cannot obey rules that they cannot understand). And still others felt that the exclusionary rule was a vital safeguard to essential liberties and should be kept intact. The court has refused to let Congress abolish Miranda because it is a Constitutional rule.*

The courts themselves began to adopt the second position, deciding a number of cases in ways that retained the exclusionary rule but modified it by limiting its coverage (police were given greater freedom to question juveniles)[88] and by incorporating what was called a **good-faith exception.** For example, if the police obtain a search warrant that they believe is valid, the evidence that they gather will not be excluded if it later turns out that the warrant was defective for some reason (such as the judge's having used the wrong form).[89] And the Court decided that "overriding considerations of public safety" may justify questioning a person without first reading the person his or her rights.[90] Moreover, the Court changed its mind about the killer who led the police to the place where he had disposed of his victim's body. After the man was convicted a second time and again appealed, the Court in 1984 held that the body would have been discovered anyway; thus evidence will not be excluded if it can be shown that it would "inevitably" have been found.[91]

---

*Dickerson v. United States, 120 S. Ct. 2326 (2000).

Summary

Civil liberties questions are in some ways like and in some ways unlike ordinary policy debates. Like most issues, civil liberties problems often involve competing interests—in this case conflicting rights or conflicting rights and duties— and so we have groups mobilized on both sides of issues involving free speech and crime control. Like some other issues, civil liberties problems can also arise from the successful appeals of a policy entrepreneur, and so we have periodic reductions in liberty resulting from popular fears, usually aroused during or just after a war.

But civil liberties are unlike many other issues in at least one regard: more than struggles over welfare spending or defense or economic policy, debates about civil liberties reach down into our fundamental political beliefs and political culture, challenging us to define what we mean by religion, Americanism, and decency.

The most important of these challenges focuses on the meaning of the First Amendment: What is "speech"? How much of it should be free? How far can the state go in aiding religion? How do we strike a balance between national security and personal expression? The zigzag course followed by the courts in judging these matters has, on balance, tended to enlarge freedom of expression.

Almost as important has been the struggle to strike a balance between the right of society to protect itself from criminals and the right of people (including criminals) to be free from unreasonable searches and coerced confessions. As with free speech cases, the courts have generally broadened the rights at some expense to the power of the police. But in recent years the Supreme Court has pulled back from some of its more sweeping applications of the exclusionary rule.

The resolution of these issues by the courts is political in the sense that differing opinions about what is right or desirable compete, with one side or another prevailing (often by a small majority). In this competition of ideas federal judges, though not elected, are often sensitive to strong currents of popular opinion. When entrepreneurial politics has produced new action against apparently threatening minorities, judges are inclined, at least for a while, to give serious consideration to popular fears and legislative majorities. And when no strong national mood is discernible, the opinions of elites influence judicial thinking (as described in Chapter 14).

At the same time, courts resolve political conflicts in a manner that differs in important respects from the resolution of conflicts by legislatures or executives. First, the very existence of the courts, and the relative ease with which one may enter them to advance a claim, facilitates challenges to accepted values. An unpopular political or religious group may have little or no access to a legislature, but it will have substantial access to the courts. Second, judges often settle controversies about rights not simply by deciding the case at hand but by formulating a general rule to cover like cases elsewhere. This has an advantage (the law tends to become more consistent and better known) but a disadvantage as well: a rule suitable for one case may be unworkable in another. Judges reason by analogy and sometimes assume that two cases are similar when in fact there are important differences. A definition of "obscenity" or of "fighting words" may suit one situation but be inadequate in another. Third, judges interpret the Constitution, whereas legislatures often consult popular preferences or personal convictions. However much their own beliefs influence what judges read into the Constitution, almost all of them are constrained by its language.

Taken together, the desire to find and announce rules, the language of the Constitution, and the personal beliefs of judges have led to a general expansion of civil liberties. As a result, even allowing for temporary reversals and frequent redefinitions, any value that is thought to hinder freedom of expression and the rights of the accused has generally lost ground to the claims of the First, Fourth, Fifth, and Sixth Amendments.

World Wide Web Resources

- Court cases: www.law.cornell.edu
- Civil Rights Division of the Department of Justice: www.usdoj.gov
- American Civil Liberties Union: www.aclu.org

Key Terms

McCarthyism *p. 438*
freedom of expression
p. 440
freedom of religion *p. 441*
prior restraint *p. 441*

clear-and-present-danger
test *p. 441*
due-process clause *p. 442*
libel *p. 443*
symbolic speech *p. 446*

free-exercise clause *p. 448*
establishment clause
p. 448
wall-of-separation principle *p. 449*

exclusionary rule *p. 452*
search warrant *p. 452*
probable cause *p. 452*
good-faith exception
p. 457

Suggested Readings

Abraham, Henry J., and Barbara A. Perry, *Freedom and the Court*. 7th ed. New York: Oxford University Press, 1998. Analysis of leading Supreme Court cases on civil liberties and civil rights.

Amar, Akhil Reed. *The Constitution and Criminal Procedure: First Principles*. New Haven, Conn.: Yale University Press, 1997. A brilliant critique of how the Supreme Court has interpreted those parts of the Constitution bearing on search warrants, the exclusionary rule, and self-incrimination.

Berns, Walter. *The First Amendment and the Future of American Democracy*. New York: Basic Books, 1976. A look at what the Founders intended by the First Amendment that takes issue with contemporary Supreme Court interpretations of it.

Clor, Harry M. *Obscenity and Public Morality*. Chicago: University of Chicago Press, 1969. Argues for the legitimacy of legal restrictions on obscenity.

Levy, Leonard W. *Legacy of Suppression: Freedom of Speech and Press in Early American History*. Rev. ed. New York: Oxford University Press, 1985. Careful study of what the Founders and the early leaders meant by freedom of speech and press.

Civil Rights

Enduring Questions

1. Should children be bused to schools outside their neighborhoods in order to ensure that every school is racially mixed?
2. Under what circumstances, if any, should numerical goals be used to ensure that students or workers are drawn from every racial group?
3. To what extent should the government be able to limit the opportunity to have an abortion?

The Black Predicament

The Campaign in the Courts
   "Separate but Equal" • Can Separate Schools Be
   Equal? • *Brown v. Board of Education*

The Campaign in Congress

Women and Equal Rights
   Sexual Harassment • Abortion

Affirmative Action
   Equality of Results • Equality of Opportunity

Gays and the Supreme Court

I n 1830 Congress passed a law requiring all
Indians east of the Mississippi River to move
to the Indian Territory west of the river, and
the army set about implementing it. In the
1850s a major political fight broke out in Boston
over whether the police department should be
obliged to hire an Irish officer. Until 1920 women
could not vote in most elections. In the 1930s the
Cornell University Medical School had a strict
quota limiting the number of Jewish students who
could enroll. In the 1940s the army, with the
approval of President Franklin D. Roosevelt, removed all Japanese Americans from their homes in
California and placed them in relocation centers
far from the coast.

In all such cases some group, usually defined
along racial or ethnic lines, was denied access to
facilities, opportunities, or services that were available to other groups. Such cases raise the issue of
civil rights. The pertinent question regarding civil
rights is not whether the government has the
authority to treat different people differently; it is
whether such differences in treatment are reasonable. All laws and policies make distinctions among

461

people—for example, the tax laws require higher-income people to pay taxes at a higher rate than lower-income ones—but not all such distinctions are defensible. The courts have long held that classifying people on the basis of their income and taxing them at different rates is quite permissible because such classifications are not arbitrary or unreasonable and are related to a legitimate public need (that is, raising revenue). Increasingly, however, the courts have said that classifying people on the basis of their race or ethnicity is unreasonable. These are **suspect classifications,** and while not every law making such classifications has been ruled unconstitutional, they have all become subject to especially strict scrutiny.[1]

Given the theory of policy-making described so far in this book, it may seem surprising that specific groups, particularly those that constitute only a small minority of the population, should require any special protection at all. We have seen how easy it is

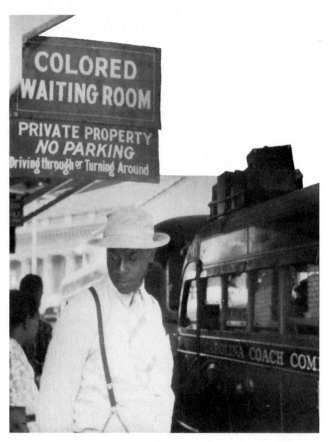

A segregated bus station in Durham, North Carolina, in 1940.

for many small groups—businesses, occupations, unions—to practice client politics. They can obtain some special advantage (a grant, a license, a subsidy) or avoid some threatened regulation because, being small, they find it easy to organize and to escape general public notice. Yet Native Americans, African Americans, Japanese Americans, and Mexican Americans are also relatively small groups whose demands seemingly place little burden on the majority population. Despite this, they have been more often the victims than the clients of the policy-making process.

To explain the victimization of certain groups and the methods by which they have begun to overcome it, we shall consider chiefly the case of African Americans. Black-white relations have in large measure defined the problem of civil rights in this country; most of the landmark laws and court decisions have involved black claims. The strategies employed by or on behalf of African Americans have typically set the pattern for the strategies employed by other groups. At the end of this chapter we shall look at the related but somewhat different issues of women's rights and gay rights.

The Black Predicament

Though constituting more than 12 percent of the population, African Americans until fairly recently could not in many parts of the country vote, attend integrated schools, ride in the front seats of buses, or buy homes in white neighborhoods.

One reason is that the perceived costs of granting these rights to blacks were not widely distributed among the public at large but instead fell on some relatively small and readily organized group. Although today white citizens generally do not feel threatened when a black family moves into Cicero, Illinois, a black child goes to school at Little Rock Central High School, or a black group organizes voters in Neshoba County, Mississippi, at one time most whites in Cicero, Little Rock, and Neshoba County felt deeply threatened by these things (and some whites still do). In the language of this book, civil rights in these places was not a matter of client politics but of competitive or interest group politics. This was especially the case in those parts of the country, notably the Deep South, where blacks were often in the majority. There the politically dominant white minority felt keenly the potential competition for jobs, land, public services, and living space posed by large numbers of people of another race. But even in the North, black gains often appeared to be at the expense of lower-income whites who lived or worked near them, not at the expense of upper-status whites who lived in suburbs.

The interest group component of racial politics put African Americans at a decided disadvantage: they were not allowed to vote at all in many areas; they could vote only with great difficulty in others; and even in those places where voting was easy, they often lacked the material and institutional support for effective political organization. If your opponent feels deeply threatened by your demands and in addition can deny you access to the political system that will decide the fate of those demands, you are, to put it mildly, at a disadvantage. Yet from the end of Reconstruction to the 1960s—for nearly a century— many blacks in the South found themselves in just such a position.

A second reason why the restrictions on African Americans continued for so long is that majoritarian politics worked to the disadvantage of blacks. Because of white attitudes, this was the case even when white and black interests were not directly in competition. To the dismay of those who prefer to explain political action in terms of economic motives, people often attach greater importance to the intangible costs and benefits of policies than to the tangible ones. Thus, even though the average black represented no threat to the average white, antiblack attitudes—racism— produced some appalling actions. Between 1882 and 1946, 4,715 people, about three-fourths of them African Americans, were lynched in the United States.[2] Some lynchings were carried out by small groups of vigilantes acting with much ceremony, but others were the actions of frenzied mobs. In the summer of 1911 a black man charged with murdering a white man in Livermore, Kentucky, was dragged by a mob to the local theater, where he was hanged. The audience, which had been charged admission, was invited to shoot the swaying body (those in the orchestra seats could empty their revolvers; those in the balcony were limited to a single shot).[3]

Though the public in other parts of the country was shocked by such events, little was done: lynching was a local, not a federal, crime. It obviously would not require many lynchings to convince

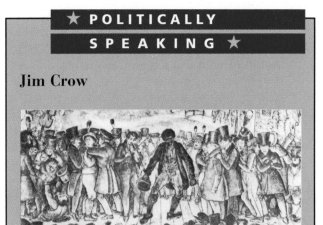

★ POLITICALLY SPEAKING ★

Jim Crow

Thomas D. ("Daddy") Rice, a white entertainer, began around 1828 to stage a vaudeville sketch in which he blacked his face with burned cork and sang a ditty that acquired the title "Wheel About and Turn About and Jump, Jim Crow." Thus was born what later became the immensely popular minstrel shows, a burlesque by whites of black songs and speech mannerisms. The term **Jim Crow**, from Rice's song, soon came to be a slang expression for blacks and was later applied to laws and practices that segregated blacks from whites.

African Americans in these localities that it would be foolhardy to try to vote or enroll in a white school. And even in those states where blacks did vote, popular attitudes were not conducive to blacks' buying homes or taking jobs on an equal basis with whites. Even among those professing to support equal rights, a substantial portion opposed African Americans, efforts to obtain them and federal action to secure them. In 1942 a national poll showed that only 30 percent of whites thought that black and white children should attend the same schools; in 1956 the proportion had risen, but only to 49 percent, still less than a majority. (In the South white support for school integration was even lower—14 percent favored it in 1956, about 31 percent in 1963.) As late as 1956 a majority of southern whites were opposed to integrated public transportation facilities. Even among whites who generally favored integration, there was in 1963 (*before* the ghetto riots) considerable opposition to the black civil rights movement: nearly half of the whites who were classified in a survey as moderate integrationists thought that demonstrations hurt the black cause; nearly two-thirds disapproved of actions taken by the civil rights movement; and over a third felt that civil rights should be left to the states.[4]

In short the political position in which African Americans found themselves until the 1960s made it difficult for them to advance their interests through a feasible legislative strategy: their opponents were aroused, organized, and powerful. Thus if black interests were to be championed in Congress or state legislatures, blacks would have to have white allies. Though some such allies could be found, they were too few to make a difference in a political system that gives a substantial advantage to strongly motivated opponents of any new policy. For that to change, one or both of two things would have to happen: additional allies would have to be recruited (a delicate problem, given that many white integrationists disapproved of aspects of the civil rights movement), or the struggle would have to be shifted to a policy-making arena in which the opposition enjoyed less of an advantage.

Partly by plan, partly by accident, black leaders followed both of these strategies simultaneously. By publicizing their grievances and organizing a civil rights movement that (at least in its early stages) concentrated on dramatizing the denial to blacks of essential and widely accepted liberties, African Americans were able to broaden their base of support both among political elites and among the general public and thereby to raise civil rights matters from a low to a high position on the political agenda. By waging a patient, prolonged, but carefully planned legal struggle, black leaders shifted decision-making power on key civil rights issues from Congress, where they had been stymied for generations, to the federal courts.

After this strategy had achieved some substantial successes—after blacks had become enfranchised and legal barriers to equal participation in political and economic affairs had been lowered—the politics of civil rights became more conventional. African Americans were able to assert their demands directly in the legislative and executive branches of government with reasonable (though scarcely certain) prospects of success. Civil rights became less a matter of gaining entry into the political system and more one of waging interest group politics within that system. At the same time, the goals of civil rights politics were broadened. The struggle to gain entry into the system had focused on the denial of fundamental rights (to vote, to organize, to obtain equal access to schools and public facilities); later the dominant issues were manpower development, economic progress, and the improvement of housing and neighborhoods.

The Campaign in the Courts

The Fourteenth Amendment was both an opportunity and a problem for black activists. Adopted in 1868, it seemed to guarantee equal rights for all: "No state shall make or enforce any law which shall abridge the privileges or immunities of citizens of the United States; nor shall any state deprive any person of life, liberty, or property, without due process of law; nor deny to any person within its jurisdiction the equal protection of the laws."

The key phrase was "equal protection of the laws." Read broadly, it might mean that the Constitution should be regarded as color-blind: no state law could have the effect of treating whites and blacks differently. Thus a law segregating blacks and whites into separate schools or neighborhoods would be unconstitutional. Read narrowly, "equal protection" might mean only that blacks and whites had certain fundamental legal rights in common, among them the right to sign contracts, to serve on juries, or to buy and sell property, but otherwise they could be treated differently.

Historians have long debated which view Congress held when it proposed the Fourteenth Amendment. What forms of racial segregation, if any, were still permissible? Segregated trains? Hotels? Schools? Neighborhoods?

The Supreme Court took the narrow view. Though in 1880 it declared unconstitutional a West Virginia law requiring juries to be composed only of white males,[5] it decided in 1883 that it was unconstitutional for Congress to prohibit racial discrimination in public accommodations such as hotels.[6] The difference between the two cases seemed, in the eyes of the Court, to be this: serving on a jury was an essential right of citizenship that the state could not deny to any person on racial grounds without violating the Fourteenth Amendment, but registering at a hotel was a convenience controlled by a private person (the hotel owner), who could treat blacks and whites differently if he or she wished.

The major decision that was to determine the legal status of the Fourteenth Amendment for over half a century was *Plessy v. Ferguson*. Louisiana had passed a law requiring blacks and whites to occupy separate cars on railroad trains operating in that state. When Adolph Plessy, who was seven-eighths white and one-eighth black, refused to obey the law, he was arrested. He appealed his conviction to the Supreme Court, claiming that the law violated the Fourteenth Amendment. In 1896 the Court rejected his claim, holding that the law treated both races equally even though it required them to be separate. The equal-protection clause guaranteed political and legal but not social equality. "Separate-but-equal" facilities were constitutional because if "one race be inferior to the other socially, the Constitution of the United States cannot put them on the same plane."[7]

"Separate but Equal"

Thus began the **separate-but-equal doctrine.** Three years later the Court applied it to schools as well, declaring in *Cumming v. Richmond County Board of Education* that a decision in a Georgia community to close the black high school while keeping open the white high school was not a violation of the Fourteenth Amendment because blacks could always go to private schools. Here the Court seemed to be saying that not only could schools be separate, they could even be unequal.[8]

What the Court has made, the Court can unmake. But to get it to change its mind requires a long, costly, and uncertain legal battle. The National Association for the Advancement of Colored People (NAACP) was the main organization that waged that battle. Formed in 1909 by a group of whites and blacks in the aftermath of a race riot, the NAACP did many things—lobbying in Washington and publicizing black grievances, especially in the pages of *The Crisis,* a magazine edited by W.E.B. Du Bois—but its most influential role was played in the courtroom.

It was a rational strategy. Fighting legal battles does not require forming broad political alliances or changing public opinion, tasks that would have been very difficult for a small and unpopular organization. A court-based approach also enabled the organization to remain nonpartisan.

The cover of the first issue of The Crisis, *the magazine started by the NAACP in 1910 to raise African American consciousness and publicize racist acts.*

But it was a slow and difficult strategy. The Court had adopted a narrow interpretation of the Fourteenth Amendment. To get the Court to change its mind would require the NAACP to bring before it cases involving the strongest possible claims that a black had been unfairly treated—and under circumstances sufficiently different from those of earlier cases that the Court could find some grounds for changing its mind.

The steps in that strategy were these: First, persuade the Court to declare unconstitutional laws creating schools that were separate but obviously unequal. Second, persuade it to declare unconstitutional laws supporting schools that were separate but unequal in not-so-obvious ways. Third, persuade it to rule that racially separate schools were inherently unequal and hence unconstitutional.

What would you do?

MEMORANDUM

To: Justice Murray
From: Ella Fitzgerald, law clerk

Until school segregation ended, southern blacks could attend only all-black colleges. Now they are free to apply to previously all-white colleges, and these schools are integrated. But the traditional black colleges still exist, and very few whites apply to them. In 1992 the Supreme Court held that the state could not solve the problem by requiring a race-neutral admissions policy.* Now the Court must decide whether a predominantly black college can receive state support.

Arguments for all-black colleges:

1. These schools have a long tradition that ought to be preserved.
2. Many black students will learn better in an all-black environment.
3. African American organizations, in particular the United Negro College Fund, raise money for these schools.

Arguments against all-black colleges:

1. If the state once required single-race schools, it now has an obligation to dismantle them.
2. Race is a suspect classification, and no state program that chiefly serves one race can be allowed.

Your decision:
Allow all-black colleges _____
Ban all-black colleges _____

*United States v. Fordice, 505 U.S. 717 (1992).

Court to Rule on Black Colleges

January 19
WASHINGTON
The Supreme Court has announced that it will decide whether all-black colleges in the South can receive state support if there are too few whites attending them. The case began in Mississippi, where . . .

Can Separate Schools Be Equal?

The first step was accomplished in a series of court cases stretching from 1938 to 1948. In 1938 the Court held that Lloyd Gaines had to be admitted to an all-white law school in Missouri because no black law school of equal quality existed in that state.[9] In 1948 the Court ordered the all-white University of Oklahoma Law School to admit Ada Lois Sipuel, a black, even though the state planned to build a black law school later. For education to be equal, it had to be equally available.[10] It still could be separate, however: the university admitted Ms. Sipuel but required her to attend classes in a section of the state capitol, roped off from other students, where she could meet with her law professors.

The second step was taken in two cases decided in 1950. Heman Sweatt, an African American, was treated by the University of Texas Law School much as Ada Sipuel had been treated in Oklahoma: "admitted" to the all-white school but relegated to a separate building. Another African American, George McLaurin, was allowed to study for his Ph.D. in a "colored section" of the all-white University of Oklahoma. The Supreme Court unanimously decided that these arrangements were unconstitutional because, by imposing racially based barriers on the black students' access to professors, libraries, and other students, they created unequal educational opportunities.[11]

The third step, the climax of the entire drama, began in Topeka, Kansas, where Linda Brown wanted to enroll in her neighborhood school but could not because she was black and the school was by law reserved exclusively for whites. When the NAACP took her case to the federal district court in Kansas, the judge decided that the black school that Linda could attend was substantially equal in quality to the white school that she could not attend. Thus denying her access to the white school was constitutional. To change that the lawyers would have to persuade the Supreme Court to overrule the district judge on the grounds that racially separate schools were unconstitutional even if they were equal. In other words, the separate-but-equal doctrine would have to be overturned by the Court.

It was a risky and controversial step to take. Many states, Kansas among them, were trying to make their all-black schools equal to those of whites by launching expensive building programs. If the NAACP succeeded in getting separate schools declared unconstitutional, the Court might well put a stop to the building of these new schools. Blacks could win a moral and legal victory but suffer a practical defeat—the loss of these new facilities. Despite these risks, the NAACP decided to go ahead with the appeal.

Brown v. Board of Education

On May 17, 1954, a unanimous Supreme Court, speaking through an opinion written and delivered by Chief Justice Earl Warren, found that "in the field of public education the doctrine of 'separate but equal' has no place" because "separate educational facilities are inherently unequal."[12] *Plessy v. Ferguson* was overruled, and "separate but equal" was dead.

The ruling was a landmark decision, but the reasons for it and the means chosen to implement it were as important and as controversial as the decision itself. There were at least three issues. First, how would the decision be implemented? Second, on what grounds were racially separate schools unconstitutional? Third, what test would a school system have to meet in order to be in conformity with the Constitution?

Implementation The *Brown* case involved a class-action suit; that is, it applied not only to Linda Brown but to all others similarly situated. This meant that black children everywhere now had the right to attend formerly all-white schools. This change would be one of the most far-reaching and conflict-provoking events in modern American history. It could not be effected overnight or by the stroke of a pen. In 1955 the Supreme Court decided that it would let local federal district courts oversee the end of segregation by giving them the power to approve or disapprove local desegregation plans. This was to be done "with all deliberate speed."[13]

In the South "all deliberate speed" turned out to be a snail's pace. Massive resistance to desegregation broke out in many states. Some communities simply defied the Court; some sought to evade its edict by closing their public schools. In 1956 over one hundred southern members of Congress signed a "Southern Manifesto" that condemned the *Brown* decision as an "abuse of judicial power" and pledged to "use all lawful means to bring about a reversal of the decision."

On September 25, 1957, troops of the 101st Airborne Division escorted nine black children into Little Rock (Arkansas) Central High School to begin its integration.

In the late 1950s and early 1960s the National Guard and regular army paratroopers were used to escort black students into formerly all-white schools and universities. It was not until the 1970s that resistance collapsed and most southern schools were integrated. The use of armed force convinced people that resistance was futile; the disruption of the politics and economy of the South convinced leaders that it was imprudent; and the voting power of blacks convinced politicians that it was suicidal. In addition, federal laws began providing financial aid to integrated schools and withholding it from segregated ones. By 1970 only 14 percent of southern black schoolchildren still attended all-black schools.[14]

The Rationale   As the struggle to implement the *Brown* decision continued, the importance of the rationale for that decision became apparent. The case was decided in a way that surprised many legal scholars. The Court could have said that the equal-protection clause of the Fourteenth Amendment makes the Constitution, and thus state laws, color-blind. Or it could have said that the authors of the Fourteenth Amendment meant to ban segregated schools. It did neither. Instead it said that segregated education is bad because it "has a detrimental effect upon the colored children" by generating "a feeling of inferiority as to their status in the community" that may "affect their hearts and minds in a way unlikely ever to be undone."[15] This conclusion was supported by a footnote reference to social science studies of the apparent impact of segregation on black children.

Why did the Court rely on social science as much as or more than the Constitution in supporting its decision? Apparently for two reasons. One was the justices' realization that the authors of the Fourteenth Amendment may *not* have intended to outlaw segregated schools. The schools in Washington, D.C., were segregated when the amendment was proposed, and when this fact was mentioned during the debate, it seems to have been made clear that the amendment was not designed to abolish this segregation. When Congress debated a civil rights act a few years later, it voted down provisions that would have ended segregation in schools.[16] The Court could not easily base its decision on a constitutional provision that had, at best, an uncertain application to schools. The other reason grew out of the first. On so important a matter the chief justice wanted to speak for a unanimous court. Some justices did not agree that the Fourteenth Amendment made the Constitution color-blind. In the interests of harmony the Court found an ambiguous rationale for its decision.

Desegregation Versus Integration   That ambiguity led to the third issue. If separate schools were inherently unequal, what would "unseparate" schools look like? Since the Court had not said that race was irrelevant, an "unseparate" school could be either one that blacks and whites were free to attend if they chose or one that blacks and whites in fact attended whether they wanted to or not. The first might be called a desegregated school, the latter an integrated school. Think of the Topeka case. Was it enough that there was now no barrier to Linda Brown's attending the white school in her neighborhood? Or was it necessary that there be black children (if not Linda, then some others) actually going to that school together with white children?

As long as the main impact of the *Brown* decision lay in the South, where laws had prevented blacks from attending white schools, this question did not seem important. Segregation by law (***de jure* segregation**) was now clearly unconstitutional. But in the North laws had not kept blacks and whites apart; instead all-black and all-white schools were the result of residential segregation, preferred living patterns, informal social forces, and administrative practices (such as drawing school district lines so as to produce single-race schools). This was often called segregation in fact (***de facto* segregation**).

In 1968 the Supreme Court settled the matter. In New Kent County, Virginia, the school board had created a "freedom-of-choice" plan under which every pupil would be allowed without legal restriction to attend the school of his or her choice. As it turned out, all the white children chose to remain in the all-white school, and 85 percent of the black children remained in the all-black school. The Court rejected this plan as unconstitutional because it did not produce the "ultimate end," which was a "unitary, nonracial system of education."[17] In the opinion written by Justice William Brennan, the Court seemed to be saying that the Constitution required actual racial mixing in the schools, not just the repeal of laws requiring racial separation.

This impression was confirmed three years later when the Court considered a plan in North Carolina under which pupils in Mecklenburg County (which includes Charlotte) were assigned to the nearest neighborhood school without regard to race. As a

In 1963 Governor George Wallace of Alabama stood in the doorway of the University of Alabama to block the entry of black students. Facing him is U.S. Deputy Attorney General Nicholas Katzenbach.

result about half the black children now attended formerly all-white schools, with the other half attending all-black schools. The federal district court held that this was inadequate and ordered some children to be bused into more distant schools in order to achieve a greater degree of integration. The Supreme Court, now led by Chief Justice Warren Burger, upheld the district judge on the grounds that the court plan was necessary to achieve a "unitary school system."[18]

This case—*Swann v. Charlotte-Mecklenburg Board of Education*—pretty much set the guidelines for all subsequent cases involving school segregation. The essential features of those guidelines are as follows:

- To violate the Constitution, a school system, by law, practice, or regulation, must have engaged in discrimination. Put another way, a plaintiff must show an intent to discriminate on the part of the public schools.
- The existence of all-white or all-black schools in a district with a history of segregation creates a presumption of intent to discriminate.
- The remedy for past discrimination will not be limited to freedom of choice, or what the Court called "the walk-in school." Remedies may include racial

Antibusing protesters buried a school bus (unoccupied) to drama-tize their cause.

quotas in the assignment of teachers and pupils, redrawn district lines, and court-ordered busing.
• Not every school must reflect the social composi-tion of the school system as a whole.

Relying on *Swann*, district courts have supervised redistricting and busing plans in localities all over the nation, often in the face of bitter opposition from the community. In Boston the control of the city schools by a federal judge, W. Arthur Garrity, lasted for more than a decade and involved him in every aspect of school administration.

One major issue not settled by *Swann* was whether busing and other remedies should cut across city and county lines. In some places the central-city schools had become virtually all black. Racial integration could be achieved only by bringing black pupils to white suburban schools or moving white pupils into central-city schools. In a series of split-vote decisions the Court ruled that court-ordered intercity busing could be authorized only if it could be demonstrated that the suburban areas as well as the central city had in fact practiced school segregation. Where that could not be shown, such intercity busing would not be required. The Court was not persuaded that intent had been proved in Atlanta, Detroit, Denver, Indi-anapolis, and Richmond, but it was persuaded that it had been proved in Louisville and Wilmington.[19]

The importance that the Court attaches to intent means that if a school system that was once inte-grated becomes all black as a result of whites' mov-ing to the suburbs, the Court will not require that district lines constantly be redrawn or new busing plans adopted to adjust to the changing distribution of the population.[20] This in turn means that as long as blacks and whites live in different neighborhoods for whatever reason, there is a good chance that some schools in both areas will be heavily of one race. If mandatory busing or other integration measures cause whites to move out of a city at a faster rate than they otherwise would (a process often called "white flight"), then efforts to integrate the schools may in time create more single-race schools. Ultimately integrated schools will exist only in integrated neighborhoods or where the quality of education is so high that both blacks and whites want to enroll in the school even at some cost in terms of travel and inconvenience.

Mandatory busing to achieve racial integration has been a deeply controversial program and has generated considerable public opposition. Surveys show that a majority of people oppose it.[21] As recently as 1992 a poll showed that 48 percent of whites in the Northeast and 53 percent of southern whites felt that it was "not the business" of the fed-eral government to ensure "that black and white children go to the same schools."[22] Presidents Nixon, Ford, and Reagan opposed busing; all three sup-ported legislation to prevent or reduce it, and Rea-gan petitioned the courts to reconsider busing plans. The courts refused to reconsider, and Congress has passed only minor restrictions on busing.

The reason why Congress has not followed public opinion on this matter is complex. It has been torn between the desire to support civil rights and uphold

Chronology of Major Events in the Civil Rights Movement, 1955–1968

Dec. 5, 1955	Blacks in Montgomery, Alabama, begin yearlong boycott of bus company; the Reverend Martin Luther King, Jr., emerges as leader.
Feb. 1, 1960	First sit-in demonstration. Black students at North Carolina Agricultural and Technical College sit in at a dime-store lunch counter in Greensboro.
May 4, 1961	Freedom rides begin as blacks attempt to ride in white sections of interstate buses. Violence erupts, a bus is burned, U.S. marshals are dispatched to restore order.
Sept. 30, 1962	Violence greets effort of James Meredith, a black, to enroll in University of Mississippi.
April 3, 1963	Demonstrations by blacks begin in Birmingham, Alabama; police retaliate.
June 12, 1963	Medgar Evers, Mississippi state chairman of NAACP, murdered in Jackson.
Aug. 28, 1963	March on Washington by 250,000 whites and blacks.
Fall 1963	Blacks boycott schools in several northern cities to protest *de facto* segregation.
June 1964	Three civil rights workers killed in Neshoba County, Mississippi.
Summer 1964	First ghetto riots by blacks in northern cities, beginning in Harlem on July 18.
Jan. 2, 1965	King begins protest marches in Selma, Alabama; police attack marchers in February and March.
Aug. 11, 1965	Black riots in Watts section of Los Angeles and on West Side of Chicago.
June 6, 1966	James Meredith shot (but not killed) while on protest march in Mississippi.
Summer 1966	Black ghetto riots in Chicago, Cleveland, New York, and other cities; King leads protest marches in Chicago.
Summer 1967	Riots or violent demonstrations in 67 cities.
April 4, 1968	Martin Luther King, Jr., murdered in Memphis, Tennessee.

the courts and the desire to represent the views of its constituents. Because it faces a dilemma, Congress has taken both sides of the issue simultaneously.

During the 1970s the House of Representatives passed bills restricting busing, but the Senate amended them to allow busing ordered by a court. The result was no policy at all. In 1981 the Senate approved a bill forbidding federal judges from ordering busing except in very narrow circumstances, but it never became law. Although a House version of these bills was adopted in 1982, it, too, never became law. Throughout the 1980s Congress did enact laws forbidding the use of federal funds to bus schoolchildren for purposes of racial integration;

these laws had little effect, however, since a judge could still order states and cities to pay the costs. By the late 1980s busing was a dying issue in Congress, in part because no meaningful legislation seemed possible and in part because popular passion over busing had somewhat abated.

Then, in 1992, the Supreme Court made it easier for local school systems to reclaim control over their schools from the courts. In DeKalb County, Georgia (a suburb of Atlanta), the schools had been operating under court-ordered desegregation plans for many years. Despite this effort full integration had not been achieved, largely because the county's neighborhoods had increasingly become either all black or all white. The Court held that the local schools could not be held responsible for segregation caused solely by segregated living patterns and so the courts would have to relinquish their control over the schools.[23]

The Campaign in Congress

The campaign in the courts for desegregated schools, though slow and costly, was a carefully managed effort to alter the interpretation of a constitutional provision. But to get new civil rights laws out of Congress required a far more difficult and decentralized strategy, one that was aimed at mobilizing public opinion and overcoming the many congressional barriers to action.

The first problem was to get civil rights on the political agenda by convincing people that something had to be done. This could be achieved by dramatizing the problem in ways that tugged at the conscience of whites who were not racist but were ordinarily indifferent to black problems. Brutal lynchings of blacks had shocked these whites, but lynchings were becoming less frequent in the 1950s, and obviously black leaders had no desire to provoke more lynchings just to get sympathy for their cause.

Those leaders could, however, arrange for dramatic confrontations between blacks claiming some obvious right and the whites who denied it to them.

Beginning in the late 1950s these confrontations began to occur in the form of sit-ins at segregated lunch counters and "freedom rides" on segregated bus lines. At about the same time, efforts were made to get blacks registered to vote in counties where whites had used intimidation and harassment to prevent it.

The best-known campaign occurred in 1955–1956 in Montgomery, Alabama, where blacks, led by a young minister named Martin Luther King, Jr., boycotted the local bus system after it had a black woman, Rosa Parks, arrested because she refused to surrender her seat on a bus to a white man.

These early demonstrations were based on the philosophy of **nonviolent civil disobedience**—that is, peacefully violating a law, such as one requiring blacks to ride in a segregated section of a bus, and allowing oneself to be arrested as a result.

But the momentum of protest, once unleashed, could not be centrally directed or confined to nonviolent action. A rising tide of anger, especially among younger blacks, resulted in the formation of more militant organizations and the spontaneous eruption of violent demonstrations and riots in dozens of cities across the country. From 1964 to 1968 there were in the North as well as the South four "long, hot summers" of racial violence.

The demonstrations and rioting succeeded in getting civil rights on the national political agenda, but at a cost: many whites, opposed to the demonstra-

In 1960 black students from North Carolina Agricultural and Technical College staged the first "sit-in" when they were refused service at a lunch counter in Greensboro (left). Twenty years later graduates of the college returned to the same lunch counter (right). Though prices had risen, the service had improved.

tions or appalled by the riots, dug in their heels and fought against making any concessions to "lawbreakers," "troublemakers," and "rioters." In 1964 and again in 1968 over two-thirds of the whites interviewed in opinion polls said that the civil rights movement was pushing too fast, had hurt the black cause, and was too violent.[24]

In short there was a conflict between the agenda-setting and coalition-building aspects of the civil rights movement. This was especially a problem since conservative southern legislators still controlled many key congressional committees that had for years been the graveyard of civil rights legislation. The Senate Judiciary Committee was dominated by a coalition of southern Democrats and conservative Republicans, and the House Rules Committee was under the control of a chairman hostile to civil rights bills, Howard Smith of Virginia. Any bill that passed the House faced an almost certain filibuster in the Senate. Finally, President John F. Kennedy was reluctant to submit strong civil rights bills to Congress.

Four developments made it possible to break the deadlock. First, public opinion was changing. As Figure 16.1 shows, between 1959 and 1965 the proportion of whites who said that they were willing to

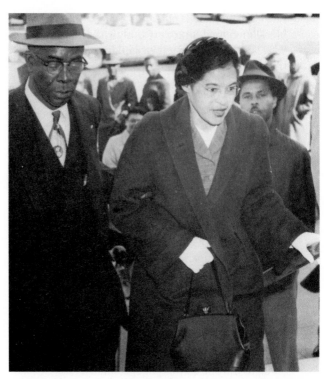

Rosa Parks was arrested for refusing to move to the black section at the back of a bus in Montgomery, Alabama.

Figure 16.1 Changing White Attitudes Toward Differing Levels of School Integration

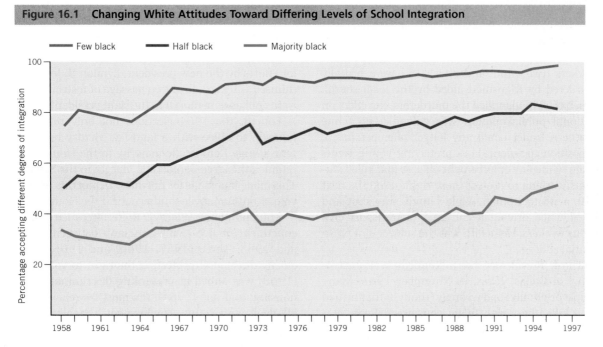

Source: Reprinted by permission of the publisher from *Racial Attitudes in America* by Howard Schuman, Cambridge, Mass.: Harvard University Press. Copyright © 1985 by the Presidents and Fellows of Harvard College.

have their children attend a school that was half black increased sharply (though the proportion of whites willing to have their children attend a school that was predominantly black increased by much less). About the same change could be found in attitudes toward allowing blacks equal access to hotels and buses.[25] Of course support in principle for these civil rights measures was not necessarily the same as support in practice; nonetheless, there clearly was occurring a major shift in popular approval of at least the principles of civil rights. At the leading edge of this change were young, college-educated people.[26]

Second, certain violent reactions by white segregationists to black demonstrators were vividly portrayed by the media, especially television, in ways that gave to the civil rights cause a powerful moral force. In May 1963 the head of the Birmingham police, Eugene "Bull" Connor, ordered his men to use attack dogs and high-pressure fire hoses to repulse a peaceful march by African Americans demanding desegregated public facilities and increased job opportunities. The pictures of that confrontation (such as the one on this page) created a national sensation and contributed greatly to the massive participation, by whites and blacks alike, in the "March on Washington" that summer. About a quarter of a million people gathered in front of the Lincoln Memorial to hear Martin Luther King, Jr., deliver a stirring and widely hailed address, often called the "I Have a Dream" speech. The following summer in Neshoba County, Mississippi, three young civil rights workers (two white and one black) were brutally murdered by Klansmen aided by the local sheriff. When the FBI identified the murderers, the effect on national public opinion was galvanic: no white southern leader could any longer offer persuasive opposition to federal laws protecting voting rights when white law enforcement officers had killed students working to protect those rights. And the next year a white woman, Viola Liuzzo, was shot and killed while driving a car used to transport civil rights workers. Her death was the subject of a presidential address.

Third, President John F. Kennedy was assassinated in Dallas, Texas, in November 1963. Many people originally (and wrongly) thought that he had been killed by a right-wing conspiracy. Even after the assassin had been caught and shown to have left-wing associations, the shock of the president's murder—in a southern city—helped build support

This picture of a police dog lunging at a black man during a racial demonstration in Birmingham, Alabama, in May 1963 was one of the most influential news photographs ever published. It was widely reprinted throughout the world and was frequently referred to in congressional debates on the civil rights bill of 1964.

for efforts by the new president, Lyndon B. Johnson (himself a Texan), to obtain passage of a strong civil rights bill as a memorial to the slain president.

Fourth, the 1964 elections not only returned Johnson to office with a landslide victory but also sent a huge Democratic majority to the House and retained the large Democratic margin in the Senate. This made it possible for northern Democrats to outvote or outmaneuver southerners in the House.

The cumulative effect of these forces led to the enactment of five civil rights laws between 1957 and 1968. Three (1957, 1960, and 1965) were chiefly directed at protecting the right to vote; one (1968) was aimed at preventing discrimination in housing; and one (1964), the most far-reaching of all, dealt with voting, employment, schooling, and public accommodations.

The passage of the 1964 act was the high point of the legislative struggle. Liberals in the House had

Key Provisions of Major Civil Rights Laws

1957   **Voting**   Made it a federal crime to try to prevent a person from voting in a federal election. Created the Civil Rights Commission.

1960   **Voting**   Authorized the attorney general to appoint federal referees to gather evidence and make findings about allegations that African Americans were being deprived of their right to vote. Made it a federal crime to use interstate commerce to threaten or carry out a bombing.

1964   **Voting**   Made it more difficult to use devices such as literacy tests to bar African Americans from voting.

        Public accommodations   Barred discrimination on grounds of race, color, religion, or national origin in restaurants, hotels, lunch counters, gasoline stations, movie theaters, stadiums, arenas, and lodging houses with more than five rooms.

        Schools   Authorized the attorney general to bring suit to force the desegregation of public schools on behalf of citizens.

        Employment   Outlawed discrimination in hiring, firing, or paying employees on grounds of race, color, religion, national origin, or sex.

        Federal funds   Barred discrimination in any activity receiving federal assistance.

1965   **Voter registration**   Authorized appointment by the Civil Service Commission of voting examiners who would require registration of all eligible voters in federal, state, and local elections, general or primary, in areas where discrimination was found to be practiced or where less than 50 percent of voting-age residents were registered to vote in 1964 election. The law was to have expired in 1970, but Congress extended it; it will expire in 2007.

        Literacy tests   Suspended use of literacy tests or other devices to prevent African Americans from voting.

1968   **Housing**   Banned, by stages, discrimination in sale or rental of most housing (excluding private owners who sell or rent their homes without the services of a real-estate broker).

        Riots   Made it a federal crime to use interstate commerce to organize or incite a riot.

1972   **Education**   Prohibited sex discrimination in education programs receiving federal aid.

1988   **Discrimination**   If any part of an organization receives federal aid, no part of that organization may discriminate on the basis of race, sex, age, or physical handicap.

1991   **Discrimination**   Made it easier to sue over job discrimination and collect damages; overturned certain Supreme Court decisions. Made it illegal for the government to adjust, or "norm," test scores by race.

---

drafted a bipartisan bill, but it was now in the House Rules Committee, where such matters had often disappeared without a trace. In the wake of Kennedy's murder a discharge petition was filed, with President Johnson's support, to take the bill out of committee and bring it to the floor of the House. But the Rules Committee, without waiting for a vote on the petition (which it probably realized it would lose), sent the bill to the floor, where it passed overwhelmingly. In the Senate an agreement between Republican minority leader Everett Dirksen and President Johnson smoothed the way for passage in several important respects. The House bill was sent directly to the Senate floor, thereby bypassing the southern-dominated Judiciary Committee. Nineteen southern senators began an eight-week filibuster against the bill. On June 10, 1964, by a vote of seventy-one to twenty-nine, cloture was invoked and the filibuster ended—the first time in history that a filibuster aimed at blocking civil rights legislation had been broken.

President Lyndon Johnson signs the Civil Rights Act of 1965 in the company of the Reverend Martin Luther King, Jr., and the Reverend Ralph Abernathy.

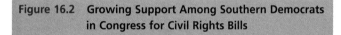

Figure 16.2   Growing Support Among Southern Democrats in Congress for Civil Rights Bills

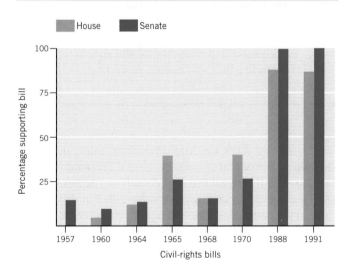

Sources: Congressional Quarterly, *Congress and the Nation,* vols. 1, 2, 3, 7, 8.

Since the 1960s congressional support for civil rights legislation has grown—so much so, indeed, that labeling a bill a civil rights measure, once the kiss of death, now almost guarantees its passage. For example, in 1984 the Supreme Court decided that the federal ban on discrimination in education applied only to the "program or activity" receiving federal aid and not to the entire school or university.[27] In 1988 Congress passed a bill to overturn this decision by making it clear that antidiscrimination rules applied to the entire educational institution and not just to that part (say, the physics lab) receiving federal money. When President Reagan vetoed the bill (because, in his view, it would diminish the freedom of church-affiliated schools), Congress overrode the veto. In the override vote every southern Democrat in the Senate and almost 90 percent of those in the House voted for the bill. This was a dramatic change from 1964, when over 80 percent of the southern Democrats in Congress voted against the Civil Rights Act (see Figure 16.2).

Table 16.1	Increase in Number of Black Elected Officials		
Office	1970	1991	1993
Congress and state legislatures	182	476	561
City and county offices	715	4,493	4,819
Judges and sheriffs	213	847	922
Boards of education	362	1,629	1,682
Total	1,472	7,445	7,984

Sources: Statistical Abstract of the United States, 1990, 260; Statistical Abstract of the United States, 1992, 267; Statistical Abstract of the United States, 1995, 287.

This change partly reflected the growing political strength of southern blacks. In 1960 less than one-third of voting-age blacks in the South were registered to vote; by 1971 more than half were, and by 1984 two-thirds were. In 1993 over nearly eight thousand blacks held elective office in the South (see Table 16.1). But this was only half of the story. Attitudes among white political elites and members of Congress had also changed. This was evident as early as 1968, when Congress passed a law barring discrimination in housing even though polls showed that only 35 percent of the public supported the measure.

Civil rights is not an issue easily confined to schools, housing, and jobs. Sometimes it is extended to crime. When crack cocaine became a popular drug, it was cheap and easily sold on street corners. When the public demanded that the police get tough on crack dealers, arrests followed. Since the great majority of arrested dealers were black, there was a sharp increase in black drug dealers going to prison. Some blacks claimed that they were being singled out by the police because of their race. The Supreme Court disagreed, holding that no evidence had been presented to show that drug dealers of other races had not been prosecuted.[28]

Women and Equal Rights

The political and legal efforts to secure civil rights for African Americans were accompanied by efforts to expand the rights of women. There was an important difference between the two movements, however: whereas African Americans were arguing against a legal tradition that explicitly aimed to keep them in a subservient status, women had to argue against a tradition that claimed to be protecting them. For example, in 1908 the Supreme Court upheld an Oregon law that limited female laundry workers to a ten-hour workday against the claim that it violated the Fourteenth Amendment. The Court justified its decision with this language:

> The two sexes differ in structure of body, in the functions to be performed by each, in the amount of physical strength, in the capacity for long-continued labor, particularly when done standing, . . . the self-reliance which enables one to assert full rights, and in the capacity to maintain the struggle for subsistence. This difference justifies a difference in legislation and upholds that which is designed to compensate for some of the burdens which rest upon her.[29]

The feminist movement that resurfaced not long after the civil rights movement questioned the claim that women differed from men in ways that justified differences in legal status. Congress responded by passing laws that required equal pay for equal work, prohibited discrimination on the basis of sex in employment and among students in any school or university receiving federal funds, and banned discrimination against pregnant women on the job.[30]

At the same time, the Supreme Court was altering the way it interpreted the Constitution. The key

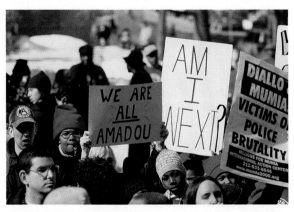

Fighting crime creates risks, as when someone is wrongly shot.

Though many women have enlisted in the armed forces, the Supreme Court in 1981 held that Congress could exclude women from the draft.

passage was the Fourteenth Amendment, which prohibits any state from denying to "any person" the "equal protection of the laws." For a long time the traditional standard, as we saw in the 1908 case, was a kind of protective paternalism. By the early 1970s, however, the Court had changed its mind. In deciding whether the Constitution bars all, some, or no sexual discrimination, the Court had a choice between two standards. The first is the *reasonableness* standard. This says that when the government treats some classes of people differently from others— for example, applying statutory rape laws to men but not to women—the different treatment must be reasonable and not arbitrary. The second is the **strict scrutiny** standard. This says that some instances of drawing distinctions between different groups of people—for example, by treating whites and blacks differently—are inherently suspect; thus the Court will subject them to strict scrutiny to ensure that they are clearly necessary to attain a legitimate state goal.

When women complained that some laws treated them unfairly, the Court adopted a standard somewhere between the reasonableness and strict scrutiny tests. Thus a law that treats men and women differently must be more than merely reasonable, but the allowable differences need not meet the strict scrutiny test.

And so in 1971 the Court held that an Idaho statute was unconstitutional because it required that males be preferred over females when choosing people to administer the estates of deceased children. To satisfy the Constitution, a law treating men and women differently "must be reasonable, not arbitrary, and must rest on some ground of difference having a fair and substantial relation to the object of legislation so that all persons similarly circumstanced shall be treated alike."[31] In later decisions some members of the Court wanted to make classifications based on sex inherently suspect and subject to the strict scrutiny test, but no majority has yet embraced this position.[32]

But sexual classifications can also be judged by a different standard. The Civil Rights Act of 1964 prohibits sex discrimination in the hiring, firing, and compensation of employees. The 1972 Civil Rights Act bans sex discrimination in local education programs receiving federal aid. These laws apply to *private* and not just government action.

Over the years the Court has decided many cases involving sexual classification. The following lists provide several examples of illegal sexual discrimination (violating either the Constitution or a civil rights act) and legal sexual distinctions (violating neither).

Illegal Discrimination

- A state cannot set different ages at which men and women legally become adults.[33]
- A state cannot set different ages at which men and women are allowed to buy beer.[34]
- Women cannot be barred from jobs by arbitrary height and weight requirements.[35]
- Employers cannot require women to take mandatory pregnancy leaves.[36]
- Girls cannot be barred from Little League baseball teams.[37]

- Business and service clubs, such as the Junior Chamber of Commerce and Rotary Club, cannot exclude women from membership.[38]
- Though women as a group live longer than men, an employer must pay them monthly retirement benefits equal to those received by men.[39]
- High schools must pay the coaches of girls' sports the same as they pay the coaches of boys' sports.[40]

Decisions Allowing Differences Based on Sex

- A law that punishes males but not females for statutory rape is permissible; men and women are not "similarly situated" with respect to sexual relations.[41]
- All-boy and all-girl public schools are permitted if enrollment is voluntary and quality is equal.[42]
- States can give widows a property-tax exemption not given to widowers.[43]
- The navy may allow women to remain officers longer than men without being promoted.[44]

The lower federal courts have been especially busy in the area of sexual distinctions. They have said that public taverns may not cater to men only and that girls may not be prevented from competing against boys in noncontact high school sports; on the other hand, hospitals may bar fathers from the delivery room. Women may continue to use their maiden names after marriage.[45]

In 1996 the Supreme Court ruled that women must be admitted to the Virginia Military Institute, until then an all-male state-supported college that had for many decades supplied what it called an "adversative method" of training to instill physical and mental discipline in cadets. In practical terms this meant being very tough on students. The Court said that for a state to justify spending tax money on a single-sex school, it must supply an "exceedingly persuasive justification" for excluding the other gender. Virginia countered by offering to support an all-female training course at another college, but this was not enough.[46] This decision came close to imposing the strict scrutiny test, and so it has raised important questions about what could happen to all-female or traditionally black colleges that accept state money.

Perhaps the most far-reaching cases defining the rights of women have involved the draft and abortion. In 1981 the Court held in *Rostker v. Goldberg* that Congress may require men but not women to register for the draft without violating the due-

process clause of the Fifth Amendment.[47] In the area of national defense the Court will give great deference to congressional policy (Congress had already decided to bar women from combat roles). For many years women could be pilots and sailors but not on combat aircraft or combat ships. In 1993 the secretary of defense opened air and sea combat positions to all persons regardless of gender; only ground-troop combat positions are still reserved for men. The issue played a role in preventing the ratification of the Equal Rights Amendment to the Constitution, because of fears that it would reverse *Rostker v. Goldberg,* and remains controversial.

Sexual Harassment

When Paula Corbin Jones accused President Clinton of sexual harassment, the judge threw the case out of court because she had not submitted enough evidence such that, if the jury believed her story, she would have made a legally adequate argument that she had been sexually harassed.

What, then, is sexual harassment? Drawing on rulings by the Equal Employment Opportunities Commission, the Supreme Court has held that harassment can take one of two forms. First, it is illegal for someone to request sexual favors as a condition of employment or promotion. This is the "quid pro quo" rule. If a person does this, the employer is "strictly liable." Strict liability means that the employer can be found at fault even if he or she did not know that a subordinate was requesting sex in exchange for hiring or promotion.

Second, it is illegal for an employee to experience a work environment that has been made hostile or intimidating by a steady pattern of offensive sexual teasing, jokes, or obscenity. But employers are not strictly liable in this case; they can be found at fault only if they were "negligent"—that is, they knew about the hostile environment but did nothing about it.

In 1998 the Supreme Court decided three cases that made these rules either better or worse, depending on your point of view. In one it determined that a school system was not liable for the conduct of a teacher who seduced a female student because the student never reported the actions. In a second it held that a city was liable for a sexually hostile work environment confronting a female lifeguard even though she did not report this to her superiors. In the third it decided that a female employee who was not

The Constitutional Position of Abortion Laws

This is what a narrow majority of the Court held in decisions made in 1992 and 2000:

1. "It is a constitutional liberty of the woman to have some freedom to terminate her pregnancy. . . . No state may prohibit a woman from terminating her pregnancy" before the fetus becomes "viable."
2. After the fetus has become viable, a state may "regulate, and even proscribe, abortion except where it is necessary . . . for the preservation of the life and the health of the mother."

3. States may put restrictions on the right to an abortion, but these restrictions must not place an "undue burden" on the exercise of a woman's rights.
4. States may not ban partial birth abortions—that is, abortions performed by removing most of the fetus from the womb and then collapsing its skull—if the procedure is performed before the fetus, if born, could live or if it is performed to "preserve the health of the mother."

Sources: Planned Parenthood v. Casey, 112 S. Ct. 291 (1992); Stenberg v. Carhart, 2000 Lexis 4484 (2000).

---

promoted after having rejected the sexual advances of her boss could recover financial damages from the firm. But, it added, the firm could have avoided paying this bill if it had put in place an "affirmative defense" against sexual exploitation, although the Court never said what such a policy might be.[48]

Sexual harassment is a serious matter, but because there are almost no federal laws governing it, we are left with somewhat vague and often inconsistent court and bureaucratic rules to guide us.

When the Supreme Court decided the abortion issue, it guaranteed endless protests, as here in front of its building.

Abortion

Until 1973 it was up to the states to decide whether and under what circumstances a woman could obtain an abortion. For example, New York allowed abortion on demand during the first twenty-four weeks of pregnancy, but Texas banned abortion except when the mother's life was threatened.

By a seven-to-two vote in the 1973 case of *Roe v. Wade*, the Supreme Court struck down the Texas law (and all similar state laws).[49] The majority argued that the due-process clause of the Fourteenth Amendment implies a "right to privacy" that protects a woman's freedom to choose, during the first three months of pregnancy, whether to have an abortion. (During the second three months, or trimester, the states are allowed to regulate abortion procedures to protect the mother's health; during the final trimester, states might ban abortions.)

In reaching this decision, the Court denied that it was trying to decide when human life began—at the moment of conception, at the moment of birth, or somewhere in between. But that is not how critics of the decision saw things. To them life begins at conception, and so the human fetus is a "person" entitled to the equal protection of the laws guaranteed by the Fourteenth Amendment. People feeling this way began to use the slogans "right to life" and "pro-life." Supporters of the Court's action saw matters differently. In their view, no one can say for certain when human life begins; what one *can* say, however, is that a woman is entitled to choose whether or not to have a baby. These people took the slogans "right to choose" and "pro-choice."

Almost immediately the congressional allies of pro-life groups introduced constitutional amendments to overturn *Roe v. Wade,* but none passed Congress. Nevertheless, abortion foes did persuade Congress, beginning in 1976, to bar the use of federal funds to pay for abortions except when the life of the mother is at stake. This provision is known as the Hyde Amendment, after its sponsor, Representative Henry Hyde. The chief effect of the amendment has been to deny the use of Medicaid funds to pay for abortions for low-income women. (In 1980 the Supreme Court upheld the constitutionality of the Hyde amendment.)[50] During the Bush administration the government carried the spirit of this amendment one step further by barring the use of federal funds for family planning clinics that provided abortion counseling. Called a "gag rule" by some, this policy was repealed by the Clinton administration.

Despite pro-life opposition, the Supreme Court for sixteen years steadfastly reaffirmed and even broadened its decision in *Roe v. Wade.* It struck down laws requiring, before an abortion could be performed, a woman to have the consent of her husband, an "emancipated" but underage girl to have the consent of her parents, or a woman to be advised by her doctor as to the facts about abortion.[51]

But in 1989, under the influence of justices appointed by President Reagan, it began in the *Webster* case to uphold some state restrictions on abortions. When that happened, many people predicted that in time *Roe v. Wade* would be overturned, especially if President Bush was able to appoint more justices. He appointed two (Souter and Thomas), but *Roe* survived. The key votes were cast by Justices O'Connor, Souter, and Kennedy. In 1992, in its *Casey* decision, the Court by a vote of five to four explicitly refused to overturn *Roe,* declaring that there was a right to abortion. At the same time, however, it upheld a variety of restrictions imposed by the state of Pennsylvania on women seeking abortions. These included a mandatory twenty-four-hour waiting period between the request for an abortion and the performance of it, the requirement that teenagers

obtain the consent of one parent (or, in special circumstances, of a judge), and a requirement that women contemplating an abortion be given pamphlets about alternatives to it. Similar restrictions had been enacted in many other states, all of which looked to the Pennsylvania case for guidance as to whether they could be enforced. In allowing these restrictions, the Court overruled some of its own earlier decisions.[52] On the other hand, the Court did strike down a state law that would have required married women to obtain the consent of their husbands before having an abortion.

In 2000 the Court visited abortion again, and by another five-to-four vote refused to allow states to ban so-called partial birth abortions. This method is usually done to fetuses that are at least twenty weeks old. The key provisions of the *Casey* and *Stenberg* cases are summarized in the box on page 480.

With the right to an abortion again, and politically secure, the struggle over its implementation took a new turn. Antiabortion activists conducted demonstrations at many abortion clinics, and a few extremists wounded or killed some abortion doctors. This led to a demand for laws protecting the clinics. Laws were passed and court orders issued, designed to strike a balance between the activists' right to protest and the clinics' right to operate.

In 1997 the Supreme Court upheld legal orders that forbid acts of physical obstruction and that provide a "buffer zone" of fifteen feet around the entrance to a clinic within which demonstrations cannot occur.[53]

Affirmative Action

A common thread running through the politics of civil rights is the argument between equality of results and equality of opportunity.

Equality of Results

One view, expressed by most civil rights and feminist organizations, is that the burdens of racism and sexism can be overcome only by taking race or sex into account in designing remedies. It is not enough to give rights to people; they must be given benefits. If life is a race, everybody must be brought up to the same starting line (or possibly even to the same finish line). This means that the Constitution is not and should not be color-blind or sex-neutral. In education this implies that the races must actually be mixed in the schools, by busing if necessary. In hiring it means that **affirmative action**—preferential hiring practices—must be used to find and hire women, African Americans, and other minorities. Women should not simply be free to enter the labor force; they should be given the material necessities (for example, free daycare) that will help them enter it. On payday workers' checks should reflect not just the results of people's competing in the marketplace but the results of plans designed to ensure that people earn comparable amounts for comparable jobs. Of late, affirmative action has been defended in the name of diversity or multiculturalism—the view that every institution (firm, school, or agency) and every college curriculum should reflect the cultural (that is, ethnic) diversity of the nation.

Equality of Opportunity

The second view holds that if it is wrong to discriminate *against* African Americans and women, it is equally wrong to give them preferential treatment over other groups. To do so constitutes **reverse discrimination.** The Constitution and laws should be color-blind and sex-neutral.[54] In this view allowing children to attend the school of their choice is sufficient; busing them to attain a certain racial mixture is wrong. Eliminating barriers to job opportunities is right; using numerical "targets" and "goals" to place minorities and women in specific jobs is wrong. If people wish to compete in the market, they should be satisfied with the market verdict concerning the worth of their work.

These two views are intertwined with other deep philosophical differences. Supporters of **equality of opportunity** tend to have orthodox beliefs; they favor letting private groups behave the way that they want (and so may defend the right of a men's club to exclude women). Supporters of the opposite view are likely to be progressive in their beliefs and insist that private clubs meet the same standards as schools or business firms. Adherents to the equality-of-opportunity view often attach great importance to traditional models of the family and so are skeptical of daycare and federally funded abortions. Adherents to the equality-of-results view

prefer greater freedom of choice in lifestyle questions and so take the opposite position on daycare and abortion.

Of course the debate is more complex than this simple contrast suggests. Take, for example, the question of affirmative action. Both the advocates of equality of opportunity and those of equality of results might agree that there is something odd about a factory or university that hires no African Americans or women, and both might press it to prove that its hiring policy is fair. Affirmative action in this case can mean *either* looking hard for qualified women and minorities and giving them a fair shot at jobs *or* setting a numerical goal for the number of women and minorities that should be hired and insisting that that goal be met. Persons who defend the second course of action call these goals "targets"; persons who criticize that course call them "quotas."

The issue has largely been fought out in the courts. Between 1978 and 1990 about a dozen major cases involving affirmative action were decided by the Supreme Court; in about half it was upheld, and in the other half it was overturned. The different outcomes reflect two things—the differences in the facts of the cases and the arrival on the Court of three justices (Kennedy, O'Connor, and Scalia) appointed by a president, Ronald Reagan, who was opposed to at least the broader interpretation of affirmative action. As a result of these decisions, the law governing affirmative action is now complex and confusing.

Consider one issue: should the government be allowed to use a quota system to select workers, enroll students, award contracts, or grant licenses? In the *Bakke* decision in 1978, the Court said that the medical school of the University of California at Davis could not use an explicit numerical quota in admitting minority students but could "take race into account."[55] So no numerical quotas, right? Wrong. Two years later the Court upheld a federal rule that set aside 10 percent of all federal construction contracts for minority-owned firms.[56] All right, maybe quotas can't be used in medical schools, but they can be used in the construction industry. Not exactly. In 1989 the Court overturned a Richmond, Virginia, law that set aside 30 percent of its construction contracts for minority owned firms.[57] Well, maybe the Court just changed its mind between

Becoming a Citizen

For persons born in the United States, the rights of U.S. citizenship have been ensured, in constitutional theory if not in everyday practice, since the passage of the Fourteenth Amendment in 1868 and the civil rights laws of the 1960s. The Fourteenth Amendment conferred citizenship upon "all persons born in the United States . . . and subject to the jurisdiction thereof." Subsequent laws also gave citizenship to children born outside the United States to parents who are American citizens.

But immigrants, by definition, are not born with the rights of U.S. citizenship. Instead those seeking to become U.S. citizens must, in effect, assume certain responsibilities in order to become citizens. The statutory requirements for naturalization, as they have been broadly construed by the courts, are as follows:

- Five years' residency, or three years if married to a citizen.
- Continuous residency since filing of the naturalization petition.

- Good moral character, which is loosely interpreted to mean no evidence of criminal activity.
- Attachment to constitutional principles. This means that potential citizens have to answer basic factual questions about American government (e.g., "Who was the first president of the United States?") and publicly denounce any and all allegiance to their native country and its leaders (e.g., Italy and the king of Italy), but devotion to constitutional principles is now regarded as being implicit in the act of applying for naturalization.
- Being favorably disposed to "the good order and happiness of the United States."*

Today about 97 percent of aliens who seek citizenship are successful in meeting these requirements and becoming naturalized citizens of the United States.

*8 U.S.C. 1423, 1427 (1970); *Girouard v. United States,* 328 U.S. 61 (1946).

Source: New York Times (July 25, 1993), 33. Copyright © 1993 by the *New York Times.* Reprinted by permission.

1980 and 1989. No. One year later it upheld a federal rule that gave preference to minority-owned firms in the awarding of broadcast licenses.[58] Then in 1993 it upheld the right of white contractors to challenge minority set-aside laws in Jacksonville, Florida.[59]

It is too early to try to make sense of these twists and turns, especially since a deeply divided Court is still wrestling with these issues and Congress (as with the Civil Rights Act of 1991) is modifying or superseding some earlier Court decisions. But a few general standards seem to be emerging. In simplified form, they are as follows:

- The courts will subject any quota system created by state or local governments to "strict scrutiny" and will look for a "compelling" justification for it.
- Quotas or preference systems cannot be used by state or local governments without first showing

that such rules are needed to correct an actual past or present pattern of discrimination.[60]
- In proving that there has been discrimination, it is not enough to show that African Americans (or other minorities) are statistically underrepresented among employees, contractors, or union members; you must identify the actual practices that have had this discriminatory impact.[61]
- Quotas or preference systems that are created by *federal* law will be given greater deference, in part because Section 5 of the Fourteenth Amendment gives to Congress powers not given to the states to correct the effects of racial discrimination.[62]
- It may be easier to justify in court a voluntary preference system (for example, one agreed to in a labor-management contract) than one that is required by law.[63]
- Even when you can justify special preferences in *hiring* workers, the Supreme Court is not likely to

The Rights of Aliens

America is a nation of immigrants. Some have arrived legally, others illegally. An illegal, or undocumented, alien is subject to being deported. With the passage in 1986 of the Immigration Reform and Control Act, illegal aliens who have resided in this country continuously since before January 1, 1982, are entitled to amnesty—that is, they can become legal residents. However, the same legislation stipulated that employers (who once could hire undocumented aliens without fear of penalty) must now verify the legal status of all newly hired employees; if they knowingly hire an illegal alien, they face civil and criminal penalties.

Aliens—people residing in this country who are not citizens—cannot vote or run for office. Nevertheless, they must pay taxes just as if they were citizens. And they are entitled to many constitutional rights, even if they are in this country illegally. This is because most of the rights mentioned in the Constitution refer to "people" or "persons," not to "citizens." For example, the Fourteenth Amendment bars a state from depriving "*any person* of life, liberty, or property, without due process of law" or from denying "to *any person* within its jurisdiction the equal protection of the laws" [italics added]. As a result, the courts have held that:

- The children of illegal aliens cannot be excluded from the public school system.[1]
- Legally admitted aliens are entitled to welfare benefits.[2]
- Illegal aliens cannot be the object of reprisals if they attempt to form a labor union where they work.[3]

- The First Amendment rights of free speech, religion, press, and assembly and the Fourth Amendment protections against arbitrary arrest and prosecution extend to aliens as well as to citizens.[4]
- Aliens are entitled to own property.

The government can make rules that apply to aliens only, but they must justify the reasonableness of the rules. For example:

- The Immigration and Naturalization Service has broader powers to arrest and search illegal aliens than police departments have to arrest and search citizens.[5]
- States can limit certain jobs, such as police officer and schoolteacher, to citizens.[6]
- The president or Congress can bar the employment of aliens by the federal government.[7]
- States can bar aliens from serving on a jury.[8]
- Illegal aliens are not entitled to obtain a Social Security card.

[1]*Plyler v. Doe,* 457 U.S. 202 (1982).

[2]*Graham v. Richardson,* 403 U.S. 365 (1971).

[3]*Sure-Tan v. National Labor Relations Board,* 467 U.S. 883 (1984).

[4]*Chew v. Colding,* 344 U.S. 590 (1953).

[5]*U.S. v. Brignoni-Ponce,* 422 U.S. 873 (1975); *INS v. Delgado,* 466 U.S. 210 (1984); *INS v. Lopez-Mendoza,* 486 U.S. 1032 (1984).

[6]*Cabell v. Chavez-Salido,* 454 U.S. 432 (1982); *Foley v. Connelie,* 435 U.S. 291 (1978); *Amblach v. Norwick,* 441 U.S. 68 (1979).

[7]*Hampton v. Mow Sun Wong,* 436 U.S. 67 (1976).

[8]*Schneider v. New Jersey,* 308 U.S. 147 (1939).

allow racial preferences to govern who gets *laid off.* A worker laid off to make room for a minority worker loses more than does a worker not hired in preference to a minority applicant.[64]

Complex as they are, these rulings still generate a great deal of passion. Supporters of the decisions

barring certain affirmative action plans hail these decisions as steps back from an emerging pattern of reverse discrimination. In contrast, civil rights organizations have denounced those decisions that have overturned affirmative action programs. In 1990 their congressional allies introduced legislation that would reverse several decisions. In particu-

The Rights of the Disabled

In 1990 the federal government passed the Americans with Disabilities Act (ADA), a sweeping law that extended many of the protections enjoyed by women and racial minorities to disabled persons.

Who Is a Disabled Person?

Anyone who *has* a physical or mental impairment that substantially limits one or more major life activities (for example, holding a job), anyone who has a *record* of such impairment, or anyone who is *regarded* as having such an impairment is considered disabled.

What Rights Do Disabled Persons Have?

Employment Disabled persons may not be denied employment or promotion if, with "reasonable accommodation," they can perform the duties of that job. (Excluded from this protection are people who currently use illegal drugs, gamble compulsively, or are homosexual or bisexual.) Reasonable accommodation need not be made if this would cause "undue hardship" on the employer.

Government Programs and Transportation Disabled persons may not be denied access to government programs or benefits. New buses, taxis, and trains must be accessible to disabled persons, including those in wheelchairs.

Public Accommodations Disabled persons must enjoy "full and equal" access to hotels, restaurants, stores, schools, parks, museums, auditoriums, and the like. To achieve equal access, owners of existing facilities must alter them "to the maximum extent feasible"; builders of new facilities must ensure that they are readily accessible to disabled persons, unless this is structurally impossible.

Telephones The ADA directs the Federal Communications Commission to issue regulations to ensure that telecommunications devices for hearing- and speech-impaired people are available "to the extent possible and in the most efficient manner."

Congress The rights under this law apply to employees of Congress.

Rights Compared The ADA does not enforce the rights of disabled persons in the same way as the Civil Rights Act enforces the rights of African Americans and women. Racial or gender discrimination must end *regardless of cost*; denial of access to disabled persons must end unless "undue hardship" or excessive costs would result.

lar this legislation would put the burden of proof on the employer, not the employee, to show that the underrepresentation of minorities in the firm's work force was the result of legitimate and necessary business decisions and not the result of discrimination. If the employer could not prove this, the aggrieved employee would be able to collect large damage awards. (In the past, he or she could collect only back pay.) In 1991 the bill was passed and was signed by President Bush.

In thinking about these matters, most Americans distinguish between compensatory action and preferential treatment. They define **compensatory action** as "helping disadvantaged people catch up, usually by giving them extra education, training, or services." A majority of the public supports this. They define preferential treatment as "giving minorities preference in hiring, promotions, college admissions, and contracts." Large majorities oppose this.[65] These views reflect an enduring element in American political culture—a strong commitment to individualism ("nobody should get something without deserving it") coupled with support for help for the disadvantaged ("somebody who is suffering through no fault of his or her own deserves a helping hand").

Where does affirmative action fit into this culture? Polls suggest that if affirmative action is defined as "helping," people will support it, but if it is defined as "using quotas," they will oppose it. On this matter blacks and whites see things differently. Blacks think that they should receive preferences in employment to create a more diverse work force and to make up for past discrimination; whites oppose

WHO GOVERNS? TO WHAT ENDS?

Federal Policy on Disability Rights

In the late 1960s federal policy on handicapped persons began to be debated as an "equal access" issue with civil rights implications. The watershed moment came on September 26, 1973, the day President Nixon signed the Rehabilitation Act into law. Section 504 of the act directed that "no otherwise qualified handicapped individual . . . shall, solely by reason of his handicap, be excluded from participation in, be denied the benefits of, or be subjected to discrimination under any program or activity receiving federal financial assistance."

Since there was virtually no discussion of this provision as the bill moved through Congress, no one really knew what was meant by phrases such as "participation in" and "subjected to discrimination under." How, for example, were these words to apply to a city transit system? Narrowly read, they might mean only that the city could not refuse to hire an otherwise qualified handicapped person to work in the transit system. Broadly read, they might mean that the buses and subway cars in the city had to be made physically accessible to all handicapped persons.

During the ensuing debate over Section 504, a host of organizations representing disabled persons (they now eschewed the term "handicapped") cut their political teeth, sinking them first into the federal bureaucrats whose job it was to interpret the law. They interpreted it broadly. Washington issued regulations requiring that city transit systems receiving federal aid equip their buses and subway cars with devices to lift wheelchairs on board. State and local government officials balked loudly at both the "federal interference" and the dollar cost. The mayor of New York City, Edward Koch, declared that rebuilding existing buses and subways would make each trip by a wheelchair user cost thirty-eight dollars. It would be cheaper, he argued, for the city to give free taxicab rides to every disabled person, but the federal regulations would not permit that. Koch, a Democrat, found a sympathetic

ear in the Republican Reagan administration, which in 1981 relaxed the requirement that buses be able to lift wheelchairs aboard. Into the mid-1980s disability rights activists attacked what they called the "Reagan rollback" of the Rehabilitation Act by lobbying to amend the Civil Rights Act of 1964.

They failed, but they did not quit. In 1975 they won passage of the Education for All Handicapped Children Act, which required public schools to accommodate the physical limitations and special educational needs of all disabled children. By the late 1980s they had coalesced around waging a campaign in Congress for a "civil rights act" of their own. The fate of this campaign would hinge on their ability to drive the politics of federal disability policy strongly in a majoritarian direction and away from any perception that "the disabled," however much sympathy they might engender, were simply another self-seeking client group.

For four main reasons, they succeeded. First, they staged media events stressing that one in six Americans had some form of disability, that every American was "only an accident away" from being disabled, and that millions of today's baby boomers were bound to join tomorrow's elderly disabled population. Apparently it worked. By 1986 surveys showed that three-quarters of Americans shared a "common identity" with "the disabled."

Second, whereas they had once relied almost exclusively on liberal House Democrats, they began to actively court members in both chambers and parties, targeting those whose own lives or families had been touched by disability. For example, they made common cause with Republican Senate minority leader Robert Dole of Kansas, whose right arm had been disabled by an injury suffered in combat during World War II.

Third, in 1986, through quietly passed amendments to the Rehabilitation Act of 1973, the fifteen-member National Council on Disability became an independent federal agency. In 1987, having assisted liberal Republican senator Lowell Weicker of Connecticut in drafting the first model federal disability rights legislation, the press hailed the council as Washington's moral conscience on the issue.

Fourth, even though they had vilified George Bush as vice president for his complicity in Reagan's "rollback" policies, disability rights activists (including members of the council) bet that Bush as president would seek a signature domestic policy initiative with which to credit his campaign call for a "kinder, gentler America."

They bet right. Neither as a House member nor as vice president had Bush ever pushed for federal disability rights. But Bush had had a three-year-old daughter die of leukemia, a son (Neil) who had had dyslexia (impaired ability to read) as a child, and another son (Marvin) who had had part of his colon removed in 1986. He put landmark changes in federal policy on disability rights at the top of his 1989–1990 legislative agenda. The only significant opposition to the first drafts of the Americans with Disabilities Act (ADA) came from small-business lobbies. Their concerns were assuaged by the granting of temporary exemptions and the insertion of an "undue hardship" clause. The final version of the ADA won by a vote of 377 to 28 in the House and 76 to 8 in the Senate. With much fanfare, President Bush signed the bill into law on July 26, 1990.

As outlined in the box on page 485, the ADA extended many of the civil rights protections enjoyed by women and minorities to disabled persons. Most of the ADA's language is quite specific. For example, Title I directs that the employment provisions of the ADA apply only to businesses that have fifteen employees or more, but Title III requires that the law's public accommodations provisions apply to all businesses, period.

Still, as one of five major federal mandates enacted in 1990 (see Chapter 3), the ADA has faced its share of controversy and confusion. No one, for example, mentioned alarm boxes during the debate over the ADA. But in 1996 federal district court judge Robert W. Sweet ordered the New York City Fire Department to halt its plan to replace the city's 16,300 antiquated alarm boxes with public telephones wired to an emergency system. Judge Sweet ruled that because deaf and hearing-impaired people may be unable to use phones to call for help, the plan violated the ADA's guarantee of equal access to public services. Likewise, golf courses are not mentioned in the ADA. There is, however, an Association of Disabled Golfers and a National Blind Golfers Association. In deference to these groups and the requirements of the ADA, some public golf course operators have built wheelchair-accessible ramps to tees, regraded bunkers, and installed special telecommunications devices in reservations offices so that hearing-impaired golfers can make tee-time reservations by phone.

As they had in response to the Rehabilitation Act of 1973, state and local government officials complained about the ADA's cost. But most have taken pains to explain that they do not mean to dispute or denigrate "disability rights" or to deny the desirability of a federal role in defining, defending, and extending these rights.

Change is the only constant in American politics, but we would be surprised if the post-1990 majoritarian politics of federal policy on disability rights changed anytime soon. Given your own general insights into the politics of who governs and to what ends, would you be surprised, too?

Sources: Sidney Milkis and Michael Nelson, *The American Presidency: Origins and Development, 1776–1998* (Washington, D.C.: Congressional Quarterly Press, 1999), 363–366; Don Vannatta, Jr., "U.S. Judge Says Removing Alarm Boxes Discriminates Against the Deaf," *New York Times* (February 14, 1986), B3; Joanne Desky, "Park Facilities Meet ADA Challenges," *PA Times* (May 1, 1993), 1, 16; Timothy J. Conlan and David R. Beam, "Federal Mandates: The Record of Reform and Future Prospects," *Intergovernmental Perspective* (Fall 1992); *Congressional Quarterly Researcher* (December 27, 1991).

The federal government subsidizes some job training programs, as for these medical assistants.

using goals to create diversity or to remedy past ills. In sum the controversy over affirmative action depends on what you mean by it and on what your racial identity is.[66]

The courts are likewise divided on this matter. In 1996 the federal appeals court for the fifth circuit (covering Louisiana, Mississippi, and Texas) decided that the University of Texas Law School's refusal to admit a white woman, Cheryl Hopwood, even though her academic record was much better than that of many black and Hispanic students who had been admitted, was unconstitutional. The school said it gave preference to racial minorities to achieve diversity among its students, but the appeals court held that diversity was not a sufficiently compelling state interest to justify racial preferences. When the school appealed the decision to the Supreme Court, it refused to hear the matter because, by then, the school had stopped using racial admissions criteria.[67] This means that no law school in Louisiana, Mississippi, and Texas can use race at all in making admissions decisions, but those in other states still can.

What may be the most important recent Supreme Court decision on affirmative action was made in 1995. A small construction company named Adarand tried to get a contract to build guardrails along a highway in Colorado. Though it was the low bidder, it lost the contract because of a government policy that favors small businesses owned by "socially and economically disadvantaged individuals"—that is, by racial and ethnic minorities. In a five-to-four decision the Court agreed with Adarand and sent the case back to Colorado for a new trial.

The essence of its decision was that *any* discrimination based on race must be subject to strict scrutiny, even if its purpose is to help, not hurt, a racial minority. Strict scrutiny means two things:

- Any racial preference must serve a "compelling government interest."
- The preference must be "narrowly tailored" to serve that interest.[68]

To serve a compelling governmental interest, it is likely that any racial preference will have to remedy a clear pattern of past discrimination. No such pattern had been shown in Colorado.

This decision prompted a good deal of political debate about affirmative action. The Republicans introduced a bill in Congress to ban it, but they later withdrew the bill. In California, however, an initiative was put on the 1996 ballot to prevent state authorities from using "race, sex, color, ethnicity, or national origin as a criterion for either discriminating against, or granting preferential treatment to, any individual or group" in public employment, public education, or public contracting. When the votes were counted, it passed. Washington has also adopted a similar measure, and other states are debating it.

Gays and the Supreme Court

As conflicts over homosexuality have risen in political importance, the Supreme Court has had to confront the issue of gay rights more frequently. Because the nation is divided about it, it shouldn't be surprising that the Court is also.

When some Georgians protested that a state law barring homosexual actions between two consenting adults was unconstitutional, the Court voted five to four that there was no constitutional reason to prevent a state from passing such a law.[69] Homosexuality in that state remained illegal.

In many cities in Colorado ordinances were passed to ban discrimination against people because of their sexual orientation. Most voters did not approve of this, and so in response they adopted a state constitutional amendment that made it illegal to pass any law to protect persons based on their "homosexual, lesbian, or bisexual orientation." The amendment did not penalize gays and lesbians; instead it said that they could not become the object of specific legal protection of the sort that has traditionally been given to racial or ethnic minorities. The Court struck down this amendment on the grounds that it violated the equal protection clause of the Constitution by singling out as unworthy of protection one specific group of citizens.[70]

So now we have an odd condition: a state can pass a law banning homosexual activities, but it cannot pass a law preventing the cities within that state from reversing that ban. (The decision that overturned the Colorado amendment did not mention the decision sustaining the Georgia law.)

In 2000 the Court was asked whether the Boy Scouts could prevent gay boys and men from being members. The majority of the Court, in a five-to-four decision, said it was not opposing homosexuality but merely reaffirming the right of a private organization to define its own membership. The dissenters did not object to the claim that private organizations could choose their own members but argued that the Boy Scouts had not published a clear opposition to homosexuality.[71] The status of civil rights for homosexuals remains unclear. Complicating matters is the role of gays in the military. In 1993 the Clinton administration instituted the policy of

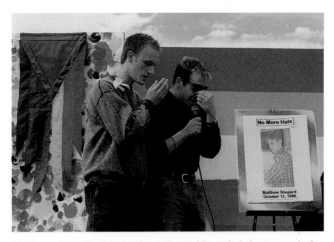

The brutal murder of Matthew Shepard horrified the nation and brought the issue of crimes against homosexuals to the forefront of the public debate.

"don't ask, don't tell" in the military, but the Court has yet to speak authoritatively about what this means in practice.

On one matter, however, the Court seems quite clear. When a private group of Irish Americans sponsored a St. Patrick's Day parade in Boston, an organization called the Irish-American Gay, Lesbian, and Bisexual Group asked for the right to march with the others. In protest the traditional sponsors of the march canceled it. The case went to the Supreme Court, which held, unanimously, that the sponsors of the march had a First Amendment right to deliver their message and that the state could not require it to alter that message by including among the marchers people with whom it disagreed.[72]

Summary

The civil rights movement in the courts and in Congress profoundly changed the nature of African American participation in politics by bringing southern blacks into the political system so that they could become an effective interest group.

The decisive move was to enlist northern opinion in this cause, a job made easier by the northern perception that civil rights involved simply an unfair contest between two minorities—southern whites and southern blacks. That perception changed when it became evident that the court rulings and legislative decisions would apply to the North as well as the South, leading to the emergence of northern opposition to court-ordered busing and affirmative action programs.

By the time this reaction developed, the legal and political system had been changed sufficiently to make it difficult if not impossible to limit the application of civil rights laws to the special circumstances of the South or to alter by legislative means the decisions of federal courts. Though the courts can accomplish little when they have no political allies (as revealed by the massive resistance to early school-desegregation decisions), they can accomplish a great deal, even in the face of adverse public opinion, when they have some organized allies (as revealed by their ability to withstand antibusing moves).

The feminist movement has paralleled in organization and tactics many aspects of the black civil rights movement, but with important differences. Women sought to repeal or reverse laws and court rulings that in many cases were ostensibly designed to protect rather than subjugate them. The conflict between protection and liberation was sufficiently intense to defeat the effort to ratify the Equal Rights Amendment.

The most divisive civil rights issues in American politics are abortion and affirmative action. From 1973 to 1989 the Supreme Court seemed committed to giving constitutional protection to all abortions within the first trimester; since 1989 it has approved various state restrictions on the circumstances under which abortions can be obtained.

There has been a similar shift in the Court's view of affirmative action. Though it will still approve some quota plans, it now insists that they pass strict scrutiny to ensure that they are used only to correct a proven history of discrimination, that they place the burden of proof on the party alleging discrimination, and that they be limited to hiring and not extended to layoffs. Congress has modified some of these rulings with new civil rights legislation.

World Wide Web Resources

- Court cases: www.law.cornell.edu
- Department of Justice: www.usdoj.gov
- Civil rights organizations:
  National Association for the Advancement of Colored People: www.naacp.org
  National Organization for Women: www.now.org

National Gay and Lesbian Task Force: www.ngltf.org
National Council of La Raza: www.nclr.org
American Arab Anti-Discrimination Committee: www.adc.org
Anti-Defamation League: www.adl.org

Key Terms

civil rights *p. 461*
suspect classifications
 p. 462
Jim Crow *p. 463*
separate-but-equal
 doctrine *p. 465*

de jure segregation
 p. 469
de facto segregation
 p. 469
nonviolent civil disobedience *p. 472*

strict scrutiny *p. 478*
affirmative action *p. 482*
reverse discrimination
 p. 482
equality of opportunity
 p. 482

compensatory action
 p. 485

Suggested Readings

Branch, Taylor. *Parting the Waters: America in the King Years*. New York: Simon & Schuster, 1988. A vivid account of the civil rights struggle.

Flexner, Eleanor. *Century of Struggle: The Women's Rights Movement in the United States*. Rev. ed. Cambridge: Harvard University Press, 1975. A historical account of the feminist movement and its political strategies.

Foreman, Christopher A. *The African-American Predicament*. Washington, D.C.: Brookings Institution, 1999. Thoughtful essays on problems faced by African Americans today.

Franklin, John Hope. *From Slavery to Freedom*. 5th ed. New York: Knopf, 1980. A survey of black history in the United States.

Kluger, Richard. *Simple Justice*. New York: Random House/Vintage Books, 1977. Detailed and absorbing account of the school-desegregation issue, from the Fourteenth Amendment to the *Brown* case.

Kull, Andrew. *The Color-Blind Constitution*. Cambridge: Harvard University Press, 1992. A history of efforts, none yet successful, to make the Constitution color-blind.

Mansbridge, Jane J. *Why We Lost the ERA*. Chicago: University of Chicago Press, 1986. Explains why the Equal Rights Amendment did not become part of the Constitution.

Thernstrom, Stephan, and Abigail Thernstrom. *America in Black and White*. New York: Simon & Schuster, 1997. Detailed history and portrait of African Americans.

Wilhoit, Francis M. *The Politics of Massive Resistance*. New York: George Braziller, 1973. The methods—and ultimate collapse—of all-out southern resistance to school desegregation.

Woodward, C. Vann. *The Strange Career of Jim Crow*. New York: Oxford University Press, 1957. Brief, lucid account of the evolution of Jim Crow practices in the South.

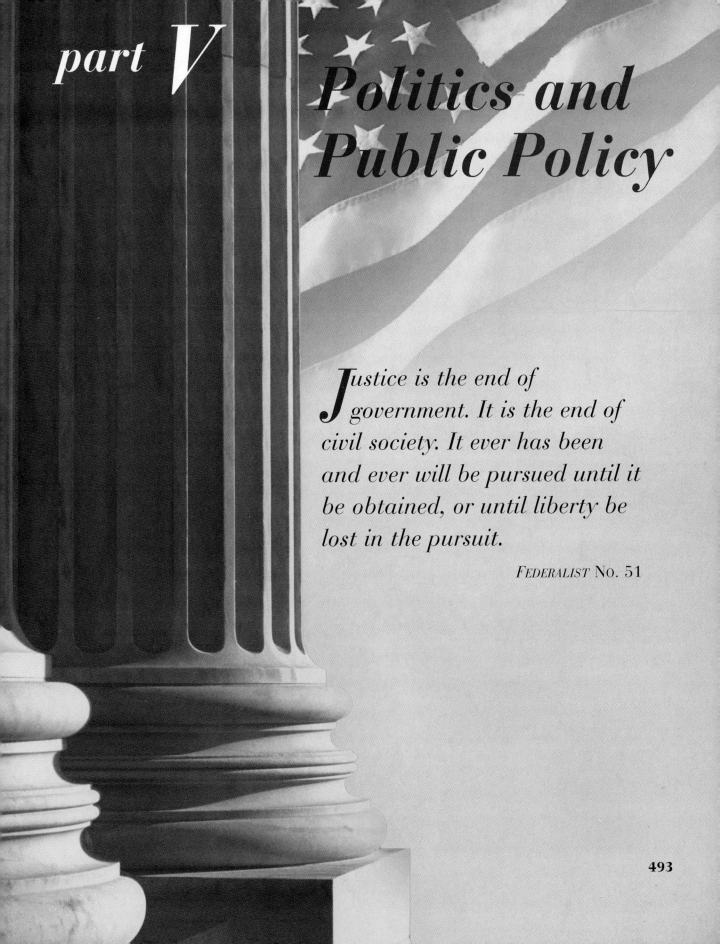

part V

Politics and Public Policy

*J*ustice is the end of
government. It is the end of
civil society. It ever has been
and ever will be pursued until it
be obtained, or until liberty be
lost in the pursuit.

FEDERALIST No. 51

Politics and Public Policy

17

Enduring Questions

1. Who, if anyone, is really in charge in American government?
2. Does every group that is affected by a government decision have a reasonable chance to be heard when it is being made?
3. Why has American government become bigger and more complicated?
4. Can we have both an efficient government and one in which almost every interest group can participate?
5. Would we be better off with a parliamentary system of government?

How the American System Affects Policy-Making

How the American System Has Changed

Restraints on Growth

Relaxing the Restraints
The Old System • The New System

Should the System Be Changed?
Reducing the Barriers to Action • Increasing the Barriers to Action • Term Limits • Who Is Right?

Talk to almost any citizen about American government and you will get a long list of complaints that generally fall into two groups. The first are gripes about politics: "Politicians are self-serving captives of special-interest groups, interested only in their own reelection. Judges are too liberal (or too conservative). The media are too interested in trivial scandals (or not interested enough in important scandals). The president and Congress are in gridlock, unable or unwilling to take decisive action." The second group are grievances about policies: "It's outrageous that we have this budget deficit; why can't we manage to live within our means? Why can't the government do something about (take your pick) crime, drug abuse, racism, poor schools, air pollution, welfare dependency, or Japanese competition?"

A lot of people think that there is a connection between our political problems and our policy failures. In their opinion we don't solve the problems of the deficit, crime, racism, or Japanese competition *because* our politicians are self-serving, the press doesn't do its job right, the courts are filled with wrong-headed judges, and special-interest

495

groups are too powerful. Many people who think that way decided to support Ross Perot when the Texas businessman announced that he would run for president as an independent in 1992 and 1996. They apparently were saying that we could solve our problems if only we had strong, dedicated leaders.

This view of how to fix the system, or of whether the system even needs fixing at all, has some truth to it, but for the most part it is too simple. Having read this book so far, you should understand that the way our system works is not mainly the result of the people in charge of it, but mainly (though not entirely) the result of the constitution that shapes it. The Constitution was written not to make governing easy but to make it hard, not to facilitate choices but to impede them, not to empower leaders but to frustrate them. The written and unwritten constitutions of European democracies are very different: they were designed to allow the government to govern, subject only to the periodic checks of a popular election. Here popular participation is encouraged; there it is discouraged. Here the courts can overturn presidential and congressional actions; there they cannot. Here many officials have the power to say no, and none has the power to say yes and make it stick; there a prime minister can say yes and make it stick.

How the American System Affects Policy-Making

This system for making policy creates quite predictable results, and among them are the very aspects of politics that so many Americans find distasteful. Consider the effects of four constitutional provisions on how we make policy:

1. *The separation of powers:* This has at least two important results. First, the president and Congress will be rivals, even when they are from the same political party. The White House and Congress will compete for power over the policies and personnel of the government. Stalemates will be the rule, not the exception, and they will only be overcome by a national crisis, a powerful tide of public opinion, or tough political bargaining. For example, if the president wants to cut the deficit by reducing spending and Congress wants to cut it by increasing taxes, a political standoff will occur, as happened during much of the Reagan and Bush administrations and during Clinton's first term. Second, members of Congress will first and foremost represent their districts and states. Virtually no bill will become a law unless it is first adjusted to reflect the differing demands of local constituencies. A president may complain that members of Congress work to get "unnecessary" benefits—roads, bridges, parks, and airports—for their districts, but he forgets that this is exactly what the voters want from their members. Calling it "pork-barrel politics" doesn't change that fundamental political reality.

2. *Federalism:* The states have an independent political position. As a result it is very hard to have a truly "national" policy on anything. And even when we do have a national policy, the states play a big role in implementing it. For

Even hateful symbols, such as this burning cross lit by members of the Ku Klux Klan, enjoy constitutional protection.

example, the states have major responsibility for enforcing pollution control programs and building major highways, even though most of the money comes from Washington. And they play the dominant role in schooling, law enforcement, and land-use controls and pay most of those bills.

3. *Judicial review:* The federal courts can declare an act of the president or Congress unconstitutional and can decide suits brought by people arguing either that a federal agency has exceeded its legal authority or that it has not done all that the law requires. The courts have obviously played a decisive role in racial integration and civil liberties cases, but they also play an important, though less visible, role in implementing laws affecting the environment, occupational safety and health, and highway construction.

4. *Freedom of speech and assembly:* The First Amendment guarantees the right of individuals to speak their minds and lobby their senators and representatives. This right cannot be preserved for individuals and denied to groups; after all, groups are just collections of like-minded individuals. As a result placing any meaningful restrictions on the activities of lobbyists is next to impossible (except, of course, to ensure that they do not engage in corruption, such as bribery).

When you add together the effects of these four features of our Constitution, you get a uniquely American system of policy-making. Though it has many distinctive features, the best word to describe our system of government is *adversarial*—that is, a system that encourages participation by people who have an incentive to fight rather than cooperate. Freedom of speech protects each person's right to participate; the separation of powers and federalism means that any participant can usually find a political ally; the decentralized structure of Congress (which is one effect of federalism and the separation of powers) gives each member an incentive to call attention to himself or herself by making speeches, taking positions, and (above all) attacking adversaries; and the courts provide a convenient (though expensive) arena in which to wage endless struggles.

One can see our adversarial system at work in many policy arenas. Business and government fight

The "Rules" of Politics

Some "Rules" of Politics

Here are some generalizations about American politics, distilled from what has been said in this book, offered in nervous awareness that our political system has a way of proving everybody wrong. (Before the 1960s it was a "rule" of politics that no Catholic could be elected president. John F. Kennedy took care of that.)

- Policies once adopted tend to persist, whatever their value. (It is easier to start new programs than to end old ones.)

- Almost all electoral politics is local politics. (Members of Congress who forget "home base" tend not to remain in Congress for long.)

- Whatever the size of their staff and budget, Congress and the White House will always be overworked. (More resources produce more work, which produces more resources.)

- Each branch of government tends to emulate the others. (Congress will become more bureaucratized to cope with an executive branch that is becoming more bureaucratized; judges will become more activist as Congress becomes more activist.)

- Proposals that seem to confer widespread and immediate benefits will be enacted, whatever their long-term costs.

- Proposals that seem to confer delayed benefits will be enacted only if their costs are unknown, concealed, or deferred.

- Nobody—businesspeople, bureaucrats, members of Congress, judges, professors—likes competition, and everybody will do whatever he or she can to reduce or eliminate it.

- "Planning" in government takes place after a crisis takes place.

- The mass media never cover a story about things that are going well. Thus the number of "problems" in society is a function of the number of reporters.

- If you want something, you are claiming a right; if your opponent wants something, he or she is protecting a vested interest.

over what environmental protection rules to enforce. (You may be surprised to learn that in much of Europe, they cooperate rather than fight in deciding these rules.) Pro-environment groups attack business, portraying it in the worst possible light; antiabortion groups attack pro-choice groups (and vice versa). Anyone offering a plan to reduce the deficit quickly discovers that every interest that might be adversely affected (either by paying higher taxes or receiving smaller benefits) is highly organized and ready to do battle. When a government agency issues an unpopular order, we don't usually respond by obeying but by claiming that our rights have been violated and threatening to sue or hold a protest march.

Not all of these situations occur as the inevitable result of the Constitution, and historical forces have intensified these problems in recent decades. But however much events have aggravated these tendencies, the tendencies themselves arise directly from the kind of government that we have chosen.

Adversarial politics puts a premium on the ability to dramatize issues, gain publicity, mount demonstrations, and attack opponents. It downplays the ability to conduct quiet negotiations, make commitments, and accept personal responsibility.

In a participatory, adversarial system, politicians have no incentive to say that the government shouldn't tackle a problem or doesn't know how to solve it, and they have every incentive to claim that government must "do something" and that they know just what to do. The more such things are done, the more interest groups will have an incentive to organize lobbying efforts and open offices in Washington. The more such offices are opened, the greater the pressure to draft more bills and the smaller the chances that any given bill will make much sense.

Adversarial politics also colors our judgment as to the actual level of corruption and misconduct in our government. The checks and balances of our constitutional system and the individualistic style of political campaigning in our country give everybody an incentive to dig up dirt and blow the whistle on a rival. By contrast, in parliamentary regimes such as those in Europe, these checks and balances and individualistic rivalries are much less common, and therefore the incentive to expose a rival also diminishes. As a result lying and corruption seem more prevalent here than abroad, when in fact we may have less; it is just that here more gets exposed—or invented.

Given these features of our system, what is surprising is that anything gets done at all. But it does. Preoccupied as we are with all the government's failings, we sometimes forget its accomplishments. Since the end of World War II our government has built an interstate highway system, passed a set of civil rights laws, created the Medicare program for the elderly, adopted a series of increasingly tough environmental laws, explored outer space, deregulated the airlines, waged and won a forty-five-year cold war against the former Soviet Union, and sustained a level of economic growth and freedom sufficient to make millions of people from all parts of the world want to immigrate to this country. It paid a price, of course, for all of this: higher taxes, more regulations, and new groups to assimilate.

Since our complex political system makes it easy for all kinds of people and groups to wield at least some power, we should not expect policies to get made in only one way. If we had a less participatory, less adversarial system, it would be much easier to explain policy-making. In Japan, for example, appointed officials—bureaucrats—have much more power than their American counterparts, and much Japanese policy is the result of government agency proposals that are only modestly changed, if changed at all, by the legislature. In Great Britain the prime minister enjoys a great deal of power for as long as his or her party has a majority in the House of Commons, and so discussing British policy-making involves explaining why the prime minister favors one policy over another.

In the United States everybody gets into the act. Some policies are proposed by the president and enacted (after many changes) by Congress; others are proposed by members of Congress and enacted despite presidential objections. (Congress may override the president's veto or sufficiently modify the proposal to get him to withhold his veto.) When a congressional majority forms around a proposal, it is not always the result of one party (say, the Democrats) outvoting the other (the Republicans); rather, the majority often consists of a coalition of Democrats and Republicans winning out over a smaller coalition of other Democrats and Republicans.

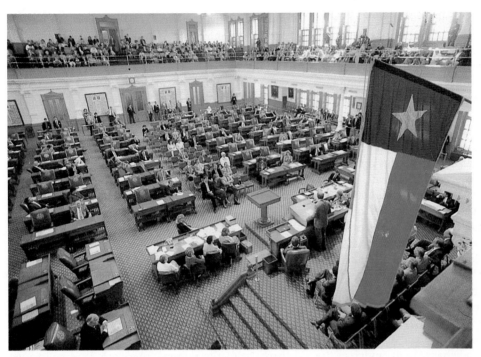

Despite the growth of the federal government, state and local governments retain more power in the United States than in almost any other nation. This is the Texas legislature.

How the American System Has Changed

Our political system has always been adversarial and participatory to some degree, but in recent decades it has become much more so. One of the main reasons for this change is that the federal government now does more things affecting more people than ever before. In 1950 Washington played little or no role in health care, civil rights, worker safety, environmental protection, or the control of crime and drug abuse. Today it plays an important role in all these matters. Since Washington touches the lives of more people than once was the case, more people try to influence Washington. And when they do, they find that everybody else has also gotten into the act. The result is an unprecedented amount of pushing and shouting. Some people find all this exciting; some are completely turned off by it.

But the Constitution was written so as to make this huge growth in government activity difficult if not impossible. For any new policy to take effect, the House and the Senate have to agree on a bill, the president has to sign it, and the courts have to accept it as constitutional. Since the president and the members of Congress are elected separately, neither branch of government can readily use a political party to control the other branch, and so no party system can (except under unusual circumstances) centralize by informal means what the Constitution has decentralized by formal ones.

Moreover, the states enjoy special constitutional protection (for a while the state legislatures even chose U.S. senators); this means that the sphere in which the federal government can act—assuming it decides to take any action at all—is quite limited. To obtain a new policy its proponents have to navigate a difficult obstacle course, persuading hundreds of independent legislators that the new policy is in their interests, does not violate states' rights, and will serve the common good. To defeat a new policy its opponents need only persuade the majority of one key committee.

If the American political system is biased against action, then how has it become so large, powerful, and expensive? If it is so hard for Congress and the president to agree, then how is it that the federal government now spends a sum one-fifth the size of the gross national product, has piled up a federal debt of around five trillion dollars, and employs more than three million civilians and over one million military personnel? If the federal government is so hedged in with constitutional restrictions, then what enables that government to manage a vast retirement system, set rules determining how factories and businesses shall operate, strike down laws banning abortions, require that private colleges allow women to participate in intercollegiate sports, search our luggage before we board an airplane, compel all eighteen-year-old males to register for the draft, and (until recently) insist that the states impose a fifty-five-mile-per-hour speed limit on all their highways?

The most striking change in the American government since its founding has been the vast increase in the scope of its activities and the reach of its powers. For the first century and a half, the government in Washington behaved pretty much as the Framers had anticipated. It regulated foreign commerce, distributed the mail, and occasionally went to war. It carried on passionate debates about slavery and the right of women to vote, but it dealt with the former only when an irrepressible conflict broke out and with the latter only after decades of agitation. Generally it spent no more money than it took in from taxes, and these taxes were mostly on imported goods, not on personal incomes. During wartime the government would get larger and run up a debt, but after the war it would shrink in size and return to pay-as-you-go financing. The standing army was minuscule. During an economic recession a major argument would arise over whether something other than gold should be the basis for American currency (if dollar bills could be redeemed for silver, for example, more dollar bills could be printed, and so money would be easier to get), but for the most part the advocates of maintaining a hard, gold-backed currency prevailed. A few efforts were made to regulate large corporations, especially the railroads, but in general government regulation of business was left to the states. And sometimes the Supreme Court prevented even the states from regulating businesses.

Until the mid–twentieth century, who ruled in Washington—and to what ends—made little differ-ence in the lives of most citizens, except in time of war or economic crisis. Governors and mayors were more in the public eye than presidents or members of Congress. Most senators and representatives served only one or two terms in office; there didn't seem to be much point in becoming a career legislator since Congress didn't do much, didn't pay much, and wasn't in session very often. If the Republicans were in power, the government tended to seek high tariffs; if the Democrats were in power, it sought lower tariffs. Today who rules and to what ends affects almost every aspect of our lives. Members of the House serve, on average, at least three terms in office. What can explain the growth of the federal government?

In a sense the question ought to be turned around. In a government whose leaders are chosen by a competitive struggle for the people's votes, candidates for office have a strong incentive to offer new programs to voters in order to win their support. It is hard to excite people by promising to do less for them; it is only natural, therefore, that politicians usually promise to do more. In acting this way politicians are not behaving badly; they are behaving democratically. If politicians foster new programs, the interesting questions become these: What kept the federal government from growing rapidly in size from its very first years of existence? Why did it not become large and powerful until nearly the middle of this century?

Restraints on Growth

There were three restraints on the growth of the U.S. government in the nineteenth and early twentieth centuries. First, the Constitution was interpreted in a way that sharply limited what policies the federal government could adopt. For a century or more the Supreme Court held that the federal government had only very limited powers to regulate business and commerce and that Congress could not delegate such powers as it had to administrative agencies. Similarly, the Supreme Court for a long time maintained that the Bill of Rights limited only what the federal government could do, and so there was little or no basis for challenging in federal court what state governments were doing. For example, not until 1963 was there a federal constitutional right to have a lawyer appointed to represent a poor person in a state criminal trial. The ratification of the Fourteenth Amendment in 1868 in theory brought more state action under federal court scrutiny (it held that no state could "deprive any person of life, liberty, or property without due process of law"), but the Court interpreted this provision narrowly, so that, for example, the amendment provided no basis for attacking school segregation as unconstitutional. The Court even held that a federal income tax was unconstitutional.

The Supreme Court could not have maintained its interpretation for as long as it did if that position had not been pretty much in accord with public opinion. This opinion was the second restraint on the growth of the federal government. There was little or no popular demand for a federal welfare or retirement system, federal aid to local public education, a federal program to deal with crime, or federal action against segregation. Not even organized labor demanded a major federal role in industrial affairs. The American Federation of Labor, led by Samuel Gompers, resisted federal involvement in labor-management disputes and was not especially outspoken in calling for a national social security program. Even as late as the 1930s, during the depths of the Great Depression, public opinion polls suggested that as many as half the voters were opposed to a federal unemployment compensation program. There were frequent popular demands by farmers for federal control over the railroads and by progressives for reforming the federal civil service, but these were matters well within the accepted limits of federal constitutional authority.

Even if people had wanted the federal government to do more, many of them lacked the political resources to back up their demands. This is the third reason that Washington had so small an agenda for so long. Although labor unions existed in the nineteenth century, it was not until after their right to organize was guaranteed in 1935 that they grew rapidly in numbers and influence. Whatever policies women might have wanted to see adopted did not stand much chance until women had won the vote, and that did not occur until 1920. Those elites who wanted to organize people concerned about the environment, consumer safety, and public health did not have the computerized mailing lists, foundation grants, and sympathetic journalists necessary to convert a cause into a campaign. Public-interest law firms, willing and able to pursue policy goals through the courts, scarcely existed.

Relaxing the Restraints

In recent decades each of these constraints on federal action has weakened or disappeared altogether. First, the courts have altered their interpretation of the Constitution in ways that have not only permitted but sometimes even required government action. The Bill of Rights has been extended so that almost all of its important provisions are now regarded as applying to the states (by having been incorporated into the due-process clause of the Fourteenth Amendment). This means that a citizen can use the federal courts to alter state policy to a greater degree than ever before. (Overturning state laws that ban abortions or require racially separate schools are two important examples of this change.) The special protection that the courts once granted property rights has been substantially reduced so that business can be regulated to a greater degree than previously. The Court has permitted Congress to give broad discretionary powers to administrative agencies, allowing bureaucrats to make decisions that once only Congress could make.

Second, public opinion has changed in ways that support an expanded role for the federal government. The public demanded action to deal with the Great Depression (the programs that resulted, such as Social Security, survived in part because the Supreme Court changed its mind about the permissible scope of federal action). Political elites changed their minds faster than the average citizen. Well-educated, politically active people began demanding federal policies regarding civil rights, public welfare, environmental protection, consumer safety, and foreign aid well before the average citizen became concerned with such things.

Once in place most of these programs proved popular, and so their continuance was supported by mass as well as elite opinion. The cumulative effect of this process was to blur, if not erase altogether, the line that once defined what the government had the authority to do. At one time a new proposal was debated in terms of whether it was legitimate for the federal government to do it at all. Federal aid to education, for example, was usually opposed, because many people feared it would lead to federal control of local schools. But after so many programs (including federal aid to education) had been passed, people stopped arguing about whether a certain policy was *legitimate* and argued instead about whether it was *effective*.

Third, political resources have become more widely distributed. The number and variety of interest groups have increased enormously. The funds available from foundations for organizations pursuing specific causes have grown. It is now easier to get access to the federal courts than formerly was the case, and once in the courts, plaintiffs are more likely to encounter judges who believe that the law and the Constitution should be interpreted broadly to permit particular goals (for example, prison reform) to be attained by legal rather than legislative means. Hundreds of magazines and newsletters have arisen to provide policy information to specialized segments of the public. The techniques of mass protest, combined with the desire of television to show pictorially interesting accounts of social conflict, have been perfected in ways that convey the beliefs of a few into the living rooms of millions.

Campaign finance laws and court rulings have given legal status and constitutional protection to thousands of political action committees (PACs) that raise and spend tens of millions of dollars from millions of small contributors. A college education, once the privilege of a tiny minority, has become the common experience of millions of people, so that the effects of college—in encouraging political participation and in shaping political beliefs—are now widespread. The ability of candidates to win nomination for office no longer depends on their ability to curry favor with a few powerful bosses; it now reflects their skill at raising money, mobilizing friends and activists, cultivating a media image, and winning a primary election.

So great have been the changes in the politics of policy-making in this country starting in the 1930s that we can refer, with only slight exaggeration, to one policy-making system having been replaced by another (see the box on page 503).

The Old System

The Old System had a small agenda. Though people voted at a high rate and often took part in torchlight parades and other mass political events, political leadership was professionalized, in the sense that the leadership circle was small, access to it was difficult, and the activists in social movements were generally kept out. Only a few major issues were under discussion at any time. A member of Congress had a small staff (if any at all), dealt with his or her colleagues on a personal basis, deferred to the prestige of House and Senate leaders, and tended to become part of some stable coalition (the farm bloc, the labor bloc, the southern bloc) that persisted across many issues.

When someone proposed adding a new issue to the public agenda, a major debate often arose over whether it was legitimate for the federal government to take action at all on the matter. A dominant theme in this debate was the importance of "states' rights." Except in wartime, or during a very brief period when the nation expressed an interest in acquiring colonies, the focus of policy debate was on domestic affairs. Members of Congress saw these domestic issues largely in terms of their effect on local constituencies. During this time the presidency was small and somewhat personal; there was only a rudimentary White House staff. The president would cultivate the press, but there was a clear understanding that what he said in a press conference was never to be quoted directly.

For the government to take bold action under this system, the nation usually had to be facing a crisis. War presented such a crisis, and so the federal government during the Civil War and World Wars I and II acquired extraordinary powers to conscript soldiers, control industrial production, regulate the flow of information to citizens, and restrict the scope of personal liberty. Each succeeding crisis left the government bureaucracy somewhat larger than it had been before, but when the crisis ended, the exercise of extraordinary powers ended. Once again the agenda of political issues became small, and legislators argued about whether it was legitimate for the government to enter some new policy area, such as civil rights or industrial regulation.

The New System

The New System began in the 1930s but did not take its present form until the 1970s. It is characterized by a large policy agenda, the end of the debate over the legitimacy of government action (except in the area of First Amendment freedoms), the diffusion and decentralization of power in Congress, and the multiplication of interest groups. The government

How American Politics and Government Have Changed

Old System	New System
Congress	
Chairmen relatively strong	Chairmen relatively weak
Small staffs	Large staffs
Few subcommittees	Many subcommittees
Interest Groups	
A few large blocs (farmers, business, labor)	Many diverse interests that form ad hoc coalitions
Rely on "insider" lobbying	Mobilize grassroots
Presidency	
Small staff	Large staff
Reaches public via press conferences	Reaches public via radio and television
Courts	
Allow government to exercise few economic powers	Allow government to exercise broad economic powers
Take narrow view of individual freedoms	Take broad view of individual freedoms
Political Parties	
Dominated by state and local party leaders meeting in conventions	Dominated by activists chosen in primaries and caucuses
Policy Agenda	
Brief agenda	Long agenda
Key Questions	
Should the federal government enter a new policy area?	How can we fix or pay for an existing policy?
Key Issue	
Would a new federal program abridge states' rights?	Would a new federal program prove popular?

has grown so large that it has a policy on almost every conceivable subject, and so the debate in Washington is less often about whether it is right and prudent to take some bold new step and more often about how the government can best cope with the strains and problems that arise from implementing existing policies. As someone once said, the federal government is now more concerned with managing than with ruling.

For example: In 1935 Congress debated whether the nation should have a Social Security retirement system at all; in the 1980s and 1990s it debated whether the system could best be kept solvent by raising taxes or by cutting benefits. In the 1960s Congress argued over whether there should be any federal civil rights laws at all; by the 1980s it was arguing over whether those laws should be administered in a way that simply eliminated legal barriers to equal opportunity for racial minorities or in a way that through affirmative action would make up for the disadvantages that had burdened such minorities in the past. As late as the 1950s

On September 25, 1957, troops of the 101st Airborne Division escorted nine black children into Little Rock (Arkansas) Central High School to begin its integration.

the president and Congress argued over whether it was right to adopt a new program if it meant that the government had to borrow money to pay for it. During the 1970s and 1980s the existence of a huge federal deficit was taken for granted, and the debate in Washington focused on the best way to slow its rate of growth or cut it back slightly. As late as the 1960s many members of Congress believed that the federal government had no business paying for the health care of its citizens; today hardly anyone argues against having Medicare, but many worry about how best to control its rising cost.

The differences between the Old and New Systems should not be exaggerated. The Constitution still makes it easier for Congress to block the proposals of the president, or for some committee of Congress to defeat the preferences of the majority of Congress, than is true in almost any other democratic government. The system of checks and bal-

ances operates as before. The essential differences between the Old and the New Systems are these:

1. Under the Old System the checks and balances made it difficult for the federal government to *start* a new program, and so the government remained relatively small. Under the New System these checks and balances make it hard to *change* what the government is already doing, and so the government remains large.

2. Under the Old System power was *somewhat centralized* in the hands of party and congressional leaders. There was still plenty of conflict, but the number of people who had to agree before something could be done was not large. Under the New System power is much more *decentralized*, and so it is harder to resolve conflict, because so many more people—party activists, interest group leaders, individual members of Congress, heads of government agencies—must agree.

The transition from the Old to the New System occurred chiefly during two periods in American politics. The first was in the early 1930s, when a catastrophic depression led the government to explore new ways of helping the needy, regulating business, and preventing a recurrence of the disaster. Franklin Roosevelt's New Deal was the result. The huge majorities enjoyed by the Democrats in Congress, coupled with popular demands to solve the problem, led to a vast outpouring of new legislation and the creation of dozens of new government agencies. Though initially the Supreme Court struck down some of these measures as unconstitutional, a key member of the Court changed his mind, and others retired from the bench; by the late 1930s the Court had virtually ceased opposing any economic legislation.

The second period was in the mid-1960s, a time of prosperity. There was no crisis akin to the Great Depression or World War II, but two events helped change the face of American politics. One was an intellectual and popular ferment that we now refer to as the spirit of "the sixties"—a militant civil rights movement, student activism aimed at resisting the Vietnam War, growing concern about threats to the environment, the popular appeal of Ralph Nader and his consumer protection movement, and an optimism among many political and intellectual leaders that the government could solve whatever problems it was willing to address. The other was the 1964 election that returned Lyndon Johnson to the presidency with a larger share of the popular vote than any other president in modern times. Johnson swept into office with huge Democratic majorities in both the House and Senate.

The combination of organized demands for new policies, elite optimism about the likely success of those policies, and extraordinary majorities in Congress meant that President Johnson was able, for a few years, to get almost any program he wanted enacted into law. So large were his majorities in Congress that the conservative coalition of Republicans and southern Democrats was no longer large enough to block action; northern Democratic liberals were sufficiently numerous in the House and Senate to take control of both bodies. Thus much of Johnson's "Great Society" legislation became law. This included (1) the passage of Medicare (to help pay the medical bills of retired people) and Medicaid (to help pay the medical bills of people on welfare); (2) greatly expanded federal aid to the states to assist them in fighting crime, rebuilding slums, and running transit systems; (3) the enactment of major civil rights laws and of a program to provide federal aid to local schools; (4) the creation of a "War on Poverty" that included various job-training and community-action agencies; and (5) the enactment of a variety of laws regulating business for the purpose of reducing auto fatalities, improving the safety and health of industrial workers, cutting back on pollutants entering the atmosphere, and safeguarding consumers from harmful products.

These two periods—the early 1930s and the mid-1960s—changed the political landscape in America. Of the two the latter was perhaps the more important, for not only did it witness the passage of so much unprecedented legislation, but it also saw major changes in the pattern of political leadership. It was during this time that the great majority of the members of the House of Representatives came to enjoy relatively secure seats, primary elections came to supplant party conventions as the decisive means of selecting presidential candidates, interest groups increased greatly in number, and television began to play an important role in shaping the political agenda and perhaps influencing the kinds of candidates that are nominated. (At least one major change in the political process occurred after the 1960s—the passage of the campaign finance laws).

Some people believed that the election of Ronald Reagan in 1981 meant that we had begun a new era of bold changes. No doubt the Reagan administration was more conservative than any other in a half a century; no doubt it made a major effort to alter how certain laws (such as in the area of civil rights) are administered. But rather little in the way of a legislative breakthrough occurred compared to the breakthroughs of Franklin Roosevelt and Lyndon Johnson. Domestic spending was cut in certain areas, and though the effect of a few of these cuts has been keen, there was no reduction in total outlays. (Federal spending, domestic as well as military, *increased* during the Reagan years.) There was a significant personal income tax cut in 1981, but it was partially offset by increases in Social Security and business taxes in subsequent years. There was a buildup in our military, but even before Reagan left office, the buildup had ended.

The politics of the deficit illustrate the features of the New System. The huge gap between what the

The "Rules" of Politics

Three Simple Rules for Improving Government

1. **No law is valid unless the members of Congress voting for it have read it.** The Ninety-seventh Congress considered over ten thousand bills and enacted over five hundred. The tax bill alone ran to several hundred pages. What is your guess as to the number of these bills that the average member of Congress read?

2. **No law or regulation is valid if it is incomprehensible to the average citizen.** Section 509(a) of the Internal Revenue Code reads as follows: "For purposes of paragraph (3), an organization described in paragraph (2) shall be deemed to include an organization described in section 501 (c) (4), (5), or (6) which would be an organization described in paragraph (2) if it were an organization described in section 501 (c) (3)." Any questions?

3. **No law is valid if it does not clearly state its goals and the means to attain them.** The law creating the Federal Communications Commission instructs it to award radio and television licenses on the following principle: to serve "the public interest, convenience, or necessity." Now you know.

Source: Adapted from Irving Younger, "Socrates and Us," *Commentary* (December 1980), 46–49. Reprinted by permission. All rights reserved.

government took in from taxes and what it spent on programs in the 1980s and early 1990s would not exist in a government that had not acquired a large policy agenda—an expensive medical care program, high levels of peacetime military spending, and many subsidies to various domestic interest groups. But the great difficulty the government experienced in trying to cut the deficit revealed, among other things, the effects of decentralized and fragmented political power: no group of officials could impose its preferences on the others.

Should the System Be Changed?

Almost from the day it was ratified, the Constitution has been the object of debate over ways in which it might be improved. These debates have rarely involved the average citizen, who tends to revere the document even if he or she cannot recall all of its details. Because of this deep and broad popular support, scholars and politicians have been wary of attacking it or suggesting many wholesale changes. But such attacks have occurred, and during 1987, when we celebrated the bicentennial of its adoption, we heard a variety of suggestions for improving the Constitution, ranging from particular amendments to wholesale revisions. In general there are today, as in the eighteenth century, two kinds of critics—those who think the federal government is too weak and those who think it is too strong.

Reducing the Barriers to Action

To the first kind of critic, the chief difficulty with the Constitution is the separation of powers. By making every decision the uncertain outcome of the pulling and hauling between the president and Congress, the Constitution precludes the emergence, except perhaps in times of crisis, of the kind of effective national leadership the country needs. In this view our nation today faces a number of challenges that require prompt, decisive, and comprehensive action. Our position of international leadership and the need to find ways of stimulating economic growth (while reducing our dependence on foreign oil and conserving our environment) all require that the president be able to formulate and carry out policies free of numerous pressures and delays from interest groups and local-minded members of Congress.

Such an increase in presidential authority would not only make for better policies, these critics argue, but also would help the voters hold the president and his party accountable for their actions. As matters now stand, nobody in government can be held responsible for policies: everybody takes the credit for successes, and nobody takes the blame for failures. This is because the president, who tends to be the major source of new programs, cannot get his policies adopted by Congress without long delays and much bargaining, the result of which may be some watered-down compromise that neither the president nor Congress really likes but which each must settle for if anything is to be done at all.

Finally, critics of the separation of powers complain that the government agencies responsible for implementing a program are exposed to undue interference from members of Congress and the special interests that can capture a member's ear. In this view the president is supposed to be in charge of the bureaucracy, but in fact he has to share that authority with countless legislators and legislative committees.

Not all critics of the separation of powers agree with all these points, nor do they all agree on what should be done about the problems. But they all have in common a fear that the separation of powers makes the president too weak and insufficiently accountable.

Their proposals for reducing the separation of powers include the following:

- Allow the president to appoint members of Congress to serve in the cabinet (the Constitution forbids members from holding any federal appointive office while in Congress).
- Allow the president to dissolve Congress and call for a special election (elections now can be held only on the schedule determined by the calendar).
- Allow Congress to require a president who has lost its confidence to face the country in a special election before his term would normally end.
- Require the presidential and congressional candidates to run as a team in each congressional district so that each voter would have to vote for the team as a whole. Thus a presidential candidate who carries a given district could be sure that the congressional candidate of his party would also win in the district.
- Have the president serve a single six-year term instead of being eligible for up to two four-year terms; this would presumably free him to lead without having to worry about reelection.
- Lengthen the terms of members of the House of Representatives from two to four years so that the entire House would stand for reelection at the same time as the president.

Some of these proposals are offered out of a desire to make the American system of government work a bit more like the British parliamentary system, in which the prime minister is the undisputed leader of the majority in the British Parliament. The parliamentary system is the major democratic alternative to the American separation-of-powers system in the world today. Another way of describing the aims of these reforms is that they would combine the somewhat greater centralization of power characteristic of the Old System of making policy with the larger agenda and bigger government characteristic of the New System.

Both the diagnosis and the remedies proposed by these critics of the separation of powers have been challenged. Many defenders of the Constitution believe that other nations with a more unified political system, such as Great Britain, have done no better than the United States in dealing with the problems of economic growth, national security, and environmental protection. Moreover, they argue, close congressional scrutiny of presidential proposals has improved those policies more often than it has weakened them. Finally, congressional "interference" in the work of government agencies is a good way of ensuring that the average citizen can fight back against the bureaucracy. Without that so-called interference citizens and interest groups might be helpless before big, powerful agencies.

Each of the specific proposals, defenders of the present system argue, would either make matters worse or have at best uncertain effects. Adding a few members of Congress to the president's cabinet would not help him much in getting his programs through Congress: of the 535 senators and representatives, only about half a dozen would probably be in the cabinet. Giving either the president or Congress the power to call a special election between the regular elections (every two or four years) would cause needless confusion and great expense; the country would live under the threat of being in a perpetual political campaign, with even weaker political parties. Linking the fate of the president and representatives by having them run as a team in each district would reduce the stabilizing and moderating effect of having them separately elected: if a Republican presidential candidate won, he would have a Republican majority in the House; if a Democratic candidate won, he would have a Democratic majority. With a linked ticket we might expect dramatic changes in policy as the political pendulum swung back and forth.

Giving the president a single six-year term would indeed free him from the need to worry about re-election, but it is precisely that worry that keeps the president reasonably concerned about what the American people want.

Finally, defenders of the present system simply do not agree that the separation of powers makes government inert. They marvel at the sweeping domestic- and foreign-policy initiatives taken during this century. How, they ask, can a government system capable of launching a New Deal, a Great Society, and a rocket to the moon; of mobilizing for World War I, World War II, and Vietnam; and of readying to impeach a president for violating his oath of office be characterized as antiquated or prone to inaction?

Defenders believe that problems in the system may result less from the separation of powers and more from the inability (or unwillingness) of key political leaders to work within it. They point, for example, to the early years of the Carter and Clinton administrations. These presidents found it hard to persuade Congress to support their domestic initiatives. Their party had a majority in both houses of Congress, but that did not seem to matter. If the separation of powers, and not a lack of political skills, explains the policy stalemate suffered by Carter and Clinton, then how, defenders ask, did Ronald Reagan

succeed in getting Congress to act quickly on his major domestic proposals?

Increasing the Barriers to Action

The second kind of critic of the Constitution thinks the government does too much, not too little. Though the separation of powers at one time may have slowed the growth of government and moderated the policies it adopted, in the last few decades government has grown helter-skelter. The problem, these critics argue, is not that democracy is a bad idea but that democracy can produce bad, or at least unintended, results if the government caters to the special-interest claims of the citizens rather than to their long-term values.

To see how these unintended results might occur, imagine a situation in which every citizen thinks the government is too big, taxes too heavily, and spends too much. Each citizen wants the government made smaller by reducing the benefits other people get—but not by reducing the benefits he or she gets. In fact the citizen may even be willing to see his or her own benefits cut, provided everybody else's are cut as well, and by a like amount.

But the political system attends to individual wants, which may or may not be in the public interest. It gives aid to farmers, contracts to industry,

Senior citizens rallying to get prescription drugs included in Medicare.

grants to professors, pensions to the elderly, and loans to students. As someone once said, the government is like an adding machine: during elections candidates campaign by promising to do more for whatever group is dissatisfied with what the present officeholders are doing for it. As a result most elections bring to office men and women who are committed to doing more for somebody. The grand total of all these additions is more for everybody. No politician has an incentive to do less for anybody.

Moreover, a big government is hard to manage. When the government tries to do too much, it does nothing well. To the critics our government is big without being strong, fat but not effective.

To remedy this state of affairs these critics suggest various mechanisms, but principally a constitutional amendment that would either set a limit on the amount of money the government could collect in taxes each year or require that each year the government have a balanced budget (that is, not spend more than it collects in taxes), or both. In some versions of these plans an extraordinary majority (say, 60 percent) of Congress could override these limits, and the limits would not apply in wartime.

The effect of such amendments, the proponents claim, would be to force Congress and the president to look at the big picture—the grand total of what they are spending—rather than just to operate the adding machine by repeatedly pushing the "add" button. If they could spend only so much during a given year, they would have to allocate what they spend among all the rival claimants, comparing the worth of each claimant to that of every other one. For example, if more money were spent on the poor, less would be spent on the military, and vice versa. In this way we could no longer add to the national debt by continuing to run up big deficits.

Some critics of an overly powerful federal government think these amendments will not be passed or may prove unworkable. Instead they favor enhancing the president's power to block spending through the line-item veto. The theory is that this power will better equip the president to stop unwarranted spending without vetoing the other provisions of a bill that he approves of.

Finally, some of these critics of a powerful government feel that the real problem arises not only from an excess of "adding machine" democracy but also from the growth in the power of the federal courts. These critics would like to devise a set of laws

or constitutional amendments that would narrow the authority of federal courts.

Congress and Clinton agreed on a law that would give the President a kind of line-item veto, but the Supreme Court has declared the law to be unconstitutional. Others argue that to restrict the level of

POLITICALLY SPEAKING

Political Proverbs

"If you can't stand the heat, get out of the kitchen."
—President Harry S Truman

"You scratch my back, I'll scratch yours."
—Attributed to Simon Cameron, secretary of war in the cabinet of Abraham Lincoln

"To the victor belong the spoils of the enemy."
—Senator William Marcy of New York, 1832

"How you stand depends on where you sit."
—Attributed to Rufus Miles, formerly of the U.S. Budget Bureau

"If it ain't broke, don't fix it."
—Bert Lance, director of the Office of Management and Budget under President Jimmy Carter

"Whenever you have to start explaining—you're in trouble."
—Representative Barber Conable of New York

Source: Adapted from *Safire's Political Dictionary* by William Safire. Copyright © 1968, 1972, 1978 by William Safire. Reprinted by permission of Random House, Inc. and the author.

taxes and to require a balanced budget are unworkable suggestions, even assuming—which these opponents do not—that a smaller government is desirable. There is no precise, agreed-upon way to measure how much the government spends or to predict in advance how much it will receive in taxes during the year; thus defining and enforcing a "balanced budget" is no easy matter. The government has shown great ingenuity in spending money in ways that never appear as part of the regular budget (for example, Social Security).

The line-item veto may or may not be a good idea, these people argue. We may discover that the president will use it not to spend less but to spend more—by threatening to veto something of a modest cost that Congress wants in order to get Congress to vote for something expensive that the president wants.

Finally, some argue that proposals to curtail judicial power are thinly veiled attacks on the ability of the courts to protect essential citizen rights. If Congress and the people do not like the way the Supreme Court has interpreted the Constitution in a particular case, they can always amend the Constitution to change the specific ruling. There is no need to adopt some general, across-the-board limitation on court powers.

Term Limits

A change that might make our system either more or less democratic is to limit the number of terms that people can serve in Congress. Already the president is limited to two terms. The most common proposal is to limit members of the House to six terms (a total of twelve years) and members of the Senate to two (also a total of twelve years).

Between 1992 and 1994 the people in twenty-two states adopted proposals that would have imposed term limits on their delegations to Congress. But federal courts have held these limits to be unconstitutional. The Constitution makes Congress the sole judge of the qualifications of its members and limits the states to determining the time, place, and manner of holding congressional elections.

It is also not clear what effect such limits might have, even if they were constitutional. Proponents argue that they would once again make members of Congress "citizen legislators," not career politicians. Knowing that they could serve for only twelve years, they would be free, at least during their last term in office, to do what is right rather than what is

demanded by interest groups or required by their own desire for reelection.

But opponents argue that short-term legislators will never master the intricacies of federal politics and policies, and so they will become dependent on unelected staff members and Washington lobbyists. And they point to the many long-term legislators who are widely admired. Finally, they argue that the voters are the best judges of who should stay in office and so should have the right to keep reelecting their own representatives and senators if they wish.

There is no way to settle this issue by arguments or theories. We will learn what difference term limits make only if we try them. But there is a risk: if we try them and don't like them, it will be very hard to get rid of them. In any event term limits may be hard to try, because Congress doesn't like them and Congress must approve a constitutional amendment to impose them (unless, of course, two-thirds of the state legislatures demand the calling of a constitutional convention to consider them). We can, of course, learn something about term limits in the states that impose them on state officials.

Who Is Right?

Some of the arguments of these various critics of the Constitution may strike you as plausible or even entirely convincing. But one should not make or remake a Constitution based entirely on abstract reasoning or unproven factual arguments. Even when the Constitution was first written in 1787, it was not an exercise in abstract philosophy but rather an effort by the Framers to solve pressing, practical problems in the light of a theory of human nature, the lessons of past experience, and a close consideration of how governments in other countries had worked.

Just because the Constitution is now over two hundred years old does not mean that it is out-of-date. The crucial questions are these: How well has it worked over the long sweep of American history? And how well has it worked compared to the constitutions of other democratic nations?

The only way to answer these questions is to study American government closely, with special attention to its historical evolution, the way it makes particular policies, and the practices of other nations. This book has provided only the briefest introduction to the workings of American government and has said very little about how it works in comparison to other governments or how it handles particular policy issues. Therefore you should not try to make up your mind about what, if anything, needs to change in our Constitution from what you have learned here. Learn more.

Nonetheless, by reviewing these competing proposals for revising the Constitution, you will at least be able to understand the central features of our system of government and the controversies that system has engendered, as well as how that system has changed over the past half century.

World Wide Web Resources

- Nonpartisan reviews of public policy issues:
  www.policy.com
  www.publicagenda.org

- For partisan discussion of issues, use the World Wide Web addresses of the Washington, D.C., think tanks listed in Chapter 14.

·The Declaration of Independence

In Congress, July 4, 1776

The Unanimous Declaration of the Thirteen United States of America

When, in the course of human events, it becomes necessary for one people to dissolve the political bands which have connected them with another, and to assume, among the powers of the earth, the separate and equal station to which the laws of nature and of nature's God entitle them, a decent respect to the opinions of mankind requires that they should declare the causes which impel them to the separation.

We hold these truths to be self-evident: That all men are created equal; that they are endowed by their Creator with certain unalienable rights; that among these are life, liberty, and the pursuit of happiness; that, to secure these rights, governments are instituted among men, deriving their just powers from the consent of the governed; that whenever any form of government becomes destructive of these ends, it is the right of the people to alter or to abolish it, and to institute new government, laying its foundation on such principles, and organizing its power in such form, as to them shall seem most likely to effect their safety and happiness. Prudence, indeed, will dictate that governments long established should not be changed for light and transient causes; and accordingly all experience hath shown that mankind are more disposed to suffer, while evils are sufferable, than to right themselves by abolishing the forms to which they are accustomed. But when a long train of abuses and usurpations, pursuing invariably the same object, evinces a design to reduce them under absolute despotism, it is their right, it is their duty, to throw off such government, and to provide new guards for their future security. Such has been the patient sufferance of these colonies; and such is now the necessity which constrains them to alter their former systems of government. The history of the present King of Great Britain is a history of repeated injuries and usurpations, all having in direct object the establishment of an absolute tyranny over these states. To prove this, let facts be submitted to a candid world.

He has refused to assent to laws, the most wholesome and necessary for the public good.

He has forbidden his governors to pass laws of immediate and pressing importance, unless suspended in their operation till his assent should be obtained; and, when so suspended, he has utterly neglected to attend to them.

He has refused to pass other laws for the accommodation of large districts of people, unless those people would relinquish the right of representation in the legislature, a right inestimable to them, and formidable to tyrants only.

He has called together legislative bodies at places unusual, uncomfortable, and distant from the depository of their public records, for the sole purpose of fatiguing them into compliance with his measures.

He has dissolved representative houses repeatedly, for opposing, with manly firmness, his invasions on the rights of the people.

He has refused for a long time, after such dissolutions, to cause others to be elected; whereby the legislative powers, incapable of annihilation, have returned to the people at large for their exercise; the state remaining, in the mean time, exposed to all dangers of invasions from without and convulsions within.

He has endeavored to prevent the population of these states; for that purpose obstructing the laws for naturalization of foreigners; refusing to pass others to encourage their migration hither, and raising the conditions of new appropriations of lands.

He has obstructed the administration of justice, by refusing his assent to laws for establishing judiciary powers.

He has made judges dependent on his will alone, for the tenure of their offices, and the amount and payment of their salaries.

He has erected a multitude of new offices, and sent hither swarms of officers to harass our people, and eat out their substance.

He has kept among us, in times of peace, standing armies, without the consent of our legislatures.

He has affected to render the military independent of, and superior to, the civil power.

He has combined with others to subject us to a jurisdiction foreign to our constitution, and unacknowledged by our laws, giving his assent to their acts of pretended legislation:

For quartering large bodies of armed troops among us:

For protecting them, by a mock trial, from punishment for any murders which they should commit on the inhabitants of these states;

For cutting off our trade with all parts of the world;

For imposing taxes on us without our consent;

For depriving us, in many cases, of the benefits of trial by jury;

For transporting us beyond seas, to be tried for pretended offenses;

For abolishing the free system of English laws in a neighboring province, establishing therein an arbitrary government, and enlarging its boundaries, so as to render it at once an example and fit instrument for introducing the same absolute rule into these colonies;

For taking away our charters, abolishing our most valuable laws, and altering fundamentally the forms of our governments;

For suspending our own legislatures, and declaring themselves invested with power to legislate for us in all cases whatsoever.

He has abdicated government here, by declaring us out of his protection and waging war against us.

He has plundered our seas, ravaged our coasts, burned our towns, and destroyed the lives of our people.

He is at this time transporting large armies of foreign mercenaries to complete the works of death, desolation, and tyranny already begun with circumstances of cruelty and perfidy scarcely paralleled in the most barbarous ages, and totally unworthy the head of a civilized nation.

He has constrained our fellow-citizens, taken captive on the high seas, to bear arms against their country, to become the executioners of their friends and brethren, or to fall themselves by their hands.

He has excited domestic insurrection among us, and has endeavored to bring on the inhabitants of our frontiers the merciless Indian savages, whose known rule of warfare is an undistinguished destruction of all ages, sexes, and conditions.

In every stage of these oppressions we have petitioned for redress in the most humble terms; our repeated petitions have been answered only by repeated injury. A prince, whose character is thus marked by every act which may define a tyrant, is unfit to be the ruler of a free people.

Nor have we been wanting in our attentions to our British brethren. We have warned them, from time to time, of attempts by their Legislature to extend an unwarrantable jurisdiction over us. We have reminded them of the circumstances of our emigration and settlement here. We have appealed to their native justice and magnanimity; and we have conjured them, by the ties of our common kindred, to disavow these usurpations, which would inevitably interrupt our connections and correspondence. They, too, have been deaf to the voice of justice and of consanguinity. We must, therefore, acquiesce in the necessity which denounces our separation, and hold them, as we hold the rest of mankind, enemies in war, in peace friends.

We, therefore, the representatives of the United States of America, in General Congress assembled, appealing to the Supreme Judge of the world for the rectitude of our intentions, do, in the name and by the authority of the good people of these colonies, solemnly publish and declare, that these United Colonies are, and of right ought to be, FREE AND INDEPENDENT STATES; that they are absolved from all allegiance to the British crown, and that all political connection between them and the state of Great Britain is, and ought to be, totally dissolved; and that, as free and independent states, they have full power to levy war, conclude peace, contract alliances, establish commerce, and do all other acts and things which independent states may of right do. And for the support of this declaration, with a firm reliance on the protection of Divine Providence, we mutually pledge to each other our lives, our fortunes, and our sacred honor.

JOHN HANCOCK [*President*]
[*and fifty-five others*]

The Constitution of the United States

Preamble

We the People of the United States, in Order to form a more perfect Union, establish Justice, insure domestic Tranquility, provide for the common defence, promote the general Welfare, and secure the Blessings of Liberty to ourselves and our Posterity, do ordain and establish this Constitution for the United States of America.

ARTICLE I.

Bicameral Congress

Section 1.   All legislative Powers herein granted shall be vested in a Congress of the United States, which shall consist of a Senate and House of Representatives.

Membership of the House

Section 2.   The House of Representatives shall be composed of Members chosen every second Year by the People of the several States, and the Electors in each State shall have the Qualifications requisite for Electors of the most numerous Branch of the State Legislature.

No person shall be a Representative who shall not have attained to the age of twenty five Years, and been seven Years a Citizen of the United States, and who shall not, when elected, be an Inhabitant of that State in which he shall be chosen.

Representatives and direct Taxes shall be apportioned among the several States which may be included within this Union, according to their respective Numbers, which shall be determined by adding to the whole Number of free Persons, including those bound to Service for a Term of Years, and excluding Indians not taxed, three fifths of all other Persons.[1] The actual Enumeration shall be made within three Years after the first Meeting of the Congress of the United States, and within every subsequent Term of ten Years, in such Manner as they shall by Law direct. The Number of Representatives shall not exceed one for every thirty Thousand, but each State shall have at Least one Representative; and until such enumeration shall be made, the State of New Hampshire shall be entitled to chuse three, Massachusetts eight, Rhode-Island and Providence Plantations one, Connecticut five, New-York six, New Jersey four, Pennsylvania eight, Delaware one, Maryland six, Virginia ten, North Carolina five, South Carolina five, and Georgia three.

When vacancies happen in the Representation from any State, the Executive Authority thereof shall issue Writs of Election to fill such Vacancies.

Power to impeach

The House of Representatives shall chuse their Speaker and other Officers; and shall have the sole Power of Impeachment.

Membership of the Senate

Section 3.   The Senate of the United States shall be composed of two Senators from each State, *chosen by the Legislature thereof,*[2] for six Years; and each Senator shall have one Vote.

NOTE: The topical headings are not part of the original Constitution. Excluding the Preamble and Closing, those portions set in italic type have been superseded or changed by later amendments.
1. Changed by the Fourteenth Amendment, section 2.
2. Changed by the Seventeenth Amendment.

Immediately after they shall be assembled in Consequence of the first Election, they shall be divided as equally as may be into three Classes. The Seats of the Senators of the first class shall be vacated at the Expiration of the second Year, of the second Class at the Expiration of the fourth Year, and of the third Class at the Expiration of the sixth Year, so that one third may be chosen every second Year; *and if Vacancies happen by Resignation, or otherwise, during the Recess of the Legislature of any State, the Executive thereof may make temporary Appointments until the next Meeting of the Legislature, which shall then fill such Vacancies.*[3]

No Person shall be a Senator who shall not have attained to the Age of thirty Years, and been nine Years a Citizen of the United States, and who shall not, when elected, be an Inhabitant of that State for which he shall be chosen.

The Vice President of the United States shall be President of the Senate, but shall have no Vote, unless they be equally divided.

The Senate shall chuse their other Officers, and also a President pro tempore, in the Absence of the Vice President, or when he shall exercise the Office of President of the United States.

Power to try impeachments

The Senate shall have the sole Power to try all Impeachments. When sitting for that Purpose, they shall be on Oath or Affirmation. When the President of the United States is tried the Chief Justice shall preside: And no Person shall be convicted without the Concurrence of two thirds of the Members present.

Judgment in Cases of Impeachment shall not extend further than to removal from Office, and disqualification to hold and enjoy any Office of honor, Trust or Profit under the United States: but the Party convicted shall nevertheless be liable and subject to Indictment, Trial, Judgment and Punishment, according to Law.

Laws governing elections

Section 4.   The Times, Places and Manner of holding Elections for Senators and Representatives, shall be prescribed in each State by the Legislature thereof; but the Congress may at any time by Law make or alter such Regulations, except as to the Places of chusing Senators.

The Congress shall assemble at least once in every Year, and such Meeting shall be on the *first Monday in December, unless they shall by Law appoint a different Day.*[4]

Rules of Congress

Section 5.   Each House shall be the Judge of the Elections, Returns and Qualifications of its own Members, and a Majority of each shall constitute a Quorum to do Business; but a smaller number may adjourn from day to day, and may be authorized to compel the Attendance of absent Members, in such Manner, and under such Penalties as each House may provide.

Each House may determine the Rules of its Proceedings, punish its Members for disorderly Behaviour, and, with the Concurrence of two thirds, expel a Member.

Each House shall keep a Journal of its Proceedings, and from time to time publish the same, excepting such Parts as may in their Judgment require Secrecy; and the Yeas and Nays of the Members of either House on any question shall, at the Desire of one fifth of those Present, be entered on the Journal.

---

3. Changed by the Seventeenth Amendment.
4. Changed by the Twentieth Amendment, section 2.

Neither House, during the Session of Congress, shall, without the Consent of the other, adjourn for more than three days, nor to any other Place than that in which the two Houses shall be sitting.

Salaries and immunities of members

Section 6.   The Senators and Representatives shall receive a Compensation for their Services, to be ascertained by Law, and paid out of the Treasury of the United States. They shall in all Cases, except Treason, Felony and Breach of the Peace, be privileged from Arrest during their Attendance at the Session of their respective Houses, and in going to and returning from the same; and for any Speech or Debate in either House, they shall not be questioned in any other Place.

Bar on members of Congress holding federal appointive office

No Senator or Representative shall, during the Time for which he was elected, be appointed to any civil Office under the Authority of the United States, which shall have been created, or the Emoluments whereof shall have been encreased during such time; and no Person holding any Office under the United States, shall be a Member of either House during his Continuance in Office.

Money bills originate in House

Section 7.   All Bills for raising Revenue shall originate in the House of Representatives; but the Senate may propose or concur with Amendments as on other Bills.

Procedure for enacting laws; veto power

Every Bill which shall have passed the House of Representatives and the Senate, shall, before it become a Law, be presented to the President of the United States; If he approve he shall sign it, but if not he shall return it, with Objections to that House in which it shall have originated, who shall enter the Objections at large on their Journal, and proceed to reconsider it. If after such Reconsideration two thirds of that House shall agree to pass the Bill, it shall be sent, together with the Objections, to the other House, by which it shall likewise be reconsidered, and if approved by two thirds of that House, it shall become a Law. But in all such Cases the Votes of both Houses shall be determined by yeas and Nays, and the Names of the Persons voting for and against the Bill shall be entered on the Journal of each House respectively. If any Bill shall not be returned by the President within ten Days (Sundays excepted) after it shall have been presented to him, the Same shall be a Law, in like Manner, as if he had signed it, unless the Congress by their Adjournment prevent its Return, in which Case it shall not be a Law.

Every Order, Resolution, or Vote to which the Concurrence of the Senate and House of Representatives may be necessary (except on a question of Adjournment) shall be presented to the President of the United States; and before the Same shall take Effect, shall be approved by him, or being disapproved by him, shall be repassed by two thirds of the Senate and House of Representatives, according to the Rules and Limitations prescribed in the Case of a Bill.

Powers of Congress
—taxes

Section 8.   The Congress shall have Power To lay and Collect Taxes, Duties, Imposts and Excises, to pay the Debts and provide for the common Defence and general Welfare of the United States; but all Duties, Imposts and Excises shall be uniform throughout the United States.

—borrowing

To borrow Money on the credit of the United States;

—regulation of commerce

To regulate Commerce with foreign Nations, and among the several States, and with the Indian Tribes;

—naturalization and bankruptcy

To establish an uniform Rule of Naturalization, and uniform Laws on the subject of Bankruptcies throughout the United States;

—money

To coin Money, regulate the Value thereof, and of foreign Coin, and fix the Standard of Weights and Measures;

—counterfeiting

To provide for the Punishment of counterfeiting the Securities and current Coin of the United States;

—post office

To establish Post Offices and post Roads;

—patents and copyrights

To promote the Progress of Science and useful Arts, by securing for limited Times to Authors and Inventors the exclusive Right to their respective Writings and Discoveries;

—create courts

To constitute Tribunals inferior to the Supreme Court;

—punish piracies

To define and punish Piracies and Felonies committed on the high Seas, and Offences against the Law of Nations;

—declare war

To declare War, grant Letters of Marque and Reprisal, and make Rules concerning Captures on Land and Water;

—create army and navy

To raise and support Armies, but no Appropriation of Money to that Use shall be for a longer Term than two Years;

To provide and maintain a Navy;

To make Rules for the Government and Regulation of the land and naval Forces;

—call the militia

To provide for calling forth the Militia to execute the Laws of the Union, suppress Insurrections and repel Invasions;

To provide for organizing, arming, and disciplining, the Militia, and for governing such Part of them as may be employed in the Service of the United States, reserving to the States respectively, the Appointment of the Officers, and the Authority of training the Militia according to the discipline prescribed by Congress;

—govern District of Columbia

To exercise exclusive Legislation in all Cases whatsoever, over such District (not exceeding ten Miles square) as may, by Cession of Particular States, and the Acceptance of Congress, become the Seat of the Government of the United States, and to exercise like Authority over all Places purchased by the Consent of the Legislature of the State in which the Same shall be, for the Erection of Forts, Magazines, Arsenals, dock-Yards and other needful Buildings;—And

 —"necessary-and-proper" clause

To make all Laws which shall be necessary and proper for carrying into Execution the foregoing Powers, and all other Powers vested by this Constitution in the Government of the United States, or in any Department or Officer thereof.

Restrictions on powers of Congress

Section 9.   The Migration or Importation of such Persons as any of the States now existing shall think proper to admit, shall not be prohibited by the Congress prior to the Year one thousand eight hundred and eight, but a Tax or duty may be imposed on such Importation, not exceeding ten dollars for each Person.

—slave trade

—habeas corpus

The Privilege of the Writ of Habeas Corpus shall not be suspended, unless when in Cases of Rebellion or Invasion the public Safety may require it.

—no bill of attainder or ex post facto law

No bill of Attainder or ex post facto Law shall be passed.

No Capitation, or other direct, Tax shall be laid, *unless in Proportion to the Census or Enumeration herein before directed to be taken.*[5]

—no interstate tariffs

No Tax or Duty shall be laid on Articles exported from any State.

—no preferential treatment for some states

No Preference shall be given by any Regulation of Commerce or Revenue to the Ports of one State over those of another; nor shall Vessels bound to, or from, one State, be obliged to enter, clear or pay Duties in another.

———

5. Changed by the Sixteenth Amendment.

—*appropriations*

No Money shall be drawn from the Treasury, but in Consequence of Appropriations made by Law; and a regular Statement and Account of the Receipts and Expenditures of all public Money shall be published from time to time.

—*no titles of nobility*

No Title of Nobility shall be granted by the United States: And no Person holding any Office of Profit or Trust under them, shall, without the Consent of the Congress, accept of any present, Emolument, Office, or Title, of any kind whatever, from any King, Prince, or foreign State.

Restrictions on powers of states

Section 10.   No State shall enter into any Treaty, Alliance, or Confederation; grant Letters of Marque and Reprisal; coin Money; emit Bills of Credit; make any Thing but gold and silver Coin a Tender in Payment of Debts; pass any Bill of Attainder, ex post facto Law, or Law impairing the Obligation of Contracts, or grant any Title of Nobility.

No State shall, without the Consent of Congress, lay any Imposts or Duties on Imports or Exports, except what may be absolutely necessary for executing its inspection Laws; and the net Produce of all Duties and Imposts, laid by any State on Imports or Exports, shall be for the Use of the Treasury of the United States; and all such Laws shall be subject to the Revision and Controul of the Congress.

No State shall, without the Consent of Congress, lay any Duty of Tonnage, keep Troops, or Ships of War in time of Peace, enter into any Agreement or Compact with another State, or with a foreign Power, or engage in War, unless actually invaded, or in such imminent Danger as will not admit of delay.

ARTICLE II.

Office of president

Section 1.   The executive Power shall be vested in a President of the United States of America. He shall hold his Office during the Term of four Years, and, together with the Vice President, chosen for the same Term, be elected, as follows

Election of president

Each State shall appoint, in such Manner as the Legislature thereof may direct, a Number of Electors, equal to the whole Number of Senators and Representatives to which the State may be entitled in the Congress: but no Senator or Representative, or Person holding an Office of Trust or Profit under the United States, shall be appointed an Elector.

The Electors shall meet in their respective States, and vote by Ballot for two Persons, of whom one at least shall not be an Inhabitant of the same State with themselves. And they shall make a List of all the Persons voted for, and of the Number of Votes for each; which List they shall sign and certify, and transmit sealed to the Seat of the Government of the United States, directed to the President of the Senate. The President of the Senate shall, in the Presence of the Senate and House of Representatives, open all the Certificates, and the Votes shall then be counted. The Person having the greatest Number of Votes shall be the President, if such Number be a Majority of the whole Number of Electors appointed; and if there be more than one who have such Majority, and have an equal Number of Votes, then the House of Representatives shall immediately chuse by Ballot one of them for President; and if no Person have a Majority, then from the five highest on the List said House shall in like Manner chuse the President. But in chusing the President, the Votes shall be taken by States, the Representation from each State having one Vote; a quorum for this Purpose shall consist of a Member or Members from two thirds of the States, and a Majority of all the States shall be necessary to a Choice. In every Case, after the Choice of the President, the Person having the greatest Number of Votes of the Electors shall be the Vice President. But if there should remain two or more who have equal Votes, the Senate shall chuse from them by Ballot the Vice President.[6]

The Congress may determine the Time of chusing the Electors, and the Day on which they shall give their Votes, which Day shall be the same throughout the United States.

Requirements to be president

No Person except a natural born Citizen, or a Citizen of the United States, at the time of the Adoption of this Constitution, shall be eligible to the Office of President; neither shall any person be eligible to that Office who shall not have attained to the Age of thirty five Years, and been fourteen Years a Resident within the United States.

In Case of the Removal of the President from Office, or of his Death, Resignation, or Inability to discharge the Powers and Duties of the said Office, the Same shall devolve on the Vice President, and the Congress may by Law provide for the Case of Removal, Death, Resignation or Inability, both of the President and Vice President, declaring what Officer shall then act as President, and such Officer shall act accordingly, until the Disability be removed, or a President shall be elected.[7]

Pay of president

The President shall, at stated Times, receive for his Services, a Compensation, which shall neither be increased nor diminished during the Period for which he shall have been elected, and he shall not receive within that Period any other Emolument from the United States, or any of them.

Before he enter on the Execution of his Office, he shall take the following Oath or Affirmation:—"I do solemnly swear (or affirm) that I will faithfully execute the Office of President of the United States, and will to the best of my Ability preserve, protect and defend the Constitution of the United States."

Powers of president
—commander in chief

Section 2.   The President shall be Commander in Chief of the Army and Navy of the United States, and of the Militia of the several States, when called into the actual Service of the United States; he may require the Opinion, in writing, of the principal Officer in each of the executive Departments, upon any Subject relating to the Duties of their respective Offices, and he shall have Power to grant Reprieves and Pardons for Offences against the United States, except in Cases of Impeachment.

—pardons

—treaties and appointments

He shall have Power, by and with the Advice and Consent of the Senate, to make Treaties, provided two thirds of the Senators present concur; and he shall nominate, and by and with the Advice and Consent of the Senate, shall appoint Ambassadors, other public Ministers and Consuls, Judges of the supreme Court, and all other Officers of the United States, whose Appointments are not herein otherwise provided for, and which shall be established by Law: but the Congress may by Law vest the Appointment of such inferior Officers, as they think proper, in the President alone, in the Courts of Law, or in the Heads of Departments.

The President shall have Power to fill up all Vacancies that may happen during the Recess of the Senate, by granting Commissions which shall expire at the End of their next Session.

Relations of president with Congress

Section 3.   He shall from time to time give to the Congress Information of the State of the Union, and recommend to their Consideration such Measures as he

---

6. Superseded by the Twelfth Amendment.
7. Modified by the Twenty-fifth Amendment.

shall judge necessary and expedient; he may, on extraordinary Occasions, convene both Houses, or either of them, and in Case of Disagreement between them, with Respect to the Time of Adjournment, he may adjourn them to such Time as he shall think proper; he shall receive Ambassadors and other public Ministers; he shall take Care that the Laws be faithfully executed, and shall Commission all the Officers of the United States.

Impeachment

Section 4.   The President, Vice President and all civil Officers of the United States, shall be removed from Office on Impeachment for, and Conviction of, Treason, Bribery, or other high Crimes and Misdemeanors.

ARTICLE III.

Federal courts

Section 1.   The judicial Power of the United States, shall be vested in one supreme Court, and in such inferior Courts as the Congress may from time to time ordain and establish. The Judges, both of the supreme and inferior Courts, shall hold their Offices during good Behaviour, and shall, at stated Times, receive for their Services, a Compensation, which shall not be diminished during their Continuance in Office.

Jurisdiction of courts

Section 2.   The judicial Power shall extend to all Cases, in Law and Equity, arising under this Constitution, the Laws of the United States, and Treaties made, or which shall be made, under their Authority;—to all Cases affecting Ambassadors, other public Ministers and Consuls;—to all Cases of admiralty and maritime Jurisdiction;—to Controversies to which the United States shall be a Party;—to Controversies between two or more States;—*between a State and Citizens of another State;*[8]—between Citizens of different States;—between Citizens of the same State claiming Lands under Grants of different States, and between a State, or the Citizens thereof, and foreign States, Citizens or Subjects.

—original

In all Cases affecting Ambassadors, other public Ministers and Consuls, and those in which a State shall be Party, the supreme Court shall have original Jurisdiction. In all the other Cases before mentioned, the supreme Court shall have appellate Jurisdiction, both as to Law and Fact, with such Exceptions, and under such Regulations as the Congress shall make.

—appellate

The Trial of all Crimes, except in Cases of Impeachment, shall be by Jury; and such Trial shall be held in the State where the said Crimes shall have been committed; but when not committed within any State, the Trial shall be at such Place or Places as the Congress may by Law have directed.

Treason

Section 3.   Treason against the United States, shall consist only in levying War against them, or in adhering to their Enemies, giving them Aid and Comfort. No Person shall be convicted of Treason unless on the Testimony of two Witnesses to the same overt Act, or on Confession in open Court.

The Congress shall have Power to declare the Punishment of Treason, but no Attainder of Treason shall work Corruption of Blood, or Forfeiture except during the Life of the Person attainted.

---

8. Modified by the Eleventh Amendment.

ARTICLE IV.

Full faith and credit

Section 1.   Full Faith and Credit shall be given in each State to the public Acts, Records, and judicial Proceedings of every other State. And the Congress may by general Laws prescribe the Manner in which such Acts, Records and Proceedings shall be proved, and the Effect thereof.

Privileges and immunities

Section 2.   The Citizens of each State shall be entitled to all Privileges and Immunities of Citizens in the several States.

Extradition

A person charged in any State with Treason, Felony, or other Crime, who shall flee from Justice, and be found in another State, shall on Demand of the executive Authority of the State from which he fled, be delivered up, to be removed to the State having Jurisdiction of the Crime.

No Person held to Service or Labour in one State, under the Laws thereof, escaping into another, shall, in Consequence of any Law or Regulation therein, be discharged from such Service or Labour, but shall be delivered up on Claim of the Party to whom such Service or Labour may be due.[9]

Creation of new states

Section 3.   New States may be admitted by the Congress into this Union; but no new State shall be formed or erected within the Jurisdiction of any other State; nor any State be formed by the Junction of two or more States, or Parts of States, without the Consent of the Legislatures of the States concerned as well as of the Congress.

Governing territories

The Congress shall have Power to dispose of and make all needful Rules and Regulations respecting the Territory or other Property belonging to the United States; and nothing in this Constitution shall be so construed as to Prejudice any Claims of the United States, or of any particular State.

Protection of states

Section 4.   The United States shall guarantee to every State in this Union a Republican Form of Government, and shall protect each of them against Invasion; and on Application of the Legislature, or of the Executive (when the Legislature cannot be convened) against domestic Violence.

ARTICLE V.

Amending the Constitution

The Congress, whenever two thirds of both Houses shall deem it necessary, shall propose Amendments to this Constitution, or, on the Application of the Legislatures of two thirds of the several States, shall call a Convention for proposing Amendments, which, in either Case, shall be valid to all Intents and Purposes, as Part of this Constitution, when ratified by the Legislatures of three fourths of the several States, or by Conventions in three fourths thereof, as the one or the other Mode of Ratification may be proposed by the Congress; Provided that no Amendment which may be made prior to the Year One thousand eight hundred and eight shall in any Manner after the first and fourth Clauses in the Ninth Section of the first Article; and that no State, without its Consent, shall be deprived of its equal Suffrage in the Senate.

---

9. Changed by the Thirteenth Amendment.

ARTICLE VI.

Assumption of debts of
Confederation

All Debts contracted and Engagements entered into, before the Adoption of this Constitution, shall be as valid against the United States under this Constitution, as under the Confederation.

 Supremacy of federal laws and
treaties

This Constitution, and the Laws of the United States which shall be made in Pursuance thereof; and all Treaties made, or which shall be made, under the Authority of the United States, shall be the Supreme Law of the Land; and the Judges in every State shall be bound thereby, any Thing in the Constitution or Laws of any State to the Contrary notwithstanding.

No religious test

The Senators and Representatives before mentioned, and the Members of the several State Legislatures, and all executive and judicial Officers, both of the United States and of the several States, shall be bound by Oath or Affirmation, to support this Constitution; but no religious Test shall ever be required as a Qualification to any Office or public Trust under the United States.

ARTICLE VII.

Ratification procedure

The Ratification of the Conventions of nine States, shall be sufficient for the Establishment of this Constitution between the States so ratifying the Same.

Done in Convention by the Unanimous Consent of the States present the Seventeenth Day of September in the Year of our Lord one thousand seven hundred and Eighty seven and of the Independence of the United States of America the Twelfth In witness whereof We have hereunto subscribed our Names,

G⁰. ASHINGTON—*Presid ͭ.*
and deputy from Virginia

New Hampshire	JOHN LANGDON NICHOLAS GILMAN	*Connecticut*	Wᴹ. SAMᴸ. JOHNSON ROGER SHERMAN
Massachusetts	NATHANIEL GORHAM RUFUS KING	*New York*	ALEXANDER HAMILTON
New Jersey	WIL: LIVINGSTON DAVID BREARLEY Wᴹ. PATERSON JONA: DAYTON	*Maryland*	JAMES Mᶜ HENRY DAN OF Sᵀ THOˢ. JENIFER DANᴸ. CARROLL
		Virginia	JOHN BLAIR— JAMES MADISON JR.
Pennsylvania	B FRANKLIN THOMAS MIFFLIN ROBᵀ. MORRIS GEO. CLYMER THOˢ. FITZSIMONS JARED INGERSOLL JAMES WILSON GOUV MORRIS	*North Carolina*	Wᴹ. BLOUNT RICHᴰ. DOBBS SPAIGHT HU WILLIAMSON
		South Carolina	J. RUTLEDGE CHARLES COTESWORTH PINCKNEY CHARLES PINCKNEY PIERCE BUTLER

Delaware
{
GEO: READ
GUNNING BEDFORD jun
JOHN DICKINSON
RICHARD BASSETT
JACO: BROOM
}

Georgia
{
WILLIAM FEW
ABR BALDWIN
}

[The first ten amendments, known as the "Bill of Rights," were ratified in 1791.]

AMENDMENT I.

Freedom of religion, speech, press, assembly

Congress shall make no law respecting an establishment of religion, or prohibiting the free exercise thereof, or abridging the freedom of speech, or of the press; or the right of the people peaceably to assemble, and to petition the Government for a redress of grievances.

AMENDMENT II.

Right to bear arms

A well regulated Militia, being necessary to the security of a free State, the right of the people to keep and bear Arms, shall not be infringed.

AMENDMENT III.

Quartering troops in private homes

No Soldier shall, in time of peace be quartered in any house without the consent of the Owner, nor in time of war, but in a manner to be prescribed by law.

AMENDMENT IV.

Prohibition against unreasonable searches and seizures

The right of the people to be secure in their persons, houses, papers, and effects, against unreasonable searches and seizures, shall not be violated, and no Warrants shall issue, but upon probable cause, supported by Oath or affirmation, and particularly describing the place to be searched, and the persons or things to be seized.

AMENDMENT V.

Right when accused; "due-process" clause

No person shall be held to answer for a capital, or otherwise infamous crime, unless on a presentment or indictment of a Grand Jury, except in cases arising in the land or naval forces, or in the Militia, when in actual service in time of War or public danger; nor shall any person be subject for the same offence to be twice put in jeopardy of life or limb; nor shall be compelled in any criminal case to be a witness against himself, nor be deprived of life, liberty, or property, without due process of law, nor shall private property be taken for public use, without just compensation.

AMENDMENT VI.

Rights when on trial

In all criminal prosecutions, the accused shall enjoy the right to a speedy and public trial, by an impartial jury of the State and district wherein the crime shall have been committed, which district shall have been previously ascertained by law, and to be informed of the nature and cause of the accusation; to be confronted with the witnesses against him; to have compulsory process for obtaining witnesses in his favor, and to have the Assistance of Counsel for his defence.

AMENDMENT VII.

Common-law suits

In Suits at common law, where the value in controversy shall exceed twenty dollars, the right of trial by jury shall be preserved, and no fact tried by a jury, shall be otherwise reexamined in any Court of the United States, than according to the rules of the common law.

AMENDMENT VIII.

Bail; no "cruel and unusual" punishments

Excessive bail shall not be required, nor excessive fines imposed, nor cruel and unusual punishments inflicted.

AMENDMENT IX.

Unenumerated rights protected

The enumeration in the Constitution, of certain rights, shall not be construed to deny or disparage others retained by the people.

AMENDMENT X.

Powers reserved for states

The powers not delegated to the United States by the Constitution, nor prohibited by it to the States, are reserved to the States respectively, or to the people.

AMENDMENT XI.
[*Ratified in 1795.*]

Limits on suits against states

The Judicial power of the United States shall not be construed to extend to any suit in law or equity, commenced or prosecuted against one of the United States by Citizens of another state, or by Citizens or Subjects of any Foreign State.

AMENDMENT XII.
[*Ratified in 1804.*]

Revision of electoral-college procedure

The Electors shall meet in their respective states and vote by ballot for President and Vice President, one of whom, at least, shall not be an inhabitant of the same state with themselves; they shall name in their ballots the person voted for as President, and in distinct ballots the person voted for as Vice President, and they shall make distinct lists of all persons voted for as President, and of all persons voted for as Vice President, and of the number of votes for each, which lists they shall sign and certify, and transmit sealed to the seat of government of the United States, directed to the President of the Senate;—The President of the Senate shall, in the presence of the Senate and House of Representatives, open all the certificates and the votes shall then be counted;—The person having the greatest number of votes for President, shall be the President, if such number be a majority of the whole number of Electors appointed; and if no person have such majority, then from the persons having the highest numbers not exceeding three on the list of those voted for as President, the House of Representatives shall choose immediately, by ballot, the President. But in choosing the President, the votes shall be taken by states, the representation from each state having one vote; a quorum for this purpose shall consist of a member or members from two-thirds of the states, and a majority of all the states shall be necessary to a choice. *And if the House of Representatives shall not choose a President whenever the right of choice shall devolve upon them, before the fourth day of March next following, then the Vice President shall act as President, as in the case of the death or other constitutional disability of the President.*—[10] The person having the greatest number of votes as Vice President, shall be the Vice President, if such number be a majority of the whole number of Electors appointed, and if no person have a majority, then from the two highest numbers on the list, the Senate shall choose the Vice President; a quorum for the purpose shall consist of two-thirds of the whole number of Senators, and a majority of the whole number shall be necessary to a choice. But no person constitutionally ineligible to the office of President shall be eligible to that of Vice President of the United States.

AMENDMENT XIII.
[*Ratified in 1865.*]

Slavery prohibited

Section 1.   Neither slavery nor involuntary servitude, except as a punishment for crime whereof the party shall have been duly convicted, shall exist within the United States, or any place subject to their jurisdiction.

Section 2.   Congress shall have power to enforce this article by appropriate legislation.

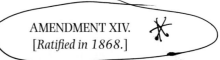

AMENDMENT XIV.
[*Ratified in 1868.*]

Ex-slaves made citizens

"Due-process" clause applied to states

"Equal-protection" clause

Section 1.   All persons born or naturalized in the United States and subject to the jurisdiction thereof, are citizens of the United States and of the State wherein they reside. No State shall make or enforce any law which shall abridge the privileges or immunities of citizens of the United States; nor shall any State deprive any person of life, liberty, or property, without due process of law; nor deny to any person within its jurisdiction the equal protection of the laws.

Reduction in congressional representation for states denying adult males the right to vote

Section 2.   Representatives shall be apportioned among the several States according to their respective numbers, counting the whole number of persons in each State, excluding Indians not taxed. But when the right to vote at any election for the choice of electors for President and Vice President of the United States, Representatives in Congress, the Executive and Judicial officers of a State, or the members of the Legislature thereof, is denied to any of the male inhabitants of such State, being *twenty-one*[11] years of age and citizens of the United States, or in any way abridged, except for participation in rebellion, or other crime, the basis of representation therein shall be reduced in the proportion which the number of such male citizens shall bear to the whole number of male citizens twenty-one years of age in such State.

Southern rebels denied federal office

Section 3.   No person shall be a Senator or Representative in Congress, or elector of President and Vice President, or hold any office, civil or military, under the

---

10. Changed by the Twentieth Amendment, section 3.
11. Changed by the Twenty-sixth Amendment.

United States, or under any State, who, having previously taken an oath, as a member of Congress, or as an officer of the United States, or as a member of any State legislature, or as an executive or judicial officer of any State, to support the Constitution of the United States, shall have engaged in insurrection or rebellion against the same, or given aid or comfort to the enemies thereof. But Congress may by a vote of two-thirds of each House, remove such disability.

Rebel debts repudiated

Section 4.   The validity of the public debt of the United States, authorized by law, including debts incurred for payment of pensions and bounties for services in suppressing insurrection or rebellion, shall not be questioned. But neither the United States nor any State shall assume or pay any debt or obligation incurred in aid of insurrection or rebellion against the United States, or any claim for the loss or emancipation of any slave; but all such debts, obligations and claims shall be held illegal and void.

Section 5.   The Congress shall have power to enforce, by appropriate legislation, the provisions of this article.

AMENDMENT XV.
[Ratified in 1870.]

Blacks given right to vote

Section 1.   The right of citizens of the United States to vote shall not be denied or abridged by the United States or by any State on account of race, color, or previous condition of servitude.

Section 2.   The Congress shall have power to enforce this article by appropriate legislation.

AMENDMENT XVI.
[Ratified in 1913.]

Authorizes federal income tax

The Congress shall have power to lay and collect taxes on incomes, from whatever source derived, without apportionment among the several States, and without regard to any census or enumeration.

AMENDMENT XVII.
[Ratified in 1913.]

Requires popular election of senators

The Senate of the United States shall be composed of two Senators from each State, elected by the people thereof, for six years; and each Senator shall have one vote. The electors in each State shall have the qualifications requisite for electors of the most numerous branch of the State legislatures.

When vacancies happen in the representation of any State in the Senate, the executive authority of such State shall issue writs of election to fill such vacancies: Provided, That the legislature of any State may empower the executive thereof to make temporary appointments until the people fill the vacancies by election as the legislature may direct.

This amendment shall not be so construed as to affect the election or term of any Senator chosen before it becomes valid as part of the Constitution.

AMENDMENT XVIII.
[*Ratified in 1919.*]

Prohibits manufacture and sale
of liquor

Section 1.   *After one year from the ratification of this article the manufacture, sale, or transportation of intoxicating liquors within, the importation thereof into, or the exportation thereof from the United States and all territory subject to the jurisdiction thereof for beverage purposes is hereby prohibited.*

Section 2.   *The Congress and the several States shall have concurrent power to enforce this article by appropriate legislation.*

Section 3.   *This article shall be inoperative unless it shall have been ratified as an amendment to the Constitution by the legislatures of the several States, as provided in the Constitution, within seven years from the date of the submission hereof to the States by the Congress.*[12]

AMENDMENT XIX.
[*Ratified in 1920.*]

Right to vote for women

The right of citizens of the United States to vote shall not be denied or abridged by the United States or by any State on account of sex.

Congress shall have power to enforce this article by appropriate legislation.

AMENDMENT XX.
[*Ratified in 1933.*]

Federal terms of office to begin
in January

Section 1.   The terms of the President and Vice President shall end at noon on the 20th day of January, and the terms of Senators and Representatives at noon on the 3d day of January, of the years in which such terms would have ended if this article had not been ratified; and the terms of their successors shall then begin.

Section 2.   The Congress shall assemble at least once in every year, and such meeting shall begin at noon on the 3d day of January, unless they shall by law appoint a different day.

Emergency presidential
succession

Section 3.   If, at the time fixed for the beginning of the term of the President, the President elect shall have died, the Vice President elect shall become President. If a President shall not have been chosen before the time fixed for the beginning of his term, or if the President elect shall have failed to qualify, then the Vice President elect shall act as President until a President shall have qualified; and the Congress may by law provide for the case wherein neither a President elect nor a Vice President elect shall have qualified, declaring who shall then act as President, or the manner in which one who is to act shall be selected, and such person shall act accordingly until a President or Vice President shall have qualified.

---

12. Repealed by the Twenty-first Amendment.

Section 4.   The Congress may by law provide for the case of the death of any of the persons from whom the House of Representatives may choose a President whenever the right of choice shall have devolved upon them, and for the case of the death of any of the persons from whom the Senate may choose a Vice President whenever the right of choice shall have devolved upon them.

Section 5.   Sections 1 and 2 shall take effect on the 15th day of October following the ratification of this article.

Section 6.   This article shall be inoperative unless it shall have been ratified as an amendment to the Constitution by the legislatures of three-fourths of the several States within seven years from the date of its submission.

AMENDMENT XXI.
[*Ratified in 1933.*]

Repeals Prohibition

Section 1.   The eighteenth article of amendment to the Constitution of the United States is hereby repealed.

Section 2.   The transportation or importation into any State, Territory, or possession of the United States for delivery or use therein of intoxicating liquors, in violation of the laws thereof, is hereby prohibited.

Section 3.   This article shall be inoperative unless it shall have been ratified as an amendment to the Constitution by conventions in the several States, as provided in the Constitution, within seven years from the date of submission hereof to the States by the Congress.

AMENDMENT XXII.
[*Ratified in 1951.*]

Two-term limit for president

Section 1.   No person shall be elected to the office of the President more than twice, and no person who has held the office of President, or acted as President, for more than two years of a term to which some other person was elected President shall be elected to the office of President more than once. But this Article shall not apply to any person holding the office of President when this Article was proposed by the Congress, and shall not prevent any person who may be holding the office of President, or acting as President, during the term within which this Article becomes operative from holding the office of President or acting as President during the remainder of such term.

Section 2.   This Article shall be inoperative unless it shall have been ratified as an amendment to the Constitution by the legislatures of three-fourths of the several States within seven years from the date of its submission to the States by the Congress.

AMENDMENT XXIII.
[*Ratified in 1961.*]

Right to vote for president in District of Columbia

Section 1.   The District constituting the seat of Government of the United States shall appoint in such manner as the Congress may direct:

A number of electors of President and Vice President equal to the whole number of Senators and Representatives in Congress to which the District would be entitled if it were a State, but in no event more than the least populous State; they shall be in addition to those appointed by the States, but they shall be considered, for the purposes of the election of President and Vice President, to be electors appointed by a State; and they shall meet in the District and perform such duties as provided by the twelfth article of amendment.

Section 2.   The Congress shall have power to enforce this article by appropriate legislation.

AMENDMENT XXIV.
[*Ratified in 1964.*]

Prohibits poll taxes in federal elections

Section 1.   The right of citizens of the United States to vote in any primary or other election for President or Vice President, for electors for President or Vice President, or for Senator or Representative in Congress, shall not be denied or abridged by the United States or any State by reason of failure to pay any poll tax or other tax.

Section 2.   The Congress shall have the power to enforce this article by appropriate legislation.

AMENDMENT XXV.
[*Ratified in 1967.*]

Presidential disability and succession

Section 1.   In case of the removal of the President from office or of his death or resignation, the Vice President shall become President.

Section 2.   Whenever there is a vacancy in the office of the Vice President, the President shall nominate a Vice President who shall take office upon confirmation by a majority vote of both Houses of Congress.

Section 3.   Whenever the President transmits to the President pro tempore of the Senate and the Speaker of the House of Representatives his written declaration that he is unable to discharge the powers and duties of his office, and until he transmits to them a written declaration to the contrary, such powers and duties shall be discharged by the Vice President as Acting President.

Section 4.   Whenever the Vice President and a majority of either the principal officers of the executive departments or of such other body as Congress may by law provide, transmit to the President pro tempore of the Senate and the Speaker of the House of Representatives their written declaration that the President is unable to discharge the powers and duties of his office, the Vice President shall immediately assume the powers and duties of the office as Acting President.

Thereafter, when the President transmits to the President pro tempore of the Senate and the Speaker of the House of Representatives his written declaration that no inability exists, he shall resume the powers and duties of his office unless the Vice President and a majority of either the principal officers of the executive department[s] or of such other body as Congress may by law provide, transmit within four days to the President pro tempore of the Senate and the Speaker of the House of Representatives their written declaration that the President is unable to discharge the powers and duties of his office. Thereupon Congress shall decide the issue, assembling within forty-eight hours for that purpose if not in session. If the Congress, within twenty-one days after receipt of the latter written declaration, or, if Congress is not in session, within twenty-one days after Congress is required to assemble, determines by two-thirds vote of both Houses that the President is unable to discharge the powers and duties of his office, the Vice President shall continue to discharge the same as Acting President; otherwise, the President shall resume the powers and duties of his office.

AMENDMENT XXVI.
[*Ratified in 1971.*]

Voting age lowered to eighteen

Section 1.   The right of citizens of the United States, who are eighteen years of age or older, to vote shall not be denied or abridged by the United States or by any State on account of age.

Section 2.   The Congress shall have power to enforce this article by appropriate legislation.

AMENDMENT XXVII.
[*Ratified in 1992.*]

Congressional pay raises

No law varying the compensation for the services of the Senators and Representatives shall take effect, until an election of Representatives shall have intervened.

The Federalist No. 10

——

November 22, 1787

James Madison

TO THE PEOPLE OF THE STATE OF NEW YORK.

Among the numerous advantages promised by a well constructed Union, none deserves to be more accurately developed than its tendency to break and control the violence of faction. The friend of popular governments, never finds himself so much alarmed for their character and fate, as when he contemplates their propensity to this dangerous vice. He will not fail therefore to set a due value on any plan which, without violating the principles to which he is attached, provides a proper cure for it. The instability, injustice and confusion introduced into the public councils, have in truth been the mortal diseases under which popular governments have every where perished; as they continue to be the favorite and fruitful topics from which the adversaries to liberty derive their most specious declamations. The valuable improvements made by the American Constitutions on the popular models, both ancient and modern, cannot certainly be too much admired; but it would be an unwarrantable partiality, to contend that they have as effectually obviated the danger on this side as was wished and expected. Complaints are every where heard from our most considerate and virtuous citizens, equally the friends of public and private faith, and of public and personal liberty; that our governments are too unstable; that the public good is disregarded in the conflicts of rival parties; and that measures are too often decided, not according to the rules of justice, and the rights of the minor party; but by the superior force of an interested and over-bearing majority. However anxiously we may wish that these complaints had no foundation, the evidence of known facts will not permit us to deny that they are in some degree true. It will be found indeed, on a candid review of our situation, that some of the distresses under which we labor, have been erroneously charged on the operation of our governments; but it will be found, at the same time, that other causes will not alone account for many of our heaviest misfortunes; and particularly, for that prevailing and increasing distrust of public engagements, and alarm for private rights, which are echoed from one end of the continent to the other. These must be chiefly, if not wholly, effects of the unsteadiness and injustice, with which a factious spirit has tainted our public administrations.

By a faction I understand a number of citizens, whether amounting to a majority or minority of the whole, who are united and actuated by some common impulse of passion, or of interest, adverse to the rights of other citizens, or to the permanent and aggregate interests of the community.

There are two methods of curing the mischiefs of faction: the one, by removing its causes; the other, by controlling its effects.

There are again two methods of removing the causes of faction: the one by destroying the liberty which is essential to its existence; the other, by giving to every citizen the same opinions, the same passions, and the same interests.

It could never be more truly said than of the first remedy, that it is worse than the disease. Liberty is to faction, what air is to fire, an aliment without which it instantly expires. But it could not be a less folly to abolish liberty, which is essential to political life, because it nourishes faction, than it would be to wish the annihilation of air, which is essential to animal life, because it imparts to fire its destructive agency.

The second expedient is as impracticable, as the first would be unwise. As long as the reason of man continues fallible, and he is at liberty to exercise it, different opinions will be formed. As long as the connection subsists between his reason and his self-love, his opinions and his passions will have a reciprocal influence on each other; and the former will be objects to which the latter will attach themselves. The diversity in the faculties of men from which the rights of property originate, is not less an insuperable obstacle to a uniformity of interests. The protection of these faculties is the first object of Government. From the protection of different and unequal faculties of acquiring property, the possession of different degrees and kinds of property immediately results: and from the influence of these on the sentiments and views of the respective proprietors, ensues a division of the society into different interests and parties.

The latent causes of faction are thus sown in the nature of man; and we see them every where brought into different degrees of activity, according to the different circumstances of civil society. A zeal for different opinions concerning religion, concerning Government and many other points, as well of speculation as of practice; an attachment to different leaders ambitiously contending for pre-eminence and power; or to persons of other descriptions whose fortunes have been interesting to the human passions, have in turn divided mankind into parties, inflamed them with mutual animosity, and rendered them much more disposed to vex and oppress each other, than to cooperate for their common good. So strong is this propensity of mankind to fall into mutual animosities, that where no substantial occasion presents itself, the most frivolous and fanciful distinctions have been sufficient to kindle their unfriendly passions, and excite their most violent conflicts. But the most common and durable source of factions, has been the various and unequal distribution of property. Those who hold, and those who are without property, have ever formed distinct interests in society. Those who are creditors, and those who are debtors, fall under a like discrimination. A landed interest, a manufacturing interest, a mercantile interest, a monied interest, with many lesser interests, grow up of necessity in civilized nations, and divide them into different classes, actuated by different sentiments and views. The regulation of these various and interfering interests forms the principal task of modern Legislation, and involves the spirit of party and faction in the necessary and ordinary operations of Government.

No man is allowed to be judge in his own cause; because his interest would certainly bias his judgment, and, not improbably, corrupt his integrity. With equal, nay with greater reason, a body of men, are unfit to be judges and parties, at the same time; yet, what are many of the most important acts of legislation, but so many judicial determinations, not indeed concerning the rights of single persons, but concerning the rights of large bodies of citizens, and what are the different classes of legislators, but advocates and parties to the causes which they determine? Is a law proposed concerning private debts? It is a question to which the creditors are parties on one side, and the debtors on the other. Justice ought to hold the balance between them. Yet the parties are and must be themselves the judges; and the most numerous party, or, in other words, the most powerful faction must be expected to prevail. Shall domestic manufactures be encouraged, and in what degree, by restrictions on foreign manufactures? are questions which would be differently decided by the landed and the manufacturing classes; and probably by neither, with a sole regard to justice and the public good. The apportionment of taxes on the various descriptions of property, is an act which seems to require the most exact impartiality; yet, there is perhaps no legislative act in which greater opportunity and temptation are given to a predominant party, to trample on the rules of justice. Every shilling with which they over-burden the inferior number, is a shilling saved to their own pockets.

It is in vain to say, that enlightened statesmen will be able to adjust these clashing interests, and render them all subservient to the public good. Enlightened statesmen will not always be at the helm: Nor, in many cases, can such an adjustment be made at all, without taking into view indirect and remote considerations, which will rarely prevail over the immediate interest which one party may find in disregarding the rights of another, or the good of the whole.

The inference to which we are brought, is, that the *causes* of faction cannot be removed; and that relief is only to be sought in the means of controlling its *effects*.

If a faction consists of less than a majority, relief is supplied by the republican principle, which enables the majority to defeat its sinister views by regular vote: It may clog the administration, it may convulse the society; but it will be unable to execute and mask its violence under the forms of the Constitution. When a majority is included in a faction, the form of popular government on the other hand enables it to sacrifice to its ruling passion or interest, both the public good and the rights of other citizens. To secure the public good, and private rights, against the danger of such a faction, and at the same time to preserve the spirit and the form of popular government, is then the great object to which our inquiries are directed: Let me add that it is the great desideratum, by which alone this form of government can be rescued from the opprobrium under which it has so long labored, and be recommended to the esteem and adoption of mankind.

By what means is this object attainable? Evidently by one of two only. Either the existence of the same passion or interest in a majority at the same time, must be prevented; or the majority, having such co-existent passion or interest, must be rendered, by their number and local situation, unable to concert and carry into effect schemes of oppression. If the impulse and the opportunity be suffered to coincide, we well know that neither moral nor religious motives can be relied on as an adequate control. They are not found to be such on the injustice and violence of individuals, and lose their efficacy in proportion to the number combined together; that is, in proportion as their efficacy becomes needful.

From this view of the subject, it may be concluded, that a pure Democracy, by which I mean, a Society, consisting of a small number of citizens, who assemble and administer the Government in person, can admit of no cure for the mischiefs of faction. A common passion or interest will, in almost every case, be felt by a majority of the whole; a communication and concert results from the form of Government itself; and there is nothing to check the inducements to sacrifice the weaker party, or an obnoxious individual. Hence it is, that such Democracies have ever been spectacles of turbulence and contention; have ever been found incompatible with personal security, or the rights of property; and have in general been as short in their lives, as they have been violent in their deaths. Theoretic politicians, who have patronized this species of Government, have erroneously supposed, that by reducing mankind to a perfect equality in their political rights, they would, at the same time, be perfectly equalized and assimilated in their possessions, their opinions, and their passions.

A republic, by which I mean a government in which the scheme of representation takes place, opens a different prospect, and promises the cure for which we are seeking. Let us examine the points in which it varies from pure democracy, and we shall comprehend both the nature of the cure and the efficacy which it must derive from the union.

The two great points of difference, between a democracy and a republic, are, first, the delegation of the government, in the latter, to a small number of citizens, elected by the rest; secondly, the greater number of citizens, and greater sphere of country, over which the latter may be extended.

The effect of the first difference is, on the one hand, to refine and enlarge the public views, by passing them through the medium of a chosen body of citizens, whose wisdom may best discern the true interest of their country, and whose patriotism and love of justice, will be least likely to sacrifice it to temporary or partial considerations. Under such a regulation, it may well happen, that the public voice, pronounced by the representatives of the people, will be more consonant to the public good, than if pronounced by the people themselves, convened for the purpose. On the other hand the effect may be inverted. Men of factious tempers, of local prejudices, or of sinister designs, may by intrigue, by corruption, or by other means, first obtain the suffrages, and then betray the interest of the people. The question resulting is, whether small or extensive republics are most favorable to the election of proper guardians of the public weal, and it is clearly decided in favor of the latter by two obvious considerations.

In the first place, it is to be remarked that, however small the republic may be, the representatives must be raised to a certain number, in order to guard against the cabals of a few; and that however large it may be, they must be limited to a certain number, in order to guard against the confusion of a multitude. Hence, the number of representatives in the two cases not being in proportion to that of the constituents, and being proportionally greatest in the small republic, it follows, that if the proportion of fit characters be not less in the large than in the small republic, the former will present a greater option, and consequently a greater probability of a fit choice.

In the next place, as each Representative will be chosen by a greater number of citizens in the large than in the small Republic, it will be more difficult for unworthy candidates to practise with success the vicious arts, by which elections are too often carried; and the suffrages of the people being more free, will be more likely to center on men who possess the most attractive merit, and the most diffusive and established characters.

It must be confessed, that in this, as in most other cases, there is a mean, on both sides of which inconveniences will be found to lie. By enlarging too much the number of electors, you render the representatives too little acquainted with all their local circumstances and lesser interests; as by reducing it too much, you render him unduly attached to these, and too little fit to comprehend and pursue great and national objects. The Federal Constitution forms a happy combination in this respect; the great and aggregate interests being referred to the national, the local and particular, to the state legislatures.

The other point of difference is, the greater number of citizens and extent of territory which may be brought within the compass of Republican, than of Democratic Government; and it is this circumstance principally which renders factious combinations less to be dreaded in the former, than in the latter. The smaller the society, the fewer probably will be the distinct parties and interests composing it; the fewer the distinct parties and interests, the more frequently will a majority be found of the same party; and the smaller the number of individuals composing a majority, and the smaller the compass within which they are placed, the more easily they will concert and execute their plans of oppression. Extend the sphere, and you take in a greater variety of parties and interests; you make it less probable that a majority of the whole will have a common motive to invade the rights of other citizens; or if such a common motive exists, it will be more difficult for all who feel it to discover their own strength, and to act in unison with each other. Besides other impediments, it may be remarked, that where there is a consciousness of unjust or dishonorable purposes, communication is always checked by distrust, in proportion to the number whose concurrence is necessary.

Hence it clearly appears, that the same advantage, which a Republic has over a Democracy, in controlling the effects of factions, is enjoyed by a large over a small Republic—is enjoyed by the Union over the States composing it. Does this advantage consist in the substitution of Representatives, whose enlightened views and virtuous sentiments render them superior to local prejudices, and to schemes of injustice? It will not be denied, that the Representation of the Union will be most likely to possess these requisite endowments. Does it consist in the greater security afforded by a greater variety of parties, against the event of any one party being able to outnumber and oppress the rest? In an equal degree does the increase variety of parties, comprised within the Union, increase this security? Does it, in fine, consist in the greater obstacles opposed to the concert and accomplishment of the secret wishes of an unjust and interested majority? Here, again, the extent of the Union gives it the most palpable advantage.

The influence of factious leaders may kindle a flame within their particular States, but will be unable to spread a general conflagration through the other States: a religious sect, may degenerate into a political faction in a part of the Confederacy but the variety of sects dispersed over the entire face of it, must secure the national Councils against any danger from that source: a rage for paper money, for an abolition of debts, for an equal division of property, or for any other improper or wicked project, will be less apt to pervade the whole body of the Union, than a particular member of it; in the same proportion as such a malady is more likely to taint a particular county or district, than an entire State.

In the extent and proper structure of the Union, therefore, we behold a Republican remedy for the diseases most incident to Republican Government. And according to the degree of pleasure and pride, we feel in being Republicans, ought to be our zeal in cherishing the spirit, and supporting the character of Federalists.

PUBLIUS

The Federalist No. 51

February 6, 1788

James Madison

TO THE PEOPLE OF THE STATE OF NEW YORK.

To what expedient then shall we finally resort for maintaining in practice the necessary partition of power among the several departments, as laid down in the constitution? The only answer that can be given is, that as all these exterior provisions are found to be inadequate, the defect must be supplied, by so contriving the interior structure of the government, as that its several constituent parts may, by their mutual relations, be the means of keeping each other in their proper places. Without presuming to undertake a full development of this important idea, I will hazard a few general observations, which may perhaps place it in a clearer light, and enable us to form a more correct judgment of the principles and structure of the government planned by the convention.

In order to lay a due foundation for that separate and distinct exercise of the different powers of government, which to a certain extent, is admitted on all hands to be essential to the preservation of liberty, it is evident that each department should have a will of its own; and consequently should be so constituted, that the members of each should have as little agency as possible in the appointment of the members of the others. Were this principle rigorously adhered to, it would require that all the appointments for the supreme executive, legislative, and judiciary magistracies, should be drawn from the same fountain of authority, the people, through channels, having no communication whatever with one another. Perhaps such a plan of constructing the several departments would be less difficult in practice than in it may in contemplation appear. Some difficulties however, and some additional expense, would attend the execution of it. Some deviations therefore from the principle must be admitted. In the constitution of the judiciary department in particular, it might be inexpedient to insist rigorously on the principle; first, because peculiar qualifications being essential in the members, the primary consideration ought to be to select that mode of choice, which best secures these qualifications; secondly, because the permanent tenure by which the appointments are held in that department, must soon destroy all sense of dependence on the authority conferring them.

It is equally evident that the members of each department should be as little dependent as possible on those of the others, for the emoluments annexed to their offices. Were the executive magistrate, or the judges, not independent of the legislature in this particular, their independence in every other would be merely nominal.

But the great security against a gradual concentration of the several powers in the same department, consists in giving to those who administer each department, the necessary constitutional means, and personal motives, to resist encroachments of the others. The provision for defense must in this, as in all other cases, be made commensurate to the danger of attack. Ambition must be made to counteract ambition. The interest of the man must be connected with the constitutional right of the place. It may be a reflection on human nature, that such devices should be necessary to control the abuses of government. But what is government itself but the greatest of all reflections on human nature? If men were angels, no government would be necessary. If angels were to govern men, neither external nor internal controls on government would be necessary. In framing a government which is to be administered by men over men, the great difficulty lies in this: You must first enable the government to control the governed; and in the next place, oblige it to control itself. A dependence on the people is no doubt the primary control on the government; but experience has taught mankind the necessity of auxiliary precautions.

This policy of supplying by opposite and rival interests, the defect of better motives, might be traced through the whole system of human affairs, private as well as public. We see it particularly displayed in all the subordinate distributions of power; where the constant aim is to divide and arrange the several offices in such a manner as that each may be a check on the other; that the private interest of every individual, may be a sentinel over the public rights. These inventions of prudence cannot be less requisite in the distribution of the supreme powers of the state.

But it is not possible to give each department an equal power of self defense. In republican government the legislative authority, necessarily, predominates. The remedy for this inconvenience is, to divide the legislative into different branches; and to render them by different modes of election, and different principles of action, as little connected with each other, as the nature of their common functions, and their common dependence on the society, will admit. It may even be necessary to guard against dangerous encroachments by still further precautions. As the weight of the legislative authority requires that it should be thus divided, the weakness of the executive may require, on the other hand, that it should be fortified. An absolute negative, on the legislature, appears at first view to be the natural defense with which the executive magistrate should be armed. But perhaps it would be neither altogether safe, nor alone sufficient. On ordinary occasions, it might not be exerted with the requisite firmness, and on extraordinary occasions, it might be prefidiously abused. May not this defect of an absolute negative be supplied, by some qualified connection between this weaker department, and the weaker branch of the stronger department, by which the latter may be led to support the constitutional rights of the former, without being too much detached from the rights of its own department?

If the principles on which these observations are founded be just, as I persuade myself they are, and they be applied as a criterion, to the several state constitutions, and to the federal constitution, it will be found, that if the latter does not perfectly correspond with them, the former are infinitely less able to bear such a test.

There are moreover two considerations particularly applicable to the federal system of America, which place the system in a very interesting point of view.

First. In a single republic, all the power surrendered by the people, is submitted to the administration of a single government; and usurpations are guarded against by a division of the government into district and separate departments. In the compound republic of America, the power surrendered by the people, is first divided between two distinct governments, and then the portion allotted to each, subdivided among distinct and separate departments. Hence a double security arises to the rights of the people. The different governments will control each other; at the same time that each will be controlled by itself.

Second. It is of great importance in a republic, not only to guard the society against the oppression of its rulers; but to guard one part of the society against the injustice of the other part. Different interests necessarily exist in different classes of citizens. If a majority be united by a common interest, the rights of the minority will be insecure. There are but two methods of providing against this evil: The one by creating a will in the community independent of the majority, that is, of the society itself, the other by comprehending in the society so many separate descriptions of citizens, as will render an unjust combination of a majority of the whole, very improbable, if not impracticable. The first method prevails in all governments possessing an hereditary or self appointed authority. This at best is but a precarious security; because a power independent of the society may as well espouse the unjust views of the major, as the rightful interests, of the minor party, and may possibly be turned against both parties. The second method will be exemplified in the federal republic of the United States. While all authority in it will be derived from and dependent on the society, the society itself will be broken into so many parts, interests and classes of citizens, that the rights of individuals or of the minority, will be in little danger from interested combinations of the majority. In a free government, the security for civil rights must be the same as for religious rights. It consists in the one case in the multiplicity of interests, and in the other, in the multiplicity of sects. The degree of security in both cases will depend on the number of interests and sects; and this may be presumed to depend on the extent of country and number of people comprehended under the same government. This view of the subject must particularly recommend a proper federal system to all the sincere and considerate friends of republican government: Since it shows that in exact proportion as the territory of the union may be formed into more circumscribed confederacies or states, oppressive combinations of a majority will be facilitated, the best security under the republican form, for the rights of every class of citizens, will be diminished; and consequently, the stability and independence of some member of the government, the only other security, must be proportionally increased. Justice is the end of government. It is the end of civil society. It ever has been, and ever will be pursued, until it be obtained, or until liberty be lost in the pursuit. In a society under the forms of which the stronger faction can readily unite and oppress the weaker, anarchy may as truly be said to reign, as in a state of nature where the weaker individual is not secured against the violence of the stronger: And as in the latter state even the stronger individuals are prompted by the uncertainty of their condition, to submit to a government which may protect the weak as well as themselves: So in the former state, will the more powerful factions or parties be gradually induced by a like motive, to wish for a government which will protect all parties, the weaker as well as the more powerful. It can be little doubted, that if the state of Rhode Island was separated from the confederacy, and left to itself, the insecurity of rights under the popular form of government within such narrow limits, would be displayed by such reiterated oppressions of factious majorities, that some power altogether independent of the people would soon be called for by the voice of the very factions whose misrule had proved the necessity of it. In the extended republic of the United States, and among the great variety of interests, parties and sects which it embraces, a coalition of a majority of the whole society could seldom take place on any other principles than those of justice and the general good; and there being thus less danger to a minor from the will of the major party, there must be less pretext also, to provide for the security of the former, by introducing into the government a will not dependent on the latter; or in other words, a will independent of the society itself. It is no less certain than it is important, notwithstanding the contrary opinions which have been entertained, that the larger the society, provided it lie within a practicable sphere, the more duly capable it will be of self government. And happily for the *republican cause,* the practicable sphere may be carried to a very great extent, by a judicious modification and mixture of the *federal principle.*

PUBLIUS

Presidents and Congresses, 1789–2000

Year	President and vice president	Party of president	Congress	House Majority party	House Minority party	Senate Majority party	Senate Minority party
1789–1797	**George Washington** John Adams	None	1st	38 Admin	26 Opp	17 Admin	9 Opp
			2d	37 Fed	33 Dem-Rep	16 Fed	13 Dem-Rep
			3d	57 Dem-Rep	48 Fed	17 Fed	13 Dem-Rep
			4th	54 Fed	52 Dem-Rep	19 Fed	13 Dem-Rep
1797–1801	**John Adams** Thomas Jefferson	Federalist	5th	58 Fed	48 Dem-Rep	20 Fed	12 Dem-Rep
			6th	64 Fed	42 Dem-Rep	19 Fed	13 Dem-Rep
1801–1809	**Thomas Jefferson** Aaron Burr (to 1805) George Clinton (to 1809)	Dem-Rep	7th	69 Dem-Rep	36 Fed	18 Dem-Rep	13 Fed
			8th	102 Dem-Rep	39 Fed	25 Dem-Rep	9 Fed
			9th	116 Dem-Rep	25 Fed	27 Dem-Rep	7 Fed
			10th	118 Dem-Rep	24 Fed	28 Dem-Rep	6 Fed
1809–1817	**James Madison** George Clinton (to 1813) Elbridge Gerry (to 1817)	Dem-Rep	11th	94 Dem-Rep	48 Fed	28 Dem-Rep	6 Fed
			12th	108 Dem-Rep	36 Fed	30 Dem-Rep	6 Fed
			13th	112 Dem-Rep	68 Fed	27 Dem-Rep	9 Fed
			14th	117 Dem-Rep	65 Fed	25 Dem-Rep	11 Fed
1817–1825	**James Monroe** Daniel D. Tompkins	Dem-Rep	15th	141 Dem-Rep	42 Fed	34 Dem-Rep	10 Fed
			16th	156 Dem-Rep	27 Fed	35 Dem-Rep	7 Fed
			17th	158 Dem-Rep	25 Fed	44 Dem-Rep	4 Fed
			18th	187 Dem-Rep	26 Fed	44 Dem-Rep	4 Fed
1825–1829	**John Quincy Adams** John C. Calhoun	Nat-Rep	19th	105 Admin	97 Jack	26 Admin	20 Jack
			20th	119 Jack	94 Admin	28 Jack	20 Admin
1829–1837	**Andrew Jackson** John C. Calhoun (to 1833) Martin Van Buren (to 1837)	Democrat	21st	139 Dem	74 Nat Rep	26 Dem	22 Nat Rep
			22d	141 Dem	58 Nat Rep	25 Dem	21 Nat Rep
			23d	147 Dem	53 AntiMas	20 Dem	20 Nat Rep
			24th	145 Dem	98 Whig	27 Dem	25 Whig
1837–1841	**Martin Van Buren** Richard M. Johnson	Democrat	25th	108 Dem	107 Whig	30 Dem	18 Whig
			26th	124 Dem	118 Whig	28 Dem	22 Whig
1841	**William H. Harrison*** John Tyler	Whig					
1841–1845	**John Tyler** (VP vacant)	Whig	27th	133 Whig	102 Dem	28 Whig	22 Dem
			28th	142 Dem	79 Whig	28 Whig	25 Dem
1845–1849	**James K. Polk** George M. Dallas	Democrat	29th	143 Dem	77 Whig	31 Dem	25 Whig
			30th	115 Whig	108 Dem	36 Dem	21 Whig
1849–1850	**Zachary Taylor*** Millard Fillmore	Whig	31st	112 Dem	109 Whig	35 Dem	25 Whig
1850–1853	**Millard Fillmore** (VP vacant)	Whig	32d	140 Dem	88 Whig	35 Dem	24 Whig
1853–1857	**Franklin Pierce** William R. King	Democrat	33d	159 Dem	71 Whig	38 Dem	22 Whig
			34th	108 Rep	83 Dem	40 Dem	15 Rep

NOTES: Only members of two major parties in Congress are shown; omitted are independents, members of minor parties, and vacancies.

Party balance as of beginning of Congress.

Congresses in which one or both houses are controlled by party other than that of the president are shown in color.

During administration of George Washington and (in part) John Quincy Adams, Congress was not organized by formal parties; the split shown is between supporters and opponents of the administration.

ABBREVIATIONS: **Admin** = Administration supporters; **AntiMas** = Anti-Masonic; **Dem** = Democratic; **Dem-Rep** = Democratic-Republican; **Fed** = Federalist; **Jack** = Jacksonian Democrats; **Nat Rep** = National Republican; **Opp** = Opponents of administration; **Rep** = Republican; **Union** = Unionist; **Whig** = Whig.

* Died in office.

Year	President and vice president	Party of president	Congress	House Majority party	House Minority party	Senate Majority party	Senate Minority party
1857–1861	**James Buchanan** John C. Breckinridge	Democrat	35th 36th	118 Dem 114 Rep	92 Rep 92 Dem	36 Dem 36 Dem	20 Rep 26 Rep
1861–1865	**Abraham Lincoln*** Hannibal Hamlin (to 1865) Andrew Johnson (1865)	Republican	37th 38th	105 Rep 102 Rep	43 Dem 75 Dem	31 Rep 36 Rep	10 Dem 9 Dem
1865–1869	**Andrew Johnson** (VP vacant)	Republican	39th 40th	149 Union 143 Rep	42 Dem 49 Dem	42 Union 42 Rep	10 Dem 11 Dem
1869–1877	**Ulysses S. Grant** Schuyler Colfax (to 1873) Henry Wilson (to 1877)	Republican	41st 42d 43d 44th	149 Rep 134 Rep 194 Rep 169 Dem	63 Dem 104 Dem 92 Dem 109 Rep	56 Rep 52 Rep 49 Rep 45 Rep	11 Dem 17 Dem 19 Dem 29 Dem
1877–1881	**Rutherford B. Hayes** William A. Wheeler	Republican	45th 46th	153 Dem 149 Dem	140 Rep 130 Rep	39 Rep 42 Dem	36 Dem 33 Rep
1881	**James A. Garfield*** Chester A. Arthur	Republican	47th	147 Rep	135 Dem	37 Rep	37 Dem
1881–1885	**Chester A. Arthur** (VP vacant)	Republican	48th	197 Dem	118 Rep	38 Rep	36 Dem
1885–1889	**Grover Cleveland** Thomas A. Hendricks	Democrat	49th 50th	183 Dem 169 Dem	140 Rep 152 Rep	43 Rep 39 Rep	34 Dem 37 Dem
1889–1893	**Benjamin Harrison** Levi P. Morton	Republican	51st 52d	166 Rep 235 Dem	159 Dem 88 Rep	39 Rep 47 Rep	37 Dem 39 Dem
1893–1897	**Grover Cleveland** Adlai E. Stevenson	Democrat	53d 54th	218 Dem 244 Rep	127 Rep 105 Dem	44 Dem 43 Rep	38 Rep 39 Dem
1897–1901	**William McKinley*** Garret A. Hobart (to 1901) Theodore Roosevelt (1901)	Republican	55th 56th	204 Rep 185 Rep	113 Dem 163 Dem	47 Rep 53 Rep	34 Dem 26 Dem
1901–1909	**Theodore Roosevelt** (VP vacant, 1901–1905) Charles W. Fairbanks (1905–1909)	Republican	57th 58th 59th 60th	197 Rep 208 Rep 250 Rep 222 Rep	151 Dem 178 Dem 136 Dem 164 Dem	55 Rep 57 Rep 57 Rep 61 Rep	31 Dem 33 Dem 33 Dem 31 Dem
1909–1913	**William Howard Taft** James S. Sherman	Republican	61st 62d	219 Rep 228 Dem	172 Dem 161 Rep	61 Rep 51 Rep	32 Dem 41 Dem
1913–1921	**Woodrow Wilson** Thomas R. Marshall	Democrat	63d 64th 65th 66th	291 Dem 230 Dem 216 Dem 240 Rep	127 Rep 196 Rep 210 Rep 190 Dem	51 Dem 56 Dem 53 Dem 49 Rep	44 Rep 40 Rep 42 Rep 47 Dem
1921–1923	**Warren G. Harding*** Calvin Coolidge	Republican	67th	301 Rep	131 Dem	59 Rep	37 Dem
1923–1929	**Calvin Coolidge** (VP vacant, 1923–1925) Charles G. Dawes (1925–1929)	Republican	68th 69th 70th	225 Rep 247 Rep 237 Rep	205 Dem 183 Dem 195 Dem	51 Rep 56 Rep 49 Rep	43 Dem 39 Dem 46 Dem
1929–1933	**Herbert Hoover** Charles Curtis	Republican	71st 72d	267 Rep 220 Dem	167 Dem 214 Rep	56 Rep 48 Rep	39 Dem 47 Dem
1933–1945	**Franklin D. Roosevelt*** John N. Garner (1933–1941) Henry A. Wallace (1941–1945) Harry S Truman (1945)	Democrat	73d 74th 75th 76th 77th 78th	310 Dem 319 Dem 331 Dem 261 Dem 268 Dem 218 Dem	117 Rep 103 Rep 89 Rep 164 Rep 162 Rep 208 Rep	60 Dem 69 Dem 76 Dem 69 Dem 66 Dem 58 Dem	35 Rep 25 Rep 16 Rep 23 Rep 28 Rep 37 Rep
1945–1953	**Harry S Truman** (VP vacant, 1945–1949) Alben W. Barkley (1949–1953)	Democrat	79th 80th 81st 82d	242 Dem 245 Rep 263 Dem 234 Dem	190 Rep 188 Dem 171 Rep 199 Rep	56 Dem 51 Rep 54 Dem 49 Dem	38 Rep 45 Dem 42 Rep 47 Rep

* Died in office.

Year	President and vice president	Party of president	Congress	House		Senate	
				Majority party	Minority party	Majority party	Minority party
1953–1961	**Dwight D. Eisenhower**	Republican	83d	221 Rep	211 Dem	48 Rep	47 Dem
	Richard M. Nixon		84th	232 Dem	203 Rep	48 Dem	47 Rep
			85th	233 Dem	200 Rep	49 Dem	47 Rep
			86th	283 Dem	153 Rep	64 Dem	34 Rep
1961–1963	**John F. Kennedy***	Democrat	87th	263 Dem	174 Rep	65 Dem	35 Rep
	Lyndon B. Johnson						
1963–1969	**Lyndon B. Johnson**	Democrat	88th	258 Dem	177 Rep	67 Dem	33 Rep
	(VP vacant, 1963–1965)		89th	295 Dem	140 Rep	68 Dem	32 Rep
	Hubert H. Humphrey		90th	247 Dem	187 Rep	64 Dem	36 Rep
	(1965–1969)						
1969–1974	**Richard M. Nixon†**	Republican	91st	243 Dem	192 Rep	57 Dem	43 Rep
	Spiro T. Agnew††		92d	254 Dem	180 Rep	54 Dem	44 Rep
	Gerald R. Ford§						
1974–1977	**Gerald R. Ford**	Republican	93d	239 Dem	192 Rep	56 Dem	42 Rep
	Nelson A. Rockefeller§		94th	291 Dem	144 Rep	60 Dem	37 Rep
1977–1981	**Jimmy Carter**	Democrat	95th	292 Dem	143 Rep	61 Dem	38 Rep
	Walter Mondale		96th	276 Dem	157 Rep	58 Dem	41 Rep
1981–1989	**Ronald Reagan**	Republican	97th	243 Dem	192 Rep	53 Rep	46 Dem
	George Bush		98th	269 Dem	165 Rep	54 Rep	46 Dem
			99th	253 Dem	182 Rep	53 Rep	47 Dem
			100th	257 Dem	178 Rep	54 Dem	46 Rep
1989–1993	**George Bush**	Republican	101st	262 Dem	173 Rep	55 Dem	45 Rep
	Dan Quayle		102d	267 Dem	167 Rep	56 Dem	44 Rep
1993–2000	**Bill Clinton**	Democrat	103d	258 Dem	176 Rep	57 Dem	43 Rep
	Albert Gore, Jr.		104th	230 Rep	204 Dem	53 Rep	47 Dem
			105th	228 Rep	206 Dem	55 Rep	45 Dem
			106th	223 Rep	211 Dem	54 Rep	46 Dem
2000	Unknown at time of printing		107th	Unknown at time of printing			

*Died in office. †Resigned from the presidency. ††Resigned from the vice presidency. §Appointed vice president.

Glossary

Activist approach   The view that judges should discern the general principles underlying the Constitution and its often vague language and assess how best to apply them in contemporary circumstances, in some cases with the guidance of moral or economic philosophy. (14)

Activists   Individuals, usually outside of government, who actively promote a political party, philosophy, or issue they care about. (6)

Ad hoc structure   A method of organizing a president's staff in which several task forces, committees, and informal groups of friends and advisers deal directly with the president. (12)

Adversarial press   A national press that is suspicious of officialdom and eager to break an embarrassing story about a public official. (10)

Affirmative action   The requirement, imposed by law or administrative regulation, that an organization (business firm, government agency, labor union, school, or college) take positive steps to increase the number or proportion of women, African Americans, or other minorities in its membership. (16)

Amendments   Changes in, or additions to, the U.S. Constitution. Amendments are proposed by a two-thirds vote of both houses of Congress or by a convention called by Congress at the request of two-thirds of the state legislatures and ratified by approval of three-fourths of the states. (2)

Amicus curiae   A Latin term meaning "a friend of the court." Refers to interested groups or individuals, not directly involved in a suit, who may file legal briefs or make oral arguments in support of one side. (14)

Annual authorizations   *See* Authorization legislation (13)

Antifederalists   Opponents of a strong central government who campaigned against ratification of the Constitution in favor of a confederation of largely independent states. Antifederalists successfully marshaled public support for a federal bill of rights. After ratification, they formed a political party to support states' rights. *See also* Federalists (2)

Appropriation   A legislative grant of money to finance a government program. *See also* Authorization legislation (13)

Articles of Confederation   A constitution drafted by the newly independent states in 1777 and ratified in 1781. It created a weak national government that could not levy taxes or regulate commerce. In 1789 it was replaced by our current Constitution in order to create a stronger national government. (2)

Australian ballot   A government-printed ballot of uniform size and shape to be cast in secret that was adopted by many states around 1890 in order to reduce the voting fraud associated with party-printed ballots cast in public. (6)

Authority   The right to use power. (1)

Authorization legislation   Legislative permission to begin or continue a government program or agency. An authorization bill may grant permission to spend a certain sum of money, but that money does not ordinarily become available unless it is also appropriated. Authorizations may be annual, multiyear, or permanent. *See also* Appropriation (13)

Background story (news)   A public official's explanation of current policy provided to the press on the condition that the source remain anonymous. (10)

Bicameral legislature   A lawmaking body made up of two chambers or parts. The U.S. Congress is a bicameral legislature composed of the Senate and the House of Representatives. (11)

Bill of attainder   A law that declares a person, without a trial, to be guilty of a crime. The state legislatures and Congress are forbidden to pass such acts by Article I of the Constitution. (2)

Bill of rights   A list of individual rights and liberties, such as freedom of speech, religion, and the press. (2)

Blanket primary   A primary election that permits all voters, regardless of party, to choose candidates. A Democratic voter, for example, can vote in a blanket primary for both Democratic and Republican candidates for nomination. (8)

Block grants   Grants of money from the federal government to states for programs in certain general areas rather than for specific kinds of programs. *See also* Grants-in-aid; Categorical grants (3)

Brief   A legal document prepared by an attorney representing a party before a court. The document sets forth the facts of the case, summarizes the law, gives the arguments for its side, and discusses other relevant cases. (14)

Bureaucracy   A large, complex organization composed of appointed officials. The department and agencies of the U.S. government make up the federal bureaucracy. (13)

Bureaucrats   The appointed officials who operate government agencies from day to day. (1)

Cabinet   By custom, the cabinet includes the heads of the fourteen major executive departments. (12)

Categorical grants   Federal grants for specific purposes defined by federal law: to build an airport, for example, or to make welfare payments to low-income mothers. Such grants usually require that the state or locality put up money to "match" some part of the federal grants, though the amount of matching funds can be quite small. *See also* Grants-in-aid; Block grants (3)

Caucus (congressional)   An association of members of Congress created to advocate a political ideology or a regional, ethnic, or economic interest. (7, 11)

Checks and balances   The power of the legislature, executive, and judicial branches of government to block some acts by the other two branches. *See also* Separation of powers (2)

Christmas tree bill   *See* Rider (11)

Circular structure   A method of organizing a president's staff in which several presidential assistants report directly to the president. (12)

City   A municipal corporation or municipality that has been chartered by a state to exercise certain defined powers and provide certain specific services. (3)

Civic competence   A belief that one can affect government policies. (4)

Civic duty   A belief that one has an obligation to participate in civic and political affairs. (4)

Civil law   The body of rules defining relationships among private citizens. It consists of both statutes and the accumulated customary law embodied in judicial decisions (the "common law"). *See also* Criminal law (14)

Civil rights   The rights of citizens to vote, to receive equal treatment before the law, and to share equally with other citizens the benefits of public facilities (such as schools). (16)

Class-action suit   A case brought into court by a person on behalf of not only himself or herself but all other persons in the country under similar circumstances. For example, in *Brown v. Board of Education of Topeka, Kansas*, the Supreme Court decided that not only Linda Brown but all others similarly situated had the right to attend a local public school of their choice without regard to race. (14)

Class consciousness   An awareness of belonging to a particular socioeconomic class whose interests are different from those of others. Usually used in reference to workers who view their interests as opposite those of managers and business owners. (4)

Clear-and-present-danger test   A legal interpretation that reconciled two views of the First Amendment right of free speech, the first that Congress could not pass any law to restrict speech and the second that it could punish harms caused by speech. Proposed by Supreme Court justice Oliver Wendell Holmes in 1919, it held that Congress could punish only speech that created a "clear and present danger" of bringing about the actions that Congress is authorized to prevent. (15)

Closed primary   A primary election limited to registered party members. Prevents members of other parties from crossing over to influence the nomination of an opposing party's candidate. *See also* Open primary; Primary election (8)

Closed rule   An order from the House Rules Committee that sets a time limit on debate and forbids a particular bill from being amended on the legislative floor. *See also* Open rule; Restrictive rule (11)

Cloture rule   A rule used by the Senate to end or limit debate. Designed to prevent "talking a bill to death" by filibuster. For a bill to pass in the Senate, three-fifths of the entire Senate membership (or sixty senators) must vote for it. *See also* Filibuster (11)

Coalition   An alliance among different interest groups (factions) or parties to achieve some political goal. An example is the coalition sometimes formed between Republicans and conservative Democrats. (2)

Coattails   The tendency of lesser-known or weaker candidates to profit in an election by the presence on the ticket of a more popular candidate. (8)

Committee clearance   The ability of a congressional committee to review and approve certain agency decisions in advance and without passing a law. Such approval is not legally binding on the agency, but few agency heads will ignore the expressed wishes of committees. (13)

Compensatory action   An action designed to help members of disadvantaged groups, especially minorities and women, catch up, usually by giving them extra education, training, or services. (16)

Competitive service   The government offices to which people are appointed on the grounds of merit as ascertained by a written examination or by having met certain selection criteria (such as training, educational attainments, or prior experience). (13)

Concurrent resolution   An expression of congressional opinion without the force of law that requires the approval of both the House and Senate but not of the president. Used to settle housekeeping and procedural matters that affect both houses. *See also* Simple resolution; Joint resolution (11)

Concurring opinion   A Supreme Court opinion by one or more justices who agree with the majority's conclusion but for different reasons. *See also* Opinion of the Court; Dissenting opinion (14)

Conditions of aid   Federal rules attached to the grants that states receive. States must agree to abide by these rules in order to receive the grants. (3)

Confederation or confederal system   A political system in which states or regional governments retain ultimate authority except for those powers that they expressly delegate to a central government. The United States was a confederation from 1776 to 1787 under the Articles of Confederation. *See also* Federalism; Unitary system (3)

Conference committee   *See* Joint committees (11)

Congressional campaign committee   A party committee in Congress that provides funds to members who are running for reelection or to would-be members running for an open seat or challenging a candidate from the opposition party. (7)

Conservative   In general a person who favors more limited and local government, less government regulation of markets, more social conformity to traditional norms and values, and tougher policies toward criminals. *See also* Liberal (5)

Conservative coalition   An alliance between Republicans and conservative Democrats. (11)

Constitutional Convention   A meeting of delegates in 1787 to revise the Articles of Confederation, which produced a totally new constitution still in use today. (2)

Constitutional court   A federal court exercising the judicial powers found in Article III of the Constitution and whose judges are given constitutional protection: they may not be fired (they serve during "good behavior"), nor may their salaries be reduced while they are in office. The most important constitutional courts are the Supreme Court, the ninety-four district courts, and the courts of appeals (one in each of eleven regions plus one in the District of Columbia). *See also* District courts; Courts of appeals; Federal-question cases (14)

County   The largest territorial unit between a city and a town. (3)

Courts of appeals   The federal courts with authority to review decisions by federal district courts, regulatory commissions, and certain other federal courts. Such courts have no original jurisdiction; they can hear only appeals. There are a total of twelve courts of appeals in the United states and its territories. *See also* Constitutional court; District courts (14)

Criminal law   The body of rules defining offenses that, though they harm an individual (such as murder, rape, and robbery), are considered to be offenses against society as a whole and as a consequence warrant punishment by and in the name of society. *See also* Civil law (14)

Critical or realigning periods   Periods during which a sharp, lasting shift occurs in the popular coalition supporting one or both parties. The issues that separate the two parties change, and so the kinds of voters supporting each party change. (8)

Cue (political)   A signal telling a congressional representative what values (e.g., liberal or conservative) are at stake in a vote—who is for, who against a proposal—and how that issue fits into his or her own set of political beliefs or party agenda. (9)

***De facto* segregation**   Racial segregation in schools that occurs not because of laws or administrative decisions, but as a result of patterns of residential settlement. To the extent that blacks and whites live in separate neighborhoods, neighborhood schools will often be segregated *de facto*. *See also De jure* segregation (16)

***De jure* segregation**   Racial segregation that occurs because of laws or administrative decisions by public agencies. When state laws, for example, required blacks and whites to attend separate schools or sit in separate sections of a bus, *de jure* segregation resulted. *See also De facto* segregation (16)

Delegate model   The view that an elected representative should represent the opinions of his or her constituents. (12)

Democracy   A term used to describe a political system in which the people are said to rule, directly or indirectly. *See also* Democratic centralism; Direct or participatory democracy; Representative democracy (1)

Democratic centralism   A government said to be democratic if its decisions will serve the "true interests" of the people whether or not the people affect the decision-making or select the decision-makers. Using this definition, various authoritarian regimes have claimed to be "democratic." *See also* Direct or participatory democracy; Representative democracy (1)

Descriptive representation   A correspondence between the demographic characteristics of representatives and those of their constituents. (11)

Devolution   The current effort to scale back the size and activities of the national government and to shift responsibility for a wide range of domestic programs from Washington to the states. In recent years these areas have included welfare, health care, and job training. (3)

Dillon's rule   A legal principle that holds that the terms of city charters are to be interpreted narrowly. Under this rule (named after a lawyer who wrote a book on the subject in 1911) a municipal corporation can exercise only those powers expressly given it or those powers necessarily implied by, or essential to the accomplishment of, these stated powers. (3)

Direct or participatory democracy   A political system in which all or most citizens participate directly by either holding office or making policy. The town meeting, in which citizens vote on major issues, is an example of participatory democracy. (1, 12)

Discharge petition   A device by which any member of the House, after a committee has had a bill for thirty days, may petition to have it brought to the floor. If a majority of the members agree, the bill is discharged from the committee. The discharge petition was designed to prevent a committee from killing a bill by holding it for too long. (11)

Discretionary authority   The extent to which appointed bureaucrats can choose courses of action and make policies that are not spelled out in advance by laws. (13)

Dissenting opinion   A Supreme Court opinion by one or more justices in the minority to explain the minority's disagreement with the Court's ruling. *See also* Opinion of the Court; Concurring opinion (14)

District courts   The lowest federal courts where federal cases begin. They are the only federal courts where trials are held. There are a total of ninety-four district courts in the United States and its territories. *See also* Courts of appeals; Constitutional court; Federal-question cases (14)

Diversity cases   Cases involving citizens of different states over which the federal courts have jurisdiction as described in the Constitution. *See also* Federal-question cases (14)

Divided government   A government in which one party controls the White House and another party controls one or both houses of Congress. *See also* Unified government (12)

Division vote   A congressional voting procedure in which members stand and are counted. *See also* Voice vote; Teller vote; Roll-call vote (11)

Double-tracking   A procedure to keep the Senate going during a filibuster in which the disputed bill is shelved temporarily so that the Senate can get on with other business. *See also* Filibuster; Cloture rule (11)

Dual federalism   A constitutional theory that the national government and the state governments each have defined areas of authority, especially over commerce. (3)

Due-process clause   Protection against arbitrary deprivation of life, liberty, or property as guaranteed in the Fifth and Fourteenth Amendments. (15)

Elite   An identifiable group of persons who possess a disproportionate share of some valued resource—such as money or political power. (1)

Equality of opportunity   A view that it is wrong to use race or sex either to discriminate against or give preferential treatment to minorities or women. *See also* Reverse discrimination (16)

Equal time rule   A rule of the Federal Communications Commission (FCC) stating that if a broadcaster sells time to one candidate for office, he or she must be willing to sell equal time to opposing candidates. (10)

Establishment clause   A clause in the First Amendment to the Constitution stating that Congress shall make no law "respecting an establishment of religion." (15)

Exclusionary rule   A rule that holds that evidence gathered in violation of the Constitution cannot be used in a trial. The rule has been used to implement two provisions of the Bill of Rights—the right to be free from unreasonable searches or seizures (Fourth Amendment) and the right not to be compelled to give evidence against oneself (Fifth Amendment). *See also* Good-faith exception (15)

Ex post facto law   *Ex post facto* is a Latin term meaning "after the fact." A law that makes criminal an act that was legal when it was committed, that increases the penalty for a crime after it has been committed, or that changes the rules of evidence to make conviction easier; a retroactive criminal law. The state legislatures and Congress are forbidden to pass such laws by Article I of the Constitution. (2)

External efficacy   *See* Political efficacy. (4)

Faction   According to James Madison, a group of people who seek to influence public policy in ways contrary to the public good. (2)

Fairness doctrine   A former rule of the Federal Communications Commission (FCC) that required broadcasters to give time to opposing views if they broadcast a program giving one side of a controversial issue. (10)

Feature stories   Media reports about public events knowable to any reporter who cares to inquire, but involving acts and statements not routinely covered by a group of reporters. Thus a reporter must take the initiative and select a particular event as newsworthy, decide to write about it, and persuade an editor to run it. (10)

Federalism   A political system in which ultimate authority is shared between a central government and state or regional governments. *See also* Confederation; Unitary system (2, 3)

Federalist papers   A series of eighty-five essays written by Alexander Hamilton, James Madison, and John Jay (all using the name "Publius") that were published in New York newspapers in 1787–1788 to convince New Yorkers to adopt the newly proposed Constitution. They are classics of American constitutional and political thought. (2)

Federalists   Supporters of a stronger central government who advocated ratification of the Constitution. After ratification they founded a political party supporting a strong executive and Alexander Hamilton's economic policies. *See also* Antifederalists (2)

Federal-question cases   Cases concerning the Constitution, federal law, or treaties over which the federal courts have jurisdiction as described in the Constitution. *See also* Diversity cases (14)

Federal regime   A political system in which local units of government have a specially protected existence and can make final decisions over some governmental activities. (3)

Federal system   A system in which sovereignty is shared so that on some matters the national government is supreme and on others the state, regional, or provincial governments are supreme. (3)

Fee shifting   A law or rule that allows the plaintiff (the party that initiates the lawsuit) to collect its legal costs from the defendant if the defendant loses. *See also* Plaintiff (14)

Filibuster   An attempt to defeat a bill in the Senate by talking indefinitely, thus preventing the Senate from taking action on it. From the Spanish *filibustero*, which means "freebooter," a military adventurer. (11)

Franking privilege   The ability of members of Congress to mail letters to their constituents free of charge by substituting their facsimile signature (frank) for postage. (11)

Freedom of expression   The constitutional rights of Americans to "freedom of speech, or of the press, or the right of people peaceably to assemble, and to petition the government for a redress of grievances" as outlined in the First Amendment to the Constitution. (15)

Freedom of religion   The religious rights of Americans outlined in the First Amendment to the Constitution. The amendment states that "Congress shall make no law respecting an establishment of religion; or abridging the free exercise thereof." (15)

Free-exercise clause   A clause in the First Amendment to the Constitution stating that Congress shall make no law prohibiting the "free exercise" of religion. (15)

Gender gap   Differences in the political views and voting behavior of men and women. (5)

General-act charter   A charter that applies to a number of cities that fall within a certain classification, usually based on city population. Thus in some states all cities with populations over 100,000 are governed on the basis of one charter, while all cities with populations between 50,000 and 99,999 are governed by a different one. *See also* Special-act charter (3)

General election   An election used to fill an elective office. *See also* Primary election (8)

Gerrymandering   Drawing the boundaries of political districts in bizarre or unusual shapes to make it easy for candidates of the party in power to win elections in those districts. (11)

Good-faith exception   Admission at a trial of evidence that is gathered in violation of the Constitution if the violation results from a technical or minor error. *See also* Exclusionary rule (15)

Grandfather clause   A clause added to registration laws allowing people who did not meet registration requirements to vote if they or their ancestors had voted before 1867 (before African Americans were legally allowed to vote). This was to exempt poor and illiterate whites from registration requirements established to keep former slaves from voting. The Supreme Court declared the practice unconstitutional in 1915. (6)

Grants-in-aid   Federal funds provided to states and localities. Grants-in-aid are typically provided for airports, highways, education, and major welfare services. *See also* Categorical grants; Block grants (3)

Great Compromise   A compromise at the Constitutional Convention in 1787 that reconciled the interests of small and large states by allowing the former to predominate in the Senate and the latter in the House. Under the agreement each state received two representatives in the Senate, regardless of size, but was allotted representatives on the basis of population in the House. (2)

Home-rule charter   A charter that allows the city government to do anything that is not prohibited by the charter or by state law. (3)

Ideological interest groups   Political organizations that attract members by appealing to their political convictions with coherent sets of (usually) controversial principles. (9)

Ideological party   A party that values principled stands on issues above all else, including winning. It claims to have a comprehensive view of American society and government radically different from that of the established parties. (7)

Impeachment   A formal accusation against a public official by the lower house of a legislative body. Impeachment is merely an accusation and not a conviction. Only two presidents, Andrew Johnson in 1868 and Bill Clinton in 1998, were ever impeached. They were not, however, convicted, for the Senate failed to obtain the necessary two-thirds vote required for conviction. (12)

Incentive   A valued benefit obtained by joining a political organization. (9)

Incumbent   The person currently in office. (8)

In forma pauperis   A procedure whereby a poor person can file and be heard in court as a pauper, free of charge. (14)

Initiative   A procedure allowing voters to submit a proposed law to a popular vote by obtaining a required number of signatures. *See also* Referendum (3)

Insider stories   Information not usually made public that becomes public because someone with inside knowledge tells a reporter. The reporter may have worked hard to learn these facts, in which case it is called "investigative reporting," or some official may have wanted a story to get out, in which case it is called a "leak." (10)

Interest group   An organization of people sharing a common interest or goal that seeks to influence the making of public policy. (9)

Internal efficacy   *See* Political efficacy (4)

Iron triangle   A close relationship between an agency, a congressional committee, and an interest group that often becomes a mutually advantageous alliance. *See also* Issue network (13)

Issue network   A network of people in Washington-based interest groups, on congressional staffs, in universities and think tanks, and in the mass media who regularly discuss and advocate public policies—say, health care or auto safety. Such networks are split along political, ideological, and economic lines. (13)

Jim Crow   A slang expression for African Americans that emerged in the 1820s and came to signify the laws and governmental practices designed to segregate blacks from whites, especially in the American South. (16)

John Q. Public   Colloquial term for average citizens and what they want or believe. (5)

Joint committees   Committees on which both representatives and senators serve. An especially important kind of joint committee is the *conference committee*, made up of representatives and senators appointed to resolve differences in the Senate and House versions of the same piece of legislation before final passage. *See also* Standing committees (11)

Joint resolution   A formal expression of congressional opinion that must be approved by both houses of Congress and by the president. Joint resolutions proposing a constitutional amendment need not be signed by the president. *See also* Concurrent resolution; Simple resolution (11)

Judicial review   The power of the courts to declare acts of the legislature and of the executive to be unconstitutional and hence null and void. (2, 14)

Laissez-faire   An economic theory that government should not regulate or interfere with commerce. (13)

Lame duck   A politician who is still in office after having lost a reelection bid. (12)

Legislative court   A court that is created by Congress for some specialized purpose and staffed with judges who do not enjoy the protection of Article III of the Constitution. Legislative courts include the Court of Military Appeals and the territorial courts. (14)

Legislative veto   The rejection of a presidential or administrative-agency action by a vote of one or both houses of Congress without the consent of the president. In 1983 the Supreme Court declared the legislative veto to be unconstitutional. (12, 13)

Legitimacy   Political authority conferred by law, public opinion, or constitution. (1)

Libel   A written statement that falsely injures the reputation of another person. (15)

Liberal   In general a person who favors a more active federal government for regulating business, supporting social welfare, and protecting minority rights, but who prefers less regulation of private social conduct. *See also* Conservative (5)

Libertarians   People who wish to maximize personal liberty on both economic and social issues. They prefer a small, weak government that has little control over either the economy or the personal lives of citizens. (5)

Line-item veto   The power of an executive to veto some provisions in an appropriations bill while approving others. The president does not have the right to exercise a line-item veto and must approve or reject an entire appropriations bill. *See also* Pocket veto; Veto message (2, 12)

Literacy test   A requirement that citizens pass a literacy test in order to register to vote. It was established by many states to prevent former slaves (most of whom were illiterate) from voting. Illiterate whites were allowed to vote by a "grandfather clause" added to the law saying that a person could vote, even though he did not meet the legal requirements, if he or his ancestors voted before 1867. (6)

Litmus test   In chemistry a way of finding out whether a liquid is acid or alkaline. The term is used in politics to mean a test of ideological purity, a way of finding out whether a person is a dyed-in-the-wool liberal or conservative or what his or her views are on a controversial question. (14)

Loaded language   Words that reflect a value judgment, used to persuade the listener without making an argument. For example, if someone likes a politician, he might call him "the esteemed Senator Smith"; if he doesn't like him, he might refer to him as "that right-wing or radical senator." (10)

Lobby   An interest group organized to influence government decisions, especially legislation. To *lobby* is to attempt to influence such decisions. A *lobbyist* is a person attempting to influence government decisions on behalf of the group. (9)

Lobbyist   *See* Lobby (9)

Majority leader   The legislative leader elected by party members holding the majority of seats in the House of Representatives or the Senate. *See also* Minority leader (11)

Majority-minority districts   Congressional districts designed to make it easier for citizens of a racial or ethnic minority to elect representatives. (11)

Malapportionment   Drawing the boundaries of political districts so that districts are very unequal in population. (11)

Mandates   Rules imposed by the federal government on the states as conditions for obtaining federal grants or requirements that the states pay the costs of certain nationally defined programs. (3)

Marginal districts   Political districts in which candidates elected to the House of Representatives win in close elections, typically with less than 55 percent of the vote. (11)

Market (television)   An area easily reached by a television signal. There are about two hundred such markets in the country. (10)

Marxists   People who believe that those who control the economic system also control the political one. (1)

Material incentives   Benefits that have monetary value, including money, gifts, services, or discounts received as a result of one's membership in an organization. (9)

McCarthyism   Charges that unfairly or dishonestly tarnish the motives, attack the patriotism, or violate the rights of individuals, especially of political opponents. Refers to the numerous unsubstantiated accusations of communism made against public and private individuals by Senator Joseph McCarthy in the 1950s. (15)

Middle America   A phrase coined by Joseph Kraft in a 1968 newspaper column to refer to Americans who have moved out of poverty but are not yet affluent and who cherish traditional middle-class values. (5)

Minority leader   The legislative leader elected by party members holding a minority of seats in the House of Representatives or the Senate. *See also* Majority leader (11)

Motor-voter bill   A bill passed by Congress in 1993 to make it easier for Americans to register to vote. The law, which went into effect in 1995, requires states to allow voter registration by mail, when one applies for a driver's license, and at state offices that serve the disabled or poor. (6)

Muckraker   A journalist who searches through the activities of public officials and organizations seeking to expose conduct contrary to the public interest. The term was first used by President Theodore Roosevelt in 1906 to warn that antibusiness journalism, while valuable, could be excessively negative. (10)

Mugwumps or progressives   The faction in the Republican party of the 1890s to the 1910s composed of reformers who opposed the use of patronage and party bosses and favored the leadership of experts. After 1910 they evolved into a nonpartisan "good government" movement that sought to open up the political system and curb the abuses of parties. *See also* Political machine (7)

Multiple referral   A congressional process whereby a bill may be referred to several committees that consider it simultaneously in whole or in part. For instance, the 1988 trade bill was considered by fourteen committees in the House and nine in the Senate simultaneously. (11)

Municipal corporation or municipality   A legal term for a city. It is chartered by the state to exercise certain powers and provide certain services. *See also* Special-act charter; General-act charter (3)

Name-request job   A job to be filled by a person whom a government agency has identified by name. (13)

National chairman   A paid, full-time manager of a party's day-to-day work who is elected by the national committee. (7)

National committee   A committee of delegates from each state and territory that runs party affairs between national conventions. (7)

National convention   A meeting of party delegates elected in state primaries, caucuses, or conventions that is held every four years. Its primary purpose is to nominate presidential and vice-presidential candidates and to ratify a campaign platform. (7)

"Necessary and proper" clause   The final paragraph of Article I, section 8, of the Constitution, which authorizes Congress to pass all laws "necessary and proper" to carry out the enumerated powers. Sometimes called the "elastic clause" because of the flexibility that it provides to Congress. (3)

Nonviolent civil disobedience   A philosophy of opposing a law one considers unjust by peacefully violating it and allowing oneself to be punished as a result. (16)

Norm   A standard of right or proper conduct that helps determine the range of acceptable social behavior and policy options. (5)

Nullification   A theory first advanced by James Madison and Thomas Jefferson that the states had the right to "nullify" (that is, declare null and void) a federal law that, in the states' opinion, violated the Constitution. The theory was revived by John C. Calhoun of South Carolina in opposition to federal efforts to restrict slavery. The North's victory in the Civil War determined once and for all that the federal Union is indissoluble and that states cannot declare acts of Congress unconstitutional, a view later confirmed by the Supreme Court. (3)

Office-bloc ballot   A ballot listing all candidates for a given office under the name of that office; also called a "Massachusetts" ballot. *See also* Party-column ballot (8)

Open primary   A primary election that permits voters to choose on election day the primary in which they wish to vote. They may vote for candidates of only one party. *See also* Blanket primary; Closed primary; Primary election (8)

Open rule   An order from the House Rules Committee that permits a bill to be amended on the legislative floor. *See also* Closed rule; Restrictive rule (11)

Opinion of the Court   A Supreme Court opinion written by one or more justices in the majority to explain the decision in a case. *See also* Concurring opinion; Dissenting opinion (14)

Ordinance   A law passed and enforced by a city government. (3)

Orthodox   People who believe that moral rules are derived from the commands of God or the laws of nature; these commands and laws are relatively clear, unchanging, and independent of individual moral preferences. They are likely to believe that traditional morality is more important than individual liberty and should be enforced by government and communal norms. *See also* Progressive (4)

Party-column ballot   A ballot listing all candidates of a given party together under the name of that party; also called an "Indiana" ballot. *See also* Office-bloc ballot (8)

Party polarization   A vote in which a majority of Democratic legislators oppose a majority of Republican legislators. (11)

Per curiam opinion   A brief, unsigned opinion issued by the Supreme Court to explain its ruling. *See also* Opinion of the Court (14)

Perks   A short form of *perquisites*, meaning "fringe benefits of office." Among the perks of political office for high-ranking officials are limousines, expense accounts, free air travel, fancy offices, and staff assistants. (12)

Personal following   The political support provided to a candidate on the basis of personal popularity and networks. (7)

Plaintiff   The party that initiates a lawsuit to obtain a remedy for an injury to his or her rights. (14)

Pluralist   A theory that competition among all affected interests shapes public policy. (1)

Plurality system   An electoral system, used in almost all American elections, in which the winner is the person who gets the most votes, even if he or she does not receive a majority of the votes. (7)

Pocket veto   One of two ways for a president to disapprove a bill sent to him by Congress. If the president does not sign the bill within ten days of his receiving it and Congress has adjourned within that time, the bill does not become a law. *See also* Veto message; Line-item veto (12)

Police power   The power of a state to promote health, safety, and morals. (3)

Political action committee   A committee set up by and representing a corporation, labor union, or special-interest group that raises and spends campaign contributions on behalf of one or more candidates or causes. (8)

Political cue   *See* Cue (political) (9)

Political culture   A broadly shared way of thinking about political and economic life that reflects fundamental assumptions about how government should operate. It is distinct from *political ideology*, which refers to a more or less consistent set of views about the policies government ought to follow. Up to a point people sharing a common political culture can disagree about ideology. *See also* Political ideology (4)

Political editorializing rule   A rule of the Federal Communications Commission that if a broadcaster endorses a candidate, the opposing candidate has a right to reply. (10)

Political efficacy   A citizen's belief that he or she can understand and influence political affairs. This sense is divided into two parts—internal efficacy (confidence in a citizen's own abilities to understand and take part in political affairs) and external efficacy (a belief that the system will respond to a citizen's demands). (4)

Political elite   *See* Elite (5)

Political ideology   A more or less consistent set of views as to the policies government ought to pursue. *See also* Political culture (4, 5)

Political machine   A party organization that recruits its members by dispensing *patronage*—tangible incentives such as money, political jobs, or an opportunity to get favors from government—and that is characterized by a high degree of leadership control over member activity. (7)

Political party   A group that seeks to elect candidates to public office by supplying them with a label—a "party identification"—by which they are known to the electorate. (7)

Political question   An issue that the Supreme Court refuses to consider because it believes the Constitution has left it entirely to another branch to decide. Its view of such issues may change over time, however. For example, until the 1960s the Court refused to hear cases about the size of congressional districts, no matter how unequal their populations. In 1962, however, it decided that it was authorized to review the constitutional implications of this issue. (14)

Political subculture   Fundamental assumptions about how the political process should operate that distinguish citizens by region, religion, or other characteristics. (4)

Poll   A survey of public opinion. *See also* Random sample (5)

Poll tax   A requirement that citizens pay a tax in order to register to vote. It was adopted by many states to prevent former slaves (most of whom were poor) from voting. It is now unconstitutional. *See also* Grandfather clause; Literacy test (6)

Populists   People who hold liberal views on economic matters and conservative ones on social matters. They prefer a strong government that will reduce economic inequality, regulate businesses, and impose stricter social and criminal sanctions. The name and views have their origins in an agriculturally based social movement and party of the 1880s and 1890s that sought to curb the power of influential economic interests. (5)

Pork-barrel legislation   Legislation that gives tangible benefits (highways, dams, post offices) to constituents in several districts or states in the hope of winning their votes in return. (11)

Position issue   An issue dividing the electorate on which rival parties adopt different policy positions to attract voters. *See also* Valence issue (8)

Power   The ability of one person to get another person to act in accordance with the first person's intentions. (1)

Presidential primary   *See* Primary election (8)

Primary election   An election prior to the general election in which voters select the candidates who will run on each party's ticket. Before presidential elections, a *presidential primary* is held to select delegates to the presidential nominating conventions of the major parties. *See also* Closed primary; Open primary (8)

Prior restraint   The traditional view of the press's free speech rights as expressed by William Blackstone, the great English jurist. According to this view the press is guaranteed freedom from censorship—that is, rules telling it in advance what it can publish. After publication, however, the government can punish the press for material that is judged libelous or obscene. (15)

Private bill   A legislative bill that deals only with specific, private, personal, or local matters rather than with general legislative affairs. The main kinds include immigration and naturalization bills (referring to particular individuals) and personal-claim bills. *See also* Public bill (11)

Probable cause   *See* Search warrant (15)

Progressive   A person who believes that moral rules are derived in part from an individual's beliefs and the circumstances of modern life. Progressives are likely to favor government tolerance and protection of individual choice. (4)

Prospective voting   Voting for a candidate because one favors his or her ideas for addressing issues after the election. (*Prospective* means "forward-looking.") *See also* Retrospective voting (8)

Public bill   A legislative bill that deals with matters of general concern. A bill involving defense expenditures is a public bill; a bill pertaining to an individual's becoming a naturalized citizen is not. *See also* Private bill (11)

Public-interest lobby   A political organization the stated goals of which will principally benefit nonmembers. (9)

Purposive incentive   The benefit that comes from serving a cause or principle from which one does not personally benefit. (9)

Pyramid structure   A method of organizing a president's staff in which most presidential assistants report through a hierarchy to the president's chief of staff. (12)

Quorum   The minimum number of members who must be present for business to be conducted in Congress. (11)

Quorum call   A calling of the roll in either house of Congress to see whether the number of representatives in attendance meets the minimum number required to conduct official business. (11)

Random sample   A sample selected in such a way that any member of the population being surveyed (e.g., all adults or voters) has an equal chance of being interviewed. (5)

Ratings   An assessment of a representative's voting record on issues important to an interest group. Such ratings are designed to generate public support for or opposition to a legislator. (9)

Recall   A procedure, in effect in fifteen states, whereby the voters can vote to remove an elected official from office. (3)

Red tape   Complex bureaucratic rules and procedures that must be followed to get something done. (13)

Referendum   The practice of submitting a law to a popular vote at election time. The law may be proposed by a voter's initiative or by the legislature. *See also* Initiative (3)

Registered voters People who are registered to vote. While almost all adult American citizens are theoretically eligible to vote, only those who have completed a registration form by the required date may do so. (6)

Religious tradition The moral teachings of religious institutions on religious, social, and economic issues. (5)

Remedy A judicial order preventing or redressing a wrong or enforcing a right. (14)

Representative democracy A political system in which leaders and representatives acquire political power by means of a competitive struggle for the people's vote. This is the form of government used by nations that are called democratic. (1, 12)

Republic A form of democracy in which power is vested in representatives selected by means of popular competitive elections. *See also* Representative democracy (2)

Restrictive rule An order from the House Rules Committee that permits certain kinds of amendments but not others to be made into a bill on the legislative floor. *See also* Closed rule; Open rule (11)

Retrospective voting Voting for or against the candidate or party in office because one likes or dislikes how things have gone in the recent past. (*Retrospective* means "backward-looking.") *See also* Prospective voting (8)

Revenue sharing A law providing for the distribution of a fixed amount or share of federal tax revenues to the states for spending on almost any government purpose. Distribution was intended to send more money to poorer, heavily taxed states and less to richer, lightly taxed ones. The program was ended in 1986. (3)

Reverse discrimination Using race or sex to give preferential treatment to some people. (16)

Rider An amendment on a matter unrelated to a bill that is added to the bill so that it will "ride" to passage through the Congress. When a bill has lots of riders, it is called a Christmas tree bill. (11)

Right-of-reply rule A rule of the Federal Communications Commission that if a person is attacked on a broadcast (other than in a regular news program), that person has the right to reply over that same station. (10)

Roll-call vote A congressional voting procedure that consists of members answering "yea" or "nay" to their names. When roll calls were handled orally, it was a time-consuming process in the House. Since 1973 an electronic voting system permits each House member to record his or her vote and learn the total automatically. *See also* Voice vote; Division vote; Teller vote (11)

Routine stories Media reports about public events that are regularly covered by reporters and that involve simple, easily described acts or statements. For example, the president takes a trip or Congress passes a bill. (10)

Runoff primary A second primary election held in some states when no candidate receives a majority of the votes in the first primary; the runoff is between the two candidates with the most votes. Runoff primaries are common in the South. (8)

Safe districts Districts in which incumbents win by margins of 55 percent or more. (11)

Sampling error The difference between the results of two surveys or samples. For example, if one random sample shows that 60 percent of all Americans like cats and another random sample taken at the same time shows that 65 percent do, the sampling error is 5 percent. (5)

School district A special-district government responsible for administering public schools. (3)

Search warrant An order from a judge authorizing the search of a place; the order must describe what is to be searched and seized, and the judge can issue it only if he or she is persuaded by the police that good reason (probable cause) exists that a crime has been committed and that the evidence bearing on the crime will be found at a certain location. (15)

Second-order devolution The flow of power and responsibility from states to local governments. (3)

Select committees Congressional committees appointed for a limited time and purpose. *See also* Standing committees; Joint committees (11)

Selective attention Paying attention only to those parts of a newspaper or broadcast story with which one agrees. Studies suggest that this is how people view political ads on television. (10)

Separate-but-equal doctrine The doctrine established in *Plessy v. Fergusson* (1896), in which the Supreme Court ruled that a state could provide "separate but equal" facilities for African Americans. (16)

Separation of powers A principle of American government whereby constitutional authority is shared by three separate branches of government—the legislative, the executive, and the judicial. *See also* Checks and balances (2)

Sequential referral A congressional process by which a Speaker may send a bill to a second committee after the first is finished acting, or may refer parts of a bill to separate committees. (11)

Shays's Rebellion A rebellion in 1787 led by Daniel Shays and other ex–Revolutionary War soldiers and officers to prevent foreclosures of farms as a result of high interest rates and taxes. The revolt highlighted the weaknesses of the Confederation and bolstered support for a stronger national government. (2)

Silent majority A phrase used to describe people, whatever their economic status, who uphold traditional values, especially against the counterculture of the 1960s. (5)

Simple resolution An expression of opinion either in the House of Representatives or the Senate to settle housekeeping or procedural matters in either body. Such expressions are not signed by the president and do not have the force of law. *See also* Concurrent resolution; Joint resolution (11)

Social movement A widely shared demand for change in some aspect of the social or political order. The civil rights movement of the 1960s was such an event, as are broadly based religious revivals. A social movement may have liberal or conservative goals. (9)

Social status A measure of one's social standing obtained by combining factors such as education, income, and occupation. (5)

Soft money Funds solicited from individuals, corporations, and unions that are spent on party activities, such as voter-registration campaigns and voting drives, rather than on behalf of a specific candidate. These funds need not be reported to the Federal Election Commission. (8)

Solidary incentives The social rewards that lead people to join local or state political organizations. People who find politics fun and want to meet others who share their interests are said to respond to solidary incentives. (7, 9)

Sophomore surge   An increase in the votes that congressional candidates usually get when they first run for reelection. (11)

Sound bite   A brief statement no longer than a few seconds used on a radio or television news broadcast. (10)

Sovereign immunity   A doctrine that a citizen cannot sue the government without its consent. By statute Congress has given its consent for the government to be sued in many cases involving a dispute over a contract or damage done as a result of negligence. (14)

Sovereignty   Supreme or ultimate political authority; a sovereign government is one that is legally and politically independent of any other government. (3)

Special-act charter   A charter that denies the powers of a certain named city and lists what the city can and cannot do. *See also* General-act charter (3)

Special-district government or authority   A local or regional government with responsibility for some single function such as administering schools, handling sewage, or managing airports. (3)

Split ticket   Voting for candidates of different parties for various offices in the same election. For example, voting for a Republican for senator and a Democrat for president. *See also* Straight ticket (8)

Spoils system   Another phrase for political patronage—that is, the practice of giving the fruits of a party's victory, such as jobs and contracts, to the loyal members of that party. (13)

Sponsored party   A local or state political party that is largely staffed and funded by another organization with established networks in the community. One example is the Democratic party in and around Detroit, which has been developed, led, and to a degree financed by the political-action arm of the United Auto Workers. (7)

Standing   A legal concept establishing who is entitled to bring a lawsuit to court. For example, an individual must ordinarily show personal harm in order to acquire standing and be heard in court. (14)

Standing committees   Permanently established legislative committees that consider and are responsible for legislation within a certain subject area. Examples are the House Ways and Means Committee and the Senate Judiciary Committee. *See also* Select committees; Joint committees (11)

Stare decisis   A Latin term meaning "let the decision stand." The practice of basing judicial decisions on precedents established in similar cases decided in the past. (14)

Straight ticket   Voting for candidates who are all of the same party. For example, voting for Republican candidates for senator, representative, and president. *See also* Split ticket (8)

Strict-constructionist approach   The view that judges should decide cases on the basis of the language of the Constitution. (14)

Strict scrutiny   The standard by which the Supreme Court judges classifications based on race. To be accepted such a classification must be closely related to a "compelling" public purpose. (16)

Substantive representation   The correspondence between representatives' opinions and those of their constituents. *See also* Descriptive representation (11)

Superdelegates   Party leaders and elected officials who become delegates to the national convention without having to run in primaries or caucuses. Party rules determine the percentage of delegate seats reserved for party officials. (7)

Suspect classifications   Classifications of people on the basis of their race and ethnicity. The courts have ruled that laws classifying people on these grounds will be subject to "strict scrutiny." (16)

Symbolic speech   An act that conveys a political message, such as burning a draft card to protest the draft. (15)

Teller vote   A congressional voting procedure in which members pass between two tellers, the "yeas" first and then the "nays." Since 1971 the identities of members in a teller vote can be "recorded." *See also* Voice vote; Division vote; Roll-call vote (11)

Third-order devolution   The use of non-governmental organizations to implement public policy. (3)

Town or township   A subunit of county government in many eastern and Midwestern states. (3)

Trial balloon   Information provided to the media by an anonymous public official as a way of testing the public reaction to a possible policy or appointment. (10)

Trustee approach   The view that an elected representative should act on his or her own best judgment of what public policy requires. (12)

Trust funds   Funds for government programs that are collected and spent outside the regular government budget; the amounts are determined by preexisting law rather than by annual appropriations. The Social Security trust fund is the largest of these. *See also* Appropriation (13)

Two-party system   An electoral system with two dominant parties that compete in state or national elections. Third parties have little chance of winning. (7)

Unalienable   Based on nature and Providence rather than on the preferences of people. (2)

Unified government   A government in which the same party controls both the White House and both houses of Congress. When Bill Clinton became president in 1993, it was the first time since 1981 (and only the second time since 1969) that the same party was in charge of the presidency and Congress. *See also* Divided government (12)

Unitary system   A system in which sovereignty is wholly in the hands of the national government so that subnational political units are dependent on its will. *See also* Federalism; Federal system (3)

Valence issue   An issue on which voters distinguish rival parties by the degree to which they associate each party or candidate with conditions, goals, or symbols the electorate universally approves or disapproves of. Examples of such issues are economic prosperity and political corruption. *See also* Position issue (8)

Veto message   One of two ways for a president to disapprove a bill sent to him by Congress. The veto message must be sent to Congress within ten days after the president receives it. *See also* Pocket veto; Line-item veto (12)

Voice vote   A congressional voting procedure in which members shout "yea" in approval or "nay" in disapproval; allows members to vote quickly or anonymously on bills. *See also* Division vote; Teller vote; Roll-call vote (11)

Voting-age population   The citizens who are eligible to vote after reaching a minimum age requirement. In the United States a citizen must be at least eighteen years old in order to vote. (6)

Wall-of-separation principle   A Supreme Court interpretation of the establishment clause in the First Amendment that prevents government involvement with religion, even on a non-preferential basis. (15)

Whip   A senator or representative who helps the party leader stay informed about what party members are thinking, rounds up members when important votes are to be taken, and attempts to keep a nose count on how the voting on controversial issues is likely to go. (11)

White primary   The practice of keeping African Americans from voting in primary elections (at the time, the only meaningful election in the one-party South was the Democratic primary) through arbitrary implementation of registration requirements and intimidation. Such practices were declared unconstitutional in 1944. (6)

Work ethic   A belief in the importance of hard work and personal achievement. (4)

Writ of certiorari   A Latin term meaning "made more certain." An order issued by a higher court to a lower court to send up the record of a case for review. Most cases reach the Supreme Court through the writ of certiorari, issued when at least four of the nine justices feel that the case should be reviewed. (14)

Writ of habeas corpus   A Latin term meaning "you shall have the body." A court order directing a police officer, sheriff, or warden who has a person in custody to bring the prisoner before a judge and show sufficient cause for his or her detention. The writ of habeas corpus was designed to prevent illegal arrests and imprisonment. (2)

Notes

Chapter 1 *The Study of American Government*

1. Aristotle, *Politics*, iv, 4, 1290^b. More precisely, Aristotle's definition was this: democracy is a "constitution in which the free-born and poor control the government—being at the same time a majority." He distinguished this from an oligarchy, "in which the rich and well-born control the government—being at the same time a minority." Aristotle listed several varieties of democracy, depending on whether, for example, there was a property qualification for citizenship.
2. Joseph A. Schumpeter, *Capitalism, Socialism, and Democracy*, 3d ed. (New York: Harper Torchbooks, 1950), 269. (First published in 1942.)
3. Karl Marx and Friedrich Engels, "The Manifesto of the Communist Party," in *The Marx-Engels Reader*, 2d ed., ed. Robert C. Tucker (New York: Norton, 1978), 469–500.
4. C. Wright Mills, *The Power Elite* (New York: Oxford University Press, 1956).
5. Richard Rovere, *The American Establishment* (New York: Harcourt Brace, 1962).
6. H. H. Gerth and C. Wright Mills, eds., *From Max Weber: Essays in Sociology* (London: Routledge & Kegan Paul, 1948), 232–235.
7. Among the authors whose interpretations of American politics are essentially pluralist is David B. Truman, *The Governmental Process*, 2d ed. (New York: Knopf, 1971).
8. Alexis de Tocqueville, *Democracy in America*, vol. 2, ed. Phillips Bradley (New York: Knopf, 1951), book 2, ch. 8, 122.
9. Derek C. Bok and John T. Dunlop, *Labor and the American Community* (New York: Simon & Schuster, 1970), 134.

Chapter 2 *The Constitution*

1. Quoted in Bernard Bailyn, *The Ideological Origins of the American Revolution* (Cambridge: Harvard University Press, 1967), 61, n. 6.
2. Quoted in Bailyn, ibid., 135–137.
3. Quoted in Bailyn, ibid., 77.
4. Quoted in Bailyn, ibid., 160. Italics in the original.
5. *Federalist* No. 37.
6. Gordon S. Wood, *The Creation of the American Republic* (Chapel Hill: University of North Carolina Press, 1969). See also *Federalist* No. 49.
7. Letter of George Washington to Henry Lee (October 31, 1787), in *Writings of George Washington*, vol. 29, ed. John C. Fitzpatrick (Washington, D.C.: Government Printing Office, 1939), 34.
8. Letters of Thomas Jefferson to James Madison (January 30, 1787) and to Colonel William S. Smith (November 13, 1787), in *Jefferson Himself*, ed. Bernard Mayo (Boston: Houghton Mifflin, 1942), 145.
9. *Federalist* No. 51.
10. *Federalist* No. 48.
11. *Federalist* No. 51.
12. Ibid.
13. Ibid.
14. "The Address and Reasons of Dissent of the Minority of the State of Pennsylvania to Their Constituents," in *The Anti-Federalist*, ed. Cecelia Kenyon (Indianapolis: Bobbs-Merrill, 1966), 39.
15. Max Farrand, *The Framing of the Constitution of the United States* (New Haven, Conn.: Yale University Press, 1913), 185.
16. See, for example, John Hope Franklin, *Racial Equality in America* (Chicago: University of Chicago Press, 1976), ch. 1, esp. 12–20.
17. Max Farrand, *The Records of the Federal Convention of 1787*, 4 vols. (New Haven, Conn.: Yale University Press, 1911–1937).
18. Theodore J. Lowi, *American Government: Incomplete Conquest* (Hinsdale, Ill.: Dryden Press, 1976), 97.
19. Article I, section 2, para. 3.
20. Article I, section 9, para. 1.
21. Article IV, section 2, para. 3
22. Charles A. Beard, *An Economic Interpretation of the Constitution* (New York: Macmillan, 1913), esp. 26–51, 149–151, 324–325.
23. Forrest McDonald, *We the People* (Chicago: University of Chicago Press, 1958); Robert E. Brown, *Charles Beard and the Constitution* (Princeton: Princeton University Press, 1956).
24. Robert A. McGuire, "Constitution Making: A Rational Choice Model of the Federal Convention of 1787," *American Journal of Political Science* 32 (May 1988): 483–522. See also Forrest McDonald, *Novus Ordo Seclorum* (Lawrence: University of Kansas Press, 1985), 221.
25. McDonald, *Novus Ordo Seclorum*, 202–221.
26. Robert A. McGuire and Robert L. Ohsfeldt, "Economic Interests and the American Constitution: A Quantitative Rehabilitation of Charles A. Beard," *Journal of Economic History* 44 (June 1984): 509–519.
27. Lloyd N. Cutler, "To Form a Government," *Foreign Affairs* (Fall 1980), 126–143.

Chapter 3 *Federalism*

1. Woodrow Wilson, *Constitutional Government in the United States* (New York: Columbia University Press, 1961), 173. (First published in 1908.)
2. David B. Truman, "Federalism and the Party System," in *Federalism: Mature and Emergent*, ed. Arthur MacMahon (Garden City, N.Y.: Doubleday, 1955), 123.
3. Truman, op. cit.
4. Harold J. Laski, "The Obsolescence of Federalism," *New Republic* (May 3, 1939): 367–369.
5. Riker, op. cit., 154.
6. Daniel J. Elazar, *American Federalism: A View from the States* (New York: Crowell, 1966), 216.
7. Martin Diamond, "The Federalists' View of Federalism," in *Essays in Federalism*, ed. George C. S. Benson (Claremont, Calif.: Institute for Studies in Federalism, 1961), 21–64; and Samuel H. Beer, "Federalism, Nationalism, and Democracy in America," *American Political Science Review* 72 (March 1978): 9–21.
8. *United States v. Sprague*, 282 U.S. 716 (1931).
9. *Garcia v. San Antonio Metropolitan Transit Authority*, 105 S. Ct. 1005 (1985), overruling *National League of Cities v. Usery*, 426 U.S. 833 (1976).
10. *McCulloch v. Maryland*, 4 Wheat. 316 (1819).
11. This was in part overruled in *Pollock v. Farmers' Loan & Trust Co.*, 157 U.S. 429 (1895); overruled in *South Carolina v. Baker*, No. 94 (1988).
12. *Texas v. White*, 7 Wall. 700 (1869).
13. *Champion v. Ames*, 188 U.S. 321 (1903).
14. *Hoke v. United States*, 227 U.S. 308 (1913).
15. *Clark Distilling Co. v. W. Md. Ry.*, 242 U.S. 311 (1917).
16. *Hipolite Egg Co. v. United States*, 220 U.S. 45 (1911).
17. *United States v. E. C. Knight Co.*, 156 U.S. 1 (1895).
18. *Paul v. Virginia*, 8 Wall. 168 (1869).
19. *Veazie Bank v. Fenno*, 8 Wall. 533 (1869).
20. *Brown v. Maryland*, 12 Wheat. 419 (1827).
21. *Wickard v. Filburn*, 317 U.S. 111 (1942); *NLRB v. Jones & Laughlin Steel Corp.*, 301 U.S. 58 (1937).
22. *Kirschbaum Co. v. Walling*, 316 U.S. 517 (1942).
23. *Goldfarb v. Virginia State Bar*, 421 U.S. 773 (1975); *Flood v. Kuhn*, 407 U.S. 258 (1972).
24. *United States v. California*, 332 U.S. 19 (1947).
25. Morton Grodzins, *The American System* (Chicago: Rand McNally, 1966), 49–50.
26. Morton Keller, *Affairs of State* (Cambridge: Harvard University Press, 1977), 310, 381–382.
27. Edward C. Banfield, "Making a New Federal Program: Model Cities, 1964–1968," in *Policy and Politics in America*, ed. Allan P. Sindler (Boston: Little, Brown, 1973), 124–158.

28. Neal R. Pierce, "Partnership for City Aid," *Boston Globe* (March 30, 1978).

29. Samuel H. Beer, "The Modernization of American Federalism," *Publius* 3 (Fall 1973): esp. 74–79; and Beer, "Federalism," op. cit., 18–19.

30. Calculated from *Special Analyses: Budget of the U.S. Government, Fiscal Year 1979* (Washington, D.C.: Government Printing Office, 1978), 187.

31. Quoted in *National Journal* (September 18, 1976): 1321.

32. R. Douglas Arnold, "The Local Roots of Domestic Policy," in *The New Congress*, ed. Thomas E. Mann and Norman J. Ornstein (Washington, D.C.: American Enterprise Institute, 1981), 268.

33. Congressional Budget Office, *Federal Constraints on State and Local Government Actions* (Washington, D.C.: Government Printing Office, 1979).

34. Civil Rights Act of 1871, as amended in 1875: *United States Code*, Title 42, section 1983.

35. *Nation's Business* (December 1993): 12.

36. *Federally Induced Costs Affecting State and Local Governments* (U.S. Advisory Commission on Intergovernmental Relations, September 1994), v.

37. *United States Code*, Title 23, section 131 (1976).

38. *Congressional Record* 126 (February 5, 1980): S1009–S1013.

39. Ibid., S1010.

40. *Statistical Abstract of the United States, 1990*, 371.

41. Richard P. Nathan and Fred Doolittle, *Reagan and the States* (Princeton, N.J.: Princeton University Press, 1987), 7.

42. George Peterson et al., *The Reagan Block Grants: What Have We Learned?* (Washington, D.C.: Urban Institute Press, 1986), 21–27.

43. R. Kent Weaver, "Deficits and Devolution in the 104th Congress," unpublished draft paper, Washington, D.C., Brookings Institution, April 1996.

44. Richard P. Nathan, "Hard Road Ahead: Block Grants and 'The Devolution Revolution,'" discussion paper, Washington, D.C., Center for Public Management, Brookings Institution, October 27, 1995.

45. *The Public Perspective* (April/May 1995): 5.

Chapter 4 *American Political Culture*

1. Alexis de Tocqueville, *Democracy in America*, ed. Phillips Bradley (New York: Knopf, 1951), vol. 1, 288. (First published in 1835.)

2. Ibid., vol. 1, 319–320.

3. Ibid., 319.

4. Donald J. Devine, *The Political Culture of the United States* (Boston: Little, Brown, 1972), 185; Herbert McClosky and John Zaller, *The American Ethos: Public Attitudes Toward Capitalism and Democracy* (Cambridge: Harvard University Press, 1984), ch. 3, esp. 74–75.

5. McClosky and Zaller, op. cit., 74–77.

6. Ibid., 66.

7. Gunnar Myrdal, *An American Dilemma: The Negro Problem in Modern Democracy* (New York: Harper, 1944), intro. and ch. 1.

8. Frank R. Westie, "The American Dilemma: An Empirical Test," *American Sociological Review* 30 (August 1965): 536–537.

9. Eric L. McKitrick, "Party Politics and the Union and Confederate War Efforts," in *The American Party Systems*, ed. William Nisbet Chambers and Walter Dean Burnham, 2d ed. (New York: Oxford University Press, 1975), 117–121.

10. McClosky and Zaller, op. cit., 174.

11. Sidney Verba and Gary R. Orren, *Equality in America: The View from the Top* (Cambridge: Harvard University Press, 1985), 146–147.

12. McClosky and Zaller, op. cit., 82–84.

13. Ibid., 93, 95.

14. Verba and Orren, op. cit., 74; McClosky and Zaller, op. cit., 126.

15. Verba and Orren, op. cit., 72, 254.

16. Donald Kinder and David Sears, "Symbolic Racism Versus Racial Threats to the Good Life," *Journal of Personality and Social Psychology* 40 (1981): 414–431.

17. Paul M. Sniderman and Michael Gray Hagen, *Race and Inequality: A Study in American Values* (Chatham, N.J.: Chatham House, 1985), 111.

18. Ibid., 37–38.

19. Theodore Caplow and Howard M. Bahr, "Half a Century of Change in Adolescent Attitudes: A Replication of a Middletown Survey by the Lynds," *Public Opinion Quarterly* 43 (1979): 1–17, table 1.

20. Thomas J. Anton, "Policy-Making and Political Culture in Sweden," *Scandinavian Political Studies* 4 (1969): 88–100; M. Donald Hancock, *Sweden: The Politics of Post-Industrial Change* (Hinsdale, Ill.: Dryden Press, 1972); Sten Johansson, "Liberal-Democratic Theory and Political Processes," in *Readings in the Swedish Class Structure*, ed. Richard Scarse (New York: Pergamon Press, 1976); Steven J. Kelman, *Regulating America, Regulating Sweden: A Comparative Study of Occupational Safety and Health Policy* (Cambridge, Mass.: MIT Press, 1981), 118–123.

21. Lewis Austin, *Saints and Samurai: The Political Culture of American and Japanese Elites* (New Haven, Conn.: Yale University Press, 1975).

22. Gabriel Almond and Sidney Verba, *The Civic Culture* (Princeton, N.J.: Princeton University Press, 1963), 169, 185. See also Gabriel Almond and Sidney Verba, eds., *The Civic Culture Revisited* (Boston: Little, Brown, 1980).

23. Sidney Verba et al., *Voice and Equality: Civic Voluntarism in American Politics* (Cambridge: Harvard University Press, 1995), 69, 70.

24. Gordon Heald, "A Comparison Between American, European, and Japanese Values," as quoted in Richard Rose, "Public Confidence, Popular Consent: A Comparison of Britain and the United States," *Public Opinion* (February–March 1984): 11.

25. Gallup International Poll for the European Value System Study, 1982.

26. Paul M. Sniderman, *A Question of Loyalty* (Berkeley: University of California Press, 1981).

27. Seymour Martin Lipset, *The First New Nation* (New York: Doubleday Anchor Books, 1967), 170–171.

28. Verba and Orren, op. cit., 255.

29. Max Weber, *The Protestant Ethic and the Spirit of Capitalism*, trans. Talcott Parsons (New York: Scribner's, 1930). (First published in 1904.)

30. Erik H. Erikson, *Childhood and Society* (New York: Norton, 1950), ch. 8.

31. The phrase "culture war" is from James Davison Hunter, *Culture Wars: The Struggle to Define America* (New York: Basic Books, 1991). This discussion draws heavily on Professor Hunter's analysis.

32. Ibid., 96–97, 116–117. See also Robert Lerner, Stanley Rotham, and S. Robert Lichter, "Christian Religious Elites," *Public Opinion* 11 (March/April 1989): 54–58.

33. Schlozman and Verba, op. cit., 218–224, 237.

34. Jack Citrin, "Comment: The Political Relevance of Trust in Government," *American Political Science Review* 68 (September 1974): 973–988; James S. House and William M. Mason, "Political Alienation in America, 1958–1968," *American Sociological Review* 40 (April 1975): 123–147; Seymour Martin Lipset and William Schneider, *The Confidence Gap: Business, Labor, and Government in the Public Mind* (New York: Free Press, 1983), ch. 12.

35. Citrin, op. cit., 975.

36. The Gallup Organization, *Poll Releases* (June 19, 1997), 3–6.

37. Robert E. Lane, "The Politics of Consensus in the Age of Affluence," *American Political Science Review* 59 (December 1965): 874–875; Lane, "The Decline of Politics and Ideology in a Knowledgeable Society," *American Sociological Review* 31 (October 1966): 649–662; Lipset and Schneider, op. cit., 14–15.

38. Arthur Miller, "Is Confidence Rebounding?" *Public Opinion* (June–July 1983): 16–20.

39. The Gallup Organization, *Social Audit* (June 1997), 14; George Gallup, Jr., and D. Michael Lindsay, *Surveying the Religious Landscape: Trends in U.S. Beliefs* (Harrisburg, Pa.: Morehouse Publishing, 1999), 53.

40. *The Public Perspective*, 8 (February/March 1997): 6–7.

41. Lipset and Schneider, op. cit., 21–22; Warren E. Miller, "Crisis in Confidence II—Misreading the Public Pulse," *Public Opinion* (October–November 1979): 12–13.

42. Data from the Survey Research Center, University of Michigan. See also Norman H. Nie, Sidney Verba, and John R. Petrocik, *The Changing American Voter* (Cambridge: Harvard University Press, 1976), 125–128.

43. Samuel H. Barnes and Max Kaase, eds., *Political Action: Mass Participation in Five Democracies* (Beverly Hills, Calif.: Sage, 1979), 541–542, 574.

44. James W. Prothro and Charles M. Grigg, "Fundamental Principles of Democracy: Bases of Agreement and Disagreement," *Journal of Politics* 22 (Spring 1960): 275–294.

45. Herbert McClosky and Alida Brill, *Dimensions of Tolerance: What Americans Believe About Civil Liberties* (New York: Russell Sage Foundation, 1983), 124.

46. Ibid., 62, 66, 70, 118, 131.

47. Ibid., 435; James A. Davis, "Communism, Cohorts, and Categories: American Tolerance in 1954 and 1972–1973," *American Journal of Sociology* 81 (1975): 491–513; and Clyde A. Nunn, Harry J. Crockett, Jr., and J. Allen Williams, Jr., *Tolerance for Nonconformity: A National Survey of Changing Commitment to Civil Liberties* (San Francisco: Jossey-Bass, 1978). But compare the different conclusion in John L. Sullivan, James Piereson, and George E. Marcus, *Political Tolerance and American Democracy* (Chicago: University of Chicago Press, 1982).

Chapter 5   *Public Opinion*

1. George W. Bishop, Alfred J. Tuchfarber, and Robert W. Oldendick, "1984: How Much Can We Manipulate and Control People's Answers to Public Opinion Surveys?" paper delivered at the 1984 annual meeting of the American Political Science Association; Howard Schuman and S. Presser, *Questions and Answers in Attitude Surveys* (New York: Academic Press, 1981), ch. 5.

2. M. Kent Jennings and Richard G. Niemi, "The Transmission of Political Values from Parent to Child," *American Political Science Review* 62 (March 1968): 173.

3. Robert D. Hess and Judith V. Tomey, *The Development of Political Attitudes in Children* (Chicago: Aldine, 1967), 90.

4. Several studies of child-parent agreement on party preference are summarized in David O. Sears, "Political Behavior," in *The Handbook of Social Psychology*, ed. Gardner Lindzey and Elliot Aronson, 2d ed. (Reading, Mass.: Addison-Wesley, 1969), vol. 5, 376.

5. Norman H. Nie, Sidney Verba, and John R. Petrocik, *The Changing American Voter* (Cambridge: Harvard University Press, 1976), ch. 4.

6. Robert S. Erikson and Norman R. Luttbeg, *American Public Opinion: Its Origins, Content, and Impact* (New York: Wiley, 1973), 197; and Seymour Martin Lipset, *Revolution and Counterrevolution*, rev. ed. (Garden City, N.Y.: Doubleday Anchor Books, 1970), 338–342.

7. Karen M. Kaufman and John R. Petrocik, "The Changing Politics of American Men: Understanding the Sources of the Gender Gap," *American Journal of Political Science* 43 (1999): 864–887.

8. Alexander M. Astin, *Four Critical Years: Effects of College on Beliefs, Attitudes, and Knowledge* (San Francisco: Jossey-Bass, 1978), 36–38.

9. Institute of Politics, Harvard University, *Campaign '84 and Beyond* (1986), 12.

10. Erikson and Luttbeg, op. cit., 138; Terry S. Weiner and Bruce K. Eckland, "Education and Political Party: The Effects of College or Social Class?" *American Journal of Sociology* 84 (1979): 911–928.

11. Astin, op. cit., 38.

12. John Zaller, "Information, Values, and Opinion," *American Political Science Review*, 85 (1991): 1215–38.

13. Everett Carl Ladd, Jr., and Seymour Martin Lipset, *The Divided Academy: Professors and Politics* (New York: McGraw-Hill, 1975), 26–27, 55–67, 184–190.

14. *Statistical Abstract of the United States, 1984*, 144.

15. J. L. Spaeth and Andrew M. Greeley, *Recent Alumni and Higher Education* (New York: McGraw-Hill, 1970), 100–110; and Erland Nelson, "Persistence of Attitudes of College Students Fourteen Years Later," *Psychological Monographs* 68 (1954): 1–13.

16. Kenneth A. Feldman and Theodore M. Newcomb, *The Impact of College on Students* (San Francisco: Jossey-Bass, 1969), vol. 1, 99–100, 312–320.

17. John McAdams, "Testing the Theory of the New Class," *Sociological Quarterly* 28 (1987): 23–49.

18. M. Kent Jennings, "Residues of a Movement: The Aging of the American Protest Generation," *American Political Science Review* 81 (1987): 367–382.

19. Kay Lehman Schlozman and Sidney Verba, *Insult to Injury: Unemployment, Class, and Political Response* (Cambridge: Harvard University Press, 1979), 115–118; David Butler and Donald Stokes, *Political Change in Great Britain* (New York: St. Martin's Press, 1969), 70, 77; Erikson and Luttbeg, op. cit., 184; *National Journal* (November 8, 1980): 1878.

20. V. O. Key, Jr., *Public Opinion and American Democracy* (New York: Knopf, 1961), 122–138.

21. Richard E. Dawson, *Public Opinion and Contemporary Disarray* (New York: Harper & Row, 1973), ch. 4.

22. Paul Starobin, "Party Hoppers," *National Journal* (February 7, 1998): 277, 278.

23. David A. Bostis, *Public Opinion 1998: Political Attitudes* (Washington, D.C.: Joint Center for Political and Economic Studies (October 1998), table 18A.

24. *The American Enterprise* (November/December 1998): 91, reporting data from a *Time*/CNN survey, August 1997.

25. Bruce Cain and Roderick Kiewiet, "California's Coming Minority Majority," *Public Opinion* (February–March 1986): 50–52.

26. F. Chris Garcia et al., "The Effects of Ethnic Partisanship on Electoral Behavior: An Analysis and Comparison of Latino and Anglo Voting in the 1988 United States Presidential Election," paper delivered at the Annual Meeting of the American Political Science Association, September 3–6, 1992.

27. Robert Suro, "Poll Finds Hispanic Desire to Assimilate," *New York Times* (December 15, 1992): A18, citing the findings of the National Latino Survey led by Rodolfo O. de la Garza.

28. Michael Barone, "We've Been Here Before: Ethnicity and America, 1900 and 2000," Bradley Lecture, American Enterprise Institute, October 4, 1999, 21, 22.

29. Nie, Verba, and Petrocik, op. cit., 247–250.

30. *The American Enterprise* (January/February 1999): 51, citing surveys by CBS/*New York Times*.

31. Philip E. Converse, "The Nature of Belief Systems in Mass Publics," in *Ideology and Discontent*, ed. David Apter (Glencoe, Ill.: Free Press, 1964), 206–261.

32. Christopher H. Achen, "Mass Political Attitudes and the Survey Response," *American Political Science Review* 69 (December 1975): 1218–1231.

33. Seymour Martin Lipset and Earl Raab, *The Politics of Unreason* (New York: Harper & Row, 1970), ch. 11; James A. Stimson, "Belief Systems: Constraint, Complexity, and the 1972 Election," *American Journal of Political Science* 19 (1975): 393–417; and Herbert McClosky and John Zaller, *The American Ethos* (Cambridge: Harvard University Press, 1984), ch. 8.

34. Estimates of size of four groups averaged from 1993–1994 data presented by Everett Carll Ladd, "A New View of the Electorate," *The American Enterprise* (May/June 1994): 91.

35. Zaller, op. cit.; and Stimson, op. cit. See also Allen H. Barton and R. Wayne Parsons, "Measuring Belief System Structures," *Public Opinion Quarterly* 41 (1977): 159–180.

36. McAdams, op. cit.

37. Seymour Martin Lipset and David Riesman, *Education and Politics at Harvard* (New York: McGraw-Hill, 1975), ch. 8.

38. McAdams, op. cit.

39. Ibid.

40. John Zaller, *The Nature and Origins of Mass Opinion* (Cambridge: Cambridge University Press, 1992).

41. Lawrence R. Jacobs and Robert Y. Shapiro, "Debunking the Myth of the Pandering Politician," *The Public Perspective* (April/May 1997): 3–5.

Chapter 6   *Political Participation*

1. David Glass, Peverill Squire, and Raymond Wolfinger, "Voter Turnout: An International Comparison," *Public Opinion* (December–January 1984): 49–55. See also G. Bingham Powell, Jr., "Voting Turnout in Thirty Democracies: Partisan, Legal, and Socio-Economic Influences," in *Electoral Participation: A Comparative Analysis*, ed. Richard Rose (Beverly Hills, Calif.: Sage Publications, 1980).

2. Stephen Knack, "Drivers Wanted: Motor Voter and the Election of 1996," *PS: Political Science* (June 1999): 237.

3. Ibid.; and *Congressional Quarterly Weekly* (October 24, 1998): 2881.

4. Knack, op. cit., 238.

5. Ibid., 242.

6. Morton Keller, *Affairs of State* (Cambridge: Harvard University Press, 1977), 523.

7. *United States v. Reese*, 92 U.S. 214 (1876); *United States v. Cruikshank*, 92 U.S. 556 (1876); and *Ex parte Yarbrough*, 110 U.S. 651 (1884).

8. *Guinn and Beall v. United States*, 238 U.S. 347 (1915).

9. *Smith v. Allwright*, 321 U.S. 649 (1944).

10. *Schnell v. Davis*, 336 U.S. 933 (1949).

11. *Congress and the Nation, vol. 3: 1969–1972* (Washington, D.C.: Congressional Quarterly, 1973), 1006; and *Statistical Abstract of the United States, 1975*, 450.

12. U.S. Bureau of the Census; and Elizabeth Crowley, "More Young People Turn Away from Politics," *Wall Street Journal* (June 16, 1999).

13. Crowley, op. cit., citing data from the Pew Research Center.

14. Paul Wellstone, quoted in ibid.

15. *Historical Statistics of the United States: Colonial Times to 1970*, part 2, 1071–1072.

16. Walter Dean Burnham, "The Changing Shape of the American Political Universe," *American Political Science Review* 59 (March 1965): 11; and William H. Flanigan and Nancy H. Zingale, *Political Behavior of the American Electorate*, 3d ed. (Boston: Allyn and Bacon, 1975), 15.

17. Burnham, op. cit.; E. E. Schattschneider, *The Semisovereign People* (New York: Holt, Rinehart and Winston, 1960), chs. 5, 6.

18. Philip E. Converse, "Change in the American Electorate," in *The Human Meaning of Social Change*, ed. Angus Campbell and Philip E. Converse (New York: Russell Sage Foundation, 1972), 263–338.

19. Raymond Wolfinger and Benjamen Highton, "What If They Gave an Election and Everyone Came?" Public Affairs Report, Institute of Governmental Studies, University of California at Berkeley, June 1999, 11–13.

20. Ibid., 13.

21. Ibid.

22. Michael W. Traugott and John P. Katosh, "Response Validity in Surveys of Voting Behavior," *Public Opinion Quarterly* 43 (1979): 359–377; Aage R. Clausen, "Response Validity: Vote Report," *Public Opinion Quarterly* 32 (1969): 588–606.

23. Sidney Verba et al., *Voice and Equality: Civic Voluntarism in American Politics* (Cambridge: Harvard University Press, 1995), 79.

24. Ibid., 77.

25. Sidney Verba and Norman H. Nie, *Participation in America* (New York: Harper & Row, 1972), ch. 6.

26. Lester W. Milbrath and M. I. Goel, *Political Participation*, 2d ed. (Chicago: Rand McNally, 1977); Raymond E. Wolfinger and Steven J. Rosenstone, *Who Votes?* (New Haven, Conn.: Yale University Press, 1980); W. Russell Neuman, *The Paradox of Mass Voting* (Cambridge: Harvard University Press, 1986), ch. 4.

27. Wolfinger and Rosenstone, op. cit., esp. 102, and John P. Katosh and Michael W. Traugott,

"Costs and Values in the Calculus of Voting," *American Journal of Political Science* 26 (1982): 361–376.

28. David C. Leege and Lyman A Kellstedt, *Rediscovering the Religious Factor in American Politics* (Armonk, N.Y.: M. E. Sharpe, 1993), 129–131.

29. Verba and Nie, op. cit., 151–157; Milbrath and Goel, op. cit., 120.

30. Jack Citrin, "The Alienated Voter," *Taxing and Spending* (October 1978), 1–7; Austin Ranney, "Nonvoting Is Not a Social Disease," *Public Opinion* (October–November 1983): 16–19; Glass, Squire, and Wolfinger, op. cit.

31. *Dunn v. Blumstein*, 405 U.S. 330 (1972).

32. Wolfinger and Rosenstone, op. cit.

33. Richard G. Smolka, *Election Day Registration: The Minnesota and Wisconsin Experience* (Washington, D.C.: American Enterprise Institute, 1977), 5.

34. Gary R. Orren, "The Linkage of Policy to Participation," in *Presidential Selection*, ed. Alexander Heard and Michael Nelson (Durham, N.C.: Duke University Press, 1987).

35. Glass, Squire, and Wolfinger, op. cit., 52.

36. Powell, op. cit.; Robert W. Jackman, "Political Institutions and Voter Turnout in Industrial Democracies," *American Political Science Review* 81 (1987): 405–423.

37. Roy Texeira, "Will The Real Nonvoter Please Stand Up?" *Public Opinion* (July/August 1988): 43; Texeira, "Registration and Turnout," *Public Opinion* (January/February 1989): 12.

38. Richard A. Brody, "The Puzzle of Political Participation in America," in *The New American Political System*, ed. Anthony King (Washington, D.C.: American Enterprise Institute, 1978): 315–323.

39. Richard Smolka, quoted in William J. Crotty, *Political Reform and the American Experiment* (New York: Crowell, 1977): 86–87.

40. Sidney Verba, et al., "Race, Ethnicity, and the Resources for Participation: The Role of Religion," paper delivered at the 1992 annual meeting of the American Political Science Association, September 3–6, 1992.

Chapter 7   *Political Parties*

1. Leon D. Epstein, "Political Parties," in *Handbook of Political Science*, ed. Fred I. Greenstein and Nelson W. Polsby (Reading, Mass.: Addison-Wesley, 1975), vol. 4, 230.

2. Quoted in Henry Adams, *History of the United States of America During the Administrations of Jefferson and Madison*, ed. Ernest Samuels, abridged edition (Chicago: University of Chicago Press, 1967), 147.

3. Robert Kuttner, "Fat and Sassy," *The New Republic* (February 23, 1987): 21–23.

4. Morton Keller, *Affairs of State* (Cambridge: Harvard University Press, 1977), 239.

5. Quoted in Keller, ibid., 256.

6. Martin Shefter, "Parties, Bureaucracy, and Political Change in the United States," in *The Development of Political Parties*, Sage Electoral

Studies Yearbook, vol. 4, ed. Louis Maisel and Joseph Cooper (Beverly Hills, Calif.: Sage Publications, 1978).

7. James Q. Wilson, *The Amateur Democrat: Club Politics in Three Cities* (Chicago: University of Chicago Press, 1962).

8. Samuel J. Eldersveld, *Political Parties: A Behavioral Analysis* (Chicago: Rand McNally, 1964), 278, 287.

9. Robert H. Salisbury, "The Urban Party Organization Member," *Public Opinion Quarterly* 29 (Winter 1965–1966): 550–564.

10. Ibid., 557, 559.

11. Eldersveld, op. cit.; and J. David Greenstone, *Labor in American Politics* (New York: Knopf, 1969), 187.

12. David R. Mayhew, *Placing Parties in American Politics* (Princeton, N.J.: Princeton University Press, 1986), chs. 2, 3.

13. *Boston Globe* (July 9, 1984): 1.

14. William Nisbet Chambers and Walter Dean Burnham, eds., *The American Party Systems: Stages of Political Development*, 2d ed. (New York: Oxford University Press, 1975), 6.

15. *Williams v. Rhodes*, 393 U.S. 23 (1968).

16. James Q. Wilson, *Political Organizations* (New York: Basic Books, 1973), ch. 12; and Samuel Stouffer, *Communism, Conformity, and Civil Liberties* (Garden City, N.Y.: Doubleday, 1955).

17. On 1972 and 1976 see Jeane Kirkpatrick, *The New Presidential Elite* (New York: Russell Sage Foundation and Twentieth Century Fund, 1976), 297–315; on 1980 see *New York Times* (August 13, 1980).

18. Nelson W. Polsby, *Consequences of Party Reform* (New York: Oxford University Press, 1983), 9–11, 64.

19. Ibid., 158. But compare John G. Geer, "Voting in Presidential Primaries," paper delivered to the 1984 annual meeting of the American Political Science Association.

20. Center for the Study of the American Electorate, April 2000.

21. Michael J. Malbin, "Democratic Party Rules Are Made to Be Broken," *National Journal* (August 23, 1980): 1388.

22. Kirkpatrick, op. cit., ch. 4.

Chapter 8   *Elections and Campaigns*

1. Fred Barnes, "Charade on Main Street," *The New Republic* (June 15, 1987): 15–17. See also Hugh Winebrenner, *The Iowa Precinct Caucuses: The Making of a Media Event* (Ames: Iowa State University Press, 1987).

2. Arthur H. Miller et al., "A Majority Party in Disarray: Policy Polarization in the 1972 Election," *American Political Science Review* 70 (1976): 757.

3. Donald E. Stokes and John J. DiIulio, Jr., "Valence Politics in Modern Elections," in *The 1992 Elections*, ed. Michael J. Nelson (Washington, D.C.: Congressional Quarterly Press, 1993), ch. 1.

4. Michael Kelley, "The Making of a First Family: A Blueprint," *New York Times* (November 14, 1992): 1, 9.

5. Ibid.

6. Thomas E. Patterson and Robert D. McClure, *The Unseeing Eye: The Myth of Television Power in National Politics* (New York: Putnam, 1976); and Xandra Kayden, *Campaign Organization* (Lexington, Mass.: D. C. Heath, 1978), ch. 6.

7. Gerald M. Pomper et al., *The Election of 1980* (Chatham, N.J.: Chatham House, 1981), 75, 105–107.

8. *Buckley v. Valeo*, 424 U.S. 1 (1976).

9. John J. DiIulio, Jr., "Valence Voters Are Not Fools," in *The 1996 Elections*, ed. Michael J. Nelson (Washington, D.C.: Congressional Quarterly Press, 1997), ch. 10.

10. Gary C. Jacobson, *The Politics of Congressional Elections*, 2d ed. (Boston: Little, Brown, 1987), 49.

11. Donald Philip Green and Jonathan S. Krasno, "Salvation for the Spendthrift Incumbent: Reestimating the Effects of Campaign Spending in House Elections," *American Journal of Political Science* 32 (1988): 884–960; Stephen Ansolabehre, "Winning Is Easy but It Sure Ain't Cheap," Working Paper 90–1, Center for American Politics and Public Policy, UCLA, 1990; Robert S. Erickson and Thomas R. Palfrey, "The Puzzle of Incumbent Spending in Congressional Elections," Social Science Working Paper 806, California Institute of Technology, August 1992.

12. Angus Campbell, Philip E. Converse, Warren E. Miller, and Donald E. Stokes, *The American Voter* (New York: Wiley, 1960), ch. 8.

13. V. O. Key, Jr., *The Responsible Electorate* (Cambridge: Harvard University Press, 1966).

14. Morris P. Fiorina, *Retrospective Voting in American National Elections* (New Haven, Conn.: Yale University Press, 1981).

15. Jay P. Greene, "Forewarned Before Forecast: Presidential Election Forecasting Models and the 1992 Election," *P.S.: Political Science and Politics* (March 1993): 20.

16. In 1988 Dukakis led Bush by 17 percent in polls taken shortly after Dukakis was nominated, only to see Bush win handily. In 1980 Carter led Reagan in the early polls.

17. Updated by Daron Shaw from Robert Axelrod, "Where the Votes Come From: An Analysis of Electoral Coalitions, 1952–1968," *American Political Science Review* 66 (1972): 11–20; and Axelrod, "Communication," *American Political Science Review* 68 (1974): 718–719.

18. Walter Dean Burnham, *Critical Elections and the Mainsprings of American Politics* (New York: Norton, 1970), 10.

19. James L. Sundquist, *Dynamics of the Party System* (Washington, D.C.: Brookings Institution, 1973), ch. 7.

20. Edward G. Carmines and James A. Stimson, "Issue Evolution, Population Replacement, and Normal Partisan Change," *American Political Science Review* 75 (March 1981): 107–118; and Gregory Markus, "Political Attitudes in an Election Year," *American Political Science Review* 76 (September 1982): 538–560.

21. Ray Wolfinger and Michael G. Hagen, "Republican Prospects: Southern Comfort," *Public Opinion* (October–November 1985): 8–13. But compare Richard Scammon and James A. Barnes, "Republican Prospects: Southern Discomfort," *Public Opinion* (October–November 1985): 14–17.

22. Jerrold G. Rusk, "The Effect of the Australian Ballot Reform on Split-Ticket Voting: 1876–1908," *American Political Science Review* 64 (December 1970): 1220–1238.

23. Gerald M. Pomper, *Elections in America* (New York: Dodd, Mead, 1971), 178.

24. Benjamin Ginsberg, "Elections and Public Policy," *American Political Science Review* 70 (March 1976): 41–49.

Chapter 9 *Interest Groups*

1. L. Harmon Zeigler and Hendrik van Dalen, "Interest Groups in the States," in *Politics in the American States*, ed. Herbert Jacob and Kenneth N. Vines, 2d ed. (Boston: Little, Brown, 1974), 122–160; Edward C. Banfield and James Q. Wilson, *City Politics* (Cambridge: Harvard University Press, 1963), chs. 18, 19.

2. Joseph LaPalombara, *Interest Groups in Italian Politics* (Princeton, N.J.: Princeton University Press, 1964).

3. Kay Lehman Schlozman and John T. Tierney, "More of the Same: Washington Pressure Group Activity in a Decade of Change," *Journal of Politics* 45 (1983): 356.

4. The use of injunctions in labor disputes was restricted by the Norris-LaGuardia Act of 1932; the rights to collective bargaining and to the union shop were guaranteed by the Wagner Act of 1935.

5. *Historical Statistics of the United States, Colonial Times to 1970*, vol. 1, 386.

6. The distinction is drawn from Kay Lehman Schlozman and John T. Tierney, *Organized Interests and American Democracy* (New York: Harper & Row, 1985).

7. Jeffrey M. Berry, *The Interest Group Society* (Boston: Little, Brown, 1984), 20–21.

8. Ibid., 24, 130.

9. Gabriel A. Almond and Sidney Verba, *The Civic Culture* (Princeton, N.J.: Princeton University Press, 1963), 302; Derek C. Bok and John T. Dunlop, *Labor and the American Community* (New York: Simon & Schuster, 1970), 49; *Statistical Abstract of the United States, 1975*, 373.

10. Almond and Verba, op. cit., 194.

11. Ibid., 207.

12. Mancur Olson, Jr., *The Logic of Collective Action* (Cambridge: Harvard University Press, 1965), 153–157.

13. Bok and Dunlop, op. cit., 134.

14. Henry J. Pratt, *The Liberalization of American Protestantism* (Detroit: Wayne State University Press, 1972), ch. 12; Gerhard Lenski, *The Religious Factor* (Garden City, N.Y.: Doubleday, 1961), ch. 4.

15. Jane J. Mansbridge, *Why We Lost the ERA* (Chicago: University of Chicago Press, 1986), ch. 10.

16. Joyce Gelb and Marian Lief Palley, *Women and Public Choices* (Princeton, N.J.: Princeton University Press, 1982), ch. 3; Jo Freeman, *The Politics of Women's Liberation* (New York: McKay, 1975), ch. 3; Maren Lockwood Carden, "The Proliferation of a Social Movement: Ideology and Individual Incentives in the Contemporary Feminist Movement," *Research in Social Movements* 1 (1978): 179–196; and Dom Bonafede, "Still a Long Way to Go," *National Journal* (September 13, 1986): 2175–2179.

17. Mansbridge, op. cit., 130–131.

18. Jeffrey M. Berry, *Lobbying for the People* (Princeton, N.J.: Princeton University Press, 1977), 71–76.

19. Berry, *Interest Group Society*, op. cit., 88.

20. Schlozman and Tierney, *Organized Interests and American Democracy*, op. cit., table 5-4.

21. *New York Times* (December 8, 1983): 1.

22. Raymond A. Bauer, Ithiel de Sola Pool, and Lewis Anthony Dexter, *American Business and Public Policy* (New York: Atherton, 1963), ch. 30.

23. Berry, *Lobbying for the People*, op. cit., 136–140.

24. Margaret Ann Latus, "Assessing Ideological PACs: From Outrage to Understanding," in *Money and Politics in the United States*, ed. Michael J. Malbin (Chatham, N.J.: Chatham House, 1984), 143; data supplied by the Federal Election Commission, March 1992.

25. Latus, op. cit., 144.

26. Malbin, op. cit., table A.8, 290–291.

27. Michael J. Malbin, "Looking Back at the Future of Campaign Finance Reform: Interest Groups and American Elections," in Malbin, *Money and Politics*, op. cit., 248; James B. Kau and Paul H. Rubin, *Congressmen, Constituents and Contributors* (Boston: Martinus Nijhoff, 1982); Henry W. Chappell, Jr., "Campaign Contributions and Voting on the Cargo Preference Bill: A Comparison of Simultaneous Models," *Public Choice* 36 (1981): 301–312; W. P. Welch, "Campaign Contributions and Voting: Milk Money and Dairy Price Supports," *Western Political Quarterly* 35 (1982): 478–495; John R. Wright, "PACs, Contributions, and Roll Calls: An Organizational Perspective," *American Political Science Review* 79 (1985): 400–414. But compare Benjamin Ginsberg and John C. Green, "The Best Congress Money Can Buy," in *Do Elections Matter?*, ed. Benjamin Ginsberg and Alan Stone (Armonk, N.Y.: M. E. Sharpe, 1986), 75–89.

28. William T. Gormley, "A Test of the Revolving Door Hypothesis at the FCC," *American Journal of Political Science* 23 (1979): 665–683; Paul J. Quirk, *Industry Influence in Federal Regulatory Agencies* (Princeton, N.J.: Princeton University Press, 1981); Jeffrey E. Cohen, "The Dynamics of the 'Revolving Door' on the FCC," *American Journal of Political Science* 30 (1986): 689–708.

29. Suzanne Weaver, *Decision to Prosecute* (Cambridge, Mass.: MIT Press, 1977), 154–163.

30. *United States v. Harriss*, 347 U.S. 612 (1954).
31. *United States Code*, Title 26, section 501(c)(3).

Chapter 10   *The Media*

1. R. L. Lowenstein, *World Press Freedom, 1966* (Columbia, Mo.: Freedom of Information Center, 1967), publication No. 11.
2. D. E. Butler, "Why American Political Reporting Is Better Than England's," *Harper's* (May 1963), 15–25.
3. *New York Times* (March 15, 1975).
4. *New York Times* (January 28, 1974).
5. Douglass Cater, *The Fourth Branch of Government* (Boston: Houghton Mifflin, 1959), 76; and William L. Rivers, "The Press as a Communication System," in *Handbook of Communication*, ed. Ithiel de Sola Pool et al. (Chicago: Rand McNally, 1973), 522–526.
6. Quoted in F. L. Mort, *American Journalism, 1690–1960*, 3d ed. (New York: Macmillan, 1962), 529, as cited in Rivers, op. cit., 526.
7. Kiko Adatto, *Picture Perfect: The Art and Artifice of Public Image Making* (New York: Basic Books, 1993).
8. Edward Jay Epstein, *News from Nowhere: Television and the News* (New York: Random House, 1973), 37.
9. Allen H. Barton, "Consensus and Conflict Among American Leaders," *Public Opinion Quarterly* 38 (Winter 1974–1975): 507–530.
10. Paul H. Weaver, "The New Journalism and the Old—Thoughts After Watergate," *The Public Interest* (Spring 1974), 67–88.
11. *Near v. Minnesota*, 283 U.S. 697 (1931).
12. *New York Times v. United States*, 403 U.S. 713 (1971).
13. *New York Times v. Sullivan*, 376 U.S. 254 (1964).
14. *Miami Herald Publishing Co. v. Tornillo*, 418 U.S. 241 (1974).
15. *Yates v. United States*, 354 U.S. 298 (1957).
16. *Branzburg v. Hayes*, 408 U.S. 665 (1972).
17. *Zurcher v. Stanford Daily*, 436 U.S. 547 (1978), overturned by the Privacy Protection Act of 1980 (P.L. 96–440).
18. *National Journal* (April 16, 1983), 787.
19. Benjamin I. Page, "The Media as Political Actors," *PS: Political Science & Politics* (March 1996), p. 21.
20. Thomas E. Patterson and Robert D. McClure, *The Unseeing Eye: The Myth of Television Power in National Elections* (New York: Putnam, 1976); and Herbert Asher, *Presidential Elections and American Politics* (Homewood, Ill.: Dorsey Press, 1976), 239–240 (and studies cited therein).
21. David O. Sears and Richard E. Whitney, "Political Persuasion," in Pool, op. cit., 253–289.
22. Robert S. Erickson, "The Influence of Newspaper Endorsements in Presidential Elections: The Case of 1964," *American Journal of Political Science* 20 (May 1976): 207–233.
23. Maxwell E. McCombs and Donald R. Shaw, "The Agenda Setting Function of the Mass Media," *Public Opinion Quarterly* 36 (Summer 1972): 176–187; Shanto Iyengar and Donald

R. Kinder, *News That Matters* (Chicago: University of Chicago Press, 1987).
24. G. Ray Funkhouser, "The Issues of the Sixties," *Public Opinion Quarterly* 37 (Spring 1973): 62–75.
25. Joseph Wagner, "Media Do Make a Difference: The Differential Impact of Mass Media in the 1976 Presidential Race," *American Journal of Political Science* 27 (August 1983): 407–430.
26. Benjamin I. Page, Robert Y. Shapiro, and Glenn R. Dempsey, "What Moves Public Opinion?" *American Political Science Review* 81 (March 1987): 23–43.
27. George Jergens, "Theodore Roosevelt and the Press," *Daedalus* (Fall 1982), 113–133; and Henry Fairlie, "The Rise of the Press Secretary," *New Republic* (March 18, 1978), 20–23.
28. Michael J. Robinson, "A Twentieth Century Medium in a Nineteenth Century Legislature: The Effects of Television on the American Congress," in *Congress in Change*, ed. Norman J. Ornstein (New York: Praeger, 1975), 240–261.
29. S. Robert Lichter and Stanley Rothman, "Media and Business Elites," *Public Opinion* (October–November 1981), 42–46.
30. Robert Lichter, "Consistently Liberal: But Does It Matter?," unpublished draft paper, forthcoming in *Media Critic*, p. 26.
31. Michael J. Robinson, "Just How Liberal Is the News? 1980 Revisited," *Public Opinion* (February–March 1983), 55–60; Maura Clancey and Michael J. Robinson, "The Media in Campaign '84: General Election Coverage," *Public Opinion* (December–January 1985); Elizabeth Kolbet, "Maybe the Media Did Treat Bush Harshly," *New York Times* (November 22, 1992), E2.
32. Peter Braestrup, *Big Story*, 2 vols. (Boulder, Colo.: Westview Press, 1977).
33. S. Robert Lichter, Stanley Rothman, and Linda S. Lichter, *The Media Elite* (Bethesda, MD: Adler and Adler, 1986).
34. *Media Monitor* 12 (March/April):1

Chapter 11   *Congress*

1. *Congressional Quarterly Weekly* (January 7, 1995): 18.
2. H. Douglas Price, "Careers and Committees in the American Congress," in *The History of Parliamentary Behavior*, ed. William O. Aydelotte (Princeton, N.J.: Princeton University Press, 1977), 28–62; John F. Bibby, Thomas E. Mann, and Norman J. Ornstein, *Vital Statistics on Congress, 1980* (Washington, D.C.: American Enterprise Institute, 1980), 53–54; Thomas E. Cavanaugh, "The Dispersion of Authority in the House of Representatives," *Political Science Quarterly* 97 (1982–1983): 625–626; *Congressional Quarterly Weekly Reports*.
3. David R. Mayhew, *Congress: The Electoral Connection* (New Haven, Conn.: Yale University Press, 1974); Bibby, Mann, and Ornstein, op. cit., 14–15.

4. Mayhew, op. cit.; Morris P. Fiorina, *Congress: Keystone of the Washington Establishment* (New Haven, Conn.: Yale University Press, 1977).
5. Rhodes Cook, "House Republicans Scored a Quiet Victory in '92," *Congressional Quarterly* (April 17, 1993): 966.
6. Bruce E. Cain and David Butler, "Redrawing District Lines: What's Going On and What's at Stake," *The American Enterprise* (July/August 1991): 37.
7. Gary C. Jacobson, "The Persistence of Democratic House Majorities: Structure or Politics," paper delivered at the 1990 Annual Meeting of the American Political Science Association, San Francisco, August 30–September 2, 1990, 2.
8. *Wesberry v. Sanders*, 376 U.S. 1 (1964).
9. Linda Greenhouse, "Court Questions Districts Drawn to Aid Minorities," *New York Times* (June 29, 1993): A1, A12.
10. Dave Kaplan, "Constitutional Doubt Is Thrown on Bizarre-Shaped Districts," *Congressional Quarterly* (July 3, 1993): 1761–1763.
11. John Leo, "Electioneering by Race," *U.S. News and World Report* (September 28, 1992): 33.
12. Kaplan, op. cit.; Greenhouse, op. cit.
13. Holly Idelson, "Supreme Court Considers Racially Conscious Map," *Congressional Quarterly* (April 24, 1993): 1034; Kaplan, op. cit.; Greenhouse, op. cit.
14. Hannah F. Pitkin, *The Concept of Representation* (Berkeley: University of California Press, 1967).
15. Carol M. Swain, *Black Faces, Black Interests: The Representation of African-Americans in Congress* (Cambridge: Harvard University Press, 1993), 207.
16. Richard F. Fenno, Jr., "U.S. House Members and Their Constituencies: An Exploration," *American Political Science Review* 71 (September 1977): 883–917, esp. 914.
17. John A. Ferejohn, *Pork Barrel Politics* (Stanford, Calif.: Stanford University Press, 1974).
18. Douglas Arnold, *Congress and the Bureaucracy* (New Haven, Conn.: Yale University Press, 1979).
19. Warren E. Miller and Donald E. Stokes, "Constituency Influence in Congress," in *Elections and the Political Order*, ed. Angus Campbell et al. (New York: Wiley, 1966), 359.
20. John E. Jackson, *Constituencies and Leaders in Congress* (Cambridge: Harvard University Press, 1974).
21. Jerrold E. Schneider, *Ideological Coalitions in Congress* (Westport, Conn.: Greenwood Press, 1979), 134, 195.
22. Michael Foley, *The New Senate: Liberal Influence on a Conservative Institution, 1959–1972* (New Haven, Conn.: Yale University Press, 1980), 242.
23. Tim Groseclose, Steven D. Levitt, and James M. Snyder, Jr., "Comparing Interest Group Scores Across Time and Chambers," *American Political Science Review* 93 (1999): 33–50.
24. *Congressional Quarterly Weekly Report* (December 3, 1994): 3430–3435.

25. In 1993 the 103d Congress also contained a lot of newly elected Democratic members eager to change House rules. They voted for the old rules and procedures, however, because that is what their party leaders wanted.

26. Barbara Sinclair, *The Transformation of the United States Senate* (Baltimore: Johns Hopkins University Press, 1989).

27. Norman J. Ornstein, Thomas E. Mann, and Michael J. Malbin, *Vital Statistics on Congress, 1995–1996* (Washington, D.C.: Congressional Quarterly Press, 1996), 199–200.

28. Gary C. Cox and Matthew D. McCubbins, *Legislative Leviathan* (Berkeley: University of California Press, 1993); David W. Rhode, *Parties and Leaders in the Postreform House* (Chicago: University of Chicago Press, 1991).

29. Susan Webb Hammond, "Congressional Caucuses in the 104th Congress," chapter in *Congress Reconsidered*, ed. Lawrence C. Dodd and Bruce I. Oppenheimer, 6th ed. (Washington, D.C.: Congressional Quarterly Press, 1997), 6.

30. Ibid., 34.

31. Steven S. Smith, "Revolution in the House: Why Don't We Do It on the Floor?" discussion paper no. 5, Brookings Institution, Washington, D.C., September 1986.

32. Richard F. Fenno, Jr., *Congressmen in Committees* (Boston: Little, Brown, 1973).

33. Michael J. Malbin, "Delegation, Deliberation, and the New Role of Congressional Staff," in *The New Congress*, ed. Thomas E. Mann and Norman J. Ornstein (Washington, D.C.: American Enterprise Institute, 1981), 134–177, esp. 170–171.

34. Lawrence H. Chamberlain, "The President, Congress, and Legislation," in *The Presidency*, ed. Aaron Wildavsky (Boston: Little, Brown, 1969), 444–445; Ronald C. Moe and Steven C. Teel, "Congress as a Policy-Maker: A Necessary Reappraisal," *Political Science Quarterly* 85 (September 1970): 443–470.

35. Richard E. Cohen, "Challenging the House's Traffic Cop," *National Journal* (April 4, 1993): 1002.

36. Thomas E. Mann and Norman J. Ornstein, *Renewing Congress: A Second Report* (Washington, D.C.: American Enterprise Institute, 1993), 49.

37. Malcolm E. Jewell and Samuel C. Patterson, *The Legislative Process in the United States*, 3d ed. (New York: Random House, 1977), 439.

38. Based on results of interviews with one thousand randomly selected Americans conducted by the American Talk Issues Foundation, March 10–15, 1993.

39. Survey by NBC News/*Wall Street Journal*, April 11–14, 1992, as reported in *The American Enterprise* (January/February 1993): 97.

40. *Decisionmaking in the Federal Government: The Wallace S. Sayre Model*, 20–21.

41. Mann and Ornstein, *Renewing Congress*, op. cit., 71–72.

42. Mann and Ornstein, *Renewing Congress*, op. cit., 72.

43. Dennis F. Thompson, *Ethics in Congress: From Individual to Institutional Corruption* (Washington, D.C.: Brookings Institution, 1995), 191.

44. Ibid., 3.

Chapter 12   *The Presidency*

1. Jean Blondel, *An Introduction to Comparative Government* (New York: Praeger, 1969), as cited in Nelson W. Polsby, "Legislatures," in *Handbook of Political Science*, ed. Fred I. Greenstein and Nelson W. Polsby (Reading, Mass.: Addison-Wesley, 1975), vol. 5, 275.

2. Donald F. Kettl, *Deficit Politics: Public Budgeting in Its Institutional and Historical Context* (New York: Macmillan, 1992), 13.

3. Morris P. Fiorina, *Divided Government* (New York: Macmillan, 1992), 86–111.

4. David Mayhew, *Divided We Govern: Party Control, Lawmaking, and Investigations, 1946–1990* (New Haven, Conn.: Yale University Press, 1991), 76.

5. Mark A. Peterson, *Legislating Together: The White House and Congress from Eisenhower to Reagan* (Cambridge: Harvard University Press, 1990).

6. Richard E. Cohen, *Washington at Work: Back Rooms and Clean Air* (New York: Macmillan, 1992), 154–155.

7. Ibid., 169.

8. Kettl, op. cit., 138.

9. Woodrow Wilson, *Congressional Government* (New York: Meridian Books, 1956), 167–168, 170. (First published in 1885.)

10. Stephen Hess, *Organizing the Presidency* (Washington, D.C.: Brookings Institution, 1976), 3; R. W. Apple, "Clinton's Refocusing," *New York Times* (May 6, 1993), A22; Michael K. Frisby, "Power Switch," *Wall Street Journal* (March 26, 1993), A1, A7.

11. David T. Stanley et al., *Men Who Govern* (Washington, D.C.: Brookings Institution, 1967), 41–42, 50.

12. Daniel J. Elazar, "Which Road to the Presidency?" in *The Presidency*, ed. Aaron Wildavsky (Boston: Little, Brown, 1969), 340.

13. James David Barber, *The Presidential Character: Predicting Performance in the White House*, 3d ed. (Englewood Cliffs, N.J.: Prentice-Hall, 1985).

14. Richard E. Neustadt, *Presidential Power*, rev. ed. (New York: Wiley, 1976), ch. 4.

15. Walter D. Burnham, "Insulation and Responsiveness in Congressional Elections," *Political Science Quarterly* 90 (Fall 1975): 412–413; George C. Edwards III, *Presidential Influence in Congress* (San Francisco: Freeman, 1980), 70–78; Warren E. Miller, "Presidential Coattails: A Study in Political Myth and Methodology," *Public Opinion Quarterly* 19 (Winter 1955–1956): 368; and Miller, "The Motivational Basis for Straight and Split Ticket Voting," *American Political Science Review* 51 (June 1957): 293–312.

16. *Clinton v. City of New York*, 118 S.Ct. 2091 (1998).

17. *Marbury v. Madison*, 1 Cranch 137 (1803).

18. *United States v. Nixon*, 418 U.S. 683 (1974).

19. *Clinton v. Jones*, 520 U.S. 681 (1997); *In Re Grand Jury Subpoena Duces Tecum*, 112 F.3d 910 (1997); *In Re Sealed Case*, 121 F.3d 729 (1997).

20. Marcus Cunliffe, *American Presidents and the Presidency* (New York: American Heritage Press/McGraw-Hill, 1972), 63, 65.

21. Ibid., 214.

22. Adapted from Paul C. Light, *The President's Agenda* (Baltimore, Md.: Johns Hopkins University Press, 1982), 217–225.

Chapter 13   *The Bureaucracy*

1. Charles E. Lindblom, *Politics and Markets* (New York: Basic Books, 1977), 114.

2. Article II, section 2, para. 2.

3. Article II, section 3.

4. Calculated from data in *Historical Statistics of the United States: Colonial Times to 1970* (Washington, D.C.: Government Printing Office, 1975), vol. 2, 1102–1103.

5. *Panama Refining Co. v. Ryan*, 293 U.S. 388 (1935).

6. *Hampton Jr. & Co. v. United States*, 276 U.S. 394 (1928).

7. Edward S. Corwin, *The Constitution and What It Means Today*, 13th ed. (Princeton, N.J.: Princeton University Press, 1973), 151.

8. Bruce D. Porter, "Parkinson's Law Revisited: War and the Growth of American Government," *Public Interest* (Summer 1980): 50–68.

9. See the cases cited in Corwin, op. cit., 8.

10. *U.S. Statutes*, vol. 84, sec. 799 (1970).

11. *Historical Statistics of the United States*, vol. 2, 1107.

12. Donald F. Kettl et al., *Civil Service Reform: Building a Government That Works* (Washington, D.C.: Brookings Institution, 1996), 18.

13. Ibid., 15.

14. Hugh Heclo, "Issue Networks and the Executive Establishment," in *The New American Political System*, ed. Anthony King (Washington, D.C.: American Enterprise Institute, 1978), 87–124.

15. Quoted in Hugh Heclo, *A Government of Strangers* (Washington, D.C.: Brookings Institution, 1977), 225.

16. Alexis Simendinger, "Of the People, for the People," *National Journal* (April 18, 1998): 852–855. Data from the Pew Charitable Trusts Research Center for the People and the Press.

17. Stanley Rothman and S. Robert Lichter, "How Liberal Are Bureaucrats?" *Regulation* (November–December, 1983): 17–18.

18. Kenneth Meier and Lloyd Nigro, "Representative Bureaucracy and Policy References: A Study of the Attitudes of Federal Executives," *Public Administration Review* 36 (July–August 1976): 458–467; Bernard Mennis, *American Foreign Policy Officials* (Columbus: Ohio State University Press, 1971).

19. Joel D. Aberbach and Bert A. Rockman, "Clashing Beliefs Within the Executive

Branch: The Nixon Administration Bureaucracy," *American Political Science Review* 70 (June 1976): 456–468.

20. David Stockman, *The Triumph of Politics* (New York: Harper and Row, 1986).

21. James Q. Wilson, *Bureaucracy* (New York: Basic Books, 1989), ch. 6.

22. Heclo, "Issue Networks and the Executive Establishment," op. cit., 87–124.

23. Richard F. Fenno, Jr., *The Power of the Purse* (Boston: Little, Brown, 1966), 450, 597.

24. John E. Schwartz and L. Earl Shaw, *The United States Congress in Comparative Perspective* (Hinsdale, Ill.: Dryden Press, 1976), 262–263; *National Journal* (July 4, 1981): 1211–1214.

25. *Immigration and Naturalization Service v. Chadha*, 103 S. Ct. 2764 (1983); *Maine v. Thiboutot*, 100 S. Ct. 2502 (1980).

26. See cases cited in Corwin, op. cit., 22.

27. Steven Kelman, "The Grace Commission: How Much Waste in Government?" *Public Interest* (Winter 1985): 62–87.

28. Daniel Katz et al., *Bureaucratic Encounters* (Ann Arbor: Survey Research Center, University of Michigan, 1975), 63–69, 118–120, 184–188.

29. *From Red Tape to Results: Creating a Government That Works Better and Costs Less*, report of the National Performance Review, Vice President Al Gore, September 7, 1993.

Chapter 14   *The Judiciary*

1. Henry J. Abraham, *The Judicial Process*, 3d ed. (New York: Oxford University Press, 1975), 279–280.

2. Robert G. McCloskey, *The American Supreme Court* (Chicago: University of Chicago Press, 1960), 27.

3. *Marbury v. Madison*, 5 U.S. 137 (1803); and *McCulloch v. Maryland*, 17 U.S. 316 (1819).

4. *Martin v. Hunter's Lessee*, 14 U.S. 304 (1816); and *Cohens v. Virginia*, 19 U.S. (1821).

5. *Gibbons v. Ogden*, 22 U.S. (1824).

6. Quoted in Albert J. Beveridge, *The Life of John Marshall* (Boston: Houghton Mifflin, 1919), vol. 4, 551.

7. *Dred Scott v. Sandford*, 60 U.S. 393 (1857).

8. Abraham, op. cit., 286.

9. *In re Debs*, 158 U.S. 564 (1895).

10. *Pollock v. Farmers' Loan & Trust Co.*, 157 U.S. 429 (1895).

11. *United States v. Knight*, 156 U.S. 1 (1895).

12. *Cincinnati, N.O. & T.P. Railway Co. v. Interstate Commerce Commission*, 162 U.S. 184 (1896).

13. *Hammer v. Dagenhart*, 247 U.S. 251 (1918).

14. *Lochner v. New York*, 198 U.S. 45 (1905).

15. McCloskey, op. cit., 151.

16. *Munn v. Illinois*, 94 U.S. 113 (1877).

17. *Dayton-Goose Creek Railway Co. v. United States*, 263 U.S. 456 (1924).

18. *Atchison, Topeka, and Santa Fe Railroad Co. v. Matthews*, 174 U.S. 96 (1899).

19. *Mugler v. Kansas*, 123 U.S. 623 (1887).

20. *St. Louis Consolidated Coal Co. v. Illinois*, 185 U.S. 203 (1902).

21. *New York Central Railroad Co. v. White*, 243 U.S. 188 (1917).

22. *German Alliance Insurance Co. v. Lewis*, 233 U.S. 389 (1914).

23. Morton Keller, *Affairs of State* (Cambridge: Harvard University Press, 1977), 369. See also Mary Cornelia Porter, "That Commerce Shall Be Free: A New Look at the Old Laissez-Faire Court," in *The Supreme Court Review*, ed. Philip B. Kurland (Chicago: University of Chicago Press, 1976), 135–159.

24. *Chief of Capitol Police v. Jeannette Rankin Brigade*, 409 U.S. 972 (1972).

25. *Aptheker v. Secretary of State*, 378 U.S. 500 (1964).

26. *Trop v. Dulles*, 356 U.S. 86 (1958); *Afroyim v. Rusk*, 387 U.S. 253 (1967); and *Schneider v. Rusk*, 377 U.S. 163 (1964).

27. *Lamont v. Postmaster General*, 381 U.S. 301 (1965); and *Blount v. Rizzi*, 400 U.S. 410 (1971).

28. *Richardson v. Davis*, 409 U.S. 1069 (1972); *U.S. Department of Agriculture v. Murry*, 413 U.S. 508 (1973); *Jimenez v. Weinberger*, 417 U.S. 628 (1974); and *Washington v. Legrant*, 394 U.S. 618 (1969).

29. *United States v. Lopez*, 514 U.S. 549 (1995).

30. *Seminole Tribe of Florida v. Florida*, 517 U.S. 44 (1996); *Alden v. Maine*, 527 U.S. 706 (1999); *Florida v. College Savings Bank*, 527 U.S. 627 (1999).

31. Robert A. Carp and C. I. Rowland, *Policymaking and Politics in the Federal District Courts* (Knoxville: University of Tennessee Press, 1983), 38; Sheldon Goldman, "Voting Behavior on the United States Courts of Appeals, Revisited," *American Political Science Review* 69 (1975): 491–506; C. Heal Tate, "Personal Attribute Models of the Voting Behavior of U.S. Supreme Court Justices," *American Political Science Review* 75 (1981): 355–367.

32. Daniel R. Pinello, "Linking Party to Judicial Ideology in American Courts: A Meta-analysis," *Justice System Journal* 20 (1999): 219–254.

33. *United States v. Lanza*, 260 U.S. 377 (1922). Cf. *Abbate v. United States*, 359 U.S. 187 (1959), and *Bartkus v. Illinois*, 359 U.S. 121 (1989).

34. *Gideon v. Wainwright*, 372 U.S. 335 (1963). The story is told in Anthony Lewis, *Gideon's Trumpet* (New York: Random House, 1964).

35. Erwin Griswold, "Rationing Justice: The Supreme Court's Case Load and What the Court Does Not Do," *Cornell Law Review* 60 (1975): 335–354.

36. Joseph Weis, Jr., "Disconnecting the Overloaded Circuits—A Plan for a Unified Court of Appeals," *St. Louis University Law Journal* 39 (1995): 455.

37. *Alyeska Pipeline Service Co. v. Wilderness Society*, 421 U.S. 240 (1975).

38. *Flast v. Cohen*, 392 U.S. 83 (1968), which modified the earlier *Frothingham v. Mellon*, 262 U.S. 447 (1923); *United States v. Richardson*, 418 U.S. 166 (1947).

39. *Brown v. Board of Education of Topeka*, 347 U.S. 483 (1954).

40. *Baker v. Carr*, 369 U.S. 186 (1962).

41. See Louise Weinberg, "A New Judicial Federalism?" *Daedalus* (Winter 1978): 129–141.

42. Quoted in Abraham, op. cit., 330.

43. Carolyn D. Richmond, "The Rehnquist Court: What Is in Store for Constitutional Precedent?" *New York Law Review* 39 (1994): 511.

44. *Colegrove v. Green*, 328 U.S. 549 (1946).

45. The Court abandoned the "political question" doctrine in *Baker v. Carr*, 369 U.S. 186 (1962), and began to change congressional-district apportionment in *Wesberry v. Sanders*, 376 U.S. 1 (1964).

46. Donald L. Horowitz, *The Courts and Social Policy* (Washington, D.C.: Brookings Institution, 1977), 6.

47. *Gates v. Collier*, 349 F. Supp. 881 (1972).

48. *Lau v. Nichols*, 414 U.S. 563 (1974).

49. Jane Burnbaum, "Guilty! Too Many Lawyers and Too Much Litigation," *Business Week* (April 13, 1992), 60–61.

50. Joel B. Grossman and Austin Sarat, "Litigation in the Federal Courts: A Comparative Perspective," *Law and Society Review* 9 (Winter 1975): 321–346.

51. Administrative Office of the U.S. Courts, *Annual Report, 1988*, 109.

52. Jack W. Peltason, *Fifty-eight Lonely Men: Southern Federal Judges and School Desegregation* (New York: Harcourt Brace, 1961).

53. Anthony Patridge and William B. Eldridge, *The Second Circuit Sentencing Study* (Washington, D.C.: Federal Judicial Center, 1974).

54. *Abington School District v. Schempp*, 374 U.S. 203 (1963).

55. Robert H. Birkby, "The Supreme Court and the Bible Belt," *Midwest Journal of Political Science* 10 (1966): 3.

56. Cless R. Sunstein, "Impeaching the President," *University of Pennsylvania Law Review* 147 (1998): 279.

57. *United States v. Butler*, 297 U.S. 1 (1936).

58. *Ex parte McCardle*, 74 U.S. 506 (1869).

59. Walter F. Murphy, *Congress and the Court* (Chicago: University of Chicago Press, 1962); and C. Herman Pritchett, *Congress Versus the Supreme Court* (Minneapolis: University of Minnesota Press, 1961).

60. Gregory A. Caldeira, "Neither the Purse nor the Sword: Dynamics of Public Confidence in the U.S. Supreme Court," *American Political Science Review* 80 (1986): 1209–1226. See also Joseph T. Tannenhaus and Walter F. Murphy, "Patterns of Public Support for the Supreme Court: A Panel Study," *Journal of Politics* 43 (1981): 24–39.

Chapter 15   *Civil Liberties*

1. *Zamora v. Pomeroy*, 639 F.2d 662 (1981); *Goss v. Lopez*, 419 U.S. 565 (1975); *Tinker v. Des Moines Community School District*, 393 U.S. 503 (1969); *Smith v. Goguen*, 415 U.S. 566 (1974); *New Jersey v. T.L.O.*, 469 U.S. 325 (1985).

2. *Sheppard v. Maxwell*, 384 U.S. 333 (1966); *New York Times Co. v. United States*, 403 U.S.

713 (1971); *Kunz v. New York,* 340 U.S. 290 (1951).

3. William Blackstone, *Commentaries,* vol. 4 (1765), 151–152.

4. Jefferson's remarks are from a letter to Abigail Adams (quoted in Walter Berns, *The First Amendment and the Future of American Democracy* [New York: Basic Books, 1976], 82) and from a letter to Thomas McKean, governor of Pennsylvania, February 19, 1803 (Paul L. Ford, ed., *The Writings of Thomas Jefferson: 1801–1806,* vol. 8 [New York: Putnam, 1897], 218).

5. *Schenck v. United States,* 249 U.S. 47 (1919), 52.

6. *Gitlow v. New York,* 268 U.S. 652 (1925), 666.

7. *Fiske v. Kansas,* 274 U.S. 380 (1927); *Stromberg v. California,* 283 U.S. 359 (1931); *Near v. Minnesota,* 283 U.S. 697 (1931); *De Jonge v. Oregon,* 299 U.S. 353 (1937).

8. *Dennis v. United States,* 341 U.S. 494 (1951), 510ff. The test was first formulated by Judge Learned Hand of the court of appeals: see *Dennis v. United States,* 183 F.2d 201 (1950), 212.

9. *Yates v. United States,* 354 U.S. 298 (1957).

10. *Brandenburg v. Ohio,* 395 U.S. 444 (1969).

11. *Village of Skokie v. National Socialist Party,* 432 U.S. 43 (1977); 366 N.E.2d 349 (1977); and 373 N.E.2d 21 (1978).

12. *R.A.V. v. City of St. Paul,* 112 S. Ct. 2538 (1992).

13. *Wisconsin v. Mitchell,* No. 92–515 (1993).

14. C. Herman Pritchett, *Constitutional Civil Liberties* (Englewood Cliffs, N.J.: Prentice-Hall, 1984), 100.

15. *New York Times v. Sullivan,* 376 U.S. 254 (1964); but compare *Time, Inc. v. Firestone,* 424 U.S. 448 (1976).

16. Henry J. Abraham, *Freedom and the Court,* 4th ed. (New York: Oxford University Press, 1982), 193, fn 189.

17. Justice Stewart's famous remark was made in his concurring opinion in *Jacobellis v. Ohio,* 378 U.S. 184 (1964), 197.

18. *Miller v. California,* 413 U.S. 15 (1973).

19. *Jenkins v. Georgia,* 418 U.S. 153 (1974).

20. *Schad v. Borough of Mt. Ephraim,* 452 U.S. 61 (1981).

21. *Barnes v. Glen Theatre,* 111 S. Ct. 2456 (1991).

22. *American Booksellers Association v. Hudnut,* 771 F.2d 323 (1985), affirmed at 475 U.S. 1001 (1986).

23. *Renton v. Playtime Theatres,* 475 U.S. 41 (1986). See also *Young v. American Mini-Theatres, Inc.,* 427 U.S. 50 (1976).

24. *Reno v. American Civil Liberties Union,* 521 U.S. 844 (1997).

25. *United States v. O'Brien,* 391 U.S. 367 (1968).

26. *Texas v. Johnson,* 109 S. Ct. 2533 (1989).

27. The Court had earlier held unconstitutional statutes that made it illegal to mutilate the flag (*Street v. New York,* 394 U.S. 576 [1967]), deface the flag (*Spence v. Washington,* 418 U.S. 405 [1974]), or treat the flag contemptuously by, for example, sewing it to the seat of your pants (*Smith v. Goguen,* 415 U.S. 566 [1974]). *U.S. v. Eichman,* 496 U.S. 310 (1990).

28. *First National Bank of Boston v. Bellotti,* 435 U.S. 765 (1978); *Federal Election Commission v. Massachusetts Citizens for Life, Inc.,* 479 U.S. 238 (1986).

29. *44 Liquormart v. Rhode Island,* 116 S. Ct. 1495 (1996); *Greater New Orleans Broadcasting Association v. United States,* 119 S. Ct. 1923 (1999).

30. *Pacific Gas and Electric Co. v. Public Utilities Commission,* 475 U.S. 1 (1986). Some limitations on corporate speech have been upheld, including a state law prohibiting a firm from spending money on candidates for elective office. *Austin v. Michigan Chamber of Commerce,* 100 S. Ct. 1391 (1990).

31. *Board of Trustees of the State University of New York v. Fox,* 492 U.S. 469 (1989).

32. *Bates v. State Bar of Arizona,* 433 U.S. 350 (1977); *Edenfield v. Bane,* 113 S. Ct. 1792 (1993).

33. *Hazelwood School District v. Kuhlmeier, et al.,* 484 U.S. 260 (1988).

34. *Murdock v. Pennsylvania,* 319 U.S. 105 (1943).

35. *Church of the Lukumi Babalu Aye v. City of Hialeah,* No. 91–948 (1993).

36. *Reynolds v. United States,* 98 U.S. 145 (1878).

37. *Jacobson v. Massachusetts,* 197 U.S. 11 (1905).

38. *Employment Division, Department of Human Resources of Oregon v. Smith,* 110 S. Ct. 1595 (1990).

39. *Society for Krishna Consciousness v. Lee,* 112 S. Ct. 2701 (1992).

40. *Welsh v. United States,* 398 U.S. 333 (1970); Pritchett, op. cit., 140–141.

41. *Sherbert v. Verner,* 374 U.S. 398 (1963); *Wisconsin v. Yoder,* 406 U.S. 205 (1972); *Hobbie v. Unemployment Appeals Commission of Florida,* 480 U.S. 136 (1987); *Estate of Thornton v. Caldor, Inc.,* 472 U.S. 703 (1985).

42. Berns, op. cit.

43. Pritchett, op. cit., 145–147.

44. *Everson v. Board of Education,* 330 U.S. 1 (1947).

45. *Engel v. Vitale,* 370 U.S. 421 (1962).

46. *Lubbock Independent School District v. Lubbock Civil Liberties Union,* 669 F.2d 1038.

47. *School District of Abington Township v. Schempp,* 374 U.S. 203 (1963).

48. *Lee v. Weisman,* 112 S. Ct. 2649 (1992).

49. *Epperson v. Arkansas,* 393 U.S. 97 (1968); *McLean v. Arkansas Board of Education,* 529 F.Supp. 1255 (1982).

50. *McCollum v. Board of Education,* 333 U.S. 203 (1948); *Zorach v. Clauson,* 343 U.S. 306 (1952).

51. *Tilton v. Richardson,* 403 U.S. 672 (1971).

52. *Board of Education v. Allen,* 392 U.S. 236 (1968).

53. *Walz v. Tax Commission,* 397 U.S. 664 (1970).

54. *Mueller v. Allen,* 463 U.S. 388 (1983).

55. *Zobrest v. Catalina Foothills School District,* 509 U.S. 1 (1993); *Mitchell v. Helms,* 2000 Lexis 4485.

56. *Lemon v. Kurtzman,* 403 U.S. 602 (1971).

57. *Committee for Public Education v. Nyquist,* 413 U.S. 756 (1973).

58. *Meek v. Pittenger,* 421 U.S. 349 (1975); *Wolman v. Walter,* 433 U.S. 229 (1977).

59. *Edwards v. Aguillard,* 482 U.S. 578 (1987); *Board of Education of Kiryas Joel Village School v. Louis Grumet,* 114 S. Ct. 2481 (1994).

60. *Agostini v. Felton,* 521 U.S. 203 (1997) overruled *Aguilar v. Felton,* 473 U.S. 402 (1985).

61. *Lemon v. Kurtzman,* 403 U.S. 602 (1971).

62. *Lynch v. Donelly,* 465 U.S. 668 (1984); *Allegheny v. ACLU,* 109 S. Ct. 3086 (1989).

63. *Marsh v. Chambers,* 492 U.S. 573 (1983).

64. Yale Kamisar, "Does (Did) (Should) the Exclusionary Rule Rest on a 'Principled Basis' Rather Than an 'Empirical Proposition'?" *Creighton Law Review* 16 (1982–1983): 565–667.

65. *Wolf v. Colorado,* 338 U.S. 25 (1949).

66. *Mapp v. Ohio,* 367 U.S. 643 (1961).

67. *Chimel v. California,* 395 U.S. 752 (1969).

68. *Washington v. Chrisman,* 455 U.S. 1 (1982).

69. *Oliver v. United States,* 466 U.S. 170 (1984).

70. *Arkansas v. Sanders,* 442 U.S. 753 (1979); *Robbins v. California,* 453 U.S. 420 (1981).

71. *United States v. Ross,* 456 U.S. 798 (1982); *Maryland v. Dyson,* 199 S. Ct. 2013 (1999); *Wyoming v. Houghton,* 119 S. Ct. 1297 (1999); *Whren v. United States,* 517 U.S. 806 (1996).

72. *Winston v. Lee,* 470 U.S. 753 (1985).

73. *South Dakota v. Neville,* 459 U.S. 553 (1983); *Schmerber v. California,* 384 U.S. 757 (1966).

74. *United States v. Dunn,* 480 U.S. 294 (1987); *California v. Ciraolo,* 476 U.S. 207 (1986); *California v. Carney,* 471 U.S. 386 (1985).

75. *O'Connor v. Ortega,* 480 U.S. 709 (1987).

76. *Bowers v. Hardwick,* 478 U.S. 186 (1986).

77. *National Treasury Employees Union v. von Rabb,* 489 U.S. 656 (1989); *Skinner v. Railway Labor Executives' Association,* 489 U.S. 602 (1989); *Michigan v. Sitz,* 496 U.S. 444 (1990); *Vernonia School District v. Acton,* 115 S. Ct. 2386 (1995).

78. *Chandler v. Miller,* 520 U.S. 305 (1997).

79. *Escobedo v. Illinois,* 378 U.S. 478 (1964); *Miranda v. Arizona,* 384 U.S. 436 (1966).

80. *Malloy v. Hogan,* 378 U.S. 1 (1964).

81. *Miranda v. Arizona,* 384 U.S. 436 (1966).

82. *Gilbert v. California,* 388 U.S. 263 (1967); *Kirby v. Illinois,* 406 U.S. 682 (1972).

83. *Estelle v. Smith,* 451 U.S. 454 (1981).

84. *Brewer v. Williams,* 430 U.S. 387 (1977).

85. *Illinois v. Perkins,* 496 U.S. 292 (1990).

86. *Dickerson v. United States,* 166 F.3d 667 (1999).

87. *Dickerson v. United States,* 120 S. Ct. 2326 (2000).

88. *Fare v. Michael C.,* 442 U.S. 707 (1979).

89. *United States v. Leon,* 468 U.S. 897 (1984); *Massachusetts v. Sheppard,* 468 U.S. 981 (1984).

90. *New York v. Quarles,* 467 U.S. 649 (1984). See also *Arizona v. Fulminante,* 111 S. Ct. 1246 (1991).

91. *Nix v. Williams,* 467 U.S. 431 (1984).

Chapter 16 *Civil Rights*

1. *United States v. Carolene Products Co.,* 304 U.S. 144 (1938); *San Antonio Independent School District v. Rodriguez,* 411 U.S. 1 (1973).

2. Gunnar Myrdal, *An American Dilemma* (New York: Harper, 1944), ch. 27.

3. Richard Kluger, *Simple Justice* (New York: Random House/Vintage Books, 1977), 89–90.

4. Paul B. Sheatsley, "White Attitudes Toward the Negro," in *The Negro American*, ed. Talcott Parsons and Kenneth B. Clark (Boston: Houghton Mifflin, 1966), 305, 308, 317.

5. *Strauder v. West Virginia*, 100 U.S. 303 (1880).

6. *Civil Rights Cases*, 109 U.S. 3 (1883).

7. *Plessy v. Ferguson*, 163 U.S. 537 (1896).

8. *Cumming v. Richmond County Board of Education*, 175 U.S. 528 (1899).

9. *Missouri ex rel. Gaines v. Canada*, 305 U.S. 337 (1938).

10. *Sipuel v. Board of Regents of the University of Oklahoma*, 332 U.S. 631 (1948).

11. *Sweatt v. Painter*, 339 U.S. 629 (1950); *McLaurin v. Oklahoma State Regents for Higher Education*, 339 U.S. 637 (1950).

12. *Brown v. Board of Education of Topeka*, 347 U.S. 483 (1954).

13. *Brown v. Board of Education of Topeka*, 349 U.S. 294 (1955). This case is often referred to as "Brown II."

14. Frederick S. Mosteller and Daniel P. Moynihan, eds., *On Equality of Educational Opportunity* (New York: Random House, 1972), 60–62.

15. *Brown v. Board of Education of Topeka*, 347 U.S. 483 (1954).

16. C. Herman Pritchett, *Constitutional Civil Liberties* (Englewood Cliffs, N.J.: Prentice-Hall, 1984), 250–251, 261.

17. *Green et al. v. County School Board of New Kent County*, 391 U.S. 430 (1968).

18. *Swann v. Charlotte-Mecklenburg Board of Education*, 402 U.S. 1 (1971).

19. Busing *within* the central city was upheld in *Armour v. Nix*, 446 U.S. 930 (1980); *Keyes v. School District No. 1*, Denver, 413 U.S. 189 (1973); *Milliken v. Bradley*, 418 U.S. 717 (1974); *Board of School Commissioners of Indianapolis v. Buckley*, 429 U.S. 1068 (1977); and *School Board of Richmond v. State Board of Education*, 412 U.S. 92 (1972). Busing *across* city lines was upheld in *Evans v. Buchanan*, 423 U.S. 963 (1975), and *Board of Education v. Newburg Area Council*, 421 U.S. 931 (1975).

20. *Pasadena City Board of Education v. Spangler*, 427 U.S. 424 (1976).

21. See, for example, Herbert McClosky and John Zaller, *The American Ethos* (Cambridge: Harvard University Press, 1984), 92, 100; and data reported in Chapter 5 of this text.

22. NES, *1952–1990 Cumulative Data File, 1992 NES Pre/Post Election Study* (1992).

23. *Freeman v. Pitts*, 112 S. Ct. 1430 (1992).

24. Robert S. Erikson and Norman R. Luttbeg, *American Public Opinion* (New York: Wiley, 1973), 49; Hazel Erskine, "The Polls: Demonstrations and Race Riots," *Public Opinion Quarterly* 31 (Winter 1967–1968): 654–677.

25. Howard Schuman, Charlotte Steeh, and Lawrence Bobo, *Racial Attitudes in America* (Cambridge: Harvard University Press, 1985), 69, 78–79.

26. Ibid., 102, 110, 127–135.

27. *Grove City College v. Bell*, 465 U.S. 555 (1984).

28. *United States v. Armstrong*, 116 S. Ct. 1480 (1996).

29. *Mueller v. Oregon*, 208 U.S. 412 (1908).

30. Equal Pay Act of 1963; Civil Rights Act of 1964, Title VII, and 1978 amendments thereto; Education Amendments of 1972, Title IX.

31. *Reed v. Reed*, 404 U.S. 71 (1971).

32. *Frontiero v. Richardson*, 411 U.S. 677 (1973).

33. *Stanton v. Stanton*, 421 U.S. 7 (1975).

34. *Craig v. Boren*, 429 U.S. 190 (1976).

35. *Dothard v. Rawlinson*, 433 U.S. 321 (1977).

36. *Cleveland Board of Education v. LaFleur*, 414 U.S. 632 (1974).

37. *Fortin v. Darlington Little League*, 514 F.2d 344 (1975).

38. *Roberts v. United States Jaycees*, 468 U.S. 609 (1984); *Board of Directors Rotary International v. Rotary Club of Duarte*, 481 U.S. 537 (1987).

39. *Arizona Governing Committee for Tax Deferred Annuity and Deferred Compensation Plans v. Norris*, 463 U.S. 1073 (1983).

40. *E.E.O.C. v. Madison Community Unit School District No. 12*, 818 F.2d 577 (1987).

41. *Michael M. v. Superior Court*, 450 U.S. 464 (1981).

42. *Vorchheimer v. School District of Philadelphia*, 430 U.S. 703 (1977).

43. *Kahn v. Shevin*, 416 U.S. 351 (1974).

44. *Schlesinger v. Ballard*, 419 U.S. 498 (1975).

45. *Bennett v. Dyer's Chop House*, 350 F.Supp. 153 (1972); *Morris v. Michigan State Board of Education*, 472 F.2d 1207 (1973); *Fitzgerald v. Porter Memorial Hospital*, 523 F.2d 716 (1975); *Kruzel v. Podell*, 226 N.W.2d 458 (1975).

46. *United States v. Virginia*, 116 S. Ct. 2264 (1996).

47. *Rostker v. Goldberg*, 453 U.S. 57 (1981).

48. *Gebser v. Lago Vista School District*, 118 S. Ct. 1989 (1998); *Faragher v. Boca Raton*, 118 S. Ct. 2275 (1998); *Burlington Industries v. Ellerth*, 118 S. Ct. 2257 (1998).

49. *Roe v. Wade*, 410 U.S. 113 (1973).

50. *Harris v. McRae*, 448 U.S. 297 (1980); *Beal v. Doe*, 432 U.S. 438 (1977); *Maher v. Roe*, 432 U.S. 464 (1977).

51. *Planned Parenthood Federation of Central Missouri v. Danforth*, 428 U.S. 52 (1976); *Bellotti v. Baird*, 443 U.S. 622 (1979); *Akron v. Akron Center for Reproductive Health*, 462 U.S. 416 (1983); *Thornburgh v. American College of Obstetricians and Gynecologists*, 476 U.S. 747 (1986). But compare with *Planned Parenthood Association of Kansas City v. Ashcroft*, 462 U.S. 476 (1983).

52. *Planned Parenthood v. Casey*, 112 S. Ct. 2791 (1992).

53. *Schenck v. Pro-Choice Network of Western New York*, 519 U.S. 357 (1997).

54. For an argument in support of a color-blind Constitution, see Andrew Kull, *The Color-Blind Constitution* (Cambridge: Harvard University Press, 1992).

55. *Regents of the University of California v. Bakke*, 438 U.S. 265 (1978).

56. *Fullilove v. Klutznick*, 448 U.S. 448 (1980).

57. *City of Richmond v. J.A. Croson Co.*, 488 U.S. 469 (1989).

58. *Metro Broadcasting v. FCC*, 497 U.S. 547 (1990).

59. *Northeastern Florida Contractors v. Jacksonville*, No. 91–1721 (1993).

60. *Firefighters Local Union No. 1784 v. Stotts*, 467 U.S. 561 (1984); *Wygant v. Jackson Board of Education*, 476 U.S. 267 (1986); *City of Richmond v. J.A. Croson Co.*, 488 U.S. 469 (1989).

61. *Local No. 28 of the Sheet Metal Workers' International Association v. Equal Employment Opportunity Commission*, 478 U.S. 421 (1986); *Wards Cove Packing Co. v. Atonio*, 490 U.S. 642 (1989); *Price Waterhouse v. Hopkins*, 490 U.S. 228 (1989). (Note: Wards Cove and Price were both superseded in part by the Civil Rights Act of 1991.)

62. *Fullilove v. Klutznick*, 448 U.S. 448 (1980); *Metro Broadcasting v. FCC*, 497 U.S. 547 (1990).

63. *United Steelworkers of America v. Weber*, 443 U.S. 193 (1979); *Johnson v. Santa Clara County Transportation Agency*, 480 U.S. 616 (1987).

64. *Wygant v. Jackson Board of Education*, 476 U.S. 267 (1986); *U.S. v. Paradise*, 480 U.S. 149 (1987).

65. Seymour Martin Lipset and William Schneider, "An Emerging National Consensus," *The New Republic* (October 15, 1977), 8–9.

66. John R. Bunzel, "Affirmative Re-Actions," *Public Opinion* (February–March 1986), 45–49; *New York Times* (December 14, 1997).

67. *Hopwood v. State of Texas*, 78 F.3d 932 (1996); *Texas v. Hopwood*, 135 L.Ed.2d 1095 (1996).

68. *Adarand Constructors v. Pena*, 115 S. Ct. 2097 (1995).

69. *Bowers v. Hardwick*, 478 U.S. 186 (1986).

70. *Romer v. Evans*, 116 S. Ct. 1620 (1996).

71. *Boy Scouts of America v. Dale*, 2000 Lexis 4487.

Index

AARP (American Association of Retired Persons), 223, 241
ABC, 250
Abernathy, Ralph, 476
Abortion, 74, 198, 479, 480–481
Acheson's rule, 392
Acid rain, 391
ACLU (American Civil Liberties Union), 243, 417, 437, 458
Acquired immunodeficiency syndrome (AIDS), 125, 455–456
"Acting" appointments, 350
Activism (activists), 123–124, 138, 174. *See also* Judicial activism; Political elites; Political participation
ADA (Americans with Disabilities Act) (1990), 67, 485, 487
Adams, John, 5, 24, 406
    on appointments, 377
    conflict with Democratic-Republicans, 88, 153, 406
    on English politics, 18
    Marbury v. Madison (1803), 405, 406–407
    presidency of, 279–280, 342, 343, 349, 353, 366, 378
    on revolution, 20
    as vice president, 377
Adams, John Quincy, 185, 340, 353
Adams, Samuel, 24, 30
Adarand, 488
Ad hoc structure, of White House Office, 346, 347
ADL (Anti-Defamation League), 219, 490
Administrative Procedure Act (1946), 390
Adversarial politics, 497–498
Adversarial press, 266
Adversary culture, 376
Advertising, 106, 259, 447. *See also* Direct-mail solicitations
    laws to limit, 193, 194, 195
    negative, 213, 268, 269
    role in presidential campaigns, 187–191
AFBF (American Farm Bureau Federation), 70, 71, 72
AFDC. *See* Aid to Families with Dependent Children
Affirmative action, 114, 116(fig.), 121, 481–488
    Clinton and, 364
    equality of opportunity and, 482–485, 488
    equality of results and, 481–482
    universities and, 413, 482, 488
Afghanistan, Soviet invasion of, 363
AFL-CIO, 10, 165, 352, 421
    as interest group, 218, 219, 229
    membership growth in, 228(fig.), 229
    ratings of legislators by, 233, 304
African Americans. *See* Blacks
Age Discrimination Act, 323
Agencies, 381. *See also* Bureaucracy; *and specific agencies*
    budgets for, 393–395

congressional oversight of, 393–395
congressional staff, 311
constraints on, 389–393
"executive," 350, 351
federal, 376, 378–379
growth in, 376, 378–379
independent and quasi-independent, 350, 351
iron triangles and, 392–393
point of view of, 385–386
recruitment and retention in, 381–383, 385
regulatory. *See* Regulatory agencies
Web sites, 401
Agency for International Development, 389
Agenda-setting process. *See* Policy-making process
Agnew, Spiro, 369
Agricultural Stabilization and Conservation Service, 395
Agriculture Department, 378, 392, 393
AIDS (acquired immunodeficiency syndrome), 125, 455–456
Aid to Families with Dependent Children (AFDC), 71, 72
    devolution and, 70, 72, 73(fig.)
    Medicaid compared with, 71, 72
    public opinion about, 72, 73(fig.)
Airline regulations, 233
Alabama, 61, 211, 423–424, 469, 471, 472, 474
Alaska, 186, 187, 290, 379
Albany, Georgia, 444
Alden v. Maine (1999), 59
Alger, Horatio, 90
Aliens, rights of, 484
All-black colleges, 466
Allocation formulas, 65–66
Almond, Gabriel, 84–85, 222
Amendments to Constitution, 28, 35, 36. *See also specific amendments*
    proposing, 41
    ratifying, 41
American Arab Anti-Discrimination Committee, 490
American Association of Retired Persons (AARP), 223, 241
American Civil Liberties Union (ACLU), 243, 417, 437, 458
American Conservative Union, 243
American Cotton Manufacturers Institute, 221
American Council on Education, 222
American Farm Bureau Federation (AFBF), 218, 219, 220
American Federation of Labor, 501
American Independent (George Wallace) party, 170
American Indians, 439
Americanism, 82, 120, 436, 439
American Jewish Committee, 219
American Legion, 223
American Medical Association, 219, 233
American Nazi party, 442–443

American ("Know-Nothing") party, 170
American Public Transit Association, 222
American Revolution. *See* Revolutionary War
Americans for Constitutional Action, 233
Americans for Democratic Action, 233, 243
Americans with Disabilities Act (ADA) (1990), 67, 485, 487
American System, 1–100. *See also* Constitution of the United States; Federalism; Political culture
American way of life, 82
Amicus curiae briefs, 225, 421, 431
Amish people, 449
Anderson, John, 123, 168
Andrus, Cecil D., 225
"Angry white males," 198
Annual authorizations, 394
Anti-abortion organizations, 163, 227, 480–481
Anti-Defamation League (ADL), 219, 490
Antifederalists, 30, 31, 34, 35, 39, 320
Antifeminist movement, 227
Antigua, 389
Anti-Jackson Republicans (1831), 154
Anti-Masonic party (1831), 154
Anti-Saloon League, 171
Antislavery organizations, 220
Antitrust regulation, 239, 418
Antiwar movement, 169, 170, 240
Apathy, of voters, 130
Appointments, presidential, 350–353, 386–387, 387(fig.), 399
    "acting," 350
    bureaucratic, 376–378, 381–382
    cabinet, 349–350, 350(fig.), 351–352, 376–377, 399
    Constitution and, 376–377
    growth of, 345–346, 346(fig.), 376–380, 384(fig.)
    parliamentary system compared with, 334–335, 351
    rule of propinquity and, 346
Appropriations, 393–394
Appropriations Committee (House), 393–394
Aristotle, 6
Arizona, 416, 456
Arkansas, 345
Armed Services Committees, congressional, 296
Arthur, Chester, 343
Article I, of Constitution, 40, 55, 132, 278, 290, 394
Article II, of Constitution, 343, 344
Article III, of Constitution, 407, 411
Articles of Confederation (1781), 21–22, 30, 37
    Constitutional Convention and, 22–25
    New Jersey Plan, 26
    Virginia Plan, 25–26
Ash Council, 398
Asian Americans, 116–117, 117(fig.)
Assassination attempts, 235, 366
Assassinations, 345, 383, 474
Associated Press (AP), 248, 253
Association of Disabled Golfers, 487

Athens (Greece), 6, 7
Atlantic Monthly, 249
Attitudes. *See* Political attitudes
Attitudinal voting, in Congress, 295, 296–298
Attorney general, 370, 421, 475
Australia, 50, 140
Australian ballot, 136
Austria, 85, 94, 219
Authority, 4–5. *See also* Power; *and specific kinds of power*
    decentralization of, 151
    discretionary, of bureaucracy, 380
    under federalism, 29, 50, 51, 52–53
    of president, 42, 43–44, 506–507
Authorization legislation, 393, 394

Background briefings, 266, 267
Background stories, 271
Baker, Howard, 182, 347
Bakke, Allan, 421
Bakke decision (1978), 421, 482
Ballot initiatives, ban on, 13
Banking, 56
Bank of the United States, 56
Barbuda, 389
Barriers to action. *See also* Separation of powers
    reducing, 506–508
Barton, Clara, 389
Bayh, Birch, 165
Bay of Pigs, 363
Beard, Charles, 38–39
Bell, Alexander Graham, 389
Bentsen, Lloyd, 299, 340
Berman, Howard L., 163
Bernstein, Carl, 255
Beverly Hills, California, 65
Bias
    of interest groups, 230–232, 230(fig.)
    in the media, 257, 263–266, 263(fig.), 264(fig.)
    upper-class, 230–232, 230(fig.)
Bicameral legislature, 279
Big 10 Tuesday (March 19), 183
Bilingual education, 117, 440
Bill of attainder, 34
Bill of Rights, 21, 34–35, 35, 500, 501. *See also specific amendments*
    broadening of, 416
    gender not mentioned, 40
    need for, 35–36
Bills, 311–312. *See also* Legislation; Legislative process
    Christmas tree, 316
    introducing, 312–313
    private and public, 313
    riders, 316
    study by committees, 313–316
Birmingham, Alabama, 471, 474
Black, Hugo, 404, 444
Black colleges, 466
Blackmun, Harry, 412, 429
Blacks
    civil rights and, 462–464. *See also* Affirmative action; Civil rights legislation; Civil-rights movement
    in Congress, 284, 285(fig.), 291–292, 477(fig.)
    employment in the Federal bureaucracy, 386, 388(fig.)
    majority-minority districts and, 291–292, 292(fig.)

political participation and, 138, 139, 144, 144(fig.)
public opinion and, 114–117, 116(fig.), 117(fig.), 463
trust in federal government, 93
voting records of, 205, 206(fig.), 207
voting rights of, 132–134, 134(fig.), 463, 474
Blackstone, William, 441
Blair, Tony, 335
Blanket primaries, 186
Block grants, 50, 62, 64–65, 66, 69–70
    for entitlements, 70–71
Blount, William, 39
"Blue Dog Democrats," 306
"Blue slip," 412
Bolton, Frances, 293
Bonds, 56
Border Patrol, 390
Boren's laws, 392
Bork, Robert, 414
Born-again Christians, 91, 107
Bosnia, 364
Boston Globe, 252
Boston Herald, 252
Boy Scouts, 489
Bradley, Bill, 173, 181
Brady, Jim, 235
Brady Bill (1993), 235, 411
Braestrup, Peter, 265
Brandeis, Louis, 427
Brandenburg, Clarence, 442–443
Brandenburg v. Ohio (1969), 445
Braun, Carol Mosely, 284
Breckinridge, John C., 208–209
Brennan, William, 469
Bribery, 239, 241, 324
Briefs, 420–421
    amicus curiae, 225, 421, 431
Brill, Alida, 95, 96
Britain. *See* Great Britain
Broad-based aid. *See* Block grants
Broder, David, 181
Brown, Linda, 419, 467, 469
Brown, Pat, 165
Brown, Ronald H., 161
Brownlow, Louis, 398
Brownlow Commission, 398
Brown v. Board of Education (1954), 419, 467–472
    desegregation versus integration, 469–472
    implementation of ruling, 467–468
    rationale behind, 468–469
Bryan, William Jennings, 155, 208, 209
Buchanan, James, 353
Buckley v. Valeo (1976), 242
Buddy system, 383–384
Budget and Accounting Act (1921), 345
Budget deficits, 72, 103, 289, 394
    New System and, 505–506
    reduction, 71, 72
Budget Reform Act (1974), 362
    Budgets
    for agencies, 393–395
    Congressional Budget Act (1974) and, 329
"Bull Moose" (Progressive) party, 170
Bunyan, John, 248
Bureaucracy, 374–401. *See also* Bureaucrats
    agency point of view of, 385–386
    attempts at reform, 397–400
    bureaucratic "pathologies," 395–397
    bureaucratic power, 381, 386, 387–389

careers in, 389
comparison with other countries, 376
congressional oversight of, 393–395
constraints on, 389–393
culture of, 389
definitions of, 375–376
discretionary authority of, 380
growth of, 345–346, 346(fig.), 376–380, 384(fig.)
minority employment in, 386, 388(fig.)
power of, 380–381
problems with, 395–397
recruitment and retention, 381–383, 385
during war time, 377–378, 379–380
Web sites, 401
of White House, 345–346, 346(fig.), 347
Bureaucrats, 9–10
    appointment of, 381–383
    firing, 384–385, 390–391
    personal attributes of, 386–387, 387(fig.)
    political sabotage by, 387–389
    trivia about, 389
    typical daily schedule, 383
Bureau of Competition (FTC), 388
Bureau of Economics (FTC), 388
Bureau of the Budget, 345, 349. *See also* Office of Management and Budget
Burger, Warren, 412, 429, 469
Burnett, Carol, 443
Burr, Aaron, 340
Bush, George H. W., 339
    abortion and, 481
    affirmative action and, 481, 485, 487
    approval rating of, 357
    books on, 373
    character of, 354
    crises of, 364
    mandates and, 67, 67(fig.)
    presidency of, 334, 336, 343, 365, 393, 481
    presidential campaign of 1988, 182, 183, 184, 186, 202, 203, 211
    presidential campaign of 1992, 115, 137, 165, 182, 190, 264, 336
    Supreme Court nominations, 403, 414
    as vice president, 366
Bush, George W., 117, 165, 173, 187, 255
Bush, John Ellis ("Jeb"), 165
Bush family, 165, 487
Business
    civil liberties for corporations, 447–448
    interest groups representing, 219, 221–222, 229, 230
    interstate versus intrastate commerce and, 57
    PACs sponsored by, 237
    public confidence in big, 267, 268(fig.)
    Republican party and, 205, 209
Business regulation, 83, 239
    majoritarian politics and and, 231
Busing
    to achieve desegregation, 412, 428–429, 469–470
    Congress and, 470–471
    media coverage of, 265, 266
    opposition to, 103, 470
    Byrd family, 165

CAB (Civil Aeronautics Board), 10, 233
Cabinet, 334–335, 349–350, 349(fig.)
    appointments to, 349–350, 351–352, 376–377
    Web sites, 401

Cable News Network (CNN). *See* CNN
Cable television, 190–191, 250, 252, 253, 262, 269
Calhoun, John C., 57, 342
California, 21, 52, 65, 156, 164, 224, 297, 322
    Congress and, 287, 290, 291, 291(fig.)
    party identification and political attitudes of ethnic groups in, 116, 117, 117(fig.), 204
    Proposition 13, 6
California Public Utility Commission, 447
Calorie Control Council, 235
Cambridge, Massachusetts, 167
Cameron, Simon, 352, 509
Campaign debates, 189–191, 258
Campaigners, 138
Campaign finance rules, 192–196, 502
    major federal, 193
Campaign fund raising, 182, 183, 191–199
    comparison with Europe, 198(fig.)
    current reform proposals, 195–196
    legal constraints on, 241
    reforms of 1974, 193, 194–195
    soft money, 158–159, 194, 195, 241
    sources of money, 191–192, 192(fig.)
    Web sites, 215
    winning and, 191, 191(fig.), 196–199
Campaign issues, 185–187
Campaign oratory, 189–190
Campaigns, 180–183. *See also* Congressional campaigns; Presidential campaigns
    elections and, 178–215
    funding for, 242
Campbell, Ben Nighthorse, 284
Canada, 21, 22, 50, 428
Cannon, Joseph G., 281, 307
Capital grants, 70–71
Capitalists, 10
    Marxism and, 8–9
Capital punishment, 425
Carlyle, Thomas, 397
Carnal Knowledge (movie), 444
Carp, Robert A., 411
Carter, Jimmy, 357, 436
    on "American malaise," 92
    approval rating of, 357
    audience of, 355
    books on, 373
    campaign and election, 115, 118, 123, 182, 186, 189–190, 202, 205, 254, 258
    character of, 354
    Congress and, 393
    crises of, 363
    environmental and energy policy, 314, 318
    media and, 261, 271
    presidency of, 303, 314, 333, 334, 335, 336, 346, 347, 363
    Reagan versus, 210
    reform of government by, 398
    Supreme Court nominations by, 333, 413, 427
Casey case (1992), 480, 481
Categorical grants, 62, 64, 65
    revenue sharing versus, 62, 64
Catholics (Catholic Church; Catholicism), 89, 90, 107, 198, 205, 437, 439, 448, 449
Caucuses, 154, 173, 174, 183, 184
    congressional, 280, 281, 298–306, 306(fig.)
    list of key, 183
    primaries versus, 173
CBC (Congressional Black Caucus), 305

CBO (Congressional Budget Office), 311
CBS, 127, 250, 418
CEA (Council of Economic Advisers), 348
Censorship, 255, 441, 445
Census Bureau, U.S., 100, 115
Center for Equal Opportunity, 243
Center for Individual Rights, 417
Central Intelligence Agency (CIA), 348, 419
CETA (Comprehensive Employment and Training Act), 64
Chadha case (1983), 365, 394–395
Chamber of Commerce, 219, 220, 221–222, 233
Chapman's Rules of Committees, 392
Character of the president, 353–354
    voters and, 198, 203
Charitable Choice, 98
Chase, Salmon P., 352
Chase, Samuel, 427
Checks and balances, 29, 336, 504
    Congress and, 29, 279, 324
    judicial review, 28, 403–404, 405
Chicago, 163, 471
Chief justices, 404(fig.), 410, 411–414, 420(fig.), 421–422
China, 364
Chinese Americans, 132
Chinese Revolution, 17
Christian Coalition, 88, 108–109, 164, 233, 243
Christian Science Monitor, 253
Christmas-tree bills, 316
Churches, 89–90, 168. *See also* Religion
    public confidence in, 93, 94(fig.)
    separation of state and, 448–451
Church of England, 449
CIA (Central Intelligence Agency), 348, 419
Cicero, Illinois, 462
Circular structure, of White House Office, 346
Cities
    definition of, 58
    "Model Cities" plan (1966), 61
    sovereignty of, 59
Citizens (citizenship), 6, 8, 34, 35, 40
    rights of, 483
Civic competence, 85
Civic duty, 81, 84–85
Civic intolerance, 95–99
Civil Aeronautics Board (CAB), 10, 233
Civil disobedience, 472
Civil law, 416
Civil liberties, 434–459
    church and state, separation of, 448–451
    for corporations and groups, 447–448
    crime and due process, 451–457
    cultural conflicts and, 90–92, 439–440
    definition of person, 447–448
    definition of speech, 443–447
    establishment clause and, 448, 449–451
    First Amendment. *See* First Amendment
    free-exercise clause and, 448–449
    obscenity and, 255, 444–446
    policy entrepreneurs and, 437–439
    politics, culture, and, 436–440
    rights in conflict and, 437
    symbolic speech and, 446–447
Civil rights, 83, 460–491
    affirmative action and, 481–488
    black predicament and, 462–464
    Congress and, 282, 295, 314, 317, 472–477, 473(fig.), 476(fig.), 477(fig.)
    courts and, 464–472

definition of, 461–462
    for gays, 488–489
    groups, 243
    political ideology and, 121–122
    public opinion on, 472, 473–474, 473(fig.)
    representational view of, 295
    separate-but-equal doctrine and, 465, 467–472
    suspect classifications and, 462
    view of, in the South, 117, 118(fig.), 476(fig.)
    Web sites, 490
    for women, 477–481
Civil Rights Act (1957), 475
Civil Rights Act (1960), 475
Civil Rights Act (1964), 424, 474–475, 475, 476, 478, 486
Civil Rights Act (1965), 475
Civil Rights Act (1968), 474, 475
Civil Rights Act (1972), 475, 478
Civil Rights Act (1988), 475
Civil Rights Act (1991), 475, 483
Civil Rights Commission, 475
Civil Rights Division of the Justice Department, 458
Civil rights legislation, 67, 282, 313, 314. *See also specific laws*
    key provisions of, 475
Civil-rights movement, 93, 169, 225, 243, 472–477
    chronology of major events in (1955–1968), 471
    conflict in, 473
    disruptive tactics of, 240
    opposition to, 463–464
    role of religion, 87
Civil service, 162–163, 381–382, 384–386, 390–391
Civil Service Reform Act (1978), 385
Civil War, 5, 82, 209, 280, 502
    bureaucratic development during, 377–378
    Dred Scott decision (1857) and, 407
    effects of, 51, 55–56, 57
    sectionalism and, 154–156
    slavery issue and, 38, 155, 185, 280
Clarity, free speech and, 445
Class-action suits, 419–420, 467
Class consciousness, 90, 112
Class differences. *See* Social class
Clay, Henry, 280, 342
Clayton, Eva, 291
Clean Air Act (1970), 343
    1990 amendment, 234, 343
Clear-and-present-danger test, 441–442
Cleveland, Grover, 156, 185, 343
    presidency of, 342, 345, 382–383
    use of vetoes, 343, 360, 361(fig.)
Client-based welfare programs. *See* Aid to Families with Dependent Children; Medicaid
Client politics
    civil rights and, 462–463
    interest groups and, 233, 238
    iron triangles as examples of, 392
Clinton, Bill, 334, 335, 336, 339, 343–344, 363, 376
    abortion and, 481
    affirmative action and, 364
    appointments, 350, 382, 386
    approval rating of, 357
    character of, 354
    Congress and, 277, 296, 336

Clinton, Bill *(cont.)*
  crises of, 364
  devolution and, 70
  foreign policy, 365
  gays in the military and, 489
  health care plan, 233, 333
  impeachment of, 201, 296, 298, 369–370
  Jones and, 269, 361, 479
  Lewinsky and, 251, 269
  line-item veto, 43, 509–510
  mandates, 68
  media and, 267, 269
  presidential campaign and election of 1992,
    115, 118, 137, 167, 183, 187, 189, 190,
    263–264, 267, 336
  presidential campaign and election of 1996,
    110, 115, 118, 137, 187, 189, 198, 201
  soft money and, 158–159
  staff of, 346, 347
  Supreme Court nominations by, 413
Clinton, George, 23
Clinton, Hillary Rodham, 187, 267, 346
Clinton et al. v. New York et al. (1998), 44
Closed primaries, 186
Closed rule, 315
Clothespin vote, 184, 185
Cloture rule, 284, 317, 475
CNN (Cable News Network), 190, 250, 253, 263,
  269, 272
Coalition, the ("Blue Dog Democrats"), 306
Coalitions, Madison and, 34
Coattails, 181, 356
Colonists, American, 17–20
Colorado, 322, 488, 489
Columbus Dispatch, 254
Commander in chief, president as, 344, 405
Commentaries (Blackstone), 441
Commerce
  intrastate versus interstate, 57–58
  regulation of, 55
Commerce clause, 57–58, 58
Commerce Committee (Senate), 314
Commerce Department, 378
Committee Clearance, 394
Committee of the Whole (House), 316–317
Committee on Committees, congressional, 299,
  300
Committees, 306–309, 310. *See also* Political
    action committees; *and specific committes*
  conference, 306, 307, 308, 318
  iron triangles and, 392–393
  joint, 306
  power in, 307–309
  reduction in number of, 301, 306–307
  select, 306
  standing, 306, 307, 308, 318
  study of bills by, 313–316
  types of, 306
Common Cause, 230, 231
Communalists, 138
Communism, 438, 442
Communist Control Act (1954), 438
Communist Manifesto (Marx), 9
Communist party, 170
Community Development Block Grants, 64
Compensatory action, 485
Competing interests, 54–55
Competitive service, 381–382
Comprehensive Employment and Training Act
  (CETA), 64

Compulsory voting, 140, 145
Conable, Barber, 509
Concurrent resolutions, 313
Concurring opinions, 422
Conditions of aid, 66, 68–70
Confederal systems (confederation), 51, 53
Conference committees, 306, 307, 308, 318
Confessions, due process and, 456–457
Confidentiality of sources, 256
Conflict
  in bureaucracy, 395, 396, 397
  cultural conflicts, 90–92, 437, 439–440
  rights in conflict and, 437
Conflict of interest, 238, 239
Congress, 27, 28, 31, 274–330. *See also* House of
    Representatives; Legislation; Senate; *and spe-*
    cific laws
  104th (1994–1996), 43, 50, 67, 71, 277,
    287, 289, 305, 306–307
  abortion and, 481
  agency oversight by, 393–395
  attitudinal voting in, 295, 296–298
  blacks and, 284, 285(fig.), 291–292, 477(fig.)
  bureaucracy and, 393–395
  calendar, 315
  caucuses, 280, 281, 298–306, 306(fig.)
  changes in, 503
  checks and balances and, 29, 279, 324
  civil rights and, 282, 295, 314, 317,
    472–477, 473(fig.), 476(fig.), 477(fig.)
  committees, 306–309
  composition of, 284–289, 285(fig.), 286(fig.),
    287(fig.)
  criticisms of, 319–324
  delegation of power to agencies, 380–381
  distribution of power and, 8–11
  divided government and, 212, 280, 335–337
  elections. *See* Congressional elections
  ethics and, 324–326
  evolution of, 279–284, 342–344
  fair representation in, 290–291, 291(fig.)
  federalism and, 49–50, 72–75
  gridlock in, 42, 320, 322
  history of, 279–284, 342–344
  House-Senate differences, 319
  ideology and civility in, 298
  incumbency and, 284–288, 286(fig.),
    287(fig.), 289, 292, 293, 320
  information sources for, 327
  investigations by, 395
  judiciary and, 405, 407, 411, 426, 427–429
  legislative process in. *See* Legislative process
  local orientation of members of, 293–294
  media coverage of, 262–263, 271
  methods of raising pay, 326
  organizational voting in, 295, 296
  organization of, 298–311
  PACs and, 192, 236–238, 325
  parliamentary system compared with,
    275–276, 277, 278, 279, 304, 324
  party affiliation and, 287–289, 288(fig.)
  party leadership structure, 301
  party polarization on, 302–304, 303(fig.)
  pay in, 326
  as political career, 285
  political parties and. *See* Political parties, Con-
    gress and
  powers and perks of, 278, 294, 322–324
  president and, 305, 313, 338, 355–357,
    356(fig.), 360, 362, 400

  public interest and, 320
  public opinion and, 295–296, 297, 297(fig.)
  qualifications for entering, 294
  reforming, 319–324, 397–400
  representational voting in, 295–296
  restraints on, 499–500
  right to charter a national bank, 56
  staff and specialized offices. *See* Congressional
    staffs
  strength of party structures in, 301–302
  subjecting to law, 323
  term limits in, 285, 320, 322, 510
  trivia about, 293
  unity of parties in, 302–304
  voting in, 295–298, 318–319
  Web sites, 47, 330
Congressional Accountability Act (1995), 323
Congressional Black Caucus (CBC), 305
Congressional Budget Act (1974), 329
Congressional Budget Office (CBO), 311
Congressional campaigns, 180–183
  committees, 157
Congressional caucuses, 280, 281, 298–306,
  306(fig.)
Congressional Directory, 327
Congressional districts, 290–292, 291(fig.), 423
Congressional elections, 289–295
  fair representation in, 290–291, 291(fig.)
  incumbency and, 284–288, 286(fig.),
    287(fig.), 289, 292, 293, 320,
  majority-minority districts and, 291–292,
    292(fig.)
  marginal versus safe districts, 286, 296
  money and winning, 198–199, 199(fig.)
  presidential versus, 180–183
  primary, 292–295
Congressional Government (Wilson), 344
Congressional Quarterly, 327
Congressional Record, 327
Congressional Research Service (CRS), 311
Congressional staffs, 309–311, 310(fig.)
  tasks of members, 310–311
Connecticut, 21, 27n, 37, 58, 153, 235, 337
Connecticut ("Great") Compromise, 27
Connor, Eugene ("Bull"), 474
Conservatism (conservatives), 119, 120–122,
  122(fig.)
  analyzing consistency in, 122–123
  of college students, 110, 111, 112(fig.)
  education and, 111, 112(fig.)
  in public-interest groups, 223–224, 225, 226,
    229, 233, 243
  selection of judges and, 411, 412(fig.), 413
  in the Senate, 289, 296–297, 298
  think tanks, 226
  use of term, 118–119
Conservative coalition, 289
Conservative party, 180, 212
Conservative/strict-constructionist approach, to
  judicial review, 404–405, 413, 429
Considine, Bob, 437
Consistency of attitudes, 120
Constituents, 180, 238
Constituent services, 321, 329
Constitutional Convention (1787), 5, 22–25, 53
  economic interests at, 38–39
  the Framers and, 23–25
  Great Compromise, 27
  New Jersey Plan, 26
  Virginia Plan, 25–26

Constitutional courts, 411
Constitution of the United States, A4, 5, 16–47,
    88–89. *See also* Constitutional Convention
  Bill of Rights. *See* Bill of Rights; *and individual
    amendments*
  challenges to, 25–27
  checks and balances and, 29
  commerce clause, 57–58, 58
  competing rights and duties, 437
  court cases about, 47
  criticisms of, 41–44
  democracy and, 28–30
  Eighth Amendment to, 35
  Eleventh Amendment to, 58–59, 411, 427
  equality issue and, 39–40
  Fifteenth Amendment to, 133, 409, 427
  Fifth Amendment to, 35
  First Amendment to. *See* First Amendment
  Fourteenth Amendment to. *See* Fourteenth
    Amendment
  Fourth Amendment to, 35
  Framers of, 23–25, 38–39
  human nature as factor, 29–30
  key principles of, 28–29
  leaks in the news and, 266
  liberty and, 30–38
  Nineteenth Amendment to, 40, 134
  Ninth Amendment to, 35
  preamble to, 104
  presidency and, 355
  problem of liberty, 17–22
  ratification of, 30–31, 32, 34, 35–36, 39
  reform and, 41–46
  representative democracy and, 7–8, 28
  representative versus direct democracy, 7–8,
    319–320
  role of religion in, 88, 89
  Second Amendment to, 35
  Seventeenth Amendment to, 283
  Seventh Amendment to, 35
  Sixteenth Amendment, 427
  Sixteenth Amendment to, 380, 427
  Sixth Amendment to, 35
  slavery and, 36–38
  states and, 54
  Tenth Amendment to, 35, 53–54, 58, 66, 68
  Third Amendment to, 35
  Thirteenth Amendment to, 427
  Twelfth Amendment, 340
  Twenty-fifth Amendment, 349, 367
  Twenty-fifth Amendment to, 349, 367, 369
  Twenty-second Amendment to, 338, 365
  Twenty-sixth Amendment to, 134, 427
  Twenty-third Amendment to, 135
  voting and, 132
  women and, 40
Constitutions, 21, 44
  English, 18
  federal. *See* Constitution of the United States
  state. *See* State constitutions
Consumer advocates. *See* Policy entrepreneurs
Consumer Federation of America, 233
Consumer Product Safety Commission, 351
Continental Congress, 23, 37, 38, 39
"Contract with America," 282
Conventions. *See* National nominating conven-
    tions
Coolidge, Calvin, 343
Cornell University Medical School, 461
Corporations. *See* Business

Corruption, 156, 241, 324–325
  constituent services and, 321, 329
  Ethics in Government Act (1978), 238, 239
Cosmopolitan, 249
Cost of Living Council, 379
Council of Economic Advisers (CEA), 348
Counties, 58
Court of International Trade, 411
Court of Military Appeals, 411
Courts, 27, 28. *See also* Judiciary; Supreme
    Court
  changes in, 503
  checks and balances and, 29
  civil rights and, 464–472
  class-action suits, 419–420, 467
  constitutional, 411
  district, 410(fig.), 411, 412, 414–417, 416
  federal. *See* Federal courts
  jurisdiction of, 414–417
  legal standing and, 418–419, 420, 426
  legislative, 411
  policy making and, 422–426
  political liberties and, 409–411
  relaxing constraints on federal government
    and, 501
  state, jurisdiction of, 414–417
Courts of appeals, 411, 413
Cox Broadcasting Corp. v. Cohn (1975), 451, 454
Crack cocaine, 477
Crawford, William H., 340
Creationism, 450
Crèche, 440, 450
Crime. *See also* Police
  due process and, 451–457
Criminal law, 416
Crisis, The, 222, 465
Critical or realigning periods, 208
CRS (Congressional Research Service), 311
C-SPAN, 262, 263
Cuba, 363, 365
Cuban-Americans, 117, 204, 205
Cultural conflicts, 90–92, 437, 439–440
Cultural differences, effects on political system,
    84, 86, 87(fig.), 440
Culture, civil liberties and, 436–440
Culture wars, 90–92
Cumming v. Richmond County Board of Education
    (1899), 465
Cuomo, Mario, 181–182
Cynicism, in the media, 266–267

Dairy industry, 231
Das Kapital (Marx), 9
Davis, Gray, 117
Davis, John W., 159
DEA (Drug Enforcement Administration), 390
Death penalty, 117, 257, 425
Deaver, Michael K., 238
Debates
  floor, 309, 316–318
  on meaning of federalism, 55–59
  role in presidential campaigns, 189–191, 258
  televised, 189–191, 258
Debs, Eugene, 169
Debt. *See* National debt
Declaration of Independence (1776), A1, 17, 18,
    19–20, 21, 24
  role of religion in, 87
  slavery and, 36, 37
De facto segregation, 469, 471

Defendant, 418
Defense Department
  bureaucratic constraints on, 389–390
  spending by, 238–239, 389–390
  Web site, 401
Deficit reduction, 71, 72
De jure segregation, 469
DeKalb County, Georgia, 471–472
Delaware, 27n, 37, 153, 297
Delegate model, 364
Delegates to nominating conventions, 159–161,
    172–174
  apportioning, 159
  characteristics of, 160(fig.)
  influence of "new," 174
  primaries and, 173
  selection of, 159–161, 186
  voter attitudes and, 172–173, 173(fig.), 174,
    176, 176(fig.)
Democracy, 81
  definitions of, 5–6
  direct. *See* Direct democracy
  distribution of power in, 8–11
  representative. *See* Representative democracy
Democracy in America (de Tocqueville), 80
Democracy Network, 146
Democratic centralism, 5
Democratic National Committee (DNC), 158, 161,
    177, 192
Democratic party, 154–157. *See also* Political par-
    ties
  African Americans in, 205, 206(fig.), 207
  agencies and, 387
  antiwar movement and, 169, 170, 240
  Congress dominated by, 287–289
  donkey as symbol of, 154
  history of, 154–157
  Iowa caucus, 184–185
  modern party structure, 157–161
  national conventions. *See* National nominating
    conventions
  political machine and, 162, 163
  presidential elections and, 200–201,
    200(fig.)
    electoral coalitions, 204–205, 206(fig.),
      207, 207(fig.)
  presidential nominations, 172–173, 183–185
  public rating of, 168, 168(fig.)
  realignments of, 208–211
  reform clubs, 163–164
  reform of, 156–157, 160–161
  selection of judges and, 411, 412(fig.), 413
  sponsored parties, 164–165
  state and local parties, 161–165
  Tammany Hall (New York City), 162, 164
  voters versus, 174, 176, 176(fig.)
Democratic Party v. La Follette (1981), 186
Democratic Republican Voter Education, 237,
    237(fig.)
Democratic Study Group, 296, 305
Denmark, 198(fig.)
Departments. *See specific departments*
Deregulation, 258
Descriptive representation, 292
Desegregation, 225, 467
  integration distinguished from, 469–472
  mandates, 68
  public opinion on, 473–474, 473(fig.)
  social science as support for, 468–469
Detroit, 164–165

Devolution, 50, 70–72, 73
  child welfare spending and, 71, 72(fig.)
  drive for, 71–72
  in the polls, 72, 73(fig.)
Dickerson v. United States (2000), 457
Dickinson, John, 18
Dillon's rule, 58
Direct democracy, 6–8, 59, 319–320, 337
  paricipatory versus, 6–8
Direct-mail solicitations, 157, 158
  by interest groups, 229–230, 231
  role in presidential campaigns, 191
Dirksen, Everett, 475
"Dirty Dozen," in House of Representatives, 235
Disability of president, succession and, 366–367,
    369
Disabled person
  Americans with Disabilities Act (ADA) (1990),
    485, 487
  federal policy on, 486–487
  rights of, 485
Discharge petitions, 315, 316
Discretionary authority, of bureaucracy, 380
Discrimination, 475, 478–479
  Age Discrimination Act, 323
  in education, 475, 476
  in housing, 464–465, 475
  reverse, 482, 484
  sex, 475, 478
Disruptive tactics, of interest groups, 239–240
Dissenting opinions, 422
Distributional formulas, 65–66
Distribution of power, 8–11, 50
  congressional conflict over, 279
District courts, 410(fig.), 411, 416
  jurisdiction of, 414–417
  senatorial courtesy and, 412
Diversity cases, 414
Divided government, 212, 280, 335–337. *See also*
    Policy gridlock
Division (or standing) votes, 318
Dixiecrats, 169, 170, 171
DNC (Democratic National Committee), 158, 161,
    177, 192
Dole, Robert, 115, 137, 182, 184, 187, 486
Dominican Republic, 363, 365
Donkey, 154
Donnelly, Ignatius, 154
"Don't ask, don't tell" policy, 489
Double-tracking, 317
Douglas, Stephen A., 208
Douglass, Frederick, 159
Draft
  laws, 446–447, 448
Dred Scott decision (1857), 407, 427, 429
Drug dealing, 477
Drug Enforcement Administration (DEA), 390
Drug testing, 455–456
Drug trafficking, 390
Dual federalism, 57–58
Dual sovereignty doctrine, 58–59, 415–416
Du Bois, W.E.B., 222, 465
Due process, 451–457
  confessions and self-incrimination, 456–457
  drug and AIDS testing, 455–456
  exclusionary rule, 452, 453, 457
  Miranda rule, 456–457
  search and seizure, 452, 454–455
Due-process clause, 442, 448, 456, 479
Dukakis, Michael, 173, 182, 202, 203, 267, 340

Dunlop, John, 352
Duplication, in bureaucracy, 395, 396, 397

Economic equity. *See* Income equity
Economic individualism, 83, 84(fig.)
Economic inequality, tolerance for, 83
Economic issues
  elections and, 185–187, 201–203, 202,
    203(fig.)
  influence of political elites, 125
  interest groups and, 232–233
  ratings of legislators on, 233, 304
  retrospective voting and, 201–202
Economic policy
  the Fed and, 390
Economic-protest parties, 169, 170
Economic system (economy), 83–84
  comparision with other countries, 85–86
  Constitution and, 38–40
  regulation by Supreme Court, 407–409
Editorials, newspaper, 253, 258, 263
Education. *See also* Schools
  bilingual, 117, 440
  liberalism and, 110–111, 112(fig.), 124
  political attitudes and, 110–111, 112(fig.)
  political participation and, 138–139
Education Department, 376
Education for All Handicapped Children Act
    (1975), 486
EEOC (Equal Employment Opportunity Commis-
    sion), 351, 479
Efficacy, political, 93–94
  changes in sense of, 95(fig.)
Eighth Amendment, 35
EIS (environmental impact statements), 390
Eisenhower, Dwight D.
  books on, 373
  character of, 353
  civil rights policy, 345
  election of, 356
  foreign policy, 365
  illnesses in office, 367
  presidency of, 207, 334, 341, 346, 349, 357
  use of vetoes, 360, 361(fig.)
Elazar, Daniel J., 51, 52
Election 2000, A32, 165, 166, 185, 196–197,
    200, 206–207, 288, 298, 300, 335, 356
Elections, 178–215. *See also* Congressional elec-
    tions; Presidential elections; Primary elec-
    tions; Voting
  campaign and, 203–204
  campaigns. *See* Campaigns
  decline of parties and, 211–212
  economic issues and, 201–203, 203(fig.)
  effects on policy, 212, 214
  electoral coalitions, 204–207
  outcomes of, 207–212, 214
  party identification and, 199–201, 200(fig.)
  party realignments and, 208–211
  trivia about, 185
  types of, 186
  winner-take-all feature, 340
Electoral coalitions, 204–205, 206(fig.), 207
Electoral college, 167, 215, 338, 340–341
Electoral realignments, 208–211
Electorate, 132–137
  realignments of, 208–211
  state and federal control of, 132–135,
    134(fig.)
  voter turnout. *See* Voter turnout

Electronic media, 249–251. *See also* Radio; Televi-
    sion
Electronic town meetings, 249–250
Elephant, 154
Eleventh Amendment, 58–59, 411, 427
Elites, 123, 125. *See also* Political elites
  bias of interest groups and, 230–232,
    230(fig.)
  definition of, 123
  media, 263–264, 264(fig.)
  power, 8–11
Emancipation Proclamation, 343
Emory University Law School, 47
Employment. *See also* Unemployment
  civil rights acts and, 474, 475, 479
  preference systems in, 483
  rights of disabled person, 485
  sex discrimination in, 475, 478
Employment and Training Administration, 376
Endorsements, newspaper, 259–260, 263
England. *See* Great Britain
Enhanced rescission authority, 44. *See also* Line-
    item veto
Entitlements, 70–71. *See also* Medicare; Social
    Security
  block grants for, 70–71
Entrepreneurial politics. *See also* Policy entrepre-
    neurs
  civil liberties and, 437–439
Environmental Action, 226, 235
Environmental Defense Fund, 226, 229, 243
Environmental impact statements (EIS), 390
Environmentalism, 125
Environmental movement, 225, 226, 230, 243
Environmental Protection Agency (EPA), 376,
    386, 393, 418
Equal Employment Opportunity Commission
    (EEOC), 351, 479
Equality, 81, 82
  affirmative action and, 482–485, 488
  Constitution and, 39–40
  economic, attitudes toward, 86, 87(fig.)
Equality of opportunity, 482–485, 488
Equality of results, 481–482
Equal justice principle, 423
Equal Rights Amendment (ERA), 103, 227, 479
Equal time rule, 258
ERA (Equal Rights Amendment), 103, 227, 479
Erikson, Erik, 90
Erznoznik v. Jacksonville (1975), 451, 454
Escobedo case, 456
Espionage Act (1917), 441–442
Espionage and Sedition Acts (1917–1918), 438
"Establishment, the," 9
Establishment clause, 448, 449–451
Ethics
  Congress and, 324–326
  Ethics in Government Act (1978), 238, 239
  ethics violations, 298, 325
Ethics Committee (Senate), 325
Ethics in Government Act (1978), 238, 239
Ethnic minorities. *See also specific minorities*
  party identification and, 116–117, 117(fig.)
  political participation and, 138, 139, 144,
    144(fig.)
  public opinion and, 114–116, 116(fig.),
    117(fig.)
Europe. *See also specific countries*
  campaign fund raising in, 198(fig.)
  government programs in, 376

judicial review in, 428
political attitudes in, 112
political culture of, versus America, 84–88
political efficacy in, 94
political parties in, 151–152, 165, 167
role of religion in, 86–87
voter participation in, 140, 142(fig.), 143–144, 143(fig.)
European Court of Human Rights (Strasbourg, France), 428
Evers, Medgar, 471
Evolution, 450
Exclusionary rule, 452, 453
relaxation of, 457
Executive branch. *See* Cabinet; Presidency; President; Presidential power
Executive departments, 349–350, 349(fig.). *See also* Cabinet; *and specific departments*
Executive Office of the President, 348–349, 365
Executive privilege, 29, 358, 360–362, 395
Ex post facto law, 34
External efficacy, 94

Factional parties, 169, 170
Factions, 30, 104, 152. *See also* Interest groups
ideological, 163
Madison and, 32–33, 88, 218, 320
in political parties, 155–156, 157, 161, 163, 169, 170–171
Fairness doctrine, 258
Fair representation, 290–291, 291(fig.)
Faithless electors, 340, 341
Falwell, Jerry, 230
Family, 90
personal followings and, 165
role of, in formation of political ideology, 106–107
Family Assistance Plan (1969), 118
Farber, Myron, 256
Farm Bureau, 231
Farmers, 153, 209, 378, 393, 428
interest groups of, 218, 219, 220, 223, 231
organizations of, 219, 220, 223, 231
policy-making and, 231
voting records of, 205
Farmers' Union, 219, 233
Farm organizations, 219, 220, 223, 231
Favoritism, 381, 392, 400. *See also* Patronage
FBI (Federal Bureau of Investigation), 376, 401, 418
FDA (Food and Drug Administration), 235, 239, 386
FDIC (Federal Deposit Insurance Corporation), 351, 390
FEA (Federal Energy Administration), 233
Feature stories, 265, 266
FEC (Federal Election Commission), 193, 215
Federal bureaucracy. *See* Bureaucracy
Federal Bureau of Investigation (FBI), 376, 401, 418
Federal Communications Commission (FCC), 190, 233, 253, 256–258, 351, 393, 416
Federal controls, 66–70
conditions of aid, 66, 68–70
mandates, 66–68
Federal courts. *See also* Courts; Supreme Court
control over, 422–428
development of, 405–411
economic issues and, 407–409
getting to court, 417–420

judicial activism of, 404–405, 408, 410–411, 424, 426, 429–430
jurisdiction of, 414–417
policy-making by, 423–424
political liberty and, 409–411
power of, 422–426
public opinion and, 429–430, 430(fig.)
public policy and, 422–426
selecting judges, 411–414
slavery issue and, 405–407
state sovereignty, revival of, 411
structure of, 411–414
Web sites, 431
Federal Deposit Insurance Corporation (FDIC), 351, 390
Federal Election Commission (FEC), 193, 215
Federal Energy Administration (FEA), 233
Federal Energy Regulatory Commission, 351
Federal government. *See also* Congress; Government; House of Representatives; Judiciary; Presidency; President; Senate; Supreme Court
control of electorate, 132–135
restraints on growth of, 500–501
right to issue currency, 56, 61
states versus, 30, 49–51, 54 . *See also* Federalism; Federal-state relations
supremacy of, 405–411
Federal grants. *See* Grants-in-aid
Federal Housing Finance Board, 390
Federal income taxes
Sixteenth Amendment and, 380, 427
Supreme Court, 427
Federalism, 28, 29, 30, 48–77. *See also* Federal-state relations
Congress and, 49–50, 72–75
debate on meaning of, 55–59
definition of, 50
devolution revolution and, 70–72
dual, 57–58
federal aid and federal control, 66–70
founding of, 52–55
"free" money and, 64–66
governmental structure, 50–52
political activity, increase in, 52
pros and cons of, 51–52
Federalism, 496–497, 497
Federalist papers, 32–35
No. 10, A21, 31, 32–33, 218, 320
No. 39, 51
No. 45, 55
No. 46, 53
No. 51, A26, 31, 32, 33–34
No. 78, 405
Federalists, 30, 35, 39, 88, 153, 406. *See also* Jeffersonian Republicans
Federal judges, 68, 333, 412–413, 416, 424
attitudes of, 426
impeachment of, 350, 369, 427
Federal Judicial Center, 431
Federal Maritime Commission, 351
Federal power. *See also* Federalism; *and specific branches, offices, and agencies*
powers of courts, 422–426
Federal-question cases, 414
Federal regime, 51
Federal Regulation of Lobbying Act (1946), 240–241
Federal Reserve System (the "Fed"), 390
Federal-state relations, 30, 49–51, 59–64. *See also* Federalism

categorical grants versus revenue sharing, 62, 64
grants-in-aid, 60–61
intergovernmental lobby, 62
meeting national needs, 61–62, 63(fig.), 64(fig.)
Federal system, 50, 51. *See also* Federalism
Federal Trade Commission (FTC), 239, 351, 386, 388
Federation of Business and Professional Women, 227
FedLaw, 47
Fee shifting, 418
Feminist movement, 226–227, 240, 352, 445, 477, 490
Ferraro, Geraldine, 185
Fifteenth Amendment, 133, 409, 427
Fifth Amendment, 35
Filibusters, 283, 284, 317–318, 329, 475
Finance Committee (Senate), 299, 309
First Amendment, 35, 193–194, 255, 440–443
definition of person, 447–448
definition of speech, 443–447
establishment clause, 448, 449–451
Fourteenth Amendment and, 442, 448, 449
freedom of speech and assembly in, 497
free-exercise clause, 448–449
interest group activities and, 240
interpreting and applying, 440–443
obscenity and, 444–446
prior restraint and, 255, 441, 445
public religious displays and, 440, 450
religion clauses of, 448–451
speech and national security, 441–443
First Great Awakening, 87
First Hoover Commission, 398
First National Bank of Boston, 447
Fitness, rule of, 341
Flag burning, 446–447
Floaters, 136
Floor debates, 309, 316–318
Florida, 21, 291, 291(fig.), 451
Flowers, Gennifer, 269
Food and Drug Administration (FDA), 235, 239, 386
Ford, Gerald R., 185
assassination attempt, 366
audience of, 355
cabinet of, 352
campaign of 1976, 115, 189–190, 261
character of, 354
clumsiness of, 267
pardon of Nixon, 357, 371
school busing and, 470
as vice president, 369
Ford Foundation, 229
Foreign affairs, 11–12, 121, 125, 309, 364
Foreign Investors Act (1966), 316
Foreign Relations Committee (Senate), 299, 309
Forest Service, 235, 394
Fort Dix Military Reservation (New Jersey), 451, 454
Foundations, grants made by, 229
Fourteenth Amendment, 36, 168, 405, 408–409, 427, 442, 501
abortion and, 480–481
black civil rights movement and, 464–465, 468–469
citizenship and, 483
due-process clause, 442, 448, 456, 479

Fourteenth Amendment *(cont.)*
  First Amendment and, 442, 448, 449
  quotas and preference systems and, 83, 121, 470, 482, 483, 485
  reasonableness standard and, 478
  strict scrutiny standard and, 478, 479, 483
  women and, 478
Fourth Amendment, 35
Framers, of Constitution, 23–25
  Congress and, 278, 279
  impeachment and, 370
  on judiciary, 405
  motives of, 38–39
  political parties and, 152–153
  presidency and, 337–338
  public opinion and, 104
France, 22, 23, 50, 51, 438
  campaign fund raising, 198(fig.)
  government programs in, 376
  interest groups in, 219
  judicial review in, 428
  media in, 246, 252
  political attitudes in, 112
  political parties in, 167
Frankfurter, Felix, 423
Franking privileges, 278, 322–323
Franklin, Benjamin, 24, 26, 27
Fraternal Order of the Police, 437
Freebooter, 284
Freedom of expression, 440–441, 442–443, 447, 458
  national security and, 441–443
  testing restrictions on, 442–443, 445
Freedom of Information Act (1966), 246, 390
Freedom of religion, 441, 449
Freedom of speech and assembly, 497
Freedom of the press, 437, 451
Freedom rides, 471, 472
Free-exercise clause, 448–449
Free-Soil party, 170
Free trade, 348
French Revolution (1789), 17
Freneau, Philip, 247
FTC (Federal Trade Commission), 239, 351, 386, 388
Fulton, Robert, 406
Fundamentalism, 91, 108, 108(fig.), 204, 209
Fund for Animals, 235
Fund raising for campaigns. *See* Campaign fund raising

Gag rule, 481
Gaines, Lloyd, 467
Gallatin, Albert, 280
Gallup poll, 100, 127
GAO (General Accounting Office), 311
Gardner, John, 230
Garfield, James A., 366, 367, 383
Garner, John Nance, 366–367
Gatekeeper role, of national press, 253–254
Gay rights, 90–91, 95, 109, 488–489. *See also* Homosexuality
Gays in the military, 489
Gazette of the United States, 247
Gender. *See also* Women
  of congresspersons, 284, 285(fig.)
  female and minority judicial appointments, 413(fig.)
  omitted from Constitution, 40
  political attitudes and, 109–110, 110(fig.)

political participation and, 139
  sexual classification and, 478–479
Gender gap, 109–110, 110(fig.)
General Accounting Office (GAO), 311
General-act charters, 58
General elections, 186
General Motors, 221, 224, 388
General revenue sharing (GRS). See Revenue sharing
George III, King of England, 19, 20
Georgia, 27n, 156, 451, 455, 488
Gephardt, Richard, 181, 182
Germany, 50, 85, 94, 198(fig.), 252, 428, 438
Gerry, Elbridge, 28, 34–35, 39
Gerrymandering, 290, 291, 291(fig.)
Gettysburg Address, 103, 298
Gideon, Clarence Earl, 416, 417
Gingrich, Newt, 201, 282, 300, 301, 307, 329
  ethics violations, 298, 325
Ginsburg, Ruth Bader, 422
Gitlow, Benjamin, 442
Goldwater, Barry, 120–121, 172, 173, 174, 189
Golf courses, 487
Gompers, Samuel, 501
Good-faith exception, 457
Gore, Albert, 367
  campaign of 2000, 173, 182, 183, 185, 187
  "reinventing government," 397
  soft money and, 158–159
Government. *See also* Federal government
  competing interests and, 54–55
  human nature and, 29–30
  political change and, 11–12
  restraints on growth of, 500–501
  theories of, 8–11
Government employee unions, 228(fig.), 229
Government Printing Office, 248
Grace, J. Peter, 396
Grace Commission, 396, 398
Grand Army of the Republic, 220
Grandfather clause, 133
Grange, the, 219
Grants-in-aid, 60–62
  changing purpose of, 63(fig.)
  conditions of aid, 66, 68–70
  for interest groups, 229
  intergovernmental lobbies for, 62, 63(fig.)
  national needs and, 61–62, 63(fig.), 64(fig.)
  slowdown in, 64–66
Grassroots lobbying, 234, 235, 240
Gravel, Mike, 187, 294
Gravel v. United States (1972), 294
Great Britain, 18, 50, 180
  campaign fund raising, 198(fig.)
  free speech and free press and, 441
  interest groups in, 218, 222
  judiciary of, 404
  media in, 246, 252, 262, 266
  Official Secrets Act, 246, 266
  parliamentary system. *See* Parliamentary system
  political attitudes in, 112
  political culture of, 84–85
  political efficacy in, 94
Great (Connecticut) Compromise, 27
Great Depression, 209, 227, 379, 501
Greatest Compromise, 37
"Great Mentioner," 181
"Great Society," 364, 505
Greek city-state, 6, 7

Greenback party, 170
Green party, 177
Greer v. Spock (1976), 451, 454
Groups. *See* Interest groups
Gulf War, 365
Gun control, 235–236, 296, 411
  Brady Bill (1993), 235, 411
  NRA and, 235–236

Haddon, William, Jr., 234–235
Hagen, Michael Gray, 83
Haig, Alexander, 351
Haiti, 365
Haldeman, H. R., 347
Hamilton, Alexander, 5, 32, 280, 340, 347, 349, 352. *See also Federalist* papers
  conflict with Jefferson, 55, 88, 152–153, 247
  on English politics, 18
  on federalism, 32, 35, 53, 55
  on judiciary, 405
  on presidency, 337, 339
  role at Constitutional Convention, 27, 32, 55
  on strong national government, 22, 55
Hammond, Susan Webb, 304–305, 306
Hancock, John, 21, 22
Handgun Control, Inc., 236
Handicapped Children's Protection Act (1986), 67
Handicapped person
  Americans with Disabilities Act (ADA) (1990), 485, 487
  federal policy on, 486–487
  rights of, 485
Harding, Warren G., 163
Harkin, Tom, 182
Harlan, John, 427
Harper's, 249
Harrison, William Henry, 342, 366
Hart, Gary, 255
Harvard College, 110, 124
Harvard Law Review, 421
Hastert, Dennis, 282
Hastings, Alcee, 427
Hatch Act (1939), 162
Hawaii, 224
Hawthorne, Nathaniel, 389
Hayden, Carl, 293
Hayes, Rutherford B., 159, 343
Hazelwood High School, 447
Health and Human Services Department, 376, 401
Health care. *See also* Medicare
  Clinton proposal for, 233, 333–334, 346
Health Care Financing Administration, 376
Hearst, William Randolph, 248
Heclo, Hugh, 393
Heinz, John, III, 251
Helms, Jesse, 230
Henry, Patrick, 18, 24, 35
Henry Wallace Progressive party, 170
Hialeah, Florida, 448
Highway beautification programs, 68
Hill, Anita F., 403
Hiring practices. *See* Affirmative action
Hispanic Americans, 439–440
  bilingual education, 117, 440
  as congresspersons, 284, 285(fig.)
  majority-minority districts and, 291–292, 292(fig.)
  public opinion and, 116–117
  voter participation by, 144, 146, 204

Historical documents, Web sites for, 47
Holmes, Oliver Wendell, 412, 441–442
Homeless, 110, 110(fig.)
Home-rule charters, 58
Homosexuality, 91. *See also* Gay rights
    AIDS and, 125, 455–456
    conflict over, 455, 488–489
    media elite and, 263, 264(fig.)
    in the military, 489
    in the schools, 90–91
"Honeymoon," president and, 357, 372
Hoover, Herbert, 262, 356, 364, 398
Hoover Commissions, 398
Hopwood, Cheryl, 488
Horse-race reporting, 254, 255
Hostage crisis
    in Iran, 357, 363
House of Representatives, 27, 28, 31. *See also*
    Congress
    Appropriations Committee, 393–394
    attitudinal voting in, 295, 296–298
    calendar, 315
    caucuses, 280, 281, 298–306
    committees, 306–309
    comparison with other countries, 277–278
    composition of, 284–289, 285(fig.), 286(fig.),
        287(fig.)
    ethics rules and, 324–326
    evolution of, 279–283
    floor debates, 316–317
    history of, 279–283
    increasing size of, 321
    media and, 262–263
    minorities in, 284, 285(fig.), 291–292,
        477(fig.)
    organization of, 298–311
    party structure in, 300–301
    procedural changes made, 277, 313
    public opinion and, 297, 297(fig.)
    Rules Committee, 280–281, 300, 315–316,
        473, 475
    rules on congressional ethics, 325
    rules on gifts, 325, 348
    salaries and allowances, 326
    Senate compared with, 319
    standing committees of, 306, 308
    strength of party structures in, 301–302
    Un-American Activities Committee, 82–83
    Ways and Means Committee, 309, 314, 327
    Web site, 330
    women in, 284, 285(fig.)
Housing, discrimination in, 464–465, 475
HUD (Department of Housing and Urban Develop-
    ment), 212, 350, 376, 392
Hughes, Charles Evans, 427
Human nature, government and, 29–30
Humphrey, Herbert, 367
Humphrey, Hubert, 165, 169, 173, 189
Hunt, James B., 160
Hunt Commission, 160
Hutchinson v. Proxmire (1979), 294
Hyde, Henry, 481
Hyde Amendment, 481
Hynes v. Mayor and Council of Oradell (1976), 445

ICC (Interstate Commerce Commission), 378, 408
Idaho, 186
Ideological factions, 163
Ideological interest groups, 223
Ideological PACs, 237

Ideological parties, 163–164, 170
Ideology. *See* Political ideology
"I Have a Dream" speech (King, Jr.), 474
Illegal aliens, 484
Illegal discrimination, 478–479
Illinois, 167
Illinois Farm Bureau, 223
Immigration, 126, 439–440, 439(fig.), 440(fig.)
    becoming a citizen, 483
    nativist movements to reduce, 226
Immigration and Naturalization Service (INS),
    484
Immigration Reform and Control Act (1986), 484
Imminent danger, free speech and, 445
Impeachment, 369–371
    of Clinton, 201, 369–370
    of federal judges, 350, 369, 427
    of Nixon, 262, 354, 369
Imperialism, in bureaucracy, 395, 396, 397
Impoundment of funds, 362
"In-and-outers," 351
Incitement, 255, 256, 445
Income equity, 83, 85–86, 86(fig.), 87(fig.)
Income taxes. *See* Federal income taxes
Incumbency, 180
    campaign fund raising and, 192(fig.),
        194–195, 199, 199(fig.), 237–238,
        238(fig.)
    composition of Congress and, 284–288,
        286(fig.), 287(fig.), 289, 292, 293, 320
    economic performance and elections and, 202,
        203(fig.)
    franking privileges and, 278, 322–323
    pocketbook issues and, 197–198
Independent agencies and commissions, 350, 351
Independent counsels, 370
India, 50, 363
Indiana, 83–84, 162, 259, 279, 445
Indiana (party-column) ballot, 212
Indianapolis, Indiana, 445, 470
Indian Territory, 461
Individual contributions, 192, 193
Individualism, 83, 88
Individual responsibility. *See* Personal responsibil-
    ity
In forma pauperis, 417
Initiatives, 59
INS (Immigration and Naturalization Service),
    484
Insider stories, 265, 266
Insider strategy, 233–234
Institutional interests, 221–222
Institutions of government, 273–432. *See also*
    specific institutions
Intellectuals, 110–111
Intent to discriminate, 469, 470
Interest groups, 216–243, 320, 393. *See also* Lob-
    bies
    activities of, 232–240
    biases of, 230–232
    changes in, 503
    comparison with other countries, 218, 219,
        222
    court cases and, 417–418
    dates of founding of organizations having
        Washington offices, 221, 221(fig.)
    definition of, 221
    disruptive tactics by, 239–240
    Federal Regulation of Lobbying Act (1946),
        240–241

    funds for, 229–230
    history of, 219–221
    incentives to join, 223–225
    influence of staff on, 225
    institutional interests of, 221–222
    iron triangles and, 392–393
    legal constraints on, 240–241
    membership interests, 222
    PACs and, 236–238, 237(fig.), 238(fig.)
    president and, 355, 362, 364
    public pressure by, 233–236
    racial politics and, 463
    rankings of members of Congress by, 304
    reasons for proliferation of, 217–219
    regulating, 240–241
    relaxing constraints on federal government
        and, 502
    rise of, 219–221
    social movements and, 225–229
    types of organizations, 221–225
    upper-class bias of, 230–232, 230(fig.)
    Web sites, 243
Intergovernmental lobbies, 62, 63(fig.)
Interior Department, 392
Internal efficacy, 94
Internal Revenue Code, 506
Internal Revenue Service (IRS), 376
Internal Security Act (1950), 438
International Relations Committee (House), 309
Internet, the, 191, 234, 251
    free speech and, 445–446
Interstate commerce, 57–58
Interstate Commerce Commission (ICC), 378, 408
Intrastate commerce, 57–58
Iowa, 156, 185
    caucuses in (February 12), 183, 184–185, 254
Iran, American hostages in, 357, 363
Iran-contra affair, 364
Iraq, 364
Irish-American Gay, Lesbian, and Bisexual Group,
    489
Iron triangles, 392–393
IRS (Internal Revenue Service), 376
Irving, Washington, 389, 397
Israel, 180, 198(fig.)
Issue networks, 393
Issue public, 234
Issues, 201–203. *See also specific issues*
    economic. *See* Economic issues
    interest groups and, 232–240
    media and, 260–261
    pocketbook, 197–198
    position and valence, 186–187
    in presidential elections, 185–187, 201–203
    prospective and retrospective voting, 201–202
Italy, 50, 85, 140, 198(fig.), 219

Jackson, Andrew, 153, 181, 340, 342
    assassination attempt, 366
    attack on Supreme Court, 406, 407
    presidency of, 132, 247, 280, 342, 343
    spoils and, 378
Jackson, Jesse, 161, 170, 173, 229
Jacksonian Democrats, 153–154, 208, 324
Jacksonville, Florida, 451, 454, 483
Jacobson, Gary C., 199, 288
Japan, 84, 198(fig.), 252
Japanese Americans, 117
    internment during World War II, 461
Jay, John, 32

Jefferson, Thomas, 5, 55, 185, 349, 353
    conflict with Hamilton, 55, 88, 152–153, 247
    Constitutional Convention and, 22, 24
    Declaration of Independence and, 18, 19–20, 37
    election of 1800, 89, 340, 406
    on equality, 39–40
    founding of *National Gazette*, 247
    founding of parties, 152–153
    on freedom of religion, 449
    French Revolution and, 438
    Marbury v. Madison (1803), 405, 406–407
    presidency of, 280, 339, 342, 343, 352, 362, 366, 377, 378
    Sedition Act and, 441
    on Shays's Rebellion, 23
    on slave trade, 37
    on states' rights, 55, 57
Jeffersonian Republicans, 152–153, 153n, 208, 406–407, 429
    founding of party, 152
    Marbury v. Madison (1803), 405, 406–407
Jehovah's Witness, 436, 448
Jews (Judaism), 107–108, 205, 210, 437, 439, 440, 448
Jim Crow, 463
John Q. Public, 105
Johnson, Andrew, 185, 280
    impeachment of, 369–370
Johnson, Hiram, 156
Johnson, Lyndon B., 185
    audience of, 355
    books on, 373
    campaigns, 118, 169–170, 189, 205, 271
    character of, 353
    civil rights policy, 474–476
    crises of, 363
    "Great Society," 364, 505
    media and, 271
    "Model Cities" plan (1966), 61
    presidency of, 299, 334, 335, 336, 351, 357, 362, 365, 367
    Vietnam War and, 169–170, 262, 357
Joint Committee on Reorganization, 398
Joint committees, 306
Joint resolutions, 313
Jones, Paula, 361
Jordan, Hamilton, 347
Journalism. *See* Media; Newspapers
Judges. *See also* Courts; Judiciary; Supreme Court
    federal. *See* Federal judges
    selection of, 411–414, 412(fig.)
Judicial activism, 404–405, 408, 410–411, 424, 426, 429–430
Judicial remedies, 423
Judicial review, 28, 403–404, 405, 497
    competing views of, 404
Judiciary, 402–431. *See also* Courts; *and specific courts*
    checks on power of, 426–430
    comparison with other countries, 402–432, 424, 428
    Congress and, 405, 407, 411, 426, 427–429
    federal. *See* Federal courts; Federal judges
    getting to court, 417–420
    public opinion and, 429–430, 430(fig.)
    school prayer issue, 426–427
    Supreme Court. *See* Supreme Court
    Web sites, 431

Judiciary Act (1789), 406, 407
Judiciary Committee (Senate), 314, 317, 473
Justice Department, 241, 390, 413, 490
    Civil Rights Division, 458
Justices of Supreme Court, 404(fig.), 410, 411–414, 420(fig.), 421–422

Kamarck, Elaine, 346
Kansas-Nebraska Act (1854), 284
Kassebaum, Nancy Landon, 293
Keep Commission, 398
Kefauver, Estes, 260, 262
Kemp, Jack, 182
Kennedy, Anthony M., 59, 481
Kennedy, Edward M., 165, 230, 236, 358, 360
Kennedy, John F., 165, 334, 335, 382
    assassination of, 474
    books on, 373
    campaign of 1960, 115, 118, 163, 189, 205, 356
    character of, 353
    civil rights policy, 473
    crises of, 363
    foreign policy, 361, 362, 365
    relations with media, 269, 271, 365
    religion of, 198, 205
Kennedy, Joseph P., II, 165
Kennedy, Robert, 165
Kennedy family, 165
Kentucky, 463
Kentucky Resolution, 57
Kerrey, Bob, 182
Key, V. O., Jr., 113, 201
Kinder, Donald, 83
King, Martin Luther, Jr., 87, 269, 471, 472
    assasination of, 471
    "I Have a Dream" speech, 474
King, Rodney, 415
Kirk, Paul, 161
Kissinger, Henry, 347, 352
Klu Klux Klan, 159, 239, 442–443, 474
"Know-Nothing" (American) party, 170
Koch, Edward, 69, 486
Koppel, Ted, 263
Korean Americans, 117
Korean War, 438, 442
Kraft, Joseph, 105
Kristol, William, 233
K Street (Washington, D. C.), 217
Kunz, Carl Jacob, 437
Kunz v. New York (1951), 445
Kuwait, 364

Labor Department, 376, 378
Labor union movement, 227–229
    decline in membership, 227–228, 228(fig.)
Labor unions, 85, 85(fig.). *See also specific unions*
    as interest groups, 227–229, 228(fig.)
    PACs sponsored by, 237
    political parties and, 164–165, 170
    elections, 193, 194, 205, 207
Labour party, in Britain, 112, 180, 212
La Follette, Robert, 156, 165
La Follette Progressive party, 170
Laissez-faire, 378
Lame duck, 370
Lance, Bert, 363, 509
Land-grant colleges, 60
Land grants, 60
"Larry King Live," 190, 250

Laski, Harold, 51
Latinos. *See* Hispanic Americans
Law. *See also* Bills; Legislation; Legislative process; *and specific laws*
    civil versus criminal, 416
    ex post facto, 34
    sedition, 437–439
Law Enforcement Assistance Act, 64
Lawsuits
    class-action suits, 419–420, 467
    libel, 246, 255–256, 443–444
League of Conservation Voters, 233
League of Women Voters, 146, 223, 226–227, 258
Leaks, in the news, 266–269, 387
Least-restrictive means, free speech and, 445
Lebanon, 363, 365
Legal documents, Web sites for, 47
Legislation. *See also specific laws*
    antitrust, 239, 418
    authorization, 393, 394
    civil rights, 67, 282, 313, 314, 475
    courts and, 426
    policy gridlock, 336–337
    pork-barrel, 322, 323–324
Legislative courts, 411
Legislative process, 311–319
    floor debate, 316–318
    introducing a bill, 312–313
    study by committees, 313–316
    voting methods, 318–319
Legislative Reference Service. *See* Congressional Research Service
Legislative vetoes, 365, 394–395
Legislature. *See* Congress; House of Representatives; Parliamentary system; Senate
Legitimacy, definition of, 5
Levin, Adam K., 259
Lewinsky, Monica, 251, 269
Libel, 246, 255–256, 443–444
Libelous material, 255–256
Liberalism (liberals), 119, 120–122, 122(fig.), 124, 173(fig.)
    of agencies, 386–387
    analyzing consistency in, 122–123
    of college students, 110, 111, 112(fig.)
    education and, 110–111, 112(fig.), 124
    media bias and, 263–264, 263(fig.), 264(fig.)
    presidential appointments and, 386
    in public-interest groups, 223–224, 225, 226, 229, 233, 243
    selection of judges and, 411, 412(fig.), 413
    in Senate, 289, 296–297, 298
    think tanks, 226
    use of term, 118–119
Libertarian party, 163, 170, 177
Libertarians, 123
Liberty, 80, 88, 99. *See also* Civil liberties; First Amendment
    Antifederalist view of, 39
    Constitution and, 30–38
    federalism as protector of, 52–53
    problem of, 17–22
    restrictions during war, 438–439
    Supreme Court, 409–411
Library of Congress, 311, 330
Lilie, Stuart A., 122
Lincoln, Abraham, 339, 342, 343, 345
    assassination of, 366
    coattails and, 181

election of, 163
Gettysburg Address, 103
slavery and, 208
Lincoln Bedroom, 159
Lincoln Memorial, 474
Line-item veto, 43–44, 45, 360, 509–510
Line Item Veto Act of 1996, 43–44
Linmark Associates, Inc. v. Willingboro (1977), 451, 454
Lipset, Seymour Martin, 86–87, 122
Literacy tests, 133, 475
Litmus test, 413–414
Little Rock (Arkansas) Central High School, 345, 462, 468
Liuzzo, Viola, 474
Livermore, Kentucky, 463
Loaded languages, 257
Lobbies, 218, 221. *See also* Interest groups
activities of, 232–240
definition of, 218
Federal Regulation of Lobbying Act (1946), 240–241
intergovernmental, 62, 63(fig.)
legal constraints on, 240–241
Lobbyists, 218, 232–233
insider strategy of, 233–234
Local governance, terms of, 58
Local political parties. *See* State and local political parties
Locke, John, 25
Long, Huey, 171
Long family, 165
Los Angeles, 163, 290, 471
Los Angeles Times, 127
Lowi, Theodore, 37
Low-income families
aid to, 60, 62, 70
voting record of, 205, 206(fig.)
Lynchings, of blacks, 463, 472

McAdams, John, 124
McCain, John, 173, 195, 251, 254–255
McCardle, 428
McCarthy, Eugene, 255
McCarthy, Joseph R., 438
McCarthyism, 438
McClosky, Herbert, 95, 96, 122
McClure's, 249
McCulloch, James, 56
McCulloch v. Maryland (1819), 56, 405
McGovern, George, 134, 159, 185, 189, 255
McKinley, William, 209, 248, 345, 366
McLaurin, George, 467
McNamara, Robert S., 361
Maddox, William S., 122
Madison, James, 25, 36, 153, 280, 293
creation of State Department, 377
on equality, 39–40
on factions, 30, 32–33, 88, 218, 320
Federalist papers, 25, 31, 32–34, 51, 52, 55, 218, 320
Marbury v. Madison (1803), 405, 406–407
on nullification, 57
on public interest, 320
role at Constitutional Convention, 22, 23, 25, 27, 30, 31, 35
on self-interest, 30
Magaziner, Ira, 346
Magazines, 249, 253, 265–266. *See also* Newspapers

Maine, 140
Maine, USS, 248
Majoritarian politics, 8
civil rights and, 463
Majority leaders, congressional, 299, 300, 301, 316
Majority-minority districts, 291–292, 292(fig.)
Majority rule, 25, 28, 166–167
Malapportionment, 290, 291, 291(fig.), 419
Manchester, New Hampshire, 252
Manchester Union Leader, 252
Mandates, 66–68
major enactments regulating state and local governments, 67, 67(fig.)
Mansbridge, Jane, 227
Mansfield, Mike, 299
Mapp, Dollree, 452
Mapp v. Ohio (1961), 452
Marbury, William, 406
Marbury v. Madison (1803), 405, 406–407
"March on Washington" (Aug. 28 1963), 471, 474
Marcy, William, 509
Marginal districts, 286, 296
Markets, television, 259
Marshall, John, 56, 405–407, 429
Marshall, Thurgood, 427, 429
Marshall Plan, 336
Marx, Karl, 8–9, 10
Marxists, 8–9
Maryland, 27n, 56
Mason, George, 5, 28, 37, 39
Massachusetts, 22, 23, 27n, 35, 37, 68, 142–143, 185, 203
Massachusetts (office-bloc) ballots, 212
Massachusetts Citizens for Life, 447
Matching funds, 62–63, 64, 183, 192, 193, 242
Material incentives, 223
Mayhew, David, 165, 336
Mecklenburg County, North Carolina, 469–470
Media, 244–273. *See also* Electronic media; *and specific media*
bias in, 257, 263–266, 263(fig.), 264(fig.)
comparison with other countries, 246, 252
confidentiality of sources and, 256
Congress and, 262–263, 271
effects on politics, 259–261
as gatekeepers, 253–254
government constraints on journalists, 271
interest groups and, 235–236
interpreting news stories, 263–271, 263(fig.), 264(fig.), 268(fig.)
journalism. *See* Newspapers
presidency and, 261–262, 271
prior restraint and, 255, 441, 445
public view of, 263, 263(fig.), 268(fig.)
rules governing, 246, 255–259
as scorekeepers, 254–255
sensationalism in, 269, 271
structure of, 251–255
as watchdogs, 255
Web sites, 272
Medicaid, 71–72, 212
AFDC compared with, 71, 72
devolution and, 70, 72, 73(fig.)
reform of, 71
Medicare, 313
Membership interests, 222
Mencken, H. L., 255
Meredith, James, 471

Merit-based appointment system, 381, 382, 383
Merit Systems Protection Board (MSPB), 385
Meskimen's law, 392
Mexican Americans, 117, 204, 205, 462
Mexican War, 343
Mexico, 12, 85, 88(fig.)
Miami Herald, 255
Miami Herald Publishing Co. v. Tornillo (1974), 451, 454
Michigan, 156, 173, 186, 296
Micromanagement, 400
Middle America, 105
Middle class, 90, 124–125
Mikulski, Barbara, 159, 164
Miles, Rufus, 509
Military
homosexuals in the, 489
Military policy
on homosexuality, 489
War Powers Act, 329
Military Reform Caucus, 306
Militias, 60
Mills, C. Wright, 9
Minnesota, 140, 163, 175, 186, 443
Minority leaders, congressional, 299, 300, 301, 316
Minor parties, 169–171
types of, 170
Minstrel shows, 463
Miranda, Ernesto A., 456–457
Miranda rule, 456–457
Mississippi, 134, 427
Missouri, 167, 467
Missouri Compromise, 407
Mistrust, of government, 92–93, 93(fig.), 94(fig.)
"Model Cities" plan (1966), 61
Mondale, Walter, 110, 160, 182, 189, 367
Monetary Control Bill of 1983, 104–105
Money raising for campaigns. *See* Campaign fund raising
Monroe, James, 153, 280, 293, 339, 353
Montana, 186
Montgomery, Alabama, 471, 472
Morality, 91, 97(fig.)
Moral Majority, 88, 109, 230
Mormon Church, 448
Morris, Gouverneur, 338
Morris, Robert, 27, 39
Motor-voter law, 130
Moynihan, Daniel Patrick, 275, 299, 325–326, 352
MSPB (Merit Systems Protection Board), 385
Muckrakers, 248, 249
Mugwumps, 155–157, 171
Multi-party systems, 165
Multiple referrals, 314–315, 329
Municipal corporations (municipalities), 58
Murphy's law, 392
Muskie, Edmund, 61, 234, 255

NAACP. *See* National Association for the Advancement of Colored People
Nader, Ralph, 219, 224, 234–235, 384, 393, 505
Name recognition, 199
Name-request jobs, 383, 385
NARAL (National Abortion Rights Action League), 227
Nast, Thomas, 154
Nathan, Richard P., 70, 72

Nation, 249
National Abortion Rights Action League
  (NARAL), 227
National Alliance of Business, 229
National Association for the Advancement of Col-
  ored People (NAACP), 219, 220, 222, 223,
  233
  formation of, 465
  organization of civil rights cases, 418, 419,
    465–466, 467–472
  tax exempt status of, 241
  Web site, 243
  Web sites, 490
National Association of Counties, 221, 222
National Association of Manufacturers, 219
National banks, 56
National Blind Golfers Association, 487
National Catholic Welfare Conference, 219
National chairmans, 157
National committees, 157, 159
National Constitution Center, 47
National Council of La Raza, 490
National Council of the Churches of Christ (NCC),
  225
National Council on Disability, 486–487
National debt, 61
National Education Association (NEA), 165
National Endowment for the Arts, 91
National Environmental Policy Act (1969), 390
National Federation of Republican Women, 227
National Gay and Lesbian Task Force, 490
National Gazette, 247
National government. *See* Federal government;
  Government
National Governors' Association, 77
National Guard, 468
National Highway Traffic Safety Administration,
  235
National Independent Retail Jewelers, 221
National Intelligencer, 247
National Labor Relations Board (NLRB), 351
National Legal Center for the Public Interest, 229
National Mail Voter Registration Form, 146
National nominating conventions, 157,
    159–161, 172–174, 186
  controlling, 183
  delegates to. *See* Delegates to nominating con-
    ventions
  effects of television on, 260
  government funds for, 192
  origin of, 154, 280, 305
National Organization for Women (NOW), 165,
  227, 243, 490
National Performance Review (NPR), 397–398,
  400, 401
National press, 253–255
  as gatekeepers, 253–254
  as scorekeepers, 254–255
  as watchdogs, 255
National Resources Defense Council, 243
National Rifle Association (NRA), 235–236
National Science Foundation, 351
National Wildlife Federation, 226
National Women's Political Caucus, 227
Federal-state relations. *See* Nation-state relation-
  ship
Native Americans, 159, 448, 461
  as senators and representatives, 284, 285(fig.)
Nativist movements, 226
Naturalization requirements, 483

Natural rights, 18, 25
NBC, 250
NCC (National Council of the Churches of Christ),
  225
NEA (National Education Association), 165
Near v. Minnesota (1931), 445
NEAs (noncareer executive assignments), 382
Nebraska Press Association v. Stuart (1976), 445
"Necessary and proper" clause, 56, 278, 405
Negative advertising, 213, 268, 269
Neshoba County, Mississippi, 462, 471, 474
Netherlands, the, 85, 94, 180
Neustadt, Richard, 351, 355, 372n
Neutrality, free speech and, 445
"New class," 124–125
New Deal, 5, 209, 212, 409, 505
New Hampshire, 27n, 35
  primary (February 20), 183, 254–255
New Haven, Connecticut, 260
New Jersey, 27n, 235, 451
New Jersey Plan, 26, 30n
New Kent County, Virginia, 469
News, 263–271, 263(fig.), 264(fig.), 268(fig.).
    See also Media; *and specifc media*
  leaks, 266–269
  sensationalism in, 269, 271
  slanted stories, 264–266
Newspapers, 246–251. *See also specific newspapers*
  competition between, 252–253
  confidentiality of sources and, 256
  controlled by political parties, 246–247
  effects on politics, 259–260
  as gatekeepers, 253–254
  government constraints on journalists, 271
  interest groups and, 235–236
  national press, 253–255
  popular press, 247–249
  prior restraint and, 255, 441, 445
  reading intelligently, tips on, 257
  rules governing, 255–259
  as scorekeepers, 254–255
  as watchdogs, 255
  Web sites, 272
New System, for public policy, 502–506
New York City, 21, 32, 35, 163–164, 437
  majority-minority districts, 291
  proportional representation in, 167
  Tammany Hall, 162
New York City Fire Department, 487
New York Customhouse, 162
New York State, 27n, 32, 35, 185, 204, 297, 480
New York Times, 253, 254, 255, 256, 265, 266,
  272
Nicaragua, 364
Nie, Norman, 137, 138
Nineteenth Amendment, 40, 134
Ninth Amendment, 35
Nixon, Richard
  books on, 373
  campaigns, 115, 134, 169, 185, 186, 189, 200
  character of, 353–354
  crises of, 363
  Ford pardon of, 357, 371
  foreign policy, 365
  impeachment of, 262, 354, 369
  media and, 271
  on "new federalism," 69
  presidency of, 334, 347, 352, 356, 362, 369,
    379
  school busing and, 470

  Supreme Court appointments, 412, 429
  United States v. Nixon (1973), 361
  Watergate scandal, 92, 192, 269, 354, 357,
    361, 363, 429
Nixon, Walter, 427
NLRB (National Labor Relations Board), 351
Nofziger, Lyn, 238
Nomenklatura, 123
Nominating conventions. *See* National nominat-
  ing conventions
Noncareer executive assignments (NEAs), 382
Nonviolent civil disobedience, 472
Nonvoting, 129–131, 130(fig.), 131(fig.)
  causes of, 138–141
  fining nonvoters, 145
Norms, 125
North, Oliver, 347
North Carolina, 27n, 31, 260, 469
  majority-minority districts, 291, 292(fig.)
North Carolina Agricultural and Technical Col-
  lege, 471
North Dakota, 130, 186
North Korea, 364
NOW (National Organization for Women), 165,
  227, 243, 490
NPR (National Performance Review), 397–398,
  400, 401
NRA (National Rifle Association), 235–236
Nullification, 57

Obscenity, 255, 444–446
Occupation
  voting and, 112, 143–144, 143(fig.), 205,
    206(fig.)
Occupational Safety and Health Administration
  (OSHA), 376, 393
Ocean Dumping Ban Act (1988), 67
O'Connor, Sandra Day, 427, 429, 481
Office-bloc (Massachusetts) ballots, 212
Office of Compliance, 323
Office of Management and Budget (OMB),
  348–349, 387
Office of Personnel Management (OPM), 348,
  381–382
Office of Special Counsel, 388
Office of Technology Assessment (OTA), 311
Office of the President, 334–335, 345–350. *See
  also* White House Office
  cabinet, 334–335, 349–350, 349(fig.)
  Executive Office, 348–349, 365
  organization of, 346–347
Official Secrets Act (England), 246, 266
"Off the record," 267
Ohio, 156, 168
Oklahoma, 305, 322, 467
"Old boys" network, 384
Old System, for public policy, 502–506
OMB (Office of Management and Budget),
  348–349, 387
O'Neill, Thomas P. ("Tip"), 294, 300, 329
One-issue parties, 170
"On the record," 267
Open Meeting Law (1976), 390
Open primaries, 186
Open rules, 315
Operational grants, 70–71
Opinion, public. *See* Public opinion
Opinion of the Court, 422
OPM (Office of Personnel Management), 348,
  381–382

Ordinances, 58
Oregon, 140, 229
Organizational voting, 295, 296
Orthodox views, 91, 482
OSHA (Occupational Safety and Health Administration), 376, 393
OTA (Office of Technology Assessment), 311
Otis, James, 37
O'Toole's Corollary to Murphy's Law, 392
Outsider strategy, 234

Pacific Gas and Electric Company, 447
Packwood, Robert, 325
PACs. *See* Political action committees
Paine, Thomas, 23
Pakistan, 363
Palmer, A. Mitchell, 438
Panama Canal treaties (1978), 235, 262
Panetta, Leon E., 346
Parent Teacher Association (PTA), 223
Parkinson's laws, 392
Parks, Rosa, 472, 473
Parliamentary system, 42, 143, 275–276
    bureaucracy compared with, 376, 400
    cabinet officers in, 276, 335, 351
    Congress compared with, 275–276, 277, 278, 279, 304, 324
    effect of elections on, 212
    judiciary and, 404
    legislature in, 29
    lobbies and, 218
    policy gridlock and, 336
    prime minister in, 42, 152, 167, 179, 180, 334–335
Parochial participants, 138
Parochial schools, public aid to, 419, 437, 449, 450
Participation, in politics. *See* Activism; Political participation; Voting
Participatory democracy. *See* Direct democracy
Party affiliations, Congress and, 287–289, 288(fig.)
Party caucuses. *See* Caucuses
Party-column (Indiana) ballots, 212
Party conventions. *See* National nominating conventions
Party identification, 106–110, 150, 151
    decline in, 150(fig.), 151, 211–212
    family role and, 106–107, 106(fig.)
    formation of, 106–108, 109–110
    gender and, 109, 109(fig.)
    in presidential elections, 199–201, 200(fig.), electoral coalitions, 204–205, 206(fig.), 207
    race and ethnicity and, 116–117, 117(fig.)
    region and, 117, 118, 118(fig.)
Party polarization, 302–304, 303(fig.)
Party symbols, 154
Party unity, 302–304
Paterson, William, 26
Patriotism, 85, 86(fig.)
Patronage, 155, 162, 164, 378, 381, 382–383. *See also* Spoils system
Paw Paw, West Virginia, 65
Pawtucket, Rhode Island, 450
Peckham, Rufus, 405
Pendleton Act (1883), 383
Pennsylvania, 22, 23, 25, 27n, 35, 37, 155, 290, 481
Pension Office, 378

Pentagon Papers, 255, 294, 437
Penthouse (magazine), 443
Per curiam opinions, 422
Perks, 322, 348
Perot, Ross, 115, 168, 171, 175, 190, 202, 336
Persian Gulf War, 365
Person, definition of, 447–448
Personal conduct, 122, 123
Personal followings, 165
Personal responsibility, 81, 83
Personal Responsibility and Work Opportunity Reconciliation Act (1996). *See* Welfare Reform Act
Peter Principle, 392
Peterson, Mark A., 343
Pilgrim's Progress (Bunyan), 248
Pitkin, Hannah F., 292
Plaintiff, 418
Planned Parenthood v. Casey (1992), 480, 481
Plessy, Adolph, 465
Plessy v. Ferguson (1896), 465, 467
Pluralist theory, 10
Plurality system, 166–167
Pocketbook issues, 197–198
Pocket veto, 358, 360, 361(fig.)
Poindexter, John, 347
Poland, 22, 189, 339, 363
Police
    due process and, 451–457
    exclusionary rule, 452
    Fraternal Order of the Police, 437
    Miranda rule, 456–457
    protections against, 35, 415
    search and seizure, 452, 454–455
    Supreme Court rulings, 256
Police powers, 59, 437
Policy. *See also* Policy-making process
    economic. *See* Economic policy
    effects of elections on, 212, 214
    federal courts and, 422–426
    military. *See* Military policy
    political elites and, 125
Policy Committees, congressional, 299, 300
Policy entrepreneurs. *See also* Entrepreneurial politics
    civil liberties and, 437–439
Policy gridlock, 336–337
Policy-making process, 496–511
    changing the system for, 506–511
    constitutional provisions effect on, 496–497
    deregulation and, 258
    increasing barriers to action, 508–510
    Old System versus New System, 502–506
    reducing barriers to action, 506–508
    relaxing the restraints on, 501–506
Polis, 6, 7
Political action committees (PACs), 182, 192, 193, 194–195, 195(fig.), 325, 502
    ideological, rise of, 237
    interest groups and, 236–238, 237(fig.), 238(fig.)
    spending by, 237, 237(fig.), 238(fig.)
Political associations. *See* Interest groups
Political attitudes, 106–112
    education and, 110–111, 112(fig.)
    family and, 106–107, 106(fig.)
    gender and, 109–110, 109(fig.), 110(fig.)
    origins of, 106–111
    religion and, 107–109, 108(fig.)
Political change, 11–12

Political cues, 233
Political culture, 78–100, 152
    civil liberties and, 436–440
    comparision with other countries, 84–88, 85(fig.), 86(fig.), 87(fig.)
    cultural conflict and, 90–92
    definition of, 80, 81
    economic system and, 83–84, 84(fig.)
    mistrust of government, 92–93, 93(fig.), 94(fig.)
    political efficacy and, 93–94, 95(fig.)
    political systems, 80–83
    political tolerance in, 94–99, 96(fig.), 97(fig.), 99(fig.)
    religion and, 86–88, 87(fig.), 88(fig.)
    sources of, 88–92
Political editorializing rule, 258
Political efficacy, 93–94
    changes in sense of, 94, 95(fig.)
Political elites, 8, 123–124. *See also* Activism
    bias of interest groups and, 230–232, 230(fig.)
    explanatory theories, 8–11
    ideology of, 123–125
    media and, 263–264, 264(fig.)
    as "new class," 124–125
    public policy and, 125
    relaxing constraints on federal government and, 501–502
Political ideology, 81, 118–125, 120(fig.)
    of agencies, 386–387
    analyzing consistency in, 122–123
    civil rights and, 121–122
    consistent attitudes and, 120
    definition of, 81, 119
    liberalism and conservatism, 120–121
    members of Congress and, 296–298
    of political elites, 123–125
    role of family in, 106–107
    selection of judges and, 411–412, 412(fig.), 413
    welfare and, 120–121
Political liberties, 409–411
Political machines, 161–163
Political movements. *See* Social movements
Political participation, 128–147, 142(fig.). *See also* Activism; Voting
    causes of, 138–141, 139(fig.)
    forms of, 137–138, 138(fig.)
    meaning of participation rates, 141–146, 142(fig.), 144(fig.)
    nonvoting and, 129–131
    rise of the American electorate and, 132–137
Political parties, 75, 148–177, 328. *See also* Party identification; *specific parties*
    changes in, 503
    comparison with other countries, 151–152, 167
    Congress and, 298–306
        caucuses, 304–306, 306(fig.)
        composition of members, 287–289, 288(fig.)
        House of Representatives, 300–301
        party polarization, 302–304, 303(fig.)
        Senate, 298–300
        strength of parties, 301–302
        unity of parties, 302–304
    convention delegates. *See* Delegates to nominating conventions
    definition of, 150

Political parties *(cont.)*
  effects of Civil War on, 154–156
  factions in, 155–156, 157, 161, 163, 169, 170–171
  founding of, 152–153
  history of, 152–157
  ideological factions in, 163–164, 170
  Jacksonian Democrats, 153–154, 208, 324
  minor (third), 169–171
  modern party structure, 157–161
  national conventions. *See* National nominating conventions
  newspapers controlled by, 246–247
  organization of, 161–165
  platforms, 214
  political culture of, 152
  presidential nominations, 172–174, 183–185
  primaries. *See* Primary elections
  realignments, 208–211
  reform of, 156–157, 160–161
  rise and decline of, 152–157, 211–212, 218
  selection of judges and, 411, 412(fig.), 413
  state and local. *See* State and local political parties
  symbols of, 154
  trivia about, 159
  two-party system, 165–168
  voters versus, 174, 176, 176(fig.)
Political party machine, 161–163
Political power. *See also* Presidential power; *and specific powers and kinds of power*
  checks on judiciary power, 426–430
  definition of, 4–5
  distribution of. *See* Distribution of power
  of federal courts, 422–426
  pluralist theory of, 10
Political proverbs, 509
Political questions, 423
Political subculture, 81
Political systems, 80–83
  comparison with other countries, 84–85
Political tolerance, 94–99, 96(fig.), 97(fig.), 99(fig.)
Politics
  civil liberties and, 436–440
  client. *See* Client politics
  entrepreneurial. *See* Entrepreneurial politics
  interest group. *See* Interest groups
  majoritarian. *See* Majoritarian politics
Polk, James K., 342
Polling organizations, Web sites for, 100, 127
Polls. *See* Public opinion polls
Poll taxes, 133
Polygamy, 448
Popular press, 247–249
Popular rule, 28, 104
Popular votes, 167
Populist party, 123, 170
Pork barrel, 323
Pork-barrel legislation, 322, 323–324
Pornography, 444–446
Position issues, 185
Postal Service, 376, 382
Post Office Department, 377
Poverty. *See* Low-income families
Power. *See also* Political power; Presidential power
  bureaucratic, 381, 386, 387–389
  of Congress, 380–381
  definition of, 4
  distribution of. *See* Distribution of power

federal. *See* Federal power
  of federal courts, 422–426
  in unitary systems, 50, 51–52
  veto power. *See* Veto power
Power Elite, The (Mills), 9
Power elites, 9
Prayer
  in Congress, 450
  in public schools, 426–427, 450
Preamble to the Constitution, 104
Precedents, 423
Preferential treatment, 83, 482, 485, 488
Preferred position, free speech and, 445
Presidency, 332–373. *See also* Office of the President; President; *and specific presidents*
  appointive powers of. *See* Appointments, presidential
  changes in, 503
  comparison with other countries, 334–335
  concerns of Founders about, 337–338
  divided government and, 212, 280, 335–337
  electoral college and, 167, 215, 338, 340–341
  evolution of, 337–344
  executive privilege, 29, 358, 360–362, 395
  history of, 337–344
  impeachment, 369–371
  peaceful transitions, 365–371
  persuasive powers of, 354–358
  powers of. *See* Presidential power
  succession and, 366–367, 369
  term of office issue, 338–339, 365, 368
  two-party system and, 165–168
  veto. *See* Veto power
President, 27, 28, 31. *See also* Office of the President; Presidency; *and specific presidents*
  access to, 348
  agenda of, 362–365
  appointments by. *See* Appointments, presidential
  audiences, 355–356
  character of, 353–354
  checks and balances and, 29
  as commander in chief, 344, 405
  Congress and, A30, 305, 313, 338, 355–357, 356(fig.), 360, 362, 400
  constraints on policy, 362–364
  crises of, 363–364
  executive privilege, 29, 358, 360–362, 395
  impoundment of funds by, 362
  interest groups and, 355, 362, 364
  legislative process and, 313, 343–344
  media and, 261–262, 271
  nomination of, 172–174, 183–184
  persuasive powers of, 354–358
  popularity and influence of, 261, 300, 356–358, 358(fig.), 371
  programs of, 362–365
  qualifications and benefits, 345
  reorganization by, 364–365
  restraints on, 499–500
  signature or veto of bills. *See* Veto power
  succession problems, 367, 369
  Supreme Court nominations by, 412, 413–414
  trivia about, 353
  Web sites about, 372
Presidential campaigns, 180–199, 203–207
  campaign issues, 185–187
  congressional versus, 180–183
  debates, 189–191, 258
  direct-mail solicitations, 157, 158, 191
  fund raising for. *See* Campaign fund raising

getting "mentioned," 181–182
  money for, 182, 183, 191–199. *See also* Campaign fund raising
  organizations for, 182, 183
  primary versus general, 183–191
  role of media in, 187–191, 258–259
  slips of the tongue in, 189–190
  strategy and themes, 182–183
  tone, timing, and targets of, 182–183
Presidential elections, 199–207
  of 1800, 208
  of 1828, 208
  of 1860, 208–209, 212
  of 1896, 207, 208, 209, 212
  of 1912, 207
  of 1916, 207
  of 1932, 207, 208, 209–210, 211, 212
  of 1952, 207
  of 1964, 212, 474
  of 1980, 210, 212, 214
  of 1984, 210
  of 1992, 267
  of 1998, 237
  of 2000, 185, 196–197
  debates, 189–191, 258
  deciding factors in, 199–203
  economy as issue in, 201–203, 203(fig.)
  effects of media on, 187–191, 259–261
  effects on policy, 212, 214
  electoral coalitions, 204–205, 206(fig.), 207
  electoral realignments following, 208–211
  issues and, 201–203
  money and winning, 196–198
  outcome of, 207–212
  partisan gains or losses in Congress during, 350(fig.), 356(fig.)
  party identification and, 199–201, 200(fig.)
  party voting in, 167–168, 167(fig.)
  popular vote, trend in, 207, 207(fig.)
  voter participation in, 135–137, 135(fig.), 139(fig.)
Presidential nominations. *See* Delegates to nominating conventions; National nominating conventions
Presidential power, 344–345, 358–362
  appointive. *See* Appointments, presidential
  under Constitution, 358
  executive privilege, 29, 358, 360–362, 395
  impoundment of funds, 362
  persuasion and, 354–358
  veto power. *See* Veto power
  War Powers Act (1973), 329
Presidential Power (Neustadt), 355
Presidential primary. *See* Primary elections
President pro tempore of the Senate, 298–299, 367, 369
President's Commission on Administrative Management, 347, 398
President's Commission on Economy and Efficiency, 398
Press, the. *See* Magazines; Newspapers
Press secretary, 262
Primary elections, 173, 174, 183–191
  of 1972, 185
  of 2000, 185, 195
  caucuses versus, 173
  congressional, 292–295
  list of key, 183
  money for, 192, 193
  types of, 186

Prime minister, in parliamentary system, 42, 152, 167, 179, 180, 334–335
Print media. *See* Magazines; Newspapers
Printz v. United States (1997), 58
Prior restraint, 255, 441, 445
Privacy Act (1974), 390
Private bills, 313
Privileged speech doctrine, 294
Probable cause, 452, 454–455
Professional societies, 220
Progressive ("Bull Moose") party, 170
Progressives, 155–157, 212
Progressive views, 91
Prohibition party, 170, 171
Project Vote Smart, 215
Pro-life movement, 163, 227, 480–481
Property rights, 18, 19, 33, 407–408, 445
Proportional representation, 167
Proposition 13 (California), 6
Prospective voting, 201–202
Prostitution, 59
Protestants (Protestant Church), 89–90, 91, 107–108, 117–118, 225, 437, 439
Protest marches, 141–142, 239–240
Proverbs, political, 509
Proxmire, William, 294
Public accommodations, civil rights and, 464–465, 475, 485
Public bills, 313
Public Citizen, 224
Public figures, libel and, 256, 443–444
Public financial disclosure report, 239
Public interest, 12, 320
Public-interest groups. *See* Interest groups
Public-interest law firms, 225
Public-interest lobbies, 223–225
Public Interest Research Groups (PIRGs), 224
Public opinion, 102–127. *See also* Political ideology
  on civil rights, 472, 473–474, 473(fig.)
  cleavages in, 112–118
  congressional voting and, 295–296, 297, 297(fig.)
  courts and, 429–430
  definitions of, 104–106
  formation of, 106–112
  government and the news, 261–263
  origins of political attitudes and, 106–112
  political elites and public policy and, 125–126
  relaxing constraints on federal government and, 501
Public opinion polls, 81, 95, 104–105, 114–115, 234, 364
  designing and interpreting, key criteria for, 114–115
  by president, 364
  RNC money for, 158
  on the Supreme Court, 429, 430(fig.)
  Web sites, 100, 127
Public policy. *See also* Policy; Policy-making process; *and specific policies and kinds of policy*
  changes in system, 499–500
  changing the system for, 506–511
  constitutional provisions effect on, 496–497
  increasing barriers to action, 508–510
  Old System versus New System, 502–506
  reducing barriers to action, 506–508
  relaxing the restraints on, 501–506
  restraints on, 500–501
  reviews of, Web sites, 511

Public pressure, by interest groups, 233–236
Public religious displays, 440, 450
Public schools. *See* Schools
Pulitzer, Joseph, 248
Pure conservatives, 122–123
Pure liberals, 122
Puritanism, 89
Purposive incentives, 223, 224, 225, 226, 227
PUSH, 229
Pyramid structure, of White House Office, 346

Quasi-independent agencies, 350, 351
Quorum, 316–317
Quorum call, 317
Quotas, discrimination and, 83, 121, 470, 482, 483, 485

Raab, Earl, 122
Race
  Congress and, 284, 285(fig.), 291
  judicial appointments and, 413(fig.)
  majority-minority districts and, 291–292, 292(fig.)
  minority employment in the Federal bureaucracy, 386, 388(fig.)
  party identification and, 116–117, 117(fig.)
  political participation and, 138, 139, 144, 144(fig.)
  public opinion and, 114–116, 116n, 117(fig.)
  voting rights and, 132–134, 134(fig.)
Racial discrimination, 475. *See also Brown v. Board of Education*; Desegregation; Segregation
  black colleges and, 466
  intent to discriminate, 469, 470
  majority-minority districts and, 291–292, 292(fig.)
  reverse discrimination and, 482, 484
  separate-but-equal doctrine, 465, 467–472
Racism, 51, 83, 125, 463
"Radical Republicans," 280, 370
Radio, 246, 249–250
  competition between stations, 252
  deregulation of, 258
  regulation of, 256–258
Rainey, Joseph H., 293
Randolph, Edmund, 25, 27, 337
Random sample polls, 114
Rangel, Charles, 237
Rankin, Jeannette, 293
Rather, Dan, 263
Ratification of Constitution, 30–31, 32, 34, 35–36
Ratings of legislators, 233, 304
Rayburn, Sam, 300, 304
Reagan, Ronald, 185, 353, 505
  abortion and, 481
  affirmative action, 482
  AIDS and, 455
  appointments, 238, 351, 386, 393
  assassination attempt, 235, 366, 367
  attempt to abolish SBA, 392
  block grants, 69–70, 71
  books on, 373
  campaigns, 182, 183, 189, 190, 258
  character of, 354
  civil rights policy, 476
  congressional elections of 1986, 356, 357
  crises of, 363–364
  drug testing and, 455

  election of 1980, 92, 112, 115, 151, 189, 190, 202, 210, 211, 258
  election of 1984, 110, 112, 186, 200, 202
  foreign policy, 365
  judicial appointments, 333, 413, 414, 420(fig.), 427, 429
  political ideology and, 122, 123
  popularity of, 357, 358(fig.)
  presidency of, 297, 334, 346, 347, 351, 363, 429–430
  school busing and, 470
  Stockman and, 387
  trust for, 93
  use of vetoes, 360, 361(fig.)
Reagan administration, 505
  block grants, 69–70, 71
  disability rights, 486–487
  efforts to cut federal power, 11, 69–70, 212, 229
  opposition to mandates, 67
  personal income and, 113
  polls of, 158
  scandals of, 203, 269, 363
  Supreme Court nominations by, 414, 427, 429
Realigning periods, 208
Reapportionment, 290–291, 291(fig.)
Reasonable expectation of privacy, 455
Reasonableness standard, 478
Recalls, 59
Recession, 202, 500
Reconstruction, 343, 366, 428
Redistricting, 290–292, 291(fig.)
Red Scare, 438, 442
Red tape, 395, 396–397, 398
Reed, Ralph, 109
Reed, Thomas B., 280–381, 307
Referendum, 6, 59, 156
Referrals
  multiple, 314–315, 329
  sequential, 315
Reform clubs, 163–164
Reform party, 170, 171, 177
Regan, Donald, 347
Region, public opinion by, 117–118, 118(fig.), 119(fig.)
Registered voters, 130, 139–140
Regulatory agencies, 378–380
  "revolving door" in, 238–239
Rehabilitation Act (1973), 396, 486–487
Rehnquist, William, 58, 404, 414, 420, 429
Religion, 198
  belief in America and Europe, 87, 87(fig.)
  civil liberties and, 448–451
  comparison with other countries, 87, 87(fig.)
  culture war and, 90–91
  diversity in, 89–90
  establishment clause, 448, 449–451
  First Amendment clauses and, 448–451
  First Great Awakening, 87
  free-exercise clause, 448–449
  in industrial nations, 87, 88(fig.)
  political attitudes and, 107–109
  political participation and, 139
  public religious displays, 440, 450
  role of, 86–87, 87(fig.), 88(fig.), 89–90
  voting and, 205, 206(fig.)
Religious orientation, 108(fig.)
"Religious Right," 91
Religious tradition, 107–108
Remedies (judicial), 423
Reorganization Act (1939), 365

Repeaters, 136
Representational voting, 295–296
Representative democracy, 6–8, 319–320, 337
the Constitution and, 7–8, 28
direct versus, 6–8
distribution of power in, 8–11
Republic, 22, 28
Republican National Committee (RNC), 157–158, 177
Republican party. *See also* Jeffersonian Republicans
Christian Coalition and, 88, 108–109, 164, 233, 243
"Contract with America," 282
electoral coalitions, 204–205, 207, 207(fig.)
elephant as symbol of, 154
founding of, 152–153
history of, 154–157
Iowa caucus and, 184–185
minor parties split off from, 170
modern party structure, 157–161
national conventions. *See* National nominating conventions
newspaper endorsements and, 259–260, 263
political machine and, 163
presidential elections and, 200–201, 200(fig.)
presidential nominations, 172–173, 183–185
public rating of, 168, 168(fig.)
realignments, 208–211
reform clubs, 164
reform of, 156–157, 160–161
selection of judges and, 411, 412(fig.), 413
state and local parties, 161–165
voters versus, 174, 176, 176(fig.)
Republican Study Committee (House), 296
Residential segregation, 469
Resolution Funding Corporation, 390
Resolutions, 313
Resolution Trust Corporation, 390
Restrictive rules, 308, 315, 329
Retrospective voting, 202
Revenue sharing, 64–65, 66, 69
categorical grants versus, 62, 64
Reverse discrimination, 482, 484
Revolutionary War, 17–21, 38, 88, 340
goals of, 17–18
"Revolving door," 238–239
Rhode Island, 21, 23, 27n, 31, 37, 58
Rice, Donna, 255
Rice, Thomas D. ("Daddy"), 463
Richmond, Virginia, 482–483
Riders, 316
Right-of-reply rule, 258
Right-to-life movement, 163, 227, 480–481
Riker, William H., 51, 52
Riots, 363, 471, 472–473, 475
RNC (Republican National Committee), 157–158, 177
Roberts, Owen, 410
Robertson, Pat, 109, 173
Robertson's rule, 392
Rockefeller, Nelson, 190, 369
Rockefeller Family Fund, 229
Rockne, Knute, 389
Roemer, Tim, 259
Roe v. Wade (1973), 480–481
Roll Call (magazine), 330
Roll calls, 317, 318, 319
Roll-call votes, 318
Roosevelt, Franklin Delano, 159, 334, 353

assasination attempt, 366
attempt to "pack" Supreme Court, 409–410, 427, 428
audience of, 355
books on, 373
campaigns and elections, 118, 163, 209, 210
Congress and, 335
crises of, 363
internment of Japanese-Americans, 461
New Deal, 5, 170–171, 207, 209, 210, 409, 505
polls used by, 364
popularity of, 356
presidency of, 336, 346, 349, 351, 352, 356, 357, 365, 367, 372, 409
press and, 262, 269, 356
Social Security Act (1935), 371
term of office, 338
use of liberal term, 120
use of vetoes, 343, 360, 361n
Roosevelt, Theodore, 353
assasination attempt, 366
campaigns and elections, 343
libel and, 443
muckrakers, 248
press and, 261–262
Supreme Court appointments, 412
Rostker v. Goldberg (1981), 479
Rotary Club, 223
Routine stories, 265–266
Rowland, C. K., 411
Rule 22, 283–284
Rule of propinquity, 346
Rules Committee (House), 280–281, 300, 315–316, 473, 475
Runoff primaries, 186
Ruritania, 270
Russian Revolution (1917), 17

Saccharin ban, 235
Safe districts, 286, 296
St. Patrick's Day parade (Boston), 489
Sampling, 114–115
Sampling errors, 115
Santeria religion, 448
SBA (Small Business Administration), 392
Scaife foundations, 229
Scalia, Antonin, 58, 422, 429
Scandals, 325
of Clinton, 269, 370
in Congress, 324–325
media focus on, 255, 266, 271, 298
of Reagan administration, 203, 269, 363
Watergate, 92, 192, 269, 354, 357, 361, 363, 429
"Schedule C" appointments, 382
Schenck, Charles T., 441–442
Schlozman, Daniel Aaron, 231
School districts, 58
Schools. *See also* Busing; Desegregation; Education; Segregation
civil rights and, 462–464
First Amendment rights and, 447–448
parochial, public aid to, 419, 437, 449, 450
prayer in public, 426–427, 450
school districts, 58
separate-but-equal doctrine and, 465, 467–472
single-sex, 479
Schumpeter, Joseph, 6

Scorekeeper role, of media, 254–255
Scott, Dred, 407, 427, 429
Scribner's, 249
Search and seizure, 452, 454–455
Search warrants, 452
Sears, David, 83
SEC (Securities and Exchange Commission), 351
Second Amendment, 35
Second Hoover Commission, 398
Second-order devolution, 71
Secretary of State, 352
Secret Service, 345, 361
Section 504 of Rehabilitation Act (1973), 486
Section 509(a) of the Internal Revenue Code, 506
Section 1983, 418
Sectionalism, Civil War and, 154–156
Securities and Exchange Commission (SEC), 351
Sedition, 437–439
Sedition Act (1798), 437–438, 441
Sedition Act (1917–1918), 438, 442
Segregation. *See also Brown v. Board of Education;* Civil rights; Civil-rights movement; Desegregation
colleges and universities, 466, 467
de facto and de jure, 469, 471
of public accommodations, 464–465, 475
of public transportation, 465
residential, 469
separate-but-equal doctrine, 465, 467–472
Select committees, 306
Selective attention, 259
Self-incrimination, due process and, 456–457
Self-interest, principal of, 10–11, 29–30, 38
Senate, 27. *See also* Congress
attitudinal voting in, 295, 296–298
calendar, 315
committees, 306–309
composition of, 284–289, 285(fig.), 286(fig.), 287(fig.)
ethics rules and, 324–326
evolution of, 283–284
filibusters, 283, 284, 317–318, 329, 475
floor debates, 317–318
history of, 283–284
House compared with, 319
media and, 262–263
minorities in, 284, 285(fig.), 291–292, 477(fig.)
organization of, 298–311
party organization of, 298–300
public opinion and, 297, 297(fig.)
Rule 22, 283–284
rules on congressional ethics, 325
rules on gifts, 325, 348
salaries and allowances, 326
standing committees of, 306, 307
Web site, 330
women in, 284, 285(fig.)
Senatorial courtesy, 412, 414
Senior Executive Service (SES), 385
Sensationalism, in the media, 269, 271
Separate-but-equal doctrine, 465, 467–472
Separation of church and state, 448–451
Separation of powers, 30, 41, 336, 360–361, 496, 497, 506
criticism of, 41–42
ethics and, 323, 324
increasing, proposals for, 508–510
reducing, proposals for, 42–43, 506–508
Sequential referrals, 315

SES (Senior Executive Service), 385
Seventeenth Amendment, 283
Seventh Amendment, 35
Seventh-Day Adventists, 448–449
Sex discrimination, 475, 478
Sexual classifications, 478–479
Sexual harassment, 325, 403, 479–480
Shalala, Donna E., 346
Shapp, Milton, 187
Sharon, Ariel, 256, 443–444
Shaw v. Reno (1993), 291–292
Shays, Daniel, 23
Shays's Rebellion (1787), 23, 25
Sheppard, Samuel H., 437
Sherman, Roger, 28, 35
Sierra Club, 222, 226, 241, 243
Silent majority, 105
Simon, Paul, 182
Simple resolutions, 313
Simpson, O. J., 114
Sinclair, Barbara, 302
Sipuel, Ada Lois, 467
Sit-ins, 141, 239–240, 471, 472
Sitting duck, 370
Sixteenth Amendment, 380, 427
Sixth Amendment, 35
Slanted news stories, 264–266
Slavery, 49, 57
    Constitution and, 36–38
    federal courts and, 405–407
    history of political parties and, 155
    party realignments and, 208–209
    Supreme Court on, 407, 427, 429
Small Business Administration (SBA), 392
Smith, Al, 159
Smith, Howard, 473
Smith, Samuel Harrison, 247
Smith Act (1940), 438, 442
Smith's Principle, 392
Sniderman, Paul M., 83
"Soccer moms," 198
Social class, 8
    interest-group bias and, 230–232, 230(fig.)
    organizational membership and, 230–232,
      230(fig.)
    political elites as "new class," 124–125
    political participation and, 139
    public opinion and, 112–114
Socialist Labor party, 170
Socialist party, 163, 169, 170–171
Socialist Workers party, 163, 170
Social movements, 225–229
    for civil rights. *See* Civil-rights movement
    environmental movement, 225, 226, 230,
      243
    feminist movement, 226–227, 240, 352, 477,
      490
    interest groups and, 225–229
Social science, desegregation and, 468–469
Social Security, 426
    Congress and, 503–504
    trust fund for, 394
Social Security Act (1935), 371
Social status, of religious groups, 107
Social welfare, 14. See also . *See also* Welfare; *and
    specific welfare programs*
    devolution of, 70, 71–72
Soft money, 158–159, 194, 195, 241
Soil Conservation Service, 389
Solarz, Stephen, 291

Solicitor general, 421
Solidary groups, 164
Solidary incentives, 164, 223
Sophomore surge, 293, 329
Sound bites, 250
Sources of news, 257
confidentiality of, 256
Souter, David, 414, 481
South, the, 132, 133, 136, 209, 211
    civil rights, view of, 117, 118(fig.), 476(fig.)
    Democratic party and, 117–118, 118(fig.),
      119(fig.), 136, 166
    Jeffersonian Republicans in, 152–153, 153n,
      208, 406–407, 429
    majority-minority districts in, 291
    public opinion in, 117–118, 118(fig.),
      119(fig.)
    Republican politics in, rise of, 153, 157,
      166(fig.), 289
    slavery and, 37, 280
    voter registration in, 133–134, 134(fig.)
South Carolina, 27n, 155
"Southern Manifesto" (1956), 467–468
Sovereign immunity, 418–419
Sovereignty, 51
Soviet Union (former), 5–6, 50
collapse of, 364
Spain, 21, 85, 88(fig.), 248
Speaker of the House, 279, 300, 367, 369
    evolution of position, 280–282
Special-act charters, 58
Special-district governments (authorities), 58
Special interests, 32, 320. See also Factions; Inter-
    est groups
    PACs and, 194
Special revenue sharing. *See* Block grants
Speech, 441–443
    nature of, 443–447
    symbolic, 446–447
Split tickets, 211–212, 211(fig.), 337
Spock, Benjamin, 451, 454
Spoils system, 378, 383
Sponsored parties, 164–165
Spots (television ads), 187–188, 189
Staff agencies, 311
Staffs, congressional. *See* Congressional staffs
Standing, in the courts, 418–419, 420, 426
Standing committees, 306, 307, 308, 318
Stare decisis, 423
Starr, Kenneth, 269, 271, 370
State and Local Fiscal Assistance Act (1972), 64
State and local political parties, 161–165
    ideological parties, 163–164
    personal followings, 165
    political machine and, 161–163
    solidary groups, 164
    sponsored parties, 164–165
    two-party system and, 165–168
State constitutions, 21, 22–23, 59
State courts, jurisdiction of, 414–417
State Department, 377, 386, 389, 401
State Farm, 420
State government, national versus, 30, 49–51.
    See also Federalism; Federal-state relations
State militias, 60
States
    federal government and. *See* Federal-state rela-
     tions
    rivalry among, 65–66
    voting rights and, 132–135, 140

State sovereignty, 54, 58–59
    revival of, 411
States' Rights ("Dixiecrat") party, 170
Steel industry, 82, 348, 427
Steering Committee (Senate), 299
Steffens, Lincoln, 249
Stenberg v. Carhart (2000), 480, 481
Stephanopoulos, George, 347
Stevens, Thaddeus, 280
Stevenson, Adlai, 154, 173, 260
Stewart, Potter, 444
Stockman, David, 349, 387
STOP ERA, 227
Straight tickets, 211
Strict-constructionist approach, to judicial review,
    404–405, 413, 426
Strict scrutiny standard, 478, 479, 483
Study by committees, 313–316
Study commission on executive reorganization,
    398
Subcommittees, 306, 307, 308
Subsidies, 380–381
Substantive representation, 292
Succession Act (1886), 367
Succession to presidency, 366–367, 369
Suffrage, 132–133
Superdelegates, 160, 161
Super Tuesday (March 12), 183
Supreme Court, 27, 28, 31, 404, 411, 420–422.
    See also Courts; Federal courts; *and specific
    decisions*
    on abortion, 480, 481
    on affirmative action, 482–485, 488
    attemp to define obscenity, 255, 444–446
    attempt of FDR to "pack," 409–410, 427, 428
    on campaign financing, 193–194
    case getting to court, 417–420
    on civil rights, 464–472
    on class-action suits, 420
    commerce and, 57–58
    on confidentiality of sources, 256
    on congressional investigative powers, 395
    decisions, Web site for, 77, 431
    development of, 405–411
    on drug testing, 455–456
    on dual sovereignty doctrine, 415–416
    economy and regulation by, 407–409
    on Espionage Act, 441–442
    on exclusionary rule, 452
    on executive privilege, 361
    on fair representation, 291
    on federal-state relationship, 56–57, 58–59,
      405–407, 411
    on First Amendment rights, 441–443, 444,
      446–450, 451, 454
    on flag burning, 446–447
    on freedom of expression, 441–443
    on free-exercise clause, 448–449
    on gay rights, 455, 488–489
    on income taxes, 427
    increase in workload of, 408, 417
    influence of law clerks on, 417
    influences on, 421
    judicial activism of, 404–405, 408, 410–411,
      424, 426, 429–430
    jurisdiction of, 414–417
    justices, selection of, 411–414
    justices of, 404(fig.), 420(fig.)
    on legislative veto, 365, 394–395
    litmus test issue and, 413–414

Supreme Court *(cont.)*
  on lobbying, 240
  on majority-minority redistricting, 291–292
  on malapportionment, 290, 291, 291(fig.), 419
  on male/female differences, 478–479
  on mandatory busing, 470
  on Miranda rule, 456–457
  on national convention selections, 186
  on national supremacy, 405–407
  national-supremacy view of, 56–57
  nullification and, 57
  on political liberty, 409–411
  on prayer in schools, 426–427
  on private property, 407–408, 409
  public opinion on, 429, 430(fig.)
  on regulations, 408–409
  on regulatory agencies, 379
  rejection of nominees, 414
  as restraint on government, 500–501
  on restrictions on liberty during war, 438–439
  school desegregation ruling, 467–469
  school prayer issue, 426–427
  on separate-but-equal doctrine, 465, 467–472
  on sexual classifications, 478–479
  on sexual harassment, 479–480
  on slavery, 407, 427, 429
  on state sovereignty, 54, 58–59, 411
  Tenth Amendment and, 54
  on term limits, 285
  trivia about, 427
  typical court case in, 420–422
  on unreasonable search and seizure, 452, 454–455
  on voting rights, 133–134, 140
  wall-of-separation principle, 449–450
  writ of certiorari and, 416–417, 420
  written opinion by, 422
Suspect classifications, 462
Swain, Carol M., 292
Swann v. Charlotte-Mecklenburg Board of Education (1971), 469–470
Sweatt, Heman, 467
Sweden, 50, 84, 85–86, 252, 376
Sweet, Robert W., 487
Switzerland, 22, 50, 130
Symbolic racism, 83
Symbolic speech, 446–447
Symbols, 154

Taft, William Howard, 220, 427
Talmadge family, 165
Tammany Hall (New York City), 162, 164
Taney, Roger B., 407, 427
Tariffs, 222
Taxation. *See also* Federal income taxes
  Sixteenth Amendment and, 380, 427
Tax-exempt status, 241, 450
Tax Reform Act (1986), 181, 336
Taylor, Zachary, 181, 342, 366
Teamsters Union, 218
Telecommunications Act (1996), 258
Television, 246, 249–250
  cable, 190, 250, 252, 253, 262, 269
  competition between stations, 252
  debates, 189–191, 258
  deregulation of, 258
  effects on politics, 259–261
  free time on, 190–191
  interpreting news stories, 263

  major networks, 190, 250, 250(fig.), 269
  regulation of, 256–258
  role in presidential campaigns, 187–191, 258–259
  spots, 187–188, 189
  visuals, 187, 188–189, 251
  as watchdogs, 255
Teller votes, 318
Tennessee Valley Authority, 351
Tenth Amendment, 35, 53–54, 58, 66, 68
Term limits, 27, 42, 510. *See* Incumbency
  in Congress, 285, 320, 322
  the presidency, 338–339, 365
  Twenty-second Amendment and, 338, 365
Tet Offensive, 265
Texas, 62, 204, 480
  Congress and, 287, 290, 291, 291(fig.)
Think tanks, 226, 511
Third Amendment, 35
Third-order devolution, 71
Third parties, 163, 169, 175, 340. *See also* Minor parties
Thirteenth Amendment, 427
Thomas, Clarence, 403, 404, 414
Thurber, James, 389
Thurmond, J. Strom, 169, 293
Tiananmen Square (China), 364
Ticket splitting, 211–212, 211(fig.), 337
Tilden, Samuel J., 159
Time (magazine), 256, 265, 266, 444
Tocqueville, Alexis de, 10, 79, 80, 86
Tolerance, political, 94–99, 96(fig.), 97(fig.), 99(fig.)
Topeka (Kansas) Board of Education, 419, 467, 469
Treasury, secretary of the, 348
Treasury Department, 340, 377, 379, 390
Trial balloons, 257, 363
Trouble making, by interest groups, 239–240
Truman, David B., 50
Truman, Harry S., 362, 365, 509
  assassination attempt, 366
  audience of, 355
  books on, 373
  campaign and election, 118, 169, 173
  decline in popularity, 357
  impoundment of funds, 362
  seizure of steel mills, 427
  use of vetoes, 360, 361(fig.)
  as vice president, 367
Trust. *See also* Mistrust
  in government, 85, 92–93, 93(fig.), 94(fig.), 139
Trustbusting, 249
Trustee approach, 364
Trust funds, 394
Tuskegee Institute (Alabama), 211
Twelfth Amendment, 340
Twenty-fifth Amendment, 349, 367, 369
Twenty-second Amendment, 338, 365
Twenty-sixth Amendment, 134, 427
Twenty-third Amendment, 135
Two-party system, 165–168
  persistence of, 167–168, 167(fig.), 168(fig.)
Tyler, John, 366, 367
Tyner, James N., 162

UAW (United Auto Workers), 164–165
UI (unemployment insurance), 72, 449
Unalienable rights, 19

Unemployment, 90. *See also* Employment
Unemployment insurance (UI), 72, 449
Unified government, 335, 336, 337
Unions. *See* Labor unions
Unitary political systems, 50, 51–52, 58
United Auto Workers (UAW), 164–165
United Kingdom. *See* Great Britain
United States Code, 418
United States v. Carolene Products (1938), 445
United States v. Fordice (1992), 466
United States v. Lopez (1995), 58
United States v. Morrison, 58
United States v. Nixon (1973), 361
United We Stand America, 171. *See also* Reform party
Universal enrollment (voting registration), 140
University of California, 421, 482
University of Mississippi, 471
University of Oklahoma, 467
University of Oklahoma Law School, 467
University of Texas Law School, 467, 488
Unreasonable search and seizure, 452, 454–455
Urban League, 219
USA Today, 253
U.S. Forest Service, 235, 394
USS *Maine*, 248
Utah, 186

Valence issues, 186–187
Van Buren, Martin, 154, 366, 378
Vance, Cyrus, 351
Vanishing Voter, 146
Velasquez, Nydia M., 291
Ventura, Jesse, 175
Verba, Sidney, 84–85, 137, 138, 222
Vermont, 22, 173, 186
Veterans Affairs, Department of, 392
Veterans organizations, 220
Veto message, 358, 360
Veto power, 26, 45, 319, 351(fig.), 358–360, 359(fig.)
  legislative, 365, 394–395
  line-item vetos, 43–44, 45, 360
  pocket veto, 358, 360, 361(fig.)
Vice presidency, 355, 366–367
  succession of, 366–367, 369
Vice president, in the Senate, 298–299, 367
Vietnam War, 169, 185, 299
  Johnson and, 169–170, 262, 357
  media coverage of, 261, 265, 266, 269
  Pentagon Papers, 255, 294, 437
  public opinion on, 253
Violence Against Women Act (1994), 58
Virginia, 22, 25, 27(fig.), 153, 235, 406
Virginia and Kentucky Resolutions, 57
Virginia Military Institute, 479
Virginia Plan, 25–26
Virginia Resolution, 57
Visuals, 187, 188–189, 251
Voice votes, 318
Voluntary activity, 138
  nonpolitical, among citizens, 138(fig.)
Voter Information Services, 146
Voter registration, 130, 139–141, 475
  sources of, 131(fig.)
Voter registration form, 146
Voters. *See also* Voting
  apathy of, 130
  attitudes of, delegate opinion and, 172–173, 173(fig.)

political parties versus, 174, 176, 176(fig.)
in primary elections, 173
Voter turnout, 129–131, 130(fig.), 131(fig.), 135–137, 135(fig.)
calculating, 129–130, 130(fig.)
causes of, 138–141
comparison with Europe, 140, 142(fig.), 143–144, 143(fig.)
meaning of participation rates, 141–146
myths and realities about, 137
in presidential elections, 135(fig.), 139(fig.)
statistics on, Web sites, 146
Voting, 129–146. *See also* Nineteenth Amendment
causes of, 138–141
comparison with other countries, 140, 142(fig.), 143–144, 143(fig.)
in Congress, 295–298, 318–319
economic issues and, 202, 203(fig.)
meaning of participation rates, 141–146
nonvoting, 129–131, 130(fig.), 131(fig.), 145
pocketbook issues and, 197–198
prospective, 201–202
retrospective, 202
split tickets, 211–212, 211(fig.), 337
from state to federal control, 132–135
Web sites, 146
Voting age, 134–135, 427
Voting-age population, 129–130, 130(fig.)
Voting fraud, 136, 140, 156, 162, 163
Voting Rights Act (1965), 212
Voting Rights Act (1970), 134
Voting Rights Act Amendments (1982), 67
Voting specialists, 138

Wallace, George, 118. 134, 165, 168, 169
Wallace, Henry, 169, 170
Wall-of-separation principle, 449–450
Wall Street Journal, 253
Walsh, Lawrence, 269, 271
War. *See also specific wars*
restrictions on liberty during, 437–439, 441–443
War Department, 377
War of Independence, 18, 20
"War on Poverty," 505
War Powers Act (1973), 329
Warren, Earl, 410–411, 467
Wars, 500
Washington, George, 5
American Revolution and, 21, 22
Farewell Address, 152
presidency of, 36, 152, 153, 247, 280, 337, 338, 339, 341–342, 349, 352, 371

role at Constitutional Convention, 25, 36, 39
on Shays's Rebellion, 23
on strong national government, 22
Washington Globe, 247
Washington Post, 47, 253, 254, 255, 266, 269, 272
Washington Times, 47, 272
Waste, in bureaucracy, 395, 396, 397
Wasteful duplication, in bureaucracy, 395, 396, 397
Watchdog role of media, 255
Watergate, 92, 192, 269, 354, 357, 361, 363, 429
Watt, James, 225, 230
Watt, Melvin, 291
Watts, J. C., 305
Waxman, Henry A., 163
"Waxman-Berman organization," 163
Ways and Means Committee (House), 309, 314, 327
WEAL (Women's Equity Action League), 227
Weather Underground, 239
Weaver, R. Kent, 71
Weaver, Robert, 352
Weber, Max, 9–10, 90
Webster, Daniel, 342, 366
Webster case (1989), 481
Wednesday Club, 296
Weicker, Lowell, 487
Welfare, 71. *See also* Social welfare; *and specific programs*
devolution of, 70, 71–72
number of people on, 71, 72(fig.)
political ideology and, 120–121
public perceptions of, 83, 110, 117, 117(fig.), 118(fig.)
suing for payments, 423
Supreme Court rulings on programs, 59
Welfare Reform Act (1996), 71, 343–344
Wellstone, Paul, 134–135
Westmoreland, William, 418
Whig party, 155, 167, 181, 208
Whips, 299, 300, 301
Whistle Blower Protection Act (1989), 388
Whistler, James, 389
"Whistle-stop" tours, 187
White Anglo-Saxon Protestants, 439
White flight, 451, 454, 470
White House, Web site for, 372, 401
White House Office, 346–348. *See also* Office of the President
appointments to, 352–353
growth of, 346(fig.)

myth and reality of, 347
organization of, 346–347
White House press corps, 262, 271
White primary, 133
Whitewater, 267, 364
Whitman, Walt, 389
Wilderness Society, 226
Wilson, James, 27, 28, 337
Wilson, Woodrow, 50, 169, 283, 343, 344, 367
Winchell, Walter, 437
Winograd, Morley, 159–160
Wire services, 253, 265
Wirthlin, Richard, 158
Wisconsin, 140, 156, 163, 186
Woman's party, 170
Women
in bureaucracy, 384
cabinet appointments of, 351, 352
civil rights and, 477–481. *See also* Affirmative action
in Congress, 284, 285(fig.)
illegal discrimination, 478–479
judicial appointments, 413(fig.)
omitted from Constitution, 40
political attitudes of, 109–110, 110(fig.)
sexual classification and, 478–479
sexual harassment, 325, 403, 479–480
valence issues and, 186–187
voting restrictions, 132–133, 134
Women's Equity Action League (WEAL), 227
Women's Voting Guide, 146
Woodward, Bob, 255
Workers, 10
Marxism and, 8–9
Work ethic, 90
World War I, 438, 502
World War II, 438, 442, 502
bureaucratic development during, 379–380
World Wide Web, 251
Wright, Jim, 325
Writ of certiorari, 416–417, 420
Writ of habeas corpus, 34

Yale Law Journal, 421
Yale University Law School, 47
Yellow journalism, 445
Younger, Irving, 506
Yugoslavia, 364

Zacchini v. Scripps-Howard Broadcasting Co. (1977), 451, 454
Zaller, John, 110, 122
Zoning ordinances, 249
pornography and, 445

Photo Credits

Chapter 1

p. 3: Frank White/Liaison Agency; p. 5: Bob Daemmrich/Stock Boston; p. 6: Wang Jianmin, Xinhua/AP/Wide World; p. 7: Randy Taylor/Corbis-Sygma; p. 9 *left*: The Granger Collection, New York; p. 9 *right*: German Information Center; p. 11: Topham/The Image Works.

Chapter 2

p. 17: Pete Souze/Folio; p. 18: Library of Congress; p. 19: William Walcutt, "Pulling Down the Statue of George III at Bowling Green, 1857" oil on canvas, 51–5/8" × 77–5/8". Lafayette College Art Collection, Easton, Pennsylvania; p. 21: Rare Books Division, the New York Public Library, Astor, Lenox and Tilden Foundations; p. 23: The Print and Picture Collection, the Free Library of Philadelphia; p. 24 *left*: Corbis-Bettmann; p. 24 *right*: American Antiquarian Society; p. 26: Dennis Degnan/Pictor; p. 32 *top left*: U.S. Government Printing Office; p. 32 *top right*: New-York Historical Society; p. 32 *bottom*: Library of Congress; p. 33: American Antiquarian Society; p. 36: Chicago Historical Society; p. 37: "Doonesbury" ©G. B. Trudeau. Reprinted with permission of Universal Press Syndicate. All rights reserved; p. 38 *left*: the Bostonian Society/Old State House; p. 38 *right*: National Collection of Fine Arts, Smithsonian Institution/Art Resource, NY.

Chapter 3

p. 49: Bob Daemmrich/Stock Boston; p. 52: The Granger Collection, New York; p. 55: Bowdoin College Museum of Art. Brunswick, ME. Bequest of the Honorable James Bowdoin III; p. 56: The Granger Collection, New York; p. 60: David Weintraub/Stock Boston; p. 64: Bob Daemmrich/The Image Works; p. 66: Paul S. Conklin; p. 69: Bob Daemmrich/Stock Boston.

Chapter 4

p. 79: Clint Clemens/Liaison Agency; p. 80: The Granger Collection, New York; p. 82: Corbis-Bettmann; p. 83: UPI/Corbis-Bettmann; p. 85: Itsuo Inouye/AP/Wide World; p. 87: Myrleen Ferguson/PhotoEdit; p. 89 *top right*: Elizabeth Crews/The Image Works; p. 89 *bottom right*: Mark Richards/PhotoEdit; p. 89 *right*: S. Gazin/The Image Works; p. 92 *left*: UPI/Corbis-Bettmann; p. 92 *left*: Chronicle-Tribune, Christina Dicken/AP/Wide World.

Chapter 5

p. 103: Billy E. Barnes/PhotoEdit; p. 104: Drew Harmon/Folio; p. 107, Drawing by Richter;

©1991 The New Yorker Magazine; p. 108: Les Stone/Corbis-Sygma; p. 111: Najilah Feanny/Stock Boston; p. 113: Les Stone/Corbis-Sygma; p. 123: Tony Savino/Corbis-Sygma; p. 125: Bob Bird/AP/Wide World Photos.

Chapter 6

p. 129: Bob Daemmrich/Corbis-Sygma; p. 131: Washington Secretary of State; p. 132: Abby Aldrich Rockefeller Folk Art Center; p. 133 *right*: The Granger Collection, New York; p. 133 *right*: Department of Social History/Smithsonian Institution; p. 135: Library of Congress; p. 140: Bob Daemmrich/Stock Boston; p. 141: Joe Sohm/The Image Works.

Chapter 7

p. 149: Philip Gould/Corbis; p. 151: Ajit Kumar/AP/Wide World Photos; p. 153: Tennessee Historical Society; p. 155: UPI/Corbis-Bettmann; p. 157: The Image Works; p. 158: Jonathan Nourok/PhotoEdit; p. 162: By permission of the Houghton Library, Harvard University; p. 163: Reuters/Robert Giroux/Archive Photos; p. 165: Corbis -Bettmann; p. 169: Corbis-Sygma; p. 171 *top*: Library of Congress; p. 171 *bottom*: Corbis-Bettmann; p. 172: Victoria Arocho/AP/Wide World Photos; p. 173: Joel Page/AP/Wide World Photos.

Chapter 8

p. 179: M. Granitsas/The Image Works; p. 182: Tomas Muscionico/Contact Press Images; p. 184: Stephen Savoia/AP/Wide World Photos; p. 187: Andrew Lichtenstein/Corbis-Sygma; p. 188 *top*: Library of Congress; p. 188 *bottom*: Corbis-Bettmann; p. 189: UPI/Corbis-Bettmann; p. 190 *top*: NBC/Globe Photos, Inc.; p. 190 *bottom*: Ron Edwards/AP Wide World Photos; p. 202: Michael Newman/PhotoEdit p. 204: A Ramey/Stock Boston; p. 205: Michael Evans/Corbis-Sygma; p. 210 *left*: The Granger Collection, New York; p. 210 *right*: Stock Montage; p. 211: UPI/Corbis Bettmann.

Chapter 9

p. 217: Bob Daemmrich; p. 219 *both*: Michael Schumann/Saba Press; p. 220: Reuters NewMedia Inc./Corbis; p. 222: Stock Montage; p. 223: Barry Staver; p. 224: copyright© 1978 The New York Times Co. Reprinted by permission; p. 227: Toby Talbot/AP/Wide World Photos; p. 232: J. P. Laffont/Corbis-Sygma; p. 234: David Burnett/Contact Press Images; p. 235: Matt Freedman; p. 236: Courtesy National Educational Association; p. 240: Bruce Allen/IPOL.

Chapter 10

p. 245: John Newbauer/PhotoEdit; p. 247: By permission of the Houghton Library, Harvard University; p. 250 *left*: UPI/Corbis-Bettmann; p. 250 *right*: Paul S. Conklin/Pictor; p. 251: David Young-Wolff/PhotoEdit; p. 253: ©Reuters Newmedia Inc./CORBIS; p. 254: Lyndon Baines Johnson Library; p. 256: Molly Lynch/WCVB TV; p. 258: Democrat National Comittee; p. 261: UPI/Corbis-Bettmann; p. 262: Andrew Kaufman/Contact Press Images; p. 262 *top*: Brown Brothers; p. 269: ©The New Yorker Collection 1991 Dana Fradon from cartoonbank.com. All Rights Reserved; p. 271: CNN/CORBIS Sygma.

Chapter 11

p. 275: Mark C. Burnett/Stock Boston; p. 276: AP/Wide World Photos; p. 277: J. Ficara/Corbis-Sygma; p. 280: Library of Congress; p. 280 *left and middle*: Library of Congress; p. 280 *right*: AP/Wide World photos; p. 283: The New York Public Library, Astor, Lenox and Tilden Foundations; p. 290: Corbis-Bettmann; p. 295: Bob Briendenbach/Providence Journal; p. 300: Brad Markel/Liaison Agency; p. 304: Office of the Congressional Black Caucus; p. 309: Ficara/Corbis-Sygma; p. 313: U.S. House of Representatives; p. 314: Brad Markel/Liaison Agency; p. 318: Keith Jewell. U.S. House of Representatives; p. 322: Cartoon by Newstaff/Cullum. Copyright The Birmingham News. Reprinted with permission.

Chapter 12

p. 333: Mark E. Gibson/Folio; p. 334: Corbis-Bettmann; p. 335: Corbis-Bettmann; p. 339 *left*: Library of Congress; p. 339 *right*: AP/Wide World Photos; p. 342: The Granger Collection, New York; p. 344: M. Reinstein/Pictor; p. 352 *left*: Franklin D. Roosevelt Library; p. 352 *right*: Lyndon Baines Johnson Library; p. 354: Reuters/Luc Novovitch/Archive Photos; p. 355 *left*: UPI/Corbis-Bettmann; p. 355 *right*: ©1997, The Washington Post. Reprinted with permission; p. 365: ©Schwadron-Rothco Cartoons; p. 366: Michael Evans/The White House; p. 367: Stock Montage; p. 369: Corbis Sygma.

Chapter 13

p. 375: P. Chauvel/Corbis-Sygma; p. 379 *left*: Smithsonian Institution; p. 379 *right*: Mark Mangold/Bureau of the Census; p 382: AP/Wide World Photos; p. 384: ©Tribune Media Services Inc. All rights reserved. Reprinted with permission; p. 391: With permission of Bob Thaves; p. 393: Michael Schwarz/Liaison Agency; p. 396: Stephen Freey/Liaison Agency; p. 400: Mary Kate Denny/PhotoEdit.